Bisk Education

CPA REVIEW™

AMERICA'S BEST CPA REVIEW SINCE 1971

GET READY TO PASS THE CPA EXAM

SAVE HUNDREDS OF DOLLARS!

See coupons at back of book for special offers on AUDIO, VIDEO, ONLINE and SOFTWARE exam reviews.

WITH BISK'S ONLINE or CLASSIC CPA REVIEW

CPA

Comprehensive Exam Review

Regulation

Nathan M. Bisk, JD, CPA

ACKNOWLEDGEMENTS

CONTRIBUTING EDITORS

J. Ralph Byington
PhD, CPA
University of South Carolina, Aiken

Anne Keaty
JD
University of Louisiana at Lafayette

Robert L. Monette
JD, CPA
Philadelphia CPA Review

Paul Munter
PhD, CPA
KPMG

Thomas A. Ratcliffe
PhD, CPA
Troy University

C. William Thomas
MBA, PhD, CPA
Baylor University

Mark A. Turner
DBA, CPA, CMA
Texas State University

We wish to thank the **American Institute of Certified Public Accountants** and other organizations for permission to reprint or adapt the following copyrighted © materials:

1. Uniform CPA Examination Questions and Unofficial Answers, Copyright © American Institute of Certified Public Accountants, Inc., Harborside Financial Center, 201 Plaza Three, Jersey City, NJ 07311-3881.
2. Accounting Research Bulletins, APB Opinions, Audit and Accounting Guides, Auditing Procedure Studies, Risk Alerts, Statements of Position, and Code of Professional Conduct, Copyright © American Institute of Certified Public Accountants, Inc., Harborside Financial Center, 201 Plaza Three, Jersey City, NJ 07311-3881.
3. FASB Statements, Interpretations, Technical Bulletins, and Statements of Financial Accounting Concepts, Copyright © Financial Accounting Standards Board, 401 Merrit 7, P.O. Box 5116, Norwalk, CT 06856.
4. GASB Statements, Interpretations, and Technical Bulletins, Copyright © Governmental Accounting Standards Board, 401 Merritt 7, P.O. Box 5116, Norwalk CT 06856-5116.
5. Statements on Auditing Standards, Statements on Standards for Consulting Services, Statements on Responsibilities in Personal Financial Planning Practice, Statements on Standards for Accounting and Review Services, Statements on Quality Control Standards, Statements on Standards for Attestation Engagements, and Statements on Responsibilities in Tax Practice, Copyright © American Institute of Certified Public Accountants, Inc., Harborside Financial Center, 201 Plaza Three, Jersey City, NJ 07311-3881.
6. ISB Standards, Copyright © Independence Standards Board, 6th Floor, 1211 Avenue of the Americas, New York, NY 10036-8775

THIRTY-NINTH EDITION

PREFACE

Our texts provide comprehensive, complete coverage of all the topics tested on all four sections of the CPA Examination, including **Financial Accounting & Reporting, Auditing & Attestation, Regulation,** and **Business Environment & Concepts.** Used effectively, our materials will enable you to achieve maximum preparedness for the Uniform CPA Examination. Here is a brief summary of the **features** and **benefits** that our texts will provide for you:

1. **Information on the Computer-Based Exam**...The Uniform CPA Examination is administered at secure testing centers on computers. See Appendix B for a full discussion of this issue. This edition contains up-to-date coverage, including complete coverage of all exam changes. This edition also includes all the latest pronouncements of the AICPA and FASB, the current tax rates, governmental and nonprofit accounting, and other topics that are tested on the CPA exam. Our coverage is based on the most recent **AICPA Content Specification Outlines for the Uniform CPA Exam.**

2. **Separate and Complete Volumes**...Each volume includes text, multiple choice questions, and case-based simulations with solutions. There is no need to refer to any other volume.

3. **Approximately 3,600 Pages of Text**...Including a selection of more than 4,500 recent CPA Examination and exclusive Bisk Education multiple choice questions and simulations with Unofficial Answers from past CPA exams. Solving these questions under test conditions with immediate verification of results instills confidence and reinforces our **SOLUTIONS APPROACH**™ to solving exam questions.

4. **Complete Coverage**...No extra materials are required to be purchased. We discuss and explain all important AICPA, FASB, GASB, and ISB pronouncements, including all significant ARBs, APBs, SASs, SSARs, SFACs, and FASB materials. We also cite and identify all authoritative sources including the dates of all AICPA Questions and Unofficial Answers covered in our materials.

5. **Detailed Summaries**...We set forth the significant testable concepts in each CPA exam topic. These highly readable summaries are written in complete sentences using an outline format to facilitate rapid and complete comprehension. The summaries isolate and emphasize topics historically tested by the CPA examiners.

6. **Emphasis on "How to Answer Questions" and "How to Take the Exam"**...We teach you to solve free-response and simulations using our unique and famous **SOLUTIONS APPROACH**™.

7. **Discussion and Development of**...AICPA grading procedures, grader orientation strategies, examination confidence, and examination success.

8. **Unique Objective Question Coverage and Unofficial Answers Updated**...We explain ***why*** the multiple choice alternatives are either right or wrong. Plus, we clearly indicate the changes that need to be made in the Unofficial Answers to correctly reflect current business and tax laws and AICPA, FASB, GASB, and other authoritative pronouncements.

9. **Writing Skills**...Each volume contains a section to help you brush up on your writing skills for the CPA exam.

10. **Indexes**...We have included a comprehensively compiled index for easy topic reference in all four sections.

11. **Cross References**...If you do decide to use our other materials, the software uses the same chapter numbering system as the book to allow for easy synchronization between the two formats. Our video and audio programs also are referenced to those same chapters.

12. **Diagnostic Exam to Test Your Present Level of Knowledge**...And we include a **Practice Exam** to test your exam preparedness under actual exam conditions. These testing materials are designed to help you single out for concentrated study the exam topic areas in which you are dangerously deficient.

Our materials are designed for the candidate who previously has studied accounting. Therefore, the rate at which a candidate studies and learns (not merely reads) our material will depend on a candidate's background and aptitude. Candidates who have been out of school for a period of years might need more time to study than recent graduates. The point to remember is that all the material you will need to know to pass the exam is here, except for the professional databases available for free from www.cpa-exam.org to candidates with a *Notice to Schedule.* All you need to do is apply yourself and learn this material at a rate that is appropriate to your situation. **As a final thought,** keep in mind that test confidence gained through disciplined preparation equals success.

OUR EDITORIAL BOARD INCLUDES THE NATION'S LEADING CPAs, ATTORNEYS AND EDUCATORS!

The Only CPA Review Texts Developed By Full-Time Experts.

YOU WILL LEARN FROM OUR OUTSTANDING EXPERTS... WITHOUT LEAVING YOUR HOME OR OFFICE.

Consulting Editor
RICHARD M. FELDHEIM, MBA, JD, LLM, CPA (NY), is a New York CPA as well as an attorney in New York and Arizona. He holds a Master's in Tax Law from New York University Law School. Mr. Feldheim is a member of the AICPA, New York State Society of CPAs, American Bar Association, New York State Bar Association, and Association of the Bar of the City of New York. His background includes practice as both a CPA with Price Waterhouse & Co. and as a Senior Partner with the Arizona law firm of Wentworth & Lundin. He has lectured for the AICPA, the Practising Law Institute, Seton Hall University, and the University of Arizona.

Consulting Editor
WILLIAM J. MEURER, CPA (FL), is former Managing Partner for both the overall operations in Central Florida and the Florida Audit and Business Advisory Services sector of Arthur Andersen LLP. During his 35-year career with the firm, Mr. Meurer developed expertise in several industries, including high technology, financial services, real estate, retailing/distribution, manufacturing, hospitality, professional services, and cable television. A graduate of Regis University, Mr. Meurer is a member of both the American Institute of CPAs and the Florida Society of CPAs.

Consulting Editor
THOMAS A. RATCLIFFE, PhD, CPA (TX), is the Director of Accounting and Auditing at Wilson, Price, Barranco, Blankenship & Billingsley, P.C. [Montgomery, AL]. In that role, Dr. Ratcliffe is responsible for quality control within the firm. Dr. Ratcliffe is Director Emeritus of the School of Accountancy at Troy University and also serves as accounting/auditing technical advisor to several different associations of CPA firms. Continuing his involvement in service roles within the accounting profession, Dr. Ratcliffe serves on the AICPA Council and the Auditing Standards Board. He is the former chair of the AICPA Accounting and Review Services Committee. He is also a former member of the Private Company Financial Reporting Committee.

Consulting Editor
C. WILLIAM THOMAS, MBA, PhD, CPA (TX), is J.E. Bush Professor and former chairman of the Department of Accounting and Business Law at Baylor University. He is a member of the AICPA, the Texas Society of CPAs, the Central Texas Chapter of CPAs, and the American Accounting Association, where he is past Chairperson for the Southwestern Regional Audit Section. In addition, he has received recognition for special Audit Education and Curriculum projects he developed for Coopers & Lybrand. His background includes public accounting experience with KPMG Peat Marwick.

CHANGE ALERTS

The **American Recovery & Reinvestment Act of 2009** (ARRA '09) was passed in February, 2009, making it first eligible to be tested starting in October, 2009.

The **Emergency Economic Stabilization Act of 2008** (EESA '09) was passed in October, 2008, making it first eligible to be tested starting in July, 2009.

These changes are integrated into this volume to the extent they are within the scope of the CPA exam.

REGULATION

VOLUME III of IV

TABLE OF CONTENTS

The percentages on this page refer to the percent of exam coverage as outlined in the AICPA Examination Content Specification Outline (CSO) dated June 2002. See the Practical Advice appendix for more information on the CSO.

The editors recommend that candidates remain cognizant of the depth of coverage of a topic and their proficiency with it when studying for the exam. Make informed decisions about your study plan by reading the information in the **Getting Started** and **Practical Advice** sections of this volume.

QUICK TEXT REFERENCE

The editors strongly recommend that candidates read the entire **Getting Started, Practical Advice,** and **Writing Skills** sections of this volume, unless already they have read these sections in the *Financial Accounting & Reporting* or *Auditing & Attestation* volumes. The references on this page are intended only for conveniently relocating selected parts of the volume. Add items to this list that you find yourself revisiting frequently.

FOREWORD: GETTING STARTED

Step One: Read Section One of the Practical Advice Section

Section One of the **Practical Advice** section (Appendix B) is designed to familiarize you with the CPA examination. Included in **Practical Advice** are general comments about the exam, a schedule of exam dates, contact information for state boards of accountancy, and attributes required for exam success.

Step Two: Take the Diagnostic Exam

The diagnostic exam in this foreword is designed to help you determine your strong and weak areas. This in turn will help you design your personalized training plan so that you spend more time in your weak areas and do not waste precious study time in areas where you are already strong. You can take the exams using either the books or the Bisk CPA Review Software. Don't mark answers in the book; then you can use the diagnostic as a second practice exam, if you want. The books provide you with a worksheet that makes self-diagnosis fast and easy. The Bisk CPA Review Software automatically scores your exams and gives you a personalized analysis of your strong and weak areas.

NOTE: If you sat for one or more CPA exam sections, also analyze your performance on these exam sections to help you determine how to refine your efforts for the remaining exam sections.

NOTE: If you purchase a package that includes software, you also will want to go through all of the software tutorials prior to beginning intensive study. They are each only a few minutes long, but they are loaded with valuable information. There is simply no better way to acquaint yourself with the software. The software programmers assumed candidates would take the diagnostic exam before beginning studying; take the diagnostic exam to get full benefit from the software.

Step Three: Develop a Personalized Training Plan

Based on the results from your diagnostic exams, develop your personalized training plan. If you are taking all four exam sections, are sitting for the exam for the first time, and are an "average" CPA candidate, we recommend that you train for 20 weeks at a minimum of 20 hours per week. This level of intensity should increase during the final four weeks of your training and peak at 40 hours the final week before the exam. Designed to complete your study program, our Intensive Video Series is a concentrated and effective "cram course" that targets the information you must know to pass. The videos will refresh your memory on subjects you covered weeks earlier and clarify topics you haven't yet grasped fully.

The Bisk Education editors expect that most candidates will take less than four sections at once. If you are taking less than four sections, you should adjust these guidelines accordingly.

Also adjust these guidelines for your pre-review level of knowledge. For instance, if your work is mainly tax preparation, you likely will need less time to review REG topics and, perhaps, more time to review AUD topics.

You may wonder what we mean by an "average" candidate. We are referring to a candidate who is finishing or recently has finished academic training, attended a school that has a solid accounting curriculum, and received above average grades in accounting and other business courses. (An "average" candidate's native language is English.) Remember, "average" is a benchmark. Many candidates are not "average," so adjust your training plan accordingly.

Time Availability

	Mon.	Tues.	Wed.	Thurs.	Fri.	Sat.	Sun.
1:00 a.m.							
2:00 a.m.							
3:00 a.m.							
4:00 a.m.							
5:00 a.m.							
6:00 a.m.							
7:00 a.m.							
8:00 a.m.							
9:00 a.m.							
10:00 a.m.							
11:00 a.m.							
12:00 p.m.							
1:00 p.m.							
2:00 p.m.							
3:00 p.m.							
4:00 p.m.							
5:00 p.m.							
6:00 p.m.							
7:00 p.m.							
8:00 p.m.							
9:00 p.m.							
10:00 p.m.							
11:00 p.m.							
12:00 a.m.							

How to Find 20 Hours a Week to Study

The typical CPA candidate is a very busy individual. He or she goes to school and/or works full or part time. Some candidates have additional responsibilities such as a spouse, children, a house to take care of—the list can go on and on. Consequently, your first reaction may be, "I don't have 20 hours a week to devote to training for the CPA exam." Using the chart on the previous page, we will show you how to "find" the time that you need to develop your training schedule.

1. Keeping in mind what you would consider to be a typical week, first mark out in black the time that you know you won't be able to study. For example, mark an "X" in each block which represents time that you normally sleep, have a class, work, or have some other type of commitment. Be realistic.

2. Next, in a different color, put a "C" in each block that represents commute time, an "M" in each block that represents when you normally eat, and an "E" in each block that represents when you exercise.

3. Now pick one hour each day to relax and give your mind a break. Write "BREAK" in one block for each day. Do not skip this step. By taking a break, you will study more efficiently and effectively.

4. In a third color, write "STUDY" in the remaining blocks. Count the "STUDY" blocks. Are there 20? If not, count your "C", "M", and "E" blocks; if needed, these blocks of time can be used to gain additional study time by using Bisk Education CPA Review audio lectures and video programs. For example, our audio tutor is ideal for candidates on the go, you can listen to lectures whenever you're in the car or exercising and gain valuable study time each week.

5. If you still do not have 20 "STUDY" blocks, and you scored 70% or more on your diagnostic exams, you may still be able to pass the exam even with your limited study time. If, however, you scored less than 70% on your diagnostic exams, you have several options: (1) re-prioritize and make a block that has an "X" in it available study time; (2) concentrate on fewer exam sections; or (3) study more weeks but fewer hours per week.

How to Allocate Your 20 Weeks

Develop your overall training plan. We outline a sample training plan based on 20 hours per week and 20 weeks of study for all four sections. The time allocated to each topic was based on the length of the chapter, the difficulty of the material, and how heavily the topic is tested on the exam (refer to the exam content specifications found in the **Practical Advice** section of this book). Keep in mind that this plan is for the "average" CPA candidate. You should **customize one of these plans** based on the results of your diagnostic exams and level of knowledge in each area tested. Given the AICPA examiner's stated intent to make the BEC exam section integrative, the editors recommend that candidates review for the BEC section after, or concurrently with, other exam sections. **Warning:** When studying, be careful not to fall into the trap of spending too much time on an area that rarely is tested. Note: There are Hot•Spot™ videos and audio lectures corresponding to each chapter for more in-depth study. Call 1-888-CPA-BISK.

Sample Training Plan (all 4 sections)*

		Hours
Week 1:	Read **Getting Started** and **Practical Advice** sections	1
	Take Diagnostic Exams under exam conditions (see page F-19)	10
	Read **Writing Skills** section and get organized	1
	Chapter 1—Overview	2
	Chapter 2—Cash, Receivables & Investments	6

* Candidates should make modifications to this plan to suit their individual circumstances. For instance, this plan repeats Chapter 18. Candidates may not need to return to Chapter 18, particularly those who took a governmental accounting course. Training plans for candidates sitting for one or two sections start on page F-14. The Online and Classic classes incorporate different training plans within the weekly assignments. These different plans take advantage of the additional material provided for Online and Classic reviews.

		Hours
Week 2:	Chapter 2—Cash, Receivables & Investments	4
	Chapter 3—Inventory	5
	Chapter 4—Property, Plant & Equipment	6
	Chapter 5—Intangible Assets, R&D Costs & Other Assets	4
	Chapter 6—Bonds	1
Week 3:	Weekly review of weeks 1 - 2	1
	Chapter 6—Bonds	5
	Chapter 7—Liabilities	6
	Chapter 8—Leases	5
	Chapter 9—Postemployment Benefits	3
Week 4:	Weekly review of weeks 1 - 3	1
	Chapter 9—Postemployment Benefits	2
	Chapter 10—Owners' Equity	8
	Chapter 21—Standards & Related Topics	4
	Chapter 22—Planning	5
Week 5:	Weekly review of weeks 1 - 4	1
	Chapter 22—Planning	2
	Chapter 23—Internal Control	11
	Chapter 24—Evidence & Procedures	6
Week 6:	Weekly review of weeks 1 - 5	1
	Chapter 11—Reporting the Results of Operations	8
	Chapter 24—Evidence & Procedures	4
	Chapter 25—Audit Programs	7
Week 7:	Weekly review of weeks 1 - 6	1
	Chapter 11—Reporting the Results of Operations	4
	Chapter 12—Reporting: Special Areas	2
	Chapter 26—Audit Sampling	7
	Chapter 27—Auditing IT Systems	6
Week 8:	Weekly review of weeks 1 - 7	1
	Chapter 12—Reporting: Special Areas	4
	Chapter 13—Accounting for Income Taxes	6
	Chapter 14—Statement of Cash Flows	6
	Chapter 16—Foreign Operations	3
Week 9:	Weekly review of weeks 1 - 8	1
	Chapter 15—Financial Statement Analysis	4
	Chapter 28—Reports on Audited Financial Statements	12
	Chapter 29—Other Auditing Standards	3
Week 10:	Weekly review of weeks 1 - 9	1
	Chapter 17—Consolidated Financial Statements	8
	Chapter 29—Other Auditing Standards	1
	Chapter 30—Other Types of Reports	3
	Chapter 31—Other Professional Services	7

		Hours
Week 11:	Weekly review of weeks 1 - 10	1
	Chapter 18—Governmental Overview	3
	Chapter 19—Governmental Funds & Transactions	9
	Chapter 32—Accountant's Professional Responsibilities	3
	Chapter 33—Accountant's Legal Responsibilities	4
Week 12:	Weekly review of weeks 1 - 11	1
	Chapter 18—Governmental Overview (after Chapter 19)	3
	Chapter 20—Nonprofit Accounting	6
	Chapter 34—Contracts	8
	Chapter 35—Sales	2
Week 13:	Weekly review of weeks 1 - 12	1
	Chapter 35—Sales	4
	Chapter 36—Negotiable Instruments & Documents of Title	5
	Chapter 37—Secured Transactions	2
	Chapter 50—Economic Theory	8
Week 14:	Weekly review of weeks 1 - 13	1
	Chapter 38—Debtor & Creditor Relationships	7
	Chapter 42—Property	1
	Chapter 51—Financial Management	11
Week 15:	Weekly review of weeks 1 - 14	1
	Chapter 41—Other Regulations	2
	Chapter 42—Property	4
	Chapter 51—Financial Management	2
	Chapter 52—Decision Making	4
	Chapter 53—Cost Accounting	7
Week 16:	Weekly review of weeks 1 - 15	1+
	Chapter 39—Agency	2
	Chapter 43—Federal Taxation: Property & Other Topics	5
	Chapter 44—Federal Taxation: Individuals	4
	Chapter 52—Decision Making	2
	Chapter 54—Planning & Control	6
Week 17:	Weekly review of weeks 1 - 16	1+
	Chapter 44—Federal Taxation: Individuals	6
	Chapter 46—Federal Taxation: Corporations	7
	Chapter 49—Corporations	6
Week 18:	Weekly review of weeks 1 - 17	1
	Chapter 45—Federal Taxation: Estates & Trusts	6
	Chapter 46—Federal Taxation: Corporations	3
	Chapter 47—Federal Taxation: Partnerships	5
	Chapter 48—Partnerships	5
Week 19:	Review areas in which you still feel weak	10+
	Chapter 40—Federal Securities Regulation	3
	Chapter 55—Information Technology	7
Week 20:	Take Practice Exams under exam conditions (see page A-1)	10
	Do final reviews and check for updating supplements	10+

Your Personalized Training Plan:

Week	Task	Diagnostic Score	Est. Hours	Date Complete	Chapter Score	Final Score
1						
2						
3						
4						
5						
6						
7						
8						
9						

Week	Task	Diagnostic Score	Est. Hours	Date Complete	Chapter Score	Final Score
10						
11						
12						
13						
14						
15						
16						
17						

Week	Task	Diagnostic Score	Est. Hours	Date Complete	Chapter Score	Final Score
18						
19						
20						

Step Four: Read the Rest of the Practical Advice Section

In Section Two of the **Practical Advice** section of the book, we discuss examination strategies. Section Three will familiarize you with how the CPA examination is graded and tell you how you can earn extra points on the exam simply by knowing what the grader is going to seek. In addition, in Section Four we explain our Solutions Approach™, an approach that will help you maximize your grade. In Section Five, we provide information on the AICPA exam content specifications and point distribution.

Step Five: Integrate Your Review Materials

In this step, we demonstrate how to integrate the Bisk Education CPA Review products to optimize the effectiveness of your training plan. Find and read the section that corresponds to the package that you purchased. (To facilitate easy reference to your package guidance, you may want to strike through the sections corresponding to other packages.)

Videos

The video programs are designed to supplement all of the study packages. Note how we recommend using the audio lectures in the following review plans. These recommendations also apply to the Hot•Spot™ video lectures. FYI: The videos have similar content as the Online and Classic review video lectures, but they are not exactly the same. Each of the Hot•Spot™ video programs concentrates on a few topics. Use them to help you study the areas that are most troubling for you. Each of the Intensive video programs is designed for a final, intensive review, after a candidate already has done considerable work. If time permits, use the Intensive programs at both the very beginning (for an overview) and set them aside until the final review one or two weeks before your exam. They contain concise, informative lectures, as well as CPA exam tips, tricks, and techniques that will help you to learn the material needed to pass the exam. See study tips in Step Six on effective use of the video lectures.

Online and Classic Reviews

Our most comprehensive review packages, the Online and Classic reviews provide the discipline and learning experience of a classroom setting with the convenience of self-study. The Online reviews also provide personal attention from a faculty advisor for about seven weeks. They include video lectures, weekly assignments, a full set of comprehensive CPA review textbooks and powerful software study tools not found in other packages available on the market. These packages are intended for those candidates who want to make sure that they pass the exam the first time, and may be purchased as a full set or individually by section. By using one of these packages, you are eligible to qualify for Bisk Education's money-back guarantee. Contact a customer representative for details on the components of these packages. Online students may contact their faculty advisor with questions about integrating materials after viewing the web-site guidance. (The editors strongly recommend that candidates working full-time take a maximum of 2 sections concurrently.)

Books, Audio Tutor & CPA Review Multimedia

Another comprehensive self-study review package. This combination is designed expressly for the serious CPA candidate. It is intended for those candidates who want to make sure that they pass the exam the **first** time (or *this* time, if you already have taken the exam). By using this package, you are eligible to qualify for Bisk Education's money-back guarantee.

How to Use This Package:

1. First take the diagnostic exam using the Bisk CPA Review Software. The Bisk CPA Review Software scores your exam and tells you what your strong and weak areas are. Then view the short tutorial to learn how to use the software features to their fullest.

In chapters where you are strong (i.e., you scored 65% or better on the diagnostic exam):

2. Answer the multiple choice questions using the Bisk CPA Review Software.

3. Read the subsections of the chapter that correspond to your weak areas.

4. Listen to the audio tutor for topics covered in this chapter to reinforce your weak areas and review your strong areas.

5. Now, using the Bisk CPA Review Software, answer the multiple choice questions that you previously answered incorrectly. If you answer 70% or more correctly, you are ready to move to the next chapter. If you answer less than 70% correctly, handle this chapter as if you scored less than 65% on the diagnostic exam.

6. Answer at least one simulation (if there are any) and review written communication questions and solutions in any other simulations.

In chapters where you are weak (i.e., you scored less than 65% on the diagnostic exam):

2. Read the chapter in the book.

3. Listen to the audio tutor on topics covered in the chapter.

4. Re-read the subsections of the chapter that correspond to your weak subtopics.

5. Using the Bisk CPA Review Software, answer the multiple choice questions for this chapter. If you answer 70% or more correctly, you are ready to move on to the next chapter. If you get less than 70% of the questions correct, review the subtopics where you are weak and then answer the questions that you previously answered incorrectly. If you still get less than 70% correct, check the exam specifications in the Practical Advice section to see how heavily the area is tested. If this is an area that is heavily tested, continue reviewing the material and answering multiple choice questions until you can answer at least 70% correctly. Allocate more time than you originally budgeted, if necessary. If the area is not heavily tested, move on, but make a note to come back to this area later as time allows.

6. Answer at least one simulation (if there are any) and review written communication questions and solutions in any other simulations.

Books & CPA Review Multimedia

This combination allows you to use the books to review the material and the Bisk CPA Review Software to practice exam questions. You can also use the books to practice exam questions when you do not have access to a computer. Using this package, you are eligible to qualify for Bisk Education's money-back guarantee.

How to Use This Package:

1. Take the diagnostic exam using the Bisk CPA Review Software. The Bisk CPA Review Software scores your exam and tells you what your strong and weak areas are. Then view the short tutorial to learn how to use the software features to their fullest.

In chapters where you are strong (i.e., you scored 65% or better on the diagnostic exam):

2. Answer the multiple choice questions using the Bisk CPA Review Software.

3. Read the subsections of the chapter that correspond to your weak areas.

4. Now using the Bisk CPA Review Software, answer the multiple choice questions that you previously answered incorrectly. If you answer 70% or more correctly, you are ready to move on to the next chapter. If you answer less than 70% correctly, handle this chapter as if you scored less than 65% on the diagnostic exam.

5. Answer at least one simulation (if there are any) and review written communication questions and solutions in any other simulations.

In chapters where you are weak (i.e., you scored less than 65% on the diagnostic exam):

2. Read the chapter in the book.

3. Using the Bisk CPA Review Software answer the multiple choice questions for this chapter. If you answer 70% or more of the questions correctly, you are ready to move to the next chapter. If you get less than 70% of the questions correct, review the subtopics where you are weak. Then answer the questions that you previously answered incorrectly. If you still get less than 70% correct, check the exam specifications in the Practical Advice section to see how heavily the area is tested. If this is an area that is heavily tested, continue reviewing the material and answering multiple choice questions until you can answer at least 70% correctly. Allocate more time than you originally budgeted, if necessary. If this is not a heavily tested area, move on, but make a note to come back to this area later as time allows.

4. Answer at least one simulation (if there are any) and review written communication questions and solutions in any other simulations.

Books & Audio Tutor

This combination is designed for the candidate who has a strong preference for hard copy, who spends time commuting or doing other activities that could take valuable time away from studying, and for those who like to reinforce what they read by listening to a lecture.

How to Use This Package:

1. Take the diagnostic exam found in this volume. Using the worksheet provided, score your exam to determine your strong and weak areas.

In chapters where you are strong (i.e., you scored 65% or better on the diagnostic exam):

2. Answer the multiple choice questions for that chapter. Using the worksheet provided, analyze your strong and weak areas.

3. Read the subsections of the chapter that correspond to your weak subtopics.

4. Listen to the audio tutor on topics covered in this chapter to reinforce weak areas and review strong areas.

5. Answer the multiple choice questions that you previously answered incorrectly. If you answer 70% or more correctly, you are ready to move on to the next chapter. If you answer less than 70% correctly, handle this chapter as if you scored 65% or less on the diagnostic exam.

6. Answer at least one simulation (if there are any) and review written communication questions and solutions in any other simulations.

In chapters where you are weak (i.e., you scored less than 65% on the diagnostic exam):

2. First read the chapter in the book.

3. Now listen to the audio tutor covering topics in this chapter.

4. Re-read the subsections of the chapter that correspond to your weak subtopics.

5. Do the multiple choice questions and score yourself using the worksheet provided. If you answer 70% or more of the questions correctly, you are ready to move to the next chapter. If you answer less than 70% of the questions correctly, review the subtopics that are still giving you trouble. Then answer the questions that you previously answered incorrectly. If you still get less than 70% of the questions correct, check the exam specifications in the Practical Advice section to see how heavily this area is tested. If this is an area that is heavily tested, continue reviewing the material and answering questions until you can answer at least 70% of them correctly. Allocate more time than you originally budgeted, if necessary. If this area is not heavily tested, move on, but make a note to come back to this topic later as time allows.

6. Answer at least one simulation (if there are any) and review written communication questions and solutions in any other simulations.

Step Six: Use These Helpful Hints as You Study

- MAKE FLASHCARDS OR TAKE NOTES AS YOU STUDY

  Make flashcards for topics that are tested heavily on the exam or that are giving you trouble. By making your own flashcards, you learn during their creation plus you can tailor them to your individual learning style and problem areas. You will find these very useful for weekly reviews and your final review. Replace flashcards of information you know with new material as you progress through your study plan. Keep them handy and review them when you are waiting in line or on hold. This will turn nonproductive time into valuable study time. Review your complete set during the last two weeks before the exam.

  Make notes and/or highlight when you read the chapters in the book. When possible, make notes when you listen to the lectures. You will find these notes very useful for weekly reviews and your final review.

- DO NOT MARK THE OBJECTIVE QUESTION ANSWERS IN THE BOOK.

  Do not circle the answer to objective questions in the book. You should work every multiple-choice question at least twice and you do not want to influence later answers by knowing how you previously answered.

  Date your answer sheets to facilitate tracking your progress.

- SPEND YOUR WEEKLY REVIEW TIME EFFECTIVELY. DURING EACH WEEKLY REVIEW:

  Answer the objective questions that you previously answered incorrectly or merely guessed correctly.

  Go through your flashcards or notes.

  Pick at least one simulation to work, except for the BEC exam section. (Do not wait until the end of your review to attempt a simulation with a written communication question.) Read the written communication questions and solutions for this week's topics that you do not answer this week.

- MARK THE OBJECTIVE QUESTIONS THAT YOU ANSWER INCORRECTLY OR MERELY GUESS CORRECTLY.

  This way you know to answer these questions again at a later time.

- EFFECTIVELY USE THE VIDEO PROGRAMS

  Watch video lectures in an environment without distractions. Be prepared to take notes and answer questions just as if you were attending a live class. Frequently, the instructors will have you stop the program to work a question on your own. This means a 2-hour program may take 2½ hours or more to view.

  If you are strong in a topic, the editors suggest that you read the chapter in the book or software, then watch the related Hot•Spot™ video, and finally, answer the questions. If you are not particularly strong in a topic, watch the related video, then read the chapter and answer the questions. If you are weak in a topic, watch the related video, read the chapter, watch the video again, and then answer the questions. Amend these plans to suit your particular learning style as well as your strengths and weaknesses.

- EFFECTIVELY USE THE AUDIO TUTOR

  Use Audio Tutor to turn nonproductive time into valuable study time. For example, play the lectures when you are commuting, exercising, getting ready for school or work, doing laundry, etc. Audio Tutor will help you to memorize and retain key concepts. It also will reinforce what your reading and question drill. The more times that you listen to each lecture, the more familiar you will become with the material and the easier it will be for you to recall it during the exam.

Step Seven: Implement Your Training Plan

This is it! You are primed and ready. You have decided which training tools will work best for you and you know how to use them. As you implement your personalized training plan, keep yourself focused. Your goal is to obtain a grade of 75 or better on each section and, thus, pass the CPA exam. Therefore, you should concentrate on learning new material and reviewing old material only to the extent that it helps you reach this goal. Also, keep in mind that now is not the time to hone your procrastination skills. Utilize the personalized training plan that you developed in step three so that you do not fall behind schedule. Adjust it when necessary if you need more time in one chapter or less time in another. Refer to the AICPA content specifications to make sure that the adjustment is warranted. Above all else, remember that passing the exam is an **attainable** goal. Good luck!

Video Cross-Reference

The video programs are designed to supplement all of our study packages. They contain concise, informative lectures, as well as CPA exam tips, tricks, and techniques to help you learn the material needed to pass the exam. The **Hot•Spot**™ videos concentrate on particular topics. Use them to study the areas that are most troubling for you. Each of the **Intensive** video programs covers one of the four exam sections. The Intensive videos are designed for a final review, after you already have done considerable work. Alternatively, the Intensive videos may be used as both a preview and a final review. Please see page F-8 of this volume and page iii of any Hot•Spot™ or Intensive viewer guide for a discussion on integrating videos into your study plan. This information, with approximate times, is accurate as we go to press, but it is subject to change without notice.

Video Title	Text Chapter	Time
Hot•Spot™ Cash, Receivables & Marketable Securities	2	2:30
Hot•Spot™ Inventory, Fixed Assets & Intangible Assets	3, 4, 5	2:25
Hot•Spot™ Bonds & Other Liabilities	6, 7	3:00
Hot•Spot™ Leases & Pensions	8, 9	3:05
Hot•Spot™ Owners' Equity & Miscellaneous Topics	10, 15, 16	2:10
Hot•Spot™ Revenue Recognition & Income Statement Presentation	1, 11, 12	3:55
Hot•Spot™ Accounting for Income Taxes	13	2:00
Hot•Spot™ Statement of Cash Flows	14	2:00
Hot•Spot™ Consolidations	2, 17	3:30
Hot•Spot™ Governmental & Nonprofit Accounting	18 - 20	3:50
Hot•Spot™ Audit Standards & Planning	21, 22, 29	2:45
Hot•Spot™ Internal Control	23, 27	2:00
Hot•Spot™ Audit Evidence	24, 25	2:30
Hot•Spot™ Statistical Sampling	26	1:30
Hot•Spot™ Standard Audit Reports	28	1:40
Hot•Spot™ Other Reports, Reviews & Compilations	30, 31	1:50
Hot•Spot™ Professional & Legal Responsibilities	32, 33	2:00
Hot•Spot™ Contracts	34	3:00
Hot•Spot™ Sales	35	2:20
Hot•Spot™ Commercial Paper & Documents of Title	36	2:05
Hot•Spot™ Secured Transactions	37	1:15
Hot•Spot™ Bankruptcy & Suretyship	38	2:10
Hot•Spot™ Fiduciary Relationships	39, 45	2:00
Hot•Spot™ Government Regulation of Business	40, 41	2:10
Hot•Spot™ Property & Insurance	42	1:20
Hot•Spot™ Property Taxation	43	2:05
Hot•Spot™ Individual Taxation	44	3:10
Hot•Spot™ Gross Income, Tax Liabilities & Credits	44, 46	3:00
Hot•Spot™ Corporate Taxation	46	3:00
Hot•Spot™ Partnerships & Other Tax Topics	45, 47	2:30
Hot•Spot™ Business Entities	48, 49	2:25
Hot•Spot™ Economics	50	3:25
Hot•Spot™ Financial Management	51	3:00
Hot•Spot™ Cost & Managerial Accounting	52 - 54	3:30
Hot•Spot™ Information Technology	55	3:00

Intensive Video Review	FAR	AUD	REG	BEC
Text Chapters	1 - 20	21 - 31	32 - 47	48 - 55
Approximate Time	9:40	4:20	5:50	4:45

Supplement to Step Three: Alternative Sample Training Plans

The editors strongly recommend that candidates develop personalized training plans. Several training plans are outlined for candidates to modify. The time allocated to each topic was based on the length of the chapter, the difficulty of the material, and how heavily the topic is tested on the exam (refer to the exam specifications found in the **Practical Advice** section). You should **customize** one of these plans based on the results of your diagnostic exams and level of knowledge in each area tested.

REG Sample Training Plan (1 exam section)

		Hours
Week 1:	Take Diagnostic Exam under exam conditions (see page F-19)	3
	Read **Getting Started** and **Practical Advice** sections (if not yet done)	1
	Read **Writing Skills** section and get organized (if not yet done)	1
	Chapter 32—Accountant's Professional Responsibilities	3
	Chapter 33—Accountant's Legal Responsibilities	4
	Chapter 34—Contracts	8
Week 2:	Weekly review of week 1	1
	Chapter 35—Sales	6
	Chapter 36—Negotiable Instruments & Documents of Title	5
	Chapter 37—Secured Transactions	2
	Chapter 38—Debtor & Creditor Relationships	6
Week 3:	Weekly review of weeks 1 - 2	1
	Chapter 39—Agency	2
	Chapter 41—Other Regulations	2
	Chapter 42—Property	5
	Chapter 43—Federal Taxation: Property & Other Topics	5
	Chapter 44—Federal Taxation: Individuals	5
Week 4:	Weekly review of weeks 1 - 3	1+
	Chapter 44—Federal Taxation: Individuals	5
	Chapter 46—Federal Taxation: Corporations	8
	Chapter 45—Federal Taxation: Estates & Trusts	6
Week 5:	Review areas in which you still feel weak	10+
	Chapter 40—Federal Securities Regulation	3
	Chapter 46—Federal Taxation: Corporations	2
	Chapter 47—Federal Taxation: Partnerships	5
Week 6:	Take Practice Exams under exam conditions (see page A-1)	3
	Do final reviews and check for updating supplements	17+

Note the BEC exam section currently does not have simulations. The AICPA originally planned to have BEC simulations at a future undisclosed date. This date likely will be no earlier than late 2010. Bisk Education's updating supplements will notify candidates when simulations will be on the BEC exam section.

UPDATING SUPPLEMENTS

Bisk Education's updating supplements are small publications available from either customer representatives or our CPA Review website (http://www.cpaexam.com/content/support.asp). The editors recommend checking the website for new supplements a month and again a week before your exam. Version 39 (and higher) updating supplements are appropriate for candidates with the 39th edition. Information from earlier supplements (for instance, Version 38.3) are incorporated into this edition. Supplements are issued no more frequently than every three months. Supplements are not necessarily issued every three months; supplements are issued only as information appropriate for supplements becomes available.

FAR & REG Sample Training Plan (2 exam sections)

		Hours
Week 1:	Take Diagnostic Exams under exam conditions (see page F-19)	5
	Read **Getting Started** and **Practical Advice** sections (if not yet done)	1
	Read **Writing Skills** section and get organized (if not yet done)	1
	Chapter 1—Overview	2
	Chapter 2—Cash, Receivables & Investments	10
	Chapter 3—Inventory	1
Week 2:	Chapter 3—Inventory	4
	Chapter 4—Property, Plant & Equipment	6
	Chapter 5—Intangible Assets, R&D Costs & Other Assets	4
	Chapter 6—Bonds	6
Week 3:	Weekly review of weeks 1 - 2	1
	Chapter 7—Liabilities	6
	Chapter 8—Leases	5
	Chapter 9—Postemployment Benefits	5
	Chapter 10—Owners' Equity	3
Week 4:	Weekly review of weeks 1 - 3	1
	Chapter 10—Owners' Equity	5
	Chapter 11—Reporting the Results of Operations	12
	Chapter 12—Reporting: Special Areas	2
Week 5:	Weekly review of weeks 1 - 4	1
	Chapter 12—Reporting: Special Areas	4
	Chapter 13—Accounting for Income Taxes	2
	Chapter 42—Property	5
	Chapter 43—Federal Taxation: Property & Other Topics	5
	Chapter 44—Federal Taxation: Individuals	3
Week 6:	Weekly review of weeks 1 - 5	1
	Chapter 13—Accounting for Income Taxes	4
	Chapter 14—Statement of Cash Flows	6
	Chapter 15—Financial Statement Analysis	2
	Chapter 44—Federal Taxation: Individuals	7
Week 7:	Weekly review of weeks 1 - 6	1
	Chapter 15—Financial Statement Analysis	2
	Chapter 16—Foreign Operations	3
	Chapter 17—Consolidated Financial Statements	8
	Chapter 46—Federal Taxation: Corporations	6
Week 8:	Weekly review of weeks 1 - 7	1
	Chapter 18—Governmental Overview	3
	Chapter 19—Governmental Funds & Transactions	9
	Chapter 32—Accountant's Professional Responsibilities	3
	Chapter 33—Accountant's Legal Responsibilities	4
Week 9:	Weekly review of weeks 1 - 8	1+
	Chapter 18—Governmental Overview (after Chapter 19)	3
	Chapter 20—Nonprofit Accounting	6
	Chapter 34—Contracts	8
	Chapter 35—Sales	2

		Hours
Week 10:	Weekly review of weeks 1 - 9	1+
	Chapter 35—Sales	4
	Chapter 36—Negotiable Instruments & Documents of Title	5
	Chapter 37—Secured Transactions	2
	Chapter 38—Debtor & Creditor Relationships	7
	Chapter 39—Agency	1
Week 11:	Weekly review of weeks 1 - 10	1+
	Chapter 39—Agency	1
	Chapter 40—Federal Securities Regulation	3
	Chapter 41—Other Regulations	2
	Chapter 45—Federal Taxation: Estates & Trusts	6
	Chapter 46—Federal Taxation: Corporations	4
	Chapter 47—Federal Taxation: Partnerships	3
Week 12:	Review areas in which you still feel weak	8+
	Chapter 47—Federal Taxation: Partnerships	2
	Take Practice Exams under exam conditions (see page A-1)	5
	Do final reviews and check for updating supplements	5+

AUD & REG Sample Training Plan (2 exam sections)

Week 1:	Take Diagnostic Exams under exam conditions (see page F-19)	5
	Read **Getting Started** and **Practical Advice** sections (if not yet done)	1
	Read **Writing Skills** section and get organized (if not yet done)	1
	Chapter 21—Standards & Related Topics	3
	Chapter 22—Planning	3
	Chapter 32—Accountant's Professional Responsibilities	3
	Chapter 33—Accountant's Legal Responsibilities	4
Week 2:	Chapter 22—Planning	3
	Chapter 23—Internal Control	11
	Chapter 24—Evidence & Procedures	6
Week 3:	Weekly review of weeks 1 - 2	1
	Chapter 24—Evidence & Procedures	4
	Chapter 25—Audit Programs	7
	Chapter 26—Audit Sampling	7
	Chapter 27—Auditing IT Systems	1
Week 4:	Weekly review of weeks 1 - 3	1
	Chapter 27—Auditing IT Systems	5
	Chapter 34—Contracts	8
	Chapter 35—Sales	6
Week 5:	Weekly review of weeks 1 - 4	1
	Chapter 36—Negotiable Instruments & Documents of Title	5
	Chapter 37—Secured Transactions	2
	Chapter 38—Debtor & Creditor Relationships	7
	Chapter 42—Property	5

		Hours
Week 6:	Weekly review of weeks 1 - 5	1
	Chapter 39—Agency	2
	Chapter 41—Other Regulations	2
	Chapter 43—Federal Taxation: Property & Other Topics	5
	Chapter 44—Federal Taxation: Individuals	10
Week 7:	Weekly review of weeks 1 - 6	1+
	Chapter 45—Federal Taxation: Estates & Trusts	6
	Chapter 46—Federal Taxation: Corporations	10
	Chapter 47—Federal Taxation: Partnerships	3
Week 8:	Weekly review of weeks 1 - 7	1+
	Chapter 47—Federal Taxation: Partnerships	2
	Chapter 28—Reports on Audited Financial Statements	12
	Chapter 29—Other Auditing Standards	4
	Chapter 30—Other Types of Reports	1
Week 9:	Review areas in which you still feel weak	8+
	Chapter 30—Other Types of Reports	2
	Chapter 31—Other Professional Services	7
	Chapter 40—Federal Securities Regulation	3
Week 10:	Take Practice Exams under exam conditions (see page A-1)	5
	Do final reviews and check for updating supplements	15+

REG & BEC Sample Training Plan (2 exam sections)

Week 1:	Take Diagnostic Exams under exam conditions (see page F-19)	5
	Read **Getting Started** and **Practical Advice** sections (if not yet done)	1
	Read **Writing Skills** section and get organized (if not yet done)	1
	Chapter 32—Accountant's Professional Responsibilities	3
	Chapter 33—Accountant's Legal Responsibilities	4
	Chapter 34—Contracts	6
Week 2:	Chapter 34—Contracts	2
	Chapter 35—Sales	6
	Chapter 36—Negotiable Instruments & Documents of Title	5
	Chapter 37—Secured Transactions	2
	Chapter 50—Economic Theory	5
Week 3:	Weekly review of weeks 1 - 2	1
	Chapter 38—Debtor & Creditor Relationships	7
	Chapter 39—Agency	2
	Chapter 50—Economic Theory	3
	Chapter 51—Financial Management	7
Week 4:	Weekly review of weeks 1 - 3	1
	Chapter 41—Other Regulations	2
	Chapter 42—Property	5
	Chapter 43—Federal Taxation: Property & Other Topics	5
	Chapter 51—Financial Management	6
	Chapter 52—Decision Making	1

		Hours
Week 5:	Weekly review of weeks 1 - 4	1
	Chapter 44—Federal Taxation: Individuals	10
	Chapter 45—Federal Taxation: Estates & Trusts	4
	Chapter 52—Decision Making	5
Week 6:	Weekly review of weeks 1 - 5	1
	Chapter 45—Federal Taxation: Estates & Trusts	2
	Chapter 46—Federal Taxation: Corporations	4
	Chapter 47—Federal Taxation: Partnerships	2
	Chapter 48—Partnerships	5
	Chapter 49—Corporations	6
Week 7:	Weekly review of weeks 1 - 6	1
	Chapter 40—Federal Securities Regulation	3
	Chapter 46—Federal Taxation: Corporations	6
	Chapter 47—Federal Taxation: Partnerships	3
	Chapter 53—Cost Accounting	7
Week 8:	Review areas in which you still feel weak	7+
	Chapter 54—Planning & Control	6
	Chapter 55—Information Technology	7
Week 9:	Take Practice Exams under exam conditions (see page A-1)	5
	Do final reviews and check for updating supplements	15+

Exam Scheduling Strategies

Most candidates likely will split the exam between two or more windows. Sitting for all four exam sections during one exam window is preferable for candidates who want to pass the exam quickly or who travel far to take the exam.

Sitting for one exam section during one exam window is the best means of ensuring a passing score; however it does take a long time. Further, the synergy resulting from studying more than one exam section at a time is lost. The following are number of weeks from the Bisk Education one-exam-section-at-a-time study plans.

Financial Accounting & Reporting	8	Regulation	6
Auditing & Attestation	5	Business Environment & Concepts	4

Sitting for two exam sections during one exam window halves the number of exam windows and takes advantage of the synergy resulting from studying more than one exam section at a time. By scheduling one exam toward the beginning of a window and the second toward the end of a window, several weeks may separate the two exam sections.

You may want to sit for one exam section during your first exam window to get some idea of the preparation involved for your circumstances. Bear in mind, these study plans are **rigorous** schedules that assume the candidate has recently graduated from a school with a strong accounting program, etc. Once you have the experience of one exam section behind you, sitting for two or even three exam sections in the next window will be facilitated by the study habits that you have developed.

DIAGNOSTIC EXAMINATION

Editor's Note: There is only one practice (or final) examination. If you mark answers for the diagnostic exam on a separate sheet of paper, you can use these questions as a second "final" exam at the end of your review.

Problem 1 MULTIPLE CHOICE QUESTIONS (90 to 120 minutes)

1. According to the profession's ethical standards, which of the following events may justify a departure from a Statement of Financial Accounting Standards?

	New legislation	*Evolution of a new form of business transaction*
a.	No	Yes
b.	Yes	No
c.	Yes	Yes
d.	No	No

(5181)

2. A CPA is permitted to disclose confidential client information without the consent of the client to

I. Another CPA firm if the information concerns suspected tax return irregularities
II. A state CPA society voluntary quality control review board

a. I only
b. II only
c. Both I and II
d. Neither I nor II (5339)

3. A member would be in violation of the Standards for Tax Services if the member recommends a return position under which of the following circumstances?
a. It does **not** meet the realistic possibility standard but is **not** frivolous and is disclosed on the return.
b. It might result in penalties and the member advises the taxpayer and discusses avoiding such penalties through disclosing the position.
c. It does **not** meet the realistic possibility standard but the member feels the return has a minimal likelihood for examination by the IRS.
d. It meets the realistic possibility standard based on the well-reasoned opinion of the taxpayer's attorney. (7884)

4. Burrow & Co., CPAs, have provided annual audit and tax compliance services to Mare Corp. for several years. Mare has been unable to pay Burrow in full for services Burrow rendered 19 months ago. Burrow is ready to begin fieldwork for the current year's audit. Under the ethical standards of the profession, which of the following arrangements will permit Burrow to begin the fieldwork on Mare's audit?
a. Mare sets up a two-year payment plan with Burrow to settle the unpaid fee balance.
b. Mare commits to pay the past due fee in full before the audit report is issued.
c. Mare gives Burrow an 18-month note payable for the full amount of the past due fees before Burrow begins the audit.
d. Mare engages another firm to perform the fieldwork, and Burrow is limited to reviewing the workpapers and issuing the audit report. (7114)

5. In which of the following situations would a CPA's independence be considered to be impaired?

I. The CPA maintains a checking account that is fully insured by a government deposit insurance agency at an audit-client financial institution.
II. The CPA has a direct financial interest in an audit client, but the interest is maintained in a blind trust.
III. The CPA owns a commercial building and leases it to an audit client. The lease qualifies as a capital lease.

a. I and II
b. II and III
c. I and III
d. I, II, and III (2936)

6. Which of the following penalties is usually imposed against an accountant who, in the course of performing professional services, breaches contract duties owed to a client?
a. Specific performance
b. Punitive damages
c. Money damages
d. Rescission (8464)

7. A CPA firm must do which of the following before it can participate in the preparation of an audit report of a company registered with the Securities and Exchange Commission (SEC)?
a. Join the SEC Practice Section of the AICPA
b. Register with the Public Company Accounting Oversight Board
c. Register with the Financial Accounting Standards Board (FASB)
d. Register with the SEC pursuant to the Securities Exchange Act of 1934 (8462)

8. Which of the following statements is correct regarding an accountant's working papers?
a. The accountant owns the working papers and generally may disclose them as the accountant sees fit.
b. The client owns the working papers but the accountant has custody of them until the accountant's bill is paid in full.
c. The accountant owns the working papers but generally may **not** disclose them without the client's consent or a court order.
d. The client owns the working papers but, in the absence of the accountant's consent, may not disclose them without a court order. (7039)

9. The quarterly data required by SEC Regulation S-K have been omitted. Which of the following statements must be included in the auditor's report?
a. The auditor was unable to review the data.
b. The company's internal control provides an adequate basis to complete the review.
c. The company has not presented the selected quarterly financial data.
d. The auditor will review the selected data during the review of the subsequent quarterly financial data. (8208)

10. If management of a public company does not document its evaluation of the effectiveness of the company's internal control over financial reporting sufficiently, what must the auditor report to the audit committee in writing?

I. The auditor must disclaim an opinion.
II. The audit of internal control over financial reporting cannot be completed.

a. I only
b. II only
c. Both I and II
d. Neither I nor II (8275)

11. The president of Deal Corp. wrote to Boyd, offering to sell the Deal factory for $300,000. The offer was sent by Deal on June 5 and was received by Boyd on June 9. The offer stated that it would remain open until December 20. The offer
a. Constitutes an enforceable option
b. May be revoked by Deal any time prior to Boyd's acceptance
c. Is a firm offer under the UCC but will be irrevocable for only three months
d. Is a firm offer under the UCC because it is in writing (8011)

12. Castle borrowed $5,000 from Nelson and executed and delivered to Nelson a promissory note for $5,000 due on April 30. On April 1 Castle offered, and Nelson accepted, $4,000 in full satisfaction of the note. On May 15, Nelson demanded that Castle pay the $1,000 balance on the note. Castle refused. If Nelson sued for the $1,000 balance, Castle would
a. Win, because the acceptance by Nelson of the $4,000 constituted an accord and satisfaction
b. Win, because the debt was unliquidated
c. Lose, because the amount of the note was not in dispute
d. Lose, because no consideration was given to Nelson in exchange for accepting only $4,000 (3096)

13. Under the UCC Sales Article, a plaintiff who proves fraud in the formation of a contract may
a. Elect to rescind the contract and need **not** return the consideration received from the other party
b. Be entitled to rescind the contract and sue for damages resulting from fraud
c. Be entitled to punitive damages provided physical injuries resulted from the fraud
d. Rescind the contract even if there was **no** reliance on the fraudulent statement (2350)

14. Under the Negotiable Instruments Article of the UCC, which of the following instruments meets the negotiability requirement of being payable on demand or at a definite time?
a. A promissory note payable one year after a person's marriage
b. A promissory note payable June 30, year 1, whose holder can extend the time of payment until the following June 30 if the holder wishes
c. A promissory note payable June 30, year 1, whose maturity can be extended by the maker for a reasonable time
d. An undated promissory note payable one month after date (8436)

15. Burke stole several negotiable warehouse receipts from Grove Co. The receipts were deliverable to Grove's order. Burke endorsed Grove's name and sold the warehouse receipts to Federated Wholesalers, a bona fide purchaser. In an action by Federated against Grove,

a. Grove will prevail, because Burke **cannot** validly negotiate the warehouse receipts.
b. Grove will prevail, because the warehouser must be notified before any valid negotiation of a warehouse receipt is effective.
c. Federated will prevail, because the warehouse receipts were converted to bearer instruments by Burke's endorsement.
d. Federated will prevail, because it took the negotiable warehouse receipts as a bona fide purchaser for value. (3124)

16. In what order are the following obligations paid after a secured creditor rightfully sells the debtor's collateral after repossession?

I. Debt owed to any junior security holder
II. Secured party's reasonable sale expenses
III. Debt owed to the secured party

a. I, II, III
b. II, I, III
c. II, III, I
d. III, II, I (4350)

17. On June 5, Year 3, Gold rented equipment under a four-year lease. On March 8, Year 4, Gold was petitioned involuntarily into bankruptcy under the Federal Bankruptcy Code's liquidation provisions. A trustee was appointed. The fair market value of the equipment exceeds the balance of the lease payments due. The trustee

a. May **not** reject the equipment lease because the fair market value of the equipment exceeds the balance of the lease payments due
b. May elect **not** to assume the equipment lease
c. Must assume the equipment lease because its term exceeds one year
d. Must assume and subsequently assign the equipment lease (0613)

18. A debtor may attempt to conceal or transfer property to prevent a creditor from satisfying a judgment. Which of the following actions will be considered an indication of fraudulent conveyance?

	Debtor remaining in possession after conveyance	*Secret conveyance*	*Debtor retains an equitable benefit in the property conveyed*
a.	Yes	Yes	Yes
b.	No	Yes	Yes
c.	Yes	Yes	No
d.	Yes	No	Yes

(4776)

19. Blue, a used car dealer, appointed Gage as an agent to sell Blue's cars. Gage was authorized by Blue to appoint subagents to assist in the sale of the cars. Vond was appointed as a sub-agent. To whom does Vond owe a fiduciary duty?

a. Gage only
b. Blue only
c. Both Blue and Gage
d. Neither Blue nor Gage (7041)

20. The prospectus for the sale of securities of a not-for-profit corporation contained material misrepresentations due to the negligence of the person who prepared the financial statements. As a result of the misrepresentations, purchasers of the shares lost their investment. Do the anti-fraud provisions of the Securities Act of 1933 apply in this situation?

a. Yes, because the securities are required to be registered
b. Yes, because the misrepresentations were material
c. No, because the securities are exempt from registration
d. No, because only the issuer was negligent (7118)

21. Lux Limited Partnership intends to offer $600,000 of its limited partnership interests under Rule 504 of Regulation D of the Securities Act of 1933. Which of the following statements is correct?

a. The resale of the limited partnership interests by a purchaser may be restricted.
b. The limited partnership interests may be sold only to accredited investors.
c. The exemption under Rule 504 is **not** available to an issuer of limited partnership interests.
d. The limited partnership interests may **not** be sold to more than 35 investors. (4335)

22. Under the Federal Insurance Contributions Act (FICA), which of the following acts will cause an employer to be liable for penalties?

	Failure to supply taxpayer identification numbers	*Failure to make timely FICA deposits*
a.	Yes	Yes
b.	Yes	No
c.	No	Yes
d.	No	No

(5900)

23. Marvel Company manufacturers and sells distinctive clocks. Tinker Company purchased 100 of these clocks from Marvel at $99 each. One of Tinker's competitors, Soldier Company, also purchased 100 of the same model of clock from Marvel at $94 per clock. Marvel gives such discounts to all customers who, like Soldier, have done business with it continuously for ten years or more. In the event that Tinker litigates the issue,

a. Tinker must either show that Marvel has engaged in predatory pricing with intent to harm competition or present a detailed market analysis that demonstrates how the defendant's price discrimination actually harmed competition.
b. Marvel will prevail if Tinker cannot show that Marvel has engaged in predatory pricing with intent to harm competition.
c. Marvel will prevail if it can show that it sold clocks at the lower price to all customers that had done business with it continuously for ten years or more.
d. Marvel will prevail if it can establish that there were several other clock companies with which Tinker could deal if dissatisfied with Marvel.

(8528)

24. Mason Co. maintained two standard fire insurance policies on one of its warehouses. Both policies included an 80% coinsurance clause and a typical "other insurance" clause. One policy was with Ace Fire Insurance, Inc., for $24,000, and the other was with Thrifty Casualty Insurance Co., for $16,000. At a time when the warehouse was worth $100,000, a fire in the warehouse caused a $40,000 loss. What amounts can Mason recover from Ace and Thrifty, respectively?

a. $0 and $0
b. $10,000 and $10,000
c. $12,000 and $8,000
d. $24,000 and $16,000 (2388)

25. Fred Berk bought a plot of land with a cash payment of $40,000 and a purchase money mortgage of $50,000. In addition, Berk paid $200 for a title insurance policy. Berk's basis in this land is

a. $40,000
b. $40,200
c. $90,000
d. $90,200 (1613)

26. Fuller was the owner and beneficiary of a $200,000 life insurance policy on a parent. Fuller sold the policy to Decker, for $25,000. Decker paid a total of $40,000 in premiums. Upon the death of the parent, what amount must Decker include in gross income?

a. $0
b. $135,000
c. $160,000
d. $200,000 (7083)

27. In Year 3, Bach sold a painting for $50,000 purchased for his personal use in Year 0 at a cost of $20,000. In Bach's Year 3 income tax return, the sale of the painting should be treated as a transaction resulting in

a. No taxable gain
b. Section 1231 (capital gain–ordinary loss rule) gain
c. Long-term capital gain
d. Ordinary income (7643)

28. Among which of the following related parties are losses from sales and exchanges **not** recognized for tax purposes?

a. Father-in-law and son-in-law
b. Brother-in-law and sister-in-law
c. Grandfather and granddaughter
d. Ancestors, lineal descendants, and all in-laws

(3352)

29. Jackson, a single individual, inherited Bean Corp. common stock from Jackson's parents. Bean is a qualified small business corporation under Code Sec. 1244. The stock cost Jackson's parents $20,000 and had a fair market value of $25,000 at the parents' date of death. During the year, Bean declared bankruptcy and Jackson was informed that the stock was worthless. What amount may Jackson deduct as an ordinary loss in the current year?

a. $0
b. $ 3,000
c. $20,000
d. $25,000 (7081)

30. To avoid tax return preparer penalties for a return's understated tax liability due to an intentional disregard of the regulations, which of the following actions must a tax preparer take?
a. Audit the taxpayer's corresponding business operations
b. Review the accuracy of the taxpayer's books and records
c. Make reasonable inquiries if the taxpayer's information is incomplete
d. Examine the taxpayer's supporting documents (6686)

31. A husband and wife can file a joint return even if
a. The spouses have different tax years, provided that both spouses are alive at the end of the year.
b. The spouses have different accounting methods.
c. Either spouse was a nonresident alien at any time during the tax year, provided that at least one spouse makes the proper election.
d. They were divorced before the end of the tax year. (1560)

32. Jim and Kay Ross contributed to the support of their two children, Dale and Kim, and Jim's widowed parent, Grant. Dale, a 19-year-old full-time college student, earned $4,500 as a baby-sitter. Kim, a 23-year-old bank teller, earned $12,000. Grant received $5,000 in dividend income and $4,000 in nontaxable social security benefits. Grant, Dale, and Kim are U.S. citizens and were over one-half supported by Jim and Kay. How many exemptions can Jim and Kay claim on their joint income tax return?
a. Two
b. Three
c. Four
d. Five (4619)

33. A claim for refund of erroneously paid income taxes, filed by an individual before the statute of limitations expires, must be submitted on Form
a. 1139
b. 1045
c. 1040X
d. 843 (5438)

34. On April 15, Year 1, a married couple filed their joint Year 0 calendar-year return showing gross income of $120,000. Their return had been prepared by a professional tax preparer who mistakenly omitted $45,000 of income, which the preparer in good faith considered to be nontaxable. No information with regard to this omitted income was disclosed on the return or attached statements. By what date must the Internal Revenue Service assert a notice of deficiency before the statute of limitations expires?
a. April 15, Year 7
b. December 31, Year 6
c. April 15, Year 4
d. December 31, Year 3 (3340)

35. Harold sustained a serious injury in the course of his employment. As a result of this injury, Harold received the following payments during the current year:

Workers' compensation	$ 6,500
Reimbursement from his employer's insurance plan for medical expenses paid by Harold and not deducted by him	4,000
Damages for personal injuries	16,000

The amount to be included in Harold's gross income for the current year should be
a. $26,500
b. $16,000
c. $ 4,000
d. $0 (1601)

36. Adams owns a second residence that is used for both personal and rental purposes. During Year 1, Adams used the second residence for 50 days and rented the residence for 200 days. Which of the following statements is correct?
a. Depreciation may not be deducted on the property under any circumstances.
b. A rental loss may be deducted if rental-related expenses exceed rental income.
c. Utilities and maintenance on the property must be divided between personal and rental use.
d. All mortgage interest and taxes on the property will be deducted to determine the property's net income or loss. (7007)

37. Which allowable deduction can be claimed in arriving at an individual's adjusted gross income?
a. Alimony payment
b. Charitable contribution
c. Personal casualty loss
d. Unreimbursed business expense of an outside salesperson (4456)

38. During Year 2, Scott charged $4,000 on his credit card for his dependent son's medical expenses. Payment to the credit card company had not been made by the time Scott filed his income tax return in Year 3. However, in Year 2, Scott paid a physician $2,800 for medical expenses of his wife, who died in Year 1. Disregarding the adjusted gross income percentage threshold, what amount could Scott claim in his Year 2 income tax return for medical expenses?
a. $0
b. $2,800
c. $4,000
d. $6,800 (1557)

39. With regard to the passive loss rules involving rental real estate activities, which one of the following statements is correct?
a. The term "passive activity" includes any rental activity without regard as to whether or not the taxpayer materially participates in the activity.
b. Passive rental activity losses may be deducted only against passive income, but passive rental activity credits may be used against tax attributable to nonpassive activities.
c. Gross investment income from interest and dividends **not** derived in the ordinary course of a trade or business is treated as passive activity income that can be offset by passive rental activity losses when the "active participation" requirement is **not** met.
d. The passive activity rules do **not** apply to taxpayers whose adjusted gross income is $300,000 or less. (4596)

40. Taylor, an unmarried taxpayer, had $90,000 in adjusted gross income for the year. Taylor donated land to a church and made no other contributions. Taylor purchased the land ten years ago as an investment for $14,000. The land's fair market value was $25,000 on the day of the donation. What is the maximum amount of charitable contribution that Taylor may deduct as an itemized deduction for the land donation for the current year?
a. $25,000
b. $14,000
c. $11,000
d. $0 (6911)

41. In 2007, Sayers, who is single, gave an outright gift of $50,000 to a friend, Johnson, who needed the money to pay medical expenses. In filing the gift tax return, Sayers was entitled to a maximum exclusion of
a. $0
b. $12,000
c. $24,000
d. $50,000 (4638)

42. The standard deduction for a trust or an estate in the fiduciary income tax return is
a. $0
b. $100
c. $300
d. $600 (2472)

43. For income tax purposes, the estate's initial taxable period for a decedent who died on October 24
a. May be either a calendar year, or a fiscal year beginning on the date of the decedent's death
b. Must be a fiscal year beginning on the date of the decedent's death
c. May be either a calendar year, or a fiscal year beginning on October 1 of the year of the decedent's death
d. Must be a calendar year beginning on January 1 of the year of the decedent's death (6914)

44. For federal estate taxation, the alternate valuation date
a. If elected on the first return filed for the estate, may be revoked in an amended return provided that the first return was filed on time
b. Is required to be used if the fair market value of the estate's assets has increased since the decedent's date of death
c. Must be used for valuation of the estate's liabilities if such date is used for valuation of the estate's assets
d. Can be elected only if its use decreases both the value of the gross estate and the estate tax liability (1731)

45. Jackson Corp., a calendar year corporation, mailed its Year 1 tax return to the Internal Revenue Service by certified mail on Friday, March 10, Year 2. The return, postmarked March 10, Year 2, was delivered to the Internal Revenue Service on March 20, Year 2. The statute of limitations on Jackson's corporate tax return begins on
a. December 31, Year 1
b. March 10, Year 2
c. March 16, Year 2
d. March 20, Year 2 (5030)

46. Krol Corp. distributed marketable securities in redemption of its stock in a complete liquidation. On the date of distribution, these securities had a basis of $100,000 and a fair market value of $150,000. What gain does Krol have as a result of the distribution?

a. $0
b. $50,000 capital gain
c. $50,000 Section 1231 gain
d. $50,000 ordinary gain (1652)

47. Kisco Corp.'s taxable income before taking the dividends received deduction was $70,000. This includes $10,000 in dividends from an unrelated taxable domestic corporation. Given the following tax rates, what would Kisco's income tax be before any credits?

Partial rate table	Tax rate
Up to $50,000	15%
Over $50,000 but not over $75,000	25%

a. $10,000
b. $10,750
c. $12,500
d. $15,750 (4629)

48. Media Corp. is an accrual-basis, calendar-year C corporation. Its reported book income included $6,000 in municipal bond interest income. Its expenses included $1,500 of interest incurred on indebtedness used to carry municipal bonds and $8,000 in advertising expense. What is Media's net M-1 adjustment on its Form 1120, U.S. Corporation Income Tax Return, to reconcile to its taxable income?
a. $(4,500)
b. $ 1,500
c. $ 3,500
d. $ 9,500 (6675)

49. Prin Corp., the parent corporation, and Strel Corp., both accrual-basis, calendar-year C corporations, file a consolidated return. During the current year, Strel made dividend distributions to Prin as follows:

	Adjusted tax basis	*Fair market value*
Cash	$4,000	$4,000
Land	2,000	9,000

What amount of dividend income should be reported on Prin and Strel's consolidated income tax return for the current year?
a. $13,000
b. $11,000
c. $ 6,000
d. $0 (7652)

50. Which of the following conditions will prevent a corporation from qualifying as an S corporation?
a. The corporation has both common and preferred stock.
b. The corporation has one class of stock with different voting rights.
c. One shareholder is an estate.
d. One shareholder is a grantor trust. (4156)

51. Bass Corp., a calendar year C corporation, made qualifying Year 1 estimated tax deposits based on its actual Year 0 tax liability. On March 15, Year 2, Bass filed a timely automatic extension request for its Year 1 corporate income tax return. Estimated tax deposits and the extension payment totaled $7,600. This amount was 95% of the total tax shown on Bass' final Year 1 corporate income tax return. Bass paid $400 additional tax on the final Year 1 corporate income tax return filed before the extended due date. For the Year 1 calendar year, Bass was subject to pay

I. Interest on the $400 tax payment made in Year 2
II. A tax delinquency penalty

a. I only
b. II only
c. Both I and II
d. Neither I nor II (5767)

52. Boles Corp., an accrual-basis, calendar-year S corporation, has been an S corporation since its inception and is not subject to the uniform capitalization rules. In Year 3, Boles recorded the following:

Gross receipts	$50,000
Dividends income from investments	5,000
Supplies expense	2,000
Utilities expense	1,500

On Boles's Year 3 S corporation Form Schedule K, *Shareholders' Shares of Income, Credits, Deductions, etc.*, what amount of income should be separately stated from business income?
a. $50,000
b. $48,000
c. $ 5,000
d. $0 (7872)

53. Packer Corp., an accrual-basis, calendar-year S corporation, has been an S corporation since its inception. Starr was a 50% shareholder in Packer throughout the current year and had a $10,000 tax basis in Packer stock on January 1. During the current year, Packer had a $1,000 net business loss and made an $8,000 cash distribution to each shareholder. What amount of the distribution was includible in Starr's gross income?
a. $8,000
b. $7,500
c. $4,000
d. $0 (7650)

54. A corporation may reduce its regular income tax by taking a tax credit for
a. Dividends-received exclusion
b. Foreign income taxes
c. State income taxes
d. Accelerated depreciation (5761)

55. At partnership inception, Black acquires a 50% interest in Decorators Partnership by contributing property with an adjusted basis of $250,000. Black recognizes a gain if

I. The fair market value of the contributed property exceeds its adjusted basis.
II. The property is encumbered by a mortgage with a balance of $100,000.

a. I only
b. II only
c. Both I and II
d. Neither I nor II (5772)

56. Dean is a 25% partner in Target Partnership. Dean's tax basis in Target on January 1, Year 1, was $20,000. At the end of Year 1, Dean received a nonliquidating cash distribution of $8,000 from Target. Target's accounts recorded municipal bond interest income of $12,000 and ordinary income of $40,000 for the year. What was Dean's tax basis in Target on December 31, Year 1?
a. $15,000
b. $23,000
c. $25,000
d. $30,000 (5444)

57. Stone and Frazier decided to terminate the Woodwest Partnership as of December 31. On that date, Woodwest's balance sheet was as follows:

Cash	$2,000
Equipment (adjusted basis)	2,000
Capital—Stone	3,000
Capital—Frazier	1,000

The fair market value of the equipment was $3,000. Frazier's outside basis in the partnership was $1,200. Upon liquidation, Frazier received $1,500 in cash. What gain should Frazier recognize?
a. $0
b. $250
c. $300
d. $500 (7090)

58. On December 31, after receipt of his share of partnership income, Clark sold his interest in a limited partnership for $30,000 cash and relief of all liabilities. On that date, the adjusted basis of Clark's partnership interest was $40,000, consisting of his capital account of $15,000 and his share of the partnership liabilities of $25,000. The partnership has no unrealized receivables or substantially appreciated inventory. What is Clark's gain or loss on the sale of his partnership interest?
a. Ordinary loss of $10,000
b. Ordinary gain of $15,000
c. Capital loss of $10,000
d. Capital gain of $15,000 (8446)

59. Acme and Buck are equal members in Dear, an LLC. Dear has not elected to be taxed as a corporation. Acme contributed $7,000 cash and Buck contributed a machine with an adjusted basis of $5,000 and a fair market value of $10,000, subject to a liability of $3,000. What is Acme's basis in Dear?
a. $ 4,000
b. $ 7,000
c. $ 8,500
d. $10,000 (7656)

60. On January 3, the partners' percentage interest in the capital, profits, and losses of Able Partnership were:

Dean	25%
Poe	30%
Ritt	45%

On February 4, of the same year, Poe sold her entire interest to an unrelated party. Dean sold his 25% interest in Able to another unrelated party on December 20, of the same year. No other transactions took place in this year. For tax purposes, which of the following statements is correct with respect to Able?
a. Able terminated as of February 4.
b. Able terminated as of December 20.
c. Able terminated as of December 31.
d. Able did **not** terminate. (5777)

SIMULATIONS

Problem 2 (20 to 30 minutes)

Alex and Myra Burg, married and filing joint income tax returns, derive their entire income from the operation of their retail candy shop. The Burg's received the following in Year 0.

Net income from retail candy shop	$50,000
Interest on:	
Refund from amended tax return	175
Savings account and certificates of deposit	425
Municipal bonds	90
Gift	4,000
Jury duty pay	250
Gambling winnings	500
Life insurance proceeds (Paid on account of Mrs. Burg's father's death)	10,000

The Burg's itemized their deductions on Schedule A for Year 0. The following unreimbursed cash expenditures were among those made by the Burgs during Year 0.

Taxes:	
State income tax	$1,200
Self-employment tax	7,650
Repair of glass vase accidentally broken by dog (Vase cost $500 and had FMV of $600 before accident and $200 after accident)	90
Fee for breaking lease on prior apartment residence located 20 miles from new residence	500
Repair and maintenance of motorized wheelchair for physically handicapped dependent child	300
Four tickets to a theater party sponsored by a qualified charitable organization; not considered a business expense (Similar tickets would cost $25 each at the box office)	160
Security deposit placed on apartment at new location	900

(9911)

For items 1 through 5, determine the taxable amount, if any, that should be included in Adjusted Gross Income (AGI) on the Burg's Year 0 federal income tax return.

Income	Amount
1. Interest income	
2. Gift	
3. Life insurance proceeds	
4. Jury duty pay	
5. Gambling winnings	

For items 6 through 10, determine the amount of the deduction, if any, that would be included on the Burg's Year 0 federal income tax return.

Deduction	Amount
6. Without regard to the adjusted gross income percentage threshold, what amount may the Burgs claim in their return as qualifying medical expenses?	
7. What amount should the Burgs deduct for taxes in their itemized deductions on Schedule A?	
8. What amount should the Burgs deduct for gifts to charity in their itemized deductions on Schedule A?	
9. Without regard to the $100 "floor" and the adjusted gross income percentage threshold, what amount should the Burgs deduct for the casualty loss in their itemized deductions on Schedule A?	
10. What amount should the Burgs deduct for moving expenses for adjusted gross income?	

Write a memo to the Burgs, outlining the appropriate tax treatment from the list for payments or losses incurred during Year 0.

1. Legal fees paid to collect alimony
2. Sewer system assessment imposed by the city
3. Penalty for early withdraw of funds from a certificate of deposit
4. Casualty insurance premium
5. Self-employed health insurance premium paid

Research Question: What code section and subsection, if applicable, provides guidance on the amount of the alternative minimum tax (AMT)?

Section & Subsection Answer: §_____ (___)

Problem 3 (20 to 30 minutes)

Melvin, Otto, and Patricia formed the MOP Disaster Recovery Partnership on January 2, Year 2. Melvin contributed $50,000 in cash for a 40% share in capital and profits. Otto contributed land with an adjusted basis of $14,000 and a fair market value of $26,250 for a 20% share. The land was a capital asset to Otto, subject to a $6,250 mortgage, which was assumed by the partnership. Patricia contributed equipment with an adjusted basis of $30,000 and a fair market value of $32,000 for a 30% share.

The partners are unrelated outside of the general partnership.

In Year 2, the partnership had a $20,000 loss.

In Year 3, Melvin sold several pieces of antique furniture that he previously used in his home to the partnership at fair market value, $18,750. Melvin had an adjusted basis in the furniture of $6,250. The antiques subsequently were used as office furniture. The partners are concerned about tax issues due to transactions with a related party. (5038)

For items 1 through 3, determine the amount.

Partner	Amount
1. Determine Otto's initial basis in MOP.	
2. Determine Patricia's initial basis in MOP.	
3. Determine Melvin's basis in MOP at the end of Year 2.	

During Year 3, the MOP Partnership breaks even but decides to make distributions to each partner.

For items 4 through 8, determine whether the statement is true (T) or false (F).

Statement	Answer
4. A nonliquidating cash distribution may reduce the recipient partner's basis in her/his partnership interest below zero.	
5. A nonliquidating distribution of unappreciated inventory reduces the recipient partner's basis in her/his partnership interest.	
6. In a liquidating distribution of property other than money, where the partnership's basis of the distributed property exceeds the basis of the partner's interest, the partner's basis in the distributed property is limited to her/his predistribution basis in the partnership interest.	
7. Gain is recognized by the partner who receives a nonliquidating distribution of property, where the adjusted basis of the property exceeds her/his basis in the partnership interest before the distribution.	
8. In a nonliquidating distribution of inventory, where the partnership has no unrealized receivables or appreciated inventory, the basis of inventory that is distributed to a partner cannot exceed the inventory's adjusted basis to the partnership.	

Write a memo to the partnership explaining how Melvin's sale of furniture to the partnership is handled for tax purposes for both the partnership and Melvin.

Research Question: What code section and subsection, if applicable, provides guidance regarding the affect on the other partners' bases in their partnership interests when the partnership makes a nonliquidating distribution of encumbered property to a partner who assumes the mortgage.

Section & Subsection Answer: §_____ (___)

MULTIPLE CHOICE ANSWERS

The editors strongly recommend that candidates **not** spend much time on the answers to specific questions that they answered incorrectly on the diagnostic exam, particularly at the beginning of their review. Instead, study the related chapters.

Solution 1

Chapter 32: Accountant's Professional Responsibilities

1. (c) ET 203 provides that a CPA must use professional judgment in deciding when a deviation from GAAP is appropriate. Circumstances that may justify a departure include new legislation or the evolution of a new form of business.

2. (b) ET 301 prohibits the disclosure of confidential information obtained in the course of the professional engagement without the consent of the client, but does not prohibit review of a CPA's professional practices (including pertinent information) as a part of an AICPA authorized voluntary quality review program.

3. (c) The Statement on Standards for Tax Services No. 1, *Tax Return Positions,* contains the standards a member should follow in recommending tax return positions and in preparing or signing tax returns. In general, a member should have a good-faith belief that the tax return position being recommended has a realistic possibility of being sustained administratively or judicially on its merits, if challenged. A member may recommend a tax return position that the member concludes is not frivolous as long as the member advises the taxpayer to appropriately disclose. When recommending tax return positions and preparing or signing a return on which a tax return position is taken, a member should advise the taxpayer regarding potential penalty consequences of such tax return position and the opportunity, if any, to avoid such penalties through disclosure.

4. (b) Independence is considered impaired if fees for professional services rendered for more than one year prior are not collected before the issuance of the CPA's report for the current year. This includes billed and unbilled fees and notes receivable arising from such fees (ET 191-52).

5. (b) A CPA's independence would not be considered to be impaired by her/his maintaining a checking account that is fully insured by a government deposit insurance agency at an audit-client financial institution (ET 191-70). Independence is considered impaired if a CPA has a direct financial interest in a client, whether or not it is placed in a blind trust (ET 191-68). Independence generally is considered impaired if a lease meets the criteria of a capital lease as defined by GAAP and independence is not considered impaired if a lease meets the criteria of an operating lease as long as the terms and conditions are comparable with other leases of a similar nature and all amounts are paid in accordance with the terms of the lease (ET 191-91).

Chapter 33: Accountant's Legal Responsibilities

6. (c) Failure to fulfill the terms of a contract usually constitutes a breach of the contract and may subject the accountant to liability in the form of money damages. Specific performance is not granted for a personal services contract. Punitive damages are not allowed even if the breach is willful. A rescission involves undoing the contract on both sides and placing the parties in their original positions; such a resolution would be difficult following the breach of a professional services contract.

7. (b) The Sarbanes-Oxley Act requires firms that perform audits of public companies to register with the Public Company Accounting Oversight Board (PCAOB). Membership in the AICPA or its practice sections is not necessary to audit any company. The FASB sets accounting standards; it does not register firms, accountants, or auditors. Issuers of publicly traded securities, not auditors, register with the SEC pursuant to the 1934 Act.

8. (c) The accountant's ownership of working papers is of a custodial interest.

9. (c) A company registering under the 1934 Act must supply certain information. When reporting on financial statements submitted to a government agency, the auditor generally should note any exceptions to that agency's requirements in the audit report. Candidates with concerns regarding the placement of this question in the REG, rather than the AUD, exam section should contact the AICPA.

10. (c) Management must support its evaluation of internal control over financial reporting (ICOFR) with sufficient evidence, including documentation. If the auditor concludes that management has not fulfilled these responsibilities, the PCAOB requires the auditor to report, in writing, to

management and the audit committee that the audit of ICOFR cannot be completed and that the auditor must disclaim an opinion.

Chapter 34: Contracts

11. (b) Under the law of contracts, an offer that states it will be held open for a period of time may, without consideration, be revoked any time before its acceptance. In contrast, under the UCC, a signed written offer by a merchant to buy or sell goods in which the merchant gives assurance that the offer will be held open is irrevocable, even without consideration, for a period not exceeding three months. However, the UCC does not apply to this situation since a sale of realty is involved; the law of contracts applies instead. An option contract requires that the offeror receive consideration for his promise to keep his offer open.

12. (a) An accord and satisfaction is the settlement of a dispute or the satisfaction of a claim through the creation of a new contract between the parties to the original contract. In this case, a new contract was created. The consideration given by Castle to Nelson, who agreed to accept $1,000 less than the originally agreed upon amount, was Castle's offer to pay the note on April 1 instead of the originally contracted date of April 30. An unliquidated debt is one in which the specific amount of the debt has not been determined by the parties involved. In this question, an amount of $5,000 had been specified. Castle would win if Nelson sued.

Chapter 35: Sales

13. (b) Under the UCC Sales Article, if fraud in the inducement (i.e., in the formation of a contract) is present, the resulting contract is *voidable* at the option of the defrauded party, thereby, allowing that party to rescind the contract and sue for damages. The plaintiff may elect to rescind the contract, but in doing so must return any consideration received. Punitive damages normally are not allowed. There must have been reliance on the fraudulent statement.

Chapter 36: Negotiable Statements & Documents of Title

14. (b) For an instrument to be payable on demand or at a definite time, it must be possible to determine the last possible date that the holder of the instrument will be paid from the face of the instrument. The date of a person's marriage, a reasonable time for an extension, and one month after an undated note are not definite (objectively known) times.

15. (a) A negotiable warehouse receipt "duly negotiated" can give certain good-faith purchasers greater rights than those possessed by the transferor (similar to the rules of a holder in due course). In this question, the warehouse receipt was not duly negotiated since a proper endorsement is required for negotiation, and a forged document is not valid. Grove will prevail since Burke cannot validly negotiate the warehouse receipt. There is no rule that a warehouser must be notified before any valid negotiation of a warehouse receipt is effective. Burke's endorsement is invalid and does not convert the instrument to a bearer instrument.

Chapter 37: Secured Transactions

16. (c) Proceeds from the disposition of collateral must be applied in the following order.

1. Reasonable expenses incurred in retaking, holding, and selling the collateral.
2. Satisfaction of the debt owed the secured party.
3. Subordinate security interests in the property.
4. Any surplus goes back to the debtor.

Chapter 38: Debtor & Creditor Relationships

17. (b) In the administration of the bankrupt's estate, the trustee can assume or reject executory contracts and unexpired leases subject to the approval of the court or judge. A trustee may elect not to assume the equipment lease. The lease may be rejected even if it is for more than one year.

18. (a) A debtor's remaining in possession of property transferred, a debtor's retention of an equitable benefit in property conveyed, and the fact that a conveyance occurred in secret are all indicators of a fraudulent conveyance.

Chapter 39: Agency

19. (c) An agent owes a duty to her/his principal. The appointing agent is a like a "sub-principal" to a sub agent.

Chapter 40: Federal Securities Regulation

20. (b) The 1933 Act generally prohibits the use of fraud by any person who offers or sells a security in interstate commerce. This prohibition applies to all securities, whether or not those securities must be registered. The Act specifically prohibits (1) use of any device, scheme, or artifice to defraud; (2) obtaining money or property by means of an untrue

statement of material fact or by an omission of a material fact; and (3) engaging in any transaction or practice that would operate as a fraud or deceit on the purchaser. Material misrepresentation is gross negligence; gross negligence is fraud.

21. (a) Rule 504 only allows resale within the first two years under certain conditions. Rule 504 allows resale within the first two years only within certain restrictions. Rule 504 does not disallow the sale of securities to any class of investors. The Rule 504 exemption is available to the issuers of limited partnership interests. Rule 504 does not place restrictions on the class or number of investors to whom the securities may be sold.

Chapter 41: Other Regulations

22. (a) Under the Federal Insurance Contributions Act (FICA) an employer will be liable for penalties both for failure to supply taxpayer identification numbers and for failure to make timely FICA deposits.

23. (a) The Robinson-Patman Act prohibits price discrimination by prohibiting sellers from charging different prices to buyers for commodities of similar grade and quality. A plaintiff must either show that the defendant has engaged in predatory pricing with intent to harm competition or present a detailed market analysis that demonstrates how the defendant's price discrimination actually harmed competition. Permissible price differentials are justified by proof of either a cost savings to the seller or a good-faith price reduction to meet the lawful price of a competitor, but not the length of time of a business relationship. The existence of other inventory sources are immaterial.

Chapter 42: Property

24. (c) A coinsurance clause provides that if the insured fails to carry an amount of insurance equal to the stated percentage (80% in this case) of the value of the property insured, then the insured becomes a coinsurer and must proportionally bear the loss. The *total* amount of loss borne by the insurers is the lower of (1) the $40,000 face value of the policies, (2) the $100,000 fair market value of property at date of loss, or (3) the coinsurance amount of $20,000 [($40,000/$80,000) × $40,000]. Thus, the loss borne by the insurers is $20,000. Ace is responsible for 60% of the loss ($12,000) because it provided 60% of the total insurance ($24,000/ $40,000). Thrifty is responsible for 40% of the loss ($8,000) because it provided 40% of the total insurance ($16,000/$40,000).

Chapter 43: Federal Taxation: Property & Other Tax Topics

25. (d) When mortgaged property is purchased, its basis is the cash paid, or FMV of other property given, the amount of any mortgage assumed, plus any other costs connected with the purchase.

26. (b) Generally, life insurance proceeds (face value of the policy) paid by reason of death of the insured are excluded from gross income. When the life insurance policy subsequently is transferred in exchange for consideration, it is purchased asset. The sale or disposition of property generally results in the recognition of gain or loss. Thus, payments by reason of death of the insured are income to the assignee to the extent they exceed the consideration and premiums paid. In a taxable exchange, the gain or loss on the disposal of property generally is equal to the difference between the amount realized in the transaction and the adjusted basis of the property relinquished.

Insurance proceeds of transferred policy	$200,000
Less: Cost	(25,000)
Premiums paid	(40,000)
Included in gross income	$135,000

27. (c) The painting is considered a capital asset because it does not fall within one of the five categories that would exclude it from being a capital asset under §1221. The sale of the painting is taxable as it was sold for an amount that was greater than its basis. The painting is not §1231 property because it was not depreciable property used in the taxpayer's trade or business. Nor is the painting ordinary income property because it was not held primarily for sale to customers in the ordinary course of the business.

28. (c) In-laws are not related parties. Ancestors and lineal descendants are related parties.

29. (a) When investments in a small business investment company become worthless, §1244 allows for an ordinary rather than a capital loss deduction. Qualified small business stock must be acquired by the taxpayer at the original issuance in exchange for money, other property (not stock), or as compensation for services provided to the corporation. Thus, Jackson cannot take an ordinary deduction for the worthless stock, but would be entitled to a long-term capital loss of $25,000 (his basis in the stock at the time of the inheritance).

30. (c) A preparer generally may rely in good faith without verification upon information furnished

by a taxpayer. The preparer is not required to audit, examine, or review the taxpayer's records or operations. The preparer must make reasonable inquiries if the furnished information appears to be incorrect or incomplete.

31. (b) The same accounting method does not have to be used by both husband and wife. For example, if the husband regularly uses the accrual method, and the wife the cash basis, each one computes her/his own income according to the appropriate accounting method, and the amounts so determined are aggregated for the purposes of the joint return. In order to file a joint return, the taxable years of both spouses must begin and end on the same day. As indicated in §6013(g), one spouse may be a nonresident alien, but *both* must make the election which subjects their worldwide income to U.S. taxation. Only married couples may file joint returns, and marital status is determined as of the last day of the taxable year.

Chapter 44: Federal Taxation: Individuals

32. (b) Jim and Kay may each claim an exemption for themselves under §151(a) and §151(b). Dale passes all four tests (relationship, residence, age and support) and the two additional general tests (martial status and citizenship) under the uniform definition, allowing Jim and Kay to claim a dependency exemption for him. No exemption is allowed on Jim and Kay's joint return for Kim. Kim fails the gross income test of §151(d)(1)(B). Kim is neither a qualifying child (age test) nor a qualifying relative (gross income test). Neither is an exemption allowed for Grant because he fails the gross income test of §151(d)(1)(B). Thus, Jim and Kay may claim three exemptions on their joint return.

33. (c) Form 1040X is an amended income tax return for individuals. Form 1139 is a claim for tentative refund of a corporation's income taxes for, among other things, a carryback of net operating losses. Form 1045 is a tentative claim for refund for an individual's income taxes for, among other things, a carryback of net operating losses. Form 843 is a claim for refund that is used for other types of taxes.

34. (a) The general rule is that all income taxes must be assessed within three years after the later of the due date or the filing date of the original return. However, if income is understated by more than 25% of the amount stated on the return, then there is a 6-year statute of limitations period. The Burgs omitted $45,000 which is equal to 37.5% of the gross income stated on their return. Therefore, the statute of limitations expires on April 15, Year 7.

35. (d) Section 104 provides for the exclusion from gross income of certain types of compensation received for injury or sickness. The types of compensation which are excluded include amounts received under workers' compensation acts as compensation for personal injury or sickness, and the amount of any damages received on account of personal physical injuries or physical sickness. Furthermore, §105(b) generally states "gross income does not include... (amounts that are received by an employee through accident or health insurance plans that are attributable to employer contributions which were not includible in the gross income of the employee)...if such amounts are paid, directly or indirectly, to the taxpayer to reimburse the taxpayer for expenses incurred by him for...medical care..." and for which no deduction was taken under §213. Therefore, none of the amounts received by Harold are includible in his gross income.

36. (c) The deductibility of a vacation home's expenses depends on the allocation of personal and rental use of the property. Depreciation may be allowed, but losses are not.

37. (a) Alimony paid is deductible in arriving at AGI under §62(a)(10). The other items are deductible **from** AGI as itemized deductions.

38. (d) The use of bank credit cards is deemed to be payment for purposes of timing the deductibility of charitable and medical expenses. Therefore, the $4,000 Scott charged on his credit card for his dependent son's medical expenses can be claimed by Scott as a medical expense in the year charged. Scott can also claim the $2,800 of medical expenses Scott paid in Year 2 on his Year 2 tax return because medical expenses are deductible in the year paid and the medical expenses were for his spouse at the time the expenses were incurred.

39. (a) Section 469(c)(2) defines a passive activity to include *any* rental activity. However, a taxpayer is allowed to deduct a certain amount of a rental property's losses if he materially participates in the rental activity. Interest and dividends are *never* treated as passive activity income. Passive activity credits *are* subject to the same rules as passive activity losses (e.g., the credits have to be used against tax that is attributable to passive activity income). The passive activity rules apply to *everyone*. (Section 469(c)(2) provides an exception for qualified real estate professionals.)

40. (a) Generally, the fair market value of appreciated property donated to a qualified charity may be deducted if it doesn't exceed 30% of the donor's AGI. [$25,000 < (30% × $90,000)].

Chapter 45: Federal Taxations: Estates & Trusts

41. (b) Section 2503(b) provides for an exclusion from taxable gifts of $12,000 per donee in 2007. Section 2503(e)(2)(B) provides that all of the gift is excluded from taxable gifts if the gift was made on behalf of an individual to any person who provides medical care. Sayers is not entitled to exclude the entire gift because the amount was paid directly to Johnson and not to a person who provided Johnson with medical care. Sayers could exclude $24,000 if Sayers and Sayers' spouse consented under §2513 to have the gift treated as made one half by each. However, Sayers is single and therefore is entitled to only one annual exclusion under §2503(b).

42. (a) The standard deduction is not available to estates, trusts, corporations, or partnerships. Estates and trusts may have a personal exemption.

43. (a) Estates have the option of choosing a calendar year or a fiscal year based on the date of the decedent's death. Most trusts established after 1986 must use a calendar year.

44. (d) Under §2032, the alternative valuation date can be used only to value a decedent's estate if the election will decrease the value of the estate and if it will reduce any estate tax liability. The election can be used only if the election will decrease the value of the estate. The election once made is irrevocable and cannot be changed by filing an amended return. The election applies only to the gross estate and not to the net value of the estate (e.g., after liabilities and allowable deductions).

Chapter 46: Federal Taxation: Corporations

45. (c) Under §6072, the due date for a calendar year corporation's income tax return is March 15 following the close of the tax year. Under §7502, the return is deemed to have been filed when it is postmarked. Thus, Jackson's return is deemed to have been filed on March 10. Section 6501 states that for purposes of determining the statute of limitations, an early return is treated as if filed on its due date. Thus, for determining the statute of limitations on assessment, Jackson's return is deemed to have been filed on March 15. The statute of limitations begins to run the day after the due date, which is March 16.

46. (b) A corporation recognizes gain or loss on the distribution of property in complete liquidation as if such property had been sold to the distributee at fair market value. The type of gain which is recognized depends on the type of property sold. Krol recognizes $50,000 (e.g., $150,000 – $100,000) of capital gain since it is assumed that the securities were a capital asset in the hands of Krol.

47. (b) Section 243(a)(1) provides for a 70% dividend-received deduction for corporations that received dividends from taxable domestic corporations. This deduction is limited to 70% of taxable income determined without regard to the DRD and other specified deductions. In this case, the taxable income limitation of §246(b)(1) is greater than the tentative DRD: $70,000 × 70% = $49,000. Thus, the DRD is $7,000.

Taxable income before DRD	$70,000
Dividends received deduction ($10,000 × 70%)	(7,000)
Taxable Income [Sec. 63(a)]	$63,000
First tier ($50,000 × 15%)	$ 7,500
($63,000 – $50,000 = $13,000; $13,000 × 25%)	3,250
Income Tax [Sec. 11(b)]	$10,750

48. (a) The $6,000 in municipal bond interest income must be removed from book income to reconcile to taxable income, as it is not taxable income. The $1,500 of interest incurred to carry a tax-exempt investment is not an expense deductible for taxes and thus must be included in book income to reconcile to taxable income. The advertising expense is deductible for both tax and book purposes; no adjustment need be made for it.

49. (d) Prin must include the dividends in its gross income under §61(a)(7). However, under §243(a)(3) and §243(b) Prin is allowed a deduction for 100% of the dividends received from a corporation that is a member of the same affiliated group. The net result is that the dividends are not taxed on the consolidated return.

50. (a) An S corporation may only have one class of stock. Stock may have different voting rights and still be classified as one class of stock. An estate may be an S corporation shareholder. A grantor trust may be an S corporation shareholder.

51. (a) Section 6601(a) imposes interest as an addition to tax when the tax is not paid on or before the last date prescribed for payment. Section 6601(b)(1) states that the last date prescribed for payment is to be determined without regard to extensions of time for payment. Under §6651(a)(2), there is a penalty for failure to pay tax when due equal to 0.5% of the net tax due for each month or fraction thereof that the tax is not paid. This penalty in the aggregate may not exceed 25% of the net tax due. However, this provision states that the penalty will not apply if the taxpayer shows reasonable cause for not paying the tax on time. Reg. §301.6651-1(c)(4) provides that reasonable cause will be presumed if a

corporation files a timely request for extension to file its return, pays in at least 90% of the tax due by the due date without regard to the extension, and pays the balance due on or before the extended due date. Thus, Bass Corp. must pay interest on the $400 balance due. However, Bass Corp. demonstrated reasonable cause for late payment and thereby avoids the tax delinquency penalty of §6651(a)(2).

52. (c) Section 1566(a)(2) requires that the S corporation take into account the shareholder's *pro rata* share of non-separately computed income or loss. Section 1366(a)(1) requires that an S corporation take into account the shareholder's pro rata share of items of income, deduction, loss, or credit that could affect the liability for tax of any shareholder. The $5,000 of dividend income is stated separately because it is necessary to determine those dividends that qualify to be taxed at capital gain rates under §1(h)(11).

53. (d) Generally, a corporation that has been an S corporation since its inception would not have Earnings & Profits (E&P). Therefore, the distributions from the S corporation are tax-free to the extent of the shareholder's basis in the stock of the S corporation. Any excess distributions are treated as gain from the sale of stock.

54. (b) Section 27(a) allows a tax credit for foreign income taxes paid. The other answers are allowed as deductions, not credits.

Chapter 47: Federal Taxation: Partnerships

55. (d) Section 721(a) provides that no gain or loss is recognized by the partnership or by any partner on the contribution of property to the partnership in exchange for a partnership interest. The net debt relief is less than the adjusted basis of the property.

56. (c) Dean's basis in his partnership interest is increased by his distributive share of the partnership's ordinary income. His basis in the partnership interest is increased by his distributive share of the partnership's tax-exempt income. His basis in the partnership interest is reduced, but not below zero, by cash distributions.

57. (c) The $1,500 cash distribution received by Frazier is comprised of his portion of the partnership cash ($2,000 × 50%) and his portion of the gain from the sale of equipment ($3,000 – $2,000) × 50%. Gain is recognized to the extent that money distributed exceeds the partner's adjusted basis in the partnership interest.

Cash distribution	$ 1,500
Less: Basis in partnership	(1,200)
Gain recognized	$ 300

58. (d) The amount that a partner realizes on the sale of a partnership interest includes any cash received, plus any partnership liabilities that are assumed by the buyer. $30,000 cash plus $25,000 liability relief equals $55,000 amount realized. $55,000 amount realized less $40,000 basis equals $15,000 gain. Gains from the sale of partnership interests generally are characterized as capital gains, unless attributable to unrealized receivables or inventory items.

59. (c) Acme's initial basis in the partnership interest is Acme's adjusted basis in the cash plus Acme's portion of the debt assumed by the partnership. [$7,000 + (50% × $3,000) = $8.500]

60. (b) Section 708(b)(1) provides that a partnership is considered as terminated if within a 12-month period there is a sale or exchange of 50% or more of the total interest in partnership capital and profits. Poe sold a 30% interest on February 4, and Dean sold his 25% interest on December 20. Thus, on December 20, 55% of the interest in the partnership's capital and profits had been sold within a 12-month period.

PERFORMANCE BY TOPICS

Diagnostic exam questions corresponding to each chapter of the Regulation text are listed below. To assess your preparedness for the CPA exam, record the number and percentage of questions you correctly answered in each topic area. To simplify the self-evaluation, the simulations are excluded from the Performance By Topic. The point distribution of the multiple choice questions (not including the simulations) approximates that of the exam.

Chapter 32: Accountant's Professional Responsibilities

Question #	Correct √
1	
2	
3	
4	
5	
# Questions	5
# Correct	
% Correct	

Chapter 33: Accountant's Legal Responsibilities

Question #	Correct √
6	
7	
8	
9	
10	
# Questions	5
# Correct	
% Correct	

Chapter 34: Contracts

Question #	Correct √
11	
12	
# Questions	2
# Correct	
% Correct	

Chapter 35: Sales

Question #	Correct √
13	
# Questions	1
# Correct	
% Correct	

Chapter 36: Negotiable Instruments & Documents of Title

Question #	Correct √
14	
15	
# Questions	2
# Correct	
% Correct	

Chapter 37: Secured Transactions

Question #	Correct √
16	
# Questions	1
# Correct	
% Correct	

Chapter 38: Debtor & Creditor Relationships

Question #	Correct √
17	
18	
# Questions	2
# Correct	
% Correct	

Chapter 39: Agency

Question #	Correct √
19	
# Questions	1
# Correct	
% Correct	

Chapter 40: Federal Securities Regulation

Question #	Correct √
20	
21	
# Questions	2
# Correct	
% Correct	

Chapter 41: Other Regulations

Question #	Correct √
22	
23	
# Questions	2
# Correct	
% Correct	

Chapter 42: Property

Question #	Correct √
24	
# Questions	1
# Correct	
% Correct	

Chapter 43: Federal Taxation: Property & Other Tax Topics

Question #	Correct √
25	
26	
27	
28	
29	
30	
31	
# Questions	7
# Correct	
% Correct	

Chapter 44: Federal Taxation: Individuals

Question #	Correct √
32	
33	
34	
35	
36	
37	
38	
39	
40	
# Questions	9
# Correct	
% Correct	

Chapter 45: Federal Taxation: Estates & Trusts

Question #	Correct √
41	
42	
43	
44	
# Questions	4
# Correct	
% Correct	

Chapter 46: Federal Taxation: Corporations

Question #	Correct √
45	
46	
47	
48	
49	
50	
51	
52	
53	
54	
# Questions	10
# Correct	
% Correct	

Chapter 47: Federal Taxation: Partnerships

Question #	Correct √
55	
56	
57	
58	
59	
60	
# Questions	6
# Correct	
% Correct	

PERFORMANCE BY CONTENT SPECIFICATIONS

Diagnostic exam questions corresponding to the Regulation portion of the AICPA Content Specification Outline are listed below. To assess your preparedness for the CPA exam, record the number and percentage of questions you correctly answered in each topic area. To simplify the self-evaluation, the simulations are excluded from the Performance By Content Specifications. The point distribution of the multiple choice questions (not including the simulations) approximates that of the exam.

CSO I

Question #	Correct √
1	
2	
3	
4	
5	
6	
7	
8	
9	
10	
# Questions	10
# Correct	______
% Correct	______

CSO II

Question #	Correct √
11	
12	
13	
14	
15	
16	
17	
18	
19	
20	
21	
22	
23	
24	
# Questions	14
# Correct	______
% Correct	______

CSO III

Question #	Correct √
30	
31	
33	
34	
43	
45	
51	
# Questions	7
# Correct	______
% Correct	______

CSO IV

Question #	Correct √
25	
26	
27	
28	
29	
# Questions	5
# Correct	______
% Correct	______

CSO V

Question #	Correct √
32	
35	
36	
37	
38	
39	
40	
# Questions	7
# Correct	______
% Correct	______

CSO VI

Question #	Correct √
41	
42	
44	
46	
47	
48	
49	
50	
52	
53	
54	
55	
56	
57	
58	
59	
60	
# Questions	17
# Correct	______
% Correct	______

SIMULATION SOLUTIONS

Solution 2 Federal Taxation: Individuals

Income (2 points)

1. $600

The interest from a refund from an amended tax return and interest on a savings account are included in gross income under §61(a)(4). Interest on the municipal bonds is excluded from gross income under §103(a).

2. $0

Gifts are excluded from gross income as long as the gift is not from the taxpayer's employer.

3. $0

The life insurance proceeds are excluded from gross income because they were paid on account of the death of Mrs. Burg's insured father.

4. $250

The jury duty pay is included in gross income. Gross income includes all income unless specifically excluded. If jury duty pay is surrendered to the taxpayer's employer because the employer compensated the employee during the period of jury service, the taxpayer is entitled to deduct such amount from gross income in arriving at AGI under §62(a)(13).

5. $500

The gambling winnings are included in gross income under §61(a) and Reg. §1.61-14(a).

Deductions (2 points)

6. $300

The repair and maintenance of the motorized wheelchair qualify as a medical expense.

7. $1,200

The state income taxes paid by the Burgs are deductible on Schedule A. The self-employment tax, however, is not deductible on Schedule A. Half of the amount of self-employment tax paid is allowed as a deduction for arriving at adjusted gross income.

8. $60

A charitable deduction is allowed for the purchase of the theater tickets to the extent that the purchase price exceeds the fair market value of the tickets. Since the four tickets would cost a total of $100 if purchased at the box office, only the excess $60 is allowed as a charitable deduction.

9. $0

A casualty loss is a loss that is caused by a sudden, unexpected, or unusual event such as a fire, storm, or shipwreck. Although the Burgs may consider the broken vase to be a casualty, the repair costs are not deductible on their tax return.

10. $0

Moving expenses are deductible for AGI if the move is related to the commencement of work in a new location and the amount deducted is reasonable. To qualify for the moving deduction, the new work place must be at least 50 miles away from the taxpayer's old residence. The facts do not specify that the reason for the move was work related. In addition, the mileage requirement is not met.

Written Communication (5 points)

To: Myra and Alex **Burg**
From: A. Candidate
Re: Tax Treatments

1. **Legal fees** attributable to the **production** or **collection** of taxable **alimony** are deductible by the payee. Expenses of producing such income are considered miscellaneous itemized deductions **subject** to the **2%** of AGI limitation. Legal expenses related to divorce, separation or support decree are nondeductible personal expenses *except* for those attributable to the production or collection of alimony. This deduction is available only if you itemize your deductions, instead of using the **standard deduction.**

2. **Special assessment** taxes paid for local benefits, such as streets and sewer systems are ***not*** deductible, except to the extent the tax assessment is made for **maintenance** or repair purposes.

3. The **forfeited interest penalty** for premature withdrawal of time deposits is a deduction from gross income in arriving at **adjusted gross income** whether or not you itemize other deductions.

4. No deduction is allowed for **personal**, living, or family expenses, except as specifically provided for in the Internal Revenue Code. No provision exists to allow a deduction for insurance premiums to cover a taxpayer's residence against **casualty** loss.

5. The premiums paid by a **self-employed** person for **health insurance** are deductible in arriving at **adjusted gross income** whether or not you itemize other deductions.

Research (1 point)

Code Section Answer: §55(a)

Code §55(a) states, "There is hereby imposed (in addition to any other tax imposed by this subtitle) a tax equal to the excess (if any) of (1) the tentative minimum tax for the taxable year, over (2) the regular tax for the taxable year."

Solution 3 Federal Taxation: Partnerships

Basis (1.5 points)

1. $10,000

Otto's basis in the partnership interest includes the $15,000 adjusted basis of property contributed in exchange for such interest under §722. The $6,250 mortgage assumed by the partnership on the land contributed by Otto reduces Otto's basis in the partnership interest by $6,250 under §733. Otto's 20% share of the mortgage assumed by the partnership is a deemed contribution of money to the partnership by Otto.

Adjusted basis of property transferred	$15,000
Less: Debt assumed by partnership	(6,250)
Add: Share of partnership's debt ($6,250 × 20%)	1,250
Initial basis in MOP partnership interest	$10,000

2. $31,875

Patricia obtains a basis in the partnership interest equal to the $30,000 adjusted basis of the equipment contributed under §722. In addition, Patricia is deemed to have contributed money to the partnership equal to Patricia's share of the partnership's debts. Thus, Patricia is deemed to have contributed $1,875 ($6,250 × 30%) in money for which Patricia obtains additional basis. Therefore, Patricia's initial basis in the MOP partnership interest is $31,875 ($30,000 + $1,875).

3. $43,125

Melvin's initial basis in the partnership interest is his $50,000 initial cash investment plus his share of the debt assumed (50% × $6,250). A partner's basis is increased by the partner's share of income as well as reduced by the partner's share of losses and actual distributions to the partner. In the absence of an agreement to the contrary, losses are allocated on the same basis as profits: $53,125 – 0.50 × $20,000 = $43,125.

Distributions (2.5 points)

4. F

Section 733 states that a partner's basis in her/his partnership interest is to be reduced—but not below zero—by money distributed to the partner in a nonliquidating distribution.

5. T

Section 733 states that a partner's basis in her/his partnership interest is to be reduced—but not below zero—by a nonliquidating distribution of property other than money by the amount of the basis to such partner of distributed property, as determined under §732. Section 732(a)(1) provides that in the case of a nonliquidating distribution, the partner's basis in distributed property is the adjusted basis of the distributed property in the hands of the partnership. However, §732(a)(2) limits the partner's basis in the distributed property to the adjusted basis in the partnership interest.

6. T

Section 732(b) provides that in a liquidating distribution, the partner's basis in distributed property is equal to the adjusted basis in her/his partnership interest reduced by any money distributed in the same transaction.

7. F

Section 731(a)(1) provides that gain will not be recognized on a distribution to a partner, except to the extent that money distributed exceeds the adjusted basis of the partnership interest immediately before the distribution. If the adjusted basis of the property distributed exceeds the adjusted basis in the partnership interest, no gain is recognized, and the adjusted basis in the partnership interest becomes the partner's adjusted basis in the distributed property. The partner's adjusted basis in the partnership interest would then be reduced to zero.

8. T

The basis of inventory distributed to a partner in a nonliquidating distribution is the partnership's adjusted basis in the inventory, not to exceed the partner's adjusted basis in the partnership interest under §732(a). The partnership's adjusted basis in the inventory cannot exceed itself.

Communication (5 points)

October 10, Year 3

To: MOP Partnership
From: Jean Preparer
Re: Related-Party Transactions

Generally, a partner may engage in a transaction with his or her partnership and it will be deemed as occurring between two **independent entities.**

Exceptions include gains and losses from the sale of property between related parties, such as between a **controlling partner** and her partnership. For this purpose, a controlling partner is defined as a partner with a **more than 50%** ownership interest in his partnership. Such gains are **re-characterized** as **ordinary income.** Such losses are **not recognized.**

As Melvin held a 50% ownership interest at the time of the furniture transaction, he is not a controlling partner. Hence, the furniture transaction is not considered to be a related-party transaction. Accordingly, MOP Partnership recognizes this transaction as a **fixed asset** purchase and Melvin recognizes this transaction as a **capital gain.**

Research (1 point)

Code Section Answer: §752(b)

Code §752(b) states, "Any decrease in a partner's share of the liabilities of a partnership, or any decrease in a partner's individual liabilities by reason of the assumption by the partnership of such individual liabilities, shall be considered as a distribution of money to the partner by the partnership." [§733 "In the case of a distribution by a partnership to a partner other than in liquidation of a partner's interest, the adjusted basis to such partner of his interest in the partnership shall be reduced (but not below zero) by (1) the amount of any money distributed to such partner, and (2) the amount of the basis to such partner of distributed property other than money…."]

Time Management

Approximately 20 percent of the multiple choice questions in every section of every exam given after November 2003 are questions that are being pre-tested. These questions are **not** included in candidates' final grades; they are presented only so that the Board of Examiners may evaluate them for effectiveness and possible ambiguity.

The Scholastic Achievement Test and the Graduate Record Exam both employ similar but not identical strategies. Those tests include an extra section, which is being pre-tested, and test-takers do not know which section is the one that will not be graded. On the Uniform CPA Examination, however, the extra questions are mixed in among the graded questions.

This makes time management crucial. Candidates who are deciding how much time to spend on a difficult multiple choice question must keep in mind that there is a 20 percent chance that the answer to the question will not affect them either way. Also, candidates should not allow a question that seems particularly difficult or confusing to shake their confidence or affect their attitude towards the rest of the test; it may not even count.

This experimental 20 percent works against candidates who are not sure whether they have answered enough questions to earn 75 points. Candidates should try for a safety margin, so that they will have accumulated enough correct answers to pass, even though some of their correctly answered questions will not be scored.

See the **Practical Advice** appendix for more information regarding the exam.

CHAPTER 32

ACCOUNTANT'S PROFESSIONAL RESPONSIBILITIES

EXAM COVERAGE: The ethics and professional and legal responsibilities portion of the Regulation section of the CPA exam is designated by the examiners to be 15-20 percent of the section's point value. More information about point distribution and information eligible to be tested is included in the **Practical Advice** section of this volume.

CHAPTER 32

ACCOUNTANT'S PROFESSIONAL RESPONSIBILITIES

I. Governing Entities

A. Government Organizations

1. **State Boards of Accountancy** Certified public accountants (CPAs) are licensed to practice by individual state boards of accountancy. Requirements for license and the renewal of licenses, including continuing professional education, are regulated at the state level. The boards also have the power to suspend or revoke licenses or otherwise sanction CPAs. Note that the right to practice public accounting requires only a valid CPA license.

2. **Securities & Exchange Commission (SEC)** The SEC Rules of Practice include provisions governing the conduct of accountants and other professionals performing audits for public companies or otherwise practicing before the commission. (The term "public companies" commonly refers to issuers of publicly traded securities.)

   a. **General** Rule 102(e) authorizes the commission to censure, suspend, or bar from practice before the commission any professional it finds:

      (1) Lacking the requisite qualifications to represent others; or

      (2) Lacking in character or integrity or having engaged in unethical or improper professional conduct; or

      (3) Has willfully violated, or willfully aided and abetted the violation of, any provision of the federal securities laws or its rules and regulations.

   b. **Improper Professional Conduct** The SEC amended this rule to officially define "improper professional conduct" as either one of the following. This definition requires greater than simple negligence, but less than recklessness, to constitute improper professional conduct.

      (1) Intentional or knowing conduct, including reckless conduct, resulting in a violation of applicable professional standards.

      (2) Negligent conduct that either is a single instance of highly unreasonable conduct resulting in a violation of applicable professional standards in circumstances in which an accountant knows, or should know, that heightened scrutiny is warranted; or repeated instances of unreasonable conduct that each result in a violation of applicable professional standards that indicate a lack of competence to practice before the commission.

3. **Public Company Accounting Oversight Board (PCAOB)** The Sarbanes-Oxley Act (SOX) established the PCAOB and charged it with the responsibility of overseeing the audits of public companies. The Securities and Exchange Commission (SEC) has oversight and enforcement authority over the PCAOB.

   a. **Responsibilities** The PCAOB's duties include registering accounting firms that audit public companies; establishing auditing, quality control, ethics, independence and other standards relating to public company audits; conducting inspections, investigations and disciplinary proceedings of registered accounting firms; and enforcing compliance with SOX.

b. **Registration** Public accounting firms that perform or participate in the performance of audits of public companies, or their subsidiaries, must be registered with the PCAOB; registrations must be updated annually.

4. **Internal Revenue Service (IRS)** The IRS may bar an accountant from practicing before the IRS based upon incompetency or noncompliance with tax rules and regulations. IRS regulations also provide for assessing fines for various violations.

B. Professional Organizations

CPAs are not required to join a state CPA society or the AICPA.

1. **American Institute of Certified Public Accountants (AICPA)** Requirements for full membership in the AICPA include passing the uniform CPA exam and possession of a valid and unrevoked CPA certificate issued by a legal state authority. Additional requirements of CPAs engaged in the practice of public accounting include participation in an AICPA-approved practice-monitoring program, if applicable.

a. **Non-Compliance** AICPA membership may be terminated for failure to pay dues or other financial obligations to the AICPA within 5 months of becoming due or for failure to comply with practice-monitoring or continuing education requirements. Members whose licenses/certificates are on inactive status with their state boards of accountancy are exempt from the AICPA's continuing professional education requirements, as long as they are compliant with the regulations of their state boards.

b. **Criminal Acts** AICPA membership may be suspended or terminated without a hearing for a criminal conviction of the member for a crime punishable by imprisonment for more than one year, the willful failure to file a required personal income tax return, or the filing of, or the willful aiding in the preparation of, a false or fraudulent income tax return for a client.

c. **Suspension** AICPA membership is suspended automatically without a hearing if the member's CPA license, certificate, or permit to practice public accounting is suspended, revoked, withdrawn, or canceled as a disciplinary measure by any governmental authority. In the case of suspension of license, the automatic suspension of AICPA membership ceases once the period of license suspension has expired.

d. **Disciplinary Matters** The professional ethics executive committee investigates potential disciplinary matters involving members.

(1) **Informal Action** When the committee determines that a *prima facie* violation of the Code of Professional Conduct or bylaws is not of sufficient gravity to bring formal action, the committee may direct the member in violation to complete specific continuing professional education or take other remedial or corrective action as appropriate. In such case, no notice is included in the AICPA's membership periodical. The offending member may reject such direction, in which case the committee then must determine whether to take the case to the trial board for a hearing.

(2) **Settlement** The executive committee may offer a violating member a settlement agreement to avoid further investigation and possible hearing before the trial board. Terms of the settlement agreement may include resignation from membership, completion of continuing professional education courses, submission to preissuance independent review of financial reports, submission to accelerated quality or peer review, or termination or suspension of membership with publication in the membership periodical.

(3) **Joint Trial Board** The committee is empowered to arrange for cases to be presented before the Joint Trial Board. The trial board consists of at least

36 members elected for no more than 2 successive 3-year terms. Panels of not less than 5 members are appointed by the trial board chairman to hear and adjudicate charges against members. Decisions of any hearing panel are subject to review only by the trial board.

(4) **Formal Action** The Joint Trial Board hears cases of infringements of the bylaws or rules of the Code of Professional Conduct; conviction of fraud; court declaration of insanity or incompetence; suspension, revocation, withdrawal, or cancellation of license as a disciplinary measure by a governmental authority; and failure to cooperate with a disciplinary investigation by the professional ethics division. The trial board may expel a member, suspend the member for not more than 2 years, or may impose lesser sanctions. Notices of disciplinary action are published in the AICPA membership periodical.

(5) **Peer Review** The Joint Trial Board also may act on petitions for review of peer review decisions terminating a firm's participation in the practice-monitoring program. The trial board may affirm, modify, or reverse all or any part of a peer review board decision, however it may not increase the severity of a peer review board's sanction.

2. **State CPA Societies** Membership in a state CPA society is governed by each individual society, including suspension or termination of membership. The AICPA trial board may hear and rule on alleged violations of a state CPA society's bylaws or code of professional conduct as long as a valid written agreement for this procedure exists between the AICPA and the state society.

II. AICPA Code of Professional Conduct

A. Background

The AICPA recognizes that a distinguishing mark of a profession is its acceptance of a high degree of responsibility to the public. The Code of Professional Conduct requires an unswerving commitment to honorable behavior even if it means sacrificing personal advantages.

1. **AICPA Membership** Membership in the American Institute of Certified Public Accountants (AICPA) is voluntary, and assumes an obligation of self-discipline above and beyond the requirements of laws and regulations. Reference to "member" in this chapter means a member or international associate of the AICPA.

2. **Uniform Accountancy Act** The AICPA and NASBA (National Association of State Boards of Accountancy) have a history of working together to enhance the regulation of the accounting profession to benefit the public and to promote uniformity of regulation among the U.S. jurisdictions. In 1992, the AICPA/NASBA Uniform Accountancy Act (UAA) became effective and subsequently was revised. Uniform Accountancy Rules were added to assist states in implementing the UAA's provisions.

3. **Compliance With All Applicable Regulations & Standards** The AICPA Professional Standards are summarized in this chapter. Regulations, however, vary from state to state and often differ from the AICPA Professional Standards. CPAs, as members of the AICPA, are required to comply with the AICPA Professional Standards, and also must comply with the regulations effective in the states in which they practice.

B. Principles of Conduct

Six articles compose the Principles of Conduct section of the AICPA Code of Professional Conduct. They stress the CPA's responsibility to the public, to clients, and to colleagues. Their purpose is to provide a level of conduct toward which CPAs should strive, and to provide a basis for the Rules of Conduct.

1. **Code Components**

    a. **Rules of Conduct** The rules of conduct govern the performance of professional services by members, within the framework provided by the Principles of Conduct.

    b. **Interpretations of Rules of Conduct** The Interpretations provide guidelines as to the scope and application of the Rules of Conduct. A CPA who departs from these guidelines shall have the burden of justifying such departures in any disciplinary hearing.

    c. **Ethics Rulings** The Ethics Rulings are formal rulings that summarize the application of the Rules of Conduct and Interpretations to particular circumstances. A CPA who departs from these rulings in similar circumstances may be requested to justify such departure. Note: Although there are numerous ethics rulings, only the more heavily tested ones are summarized in the Exhibits included in this chapter. Rather than memorizing a long list of situations, many quite complex, in which rulings have established precedents, knowing the more heavily tested situations and using judgment in the case of any other questions, has proven to be the most effective approach considering the amount of material to cover in preparation for the exam.

2. **Responsibilities (Article I)** In carrying out their responsibilities as professionals, members should exercise sensitive professional and moral judgments in all their activities. Members have responsibilities to all who use their professional services. Members also have a responsibility to cooperate with each other to continually improve the art of accounting, maintain the public's confidence, and carry out the responsibilities of self-governance.

3. **Public Interest (Article II)** Members should accept the obligation to act in a way that will **serve the public interest,** honor the public trust, and demonstrate a commitment to professionalism. A distinguishing mark of a profession is acceptance of its **responsibility to the public.** Members have a duty to discharge their responsibilities with integrity, objectivity, due professional care, and a genuine interest in serving the public. The public relies on the integrity and objectivity of certified public accountants to maintain the orderly functioning of commerce.

4. **Integrity (Article III)** To maintain and broaden public confidence, members should perform all professional responsibilities with the highest sense of integrity. Integrity requires a member to be honest and candid within the constraints of client confidentiality. Integrity also requires a member to observe the principles of objectivity and independence and of due care. **Service and the public trust** should not be subordinated to personal gain and advantage.

5. **Objectivity & Independence (Article IV)** Independence is required for audit and attest services only. Objectivity always is required.

    a. **Maintain Objectivity & Independence** A member should maintain objectivity and be free of conflicts of interest in discharging professional responsibilities.

    b. **Independence in Fact & Appearance** A member in public practice should be independent in fact and appearance when providing auditing and other attestation services. It is of utmost importance to the profession that the general public maintain confidence in the auditor's independence. Public confidence would be impaired by evidence that independence was actually impaired and it might also be impaired by the existence of circumstances that reasonable people might believe likely to influence independence.

    c. **Objectivity** Members in public practice providing services other than auditing and attestation, and members not in public practice have the responsibility to maintain objectivity in rendering professional services.

6. **Due Care (Article V)** A member should observe the profession's technical and ethical standards, strive continually to improve competence and the quality of services, and discharge professional responsibility to the best of the member's ability.

a. **Quest for Excellence** The essence of due care is the quest for excellence. Members are required to carry out their professional responsibilities with competence and diligence, with concern for the best interest of those for whom the services are performed and the public. Services should be rendered promptly, carefully, thoroughly, and in accordance with applicable technical and ethical standards.

b. **Competence** The maintenance of competence requires a commitment to learning and professional improvement throughout a member's professional life.

c. **Plan & Supervise** A member is required to plan and supervise adequately all professional activities for which the member has responsibility.

7. **Scope & Nature of Services (Article VI)** A member in public practice should observe the Principles of the Code of Professional Conduct in determining the scope and nature of services to be provided. Members of the AICPA should practice in **firms** that maintain adequate internal quality control procedures, determine whether the scope and nature of other services provided to an audit client would create a conflict of interest, and assess whether an activity is consistent with their role as professionals.

C. **Independence (Rule 101)**
A member in public practice shall be independent in the performance of professional services. In the performance of professional services requiring independence, a member should consult the rules of the appropriate state board of accountancy; state CPA society; the Public Company Accounting Oversight Board (PCAOB) and the U.S. Securities and Exchange Commission (SEC), if the member's report will be filed with the SEC; the U.S. Department of Labor (DOL), if the report will be filed with the DOL; the Government Accountability Office (GAO), if law, regulation, agreement, policy, or contract requires the member's report to be filed under GAO regulations; and any organization that issues or enforces standards of independence applicable to the engagement. Such organizations may have independence requirements or rulings that differ from (and may be more restrictive than) those of the AICPA.

Exhibit 1 ▸ Ethics Rulings on Independence Not Impaired

Independence is **not** considered to be impaired in these following situations:
- A member provides extensive advisory services to a client. (ET 191-8)
- A member holds a membership in a social club, providing the membership is essentially a social matter and the member does not take part in its management. (ET 191-17)
- A member has a checking or savings account, or a certificate of deposit or money market accounts at a client financial institution, providing the accounts are fully insured by the appropriate state or federal government deposit insurance agencies, or the amount uninsured is immaterial to the member or the member's firm. (ET 191-70)
- A member leases property to or from a client and the lease qualifies as an operating lease under GAAP, providing the lease is comparable to other similar leases and all the terms of the lease are currently met. (ET 191-91)

1. **Independence Impaired (Interpretation 101-1)** Certain transactions, interests, or relationships are considered to impair independence.

a. **Transactions & Interest** During the period of the professional engagement, or at the time of expressing an opinion, the following are considered to impair independence.

(1) **Financial Interest** Direct or material indirect financial interest in the client. A direct financial interest will impair independence even if it is immaterial. This applies also to a situation where the member or the member's firm is trustee, executor, or administrator of any estate that had acquired or was committed to acquire any direct or material indirect financial interest in the client and

(a) Member (individually or with others) had investment decision authority for the trust or estate or

(b) Trust or estate owned or was committed to acquire more than 10 percent of the client's outstanding equity securities or other ownership interests or

(c) Trust's or estate's holdings value in the client exceeded 10 percent of the total assets of the trust or estate.

(2) **Business Investment** Business investment with the client, any of its officers, directors, or principal stockholders that is material in relation to the member's net worth or to the net worth of the member's firm.

(3) **Loans** Loan to or from the client or any officer, director, or principal stockholder of the client except in the case of certain grandfathered loans and certain other permitted loans.

Exhibit 2 ▸ Ethics Rulings on Impaired Independence

Independence is considered to be impaired in the following situations:

- An employee or partner of a member firm accepts more than a token gift from a client, even with the knowledge of the firm. (ET 191-1)
- Fees for professional services rendered for more than one year prior are not collected before the issuance of the CPA's report for the current year. This includes billed and unbilled fees and notes receivable arising from such fees. (ET 191-52)
- A member should ensure that any blind trust for which s/he is a beneficiary of does not hold a direct or material indirect financial interest in any of the member's clients. (ET 191-68)
- A member leases property to or from a client and the lease qualifies as a capital lease under GAAP that would be considered a loan. (ET 191-91)
- Investments in a client through a financial services product such as an insurance contract or other investment arrangement, as follows: (ET 191-109)
    - If the member has the ability to direct the investment to a client and does so, the investment is considered a direct financial interest.
    - If the member has the ability to direct the investments but does not exercise this ability and the financial services product directs the investment to the member's client, the investment is still considered a direct financial interest.
    - If the member does not have the ability to direct the investments, an investment in a client through the financial services product is considered an indirect financial interest and, if material, impairs independence. If the member has significant influence over a mutual fund, independence would be considered to be impaired. (ET 191-35)
    - If a member invests in a financial services product that invests only in clients of the member, the investment is considered a direct financial interest.
- A member is an officer, director, or principal shareholder of an entity that has a loan to or from the member's client and the member has control over the entity, unless the loan is a permitted loan under Interpretation 101-5. (ET 191-110)

b. **Relationship** During the period covered by the financial statements, in addition to the time periods covered (see a., above), the following also are considered to impair independence.

(1) **Management** Director, officer, or employee, or in any capacity equivalent to that of a member of management.

(2) **Client** A relationship with the client as a promoter, underwriter, voting trustee.

(3) **Trustee** Trustee for any pension or profit-sharing trust of the client.

c. **Application of Independence Rules** A key position is a position in which an individual has: primary responsibility for significant accounting functions that support material components of the financial statements; primary responsibility for the preparation of the financial statements; or the ability to exercise influence over the contents of the financial statements, including when the individual is a member of the board of directors or similar governing body, chief executive officer, president, chief financial officer, chief operating officer, general counsel, chief accounting officer, controller, director of internal audit, director of financial reporting, treasurer, or any equivalent position. For purposes of attest engagements not involving a client's financial statements, a key position is one in which an individual is primarily responsible for, or able to influence, the subject matter of the attest engagement.

(1) **Members Formerly Employed by, or Otherwise Associated With, Client** An individual who formerly was employed by a client or associated with a client as an officer, director, promoter, underwriter, voting trustee, or trustee for a pension or profit-sharing trust of the client would impair the firm's independence if the individual:

(a) Participated on the attest engagement team or was an individual in a position to influence the attest engagement for the client when the attest engagement covers any period that includes the former employment or association with that client; or

(b) Was otherwise a member with respect to the client, unless the individual first dissociates from the client by: (1) terminating any relationships with the client; (2) disposing of any direct or material indirect financial interest in the client; (3) collecting or repaying any loans to or from the client, except for loans specifically permitted or grandfathered; (4) ceasing to participate in all employee benefit plans sponsored by the client, unless the client is legally required to allow the individual to participate in the plan (for example, COBRA) and the individual pays 100% of the cost of the participation on a current basis; and (5) liquidating or transferring all vested benefits in the client's defined benefit plans, defined contribution plans, deferred compensation plans, and other similar arrangements at the earliest date permitted under the plan. (However, liquidation or transfer is not required if a penalty significant to the benefits is imposed upon liquidation or transfer.)

(2) **Member's Immediate Family** A member's immediate family (spouse, spousal equivalent, or dependent) is subject to Rule 101, Independence (and its interpretations and rulings), but with some exceptions. The exceptions are that independence would not be considered impaired solely as a result of the following.

(a) An individual in a member's immediate family was employed by the client in a position other than a key position.

(b) In connection with her/his employment, an individual in the immediate family of one of the following members participated in a retirement, savings, compensation, or similar plan that is a client, is sponsored by a client, or that invests in a client (provided such plan normally is offered to all employees in similar positions): (1) a partner or manager who provides ten or more hours of nonattest services to the client; or (2) any partner in the office in which the lead attest engagement partner primarily practices in connection with the attest engagement.

(3) **Close Relatives** Independence would be considered impaired with respect to close relatives (parent, sibling, or nondependent child) if:

(a) An individual participating on the attest engagement team has a close relative who had a key position with the client, or a financial interest in the client that was material to the close relative and of which the individual has knowledge or enabled the close relative to exercise significant influence over the client.

(b) An individual in a position to influence the attest engagement or any partner in the office in which the lead attest engagement partner primarily practices in connection with the attest engagement has a close relative who had a key position with the client, or a financial interest in the client that was material to the close relative and of which the individual or partner has knowledge and enabled the close relative to exercise significant influence over the client.

2. **Employment or Association With Attest Clients (Interpretation 101-2)** If a partner or professional employee leaves the firm and subsequently is employed by or associated with that client in a key position, then the firm's independence would be impaired, unless these conditions are met.

a. **Payments for Prior Services** Payment of amounts owed to a former partner or professional employee for a prior interest in the firm or for unfunded, vested retirement benefits. The amounts may not be material to the firm and the formula used to calculate the payments should be fixed during the payout period.

b. **No Influence in Firm's Operations** The former partner and professional employee are not in a position to influence the accounting firm's operations or financial policies.

c. **No Participation With Former Firm** The former partner and professional employee may not participate or appear to participate, and is not associated with the firm. An appearance of participation includes: individual provides consultation to the firm; firm provides the individual with an office and related amenities (for example, secretarial and telephone services); individual's name is included in the firm's office directory or as a member of the firm in other membership lists of business, professional, or civic organizations unless the individual clearly is designated as retired.

d. **Engagement Procedure Modification** The ongoing attest engagement team considers the appropriateness or necessity of engagement procedures modification to adjust for the risk that audit effectiveness could be reduced as a result of the former partner or professional employee's prior knowledge of the audit plan. Procedures adopted will depend on several factors, including whether the former partner or professional employee was a member of the engagement team, the positions held at the firm and accepted with the client, the time that lapsed since the professional left the firm, and circumstances of the departure. When the former professional will have significant interaction with the attest engagement team, the firm should perform the following.

(1) Assessment of existing attestation engagement team members to determine their effectiveness in dealing with the former partner or professional employee.

(2) Review of subsequent attestation engagement to determine whether the engagement team members maintained the appropriate level of skepticism when evaluating the representations and work of the former partner or professional employee, when the person joins the client in a key position within one year of disassociating from the firm.

e. **Considering Employment or Association With Client** When a covered member becomes aware that a member of the attest engagement team or an individual in a position to influence the attest engagement is considering employment or association with a client, the covered member should notify an appropriate person in the firm.

(1) Independence will be impaired for an attest engagement team member or an individual in a position to influence the attest engagement who seeks, discusses, or is in receipt of potential employment or association with an attest client, unless the person promptly reports such consideration or offer to an appropriate person in the firm and removes her/himself from the engagement until the employment offer is rejected or employment is no longer being sought.

(2) A member should notify an appropriate person in the firm when that member becomes aware of a member of or an individual in a position to influence the attest engagement team whom is considering employment or association with a client.

3. **Performance of Nonattest Services (Interpretation 101-3)** A member in public practice or the member's firm who performs attest services for a client (which requires independence) also may perform other nonattest services for the same client. The member must evaluate the effect of such services on the member's independence, including compliance with independence regulations of authoritative regulatory bodies.

a. **General Requirements**

(1) **Management Functions** A member may provide advice, research materials, and recommendations to assist the client's management in performing its functions and making decisions.

(2) **Understanding of Client's Responsibility** An understanding with the client, preferably documented in an engagement letter, should be established regarding the objectives of the engagement and the client's responsibility to:

(a) Make all management decisions and perform all management functions;

(b) Designate an individual who possesses suitable skill, knowledge, and/or experience, preferably within senior management, to oversee the services;

(c) Evaluate the adequacy and results of the services performed;

(d) Accept responsibility for the result of the services; and

(e) Establish and maintain internal controls that include monitoring ongoing activities.

(3) **Prior to Nonattest Services** Before performing nonattest services, the member should establish and document in writing the understanding with the client (board of directors, audit committee, or management, or appropriate in the circumstances) concerning the: objectives of the engagement; services to be performed; client's acceptance of responsibilities; member's responsibilities; and any engagement limitations. The documentation requirement does not apply to nonattest services performed prior to the client becoming an attest client.

(4) **Routine Responsibilities** The understanding of client's responsibilities and prior to nonattest services requirements do not apply to certain routine activities performed by the member such as providing advice and responding to the client's questions as part of the normal client-member relationship.

b. **General Activities** Activities that would impair a member's independence include the following.

(1) Having or exercising authority on behalf of the client to authorize, execute or consummate a transaction.

(2) Preparing source documents in electronic form evidencing the occurrence of a transaction.

(3) Having custody of client assets.

(4) Supervising client employees in the performance of their normal recurring activities.

(5) Determining which recommendations of the member should be implemented.

(6) Reporting to the board of directors on behalf of management.

(7) Serving as a client's stock transfer or escrow agent, registrar, general counsel or its equivalent.

c. **Bookkeeping**

(1) Independence would be impaired if the CPA did any of the following.

(a) Determined or changed journal entries, account codings or classification for transactions or other client records without obtaining client approval.

(b) Authorized or approved transactions.

(c) Prepared source documents.

(d) Made changes to source documents without client approval.

(2) Independence would **not** be impaired if the CPA did the following.

(a) Posted client-approved entries to a client's trial balance.

(b) Prepared financial statements based on information in the trial balance.

(c) Proposed standards, adjusting, or correcting journal entries or other changes affecting the financial statements to the client, provided the client reviews the entries and the member is satisfied that management understands the nature of the proposed entries and the impact the entries have on the financial statements.

(d) Recorded transactions for which management determined or approved the appropriate account classifications, or posted coded transactions to a client's general ledger.

d. **Payroll & Other Disbursement**

(1) Independence would be impaired if the CPA did any of the following.

(a) Accepted responsibility to authorize payment of client funds.

(b) Accepted responsibility to sign or cosign client checks, even only in emergency situations.

(c) Maintained a client's bank account or had custody of a client's funds or made credit or banking decisions for the client.

(d) Signed payroll tax returns on behalf of client management.

(e) Approved vendor invoices for payment.

(2) Independence would **not** be impaired if the CPA did the following.

(a) Generated unsigned checks or processed client's payroll using payroll time records provided and approved by the client.

(b) Transmitted client-approved payroll or other disbursement information to a financial institution, as long as the CPA was authorized to do so by the client and the client had appropriately authorized the financial institution to process that information.

(c) Made electronic payroll tax payments in accordance with U.S. Treasury Department or comparable guidelines as long as the client made arrangements for its financial institution to limit such payments to a named payee.

e. **Benefit Plan Administration** (Note: Department of Labor regulations, which may be more restrictive, must be followed when auditing plans subject to ERISA, the Employee Retirement Income Security Act.)

(1) Independence would be impaired if the CPA did any of the following: made policy decisions on behalf of client management, interpreted plan documents on behalf of management to plan participants without first obtaining management's concurrence, made disbursements on behalf of the plan, had custody of assets of a plan, or served as a fiduciary to a plan as defined by ERISA.

(2) Independence would **not** be impaired if the CPA did the following.

(a) Communicated summary plan data to the plan trustee.

(b) Advised client management regarding the application or impact of provisions of the plan document.

(c) Processed transactions initiated by plan participants through the member's electronic medium, such as an interactive voice response system or Internet connection or other media.

(d) Prepared account valuations for plan participants using data collected through the member's electronic or other media.

(e) Prepared and transmitted participant statements to plan participants based on data collected through the member's electronic or other media.

f. **Investment—Advisory or Management**

(1) Independence would be impaired if the CPA did any of the following: made investment decisions on behalf of client management or otherwise had discretionary authority over a client's investments; executed a transaction to buy or sell a client's investments; or had custody of client assets, such as taking temporary possession of securities purchased by a client.

(2) Independence would **not** be impaired if the CPA did the following.

(a) Recommended the allocation of funds that a client should invest in various asset classes, depending upon the client's desired rate of return, risk tolerance, etc.

(b) Performed recordkeeping and reporting of a client's portfolio balances including providing a comparative analysis of the client's investments to third-party benchmarks.

(c) Reviewed the manner in which a client's portfolio is being managed by investment account managers, including determining whether the managers are following the client's investment policy statement guidelines, are meeting the client's investment objectives and are conforming to the client's stated investment styles.

(d) Transmitted a client's investment selection to a broker-dealer or equivalent provided the client had authorized the broker-dealer or equivalent to execute the transaction.

g. Corporate Finance—Consulting or Advisory

(1) Independence would be impaired if the CPA did any of the following: committed the client to the terms of a transaction or consummated a transaction on behalf of the client; acted as a promoter, underwriter, broker, dealer, or guarantor of client securities, or distributor of private placement memoranda or offering documents; or maintained custody of client securities.

(2) Independence would **not** be impaired if the CPA did the following.

(a) Assisted in developing corporate strategies.

(b) Assisted in identifying or introducing the client to possible sources of capital that meet the client's specifications or criteria.

(c) Assisted in analyzing the effects of proposed transactions including providing advice to a client during negotiations with potential buyers, sellers, or capital sources.

(d) Assisted in drafting an offering document or memorandum.

(e) Participated in transaction negotiations in an advisory capacity.

(f) Was named as a financial adviser in a client's private placement memoranda or offering documents.

h. Executive or Employee Search

(1) Independence would be impaired if the CPA either: committed the client to employee compensation or benefit arrangements or hired or terminated client employees.

(2) Independence would **not** be impaired if the CPA did the following: recommended a position description or candidate specifications, solicited and performed screening of candidates, and recommended qualified candidates to a client based on the client-approved criteria, or participated in employee hiring or compensation discussions in an advisory capacity.

i. Business Risk Consulting

(1) Independence would be impaired if the CPA either made or approved business risk decisions or presented business risk considerations to the board or others on behalf of management.

(2) Independence would **not** be impaired if the CPA either provided assistance in assessing the client's business risks and control processes or recommended a plan for making improvements to a client's control processes and assisted in implementing these improvements.

j. **Information Systems—Design, Installation or Integration**

(1) Independence would be impaired if the CPA did any of the following: designed or developed a client's financial information system, made other than insignificant modifications to source code underlying a client's existing financial information system, supervised client personnel in the daily operation of a client's information system, or operated a client's local area network (LAN) system.

(2) Independence would **not** be impaired if the CPA did the following.

(a) Installed or integrated a client's financial information system that was not designed or developed by the member (e.g., an off-the-shelf accounting package).

(b) Assisted in setting up the client's chart of accounts and financial statement format with respect to the client's financial information statement.

(c) Designed, developed, installed, or integrated a client's information system that is unrelated to the client's financial statements or accounting records.

(d) Provided training and instruction to client employees on an information and control system.

k. **Appraisal, Valuation, or Actuarial Service**

(1) Independence would be impaired if the CPA performed services, individually or in the aggregate, that:

(a) Would be material to an attest client's financial statements.

(b) Involve a significant degree of subjectivity (for example, employee stock ownership plans, business combinations, or appraisals of assets or liabilities).

(2) Independence would **not** be impaired if the CPA either performed valuation of a client's pension or postemployment benefit liabilities or performed services for nonfinancial statement purposes.

l. **Internal Audit Assistance Services**

(1) Independence would be impaired if the CPA did any of the following.

(a) Performed ongoing monitoring or control activities that affect the execution of transactions or ensure that transactions are properly executed, accounted for, or both, and performed routine activities in connection with the client's operating or production processes that are equivalent to those of an ongoing compliance or quality control function.

(b) Determined which, if any, recommendations for improving the internal control system should be implemented.

(c) Reported to the board of directors or audit committee on behalf of management or the individual responsible for the internal audit function.

(d) Approved or responsible for the overall internal audit work plan, including the determination of the internal audit risk and scope, project priorities, and frequency of performance of audit procedures.

(e) Connected with the client as an employee or in any capacity equivalent to a member of client management.

(2) Independence would **not** be impaired if the CPA did the following.

(a) Performed services involving an extension of the procedures that are generally of the type considered to be extensions of the member's audit scope applied in the audit of the client's financial statements (for example, confirming of accounts receivable and analyzing fluctuations in account balances).

(b) Performed engagements under the attestation standards.

(3) The member should be satisfied that the client's board of directors, audit committee, or other governing body is informed about the member's and management's respective roles and responsibilities in connection with the engagement. The member also should ensure that client management:

(a) Designates a competent individual or individuals, preferably within senior management, to be responsible for the internal audit function;

(b) Determines the scope, risk, and frequency of internal audit activities, including those to be performed by the member providing internal audit assistance services;

(c) Evaluates the findings and results arising from the internal audit activities, including those performed by the member providing internal audit assistance services; and

(d) Evaluates the adequacy of the audit procedures performed and the findings resulting from the performance of those procedures by, among other things, obtaining reports from the member.

4. **Honorary Directorships & Trusteeships of NPOs (Interpretation 101-4)** A not-for-profit organization that limits its activities to performing charitable, religious, civic, or similar functions may seek to gain the prestige of a member's name by asking the member to serve on its board of directors or trustees. The member may do so and be associated with the organization's financial statements as long as the position is purely honorary, all letterheads and material circulated to outside parties that identify the member as a director or trustee clearly indicate that the position is honorary, and the member does not vote or in any other way participate in management functions.

5. **Permitted Loans From Financial Institution Clients (Interpretation 101-5)** Generally, independence is considered to be impaired if, after May 2002, a member obtains a loan from an entity that is a client requiring independence at the time of obtaining the loan.

a. **Grandfathered Loans** Certain loans are grandfathered in the interpretations and are not considered to impair independence. The grandfathered loans must have been obtained from a financial institution under its normal lending procedures, terms, and requirements, and be current as to all terms. The types of grandfathered loans include home mortgages, other fully collateralized, secured loans and unsecured loans that are immaterial to the member's net worth. Grandfathered loans include loans that were obtained: (1) from a financial institution prior to its becoming a client requiring independence, (2) from a financial institution client not requiring independence, or (3) after May 2002, from a financial institute client requiring independence by a borrower prior to becoming a member in respect to the client.

b. **Other Permitted Loans** Only the following personal loans are permitted from a financial institution client for which independence is required. These loans and leases must be obtained under normal lending procedures, terms, and requirements, and must be kept current as to all terms, at all times.

(1) Car loans and leases collateralized by the vehicles.

(2) Loans fully collateralized by the cash surrender value of an insurance policy.

(3) Loans fully collateralized by cash deposits at the same financial institute.

(4) Aggregate outstanding balances from credit cards and overdraft reserve accounts that are reduced to $10,000 or less on a current basis, taking into consideration the payment due date and any grace period.

6. **Actual or Threatened Litigation (Interpretation 101-6)** When the auditor concludes that independence is impaired, the auditor should either resign from the engagement or cease any audit work then in progress until the issues can be resolved between the parties, or disclaim an opinion because of a lack of independence. Independence is no longer impaired when a resolution is reached and the matters at issue no longer have any effect on the relationship between the auditor and the client.

a. **Client & Member** Threatened or actual litigation may create an adverse relationship between the client and the CPA. This situation may affect management's willingness to disclose data to the CPA, as well as the CPA's objectivity in regard to the client. Since this is a complex area, it is impossible to pinpoint where independence becomes impaired. However, the Interpretation offers the following guidelines.

(1) Independence would be impaired when:

(a) Current management begins litigation alleging deficiencies in the audit work the CPA performed for the client.

(b) The auditor begins litigation against current management alleging management fraud or deceit.

(c) Current management has expressed the intention to begin litigation against the auditor alleging deficiencies in the audit work the CPA performed for the client as long as the CPA feels that it is probable that the claim will be filed.

(2) Independence usually will not be impaired in the case of threatened or actual litigation that is not related to the audit performed for the client for an amount that is not material to the CPA's firm or to the financial statements of the client. Examples include disputes over billings for services or results of tax or consulting advice.

b. **Security Holders** Independence is not impaired solely because of primary litigation in which the CPA and the client are defendants, for example, in the case of a *class action* suit. However, if there are cross-claims alleging that the auditor is responsible for the deficiencies that gave rise to the suit or alleging fraud or deceit by current management, the issue of independence should be examined carefully. The Interpretation provides the following guidelines. Independence usually is not impaired by:

(1) Cross-claims filed to protect a right to legal redress in the event of a future adverse decision in the primary litigation. However, if there is a significant risk that the cross-claim will result in a settlement or judgment that is material to either the CPA's firm or the financial statements, independence is impaired.

(2) The assertion of cross-claims against the auditor by underwriters if no such claims are asserted by the company or its current management.

(3) A cross-claim filed against the auditor by someone who is also an officer or director of one of the auditor's other clients.

c. **Third Parties** Independence usually will not be impaired because of third-party litigation against the auditor by a lending institution, other creditor, security holder, or insurance company alleging reliance on the financial statements examined by the auditor as a basis for extending credit or insurance coverage to the client. In cases where the real party in interest in the litigation (e.g., the other creditor) is also a client of the auditor (*the plaintiff client*), independence with respect to the plaintiff client may be impaired if the litigation involves an amount that would be material to either the CPA's firm or the plaintiff client's financial statements.

7. **Financial Interests in Nonclients (Interpretation 101-8)**

a. **Client Parent/Nonclient Subsidiary** A member's independence is considered impaired when the member owns any direct or material indirect financial interest in a nonclient subsidiary that is material to the client parent. If the nonclient subsidiary is immaterial to the client, a member's material investment that allows the member to exercise significant influence over the nonclient subsidiary impairs independence.

b. **Client Subsidiary/Nonclient Parent** Where a client investee (subsidiary) is material to nonclient investor (parent), any direct or material indirect financial interest of a member in the nonclient investor would be considered to impair the member's independence. If the client investee is immaterial to the nonclient investor, and if a member's financial interest in the nonclient investor allows the member to exercise significant influence over the actions of the nonclient investor, the member's independence would be considered impaired.

c. **Other** Other relationships, such as those involving brother-sister common control or client-nonclient joint ventures, may affect the appearance of independence. Considerations include materiality of financial interest, the degree of influence the member may exercise, and the degree of influence to which the member may be subject.

8. **Governmental Financial Statements (Interpretation 101-10)** A financial reporting entity's basic financial statements, issued in conformity with U.S. GAAP (generally accepted accounting principles) include the government-wide financial statements, the fund financial statements and other entities disclosed in the notes to the basic financial statements. Entities that should be disclosed in the notes to the basic financial statements include, but are not limited to, related organizations, joint ventures, jointly governed organizations, and component units of another government with characteristics of a joint venture or jointly governed organization.

a. **Auditor of Financial Reporting Entity** A member issuing a report on the basic financial statements of the financial reporting entity must be independent of the financial reporting entity. A member and her/his immediate family should not hold a key position with a major fund, nonmajor fund, internal service fund, fiduciary fund, or component unit of the financial reporting entity or other entity that should be disclosed in the notes to the basic financial statements. Independence is not required with respect to:

(1) Any major or nonmajor fund, internal service fund, fiduciary fund, or component unit or other entities disclosed in the financial statements, where the primary auditor explicitly states reliance on other auditors reports thereon.

(2) An entity disclosed in the notes to the basic financial statements, if the financial reporting entity is not financially accountable for the organization and the required disclosure does not include financial information.

b. **Auditor of Fund or Component Unit**

(1) A member who is auditing the financial statements of a fund or component unit of the financial reporting entity that should be disclosed in the notes to the basic financial statements of the financial reporting entity, but is not auditing the primary government, should be independent with respect to those financial statements that the member is reporting upon.

(2) The member is not required to be independent of the primary government or other funds or component units of the reporting entity or entities that should be disclosed in the notes to the basic financial statements.

(3) The member and her/his immediate family should not hold a key position within the primary government.

9. **Cooperative Arrangements With Clients (Interpretation 101-12)** Independence will be considered to be impaired if a member's firm had any cooperative arrangement with the client that was material to the member's firm or to the client.

a. **Examples** Examples of cooperative arrangements are a prime contractor/subcontractor agreement to provide services or products to a third party, and a joint venture to develop or market production services.

b. **Joint Participation** Joint participation is not ordinarily a cooperative arrangement, if the participation of the firm and the client are governed by separate agreements or arrangements **and** they assume no responsibility for each other **and** neither party has the authority to act as the representative or agent of the other party.

10. **Alternative Practice Structures (Interpretation 101-14)** The Professional Ethics Executive Committee has issued additional independence rules for alternative practice structures (APSs) which are intended to be conceptual and applicable, in spirit and in substance, to all structures where the "traditional firm" engaged in attest services is aligned closely with another organization, public or private, that performs other professional services.

a. In many nontraditional structures, a substantial (the nonattest) portion of a CPA's practice is conducted under public or private ownership, and the attest portion of the practice is conducted through a separate firm owned and controlled by the CPA. All such structures must comply with applicable state laws and regulations and Rule 505 of the Code of Professional Conduct (*Form of Organization and Name*) and the elements of quality control are required to ensure that the public interest is protected adequately. This means that all services performed by CPAs and persons over whom they have control must be in compliance with applicable standards, and all other firms providing attest services must be enrolled in an AICPA-approved practice-monitoring program. Most importantly, the CPAs are responsible, financially and otherwise, for all the attest work performed.

b. Additional rules specified in this interpretation apply to direct superiors and indirect superiors and other entities. Direct superiors are those persons that can directly control the activities of the owner or managerial employee involved in the alternative practice structure. Persons considered direct superiors and entities over whose activities such persons can exercise significant influence are subject to all the same independence requirements as a member.

c. Indirect superiors and other entities are those persons who are one or more levels above the persons included in the category of direct superior, and includes the spouses, cohabitants, and dependent persons of the indirect superior. Indirect superiors and other entities may not have a relationship with an attest client of a member that is material or allows such persons or entities to exercise significant influence over the attest client. Further, the other entities may not be connected with an attest client as a promoter, underwriter, voting trustee, director or officer. Otherwise, the indirect superiors and other entities may provide services to an attest client of the member that would impair independence if performed by the member.

D. Independence Standards Board Statements

The ISB dissolved in 2001, after the SEC revised independence rules applicable to auditors of SEC-registered entities. Three ISB pronouncements remain in effect; however, only two are relevant to the CPA exam.

1. **Independence Discussions With Audit Committees (ISB 1)** ISB 1 is applicable to any auditor intending to be considered an independent accountant with regard to an entity according to the securities acts administered by the SEC (the Acts). Annually, an independent accountant must perform three duties.

   a. The auditor must disclose, in writing, to the audit committee (or replacement), all relationships between the auditor and its related entities and the client entity and its related entities that, in the auditor's judgment, may be considered to bear on independence.

   b. The auditor must confirm in writing that, in the auditor's judgment, it is independent of the client entity according to the Acts.

   c. The auditor must discuss the auditor's independence with the audit committee.

2. **Employment With Audit Clients (ISB 3)** ISB 3 was issued as a result of concern that independence may be or appear to be threatened when an audit professional leaves the audit firm to join an audit client. The audit professional may not have exercised an appropriate level of skepticism during the audit process prior to leaving the audit firm. The professional may be familiar enough with the audit approach and testing strategy to be able to circumvent the audit process as an employee of the audit client. The remaining members of the audit team may be reluctant to challenge the decision of former colleagues and may not exercise appropriate skepticism or maintain objectivity. ISB 3 describes the following safeguards that firms should implement when their professionals join firm audit clients.

   a. Prior to a professional leaving the audit firm:

      (1) The professional is required to report promptly to the audit firm conversations with the audit client about possible employment. Any professional negotiating possible employment with an audit client must be removed immediately from the audit engagement.

      (2) After the professional has been removed from the audit engagement, the audit firm must review the professional's work to assess whether the professional on the audit engagement exercised appropriate skepticism.

   b. After a professional is employed by the audit client:

      (1) The on-going engagement team must consider the appropriateness or necessity of modifying the audit plan to adjust for risk of circumvention.

      (2) If the professional will have significant interaction with the audit team, the audit firm must take appropriate steps to provide that the existing audit team members have the stature and objectivity to deal effectively with the professional and the professional's work.

   c. When a professional joins an audit client within one year of disassociating from the audit firm and the professional has significant interaction with the audit team, the next annual audit must be reviewed separately by an audit firm professional uninvolved in the audit. This review should be tailored based on the position that the former audit firm professional has assumed with the audit client and any other facts and circumstances that might threaten independence.

E. Integrity & Objectivity (Rule 102)

In the performance of any professional service, a member shall maintain objectivity and integrity, shall be free of conflicts of interest, and shall not knowingly misrepresent facts or subordinate her/his judgment to others.

Exhibit 3 ▸ Ethics Ruling on Use of CPA Designation by Member Not in Public Practice

> A member not in public practice may use the CPA designation in connection with financial statements and correspondence of the member's employer and also use the designation along with employment title on business cards. However, the member should be careful not to imply that the member is independent of the employer or it would be considered as knowingly misrepresenting facts in violation of Rule 102. (ET 191-65)

1. **Knowing Misrepresentations in Preparation (Interpretation 102-1)** Knowingly making, permitting, or directing another to make materially false and misleading entries in an entity's financial statements or records is in violation of Rule 102. In addition, knowingly failing to correct materially false and misleading financial statements or records while having the authority to do so is in violation of Rule 102. Knowingly signing, or permitting or directing another to sign a document containing materially false and misleading information violates Rule 102.

2. **Conflicts of Interest (Interpretation 102-2)** A conflict of interest may occur if a member performs a professional service for a client or employer and the member or the member's firm has a relationship that could be viewed as impairing the member's objectivity.

   Exhibit 4 ▸ Ruling on Connection With Client Debtor or Creditor

   > A member is an officer, director, or principal shareholder of an entity, but does not control the entity that has a loan to or from the member's client. If the member believes that the professional service can be performed with objectivity, and the relationship is disclosed to the client and consent is obtained from the client and other appropriate parties, the rule shall not prohibit the performance of the professional service. (ET 191-110)

   a. **Objectivity** If the member believes that objectivity can be maintained, discloses the relationship to the client, and obtains consent from the client, the rule shall not prohibit the performance of the professional service.

   b. **Independence** Independence impairments cannot be eliminated by such disclosure and consent in audits, reviews, and attest engagements requiring independence.

3. **Obligations to Employer's External Accountant (Interpretation 102-3)** A member must be candid and not knowingly misrepresent facts or knowingly fail to disclose material facts in dealing with her/his employer's external accountant.

4. **Subordination of Judgment (Interpretation 102-4)** If a member and the member's supervisor have a disagreement or dispute relating to the preparation of financial statements or the recording of transactions, the member should take the following steps to ensure that the situation does not constitute a subordination of judgment.

   a. **Acceptable Statements** If, upon consideration, the member concludes the financial statements, as proposed, represent an acceptable alternative and do not misrepresent the facts materially, the member need do nothing further.

   b. **Materially Misstated Statements** If the member concludes that the financial statements or records could be materially misstated, the member should make her/his concerns known to the appropriate level of management within the organization. The member should consider preparing appropriate documentation.

c. **Further Action** If appropriate action is not taken, the member should consider her/his continuing relationship with the employer, and any responsibility to communicate to third parties, such as regulatory authorities. The member may wish to consult with legal counsel.

5. **Educational Services (Interpretation 102-5)** Educational services are professional services and are subject to the rules of objectivity and integrity. This includes teaching at a university, teaching a continuing professional education course, and engaging in research and scholarship.

6. **Client Advocacy (Interpretation 102-6)** A member may be requested by a client to perform a tax or consulting services engagement that involves acting as an advocate for the client or the client's position on accounting or financial reporting issues, either within the firm or outside the firm with standard setters, regulators or others.

   a. **Objectivity and Integrity** These services are considered professional services and the member shall comply with the rules of objectivity and integrity.

   b. **Standards** If the client advocacy appears to stretch the bounds of performance standards, the member should consider whether it is appropriate to perform the service.

III. General & Technical Standards

A. General Standards (Rule 201)

1. **Professional Competence** A member will undertake only those professional services that the CPA or the CPA's firm has reasonable expectations of being able to complete with professional competence. The member does not assume responsibility for infallibility of knowledge or judgment.

   a. Competence involves the technical knowledge of the CPA and the staff, the ability to apply this knowledge to the particular engagement, and the ability to supervise and evaluate the work performed.

   b. In some cases, additional research and/or consultation with others may be necessary as a normal part of the performance of professional services, and ordinarily does not represent a lack of competence. If the CPA cannot acquire the knowledge, the client should be advised that a competent individual must be engaged to perform the service either independently or as an associate.

2. **Due Professional Care** A member must exercise due professional care in the performance of professional services.

3. **Planning & Supervision** A member will adequately plan and supervise the performance of professional services.

Exhibit 5 ▸ Ethics Rulings on General & Technical Standards

Supervision of Technical Specialist on Management Consulting Services Engagements—A member must be qualified to supervise and evaluate the work of specialists employed by the member. The member need not be qualified to perform each of the specialist's tasks, however, the member should be able to define the tasks and evaluate the end product. (ET 291-9)

4. **Sufficient Relevant Data** A member must obtain sufficient relevant data to provide a reasonable basis for reaching conclusions or making recommendations in relation to any professional services performed.

B. **Compliance With Standards (Rule 202)**
A member who performs auditing, review, compilation, management consulting, tax, or other professional services shall comply with standards promulgated by bodies designated by Council of the AICPA.

C. **Accounting Principles (Rule 203)**
A member will not express an opinion that financial statements are presented in conformity with GAAP or state that the member is not aware of any material modifications that should be made to such statements or data in order for them to be in conformity with GAAP, if the statements contain a deviation from GAAP that has a material effect on the financial statements taken as a whole, unless the CPA can demonstrate that because of unusual circumstances the financial statements would have been misleading.

1. **Departures From GAAP (Interpretation 203-1)** Proper accounting treatment is that which will render the financial statements not misleading. The member must use professional judgment in deciding when a deviation from GAAP is appropriate. Circumstances justifying a departure include new legislation or the evolution of a new form of business transaction.

2. **Status of FASB & GASB Interpretations (Interpretation 203-2)** The Financial Accounting Standards Board (FASB) has been designated as the body to establish accounting principles. FASB Statements of Financial Accounting Standards and those Accounting Research Bulletins and APB Opinions that have not been superseded by the FASB constitute accounting principles. The Governmental Accounting Standards Board (GASB) has been designated as the body to establish accounting principles for state and local governmental entities.

3. **Employees' Responsibility for Conformity With GAAP (Interpretation 203-4)** A member shall not state affirmatively that financial statements or other financial data are presented in conformity with GAAP if the statements or data contain any departure from a promulgated accounting principle that has a material effect on the statements or data taken as a whole. Representation regarding GAAP conformity included in a letter or other communication from a client may be considered an affirmative statement within the meaning of this rule.

IV. Responsibilities to Clients

A. **Confidential Client Information (Rule 301)**
A member in public practice will not disclose confidential information obtained in the course of the professional engagement without the consent of the client.

1. **Without Consent** Confidential client information that may be disclosed without the client's permission include the following.

   a. To comply with a validly issued and enforceable subpoena or summons.

   b. To comply with applicable laws and government regulations.

   c. To comply with professional practice review procedures under AICPA or state CPA society or Board of Accountancy authorization.

   d. To initiate a complaint with the professional ethics division or trial board of the AICPA or other appropriate investigative or disciplinary body. The members of these bodies may not use to their advantage or disclose any member's confidential client information obtained in these activities.

   e. To initiate, pursue, or defend against in an actual or threatened lawsuit or alternative dispute resolution proceeding relating to the client.

2. **Purchase, Sale, or Merger of Practice (Interpretation 301-3)** A review of a member's professional practice is authorized in conjunction with a prospective purchase, sale, or merger of all or part of a member's practice. The member must take appropriate precautions, such as through a written confidentiality agreement, so that the prospective purchaser does not disclose any confidential client information obtained in the course of the review. Members reviewing a practice in such a case shall not use to their advantage or disclose any confidential client information obtained in the review.

B. Contingent Fees (Rule 302)

A member in public practice shall not offer or render services under an agreement whereby the fee is contingent upon the findings or results. Specified services that a member in public practice or the member's firm shall not perform for a contingent fee include an audit or review of a financial statement, a compilation of a financial statement when the member reasonably might expect that a third party will use the statement, or an examination of prospective financial information. A member also is precluded from preparing an original or amended tax return or claim for a tax refund for a contingent fee.

1. **Dependent on Complexity of Service** A CPA's fees may depend on the complexity of the service rendered. Fees that are fixed by the courts or public authorities or which are determined in tax matters by judicial proceedings or governmental agency findings are not considered contingent and, therefore, are permitted.

2. **Certain Tax Matters (Interpretation 302-1)** In some cases, contingent fees in certain tax matters are permitted. A contingent fee would be permitted when a member represents a client in an examination by a revenue agent of the client's federal or state income tax return, when the member represents a client in connection with obtaining a private letter ruling, when filing an amended return claiming a refund that exceeds the threshold for review by the appropriate taxing authority, or when filing an amended return based on a tax issue that is the subject of a test case involving a different taxpayer or on which the taxing authority is developing a position.

V. Other Responsibilities & Practices

A. Acts Discreditable (Rule 501)

A member will not commit an act that is discreditable to the profession. (This and objectivity are two rules that a member who is not engaged in the practice of public accounting must follow.)

1. **Retention of Client's Records (Interpretation 501-1)** A member commits an act discreditable to the profession by refusing to return a client's records after the client has demanded them. A member's audit documentation, or working papers, including analyses and schedules prepared by the client at the request of the member, are the member's property, not client records, and need not be made available to the client. If the relationship of a member who is not the owner of a firm is terminated, the member may not take or retain originals or copies of the firm's client files or proprietary information unless permitted by a contractual arrangement. (ET 591-191)

   a. In some instances, workpapers contain information that is not reflected in the client's records, with the result that the client's financial information is incomplete. This would include, for example, adjusting, closing, combining, or consolidating journal entries, information normally contained in books of original entry and general or subsidiary ledgers, and tax and depreciation carryforward information.

   b. In those instances when an engagement has been completed, such information also should be made available to the client upon request. The information should be provided in the requested medium, provided it exists in that medium. The member is not required to convert information that is not in electronic form to an electronic form. Once the member has complied with the initial request, the member need not comply with subsequent requests to provide such information again.

c. The member may require that all fees due the member, including the fees for the services (described in a., above), be paid before such information is provided.

2. **Discrimination & Harassment in Employment Practices (Interpretation 501-2)** Violation of any anti-discrimination law, including sexual and other forms of harassment, is presumed to be an act discreditable to the profession.

3. **Failure to Follow Standards and/or Procedures in Government Audits (Interpretation 501-3)** In audits of government grants, government units, or other recipients of government monies, the auditor is obligated to follow government audit standards, guides, procedures, statutes, rules, and regulations, in addition to GAAS. Failure to do so is an act discreditable to the profession unless the member discloses the fact that such requirements were not followed and includes the reasons in the report.

4. **Negligence in Preparation of Financial Statements or Records (Interpretation 501-4)** A member who negligently makes, or permits or directs another to make materially false and misleading entries in the financial statements or records of an entity or fails to correct an entity's materially false and misleading financial statements when having the authority to record an entry, or signs or permits or directs another to sign a document containing materially false and misleading information has committed an act discreditable to the profession.

5. **Failure to Follow Requirements of Governmental Bodies (Interpretation 501-5)** If a member prepares financial statements or related information for purposes of reporting to bodies, commissions, or regulatory agencies, the CPA must follow the requirements of the entity in addition to GAAP. If a member agrees to perform an attest or similar service for the purpose of reporting to governmental bodies, commissions, or other regulatory agencies, the CPA should follow such requirements, in addition to applicable GAAS. A material departure from such requirements is an act discreditable to the profession, unless the CPA discloses that such requirements were not followed and includes the reasons in the report. Examples of governmental bodies, commissions, or other regulatory agencies include the SEC, Federal Communications Commission (FCC), state insurance commissions, and other regulatory agencies, such as the Public Company Accounting Oversight Board (PCAOB).

6. **Solicitation or Disclosure of CPA Examination Questions & Answers (Interpretation 501-6)** A member who solicits or knowingly discloses any May 1996 or later Uniform CPA Examination question and/or answer without the written authorization of the AICPA shall be considered to have committed an act discreditable to the profession.

7. **Failure to File Tax Return or Pay Tax Liability (Interpretation 501-7)** A member who fails to comply with applicable federal, state, or local laws regarding the timely filing of the member's personal tax returns or the member's firm's returns, or the timely remittance of payroll and other taxes collected on behalf of others, may be considered to have committed an act discreditable to the profession.

B. **Advertising & Other Forms of Solicitation (Rule 502)**
A member in public practice will not seek to obtain clients by advertising or other forms of solicitation in a manner that is false, misleading, or deceptive. Solicitation by the use of coercion, over-reaching, or harassing conduct is prohibited.

1. **False, Misleading, or Deceptive Acts (Interpretation 502-2)** Advertising or other forms of solicitation that are false, misleading, or deceptive are prohibited since they are not in the public interest. Examples of such activities include those that

   a. Create false or unjustified expectations of favorable results;

   b. Imply the ability to influence any court, tribunal, regulatory agency, or similar body or official;

c. Contain a representation that specific professional services will be performed for a stated fee, estimated fee, or fee range when it was likely at the time of representation that such fees would be substantially increased and the prospective client was not advised of that likelihood; or

d. Contain any other representations that would be likely to cause a reasonable person to misunderstand or be deceived.

2. **Engagements Obtained Through Efforts of Third Parties (Interpretation 502-5)** Members are permitted to render professional services to clients or customers of third parties who were obtained through the advertising and solicitation efforts of the third parties. The member has the responsibility to determine that all promotional efforts are consistent with the Code of Professional Conduct. The reason is that the CPA will receive the benefits of the advertising and solicitation efforts of the third parties. Members cannot do through others what they are prohibited from doing.

C. **Commissions & Referral Fees (Rule 503)**
A member in public practice is prohibited from recommending or referring, for a commission, any product or service to a client or to be supplied by a client, when that member or member's firm provides certain services to the client. Specified services include an audit or review of a financial statement, a compilation of a financial statement when the member might reasonably expect that a third party will use the statement, or an examination of prospective financial information.

1. **Disclosure of Commissions** A member who receives or expects to receive a commission from a nonprohibited act should disclose that fact to the client.

2. **Referral Fees** Any member who accepts or pays a referral fee in relation to a client must disclose such acceptance or payment to the client.

D. **Form of Organization & Name (Rule 505)**
A member may practice public accounting in the form of organization permitted by law whose characteristics conform to resolutions of the Council of the AICPA. The name of the firm will not be misleading. The names of one or more past owners may be included in the firm name.

1. **AICPA Membership Designation** A firm cannot designate itself as *Members of the AICPA* unless all of its CPA owners are members of the AICPA.

2. **Separate Business (Interpretation 505-2)** A member in public practice also may own a controlling interest, as defined by GAAP, in a separate business offering to clients the type of services rendered by public accountants.

   a. In order for independence not to be considered impaired, the separate business, including the owners and the employees, must comply with all the provisions of the Code of Professional Conduct in the operation of the separate business.

   b. If a member owns an interest in such a business, but does not control the separate business, the provisions of the Code of Professional Conduct apply to the member, but not to the separate business or its other owners or employees.

3. **Application of Rule 505 to Alternative Practice Structures** The overriding focus is that CPAs remain responsible, financially and otherwise, for the attest work performed to protect the public interest.

   a. The Council Resolution requires that a majority of the financial interests in a firm engaged in attest services be owned by CPAs. Questions have arisen about alternative practice structures in which the majority of the financial interests in the attest firm is owned by CPAs and all or substantially all of the revenues are paid to another entity in return for services and the lease of employees, equipment, and office space.

b. As long as the CPAs owning the attest firm remain financially responsible, and comply with the other provisions of the Code of Professional Conduct and bylaws (including compliance with state laws, enrollment in practice monitoring program, membership in SEC practice section if attest work is for SEC clients, compliance with independence rules, and compliance with other applicable standards), then the member is considered to be in compliance with the financial interests provision of the Resolution.

Exhibit 6 ▸ Ethics Rulings on Other Responsibilities & Practices

- Fees: Collection of Notes Issued in Payment—A member may make arrangements with a bank to collect notes issued by a client in payment of a fee due. (ET 591-2)
- Newsletters & Publications—A newsletter, booklet, or similar publication may be attributed to a member even if it was not prepared by the member provided the member has a reasonable basis to conclude that the information is not false, misleading, or deceptive. (ET 591-176)
- Termination of Engagement Prior to Completion—If an engagement is terminated by either the member or the client prior to completion, the member is required to return only those records originally given to the member by the client. (ET 591-182)
- Sale of Products to Clients—A member may purchase a product from a third-party and resell the product to a client at a profit. (ET 591-185)
- Non-CPA Partner—A member in partnership with non-CPAs may sign reports with the firm name, the member's signature and the CPA designation, provided it is clear that the partnership itself is not being held out as composed entirely of CPAs. (ET 591-190)

VI. Consulting Services

A. Overview

Consulting services provided by CPAs have grown in the overall importance of the activity to the CPA profession and the scope of services performed. Services are no longer limited to advice on accounting related matters, but now include a tremendous range of technical disciplines, industry knowledge, and consulting skills.

1. **Consulting Process** This process includes the analytical approach and process applied in a consulting service. It involves some combination of activities relating to a determination of client objectives, definition of problems and solutions, fact finding, evaluation of alternatives, formulation of proposed actions, communication of results, implementation, and follow-up.

2. **Consulting Services** These services are composed of professional services that use the CPA's technical skills, education, observations and experience, and knowledge of the consulting process. Such services include the following.

   a. **Consultations** The practitioner provides advice or information based mostly, if not entirely, on existing personal knowledge about the client, the circumstances, the technical matters involved, and the mutual intent of the parties. Examples of consultations include reviewing and commenting on a client-prepared business plan and making recommendations for computer software for further analysis by the client.

   b. **Advisory Services** The practitioner develops findings, conclusions, and recommendations for client consideration and decision making. Examples include operational review and improvement study, analysis of an accounting system, assistance with strategic planning, and defining requirements for an information system.

   c. **Implementation Services** The practitioner puts an action plan into effect. In an engagement of this type, client personnel may be pooled with those of the practitioners. The overall responsibility of all the activities rests with the practitioner. Examples include providing computer system installation and support, effecting steps to improve productivity, and assisting with the merger of organizations.

d. **Transaction Services** The practitioner provides services concerning a specific client transaction, usually with a third party. Examples include insolvency services, valuation services, preparation of information to secure financing, analysis of a potential merger or acquisition, and litigation services.

e. **Staff & Other Support Services** The practitioner provides staff and other support, as needed, to accomplish tasks specified by the client. Examples include the management of data processing facilities, computer programming, trustees in a bankruptcy situation, and controllership activities.

f. **Product Services** The practitioner provides a product to the client along with professional services to support, use, or maintain the product provided. Examples of product services include the sale and delivery of a packaged training program or the sale and implementation of computer software.

B. General Standards for Consulting Services

The AICPA Management Consulting Services Executive Committee issues Statements on Standards for Consulting Services (SSCS). SSCS 1 supersedes the previous series of Statements on Standards for Management Advisory Services, and provides standards for practice for a wider variety of professional services.

1. **Applicability** The general standards of Professional Competence, Due Professional Care, Planning and Supervision, and Sufficient Relevant Data apply to all services performed by members of the AICPA and are contained in Rule 201 of the AICPA Code of Professional Conduct.

2. **Professional Judgment** Professional judgment is to be used in applying the Standards for Consulting Services to specific situations, since the understanding established with the client may impose some constraints within which the services are to be performed. The CPA is not required to decline or withdraw from a consulting engagement when such limitations are imposed. An example is limitations on the CPA's efforts to gather relevant information.

C. Additional General Standards

The following additional general standards address the distinctive nature of consulting services. These Standards are established under Rule 202 of the AICPA Code of Professional Conduct.

1. **Client Interest** The member shall serve the client's interest by seeking to accomplish the objectives established by the understanding with the client while maintaining integrity and objectivity. Independence is not required for consulting services.

2. **Understanding With Client** An oral or written understanding should be reached with the client concerning the nature, scope, and limitations of the services to be performed, and modifications should be made to the understanding if circumstances require a significant change during the engagement.

3. **Communication With Client** The client should be informed of the following.

   a. Conflicts of interest that may occur that could be viewed as impairing the CPA's objectivity. The CPA may still perform the consulting services if the client consents

   b. Significant reservations concerning the scope or benefits of the engagement

   c. Significant engagement findings or events

D. Consulting Services for Attest Clients

The performance of consulting services for an attest client does not impair independence. Members performing attest services for a client should comply with applicable independence standards, rules and regulations issued by the AICPA, the state boards of accountancy, state CPA societies, and other regulatory agencies.

VII. Specialty Practices

A. Personal Financial Planning Services

Statements on Responsibilities in Personal Financial Planning Practice are published for the guidance of members and are not enforceable standards. The statements are approved by the Personal Financial Planning Executive Committee of the AICPA.

1. **Basic Functions & Responsibilities (PFP 100)** Personal financial planning engagements are those involving the development of strategies and recommendations to help clients define and achieve personal financial goals. Such engagements may involve all of a client's personal financial goals or may focus on a limited set of goals, in which case the CPA should consider the client's overall financial circumstances in the development of recommendations.

   a. **Activities** Personal financial planning engagement activities include defining the engagement objectives, planning specific procedures, developing a basis for recommendations, communicating recommendations to the client, and identifying action tasks for planning decisions. Personal financial planning engagements also may include assisting a client in taking action on planning decisions, monitoring the client's progress in achieving goals, and updating recommendations and assisting the client in the revision of planning decisions. Some of the existing standards and guidance apply, including:

      (1) Integrity and objectivity (Rule 102) must be maintained. Note that independence is **not** required.

      (2) Professional competence, due professional care, planning and supervision, and sufficient relevant data (Rule 201).

      (3) Confidential client information (Rule 301).

      (4) Contingent fees (Rule 302) and commissions and referral fees (Rule 503).

      (5) When an engagement involves tax advice, the guidance in the Statements on Responsibilities in Tax Practice, especially Statement 8, *Form and Content of Advice to Clients,* should be considered.

      (6) When an engagement involves assistance in the preparation of personal financial statements or financial projections, the applicable AICPA pronouncements should be considered, including Statements on Standards for Accounting and Review Services, Statement on Standards for Attestation Engagements *Financial Forecasts and Projections, Guide for Prospective Financial Information,* and *Personal Financial Statements Guide.*

      (7) When the engagement involves business valuation services, the applicable provisions of the Statement on Standards for Consulting Services should be considered.

   b. **Non-Activities** Personal financial planning activities do **not** include such services as the compilation of personal financial statements, projecting future taxes, the preparation of tax returns, other tax compliance activities, and tax advice or consultations.

2. **Working With Other Advisers (PFP 200)** The CPA may use advice from others in the development of recommendations, and may refer a client to other advisers for assistance with other products or services. Appropriate evaluation, communication, and documentation guidance should be considered.

3. **Implementation Engagement Functions & Responsibilities (PFP 300)** Implementation engagement activities include selecting investment advisers, restructuring debt, creating estate documents, establishing cash reserves, preparing budgets, and selecting and acquiring

specific investments and insurance products. The CPA should apply applicable standards and consider guidance in these activities.

4. **Monitoring & Updating Engagements—Functions & Responsibilities (PFP 400)** Monitoring engagements involve determining the client's progress in achieving established personal financial planning goals. Updating engagements involve revising the client's existing financial plan and recommendations to conform to the client's current goals, circumstances, and external factors.

5. **Developing a Basis for Recommendations (PFP 500)** Activities included in this guidance section include collecting relevant quantitative and qualitative information, analyzing information, and formulating strategies and recommendations.

B. Tax Services

1. **Tax Return Positions (SSTS 1)** A member should not recommend a tax return position or prepare or sign a return reflecting a position that the member knows it exploits the audit selection process of a taxing authority or serves as a mere arguing position advanced solely to obtain leverage in the bargaining process of settlement negotiation with a taxing authority. When recommending a tax return position, a member has both the right and responsibility to be an advocate for the taxpayer with respect to any position satisfying the following standards. These apply to a member when providing professional services that involve tax return positions.

   a. **Realistic** A member should not recommend that a tax return position be taken with respect to any item, nor sign or prepare a return, unless the member has a good faith belief that the position has a realistic possibility of being sustained administratively or judicially on its merits if challenged.

   b. **Non-Frivolous** A member may recommend a tax return position that the member concludes is not frivolous as long as the member advises the taxpayer to appropriately disclose. The member may prepare or sign a return that reflects a position that the member concludes is not frivolous as long as the position is disclosed appropriately.

   c. **Penalties** When recommending tax return positions and preparing or signing a return on which a tax return position is taken, a member should, when relevant, advise the taxpayer regarding potential penalty consequences of such tax return position and the opportunity, if any, to avoid such penalties through disclosure.

2. **Answers to Questions on Returns (SSTS 2)** A member should make a reasonable effort to obtain from the taxpayer the information necessary to provide appropriate answers to all questions on a tax return before signing as preparer.

3. **Certain Procedural Aspects of Preparing Returns (SSTS 3)** In preparing or signing a return, a member may in good faith rely, without verification, on information furnished by the taxpayer or by third parties. However, a member should not ignore the implications of information furnished and should make reasonable inquiries if the information furnished appears to be incorrect, incomplete, or inconsistent either on its face or on the basis of other facts known to a member. Further, a member should refer to the taxpayer's returns for one or more prior years whenever feasible.

   a. **Inquiry** If the tax law or regulations impose a condition with respect to deductibility or other tax treatment of an item, such as taxpayer maintenance of books and records or substantiating documentation to support the reported deduction or tax treatment, a member should make appropriate inquiries to determine to the member's satisfaction whether such condition has been met.

   b. **Another's Return** When preparing a tax return, a member should consider information actually known to that member from the tax return of another taxpayer if the information is relevant to that tax return and its consideration is necessary to properly prepare that tax return. In using such information, a member should consider any limitations imposed by any law or rule relating to confidentiality.

4. **Use of Estimates (SSTS 4)** Unless prohibited by statute or by rule, a member may use the taxpayer's estimates in the preparation of a tax return if it is not practical to obtain exact data and if the member determines that the estimates are reasonable based on the facts and circumstances known to the member. If the taxpayer's estimates are used, they should be presented in a manner that does not imply greater accuracy than exists.

5. **Departure From a Position Previously Concluded in an Administrative Proceeding or Court Decision (SSTS 5)** The tax return position with respect to an item as determined in an administrative proceeding or court decision does not restrict a member from recommending a different tax position in a later year's return, unless the taxpayer is bound to a specified treatment in the later year, such as by a formal closing agreement. Therefore, as provided in SSTS No. 1, *Tax Return Positions,* the member may recommend a tax return position or prepare or sign a tax return that departs from the treatment of an item as concluded in an administrative proceeding or court decision with respect to a prior return of the taxpayer.

6. **Knowledge of Error: Return Preparation (SSTS 6)** A member should inform the taxpayer promptly upon becoming aware of an error in a previously filed return or upon becoming aware of a taxpayer's failure to file a required return. The member is not obligated to inform the taxing authority, and a member may not do so without the taxpayer's permission, except when required by law.

    a. **Recommendation** A member should recommend (oral or written) the corrective measures to be taken.

    b. **Withdrawal** If the taxpayer has not taken appropriate action to correct an error in a prior year's return, the member should consider whether to withdraw from preparing the current year's return and whether to continue a professional or employment relationship with the taxpayer.

7. **Knowledge of Error: Administrative Proceedings (SSTS 7)** If a member is representing a taxpayer in an administrative proceeding with respect to a return that contains an error of which the member is aware, the member should inform the taxpayer promptly upon becoming aware of the error. A member is neither obligated to inform the taxing authority nor allowed to do so without the taxpayer's permission, except where required by law. Special considerations may apply when a member has been engaged by legal counsel to provide assistance in a matter relating to the counsel's client.

    a. **Recommendation** The member should recommend (oral or written) the corrective measures to be taken.

    b. **Withdrawal** A member should request the taxpayer's agreement to disclose the error to the taxing authority. Lacking such agreement, the member should consider whether to withdraw from representing the taxpayer in the administrative proceeding and whether to continue a professional or employment relationship with the taxpayer.

8. **Form & Content of Advice to Taxpayers (SSTS 8)** A member should use judgment to ensure that tax advice provided to a taxpayer reflects professional competence and appropriately serves the taxpayer's needs. A member is not required to follow a standard format or guidelines in communicating written or oral advice to a taxpayer.

    a. **Advice** A member should assume that tax advice provided to a taxpayer will affect the manner in which the matters or transactions considered would be reported on the taxpayer's tax returns. Thus, for all tax advice given to a taxpayer, a member should follow the standards in SSTS 1, *Tax Return Positions.*

b. **Communication** A member has no obligation to communicate with a taxpayer when subsequent developments affect advice previously provided with respect to significant matters, except while assisting a taxpayer in implementing procedures or plans associated with the advice provided or when a member undertakes this obligation by specific agreement.

C. AICPA Assurance Service Programs

1. **WebTrust^{SM}** The WebTrust^{SM} seal informs potential customers that a CPA has evaluated a website's business practices and controls to verify that they conform to WebTrust^{SM} principles and criteria for business-to-consumer electronic commerce. Included in the requirements are privacy disclosures and testing.

2. **SysTrust^{SM}** In a SysTrust^{SM} engagement, a CPA firm issues an attestation report that evaluates whether management of an e-business has maintained effective controls to ensure that its systems function reliably within a specified period of time. A SysTrust^{SM} report uses four essential principles as benchmarks of the reliability of a system: availability, security, integrity, and maintainability.

AICPA Professional Literature Database Subscription

Please note portions of the AICPA press release (reproduced below) regarding databases of professional literature.

The American Institute of Certified Public Accountants (AICPA) and the National Association of State Boards of Accountancy (NASBA) have teamed up to offer eligible CPA Exam candidates a free six-month subscription to professional audit and accounting literature. The on-line package includes AICPA Professional Standards, FASB Current Text, and FASB Original Pronouncements. The new computerized Uniform CPA Examination requires exam candidates to know how to search electronic professional literature.

Further information may be found at www.cpa-exam.org. From the menu across the top of the site, select "Prepare for the Exam" and then "Access to Prof. Literature."

FAQ: *Where should I perform the research for the REG ethics and professional responsibilities simulation questions in the Bisk software?*

Candidates research the AICPA Professional Standards for the REG ethics and professional responsibilities simulation research elements. As qualified candidates may get a free subscription to the professional standards directly from the AICPA exam web-site, the Bisk software does not include this full database.

FAQ: *Where should I perform the research for the REG tax simulation questions?*

The AICPA does not provide candidates with pre-exam access to a database containing the tax code, nor has it designated a commercially available database as the one it provides during the exam. Candidates have no means to know which database or search functionality will be available for this exam section. The editors recommend that candidates (1) familiarize themselves with the exam interface with the AICPA's tutorial, and (2) use the electronic edition of the U.S. Code prepared and published by the Office of the Law Revision Counsel of the U.S. House of Representatives at: http://uscode.house.gov. Select the "search" feature of this site. Limit your search to the Internal Revenue Code (IRC) by specifying Title 26 in the title field.

The Bisk software does not include a full database of the tax code. A partial database is available so that candidates may practice off-line; however, the editors strongly suggest practicing research skills with a full database as well.

CHAPTER 32—ACCOUNTANT'S PROFESSIONAL RESPONSIBILITIES

Problem 32-1 MULTIPLE CHOICE QUESTIONS (38 to 50 minutes)

1. Which of the following bodies ordinarily would have the authority to suspend or revoke a CPA's license to practice public accounting?
a. The SEC
b. The AICPA
c. A state CPA society
d. A state board of accountancy
(5/96, Law, #2, 6258)

2. Which of the following statements best explains why the CPA profession has found it essential to promulgate ethical standards and to establish means for ensuring their observance?
a. A distinguishing mark of a profession is its acceptance of responsibility to the public.
b. A requirement for a profession is to establish ethical standards that stress primary responsibility to clients and colleagues.
c. Ethical standards that emphasize excellence in performance over material rewards establish a reputation for competence and character.
d. Vigorous enforcement of an established code of ethics is the best way to prevent unscrupulous acts. (5/94, Law, #2, 4757)

3. Must a CPA, in public practice, be independent in fact and appearance when providing the following services?

	Compilation of personal financial statements	*Preparation of a tax return*	*Compilation of a financial forecast*
a.	Yes	No	No
b.	No	Yes	No
c.	No	No	Yes
d.	No	No	No

(11/94, Law, #4, 5182)

4. The auditor with final responsibility for an engagement and one of the assistants have a difference of opinion about the results of an auditing procedure. If the assistant believes it is necessary to be disassociated from the matter's resolution, the CPA firm's procedures should enable the assistant to
a. Refer the disagreement to the AICPA's Quality Review Committee
b. Document the details of the disagreement with the conclusion reached
c. Discuss the disagreement with the entity's management or its audit committee
d. Report the disagreement to an impartial peer review monitoring team (11/93, AUD, #4, 4241)

5. To exercise due professional care, which **two** should an auditor do?
a. Critically review the judgment exercised by those assisting in the audit
b. Examine all available corroborating evidence supporting management's assertions
c. Design the audit to detect all instances of illegal acts
d. Notify the client when outside consultation is necessary
e. Attain the proper balance of professional experience and formal education
(11/94, Law, #3, amended, 8007)

6. A violation of the profession's ethical standards most likely would have occurred when a CPA
a. Issued an unqualified opinion on the Year 3 financial statements when fees for the Year 1 audit were unpaid
b. Recommended a controller's position description with candidate specifications to an audit client
c. Purchased a CPA firm's practice of monthly write-ups for a percentage of fees to be received over a three-year period
d. Made arrangements with a financial institution to collect notes issued by a client in payment of fees due for the current year's audit
(5/93, AUD, #1, amended, 3897)

7. Kar, CPA, is a staff auditor participating in the audit engagement of Fort, Inc. Which of the following circumstances impairs Kar's independence?
a. During the period of the professional engagement, Fort gives Kar tickets to a football game worth $25.
b. Kar owns stock in a corporation that Fort's 401(k) plan also invests in.
c. Kar's friend, an employee of another local accounting firm, prepares Fort's tax returns.
d. Kar's sibling is an internal auditor employed part-time by Fort. (R/01, Law, #1, amended, 7036)

8. On June 1, Year 1, a CPA obtained a $100,000 personal loan from a financial institution client for whom the CPA provided compilation services. The loan was fully secured and considered material to the CPA's net worth. The CPA paid the loan in full on December 31, Year 1. On April 3, Year 2, the client asked the CPA to audit the client's financial statements for the year ended December 31, Year 2. Is the CPA considered independent with respect to the audit of the client's December 31, Year 2, financial statements?
a. Yes, because the loan was fully secured
b. Yes, because the CPA was **not** required to be independent at the time the loan was granted
c. No, because the CPA had a loan with the client during the period of a professional engagement
d. No, because the CPA had a loan with the client during the period covered by the financial statements (R/01, Law, #2, amended, 7037)

9. The concept of materiality would be **least** important to an auditor when considering the
a. Adequacy of disclosure of a client's illegal act
b. Discovery of weaknesses in a client's internal control structure
c. Effects of a direct financial interest in the client on the CPA's independence
d. Decision whether to use positive or negative confirmations of accounts receivable (5/91, AUD, #52, 0003)

10. According to the profession's ethical standards, which of the following events may justify a departure from a Statement of Financial Accounting Standards?

	New legislation	*Evolution of a new form of business transaction*
a.	No	Yes
b.	Yes	No
c.	Yes	Yes
d.	No	No

(11/94, Law, #2, 5181)

11. Which of the following is(are) a correct definition of professional standards?

I. Procedures used by an auditor to gather evidence on which to base an opinion
II. Measures of the quality of the auditor's performance

a. I only
b. II only
c. Both I and II
d. Neither I nor II (R/03, REG, 0257L, #3, 7645)

12. According to the ethical standards of the profession, which of the following acts generally is prohibited?
a. Accepting a contingent fee for representing a client in connection with obtaining a private letter ruling from the Internal Revenue Service
b. Retaining client records after the client has demanded their return
c. Revealing client tax returns to a prospective purchaser of the CPA's practice
d. Issuing a modified report explaining the CPA's failure to follow a governmental regulatory agency's standards when conducting an attest service for a client (R/05, REG, 0808L, #16, 7862)

13. A CPA is permitted to disclose confidential client information without the consent of the client to

I. Another CPA firm if the information concerns suspected tax return irregularities
II. A state CPA society voluntary quality control review board

a. I only
b. II only
c. Both I and II
d. Neither I nor II (5/95, Law, #5, 5339)

14. The profession's ethical standards most likely would be considered to have been violated when a CPA represents that specific consulting services will be performed for a stated fee, and it is apparent at the time of the representation that the
a. Actual fee would be substantially higher.
b. Actual fee would be substantially lower than the fees charged by other CPAs for comparable services.
c. CPA would **not** be independent.
d. Fee was a competitive bid. (11/94, Law, #1, 5180)

15. May a CPA hire for the CPA's public accounting firm a non-CPA systems analyst who specializes in developing computer systems?
a. Yes, provided the CPA is qualified to perform each of the specialist's tasks
b. Yes, provided the CPA is able to supervise the specialist and evaluate the specialist's end product
c. No, because non-CPA professionals are **not** permitted to be associated with CPA firms in public practice
d. No, because developing computer systems is **not** recognized as a service performed by public accountants (11/93, AUD, #3, 4240)

16. Which of the following fee arrangements generally would **not** be permitted under the ethical standards of the profession?
a. A referral fee paid by a CPA to obtain a client
b. A commission for compiling a client's internal-use financial statements
c. A contingent fee for preparing a client's income tax return
d. A contingent fee for representing a client in tax court (R/03, REG, 1437L, #18, 7660)

17. A pervasive characteristic of a CPA's role in a consulting services engagement is that of being a(n)
a. Objective advisor
b. Independent practitioner
c. Computer specialist
d. Confidential reviewer
(5/93, AUD, #5, amended, 3901)

18. According to the standards of the profession, which of the following would be considered a part of a consulting services engagement?

I. Expressing a conclusion about the reliability of a client's financial statements
II. Reviewing and commenting on a client-prepared business plan

a. I only
b. II only
c. Both I and II
d. Neither I nor II (5/98, Law, #1, 6618)

19. Nile, CPA, on completing an audit, was asked by the client to provide technical assistance in integrating a new IT system. The set of pronouncements designed to guide Nile in this engagement is the Statement(s) on
a. Quality Control Standards
b. Auditing Standards
c. Standards for Accountants' IT Services
d. Standards for Consulting Services
(5/94, Law, #6, amended, 4761)

20. Under the Statements on Standards for Consulting Services, which of the following statements best reflects a CPA's responsibility when undertaking a consulting services engagement? The CPA must
a. Not seek to modify any agreement made with the client
b. Not perform any attest services for the client
c. Inform the client of significant reservations concerning the benefits of the engagement
d. Obtain a written understanding with the client concerning the time for completion of the engagement (11/95, Law, #5, 5874)

21. According to the standards of the profession, which of the following events would require a CPA performing a consulting services engagement for a nonaudit client to withdraw from the engagement?

I. The CPA has a conflict of interest that is disclosed to the client and the client consents to the CPA continuing the engagement.
II. The CPA fails to obtain a written understanding from the client concerning the scope of the engagement.

a. I only
b. II only
c. Both I and II
d. Neither I nor II (5/95, Law, #3, 5337)

22. According to the profession's standards, which of the following is **not** required of a CPA performing a consulting engagement?
a. Complying with Statements on Standards for Consulting Services
b. Obtaining an understanding of the nature, scope, and limitations of the engagement
c. Supervising staff who are assigned to the engagement
d. Maintaining independence from the client
(11/94, Law, #5, 5183)

23. Which of the following services is a CPA generally required to perform when conducting a personal financial planning engagement?
a. Assisting the client to identify tasks that are essential in order to act on planning decisions
b. Assisting the client to take action on planning decisions
c. Monitoring progress in achieving goals
d. Updating recommendations and revising planning decisions (R/99, Law, #1, 6852)

24. A member would be in violation of the Standards for Tax Services if the member recommends a return position under which of the following circumstances?
a. It does **not** meet the realistic possibility standard but is **not** frivolous and is disclosed on the return.
b. It might result in penalties and the member advises the taxpayer and discusses avoiding such penalties through disclosing the position.
c. It does **not** meet the realistic possibility standard but the member feels the return has a minimal likelihood for examination by the IRS.
d. It meets the realistic possibility standard based on the well-reasoned opinion of the taxpayer's attorney. (R/05, REG, 1519T, #18, 7884)

25. Which of the following is a term for an attest engagement in which a CPA assesses a client's commercial Internet site for predefined criteria that are designed to measure transaction integrity, information protection, and disclosure of business practices?
a. ElectroNet
b. EDIFACT
c. TechSafe
d. WebTrust (R/99, AUD, #2, 8006)

Problem 32-2 ADDITIONAL MULTIPLE CHOICE QUESTIONS (33 to 44 minutes)

26. According to the standards of the profession, which of the following activities may be required in exercising due care?

	Consulting with experts	*Obtaining specialty accreditation*
a.	Yes	Yes
b.	Yes	No
c.	No	Yes
d.	No	No

(11/95, Law, #3, 5872)

27. Burrow & Co., CPAs, have provided annual audit and tax compliance services to Mare Corp. for several years. Mare has been unable to pay Burrow in full for services Burrow rendered 19 months ago. Burrow is ready to begin fieldwork for the current year's audit. Under the ethical standards of the profession, which of the following arrangements will permit Burrow to begin the fieldwork on Mare's audit?
a. Mare sets up a two-year payment plan with Burrow to settle the unpaid fee balance.
b. Mare commits to pay the past due fee in full before the audit report is issued.
c. Mare gives Burrow an 18-month note payable for the full amount of the past due fees before Burrow begins the audit.
d. Mare engages another firm to perform the fieldwork, and Burrow is limited to reviewing the workpapers and issuing the audit report.
(R/02, Law, #4, 7114)

28. According to the standards of the profession, which of the following activities would most likely **not** impair a CPA's independence?
a. Providing extensive advisory services for a client
b. Contracting with a client to supervise the client's office personnel
c. Signing a client's checks in emergency situations
d. Accepting a luxurious gift from a client
(11/95, Law, #4, 5873)

29. Under the ethical standards of the profession, which of the following business relationships would generally not impair an auditor's independence?
a. Promoter of a client's securities
b. Member of a client's board of directors
c. Client's general counsel
d. Advisor to a client's board of trustees
(R/06, REG, 1454L, #5, 8175)

30. Under the ethical standards of the profession, which of the following positions would be considered a position of significant influence in an audit client?
a. A marketing position related to the client's primary products
b. A policy-making position in the client's finance division
c. A staff position in the client's research and development division
d. A senior position in the client's human resources division (R/05, REG, 1338L, #17, 7883)

31. In which of the following situations would a CPA's independence be considered to be impaired?

I. The CPA maintains a checking account that is fully insured by a government deposit insurance agency at an audit-client financial institution.
II. The CPA has a direct financial interest in an audit client, but the interest is maintained in a blind trust.
III. The CPA owns a commercial building and leases it to an audit client. The lease qualifies as a capital lease.

a. I and II
b. II and III
c. I and III
d. I, II, and III (11/92, AUD, #2, amended, 2936)

32. According to the profession's ethical standards, an auditor would be considered independent in which of the following instances?

a. The auditor is the officially appointed stock transfer agent of a client.
b. The auditor's checking account that is fully insured by a federal agency is held at a client financial institution.
c. The client owes the auditor fees for more than two years prior to the issuance of the audit report.
d. The client is the only tenant in a commercial building owned by the auditor. The lease qualifies as a capital lease under GAAP.

(5/94, Law, #4, amended, 4759)

33. Under the ethical standards of the profession, which of the following investments in a client is **not** considered to be a direct financial interest?

a. An investment held through a non-regulated mutual fund
b. An investment held through a nonclient investment club
c. An investment held in a blind trust
d. An investment held by the trustee of a trust

(R/02, Law, #3, amended, 7113)

34. An auditor's independence is considered impaired if the auditor has

a. An immaterial, indirect financial interest in a client
b. An automobile loan from a client bank, collateralized by the automobile
c. A joint, closely-held business investment with the client that is material to the auditor's net worth
d. A mortgage loan, executed with a financial institution client on March 1,1990, that is material to the auditor's net worth

(R/05, REG, 0903L, #18, 7864)

35. According to the standards of the profession, which of the following circumstances will prevent a CPA performing audit engagements from being independent?

a. Obtaining a collateralized automobile loan from a financial institution client
b. Litigation with a client relating to billing for consulting services for which the amount is immaterial
c. Employment of the CPA's spouse as a client's internal auditor
d. Acting as an honorary trustee for a not-for-profit organization client (5/95, Law, #1, 5335)

36. Under the ethical standards of the profession, which of the following situations involving nondependent members of an auditor's family is most likely to impair the auditor's independence?

a. A parent's immaterial investment in a client
b. A first cousin's loan from a client
c. A spouse's employment with a client
d. A sibling's loan to a marketing manager of a client (R/02, Law, #2, amended, 7112)

37. According to the ethical standards of the profession, a CPA's independence would most likely be impaired if the CPA

a. Accepted any gift from a client
b. Became a member of a trade association that is a client
c. Contracted with a client to supervise the client's office personnel
d. Served, with a client bank, as a cofiduciary of an estate or trust (R/07, REG, 0364L, #19, 8443)

38. Which of the following best describes what is meant by the term generally accepted auditing standards?

a. Rules acknowledged by the accounting profession because of their universal application
b. Pronouncements issued by the Auditing Standards Board
c. Measures of the quality of the auditor's performance
d. Procedures to be used to gather evidence to support financial statements (5/95, Law, #2, 5336)

39. Under which of the following circumstances may a CPA charge fees that are contingent upon finding a specific result?

a. For an examination of prospective financial statements
b. For an audit or a review if agreed upon by both the CPA and the client
c. For a compilation if a third party will use the financial statement and disclosure is not made in the report
d. If fixed by courts, other public authorities, or in tax matters if based on the results of judicial proceedings (R/07, REG, C01362R, #18, 8442)

40. According to the ethical standards of the profession, which of the following acts is generally prohibited?
a. Purchasing a product from a third party and reselling it to a client
b. Writing a financial management newsletter promoted and sold by a publishing company
c. Accepting a commission for recommending a product to an audit client without informing the client's management
d. Accepting engagements obtained through the efforts of third parties
(11/95, Law, #1, amended, 5870)

41. A CPA who is **not** in public practice is obligated to follow which of the following rules of conduct?
a. Independence
b. Integrity and objectivity
c. Contingent fees
d. Commissions (R/05, REG, A0564L, #19, 7885)

42. According to the profession's ethical standards, a CPA would be considered independent in which of the following instances?
a. A client leases a warehouse from the CPA under a lease that qualifies as a capital lease.
b. The CPA has a material direct financial interest in a client, but transfers the interest into a blind trust.
c. The CPA owns an office building and the mortgage on the building is guaranteed by a client.
d. The CPA belongs to a country club client in which membership requires the acquisition of a pro rata share of equity.
(11/93, AUD, #46, amended, 4238)

43. Which of the following statements best describes the ethical standard of the profession pertaining to advertising and solicitation?
a. All forms of advertising and solicitation are prohibited.
b. There are **no** prohibitions regarding the manner in which CPAs may solicit new business.
c. A CPA may advertise in any manner that is **not** false, misleading, or deceptive.
d. A CPA may only solicit new clients through mass mailings. (R/02, Law, #1, 7111)

44. Which of the following actions by a CPA most likely violates the profession's ethical standards?
a. Arranging with a financial institution to collect notes issued by a client in payment of fees due
b. Compiling the financial statements of a client that employed the CPA's spouse as a bookkeeper
c. Retaining client records after the client has demanded their return
d. Purchasing a segment of an insurance company's business that performs actuarial services for postemployment benefit plans
(5/94, Law, #1, amended, 4756)

45. Which of the following services may a CPA perform in carrying out a consulting service engagement for a client?

I. Review of the client-prepared business plan
II. Preparation of information for obtaining financing

a. I only
b. II only
c. Both I and II
d. Neither I nor II (5/96, Law, #1, 6257)

46. According to the profession's standards, which of the following would be considered consulting services?

	Advisory services	*Implementation services*	*Product services*
a.	Yes	Yes	Yes
b.	Yes	Yes	No
c.	Yes	No	Yes
d.	No	Yes	Yes

(11/94, Law, #6, 5184)

47. While preparing a client's individual federal tax return, the CPA noticed that there was an error in the previous year's tax return that was prepared by another CPA. The CPA has which of the following responsibilities to this client?
a. Inform the client and recommend corrective action
b. Inform the client and the previous CPA in writing, and leave it to their discretion whether a correction should be made
c. Discuss the matter verbally with the former CPA and suggest that corrective action be taken for the client
d. Notify the IRS if the error could be considered fraudulent or could involve other taxpayers
(R/06, REG, C03929R, #39, 8209)

SIMULATIONS

Note: The editors recommend that candidates who are unfamiliar with researching the AICPA's database of professional literature review the sample research question in the Practical Advice appendix before answering their first research question. Candidates typically should start developing their research skills at least a month before their exams. While written communication responses must be on the specified topic and should not conflict with guidance, essays on the computer-based exam are scored mainly for writing skills, rather than content. The content may be tested in any question format, either in multiple choice questions or within simulations.

Problem 32-3 (20 to 30 minutes)

Fox Corp. is an audit client of Sullivan Associates, CPAs. In Year 5, Fox's audit committee engaged Sullivan to perform litigation support services. The services were completed in January Year 5, and Sullivan billed Fox in February Year 5.

In February Year 6, Sullivan began its annual audit of Fox's financial statements. During the course of the audit, Sullivan discovered that Fox's officers had committed management fraud. The officers' fraud resulted in material misstatements in the financial statements. In March Year 6, Sullivan issued an auditor's report containing an unqualified opinion on the financial statements. As of that date, Fox had not paid Sullivan's outstanding February Year 5 bill. (11/98, Law, #3, amended, 8551)

Indicate whether the following statements are true or false.

Statement	True/False
1. Requirements for certified public accountant (CPA) licenses and permits are regulated by the Securities and Exchange Commission (SEC).	
2. The Public Company Accounting Oversight Board (PCAOB) registers accounting firms that audit issuers of publicly traded securities.	
3. The Internal Revenue Service (IRS) may fine a CPA for violations of tax rules and regulations.	
4. The IRS may bar a CPA from practicing before the IRS based on noncompliance with tax rules and regulations.	
5. A CPA must join either a state CPA society or the American Institute of Certified Public Accountants (AICPA) to practice public accounting.	
6. If an AICPA member's CPA license to practice public accounting is suspended as a disciplinary measure by any governmental authority, AICPA membership may be terminated automatically without a hearing, with automatic suspension ceasing once the period of license suspension has expired.	
7. AICPA membership may be terminated for failure to comply with continuing education requirements.	
8. The AICPA Joint Trial Board may hear and rule on alleged violations of a state CPA society's code of professional conduct in cases when a valid written agreement for this procedure exists between the AICPA and the state society.	

Write an internal memorandum as a member of a review board to your fellow members stating whether Sullivan committed any violations of the standards of the profession in the areas of independence and due care. Explain your conclusions and indicate what, if any, additional actions Sullivan should have taken.

Scenario | Practice | Communication | **Research**

Research Question: What authoritative reference considers having the authority to execute a transaction on behalf of a client an activity that would impair the independence of a member of the profession?

Paragraph Reference Answer: ____________

Problem 32-4 (20 to 30 minutes)

Merlot Corp. engaged Doyle, a CPA licensed by a state board of accountancy, to perform an audit of Merlot's financial statements so that Merlot could obtain a large capital improvement loan. During the audit, Stevens, Merlot's CFO, asked Doyle to accept a consulting engagement to assist Merlot with the installation of a new computerized accounting system. Doyle accepted the consulting engagement and performed it simultaneously with the audit.

While performing the audit, Doyle discovered material misstatements in Merlot's financial statements resulting from management fraud committed by Stevens. Doyle notified Stevens of the discovery and was told to disregard it or Doyle would lose the consulting engagement. Believing that the consulting engagement would be lost, Doyle intentionally did not notify Merlot's audit committee of the fraud, and rendered an unqualified opinion on Merlot's financial statements.

Merlot submitted to Ocean Bank the materially misstated financial statements together with Doyle's auditor's report. Ocean relied on the opinion in agreeing to finance Merlot's capital improvement.

While performing the consulting engagement, Doyle failed to discover that Merlot's new computerized accounting system had insufficient control procedures because Doyle omitted steps in order to complete the engagement on time. The insufficient control procedures had allowed and were allowing employees to steal from the corporation.

As a result of Stevens's fraud, Merlot defaulted on the Ocean loan and was petitioned into bankruptcy under Chapter 11 of the Federal Bankruptcy Code.

The following events resulted from the above situation:

- Merlot Corp. reported Doyle's actions to the state board of accountancy that licensed Doyle.
- Merlot Corp. sued Doyle for negligence in performing the consulting engagement.
- Ocean Bank sued Doyle for common law fraud for giving an unqualified opinion on Merlot's financial statements. (11/96, Law, #2a, 8550)

Poole & Sterns, CPAs, performed an audit of Flight, a privately held corporation. Poole & Sterns are AICPA members.

While performing the audit, Poole & Sterns, developed and included in its electronic working papers adjusting and closing journal entries, without which Flight's financial information is incomplete.

Flight's management requested copies of the adjusting and closing journal entries in XBML form. Poole & Sterns' audit software prints adjusting and closing journal entries to *.txt files, but doesn't provide them in XBML form.

Indicate whether the following statements are true or false.

Statement	True/False
1. Poole & Sterns, CPAs', working papers must be made available to the Flight.	
2. Poole & Sterns, CPAs, should provide the adjusting and closing journal entries to Flight regardless of whether the fees related to the audit are unpaid.	
3. Poole & Sterns, CPAs, must provide the adjusting and closing journal entries to Flight regardless of whether any fees related to other work are unpaid.	
4. Poole & Sterns, CPAs, must provide the adjusting and closing journal entries to Flight in XBML form.	
5. Once Poole & Sterns, CPAs, have provided the adjusting and closing journal entries to Flight, it need not comply with subsequent for the same information.	
6. If the engagement is ended before completion and fees incurred to that point are paid, Poole & Sterns, CPAs, must provide such adjusting and closing journal entries to Flight as are known to it at that point.	
7. As Flight is a privately held corporation, Poole & Sterns, CPAs, must keep working papers related to the audit for one year and no longer.	
8. Poole & Sterns, CPAs, may disclose information in the working papers without Flight's consent to comply with professional practice review procedures under AICPA authorization.	

Write an internal memorandum as a member of a review board to your fellow members stating whether or not Doyle violated the profession's standards in the areas of independence (when accepting the engagements), due care, and acts discreditable to the profession. Give the reasons for your conclusions.

Research Question: What authoritative reference permits a member in public practice to disclose confidential client information during a review in conjunction with a prospective purchase, sale, or merger of all or part of a member's practice without the specific consent of the client?

Paragraph Reference Answer: ____________

Problem 32-5 (20 to 30 minutes)

Sienna, CPA, performed an audit of Lintel, a privately held corporation. Sienna doesn't audit any public companies. Sienna violated the profession's standards in the areas of independence (when accepting the engagement), due care, and acts discreditable to the profession. (Editors, 8552)

Peirce & Hinds, CPAs, are reviewing issues of independence with regard to potential audit clients. Peirce & Hinds are AICPA members. Except as noted, Peirce & Hinds do not have any other association with these potential clients.

Indicate whether Peirce & Hinds, CPAs, may accept an engagement to audit each potential client.

Statement	Yes/No
1. Hinds was the controller of Amos, Inc., resigning in January, Year 3, to partner with Peirce. Amos, Inc. is seeking an auditor for its Year 3 financial statements. Hinds no longer has any financial interest in Amos' pension plan.	
2. Worth, a former audit employee of Peirce & Hinds, quit last year and now is internal auditor at Claire Cosmetics. Worth is not owed any payments by Peirce & Hinds. Worth does not influence or participate in any of Peirce & Hinds, CPAs' activities. Peirce & Hinds, CPAs' ongoing attest engagement team plans to consider the appropriateness and necessity of engagement procedures modification to adjust for the risk that audit effectiveness could be reduced as a result of Worth's prior knowledge of the audit plan.	
3. Elegance, Inc. authorized Peirce & Hinds to sign payroll checks for it in emergency situations.	
4. Yost, a professional employee of Peirce & Hinds, is a motorcycle enthusiast. This year, he received the gift of a prototype motorcycle from Gremlin Motors, Inc. When he realized Gremlin was seeking a new auditor, Yost suggested Peirce & Hinds as auditors to Gremlin and promptly reported the gift to Peirce & Hinds.	
5. Peirce & Hinds operate a local area network for Ingot, Inc.	
6. Peirce's husband is Director of Marketing at Kelpie, Inc., but does not influence the financial reporting process in this position.	
7. Hinds interviewed applicants for controller and recommended qualified candidates to Mole, Inc.	
8. Within the last year, Peirce & Hinds performed an engagement to provide assistance in assessing business risks and control processes for Optimal Solutions, Inc.	

Write an internal memorandum as a member of a review board to your fellow members stating the actions the state board of accountancy, the Public Company Accounting Oversight Board, and the Internal Revenue Service may take against Sienna as a result of Sienna's violations.

Scenario | Independence | Communication | Research

Research Question: What authoritative reference permits a member in public practice to disclose confidential client information in conjunction with an enforceable subpoena?

Paragraph Reference Answer: ___________

Solution 32-1 MULTIPLE CHOICE ANSWERS

Governing Entities

1. (d) It is the individual state boards of accountancy which have the authority to grant CPA licenses to practice public accounting, and, thus, would ordinarily be the bodies to suspend or revoke such a license. The SEC, the AICPA, and state CPA societies do not have authority to grant, suspend, or revoke CPA licenses.

Code of Professional Conduct

2. (a) The AICPA's Code of Professional Conduct states that a distinguishing mark of a profession is its acceptance of responsibility to the general public.

3. (d) A CPA who provides auditing and other attestation services should be independent in fact and appearance. In providing all other services, an accountant should maintain objectivity and avoid conflicts of interest. Thus, an accountant need not be independent when providing compilation services or when preparing a tax return.

4. (b) A CPA firm's procedures should enable an assistant to document the details of the disagreement with the conclusion reached. If the assistant concludes that the financial statements could be materially misstated, the assistant should make the concerns known to the appropriate level of management within the organization and should consider preparing appropriate documentation. If appropriate action is not taken, the assistant should consider her/his continuing relationship with the employer and any responsibility to communicate to third parties, such as regulatory authorities. The assistant may wish to consult with legal counsel (Interpretation 102-4).

5. (a, d) Two responses are required for full credit. The standard of due care requires a critical review of the work done and the judgment exercised by those assisting in the audit. It also requires that the client be advised when a consultant must be engaged to perform the audit.

Independence

6. (a) Independence is considered to be impaired if, when the report on the client's current year is issued, fees remain unpaid for professional services provided more than one year prior to the date of the report. Such amounts assume the characteristics of a loan within the meaning of Rule 101 (ET 191-52). Recommending a controller's position description is not a violation of the ethical standards as long as the final hiring decision is made by management of the client (ET 101-3). Purchasing a CPA firm's practice of monthly write-ups does not violate any provisions of the Code or client confidentiality. A member firm may make arrangements with a bank to collect notes issued by a client in payment of fees due (ET 591-2).

7. (d) The independence of a member or firm may be impaired because of nondependent close relatives, which includes parent, sibling, or nondependent children that are in a position to influence the attest arrangement.

8. (b) Independence is impaired if a member obtains a loan from an entity that, at the time of obtaining the loan, is a client requiring independence, except for certain personal loans obtained under normal lending procedures, terms, and requirements, and kept current as to terms.

9. (c) Independence will be considered to be impaired if during the period of the professional engagement, or at the time of expressing an opinion, the member or the member's firm had or was committed to acquire any direct or material indirect financial interest in the enterprise (ET 101-1). In other words, if a direct financial interest exists, materiality is not a factor.

General & Technical Standards

10. (c) ET 203 provides that a CPA must use professional judgment in deciding when a deviation from GAAP is appropriate. Circumstances that may justify a departure include new legislation or the evolution of a new form of business.

11. (b) AU 150 states, "Auditing standards differ from auditing procedures in that procedures relate to acts to be performed, whereas standards deal with measures of the quality of the performance of those acts and the objectives to be attained by the use of the procedures undertaken."

Other Professional Responsibilities

12. (b) Interpretation 501-1 requires an auditor to return a client's records after the client has demanded them. Representing a client in connection with obtaining a private letter ruling is one of the specific tax matters for which an accountant may charge a contingent fee. Confidential client information may be disclosed without the client's permission in conjunction with a prospective purchase, sale, or merger of the accountant's practice. If an auditor

does not follow requirements of government audits, this lapse must be disclosed in the auditor's report.

13. (b) ET 301 prohibits the disclosure of confidential information obtained in the course of the professional engagement without the consent of the client, but does not prohibit review of a CPA's professional practices (including pertinent information) as a part of an AICPA authorized voluntary quality review program.

14. (a) ET 502-2 provides, "Advertising or other forms of solicitation that are false, misleading, or deceptive are not in the public interest and are prohibited." A prohibited activity is one that contains a representation that specific professional services in current or future periods will be performed for a stated fee, estimated fee, or fee range when it is likely at the time of representation that such fees would be substantially increased and the prospective client was not advised of such likelihood.

15. (b) The service in question constitutes a type of service performed by public accountants, and the member may hire such an employee as long as the CPA is able to supervise the specialist and evaluate her/his results (ET 291-9). The CPA is not required to be a specialist outside of the realm of accounting and tax services. The CPA is permitted to be associated with non-CPA professionals, as long as the association is not misleading and the client is aware of the relationship.

16. (c) A contingent fee for preparing a client's income tax return would not be permitted under the ethical standards of the profession. However, a contingent fee for representing a client in tax court would be permitted under the ethical standards, because the tax authority initiated the proceedings. A member who accepts or pays a referral fee in relation to a client must disclose such acceptance or payment to the client. A member is prohibited from recommending or referring, for a commission, any product or service to a client when that member or member's firm performs a financial statement compilation where the member might reasonably expect that a third party will use the statement. Since the financial statement compilation was for internal-use only, it would be permitted under the ethical standards.

Consulting Services

17. (a) The Bylaws of the AICPA include general definitions which state that in addition to furnishing advice in conjunction with their independent examinations of financial statements, CPAs are engaged to provide objective advice and consultation on various management problems (BL 921.09). Statements on Standards for Consulting Services (CS 100.07) state that the CPA is to serve the client interest by seeking to accomplish the objectives established by the understanding with the client while maintaining integrity and objectivity.

18. (b) According to the Statement on Standards for Consulting Services, consulting services include reviewing and commenting on a client-prepared business plan. Expressing a conclusion about the reliability of a client's financial statements is an attest engagement, not a consulting services engagement.

19. (d) Under the Standards for Consulting Services, advisory services are used to develop findings, conclusions and recommendations for client consideration and decision making. A stated example of advisory services is the defining of requirements for an information system.

20. (c) Under the Statements of Standards for Consulting Services, a CPA has the responsibility to inform the client of significant reservations concerning the benefits of the engagement. The Standards for Consulting Services do not require a CPA to obtain a written understanding with the client concerning the time for completion of the engagement. Nor do the Standards prohibit a CPA from modifying a client agreement or from performing attest services.

21. (d) ET 202 requires that the client be informed of any conflict of interest or significant reservations concerning the scope or benefits of the engagement. However, independence is *not* required. This rule also requires a written *or oral* understanding between consultant and client.

22. (d) ET 201 requires a CPA performing a consulting engagement to comply with Standards on Consulting Services and to supervise staff assigned to the engagement. ET 202 requires that the CPA obtain an understanding of the nature, scope, and limitations of the engagement. ET 202 also states that performing a consulting service does not, of itself, impair independence.

Personal Financial Planning

23. (a) Personal financial planning engagement activities include defining the engagement objectives, planning specific procedures, developing a basis for recommendations, communicating recommendations to the client, and identifying action tasks for planning decisions. Assisting the client to take action on planning decisions, monitoring progress in achieving goals, and updating recommendations and revising planning decisions could also be part of a personal financial planning engagement but are not necessarily required.

Tax Services

24. (c) The Statement on Standards for Tax Services No. 1, *Tax Return Positions,* contains the standards a member should follow in recommending tax return positions and in preparing or signing tax returns. In general, a member should have a good-faith belief that the tax return position being recommended has a realistic possibility of being sustained administratively or judicially on its merits, if challenged. A member may recommend a tax return position that the member concludes is not frivolous as long as the member advises the taxpayer to appropriately disclose. When recommending tax return positions and preparing or signing a return on which a tax return position is taken, a member should advise the taxpayer regarding potential penalty consequences of such tax return position and the opportunity, if any, to avoid such penalties through disclosure.

AICPA Assurance Service

25. (d) The CPA WebTrust symbol on a web site indicates that the organization meets AICPA business practice disclosures, transaction integrity, and information protection criteria. A specially trained and licensed CPA reviews compliance with these criteria every 90 days. EDIFACT is an international EDI format. (ANSI X12 is a domestic EDI format.) ElectroNet and TechSafe are not terms that are used widely.

Solution 32-2 ADDITIONAL MULTIPLE CHOICE ANSWERS

Code of Professional Conduct

26. (b) According to the standards of the profession, exercise in due care may require consulting with experts, but would not require obtaining specialty accreditation.

27. (b) Independence is considered impaired if fees for professional services rendered for more than one year prior are not collected before the issuance of the CPA's report for the current year. This includes billed and unbilled fees and notes receivable arising from such fees (ET 191-52).

Independence

28. (a) According to the standards of the profession (ET 191-8), providing extensive advisory services for a client would not impair the CPA's independence. Contracting with a client to supervise the client's office personnel, signing client checks, and accepting luxurious gifts would all impair a CPA's independence.

29. (d) Several relationships impair independence, including being a member of management (including the board of directors) or promoter. Serving as a client's general counsel, stock transfer, escrow agent, or registrar also impairs independence. Under the ethical standards of the profession, an advisor relationship in and of itself doesn't impair an auditor's independence.

30. (b) Independence is considered impaired if a spouse or dependent person (immediate family) of the member is employed in a position that allows significant influence over the client's operating, financial, or accounting policies. Independence is considered impaired if the position with the client involves activities that are audit-sensitive, even though the position is not one that allows significant influence. A person's activities would be considered audit sensitive if such activities are normally an element of, or subject to, significant internal controls; for example, the positions of cashier, internal auditor, accounting or finance supervisor, purchasing agent, or inventory warehouse supervisor.

31. (b) A CPA's independence would not be considered to be impaired by her/his maintaining a checking account that is fully insured by a government deposit insurance agency at an audit-client financial institution (ET 191-70). Independence is considered impaired if a CPA has a direct financial interest in a client, whether or not it is placed in a blind trust (ET 191-68). Independence generally is considered impaired if a lease meets the criteria of a capital lease as defined by GAAP and independence is not considered impaired if a lease meets the criteria of an operating lease as long as the terms and conditions are comparable with other leases of a similar nature and all amounts are paid in accordance with the terms of the lease (ET 191-91).

32. (b) ET 191-70 states that the independence of an auditor with respect to a financial institution is not impaired if the accounts are fully insured by the appropriate state or federal insurance agency. General activities under ET 101-3 states that a member who serves as a client's stock transfer or escrow agent, registrar, general counsel or its equivalent would impair independence. ET 191-52 provides that independence is impaired when fees for professional services rendered for more than one prior year are not collected before the issuance of the report for

the current year. ET 191-91 states that independence generally is considered impaired if a lease meets the criteria of a capital lease as defined by GAAP and independence is not considered impaired if a lease meets the criteria of an operating lease as long as the terms and conditions are comparable with other leases of a similar nature and all amounts are paid in accordance with the terms of the lease.

33. (a) If a member does not have the ability to direct investments, an investment in a client through a financial service product (such as a mutual fund) is considered an indirect financial interest and, hence, doesn't necessarily impair independence (ET 191-109). Direct or material indirect financial interest in a client impairs independence. In addition, if a member has significant influence over the non-regulated mutual investment fund, independence would be considered to be impaired (ET 191-35). Independence is considered impaired if a covered member owns stock in a client through an investment club, where presumably the member has the ability to direct investments, whether or not exercised, resulting in a direct financial interest (ET 191-109). Accordingly, any of the club's investments in a client are deemed to impair independence regardless of materiality (ET 191-36). Independence is considered impaired even if a CPA has a material indirect financial interest in a client, whether or not it is placed in a blind trust. Furthermore, the member should ensure that any blind trust that s/he is a beneficiary of does not hold a direct or material indirect financial interest in any of the member's client's (ET 191-68). The requirements for independence with regard to ordinary trusts are not less restrictive.

34. (c) A direct financial interest (business investment) always impairs an accountant's independence, regardless of materiality. Independence is impaired when a CPA holds a direct or material indirect financial interest. A loan to or from a client generally impairs independence; however, Interpretation 101-5 permits certain loans. These loans include car loans collateralized by the vehicles from financial institution clients when the loans are current as to all terms at all times and obtained under normal lending terms, requirements, and procedures. Interpretation 101-5 also permits grandfathered mortgages that are current as to all terms obtained under normal lending procedures, terms, and requirements before the institution became a client requiring independence. With a twenty-first century question mentioning a 1990 date, the candidate may assume this loan meets these requirements. Candidates may have to make similar assumptions to answer other exam questions.

35. (c) ET 101-1 states that independence is impaired if a spouse's employment is in a position where the spouse's activities are audit sensitive, and specifically mentions *internal auditors.* Obtaining a collateralized car loan from an institutional client is a permitted loan (ET 101-5). Independence is usually not considered impaired in the case of threatened or actual litigation that is not related to the audit performed for the client for an amount that is immaterial (ET 101-6). Independence is also not considered impaired for a CPA to be an honorary trustee for a not-for-profit organization client (ET 101-4).

36. (c) Independence is considered impaired if a spouse or dependent person (immediate family) of the member is employed in a position that allows significant influence over the client's operating, financial, or accounting policies. Independence is considered impaired if the position with the client involves activities that are audit-sensitive, even though the position is not one that allows significant influence. A person's activities would be considered audit sensitive if such activities are normally an element of, or subject to, significant internal controls; for example, the positions of cashier, internal auditor, accounting supervisor, purchasing agent, or inventory warehouse supervisor.

37. (c) Serving in any capacity equivalent to that of a member of management during the period covered by the financial statements is considered to impair independence. A CPA ordinarily may accept a *de minimis* gift from a client, become a member of a trade association that is a client, or serve as a cofiduciary or an estate or trust with a client bank.

General & Technical Standards

38. (c) AU 150 states, "Auditing standards differ from auditing procedures in that *procedures* relate to acts to be performed, whereas *standards* deal with measures of the quality of the performance of those acts and the objectives to be attained by the use of the procedures undertaken."

Other Professional Responsibilities

39. (d) An AICPA member in public practice shall not offer or render services under an agreement whereby the fee is contingent upon the findings or results, specifically including an examination of prospective financial information; an audit or review or financial statements; or a compilation of financial statements, when the member reasonably might expect that a third party will use the statement. Fees that are fixed by the courts or public authorities or which are determined in tax matters by judicial proceedings or governmental agency findings are not considered contingent and, therefore, are permitted.

40. (c) ET 503 prohibits a CPA from accepting a commission for recommending a product to a client, unless the CPA informs management. The other activities are not prohibited.

41. (b) A CPA who is not in public practice is obligated to integrity and objectivity, was well as the discreditable acts, rules of conduct.

42. (d) As long as membership in a club is essentially a social matter, independence of the member's firm would not be considered to be impaired because such equity or debt ownership is not considered to be a direct financial interest (ET 191-36). ET 191-91 states that independence is considered impaired if a lease meets the criteria of a capital lease as defined by GAAP and independence is not considered impaired if a lease meets the criteria of an operating lease as long as the terms and conditions are comparable with other leases of a similar nature and all amounts are paid in accordance with the terms of the lease. The independence of the member would be considered impaired whether or not the direct financial interest is placed in a blind trust (ET 191-68). The client's guarantee of the CPA's loan creates a material indirect financial relationship between the CPA and the client.

43. (c) Advertising or other forms of solicitation that are false, misleading, or deceptive are prohibited since they are not in the public interest.

44. (c) ET 501 specifically states that a CPA would be in violation of ET 501 should the CPA refuse to return a client's records after the client has demanded them. ET 591-02 allows note collection for fees. ET 191-74 allows the issuance of a compilation report provided the report specifically discloses the lack of independence. The CPA's purchase of a segment of an insurance company's business that performs actuarial services for post employment benefit plans would not impair independence (ET 101-3).

Consulting Services

45. (c) In the standards for consulting services (SSCS 1), reviewing and commenting on a client-prepared business plan is cited as an example of a consultation service. An example of a transaction consulting service is the preparation of information for obtaining financing.

46. (a) The Statement of Standards for Consulting Services (SSCS 1) defines advisory services, implementation services, and product services as consulting services.

Tax Services

47. (a) The internal revenue code (IRC) provides penalties for disclosure of confidential information to person unnecessary to the preparation or filing of a taxpayer's return.

PERFORMANCE BY SUBTOPICS

Each category below parallels a subtopic covered in Chapter 32. Record the number and percentage of questions you correctly answered in each subtopic area.

Governing Entities

Question #	Correct √
1	
# Questions	1
# Correct	______
% Correct	______

Code of Professional Conduct

Question #	Correct √
2	
3	
4	
5	
# Questions	4
# Correct	______
% Correct	______

Independence

Question #	Correct √
6	
7	
8	
9	
# Questions	4
# Correct	______
% Correct	______

General & Technical Standards

Question #	Correct √
10	
11	
# Questions	2
# Correct	______
% Correct	______

Other Professional Responsibilities

Question #	Correct √
12	
13	
14	
15	
16	
# Questions	5
# Correct	______
% Correct	______

Consulting Services

Question #	Correct √
17	
18	
19	
20	
21	
22	
# Questions	6
# Correct	______
% Correct	______

Personal Financial Planning

Question #	Correct √
23	
# Questions	1
# Correct	______
% Correct	______

Tax Services

Question #	Correct √
24	
# Questions	1
# Correct	______
% Correct	______

AICPA Assurance Service

Question #	Correct √
25	
# Questions	1
# Correct	______
% Correct	______

SIMULATION SOLUTIONS

Solution 32-3 Independence & Due Care

Practice (4 points)

1. False

CPAs are licensed to practice by individual state boards of accountancy. Requirements for licensing are regulated at the state level. The SEC governs the conduct of professionals practicing before it, which does not include all accountants.

2. True

The Sarbanes-Oxley Act established the PCAOB and charged it with the responsibility of overseeing the audits of issuers of publicly traded securities. The SEC has oversight and enforcement authority over the PCAOB.

3. True

IRS regulations provide for assessing fines for various violations.

4. True

The IRS may bar a CPA from practicing before the IRS based on incompetency or noncompliance with tax rules and regulations.

5. False

The right to practice public accounting requires only a valid CPA license.

6. True

If an AICPA member's CPA license or permit to practice public accounting is suspended, revoked, withdrawn, or cancelled as a disciplinary measure by any governmental authority, AICPA membership may be terminated automatically without a hearing. In the case of a suspension, automatic suspension ceases once the period of license or permit suspension has expired.

7. True

AICPA membership may be terminated for failure to comply with continuing education or practice-monitoring requirements.

8. True

The AICPA Joint Trial Board may hear and rule on alleged violations of a state CPA society's code of professional conduct in cases when a valid written agreement for this procedure exists between the AICPA and the state society.

Communication (5 points)

Date: August 1, Year 6

To: Review Board Members
From: J. Doe
Re: Confidential—Sullivan Review

Sullivan **did not violate the standards of the profession in the area of independence** by accepting the litigation support services engagement. A CPA may perform litigation support services for an attest client at the same time the CPA performs an audit. However, when Sullivan did not receive payment of the bill for the litigation support services within one year and prior to issuing an audit report, Sullivan's **independence was impaired**. Sullivan should not have issued the report.

Sullivan **violated the standards of the profession in the area of due care** in two ways. First, Sullivan did this by **knowingly and intentionally** giving an unqualified opinion on the **materially misstated** financial statements.

Second, Sullivan also violated due care by failing to comply with the standards of the profession **regarding the discovery of management fraud**. Under the standards of the profession, Sullivan, on discovering the fraud committed by Fox's officers, should have reported it directly to Fox's **audit committee**. Sullivan should have **insisted that the financial statements be revised**.

If the client did not revise the financial statements, Sullivan should have **either issued a nonstandard report or withdrawn from the engagement**. Sullivan should then have reported its action (in either case) to the client's **board of directors**. By failing to take these steps, Sullivan violated due care.

Research (1 point)

Paragraph Reference Answer: ET 101.05 101-3

Paragraph ET 101.05 101-3 states, "The following are some general activities that would be considered to impair a member's independence: authorizing, executing or consummating a transaction, or otherwise exercising authority on behalf of a client or having the authority to do so; or preparing source documents, in electronic or other form, evidencing the occurrence of a transaction; or having custody of client assets; or supervising client employees in the performance of their normal recurring activities; or determining which recommendations of the member should be implemented; or reporting to the board of directors on behalf of management; or serving as a client's stock transfer or escrow agent, registrar, general counsel or its equivalent."

Solution 32-4 Professional Responsibility

Work Papers (4 points)

1. False

All of an auditor's working papers need not be made available to a client. Information in an auditor's work papers that completes the client's incomplete financial information need not be made available to the client in all circumstances.

2. False

Information in an auditor's work papers that completes the client's incomplete financial information need not be made available to the client if any fees from that client are unpaid.

3. False

Information in an auditor's work papers that completes the client's incomplete financial information need not be made available to the client if any fees from that client are unpaid.

4. False

Information in an auditor's work papers that completes the client's incomplete financial information need not be converted into another medium when providing it to the client.

5. True

Once an AICPA member has complied with an initial request for information from an auditor's work papers that completes the client's incomplete financial information, the member need not comply with subsequent requests to provide such information again.

6. False

If an engagement has been completed, ordinarily a member should provide information in the work papers that completes the client's incomplete financial information to the client upon request. There is no requirement to do so for an incomplete engagement.

7. False

An auditor must retain working papers for an audit for a reasonable period of time. One year is unlikely to meet this requirement as this doesn't have the auditor retaining work papers during the period when the audit could be selected for a peer review nor when the financial statements are likely to be circulating as part of comparative financial statements.

8. True

Auditors may disclose information in work papers without the client's consent in select circumstances only; compliance with professional practice review procedures under AICPA authorization is one of these circumstances.

Communication (5 points)

Date: April 1, Year 1

To: Review Board Members
From: J. Doe
Re: Confidential—Doyle Review

Doyle **did not violate** the profession's standards regarding **independence** when the engagements were accepted. A CPA **may perform consulting services simultaneously with an audit** engagement.

Doyle **violated** the profession's standards in **failing to perform** the consulting engagement and the audit with **due care**. Doyle acted without due care by **failing to discover** the **insufficient control procedures** because of **omitting steps** in the engagement and by **issuing an unqualified opinion** on the financial statements.

Doyle committed **acts discreditable to the profession** by **failing to notify Merlot's audit committee** of the material misstatements contained in the financial statements, **failing to disclose** Stevens's fraudulent activities, and **profiting** from withholding the information.

Research (1 point)

Paragraph Reference Answer: ET 301.04 301-3

Paragraph ET 301.04 301-3 states, "A review of a member's professional practice is hereby authorized to include a review in conjunction with a prospective purchase, sale, or merger of all or part of a member's practice. The member must take appropriate precautions (for example, through a written confidentiality agreement) so that the prospective purchaser does not disclose any information obtained in the course of the review, since such information is deemed to be confidential client information."

Solution 32-5 Independence

Independence (4 points)

1. No

Independence would be impaired. An individual who formerly was employed by a client or associated with a client as an officer, director, promoter, underwriter, voting trustee, or trustee for a pension or profit-sharing trust of the client would impair the firm's independence if the individual was an individual in a position to influence the attest engagement for the client when the attest engagement covers any period that includes the former employment or association with that client. By accepting this engagement, Hinds would be auditing his or her own work. A key position is a position in which an individual has: primary responsibility for significant accounting functions that support material components of the financial statements; primary responsibility for the preparation of the financial statements; or the ability to exercise influence over the contents of the financial statements, including when the individual is a controller or any equivalent position.

2. Yes

Independence would **not** be impaired. If a partner or professional employee leaves the firm and subsequently is employed by or associated with that client in a key position, then the firm's independence would be impaired, unless among other conditions, the ongoing attest engagement team considers the appropriateness or necessity of engagement procedures modification to adjust for the risk that audit effectiveness could be reduced as a result of the former partner or professional employee's prior knowledge of the audit plan.

3. No

Independence would be impaired if the CPA accepted responsibility to sign or co-sign client checks, even only in emergency situations.

4. No

Independence would be impaired if an employee or partner accepts more than a token gift from a client, even with the knowledge of the firm.

5. No

Independence would be impaired if the CPA designed or developed a client's financial information system, made other than insignificant modifications to source code underlying a client's existing financial information system, supervised client personnel in the daily operation of a client's information system, or operated a client's local area network (LAN) system.

6. Yes

Independence would **not** be impaired. A member's independence is not considered impaired solely as a result of the following: (1) an individual in a member's immediate family was employed by the client in a position other than a key position; or (2) in connection with his or her employment, an individual in the immediate family of one of the following members participated in a retirement, savings, compensation, or similar plan that is a client, is sponsored by a client, or that invests in a client, provided such plan normally is offered to all employees in similar positions: (a) a partner or manager who provides ten or more hours of nonattest services to the client; or (b) any partner in the office in which the lead attest engagement partner primarily practices in connection with the attest engagement.

7. Yes

Independence would **not** be impaired if the CPA recommended a position description or candidate specifications, solicited and performed screening of candidates, and recommended qualified candidates to a client based on the client-approved criteria, or participated in employee hiring or compensation discussions in an advisory capacity.

8. Yes

Independence would **not** be impaired if the CPA either provided assistance in assessing the client's business risks and control processes or recommended a plan for making improvements to a client's control processes and assisted in implementing these improvements. Independence would be impaired if the CPA either made or approved business risk decisions or presented business risk considerations to the board or others on behalf of management.

Communication (5 points)

Date: April 1, Year 1

To: Review Board Members
From: J. Doe
Re: Sienna Review

The **state board of accountancy** may permanently **revoke** Sienna's license to practice or may **suspend** or **restrict** it for a period of time. If suspended or restricted, Sienna may be required to take additional CPE **courses** as a condition of reinstatement.

The **Public Company Accounting Oversight Board** (PCAOB) may **censure,** suspend, or bar from practice any professional that it finds incompetent or **lacking** in character or **integrity**; however, the PCAOB is unlikely to take action against Sienna as its mandate is to oversee the audits of public companies. As Sienna does not audit public companies, it is unlikely that Sienna is registered with the PCAOB.

The **Internal Revenue Service** may **bar** an accountant from practicing before it based upon **incompetence** or **noncompliance** with tax rules and regulations. It is unlikely that Sienna's violations in connection with a financial statement audit would fall under IRS jurisdiction, although they may **influence** decisions relating to Sienna's practice before the IRS, if any.

Research (1 point)

Paragraph Reference Answer: ET 301.01

Paragraph ET 301.01 states, "A member in public practice shall not disclose any confidential client information without the specific consent of the client. This rule shall not be construed (1) to relieve a member of his or her professional obligations under rules 202 [ET section 202.01] and 203 [ET section 203.01], (2) to affect in any way the member's obligation to comply with a validly issued and enforceable subpoena or summons, or to prohibit a member's compliance with applicable laws and government regulations, (3) to prohibit...." Search terms: confidential disclose, refined to *Code of Professional Conduct.*

Research Skills

Expect all simulations on the CPA exam to include a research element. This type of element probably will be about 2% of the point value for an exam section with simulations. (The BEC exam section does not have simulations.)

The research element of the simulation is completed when the candidate narrows the search (to answer the question asked) down to a paragraph. In other words, the paragraph or the paragraph reference is the answer that the examiners seek. The candidate doesn't provide commentary or conclusions.

Candidates cannot avoid the research merely by answering the question; they must provide the reference to the authoritative literature that answers the question. The search can be made by using the table of contents feature (if provided with the database of authoritative literature) or using the search engine and Boolean operators. The design of questions probably will tend to make use of the search engine and Boolean operators the most efficient means of completing the research elements for most candidates. The three Boolean operators are OR, AND, and NOT. A brief review of these operators is provided here.

A search using "accounting OR auditing" will find all documents containing either the word "accounting" or the word "auditing." All other things being equal, a search using OR typically will find the most documents. OR typically is used to search for terms that are used as synonyms, such as "management" and "client." As more terms are combined in an OR search, more documents are included in the results.

A search using "accounting AND auditing" will find all documents containing both the word "accounting" and the word "auditing." All other things being equal, a search using AND typically will find fewer documents than a search using OR, but more than a search using NOT. As more terms are combined in an AND search, fewer documents are included in the results.

A search using "accounting NOT auditing" will find all documents containing the word "accounting" except those that also contain the word "auditing." All other things being equal, a search using NOT typically will find the fewest documents. As more terms are combined in a NOT search, fewer documents are included in the results.

Boolean operators can be combined to refine searches. For example, the following parameters would find information on letters to a client's attorney inquiring about litigation, claims, and assessments: (attorney OR lawyer) AND (letter OR inquiry).

If you get too many or too few results from a search, refine your search parameters until you find what you need. The exam doesn't limit candidates from repeating searches with refined parameters.

Candidates should visit the AICPA's website (www.cpa-exam.org) and practice the free tutorial there. For more information about simulations, also see the **Practical Advice** section of this volume.

Using Videos to Study

Actively watch video classes, taking notes and answering questions as if it were a live class. If the lecturer recommends that you work an example as the video plays, write the information in the viewer guide, rather than merely following along. If the lecturer instructs you to stop the video to answer questions, stop the video. If the lecturer advises you to take notes, personalize your copy of the viewer guide. The lecturers provide these instructions with the insight gained from years of CPA review experience.

Each of the Hot•Spot™ videos concentrates on a few topics. Use them to help you study the areas that are most troubling for you. If you are strong in a topic, watching the video and answering the questions may be sufficient review. If your strength is moderate in a topic, you probably should read the related text before watching the video. If you are weak in a topic, one successful strategy is to watch the video (including following all of the lecturer's instructions), read the book, and then watch the video again.

Each of the Intensive videos is designed for a final, intensive review, after a candidate already has done considerable work. If time permits, use the Intensive videos at both the very beginning (for an overview) and set them aside until the final review in the last weeks before the exam. They contain concise, informative lectures, as well as CPA exam tips, tricks, and techniques that will help you to learn the material needed to pass the exam.

FYI: The Hot•Spot™ and Intensive video programs have similar content as the audio tutor and online video lectures, but they are not exactly the same.

For more information about video programs and passing the exam, contact a customer service representative about getting a copy of Bisk Education's video, *How to Pass the CPA Exam,* featuring Robert Monette, JD, CPA. Limited numbers of complimentary copies are available to qualified candidates.

CHAPTER 33

ACCOUNTANT'S LEGAL RESPONSIBILITIES

EXAM COVERAGE: The ethics and professional and legal responsibilities portion of the Regulation section of the CPA exam is designated by the examiners to be 15-20 percent of the section's point value. More information about point distribution and information eligible to be tested is included in the **Practical Advice** section of this volume.

CHAPTER 33

ACCOUNTANT'S LEGAL RESPONSIBILITIES

I. Civil Liability to Clients

A. Contractual Liability

Generally, an accountant occupies the position of an independent contractor in her/his relationships with clients. Consequently, an accountant's liability to a client usually stems from a violation of a contractual duty owed to the client.

1. **Contractual Duties** An accountant's contractual duties may be either express or implied.

   a. **Express Duties** Express duties are those which are spelled out by the terms of the contract. For example, if the terms of the engagement letter call for the accountant to perform particular services for the client, the accountant has an express contractual duty to perform those services.

   b. **Implied Duties** Implied duties are those which the courts have determined to be a part of every contract, whether or not the duty is expressed in the terms of the contract. For example, an accountant normally has an implied contractual duty not to perform in a negligent or fraudulent manner. This duty exists even though it is not mentioned in the contract.

2. **Duty to Perform** An accountant's duty to perform under a contract may not be delegated. That is, since the contract is one for a personal service, an accountant cannot escape liability by delegating to another the duty to perform under the contract. Therefore, partners in accounting firms may be held liable for the wrongful acts of their subordinates or employees committed in the course of their employment.

3. **Failure to Fulfill Contract Terms** An accountant generally will be held liable for her/his failure to fulfill the terms of a contract with a client. Failure to fulfill the terms of a contract usually constitutes a breach of the contract and may subject the accountant to liability in the form of money damages.

   a. If the accountant's failure to fulfill her/his contractual duties is so substantial that the client receives no real benefit from the accountant's performance, a material breach of contract has occurred. For example, a material breach is committed when an accountant fails to complete an audit or finishes late when time is of the essence. When an accountant commits a material breach, s/he is not entitled to compensation for whatever work may have been performed.

   b. Minor inaccuracies and insignificant errors or omissions normally will not constitute a material breach of contract. If the accountant's breach of contract is a minor one, s/he is entitled to be compensated for her/his services. However, the client probably will be permitted to reduce or offset the accountant's compensation by the amount of damage or loss attributable to the breach.

   c. In determining the adequacy of an accountant's performance under the terms of a contract, the law imposes upon the accountant the profession's generally accepted standards of competence and care. Thus, an accountant must demonstrate the average degree of learning and skill generally possessed by accountants.

4. **Fraud Discovery** An accountant's duties under a contract with a client normally do not include a duty to discover fraud, unless the accountant's own negligence prevents her/him

from discovering the fraud. For example, in an audit, a CPA would be negligent if s/he did not perform tests of controls to verify controls on which s/he planned to rely.

5. **Client Interference** An accountant will not incur contractual liability if her/his performance under the contract was prevented by the client's interference. The client has an implied contractual duty not to interfere with or prevent the accountant's performance.

6. **Nature of Damages** An accountant who breaches her/his contract with a client may be subject to liability for damages and losses that the client suffers as a direct result of the breach. However, punitive damages normally will not be awarded for a simple breach of contract. In contrast, punitive damages may be awarded in a tort action for negligence or constructive fraud against the accountant.

B. Liability for Negligence

As a general rule, an accountant may incur liability to a client for negligence. Liability may be based on an accountant's failure to exercise reasonable care under the circumstances.

1. **Negligence** Negligence is the failure to exercise that degree of care that a reasonable person would exercise under the same or similar circumstances. Negligent conduct falls below the standard established by law for the protection of others against unreasonable risk of loss or damage.

2. **Standard of Reasonable Care** The standard of reasonable care to which accountants are held is measured by that degree of quality, accuracy, and completeness that is demonstrated by the average accountant when performing her/his work with reasonable care.

   a. Honest inaccuracies and judgmental errors will not give rise to negligence liability so long as the accountant exercised reasonable care in performing her/his work.

   b. It is not necessary that an error or inaccuracy be intentional in order to give rise to negligence liability. Negligence may be based on unintentional errors resulting from failure to exercise reasonable care.

3. **Contributory Negligence** An accountant's liability for negligence may be reduced or eliminated if it can be shown that the client's own negligence contributed to the error or inaccuracy. For example, if an inaccuracy in a financial statement is due to the client's own error or omission, and the nature of it is such that the CPA cannot reasonably be expected to find it, the client's error may amount to contributory negligence that may mitigate the accountant's potential liability.

4. **Actual Damages** Actual damages are those losses that can be proven to have been caused directly by the wrongful acts of the defendant.

5. **Damages** Damages for negligence usually are calculated on the basis of the amount of loss or damage that would have been avoided by the exercise of reasonable care. As a general rule, punitive damages normally are not awarded in simple negligence cases.

C. Liability for Fraud

An accountant may be held liable for acts or omissions that amount to actual (intentional) fraud or constructive (unintentional) fraud.

1. **Actual Fraud** Actual fraud consists of an intentional act or omission that is designed to deceive. In order to constitute actual fraud, the following must occur:

   a. The act or omission itself must have been intentionally committed.

   b. The act or omission must have been accompanied by an intent to deceive.

Exhibit 1 ▸ Elements of Actual Fraud

ACTUAL FRAUD "MS RID"	
M	**M**isrepresentation: Material misrepresentation of fact
S	**S**cienter: Intent to deceive
R	**R**eliance
I	**I**ntent to Rely
D	**D**amages

2. **Constructive Fraud** Constructive fraud consists of acts or omissions characterized by **gross negligence** or lack of even slight care.

Exhibit 2 ▸ Elements of Constructive Fraud (Gross Negligence)

CONSTRUCTIVE FRAUD "MR RID"	
M	**M**isrepresentation
R	**R**eckless Disregard for Truth
R	**R**eliance
I	**I**ntent to Rely
D	**D**amages

a. In order to prove constructive fraud, it is not necessary to prove a conscious intent to deceive; in situations involving gross negligence, the law infers an intent to deceive. For example, an accountant who takes an unauthorized shortcut in order to save time may be guilty of gross negligence and constructive fraud, but not of actual fraud, since there was a lack of conscious intent to deceive.

b. Gross negligence (constructive fraud) also has been defined as "reckless disregard for the truth" (comparable to, but not, scienter).

3. **Punitive Damages** Punitive damages are compensation in excess of actual damages, usually awarded as a means of punishing the wrongdoer. Punitive damages may be imposed on an accountant who has committed actual fraud or constructive fraud.

II. Civil Liability to Third Parties

A. Common Law

Under certain circumstances, an accountant may be held civilly liable to persons who are not clients. Such liability to third parties generally arises under the common law notions of negligence and fraud or under federal statutes. In addition, an accountant may incur contractual liability to third parties in some cases.

1. **Negligence** An accountant's tort liability to third parties for ordinary negligence normally extends only to those third parties whom the accountant knew (or should have known) would be users or beneficiaries of the accountant's work product. Thus, an accountant normally will not be held liable to third parties for ordinary negligence if the accountant was unaware that the particular third parties would be using her/his work product.

a. **General Rule** If a CPA prepares financial statements for the client's personal use only, there would be no contractual or tort liability to a bank for misstatements or omissions, as the bank was an unknown and unintended user. Conversely, if the financial statements were prepared to enable the client to obtain a bank loan, there would be contractual liability (bank is an intended beneficiary), as well as tort liability (use by bank was foreseeable at time of engagement).

b. ***Ultramares* Doctrine** In the *Ultramares* case (1931), the courts held that the accountants owed a duty of care only to those persons whose specific identity is known for which the primary benefit financial statements were intended, and that only parties in privity (contractual relationship) could hold the accountants liable for negligence.

2. **Fraud** The courts have held that accountants owe a duty to all third parties to make their reports without fraud (actual or constructive). This third-party liability for fraud exists regardless of whether the work product was intended primarily for the benefit of third parties or for the benefit of the client.

a. In order for a third party to recover damages from an accountant for actual or constructive fraud, the third party must show that s/he reasonably relied on the accountant's work.

b. There is no need for the third party to show privity of contract in the case of fraud or gross negligence.

3. **Third-Party Beneficiary** A third-party beneficiary is a person who may enforce the terms of a contract even though s/he is not a party to the contract. In order to create a valid third-party beneficiary contract, the parties to the contract must intend that the third party receive the primary benefit of performance under the contract. A third-party beneficiary of a contract is a person whom the contracting parties intended to receive the primary benefits of the accountant's services. For example, if an accountant is hired by a client to prepare financial statements for purposes of securing a loan from a particular identified bank, the bank is an intended third-party beneficiary of the contract between the accountant and her/his client.

4. **Contractual Liability** An accountant's contractual liability to persons who are not parties to the contract extends only to third-party beneficiaries of the contract.

5. **Damages** Third parties may recover actual damages and, in some cases, punitive damages.

a. Actual damages may be awarded to the extent that a third party can prove the losses were caused by the accountant's fraud, negligence, or breach of contract.

b. Punitive damages may be awarded for an accountant's fraudulent or grossly negligent acts. However, ordinary negligence or breach of contract usually will not support an award of punitive damages.

B. **Federal Law**
An accountant's liability to third parties under federal statutes is defined in the Securities Act of 1933 and the Securities Exchange Act of 1934, as amended by the Private Securities Litigation Reform Act of 1995 and the Sarbanes-Oxley Act. [For more information, see the *Federal Securities Regulation* chapter (Chapter 40).]

1. **Securities Act of 1933** The Securities Act of 1933 ("Truth in Securities Law") is designed to provide the investing public with sufficient information to enable them to adequately evaluate the merits of new securities.

a. **Registration Statement** The Act requires the filing of a registration statement with the Securities and Exchange Commission (SEC) *prior* to the public offering of any securities in interstate commerce. The registration statement must make a full disclosure of all material facts concerning the securities to be issued and must include financial statements audited by independent public accountants.

b. **Prospectus** In addition, each potential investor must be furnished with a prospectus that must contain essentially the same financial information as is required in the registration statement.

c. **Liability Under Section 11 of 1933 Act** The Securities Act of 1933 makes an accountant liable for any false statements concerning material facts or material omissions in these financial statements or in the prospectus. The risk and extent of liability under the 1933 Act is quite significant.

(1) Any purchaser of the initial issue of securities covered by the registration statement may sue the accountant. This includes third parties (investors) who are not clients of the accountant.

(2) The investor is required only to prove the existence of a false statement or material omission and that the security purchased was offered through the inaccurate registration statement. The investor does not have the burden of proving that the accountant was fraudulent or negligent. It is not necessary for the purchaser to prove that s/he relied on the accountant's error or that s/he had a contractual relationship with the accountant.

(3) An accountant charged under this Act may assert the due diligence defense. The accountant's defense of "due diligence" is established by proving that after reasonable investigation, the accountant had a reasonable basis for the belief that all statements in the registration statement were accurate and complete. A "reasonable investigation" is measured against the standard of care observed by a prudent person in the management of her/his own financial affairs.

(4) The truth and accuracy of the registration statement is determined as of the date the statement becomes effective, **not** as of the date the accountant prepared the statement. As a result, the accountant is responsible for errors resulting from changes that occurred between the time of statement preparation and its effective date.

(5) The following statutory periods of limitation are applicable to suits brought under the Securities Act of 1933:

(a) An action against an accountant must be commenced within **one year** of the time when the error or omission was (or should have been) discovered.

(b) In any event, an action against an accountant must be commenced no later than three years after the initial offering of the security.

(6) The amount of damages generally recoverable under the Act is measured by the difference between the amount paid for the security and the market value of the security at the time of the suit.

(a) If the investor already has sold the security at the time s/he brings suit, the damages are measured by the difference between the amount that s/he paid for the security and the amount for which s/he subsequently sold it.

(b) In no event can the amount of damages exceed the price at which the security was offered to the public.

(c) The investor's recovery does not include any decrease in the price of the security during the course of the suit.

2. **Securities Exchange Act of 1934** The Securities Exchange Act of 1934 regulates national securities exchanges and the securities that are traded on national exchanges. In addition, most provisions of the Act apply to securities of companies that have more than $10 million in assets and equity stock that is held by 500 or more persons as of the last day of the fiscal year.

   a. **Annual Report (Form 10-K)** The Act requires each company to submit an annual report (Form 10-K) to the SEC that includes financial statements that have been audited by an independent public accountant. These financial statements are the chief source of an accountant's liability under the Act. Form 10-K differs from the company's annual report to shareholders. (The provisions of the Securities Exchange Act do not apply to reports to shareholders.)

   b. **Civil Liability** The Act imposes civil liability on any person (including the auditor) who, in any SEC annual report, makes a false or misleading statement with respect to a material fact. This liability extends to any application, report, or document filed with the SEC.

   c. **Investor's Burden of Proof** Unlike the Securities Act of 1933, the 1934 Act places the burden on the investor to prove the following:

      (1) That s/he bought or sold the security at a price that was affected by the false or misleading statement.

      (2) That s/he was not aware that the statement was false or inaccurate.

      (3) That s/he relied on the statement.

   d. **Scienter Required** Liability under the 1934 Act requires proof that the accountant made the false or misleading statement with the intent to deceive or defraud (scienter).

      (1) As a result, the accountant's good faith or lack of knowledge of her/his statement's falsity is a valid defense under the 1934 Act.

      (2) Mere negligence will not give rise to liability under the 1934 Act.

   e. **Statutory Periods of Limitation** The statutory limitations periods for the 1934 Act are the same as under the 1933 Act. An action against an accountant must be commenced within **one year** of the time when the error or omission was (or should have been) discovered. In any event, an action against an accountant must be commenced no later than three years after the initial offering of the security.

3. **Private Securities Litigation Reform Act of 1995** This Act amends the 1933 and 1934 Acts and establishes guidelines for CPAs to disclose corporate fraud.

   a. Under Title III of this Act, *Auditor Disclosure of Corporate Fraud,* independent public accountants must include procedures to (1) detect illegal acts that would have a direct and material effect on the financial statements, (2) identify related party transactions that would have a material effect on the financial statements, and (3) evaluate an issuer's ability to continue as a going concern.

   b. An independent public accountant who, during the course of an audit, becomes aware of possible illegal activities must inform the entity's management and ensure that the audit committee or the board of directors is adequately informed. If the auditor concludes that the illegal act has a material effect on the financial statements and management has not taken appropriate remedial actions, and this failure reasonably warrants departure from a standard report, the auditor shall report this directly to the board of directors. The entity is required to notify the SEC not later than 1 business day after receipt of such report.

c. If the entity fails to notify the SEC within 1 business day, the independent public accountant must resign from the engagement and/or report to the SEC within 1 business day.

d. An auditor may face **civil penalties** for noncompliance with this Act. An auditor shall **not** be liable in a **private** action for complying with the guidelines of this act.

4. **Sarbanes-Oxley Act** The Sarbanes-Oxley Act contains provisions that impact auditors, directors, senior management, standard-setters, and regulators. **Editor's Note:** While the editors expect the examiners to test SOX and PCAOB in the *Auditing & Attestation* exam, technically, it is eligible to be tested in the *Regulation* exam section.

   a. **Public Company Accounting Oversight Board (PCAOB)** The Public Company Accounting Oversight Board is composed of five full-time members, only two of which may be CPAs. The Board is overseen by the SEC and is charged with the following duties.

      (1) Registering public accounting firms that perform audit functions for issuers.

      (2) Establishing standards to be used in the preparation and issuance of audit reports for issuers.

      (3) Conducting inspections and investigations, and imposing penalties on publicly registered accounting firms.

   b. **Auditor Independence**

      (1) **Prohibited Services** The Act prohibits registered public accounting firms from providing the following nonaudit services to an audit client that issues publicly traded securities: bookkeeping; financial information system design and implementation; appraisal or valuation services; actuarial services; internal audit outsourcing services; management functions or human resources; broker or dealer investment advisor or investment banking services; and legal and expert services.

      (2) **Audit Partner Rotation** The lead audit partner or audit partner responsible for reviewing the audit (not the audit firm) must be changed at least after every five years.

      (3) **Conflict of Interest** The issuer's CEO, controller, CFO, or CAO can not have been employed by the audit firm for one year period prior to the audit. Also, an audit firm lacks independence with respect to an issuer if a former lead partner, former concurring partner, or any former audit engagement team member who provided more than 10 hours of audit, review, or attest services to the issuer during the one-year period preceding the audit's initiation is employed by the issuer in a financial reporting oversight role.

      (4) **Audit Committee** Accounting firms must report to the audit committee of the client company the methods, practices and policies behind the audit work. The issuer's audit committee must approve all auditing and nonauditing services provided to an issuer.

   c. **Client Responsibility** The issuer's directors and officers must not provide false or misleading information about the financial condition to an audit firm conducting an audit.

      (1) **Audit Committee** The audit committee is responsible for the appointment and oversight of any audit work performed by the audit firm. The audit committee, not management, is responsible for hiring, retaining, and firing the audit firm.

(2) **Executives** Principal executive and financial officers are required to certify annual (Form 10-K) and quarterly (Form (10-Q) reports to the SEC. The issuer's executives are required to forfeit any bonus, incentive based pay, or profits from the sale of stock received in the twelve months prior to a restatement of earnings.

III. Duty of Nondisclosure

A. Work Papers

An accountant's work papers (also known as audit documentation) generally include the notes, computations, memoranda, copies, and other papers that represent the by-product of the accountant's services to the client.

1. **Ownership** Under common law and in the absence of an express agreement to the contrary, ownership of an accountant's work papers rests with the accountant.

2. **Custodial Interest** The accountant's ownership, however, is in the nature of a custodial interest, since the accountant normally may not disclose the contents of her/his work papers without the client's consent. This custodial arrangement serves the dual purpose of permitting the client to control the confidentiality of the information contained in the papers, while at the same time permitting the accountant to retain possession of the papers for use as evidence of the nature and extent of her/his services.

3. **Relinquishment** An accountant must relinquish possession of the work papers in response to an enforceable subpoena or court order.

4. **Privacy Disclosure** The provisions of the 1999 Gramm-Leach-Bliley Act apply to a broad definition of financial services, including tax planning, financial planning and tax return preparation. The Federal Trade Commission (FTC) has authority to regulate privacy practices for financial services provided to consumers, other than those provided by banks, credit unions, securities companies, investment advisers registered with the SEC, and insurance companies. CPAs who are "significantly engaged" in the preparation of personal tax returns or who provide personal financial or tax planning are subject to the FTC's privacy regulations. The rules require that certain disclosures be made to consumer clients, including one-time disclosures to new clients and annual disclosures to all clients. The disclosures must provide a clear and conspicuous notice that accurately reflects the CPA's privacy policy and practices. The disclosures must be in writing or, if the client agrees, electronically. Although there is no prescribed form for this notice, it must include the following information.

    a. The categories of non-public personal information collected by the CPA.

    b. The categories of non-public personal financial information that the CPA might disclose.

    c. The categories of affiliates and non-affiliated third parties to whom the CPA discloses information, or that the CPA does not make such disclosures.

    d. The CPA's policies with respect to sharing information on a person no longer a client.

    e. The categories of information disclosed pursuant to agreements with third-party service providers and joint marketers and the categories of third parties providing these services, or that the CPA does not do so.

    f. The client's right to opt out of the disclosure of non-public personal information, if such disclosures are made.

    g. Disclosures that the CPA makes under the Fair Credit Reporting Act, if any.

h. The CPA's practices with regard to protecting the confidentiality, security and integrity of non-public personal information.

B. **Privileged Communications**
A few states have promulgated statutes asserting that communications between an accountant and her/his clients may be regarded as privileged. This privilege protects the accountant from being compelled to testify in court with regard to privileged matters. However, the purpose of the privilege is to protect the client, and therefore, the client is free to waive it. The IRS Restructuring and Reform Act of 1998 extended the attorney-client privilege to federally authorized tax practitioners, which include CPAs. This privilege relates to noncriminal tax matters (except tax shelters) before the IRS or in federal courts.

C. **Ethical Protection From Disclosure**
In addition to the protection of legal privilege, confidential communications between accountants and their clients also are protected from unauthorized disclosure by professional ethical considerations.

1. **Confidential Communications** Confidential communications include both written and oral communications between an accountant and a client relating to professional advice and services.

2. **Exceptions** Professional ethics discourage disclosure by an accountant of confidential information **except** in the following circumstances:

a. Where disclosure is pursuant to a voluntary quality review under AICPA authorization or in response to an AICPA trial board request.

b. Where disclosure is in compliance with an enforceable subpoena or court order.

c. Where the client consents to the disclosure.

d. Where disclosure is in compliance with generally accepted accounting principles or generally accepted auditing standards.

IV. **Situations in Which Accountants May Incur Liability**

A. **Audits**
An accountant may incur civil liability for acts or omissions occurring in the course of an audit. Unless such performance specifically is contracted for, an accountant has no contractual duty to discover fraud. An accountant may be held liable for failure to discover fraud only if the failure to discover was the result of the accountant's own negligence or fraud. For example, if an accountant fails to adequately investigate an obvious indication of fraud, s/he may be liable for negligence or fraud.

1. **Contract to Discover** Where an accountant expressly has contracted to discover shortages and defalcations, her/his failure to take reasonable and adequate discovery measures may be treated as either a breach of contract or negligence.

2. **Another Auditor's Work** An accountant may be held liable for the work of another auditor if s/he relies on the other auditor's work and no mention is made of the other auditor in the audit report.

a. **Divided Responsibilities** If the audit report clearly indicates that responsibility for the audit was divided, then each auditor may be held liable only for her/his own inaccuracies.

b. **Unaudited Data** An auditor may not rely on unaudited data. If such data is included in audited financial statements, s/he must qualify or disclaim an opinion on those statements.

3. **Inadequate Disclosure** An accountant may incur liability for inadequate disclosure. For example, liability may result if the accountant fails to reveal the existence of inadequate insurance or excessive political contributions. However, liability may be avoided through the issuance of a qualified, adverse, or disclaimed opinion.

4. **Subsequent Changes** An accountant generally is not liable for inaccuracies resulting from changes that occur after the last day of field work. However, liability may result if the report is dated subsequent to the changes that caused the inaccuracy.

   a. **SEC Registration** Under the Securities Act of 1933, the accountant is responsible for changes occurring up to the effective date of the registration statement.

   b. **Misleading Statements** An accountant may be held liable if subsequently discovered facts indicate that the statements were misleading at the time they were issued. Such liability may be avoided in certain conditions.

      (1) An immediate investigation is conducted.

      (2) The statements are revised promptly.

      (3) The SEC and persons known to be relying on the statements are notified promptly.

B. Unaudited Financial Statements

An accountant may incur liability in the preparation of an unaudited financial statement. A financial statement is considered unaudited if no auditing procedures have been applied or if insufficient procedures have been applied to justify an opinion. Liability in conjunction with an unaudited financial statement may arise in certain conditions.

1. The accountant fails to mark each page "unaudited."

2. The accountant fails to issue a disclaimer.

3. The accountant fails to inform the client of discrepancies or defalcations.

C. Criminal Liability

In addition to the laws specifically mentioned, federal and state laws impose severe criminal penalties for such activities as perjury, conspiracy to defraud, and fraudulent use of the mails.

1. **Federal Securities Acts** Willful violations of the provisions of either the Securities Act of 1933 or the Securities Exchange Act of 1934 can subject the offender to criminal penalties of fines and/or imprisonment.

2. **Internal Revenue Code** The Internal Revenue Code provides criminal penalties (fines and/or imprisonment) for persons convicted of violating its provisions. Examples of types of violations particularly applicable to accountants include the following.

   a. **Willful Perjury & Evasion** Willfully preparing false returns (perjury) and willfully assisting others to evade taxes.

   b. **Fraudulent Documents** Fraudulently executing or procuring the fraudulent execution of documents required to be executed under the Internal Revenue Code.

   c. **Inventory Fraud** Removing and/or concealing goods with the intent to evade taxes.

   d. **Delivery of False Documents** Willfully delivering documents that the accountant knows to be fraudulent or false.

3. **State Laws** Each state has enacted laws imposing criminal sanctions on certain activities closely connected with an accountant's normal duties. For example, criminal penalties may be imposed in most states for activities such as the following.

   a. Knowingly certifying false or fraudulent reports.

   b. Falsifying, altering, or destroying books of account.

   c. Obtaining property or credit through the use of false financial statements.

CHAPTER 33—ACCOUNTANT'S LEGAL RESPONSIBILITIES

Problem 33-1 MULTIPLE CHOICE QUESTIONS (45 to 60 minutes)

1. When performing an audit, a CPA will most likely be considered negligent when the CPA fails to
a. Detect all of a client's fraudulent activities
b. Include a negligence disclaimer in the client engagement letter
c. Warn a client of known internal control weaknesses
d. Warn a client's customers of embezzlement by the client's employees (11/95, Law, #9, 5878)

2. A CPA's duty of due care to a client most likely will be breached when a CPA
a. Gives a client an oral instead of a written report
b. Gives a client incorrect advice based on an honest error of judgment
c. Fails to give tax advice that saves the client money
d. Fails to follow generally accepted auditing standards (5/93, Law, #4, 3973)

3. When performing an audit, a CPA
a. Must exercise the level of care, skill, and judgment expected of a reasonably prudent CPA under the circumstances
b. Must strictly adhere to generally accepted accounting principles
c. Is strictly liable for failing to discover client fraud
d. Is **not** liable unless the CPA commits gross negligence or intentionally disregards generally accepted auditing standards (11/91, Law, #2, 2330)

4. A client suing a CPA for negligence must prove each of the following factors **except**
a. Breach of duty of care
b. Proximate cause
c. Reliance
d. Injury (R/05, REG, 1284L, #16, 7882)

5. Which of the following penalties is usually imposed against an accountant who, in the course of performing professional services, breaches contract duties owed to a client?
a. Specific performance
b. Punitive damages
c. Money damages
d. Rescission (R/07, REG, 2344L, #40, 8464)

6. Which of the following statements is(are) correct regarding the common law elements that must be proven to support a finding of constructive fraud against a CPA?

I. The plaintiff has justifiably relied on the CPA's misrepresentation.
II. The CPA has acted in a grossly negligent manner.

a. I only
b. II only
c. Both I and II
d. Neither I nor II (R/99, Law, #2, 6853)

7. Which of the following statements is generally correct regarding the liability of a CPA who negligently gives an opinion on an audit of a client's financial statements?
a. The CPA is only liable to those third parties who are in privity of contract with the CPA.
b. The CPA is only liable to the client.
c. The CPA is liable to anyone in a class of third parties who the CPA knows will rely on the opinion.
d. The CPA is liable to all possible foreseeable users of the CPA's opinion. (5/97, Law, #1, 6442)

8. Which of the following facts must be proven for a plaintiff to prevail in a common law negligent misrepresentation action?
a. The defendant made the misrepresentations with a reckless disregard for the truth.
b. The plaintiff justifiably relied on the misrepresentations.
c. The misrepresentations were in writing.
d. The misrepresentations concerned opinion. (5/95, Law, #16, 5350)

9. If a CPA recklessly departs from the standards of due care when conducting an audit, the CPA will be liable to third parties who are unknown to the CPA based on
a. Negligence
b. Gross negligence
c. Strict liability
d. Criminal deceit (5/94, Law, #9, 4764)

10. Beckler & Associates, CPAs, audited and gave an unqualified opinion on the financial statements of Queen Co. The financial statements contained misstatements that resulted in a material overstatement of Queen's net worth. Queen provided the audited financial statements to Mac Bank in connection with a loan made by Mac to Queen. Beckler knew that the financial statements would be provided to Mac. Queen defaulted on the loan. Mac sued Beckler to recover for its losses associated with Queen's default. Which of the following must Mac prove in order to recover?

I. Beckler was negligent in conducting the audit.
II. Mac relied on the financial statements.

a. I only
b. II only
c. Both I and II
d. Neither I nor II (11/93, Law, #1, 4298)

Items 11 and 12 are based on the following:

While conducting an audit, Larson Associates, CPAs, failed to detect material misstatements included in its client's financial statements. Larson's unqualified opinion was included with the financial statements in a registration statement and prospectus for a public offering of securities made by the client. Larson knew that its opinion and the financial statements would be used for this purpose.

11. In a suit by a purchaser against Larson for common law negligence, Larson's best defense would be that the
a. Audit was conducted in accordance with generally accepted auditing standards.
b. Client was aware of the misstatements.
c. Purchaser was **not** in privity of contract with Larson.
d. Identity of the purchaser was **not** known to Larson at the time of the audit.
(11/93, Law, #4, 4301)

12. In a suit by a purchaser against Larson for common law fraud, Larson's best defense would be that
a. Larson did **not** have actual or constructive knowledge of the misstatements.
b. Larson's client knew or should have known of the misstatements.
c. Larson did **not** have actual knowledge that the purchaser was an intended beneficiary of the audit.
d. Larson was **not** in privity of contract with its client. (11/93, Law, #5, 4302)

13. Which of the following is the best defense a CPA firm can assert in a suit for common law fraud based on its unqualified opinion on materially false financial statements?
a. Contributory negligence on the part of the client
b. A disclaimer contained in the engagement letter
c. Lack of privity
d. Lack of scienter (11/95, Law, #10, 5879)

14. Under the liability provisions of Section 11 of the Securities Act of 1933, a CPA may be liable to any purchaser of a security for certifying materially misstated financial statements that are included in the security's registration statement. Under Section 11, which of the following must be proven by a purchaser of the security?

	Reliance on the financial statements	*Fraud by the CPA*
a.	Yes	Yes
b.	Yes	No
c.	No	Yes
d.	No	No

(11/94, Law, #13, 5191)

15. Under the liability provisions of Section 11 of the Securities Act of 1933, an auditor may help to establish the defense of due diligence if

I. The auditor performed an additional review of the audited statements to ensure that the statements were accurate as of the effective date of a registration statement.
II. The auditor complied with GAAS.

a. I only
b. II only
c. Both I and II
d. Neither I nor II (R/99, Law, #3, 6854)

16. Under the liability provisions of Section 11 of the Securities Act of 1933, which of the following must a plaintiff prove to hold a CPA liable?

I. The misstatements contained in the financial statements certified by the CPA were material.
II. The plaintiff relied on the CPA's unqualified opinion.

a. I only
b. II only
c. Both I and II
d. Neither I nor II (R/00, Law, #1, 6966)

17. Which of the following circumstances is a defense to an accountant's liability under Section 11 of the Securities Act of 1933 for misstatements and omissions of material facts contained in a registration statement?

a. The absence of scienter on the part of the accountant
b. The absence of privity between purchasers and the accountant
c. Due diligence on the part of the accountant
d. Nonreliance by purchasers on the misstatements (R/07, REG, 2359L, #14, 8438)

18. Under Section 11 of the Securities Act of 1933, which of the following standards may a CPA use as a defense?

	Generally accepted accounting principles	*Generally accepted fraud detection standards*
a.	Yes	Yes
b.	Yes	No
c.	No	Yes
d.	No	No

(11/95, Law, #12, 5881)

Items 19 and 20 are based on the following:

Dart Corp. engaged Jay Associates, CPAs, to assist in a public stock offering. Jay audited Dart's financial statements and gave an unqualified opinion, despite knowing that the financial statements contained misstatements. Jay's opinion was included in Dart's registration statement. Larson purchased shares in the offering and suffered a loss when the stock declined in value after the misstatements became known.

19. If Larson succeeds in the Section 11 suit against Dart, Larson would be entitled to

a. Damages of three times the original public offering price
b. Rescind the transaction
c. Monetary damages only
d. Damages, but only if the shares were resold before the suit was started (5/92, Law, #3, 2816)

20. If Larson succeeds in the Section 10(b) and Rule 10b-5 suit, Larson would be entitled to

a. Only recover the original public offering price
b. Only rescind the transaction
c. The amount of any loss caused by the fraud
d. Punitive damages (5/92, Law, #5, 2818)

21. Ocean and Associates, CPAs, audited the financial statements of Drain Corporation. As a result of Ocean's negligence in conducting the audit, the financial statements included material misstatements. Ocean was unaware of this fact. The financial statements and Ocean's unqualified opinion were included in a registration statement and prospectus for an original public offering of stock by Drain. Sharp purchased shares in the offering. Sharp received a copy of the prospectus prior to the purchase but did not read it. The shares declined in value as a result of the misstatements in Drain's financial statements becoming known. Under which of the following Acts is Sharp most likely to prevail in a lawsuit against Ocean?

	Securities Exchange Act of 1934, Section 10(b), Rule 10b-5	*Securities Act of 1933, Section 11*
a.	Yes	Yes
b.	Yes	No
c.	No	Yes
d.	No	No

(11/95, Law, #13, 5882)

22. An accountant will be liable for damages under Section 10(b) and Rule 10b-5 of the Securities Exchange Act of 1934 only if the plaintiff proves that

a. The accountant was negligent.
b. There was a material omission.
c. The security involved was registered.
d. The security was part of an original issuance.

(5/93, Law, #10, 3979)

23. A CPA firm must do which of the following before it can participate in the preparation of an audit report of a company registered with the Securities and Exchange Commission (SEC)?

a. Join the SEC Practice Section of the AICPA
b. Register with the Public Company Accounting Oversight Board
c. Register with the Financial Accounting Standards Board (FASB)
d. Register with the SEC pursuant to the Securities Exchange Act of 1934

(R/07, REG, C03934R, #38, 8462)

24. The Sarbanes-Oxley Act prohibits an accounting firm from providing audit services for an issuer if the CEO, Controller, CFO, CAO, or any person serving in the equivalent capacity for the issuer was employed in the audit practice of the accounting firm:

a. During the one-year period prior to the audit
b. During the three-year period prior to the audit
c. During the five-year period prior to the audit
d. During the six-year period prior to the audit

(Editors, 7481)

25. Which **two** does the Sarbanes-Oxley Act **not** prohibit a registered public accounting firm from providing?

a. Actuarial services to a public issuer that it audits
b. Internal audit outsourcing services to a public issuer that it audits
c. Bookkeeping services related to the accounting records of financial statements of a non-audit client
d. Legal services to a public issuer that it audits
e. Financial information system design and implementation services for a non-audit client

(Editors, 7480)

26. A CPA is permitted to disclose confidential client information without the consent of the client to

I. Another CPA who has purchased the CPA's tax practice
II. Another CPA firm if the information concerns suspected tax return irregularities
III. A state CPA society voluntary quality control review board

a. I and III only
b. II and III only
c. II only
d. III only (5/93, Law, #6, 3975)

27. Thorp, CPA, was engaged to audit Ivor Co.'s financial statements. During the audit, Thorp discovered that Ivor's inventory contained stolen goods. Ivor was indicted and Thorp was subpoenaed to testify at the criminal trial. Ivor claimed accountant-client privilege to prevent Thorp from testifying. Which of the following statements is correct regarding Ivor's claim?

a. Ivor can claim an accountant-client privilege only in states that have enacted a statute creating such a privilege.
b. Ivor can claim an accountant-client privilege only in federal courts.
c. The accountant-client privilege can be claimed only in civil suits.
d. The accountant-client privilege can be claimed only to limit testimony to audit subject matter.

(11/95, Law, #15, 5884)

28. Which of the following statements is (are) correct regarding a CPA employee of a CPA firm taking copies of information contained in client files when the CPA leaves the firm?

I. A CPA leaving a firm may take copies of information contained in client files to assist another firm in serving that client.
II. A CPA leaving a firm may take copies of information contained in client files as a method of gaining technical expertise.

a. I only
b. II only
c. Both I and II
d. Neither I nor II (R/01, Law, #3, 7038)

29. Which of the following statements is correct regarding an accountant's working papers?

a. The accountant owns the working papers and generally may disclose them as the accountant sees fit.
b. The client owns the working papers but the accountant has custody of them until the accountant's bill is paid in full.
c. The accountant owns the working papers but generally may **not** disclose them without the client's consent or a court order.
d. The client owns the working papers but, in the absence of the accountant's consent, may **not** disclose them without a court order.

(R/01, Law, #4, 7039)

30. Under the Securities Act of 1933, which of the following acts by an accountant may subject the accountant to criminal penalties?

a. Negligently making a false entry in financial statements included in a registration statement
b. Giving an unqualified opinion on negligently prepared financial statements in an audit report included in a registration statement
c. Willfully including materially misstated financial statements in a registration statement
d. Failing to use due diligence in the preparation of financial statements included in a registration statement (R/03, REG, 0818L, #17, 7659)

Problem 33-2 ADDITIONAL MULTIPLE CHOICE QUESTIONS (45 to 60 minutes)

31. When CPAs fail in their duty to carry out their contracts for services, liability to clients may be based on

	Breach of contract	*Strict liability*
a.	Yes	Yes
b.	Yes	No
c.	No	No
d.	No	Yes

(5/89, Law, #6, 0791)

32. Sun Corp. approved a merger plan with Cord Corp. One of the determining factors in approving the merger was the financial statements of Cord that were audited by Frank & Co., CPAs. Sun had engaged Frank to audit Cord's financial statements. While performing the audit, Frank failed to discover certain irregularities that later caused Sun to suffer substantial losses. For Frank to be liable under common law negligence, Sun at a minimum must prove that Frank

a. Knew of the irregularities
b. Failed to exercise due care
c. Was grossly negligent
d. Acted with scienter (5/93, Law, #1, 3970)

33. Which of the following statements best describes whether a CPA has met the required standard of care in conducting an audit of a client's financial statements?

a. The client's expectations with regard to the accuracy of audited financial statements
b. The accuracy of the financial statements and whether the statements conform to generally accepted accounting principles
c. Whether the CPA conducted the audit with the same skill and care expected of an ordinarily prudent CPA under the circumstances
d. Whether the audit was conducted to investigate and discover all acts of fraud

(11/93, Law, #2, 4299)

34. Which of the following elements, if present, would support a finding of constructive fraud on the part of a CPA?

a. Gross negligence in applying generally accepted auditing standards
b. Ordinary negligence in applying generally accepted accounting principles
c. Identified third party users
d. Scienter (5/93, Law, #3, 3972)

35. Cable Corp. orally engaged Drake & Co., CPAs, to audit its financial statements. Cable's management informed Drake that it suspected the accounts receivable were materially overstated. Though the financial statements Drake audited included a materially overstated accounts receivable balance, Drake issued an unqualified opinion. Cable used the financial statements to obtain a loan to expand its operations. Cable defaulted on the loan and incurred a substantial loss. If Cable sues Drake for negligence in failing to discover the overstatement, Drake's best defense would be that Drake did **not**

a. Have privity of contract with Cable
b. Sign an engagement letter
c. Perform the audit recklessly or with an intent to deceive
d. Violate generally accepted auditing standards in performing the audit (11/91, Law, #1, 2329)

36. Ford & Co., CPAs, issued an unqualified opinion on Owens Corp.'s financial statements. Relying on these financial statements, Century Bank lent Owens $750,000. Ford was unaware that Century would receive a copy of the financial statements or that Owens would use them to obtain a loan. Owens defaulted on the loan. To succeed in a common law fraud action against Ford, Century must prove, in addition to other elements, that Century was

a. Free from contributory negligence
b. In privity of contract with Ford
c. Justified in relying on the financial statements
d. In privity of contract with Owens

(11/91, Law, #3, 2331)

37. Hark, CPA, failed to follow generally accepted auditing standards in auditing Long Corp.'s financial statements. Long's management had told Hark that the audited statements would be submitted to several banks to obtain financing. Relying on the statements, Third Bank gave Long a loan. Long defaulted on the loan. In a jurisdiction applying the *Ultramares* decision, if Third sues Hark, Hark will

a. Win, because there was **no** privity of contract between Hark and Third
b. Lose, because Hark knew that banks would be relying on the financial statements
c. Win, because Third was contributorily negligent in granting the loan
d. Lose, because Hark was negligent in performing the audit (11/91, Law, #4, 2332)

38. Under common law, which of the following statements most accurately reflects the liability of a CPA who fraudulently gives an opinion on an audit of a client's financial statements?

a. The CPA is liable only to third parties in privity of contract with the CPA.
b. The CPA is liable only to known users of the financial statements.
c. The CPA probably is liable to any person who suffered a loss as a result of the fraud.
d. The CPA probably is liable to the client even if the client was aware of the fraud and did **not** rely on the opinion. (11/94, Law, #10, 5188)

39. In a common law action against an accountant, lack of privity is a viable defense if the plaintiff

a. Is the client's creditor who sues the accountant for negligence
b. Can prove the presence of gross negligence that amounts to a reckless disregard for the truth
c. Is the accountant's client
d. Bases the action upon fraud

(11/94, Law, #9, 5187)

40. If a stockholder sues a CPA for common law fraud based on false statements contained in the financial statements audited by the CPA, which of the following, if present, would be the CPA's best defense?

a. The stockholder lacks privity to sue
b. The false statements were immaterial
c. The CPA did **not** financially benefit from the alleged fraud
d. The contributory negligence of the client

(5/89, Law, #2, 0787)

41. An accounting firm was hired by a company to perform an audit. The company needed the audit report in order to obtain a loan from a bank. The bank lent $500,000 to the company based on the auditor's report. Fifteen months later, the company declared bankruptcy and was unable to repay the loan. The bank discovered that the accounting firm failed to discover a material overstatement of assets of the company. Which of the following statements is correct regarding a suit by the bank against the accounting firm? The bank

a. Cannot sue the accounting firm because of the statute of limitations
b. Can sue the accounting firm for the loss of the loan because of negligence
c. Cannot sue the accounting firm because there was **no** privity of contact
d. Can sue the accounting firm for the loss of the loan because of the rule of privilege

(R/06, REG, C00276R, #14, 8184)

42. Under the "*Ultramares*" rule, to which of the following parties will an accountant be liable for negligence?

	Parties in privity	*Foreseen parties*
a.	Yes	Yes
b.	Yes	No
c.	No	Yes
d.	No	No

(11/95, Law, #8, 5877)

43. To be successful in a civil action under Section 11 of the Securities Act of 1933 concerning liability for a misleading registration statement, the plaintiff must prove the

	Defendant's intent to deceive	*Plaintiff's reliance on the registration statement*
a.	No	Yes
b.	No	No
c.	Yes	No
d.	Yes	Yes

(5/93, Law, #5, 3974)

44. The quarterly data required by SEC Regulation S-K have been omitted. Which of the following statements must be included in the auditor's report?

a. The auditor was unable to review the data.
b. The company's internal control provides an adequate basis to complete the review.
c. The company has not presented the selected quarterly financial data.
d. The auditor will review the selected data during the review of the subsequent quarterly financial data. (R/06, REG, C00288R, #38, 8208)

45. Under the provisions of Section 10(b) and Rule 10b-5 of the Securities Exchange Act of 1934, which of the following activities must be proven by a stock purchaser in a suit against a CPA?

I. Intentional conduct by the CPA designed to deceive investors
II. Negligence by the CPA

a. I only
b. II only
c. Both I and II
d. Neither I and II (11/94, Law, #11, 5189)

46. Under the anti-fraud provisions of Section 10(b) of the Securities Exchange Act of 1934, a CPA may be liable if the CPA acted

a. Negligently
b. With independence
c. Without due diligence
d. Without good faith (11/95, Law, #11, 5880)

47. The Sarbanes-Oxley Act of 2002 requires audit committees to be directly responsible for which of the following activities?

	Hiring auditor	*Negotiating fees*	*Overseeing audit work*
a.	Yes	No	Yes
b.	Yes	Yes	No
c.	No	Yes	Yes
d.	Yes	Yes	Yes

(Editors, 8292)

48. Which of the following statements is correct concerning the Sarbanes-Oxley Act of 2002 and publicly-traded audit clients?

a. The lead engagement and reviewing audit partners must change every seven years.
b. An audit firm may not perform an audit for a client whose controller was previously employed by the audit firm and participated in the audit of the client within the client's previous fiscal year.
c. The audit firm may not also provide tax services to an audit client.
d. The audit firm may also provide tax services to an audit client without the pre-approval of the audit committee. (Editors, 8293)

49. Under the Sarbanes-Oxley Act of 2002, a registered public accounting firm may perform which of the following services with pre-approval from the audit committee for an audit client that is a publicly-traded company?

a. Internal audit outsourcing services
b. Tax services
c. Bookkeeping services
d. Financial information systems design

(Editors, 8291)

50. If management of a public company does not document its evaluation of the effectiveness of the company's internal control over financial reporting sufficiently, what must the auditor report to the audit committee in writing?

I. The auditor must disclaim an opinion.
II. The audit of internal control over financial reporting cannot be completed.

a. I only
b. II only
c. Both I and II
d. Neither I nor II (Editors, 8275)

51. Which of the following requirements must an auditor meet to express an opinion on a public company's effectiveness of internal control over financial reporting as of a point in time and taken as a whole?

I. The auditor must obtain evidence that internal control over financial reporting has operated effectively for the entire period covered by the company's financial statements.
II. The auditor must test the design and operation effectiveness of controls that the auditor ordinarily would not test if expressing an opinion only on the financial statements.

a. I only
b. II only
c. Both I and II
d. Neither I nor II (Editors, 8278)

52. In an audit conducted in accordance with the standards of the *Public Company Accounting Oversight Board* (PCAOB), the auditor must communicate in writing to the audit committee

a. Significant deficiencies only
b. Material weaknesses only
c. Significant deficiencies and material weaknesses, but need not distinguish between them
d. Significant deficiencies and material weaknesses, distinguishing between them

(Editors, 8282)

53. In connection with an audit of internal control over financial reporting that meets the requirements of the *Public Company Accounting Oversight Board* (PCAOB), which of the following must an auditor document?

I. The effect of a conclusion that control risk is other than low for any relevant assertion related to any significant accounts in connection with the audit of financial statements
II. The identification of the points at which misstatements related to relevant financial statement assertions could occur within significant accounts and disclosures and major classes of transactions

a. I only
b. II only
c. Both I and II
d. Neither I nor II (Editors, 8279)

54. In forming a basis for expressing an unqualified opinion on management's assessment of the effectiveness of a public company's internal control over financial reporting, the auditor need not

a. Audit the company's financial statements as of that date
b. Evaluate the assessment performed by management
c. Obtain reasonable assurance that no material weaknesses exist as of the date specified in management's assessment
d. Use the work performed by others as evidence

(Editors, 8272)

55. Page, CPA, has T Corp. and W Corp. as audit clients. T Corp. is a significant supplier of raw materials to W Corp. Page also prepares individual tax returns for Time, the owner of T Corp. and West, the owner of W Corp. When preparing West's return, Page finds information that raises going-concern issues with respect to W Corp. May Page disclose this information to Time?

a. Yes, because Page has a fiduciary relationship with Time
b. Yes, because there is **no** accountant-client privilege between Page and West
c. No, because the information is confidential and may **not** be disclosed without West's consent
d. No, because the information should only be disclosed in Page's audit report on W Corp.'s financial statements

(R/06, REG, 0918L, #23, 8193)

56. Which of the following statements is correct with respect to ownership, possession, or access to a CPA firm's audit working papers?

a. Working papers may **never** be obtained by third parties unless the client consents.
b. Working papers are **not** transferable to a purchaser of a CPA practice unless the client consents.
c. Working papers are subject to the privileged communication rule which, in most jurisdictions, prevents any third-party access to the working papers.
d. Working papers are the client's exclusive property. (5/94, Law, #10, 4765)

57. To which of the following parties may a CPA partnership provide its working papers without either the client's consent or a lawful subpoena?

	The IRS	*The FASB*
a.	Yes	Yes
b.	Yes	No
c.	No	Yes
d.	No	No

(R/00, Law, #2, 6967)

58. Which of the following statements is correct regarding a CPA's working papers? The working papers must be

a. Transferred to another accountant purchasing the CPA's practice even if the client hasn't given permission
b. Transferred permanently to the client if demanded
c. Turned over to any government agency that requests them
d. Turned over pursuant to a valid federal court subpoena (11/95, Law, #14, 5883)

59. At a confidential meeting, an audit client informed a CPA about the client's illegal insider-trading actions. A year later, the CPA was subpoenaed to appear in federal court to testify in a criminal trial against the client. The CPA was asked to testify to the meeting between the CPA and the client. After receiving immunity, the CPA should do which of the following?

a. Take the Fifth Amendment and **not** discuss the meeting
b. Site the privileged communications aspect of being a CPA
c. Discuss the entire conversation including the illegal acts
d. Discuss only the items that have a direct connection to those items the CPA worked on for the client in the past

(R/06, REG, C03939R, #19, 8189)

60. Which of the following statements concerning an accountant's disclosure of confidential client data is generally correct?

a. Disclosure may be made to any state agency without subpoena
b. Disclosure may be made to any party on consent of the client
c. Disclosure may be made to comply with an IRS audit request
d. Disclosure may be made to comply with generally accepted accounting principles

(11/94, Law, #14, 5192)

Problem 33-3 EXTRA MULTIPLE CHOICE QUESTIONS (21 to 28 minutes)

61. The *Public Company Accounting Oversight Board* (PCAOB) uses the term "internal control over financial reporting" to describe a process that does **not** include which of the following procedures?
a. Procedures performed by the auditor
b. Procedures that pertain to the maintenance of reasonably detailed records that accurately and fairly reflect the transactions and disposition of the company's assets
c. Procedures that provide reasonable assurance that company receipts and expenditures are made only in accordance with company management and director authorization
d. Procedures that provide reasonable assurance regarding timely detection of unauthorized disposition of company assets (Editors, 8271)

62. Which of the following statements apply to an audit conducted in accordance with the standards of the *Public Company Accounting Oversight Board* (PCAOB)?

I. The auditor should focus on combinations of controls in assessing whether the objectives of internal control over financial reporting have been achieved.
II. While management is responsible for the company's internal control, the auditor still should assess the effectiveness of the audit committee's oversight as part of understanding and evaluating the control environment and monitoring components of internal control over financial reporting.

a. I only
b. II only
c. Both I and II
d. Neither I nor II (Editors, 8276)

63. The *Public Company Accounting Oversight Board* (PCAOB) standards recognize that a public company's internal control over financial reporting cannot provide absolute assurance of achieving financial reporting objectives due to inherent limitation. Which of the following is **not** such an inherent limitation?
a. Breakdowns from human failures
b. Circumvention by collusion
c. Improper management override
d. Lack of controls over information technology
e Lapses in judgment (Editors, 8274)

64. Which of the following is **not** identified by the Committee of Sponsoring Organizations (COSO) framework as one of the three primary objectives of internal control?
a. Availability to users of management's reports
b. Compliance with laws and regulations
c. Efficiency and effectiveness of operations
d. Financial reporting (Editors, 8273)

65. Mammoth Co. plans to present comparative financial statements for the years ended December 31, Year 5, and Year 6, respectively. Brown, CPA, audited Mammoth's financial statements for both years and plans to report on the comparative financial statements on March 1, Year 7. Brown's audit is subject to the requirements of the *Public Company Accounting Oversight Board* (PCAOB). Mammoth's current management team was not present until January 1, Year 6. What period of time should be covered by Mammoth's management representation letter?
a. January 1, Year 5, through December 31, Year 6
b. January 1, Year 5, through March 1, Year 7
c. January 1, Year 6, through December 31, Year 6
d. January 1, Year 6, through March 1, Year 7 (Editors, 8277)

66. Which of the following statements apply to walkthroughs performed as part of an audit of internal control over financial reporting conducted in accordance with the standards of the *Public Company Accounting Oversight Board* (PCAOB)?

I. The auditor may issue an unqualified opinion only when there are no identified material weaknesses.
II. The auditor may issue an unqualified opinion only when there was no restrictions on the scope of the auditor's work.
III. The auditor must determine whether any identified control deficiencies, individually or in combination are significant deficiencies or material weaknesses.

a. Only I
b. Only II
c. Only I and II
d. Only II and III
e. I, II, and III (Editors, 8288)

67. Wale Company plans to present comparative financial statements for the years ended December 31, Year 7, and Year 8, respectively. Dauphin, CPA, audited Wale's financial statements for both years and plans to report on the comparative financial statements on March 1, Year 9. Dauphin's audit is subject to the requirements of the *Public Company Accounting Oversight Board* (PCAOB). What time is covered by Dauphin's opinion on the effectiveness of internal control over financial reporting and management's assessment of the effectiveness of internal control over financial reporting?
a. The end of Year 7 and the end of Year 8
b. The end of Year 8
c. Year 7 and Year 8
d. Year 8 (Editors, 8280)

68. Section 302 of the Sarbanes-Oxley Act and Securities Exchange Act rules require a company's management to make quarterly certifications with respect to the company's internal control over financial reporting. Which of the following are true with regard to these certifications?

I. The auditor should perform procedures to provide a high level of assurance that the controls are operating effectively.
II. If the auditor communicates to the appropriate level of management that the auditor believes that modification to the disclosures about changes in internal control over financial reporting are necessary for the certifications to be accurate, but management does not respond appropriately, the auditor should inform the audit committee.

a. I only
b. II only
c. Both I and II
d. Neither I nor II (Editors, 8281)

69. What does the *Public Company Accounting Oversight Board* (PCAOB) call an combination of deficiencies of internal control that adversely affects a company's ability to initiate authorize record, process, or report external financial data reliably in accordance with GAAS such that there is more than a remote likelihood that a misstatement of the company's financial statements that is more than inconsequential will not be prevented or detected?
a. Control deficiency
b. Material deficiency
c. Material weaknesses
d. Significant deficiency (Editors, 8283)

70. Which of the following statements apply to walkthroughs performed as part of an audit of internal control over financial reporting conducted in accordance with the standards of the *Public Company Accounting Oversight Board* (PCAOB)?

I. When there have been significant changes in the flow of transactions, the auditor must walk through transactions that were processed both before and after the change.
II. The auditor must make inquires of personnel involved in significant aspects of controls rather than of a single employee.

a. I only
b. II only
c. Both I and II
d. Neither I nor II (Editors, 8285)

71. The conceptual definition of materiality that applies to an audit of a public company's internal control over financial reporting includes which of the following considerations?

	Qualitative	*Quantitative*	
a.	Yes	Yes	
b.	Yes	No	
c.	No	Yes	
d.	No	No	(Editors, 8284)

72. In an audit of internal control over financial reporting conducted in accordance with the standards of the *Public Company Accounting Oversight Board* (PCAOB), which test of controls over operating effectiveness is insufficient by itself?
a. Inquiries of appropriate personnel
b. Inspection of relevant documents
c. Observation of operations
d. Reperformance of the control procedure (Editors, 8286)

73. Which of the following statements is false in regard to an audit of internal control over financial reporting conducted in accordance with the standards of the *Public Company Accounting Oversight Board* (PCAOB)?
a. The auditor may rely upon the judgments of others regarding the sufficiency of evidence.
b. The auditor may use the work of others to alter the nature, timing, or extent of the work that the auditor performs.
c. The extent to which the auditor may use the work of others depends on their objectivity.
d. When using the work of others, the auditor may evaluate the quality and effectiveness of their work by testing similar controls not actually tested by the others. (Editors, 8287)

74. Which of the following is true with regard to the annual report of a publicly held company?

I. Management must provide a written conclusion about the effectiveness of the company's internal control over financial reporting.
II. Management may represent that internal control over financial reporting as of the end of the period is effective even if a material weakness existed during the period.

a. I only
b. II only
c. Both I and II
d. Neither I nor II (Editors, 8289)

Editor's Note: The requirements for auditors under the Sarbanes-Oxley Act and public company reporting issues probably will be tested in the AUD exam section; however, the examiners do not state explicitly where this topic will be tested. SOX and PCAOB questions are included here as a safety net in the unlikely event that the examiners test this issue in the REG exam section and you are sitting for the REG exam section before the AUD exam section.

After reviewing these questions and their explanations, if you still have concerns regarding these topics, consider reviewing your AUD materials for more in-depth information. Before you do, bear in mind that this topic is more likely to be tested in AUD. Ensure have a firm grasp on other REG topics before spending additional time with this topic.

SIMULATIONS

Problem 33-4 (20 to 30 minutes)

Malcolm Manufacturing Corp. planned to raise capital for a plant expansion by borrowing from banks and making several stock offerings. Malcolm engaged Potter, CPA, to audit its December 31, Year 4, financial statements. Malcolm told Potter that the financial statements would be given to certain named banks and included in the prospectuses for the stock offerings.

In performing the audit, Potter did not confirm accounts receivable and, as a result, failed to discover a material overstatement of accounts receivable. Also, Potter was aware of a pending class action product liability lawsuit that was not disclosed in Malcolm's financial statements. Despite being advised by Malcolm's legal counsel that Malcolm's potential liability under the lawsuit would result in material losses, Potter issued an unqualified opinion on Malcolm's financial statements.

In May Year 5, Union Bank, one of the named banks, relied on the financial statements and Potter's opinion in giving Malcolm a $500,000 loan.

Malcolm raised an additional $16,450,000 through the following stock offerings, which were sold completely:

- June Year 5—Malcolm made a $450,000 unregistered offering of Class B nonvoting common stock under Rule 504 of Regulation D of the Securities Act of 1933. This offering was sold over two years to 30 nonaccredited investors and 20 accredited investors by general solicitation. The SEC was notified eight days after the first sale of this offering.
- September Year 5—Malcolm made a $10,000,000 unregistered offering of Class A voting common stock under Rule 506 of Regulation D of the Securities Act of 1933. This offering was sold over two years to 200 accredited investors and 30 nonaccredited investors through a private placement. The SEC was notified 14 days after the first sale of this offering.
- November Year 5—Malcolm made a $6,000,000 unregistered offering of preferred stock under Rule 505 of Regulation D of the Securities Act of 1933. This offering was sold during a one-year period to 40 nonaccredited investors by private placement. The SEC was notified 18 days after the first sale of this offering.

Shortly after obtaining the Union loan, Malcolm began experiencing financial problems but was able to stay in business because of the money raised by the offerings. Malcolm was found liable in the product liability suit. This resulted in a judgment Malcolm could not pay. Malcolm also defaulted on the Union loan and was involuntarily petitioned into bankruptcy. This caused Union to sustain a loss and Malcolm's stockholders to lose their investments.

As a result:

- The SEC claimed that all three of Malcolm's offerings were made improperly and were not exempt from registration.
- Union sued Potter for negligence.
- The stockholders who purchased Malcolm's stock through the offerings sued Potter, alleging fraud under Section 10(b) and Rule 10b-5 of the Securities Exchange Act of 1934.

These transactions took place in a jurisdiction providing for accountant's liability for negligence to known and intended users of financial statements. (5/94, Law, #61, amended, 4921)

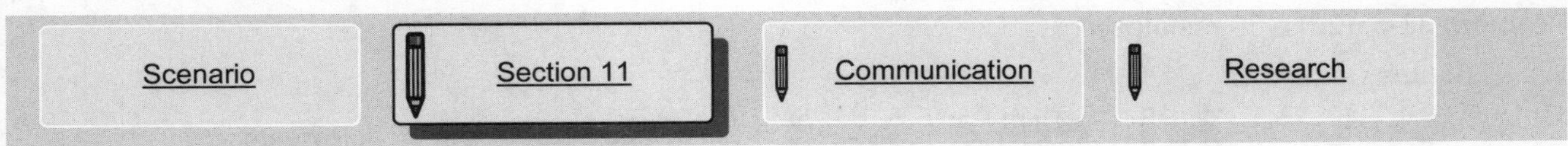

Under Section 11 of the Securities Act of 1933 and Section 10(b), Rule 10b-5 of the Securities Exchange Act of 1934, a CPA may be sued by a purchaser of registered securities.

Items 1 through 6 relate to what a plaintiff who purchased securities must prove in a civil liability suit against a CPA. For each item determine whether the statement must be proven under Section 11 of the Securities Act of 1933, under Section (10)b, Rule 10b-5 of the Securities Exchange Act of 1934, both Acts, or neither Act.

Acts

A. The item must be proven **only** under Section 11 of the Securities Act of 1933.
B. The item must be proven **only** under Section 10(b), Rule 10b-5, of the Securities Exchange Act of 1934.
C. The item must be proven under **both** Acts.
D. The item must be proven under **neither** of the Acts.

Statement	Answer
1. Material misstatements were included in a filed document.	
2. A monetary loss occurred.	
3. Lack of due diligence by the CPA	
4. Privity with the CPA	
5. Reliance on the document	
6. The CPA had scienter.	

Write an internal memorandum to your supervisor addressing the following question, giving reasons for your conclusions. Will Union be successful in its suit against Potter for negligence?

Research Question: What authoritative reference considers a member of the profession to have committed a discreditable act when the member permits another to make materially false and misleading entries in the records of an entity?

Paragraph Reference Answer: ET ____________

Problem 33-5 (20 to 30 minutes)

Malcolm Manufacturing Corp. planned to raise capital for a plant expansion by borrowing from banks and making several stock offerings. Malcolm engaged Potter, CPA, to audit its December 31, Year 4, financial statements. Malcolm told Potter that the financial statements would be given to certain named banks and included in the prospectuses for the stock offerings.

In performing the audit, Potter did not confirm accounts receivable and, as a result, failed to discover a material overstatement of accounts receivable. Also, Potter was aware of a pending class action product liability lawsuit that was not disclosed in Malcolm's financial statements. Despite being advised by Malcolm's legal counsel that Malcolm's potential liability under the lawsuit would result in material losses, Potter issued an unqualified opinion on Malcolm's financial statements.

In May Year 5, Union Bank, one of the named banks, relied on the financial statements and Potter's opinion in giving Malcolm a $500,000 loan.

Malcolm raised an additional $16,450,000 through the following stock offerings, which were sold completely:

- June Year 5—Malcolm made a $450,000 unregistered offering of Class B nonvoting common stock under Rule 504 of Regulation D of the Securities Act of 1933. This offering was sold over two years to 30 nonaccredited investors and 20 accredited investors by general solicitation. The SEC was notified eight days after the first sale of this offering.
- September Year 5—Malcolm made a $10,000,000 unregistered offering of Class A voting common stock under Rule 506 of Regulation D of the Securities Act of 1933. This offering was sold over two years to 200 accredited investors and 30 nonaccredited investors through a private placement. The SEC was notified 14 days after the first sale of this offering.
- November Year 5—Malcolm made a $6,000,000 unregistered offering of preferred stock under Rule 505 of Regulation D of the Securities Act of 1933. This offering was sold during a one-year period to 40 nonaccredited investors by private placement. The SEC was notified 18 days after the first sale of this offering.

Shortly after obtaining the Union loan, Malcolm began experiencing financial problems but was able to stay in business because of the money raised by the offerings. Malcolm was found liable in the product liability suit. This resulted in a judgment Malcolm could not pay. Malcolm also defaulted on the Union loan and was involuntarily petitioned into bankruptcy. This caused Union to sustain a loss and Malcolm's stockholders to lose their investments.

As a result, Union sued Potter for common law fraud.

These transactions took place in a jurisdiction providing for accountant's liability for negligence to known and intended users of financial statements. (Editors, 4922)

For items 1 through 8, indicate whether the statement is true (T) or false (F).

Statement	Answer
1. A CPA who negligently gives an opinion on an audit of a client's financial statements is liable only to those third parties who are in privity of contract with the CPA.	
2. For a plaintiff to prevail in a common law negligent misrepresentation action, the plaintiff must prove that the plaintiff justifiably relied on the misrepresentations.	
3. In a suit for common law fraud based on its unqualified opinion on materially false financial statements, a CPA firm can assert, as a defense, a disclaimer contained in the engagement letter.	
4. For a plaintiff to prevail in a common law negligent misrepresentation action, the plaintiff must prove that the defendant made the misrepresentations with a reckless disregard for the truth.	
5. For a plaintiff to prevail in a common law negligent misrepresentation action, the plaintiff must prove that the misrepresentations concerned opinion.	
6. For a plaintiff to prevail in a common law negligent misrepresentation action, the plaintiff must prove that the misrepresentations were in writing.	
7. In a suit for common law fraud based on its unqualified opinion on materially false financial statements, a CPA firm can assert, as a defense, contributory negligence on the part of the client.	
8. In a suit for common law fraud based on its unqualified opinion on materially false financial statements, a CPA firm can assert, as a defense, a lack of scienter.	

Write an internal memorandum to your supervisor addressing the following question, giving reasons for your conclusions. Will Union be successful in its suit against Potter for common law fraud?

Scenario | Third-Party Liability | Communication | Research

Research Question: What authoritative reference considers it appropriate for a member to require all fees due to the member for completed engagements where the member's work papers contain information that is not reflected in the client's books and records be paid before such information is made available to the client upon request?

Paragraph Reference Answer: ET ____________

Problem 33-6 (20 to 30 minutes)

Goodwin, a CPA, and Jensen, a banker, were the trustees of the Moore Family Trust. The trust was created as a spendthrift trust and provided for distribution of income annually to the four Moore adult children for life, with the principal to be distributed to their issue after the death of the last income beneficiary. The trust was funded with commercial and residential real estate and a stock portfolio.

Goodwin, in addition to being a trustee, was lawfully employed as the trust's accountant. Goodwin, as the trust's accountant, prepared and signed all trust tax returns, kept the trust's accounting records, and supervised distributions to the income beneficiaries.

In Year 5, Goodwin and Jensen, as trustees, sold a building owned by the trust for $400,000, its fair market value. The building had been valued at $250,000 when acquired by the trust. The $150,000 gain was allocated to income. In addition, the trust had rental, interest, and dividend income of $1,500,000 in Year 5. Expenses for taxes, replacement of plumbing fixtures, roof repairs, utilities, salaries, and fees and commissions totaled $1,050,000.

On December 31, Year 5, Goodwin and Jensen prepared and signed four $150,000 trust account checks and sent three of them to three of the income beneficiaries and the fourth one to a creditor of the fourth beneficiary. This beneficiary had acknowledged that the creditor was owed $200,000.

In February Year 5, Goodwin discovered that Jensen had embezzled $200,000 by secretly selling part of the trust's stock portfolio. Goodwin agreed not to reveal Jensen's embezzlement if Jensen would pay Goodwin $25,000.

In April Year 6, Goodwin prepared the Year 5 trust income tax return. The return was signed by Goodwin as preparer and by Jensen and Goodwin as trustees and was filed with the IRS. Goodwin also prepared the Year 5 income tax returns for the income beneficiaries. In an attempt to hide the embezzlement, Goodwin, in preparing the trust tax return, claimed nonexistent losses and improper credits. The beneficiaries' returns reflected the same nonexistent losses and improper credits. Consequently, the beneficiaries' taxes were underpaid. As a result of an IRS audit, the embezzlement was uncovered, the nonexistent losses and improper credits were disallowed, and the beneficiaries were assessed additional taxes, penalties, and interest.

Jensen cannot be located.

As a result of the above, the income beneficiaries sued Goodwin for negligence, fraud, and breach of fiduciary duty. (5/92, Law, #3, amended, 9690)

For items 1 through 4, determine whether the statement is true (T) or false (F).

Statement	Answer
1. An accountant must relinquish possession of work papers in response to a court order.	
2. A CPA may disclose the contents of work papers without permission from clients when disclosure is in compliance with generally accepted accounting principles.	
3. A CPA may disclose the contents of work papers without permission from the client when disclosure is pursuant to a voluntary quality review under AICPA authorization.	
4. An accountant is protected from being compelled to testify in federal tax court with regard to privileged matters under state statutes asserting that communications between the client and the accountant are privileged.	
5. In the absence of an agreement to the contrary, ownership of an accountant's work papers rests with the accountant.	
6. A group of CPAs may disclose the contents of work papers without permission from clients when the accounting firm is sold to another CPA.	
7. A CPA may disclose the contents of work papers without permission from clients when disclosure is pursuant to a voluntary quality review under AICPA authorization.	
8. A CPA may disclose the contents of work papers without permission from clients when disclosure is in compliance with generally accepted auditing standards.	
9. Work papers must be transferred permanently to the client if demanded.	

Write a memo to your supervisor answering the following questions, giving the reasons for your conclusions.

Will the income beneficiaries win their suits against Goodwin for:

a. Accountant's negligence?

b. Actual fraud?

c. Breach of fiduciary duty as a trustee?

Research Question: What authoritative reference prohibits a CPA from accepting a commission for recommending a product to a client, unless the CPA informs the client's management?

Paragraph Reference Answer: ET ____________

Problem 33-7 (20 to 30 minutes)

Feline Corp. is a public corporation whose stock is traded on a national securities exchange. Feline hired Wilcox Associates, CPAs, to audit Feline's financial statements. Feline needed the audit to obtain bank loans and to make a public stock offering so that Feline could undertake a business expansion program.

Before the engagement, Fred Hedge, Feline's president, told Wilcox's managing partner that the audited financial statements would be submitted to Feline's banks to obtain the necessary loans.

During the course of the audit, Wilcox's managing partner found that Hedge and other Feline officers had embezzled substantial amounts of money from the corporation. Those embezzlements threatened Feline's financial stability. When these findings were brought to Hedge's attention, Hedge promised that the money would be repaid and begged that the audit not disclose the embezzlements.

Hedge also told Wilcox's managing partner that several friends and relatives of Feline's officers had been advised about the projected business expansion and proposed stock offering, and had purchased significant amounts of Feline's stock based on this information.

Wilcox submitted an unqualified opinion on Feline's financial statements, which did not include adjustments for or disclosures about the embezzlements and insider stock transactions. The financial statements and audit report were submitted to Feline's regular banks including Knox Bank. Knox, relying on the financial statements and Wilcox's report, gave Feline a $2,000,000 loan.

Feline's audited financial statements were also incorporated in a registration statement prepared under the provisions of the Securities Act of 1933. The registration statement was filed with the SEC in conjunction with Feline's public offering of 100,000 shares of its common stock at $100 per share.

An SEC investigation of Feline disclosed the embezzlements and the insider trading. Trading in Feline's stock was suspended and Feline defaulted on the Knox loan.

As a result, both Knox and the general public purchasers of Feline's stock offering sued Wilcox.

(5/91, Law, #5, amended, 8553)

Billings is a publicly traded company subject to the provisions of the Sarbanes-Oxley Act and its audit must be performed in accordance with the standards of the Public Company Accounting Oversight Board (PCAOB) which is overseen by the Securities and Exchange Commission (SEC).

Indicate whether the following statements are true (T) or false (F) in this situation.

Statement	True/False
1. The lead audit partner and the audit partner responsible for reviewing the audit must be changed every seven years.	
2. Billings' audit committee must approve all services by the audit firm to the audit client.	
3. The audit firm may accept an engagement to design internal controls for Billings' financial information system.	
4. Billings' chief executive officer must be a member of the audit committee.	
5. The audit firm must register with the SEC.	
6. The audit firm may not have employed Billings's chief financial officer or controller within the last five years of the period under audit.	
7. Billings' chief executive officer and chief financial officer must certify annual (Form 10-K) and quarterly (Form 10-Q) reports to the SEC.	
8. The audit firm must keep work papers related to the audit for seven years.	

Write an internal memorandum to your supervisor addressing the following questions. Give the reasons for your conclusions.

a. Would Knox recover from Wilcox for fraud?

b. Would the general public purchasers of Feline's stock offerings recover from Wilcox:

1. Under the liability provisions of Section 11 of the Securities Act of 1933?
2. Under the anti-fraud provisions of Rule 10b-5 of the Securities Exchange Act of 1934?

Scenario | PCAOB Audit | Communication | Research

Research Question: What authoritative reference considers representing a client in an examination by a revenue agent of the client's federal or state income tax return as a circumstance where a contingent fee would be permitted?

Paragraph Reference Answer: ET ____________

Problem 33-8 (20 to 30 minutes)

Ursula Corp. is an audit client of Knightsbridge Associates, CPAs. In Year 5, Ursula's audit committee engaged Knightsbridge to perform litigation support services. The services were completed in January, Year 5, and Knightsbridge billed Ursula in February, Year 5.

In February, Year 6, Knightsbridge began its annual audit of Ursula's financial statements. During the course of the audit, Knightsbridge discovered that Ursula's officers had committed management fraud. The officers' fraud resulted in material misstatements in the financial statements that were to be submitted to the SEC with Ursula's annual report (Form 10-K). In March, Year 6, Knightsbridge issued an auditor's report containing an unqualified opinion on the financial statements. As of that date, Ursula had not paid Knightsbridge's outstanding February Year 5 bill.

(Editors, 6768)

For items 1 through 8, determine whether the statement is true (T) or false (F).

Statement	Answer
1. A CPA has met the required standard of care in conducting an audit of a client's financial statements when the client's expectations with regard to the accuracy of audited financial statements are met.	
2. A CPA has met the required standard of care in conducting an audit of a client's financial statements when the financial statements conform to generally accepted accounting principles.	
3. A CPA has met the required standard of care in conducting an audit of a client's financial statements if the CPA conducted the audit with the same skill and care expected of an ordinarily prudent CPA under the circumstances.	
4. A CPA has met the required standard of care in conducting an audit of a client's financial statements when the audit was conducted to discover all acts of fraud.	
5. While performing the audit, a CPA failed to discover irregularities that later caused stockholders to suffer substantial losses. For the CPA to be liable under common law negligence, the stockholders must prove, at a minimum, that the CPA knew of the irregularities.	
6. While performing the audit, a CPA failed to discover irregularities that later caused stockholders to suffer substantial losses. For the CPA to be liable under common law negligence, the stockholders must prove, at a minimum, that the CPA failed to exercise due care.	
7. While performing the audit, a CPA failed to discover irregularities that later caused stockholders to suffer substantial losses. For the CPA to be liable under common law negligence, the stockholders must prove, at a minimum, that the CPA was grossly negligent.	
8. While performing the audit, a CPA failed to discover irregularities that later caused stockholders to suffer substantial losses. For the CPA to be liable under common law negligence, the stockholders must prove, at a minimum, that the CPA acted with scienter.	

Write an internal memorandum as a member of a review board to your fellow members stating whether Knightsbridge committed any violations of the Securities Exchange Act of 1934, the Private Securities Litigation Reform Act of 1995, and the Sarbanes-Oxley Act of 2002. Explain your conclusions.

Scenario	True/False	Communication	Research

Research Question: What authoritative reference considers it appropriate for a member to require all fees due to the member for completed engagements where the members' workpapers contain information that is not reflected in the client's books and records be paid before such information is made available to the client upon request?

Paragraph Reference Answer: ET ____________

Problem 33-9 (20 to 30 minutes)

Editor's Note: Candidates unfamiliar with SEC regulations should consider waiting to answer this simulation until after reviewing the *Federal Securities Regulation* chapter.

Battery Associates, CPAs, were retained to perform a consulting service engagement by Akemi Corp. Battery contracted to advise Akemi on the proper computers to purchase. Battery was also to design computer software that would allow for more efficient collection of Akemi's accounts receivable. Battery prepared the software programs in a manner that allowed some of Akemi's accounts receivable to be erroneously deleted from Akemi's records. As a result, Akemi's expense to collect these accounts was increased greatly.

During the course of the engagement, a Battery partner learned from a computer salesperson that the computers Battery was recommending to Akemi would be obsolete within a year. The salesperson suggested that Battery recommend a newer, less expensive model that was more efficient. Battery intentionally recommended, and Akemi purchased, the more expensive model. Battery received a commission from the computer company for inducing Akemi to purchase that computer. Akemi sued Battery for negligence and common law fraud.

(Editors, 6163)

Coffee Corp., a publicly-held corporation, wants to make an $8,000,000 exempt offering of its shares as a private placement offering under Regulation D, Rule 506, of the Securities Act of 1933. Coffee has more than 500 shareholders and assets in excess of $1 billion, and has its shares listed on a national securities exchange.

Items 1 through 5 relate to the application of the provisions of the Securities Act of 1933 and the Securities Exchange Act of 1934 to Coffee Corp. and the offering. For each item, indicate whether only statement I is correct, only statement II is correct, both statements I and II are correct, or neither statement I nor II is correct.

A. I only
B. II only
C. Both I and II
D. Neither I nor II

Statement	Answer
1. I. Coffee Corp. may make the Regulation D, Rule 506, exempt offering. II. Coffee Corp., because it is required to report under the Securities Exchange Act of 1934, may **not** make an exempt offering.	
2. I. Shares sold under a Regulation D, Rule 506, exempt offering may only be purchased by accredited investors. II. Shares sold under a Regulation D, Rule 506, exempt offering may be purchased by any number of investors provided there are no more than 35 nonaccredited investors.	
3. I. An exempt offering under Regulation D, Rule 506, must not be for more than $10,000,000. II. An exempt offering under Regulation D, Rule 506, has no dollar limit.	

4. I. Regulation D, Rule 506, requires that all investors in the exempt offering be notified that for nine months after the last sale no resale may be made to a nonresident. II. Regulation D, Rule 506, requires that the issuer exercise reasonable care to assure that purchasers of the exempt offering are buying for investment and are not underwriters.	
5. I. The SEC must be notified by Coffee Corp. within 5 days of the first sale of the exempt offering securities. II. Coffee Corp. must include an SEC notification of the first sale of the exempt offering securities in Coffee's next filed Quarterly Report (Form 10-Q).	

Write an internal memo to a member of the board stating whether or not a negligence suit against Battery Associates, CPAs, relating to the Akemi consulting service engagement would be successful and describe the elements of negligence presented in the scenario.

Research Question: What authoritative reference considers a member who solicits or knowingly discloses the May 1996 or later Uniform CPA Examination question(s) and/or answer(s) without the written authorization of the AICPA shall be considered to have committed an act discreditable to the profession?

Paragraph Reference Answer: ET ____________

Solution 33-1 MULTIPLE CHOICE ANSWERS

Liability to Clients

1. (c) Negligence involves a breach of a duty of due care. A CPA would most likely be considered negligent while performing an audit when the CPA fails to warn a client of known internal control weaknesses. A CPA has no duty to detect all of a client's fraudulent activities nor to warn a client's customers of embezzlement by the client's employees. If no such duty is imposed, then negligence cannot exist. Failure to include a negligence disclaimer in a client engagement letter would also not result in a CPA being found negligent.

2. (d) An auditor has a responsibility to exercise due professional care in the performance of the audit and the preparation of the report. CPAs are expected to comply with generally accepted auditing standards (GAAS). Although adherence to GAAS does not guarantee that there is no negligence, failure to follow GAAS would be a breach of a CPA's duty of due care. An oral report is not necessarily a breach of due care. Depending on the type of engagement involved, an oral report may be appropriate. Honest inaccuracies and judgmental errors will not give rise to negligence liability so long as the CPA exercised reasonable care in performing her/his work. A CPA in tax practice has a responsibility to use judgment to ensure that advice given reflects professional competence and appropriately serves the clients' needs. While one goal of tax advice is to save the client money, failure to do so does not necessarily result in a breach of a CPA's duty of due care.

3. (a) The law imposes upon the accountant the profession's generally accepted standards of competence and care. Thus, an accountant must demonstrate the average degree of learning and skill possessed by accountants generally. It is the financial statements that must be in conformity with GAAP. An accountant's duties under a contract with a client normally do not include a duty to discover fraud, unless the accountant's own negligence prevents her/him from discovering the fraud. The CPA also could be held liable for ordinary negligence.

4. (c) The client need not prove reliance in a negligence action against a CPA. In a negligence action, a client must prove a loss (injury) that is caused (proximate cause) by the wrongful acts of the defendant (breach of duty of care).

5. (c) Failure to fulfill the terms of a contract usually constitutes a breach of the contract and may subject the accountant to liability in the form of money damages. Specific performance is not granted for a personal services contract. Punitive damages are not allowed even if the breach is willful. A rescission involves undoing the contract on both sides and placing the parties in their original positions; such a resolution would be difficult following the breach of a professional services contract.

6. (c) Constructive fraud is characterized by gross negligence. The plaintiff must also prove that the plaintiff justifiably relied on the CPA's work.

Common Law Liability to Third Parties

7. (c) Under common law, an accountant's tort liability to third parties for ordinary negligence normally extends only to those third parties whom the accountant knew or should have known would be users or beneficiaries of the CPA's work product. The CPA is liable to the client, to third parties in privity of contract, and also to anyone in a class of third parties who the CPA knows will rely on the opinion; however, this liability does not extend to all possible foreseeable users of the opinion.

8. (b) Negligent misrepresentation requires proof of a misstatement of material fact upon which the other party relies to their detriment. It is not necessary to show that the misrepresentations were made with a reckless disregard for the truth nor that they be in writing.

9. (b) A CPA's liability to third parties who are unknown to the CPA usually will arise only if the CPA was grossly negligent. A CPA normally is not liable for ordinary negligence to third parties of whose existence the CPA is unaware. A CPA normally would be held liable for ordinary negligence to those third parties whom the CPA knew (or should have known) to be using the CPA's work product. CPAs are not strictly liable to anyone since they are neither engaged in an ultrahazardous activity nor sellers of a good in the stream of commerce (UCC 2). There is no standard of criminal deceit by which a CPA would have liability to unknown third parties.

10. (c) In order to prove negligence under common law, Mac must prove the following:

1. A duty of care existed.
2. That duty of care was breached.
3. The injury was proximately caused by the defendant's breach of the duty of care.
4. The plaintiff suffered an injury.

Item I corresponds to the second element—"duty of care." Item II corresponds to the third element—"proximate cause." Thus, both items I and II are necessary in order for Mac to recover.

11. (a) Under common law (not under the Securities Act), the duty of care required for accountants is compliance with GAAP and GAAS. As long as an accountant conforms to generally accepted auditing standards in good faith, s/he will not be held liable to the client for incorrect judgment. Compliance with GAAS, however, does not *necessarily* relieve an accountant from all potential legal liability. Therefore, the editorial board feels that this answer is not entirely correct. "Awareness" of the misstatements is not a requirement in a negligence suit under common law. Most courts have adopted the position taken by the Restatement of Torts (in place of the *Ultramares* rule), which states that accountants will be subject to a suit by any *foreseen,* or *known,* users or class of users of the accountant's work product. The erosion of the *Ultramares* rule eliminates the necessity of privity of contract. Larson will be subject to a suit by any third party whom the accountant *knew* or *should have known* would be users of the accountant's work product.

12. (a) The four elements required in a fraud action include the following: (1) misrepresentation of a material fact; (2) intent to deceive or reckless disregard for the truth (constructive knowledge); (3) justifiable reliance by the injured party; (4) innocent party is injured. Thus, the best defense would be that the CPA did not have actual or constructive knowledge of the misstatements and so had no "intent to deceive." The client's knowledge of the misstatements does not affect the accountant's liability. Under the common law, a third party need only prove that s/he reasonably relied on the accountant's work. Privity of contract is never a defense to fraud under common law.

13. (d) A CPA is liable for common law fraud when there is (1) a misstatement of material fact, (2) scienter (which exists if the CPA acted with knowledge of the falsity or a reckless disregard for the truth and the intent to mislead), and (3) justifiable reliance by the injured party. Thus, lack of scienter would be the CPA's best defense. Contributory negligence and lack of privity are not defenses to an action for fraud. A fraud disclaimer contained in an engagement letter would not protect the CPA from liability for her/his fraudulent actions.

Section 11 (1933)

14. (d) To impose liability under Section 11 of the Securities Act of 1933, a purchaser of securities can hold a CPA liable upon proof that the financial statement either omitted or misstated a material fact. It is not necessary that the purchaser prove reliance or fraud, which requires proof of intent or scienter.

15. (c) The due diligence defense may be established by proving that after reasonable investigation, the accountant had reasonable basis for the belief that all statements and registration statements were accurate and complete. The standard of reasonableness is met by showing the auditor was as reasonably careful as the auditor's peers. Compliance with GAAS and performing an additional review would help to establish the due diligence defense.

16. (a) Under Section 11 of the 1933 Act, the plaintiff must prove that a material misstatement or omission of a material fact occurred in the registration statement, that the plaintiff purchased the securities, and that damages were suffered. Then the burden of proof switches to the defendant CPA who must prove using one of four defenses: the due diligence defense; the plaintiff knew of the material misstatement or omission; the loss was due to other causes; or the plaintiff failed to commence their law suit within the statute of limitations (one year from discovery, maximum of three years from the effective date of the registration statement).

17. (c) Under the provisions of Section 11 of the Securities Act of 1933, a CPA will be liable to a purchaser of securities if the financial statements either omit or misstate a material fact. The CPA may avoid liability by showing that s/he acted with due diligence. Pursuant to the 1933 Act, the purchaser need not prove scienter or privity to impose liability. Other defenses include that the plaintiff knew of the material misstatement or omission, the loss was due to other causes, or the plaintiff failed to commence the lawsuit within the time allowed by the statute of limitations. The purchaser's reliance on the statements is irrelevant.

18. (b) Under Section 11 of the Securities Act of 1933, a CPA charged with fraud can use the due diligence defense. Due diligence would include following GAAP. There are no generally accepted fraud detection standards.

19. (c) The amount of damages generally recoverable under the Act is measured by the difference between the amount paid for the security and the market value of the security at the time of the suit. In no event can the amount of damages exceed the price at which the security was offered to the public. Treble damages are not permitted in such cases. The transaction cannot be rescinded.

There is no requirement that the shares must have been resold before the suit was commenced.

Section 10 (1934)

20. (c) Where the defendant has violated the antifraud provisions [Section 10(b) and Rule 10b-5] of the Securities and Exchange Act of 1934, the plaintiff may recover the amount of loss caused by the fraud. The plaintiff would not be entitled to punitive damages.

21. (c) An original public offering of stock would be governed by the provisions of the Securities Act of 1933. Under section 11 of this Act, a CPA can be liable for fraud if the registration statement contains material misstatements. It is not necessary that the CPA have scienter or that the client relied on the registration materials.

22. (b) In an action brought under Section 10(b) and Rule 10b-5 of the Securities Act of 1934, a plaintiff must prove the following: (1) there was a material misrepresentation or omission, (2) the plaintiff suffered damages, (3) the plaintiff relied on the fraudulent statement, and (4) existence of scienter. Negligence alone will not subject an accountant to liability under this section. Section 10(b) and Rule 10b-5 cover transactions in both registered and unregistered securities and apply to transactions involving the purchase or sale of any security within the jurisdiction of the SEC, not just original issuances.

Sarbanes-Oxley Act

23. (b) The Sarbanes-Oxley Act requires firms that perform audits of public companies to register with the Public Company Accounting Oversight Board (PCAOB). Membership in the AICPA or its practice sections is not necessary to audit any company. The FASB sets accounting standards; it does not register firms, accountants, or auditors. Issuers of publicly traded securities, not auditors, register with the SEC pursuant to the 1934 Act.

24. (a) The Sarbanes-Oxley Act prohibits an accounting firm from providing audit services for an issuer if the CEO, Controller, CFO, CAO, or any person serving in the equivalent capacity for the issuer was employed in the audit practice of the accounting firm during the one-year period prior to the audit.

25. (c, e) Both responses are required for full credit. The Sarbanes-Oxley Act prohibits registered public accounting firms from providing the following nonaudit services to an audit client: bookkeeping; financial information system design and implementation; appraisal or valuation services; actuarial services; internal audit outsourcing services; management functions or human resources; broker or dealer, investment advisor or investment banking services; legal services and expert services. It doesn't prohibit such services being provided to non-audit clients.

Disclosure

26. (d) The Code of Professional Conduct prohibits disclosure by a CPA of confidential information except in the following circumstances: (1) where disclosure is pursuant to a voluntary quality review under AICPA authorization, (2) where disclosure is in compliance with an enforceable subpoena or court order, (3) where the client consents to the disclosure, and (4) to comply with GAAP or GAAS. A CPA must have permission from the client to disclose confidential information to another CPA who has purchased the CPA's tax practice or another CPA firm if the information concerns suspected tax return irregularities.

27. (a) The Supreme Court has held that the U.S. Constitution's Fifth Amendment rights regarding self-incrimination do not extend to the CPA-client relationship. A number of states, however, do recognize such a privilege pursuant to state constitutional protections. Thus, Ivor can claim the privilege in those states that recognize such a privilege. There are no other instances in which a CPA-client privilege is recognized. The type of suit is irrelevant.

28. (d) Ownership of an accountant's working papers rests with the accountant, not with the accountant's employees.

29. (c) The accountant's ownership of working papers is of a custodial interest.

Criminal Penalties

30. (c) Willful violations of the provisions of either the Securities Act of 1933 or the Securities Exchange Act of 1934 can subject the offender to criminal penalties of fines and/or imprisonment. On the other hand, negligence may be based on unintentional errors resulting from failure to exercise reasonable care, which usually results in civil penalties.

Solution 33-2 ADDITIONAL MULTIPLE CHOICE ANSWERS

Liability to Clients

31. (b) A CPA's contract for services to her/his client is governed by general common law contract rules. Therefore, the CPA's failure to perform as promised is a breach of contract. A CPA is not liable to her/his client under the concept of strict liability because this legal concept normally applies to merchant sellers. Strict liability provides that a merchant seller is strictly liable for the physical harm or property damage experienced by the ultimate consumer if the product was in a defective condition and unreasonably dangerous to the user.

32. (b) For an accountant to be held liable under common law negligence, a client must prove that the accountant failed to exercise due care under the circumstances. Sun need not prove that Frank knew of the irregularities, only that he failed to exercise due care. Gross negligence involves a reckless disregard for the truth and is an element of constructive fraud. Scienter is an element of fraud.

33. (c) The basic duty of care standard is that of the reasonable person. However, since CPAs have knowledge and skill beyond that of the ordinary person, they must act with a level of care of similarly situated professionals.

34. (a) The elements of constructive fraud are: (1) misrepresentation or omission of a material fact, (2) reckless disregard for the truth, (3) reasonable reliance by the injured party, and (4) injury. Proof of reckless disregard for the truth (gross negligence) satisfies the scienter requirement to support a finding of constructive fraud. All four of these elements must be present to support a finding of constructive fraud, as is the case when a CPA is grossly negligent in applying generally accepted auditing standards. Ordinary negligence is not sufficient to support a finding of constructive fraud. Third party users may recover for fraud once they establish the elements of fraud, but the identification of the third party users is not an actual element of fraud. Scienter indicates that the misrepresentation was "knowingly made" and there was actual knowledge of the misrepresentation as compared to constructive knowledge. However, in general, reckless disregard for the truth will normally support a finding of scienter for purposes of a 1934 SEC violation.

35. (d) An auditor's best defense when sued for negligence is proof that the auditor did not violate generally accepted auditing standards in performing the audit. Lack of privity is not a valid defense with the client who engaged the auditor. A signed engagement letter is not a required part of the audit and the lack of such a letter would not be a valid defense for the auditor. Even if the auditor did not perform the audit recklessly or with an intent to deceive, it is still possible that the auditor failed to exercise reasonable care, under the circumstances, in conducting the audit.

Common Law Liability to Third Parties

36. (c) Under common law an accountant may be liable to a third party for fraud in the accountant's reports regardless of whether or not the work was intended for use by the third party or for the accountant's clients. To recover damages, the third party must show that s/he reasonably relied on the accountant's work. The third party is not required to show privity with either the client or the accountant. Contributory negligence is not a defense to a charge of fraud.

37. (a) In order to prevail in a suit under the *Ultramares* doctrine the third party must show privity of contract when ordinary negligence took place. Liability extends to third parties only in case of fraud. Since, under common law, for privity of contract to exist a person must have a contractual relationship with the person sued, in this case, there is no privity of contract between Hark and Third.

38. (c) Under common law, accountants owe a duty to ALL third parties to make their reports without actual or constructive fraud. It is not necessary that the CPA have knowledge of or be in privity of contract with third parties to incur liability for fraud. The CPA will not be liable to a client who is aware of the fraud and did not rely on the opinion.

39. (a) Historically, privity of contract was a requirement for a cause of action based upon negligence. This approach was established in the landmark *Ultramares* case. Under common law, accountants owe a duty to all third parties to make their reports without actual or constructive fraud. Gross negligence amounting to a reckless disregard for the truth constitutes constructive fraud. Accountants have a contractual relationship with their clients, thus privity would not be a defense.

40. (b) In a suit based on fraud, the plaintiff must prove: (1) false statements of a *material* fact knowingly made (scienter) or made with reckless disregard for the truth (constructive fraud), and (2) the plaintiff relied on the false statements and suffered damages thereby. The suit is not based on negligence where privity is an essential element. It

does not matter if the CPA benefited from the alleged fraud or not. This is not a defense. The amount of damages suffered by the third party (the stockholder) is the important factor. Contributory negligence applies only if the suit is based on negligence.

41. (b) Negligence is the failure to exercise that degree of care that a reasonable person would exercise under similar circumstances. An auditor failing to discover a material overstatement of assets during an audit generally is such a failure. The issue of whether the accountant knew that the audit of the financial statements was undertaken to obtain a loan from specific bank is unclear in this scenario; a known, specific bank is a third-party beneficiary and contractual liability extends to third-party beneficiaries. Fifteen months after the audit is unlikely to be past the time limit for bringing action; under federal securities law, actions must be commenced within one year of the time when the error or omission was discovered, but no later than three years after the security offering. The "rule of privilege" is inapplicable in this context; typically it concerns the attorney-client privilege; there is no widespread auditor-client privilege.

42. (b) The U.S. Supreme Court's decision in the *Ultramares* case holds that an accountant is only liable for negligence to parties for whose primary benefit the work was intended. This would include only parties in privity of contract with the accountant. The CPA would not be liable in negligence to foreseen parties not in privity of contract with the accountant. Under the Ultramares Doctrine, however, accountants are liable to third parties for fraud.

Section 11 (1933)

43. (b) To be successful under Section 11 of the Securities Act of 1933, the plaintiff must establish that s/he purchased securities which had been issued under a registration statement containing a false statement or an omission of a material fact and that s/he suffered an economic loss. The plaintiff need not prove reliance on the registration statement or the defendant's intent to deceive.

Section 10 (1934)

44. (c) A company registering under the 1934 Act must supply certain information. When reporting on financial statements submitted to a government agency, the auditor generally should note any exceptions to that agency's requirements in the audit report. Candidates with concerns regarding the placement of this question in the REG, rather than the AUD, exam section should contact the AICPA.

45. (a) Section 10(b) and Rule 10b-5 of the Securities Exchange Act of 1934 impose liability on anyone (including a CPA) who intentionally (or with reckless disregard) makes an untrue statement of fact or omits a material fact in an SEC annual report. It is not necessary that the stock purchaser prove negligence.

46. (d) Under the antifraud provisions of Section 10(b) of the Securities Exchange Act of 1934, a CPA may be liable for fraud if the CPA makes a material misrepresentation of fact with knowledge of its falsity or with a reckless disregard for the truth (i.e., scienter). Acting without scienter involves acting without good faith. Negligence is not an issue with fraud. A CPA should always act with independence in auditing engagements. Due diligence is a defense for fraud under the provisions of the Securities Act of 1933.

Sarbanes-Oxley Act

47. (d) The Sarbanes-Oxley Act requires that audit committees be directly responsible for appointing, compensating and overseeing the external audit firm.

48. (b) It is prohibited for a firm to provide audit services to an issuer if the issuer's CEO, controller, CFO, CAO, or other person serving in the equivalent capacity, was employed in the audit firm and participated in the audit of that issuer during the one-year fiscal period prior to the current audit. The Sarbanes-Oxley Act also prohibits a registered public accounting firm from providing audit services to an issuer if the lead audit partner, or the audit partner responsible for reviewing the audit, has performed audit services for that issuer in each of the five previous fiscal years. An auditor may perform other services, such as tax preparation services, for audit clients that are issuers of public securities only with advance approval from the audit committee.

49. (b) The Sarbanes-Oxley Act prohibits any registered public accounting firm from providing bookkeeping, financial information system design, and internal audit outsourcing services as well as many other non-audit services to a publicly-traded audit client. However, a firm may perform tax services for a publicly-traded audit client, although only with advance approval from the audit committee.

50. (c) Management must support its evaluation of internal control over financial reporting (ICOFR) with sufficient evidence, including documentation. If the auditor concludes that management has not fulfilled these responsibilities, the PCAOB requires the auditor to report, in writing, to

management and the audit committee that the audit of ICOFR cannot be completed and that the auditor must disclaim an opinion.

51. (b) To express an opinion on ICOFR effectiveness as of a *point in time,* the auditor should obtain evidence that ICOFR has operated effectively for a sufficient period of time, which may be less than the entire period covered by the company's financial statements. To express an opinion on ICOFR effectiveness *taken as a whole,* the auditor must obtain evidence about the effectiveness of controls over all relevant assertions related to all significant accounts and financial statement disclosures. This requires the auditor to test the design and operation effectiveness of controls that the auditor ordinarily would not test if expressing an opinion only on the financial statements.

52. (d) The auditor must communicate in writing to management and the audit committee all significant deficiencies and material weaknesses identified during the audit, prior to the issuance of the auditor's report on internal control over financial reporting. The communication should distinguish clearly between significant deficiencies and material weaknesses.

53. (c) The auditor should document the effect of a conclusion that control risk is other than low for any relevant assertions related to any significant accounts in connection with the financial statement audit in the auditor's opinion on the audit of ICOFR. The auditor should document the identification of the points at which misstatements related to relevant financial statement assertions could occur within significant accounts and disclosures and major classes of transactions.

54. (d) The auditor obtains and evaluates evidence about whether the internal control over financial reporting was designed and operated effectively. This evidence may come from various sources, including work performed by the auditor and others. The auditor must audit the company's financial statements as of the date specified in management's assessment, evaluate the assessment performed by management, and obtain reasonable assurance that no material weaknesses exist as of the date specified in management's assessment.

Disclosure

55. (c) Professional ethics discourage disclosure of confidential information by a CPA except in select circumstances. These circumstances generally exclude disclosure to the client's vendors or customers.

56. (b) A CPA may not transfer working papers to a purchaser of her/his practice without the client's consent. Third parties may obtain working papers if they have an enforceable subpoena or court order. Federal law and the laws of most states do not recognize an accountant-client privilege. Under the common law, working papers are held to be the accountant's property, although the client has a right to access them.

57. (d) The IRS Restructuring and Reform Act of 1998 extended the attorney-client privilege to federally authorized tax practitioners, which include CPAs. This privilege relates to noncriminal tax matters (except tax shelters) before the IRS or in federal courts. However, the IRS cannot request disclosure of working papers without either the client's consent or a lawful subpoena. Certain states provide for an attorney-client privilege for state matters only. This state privilege is not available for federal matters. Professional ethics discourages disclosure by an accountant of confidential information, except in certain circumstances, including disclosure in pursuant to a voluntary quality review under AICPA authorization in response to an AICPA trial board request. The FASB issues standards for financial accounting and reporting. FASB, however, plays no role in conducting quality (peer) reviews of the AICPA membership.

58. (d) Since the Fifth Amendment to the U.S. Constitution does not extend to the CPA-client relationship, CPAs must turn over their working papers pursuant to a valid federal court subpoena, but need not turn over papers merely at government request. Working papers are the property of the accountant and need not be given to the client, nor may a CPA turn over working papers to another accountant without a client's permission.

59. (c) Professional ethics discourage disclosure of confidential information by a CPA except in select circumstances, such as when in compliance with an enforceable subpoena. Professional ethics require a CPA to act in a way that will serve the public interest and honor the public trust. The attorney-client privilege extends to federally authorized tax practitioners (including CPAs) relating to noncriminal tax matters (except tax shelters) before the IRS or in federal courts.

60. (b) An accountant may disclose confidential client information to any party with the consent of the client. An accountant may not make disclosure to the IRS or state agencies except in response to an enforceable subpoena or court order. Answer (d) is also potentially correct since disclosure can be made in compliance with generally

accepted accounting principles. Answer (b) is a better answer than answer (d) because an accountant may always disclose information with the client's consent.

Solution 33-3 EXTRA MULTIPLE CHOICE ANSWERS

Sarbanes-Oxley Act

61. (a) An auditor's procedures are not part of a company's ICOFR. The term *internal control over financial reporting* (ICOFR) is defined as a process designed by, or under the supervision of, the company's principal executive and financial officers, and effected by the company's personnel, to provide reasonable assurance regarding the reliability of financial reporting for external purposes in accordance with GAAP. It includes those policies and procedures that: (1) pertain to the maintenance of reasonably detailed records that accurately and fairly reflect the transactions and disposition of the company assets; (2) provide reasonable assurance that transactions are recorded as necessary to permit preparation of financial statements in accordance with GAAP and that company receipts and expenditures are made only in accordance with company management and director authorization; and (3) provide reasonable assurance regarding prevention or timely detection of unauthorized acquisition, use, or disposition of company assets that could have a material effect on the financial statements.

62. (c) The absence or inadequacy of a control specific to one criterion might not be a deficiency if other controls address the same criterion. Ineffective oversight by the audit committee of the company's external financial reporting and internal control over financial reporting (ICOFR) should be regarded as a significant deficiency and is a strong indication of a material weakness in ICOFR.

63. (d) Lack of information technology (IT) controls is not an inherent limitation of internal controls. Controls may be programmed into IT systems. Internal control over financial reporting is subject to lapses in judgment, breakdowns resulting from human failures, circumvention by collusion, and management override.

64. (a) An appropriate internal control framework is available to users of management's reports, but it is not a primary objective of internal control identified by COSO. The COSO framework identifies three primary internal control objectives: (1) efficiency and effectiveness of operations; (2) financial reporting; and (3) compliance with laws and regulations.

65. (b) Issues of who signs the representations, the period covered by the representations, and when updating representations are appropriate are the same as in a financial statement audit under GAAS. AU 333.05 states, "...if comparative financial statements are reported on, the written representations obtained at the completion of the most recent audit should address all periods being reported on." AU 333.09 states, "...the representations should be made as of a date no earlier than the date of the auditor's report." AU 333.10 states, "If current management was not present during all periods covered by the auditor's report, the auditor should nevertheless obtain written representations from current management on all such periods."

66. (e) The auditor may issue an unqualified opinion only when there are no identified material weaknesses and there were no restrictions on the scope of the auditor's work. The auditor must evaluate identified control deficiencies and determine whether the deficiencies, individually or in combination, are significant deficiencies or material weaknesses.

67. (b) The date of the reports on the company's financial statements and on internal control over financial reporting (ICOFR) should be the same, as the auditor cannot audit ICOFR without also auditing the financial statements. When the auditor elects to issue a combined report, the audit opinion will address multiple periods for the financial statements presented but only the end of the most recent fiscal year for the effectiveness of ICOFR and management's assessment of the effectiveness of ICOFR.

68. (b) The auditor's responsibility as it relates to management's quarterly certifications on internal control over financial reporting (ICOFR) is different from the auditor's responsibility as it relates to management's annual assessment of ICOFR. On a quarterly basis, the auditor should perform limited procedures to provide a basis for determining whether the auditor is aware of any material modifications that, in the auditor's judgment, should be made to the disclosures about changes in ICOFR in order for the certifications to be accurate. When the auditor believes that modification to the disclosures about changes in ICOFR are necessary for the certifications to be accurate, the auditor should

communicate this to the appropriate level of management as soon as practicable. In the auditor's judgment, if management does not respond appropriately to the auditor's communication within a reasonable period of time, the auditor should inform the audit committee.

69. (d) A *significant deficiency* is a control deficiency, or combination of control deficiencies, that adversely affects the company's ability to initiate, authorize, record, process, or report external financial data reliably in accordance with GAAP such that there is more than a remote likelihood that a misstatement of the company's annual or interim financial statements that is more than inconsequential will not be prevented or detected. A *control deficiency* exists when the design or operation of a control does not allow management or employees to prevent or detect misstatements on a timely basis in the normal course of performing their assigned functions. A *material weakness* is a significant deficiency, or combination of significant deficiencies, that results in more than a remote likelihood that a misstatement of the company's annual or interim financial statements will not be prevented or detected. The PCAOB standards generally don't use the term *material deficiency*.

70. (b) When there have been significant changes in the flow of transactions, the auditor should evaluate the nature of the changes to determine whether to walk through transactions that were processed both before and after the change. The auditor should make inquiries of personnel involved in significant aspects of the process or controls, rather than of a single person at the company.

71. (a) The same conceptual definition of materiality that applies to financial reporting applies to information on internal control over financial reporting, including the relevance of both quantitative and qualitative considerations.

72. (a) Evaluating responses to inquiries is an integral part of the inquiry procedure; inquiry alone does not provide sufficient evidence to support a control's operating effectiveness. Tests of controls over operating effectiveness include a mix of inquiries of appropriate personnel, inspection of relevant documents, observation of operations, and reperformance of the control application.

73. (a) Judgments about evidence sufficiency and other factors affecting the opinion must be the auditor's. The auditor may use the work of others (internal auditors, other company personnel, and third parties working under the direction of management or the audit committee) to alter the nature, timing, or extent of the work that that auditor performs. The extent to which the auditor may use the work of others depends on their competence and objectivity. When using the work of others, the auditor must test some of the work of others to evaluate the quality and effectiveness of their work. These tests may be accomplished by testing either some of the controls that others tested or similar controls not actually tested by others.

74. (c) In both its report on internal control over financial reporting (ICOFR) and in its representation letter to the auditor, management should provide a written conclusion about the effectiveness of the company's ICOFR. Although management is precluded from concluding that the company's ICOFR is effective if there are any material weaknesses, management may be able to represent that ICOFR as of the end of the period is effective even if a material weakness existed during the period.

PERFORMANCE BY SUBTOPICS

Each category below parallels a subtopic covered in Chapter 33. Record the number and percentage of questions you correctly answered in each subtopic area.

Liability to Clients

Question #	Correct √
1	
2	
3	
4	
5	
6	
# Questions	6
# Correct	______
% Correct	______

Common Law Liability to Third Parties

Question #	Correct √
7	
8	
9	
10	
11	
12	
13	
# Questions	7
# Correct	______
% Correct	______

Section 11 (1933)

Question #	Correct √
14	
15	
16	
17	
18	
19	
# Questions	6
# Correct	______
% Correct	______

Section 10 (1934)

Question #	Correct √
20	
21	
22	
# Questions	3
# Correct	______
% Correct	______

Sarbanes-Oxley Act

Question #	Correct √
23	
24	
25	
# Questions	3
# Correct	______
% Correct	______

Disclosure

Question #	Correct √
26	
27	
28	
29	
# Questions	4
# Correct	______
% Correct	______

Criminal Penalties

Question #	Correct √
30	
# Questions	1
# Correct	______
% Correct	______

Editor's Note: While it is unlikely that detailed questions on the PCAOB, ICOFR, and COSO will be asked on the REG exam, they appear here as a safety check. Candidates who remain uncomfortable with this topic after studying these questions should read the AUD material covering these concepts.

SIMULATION SOLUTIONS

Solution 33-4 Liability

Section 11 (4 points)

1. C

A purchaser of securities may bring a civil suit for fraud under Section 11 of the Securities Act of 1933. A purchaser or seller of securities may bring a civil action for fraud under Section 10(b), Rule 10b-5 of the Securities Exchange Act of 1934. Under both statutes, a plaintiff must prove that there were material misstatements or omissions in the filed document(s).

2. C

A plaintiff bringing a civil suit for fraud under either Section 11 of the Securities Act of 1933 or Section 10(b) of the Securities Exchange Act of 1934 must prove that they sustained a loss. If no loss can be proven, then there is nothing on which a court can base a damage award.

3. D

Lack of due diligence on the part of the CPA need not be proven by a plaintiff in a civil suit under either Section 11 of the 1933 Act or Rule 10(b) of the 1934 Act. Due diligence is a defense available to CPAs and others who are sued for violation of Section 11 of the Securities Act of 1933.

4. D

Neither Section 11 of the Securities Act of 1933 nor Rule 10(b) of the Securities Exchange Act of 1934 requires that a plaintiff in a civil suit prove that s/he was in privity of contract with the CPA.

5. B

Under Section 11 of the Securities Act of 1933, it is not necessary for a plaintiff in a civil action to prove reliance on the document. Material omissions or misstatements in the filed document are sufficient to trigger liability where a plaintiff has suffered a loss. However, under Rule 10(b) of the Securities Exchange Act of 1934, it is necessary that a plaintiff prove her/his reliance on the document.

6. B

Under Section 11 of the Securities Act of 1933, it is not necessary for a plaintiff in a civil action to prove that the CPA had scienter. Material omissions or misstatements in the filed documents are sufficient to trigger liability where a plaintiff has suffered a loss. However, under Rule 10(b) of the Securities Exchange Act of 1934, it is necessary that a plaintiff prove that the CPA had scienter.

Communication (5 points)

To: D. Boss
From: A. Candidate
Re: Union's Negligence Suit Against Potter

Union Bank will be successful in its negligence suit against Potter. To be successful in a lawsuit for accountant's **negligence** there must be:

- **duty**
- **breach**
- **plaintiff must be a known intended user**
- **reliance**
- **loss**

Potter was negligent in performing the audit by failing to confirm accounts receivable, which resulted in failing to discover the overstatement of accounts receivable. Potter's failure to confirm accounts receivable was a **violation of Potter's duty to comply with generally accepted auditing standards.** Potter knew that Union would receive the financial statements and was, thereby, an **intended user.** Union relied on Potter's opinion in granting the loan and, as a result, **suffered a loss.**

Research (1 point)

Paragraph Reference Answer: ET 501.05 501-4

Paragraph ET 501.05 501-4 states, "A member shall be considered to have committed an act discreditable to the profession in violation of Rule 501 when, by virtue of his or her negligence, such member: makes, or permits or directs another to make, materially false and misleading entries in the financial statements or records of an entity; or fails to correct an entity's financial statements that are materially false and misleading when the member has the authority to record an entry; or signs, or permits or directs another to sign, a document containing materially false and misleading information."

Solution 33-5 Fraud & Negligence

Third-Party Liability (4 points)

1. F

Under common law, an accountant's tort liability to third parties for ordinary negligence normally extends only to those third parties whom the accountant knew or should have known would be users or beneficiaries of the CPA's work product. The CPA is liable to the client, to third parties in privity of contract, and also to anyone in a class of third parties who the CPA knows will rely on the opinion.

2. T

Negligent misrepresentation requires proof of a misstatement of material fact upon which another party relies to its detriment.

3. F

A CPA is liable for common law fraud when there is (1) a misstatement of material fact, (2) scienter, and (3) justifiable reliance by the injured party. A fraud disclaimer contained in an engagement letter would not protect the CPA from liability for her/his fraudulent actions.

4. F

Negligent misrepresentation requires proof of a misstatement of material fact upon which another party relies to its detriment. It is not necessary to show that the misrepresentations were made with a reckless disregard for the truth.

5. F

Negligent misrepresentation requires proof of a misstatement of material fact, not opinion, upon which another party relies to its detriment.

6. F

Negligent misrepresentation requires proof of a misstatement of material fact upon which another party relies to its detriment. It is not necessary to show that the misrepresentations be in writing.

7. F

A CPA is liable for common law fraud when there is (1) a misstatement of material fact, (2) scienter, and (3) justifiable reliance by the injured party. Contributory negligence is not a defense to an action for fraud.

8. T

A CPA is liable for common law fraud when there is (1) a misstatement of material fact, (2) scienter (which exists if the CPA acted with knowledge of the falsity or a reckless disregard for the truth and the intent to mislead), and (3) justifiable reliance by the injured party. Thus, lack of scienter would be a valid defense.

Communication (5 points)

To: A. Supervisor
From: A. Junior
Re: Union's Fraud Suit Against Potter

Union will be successful in its common-law **fraud** suit against Potter. To be successful in a lawsuit for common law fraud there must be:

- **intentional material misstatement or omission**
- **reliance**
- **loss**

Potter was **grossly negligent** for failing to qualify its opinion after being advised of Malcolm's potential material losses from the product liability lawsuit by legal counsel. Potter will be liable to anyone who **relied** on Potter's opinion and **suffered a loss** as a result of this **fraudulent omission.**

Research (1 point)

Paragraph Reference Answer: ET 501.02 501-1

Paragraph ET 501.02 501-1 states, "In some instances a member's workpapers contain information that is not reflected in the client's books and records, with the result that the client's financial information is incomplete. In those instances when an engagement has been completed, such information should also be made available to the client upon request. The member may require that all fees due the member, including the fees for the above services, be paid before such information is provided."

Solution 33-6 Accountant & Trustee's Liability

Work Papers (4 points)

1. T

An accountant must relinquish possession of work papers in response to an enforceable subpoena or court order.

2. T

A CPA may disclose the contents of work papers without permission from clients when disclosure is in compliance with generally accepted auditing standards and with generally accepted accounting principles.

3. T

A CPA may disclose the contents of work papers without permission from clients when disclosure is pursuant to a voluntary quality review under AICPA authorization or in response to an AICPA trial board request.

4. F

An accountant is protected from being compelled to testify in state courts with regard to privileged matters under state statutes asserting that communications between the client and the accountant are privileged; however, this protection does not extend to federal courts.

5. T

Under common law, in the absence of an agreement to the contrary, ownership of an accountant's work papers rests with the accountant.

6. F

Disclosure of work papers without permission from clients rarely is permitted. The sale of an accounting firm is not an exception to the general rule.

7. T

A CPA may disclose the contents of work papers without permission from clients when disclosure is pursuant to a voluntary quality review under AICPA authorization or in response to an AICPA trial board request.

8. T

A CPA may disclose the contents of work papers without permission from clients when disclosure is in compliance with generally accepted auditing standards and with generally accepted accounting principles.

9. F

Work papers are the property of the accountant and need not be given to the client.

Communication (5 points)

To: B. Smith
From: J. Jones
Re: Suits Against Goodwin

a. The income beneficiaries will win their suit for **negligence** against Goodwin. Goodwin was negligent in **improperly allocating** trust income and in **paying a beneficiary's creditor.** The beneficiaries sustained losses due to Goodwin's **failure** to exercise the **due care** required of a reasonable accountant.

b. The income beneficiaries will win their suit for **fraud** against Goodwin. Goodwin **intentionally concealed** the **embezzlements** and **made material misstatements** in the **tax returns.** These actions are considered fraud and will permit the beneficiaries who relied on Goodwin to prepare the returns, to recover their losses.

c. The income beneficiaries will win their suit for **breach of fiduciary duty** against Goodwin. The following fiduciary duties were breached by Goodwin:

- The fiduciary duty of **loyalty** by **personally benefiting** from and **concealing** the embezzlements.
- The fiduciary duty of **obedience** by paying the beneficiary's creditor.
- The fiduciary duty of **due care** by **misallocating** trust principal and income, paying the creditor, and **falsifying** tax returns.
- The fiduciary duty to **notify** by **failing** to **inform** the **beneficiaries** of the **embezzlements.**
- The fiduciary duty to **account** by maintaining **improper** records and **profiting** from the embezzlements.

Research (1 point)

Paragraph Reference Answer: ET 503.01

Paragraph ET 503.01 states, "Rule 503—Commissions and referral fees / A. *Prohibited commissions*: A member in public practice shall not for a commission recommend or refer to a client any product or service, or for a commission recommend or refer any product or service to be supplied by a client, or receive a commission, when the member or the member's firm also performs for that client. (a) an audit or review of a financial statement; or (b) a compilation of a financial statement when the member expects, or reasonably might expect, that a third party will use the financial statement and the member's compilation report does not disclose a lack of independence; or (c) an examination of prospective financial information. This prohibition applies during the period in which the member is engaged to perform any of the services listed above and the period covered by any historical financial statements involved in such listed services. B. *Disclosure of permitted commissions:* A member in public practice who is not prohibited by this rule from performing services for or receiving a commission and who is paid or expects to be paid a commission shall disclose that fact to any person or entity to whom the member recommends or refers a product or service to which the commission relates. C. *Referral fees*: Any member who accepts a referral fee for recommending or referring any service of a CPA to any person or entity or who pays a referral fee to obtain a client shall disclose such acceptance or payment to the client."

Solution 33-7 Liability for Fraud

PCAOB Audit (4 points)

1. F

The lead audit partner and the audit partner responsible for reviewing the audit must be changed every five, not seven, years.

2. T

Billings's audit committee must approve all audit and non-audit services by the audit firm to the audit client.

3. F

Acceptance of an engagement to design or implement the financial information system of an audit client that issues publicly traded securities is prohibited.

4. F

Audit committees ideally are composed entirely of independent directors.

5. T

Audit firms that audit issuers of publicly traded securities must register with the SEC.

6. F

The audit firm may not have employed Billings's chief financial officer or controller one year prior to the period under audit.

7. T

Billings's chief executive officer and chief financial officer must certify annual (Form 10-K) and quarterly (Form 10-Q) reports to the SEC. Billings's executives must forfeit any bonus, incentive-based pay, or profits from the sale of stock received in the twelve months prior to an earnings restatement.

8. T

The audit firm must keep work papers related to the audit for seven years.

Communication (5 points)

Date: July 1, Year 7

To: D. Boss
From: J. Doe
Re: Potential Wilcox Liability

a. Knox would recover from Wilcox for fraud. The elements of fraud are: the **misrepresentation of a material fact** (because Wilcox issued an unqualified opinion on misleading financial statements. Wilcox's opinion did not include adjustments for or disclosures about the embezzlements and insider stock transactions); with knowledge or **scienter** (because Wilcox was aware of the embezzlements and insider stock transactions); and a loss sustained by Knox (because of Feline's default on the loan).

b. 1. The general public purchasers of Feline's stock offerings would recover from Wilcox under the liability provisions of Section 11 of the Securities Act of 1933. Section 11 of the Act provides that anyone, such as an accountant, who submits or contributes to a registration statement or allows **material misrepresentations or omissions** to appear in a **registration statement** is liable to **anyone purchasing the security who sustains a loss.** Under the facts presented, Wilcox could not establish a "**due diligence**" defense to a Section 11 action because it knew that the registration statement failed to disclose material facts.

2. The general public purchasers of Feline's stock offerings also would recover from Wilcox under the **anti-fraud provisions** of Section 10(b) and Rule 10b-5 of the Securities Exchange Act of 1934. Under Rule 10b-5, Wilcox's knowledge that the registration statement **failed to disclose a material fact,** such as the insider trading and the embezzlements, is considered a **fraudulent action.** The **omission was material.** Wilcox's **action was intentional** or, at a minimum, a result of **gross negligence** or recklessness (**scienter**). These

purchasers relied on Wilcox's opinion on the financial statements and **incurred a loss.**

Research (1 point)

Paragraph Reference Answer: ET 302.02 302-1

Paragraph ET 302.02 302-1 states, "The following are examples, not all-inclusive, of circumstances where a contingent fee would be permitted: (1) representing a client in an examination by a revenue agent of the client's federal or state income tax return, (2) filing an amended federal or state income tax return claiming a tax refund based on a tax issue that is either the subject of a test case (involving a different taxpayer) or with respect to which the taxing authority is developing a position…"

Solution 33-8 Fraud

True/False (4 points)

1. F

The basic duty of care standard is that of the reasonable person. The client's expectations are not necessarily adequate nor reasonable.

2. F

The client is responsible for the financial statements conforming to generally accepted accounting principles. The auditor merely audits the client's financial statements as presented.

3. T

The basic duty of care standard is that of the reasonable person. Since CPAs have knowledge and skill beyond that of the ordinary person, they must act with a level of care of similarly situated professionals.

4. F

The basic duty of care standard is that of the reasonable person. The purpose of an audit is to obtain reasonable assurance that the financial statements fairly represent the financial operations and position of the audited entity. Uncovering all acts of fraud is a different goal in terms of both scope and nature.

5. F

For an accountant to be held liable under common law negligence, a plaintiff must prove that the accountant failed to exercise due care under the circumstances. The stockholders need not prove that the CPA knew of the irregularities.

6. T

For an accountant to be held liable under common law negligence, a plaintiff must prove that the accountant failed to exercise due care under the circumstances.

7. F

For an accountant to be held liable under common law negligence, a plaintiff must prove that the accountant failed to exercise due care under the circumstances. Gross negligence (constructive fraud) which is beyond negligence—involves a reckless disregard for the truth.

8. F

For an accountant to be held liable under common law negligence, a plaintiff must prove that the accountant failed to exercise due care under the circumstances. Scienter is an element of fraud—which is beyond negligence.

Written Communication (5 points)

To: Review Board Members
From: J. Doe
Re: Confidential—Knightsbridge Review

Knightsbridge likely will be found to have **violated** the antifraud provisions of Section 10(b) and Rule 10b-5 of the Securities Exchange Act of 1934. Specifically, Knightsbridge **contributed** to the filing with the SEC of written materials (Form 10-K) containing **misstatements of material facts.**

Knightsbridge also likely will be found to have **violated** the antifraud provision of both the 19345 Act and the provisions of the Private Securities Litigation Reform Act of 1995. Specifically, Knightsbridge will be found to have **committed fraud** because **scienter** can be established. Knightsbridge **knowingly and intentionally** issued an unqualified opinion after discovering **management fraud** that caused material misstatements in the financial statements.

Knightsbridge also likely will be found to have **violated** the provisions of the Private Securities Litigation Reform Act of 1995. Specifically, Knightsbridge **failed to withdraw** from the engagement and **notify the SEC** of the material illegal acts committed by Ursula's officers.

Knightsbridge also likely will be found to have **violated** the provisions of the Sarbanes-Oxley Act of 2002. Specifically, Knightsbridge **performed legal and expert services** for an **audit client** who issues **publicly traded** securities.

Research (1 point)

Paragraph Reference Answer: ET 501-1

Paragraph ET 501-1 states, "In some instances, a member's workpapers contain information that is not reflected in the client's books and records, with the result that the client's financial information is incomplete. In those instances when an engagement has been completed, such information should also be made available to the client upon request... The member may require that all fees due the member, including the fees for the above services, be paid for before such information is provided."

Solution 33-9 Negligence

SEC Regulation D (4 points)

1. A

Regulation D, Rule 506, permits public as well as non-public corporations to raise an unlimited amount of money without full registration. Transactions exempted from the full registration requirements of the 1933 Securities Act are not exempt from the reporting requirements of the Securities Exchange Act of 1934.

2. B

Shares sold under a Regulation D, Rule 506, exempt offering may be purchased by any number of investors provided there are no more than 35 nonaccredited investors.

3. B

An exempt offering under Regulation D, Rule 506, has no dollar limit.

4. B

Regulation D, Rule 506, requires that the issuer exercise reasonable care to assure that purchasers of the exempt offering are buying for investment and are not underwriters. The purchaser must be notified that the securities are not registered and that resale of the securities is subject to the restrictions of Rule 144. The requirement that all investors be notified that sales of the securities are restricted to state residents for a period of nine months applies to securities exempt pursuant to an intra-state offering, not to transactions exempt under Regulation D, Rule 506.

5. D

Notification of a Regulation D, Rule 506, exempt offering must be made to the SEC within 15 days of the sale of the first security in the offering. There is no requirement that the issuer notify the SEC of the first sale of exempt offering securities on its next filed Quarterly Report (Form 10-Q).

Communication (5 points)

To: Review Board Member
From: Candidate
Re: Akemi: Possible Negligence

Akemi will be **successful** in its **negligence** suit against Battery. The elements of negligence are as follows:

- **duty of care owed**
- **breach of the duty**
- **loss caused by the breach of duty**

Battery Associates, CPAs, **owed a duty** to its client, Akemi Corp., to **perform** the consulting services engagement in a **competent manner** with the **expertise necessary** to perform the engagement. Battery breached this duty by **incompetently preparing** the computer software programs. **As a result of the breach,** Akemi **sustained damages** through increased accounts receivable collection costs.

Research (1 point)

Paragraph Reference Answer: ET 501.07 501-6

ET 501.07 501-6 states, "A member who solicits or knowingly discloses the May 1996 or later Uniform CPA Examination question(s) and/or answer(s) without the written authorization of the AICPA shall be considered to have committed an act discreditable to the profession in violation of rule 501." Search terms: uniform AND examination AND disclosure

Wondering how you can prepare for written communication questions?

Some candidates who are otherwise confident about the exam are overwhelmed by the written communication portion of simulations. The following tips are designed to help you increase your confidence when presented with questions requiring free-form answers.

Review the **Writing Skills** appendix. This appendix has an example of what the AICPA labels as "ideal" and "good" solutions. Notice that the gap between "ideal" and "good" is larger than the gap between "good" and "poor." This works to your benefit.

As you progress through your study plan, answer a written communication question from each major topic; waiting until the last month leaves you little time to prepare for written communication questions. The more uncomfortable that you are with written communication questions, the more important this becomes. Bear in mind, you might not realize that you are uncomfortable with written communication questions, if you don't try answering some of them.

Once you grade your written communication question in comparison to the unofficial solution, reflect on the question. Assigning a point value is probably the least important part of answering the question. Any mistakes or omissions are solid learning opportunities. Additional information about written communication techniques is in the **Practical Advice** appendix.

Read through the written communication (with their related unofficial solutions) of simulations you will not be answering within the next few days. This provides a good review of the material you have just covered, as well as acquainting you with the types of questions.

Once you know the content, you will be able to prepare a response regardless of the question format. However, exam time is limited, and you don't want the pressure of time considerations to distract you from providing your best answer to a question. To reduce the pressure, remember that you must earn 75 points to pass—it doesn't matter which format that you use to earn those 75 points. Practice more written communication questions that cover topics that have high point value; be prepared to answer a written communication question in any topic area.

Remember, with the techniques and information in your material,

A passing score is well within reach!

Hot•Spot™ Video Descriptions

(Selected subjects only; subject to change without notice.)

CPA 4115, Professional & Legal Responsibilities
Gary Laursen covers the important points that a candidate needs to know about accountants' professional responsibilities and legal liabilities in this video. Negligence, fraud, scienter, due diligence and good faith defenses, privileged communications, confidentiality, liability to clients and to third parties, privity, and liability under the Securities Acts of 1933 and 1934 and the Sarbanes-Oxley Act are highlighted.

CPA 2050, Contracts
In this video program, John Norman examines contract elements and classification. Jack covers the issues of fraud, mistake, illegality, capacity, duress, undue influence, alteration, performance, and contract termination. He elaborates on the Statute of Frauds and the parol evidence rule as well as presenting mnemonics and exam tips.

CPA 3275, Sales
In this program, John Norman details the laws governing the sale of goods. He covers what candidates need to know about Article 2 of the Uniform Commercial Code, including express and implied warranties, title, risk of loss, and various parties' rights, responsibilities, and remedies. Jack discusses firm offers, the mailbox rule, confirming letters, the Statute of Frauds, privity, transportation, sale on approval, sale or return, warranties, negligence, and strict liability.

CHAPTER 34

CONTRACTS

EXAM COVERAGE: The business law portion of the Regulation section of the CPA exam is designated by the examiners to be 20-25 percent of the section's point value. More information about point distribution and information eligible to be tested is included in the **Practical Advice** section of this volume.

CHAPTER 34

CONTRACTS

I. Overview

A. Definitions

1. **Contract** An express or implied legally binding agreement between two or more persons to perform or not to perform some specific act or undertaking. The law views the performance of a valid contract as a duty and provides a suitable remedy for its breach. One to whom performance under a contract is owed (promisee) has a contract right (the right to receive that performance), while one who must perform under a contract (obligor) has a contractual duty (the duty to perform). Assignment of a contract rebuttably is presumed to mean assignment of rights and delegation of duties.

2. **Bilateral vs. Unilateral Contract** A bilateral contract is one in which both the contracting parties are bound by their mutual promises to fulfill reciprocal obligations towards each other. For example, a contract in which an accountant promises to prepare a tax return and the accountant's client promises to pay an agreed fee would be a bilateral contract. A unilateral contract is one in which one party promises a performance in return for an act or forbearance, and a second party, without promising to do so, acts or forbears. A unilateral contract is completed upon the act or forbearance of the one party; only then is the other party obligated to render her/his performance.

   Example 1 ▸ Unilateral Contract

   A promises to pay a $100 reward to whoever finds her missing cat, and B finds the cat, the result is a completed unilateral contract. Note that B is not obligated to look for the cat. Distinguish this from a bilateral contract, wherein A hires B to look for the missing cat, and B agrees to do so.

3. **Executed vs. Executory Contract** An executed contract has been performed fully. An executory contract has not been performed fully. Note that a contract may be *executory* as to a party who has not rendered performance and *executed* as to a party who has completed performance.

4. **Express vs. Implied Contract** An express contract is created by the verbal or written expression of its terms by the parties involved. An implied contract does not exist in form, but is implied in fact from the acts and circumstances of the parties.

5. **Promise** A promise is a declaration or assurance, however expressed, to do or refrain from doing a specified act. A promise that is legally enforceable is a contract. A **promisee** is the person to whom a promise is made. A **promisor** is the person who makes a promise.

6. **Quasi-Contract** A concept or principle of law having its foundation in equity and good conscience. As implied by its name, a quasi-contract is not properly a contract. Rather, it is a legal obligation created by the law in cases in which there is no contract, but the law ought to imply a contract as a matter of equity and justice.

7. **Unenforceable Contract** A contract that cannot be enforced by legal proceedings. For example, an oral contract is unenforceable if required to be in writing by the Statute of Frauds.

8. **Void Contract** An agreement that lacks one or more of the essential elements of a contract and, therefore, does not create any legal obligations.

9. **Voidable Contract** A contract that may be avoided by rescission but that remains binding if not rescinded. For example, contracts of infants, incompetents, and contracts obtained by fraud are voidable contracts.

10. **Joint Obligees** Two or more persons who are owed performance as a single group.

11. **Joint Obligors** Two or more persons under a joint duty to a single obligee.

    a. **Entire Performance** The obligee can hold any of them responsible for the entire performance due. Between themselves, joint obligors may agree on how they are to share in the obligation, and if any pays more than her/his share, s/he is entitled to reimbursement from the others.

    b. **Surety's Rights to Recovery** A surety may recover the entire performance from the principal debtor or a *pro rata* contribution from co-sureties.

    c. **Principal Debtor's Right to Recovery** A principal debtor cannot recover from her/his surety, but is entitled to reimbursement from any other joint principal debtors.

12. **Several Obligees** Two or more persons who are owed individual performance.

13. **Several Obligors** Two or more persons who separately promise the same performance in the alternative.

    a. **Effect of Discharge** Discharge of one does not discharge others.

    b. **Obligee's Entitlement** The obligee is entitled to only one performance.

    c. **Recovery** If one obligor is required to perform more than her/his share, s/he is entitled to reimbursement from the others.

B. Assignment

A contract right ordinarily can be assigned by the person to whom it is owed (assignor) to another person (assignee).

1. **Assignment Not Allowed**

    a. **No Permission** Without permission of the obligor, if one of the following applies.

        (1) The right is personal to the promisee or involves a confidential relationship between the parties.

        (2) The duty of the obligor would be changed materially, the burden or risk increased materially, or the chances of obtaining return performance are impaired materially.

    b. **Prohibited by Contract** The contract prohibits assignment. However, in certain cases, the prohibitive clause is void as a matter of law. If a contract for the sale of goods forbids "assignment of the contract" without specifying rights or duties, the prohibition is construed to apply only to the delegation of performance unless the circumstances indicate the contrary [UCC 2-210 (3)].

2. **Assignee's Rights Against Obligor** Generally, the assignee takes whatever rights the assignor had against the obligor, but no more.

    a. **Assignor Rights** If the claim was covered by any security, the assignee gets the benefit of the security.

b. **"But No More"** The assignee takes subject to any defenses and counterclaims arising from the contract that the obligor had against the assignor.

c. **Payment as Defense** Payment of the obligation to the assignor is a defense if made before the obligor had notice of the assignment.

d. **Counterclaims** Any counterclaims against the assignor arising from collateral transactions may be asserted against the assignee, but if the assignee notifies the obligor of the assignment, the obligor can assert only those collateral counterclaims that accrued **before** notice was given.

e. **Nonconsumer Contracts Under UCC** UCC 9-403 provides that in nonconsumer contracts, an agreement by a buyer or lessee of personal property that s/he will not assert any claims or defenses s/he has against the seller or lessor is enforceable by an assignee who takes for value, in good faith, and without notice of any claim or defense. A contract for the sale of inventory or business-use equipment is an example of a nonconsumer contract.

3. **Assignee vis-à-vis Assignor**

a. **Valid Assignment** A valid assignment is effective between the parties without notice to the obligor. The assignor no longer owns the right; the assignee does. If the assignor receives the assigned performance, the assignee can recover from her/him. If the assignor causes the obligor not to perform, the assignee can recover from the assignor. If the assignor wrongfully assigns the same right to two assignees, one of two following rules generally applies.

(1) The one who first received the assignment prevails over the other.

(2) The one who first gave notice to the obligor prevails.

b. **Revocation of Assignment** An assignor can revoke a gratuitous (e.g., without consideration) assignment unless one of the following applies.

(1) There is promissory estoppel.

(2) The assignor delivers either a tangible document embodying the right assigned or a written assignment.

(3) The assignee collects the obligation prior to the attempted revocation.

C. **Delegation**

Some contract duties may be delegated by the party having the duty (delegator) to another (delegatee), so that performance by the delegatee satisfies the delegator's duty. Delegation does not strip the delegator of duty. The delegator remains liable to the obligee until someone performs. Certain duties may not be delegated.

1. **Personal Performance Duty** If the duty requires the personal performance of the original obligor-delegator (e.g., the rendering of professional services), the substitute performance would differ materially from that agreed on.

2. **Law or Contract** A statute, common law, or the contract may forbid the delegation of a particular duty.

II. Contract Elements

A. Agreement

Mutual assent by the parties. Both parties must agree to the same bargain through the medium of offer and acceptance. Under common law, the acceptance must contain all the terms and conditions included in the offer. Doctrinally, this is known as the **Mirror Acceptance Rule.**

Exhibit 1 ▸ Contract Elements

"A Cold Sip of COLA"	
A	**A**greement
C	**C**onsideration
S	**S**tatute of Frauds
C	**C**apacity
O	**O**ffer
L	**L**egal subject matter
A	**A**cceptance

1. **Expressed or Inferred** Assent may be "expressed" or may be inferred from a party's conduct.

2. **Objective Rule of Contracts** There is assent if a party's outward conduct would lead a reasonable person to believe that a party is assenting. An actual subjective "meeting of the minds" is **not** required. Instead, the courts use an objective test in which each party is bound by the intention that they manifest to the other party. For example, picking up a package of candy in a drugstore is an objective act that manifests conduct indicating an intent to purchase the candy. This is an implied contract to purchase goods as distinguished from an express contract.

3. **Offer & Acceptance** The normal manner in which parties arrive at a mutual manifestation of assent is for one to make an offer and the other to accept it.

B. Offer

An offer is a proposal made by one party (the offeror) to another (the offeree) which manifests an intent to enter into a contract. The offeree has the power to create the contract by acceptance.

1. **Requirements** The offeror (person making the offer) generally must intend the action to be an offer. Thus, an offer that is made in jest or anger is not a true offer. The courts apply the "objective rule"; therefore, they will find **intent** if a reasonable person would interpret the offeror's action as manifesting actual intent, whether or not the offeror had such actual intent. However, if the offeree (person to whom the offer is made) actually knows there is no intent to offer, then no offer has been made.

   a. **Invitations to Make Offers** Mere invitations or inquiries soliciting offers are not offers. Such language as "I would consider selling for $100" or "I quote you a price…" usually is construed as an invitation to make an offer or commence negotiations. On the other hand, language such as "I offer" or "I will sell X for $100" usually is construed as an offer. In determining whether a mere invitation or an offer exists, the courts generally will look not only to the specific language but also will consider the surrounding circumstances, the custom within the industry, and the prior practice between the parties.

(1) **Advertisements** Communications sent to large numbers of people (newspaper advertisements) normally are only invitations. However, when an ad limits the quantities or uses "first come, first served" language, it is probably an offer.

(2) **Reward** A reward is an offer to form a unilateral contract; that is, it may be accepted only by performance.

b. **Definite & Certain** The offer must be sufficiently definite and certain as to allow a court to delineate the terms and requirements of the contract that would result from acceptance. A valid offer may leave one or more terms open. Contracts often are made in which the parties intend to supply the missing terms at a later date. If the parties fail to agree on a term left open, the courts will imply a reasonable term. Terms commonly left open are time and method of delivery, method of payment, and price. **Note:** Article 2 of the UCC requires that only the **quantity** term be certain.

(1) **Identification** A certain offeree or class of offerees must be identifiable by the terms of the offer.

(2) **Subject Matter** The offer must identify the subject matter adequately. For example, an "offer" to sell "some of my farmland" is not an offer.

2. **Types** Offers may be **written, oral,** or **implied** from the offeror's actions.

a. **General or Specific** An offer is either **general** (addressed to whomever accepts) or **specific** (addressed to a particular person or persons).

b. **Continuing Offer** An offer that may result in a series of contracts by successive acceptances.

c. **Illusory Offer** An offer in which the offeror retains the unlimited option to perform the promise. Such an offer generally results in an unenforceable contract.

3. **Termination** Termination of an offer ends the offeree's power to accept it. If acceptance is attempted after the offer has terminated, it is in effect a new offer. Thus, the original offeror's treatment of it as a valid "acceptance" is actually the offeror's own acceptance of a new offer. Termination of an offer may be effected by the following means.

a. **Revocation by Offeror** Generally, an offeror can revoke an offer at any time prior to an effective acceptance even if the offeror stated it would be open for a fixed period.

(1) **Sufficiency** Any language or conduct indicating that the offer is revoked is sufficient (e.g., a statement that the property in question has been sold to someone else).

(2) **Communication** Revocation must be communicated to the offeree, and it is not effective until **received** by the offeree. However, the communication need not be direct. Thus, the offeree cannot accept if s/he learns by any reliable means that the offeror has revoked the offer. If a general offer has been made by public announcement, revocation may be made by any means reasonably certain to reach all who may have heard of the offer. Preferably, the original method of publication should be used to make the revocation. A continuing offer may be revoked as to future contracts even if some binding contracts already have been created.

(3) **Exceptions** There are several **exceptions** to this rule.

(a) **Option Contract** If there is **consideration** for the offeror's promise to keep the offer open, then that promise becomes an **option contract,** and it is irrevocable for the period of the option.

(b) **Firm Offers** These are offers made under the UCC that are irrevocable even though they are not supported by consideration.

(c) **Partial Performance**

(i) **Unilateral Contract** If an offer can be accepted only by performance so that there is no acceptance until the act is complete, the majority rule is that **partial performance** makes the offer **irrevocable.** The usual rationale is that partial performance is consideration for an implied option contract. **Minority rule:** Revocation is allowed, but the offeree can recover for her/his performance in quasi-contract.

(ii) **Bilateral Contract** If the offer can be accepted by a promise, then partial performance implies a promise to complete performance, and, therefore, a bilateral contract results.

b. **Lapse of Time**

(1) **Specified Time** If the offeror specifies a time for acceptance, the offer automatically terminates upon the expiration of that time period. If the offeror specifies a mode of communication for acceptance (e.g., "by return mail"), this usually is construed to mean that acceptance must arrive as soon as it would if communicated by that mode. If the offer specifies that the offeree must respond within a certain number of days after receiving the offer and the delivery of the offer was delayed by a person other than the offeror, then the following rules apply.

(a) If the offeree knows of the delay, s/he must accept within a time period that commences on the date the offer normally would have arrived.

(b) If the offeree has no reason to know of the delay, s/he may accept within a time period that commences on the date of actual delivery.

(2) **Nonspecified Time** If no time for acceptance is specified, the offer lapses after a reasonable time. What is reasonable under the circumstances depends on factors such as: the nature of the subject matter; the rate at which the price fluctuates (e.g., nature of the market); the time within which the offeror's purpose can be accomplished; and the manner in which the offer is communicated.

c. **Offer Provisions** The offer may specify that on the occurrence of a specific condition, the offer will terminate automatically.

d. **Rejection** Any conduct communicated to the offeror, either by word or act, that indicates the offeree's intention not to accept constitutes a rejection. A rejection is effective only **upon receipt.** Thus, the offeree can change her/his mind and accept if the offeree does so before the tendered rejection is received.

(1) **Counteroffer** A counteroffer, in which the offeree attempts to substitute different terms, is treated as a **rejection and a new offer.** However, a counteroffer may be worded so as to reserve the original offer for further consideration.

(2) **Inquiry** A mere inquiry as to the addition of other terms is not a counteroffer.

e. **Bankruptcy, Insolvency, Death, or Disability** In general, the death or supervening insanity of the offeror or a specific offeree terminates the offer. Bankruptcy or insolvency of either the offeror or offeree terminates the offer.

f. **Supervening Illegality or Impossibility** An offer terminates by operation of law if after being made, and prior to acceptance, the object of the contract or either party's performance becomes illegal. Likewise, an offer terminates automatically if a person or thing essential to the performance of the proposed contract dies or is destroyed.

C. Acceptance

The intentional manifestation of assent required by an offer to create the contract is termed an acceptance. If, for one reason or another, a party's assent to an agreement actually was not given, the contract may be voidable.

1. **Requirements** Acceptance must be made with **knowledge** of the offer and with the **intention** to accept. **Note:** This is an exception to the objective rule of contracts; that is, if it is not clear whether an act or forbearance to act is meant as an acceptance, the offeree's actual subjective intent determines whether a contract was created.

a. **Form** Acceptance must be in the form required by the offer. If it is not clear whether a promise or an act is required, the offer usually is interpreted to permit acceptance in either form.

(1) **Promise** An offer may call for acceptance by promise. Such acceptance creates a **bilateral** contract. If the offeree simply begins performance with the offeror's knowledge, a promise to complete the performance may be **implied** from the offeree's conduct.

(2) **Act** An offer may call for or permit acceptance by act or forbearance to act. Such acceptance creates a unilateral contract. If the offer requires acceptance by act, acceptance by a promise alone is not an acceptance. While partial performance may end the offeror's right to revoke, acceptance requires full performance.

b. **Unconditional** Acceptance must be unequivocal and unconditional and must comply with any terms set forth in the offer.

(1) If the offer sets forth conditions regarding acceptance, such as time, place, or manner, these must be fulfilled for the acceptance to be effective. If an offer merely **suggests** a time, place, or manner, acceptance by other means may be permitted.

(2) A reply that purports to accept an offer, but that adds material qualifications or conditions, is not an acceptance; rather, it is a rejection and a counter-offer. If the qualification is immaterial or one that would be implied by law, the acceptance is effective.

(3) Article 2 of the UCC materially changed the law stated in (2), above, as it applies to contracts for the sale of goods.

c. **Communication**

(1) **Bilateral Contract** Unless the offer provides for acceptance to be made without communication, the offeree must communicate acceptance to the offeror.

(2) **Unilateral Contract** Unless the offeror has no way of knowing that performance has been completed, the offeree need not communicate acceptance.

2. **When Effective** Generally, acceptance is effective when it is **sent** to the offeror or the offeror's agent.

a. **Mailbox Rule** If acceptance is sent by a mode of communication expressly or impliedly authorized by the offeror (e.g., mail), it is effective when sent, even if it is thereafter delayed or lost. This is known as the **mailbox rule.**

b. **Unspecified Mode** If no mode of acceptance is authorized expressly, the following modes of communication are authorized impliedly:

(1) **Common Law Rule** The same mode by which the offer was sent.

(2) **UCC Rule** Any reasonable mode dictated by business custom. (For example, if an offer is sent by mail, an acceptance by fax or by Federal Express (e.g., a faster method) generally would be considered a reasonable mode and the acceptance would be effective when sent.)

c. **Exception** If the offer is held open under an option contract, acceptance must be received in order to be effective, regardless of the mode of communication.

3. **Who May Accept**

a. **Specific Offeree** If the offer is made to a specific offeree, a valid acceptance can be made only by that person or her/his agent.

(1) If the offeror is mistaken as to the offeree's identity, the offeree still may accept if the offeree reasonably believes the offer was made to her/him intentionally.

(2) If the offer requires a promise from a third person as the consideration, acceptance must be made by that third person.

b. **General Offers** General offers (reward cases) usually can be accepted by whoever performs the specified act, provided s/he knew of the offer **and** intended the act to be her/his acceptance.

4. **Silence as Acceptance** Silence usually is not acceptance. However, it may constitute acceptance if the circumstances are such that assent may be implied. The following are some common examples.

a. The offeree accepts services that reasonably appear to be offered only for payment, when the offeree could have rejected them.

b. The offeree solicits goods "on approval" and retains them for an unreasonable length of time.

c. The offeror indicates that silence will be understood as assent, and the offeree subjectively intends her/his silence to be so understood.

d. Previous dealings lead the offeror to understand silence as assent (estoppel).

e. Acceptance of a contractual paper, such as a deed, an insurance policy, or a ticket purporting to be a contract, may be taken to imply assent to its terms.

D. Consideration

An act or a forbearance to act, or a promise to do either, given by one party to a contract in exchange for another party's act or promise; the consideration must be understood by both parties to be the "*quid pro quo,*" or purchase price. To be enforceable, contracts must be supported by consideration.

1. **Test** The party to a contract must suffer a "legal detriment." This means the party must do something or bind her/himself to do something the party is not legally or otherwise bound to do, or the party must surrender a legal right to which s/he is otherwise entitled. To constitute consideration, it is not necessary that the other party receive a legal benefit.

Example 2 ▸ Consideration

A and B enter into a contract wherein A promises to pay B $25 if B quits smoking for 6 months. B's surrender of the right to smoke is a legal detriment and, therefore, constitutes consideration even though A gains no legal benefit through B's performance. On the other hand, A's payment of $25 to B is both a legal detriment to A and a legal benefit to B.

2. **Types of Consideration**

   a. **Act or Forbearance** An **act** or **forbearance to act** given in exchange for a promise in a unilateral contract.

   b. **Promise** A promise to do something, if the action promised would itself suffice as consideration that is given in exchange for another promise in a bilateral contract. If the promises supply the consideration, there must be mutuality of obligation; in other words, both parties must be bound.

      (1) **Illusory Promise** The promisor is free to perform or not perform the promise. This type of promise will not bind the promisor because there is no mutuality of obligation.

      (2) **Conditional Promise** A conditional promise is valid consideration if the promisor is bound to perform upon the occurrence of a condition beyond the promisor's control. For example, an insurance company promises to pay B $100 a day if B is hospitalized.

      (3) **Right to Choose** If the promisor promises to do one of two or more acts but reserves the right to choose which one, there is no mutuality of obligation, unless each act is a legal detriment. However, if the promisee has the right to choose which act the promisor will perform, there is mutuality of obligation if at least one act would be a legal detriment to the promisor.

3. **Adequacy of Consideration** The general rule is that the law will not inquire into the adequacy of consideration (e.g., a contract need not be absolutely fair to both sides). Exceptions are as follows.

   a. An exceedingly disadvantageous bargain may be evidence of fraud, duress, or unconscionability, which furnishes a court with reason to refuse enforcement.

   b. A contract to exchange unequal amounts of money or fungible goods at the same time is inadequate for lack of consideration. However, unequal amounts may be exchanged at different times.

   c. Nominal consideration (e.g., $1) for an act or promise of some value may raise the question of whether it was actually the *quid pro quo.* However, nominal consideration usually is adequate for an option contract.

4. **Common Situations Lacking Consideration**

   a. **Performance or Promise to Perform Preexisting Duty** There is no legal detriment if one does or promises to do that which one is already bound to do. Any change in the preexisting duty may supply sufficient consideration to support the amended contract. For example, a promise to accept $400 as full payment for a $500 debt—provided the $400 is tendered one week before the $500 is due—would be enforceable. The following acts are not sufficient consideration.

      (1) Refraining from criminal or tortious conduct.

(2) Performing acts that one is required to perform by law (for example, a promise to pay a policeman money for solving a crime is unenforceable for lack of consideration since the policeman has a preexisting duty to perform).

(3) Performing acts that the promisee already is under contract to the promisor to perform (for example, a promise to pay a contractor more than originally agreed upon in exchange for the completion of a building by the time set forth in the contract is not enforceable because the contractor assumed no additional legal detriment in return for the additional payment).

(4) Payment of a liquidated debt at or after the time it is due (for example, a promise to take $400 as full payment for a debt of $500 is not enforceable since the debtor was already obligated to pay the money).

b. **Past Consideration** A promise in exchange for an act completed prior to the making of the promise (past consideration) will not be enforced because the act was not done in exchange for the promise, but independent of it.

c. **Moral Obligation** A moral obligation is insufficient consideration to support a contract under the past consideration rationale, except in certain cases in which a former promise (for which good consideration once was given) is renewed or slightly qualified. For example, a new promise to pay a debt barred by the statute of limitations is enforceable without additional consideration because the debt barred by the statute has been renewed.

5. **Exceptions**

a. **Commercial Paper** If executed and delivered, consideration for commercial paper is rebuttably presumed between the parties. When commercial paper is negotiated, consideration conclusively is presumed.

b. **Contracts Under Seal** Under common law, a contract under seal required no consideration to be enforceable; consideration was presumed conclusively. However, today most states have abolished this rule. Article 2 of the UCC has abolished the effect of a seal with regard to the sale of goods.

c. **Other UCC Exceptions** There are other specific exceptions under the UCC. The *Sales* chapter discusses the UCC in greater detail.

d. **Promissory Estoppel** The promisor is "estopped" (prevented) from asserting the lack of consideration for the promise if the following elements are present.

(1) The promisor makes an express promise.

(2) The promisor expects or should expect the promise to induce and it does induce the promisee to act or forbear to act in a substantial way.

(3) The promisee in fact relied on the promise and this reliance was justifiable.

(4) An injustice (not merely a legal detriment) will result to the promisee, unless the promise is enforced.

6. **Special Contracts** Consideration must exist on both sides in order to have a valid contract. However, in certain situations, the courts have recognized mutual consideration when one party has substantial discretion while the other party essentially is bound.

a. **Requirement Contract** A requirement contract is an agreement by one party to buy her/his "requirements" of a certain product from a certain supplier. The supplier is bound to meet these requirements while the other party is bound to purchase only what s/he needs. The law generally recognizes, however, that the purchasing party is under a "good faith" requirement to stay in business and continue to use the product that is the subject of the contract. Consideration also is recognized on the part of the purchaser in that, generally, the purchaser has given up the right to purchase her/his requirements from other suppliers.

b. **Output Contract** An output contract is an agreement by a supplier to sell all or a specified part of the products that s/he manufactures to the purchasing party. The purchaser is bound to purchase a specified portion or all that is produced, while the producer is not required to produce any fixed amount. The law places a "good faith" requirement on the producer, however, to stay in the business of making her/his product and to continue production at a steady rate. The producer's consideration is recognized to be the surrender of her/his freedom to sell to others.

c. **UCC Sale of Goods** Article 2 of the UCC has the following provisions concerning output, requirement, and exclusive dealing contracts. Article 2 governs contracts for the sale of goods only.

(1) **Good Faith** A term that measures the quantity by the output of the seller or the requirements of the buyer means such actual output or requirements as may occur in "good faith," except that no quantity unreasonably disproportionate to any stated estimate, or in the absence of a stated estimate to any normal or prior output or requirements, may be tendered or demanded.

(2) **Best Efforts** A lawful agreement by the seller or the buyer for exclusive dealing in the kind of goods concerned imposes an obligation by the seller to use best efforts to supply the goods and by the buyer to use best efforts to promote their sale unless there is an express agreement to the contrary.

E. Capacity

1. **Infants (Minors)** A contract made by an infant is **voidable** by the infant (e.g., s/he may avoid performance). The one **exception** to this rule is that an infant may not avoid contracts that supplied her/him with necessities, such as food, shelter, and clothing. The other party to a contract with an infant has no power to void the contract on the basis of infancy.

   a. **Age** Under common law, infants or minors are defined as persons less than 21. State law supersedes common law. Court action also may make an infant an adult. Currently, 18 is the age of majority in most states.

   b. **Marriage** A statute may provide that marriage removes the disability of infancy.

2. **Incompetent Persons** A test of capacity to contract is the question: Does the disability render the person incapable of understanding the nature and consequences of the transaction? There are two kinds of incompetent persons.

   a. Persons adjudicated insane by a court. Contracts made by such persons are void from the beginning. Such incompetents still are liable for necessaries furnished to them.

   b. Persons who are *de facto* insane. Contracts made by insane persons not judicially declared incompetent generally are voidable.

3. **Intoxication** Intoxicated persons are treated like incompetents; a contract made by an intoxicated individual when s/he is unable to understand the nature of the transaction generally is voidable by the intoxicated individual.

F. Legal Subject Matter

An agreement may be unenforceable if performance of it would be illegal or if the object of the contract is illegal. Related to illegal contracts, **unconscionable** contracts occur when one party takes unfair advantage of another party. Types of illegality include the following.

1. **Contrary to Public Policy** A contract may be illegal because courts have declared it to be contrary to public policy. Examples include the following.

   a. Agreements that interfere with the administration of government; for example, an agreement inducing a public official to deviate from her/his duty.

   b. Agreements that interfere with the administration of justice; for example, agreements tending to hinder prosecution for crime, agreements to give false testimony, and agreements to extend the statute of limitations.

   c. Agreements that unreasonably restrain trade or interfere with competition.

   d. Agreements containing exculpatory clauses tending to absolve one from negligence (if the party being exculpated has a superior bargaining position) or from willful wrongdoing.

2. **Violation of Law** A contract may be illegal because it violates a statute or a rule of common law. Examples include the following.

   a. Contracts for the performance of a crime or tort.

   b. Usurious contracts (e.g., those charging more than the statutorily permissible rate of interest for the loan of money).

G. Statute of Frauds

Contracts that fall within the Statute of Frauds must be in writing; contracts that fall outside the Statute of Frauds may be oral. A party may be **estopped** from pleading the Statute of Frauds. For example, under the theory of promissory estoppel, a party who promises to waive the statute and thereby induces the other party to reasonably rely on that promise to her/his detriment cannot later plead the statute.

1. **Enforceability** The Statute of Frauds provides that certain kinds of contracts cannot be enforced unless they are: (1) evidenced by a writing or writings and (2) signed by the party to be charged.

2. **Writing Requirement** If the writing is lost or destroyed before suit is brought, the requirement may be satisfied by oral proof that it existed. The writing may appear in a written contract or in letters, telegrams, receipts, memoranda, etc. The writing need not appear in a single document, so long as the several documents refer to the same transaction. The writing may be prepared at any time before suit is brought. No formal writing is required, and the contract itself need not be written; however, there must be at least a note or memorandum of the contract that contains all of the following.

   a. Identity of the parties

   b. Subject matter

   c. Essential terms and conditions

   d. Identity of the consideration

   e. Signature of the party against whom enforcement is sought

3. **Signature Requirement** Any mark can be a signature as long as the party so signing authenticates it as her/his own (e.g., initials, nickname, "X"). An agent generally can sign for her/his principal. If one party signs the memo and the other does not, the contract generally can be enforced only against the one who signed.

4. **Effect of Failure to Comply** Failure to comply makes a contract **unenforceable,** but **not** void or voidable.

   a. If one party performs, the party cannot sue on the contract for the other's breach, but the party can recover in quasi-contract for the value of benefits given.

   b. An executed contract cannot be rescinded.

   c. If suit is brought on a contract that fails to comply, and the defendant fails to plead the statute as a defense, the defendant waives the statute and the contract is enforceable.

   d. If the contract is bilateral and one promise comes within the statute (requires a writing) while the other promise does not, and the promise that comes within the statute is executed, then the promise that does not come within the statute can be enforced.

5. **Contracts Within Statute**

Exhibit 2 ▸ Contracts Covered by Statute of Frauds

	"GRIPE + Marriage"
G	Sale of **G**oods worth $500 or more; must state quantity
R	**R**eal estate contracts
I	**I**mpossible to perform within one year from date contract is made
P	**P**romise to answer for the debt of another
E	Promise of an **E**xecutor to be personally liable for the debt of the estate
+	
Marriage	A promise in consideration of marriage

   a. Contracts for the sale of goods if the price is $500 or more.

   b. Contracts for the transfer of an interest in real property including buildings, easements, mortgages, and leases longer than 1 year.

      (1) Real estate agency contracts are included.

      (2) An oral real estate contract typically will satisfy the statute if the buyer has **possession** of the land and made either **partial payment** or **improvements.**

   c. Contracts that cannot be performed within one year from the date of the agreement.

      (1) The one-year period begins to run on the day after the date the contract is **entered into,** not from the date upon which performance under the contract begins.

      (2) If performance **could** occur within the one-year period, the contract is not within the statute and need not be written. An employment contract **for life** need not be written because performance could be completely performed within a year (e.g., if the employee dies). An employment contract **for two years** is within

the statute because it cannot be performed within a year; the employee's death prior to one year merely excuses performance.

(3) If one party can and does perform within a year, most courts will enforce the other party's promise even if it cannot be performed within a year.

d. A **promise to answer** for the debt of another (surety or guarantor). In summary, if the primary purpose is to be a surety for another person's debt (when the promisor does not benefit directly), then the promise must be in writing.

(1) The promise must be **collateral** (for the benefit of another), and **not primary** (for the promisor's benefit). Thus, in order to fall within the statute, the promise both must be made for the primary purpose of paying the debt of a third person (debtor) with payment possibly coming out of the promisor's assets, and be directed to and relied on by the creditor.

Example 3 ▸ Promise to Answer for Debts of Another

A, an infant, obtains goods that are not necessaries from B, a merchant. The sale is a credit transaction. In order to convince B to part with the goods, C (an unrelated adult) agrees with B that A will pay as per the agreed credit terms. If A does not pay, then B can look to C as surety. This agreement must be in writing because it is a promise to answer for the debt of another (see and compare (2), below).

- Exception: If the primary purpose of the promisor is to serve her/his own monetary ends (e.g., to assure a continuing supply of goods from the debtor by promising to pay the debtor's obligation to its suppliers), the contract is not within the statute. Therefore, the contract of the promisor is **enforceable** even though it is oral.

(2) A **promise to pay** and not answer for the debt of another is not within the statute. For example, when C orally promises to pay the purchase price of goods to be delivered by A to B, the promise is not within the statute. The following are other examples of promises outside the Statute of Frauds.

(a) **Indemnity Contract** A contract between two parties whereby one undertakes and agrees to reimburse the other against loss or damage arising from some contemplated occurrence.

(b) **Novation** A substitution of a new contract between the same or different parties that discharges the old contract and extinguishes the outstanding obligations.

e. A promise by an executor or administrator to answer for obligations of the decedent's estate.

f. Agreements in consideration of marriage (e.g., an antenuptial contract), except for mutual promises to marry.

6. **Additional Contracts Within the Statute (Infrequently Tested)** Contracts for the sale of any face amount of securities. Contracts for the sale of intangible personal property, such as royalty rights, for $5,000 or more.

III. Written Contract Interpretation

A. General Rules

Terms in written contracts are assumed to have their ordinary and usual meanings. Technical terms are understood to have their technical meanings. If there are ambiguous terms, then the most reasonable meaning under the circumstances is ascribed to them in light of trade customs. Generally, ambiguities are construed against the party who drafted them.

B. Parol Evidence Rule

If a contract is integrated completely into a written instrument, any evidence (written or oral) of a prior or **contemporaneous agreement** offered to modify or contradict the terms of the written instrument is inadmissible. Parties are presumed to have included every material term in the completed writing.

1. **Intent** A writing is integrated if the parties intended it to represent the complete agreement at the time of writing.

2. **Evidence Not Excluded** The parol evidence rule does not exclude the following.

   a. Evidence that does not alter, vary, or contradict the terms of the written contract.

   b. Evidence showing that the contract never became effective (its taking effect was conditioned on an event that never occurred).

   c. Evidence that the contract is void or voidable because of fraud, duress, mistake, lack of capacity, or failure of consideration.

   d. Evidence of a clerical mistake in the execution of the contract.

   e. Evidence of a party's identity.

   f. Evidence of the intended meaning of an ambiguous term.

3. **Subsequent Agreements** The rule does not apply to **subsequent** agreements varying the terms of a prior integrated written contract.

4. **Sale of Goods (UCC)** With respect to the sale of goods, UCC 2-202 applies. This section allows the written contract to be explained or supplemented, **but not contradicted,** by evidence relating to course of dealing, usage of trade, or course of performance. In addition, prior or contemporaneous agreements can supplement the integrated written instrument unless the court determines that the written instrument was intended to be the exclusive and complete statement of the terms of the contract.

IV. Lacking Actual Assent

A. Mistakes

1. **Unilateral Mistake** A mistake made by only one party to the contract. The mistake is usually to the detriment of the mistaken party. In general, if the other party had no notice and acted in good faith, the mistaken party cannot avoid the contract. One major exception is that if the other party knew or had reason to know of the mistake and attempted to take advantage of it, the mistaken party may be able to avoid the contract.

2. **Mutual Mistake** A mistake made by both parties; both parties are mistaken as to the nature or existence of the subject matter, the terms of the contract, or other material facts.

   a. **No Agreement** If the result of the mistake is that there is no real agreement (hence no contract), the purported contract is void.

b. **Materiality** If the mistake is related to a material provision and materially increased one party's obligations, the contract is voidable by that party unless an innocent third party would be adversely affected, or the contract can be reformed or the loss can be compensated.

c. **Actual Agreement** If the mistake was made in reducing an oral agreement to writing, an equity court may reform the contract to make it conform to the actual agreement.

3. **Mistake in the Inducement** If either or both parties were mistaken concerning their reasons for entering into the contract, this is a mistake in the inducement which is not, in and of itself, a ground for relief.

B. Innocent Misrepresentation

A misstatement of fact made **without intent** to defraud is an innocent misrepresentation. If an innocent misrepresentation is material, such misrepresentation gives rise to the following.

1. **Defense** A defense to an action to enforce the contract.

2. **Grounds for Rescission** Grounds for rescission; that is, a restoration of each party to its original position insofar as can equitably be accomplished, including the return of any benefits received.

C. Fraud

Fraud is a **false representation** of **material fact** made by one party to the other party with the **intent** to deceive and which induces the other party to **justifiably rely** on that fact to her/his **detriment.**

1. **Elements** In order to find fraud, **all** of the following elements must be present.

a. **False Representation** Usually there must be a false statement. However, **non-disclosure** is a misrepresentation when:

(1) There is a false denial of knowledge of the facts.

(2) Truth is suppressed by active concealment or by revealing only part of the facts.

(3) Under the circumstances, there is a duty to reveal the facts. For example, there is a confidential or fiduciary relationship between the parties, or one party is known to rely upon the special knowledge or skill of the other.

b. **Material Fact** To be material, a fact must be a substantial factor in inducing someone to enter the contract. The following generally are not considered to be statements of fact.

(1) Statements of opinion, unless made by an expert

(2) Statements of value

(3) Sales "puffing"

(4) Statements of law, unless made by an expert (a lawyer)

(5) Predictions about the future

c. **Intention to Deceive (Scienter)** The knowledge that one's statement is false or made in reckless disregard as to whether it is true or false.

d. **Justifiable Reliance** The misrepresentation must have been a substantial factor inducing the person to enter into the contract. If there are means whereby the accuracy of the statement can be verified and it would be reasonable to do so, justifiable reliance requires such verification.

e. **Injury** Injury results from the deception.

2. **Types**

a. **Inducement** If fraud in the inducement (e.g., during contract negotiations) is present, the resulting contract is voidable at the option of the defrauded party.

b. **Execution** If fraud in the execution is present (e.g., when one party is induced to sign an instrument different from the one the party intended to sign), the contract is void. It is void because there was never any actual intention to enter into it on the part of the defrauded party.

3. **Remedies**

a. **Voidable** If the contract is voidable due to fraud, the defrauded party may use the fraud as a defense to an action brought against her/him on the contract. The defrauded party may affirm the contract or sue for rescission.

b. **Void** If the contract is void, it is of no legal effect. The defrauded party may seek damages in tort.

D. **Duress**
Duress is the threat of harm to a party or to a member of a party's family that forces her/him to enter into a contract with the person initiating the threat or on whose behalf the threat is made.

1. **Effect** Contract is voidable by the victim.

2. **Examples** Examples of duress include the threat of physical violence and the threat of criminal prosecution, whether the victim is guilty or not, but not threat of civil suit. The threat of economic loss is generally not duress, but under some circumstances unlawful detention of another's goods or the threatened destruction of them may constitute duress.

E. **Undue Influence**
Undue influence is the mental coercion of one person by another person so that the will of the influencing party is substituted for that of the victim. Consequently, the unduly influenced party's assent to the contract is not voluntary. The usual case occurs when a person in a position of trust (e.g., an accountant or a lawyer) exerts influence over a person with a weak, susceptible mind who succumbs to such influence. The contract is voidable by the victim.

F. **Unconscionability**
Unconscionability occurs when one party takes unfair advantage of another party's ignorance, illiteracy, or greatly inferior bargaining position, so as to cause the party to enter into a contract with oppressive terms. Under UCC 2-302 (regarding contracts for the sale of goods), a court can refuse to enforce an unconscionable contract or an unconscionable clause in a contract, or may limit the application of the unconscionable clause so as to prevent an unconscionable result.

V. Third-Party Beneficiary Contracts

A. **Nature**
Third-party beneficiary contracts are contracts that are likely to benefit a person other than the contracting parties.

1. **Creditor Beneficiary** A third person to whom a debt or other duty is owed by the promisee. The debt or duty will be discharged in whole or in part by the promisor's rendering performance to the third party. For example, if the purchaser of a house (promisor) promises the seller (promisee) that s/he will assume the mortgage (debt owed to third party), the

mortgagee is a creditor beneficiary of the contract for the sale of the house. If the promisor fails to perform, the third party creditor beneficiary can do one of the following.

a. Sue the promisor on the contract.

b. Recover the original obligation from the promisee, who remains secondarily liable (unless there has been a novation). If made to perform, the promisee can then recover from the promisor for breach of contract.

2. **Donee Beneficiary** A third person to whom the promisee intends to make a gift, by having the promisor render performance to the beneficiary. In a donee beneficiary relationship, there is no debt or duty owed by the promisee to the beneficiary. For example, the promisee pays money and the promisor agrees to deliver a car as a gift to a third person, the donee beneficiary. If the promisor fails to perform, either of the following apply.

   a. The donee beneficiary can sue the promisor for breach of contract, but cannot sue the promisee because an unexecuted gift cannot be enforced, or

   b. The promisee can sue the promisor for rescission to recover any consideration paid. Alternatively, the promisee can sue the breaching promisor for specific performance. However, in this case the promisee cannot recover damages because s/he suffered no substantial harm as a result of the promisor's nonperformance.

3. **Incidental Beneficiary** A third person who benefits from a contract between others made without intent to benefit her/him. Incidental beneficiaries have no contract rights and no cause of action if the parties fail to perform.

Example 4 ▸ Incidental Beneficiary

> A contracts to have B build a house and specifies in the contract for B to use a certain type of lumber. If B fails to use the type of wood required in the contract, the local supplier of that kind of lumber has no rights under the contract even though proper performance by B of her/his duties would have benefited the supplier. The supplier is only an incidental beneficiary.

4. **Original Defenses** The promisor's original defenses against the promisee are good against the beneficiary. The promisee's failure to perform a condition precedent to promisor's performance, failure of consideration, incapacity, and failure to comply with the Statute of Frauds are all good against the beneficiary.

5. **Defenses After Rights Vested** Defenses against the promisee that arise after the rights vest in the beneficiary are not good against the beneficiary.

6. **Defenses of Promisee** Defenses of the promisee against a creditor beneficiary on the original obligation cannot be used by the promisor against the beneficiary.

B. Vesting Rights in Third-Party Beneficiaries

1. **Life Insurance Contracts** Rights vest in the beneficiary immediately, unless the parties—insurer and insured—reserve the right to modify or discharge the contract (e.g., the right to change the named beneficiary).

2. **Other Contracts** Rights vest in a third-party creditor or donee beneficiary when s/he knows of the contract and one of the following applies.

   a. Manifests assent to it

   b. Materially changes her/his position in justifiable reliance on it

c. Sues to enforce it

3. **Modification or Discharge of Contract** Until the rights vest in a beneficiary, the parties can modify or discharge the contract without the beneficiary's consent.

VI. Discharge

A. Performance

Most contracts are discharged by performance of the promises and acts that the parties have agreed to perform.

1. **Performance Types**

   a. **Complete Performance** The obligation is performed exactly as agreed or so close as to satisfy a reasonable person.

   b. **Substantial Performance** Performance that is less than complete but which satisfies the contract to the extent that there is not a failure of consideration. There must be a substantial, good faith performance of the obligation, with only minor deviations. Any loss caused by the breach, or performance as rendered, must be paid to the nonbreaching party or subtracted from the price the party was to pay for complete performance.

   c. **Material Breach** A major defect in performance that constitutes a failure of consideration and excuses the other party from her/his duty to perform.

2. **Conditions to Performance** A condition may be within the control of one party or neither party. If a condition is not met, no liability accrues unless the condition was also a promise. If a condition precedent fails to occur, the party whose performance was conditional simply is relieved of having to perform.

   a. **Condition Precedent** An uncertain future event that must occur before there is a duty to perform.

   b. **Condition Subsequent** An uncertain future event that, if it occurs, relieves a party of a previously existing duty to perform.

   c. **Condition Concurrent** Two promises that are to be performed at or about the same time, one in exchange for the other.

3. **Time of Performance**

   a. **Unspecified** If no time is specified, performance must be made within a **reasonable** time. What is reasonable depends on the circumstances.

   b. **Specified** If a time is specified, failure to perform on time is a breach of contract, giving rise to an action for damages.

   c. **Of the Essence** If time is "of the essence," then failure to perform on time is a failure of a condition, and the other party is relieved of the duty to perform. Time is of the essence if so specified by the parties or if a failure to perform in time would defeat the purpose of the contract.

4. **Performance by Means of Payment** Payment may be made by either the delivery of money or a negotiable instrument. If payment is made with a negotiable instrument, the acceptance is conditional; that is, the contract is not discharged until the instrument is paid. In the case of part payment, the following apply.

a. The debtor may specify the application of payment (e.g., to one of several debts, to principal, or to interest).

b. If the debtor does not specify, the creditor may choose the application of payment. However, some courts require payment to be applied to interest before principal.

c. If neither party chooses, the law presumes payments go to interest before principal, to older before newer debts, and to unsecured before secured debts.

5. **Tender** An attempt or offer to perform, which is proper in time, place, and manner, is a tender. If proper performance is tendered, a refusal to accept discharges the promisor and gives the promisor the right to sue for breach of contract. If the tender involves the payment of money, a refusal does **not** discharge the debt, but it does stop the accrual of interest.

B. Agreement

Contracting parties may agree to end or modify liability.

1. End

a. **Release** The discharging of a contractual right. To be effective, a release requires one of the following: seal, consideration, detrimental reliance, deed of gift, or gift of evidence of indebtedness. Mutual release discharges both parties from further performance; each release is consideration for the other.

b. **Waiver** Promise to excuse the breach of promise or failure of condition, often binding without consideration.

c. **Cancellation** Physical destruction of a written contract with intent to destroy its legal effect.

d. **Mutual Rescission** Undoing of the contract on both sides and placing the parties in their original position.

2. **Modify** Common law makes unenforceable any clause in a written contract that prohibits a future oral modification or a rescission of the contract. Under common law, the modification of a contract requires consideration.

a. **Merger** A contract duty is superseded by a higher duty (e.g., a promissory note for a debt on open account, a judicial judgment for a contract obligation).

b. **Accord & Satisfaction (Executory Accord)** An agreement to accept a performance in the future in substitution for a performance required under an existing contract. Performance of the substituted duty is the "satisfaction" that discharges the original duty. In the case of disputed or unliquidated debts where there is a question as to the amount actually owed on a contract, an accord can be used to settle the debt. In this situation, use of the words "payment in full" on a check for an amount less than that claimed by the creditor may operate as an accord. Thus, an accord, or an offer to settle for a different sum, will result if the amount is in dispute and the creditor has reasonable notice that the check is being tendered as full satisfaction. A satisfaction and acceptance of the accord occurs upon the cashing of the check.

c. **Substituted Contract** The parties agree on a different contract that supersedes and replaces the old contract.

d. **Novation** A substitution of a new contract between the same or different parties that discharges the old contract and extinguishes the outstanding obligations. If the promisor of the new contract breaches the new contract, the suit by the promisee must be against the promisor and must be based on the new contract rather than the original contract.

e. **UCC** UCC 2-209 provides that a good faith modification is binding without consideration. Although common law makes clauses prohibiting future oral modification or rescission of written contracts unenforceable, UCC 2-209 validates written clauses providing that, except as between merchants, such a clause on a form supplied by a merchant must be signed separately by the other party.

C. Operation of Law

Under certain circumstances, unperformed contracts may be excused by operation of law.

1. **Impossibility** Impossible performance is excused. This means that there is no consideration for the other party's performance, thus the other party is entitled to rescission. Performance under the contract must be objectively impossible, that is, it must be impossible for anyone to complete the required performance. There will be no excuse if the required performance is only subjectively impossible, that is, not capable of being performed by the party to the contract (e.g., due to lack of funds). Types of impossibility include the following.

   a. Subsequent to the formation of the contract, the performance contemplated becomes illegal.

   b. Subject matter necessary for performance is destroyed through no fault of the promisor.

   c. Personal performance is required and the particular person to render or receive it dies or otherwise is incapacitated.

2. **Frustration of Purpose** Performance still may be possible, but its value is destroyed by a supervening event not foreseen by the parties. The purpose of the performance must be known to both parties. The frustration of purpose acts as a failure of consideration.

3. **Impracticality** Generally, unexpected difficulty or expense does not excuse performance. However, in contracts for the sale of goods, UCC 2-615 provides there is no breach if performance becomes impracticable by the occurrence of a contingency that contradicts the assumptions upon which the contract was based.

4. **Statute of Limitations** A statute of limitations is a statutorily created period of time within which a party must bring an action to enforce its rights. The expiration of the statute of limitations technically does not discharge a party's performance, but it operates to bar the bringing of an action against a nonperforming party.

D. Breach

A breach of a contractual promise may excuse the other party's performance. A breach is an unexcused failure to perform a contractual promise. Failure to perform is a breach whether or not the breaching party was at fault. Types of breach include the following.

1. **Renunciation** Renunciation during the course of performance is any act rendering substantial performance impossible, or a statement that the promisor will not perform. The promisee is discharged from continuing performance and may sue for breach immediately.

2. **Anticipatory Breach** Anticipatory breach is the renunciation of a bilateral contract before performance is due. The promisee (obligee) has the following options.

   a. The promisee may sue immediately for damages, or rescind the contract and sue for restitution.

   b. The promisee may wait to see if the promisor (obligor) will change her/his mind and perform when performance is due.

      (1) If the promisee changes her/his position in reliance on the breach, the breaching party cannot withdraw her/his renunciation.

(2) If the breaching party withdraws her/his renunciation and performs, there is no breach.

3. **Actions to Prevent Performance** Action on the part of one party that prevents the other party from performing, discharges the other party and gives her/him the right to sue for the breach.

4. **Violation of Contract Terms** A slight breach entitles the other party to at least nominal damages. A breach discharges the other party's obligation if either of the following apply.

   a. The breach is material, so that there is essentially a failure of consideration for the other party's promise.

   b. The breach amounts to the failure of an express condition to the other party's performance.

VII. Remedies for Breach

A. Election of Remedies

1. **Common Law** Under common law, a material breach entitled the other party to either

   a. Rescind the contract and sue for restitution, in order to put the nonbreaching party in the position the party was in before the contract, or

   b. Affirm the contract and sue for damages or specific performance.

2. **UCC** UCC 2-720 provides that a breached contract for the sale of goods may be rescinded and damages recovered.

3. **Injunction** Equitable remedy in which the court orders a party to do something (mandatory injunction) or to refrain from doing something (prohibitory injunction).

4. **Specific Performance** When the injured party cannot obtain complete relief through the award of damages, a court may order the breaching party to carry out the specific terms of the breached contract.

   a. **Granted** Specific performance may be granted when the legal remedy of damages is insufficient. Following are some common examples.

      (1) A contract for the sale of unique property (land or goods that are unique or unobtainable elsewhere).

      (2) A contract for which damages would be speculative or conjectural (output or requirement contracts).

      (3) An enforceable contract not to compete.

   b. **Not Granted** Specific performance may not be granted if either specific performance would require close and complicated court supervision of complex matters or the contract requires personal services or a personal relationship (e.g., marriage or partnership).

B. Damages

Even if the breach is not material, the other party can sue for damages. The nonbreaching party has a duty to "mitigate" or minimize the losses caused by the breach. The party cannot recover damages for losses that s/he could have prevented by reasonable action or forbearance to act (e.g., by forbearing from amassing losses after the other party's material breach). If foreseeable losses result from a reasonable attempt to mitigate damages, they are recoverable. Types of damages include the following.

1. **Compensatory** Compensatory damages are awarded to compensate for losses and lost profits suffered as a result of the breach. If the promisor fails to render the promised service and the promisee must obtain it elsewhere at a higher cost, damages are the difference between the market price and the contract price.

2. **Consequential** Consequential damages are damages that predictably follow as a consequence of the breach (e.g., losses resulting from the general or specific needs of the injured party that were known or should have been known by the breaching party).

3. **Special** Special damages arise from unusual or special circumstances. Generally, special damages are excluded as not within the contemplation of the parties. They are not excluded, if they are provided for in the contract or are foreseeable by the breaching party when the contract is entered into.

4. **Punitive** Punitive damages are not allowed even if the breach is willful.

5. **Nominal** Nominal damages are allowed if there is a breach of contract, but no provable loss.

6. **Liquidated** Liquidated damages are specific amounts provided in the contract to be recoverable in the event of a breach. If the liquidated damages are excessive, a court may interpret them as a penalty and refuse enforcement.

    a. They are enforceable if actual damage would be difficult to assess and the amount appears reasonable at time of contracting.

    b. UCC 2-718 allows liquidated damages if the amount is reasonable in light of the anticipated or actual harm caused by the breach.

CHAPTER 34—CONTRACTS

Problem 34-1 MULTIPLE CHOICE QUESTIONS (60 to 80 minutes)

1. On August 1, Neptune Fisheries contracted in writing with West Markets to deliver to West 3,000 pounds of lobsters at $4.00 a pound. Delivery of the lobsters was due October 1 with payment due November 1. On August 4, Neptune entered into a contract with Deep Sea Lobster Farms which provided as follows: "Neptune Fisheries assigns all the rights under the contract with West Markets dated August 1 to Deep Sea Lobster Farms." The best interpretation of the August 4 contract would be that it was

a. Only an assignment of rights by Neptune
b. Only a delegation of duties by Neptune
c. An assignment of rights and a delegation of duties by Neptune
d. An unenforceable third-party beneficiary contract

(5/90, Law, #22, 0472)

2. Generally, which of the following contract rights are assignable?

	Option contract rights	Malpractice insurance policy rights
a.	Yes	Yes
b.	Yes	No
c.	No	Yes
d.	No	No

(5/95, Law, #21, 5355)

3. Egan contracted with Barton to buy Barton's business. The contract provided that Egan would pay the business debts Barton owed Ness and that the balance of the purchase price would be paid to Barton over a 10-year period. The contract also required Egan to take out a decreasing term life insurance policy naming Barton and Ness as beneficiaries to ensure that the amounts owed Barton and Ness would be paid if Egan died. Barton's contract rights were assigned to Vim, and Egan was notified of the assignment. Despite the assignment, Egan continued making payments to Barton. Egan died before completing payment and Vim sued Barton for the insurance proceeds and the other payments on the purchase price received by Barton after the assignment. To which of the following is Vim entitled?

	Payments on purchase price	Insurance proceeds
a.	No	Yes
b.	No	No
c.	Yes	Yes
d.	Yes	No

(5/92, Law, #34, 2847)

4. One of the criteria for a valid assignment of a sales contract to a third party is that the assignment must

a. Be supported by adequate consideration from the assignee
b. Be in writing and signed by the assignor
c. Not materially increase the other party's risk or duty
d. Not be revocable by the assignor

(5/95, Law, #22, 5356)

5. West, an Indiana real estate broker, misrepresented to Zimmer that West was licensed in Kansas under the Kansas statute that regulates real estate brokers and requires all brokers to be licensed. Zimmer signed a contract agreeing to pay West a 5% commission for selling Zimmer's home in Kansas. West did not sign the contract. West sold Zimmer's home. If West sued Zimmer for nonpayment of commission, Zimmer would be

a. Liable to West only for the value of services rendered
b. Liable to West for the full commission
c. Not liable to West for any amount because West did **not** sign the contract
d. Not liable to West for any amount because West violated the Kansas licensing requirements

(5/92, Law, #25, 2838)

6. Kay, an art collector, promised Hammer, an art student, that if Hammer could obtain certain rare artifacts within two weeks, Kay would pay for Hammer's post-graduate education. At considerable effort and expense, Hammer obtained the specified artifacts within the two-week period. When Hammer requested payment, Kay refused. Kay claimed that there was no consideration for the promise. Hammer would prevail against Kay based on

a. Unilateral contract
b. Unjust enrichment
c. Public policy
d. Quasi-contract (5/91, Law, #16, 8009)

7. Carson Corp., a retail chain, asked Alto Construction to fix a broken window at one of Carson's stores. Alto offered to make the repairs within three days at a price to be agreed on after the work was completed. A contract based on Alto's offer would fail because of indefiniteness as to the

a. Price involved
b. Nature of the subject matter
c. Parties to the contract
d. Time for performance (5/91, Law, #12, 8008)

8. On September 10, Harris, Inc., a new car dealer, placed a newspaper advertisement stating that Harris would sell 10 cars at its showroom for a special discount only on September 12, 13, and 14. On September 12, King called Harris and expressed an interest in buying one of the advertised cars. King was told that five of the cars had been sold and to come to the showroom as soon as possible. On September 13, Harris made a televised announcement that the sale would end at 10:00 p.m. that night. King went to Harris' showroom on September 14 and demanded the right to buy a car at the special discount. Harris had sold the 10 cars and refused King's demand. King sued Harris for breach of contract. Harris' best defense to King's suit would be that Harris'

a. Offer was unenforceable.
b. Advertisement was **not** an offer.
c. Television announcement revoked the offer.
d. Offer had **not** been accepted.

(5/92, Law, #21, 2834)

9. On June 15, Year 1, Alpha, Inc. contracted with Delta Manufacturing, Inc. to buy a vacant parcel of land Delta owned. Alpha intended to build a distribution warehouse on the land because of its location near a major highway. The contract stated that: "Alpha's obligations hereunder are subject to the vacant parcel being rezoned to a commercial zoning classification by July 31, Year 2." Which of the following statements is correct?

a. If the parcel is **not** rezoned by July 31, and Alpha refuses to purchase it, Alpha would **not** be in breach of contract.
b. If the parcel is rezoned by July 31, and Alpha refuses to purchase it, Delta would be able to successfully sue Alpha for specific performance.
c. The contract is **not** binding on either party because Alpha's performance is conditional.
d. If the parcel is rezoned by July 31, and Delta refuses to sell it, Delta's breach would **not** discharge Alpha's obligation to tender payment.

(11/92, Law, #25, amended, 3107)

10. Martin wrote Dall and offered to sell Dall a building for $200,000. The offer stated it would expire 30 days from April 1. Martin changed his mind and does not wish to be bound by his offer. If a legal dispute arises between the parties regarding whether there has been a valid acceptance of the offer, which one of the following is correct?

a. The offer cannot be legally withdrawn for the stated period of time.
b. The offer will **not** expire before the 30 days even if Martin sells the property to a third person and notifies Dall.
c. If Dall categorically rejects the offer on April 10, Dall cannot validly accept within the remaining stated period of time.
d. If Dall phoned Martin on May 3, and unequivocally accepted the offer, a contract would be created, provided that Dall had **no** notice of withdrawal of the offer. (5/89, Law, #21, 0479)

11. On June 15, Peters orally offered to sell a used lawn mower to Mason for $125. Peters specified that Mason had until June 20 to accept the offer. On June 16, Peters received an offer to purchase the lawn mower for $150 from Bronson, Mason's neighbor. Peters accepted Bronson's offer. On June 17, Mason saw Bronson using the lawn mower and was told the mower had been sold to Bronson. Mason immediately wrote to Peters to accept the June 15 offer. Which of the following statements is correct?

a. Mason's acceptance would be effective when received by Peters.
b. Mason's acceptance would be effective when mailed.
c. Peters' offer had been revoked and Mason's acceptance was ineffective.
d. Peters was obligated to keep the June 15 offer open until June 20. (11/92, Law, #13, 3095)

12. On February 12, Harris sent Fresno a written offer to purchase Fresno's land. The offer included the following provision: "Acceptance of this offer must be by registered or certified mail, received by Harris no later than February 18 by 5:00 p.m. CST." On February 18, Fresno sent Harris a letter accepting the offer by private overnight delivery service. Harris received the letter on February 19. Which of the following statements is correct?

a. A contract was formed on February 19.
b. Fresno's letter constituted a counteroffer.
c. Fresno's use of the overnight delivery service was an effective form of acceptance.
d. A contract was formed on February 18 regardless of when Harris actually received Fresno's letter. (11/92, Law, #11, 3093)

13. A sheep rancher agreed, in writing, to sell all the wool shorn during the shearing season to a weaver. The contract failed to establish the price and a minimum quantity of wool. After the shearing season, the rancher refused to deliver the wool. The weaver sued the rancher for breach of contract. Under the Sales Article of the UCC, will the weaver win?

a. Yes, because this was an output contract
b. Yes, because both price and quantity terms were omitted
c. No, because quantity cannot be omitted for a contract to be enforceable
d. No, because the omission of price and quantity terms prevents the formation of a contract

(R/01, Law, #19, 7054)

14. Which of the following will be legally binding despite lack of consideration?

a. An employer's promise to make a cash payment to a deceased employee's family in recognition of the employee's many years of service
b. A promise to donate money to a charity on which the charity relied in incurring large expenditures
c. A modification of a signed contract to purchase a parcel of land
d. A merchant's oral promise to keep an offer open for 60 days (5/92, Law, #23, 2836)

15. Which of the following promises is supported by legally sufficient consideration and will be enforceable?

a. A person's promise to pay a real estate agent $1,000 in return for the real estate agent's earlier act of not charging commission for selling the person's house
b. A parent's promise to pay one child $500 because that child is not as wealthy as the child's sibling
c. A promise to pay the police $250 to catch a thief
d. A promise to pay a minor $500 to paint a garage

(R/07, REG, 2054L, #13, 8437)

16. Which of the following would be unenforceable because the subject matter is illegal?

a. A contingent fee charged by an attorney to represent a plaintiff in a negligence action
b. An arbitration clause in a supply contract
c. A restrictive covenant in an employment contract prohibiting a former employee from using the employer's trade secrets
d. An employer's promise **not** to press embezzlement charges against an employee who agrees to make restitution (11/90, Law, #22, 0458)

17. On May 25, Fresno sold Bronson, a minor, a used computer. On June 1, Bronson reached the age of majority. On June 10, Fresno wanted to rescind the sale. Fresno offered to return Bronson's money and demanded that Bronson return the computer. Bronson refused, claiming that a binding contract existed. Bronson's refusal is

a. Not justified, because Fresno is **not** bound by the contract unless Bronson specifically ratifies the contract after reaching the age of majority
b. Not justified, because Fresno does **not** have to perform under the contract if Bronson has a right to disaffirm the contract
c. Justified, because Bronson and Fresno are bound by the contract as of the date Bronson reached the age of majority
d. Justified, because Fresno must perform under the contract regardless of Bronson's minority

(R/05, REG, 0395L, #14, 7860)

18. On June 1, Year 2, Decker orally guaranteed the payment of a $5,000 note Decker's cousin owed Baker. Decker's agreement with Baker provided that Decker's guaranty would terminate in 18 months. On June 3, Year 2, Baker wrote Decker confirming Decker's guaranty. Decker did not object to the confirmation. On August 23, Year 2, Decker's cousin defaulted on the note and Baker demanded that Decker honor the guaranty. Decker refused. Which of the following statements is correct?

a. Decker is liable under the oral guaranty because Decker did **not** object to Baker's June 3 letter.
b. Decker is **not** liable under the oral guaranty because it expired more than one year after June 1.
c. Decker is liable under the oral guaranty because Baker demanded payment within one year of the date the guaranty was given.
d. Decker is **not** liable under the oral guaranty because Decker's promise was **not** in writing.

(11/92, Law, #17, amended, 3099)

19. All of the following statements regarding compliance with the statute of frauds are correct except

a. Any necessary writing must be signed by all parties against whom enforcement is sought.
b. Contracts involving the sale of goods in an amount greater than $500 must be in writing.
c. Contract terms must be contained in only one document.
d. Contracts for which it is improbable to assume that performance will be completed within one year must be in writing.

(R/06, REG, 1742L, #7, 8177)

20. Nolan agreed orally with Train to sell Train a house for $100,000. Train sent Nolan a signed agreement and a down payment of $10,000. Nolan did not sign the agreement, but allowed Train to move into the house. Before closing, Nolan refused to go through with the sale. Train sued Nolan to compel specific performance. Under the provisions of the Statute of Frauds,

a. Train will win because Train signed the agreement and Nolan did **not** object.
b. Train will win because Train made a downpayment and took possession.
c. Nolan will win because Nolan did **not** sign the agreement.
d. Nolan will win because the house was worth more than $500. (5/91, Law, #14, 0451)

21. Kram sent Fargo, a real estate broker, a signed offer to sell a specified parcel of land to Fargo for $250,000. Kram, an engineer, had inherited the land. On the same day that Kram's letter was received, Fargo telephoned Kram and accepted the offer. Which of the following statements is correct under the common law statute of frauds?

a. No contract could be formed because Fargo's acceptance was oral.
b. No contract could be formed because Kram's letter was signed only by Kram.
c. A contract was formed and would be enforceable against both Kram and Fargo.
d. A contract was formed but would be enforceable only against Kram. (R/05, REG, 0054L, #5, 7851)

22. In negotiations with Andrews for the lease of Kemp's warehouse, Kemp orally agreed to pay one-half of the cost of the utilities. The written lease, later prepared by Kemp's attorney, provided that Andrews pay all of the utilities. Andrews failed to carefully read the lease and signed it. When Kemp demanded that Andrews pay all of the utilities, Andrews refused, claiming that the lease did not accurately reflect the oral agreement. Andrews also learned that Kemp intentionally misrepresented the condition of the structure of the warehouse during the negotiations between the parties. Andrews sued to rescind the lease and intends to introduce evidence of the parties' oral agreement about sharing the utilities and the fraudulent statements made by Kemp. The parol evidence rule will prevent the admission of evidence concerning the

	Oral agreement regarding who pays the utilities	*Fraudulent statements by Kemp*
a.	*Yes*	Yes
b.	No	Yes
c.	Yes	No
d.	No	No

(11/92, Law, #22, 3104)

23. Where the parties have entered into a written contract intended as the final expression of their agreement, which of the following agreements will be admitted into evidence because they are **not** prohibited by the parol evidence rule?

	Subsequent oral agreements	*Prior written agreements*
a.	Yes	Yes
b.	Yes	No
c.	No	Yes
d.	No	No

(5/95, Law, #18, 5352)

24. If a buyer accepts an offer containing an immaterial unilateral mistake, the resulting contract will be

a. Void as a matter of law
b. Void at the election of the buyer
c. Valid as to both parties
d. Voidable at the election of the seller

(5/92, Law, #29, 2842)

25. Miller negotiated the sale of Miller's liquor store to Jackson. Jackson asked to see the prior year's financial statements. Using the store's checkbook, Miller prepared a balance sheet and profit and loss statement as well as he could. Miller told Jackson to have an accountant examine Miller's records because Miller was not an accountant. Jackson failed to do so and purchased the store in reliance on Miller's financial statements. Jackson later learned that the financial statements included several errors that resulted in a material overstatement of assets and net income. Miller was not aware that the errors existed. Jackson sued Miller, claiming Miller misrepresented the store's financial condition and that Jackson relied on the financial statements in making the decision to acquire the store. Which of the following statements is correct?

a. Jackson will prevail if the errors in the financial statements were material.
b. Jackson will **not** prevail because Jackson's reliance on the financial statements was **not** reasonable.
c. Money damages is the only remedy available to Jackson if, in fact, Miller has committed a misrepresentation.
d. Jackson would be entitled to rescind the purchase even if the errors in the financial statements were **not** material.

(11/92, Law, #20, 3102)

26. On May 25, Year 1, Smith contracted with Jackson to repair Smith's cabin cruiser. The work was to begin on May 31, Year 1. On May 26, Year 1, the boat, while docked at Smith's pier, was destroyed by arson. Which of the following statements is correct with regard to the contract?

a. Smith would **not** be liable to Jackson because of mutual mistake.
b. Smith would be liable to Jackson for the profit Jackson would have made under the contract.
c. Jackson would **not** be liable to Smith because performance by the parties would be impossible.
d. Jackson would be liable to repair another boat owned by Smith.

(11/91, Law, #25, amended, 2353)

27. To prevail in a common law action for fraud in the inducement, a plaintiff must prove that the

a. Defendant was an expert with regard to the misrepresentations
b. Defendant made the misrepresentations with knowledge of their falsity and with an intention to deceive
c. Misrepresentations were in writing
d. Plaintiff was in a fiduciary relationship with the defendant (11/93, Law, #23, 4320)

28. For a purchaser of land to avoid a contract with the seller based on duress, it must be shown that the seller's improper threats

a. Constituted a crime or tort
b. Would have induced a reasonably prudent person to assent to the contract
c. Actually induced the purchaser to assent to the contract
d. Were made with the intent to influence the purchaser (11/90, Law, #23, 0459)

29. If a person is induced to enter into a contract by another person because of the close relationship between the parties, the contract may be voidable under which of the following defenses?

a. Fraud in the inducement
b. Unconscionability
c. Undue influence
d. Duress (R/00, Law, #5, 6970)

30. Egan contracted with Barton to buy Barton's business. The contract provided that Egan would pay the business debts Barton owed Ness and that the balance of the purchase price would be paid to Barton over a 10-year period. The contract also required Egan to take out a decreasing term life insurance policy naming Barton and Ness as beneficiaries to ensure that the amounts owed Barton and Ness would be paid if Egan died. Which of the following would describe Ness' status under the contract and insurance policy?

	Contract	*Insurance policy*
a.	Donee beneficiary	Donee beneficiary
b.	Donee beneficiary	Creditor beneficiary
c.	Creditor beneficiary	Donee beneficiary
d.	Creditor beneficiary	Creditor beneficiary

(5/92, Law, #33, 2846)

31. Graham contracted with the city of Harris to train and employ high school dropouts residing in Harris. Graham breached the contract. Long, a resident of Harris and a high school dropout, sued Graham for damages. Under the circumstances, Long will

a. Win, because Long is a third-party beneficiary entitled to enforce the contract
b. Win, because the intent of the contract was to confer a benefit on all high school dropouts residing in Harris
c. Lose, because Long is merely an incidental beneficiary of the contract
d. Lose, because Harris did **not** assign its contract rights to Long (5/91, Law, #22, 0456)

32. Jones owned an insurance policy on her life, on which she paid all the premiums. Smith was named the beneficiary. Jones died and the insurance company refused to pay the insurance proceeds to Smith. An action by Smith against the insurance company for the insurance proceeds will be

a. Successful, because Smith is a third party donee beneficiary
b. Successful, because Smith is a proper assignee of Jones' rights under the insurance policy
c. Unsuccessful, because Smith was **not** the owner of the policy
d. Unsuccessful, because Smith did **not** pay any of the premiums (11/89, Law, #17, 0477)

33. Which of the following types of conditions affecting performance may validly be present in contracts?

	Conditions precedent	*Conditions subsequent*	*Concurrent conditions*
a.	Yes	Yes	Yes
b.	Yes	Yes	No
c.	Yes	No	Yes
d.	No	Yes	Yes

(5/95, Law, #19, 5353)

34. Ames Construction Co. contracted to build a warehouse for White Corp. The construction specifications required Ames to use Ace lighting fixtures. Inadvertently, Ames installed Perfection lighting fixtures which are of slightly lesser quality than Ace fixtures, but in all other respects meet White's needs. Which of the following statements is correct?

a. White's recovery will be limited to monetary damages because Ames' breach of the construction contract was **not** material.
b. White will **not** be able to recover any damages from Ames because the breach was inadvertent.
c. Ames did **not** breach the construction contract because the Perfection fixtures were substantially as good as the Ace fixtures.
d. Ames must install Ace fixtures or White will **not** be obligated to accept the warehouse.

(11/93, Law, #26, 4323)

35. Wren purchased a factory from First Federal Realty. Wren paid 20% at the closing and gave a note for the balance secured by a 20-year mortgage. Five years later, Wren found it increasingly difficult to make payments on the note and defaulted. First Federal threatened to accelerate the loan and foreclose if Wren continued in default. First Federal told Wren to make payment or obtain an acceptable third party to assume the obligation. Wren offered the land to Moss, Inc., for $10,000 less than the equity Wren had in the property. This was acceptable to First Federal and at the closing Moss paid the arrearage, assumed the mortgage and note, and had title transferred to its name. First Federal released Wren. The transaction in question is a(an)

a. Purchase of land subject to a mortgage
b. Assignment and delegation
c. Third party beneficiary contract
d. Novation (5/90, Law, #25, 0475)

36. When there has been no performance by either party, which of the following events generally will result in the discharge of a party's obligation to perform as required under the original contract?

	Accord and satisfaction	*Mutual rescission*
a.	Yes	Yes
b.	Yes	No
c.	No	Yes
d.	No	No

(R/05, REG, 0060L, #3, 7869)

37. Ordinarily, in an action for breach of a construction contract, the statute of limitations time period would be computed from the date the

a. Contract is negotiated.
b. Contract is breached.
c. Construction is begun.
d. Contract is signed. (5/95, Law, #25, 5359)

38. In Year 2, Dart bought an office building from Graco under a written contract signed only by Dart. In Year 15, Dart discovered that Graco made certain false representations during their negotiations concerning the building's foundation. Dart could have reasonably discovered the foundation problems by Year 8. Dart sued Graco claiming fraud in the formation of the contract. Which of the following statements is correct?

a. The parol evidence rule will prevent the admission into evidence of proof concerning Dart's allegations.
b. Dart will be able to rescind the contract because both parties did **not** sign it.
c. Dart must prove that the alleged misrepresentations were part of the written contract because the contract involved real estate.
d. The statute of limitations would likely prevent Dart from prevailing because of the length of time that has passed. (5/91, Law, #15, amended, 0452)

39. For which of the following contracts will a court generally grant the remedy of specific performance?

a. A contract for the sale of a patent
b. A contract of employment
c. A contract for the sale of fungible goods
d. A contract for the sale of stock that is traded on a national stock exchange

(R/07, REG, 1510L, #28, 8452)

40. Master Mfg., Inc. contracted with Accur Computer Repair Corp. to maintain Master's computer system. Master's manufacturing process depends on its computer system operating properly at all times. A liquidated damages clause in the contract provided that Accur pay $1,000 to Master for each day that Accur was late responding to a service request. On January 12, Accur was notified that Master's computer system failed. Accur did not respond to Master's service request until January 15. If Master sues Accur under the liquidated damage provision of the contract, Master will

a. Win, unless the liquidated damage provision is determined to be a penalty
b. Win, because under all circumstances liquidated damage provisions are enforceable
c. Lose, because Accur's breach was **not** material
d. Lose, because liquidated damage provisions violate public policy (5/93, Law, #25, 3993)

Problem 34-2 ADDITIONAL MULTIPLE CHOICE QUESTIONS (45 to 60 minutes)

41. On February 1, Burns contracted in writing with Nagel to sell Nagel a used car. The contract provided that Burns was to deliver the car on February 15 and Nagel was to pay the $800 purchase price not later than March 15. On February 21, Burns assigned the contract to Ross for $600. Nagel was not notified of the assignment. Which of the following statements is correct?

a. By making the assignment, Burns impliedly warranted Nagel would pay the full purchase price.
b. The assignment to Ross is invalid because Nagel was **not** notified.
c. Ross will **not** be subject to any contract defenses Nagel could have raised against Burns.
d. By making the assignment, Burns impliedly warranted a lack of knowledge of any fact impairing the value of the assignment.

(5/93, Law, #24, 3992)

42. West, Inc. and Barton entered into a contract. After receiving valuable consideration from Egan, West assigned its rights under the Barton contract to Egan. In which of the following circumstances would West **not** be liable to Egan?

a. West released Barton.
b. West breached the contract.
c. Egan released Barton.
d. Barton paid West. (R/05, REG, 0399L, #7, 7873)

43. Opal offered, in writing, to sell Larkin a parcel of land for $300,000. If Opal dies, the offer will

a. Terminate prior to Larkin's acceptance only if Larkin received notice of Opal's death
b. Remain open for a reasonable period of time after Opal's death
c. Automatically terminate despite Larkin's prior acceptance
d. Automatically terminate prior to Larkin's acceptance (5/90, Law, #14, 0464)

44. On July 1, Silk, Inc. sent Blue a telegram offering to sell Blue a building for $80,000. In the telegram, Silk stated that it would give Blue 30 days to accept the offer. On July 15, Blue sent Silk a telegram that included the following statement: "The price for your building seems too high. Would you consider taking $75,000?" This telegram was received by Silk on July 16. On July 19, Tint made an offer to Silk to purchase the building for $82,000. Upon learning of Tint's offer, Blue, on July 27, sent Silk a signed letter agreeing to purchase the building for $80,000. This letter was received by Silk on July 29. However, Silk now refuses to sell Blue the building. If Blue commences an action against Silk for breach of contract, Blue will

a. Win, because Blue effectively accepted Silk's offer of July 1
b. Win, because Silk was obligated to keep the offer open for the 30-day period
c. Lose, because Blue sent the July 15 telegram
d. Lose, because Blue used an unauthorized means of communication (5/88, Law, #17, 8010)

45. The president of Deal Corp. wrote to Boyd, offering to sell the Deal factory for $300,000. The offer was sent by Deal on June 5 and was received by Boyd on June 9. The offer stated that it would remain open until December 20. The offer
a. Constitutes an enforceable option
b. May be revoked by Deal any time prior to Boyd's acceptance
c. Is a firm offer under the UCC but will be irrevocable for only three months
d. Is a firm offer under the UCC because it is in writing (11/88, Law, #10, 8011)

46. Dye sent Hill a written offer to sell a tract of land located in Newtown for $60,000. The parties were engaged in a separate dispute. The offer stated that it would be irrevocable for 60 days if Hill would promise to refrain from suing Dye during this time. Hill promptly delivered a promise not to sue during the term of the offer and to forego suit if Hill accepted the offer. Dye subsequently decided that the possible suit by Hill was groundless and therefore phoned Hill and revoked the offer 15 days after making it. Hill mailed an acceptance on the 20th day. Dye did not reply. Under the circumstances,
a. Dye's offer was supported by consideration and was **not** revocable when accepted.
b. Dye's written offer would be irrevocable even without consideration.
c. Dye's silence was an acceptance of Hill's promise.
d. Dye's revocation, **not** being in writing, was invalid. (5/89, Law, #24, 0482)

47. Dunne and Cook signed a contract requiring Cook to rebind 500 of Dunne's books at 80¢ per book. Later, Dunne requested, in good faith, that the price be reduced to 70¢ per book. Cook agreed orally to reduce the price to 70¢. Under the circumstances, the oral agreement is
a. Enforceable, but proof of it is inadmissible into evidence
b. Enforceable, and proof of it is admissible into evidence
c. Unenforceable, because Dunne failed to give consideration, but proof of it is otherwise admissible into evidence
d. Unenforceable, due to the Statute of Frauds, and proof of it is inadmissible into evidence (5/91, Law, #18, 0495)

48. Green was adjudicated incompetent by a court having proper jurisdiction. Which of the following statements is correct regarding contracts subsequently entered into by Green?
a. All contracts are voidable.
b. All contracts are valid.
c. All contracts are void.
d. All contracts are enforceable. (R/01, Law, #12, 7047)

49. Payne entered into a written agreement to sell a parcel of land to Stevens. At the time the agreement was executed, Payne had consumed alcoholic beverages. Payne's ability to understand the nature and terms of the contract was not impaired. Stevens did not believe that Payne was intoxicated. The contract is
a. Void as a matter of law
b. Legally binding on both parties
c. Voidable at Payne's option
d. Voidable at Stevens' option (5/90, Law, #17, 0467)

50. Carson agreed orally to repair Ives' rare book for $450. Before the work was started, Ives asked Carson to perform additional repairs to the book and agreed to increase the contract price to $650. After Carson completed the work, Ives refused to pay and Carson sued. Ives' defense was based on the Statute of Frauds. What total amount will Carson recover?
a. $0
b. $200
c. $450
d. $650 (5/92, Law, #26, 2839)

51. Sand orally promised Frost a $10,000 bonus, in addition to a monthly salary, if Frost would work two years for Sand. If Frost works for the two years, will the Statute of Frauds prevent Frost from collecting the bonus?
a. No, because Frost fully performed
b. No, because the contract did **not** involve an interest in real estate
c. Yes, because the contract could **not** be performed within one year
d. Yes, because the monthly salary was the consideration of the contract (5/90, Law, #18, 0468)

52. Under the parol evidence rule, oral evidence will be excluded if it relates to
a. A contemporaneous oral agreement relating to a term in the contract
b. Failure of a condition precedent
c. Lack of contractual capacity
d. A modification made several days after the contract was executed (5/92, Law, #30, 8012)

53. Which of the following offers of proof are inadmissible under the parol evidence rule when a written contract is intended as the complete agreement of the parties?

I. Proof of the existence of a subsequent oral modification of the contract
II. Proof of the existence of a prior oral agreement that contradicts the written contract

a. I only
b. II only
c. Both I and II
d. Neither I nor II (11/93, Law, #24, 4321)

54. A building subcontractor submitted a bid for construction of a portion of a high-rise office building. The bid contained material computational errors. The general contractor accepted the bid with knowledge of the errors. Which of the following statements best represents the subcontractor's liability?
a. Not liable, because the contractor knew of the errors
b. Not liable, because the errors were a result of gross negligence
c. Liable, because the errors were unilateral
d. Liable, because the errors were material (5/95, Law, #17, 5351)

55. Which of the following, if intentionally misstated by a seller to a buyer, would be considered a fraudulent inducement to make a contract?
a. Nonexpert opinion
b. Appraised value
c. Prediction
d. Immaterial fact (5/92, Law, #28, 2841)

56. Which of the following types of mistake will generally make a contract unenforceable and allow it to be rescinded?
a. A unilateral mistake of fact
b. A mutual mistake of fact
c. A unilateral mistake of value
d. A mutual mistake of value (R/06, REG, 2095L, #9, 8179)

57. Long purchased a life insurance policy with Tempo Life Insurance Co. The policy named Long's daughter as beneficiary. Six months after the policy was issued, Long died of a heart attack. Long had failed to disclose on the insurance application a known preexisting heart condition that caused the heart attack. Tempo refused to pay the death benefit to Long's daughter. If Long's daughter sues, Tempo will
a. Win, because Long's daughter is an incidental beneficiary
b. Win, because of Long's failure to disclose the preexisting heart condition
c. Lose, because Long's death was from natural causes
d. Lose, because Long's daughter is a third-party donee beneficiary (5/93, Law, #23, 3991)

58. Johns leased an apartment from Olsen. Shortly before the lease expired, Olsen threatened Johns with eviction and physical harm if Johns did not sign a new lease for twice the old rent. Johns, unable to afford the expense to fight eviction, and in fear of physical harm, signed the new lease. Three months later, Johns moved and sued to void the lease claiming duress. The lease will be held
a. Void because of the unreasonable increase in rent
b. Voidable because of Olsen's threat to bring eviction proceedings
c. Void because of Johns' financial condition
d. Voidable because of Olsen's threat of physical harm (5/91, Law, #20, 0454)

59. Maco Inc. and Kent contracted for Kent to provide Maco certain consulting services at an hourly rate of $20. Kent's normal hourly rate was $90 per hour, the fair market value of the services. Kent agreed to the $20 rate because Kent was having serious financial problems. At the time the agreement was negotiated, Maco was aware of Kent's financial condition and refused to pay more than $20 per hour for Kent's services. Kent has now sued to rescind the contract with Maco, claiming duress by Maco during the negotiations. Under the circumstances, Kent will
a. Win, because Maco refused to pay the fair market value of Kent's services
b. Win, because Maco was aware of Kent's serious financial problems
c. Lose, because Maco's actions did **not** constitute duress
d. Lose, because Maco **cannot** prove that Kent, at the time, had **no** other offers to provide consulting services (11/92, Law, #18, 3100)

60. Ferco, Inc. claims to be a creditor beneficiary of a contract between Bell and Allied Industries, Inc. Allied is indebted to Ferco. The contract between Bell and Allied provides that Bell is to purchase certain goods from Allied and pay the purchase price directly to Ferco until Allied's obligation is satisfied. Without justification, Bell failed to pay Ferco and Ferco sued Bell. Ferco will

a. Not prevail, because Ferco lacked privity of contract with either Bell or Allied
b. Not prevail, because Ferco did **not** give any consideration to Bell
c. Prevail, because Ferco was an intended beneficiary of the contract between Allied and Bell
d. Prevail, provided Ferco was aware of the contract between Bell and Allied at the time the contract was entered into (11/92, Law, #21, 3103)

61. Union Bank lent $200,000 to Wagner. Union required Wagner to obtain a life insurance policy naming Union as beneficiary. While the loan was outstanding, Wagner stopped paying the premiums on the policy. Union paid the premiums, adding the amounts paid to Wagner's loan. Wagner died and the insurance company refused to pay the policy proceeds to Union. Union may

a. Recover the policy proceeds because it is a creditor beneficiary
b. Recover the policy proceeds because it is a donee beneficiary
c. Not recover the policy proceeds because it is **not** in privity of contract with the insurance company
d. Not recover the policy proceeds because it is only an incidental beneficiary (5/90, Law, #19, 0469)

62. Parc hired Glaze to remodel and furnish an office suite. Glaze submitted plans that Parc approved. After completing all the necessary construction and painting, Glaze purchased minor accessories that Parc rejected because they did not conform to the plans. Parc refused to allow Glaze to complete the project and refused to pay Glaze any part of the contract price. Glaze sued for the value of the work performed. Which of the following statements is correct?

a. Glaze will lose because Glaze breached the contract by **not** completing performance.
b. Glaze will win because Glaze substantially performed and Parc prevented complete performance.
c. Glaze will lose because Glaze materially breached the contract by buying the accessories.
d. Glaze will win because Parc committed anticipatory breach. (11/90, Law, #25, 0460)

63. Which of the following will release all original parties to a contract but will maintain a contractual relationship between the original parties?

	Novation	*Substituted contract*
a.	Yes	Yes
b.	Yes	No
c.	No	Yes
d.	No	No

(R/99, Law, #8, 6859)

64. Which of the following actions will result in the discharge of a party to a contract?

	Prevention of performance	*Accord and satisfaction*
a.	Yes	Yes
b.	Yes	No
c.	No	Yes
d.	No	No

(5/95, Law, #23, 5357)

65. Which of the following actions if taken by one party to a contract generally will discharge the performance required of the other party to the contract?

a. Material breach of the contract
b. Delay in performance
c. Tender
d. Assignment of rights (R/01, Law, #13, 7048)

66. To cancel a contract and to restore the parties to their original positions before the contract, the parties should execute a

a. Novation
b. Release
c. Rescission
d. Revocation (5/92, Law, #32, 2845)

67. Nagel and Fields entered into a contract in which Nagel was obligated to deliver certain goods to Fields by September 10. On September 3, Nagel told Fields that Nagel had no intention of delivering the goods required by the contract. Prior to September 10, Fields may successfully sue Nagel under the doctrine of

a. Promissory estoppel
b. Accord and satisfaction
c. Anticipatory repudiation
d. Substantial performance (11/89, Law, #19, 0478)

68. Which of the following statements is correct regarding the effect of the expiration of the period of the statute of limitations on a contract?
a. Once the period of the statute of limitations has expired, the contract is void.
b. The expiration of the period of the statute of limitations extinguishes the contract's underlying obligation.
c. A cause of action barred by the statute of limitations may **not** be revived.
d. The running of the statute of limitations bars access to judicial remedies.
(11/97, Law, #11, 6509)

69. Which of the following concepts affect(s) the amount of monetary damages recoverable by the non-breaching party when a contract is breached?

	Forseeability of damages	*Mitigation of damages*
a.	Yes	Yes
b.	Yes	No
c.	No	Yes
d.	No	No

(R/99, Law, #9, 6860)

70. In general, a clause in a real estate contract entitling the seller to retain the purchaser's down payment as liquidated damages if the purchaser fails to close the transaction, is enforceable
a. In all cases, when the parties have a signed contract
b. If the amount of the down payment bears a reasonable relationship to the probable loss
c. As a penalty, if the purchaser intentionally defaults
d. Only when the seller cannot compel specific performance (5/91, Law, #24, 0457)

Problem 34-3 EXTRA MULTIPLE CHOICE QUESTIONS (26 to 34 minutes)

71. Yost contracted with Egan for Yost to buy certain real property. If the contract is otherwise silent, Yost's rights under the contract are
a. Assignable only with Egan's consent
b. Nonassignable because they are personal to Yost
c. Nonassignable as a matter of law
d. Generally assignable (11/91, Law, #24, 2352)

72. Which of the following statements is(are) correct regarding a valid assignment?

I. An assignment of an interest in a sum of money must be in writing and must be supported by legally sufficient consideration.
II. An assignment of an insurance policy must be made to another party having an insurable interest in the property.

a. I only
b. II only
c. Both I and II
d. Neither I nor II (11/97, Law, #10, 6508)

73. Which of the following contract rights can generally be assigned?
a. The right to receive personal services
b. The right to receive a sum of money
c. The right of an insured to coverage under a fire insurance policy
d. A right whose assignment is prohibited by statute
(R/06, REG, 2087L, #35, 8205)

74. Wilcox Co. contracted with Ace Painters Inc. for Ace to paint Wilcox's warehouse. Ace, without advising Wilcox, assigned the contract to Pure Painting Corp. Pure failed to paint Wilcox's warehouse in accordance with the contract specifications. The contract between Ace and Wilcox was silent with regard to a party's right to assign it. Which of the following statements is correct?
a. Ace remained liable to Wilcox despite the fact that Ace assigned the contract to Pure.
b. Ace would **not** be liable to Wilcox if Ace had notified Wilcox of the assignment.
c. Ace's duty to paint Wilcox's warehouse was nondelegable.
d. Ace's delegation of the duty to paint Wilcox's warehouse was a breach of the contract.
(11/92, Law, #24, 3106)

75. On September 27, Summers sent Fox a letter offering to sell Fox a vacation home for $150,000. On October 2, Fox replied by mail agreeing to buy the home for $145,000. Summers did not reply to Fox. Do Fox and Summers have a binding contract?
a. No, because Fox failed to sign and return Summers' letter
b. No, because Fox's letter was a counteroffer
c. Yes, because Summers' offer was validly accepted
d. Yes, because Summers' silence is an implied acceptance of Fox's letter (5/90, Law, #12, 0462)

76. In which of the following situations does the first promise serve as valid consideration for the second promise?
a. A police officer's promise to catch a thief for a victim's promise to pay a reward
b. A builder's promise to complete a contract for a purchaser's promise to extend the time for completion
c. A debtor's promise to pay $500 for a creditor's promise to forgive the balance of a $600 liquidated debt
d. A debtor's promise to pay $500 for a creditor's promise to forgive the balance of a $600 disputed debt (5/92, Law, #24, 2837)

77. Which of the following requires consideration to be binding on the parties?
a. Material modification of a contract involving the sale of real estate
b. Ratification of a contract by a person after reaching the age of majority
c. A written promise signed by a merchant to keep an offer to sell goods open for 10 days
d. Material modification of a sale of goods contract under the UCC (11/90, Law, #21, 0508)

78. In determining whether the consideration requirement to form a contract has been satisfied, the consideration exchanged by the parties to the contract must be
a. Of approximately equal value
b. Legally sufficient
c. Exchanged simultaneously by the parties
d. Fair and reasonable under the circumstances (11/92, Law, #12, 3094)

79. Grove is seeking to avoid performing a promise to pay Brook $1,500. Grove is relying on lack of consideration on Brook's part. Grove will prevail if he can establish that
a. Prior to Grove's promise, Brook had already performed the requested act.
b. Brook's only claim of consideration was the relinquishment of a legal right.
c. Brook's asserted consideration is only worth $400.
d. The consideration to be performed by Brook will be performed by a third party. (5/95, Law, #20, 5354)

80. Able hired Carr to restore Able's antique car for $800. The terms of their oral agreement provided that Carr was to complete the work within 18 months. Actually, the work could be completed within one year. The agreement is
a. Unenforceable, because it covers services with a value in excess of $500
b. Unenforceable, because it covers a time period in excess of one year
c. Enforceable, because personal service contracts are exempt from the Statute of Frauds
d. Enforceable, because the work could be completed within one year (5/89, Law, #27, 8013)

81. To prevail in a common law action for innocent misrepresentation, the plaintiff must prove
a. The defendant made the false statements with a reckless disregard for the truth.
b. The misrepresentations were in writing.
c. The misrepresentations concerned material facts.
d. Reliance on the misrepresentations was the only factor inducing the plaintiff to enter into the contract. (5/91, Law, #21, 0455)

82. Bradford sold a parcel of land to Jones who promptly recorded the deed. Bradford then resold the land to Wallace. In a suit against Bradford by Wallace, recovery will be based on the theory of
a. Bilateral mistake
b. Ignorance of the facts
c. Unilateral mistake
d. Fraud (11/89, Law, #14, 8016)

83. On June 1, Year 3, Nord Corp. engaged Milo & Co., CPAs, to perform certain management advisory services for nine months for a $45,000 fee. The terms of their oral agreement required Milo to commence performance any time before October 1, Year 3. On June 30, Year 4, after Milo completed the work to Nord's satisfaction, Nord paid Milo $30,000 by check. Nord conspicuously marked on the check that it constituted payment in full for all services rendered. Nord has refused to pay the remaining $15,000 arguing that although it believes the $45,000 fee is reasonable, it had received bids of $20,000 and $38,000 from other firms to perform the same services as Milo. Milo endorsed and deposited the check. If Milo commences an action against Nord for the remaining $15,000, Milo will be entitled to recover

a. $0, because there has been an enforceable accord and satisfaction
b. $0, because the Statute of Frauds has **not** been satisfied
c. $8,000, because $38,000 was the highest other bid
d. $15,000, because it is the balance due under the agreement (11/87, Law, #1, amended, 8015)

84. Under a personal services contract, which of the following circumstances will cause the discharge of a party's duties?

a. Death of the party who is to receive the services
b. Cost of performing the services has doubled
c. Bankruptcy of the party who is to receive the services
d. Illegality of the services to be performed

(5/95, Law, #24, 5358)

85. Castle borrowed $5,000 from Nelson and executed and delivered to Nelson a promissory note for $5,000 due on April 30. On April 1 Castle offered, and Nelson accepted, $4,000 in full satisfaction of the note. On May 15, Nelson demanded that Castle pay the $1,000 balance on the note. Castle refused. If Nelson sued for the $1,000 balance, Castle would

a. Win, because the acceptance by Nelson of the $4,000 constituted an accord and satisfaction
b. Win, because the debt was unliquidated
c. Lose, because the amount of the note was not in dispute
d. Lose, because no consideration was given to Nelson in exchange for accepting only $4,000

(11/92, Law, #14, 3096)

86. Baker fraudulently induced Able to sell Baker a painting for $200. Subsequently, Baker sold the painting for $10,000 to Gold, a good faith purchaser. Able is entitled to

a. Rescind the contract with Baker
b. Recover the painting from Gold
c. Recover damages from Baker
d. Rescind Baker's contract with Gold

(5/87, Law, #19, 8014)

87. Kaye contracted to sell Hodges a building for $310,000. The contract required Hodges to pay the entire amount at closing. Kaye refused to close the sale of the building. Hodges sued Kaye. To what relief is Hodges entitled?

a. Punitive damages and compensatory damages
b. Specific performance and compensatory damages
c. Consequential damages or punitive damages
d. Compensatory damages or specific performance

(5/92, Law, #35, 2848)

SIMULATION

Problem 34-4 (20 to 30 minutes)

On January 15, East Corp. orally offered to hire Bean, CPA, to perform management consulting services for East and its subsidiaries. The offer provided for a three-year contract at $10,000 per month. On January 20, East sent Bean a signed memorandum stating the terms of the offer. The memorandum also included a payment clause that hadn't been discussed and the provision that Bean's acceptance of the offer would not be effective unless it was received by East on or before January 25. Bean received the memorandum on January 21, signed it, and mailed it back to East the same day. East received it on January 24. On January 23, East wrote to Bean revoking the offer. Bean received the revocation on January 25.

On March 1, East Corp. orally engaged Snow Consultants to install a corporate local area network system (LAN) for East's financial operations. The engagement was to last until the following February 15 and East would pay Snow $5,000 twice a month. On March 15, East offered Snow $1,000 per month to assist in the design of East's Internet homepage. Snow accepted East's offer. On April 1, citing excess work, Snow advised East that Snow would not assist with the design of the homepage. On April 5, East accepted Snow's withdrawal from the Internet homepage design project. On April 15, Snow notified East that Snow had assigned the fees due Snow on the LAN installation engagement to Band Computer Consultants. On April 30, East notified Snow that the LAN installation agreement was canceled.

On June 1, East Corp. bought an office building from Dale for $240,000. At the time of the purchase, the building had a market value of $200,000 and the land was valued at $40,000. East assumed the recorded $150,000 mortgage Dale owed Long Bank and paid $90,000 cash. Dale gave East a quitclaim deed that failed to mention a recorded easement on the property held by Dalton, the owner of the adjacent piece of property. East purchased a title insurance policy from Periphery Title Insurance Co. Periphery's policy neither disclosed nor excepted Dalton's easement. (6623)

Items 1 through 5 are based on the transaction between East Corp. and Bean, CPA. For each item, select the **best** answer for each item. An answer may be selected once, more than once, or not at all.

Effect of Event

A. Acceptance of a counteroffer
B. Acceptance of an offer governed by the mailbox rule
C. Attempted acceptance of an offer
D. Attempted revocation of an offer
E. Formation of an enforceable contract
F. Formation of a contract enforceable only against East
G. Invalid revocation because of prior acceptance of an offer
H. Offer revoked by sending a revocation letter
I. Submission of a counteroffer
J. Submission of a written offer

Date	Answer
1. What was the effect of the event(s) that took place on January 20?	
2. What was the effect of the event(s) that took place on January 21?	
3. What was the effect of the event(s) that took place on January 23?	
4. What was the effect of the event(s) that took place on January 24?	
5. What was the effect of the event(s) that took place on January 25?	

Items 6 through 10 are based on the transaction between East Corp. and Snow Consultants. For each item, select the best answer from the list. An answer may be selected once, more than once, or not at all.

Effect of Event

A. Breach of contract
B. Discharge from performance
C. Enforceable oral contract modification
D. Formation of a voidable contract
E. Formation of an enforceable contract
F. Formation of a contract unenforceable under the statute of frauds
G. Invalid assignment
H. Mutual rescission
I. Novation
J. Unilateral offer
K. Valid assignment of rights
L. Valid assignment of duties
M. Valid assignment of rights and duties

Date	Answer
6. What was the effect of the event(s) that took place on March 1?	
7. What was the effect of the event(s) that took place on March 15?	
8. What was the effect of the event(s) that took place on April 5?	
9. What was the effect of the event(s) that took place on April 15?	
10. What was the effect of the event(s) that took place on April 30?	

On June 1, East Corp. bought an office building from Dale for $240,000. At the time of the purchase, the building had a market value of $200,000 and the land was valued at $40,000. East assumed the recorded $150,000 mortgage Dale owed Long Bank and paid $90,000 cash. Dale gave East a quitclaim deed that failed to mention a recorded easement on the property held by Dalton, the owner of the adjacent piece of property. East purchased a title insurance policy from Periphery Title Insurance Co. Periphery's policy neither disclosed nor excepted Dalton's easement. East plans to sue Dale for failing to mention Dalton's easement in the quitclaim deed. East plans to sue Periphery for failing to disclose Dalton's easement.

Write a memo to your supervisor, a member of the audit team auditing East Corporation, outlining the likely outcome of East's planned suits against Dale and Periphery. In this memo, include a discussion of the benefits of a warranty deed.

Research Question: What code section and subsection, if applicable, provides guidance on the number of required installments of estimated income tax by corporations and the related due dates?

Section & Subsection Answer: §_____ (___)

Solution 34-1 MULTIPLE CHOICE ANSWERS

Assignment & Delegation

1. (c) An assignment rebuttably is presumed to be an assignment of rights *and* a delegation of duties. Here, assignee Deep Sea Lobster Farms presumably could carry out the delivery duties.

2. (b) Contract rights generally are assignable unless the right is personal to the promisee or the duty of the obligor or the obligor's burden or risk is materially increased. If neither of these are present, option contract rights are clearly assignable. Malpractice insurance policy rights normally are not assignable since the assignee might subject the insurance company to a greater risk, and thus, the insurance company would not agree to such an assignment. It is first necessary to determine who possesses the policy rights. If the right is viewed as being owed by the insurer to the insured, the insured could not assign their rights to another without violating the rules as to assignment. If, however, the right is viewed as being owed by the insurer to a claimant injured by the insured's malpractice, the claimant's right to receive compensation should be assignable by the claimant.

3. (c) Vim, the assignee, is entitled to the payments on the purchase price and the insurance proceeds because the assignee is entitled to all the rights the assignor had under the assigned contract—including the right to the promisor's (Egan's) performance. A promisor having notice of an assignment who, nevertheless, renders performance to the assignor or to any other third party remains liable to the assignee under the assigned contract. Furthermore, an assignor who accepts performance from the promisor after the assignment receives any benefits as trustee for the assignee.

4. (c) Contract rights can be assigned unless the assignment would materially increase the obligor's risk or duty. It is not necessary that an assignment be supported by consideration, nor is it necessary to be in writing. An assignor's right to revoke the assignment will not affect its validity.

Contract Elements

5. (d) There are two types of licensing statutes—those intended primarily for revenue raising and those intended primarily to protect the public against dishonest or incompetent professionals (regulatory). An individual without a license can collect the total compensation if the primary purpose of the statute was to raise revenue. However, if the purpose was regulatory in nature (intended to protect the public), the individual can collect nothing since the contract is voidable. An unlicensed individual who enters into a contract to provide regulated services will not be allowed to enforce the contract or recover even the value of the services rendered.

6. (a) The offeror made a promise for an act. When the act was performed, a unilateral contract was created and the offeror is bound to pay. Unjust enrichment generally is considered only if there was no contract and the court wishes to provide an "equitable solution." There are no public policy issues involved. A quasi-contract applies only if there was no contract to begin with and the law implies one to prevent an unjust enrichment. Since there was a unilateral contract, there can be no quasi-contract.

7. (a) The contract based on Alto's offer would fail because of indefiniteness as to the price. The contract clearly was definite as to the nature of the subject matter, the parties to the contract, and the time for performance.

Offer & Acceptance

8. (b) Communications sent to large numbers of people such as newspaper advertisements, are normally only invitations. However, when an ad limits the quantities, it probably is an offer. In this case, the advertisement does not constitute an offer because

it does not offer 10 cars at specific prices, only at a "special discount" and is, in effect, only an invitation to negotiate. The usual form of business with car dealers is one of negotiation.

9. (a) The contract between Alpha and Delta contained the condition that the land be rezoned. Since the nonoccurrence of a condition can terminate the existing obligation and, if the condition was not met when the vacant parcel was not rezoned by the deadline set forth in the contract, then the contract was in effect terminated on July 31. If the parcel were rezoned by the deadline and Alpha refused to purchase it, Delta would be able to sue for breach of contract, but not specific performance. Specific performance typically is granted only when damages (usually, money) is insufficient. Under the contract, Delta would receive money (not a unique property) in exchange for land. (A land purchaser probably would be granted specific performance if a seller refused to honor a contract.) The rezoning was a reasonable condition set forth in the contract. The condition of the contract could have been met, and Delta's refusal then to sell the property would have breached the contract, negating any obligation of Alpha.

10. (c) Offers are terminated when rejected by the offeree (Dall). Thus, any attempt by Dall to accept an offer after termination will act only as an offer to enter into a new contract. As to this question, the only exception to this rule involves the "option" rule. If consideration is given to hold the offer open for a stated period of time, a rejection by Dall would not terminate the offer during the option period. You can revoke an offer prior to acceptance *even if you stated you would keep your offer open for a stated period of time.* The only exceptions to this rule are if the "option" rule applies or if the UCC "firm offer" rule applies. An offer terminates by the terms of the offer. In this case, the offer terminated on May 1 and any attempt to accept on May 3 would be too late.

11. (c) Peters' offer had been revoked. Since revocation notice can be received either directly or indirectly, Mason, in effect, received the revocation notice when he was told the mower had been sold to Bronson; therefore, Mason's acceptance was ineffective, even though the specified time of the oral contract had not expired. Peters' offer had been revoked prior to Mason's acceptance. There was no obligation on the part of Peters to keep the offer open, since there was no consideration for him to do so.

12. (b) The letter from Fresno (the offeree) constituted a counteroffer, because it was received by Harris (the offeror) on February 19, a day late. If the offeror specifies a time for acceptance, the offer automatically terminates upon the expiration of that time period. The termination of the offer ends the offeree's power to accept it. If acceptance is attempted after the offer has terminated, the acceptance constitutes a new offer. The offer specifically stated that the acceptance must be by registered or certified mail and received by February 18.

Consideration

13. (a) Under the UCC, when parties do not agree upon price, the contract price is deemed to be a reasonable price at time of delivery. The quantity of goods in this contact is "all the wool shorn during the shearing season."

14. (b) Under the concept of promissory estoppel, a promisor is "estopped" or prevented from asserting that her/his promise is not binding due to lack of consideration if the following elements are present: (1) the promisor makes an express promise; (2) the promisor expects or should expect her/his promise to induce and it does induce the promisee to act or forbear to act in a substantial way; (3) the promisee did in fact rely on the promise and this reliance was justifiable and; (4) an injustice will result (not merely a legal detriment) to the promisee unless the promise is enforced. It is reasonable to expect a charity to make expenditures in reliance upon promised donations, with a resulting injustice to the charity if such promises are not met.

15. (d) Consideration is an act or a forbearance to act that causes a contracting party to suffer a legal detriment. The minor suffers a legal detriment (painting the garage) for the promise to pay. A preexisting duty and past consideration are not consideration as these cause the party to suffer no legal detriment. In the incorrect answer options, the real estate agent, the child, and the police have given no consideration for the promise to pay.

Capacity & Legality

16. (d) The law requires reporting of criminal activity. Thus, the promise to not report embezzlement would be unenforceable. Answers (a), (b), and (c) all involve legal activities and thus would be enforceable.

17. (d) A contract made by an infant is voidable by the infant. A non-infant party to a contract with an infant has no power to the void the contract on the basis of infancy.

Statute of Frauds

18. (d) Decker is not liable because his promise was not in writing. When the promisor, Decker, is not benefiting directly in the transaction, but acting as the surety for another person's debt, then the promise must be in writing and signed by the person to be charged. The June 3rd letter is irrelevant. The contract length is not relevant here.

19. (c) Under the statute of frauds, certain contracts may not be enforced unless they are evidenced by a writing or writings and signed by the party to be charged. The writings need not be in only one document. While there are exceptions, generally, contracts involving the sale of goods for more than $500 or that cannot be performed within one year from the contract date must be in writing. Editor's Note: Remember, the examiners instruct candidates to select the best answer.

20. (b) Generally, an oral contract for the sale of real property is not enforceable under the Statute of Frauds. However, there are certain exceptions. For example, if the purchaser takes possession of the property or makes a partial payment on the property, an unwritten contract would be enforceable. Under the Statute of Frauds, the contract must be signed by the party to be charged. It is irrelevant that Train signed the agreement; in this case, the contract was enforceable without a signing. The sale of real estate is not affected by a $500 benchmark.

21. (d) The Statute of Frauds provides that contracts for the sale of real estate be evidenced by a writing or writings and signed by the party to be charged.

Parol Evidence Rule

22. (c) The parol evidence rule will prevent the admission of evidence concerning the oral agreement regarding who pays the utilities, since the rule excludes evidence of prior or contemporaneous oral agreements which would vary the written contract. However, the parol evidence rule will *not* prevent the admission of the fraudulent statements by Kemp during the original negotiations.

23. (b) Where a contract is completely integrated into a written agreement, the parol evidence rule will apply to prohibit any further evidence except for the following three items: (1) one can introduce evidence to show a subsequent agreement, but not a prior or contemporaneous agreement; (2) one can introduce evidence to explain an ambiguity; and (3) one can introduce evidence to show why no contract should exist due to fraud, lack of consideration, mistake, etc.

Mistake & Misrepresentation

24. (c) A unilateral mistake is a mistake made by only one party to the contract. In most cases, the mistake is to the detriment of the mistaken party. Generally, a unilateral mistake does not allow a party to void the contract; it will be binding to both sides. However, an exception to this rule concerns a contract based on a calculation that is so far off that the other party should have known of the mistake, resulting in a voidable contract by the party making the mistake.

25. (b) Jackson will not prevail. If there are any means whereby the accuracy of the statement can be verified and it would be reasonable to do so, justifiable reliance requires such verification. Miller told Jackson to have an accountant examine Miller's records, which should have indicated to Jackson that verification was in order. Therefore, Jackson could not claim justifiable reliance. To recover, Jackson must not only prove that the errors were material, but also that his reliance on the misstatements was reasonable. If an innocent misrepresentation had occurred, Jackson could rescind the contract but generally would be unable to seek monetary damages.

26. (c) Performance of a contract is objectively impossible if the subject matter necessary for performance is destroyed through no fault of the promisor. Thus, impossible performance is excused, meaning that there is no consideration for the other party's performance and the other party is entitled to rescission.

Fraud, Duress & Undue Influence

27. (b) Fraud in the inducement can be defined as a false representation of a material fact, made with knowledge of its falsity and the intent to deceive, and the representation is justifiably relied on.

28. (c) The test for duress is whether the improper threats actually caused an individual to enter into a contract against her/his will. Duress can involve conduct outside of a tort or a crime. There is no "reasonable person test" in determining duress. The intent of the person making the improper threat is not relevant.

29. (c) Undue influence is defined as the mental coercion of one person by another person so that the will of the influencing party is substituted for that of the victim. Consequently, the unduly influenced party's assent to the contract is not voluntary. The result is that the contract is voidable by the victim. Fraud in the inducement is a knowing misrepresentation or omission of a material fact with the intent to induce someone to enter into a contract, and in fact,

that person does rely upon that fraud to enter into the contract. Unconscionability is a doctrine wherein a court will deny enforcing a contract because of the unfair bargaining power held by one of the parties to the contract. Duress is mental or physical pressure against a party such that their free will is overcome and they enter into a contract as a result of such duress; a court will deny enforcing such a contract.

Beneficiaries

30. (d) A creditor beneficiary is defined as a third person to whom a debt or other duty is owed by the promisee. In a donee beneficiary relationship, there is no debt or duty owed by the promisee to the beneficiary. The primary purpose of entering into the contract and acquiring the insurance was *not* to make a gift to Ness; Ness, therefore, is not a donee beneficiary with respect to either the contract or the insurance.

31. (c) Long is merely an incidental beneficiary and has no right to enforce the contract. In this case, the purpose of the contract was not to directly benefit Long. An incidental beneficiary of a contract has no right to enforce the contract. The assignment of the contract would have no bearing on Long's being able to sue.

32. (a) In general, the insured can name anyone as the beneficiary of her/his life insurance policy. Normally, the insured can modify the beneficiary designation prior to the insured's death. Once the insured dies, the named beneficiary has a vested right to receive the insurance proceeds. If the insurance company does not pay, the beneficiary may successfully sue the insurance company as a third party donee beneficiary.

Discharge, Breach & Remedies

33. (a) Conditions precedent, conditions subsequent, and concurrent conditions are all types of conditions which validly may be present in contracts.

34. (a) For an immaterial breach of contract, the non-breaching party, White Corp., must pay the contract price less monetary damages to compensate for the immaterial breach. Equitable damages such as specific performance and injunction are available only in cases where monetary damages are not adequate. The facts of this problem illustrate an immaterial breach of contract because the injury incurred by White Corp. was relatively insignificant and would not justify an equitable remedy. White Corp. will be able to recover damages regardless of the inadvertent nature of the breach. Failure to install the brand of lighting specified in the contract does constitute a breach of contract. The immaterial nature of the breach limits the recovery to monetary damages.

35. (d) The arrangement in question is a novation, with Moss completely replacing Wren under the terms of the Wren-First Federal contract. Moss assumed liability on the mortgage. Wren has been released from liability, something an assignment and delegation does not accomplish.

36. (a) Mutual rescission is the undoing of a contract that places both the parties in their original position. An accord and satisfaction is an agreement to accept a different performance in substitution for that required under an existing contract.

Statute of Limitations

37. (b) The statute of limitations in an action for breach of contract begins to toll from the time the contract is breached.

38. (d) The statute of limitations, which runs from the time the defect reasonably could have been discovered, would likely prevent Dart from prevailing because of the length of time that has passed. The parol evidence rule does not apply to the admission into evidence of the proof of fraud. A contract can be rescinded if there was fraud. It is not necessary for the misrepresentations to be part of the written contract.

Damages

39. (a) Specific performance typically is granted only when damages are insufficient, such as a contract for the sale of unique property. Specific performance rarely is granted if the contract requires personal services, such as employment. Fungible goods and stock that is traded on a national stock exchange could be purchased with an award of money.

40. (a) A liquidated damages provision is a specific amount provided in a contract to be recoverable in the event of a breach. It is enforceable if actual damage would be difficult to assess and the amount appears reasonable at the time of contracting. UCC 2-718 allows liquidated damages if the amount is reasonable in light of the anticipated or actual harm caused by the breach. However, if the liquidated damages are excessive, a court may interpret them as a penalty and refuse enforcement. The breach was identified and specified in the contract; thus, materiality is not an issue.

Solution 34-2 ADDITIONAL MULTIPLE CHOICE ANSWERS

Assignment & Delegation

41. (d) An assignor (Burns) for value makes the following implied warranties: (1) the assignor will do nothing to destroy or impair the assigned right, (2) the right exists, (3) the right is not subject to any defense or counterclaim by the obligor (Nagel), and (4) any token or writing the assignor delivers as evidence of the assigned right is genuine. The assignor (Burns) does not warrant that the obligor (Nagel) will perform or pay or that the obligor is solvent. Failure to give notice to the obligor (Nagel) does not invalidate the assignment. The assignee (Ross) takes subject to any defenses and counterclaims arising from the contract which the obligor (Nagel) had against the assignor (Burns).

42. (c) By releasing Barton, Egan has reduced the value of the West-Barton contract to West; therefore, Egan effectively has released West. If West released Barton, then West still would owe a duty to Egan to perform. If West breached the contract, then West still would owe a duty to Egan to perform. If Barton paid West, then West still would owe a duty to Egan to perform.

Offer & Acceptance

43. (d) Death of the offeror (or offeree) will automatically terminate, by operation of law, an offer. The notice of the death is not required to effectuate a termination. Death immediately terminates the offer. However, death cannot undo an offer which already has been accepted.

44. (a) Blue's telegram on July 15 was an inquiry, not a counteroffer; it did not constitute a rejection of Silk's offer since it was so worded as to effectively reserve the original offer. As such, Blue's acceptance through the letter sent on July 27 was effective to create a valid contract. In the absence of an expressly authorized mode of acceptance, any mode dictated by business custom (e.g., mail) is authorized impliedly. The rule concerning firm offers applies to a sale of goods by a merchant in the ordinary course of business and, thus, does not apply to this situation.

45. (b) Under the law of contracts, an offer that states it will be held open for a period of time may, without consideration, be revoked any time before its acceptance. In contrast, under the UCC, a signed written offer by a merchant to buy or sell goods in which the merchant gives assurance that the offer will be held open is irrevocable, even without consideration, for a period not exceeding three months. However, the UCC does not apply to this situation since a sale of realty is involved; the law of contracts applies instead. An option contract requires that the offeror receive consideration for his promise to keep his offer open.

Consideration

46. (a) The general rule is that you can always revoke your offer prior to acceptance unless the UCC "firm offer" rule applies (it does not in this question) or there is an option (consideration has been "paid" to keep the offer open). In this situation, there is a valid option and the offer cannot be revoked during the 60 days. Forbearance to sue on a claim is valid consideration as long as the promisee has a good faith belief in the validity of the claim. The UCC "firm offer" rule does not apply in this situation. Hill's promise not to sue was acceptance of Dye's option offer. Also, silence is never acceptance unless there is a prior agreement or appropriate course of dealing. A revocation of a written offer can be oral and is effective when communicated to the offeree provided the offer is revocable. In this situation, the offer cannot be revoked for 60 days due to the option rule.

47. (c) Contracts for services are governed by common law which specifies that modifications to an agreement must be supported with consideration to be enforceable. The oral agreement is not enforceable. The Statute of Frauds does not apply in this case.

Capacity

48. (c) All contracts entered into by Green after adjudicated incompetent are void. Contracts entered into when Green was incompetent, but previous to such adjudication, are voidable.

49. (b) Since Payne's capacity was not impaired and Stevens did not believe that Payne was intoxicated, the contract is legally binding on both parties.

Statute of Frauds

50. (d) The contract between Carson and Ives does not fall under the Statute of Frauds. The fact that the contract price was renegotiated for an amount over $500 is irrelevant because the contract is not for the sale of goods. Hence, Carson is entitled to the full $650 of the contract in exchange for his repair work.

51. (a) Courts generally decide that even if the remedy is not strictly contractual, parties who have fully performed an oral contract should recover under quasi-contract, promissory estoppel, or other such principles. Although the Statute of Frauds requires written evidence for contracts which cannot be performed within one year, it would not be applicable to contracts that have been performed fully.

Parol Evidence Rule

52. (a) If a contract is completely integrated into a written instrument, any evidence, written or oral, of a prior or *contemporaneous* agreement offered to contradict the terms of the written instrument is inadmissible.

53. (b) The parol evidence rule, in general, does not allow the admission into evidence of written or oral evidence to contradict a written contract which was intended to be the final written understanding of the parties. There are three exceptions to this rule: Parol evidence can be introduced to (1) explain an ambiguity, (2) explain a subsequent agreement (not a prior or contemporaneous agreement), or (3) explain why no contract should exist due to lack of consideration, fraud, misrepresentation, duress, etc. Therefore, the rule effectively bars Item II from being admitted into evidence since it is a prior agreement. Item I, however, is not excluded by the rule as it is a subsequent modification of the contract.

Mistake & Misrepresentation

54. (a) Where a mistake is made by only one party (a unilateral mistake), the rule is that the mistaken party is bound by the contract unless the nonmistaken party knew of the mistake or should have known of the mistake. In this question, the nonmistaken party knew of the mistake; thus, the mistaken party is not bound by the contract. Whether the mistake was a result of gross negligence is irrelevant.

55. (b) Fraud is a false representation of *material* fact made by one party to the other party with the intent to deceive and which induces the other party to justifiably rely on that fact to her/his detriment. An appraisal value generally is considered to be a statement of fact. A nonexpert opinion and a prediction generally are not considered to be statements of fact. An immaterial fact does not fit the definition of fraud because such a statement of fact must be material in nature.

56. (b) A mutual mistake (when both parties are mistaken) of fact regarding a contact makes it unenforceable. A unilateral mistake is a mistake made by only one party to the contract; in most cases, the mistake is to the detriment of the mistaken party. Contracts involving a mistake in value generally are enforceable: a mistake involving the parties' reasons for entering into the contract are not a ground for relief by itself.

Fraud, Duress & Undue Influence

57. (b) Long's daughter is a third-party donee beneficiary to the insurance contract. The promisor can assert any defenses against third party beneficiaries that s/he has against the promisee. Long's failure to disclose his known preexisting heart condition was an intentional false misrepresentation resulting in fraud in the inducement, and the contract is voidable by Tempo. Thus, Tempo will win if Long's daughter sues. Long's daughter is not an incidental beneficiary, which is a third party whom a contract was not intended to benefit, but who nevertheless may receive an incidental benefit.

58. (d) The lease is voidable because of the landlord's threat of physical harm. Thus, the lease is voidable due to duress. In general, there is nothing wrong with a landlord raising the rent since the tenant, Johns, can move out. Eviction is not improper when the lease has expired. A tenant's financial condition would not cause the lease to be void.

59. (c) Kent will lose, because Maco's knowledge of Kent's financial condition did not constitute duress. Duress is the threat of physical harm to a party or to the members of the party's family. The threat of economic loss generally is not considered duress. In this case, Kent was free to refuse the contract. There is no law that a client must pay the fair market value for services. Negotiation between the two parties certainly is allowed. Maco is able to look elsewhere for its consulting needs. It is irrelevant whether Maco is aware of Kent's financial problems or whether Kent had other offers to provide consulting services.

Beneficiaries

60. (c) Ferco will prevail because Ferco was the third party creditor beneficiary. The promisor on the contract (Bell) failed to perform and, therefore, Ferco can sue Bell. Ferco does not lack privity of contract. It is an intended creditor beneficiary of the contract between Bell and Allied. The creditor beneficiary need not give consideration to have an enforceable right. Ferco need not have been aware of the contract between Bell and Allied when it was formed in order to prevail in this situation.

61. (a) Union is a creditor beneficiary under the insurance policy. It is not a donee or incidental beneficiary. Privity of contract is not the issue in this question.

Discharge, Breach & Remedies

62. (b) Glaze will win because he "substantially performed" on the contract. Glaze should receive the contract price less the cost of damages due to minor deviations from the required performance. Glaze also can collect because Parc refused to allow Glaze the opportunity to complete the contract. Glaze can recover for substantial performance of the contract. The breach was a minor breach. Glaze breached the contract by purchasing minor accessories not allowed under the contract. In response, Parc refused to allow Glaze to complete the contract. This is not deemed to be anticipatory breach by Parc.

63. (c) A novation is a substitution by agreement of a new contract for an old one, with the rights under the old one being terminated. Typically, there is a substitution of a new person who is responsible for the contract and the removal of an original party's rights and duties under the contract. A substituted contract is a different contract between the same parties that supersedes and replaces the old contract.

64. (a) Where one party to a contract prevents the other from rendering performance, the party unable to perform will be discharged from its contractual duties. An accord and satisfaction involves an agreement to accept a substitute future performance for a performance required under an existing contract. Performance of the substituted duty discharges the original duty.

65. (a) A material breach is a major defect in performance that constitutes a failure of consideration and excuses the other party from a duty to perform. Failure to perform on time may be a breach of contract, giving rise to an action for damages, but does not necessarily excuse the other party's performance. [The examiners instruct candidates to select the best answer.] Tender is an attempt or offer to perform that is proper in time, place, and manner. An assignment of rights is allowed unless it is expressly disallowed or increases the obligation of the other party.

66. (c) A rescission involves undoing the contract on both sides and placing the parties in their original positions.

67. (c) The renunciation of a bilateral contract before performance is due is an anticipatory breach which gives the non-breaching party several options (one of which is suing immediately for anticipatory repudiation). Promissory estoppel is an equitable remedy used in situations where your remedy at law is unjust (there is no indication from the facts in this problem that promissory estoppel would apply). The doctrine of accord and satisfaction applies in circumstances where there is an unliquidated debt and there is a good faith offer to settle this disputed debt. The doctrine involving substantial performance does not apply in this situation.

Statute of Limitations

68. (d) The expiration of the statute of limitations does not technically discharge a party's performance, but operates to bar the bringing of an action against a nonperforming party. The expiration of the period of the statute of limitations does not void the contract, nor does it extinguish the contract's underlying obligation. A cause of action barred by the statute of limitations may be revived. If a party makes a new promise to pay the debt discharged by the statute of limitations, the contract is revived, even without new consideration.

Damages

69. (a) The measurement of damages suffered by a party to a breached contract include the measure of consequential damages, which are damages that predictably follow as a consequence of the breach; e.g., losses resulting from the general or specific needs of the injured party that were known or should have been known by the breaching party. A non-breaching party has the duty to mitigate or minimize the losses caused by the breach. The non-breaching party cannot recover damages for losses that s/he could have prevented by reasonable action or forbearance to act.

70. (b) A liquidated damages clause will be enforceable if the amount of the penalty bears a reasonable relationship to the probable loss. It is not always necessary to have a signed writing (only if the Statute of Frauds applies). There are no punitive damages for a breach of contract. There is no requirement that liquidated damages apply only when the seller cannot compel specific performance.

Solution 34-3 EXTRA MULTIPLE CHOICE ANSWERS

Assignment & Delegation

71. (d) A contract to purchase real property is assignable. In general, a contract may be assigned unless it involves personal services or a confidential relationship or the duties of the obligor would be materially increased. In this fact situation, there is no evidence given as to why this contract could not be assigned.

72. (d) An assignment of an interest in a sum of money does not need to be in writing, and does not need to be supported by consideration. Although there generally are restrictions in the assignment of an insurance policy, the assignment of the proceeds due or payable following a loss does not have to be made to a party having an insurable interest in the property.

73. (b) The right to receive money generally may be assigned. Assignment is not allowed if it is prohibited contractually or if it is without the other party's permission if: the contract involves a right that is personal to the promisee, it involves a confidential relationship, the duty of the obligor would be changed materially, or the chance of obtaining return performance is impaired. The right to receive personal services is personal to the promisee. An insurance company duties may be changed materially depending on the insured. Assignment that is prohibited by statute means such a contract may not be assigned.

74. (a) The delegation of duties does not strip the delegator (Ace) of his duty when the delegate (Pure Painting) fails to perform, but remains liable to the obligee (Wilcox) until someone performs. Notification of the assignment does not bear on the issue of the liability of the delegate. Any duty may be delegated unless the duty requires the personal performance of the original obligor-delegator, so that the substitute performance would differ materially from that agreed on or a statute, common law, or the contract itself forbids delegation.

Offer & Acceptance

75. (b) Fox's letter was a rejection. Clearly, the difference in price was a *material* difference between Summers' offer and Fox's reply. Fox's letter served as a counteroffer.

Consideration

76. (d) Contracts, to be enforceable, must be supported by consideration. The test for consideration is whether a party to a contract suffers a "legal detriment," meaning s/he does something or binds her/himself to do something that s/he is not legally or otherwise bound to do. Regarding the promise to perform a preexisting duty, there is no legal detriment if one does or promises to do that which s/he is already bound to do. The police officer has a preexisting duty to solve crimes and thus has no legal detriment in this case. The builder is already under contract to complete the house and is not assuming any additional legal detriment in return for the additional time. A debtor's promise to settle a debt for less than the full amount on or after the time it is due does not constitute consideration since the debtor was already obligated to pay the full amount of the debt. Only the creditor would suffer a legal detriment. A debtor's promise to pay $500 for a creditor's promise to forgive the balance of a $600 disputed debt is enforceable because each party suffers a legal detriment; the debtor agrees to pay a portion of the disputed debt and the creditor agrees to accept less than the full amount of her/his claim to the debt.

77. (a) Under common law, consideration is needed to modify a contract. This is related to the "preexisting legal duty rule" where a party to a contract is not bound to modifications unless additional consideration is provided. There is no requirement to provide consideration to ratify a contract upon reaching the age of majority. Under the UCC, no consideration is necessary under the "firm offer" rule. Under the UCC, no consideration is required to modify a UCC contract; however, if the modified contract is for $500 or more, the Statute of Frauds requires written evidence of the modified UCC contract.

78. (b) Consideration must be legally sufficient. It is legally irrelevant whether consideration given by one party to the other is of approximately equal value or fair and reasonable under the circumstances. Also, the consideration must be exchanged *contemporaneously;* it need not be simultaneous.

79. (a) Past consideration is not valid consideration because the act was not done in exchange for the promise, but independent of it. Consideration requires that a party suffer a "legal detriment," which may result from the relinquishment of a legal right. Courts generally do not inquire as to the adequacy of the consideration. Contractual duties generally can be delegated to a third party.

Statute of Frauds

80. (d) The Statute of Frauds requires that contracts that cannot be performed within one year from the date of the agreement must be in writing to

be enforceable. Although Carr has 18 months to perform, it is possible for Carr to perform within one year from the date of the agreement (stated in the question). Thus, this oral contract for services was enforceable without a writing. This particular provision applies to contracts for the sale of goods, not for the performance of services. Personal service contracts may be subject to the Statute of Frauds, for instance, when the contract for personal services is for a two-year time period.

Mistake & Misrepresentation

81. (c) One element necessary to prove misrepresentation is that the misrepresentation involve material facts. It is not necessary to prove that the false statements were made with reckless disregard for the truth. It is not necessary to prove that the misrepresentations were in writing. It is not necessary to prove that the reliance on the misrepresentations was the *only factor* inducing the plaintiff to enter into the contract.

Fraud, Duress & Undue Influence

82. (d) Fraud is the false representation of a material fact made by one party with the intent to deceive and which induces the other party to justifiably rely on that fact to her/his detriment. Someone who sells land to one party and later sells the same land to another party would be found liable on the theory of fraud.

Discharge, Breach & Remedies

83. (d) The oral contract between Nord and Milo is valid since it could be performed within one year of the date it was entered into, and, thus, it did not fall within the Statute of Frauds. Since the amount owed was not in dispute, the notation on Nord's check that it constituted payment in full had no legal effect. The other bids have no relevance, since the oral contract was valid.

84. (d) When a contract is or becomes illegal, that contract becomes void, thus unenforceable. The death of the obligee will not discharge the obligor's duties because the decedent obligee's estate still may receive the services. The fact that the cost of performance has doubled does not render performance impossible and will not discharge the obligor's duties. Although the bankruptcy of the obligor may discharge the obligor's duties; the bankruptcy of the obligee will not discharge the obligor's duties.

85. (a) An accord and satisfaction is the settlement of a dispute or the satisfaction of a claim through the creation of a new contract between the parties to the original contract. In this case, a new contract was created. The consideration given by Castle to Nelson, who agreed to accept $1,000 less than the originally agreed upon amount, was Castle's offer to pay the note on April 1 instead of the originally contracted date of April 30. An unliquidated debt is one in which the specific amount of the debt has not been determined by the parties involved. In this question, an amount of $5,000 had been specified. Castle would win if Nelson sued.

Damages

86. (c) Generally, fraud in the inducement of a contract makes the resulting contract voidable at the option of the defrauded party. The defrauded party then may either affirm or rescind the contract. However, if a third party who is a good faith purchaser acquires an interest in the subject matter of the contract before the defrauded party has elected to rescind, no rescission is permitted. In such a case, the defrauded party's only recourse is to recover damages against the fraudulent party in a tort action.

87. (d) Under common law, Hodges is entitled to sue for compensatory damages *or* to obtain specific performance. Compensatory damages compensate for losses and lost profits suffered as a result of the breach. If the promisor fails to render the promised service and the promisee must obtain it *elsewhere* at a higher cost, damages are the difference between the market price and the contract price. Specific performance may be granted in cases where the contract is for the sale of unique property, meaning land or goods that are unique or unobtainable elsewhere. The building Hodges contracted to buy would, in most cases, be considered unique.

PERFORMANCE BY SUBTOPICS

Each category below parallels a subtopic covered in Chapter 34. Record the number and percentage of questions you correctly answered in each subtopic area.

Assignment & Delegation

Question #	Correct √
1	
2	
3	
4	
# Questions	4
# Correct	
% Correct	

Contract Elements

Question #	Correct √
5	
6	
7	
# Questions	3
# Correct	
% Correct	

Offer & Acceptance

Question #	Correct √
8	
9	
10	
11	
12	
# Questions	5
# Correct	
% Correct	

Consideration

Question #	Correct √
13	
14	
15	
# Questions	3
# Correct	
% Correct	

Capacity & Legality

Question #	Correct √
16	
17	
# Questions	2
# Correct	
% Correct	

Statute of Frauds

Question #	Correct √
18	
19	
20	
21	
# Questions	4
# Correct	
% Correct	

Parol Evidence Rule

Question #	Correct √
22	
23	
# Questions	2
# Correct	
% Correct	

Mistake & Misrepresentation

Question #	Correct √
24	
25	
26	
# Questions	3
# Correct	
% Correct	

Fraud, Duress & Undue Influence

Question #	Correct √
27	
28	
29	
# Questions	3
# Correct	
% Correct	

Beneficiaries

Question #	Correct √
30	
31	
32	
# Questions	3
# Correct	
% Correct	

Discharge, Breach & Remedies

Question #	Correct √
33	
34	
35	
36	
# Questions	4
# Correct	
% Correct	

Statute of Limitations

Question #	Correct √
37	
38	
# Questions	2
# Correct	
% Correct	

Damages

Question #	Correct √
39	
40	
# Questions	2
# Correct	
% Correct	

SIMULATION SOLUTION

Solution 34-4 Contracts & Real Estate

Bean, CPA (2 points)

1. J

The signed memorandum stating the terms of the oral offer is in effect the submission of a written offer. An offer is a proposal made by one party (the offeror) to another (the offeree) which manifests an intent to enter into a contract.

2. C

The signing of the offer and mailing is an attempted acceptance of the offer. Because the offer contained a provision that the acceptance would not be effective unless received by the offeror by a specified future date, the mailbox rule does not apply. Accordingly, on January 21 acceptance was attempted but not yet in effect.

3. D

The written revocation of the offer constituted an attempted revocation of the offer. Revocation is not effective until received by the offeree. There is no mailbox rule for revocations.

4. E

The receipt by the offeror of the acceptance prior to the revocation becoming effective has the effect of a formation of an enforceable contract.

5. G

The offeree's receipt of the revocation after acceptance became effective makes it an invalid revocation because of the prior acceptance of the offer.

Snow (2 points)

6. E

The oral agreement constituted the formation of an enforceable contract. All of the contract elements are present, including agreement, consideration, capacity, offer, acceptance, legal subject matter, and because it can be performed within one year, it does not fall within the Statute of Frauds and need not be written.

7. E

The new agreement constituted the formation of an enforceable contract. All of the contract elements are present, including agreement, consideration, capacity, offer, acceptance, legal subject matter, and because it can be performed within one year, it does not fall within the Statute of Frauds and need not be written.

8. H

Snow's withdrawal from the project and East's acceptance of the withdrawal constitute a mutual rescission. These events undo the contract on both sides and place the parties in their original positions.

9. K

The assignment of the fees to another party is a valid assignment of rights. A contract right can ordinarily be assigned by the person to whom it is owed (assignor) to another person (assignee), as long as the contract does not prohibit assignment and the right is not personal, does not involve a confidential relationship between the parties, would not materially change the duties, and would not materially increase the burden or risk. Snow assigned only the contract rights and not the contract duties. A novation did not occur because there was not a new contract, but merely an assignment of rights in the original contract.

10. A

The notification that the agreement was canceled was a breach of contract by renunciation during the course of performance. Because East breached the contract, Snow is effectively discharged from continuing performance and may immediately sue for breach.

Communication (5 points)

To: A. Grader
From: A. Candidate
Re: East Corporation – Office Building

East likely will not win a suit against Dale because Dale gave East a quitclaim deed as opposed to a warranty deed.

A **quitclaim** deed does not guarantee that other parties do not have claims on the property. The quitclaim deed only transfers **whatever interest** the grantor may have in the property.

In contrast, a **warranty** deed promises the grantee that the grantor has **valid title** to the property and obliges the grantor to make the grantee whole if the grantee suffers damage because of **defective** title.

Other covenants usually also are included such as title, against **encumbrances**, quiet enjoyment, and warranty. All of these assurances act to protect the purchaser against any adverse title claims that could arise.

The court likely will find that Periphery is liable to East for damages incurred as a result of the failure to disclose the recorded **easement** on the property. **Title insurance** guarantees the owner against any loss due to defects, liens, or encumbrances on the title of the property in the **record** which are **not disclosed** on the insurance policy.

Research (1 point)

Code Section Answer: §6655(c)

Code §6655 states, "IRC Section 6655 FAILURE BY CORPORATION TO PAY ESTIMATED INCOME TAX....6655(c) NUMBER OF REQUIRED INSTALLMENTS; DUE DATES.—For purposes of this section— 6655(c)(1) PAYABLE IN 4 INSTALLMENTS.—There shall be 4 required installments for each taxable year. 6655(c)(2) TIME FOR PAYMENT OF INSTALLMENTS.— In the case of the following required installments the due date is: 1st, April 15; 2nd, June 15; 3rd, September 15; [and] 4th, December 15...."

Out-of-State Candidates

Each state has separate requirements for candidates who wish to proctor within the state. Contact individual states or NASBA (www.nasba.org) for more information on individual states' requirements. Contact both the state where you plan to apply for a certificate and the state where you plan to sit for the examination.

Most states require candidates with degrees from schools outside of the United States to have their credentials evaluated by a member of the National Association of Credential Evaluation Services (NACES). View the NASBA web-site for a list of NACES members.

CHAPTER 35

SALES

EXAM COVERAGE: The business law portion of the Regulation section of the CPA exam is designated by the examiners to be 20-25 percent of the section's point value. More information about point distribution and information eligible to be tested is included in the **Practical Advice** section of this volume.

CHAPTER 35

SALES

I. Overview

A. Definitions

1. **Sale** The transfer of ownership of personal property for a price (consideration) [UCC 2-106(1)].

   a. **Contract for Sale** Sale accomplished by the making of the contract (present sale of goods) or an agreement to sell goods at a future time.

   b. **Bailment** Present transfer of possession of personal property (but not ownership) for a particular purpose.

   c. **Gift** Present transfer of ownership, requiring delivery but not consideration. On the other hand, sales require consideration, but not delivery.

2. **Goods** In general, all things moveable at the time of identification to the contract for sale [UCC 2-105(1)]. Included within the definition of goods are: unborn young of animals and growing crops and other identified things attached to realty that can be severed without harm (for example, timber). Excluded from the definition of goods are: money for payment of the purchase price; investment securities; and intangible personal property such as accounts receivable, commercial paper, and partnership interests.

   a. **Existing & Future Goods** Existing goods are those owned by the seller currently. Future goods are those to be acquired or produced by the seller. There cannot be a present sale of future goods; an attempt to make such a sale is characterized as a contract to sell in the future. [UCC 2-105(2)]

   b. **Fungible Goods** Fungible goods are goods so characterized that a unit of them is by nature, or by trade usage, considered to be equivalent to any other like unit [UCC 1-201(17)]. For example, oil in storage tanks and wheat in a storage silo are fungible goods.

3. **Firm Offer** A firm offer is a signed written offer by a merchant to buy or sell goods in which the merchant gives assurance that the offer will be held open. Such an offer will be irrevocable (even though it is not supported by consideration) for the time stated or for a reasonable time. However, in no event may this time period be longer than three months. Finally, any such term of assurance made on a form supplied by the offeree (party to whom offer is made) must be signed separately by the offeror (party making the offer) (UCC 2-205).

4. **Merchant** One who either deals in goods similar to the ones involved in the transaction or who, by occupation, represents that s/he has particular knowledge or skill relating to the practices or goods involved in the transaction [UCC 2-104(1)].

5. **Identification** The buyer obtains a special property right and an insurable interest in goods that are existing and identified. In the absence of an explicit agreement, identification occurs (UCC 2-501):

   a. When the contract is made, and the goods already exist and are referred to in the sales contract.

b. When the goods are shipped, marked, or otherwise designated by the seller as goods to which the contract refers and the contract is for the sale of future goods (other than crops or unborn young).

c. When crops are planted or when young are conceived.

6. **Tender** Tender refers to the requirement that the seller put and hold conforming goods at the buyer's disposition and give the buyer any notification reasonably necessary to take delivery.

7. **Condition Precedent** A condition that must be fulfilled before the agreement's promises or covenants are binding on the other party.

8. **Condition Subsequent** A condition, the performance or occurrence of which causes the agreement's promises or covenants to cease being binding on one or both parties.

9. **Cover** The right of the buyer, after a breach by the seller, to buy substitute goods (UCC 2-712).

B. Sale Contracts

The Uniform Commercial Code (UCC) codifies commercial practices that may differ from general contract law. Article 2 deals with contracts for the sale of goods (**not** real property, investment securities, or services) (UCC 2-102).

1. **Contract Terms Left Open** A contract for the sale of goods will be found even though some terms are left open, if the parties intended to form a contract and there is a reasonably certain basis for giving an appropriate remedy (UCC 2-204). In all cases, the parties must exercise good faith.

   a. **Price** When the price is not agreed upon by the parties, the contract price is deemed to be a "reasonable price at the time of delivery."

   b. **Delivery Place** When no place for delivery is specified, delivery shall be made at the seller's place of business; or if the seller has no place of business, then the place for delivery shall be the seller's residence. However, if the goods identified in the contract of sale are known to be located elsewhere, then that place shall be the place for delivery.

   c. **Delivery Time** When no time for delivery is specified, the time is a "reasonable time."

   d. **Payment Time** When no time for payment is specified and no credit is advanced, payment is due at the place and time the buyer is to receive the goods. This payment rule applies even though the place of business is the place of delivery.

   e. **Particulars of Performance** When not specifically stated in the contract, particulars of performance may be left open to be specified by one of the parties and the specifying party must exercise good faith in formulating particulars of performance.

   f. **Seller's Output or Buyer's Requirements** When quantity is not specified and the contract is for seller's output or buyer's requirements, the party determining the quantity is required to act in good faith so that the output or requirements will approximate a reasonably foreseeable figure.

2. **Acceptance** Unless otherwise indicated, an acceptance can be made in any manner that is reasonable under the circumstances (UCC 2-206). An acceptance containing additional terms is effective unless expressly made conditional on assent to those terms. The additional terms are treated as proposals for additions to the contract. Between merchants, the additional terms become part of the contract unless one of the following applies (UCC 2-207).

   a. The offer expressly limits acceptance to the terms of the offer.

b. The additional terms materially alter the offer.

c. Notification of objection to the additional terms is given within a reasonable time after notice of the additional terms is received.

3. **Conduct** Conduct by both parties that recognizes the existence of a contract is sufficient to establish a contract for sale although the writings of the parties (conflicting printed forms) do not otherwise establish a contract [UCC 2-207(3)].

4. **Modification or Rescission** Common law requires new consideration for any modification. An agreement to modify or rescind a sales contract need **not** be supported by consideration to be binding. However, a signed agreement that precludes modification or rescission except by a signed writing cannot otherwise be modified or rescinded. Finally, except as between merchants, such an agreement precluding modification on a form supplied by a merchant must be signed separately by the other party (UCC 2-209).

5. **Statute of Frauds** A contract for the sale of goods for a price equal to or greater than $500 is unenforceable unless there is a written memorandum signed by the party to be charged. A writing is not insufficient because it omits or incorrectly states a term agreed upon, but the contract is not enforceable under this paragraph beyond the quantity of goods shown in such writing (UCC 2-201).

Exhibit 1 ▶ Exceptions to Statute of Frauds

"SPAM"	
S	**S**pecially Manufactured Goods
P	**P**art Payment or Receipt of Goods (Enforceable only for part paid for or part delivered)
A	**A**dmission in Court (Acceptance & Receipt)
M	**M**erchant's Confirming Letter (Merchant to Merchant) (if no objections in 10 days, both bound)

a. Even if an otherwise valid contract does not satisfy the general requirements of the Statute of Frauds, it still is an enforceable contract in the following circumstances.

(1) If the goods are to be manufactured specially for the buyer and are not suitable for sale to others in the ordinary course of the seller's business, and the seller, before notice of repudiation is received and under circumstances that reasonably indicate that the goods are for the buyer, has made either a substantial beginning of their manufacture or commitments for their procurement.

(2) If the contract is partially complete, but only to the extent it has been completed with respect to goods for which payment has been made and accepted or with respect to goods that have been received and accepted.

(3) If the party against whom enforcement is sought admits in her/his pleadings, testimony, or otherwise in court that the contract was made, although the contract is not enforceable beyond the quantity of goods admitted.

b. Between merchants, the Statute of Frauds is satisfied, if within a reasonable time a writing in confirmation of the contract and sufficient against the sender is received and the receiving party has reason to know its contents, unless the receiving party gives a written notice of objection to its contents within 10 days.

C. Standard Shipping Terms

1. **F.O.B.** "Free on board" is a contract term indicating that the seller will bear that degree of risk and expense that is appropriate to the F.O.B. terms. F.O.B. terms are generally either F.O.B. shipment or F.O.B. destination.

   a. **Shipment** If the place of shipment is named ("F.O.B. seller's loading dock"), the contract is a "shipment" contract.

      (1) Under F.O.B. shipment terms, the seller must bear the risk and expense of delivering the goods to the carrier for their transportation.

      (2) The buyer must pay the costs of transportation from the place of shipment and bear the risks associated with delivery.

      (3) Title passes when the seller puts goods in the possession of the carrier.

   b. **Destination** If the place of destination is named ("F.O.B. buyer's warehouse"), the contract is a "destination" contract. Under F.O.B. destination terms, the seller must bear the risk and cost of transporting goods to the named destination. Title passes on tender at destination.

2. **F.A.S.** "Free alongside" is a delivery term indicating that the seller must, at her/his own risk and expense, deliver the goods alongside the vessel or dock named by the buyer and obtain and tender a receipt of the goods in exchange for which the carrier is under a duty to issue a bill of lading.

3. **Cost, Insurance & Freight (C.I.F.)** C.I.F. is a contract term indicating that the lump amount paid by the buyer includes the cost of the goods as well as the insurance and freight to the named destination.

   a. Since buyer pays freight, a C.I.F. contract is a shipment contract; thus, the buyer has title and bears risk of loss from the point of shipment after the seller performs her/his C.I.F. duties.

   b. The seller's duties under a C.I.F. contract are as follows.

      (1) Deliver the goods to the carrier and obtain a negotiable bill of lading

      (2) Pay the freight

      (3) Obtain insurance for the goods

      (4) Forward the documents to the buyer, who pays the lump-sum cost when the documents are tendered, unless the contract provides otherwise

   c. The buyer is obligated to pay upon tender of the documents even if the buyer has had no opportunity to inspect the goods first.

4. **Cost & Freight (C. & F.)** C. & F. is a contract term indicating that the seller is under the same obligation as with C.I.F. contracts, except that under C. & F. contracts, the seller has no obligation to insure the goods.

5. **Collect on Delivery (C.O.D.)** C.O.D. is a contract term under which the carrier is not to deliver the goods until the purchase price is paid. The buyer may **not** inspect the goods before paying for them, **unless** the contract so provides.

6. **No Arrival, No Sale** Under this type of contract, the seller must properly ship the goods and bear the risk of loss before delivery. However, if the goods are lost or destroyed en route without fault of the seller, s/he is not liable to the buyer for nondelivery (UCC 2-324).

D. Conditional Sales

If the contract provides that goods may be returned by the buyer even though they conform to the contract, this is a **conditional sale** which is characterized as either a "sale on approval" or a "sale or return" (UCC 2-326). If the contract is silent as to the type of conditional sale, then the following rules apply.

1. **Sales on Approval** There is a sale on approval, if the goods are purchased for use by the buyer. The sale is not complete until the buyer has "approved." The risk of loss is on the seller until the buyer "accepts" the goods.

   a. **Acceptance** "Acceptance" is defined as either use of the goods in a manner that is inconsistent with the purpose of the trial, or use of the goods coupled with a failure to reasonably notify the seller of the buyer's election to return the goods. Additionally, acceptance of any part of the conforming goods is acceptance of the whole.

   b. **Creditors' Claims** The goods remain free of the claims of the buyer's creditors until acceptance by the buyer.

2. **Sale or Return** There is a sale or return, if the goods are purchased for resale by the buyer. The sale is complete from inception, but is voidable at the buyer's election. The buyer has the risk of loss while the goods are in her/his possession.

   a. **Expense of Return** The risk and expense of the return are upon the buyer.

   b. **Creditors' Claims** While in the buyer's possession, the goods are subject to the claims of the buyer's creditors unless the seller files or posts a notice of consignment.

II. Title to Goods

A. Passage

Under precode law, title had substantial legal effect on many issues (e.g., risk of loss, recovery against third persons for damages, and insurable interests). Although title still determines the buyer's right to transfer the goods, the risk of loss and the right to recover damages now are covered by specific UCC provisions.

1. **Identification** Title cannot pass until goods are identified in the contract (UCC 2-401). Identification can be made (UCC 2-501) in any fashion explicitly agreed to by the parties, or in the absence of an explicit agreement, the following apply.

   a. If the goods exist and are identified, identification occurs at the making of the contract.

   b. If the goods are not existing and identified, identification occurs when goods are designated by the seller as goods to which the contract refers (e.g., by shipping or marking them).

2. **Agreement** If goods are identified in the contract at the time of contracting, the parties may agree as to when title passes. If there is no agreement as to when title passes, then title passes when the seller completes performance with respect to the physical delivery of the goods.

   a. In a shipment contract, title passes at the time and place of delivery to a carrier for shipment.

   b. In a destination contract, title passes on tender of delivery at the destination.

c. If the goods are not to be moved (e.g., goods in a warehouse) and a document of title is to be delivered, then title passes when the seller delivers such document of title.

d. If the goods are not to be moved and there is no delivery of a document, title passes at either of the following times.

(1) At the time of contracting, if the goods are identified.

(2) At the time of identification of the goods in the contract, if they have not as yet been so identified.

3. **Rejection of Goods** Rejection of the goods by the buyer revests title in the seller.

B. **Power to Transfer**
In general, a buyer of goods can acquire no better title than her/his seller (e.g., if a seller steals the goods and thus has no valid title, the seller cannot transfer valid title) [UCC 2-403].

1. **Voidable Title** If the seller has voidable title, s/he may transfer a valid title to a good faith purchaser who takes for value and without notice. Voidable title is created in a person receiving goods if any of the following apply.

a. The seller was deceived as to purchaser's identity.

b. The delivery was in exchange for a check that was later dishonored.

c. The delivery was to be for cash and no cash was paid.

d. The delivery was procured through fraud.

2. **Merchants** Entrusting the possession of goods to a merchant who deals in goods of that kind in the ordinary course of business gives the merchant the power to transfer all rights of the entruster (bailor) to a buyer who purchases in the ordinary course of the merchant's business. The theory here is that the owner/entruster or (bailor) has clothed the merchant with the apparent authority to sell the goods. Therefore, the owner is estopped from denying that authority against an innocent buyer. The owner's only remedy is against the merchant.

III. Risk of Loss

A. **Absence of Breach**
The contract for sale may include an express agreement indicating which party will bear the risk of loss. In the absence of an agreement, UCC provisions determine which party bears the loss. In the absence of breach, risk of loss is determined in the UCC (UCC 2-509) as follows.

1. **Shipment Contract** If the seller is to deliver goods to a carrier, risk of loss passes to the buyer on delivery of goods to the carrier.

2. **Destination Contract** If the seller is to deliver goods to a particular destination, risk of loss passes to the buyer when the goods are tendered.

3. **Goods Held by Bailee** If goods are held by a bailee (e.g., warehouse or carrier) and are to be delivered without being moved, the risk of loss passes to the buyer:

a. When the bailee acknowledges the buyer's right to possession of the goods.

b. When the buyer receives a negotiable document of title.

c. Within a reasonable time after the buyer receives a nonnegotiable document of title. Risk of loss still passes to the buyer even though the buyer does not present the nonnegotiable document to the bailee (to take delivery of the goods).

4. **Other Cases**

   a. Risk of loss passes to the buyer on receipt of goods if the seller is a merchant.

   b. Risk of loss passes on tender of delivery if the seller is **not** a merchant.

5. **Conditional Sales (UCC 2-327)**

   a. **Sale on Approval** Risk of loss remains with the seller until the buyer accepts the goods.

   b. **Sale or Return** Risk of loss is borne by the buyer while the goods are in her/his possession **and** during the return of the goods to the seller.

B. **Breach of Contract**
In most breach situations, the risk of loss is on the breaching party (UCC 2-510).

1. **Seller's Breach** If tender of delivery so fails to conform that the buyer has a right of rejection, the risk of loss remains on the seller until cure or acceptance.

2. **Revoked Acceptance** If the buyer rightfully revokes acceptance of the goods, the buyer may treat the risk of loss as having rested on the seller from the beginning, but only to the extent of any deficiency in the buyer's insurance coverage.

3. **Buyer's Breach** If the buyer repudiates as to conforming goods already identified to the contract or otherwise breaches before risk of loss passes to her/him, then the seller may treat the risk of loss as resting on the buyer for a commercially reasonable time. However, the seller may do so only to the extent of the deficiency in the seller's insurance coverage.

IV. Warranties

A. **Types**

1. **Warranty of Title & Against Infringement (UCC 2-312)**

   a. **Title** In any contract for sale, the seller warrants both of the following.

      (1) The title is good and the transfer rightful.

      (2) The goods will be delivered free of any security interest, lien, or encumbrance of which the buyer had no actual knowledge at the time of contracting.

   b. **Infringement** A seller, who is a merchant dealing in goods of the kind sold, warrants that the goods will be delivered free of a third person's rightful claim of infringement of patent or trademark. However, if the buyer furnishes specifications to the seller, s/he must hold the seller harmless against any such claim arising from compliance with the specifications.

2. **Express Warranties (UCC 2-313)** An express warranty may arise even if the seller does not use language such as "warrant" or "guarantee." An express warranty usually is not created by the seller's affirmation of value ("these goods are invaluable") or by the seller's opinion as to the quality of the goods ("these goods are the best of their type on the market"). An express warranty may be created in one of three ways.

   a. By affirmation of fact or promise made by the seller to the buyer that relates to the goods and becomes part of the basis of the bargain.

   b. By any description of the goods that is made part of the basis of the bargain, when such description creates a warranty that the goods will conform to the description.

c. By any sample or model that is made part of the basis of the bargain.

3. **Implied Warranty of Merchantability (UCC 2-314)** If the seller is a merchant with respect to the goods sold, the law implies a warranty of merchantability.

   a. The seller impliedly warrants that the goods are "merchantable." To be merchantable, goods must conform to the following requirements.

      (1) Pass without objection in the trade under the contract description.

      (2) If fungible, they are of fair average quality within the description.

      (3) Are fit for the ordinary purposes for which such goods are used.

      (4) Run within the variations permitted by the agreement.

      (5) Are packaged and labeled adequately.

      (6) Conform to any promises or affirmations of fact on the label.

   b. Serving food or drink for consumption on the premises or elsewhere is considered a sale of goods for purposes of this warranty.

4. **Implied Warranty of Fitness for a Particular Purpose** Warranty arises that the goods are fit for a particular purpose if (UCC 2-315) both of the following apply.

   a. The seller has actual or constructive knowledge of the particular purpose for which the goods are required.

   b. The buyer relies on the seller's skill or judgment to select goods suitable for that purpose.

B. Privity

Privity is the relationship existing between two contracting parties (e.g., buyer and seller). Under common law, a person seeking to sue another for liability under a warranty had to be "in privity" (e.g., have a contractual relationship with the person sued). For example, a buyer could sue the seller, but not the manufacturer or intermediate distributor. The UCC has three alternatives governing the rights of injured persons not in privity of contract with the seller. (UCC 2-318) A seller's warranty, whether express or implied, extends to the following.

1. Any natural person who is in the family or household of the buyer, or who is a guest in the buyer's home, if it is reasonable to expect that such person may use, consume, or be affected by the goods, and who is personally injured by breach of the warranty. A seller may not exclude or limit the operation of this section.

2. Any natural person who may reasonably be expected to use, consume, or be affected by the goods and who is personally injured by breach of the warranty. A seller may not exclude or limit the operation of this section.

3. Any person (including any individual or an organization) who may reasonably be expected to use, consume, or be affected by the goods and who is injured by breach of the warranty. A seller may not exclude or limit the operation of this section concerning injury to the person of an individual to whom the warranty extends.

C. Disclaimer of Warranties

1. **Express Warranty & Warranty of Title & Against Infringement** Express warranties, and the warranty of title and against infringement, can be modified or excluded only by specific language or circumstances (UCC 2-316). The warranty of title and against infringement can

be disclaimed only by specific language or circumstances that give the buyer reason to know that s/he is not receiving full title. The buyer is under a duty to notify the seller of any breach of the warranty of title within a reasonable time.

2. **Implied Warranties** All implied warranties are excluded by language such as "as is" or "with all faults."

   a. To limit or exclude the warranty of merchantability, the disclaimer of liability specifically must mention the word "merchantability." If written, it must be presented conspicuously in the disclaiming document (e.g., bold letter, large print).

   b. Modification of the warranty of fitness for particular use requires a conspicuous writing (no oral modification).

   c. If the buyer has an opportunity to inspect the goods or has refused to examine them despite the seller's demand that the buyer examine them, there is no implied warranty as to any defects that reasonably should have been discovered upon such examination.

   d. A course of dealing or trade usage also may modify or exclude an implied warranty.

3. **Parol Evidence Rule** When there is a final written contract, conflicting prior agreements or contemporaneous oral agreements concerning warranties will be excluded from evidence.

V. Performance

A. Seller's Rights & Duties

1. **Duty to Tender Delivery of Conforming Goods** Tender is a condition precedent to the buyer's duty to accept and pay for the goods, unless the parties agree otherwise (UCC 2-507).

2. **Right to Cure (UCC 2-508)**

   a. **General Rule** If the buyer rejects the seller's tender for nonconformance and the time for performance has not yet expired, the seller may notify the buyer of her/his intention to cure. The seller then may make a delivery of conforming goods provided s/he does so within the time for performance.

   b. **Surprise Rejection Rule** If the buyer rejects the seller's tender for nonconformance after the expiration of the time for performance, the seller may cure defects by tendering a conforming delivery within a reasonable time **if** the seller had reasonable grounds to believe the tender would be acceptable (e.g., the buyer had accepted nonconforming goods in the past).

B. Buyer's Rights & Duties

1. **Duty to Accept Conforming Goods**

   a. **Acceptance of Goods (UCC 2-606)** Acceptance occurs when the buyer does any act inconsistent with the seller's ownership.

      (1) Acceptance occurs after the buyer has an opportunity to inspect and signify that the goods are conforming or after the buyer agrees to accept them with defects (however, in the latter case, the buyer has the right to sue for damages).

      (2) Acceptance occurs impliedly when the buyer fails to make an effective rejection after a reasonable opportunity to inspect.

b. Effect of Acceptance (UCC 2-607)

(1) Duty to pay arises.

(2) Goods cannot then be rejected. Under certain circumstances, the buyer may revoke her/his acceptance; in this case, revocation is functionally the same as a rejection of the goods.

2. Duty to Pay (UCC 2-511)

a. Tender of payment is a condition to seller's duty to tender delivery, unless otherwise agreed.

b. Payment by check is conditional and is defeated by subsequent dishonor.

c. If payment is required before inspection, payment does not constitute acceptance.

3. Right to Inspect (UCC 2-513)

a. Unless otherwise agreed, the buyer may inspect prior to acceptance and payment.

b. If goods are shipped C.O.D. or the contract provides for payment against documents of title, the buyer may not inspect until after payment, unless otherwise agreed.

C. Excuses & Substitutes for Performance

1. Damage to Goods If goods identified to the contract are damaged without the fault of either party before the risk of loss passes to the buyer, then either of the following apply (UCC 2-613).

a. The contract is avoided if the loss is total.

b. If the loss is partial, or the goods have deteriorated so that they no longer conform, the buyer has the option of either of the following.

(1) Avoiding the contract.

(2) Accepting the goods with due allowance or offset from the contract price. This is in lieu of any further rights against the seller.

2. Failure of Means of Payment [UCC 2-614(2)]

a. If the agreed method of payment fails because of governmental regulation prior to delivery, the seller may withhold or stop delivery unless the buyer provides a substantially equivalent method of payment.

b. If delivery has been made, payment as provided by a foreign governmental regulation discharges the buyer's obligation unless it is discriminatory, oppressive, or predatory.

3. Failure of Means of Delivery Substitute performance must be tendered and accepted if, without the fault of either party, shipping facilities agreed upon become unavailable or commercially impracticable and a commercially reasonable substitute is available [UCC 2-614(1)].

4. Commercial Impracticability of Seller's Performance (UCC 2-615)

a. Delay in Delivery Delay in delivery or nondelivery is not a breach of the seller's duty if performance has been made impracticable by the occurrence of a contingency, the nonoccurrence of which was a basic assumption on which the contract was made.

b. **Allocation** If only part of the seller's capacity to perform is affected, the seller must allocate deliveries among the customers, and s/he must give each one reasonable notice of the quota available to her/him.

c. **Buyers' Rights** Upon notice of material delay or allocation of deliveries

(1) The buyer, by written notification as to any delivery concerned, may either terminate any unexecuted portion of the contract or modify the contract by agreeing to take her/his available quota in substitution.

(2) If the buyer fails to modify within a reasonable time, not exceeding 30 days, the contract lapses with respect to deliveries affected.

VI. Remedies for Breach

A. Buyer's Remedies

1. **Nonconforming Goods** If the seller delivers nonconforming goods, the buyer may do one of the following.

a. **Reject** The buyer may reject all or any nonconforming commercial unit(s) (UCC 2-601). Concerning the goods rejected, the following provisions apply.

(1) The buyer must reject and give notice of the rejection within a reasonable time after delivery or tender or lose the right to reject [UCC 2-602(1)].

(2) Failure to particularize defects ascertainable by reasonable inspection precludes the buyer from relying on those defects to justify rejection or to establish breach in the following cases (UCC 2-605).

(a) When the seller could have cured.

(b) As between merchants, when the seller requests in writing a full statement of defects on which the buyer proposes to rely.

(3) The buyer must not exercise ownership over the goods, but must hold the goods with reasonable care for a time sufficient to permit the seller to remove them [UCC 2-602(2)].

(4) The merchant buyer has a duty to follow the seller's reasonable instructions as to the disposition of rejected goods. In the absence of instructions, a merchant buyer must make a reasonable effort to sell the goods for the seller's account, if they are perishable or threaten to rapidly decline in value. If the goods are resold, the buyer is entitled to reimbursement for reasonable expenses of caring for and selling them (UCC 2-603).

b. **Accept** The buyer may accept any or all nonconforming commercial units (UCC 2-601). With respect to goods accepted

(1) Damages are still available if the buyer reasonably notifies the seller of the breach (UCC 2-714).

(2) Acceptance may be **revoked** if goods were accepted in either of the following situations (UCC 2-608).

(a) On the reasonable assumption that the nonconformity would be cured and it was not.

(b) Without discovery of the nonconformity, if acceptance was reasonably induced by either the difficulty of discovery before acceptance or the seller's assurances.

(3) Revocation of acceptance is similar to rejection in that the following apply.

(a) It must be done within a reasonable time.

(b) It is not effective until the buyer notifies the seller.

(c) A buyer who revokes acceptance has the same duties with regard to the goods as if s/he had rejected them.

2. **Failure to Deliver or Repudiation of Contract** If the seller unjustifiably fails to deliver or repudiates the contract before delivery, the remedies available to the buyer include the following [UCC 2-711(2)].

a. **Specific Performance** May be decreed by the court when the goods are unique or in "other proper circumstances." [UCC 2-716(1)]

b. **Replevin** The buyer may be able to recover possession if goods have been identified to the contract, and either [UCC 2-716(3)] of the following apply.

(1) The buyer is unable to *cover.*

(2) The goods have been shipped under reservation (goods shipped to the buyer under a negotiable or a nonnegotiable bill of lading).

c. **Rights on Seller's Insolvency** The buyer may recover goods identified to the contract if s/he has paid part or all of their price and the seller becomes insolvent within 10 days after receiving the first payment (UCC 2-502).

3. **Buyer's Rights Upon Seller's Breach**

a. **Cancellation of Contract** If the seller fails to deliver or repudiates the contract, or if the buyer rejects nonconforming goods or justifiably revokes her/his acceptance, the buyer may cancel the contract [UCC 2-711(2)]. Furthermore, whether the buyer cancels or not, s/he may recover the price paid and either:

(1) Cover and obtain damages.

(2) Recover damages for nondelivery.

b. **Claims & Rights** Cancellation or rescission of the contract does not discharge any claim for damages for an antecedent breach unless the cancellation expressly indicates the intention to renounce rights (UCC 2-720).

c. **Cover (UCC 2-712)** Cover means to procure substitute goods elsewhere in substitution for those due from the seller. The buyer is under no duty to cover, but if the buyer does so s/he must act reasonably and in good faith.

d. **Damages**

(1) If the buyer "covers," s/he may recover from the seller the difference between the cost of cover and the contract price, plus incidental and consequential damages, less expenses saved because of the breach [UCC 2-712(2)].

(2) If the buyer does not cover, s/he may recover damages for nondelivery from the seller. The measure of damage is the difference between the market price of the goods at the place of tender at the time the buyer learned of the breach and the

contract price, plus incidental and consequential damages, less expenses saved because of seller's breach (UCC 2-713).

(3) If the buyer accepts nonconforming goods and notifies the seller of the breach, the buyer can recover from the seller the loss resulting in the ordinary course of events from the seller's breach, determined in any reasonable manner (UCC 2-714).

(4) Incidental and consequential damages (UCC 2-715) are normally recoverable by the buyer.

(a) Incidental damages include expenses reasonably incurred as a result of the seller's delay or other breach (e.g., for inspection, receipt, transportation, care, and custody of rightfully rejected goods) and any commercially reasonable expenses incurred in effecting cover.

(b) Consequential damages include (1) losses resulting from requirements and needs the seller had reason to know of at the time of contracting which could not be prevented by cover or otherwise and (2) injuries to persons or property resulting from a breach of warranty.

(5) The buyer may notify the seller and then deduct damages for breach from any part of the price still due under the same contract (UCC 2-717).

B. Seller's Remedies

1. Buyer's Insolvency If the seller discovers that the buyer is insolvent, s/he may exercise the following rights where applicable (UCC 2-702).

a. Further Delivery The seller may refuse further delivery of goods, unless payment is in cash. Additionally, the seller may demand payment for all goods previously delivered under the contract.

b. Stoppage The seller may stop delivery of goods in transit (UCC 2-705). Generally, delivery may be stopped if the goods are in the possession of a carrier or other bailee. Stoppage is permitted until one of the following occurs.

(1) Receipt of the goods by the buyer.

(2) Acknowledgment to the buyer by a bailee other than a carrier that the bailee holds the goods for the buyer.

(3) Acknowledgment to the buyer, by a carrier as warehouseman, that s/he holds the goods for the buyer.

(4) Negotiation to the buyer of any negotiable document of title covering the goods.

c. Reclamation The seller may reclaim any goods received by the buyer on credit when s/he is insolvent.

(1) Successful reclamation of goods excludes all other remedies with respect to those goods.

(2) The seller's right to reclaim is subject to the rights of the purchasers in the ordinary course of buyer's business and other good faith purchasers from the insolvent buyer.

(3) Demand must be made by the seller within 10 days after receipt of the goods. However, if the buyer misrepresented her/his solvency to the seller in writing within the 3-month period before delivery, the 10-day limitation does not apply.

2. Buyer's Wrongful Acts If the buyer wrongfully rejects or revokes acceptance of goods, or fails to make a payment due on or before delivery, or repudiates all or part of the contract, the seller of the affected goods has the following remedies (UCC 2-703).

a. Cumulative Remedies

(1) Withhold delivery of such goods.

(2) Stop delivery by a bailee. Generally, the provision regarding stoppage of delivery to an insolvent buyer applies. In cases not involving insolvency, the seller may stop goods in transit only if such goods are in the form of a carload, truckload, planeload, or larger shipments.

(3) Resell and recover damages.

(a) A purchaser in good faith takes free of any rights of the original buyer, even if the seller fails to comply with any requirements as to resale.

(b) Method, manner, time, place, and terms of resale must be commercially reasonable, and the resale must be identified as referring to the broken contract. The resale may be public or private.

(i) If private, the seller must give the buyer reasonable notification of her/his intention to resell.

(ii) If public, goods generally must be identified and sold at a place usually used for such sales. Unless the goods are perishable or subject to a speedy decline in value, the seller must give reasonable notice to the buyer.

(c) The seller has the right to recover from the buyer the difference between the resale price and the contract price, plus incidental damages. However, expenses saved as a consequence of the buyer's breach must be taken into account.

(i) Incidental damages to a seller include the commercially reasonable costs of stopping delivery, plus those costs relating to transportation. Such damages also include costs involved in the care and custody of goods after the buyer's breach.

(ii) The seller is not accountable to the buyer for any profit made on resale.

(4) Choose to recover damages without resale. The purpose of damages is to put the seller in the position s/he would have occupied had the contract been performed.

(a) Ordinarily, in the absence of resale, the aggrieved seller is entitled to the difference between the market price at the time and place for tender, and the contract price, plus incidental damages, less expenses saved in consequence of the breach.

(b) If the damages above are inadequate to put the seller in as good a position as performance, then the damages are measured by the profit the seller would have made, plus incidental damages and costs reasonably incurred, less credit for payments or any proceeds from resale.

(5) Cancel the contract.

b. **Other Remedies** The seller may identify to the contract any conforming goods not yet identified if such goods were in the seller's possession when the seller learned of the breach [UCC 2-704(1)]. The seller, with respect to unfinished goods and to avoid a loss in the exercise of reasonable commercial judgment, can choose to do one of the following [UCC 2-704(2)].

(1) Complete the manufacture of unfinished goods and identify them to the contract.

(2) Stop manufacture and resell the unfinished goods as scrap.

(3) Proceed in any other reasonable manner.

3. **Buyer's Failure to Pay** If the buyer fails to pay the price as it becomes due, the seller may bring an action and recover the price of the goods.

a. The seller may bring an action in one of the following situations (UCC 2-709).

(1) Conforming goods were accepted.

(2) Conforming goods were lost or damaged within a commercially reasonable time after the risk of loss passed to the buyer.

(3) Goods were identified to the contract and the seller is unable after a reasonable effort to resell them at a reasonable price, or such effort reasonably appears to be unavailing.

b. If the seller sues for the price, s/he must hold for the buyer any goods identified to the contract and under her/his control. The seller may resell the goods prior to the collection of a judgment, but any excess proceeds are credited to the buyer. Furthermore, payment of the judgment entitles the buyer to any goods not resold.

C. Remedies for Buyer or Seller

1. **Right to Assurances of Performance (UCC 2-609)** If reasonable grounds for insecurity arise concerning the performance of either party (that is, it reasonably appears that performance will not be made when and as required), the other party may in writing demand adequate assurance of performance.

a. Until assurance is received, the insecure party may, if commercially reasonable, suspend any performance for which the party has not received the agreed return already.

b. If the other party fails to provide the assurances within a reasonable time (but not to exceed 30 days), the party's failure may be treated as a repudiation of the contract.

2. **Anticipatory Repudiation (UCC 2-610)** Demonstration by either party of an intention not to perform an obligation not yet due, or an action that renders that performance impossible.

a. In case of one party's anticipatory repudiation, the other party may suspend her/his own performance, plus the other party may choose to:

(1) Await performance for a commercially reasonable time.

(2) Resort to any remedy for breach, even if s/he has notified the breaching party that s/he would await performance.

b. The repudiating party may retract her/his repudiation until the time when the next performance is due, unless the other party has since canceled, materially changed her/his position, or otherwise indicated that s/he considers the repudiation final.

D. Statute of Limitations
An action for breach of warranty must be brought within four years after the cause of action accrues (UCC 2-725). Parties may agree to reduce the period to one year, but an agreement to extend the period will not be enforced. Cause accrues when the breach occurs, regardless of lack of knowledge. The cause accrues when either of the following occurs.

1. **Delivery** When tender of delivery is made.

2. **Future Performance** If the warranty extends to future performance, when the breach is or should have been discovered.

VII. Product Liability

A. Breach of Warranty
A warranty is a promise or assertion of fact concerning the quality or worth of a product sold. Warranties may arise in two ways. Express warranties are those promises actually made by the seller that are a basis of the bargain. Implied warranties are standards of quality that are established by the law.

1. **Causation** Sellers and manufacturers may be held liable for damages "caused" by their products. There are three separate theories under which product liability actions may be commenced. The law regarding actions based on the theory of *Breach of Warranty* has been codified extensively in Article 2.

   a. Under any of these theories, the plaintiff must show that the defendant's product was defective or otherwise unreasonably dangerous and that this condition caused the plaintiff harm. The plaintiff also must show that the product was in its defective or unreasonably dangerous condition before it left the defendant's hands.

   b. The plaintiff must show not only that the product caused harm or injury, but also that the harm was caused while the product was being used in a normal or foreseeable manner. For example, if a person loses her/his fingers while picking up a lawn mower to use it to trim the hedge, the person should not be able to collect for damages for any resulting injuries.

2. **Express Warranties** General code provisions have been supplemented by the Federal Consumer Product Warranty Act (FCPWA). Consumer product manufacturers and sellers who make written express warranties must comply with the provisions of this Act. Under the FCPWA, affected parties must label warranties either full, in which case they must meet express federal standards, or limited.

3. **Implied Warranties** In addition to the law as stated above, implied warranties may arise from a course of dealing or usage of trade.

4. **Disclaimer of Warranties** Remedies for breach of warranty can be limited in accordance with the provisions of Article 2.

5. **Liquidation or Limitation of Damages** Damages for breach by either party may be provided for in the agreement by insertion of a "liquidated damages" clause. The liquidated damages shall be limited to an amount that is reasonable considering the anticipated or actual harm caused by the breach, the difficulties of proof of loss, and the inconvenience or unfeasibility of otherwise obtaining an adequate remedy. A term fixing unreasonably large liquidated damages is void as a penalty.

6. **Contractual Modification or Limitation of Remedy [UCC 2-316(4)]** Consequential damages may be limited or excluded unless the limitation or exclusion is unconscionable. Limitation of consequential damages for injury to the person in the case of consumer goods is *prima facie* unconscionable. However, limitation of damages when the loss is commercial is not unconscionable. When circumstances cause an exclusive or limited remedy to fail in its essential purpose, then the general Article 2 remedies outlined above are available. Subject to the above provisions, both of the following apply.

    a. The agreement may provide for remedies in addition to or in substitution for those provided in Article 2. The agreement also may limit or alter the measure of damages recoverable under Article 2. For example, the agreement might limit the buyer's remedies to return of the goods and repayment of the price or to repair and replacement of nonconforming goods or parts.

    b. Resorting to a remedy as provided in the contract is optional unless the remedy expressly is agreed upon by the parties as being exclusive. In this case, the contractual remedy is the sole remedy.

B. Negligence Actions

A plaintiff may sue in tort for damages caused by a defective product if the plaintiff can show that the defendant failed to exercise reasonable care under the relevant circumstances. The negligence complained of need not be in the manufacture of the product; it may be in the design, packaging, inspection, or any facet of production or distribution. Negligence also may arise when the manufacturer has failed to warn of inherent dangers adequately or when the manufacturer has failed to supply adequate directions or instructions for use.

1. **Duty** In some instances, the courts require the plaintiff to show that the defendant owed a duty to the plaintiff. Presently, the law imposes a general duty on manufacturers and sellers to protect all people who may be injured while going about their normal business. However, the law does not always impose the duty to anticipate injuries occurring to a negligent party.

2. **Privity** Under the negligence theory, there is no requirement that privity of contract be established between the plaintiff and the defendant. There is **no** requirement that the plaintiff be a direct purchaser or user of the product. Therefore, any injured person may maintain an action against the negligent party.

3. **Defenses**

    a. **Disclaimer** The defendant may not avoid liability by use of a disclaimer.

    b. **Clear Warnings** In certain situations, the defendant may be able to avoid potential liability by providing adequate warning. For example, packaging lye in a protective container with clearly printed warnings and antidotes will insulate the manufacturer from liability due to human ingestion.

    c. **Contributory Negligence** In some jurisdictions, the defendant may escape liability if s/he can show that the plaintiff also was careless or at fault.

    d. **Assumption of Risk** In jurisdictions that have eliminated the contributory negligence defense, a defendant still may plead assumption of the risk. A plaintiff has assumed the risk when s/he knows of a defect but continues to use a product despite the defect and with full knowledge of the risk.

4. **Primary Uses** Negligence actions have been superseded largely by strict liability or breach of warranty actions. However, many negligence suits still are brought on the grounds that the defendant employed a defective design or failed to give adequate warnings or directions.

5. **Damages** Negligence actions may be brought to recover personal or property damages. They may not be used to recover mere economic losses caused by a product's failure to perform properly.

C. Strict Liability

A plaintiff may sue under strict liability if s/he can show that the product was sold in a defective or unreasonably dangerous condition and that this condition caused the plaintiff to suffer damages. The plaintiff further must prove that the product was defective or unreasonably dangerous before it left the defendant's hands. The plaintiff need not prove or assert that the defendant was in any way negligent or that any person connected with the manufacture, design, packaging, inspection, etc., of the product was negligent. Furthermore, the plaintiff may sue any and all of the above-mentioned persons so long as the plaintiff can show the product was defective when it left their hands.

1. **Defective or Unreasonably Dangerous** Producers and distributors are not insurers; therefore, they are not responsible for all the harm their products inflict. The courts use a subjective test when weighing whether a product is unreasonably dangerous.

   a. Some of the factors courts consider are: the usefulness and desirability of the product; the likelihood and probable extent of injury; the obviousness of the danger; the standards within the industry; the existence or absence of superior, economically feasible safety technology; and the knowledge of the public and efforts taken by the producer to further educate the consumer.

   b. Several states and the federal government have enacted consumer product safety acts. Typically, these acts (or rules promulgated under their authority) establish minimum safety standards for various products. Rules also may govern the warnings or instructions that must accompany a product. Usually, the violation of a standard is ***prima facie*** evidence that the product is either defective or unreasonably dangerous.

2. **Privity** The privity requirement for strict liability is similar to that for negligence. In the case of negligence, a manufacturer will be liable for its failure to exercise reasonable care in the manufacture of goods that, if manufactured negligently, create an unreasonable risk of bodily harm. This liability attaches regardless of whether there was a sale as long as the manufacturer was proven negligent. In the case of strict tort liability, the manufacturer need not be proved negligent. Rather, if the item would create a risk of injury if defectively made, the manufacturer and distributors are liable to specific classes of injured people.

3. **Defenses**

   a. **Disclaimer** The defendant may not escape liability by use of a disclaimer.

   b. **Clear Warnings** In certain situations, the defendant may be able to avoid potential liability by providing adequate warning.

   c. **Contributory Negligence** Contributory negligence is generally **not** a defense in strict liability. [In actions brought under a negligence theory, contributory negligence may be a defense that can be used by the defendant to avoid liability.]

   d. **Assumption of Risk** Assumption of the risk is a valid defense.

4. **Damages** Damages recoverable under strict liability are generally the same as those under negligence. That is, generally, only personal or property damages are recoverable.

What are the "minor" topics that I can ignore?

The Bisk Education instructors sometimes mention that some topics are heavily or lightly tested. Bear in mind, these comments do not apply to each specific exam. Rather, when several years' worth of exams are evaluated, some topics average more point value than others. On any one exam, candidates reasonably can expect at least one of the "minor" topics to be heavily tested. In other words, do not read too much into these evaluations; candidates are not tested on an average of several exams, but only one specific exam.

Within each exam section, some topics are emphasized more than others on a regular basis. For instance, in REG, an understanding of adjustments to gross income as well as itemized and standard deductions for individuals is essential. This topic accounts for about 10% of the point value in exam after exam. AMT usually accounts for 1% to 3% of the point value; however, the possibility of 10 points on AMT exists for any one exam.

Every now and then so-called "minor" topics show up in a simulation or in several multiple choice questions and so could count for 10 points on the section. What does this mean? You have to know these "minor" topics going into the exam. As a result, successful candidates make a point of studying everything. They concentrate on those topics that are repeatedly tested heavily while bearing in mind that any topic can be tested heavily on any one exam. In other words, any "minor" topic could be uncharacteristically heavy on your particular exam.

Having taken the exam themselves, the editors realize that candidates would like to narrow their studying down to "just what will be on the exam." Unfortunately, the examiners make a point of being unpredictable. As massive as the Bisk CPA review materials may seem, this truly is the "narrowed down" version.

Remember, with the techniques and information in your material,

A passing score is well within reach!

CHAPTER 35—SALES

Problem 35-1 MULTIPLE CHOICE QUESTIONS (45 to 60 minutes)

1. Under the UCC Sales Article, which of the following conditions will prevent the formation of an enforceable sale of goods contract?
a. Open price
b. Open delivery
c. Open quantity
d. Open acceptance (5/94, Law, #41, 4796)

2. Patch, a frequent shopper at Soon-Shop Stores, received a rain check for an advertised sale item after Soon-Shop's supply of the product ran out. The rain check was in writing and stated that the item would be offered to the customer at the advertised sale price for an unspecified period of time. A Soon-Shop employee signed the rain check. When Patch returned to the store one month later to purchase the item, the store refused to honor the rain check. Under the Sales Article of the UCC, will Patch win a suit to enforce the rain check?
a. No, because one month is too long a period of time for a rain check to be effective
b. No, because the rain check did not state the effective time period necessary to keep the offer open
c. Yes, because Soon-Shop is required to have sufficient supplies of the sale item to satisfy all customers
d. Yes, because the rain check met the requirements of a merchant's firm offer even though no effective time period was stated
(R/01, Law, #18, 7053)

3. EG Door Co., a manufacturer of custom exterior doors, verbally contracted with Art Contractors to design and build a $2,000 custom door for a house that Art was restoring. After EG had completed substantial work on the door, Art advised EG that the house had been destroyed by fire and Art was canceling the contract. EG finished the door and shipped it to Art. Art refused to accept delivery. Art contends that the contract cannot be enforced because it violated the Statute of Frauds by not being in writing. Under the Sales Article of the UCC, is Art's contention correct?
a. Yes, because the contract was not in writing
b. Yes, because the contract cannot be fully performed due to the fire
c. No, because the goods were specially manufactured for Art and cannot be resold in EG's regular course of business
d. No, because the cancellation of the contract was not made in writing (R/00, Law, #9, 6974)

4. Under the Sales Article of the UCC, which of the following statements is correct regarding risk of loss and title to the goods under a sale or return contract?
a. Title and risk of loss are shared equally between the buyer and the seller.
b. Title remains with the seller until the buyer approves or accepts the goods, but risk of loss passes to the buyer immediately following delivery of the goods to the buyer.
c. Title and risk of loss remain with the seller until the buyer pays for the goods.
d. Title and risk of loss rest with the buyer until the goods are returned to the seller.
(R/02, Law, #10, 7120)

5. Under the Sales Article of the UCC, when a contract for the sale of goods stipulates that the seller ship the goods by common carrier "F.O.B. purchaser's loading dock," which of the parties bears the risk of loss during shipment?
a. The purchaser, because risk of loss passes when the goods are delivered to the carrier
b. The purchaser, because title to the goods passes at the time of shipment
c. The seller, because risk of loss passes only when the goods reach the purchaser's loading dock
d. The seller, because risk of loss remains with the seller until the goods are accepted by the purchaser (R/99, Law, #15, 6866)

6. Under the Sales Article of the UCC, when a written offer has been made without specifying a means of acceptance but providing that the offer will only remain open for ten days, which of the following statements represent(s) a valid acceptance of the offer?

I. An acceptance sent by regular mail the day before the ten-day period expires that reaches the offeror on the eleventh day
II. An acceptance faxed the day before the ten-day period expires that reaches the offeror on the eleventh day, due to a malfunction of the offeror's printer

a. I only
b. II only
c. Both I and II
d. Neither I nor II (11/95, Law, #42, 5911)

7. Under the Sales Article of the UCC, which of the following statements is correct regarding a good faith requirement that must be met by a merchant?
a. The merchant must adhere to all written and oral terms of the sales contract.
b. The merchant must provide more extensive warranties than the minimum required by law.
c. The merchant must charge the lowest available price for the product in the geographic market.
d. The merchant must observe the reasonable commercial standards of fair dealing in the trade.
(R/02, Law, #15, 7125)

8. Webstar Corp. orally agreed to sell Northco, Inc. a computer for $20,000. Northco sent a signed purchase order to Webstar confirming the agreement. Webstar received the purchase order and did not respond. Webstar refused to deliver the computer to Northco, claiming that the purchase order did not satisfy the UCC Statute of Frauds because it was not signed by Webstar. Northco sells computers to the general public and Webstar is a computer wholesaler. Under the UCC Sales Article, Webstar's position is
a. Incorrect, because it failed to object to Northco's purchase order
b. Incorrect, because only the buyer in a sale-of-goods transaction must sign the contract
c. Correct, because it was the party against whom enforcement of the contract is being sought
d. Correct, because the purchase price of the computer exceeded $500 (5/94, Law, #46, 4801)

9. Under the Sales Article of the UCC, unless a contract provides otherwise, before title to goods can pass from a seller to a buyer, the goods must be
a. Tendered to the buyer
b. Identified to the contract
c. Accepted by the buyer
d. Paid for (11/97, Law, #14, 6512)

10. Thorn purchased a used entertainment system from Sound Corp. The sales contract stated that the entertainment system was being sold "as is." Under the Sales Article of the UCC, which of the following statements is(are) correct regarding the seller's warranty of title and against infringement?

I. Including the term "as is" in the sales contract is adequate communication that the seller is conveying the entertainment system without warranty of title and against infringement.
II. The seller's warranty of title and against infringement may be disclaimed at any time after the contract is formed.

a. I only
b. II only
c. Both I and II
d. Neither I nor II (R/07, BEC, 1850L, #11, 8435)

11. Under the Sales Article of the UCC and the United Nations Convention for the International Sale of Goods (CISG), absent specific terms in an international sales shipment contract, when will risk of loss pass to the buyer?
a. When the goods are delivered to the first carrier for transmission to the buyer
b. When the goods are tendered to the buyer
c. At the conclusion of the execution of the contract
d. At the time the goods are identified to the contract (11/98, Law, #12, 6757)

12. Under the Sales Article of the UCC, which of the following factors is most important in determining who bears the risk of loss in a sale of goods contract?
a. The method of shipping the goods
b. The contract's shipping terms
c. Title to the goods
d. How the goods were lost
(11/95, Law, #45, 5914)

13. Bond purchased a painting from Wool, who is not in the business of selling art. Wool tendered delivery of the painting after receiving payment in full from Bond. Bond informed Wool that Bond would be unable to take possession of the painting until later that day. Thieves stole the painting before Bond returned. The risk of loss
a. Passed to Bond at Wool's tender of delivery
b. Passed to Bond at the time the contract was formed and payment was made
c. Remained with Wool, because the parties agreed on a later time of delivery
d. Remained with Wool, because Bond had **not** yet received the painting (11/93, Law, #55, 4352)

14. Grill deals in the repair and sale of new and used clocks. West brought a clock to Grill to be repaired. One of Grill's clerks mistakenly sold West's clock to Hone, another customer. Under the Sales Article of the UCC, will West win a suit against Hone for the return of the clock?
a. No, because the clerk was not aware that the clock belonged to West
b. No, because Grill is a merchant to whom goods had been entrusted
c. Yes, because Grill could not convey good title to the clock
d. Yes, because the clerk was negligent in selling the clock (R/07, BEC, 1046L, #25, 8449)

15. An appliance seller promised a restaurant owner that a home dishwasher would fulfill the dishwashing requirements of a large restaurant. The dishwasher was purchased but it was not powerful enough for the restaurant. Under the Sales Article of the UCC, what warranty was violated?
a. The implied warranty of marketability
b. The implied warranty of merchantability
c. The express warranty that the goods conform to the seller's promise
d. The express warranty against infringement (R/02, Law, #13, 7123)

16. Vick bought a used boat from Ocean Marina that disclaimed "any and all warranties" in connection with the sale. Ocean was unaware the boat had been stolen from Kidd. Vick surrendered it to Kidd when confronted with proof of the theft. Vick sued Ocean. Who is likely to prevail and why?
a. Vick, because the implied warranty of title has been breached
b. Vick, because a merchant **cannot** disclaim implied warranties
c. Ocean, because of the disclaimer of warranties
d. Ocean, because Vick surrendered the boat to Kidd (5/94, Law, #43, 4798)

Items 17 and 18 are based on the following information:

On May 2, Handy Hardware sent Ram Industries a signed purchase order that stated, in part, as follows:

> "Ship for May 8 delivery 300 Model A-X socket sets at current dealer price. Terms 2/10/net 30."

Ram received Handy's purchase order on May 4. On May 5, Ram discovered that it had only 200 Model A-X socket sets and 100 Model W-Z socket sets in stock. Ram shipped the Model A-X and Model W-Z sets to Handy without any explanation concerning the shipment. The socket sets were received by Handy on May 8.

17. Assuming a contract exists between Handy and Ram, which of the following implied warranties would result?

I. Implied warranty of merchantability
II. Implied warranty of fitness for a particular purpose
III. Implied warranty of title

a. I only
b. III only
c. I and III only
d. I, II, and III (11/93, Law, #52, 4349)

18. Which of the following statements concerning the shipment is correct?
a. Ram's shipment is an acceptance of Handy's offer.
b. Ram's shipment is a counteroffer.
c. Handy's order must be accepted by Ram in writing before Ram ships the socket sets.
d. Handy's order can only be accepted by Ram shipping conforming goods. (11/93, Law, #51, 4348)

19. Smith contracted in writing to sell Peters a used personal computer for $600. The contract did not specifically address the time for payment, place of delivery, or Peters' right to inspect the computer. Which of the following statements is correct?
a. Smith is obligated to deliver the computer to Peters' home.
b. Peters is entitled to inspect the computer before paying for it.
c. Peters may **not** pay for the computer using a personal check unless Smith agrees.
d. Smith is **not** entitled to payment until 30 days after Peters receives the computer. (11/93, Law, #56, 4353)

20. Under the Sales Article of the UCC, and unless otherwise agreed to, the seller's obligation to the buyer is to
a. Deliver the goods to the buyer's place of business
b. Hold conforming goods and give the buyer whatever notification is reasonably necessary to enable the buyer to take delivery
c. Deliver all goods called for in the contract to a common carrier
d. Set aside conforming goods for inspection by the buyer before delivery (11/95, Law, #48, 5917)

21. Jefferson Hardware ordered three hundred Ram hammers from Ajax Hardware. Ajax accepted the order in writing. On the final date allowed for delivery, Ajax discovered it did not have enough Ram hammers to fill the order. Instead, Ajax sent three hundred Strong hammers. Ajax stated on the invoice that the shipment was sent only as an accommodation. Which of the following statements is correct?
a. Ajax's note of accommodation cancels the contract between Jefferson and Ajax.
b. Jefferson's order can only be accepted by Ajax's shipment of the goods ordered.
c. Ajax's shipment of Strong hammers is a breach of contract.
d. Ajax's shipment of Strong hammers is a counter-offer and **no** contract exists between Jefferson and Ajax. (5/90, Law, #46, 0514)

22. Under the UCC Sales Article, a plaintiff who proves fraud in the formation of a contract may
a. Elect to rescind the contract and need **not** return the consideration received from the other party
b. Be entitled to rescind the contract and sue for damages resulting from fraud
c. Be entitled to punitive damages provided physical injuries resulted from the fraud
d. Rescind the contract even if there was **no** reliance on the fraudulent statement
(11/91, Law, #22, 2350)

23. Under the Sales Article of the UCC, which of the following rights is(are) available to the buyer when a seller commits an anticipatory breach of contract?

	Demand assurance of performance	*Cancel the contract*	*Collect punitive damages*
a.	Yes	Yes	Yes
b.	Yes	Yes	No
c.	Yes	No	Yes
d.	No	Yes	Yes

(11/95, Law, #47, 5916)

24. Under the Sales Article of the UCC, which of the following statements regarding liquidated damages is(are) correct?

I. The injured party may collect any amount of liquidated damages provided for in the contract.
II. The seller may retain a deposit of up to $500 when a buyer defaults even if there is no liquidated damages provision in the contract.

a. I only
b. II only
c. Both I and II
d. Neither I nor II (11/95, Law, #49, 5918)

25. Cara Fabricating Co. and Taso Corp. agreed orally that Taso would custom manufacture a compressor for Cara at a price of $120,000. After Taso completed the work at a cost of $90,000, Cara notified Taso that the compressor was no longer needed. Taso is holding the compressor and has requested payment from Cara. Taso has been unable to resell the compressor for any price. Taso incurred storage fees of $2,000. If Cara refuses to pay Taso and Taso sues Cara, the most Taso will be entitled to recover is
a. $ 90,000
b. $ 92,000
c. $120,000
d. $122,000 (11/93, Law, #57, amended, 4354)

26. Under the Sales Article of the UCC, the remedies available to a seller when a buyer breaches a contract for the sale of goods may include

	The right to resell goods identified to the contract	*The right to stop a carrier from delivering the goods*
a.	Yes	Yes
b.	Yes	No
c.	No	Yes
d.	No	No

(11/98, Law, #11, 6756)

27. Under the Sales Article of the UCC, which of the following rights is available to a seller when a buyer materially breaches a sales contract?

	Right to cancel the contract	*Right to recover damages*
a.	Yes	Yes
b.	Yes	No
c.	No	Yes
d.	No	No

(11/95, Law, #50, 5919)

28. Eagle Corporation solicited bids for various parts it used in the manufacture of jet engines. Eagle received six offers and selected the offer of Sky Corporation. The written contract specified a price for 100,000 units, delivery on June 1 at Sky's plant, with payment on July 1. On June 1, Sky had completed a 200,000 unit run of parts similar to those under contract for Eagle and various other customers. Sky had not identified the parts to specific contracts. When Eagle's truck arrived to pick up the parts on June 1, Sky refused to deliver claiming the contract price was too low. Eagle was unable to cover in a reasonable time. Its production lines were in danger of shutdown because the parts were not delivered. Eagle would probably
a. Have as its only remedy the right of replevin
b. Have the right of replevin only if Eagle tendered the purchase price on June 1
c. Have as its only remedy the right to recover dollar damages
d. Have the right to obtain specific performance
(5/90, Law, #48, 0516)

29. Larch Corp. manufactured and sold Oak a stove. The sale documents included a disclaimer of warranty for personal injury. The stove was defective. It exploded causing serious injuries to Oak's spouse. Larch was notified one week after the explosion. Under the UCC Sales Article, which of the following statements concerning Larch's liability for personal injury to Oak's spouse would be correct?
a. Larch **cannot** be liable because of a lack of privity with Oak's spouse.
b. Larch will **not** be liable because of a failure to give proper notice.
c. Larch will be liable because the disclaimer was **not** a disclaimer of all liability.
d. Larch will be liable because liability for personal injury **cannot** be disclaimed.
(5/94, Law, #44, 4799)

30. To establish a cause of action based on strict liability in tort for personal injuries that result from the use of a defective product, one of the elements the injured party must prove is that the seller
a. Was aware of the defect in the product
b. Sold the product to the injured party
c. Failed to exercise due care
d. Sold the product in a defective condition
(11/95, Law, #44, 5913)

Problem 35-2 ADDITIONAL MULTIPLE CHOICE QUESTIONS (30 to 40 minutes)

31. Under the Sales Article of the UCC, in an auction announced in explicit terms to be without reserve, when may an auctioneer withdraw the goods put up for sale?

I. At any time until the auctioneer announces completion of the sale
II. If **no** bid is made within a reasonable time

a. I only
b. II only
c. Either I or II
d. Neither I nor II (R/02, Law, #17, 7127)

32. Under the Sales Article of the UCC, which **two** of the following statements are correct regarding a seller's obligation under a F.O.B. destination contract?
a. The seller is required to arrange for the buyer to pick up the conforming goods at a specified destination.
b. The seller is required to tender delivery of conforming goods at a specified destination.
c. The title passes on tender at destination.
d. The seller is required to tender delivery of conforming goods at the buyer's place of business.
e. The seller is required to tender delivery of conforming goods to a carrier who delivers to a destination specified by the buyer.
(R/02, Law, #16, amended, 7126)

33 On May 2, Mason orally contracted with Acme Appliances to buy for $480 a washer and dryer for household use. Mason and the Acme salesperson agreed that delivery would be made on July 2. On May 5, Mason telephoned Acme and requested that the delivery date be moved to June 2. The Acme salesperson agreed with this request. On June 2, Acme failed to deliver the washer and dryer to Mason because of an inventory shortage. Acme advised Mason that it would deliver the appliances on July 2 as originally agreed. Mason believes that Acme has breached its agreement with Mason. Acme contends that its agreement to deliver on June 2 was not binding. Acme's contention is
a. Correct, because Mason is **not** a merchant and was buying the appliances for household use
b. Correct, because the agreement to change the delivery date was **not** in writing
c. Incorrect, because the agreement to change the delivery date was binding
d. Incorrect, because Acme's agreement to change the delivery date is a firm offer that **cannot** be withdrawn by Acme (5/92, Law, #54, 2867)

34. Under the Sales Article of the UCC, which of the following statements is correct?
a. The obligations of the parties to the contract must be performed in good faith.
b. Merchants and nonmerchants are treated alike.
c. The contract must involve the sale of goods for a price of more than $500.
d. None of the provisions of the UCC may be disclaimed by agreement. (11/94, Law, #50, 5227)

35. Rowe Corp. purchased goods from Stair Co. that were shipped C.O.D. Under the Sales Article of the UCC, which of the following rights does Rowe have?
a. The right to inspect the goods before paying
b. The right to possession of the goods before paying
c. The right to reject nonconforming goods
d. The right to delay payment for a reasonable period of time (11/94, Law, #56, 5233)

36. Under the Sales Article of the UCC, a firm offer will be created only if the
a. Offer states the time period during which it will remain open.
b. Offer is made by a merchant in a signed writing.
c. Offeree gives some form of consideration.
d. Offeree is a merchant. (11/95, Law, #41, 5910)

Items 37 and 38 are based on the following information:

On May 2, Lace Corp., an appliance wholesaler, offered to sell appliances worth $3,000 to Parco, Inc., a household appliances retailer. The offer was signed by Lace's president, and provided that it would not be withdrawn before June 1. It also included the shipping terms: "F.O.B.—Parco's warehouse." On May 29, Parco mailed an acceptance of Lace's offer. Lace received the acceptance June 2.

37. Which of the following statements is correct if Lace sent Parco a telegram revoking its offer, and Parco received the telegram on May 25?
a. A contract was formed on May 2.
b. Lace's revocation effectively terminated its offer on May 25.
c. Lace's revocation was ineffective because the offer could **not** be revoked before June 1.
d. No contract was formed because Lace received Parco's acceptance after June 1. (5/92, Law, #51, 2864)

38. If Lace inadvertently ships the wrong appliances to Parco and Parco rejects them two days after receipt, title to the goods will
a. Pass to Parco when they are identified to the contract
b. Pass to Parco when they are shipped
c. Remain with Parco until the goods are returned to Lace
d. Revert to Lace when they are rejected by Parco (5/92, Law, #53, 2866)

39. On September 10, Bell Corp. entered into a contract to purchase 50 lamps from Glow Manufacturing. Bell prepaid 40% of the purchase price. Glow became insolvent on September 19 before segregating, in its inventory, the lamps to be delivered to Bell. Bell will **not** be able to recover the lamps because
a. Bell is regarded as a merchant.
b. The lamps were **not** identified to the contract.
c. Glow became insolvent fewer than 10 days after receipt of Bell's prepayment.
d. Bell did **not** pay the full price at the time of purchase. (5/90, Law, #47, 0515)

40. Pulse Corp. maintained a warehouse where it stored its manufactured goods. Pulse received an order from Star. Shortly after Pulse identified the goods to be shipped to Star, but before moving them to the loading dock, a fire destroyed the warehouse and its contents. With respect to the goods, which of the following statements is correct?
a. Pulse has title but **no** insurable interest.
b. Star has title and an insurable interest.
c. Pulse has title and an insurable interest.
d. Star has title but **no** insurable interest. (5/90, Law, #45, 0513)

41. Which of the following statements applies to a sale on approval under the UCC Sales Article?
a. Both the buyer and seller must be merchants.
b. The buyer must be purchasing the goods for resale.
c. Risk of loss for the goods passes to the buyer when the goods are accepted after the trial period.
d. Title to the goods passes to the buyer on delivery of the goods to the buyer. (11/93, Law, #49, 4346)

42. Under the Sales Article of the UCC, the warranty of title
a. Provides that the seller cannot disclaim the warranty if the sale is made to a bona fide purchaser for value
b. Provides that the seller deliver the goods free from any lien of which the buyer lacked knowledge when the contract was made
c. Applies only if it is in writing and signed by the seller
d. Applies only if the seller is a merchant (11/95, Law, #43, 5912)

43. Which of the following factors result(s) in an express warranty with respect to a sale of goods?

I. The seller's description of the goods as part of the basis of the bargain
II. The seller selects goods knowing the buyer's intended use

a. I only
b. II only
c. Both I and II
d. Neither I nor II (5/92, Law, #60, 2873)

44. Under the Sales Article of the UCC, most goods sold by merchants are covered by certain warranties. An example of an express warranty would be a warranty of
a. Usage of trade
b. Fitness for a particular purpose
c. Merchantability
d. Conformity of goods to sample (11/97, Law, #13, 6511)

45. Which of the following conditions must be met for an implied warranty of fitness for a particular purpose to arise in connection with a sale of goods?

I. The warranty must be in writing.
II. The seller must know that the buyer was relying on the seller in selecting the goods.

a. I only
b. II only
c. Both I and II
d. Neither I nor II (5/92, Law, #55, 2868)

46. Under the UCC Sales Article, an action for breach of the implied warranty of merchantability by a party who sustains personal injuries may be successful against the seller of the product only when
a. The seller is a merchant of the product involved.
b. An action based on negligence can also be successfully maintained.
c. The injured party is in privity of contract with the seller.
d. An action based on strict liability in tort can also be successfully maintained. (5/92, Law, #57, 2870)

47. Under the UCC Sales Article, if a buyer wrongfully rejects goods, the aggrieved seller may

	Resell the goods and sue for damages	*Cancel the agreement*
a.	Yes	Yes
b.	Yes	No
c.	No	Yes
d.	No	No

(11/89, Law, #52, 8017)

48. Under the Sales Article of the UCC, which of the following events will release the buyer from all its obligations under a sales contract?
a. Destruction of the goods after risk of loss passed to the buyer
b. Impracticability of delivery under the terms of the contract
c. Anticipatory repudiation by the buyer that is retracted before the seller cancels the contract
d. Refusal of the seller to give written assurance of performance when reasonably demanded by the buyer (11/94, Law, #55, 5232)

49. Under the Sales Article of the UCC, which of the following circumstances will relieve a buyer from the obligation of accepting a tender or delivery of goods?

I. If the goods do **not** meet the buyer's needs at the time of the tender or delivery
II. If the goods at the time of the tender or delivery do not exactly conform to the requirements of the contract

a. I only
b. II only
c. Both I and II
d. Neither I nor II (R/02, Law, #14, 7124)

50. On February 15, Mazur Corp. contracted to sell 1,000 bushels of wheat to Good Bread, Inc. at $6.00 per bushel with delivery to be made on June 23. On June 1, Good advised Mazur that it would not accept or pay for the wheat. On June 2, Mazur sold the wheat to another customer at the market price of $5.00 per bushel. Mazur had advised Good that it intended to resell the wheat. Which of the following statements is correct?
a. Mazur can successfully sue Good for the difference between the resale price and the contract price.
b. Mazur can resell the wheat only after June 23.
c. Good can retract its anticipatory breach at any time before June 23.
d. Good can successfully sue Mazur for specific performance. (5/92, Law, #56, 2869)

SIMULATION

Problem 35-3 (20 to 30 minutes)

On February 1, Grand Corp., a manufacturer of custom cabinets, contracted in writing with Axle Co., a kitchen contractor, to sell Axle 100 unique, custom-designed kitchen cabinets for $250,000. Axle had contracted to install the cabinets in a luxury condominium complex. The contract provided that the cabinets were to be ready for delivery by April 15 and were to be shipped F.O.B. sellers loading dock. On April 15, Grand had 85 cabinets complete and delivered them, together with 15 standard cabinets, to the trucking company for delivery to Axle. Grand faxed Axle a copy of the shipping invoice, listing the 15 standard cabinets. On May 1, before reaching Axle, the truck was involved in a collision and all the cabinets were damaged beyond repair. (Editors, 5407)

For items 1 through 5, determine the correct statement (A, B, or C) from within each group of statements.

Statements	Answer
1. A. The contract between Grand and Axle was a shipment contract. B. The contract between Grand and Axle was a destination contract. C. The contract between Grand and Axle was a consignment contract.	
2. A. The risk of loss for the 85 custom cabinets passed to Axle on April 15. B. The risk of loss for the 100 cabinets passed to Axle on April 15. C. The risk of loss for the 100 cabinets remained with Grand.	
3. A. The contract between Grand and Axle was invalid because no delivery date was stated. B. The contract between Grand and Axle was voidable because Grand shipped only 85 custom cabinets. C. The contract between Grand and Axle was void because the goods were destroyed.	
4. A. Grand's shipment of the standard cabinets was a breach of the contract with Axle. B. Grand would not be considered to have breached the contract until Axle rejected the standard cabinets. C. Grand made a counteroffer by shipping the standard cabinets.	
5. A. Axle is entitled to specific performance from Grand because of the unique nature of the goods. B. Axle is required to purchase substitute goods (cover) and is entitled to the difference in cost from Grand. C. Axle is entitled to punitive damages because of Grand's intentional shipment of non-conforming goods.	

Dodd performed exterminating services on behalf of Salam. Dodd suffered permanent injuries as a result of inhaling one of the chemicals used by Salam. This occurred after Dodd sprayed the chemical in a restaurant that Salam regularly services. Dodd was under the supervision of one of Salam's district managers and was trained by Salam to perform exterminating services following certain procedures, which he did. Later that day, several patrons who ate at the restaurant also suffered permanent injuries as a result of inhaling the chemical. The chemical was manufactured by Ace Chemical Corp. and sold and delivered to Salam in a closed container. It was not altered by Salam. It has now been determined that the chemical was defectively manufactured and the injuries suffered by Dodd and the restaurant patrons were a direct result of the defect.

Salam has complied with an applicable compulsory workers' compensation statute by obtaining an insurance policy from Spear Insurance Co.

As a result of the foregoing, Dodd sued Ace based on strict liability in tort.

Write a memo to your supervisor, discussing the merits of the action commenced by Dodd indicating the likely outcome and your reasons therefore.

Scenario | Statements | Communication | Research

Research Question: What code section and subsection, if applicable, provides guidance as to who is responsible for payment of estate taxes?

Section & Subsection Answer: §_____ (___)

Solution 35-1 MULTIPLE CHOICE ANSWERS

Overview

1. (d) UCC 2-306 provides that a contract for the sale of goods will not be enforceable if the acceptance is open, since if this term is left open there is no basis for determining contract existence. UCC 2-305 provides that where the price term is left open, the courts will determine a reasonable price at the time of delivery. UCC 2-308 provides that where no delivery terms are stated, the buyer will normally take delivery at the seller's place of business. The quantity may be contingent on seller's production.

2. (d) A firm offer is a signed written offer by a merchant to buy or sell goods. A firm offer is irrevocable for a reasonable or stated time, not to exceed three months.

3. (c) Art's contention is not correct. Under the Statute of Frauds as it applies to the Uniform Commercial Code, the contract need not be in writing. Generally, a contract for the sale of goods for a price equal to or greater than $500 is unenforceable unless there is a written memorandum signed by the party to be charged. However, if an otherwise valid contract does not satisfy this general requirement, the oral contract is still enforceable in the following case: if the goods are to be specially manufactured for the buyer and are not suitable for sale to others in the ordinary course of the seller's business, and the seller, before notice of repudiation is received and under circumstances that reasonably indicate that the goods are for the buyer, has made either a substantial beginning of their manufacture or commitments for their procurement.

4. (d) Title cannot pass until goods are identified. In the absence of explicit agreement, if the goods are not existing and identified at the time of the contract, identification occurs when goods are designated by the seller as goods to which the contract refers, e.g., by shipping or marking them. In a sale or return sale, risk of loss is borne by the buyer while the goods are in the buyer's possession and during the return of the goods to the seller.

5. (c) Because the shipment was sent F.O.B. purchaser's loading dock, this is a destination contract and risk of loss passes when the goods are tendered at the purchaser's loading dock. Risk of loss and title passes when the goods are delivered to the carrier under the terms of F.O.B. shipping point. Risk of loss remains with the seller until the goods are accepted by the purchaser in a sales on approval conditional sale.

6. (c) UCC 2 does not eliminate the deposited acceptance (or "mail-box") rule, which states that a properly dispatched acceptance is valid upon dispatch. Both a faxed and a mailed acceptance would be valid means of acceptance, and in each case acceptance occurred upon dispatch.

7. (d) A merchant is one who either deals in goods similar to the ones involved in the transaction or who, by occupation, represents that s/he has particular knowledge or skill relating to the practices or goods involved in the transaction [UCC 2-104 (1)]. "Good faith" in the case of a merchant means honesty in fact and the observance of reasonable commercial standards of fair dealing in the trade. Good faith requirements need not be included in the written contract.

8. (a) The Statute of Frauds requires that a contract for goods of $500 or more be in writing. UCC 2-207, however, provides that in a contract between merchants, the Statute of Frauds is satisfied if a written confirmation is sent within a reasonable time. The confirmation must be received by the other party who knows or should know the confirmation's contents. If the recipient merchant fails to object to the confirmation's contents within a reasonable time, they will be bound to the contract.

Title

9. (b) Title cannot pass until goods are identified in the contract. Title passes in a shipment contract at the time and place of delivery to a carrier for shipment, which would be before the goods are tendered to or accepted or paid for by the buyer.

10. (d) The warranty of title and against infringement may be disclaimed only by specific language or circumstances that give the buyer reason to know that the buyer is not receiving full title. The phrase "as is" may disclaim implied warranties, such as a warranty of merchantability, but not express warranties and the warranty of title and against infringement. An agreement to modify or rescind a sales contract need not be supported by consideration to be binding; however, the seller's warranties may not be unilaterally disclaimed.

Risk of Loss

11. (a) Under the Sales Article of the UCC and the CISG, absent specific terms in an international sales shipment contract, risk of loss passes to the buyer when the goods are duly delivered to the carrier. Identification of the goods is only a step towards the passing of title. To the depth tested by the examiners, the CISG is the same as the UCC. Mention of this convention is an attempt by the examiners at distraction.

12. (b) Under the Sales Article of the UCC, the contract's shipping terms would be most important in determining who bears the risk of loss. The method of shipping the goods and how the goods were destroyed is irrelevant. Although title and risk of loss frequently pass together, the UCC does not require that they do so, thus a person may hold title and not have risk of loss.

13. (a) Risk of loss passes upon *tender* of delivery when the seller is not a merchant. If the seller was a merchant, risk of loss would pass upon the buyer's receipt of the goods. In this problem, the facts clearly specify that Wool is not a merchant in the goods being sold, so we can determine that risk of loss passed to Bond upon tender of delivery.

Warranties

14. (b) Entrusting the possession of goods to a merchant who deals in goods of that kind in the ordinary course of business gives that merchant the power to transfer all of the bailor's rights to a buyer who purchases in the ordinary course of the merchant's business. While the former owner (a bailor) has a claim against the merchant, the bailor has clothed the merchant with the apparent authority to sell the goods and, thus, has no claim against the subsequent purchaser. The clerk's awareness or negligence is irrelevant. As an apparent agent, Grill may convey good title.

15. (c) An express warranty that goods conform to the seller's promise is created by an affirmation of fact or promise made by the seller to the buyer that relates to the goods and becomes part of the basis of the bargain. The "warranty of marketability" is not used commonly. The "warranty of merchantability" refers to goods that meet minimum requirements including that they are fit for the ordinary purposes for which such goods are used. This would apply if the home-use dishwasher was installed in a private residence, but not a restaurant. A warranty against infringement is a merchant's warrant that the goods are delivered free of another party's claim of patent or trademark infringement.

16. (a) UCC 2-312 provides that all sellers of goods implicitly warrant that the title they are transferring is good. The implied warranty of title can only be disclaimed with very specific language; a general disclaimer is insufficient. In this instance the warranty of title was breached and not properly disclaimed. A merchant can disclaim this as well as other warranties. The general disclaimer used by Ocean was not specific enough to disclaim the implied warranty of title. Kidd was the rightful owner. The surrender of the boat by Vick to Kidd will not affect Vick's rights against Ocean.

17. (c) An implied warranty of merchantability automatically arises in all sales of goods made by a merchant who deals in such goods. Handy Hardware did not specify a use for the goods or rely on the seller's judgment in making the purchase, so there is no implied warranty of fitness for a particular purpose. An implied warranty of title arises automatically in most sales contracts. There is no evidence to the contrary in this problem, so we can assume that the warranty of title does exist.

Performance

18. (a) The sale of goods is governed by the UCC which states that acceptance occurs if the response indicates a definite acceptance of the offer, even if the response includes different or additional terms. Handy's purchase order was an offer to purchase goods from Ram. When Ram shipped the order he effectively accepted Handy's offer even though he did change the terms of the sale when he shipped sockets of a different model number. An offeree's additional terms are considered proposals and are subject to ratification by the offeror, but they do not preclude an acceptance. The offer does not specify that a written acceptance was required.

19. (b) Unless otherwise agreed between the parties, the buyer normally has a right to inspect the goods before acceptance (there are certain minor exceptions, such as a C.O.D. purchase). Even if you have accepted, you can rightfully reject after inspection if done within a reasonable time. The seller's location is assumed when the contract is silent on the point of delivery. When a contract is silent as to the method of payment, a check is considered an acceptable form of payment. Payment is assumed to be due immediately unless specified in the contract.

20. (b) Under the Sales Article of the UCC, and unless otherwise agreed to, the seller's obligation to the buyer is to hold conforming goods and give the buyer necessary notice to take delivery. The UCC does not require, absent an agreement, that the goods be held for the buyer's inspection prior to delivery, that the goods be delivered to the buyer's place of business, or that all goods be delivered to a common carrier.

Remedies for Breach

21. (c) The perfect tender rule (UCC 2-601) has not been complied with by Ajax, and thus a breach has occurred. Of course, Jefferson can always decide to accept Ajax's attempted accommodation.

22. (b) Under the UCC Sales Article, if fraud in the inducement (i.e., in the formation of a contract) is present, the resulting contract is *voidable* at the option of the defrauded party, thereby, allowing that party to rescind the contract and sue for damages. The plaintiff may elect to rescind the contract, but in doing so must return any consideration received. Punitive damages normally are not allowed. There must have been reliance on the fraudulent statement.

23. (b) Under the Sales Article of the UCC, when a seller commits an anticipatory breach of contract, the buyer can demand assurance of performance (UCC 2-609) or cancel the contract (UCC 2-610). Punitive damages are never available in breach of contract actions.

24. (b) UCC 2-718 provides that a seller may retain a deposit of up to $500 when a buyer defaults even if there is no liquidated damages provision in the contract. Otherwise, an injured party may collect a reasonable amount of liquidated damages.

25. (d) Under the UCC, if the goods are specially manufactured goods, the seller is entitled to the contract price plus incidental damages incurred relating to the sale (storage, etc.).

26. (a) Under the Sales Article of the UCC, when a buyer breaches a contract for the sale of goods, the seller has the right to resell the goods identified to the contract and the right to stoppage of delivery of goods in the possession of a carrier or other bailee. The seller could also cancel the contract or choose to recover damages without resale.

27. (a) Under the Sales Article of the UCC, a seller has both the right to cancel the contract and the right to recover damages when the buyer materially breaches a sales contract.

28. (d) Replevin is unavailable because the goods have not been identified to specific contracts [UCC 2-716(3)]. Specific performance is always available when goods are unique or there are "other

proper circumstances" [UCC 2-716(1)], so dollar damages may not be the only remedy.

Product Liability

29. (d) The liability for personal injury is not subject to disclaimer, exclusion, or modification by contractual agreement. Under strict liability, the manufacturer of a product sold in a defective or unreasonably dangerous condition is liable for personal injuries and property damage regardless of privity. There was no failure to give proper notice (i.e., notice was given within a reasonable period). Although, Larch Corp. will be liable, the liability results due to the inability to disclaim any liability for personal injury rather than the inadequacy of the disclaimer.

30. (d) In order to prove strict liability in tort for personal injuries resulting from a defective product, the injured party must show that the product was sold in a defective condition. Knowledge and due care are irrelevant in strict liability actions, and any seller in the chain of distribution may be strictly liable for consumer injuries.

Solution 35-2 ADDITIONAL MULTIPLE CHOICE ANSWERS

Overview

31. (b) Auctioneers' statements are invitations to negotiate. Bids are offers; generally, bids may be withdrawn before acceptance. Ordinarily, an auctioneer may withdraw goods from sale if not satisfied with the bids made. An auction without reserve is defined as one where property will be sold to the highest bidder. In an auction without reserve, after the auctioneer calls for bids on property, that article or lot cannot be withdrawn unless no bid is made within a reasonable time.

32. (b, c) Both responses are required for full credit. Tender refers to the requirement that the seller put and hold conforming goods at the buyer's disposition and give the buyer any notification reasonably necessary to take delivery. If the place of destination is named, the contract is a "destination contract." Under F.O.B. destination terms, the seller must bear the risk and cost of transporting goods to the named destination. Title passes on tender at the named destination.

33. (c) Acme's contention that the agreement to change the delivery date was not binding is incorrect because an oral agreement that modifies an existing contract for the sale of goods does not need new consideration to be binding. Since the contract is for the sale of goods for a price less than $500, the Statute of Frauds does not apply, and the oral modification is enforceable.

34. (a) UCC 1-102(3) imposes an obligation on the parties to contract in good faith. Merchants are frequently treated differently under UCC 2 provisions. UCC 2 covers contracts for goods regardless of the contract price, and the UCC permits the parties to a contract to disclaim many of the UCC's provisions.

35. (c) UCC 2-513(1) provides that a buyer has a right to inspect goods before payment or acceptance occurs. UCC 2-513(3) states that where there is a C.O.D. term, the buyer is not entitled to inspect the goods before payment; however, the buyer still retains the right to inspect before acceptance. A C.O.D. term requires the buyer to pay for the goods immediately upon delivery and before obtaining possession.

36. (b) UCC 2-205 states that a merchant creates a firm offer by making an offer in a signed writing. If the offer does not state the time period for which it is open, a period of 90 days will be assumed. It is not necessary for the offeree to be a merchant, nor is it necessary that the offeree give any consideration.

37. (c) This problem illustrates the concept of a "firm offer." A firm offer is a signed written offer by a merchant to buy or sell goods in which the merchant gives assurance that the offer will be held open. Such an offer is irrevocable, even though it is not supported by consideration, for the time stated or for a reasonable period of time. However, in no event may this time period be longer than three months.

Title

38. (d) The buyer's reasonable rejection of the goods causes title to the goods to revert back to the seller.

39. (b) Under UCC 2-502(1), buyer Bell Corp. has a right to the goods if it has "a special property" under UCC 2-501. Without an identification of existing goods, no such "special property" arises. Therefore, Bell's rights do not include obtaining the goods themselves after Glow Manufacturing became insolvent.

40. (c) Under UCC 2-401(2), title passes to the buyer when the seller completes her/his delivery of the goods. Since the goods did not even get to the

place of shipment, title remained with Pulse. Under UCC 2-501(2), seller Pulse retained an insurable interest.

Risk of Loss

41. (c) Under the UCC Sales Article, a sale on approval is not a sale until the buyer accepts the offer. Until the buyer accepts, the risk of loss and title remain with the seller. Once the buyer accepts, risk of loss and title pass to the buyer. The UCC covers all sales of goods and is not limited to transactions between two merchants. The goods do not have to be for resale. Title does not pass until the offer of sale has been accepted.

Warranties

42. (b) Under UCC 2 an implied warranty of title is created anytime a good is sold, regardless of whether the seller is a merchant or whether there is a writing. The implied warranty of title may be disclaimed, but where it exists it provides that the seller deliver the goods free from any lien of which the buyer lacked knowledge.

43. (a) An express warranty may be created in several ways. One is by any description of the goods which is made part of the basis of the bargain when such description creates a warranty that the goods will conform to the description (Part I). The fact that the seller selects goods knowing the buyer's intended use (Part II) concerns the implied warranty of fitness for a particular purpose and not the creation of an express warranty.

44. (d) An express warranty may be created by any sample or model that is made part of the basis of the bargain. Fitness for a particular purpose and merchantability are implied warranties under the UCC. Usage of trade would also be an implied warranty when both parties have knowledge of a trade custom.

45. (b) The warranty of fitness for a particular purpose is created when the seller has actual or constructive knowledge of the particular purpose for which the goods are required, and also knows that the buyer is relying on the skill and judgment of the seller to select and furnish suitable goods. As this is an implied warranty, there is no requirement that it be in writing.

46. (a) UCC 2-314 implies a warranty of merchantability when the seller is a merchant with respect to the goods sold.

Remedies for Breach

47. (a) Under the UCC, if a buyer wrongfully rejects goods, the aggrieved seller may resell and recover damages *or* cancel the contract.

48. (d) UCC 2-609 provides that if reasonable grounds for insecurity arise concerning the performance of either party, the other party may in writing demand adequate assurance of performance. If the other party fails to provide the assurance within a reasonable period of time, then the party's failure to respond may be treated as a repudiation of the contract. The party requesting the assurance may then suspend their own performance. A buyer would not be released of their obligations if delivery has become impractical, nor if the goods are destroyed after risk of loss has passed to them. A repudiating buyer may retract their repudiation until the time before the next performance is due, unless the seller has changed her/his/its position or considered the repudiation to be final.

49. (b) Tender refers to the requirement that the seller put and hold conforming goods at the buyer's disposition and give the buyer any notification reasonably necessary to take delivery. If the seller delivers nonconforming goods, the buyer may reject or accept the goods (UCC 2-601). There is no general requirement that goods meet the buyer's needs at the tender time; because buyers' needs could fluctuate, such a requirement would place an unduly burdensome load on sellers.

50. (a) An anticipatory repudiation occurs when either party to a contract demonstrates an intention not to perform an obligation not yet due, or an action which renders that performance impossible. In case of one party's (Good Bread, Inc.) anticipatory repudiation, the other party (Mazur) may resort to any remedy available for breach. One remedy available to the seller is to sell the goods and to recover damages. Damages are defined in this case as the difference between the resale price and the contract price.

PERFORMANCE BY SUBTOPICS

Each category below parallels a subtopic covered in Chapter 35. Record the number and percentage of questions you correctly answered in each subtopic area.

Overview

Question #	Correct √
1	
2	
3	
4	
5	
6	
7	
8	
# Questions	8
# Correct	________
% Correct	________

Title

Question #	Correct √
9	
10	
# Questions	2
# Correct	________
% Correct	________

Risk of Loss

Question #	Correct √
11	
12	
13	
# Questions	3
# Correct	________
% Correct	________

Warranties

Question #	Correct √
14	
15	
16	
17	
# Questions	4
# Correct	________
% Correct	________

Performance

Question #	Correct √
18	
19	
20	
# Questions	3
# Correct	________
% Correct	________

Remedies for Breach

Question #	Correct √
21	
22	
23	
24	
25	
26	
27	
28	
# Questions	8
# Correct	________
% Correct	________

Product Liability

Question #	Correct √
29	
30	
# Questions	2
# Correct	________
% Correct	________

SIMULATION SOLUTION

Solution 35-3 Breach & Liability

Statements (4 points)

1. A

Under the Sales Article of the Uniform Commercial Code (UCC), if the place of shipment is named, as "F.O.B. Seller's Location," the contract is a shipment contract.

2. C

Where a contract for goods includes an F.O.B. shipment term, risk of loss usually passes from seller to buyer when the goods are delivered to the seller's loading dock. However, where a delivery fails to conform to the contract so as to result in a breach, the risk of loss remains on the seller.

3. B

The failure of a seller to ship conforming goods constitutes a breach of contract and renders the contract voidable. The Sales Article of the Uniform Commercial Code (UCC) states that if goods identified to a contract are damaged without the fault of either party before the risk of loss passes to the buyer, the contract is avoided if the loss is total (UCC 2-613). However, since the goods do not conform, this is irrelevant. Under the Sales Article, failure to include a delivery date in a contract for the sale of goods will not render the contract invalid.

4. A

The UCC Sales Article states that a shipment of non-conforming goods constitutes a breach of contract. Rejection by the buyer is not a necessary component of the seller's breach. A shipment of nonconforming goods does not result in a counteroffer.

5. A

The UCC Sales Article provides that specific performance is an appropriate remedy when the goods are unique (UCC 2-716). Where a contract is breached, the UCC does not require a non-breaching buyer to purchase substitute goods, since substitute goods may not be available, especially when the goods are unique. Punitive damages are never available in an action for breach of contract.

Communication (5 points)

To: A. Supervisor
From: A. Junior
Re: Dodd Action Against Ace

Generally, in order to establish a cause of action based on **strict liability in tort,** it must be shown that: the product was in **defective condition** when it left the possession or control of the seller; the product was **unreasonably dangerous** to the consumer or user; the **cause** of the consumer's or user's **injury** was the defect; the seller engaged in the **business** of **selling** such a product; and the product was one which the seller **expected** to, and, **did** reach the consumer or user **without substantial changes** in the condition in which it was sold.

Dodd's action against Ace based on strict liability in tort will be successful. Under the facts of this case, Ace will be liable based on strict liability in tort because all of the elements necessary to state such a cause of action have been met. The fact that Dodd is entitled to **workers' compensation** benefits does **not preclude** Dodd from recovering based on **strict liability** in tort from a **third party** (Ace).

Research (1 point)

IRC Section Answer: §2001(a)

Code §2001(a) states, "Liability for payment. The tax imposed by this chapter [CHAPTER 11—ESTATE TAX] shall be paid by the executor."

Wondering how to find 20 hours a week for study time?

Robert Monette used this method to find 20 hours a week to study while working 40 hours a week. (Ask a customer service representative about a copy of Bob's demo video, *How to Pass the CPA Exam.*) Notice how this plan leaves most of the weekend free, ensuring time for you to take care of yourself, spend time with your family, meet with friends and, in general, take care of your other commitments.

Lunch hours, Monday through Friday	5 hours
Three hours, after work, Monday through Thursday	12 hours
Three hours, Saturday morning	3 hours
Sunday, total break from studying	0 hours
Weekly total	20 hours

This plan may work for you, or it may not. Consider Bob's plan and adapt it to your situation. For example, perhaps you prefer to study an hour before work Tuesday through Thursday, and relax on Saturday as well as Sunday.

Also consider how you use time. Listening to audio lectures could transform an hour of radio listening into an hour of study time. Do you have a 30-minute commute to and from work? That could add up to 5 hours in a work week. Do you jog three times a week? That could be study time as well as exercise time.

Remember, with the techniques and information in your material,

A passing score is well within reach!

CHAPTER 36

NEGOTIABLE INSTRUMENTS & DOCUMENTS OF TITLE

EXAM COVERAGE: The business law portion of the Regulation section of the CPA exam is designated by the examiners to be 20-25 percent of the section's point value. More information about point distribution and information eligible to be tested is included in the **Practical Advice** section of this volume.

CHAPTER 36

NEGOTIABLE INSTRUMENTS & DOCUMENTS OF TITLE

I. Negotiable Instruments

A. Overview

Negotiable instruments are used to facilitate the transfer and payment of money in lieu of the money itself and to extend credit. There is a significant difference in the case of transferability of a negotiable instrument as opposed to a nonnegotiable instrument. The former is covered by the UCC while the latter is governed by the contract law of assignments. Furthermore, negotiable instruments may be transferred by negotiation (the usual case) or by assignment (occurs when the transfer falls short of a "negotiation"). Nonnegotiable instruments can be transferred only by assignment. The superiority of "negotiation" as compared to assignment can be illustrated in Exhibit 1.

Exhibit 1 ▸ Comparison of Assignment & Negotiation

ASSIGNMENT	NEGOTIATION
• Nonnegotiable instruments (e.g., contract rights) cannot be assigned if the contract right states that attempted assignments are "void."	• Negotiable instruments are fully transferable; in some cases, by delivery alone; in others, by indorsement and delivery.
• In an assignment, the assignee (person receiving the property) can take no greater interest than was owned by the assignor (person transferring the property). For example, if A steals a car and sells it to C, C can obtain no title to the car, even if C was an innocent purchaser for fair value.	• In a negotiable instrument transfer, the holder (transferee) can acquire greater rights in the property transferred than were possessed by the transferor. For example, if C was a holder in due course of a stolen negotiable instrument signed in blank, C's title would be superior to the original owner's title because the instrument was negotiable by transfer alone.
• In an assignment, the assignee takes the instrument subject to any defenses available against the assignor.	• In a transfer of a negotiable instrument, a holder in due course generally takes free of defenses available against the transferor.
• In an assignment, the assignee must give notice to the obligor (payor) in order to protect her/himself from defenses the obligor may acquire prior to notice of the assignment.	• In a negotiable instrument transfer, the holder in due course generally takes free of defenses regardless of when they arose.

1. Ambiguities

a. **Instrument Type** If there is doubt as to whether an instrument is a draft or a note, the holder may treat it as either. If the drawer and drawee of a draft are the same person, the holder may treat it as a note.

b. **Terms** Handwritten terms control typewritten and preprinted terms. Typewritten terms control preprinted terms. Words control figures, unless the words are ambiguous.

c. **Interest Provision** A provision for interest, unless otherwise specified, means interest at the legal judgment rate obtained at the place of payment. Interest runs from the date of the instrument or, if none, the date of issue.

d. **Signators' Liability** Two or more persons signing an instrument as part of one transaction in the capacity of maker, acceptor, drawer, or indorser and as part of the same transaction are **jointly and severally liable,** unless the instrument specifies otherwise, even if the words "I promise to pay" appear.

e. **Time Extension** Consent to the extension of time for payment authorizes one extension not longer than the original period, unless otherwise specified.

2. **Date** An instrument may be undated, antedated, or postdated without affecting negotiability. It is payable at the time fixed on the instrument if the instrument is payable on demand or payable at a fixed period after date.

3. **Payment Place** The omission of a place for payment does not render an instrument nonnegotiable.

   a. **Payable Through a Bank** An instrument "payable through" a bank designates that bank as a collecting bank to make presentment, but does not grant the bank authority to pay.

   b. **Payable at a Bank** An instrument "payable at" a bank is, in some states, equivalent to a draft drawn on the bank, but in most states, it is merely the designation of a place of payment.

4. **Multiple Payees**

   a. **Alternative** If an instrument is payable to the order of two or more payees in the alternative ("to A or B"), the rights with respect to that instrument may be exercised by any of them who has possession.

   b. **Joint** If an instrument is payable to the order of two or more payees **not** in the alternative ("to A and B"), any rights as to the instrument must be exercised by all of them together (thus, **both** A and B must endorse the instrument to obtain payment).

5. **Incomplete Instruments** A signed instrument that is incomplete in any necessary respect (e.g., amount payable) is unenforceable until completed. If completed in accordance with authority to complete, it is effective as completed. If completed in an unauthorized manner, the completion is treated as a material alteration. The burden of showing lack of authority is on the person asserting it.

6. **Modification of Terms** A transferor and a transferee of a negotiable instrument may modify its terms by a written agreement executed as part of the same transaction. Subsequent holders are bound by the agreement unless they are holders in due course (HDC) without notice of the modifying agreement.

7. **Alteration** An unauthorized change in an instrument that modifies the obligation of any party, such as alteration of the number or relationship of parties or completion of an incomplete instrument in any manner except as authorized. Discharge because of alteration occurs only in the case of an alteration fraudulently made.

8. **Contract Rights** An interest that is nonnegotiable, but usually is assignable.

9. **Letter of Credit** A nonnegotiable instrument that is an engagement (usually by a bank) made at the request of a bank customer that states that the bank issuer will make payments and otherwise honor its customer's obligations. The person in whose favor the letter is prepared may then draw on the bank from the account of the customer who procured the letter.

10. **Statute of Limitations** An action to enforce a liability imposed by Article 4 (*Bank Deposits and Collections*) must be commenced within three years after the cause of action accrued.

B. Draft

A written order from one person (the **drawer**) directing a second person (the **drawee**) to pay a sum certain in money to the order of a third person (the **payee**) or to the order of the bearer of the draft. An instrument is a draft if it is an **order.**

1. **Sight & Time Drafts** A draft may be a **sight** draft (payable on delivery and presentment to the drawer) or a **time** draft (payable within a certain time).

2. **Acceptance** The drawee's signed engagement to honor a draft as presented. It must be written on the draft and becomes operative when completed by delivery or notification.

   a. **Trade Acceptance** A draft drawn by the seller-drawer on the buyer-drawee that is payable to the seller at some certain future date in the amount of the purchase price. The seller transmits the draft to the buyer for "acceptance," that is, for the buyer's signed engagement written on the draft to honor the draft as presented.

   b. **Banker's Acceptance** Similar to trade acceptances **except** that the check (draft drawn on a bank) is drawn on the buyer's bank rather than on the buyer personally. Banker's acceptances are more marketable than are trade acceptances.

3. **Check** A check is a draft drawn on a bank or other financial institution (savings and loan, credit union, etc.) and payable on demand. The depositor is the drawer of the check (the bank's creditor as to the amount on deposit) and the bank's principal on the contract of deposit agreement. The bank is the drawee of the check (the depositor's debtor as to the amount on deposit) and the depositor's agent with respect to handling the account.

   a. **Conditional Payment** A check generally is a conditional payment; the obligation for which it is given is not discharged until the check has been paid.

   b. **Bank Draft** A draft (check) drawn by one bank on another bank.

   Example 1 ▸ Bank Draft

A purchaser in New York is dealing with a seller in California. In order to assure payment, the seller requires a bank draft. Purchaser obtains a bank draft from her/his bank in New York (drawer-bank). The draft is drawn on a local bank in California (drawee-bank) and is payable to the seller.

   c. **Cashier's Check** A check drawn by a bank **on itself,** ordering itself to pay a sum of money to a third person. A check may be either an ordinary check, cashier's check, or teller's check. The name on the paper is not controlling. Unless otherwise agreed, the delivery of a certified check, cashier's check, or teller's check discharges the debt for which it is given, up to the amount of the check.

   d. **Certified Check** A check accepted by the bank on which it is drawn.

C. Note

A written promise to pay a stated sum of money. The promisor is the "**maker,**" and the person receiving the sum of money is the "**payee**" or the "**bearer.**" Notes may be made payable on demand or on a stated date. An instrument is a note if it is a **promise.**

1. **Promise** A promise is an undertaking to pay, not a mere acknowledgment of a debt or obligation. For example, "I promise to pay" is a promise, but "IOU $500" is not a promise. Notes and certificates of deposit must contain a promise to pay a sum certain.

2. **Certificate of Deposit** A written acknowledgment by a bank of the receipt of a stated sum of money with a promise to repay that sum.

D. Checks

Unlike other negotiable instruments, a check need not be payable to order or bearer to be negotiable. When several checks are received on the same day, the financial institution may decide which checks to charge to the account first.

1. **Certified Check** Certification of a check is the drawee-bank's acceptance; the bank warrants that sufficient funds are on deposit and are set aside for payment. The drawee-bank ordinarily owes the depositor no duty to certify her/his checks.

   a. Certification procured by the holder discharges the drawer and any prior indorsers; the bank becomes primarily liable.

   b. Certification by holder and/or drawer discharges all indorsers and the drawer from contractual liability.

   c. Certification by drawer discharges indorsers only; the drawer is still secondarily liable.

2. **Bank's Duties to Depositor**

   a. **Honor Checks** The bank owes the depositor a duty to honor her/his checks as drawn, providing they are drawn properly and are covered by sufficient funds on deposit. This duty is owed to the drawer, not the payee. If the bank improperly dishonors a check, the payee's action is against the drawer. **Exception:** If the check has been **certified,** then the payee can compel payment by the drawee-bank. The drawee-bank is liable to the depositor for damages caused by its wrongful dishonor. If dishonor occurs by mistake, the bank's liability is limited to actual damages proved.

   b. **Stop Payment** The bank owes the depositor a duty to follow the depositor's order to stop payment. A bank that pays a check while a valid stop-payment order is in effect regarding that check cannot debit the drawer's account. A stop-payment order must be received by the bank in time to give the bank reasonable time to act. A stop-payment order may be oral or written. A written order is valid for six months unless renewed in writing. An oral order is valid for 14 days, but may be confirmed in writing before the period expires.

3. **Depositor's Duty to Bank** The depositor owes the bank a duty to examine monthly statements for possible alterations and forgeries. The bank ordinarily must recredit the drawer's account after paying a forged or altered check; its remedy is against the person making presentment and the prior transferors for breach of implied warranties.

   a. **Negligence** If the bank was negligent, the bank bears the loss even if the drawer also was negligent. If the drawer negligently fails to discover a forgery or material alteration, or fails to notify the bank within 30 days, the drawer will bear the loss of subsequent forgeries or alterations in the same series.

   b. **Time Limit** Regardless of the negligence of the drawer or bank, a drawer bears the loss on the forged or altered check if the drawer fails to report either (1) her/his unauthorized signature or any alteration within a year after receiving her/his bank statement, or (2) an unauthorized indorsement within three years.

II. Negotiability Requirements

A. Prerequisites

In order to be a negotiable instrument, the writing must possess all of the following six (6) prerequisites (UCC 3-104).

1. **Signed** The instrument must be **in writing and signed** by the maker (note) or drawer (draft, check).

2. **Promise** The instrument must contain an **unconditional** promise or order to pay.

3. **Money** The amount of money must be a fixed amount.

4. **Order or Bearer** The instrument must be payable to **order** or to **bearer** (these are the magic words of negotiability) at the time it is issued, **except** for checks. Revisions to Article 3 eliminated the requirement for a check to be payable to order or bearer to be negotiable.

5. **Time** The instrument must be payable on **demand** or at a **definite** time.

6. **Only Promise or Order** The promise or order may not have any other promise, order, obligation, or power given by the maker or drawer **except** as authorized by Article 3 of the Uniform Commercial Code.

Exhibit 2 ▸ Elements of Negotiability

"SUM BOD"

S	In writing, **S**igned by the maker or drawer
U	**U**nconditional promise or order to pay
M	Promise to pay a fixed amount of **M**oney
B	Payable to **B**earer (except checks)
	or
O	Payable to **O**rder (except checks)
D	Payable on **D**emand or at a **D**efinite time

Note: These requirements (along with holder in due course requirements) should be memorized for the CPA exam.

B. Writing & Signature

The instrument must be in writing and signed by either the maker (if a note or certificate of deposit) or drawer (if a check or other draft). Writing is handwriting, printing, typewriting, or any intentional reduction to written form. No particular form of signature is required, but there must be some symbol placed somewhere on the instrument. Additionally, the symbol must be intended to operate as a signature. No person is liable on a negotiable instrument unless her/his signature appears on it.

1. **Unauthorized Signature** An unauthorized signature (including a forgery) does not bind the person whose signature it purports to be unless that person ratifies the unauthorized signature. If not ratified, the signature operates as the signature of the unauthorized signer. The unauthorized signer is liable to any person who takes the instrument as an HDC.

2. **Authorized Agent** An authorized agent may sign for a person and the signature operates as the principal's. The agent must indicate that s/he signs in a representative capacity to avoid being personally liable on the instrument.

Example 2 ▸ Parties' Liability

Liability of agent as maker, indorser, acceptor, or drawer results if agent fails to properly sign the instrument as such.

- "P. Ball, by A. Antioch, Agent"
  The principal (P. Ball) is liable as maker, etc.; Agent (A. Antioch) has no liability.
- "P. Ball"
  The principal is liable; the agent is not. Between principal and agent, parol (oral) evidence will be admissible to show agency.
- "A. Antioch"
  The agent is liable as maker, etc., because the agent neither names the person represented nor shows the representative capacity in which s/he signed. Remember, the general rule is that no one is liable on an instrument unless her/his signature appears on it.
- "A. Antioch, Agent", or
  "P. Ball
  A. Antioch"

  The agent in both of these cases signs in a representative capacity, and parol evidence will be admissible in litigation between principal and agent to show this agency. In both cases, the agent may also introduce parol evidence of agency in a litigation between the agent and a third party. If, however, in either example, the agent is sued by an HDC, the agent is personally liable because s/he signed the instrument. However, the agent could then sue the principal for indemnification.

C. Unconditional Order or Promise to Pay

The instrument must contain an unconditional promise (note or certificate of deposit) or order (check or draft) to pay a **sum certain in money.**

1. **Promise** A promise is an undertaking to pay, not a mere acknowledgment of debt. For example, "I promise to pay" is a promise, but "IOU $500" is not a promise.

2. **Order** An order is a direction to pay, not a mere authorization or request. For example, "Pay to the order of Jones" is an order, but "I wish you (the drawee) would pay" is not an order.

3. **Unconditional** The obligation to pay must be expressed in absolute, unqualified terms.

   a. The promise or order is **conditional** (and the instrument nonnegotiable) if the instrument states that it is **subject to another agreement.** For example, a note states on its face that payment is to be made **only** if a certain act is performed. "Subject to" language will **destroy** negotiability because the terms of payment of the instrument cannot be determined by looking at the instrument alone; some other document must be consulted. However, if the note made no mention of any condition (e.g., the condition was oral), then the note would be negotiable. This results from the fact that an examination of the note itself indicated that the promise was unconditional.

   b. The promise or order is **unconditional** even though the following are present.

      (1) The instrument is subject only to implied or constructive conditions.

      (2) The instrument recites that consideration has been given and/or that the instrument arose from or refers to a separate writing. For example, if an instrument, which is otherwise negotiable, recites that it is given as payment "as per" or "in accordance with" some other contractual instrument, this reference will not destroy negotiability. Additionally, if the negotiable instrument states that it is drawn "as per a letter of credit" or that "it is secured by a mortgage," negotiability is not destroyed. In contrast, if the instrument expressly recites that it is "subject to" or "governed by" any other agreement, this conditional language will destroy negotiability.

(3) The instrument refers to a particular fund or source from which reimbursement is expected. For example, if the instrument refers to the account that is later to bear the expense, this will not destroy negotiability (e.g., "charge inventory account").

(4) The instrument requires a countersignature by a person whose specimen signature appears on the instrument. If the person whose specimen signature appears on an instrument fails to countersign the instrument, the failure to countersign is a defense to the obligation of the issuer, but the failure does not prevent a transferee of the instrument from becoming a holder of the instrument. This provision applies primarily to traveler's checks.

4. "Sum Certain" or Fixed Amount

a. The amount to be paid is a sum certain if the holder can determine the amount payable at the **time of payment.**

b. A sum payable may be certain even if it is to be paid in the following manner.

(1) With stated **interest** or "with interest" (in this case, the rate of interest is that legal judgment rate declared by law).

(2) With a stated **discount** or addition that is dependent on the date of payment.

(3) With currency **exchange rate** added or subtracted.

(4) With **attorney's fees** and/or **collection fees** on default.

5. Money Money is defined as a medium of exchange accepted as the currency of any domestic or foreign government. A promise or order to do something in addition to the payment of money renders the instrument **nonnegotiable.** However, the following do **not** affect negotiability.

a. Authorizing the sale of collateral securities on default.

b. Requiring the maintenance of collateral or the giving of additional collateral.

c. Authorizing a confession of judgment on default.

d. Waiving the benefit of a law intended to protect the obligor (e.g., presentment or notice of dishonor).

e. Stating that the payee acknowledges full satisfaction of the drawer's obligation when the payee endorses a draft.

D. Payable
The instrument must be payable on demand or at a definite time. (Most checks are payable on demand.)

1. On Demand An instrument is payable on **demand** if either of the following apply.

a. It states that it is payable on demand or at sight, or otherwise indicates that it is payable at the will of the holder.

b. No time for payment is stated.

2. **At Definite Time** An instrument is payable at a definite time, if by its terms, it is payable in accordance with any of the following.

   a. At a fixed period after sight or acceptance.

   b. At a fixed date or dates or at a time or times readily ascertainable at the time the instrument is issued, or

   c. At a definite time subject to rights of any of the following.

      (1) Prepayment, or

      (2) Acceleration (e.g., "Full amount due if any delinquency occurs," or "Full amount due 30 days after notice by holder"), or

      (3) Extension at the option of the holder, or

      (4) Extension to a further definite time at the option of the maker or acceptor, but only to a further definite time, or automatically upon or after a specified act or event.

3. **Combination** If an instrument, payable at a fixed date, is also payable upon demand made before the fixed date, the instrument is payable on demand until the fixed date and, if demand for payment is not made before that date, becomes payable at a definite time on the fixed date.

4. **Uncertainty of Time** An instrument is **not** payable at a definite time, and hence not negotiable, if it is payable only upon the occurrence of an event **uncertain** as to time of occurrence (e.g., "Payable at death" is nonnegotiable; however, "Payable on January 1, 2008, or if death occurs before that date, then on the date of death," is negotiable because the date is certain subject to acceleration).

E. Words of Negotiability

All instruments, **except checks, must** be payable to **order** or to **bearer,** or equivalent wording must be used. These are the magic words of negotiability. They must appear on the instrument for it to be negotiable.

1. **Order** Order paper is payable "to the order of any person" or "to a person or the person's order." The person must be specified with reasonable certainty (e.g., "to the order of A" or "to A or A's order"). If payable merely to a **specific person,** it is **not** payable to order and **not negotiable** (e.g., "Pay John Doe"). An instrument may be payable to the order of the following.

   a. The maker or drawer

   b. The drawee

   c. A payee other than the above

   d. Two or more payees jointly or in the alternative (jointly, "to A and B"; alternatively, "to A or B")

   e. An estate, trust, or fund

   f. An office, or an officer by her/his title as such

   g. A partnership or unincorporated association

2. **Bearer** Bearer paper is payable to the following.

   a. "Bearer" or "the order of bearer"

b. "A specified person or bearer" (e.g., "to John Jones or bearer"; however, "to John Jones, bearer" is nonnegotiable)

c. "Cash," the order of "cash," or any other indication that does not purport to designate a specific payee

3. **Order & Bearer** If the instrument states that it is payable to order **and** to bearer, it is payable to order, **unless** the bearer words are **typed or handwritten** (e.g., if the bearer words are printed, the instrument is payable to order).

III. Issue & Negotiation

A. Issue

The initial delivery of a negotiable instrument, usually by the maker or drawer, to a holder who is usually the payee (e.g., a purchaser-maker issues a 30-day promissory note upon taking delivery of goods).

B. Negotiation

Following issue, a negotiable instrument subsequently is transferred by **negotiation** or **assignment.** Negotiation is the transfer of both the title and possession of an instrument in such form that the transferee becomes a holder. If transfer is by negotiation, the transferee is a holder (or if the transferee qualifies, an HDC). If the transfer is by assignment, the transferee is an assignee.

1. **Bearer Paper** Bearer paper is negotiated by **delivery** alone (delivery is defined as the voluntary transfer of possession). Thus, a thief can deliver stolen bearer paper to an HDC. The HDC will have rights in that paper superior to the original true owner. This follows because delivery of bearer paper is negotiation of that paper.

2. **Order Paper** Order paper is negotiated by proper **indorsement plus delivery.** The proper party for indorsement always is the holder or someone authorized to sign on behalf of the holder.

3. **Holder** A holder is a person who is in possession of an instrument drawn, issued, or endorsed to her/him, to her/his order, or in blank. The result of negotiation is that the transferee becomes a "holder."

4. **Transferee by Assignment** Transfer without negotiation occurs when, for example, order paper is delivered, but not endorsed. The transferee by assignment obtains possession of the instrument. (Assignment merely requires delivery; negotiation of an order instrument requires indorsement and delivery.) The assignee only obtains the rights held by the transferor. Additionally, the assignee is subject to any claims and defenses against the assignor. The transferee-assignee has the specifically enforceable right to the unconditional indorsement of the transferor. Only at that time will a transferee for value become a holder and possibly a holder in due course (if the other requirements of HDC are satisfied).

5. **Rescission of Negotiation** Even though the right to rescind exists, the negotiation remains effective until the right is exercised. Negotiation **cannot** be rescinded against a subsequent HDC. The right to rescind negotiation may exist when negotiation was:

   a. Made by one without capacity.

   b. Obtained by fraud, duress, or mistake.

   c. Part of an illegal transaction.

   d. Made in breach of a duty.

6. **Instrument Reacquisition**

   a. **Cancellation of Indorsements** A party who reacquires an instrument may cancel any indorsement not necessary to the party's title (e.g., those following the initial indorsement to her/him).

   b. **Discharge of Liability** Intervening parties are discharged from liability against any party subsequent to the reacquirer, except an **HDC.**

   c. **Discharge Effective** If the reacquirer **cancels** the intervening indorsements, the discharge is effective even against subsequent **HDCs** because the cancellation is notice of the discharge.

   d. **Effect on Negotiation** The negotiation of commercial paper cannot be set aside if the paper is held by a person paying the instrument in good faith and without knowledge of the facts on which the rescission claim is based.

C. **Indorsement (Endorsement)**
Signing one's name on the instrument, other than as a maker, drawer, or acceptor, with or without other words, for the purpose of negotiating the instrument, or restricting payment of the instrument, or incurring the indorser's liability on the instrument. (The words "endorsement" and "indorsement" are used interchangeably.) An indorsement is a signature on an instrument, other than that of a signer as maker, drawer, or acceptor. An indorser is a person who makes an indorsement.

1. **Format** May be typewritten or rubber stamped, or an agent may indorse an instrument for the holder.

2. **Conveyance** Indorsement must convey the entire instrument; otherwise, the transfer is considered a partial assignment and not a negotiation.

3. **Errors** If the payee's name is misspelled or is incorrect, the payee may indorse in that name or her/his own or both; a purchaser for value may require her/his signature in both names.

4. **Unclear Capacity** If a signature is so placed that it is not clear in what capacity the person signed, s/he is deemed to be an indorser.

5. **Effect** Indorsement, unless qualified, will establish the indorser's secondary liability (e.g., the indorser is bound to pay the instrument if it is not honored by the maker or drawee).

   a. **Indorsement Plus Delivery** Indorsement (plus delivery) is necessary to negotiate order paper.

   b. **Indorsement & Bearer Paper** Bearer paper is paper that is bearer paper on its face (e.g., paper that is payable "to bearer," "to cash," "to a person or bearer," "to order of bearer," or "to order of cash"). Bearer paper can be transformed into order paper by making the last indorsement in the chain of indorsement a **special indorsement.** Order paper can be transformed into bearer paper by making the last indorsement in the chain of indorsement an **indorsement in blank.**

   c. **Forged Indorsement** A drawee-bank generally does not bear the loss on an instrument with a forged indorsement. A drawee cannot be expected to be able to determine the validity of any indorsements except its drawer-customer's signature. The drawee-bank, after paying a forged instrument, may be indemnified by proceeding against the party who first accepted the forged instrument.

      - Unlike the case of a forged indorsement, a drawee bank is charged with the recognition of its drawer-customer's signature. Thus, if the bank wrongfully pays an instrument on which the drawer's signature is forged, it has breached its contract with the drawer-customer and will bear the loss (in the absence of substantial contributory negligence of the drawer).

6. **Types**

a. **Blank Indorsement** The transferor's signature appears alone, without specifying any particular endorsee. A blank indorsement converts order paper into bearer paper; further negotiation may be made by delivery only (no further indorsement is necessary).

Example 3 ▸ Bearer Paper

Check is payable "to the order of cash." Drawer is A and drawee is bank Z. When A endorses the check, he signs it "A." This is a bearer instrument that has been indorsed in blank. It remains a bearer instrument.

Example 4 ▸ Order Paper

Check is payable "to the order of A." A indorses the check by signing "A." The original order paper is now a bearer instrument due to the blank indorsement.

b. **Special Indorsement** Specifies the person to whose order the instrument is now payable. A special indorsement on bearer paper converts it to order paper.

Example 5 ▸ Bearer Paper

Check is payable "to cash." A indorses the check by signing "Pay to the order of B" over her/his signature "A." The original bearer paper is now order paper due to the special indorsement.

c. **Restrictive Indorsement** Banks in the collection process may ignore restrictive indorsements **except** for those made by their immediate transferors. Aside from collecting banks, a transferee who accepts an instrument with a conditional or "deposit or collection" indorsement must give value consistent with the restriction in order to become a holder for value. A restrictive indorsement that purports to prohibit further negotiation is of no effect.

(1) Words indicating a purpose of deposit or collection (e.g., "for deposit" or "pay any bank").

(2) Conditional (e.g., "pay Robert Jones upon the completion of building X").

(3) Purporting to prohibit further transfer or negotiation (e.g., "pay A only").

(4) Payable only for the use or benefit of another (e.g., "pay A in trust for B").

d. **Qualified Indorsement** Usually characterized by writing "without recourse" on the instrument. Disclaims the indorser's secondary liability to pay the instrument in the event it is dishonored. Does not impair negotiability or prevent the transferee from becoming a holder in due course. Does not change the warranty.

e. **Multiple Indorsements** Different types of indorsements may be used together so long as they are not inconsistent.

f. **Anomalous Indorsement** An indorsement by someone who is not the holder of the instrument for the purpose of incurring liability on the instrument. Such an indorser has the status of an ordinary indorser; the signer is liable on the instrument as an indorser. Such an indorsement is normally made by an accommodation party and may be called an accommodation indorsement. An anomalous indorsement does not affect the manner in which the instrument may be negotiated.

IV. Holder in Due Course (HDC)

A. Requirements

An HDC is a holder who takes a negotiable instrument for value, in good faith, and without notice that it is overdue, has been dishonored, or that there is any defense against or claim to it on the part of any person. It is important to know about an HDC and what that status means. In order to qualify as an HDC, **all** of the requirements must be fulfilled.

Exhibit 3 ▸ Holder in Due Course

"VFW"

V Takes instrument for **V**alue.

F Takes instrument in good **F**aith.

W Takes instrument **W**ithout notice of dishonor, defense, or claim.

1. **Holder** A holder is one who takes by negotiation or issue. A holder has the right to transfer, negotiate, enforce payment, or discharge the instrument. A holder may strike out any indorsements not necessary to the holder's title. Finally, the holder is entitled to a rebuttable presumption of ownership of the instrument.

2. **Value** A holder gives value in the following ways.

Example 6 ▸ Value

A depositor opens a checking account with a $5,000 check payable to the depositor that is subsequently specially endorsed to the bank (or endorsed in blank). The bank provisionally credits the depositor's account (before collecting on the deposited check) and permits the depositor to immediately draw on the $5,000 balance. To the extent the depositor draws from the $5,000 balance, the bank has given "value" and has become an HDC (assuming the bank knows no defense to the $5,000 check).

a. To the extent the holder performs the agreed consideration.

(1) A promise to perform is not value **except** to the extent it has been performed.

(2) A negotiable instrument given for another instrument is considered to be "value" even though it is an executory promise because it can be negotiated to a holder in due course.

b. To the extent the holder acquires a security interest in the instrument, other than by legal process (e.g., the holder perfects a security interest in the instrument by taking possession of it as collateral for another debt).

c. By taking the instrument in payment of, or as security for, an antecedent claim against any person.

d. By giving a negotiable instrument in exchange for the instrument taken or by giving an irrevocable commitment to a third person in exchange for the negotiable instrument taken by the holder.

e. In the case of a bank, to the extent that the bank credits a depositor **and** permits a withdrawal of the deposited items. Thus, the bank becomes an HDC only when it permits the depositor to draw against the credited instrument.

(1) For the purpose of tracing deposits to withdrawals, the first-in, first-out rule (FIFO) is used to determine whether the credit has been withdrawn.

(2) Similarly, when a bank takes an instrument at a discount, it is giving "value" for the **face amount** of the discounted instrument.

3. **Good Faith** The HDC must take the instrument in good faith (e.g., there must be honesty in fact in the conduct or transaction at hand). This good faith test is a **subjective** test. The question is, did the holder exercise honesty in fact in taking the instrument?

4. **Without Notice** The HDC must take the instrument without notice that it is overdue, has been dishonored, or that any person has a defense against it or claim to it.

a. **Taking Without Notice** In addition to taking for value and in good faith, the holder must take without notice.

(1) The holder has notice of claim or defense when:

(a) S/he has actual knowledge of it.

(b) S/he has received notice of it.

(c) From all the facts or circumstances, s/he has reason to know of its existence.

(2) To be effective, notice must be received in time and in such manner as to give a reasonable opportunity to act on it.

(3) One who receives notice after becoming a holder, but before completing her/his performance, takes without notice only to the extent of the performance given before s/he received notice (e.g., it is possible to be a holder in due course as to **part** of the instrument and a holder not in due course as to the rest).

b. **Overdue**

(1) An instrument payable on a certain date becomes overdue at the beginning of the day after the due date.

(2) An instrument payable on demand becomes overdue after a reasonable time has lapsed after issue.

(a) "Reasonable time" depends on facts and circumstances.

(b) A domestic check is presumed overdue 90 (ninety) days after issue.

(3) The following are indications that the instrument is overdue.

(a) Notice that part of the principal (but not interest) is overdue or that there has been default in payment of another instrument of the same series.

(b) Notice that acceleration of the instrument has been made.

(c) Notice that demand has been made on a demand instrument.

c. **Dishonored** An instrument is dishonored when acceptance is necessary and cannot be obtained.

d. **Defense or Claim** A holder cannot be an HDC if s/he takes the instrument with notice that any person has a defense against it or a claim to it.

(1) The holder is on notice of a defense or claim in the following situations.

(a) The holder has notice that **any** party's obligation is voidable or that **all** parties have been discharged.

(b) The instrument is so incomplete or irregular (e.g., bearing evidence of forgery or alteration) as to call into question its validity, terms, or ownership.

(c) The holder has notice that a fiduciary has negotiated it in breach of her/his duty.

(d) A notice preserving consumer defenses is stated in a credit contract; no subsequent person can be a holder in due course.

(2) The holder is not on notice of a defense or claim in the following situations.

(a) The instrument was antedated or postdated.

(b) It was issued or negotiated in return for an executory promise or along with a separate agreement, unless the holder also knows of a defense arising from such promise or agreement.

(c) Any party has signed as an accommodation party.

(d) An incomplete instrument has been completed, unless the holder also knows it was completed improperly.

(e) Any negotiator of the instrument was a fiduciary.

B. Rights

An HDC generally takes the instrument free from all claims to it by any person and from all personal defenses of any party with whom s/he has not dealt.

Example 7 ▶ Rights

A is induced by fraud to deliver a note to B. B negotiates the note to C who in turn negotiates it to D. D strikes out the indorsements of B and C (discharging them). Because not all of the parties have been discharged (A and D are still liable as maker and indorser, respectively), D's transferee, E, can still become an HDC and cut off A's defense of fraud in the inducement (personal defense).

1. **Shelter Provision** Under the "shelter provision," the transfer of an instrument vests in the transferee such rights as the transferors had therein. In other words, because a transferee takes the rights of the transferor, a person who does not qualify as an HDC can, through the shelter provision, enjoy all of the benefits of HDC status if s/he can show that some transferor in her/his chain of ownership was an HDC. There are exceptions to the shelter provision.

Example 8 ▶ Shelter Provision

A takes a note for value and without notice of the fact that the note was originally induced by fraud by a prior possessor. A thus qualifies as an HDC and, as such, is immune from the personal defense of fraud. A then negotiates the note to B who takes with notice of the fraud. Although B is not an HDC, s/he, nevertheless, enjoys all the rights of an HDC because s/he is sheltered by A, who was an HDC.

a. A person not a HDC may **not** acquire those rights by negotiating to a holder in due course and then reacquiring the instrument so as to improve her/his status.

b. A person who is party to the fraud or illegality affecting the instrument, or who is party to any defense, cannot acquire the rights of a prior holder in due course.

2. **Not HDC or Taker Through HDC** One who is neither a holder in due course nor a taker through an HDC is subject to all valid claims to the instrument and any real or personal defenses to the instrument.

V. Defenses

A. Personal Defenses

Personal defenses are good against persons who are **not** holders in due course or takers through such holders. However, personal defenses are good against even holders in due course in favor of a person with whom the holder in due course has dealt. They typically do not go to the validity of the instrument, but are reasons that would excuse a promisor from performing the contract under contract law.

1. **Absence or Failure of Consideration or Failure of an Implied Condition Precedent** However, the UCC provides that no consideration is necessary for an instrument given in payment for an antecedent obligation (e.g., when the antecedent obligation would be considered "past consideration" under contract law).

2. **Fraud in the Inducement** In this type of fraud, (also called fraud in the procurement), the instrument fraudulently signed is what it purports to be, and the person deceived knows its terms and character (e.g., s/he knows it is a promissory note in the amount of $10,000). The fraud and deception concern some matter other than the instrument (e.g., a person is induced to sign a $10,000 note in payment for a painting that the seller fraudulently misrepresents as a Picasso, but the painting in fact is a cheap imitation worth $50).

   - **Distinguished From Fraud in the Factum** This type of fraud (also called fraud in the essence or fraud in the execution) is a real defense that is not cut off by an HDC. In fraud in the factum, the misrepresentation concerns the terms and character of the instrument itself (e.g., a person is induced to sign a $10,000 note because the procurer of the signature misrepresents that it is a $1,000 note). Fraud in the factum is a defense if the defrauded party can prove that s/he had no reasonable opportunity to learn the true character or essential terms of the instrument (e.g., the signer was blind and was induced to sign by a trusted relative).

3. **Nondelivery of Instrument** Although a person in possession of an instrument that was not delivered to her/him (e.g., a stolen bearer instrument) cannot be a holder, a rebuttable presumption is that an instrument in the possession of someone other than the maker or drawer has been delivered.

4. **Unauthorized Instrument Completion** When an instrument is **completed** by a **holder fraudulently,** the party whose contract has been **materially altered** by the unauthorized completion is discharged of all liability on it except against holders in due course (HDC) because such negligence converts this defense to a personal defense.

   Example 9 ▸ Unauthorized Instrument Completion

   A writes a check for $50 but fails to name the person to whose order the check is to be paid. S steals the check and writes "S" in the order space. Although A is not liable to S (S is not a holder), A would be liable in the amount of $50 to an HDC who took from S.

5. **Payment Before Maturity** If a note is paid to a prior holder before maturity, then that payment discharges the instrument to any subsequent holder who is not an HDC.

6. **Discharge of Parties (other than in bankruptcy or insolvency proceedings)** Distinguish these from discharge in bankruptcy or insolvency; a discharge in bankruptcy is a real defense and is a good defense against an HDC.

a. A holder is **not** barred from being an HDC by having notice upon delivery of the instrument of the discharge of one or more parties. A holder **is** barred from being an HDC if s/he takes delivery with notice that **all** parties have been discharged.

b. An HDC takes free of a discharge of any party **if** the HDC took delivery of the instrument without notice of such discharge. If the HDC had notice of such discharge at the time of delivery, then the discharge **is** good against the HDC.

c. Discharge ordinarily is a personal defense, but if the discharge shows on the face of the instrument (such as PAID, CANCELLED, or scratched out), then it is a real defense. It is not effective against a subsequent holder in due course unless the holder has notice of it when s/he takes the instrument.

B. Real Defenses

All holders, including HDCs, take subject to any real defenses of any party, regardless of whether the holder has or has not dealt with that party. Real defenses generally go to the validity of the instrument.

Exhibit 4 ▸ Real Defenses of Holder in Due Course

"MIFF'D"

M	**M**aterial alteration
I	Discharge in **I**nsolvency proceedings or bankruptcy
	Incapacity
	Illegality (if it would render the instrument void under local law)
F	**F**orgery
F	**F**raud in the factum (essence)
D	**D**uress (to the extent it would render the obligation void)

1. **Material Alteration** As a general rule, any material alteration fraudulently made by a holder that changes the original tenor (amount or number of parties) of the instrument discharges all parties whose contract changes, except as against either an HDC or that party whose negligence substantially contributed to the alteration.

   a. A material alteration is one that changes the contract of a party who has signed the instrument. Material alterations include changes in the following.

      (1) Number or relationship of the parties

      (2) Date of issue and/or of payment

      (3) Amount payable and/or medium of payment

      (4) Place of payment or the addition of one when none is specified

   b. The general rule is modified as follows.

      (1) If a **completed** instrument is altered fraudulently without any substantial contributing negligence of a party, then that party whose contract is changed has only a personal defense as to the original tenor, but a real defense (good against an HDC) as to the alteration. Thus, the HDC can enforce the instrument only up to its original amount. However, if a party's negligence substantially contributed to the alteration, that party has no real defense against an HDC.

(2) If an **incomplete** instrument is completed fraudulently (unauthorized completion), the instrument is assumed not to have had an "original tenor," and a subsequent HDC may enforce the instrument as completed. There is no real defense to the altered portion.

(3) If a party to the instrument substantially contributes to the fraudulent alteration or the unauthorized completion, s/he will be liable for the full amount to subsequent HDCs as well as to drawees and payees who pay on the instrument in good faith.

c. An unauthorized completion of an instrument is treated as a **material alteration;** however, it is **not** a real defense against an HDC.

d. A party whose substantial contributing negligence invites the material alteration is estopped from raising the alteration as a defense.

2. **Insolvency** Discharge in insolvency proceedings or bankruptcy is a real defense.

3. **Incapacity**

a. Infancy is a real defense to the extent it is a defense to a simple contract under local law, even though it renders a contract merely voidable, not void.

b. Any other type of incapacity is a real defense only if it would void a simple contract (e.g., adjudication of incompetence).

4. **Illegality** Illegality, if it would render the instrument void under local law.

5. **Forgery** No person is liable, even against an HDC as a maker, drawer, or indorser of an instrument, unless the person's authorized signature appears on it or her/his negligence substantially contributed to an unauthorized signature. A **forged signature** creates **no** liability against the person whose signature it purports to be, but instead operates as the signature of the unauthorized signer, unless the person whose name is forged is estopped by negligence from raising the defense.

a. **Agent**

(1) A valid signature may be made by an authorized representative of the person whose name is to be signed.

(2) An **unauthorized** signature may later be ratified, so that the ratifier loses the defense of forgery and becomes liable on the instrument.

b. **Exceptions** A person whose own negligence substantially contributes to the making of a forged signature is estopped from asserting the lack of a valid signature as a defense against a holder in due course or a payor who pays the instrument in good faith. Any indorsement (forged or not) **is** effective in the name of the named payee in the following circumstances.

(1) If an imposter induces the maker or drawer to issue the instrument to her/him in the name of the payee.

Example 10 ▶ Indorsement by Imposter

A introduces himself to B Company as C, one of B Company's suppliers. In fact, A is an imposter. A talks B Company into giving him an advance of $1,500 against future billings. The check from B Company is made payable to C. A endorses the check, takes the proceeds, and vanishes. Result: The loss of the $1,500 falls upon the drawer, B Company. The indorsement of an imposter is **not** considered to be a forgery; accordingly, the forgery rules do not apply.

(2) If a person signing for the maker or drawer, or supplying the name to the maker or drawer, intends the payee to have no interest (e.g., the fictitious payee will then endorse it her/himself and appropriate the proceeds).

6. **Fraud in Factum** Fraud in the factum (also called fraud in the execution or fraud in the essence) concerns the instrument itself. The fraudulent misrepresentation is of the character or terms of the instrument; it does not concern the misrepresentation of a collateral matter. In order for fraud in the factum to be a **real defense** against a subsequent HDC, the defrauded party signing the instrument must have had no reasonable opportunity to learn the true character or terms of the instrument.

7. **Duress** Duress is a real defense, to the extent it would render the obligation void. If the duress would only render the obligation voidable, it is a personal defense.

VI. Presentment, Dishonor & Notice of Dishonor

A. Presentment

Presentment is a demand for acceptance or payment made upon the maker, acceptor, drawee, or other payor by or on behalf of the holder. As conditions precedent to the activation of the maker's, drawer's, or unqualified indorser's liability, the holder must perform certain acts. The holder must first make a timely presentment of the instrument. Presentment is functionally equivalent to demanding acceptance or payment. If the instrument is dishonored, either through a refusal of the drawee or a refusal to pay on presentment, the holder's duty is fulfilled upon notifying the drawer or indorser of the dishonor. In some cases, these requirements are excused in whole or in part.

1. **For Acceptance** A drawee is not primarily liable on a draft until s/he accepts it. (The requirement for acceptance of a sight or demand draft [check] is excused—checks are presented for payment, not acceptance.) Time drafts (e.g., "Pay 30 days after sight") are the usual subjects of acceptance. Although such time drafts usually are presented for acceptance before maturity, some time drafts are not accepted until maturity. More specifically, Article 3 of the UCC provides that acceptance **is required in order to fix the secondary liability of drawers and indorsers** in the following situations.

   a. When the draft itself provides that it shall be presented for acceptance.

   b. When the draft is payable at a place other than the place of residence or business of the drawee.

   c. When the date of payment depends upon presentment for acceptance (e.g., draft payable "10 days after sight" means that the draft is payable 10 days after presentment).

2. **For Payment**

   a. Notes and accepted drafts must be presented for payment as a condition precedent to primary and secondary liability of makers and drawers, respectively.

   b. Failure to make presentment for payment discharges any indorsers. Failure to make presentment operates as a discharge of the drawer or acceptor of a draft payable at a bank only to the extent of any loss caused by the delay that is due to the insolvency of the drawee or payor.

c. Generally, payment of an instrument may be deferred without dishonor while it is examined to determine whether it is properly payable, but payment or dishonor of a check must occur by midnight of the next business day after presentment.

d. A check is overdue the day after the demand for payment has been made or 90 days after the date of the check if no demand has been made, whichever date is the earlier.

e. If the holder of the check does not present it for payment or collection within 30 days after an indorsement was made, the indorser is discharged from liability.

f. An instrument showing the date payable is due on the stated date (e.g., the primary party can be required to pay on that date). If presentment is due on a day that is not a full business day, it is due on the next full business day.

(1) An instrument may show the date payable either (a) on a specified date; (b) on a fixed period after a stated date; or (c) on a fixed period after sight (accepted instrument).

(2) An **accelerated instrument** must be presented for payment within a reasonable time after acceleration. A reasonable time is deemed to be 30 days after the issue or the date of the instrument, whichever is later, or 30 days after indorsement.

(3) A **demand instrument** presentment date depends on the purpose for which presentment is made.

(a) If the purpose is to activate the secondary liability of the drawer or indorser, presentment should be made on the date of issue.

(b) If the purpose is to move against the secondary party, presentment is timely if it is made within 30 days after the secondary party becomes liable on the instrument.

3. Methods Presentment may be as follows.

a. By mail, in which case presentment is effective on receipt of the mail.

b. Through a clearing house.

c. At the place of acceptance or payment specified in the instrument or, if none is specified, the place of business or the residence of the party to accept or pay.

d. In the case of a draft accepted or a note made payable at a bank in the United States, at such bank.

4. Conditions The party receiving presentment may impose certain requirements on the presenting party. The party presenting has a reasonable time in which to comply. Failure to comply invalidates the presentment. Requirements may include the following.

a. Exhibition of the instrument.

b. Reasonable identification of the person making presentment and evidence of her/his authority to make it.

c. Production of the instrument for acceptance or payment at a place specified in it or, if no place is specified, at any place reasonable under the circumstances.

d. A signed receipt on the instrument upon full or partial payment and its surrender upon full payment.

B. Dishonor

An instrument is dishonored when acceptance or payment cannot be obtained after making any necessary presentment. Dishonor gives the holder a right of recourse against parties who are secondarily liable, subject to any requirement of notice of dishonor and protest.

1. **Presentment Required** In the case of an instrument required to be presented for acceptance or payment, dishonor occurs when presentment is made and acceptance or payment is refused or cannot be obtained within the time allowed.

2. **Presentment Not Required** In the case of an instrument not required to be presented and not optionally presented, dishonor occurs when the instrument is not duly accepted or paid.

3. **Lack of Proper Indorsement** An instrument is not dishonored when it is returned for lack of a proper indorsement.

C. Notice of Dishonor

1. **When Necessary** Notice of dishonor is necessary unless waived in order to hold the following parties liable: the maker of a bank domiciled note, the acceptor of a bank domiciled draft, any drawer, and any indorser.

   a. Failure to give due notice of dishonor to an indorser discharges the indorser from any liability.

   b. Failure to give due notice of dishonor to any of the other parties named operates as a discharge only to the extent of any loss caused by the delay by reason of the insolvency of the drawee or payor.

2. **Time** Banks must give notice before their "midnight deadline" (midnight of the next banking day after receipt of item or receipt of notice of dishonor, whichever is later). Others must give notice within 30 days after dishonor or receipt of notice of dishonor.

3. **Form** Notice of dishonor may be oral or written. It must identify the instrument and state that the instrument has been dishonored.

4. **Effect** Notice to a party operates for the benefit of any party who has rights on the instrument against the party notified. Notice of dishonor is effective when sent, regardless of whether it is received.

D. Protest

A protest is a formal certificate of dishonor.

1. **Necessary vs. Optional** Protest is necessary for foreign drafts and **optional** for any other instrument.

2. **Method of Making Protest**

   a. Protest is made under the hand and seal of a person authorized to certify dishonor under the law of the jurisdiction (e.g., a United States consul, vice consul, or notary public).

   b. The protest must identify the instrument dishonored and certify that presentment has been made (or excused for some reason) and that notice of dishonor has been given.

3. **Due** Protest is due when notice of dishonor is due.

4. **Failure to Make a Protest** Failure to make a necessary protest by the time it is due discharges the drawer and indorsers of the foreign draft.

E. **Excuse**

1. **Delay** Delay in making presentment, in giving notice of dishonor, or in making protest **is excused** under the following circumstances:

   a. When a party is without notice that the instrument is due (e.g., acceleration of a note or demand by a prior holder without the current holder's knowledge).

   b. When caused by circumstances beyond the party's control, so long as s/he exercises reasonable diligence after the cause of delay ceases to operate.

2. **Failure** Failure to make presentment at all is excused under the following circumstances:

   a. The maker, acceptor, or drawee is dead or in insolvency proceedings that were instituted after the instrument had been issued.

   b. Acceptance or payment has already been refused for a reason other than lack of proper presentment.

3. **Other Failures** Failure to make presentment, notice of dishonor, or protest is excused under the following circumstances:

   a. If it is waived by the party to receive presentment or notice.

      (1) Waiver may be oral or written, express or implied, and made before or after presentment, notice of dishonor, or protest is due.

      (2) A waiver embodied in the instrument binds all parties; however, a waiver written above the signature of an indorser binds only the indorser.

   b. It also may be excused if a draft has been dishonored by nonacceptance and is not later accepted.

   c. If a party has dishonored the instrument or has no right to expect it to be accepted or paid; e.g., an accommodated party who breaks the accommodation agreement s/he had with the accommodation party has no right to presentment or notice of dishonor from the latter.

   d. If presentment, notice of dishonor, or protest cannot be made by reasonable diligence.

VII. Parties' Liability

A. Contractual Liability

Liability on an instrument is borne by primary and secondary parties. In order for a holder to obtain payment from a **secondary** party, the holder must fulfill certain conditions precedent. These conditions are: presentment for payment, protest if not paid, and notice of dishonor. However, these conditions precedent are **not** required in order to fix liability upon a **primary** party.

1. **Primary Parties** Makers (notes) and acceptors (drafts) are the primary parties. The maker of a note is liable on it when the note is executed; however, a drawee on a draft is not liable until s/he accepts (draft) or certifies (check) the instrument.

   a. **Maker** The maker engages that s/he will pay the instrument according to its original terms or, if incomplete at the time of making, according to its final terms if completed as authorized.

b. Drawee-Acceptor

(1) **General** Unlike the maker (who is liable when the instrument is executed), the drawee-acceptor incurs no liability on the instrument **until** it is presented for acceptance or certification. The drawee then accepts and binds her/himself by writing "accepted" or "certified" on the draft itself, along with the drawee's signature. Although the word "accepted" or like words ("good") are usually present on such drafts, the drawee's signature is absolutely required for acceptance of certification. After acceptance, the instrument will be operative when completed by delivery or notification.

(2) **Special Rules**

(a) **Certification** Certification by either holder or drawer discharges all but the drawee from contractual liability.

(b) **Subsequent Alteration** Usually, the acceptor engages that s/he will pay the draft according to its terms at the time of acceptance. Thus, the acceptor is not liable for a **subsequent** alteration or unauthorized completion. Furthermore, any such alteration discharges all parties to the instrument, except as against an HDC.

(c) **General Acceptance** The drawee accepts the draft according to its terms as originally drawn or as presented.

(d) **Acceptance Varying Draft** The drawee is unwilling to accept the draft as drawn. The drawee may change the terms of the instrument as s/he sees fit. The holder of this draft (usually a seller of goods who has obtained a draft from the purchaser-drawer payable to the seller-payee through a drawee-bank) has two choices.

(i) The holder may refuse the varying acceptance and treat the draft as dishonored.

(ii) The holder may assent to the variance. However, such assent discharges each drawer and indorser who has not affirmatively assented to the variance.

Example 11 ▸ Drawee-Acceptor

Purchaser draws a draft for $5,000 payable to seller-payee 30 days after presentment. Seller presents the draft for acceptance and the instrument is accepted and signed by drawee-bank. Seller then negotiates the draft to Forger, who raises the amount to $15,000 and subsequently negotiates the draft to Smith for value and without notice of alteration. Smith becomes an HDC.

Results:

- If Smith was **not** an HDC, the alteration by Forger, a holder, would discharge all parties (including the acceptor).
- Because Smith is an HDC, he can recover from the acceptor (drawee-bank) the amount of the draft at the time of acceptance ($5,000). Smith can recover the full $15,000 from Forger.
- If the alteration had been made before the acceptance, the drawee-bank acceptor would be liable for the full $15,000 total because that was the amount it "accepted."
- The purchaser and seller are secondarily liable for the unaltered amount ($5,000).

2. **Secondary Parties** Drawers and indorsers are secondary parties. They are secondarily liable on any instrument if the instrument is **not** paid by the primary party **and** conditions precedent to liability have been satisfied by the holder of the instrument. These conditions are presentment for acceptance or payment, notice of dishonor, and protest (in some cases).

   a. **Liability of Drawer** By drawing the instrument, the drawer contractually engages that upon dishonor of the draft and after notice of dishonor or protest (if necessary), the drawer will pay the amount of the draft to the holder or to any indorser who takes it up (assumes responsibility through her/his indorser's contract). A drawer may disclaim such secondary liability by qualifying the indorsement of the instrument using such words as "without recourse."

   b. **Liability of Indorsers** An indorser (other than a qualified indorser) engages that upon dishonor and any necessary notice of dishonor and protest, the indorser will pay the instrument according to its tenor at the time of her/his indorsement to the holder or to any subsequent holder who takes up the instrument. In the absence of an effective "without recourse" disclaimer, the indorser is jointly and severally (secondarily) liable with the drawer. Thus, a holder is not required (after presentment and dishonor) to make a demand upon or proceed against the drawer before enforcing the indorser's liability. The holder can go against an indorser immediately.

      (1) A signature appearing on an instrument is considered an indorsement unless the instrument clearly indicates that the signature is made in some other capacity.

      (2) When the indorser adds the words "payment guaranteed," it means that when the indorser's secondary liability is triggered, the indorser will become primarily liable automatically upon nonpayment by the primary party. Thus, presentment and notice are not required in a "payment guaranteed" indorsement.

      (3) When indorsement is without "payment guaranteed," any unreasonable delay by the holder in fulfilling the conditions precedent to secondary liability completely discharges any **indorser. Drawers** are discharged only to the extent of any loss covered by the delay.

         (a) Presentment of a draft must be by a holder within 30 days after the indorsement.

         (b) Because an indorsement is essential for negotiation of an order instrument and for the activation of the indorser's contractual liability, it is important to ascertain whether in fact there was an indorsement. If a bearer instrument was negotiated by delivery alone, without indorsement, the transferor bears no contractual liability. However, the transferor is still liable for certain implied warranties.

3. **Accommodation Party** An accommodation party is one who signs the instrument in any capacity for the purpose of lending her/his name to the instrument. An accommodation party may sign as a maker, acceptor, drawer, or indorser. The accommodation party is liable in the capacity in which s/he signed the instrument.

   a. If the accommodation party signs as a **maker or acceptor,** s/he is a **primary** party and is liable immediately or when accepted; the holder need **not** first present the instrument to the accommodated party (the party to whom accommodation is made). However, notice that both the accommodation party **and** the accommodated party must sign the instrument. If the accommodation party signs as an indorser, s/he is only secondarily liable.

   b. The accommodation party is treated as a **surety;** thus, s/he can be held liable on the instrument without demand being first made on the accommodated party. The normal defenses of a surety are not available to the accommodation party if the holder is an HDC. Finally, the accommodation party is liable on the instrument only and is not liable to the accommodated party. However, if the accommodation party pays the instrument, s/he is entitled to reimbursement from the accommodated party.

c. Any indorsement out of the chain of title is notice of its accommodation character.

Example 12 ▸ Accommodation Party

> B wishes to borrow money from A. However, A requires B to obtain C's signature before the loan will be made. C agrees to sign as an accommodation party to B. C will now be liable to A as an indorser of the instrument. If B later refuses to repay the loan, A can proceed against the accommodation party, C.

B. Warranty Liability

Distinctly separate from the contractual liabilities of primary and secondary parties are the warranty liabilities of the parties to an instrument. One who indorses or otherwise transfers an instrument creates an implied warranty of certain facts relating to the instrument. There are basically two groups of warranties: **transferor's warranties,** which run in favor of immediate transferees and subsequent holders, and **presenter's warranties,** which run in favor of those parties who pay or accept an instrument.

1. Transferor's Warranties

a. **General Rule** Any person who transfers and receives consideration warrants to the transferee, and if the transfer is by indorsement, to any subsequent holder who takes in good faith, the following:

(1) S/he has good title to the instrument.

(2) All signatures are genuine and authorized.

(3) The instrument has not been altered materially.

(4) No defense of any party is good against her/him.

(5) S/he has no knowledge of any insolvency proceedings instituted with respect to the maker, acceptor, or drawer of an unaccepted instrument.

b. **Transfer** Transfer means that there was a delivery; therefore, the warranties will be imposed even though the transfer was not accompanied by an indorsement (e.g., the bearer instrument was negotiated by delivery only).

c. **Consideration** The implied warranties attach only if there has in essence been a sale of the instrument through a transfer for value. For this reason, an accommodation indorser cannot be held liable on implied warranties because the accommodating party received no consideration from the transferee.

d. **Effect of Shelter Provision** It is also important to remember that transferees of HDCs who do not qualify as HDCs, nevertheless, take the warranty protection of HDCs through the shelter provision (see IV.,B.,1., above). However, if there has been a breach of the transferor's warranty of "good title," there cannot again be an HDC who is free of warranty liability when the breach of "good title" is caused by a forgery of one other than the maker or drawer.

2. Presenter's Warranties

a. **General Rule** Any person **other than an HDC** who presents an instrument for payment or acceptance warrants to the acceptor or payor that the presenter:

(1) Has good title to the instrument.

(2) Warrants that the instrument has not been altered materially.

(3) Has no knowledge that the signature of the maker or drawer is unauthorized.

b. **HDC** A **holder in due course** who presents an instrument for payment or acceptance warrants that s/he has good title to the instrument. **NOTE:** An HDC does not warrant that s/he has no knowledge that the signature of the maker or drawer is unauthorized.

c. **Prior Transferors** It is important to remember that the presenter's warranties are given not only by those specific parties who receive payment or acceptance, but also by prior transferors.

3. **Effect of Indorsement "Without Recourse"** If the indorsement is **qualified** ("without recourse"), the indorser disclaims her/his contractual secondary liability, but does not change the warranty.

4. **Validity of Instrument** A warranty does not go to the payment of the instrument, but to its validity as an instrument. If a warranty is breached, the warrantor is liable for the loss accruing as a result of the defect in the instrument. (Of course, the person liable for breach of warranty also may have contract liability for payment.)

5. **Disclaimers** Warranties may be disclaimed by an agreement between the immediate parties which is noted on the instrument.

C. **Finality of Acceptance of Payment**
If a holder in due course obtains acceptance or payment of an instrument and the signature of the maker or drawer was forged or unauthorized, the acceptance or payment is, nevertheless, final, even though the maker or drawee had no obligation to pay or accept.

1. **Reasoning** The maker or drawer was negligent in failing to detect the forgery.

2. **Forged or Unauthorized Indorsements** This rule does not apply to forged or unauthorized indorsements.

3. **Applicability** The rule applies not only to holders in due course, but also to any other person who in **good faith** changed her/his position in reliance on the payment or acceptance.

VIII. Liability Discharge

A. **Negotiable Instrument & Underlying Obligation**
The issuance of commercial paper changes the form of, and generally suspends, the underlying money obligation for varying periods depending on the negotiable instrument's maturity date. Thus, a purchaser of goods, instead of paying the seller in cash upon delivery of the goods, may convince the seller to take the purchaser's 30-day note at an acceptable interest rate. When the 30-day note is paid (perhaps after it has been negotiated to a bank for discounting), the underlying obligation (payment for goods received) is discharged. If, however, instead of being paid at maturity, the note is dishonored by the purchaser after presentment, the creditor may bring an action on either the note or the obligation underlying the note. The following rules summarize the effect of a negotiable instrument on the underlying obligation for which it is given.

1. **Suspension** Unless otherwise agreed, the obligation is suspended until the instrument is due or, if it is payable on demand, until its presentment.

2. **Discharge** The underlying obligation that is suspended during the prematurity period of the instrument is discharged totally when the obligor is discharged on the instrument.

3. **No Recourse** The obligation also is discharged if a bank is the drawer, maker, or acceptor of the instrument and there is no recourse on the instrument against the underlying obligor. For example, if the underlying obligor negotiates the instrument without indorsement, the obligation is discharged.

B. **Discharge Methods**

1. **Payment or Satisfaction** Payment or satisfaction of the instrument will discharge a party from liability on the instrument.

    a. Payment or satisfaction must be made to the holder of the instrument.

    b. However, payment or satisfaction made to a holder will **not** discharge the liability of a payor who in bad faith pays a holder whom s/he knows obtained the instrument by theft.

Example 13 ▸ Payment or Discharge

A holds B's note. After A indorses the note in blank, thief steals the note under facts that do not indicate that A was negligent. Obligor then pays T, the holder of the bearer note, without knowing of the theft. Obligor is discharged because even though the note was stolen, obligor did not act in bad faith. If obligor knew of the theft, s/he would not have been discharged upon payment to thief.

2. **Tender** If the maker or acceptor of an instrument payable other than on demand is able and ready to pay at every place of payment specified in the instrument when it is due, it is equivalent to tender.

    a. If the obligor on an instrument tenders full payment to the holder when or after the instrument is due and the holder improperly refuses payment, the obligation of the party making the tender is not discharged (except as to subsequent liability for interest, costs, and attorney's fees).

    b. The holder's refusal of such tender wholly discharges any party who has a right of recourse against the party making tender.

Example 14 ▸ Tender

A negotiates obligor's note to B. At maturity, obligor tenders payment to holder B who refuses to accept payment. A is discharged fully. The obligor is discharged to the extent of future interest, costs, and legal fees so long as the obligor continues his tender after the maturity date.

3. **Cancellation** The holder may discharge any prior party by cancellation. Cancellation may be accomplished by indicating the fact of cancellation on the face of the instrument (e.g., by intentionally canceling the instrument or party's signature by destruction or mutilation) or by striking the indorsement of a party.

    a. Cancellation usually is effected by writing "paid" on the face of the instrument.

    b. The prior party whose signature is struck is fully discharged from liability on the instrument.

    c. No consideration is needed for cancellation.

4. **Renunciation** The holder may discharge any prior party by renunciation.

    a. Renunciation may be accomplished by a signed writing stating that the holder releases the party or by the surrender of the instrument to the party to be discharged.

b. An HDC may not be bound by a discharge by renunciation because (unlike cancellation) renunciation will not appear on the face of the instrument.

5. **Reacquisition** When an instrument is returned to or reacquired by a prior party, any intervening party is discharged from liability as against the reacquiring party and as against any subsequent party who is not an HDC without notice of the discharge.

Example 15 ▸ Reacquisition

A, who is payee on a note, negotiates by delivery and indorsement to B, who in turn negotiates the note to the order of C. C then negotiates it to D who negotiates the note back to A. B, C, and D are discharged from liability on the note—they have no secondary liability (they still have transferor's warranty liability). If in these facts A negotiates the note to an HDC and the note is dishonored after presentment, the HDC may recover from **any** of the above parties.

6. **Discharge of Any Person As Surety**

   a. If the holder discharges a party, then any other party who has a right of recourse against the released party also is released.

   b. If a holder discharges the maker, **but** reserves rights against surety, then the surety's rights against the other parties on the instrument also are reserved.

7. **Activity Affecting the Validity or Terms of the Instrument** Certain acts by parties to an instrument discharge other parties from liability. These acts that discharge liability are as follows:

   a. Fraudulent and material alteration

   b. Acceptance varying a draft

   c. Unexcused delay in presentment or notice of dishonor or protest

8. **Discharge by Agreement** Parties may discharge each other by agreement. Such a discharge only affects the rights as between the parties involved.

IX. Documents of Title

A. Definitions

1. **Bailee** Party who accepts possession of the bailed property. The bailee acknowledges possession of goods and contracts to deliver them by a warehouse receipt, bill of lading, or other document [UCC 7-102(1)(a)].

2. **Bailor** Party who owns property and delivers it to the bailee.

3. **Consignee** Person named in a bill of lading to whom or to whose order the bill promises delivery [UCC 7-102(1)(b)].

4. **Consignor** Person named in a bill of lading as the person from whom the goods have been received for shipment [UCC 7-102(1)(c)].

5. **Delivery Order** Written order to deliver goods directed to a warehouseman or carrier who issues warehouse receipts or bills of lading in the ordinary course of business [UCC 7-102(1)(d)].

6. **Documents of Title** Include bills of lading, dock warrants and receipts, warehouse receipts, orders for the delivery of goods, as well as any other document that in the regular course of

business or financing is treated as adequately evidencing that the person in possession of the document is entitled to receive, hold, and dispose of the document and the goods it covers. To be a document of title, a document must purport to be issued by or addressed to a bailee and purport to cover goods in the bailee's possession [UCC 1-201(15)].

7. **Issuer** Bailee who issues a document, except that in relation to an unaccepted delivery order, it means the person who orders the possessor of goods to deliver [UCC 7-102(1)(g)].

Exhibit 5 ▸ Comparison of Commercial Paper & Documents of Title

Elements	Commercial Paper	Documents of Title
Negotiability	**S** In writing, **S**igned by the maker or drawer. **U** **U**nconditional promise or order to pay. **M** Promise to pay a fixed amount of **M**oney.	To Order or To Bearer
	B Payable to **B**earer (except checks) or **O** Payable to **O**rder (except checks). **D** Payable on **D**emand or at a **D**efinite time.	
Negotiation	Order: Endorsed & Delivered Bearer: Delivered	Same
Purchaser Entitled to Greater Rights	Holder in Due Course (HDC): **V**alue Good **F**aith **W**ithout notice of dishonor, defense, or claim	*Bona Fide* Purchaser (BFP): Present Value Good Faith Without notice of defense or claim In regular course of business
Shelter Provision	Yes	Yes
Real Defenses Subject to Claims and/or Defenses if Greater Rights	**M** **M**aterial alteration **I** Discharge in **I**nsolvency proceedings or bankruptcy **I**ncapacity **I**llegality (if it would render the instrument void under local law) **F** **F**orgery **F** **F**raud in the factum (execution / essence) **D** **D**uress (to the extent it would render the obligation void)	Forged endorsement Theft of the goods (not the paper) Buyer in ordinary course of business of fungible goods (seller-storer)

Subject to Claims and/or Defenses if no Greater Rights	Personal Defenses: Lack of consideration Fraud in the inducement Nondelivery Unauthorized completion Payment before maturity Discharge of parties	Personal Defense: Theft of document
Contract Liability	If Signed	No
Warranty Liability	Presentment & Transfer	To Immediate Purchaser: Document is genuine No knowledge of fact that would impair its worth Transfer is rightful and effective as to good title to document and goods To Bailee: Presentment

B. Warehouse Receipt

Receipt issued by a person engaged in the business of storing goods for hire. Even though one cannot become a warehouseman by storing her/his own goods, an owner-storer of goods can issue a document of title that is the equivalent of a receipt [UCC 1-201(45)]. Although no particular format is required, it must be in writing and must contain the following terms in order for the warehouseman to avoid liability for damages caused by the terms' omission.

1. **Location** Location of the warehouse in which the goods are stored
2. **Date** Date of issue of the receipt
3. **Number** Consecutive number of the receipt
4. **Delivery** Statement as to whether goods received will be delivered to the bearer, a specified person, or to a specified person on her/his order
5. **Rate** Rate of storage and handling charges
6. **Description** Description of the goods
7. **Signature** Signature of the warehouseman
8. **Ownership** Statement as to ownership, if issued for goods owned by the warehouseman
9. **Lien** Statement of the amount of advances and liabilities on which warehouseman claims a lien

C. Bill of Lading

Document evidencing the receipt of goods for shipment issued by a person engaged in the business of transporting or forwarding goods. It includes airbills and freight receipts [UCC 1-201(6)]. No particular format is required, but it must be in writing and must record adequately the fact that it was issued in receipt for goods to be shipped. Bills are regulated by Article 7 of the UCC to the extent not superseded by federal statutes and treaties. Some types of bills are as follows.

1. **Destination Bills** In the usual shipping situation, the bill is issued by the carrier at the point of shipment. If the goods subsequently arrive at the destination before the document of title, no one would be ready or able to receive them. To solve this problem, the carrier issues a "destination bill." This bill would be issued at the point of destination or other point specified by the consignor. Thus, there is no lag between issue and delivery; rather, the bill is there when the goods arrive (UCC 7-305).

2. **Through Bills** Issued by a carrier who accepts liability for the transport of goods from the point of shipment through (and over other connecting carriers) to the point of destination. Connecting carriers act as agents for the through bill carrier and are liable for loss while goods are in their possession (UCC 7-302).

3. **Freight-Forwarder Bills** Issued by a middleman who marshals less than carload amounts of goods into carload quantities. Purpose is to provide continuous title documentation while goods are in transit.

D. Negotiability

The distinction between negotiable and nonnegotiable documents is the most important aspect of Article 7, because the holder of negotiable documents may acquire more rights than the transferor had in the document. A document of title is "commodity paper"; thus, it represents the underlying goods. (In contrast, commercial paper is "money paper.") It is important to note that a holder to whom a negotiable document has been duly negotiated by endorsement and delivery acquires title to the underlying goods (UCC 7-502). However, a transferee of a negotiable or non-negotiable document to whom the document has been transferred, but not negotiated, acquires only those rights to the underlying goods that the transferor had the power and authority to transfer [UCC 7-504(1)].

1. **Negotiable Document** A warehouse receipt, bill of lading, or other document of title is negotiable if either of the following applies [UCC 7-104(1)].

   a. If by its terms, the goods are to be delivered to bearer or to the order of a named person.

   b. Where recognized in overseas trade, the document runs to a named person or assigns.

2. **Nonnegotiable Document** Any document of title not satisfying the requirements of a negotiable document. Furthermore, a bill of lading in which it is stated that the goods are consigned to a named person is **not** made negotiable by a provision that the goods are to be delivered only against a signed written order by that person. Thus, a straight bill does not become an order bill because a specific person is to be notified and must sign to take possession of goods [UCC 7-104(2)].

3. **Negotiation & Due Negotiation** It is important to keep in mind the fact that **only** a negotiable document can be negotiated (although negotiable documents also can be transferred or assigned). In contrast, a nonnegotiable document can be only transferred or assigned.

   a. **Negotiation** A special form of transfer that makes the transferee a holder. (Issuance of a negotiable document to a named person has the same effect as negotiation.)

      - **Rights Acquired by Holder** A holder to whom a document has been duly negotiated acquires title to the document, title to the goods, and right to the goods (if delivered to a bailee). Finally, the issuer of the duly negotiated document has the direct obligation to hold or deliver the goods to the holder according to the terms of the document free of any claim or defense. Moreover, these rights accrue to the holder, even though the negotiation or any prior negotiation constituted a breach of duty, or the document was obtained from a prior possessor by fraud or theft (UCC 7-502).

b. **Due Negotiation** In order to obtain the special rights of a holder, there must be either due negotiation or the transferee must take under the shelter principle.

- **Due Negotiation of a Negotiable Document** Occurs when the transferee takes **in good faith, in the regular course of business** of the transferor, and **for present (not antecedent) value** (UCC 7-501). Note the similarities (and differences) between an Article 7 holder and an Article 3 holder in due course (HDC). An Article 7 holder must take the negotiable instrument running to order of a named person in the ordinary course of business of the transferor (the HDC need not so take). Thus, there could be no due negotiation of an order document running to the order of a person who has no business holding the document. For example, there could be no holder-transferee of a document running to the order of a transient, casual friend, or person not in the business of trading in documents. (However, there would be due negotiation of an Article 3 negotiable instrument from any of the above three people.) This results from the negotiation requirements of **order** negotiable documents (negotiation accomplished by and only when **endorsement and delivery** effected) versus **bearer** negotiable documents (negotiation accomplished upon delivery) (UCC 7-501).

c. **Shelter Principle** A transferee of a negotiable or nonnegotiable document to whom the document has been delivered, but not duly negotiated, acquires the title and rights that the transferor held [UCC 7-504(1)]. In the same way that the shelter principle operates in Article 3, it operates in Article 7. When the transferee receives an unendorsed order document, the transferee has a specifically enforceable right to endorsement from the transferor. However, the transferee becomes a holder only at the instant the endorsement is obtained (UCC 7-506).

4. **Liability of Endorser or Transferor** Unlike Article 3 (commercial paper), the endorser of a negotiable document does not have liability if the bailee fails to perform. The holder-transferee's only recourse is against the bailee (UCC 7-505). However, the endorser or transferor does **warrant** the following (UCC 7-507).

   a. The document is genuine.

   b. S/he has no knowledge of any fact that would impair its worth.

   c. Her/his negotiation or transfer is rightful and fully effective with respect to the title of the document and the goods it represents.

5. **Persons Defeating Holders' & Transferees' Rights**

   a. A holder who takes an order-negotiable document with a forged endorsement has no rights in either the document or the underlying goods. This is similar to the real defense of forgery, which is good against an HDC in Article 3.

   b. A document of title conveys no rights to underlying goods in a situation in which a thief has deposited the stolen goods in a warehouse and procured a negotiable document (UCC 7-503).

   c. A buyer in the ordinary course of (the issuer's) business (e.g., a grain storer-seller) will defeat the rights of a holder of a negotiable warehouse receipt to fungible goods (UCC 7-205).

E. **Duty of Care & Risk of Loss**

1. **Warehouseman** Person engaged in the business of storing goods for hire [UCC 7-102(1)(h)].

a. **Duty of Care** Liable for damages for loss of or injury to goods caused by her/his failure to exercise such care as a reasonably careful person would exercise under like circumstances. Liability may be limited further by written agreement (UCC 7-204). Additionally, a party to, or a purchaser for value in good faith of, a warehouse receipt or other document (except bill of lading) may recover from the issuer damages caused by the nonreceipt or misdescription of the goods. However, no recovery is permitted if the description is qualified by language such as "contents, condition, and quality unknown" or "said to contain," or if the party or purchaser otherwise has notice (UCC 7-203). Furthermore, unless the warehouse receipt provides otherwise, the warehouseman has a duty to keep separate all of the goods covered by each warehouse receipt, although fungible goods may be commingled. The warehouseman will be liable for any loss caused by the commingling of nonfungible goods (UCC 7-207).

b. **Risk of Loss** When goods are held by a warehouseman or other bailee and title to the goods is to be transferred by negotiable warehouse receipt without movement of the goods, the risk of loss passes to the transferee, along with title to the document, at time of receipt of the document.

2. **Carriers**

a. **Duty of Care** Carrier must exercise that degree of care that a reasonably careful person would exercise under like circumstances. Although common carriers may limit liability to some extent (in a manner similar to warehousemen), the general view is that common carriers are strictly liable for loss or damage to goods. Contract carriers are liable only for loss or damage caused by negligence.

b. **Risk of Loss** As between buyer and seller, risk of loss is based on whether the contract is a "shipment" or "destination" contract.

How to Pass the CPA Exam

Watching this video program, CPA candidates will gain insight about the CPA exam in general and computer-based testing in particular. Robert Monette discusses when to take the exam and the content specification outline. He explains the good and bad news about computer-based testing. Bob interprets what the AICPA examiners mean by on-demand exam and adaptive testing. Bob delineates the different question types and explores exam-taking, exam-scheduling, and study strategies. Approximately 30 minutes.

Call a Bisk Education customer service representative at 1-800-874-7877 or visit Bisk Education's web-site at www.cpaexam.com. Complimentary copies of this valuable video are available for a limited time to qualified candidates.

CHAPTER 36—NEGOTIABLE INSTRUMENTS & DOCUMENTS OF TITLE

Problem 36-1 MULTIPLE CHOICE QUESTIONS (45 to 60 minutes)

1. Which of the following instruments is subject to the provisions of the Negotiable Instruments Article of the UCC?
   a. A bill of lading
   b. A warehouse receipt
   c. A certificate of deposit
   d. An investment security (R/99, Law, #14, 6865)

2. Which of the following negotiable instruments is subject to the UCC Negotiable Instruments Article?
   a. Corporate bearer bond with a maturity date of January 1, 2015
   b. Installment note payable on the first day of each month
   c. Warehouse receipt
   d. Bill of lading payable to order
   (11/92, Law, #33, amended, 3115)

3. A bank issues a negotiable instrument that acknowledges receipt of $50,000. The instrument also provides that the bank will repay the $50,000 plus 8% interest per annum to the bearer 90 days from the date of the instrument. The instrument is a
   a. Certificate of deposit
   b. Time draft
   c. Trade or banker's acceptance
   d. Cashier's check (11/88, Law, #36, 0545)

4. Under the Negotiable Instruments Article of the UCC, an instrument will be precluded from being negotiable if the instrument
   a. Fails to state the place of payment
   b. Is made subject to another agreement
   c. Fails to state the underlying consideration
   d. Is undated (R/06, REG, 0554L, #3, 8173)

5. Under the Negotiable Instruments Article of the UCC, which of the following instruments meets the negotiability requirement of being payable on demand or at a definite time?
   a. A promissory note payable one year after a person's marriage
   b. A promissory note payable June 30, year 1, whose holder can extend the time of payment until the following June 30 if the holder wishes
   c. A promissory note payable June 30, year 1, whose maturity can be extended by the maker for a reasonable time
   d. An undated promissory note payable one month after date (R/07, REG, 1988L, #12, 8436)

6. On February 15, Year 4, P. D. Stone obtained the following instrument from Astor Co. for $1,000. Stone was aware that Helco, Inc. disputed liability under the instrument because of an alleged breach by Astor of the referenced computer purchase agreement. On March 1, Year 4, Willard Bank obtained the instrument from Stone for $3,900. Willard had no knowledge that Helco disputed liability under the instrument.

> February 12, Year 4
>
> Helco, Inc. promises to pay to Astor Co. or bearer the sum of $4,900 (four thousand four hundred and 00/100 dollars) on March 12, Year 4, (maker may elect to extend due date to March 31, Year 4) with interest thereon at the rate of 12% per annum.
>
> HELCO, INC.
>
> By: *A. J. Help*
> A. J. Help, President
>
> Reference: Computer purchase agreement dated February 12, Year 4

The reverse side of the instrument is endorsed as follows:

> Pay to the order of Willard Bank, without recourse
>
> *P. D. Stone*
> P. D. Stone

The instrument is
   a. Nonnegotiable, because of the reference to the computer purchase agreement.
   b. Nonnegotiable, because the numerical amount differs from the written amount.
   c. Negotiable, even though the maker has the right to extend the time for payment.
   d. Negotiable, when held by Astor, but nonnegotiable when held by Willard Bank.
   (5/93, Law, #37, amended, 4005)

7. Under the Negotiable Instruments Article of the UCC, which of the following statements is(are) correct regarding the requirements for an instrument to be negotiable?

I. The instrument must be in writing, be signed by both the drawer and the drawee, and contain an unconditional promise or order to pay.
II. The instrument must state a fixed amount of money, be payable on demand or at a definite time, and be payable to order or to bearer.

a. I only
b. II only
c. Both I and II
d. Neither I nor II (R/00, Law, #8, 6973)

8. Under the Negotiable Instruments Article of the UCC, when an instrument is indorsed "Pay to John Doe" and signed "Faye Smith," which of the following statements is(are) correct?

	Payment of the instrument is guaranteed	*The instrument can be further negotiated*
a.	Yes	Yes
b.	Yes	No
c.	No	Yes
d.	No	No

(5/96, Law, #8, 6264)

9. Under the Documents of Title Article of the UCC, a negotiable document of title is "duly negotiated" when it is negotiated to
a. Any holder by indorsement
b. Any holder by delivery
c. A holder who takes the document in payment of a money obligation
d. A holder who takes the document for value, in good faith, and without notice of any defense or claim to it (11/97, Law, #15, 6513)

10. One of the requirements to qualify as a holder of a negotiable bearer check is that the transferee must
a. Receive the check that was originally made payable to bearer
b. Take the check in good faith
c. Give value for the check
d. Have possession of the check

(11/92, Law, #36, 3118)

11. Under the Negotiable Instruments Article of the UCC, which of the endorser's liabilities are disclaimed by a "without recourse" indorsement?
a. Contract liability only
b. Warranty liability only
c. Both contract and warranty liability
d. Neither contract nor warranty liability

(R/02, Law, #11, 7121)

12. The following endorsements appear on the back of a negotiable promissory note payable to Lake Corp.:

Pay to John Smith only

Frank Parker, President of Lake Corp.

John Smith

Pay to the order of Sharp, Inc., without recourse, but only if Sharp delivers computers purchased by Mary Harris by March 15, Year 2

Mary Harris

Sarah Sharp, President of Sharp, Inc.

Which of the following statements is correct?
a. The note became nonnegotiable as a result of Parker's endorsement.
b. Harris' endorsement was a conditional promise to pay and caused the note to be nonnegotiable.
c. Smith's endorsement effectively prevented further negotiation of the note.
d. Harris' signature was **not** required to effectively negotiate the note to Sharp.

(5/93, Law, #41, amended, 4009)

13. Under the Negotiable Instruments Article of the UCC, an endorsement of an instrument "for deposit only" is an example of what type of endorsement?
a. Blank
b. Qualified
c. Restrictive
d. Special (R/01, Law, #17, 7052)

14. Under the Negotiable Instruments Article of the UCC, which of the following requirements must be met for a person to be a holder in due course of a promissory note?
a. The note must be payable to bearer.
b. The note must be negotiable.
c. All prior holders must have been holders in due course.
d. The holder must be the payee of the note.

(5/95, Law, #46, amended, 5380)

15. Under the Negotiable Instruments Article of the UCC, which of the following parties will be a holder but not be entitled to the rights of a holder in due course?

a. A party who, knowing of a real defense to payment, received an instrument from a holder in due course
b. A party who found an instrument payable to bearer
c. A party who received, as a gift, an instrument from a holder in due course
d. A party who, in good faith and without notice of any defect, gave value for an instrument

(11/98, Law, #10, 6755)

16. A $5,000 promissory note payable to the order of Neptune is discounted to Bane by blank endorsement for $4,000. King steals the note from Bane and sells it to Ott who promises to pay King $4,500. After paying King $3,000, Ott learns that King stole the note. Ott makes no further payment to King. Ott is

a. A holder in due course to the extent of $5,000
b. An ordinary holder to the extent of $4,500
c. A holder in due course to the extent of $3,333
d. An ordinary holder to the extent of $3,000

(11/90, Law, #47, amended, 0532)

17. Under the Negotiable Instruments Article of the UCC, which of the following requirements must be met for a transferee of order paper to become a holder?

I. Possession
II. Endorsement of transferor

a. I only
b. II only
c. Both I and II
d. Neither I nor II (5/95, Law, #45, amended, 5379)

18. Cobb gave Garson a signed check with the amount payable left blank. Garson was to fill in, as the amount, the price of fuel oil Garson was to deliver to Cobb at a later date. Garson estimated the amount at $700, but told Cobb it would be no more than $900. Garson did not deliver the fuel oil, but filled in the amount of $1,000 on the check. Garson then negotiated the check to Josephs in satisfaction of a $500 debt with the $500 balance paid to Garson in cash. Cobb stopped payment and Josephs is seeking to collect $1,000 from Cobb. Cobb's maximum liability to Josephs will be

a. $0
b. $ 500
c. $ 900
d. $1,000 (11/91, Law, #49, 2377)

19. A maker of a note will have a real defense against a holder in due course as a result of any of the following conditions **except**

a. Discharge in bankruptcy
b. Forgery
c. Fraud in the execution
d. Lack of consideration (11/92, Law, #40, 3122)

20. Frank Supply Co. held the following instrument:

Clark Novelties, Inc. April 12, Year 5
29 State Street
Spokane, Washington

Pay to the order of Frank Supply Co. on April 30, Year 5, ten thousand and 00/100 dollars ($10,000.00).

Smith Industries, Inc.

J. C. Kahn
J. C. Kahn, President

ACCEPTED: Clark Novelties, Inc.
By:

Mitchell Clark
Mitchell Clark, President

Date: April 20, Year 5

As a result of an audit examination of this instrument which was properly endorsed by Frank to your client, it may be correctly concluded that

a. Smith was primarily liable on the instrument prior to acceptance.
b. The instrument is nonnegotiable and thus **no** one has rights under the instrument.
c. No one was primarily liable on the instrument at the time of issue, April 12.
d. Upon acceptance, Clark Novelties, Inc., became primarily liable and Smith was released from all liability. (5/86, Law, #28, amended, 8019)

21. Under the Negotiable Instruments Article of the UCC, in a nonconsumer transaction, which of the following are real defenses available against a holder in due course?

	Material alteration	*Discharge in bankruptcy*	*Breach of contract*
a.	No	Yes	Yes
b.	Yes	Yes	No
c.	No	No	Yes
d.	Yes	No	No

(5/95, Law, #49, amended, 5383)

22. To the extent that a holder of a negotiable promissory note is a holder in due course, the holder takes the note free of which of the following defenses?
a. Minority of the maker where it is a defense to enforcement of a contract
b. Forgery of the maker's signature
c. Discharge of the maker in bankruptcy
d. Nonperformance of a condition precedent
(5/92, Law, #47, 2860)

23. Field Corp. issued a negotiable warehouse receipt to Hall for goods stored in Field's warehouse. Hall's goods were lost due to Field's failure to exercise such care as a reasonably careful person would under like circumstances. The state in which this transaction occurred follows the UCC rule with respect to a warehouseman's liability for lost goods. The warehouse receipt is silent on this point. Under the circumstances, Field is
a. Liable, because it is strictly liable for any loss
b. Liable, because it was negligent
c. Not liable, because the warehouse receipt was negotiable
d. Not liable, unless Hall can establish that Field was grossly negligent (11/93, Law, #46, 4343)

24. Under the Documents of Title Article of the UCC, which of the following acts may excuse or limit a common carrier's liability for damage to goods in transit?
a. Vandalism
b. Power outage
c. Willful acts of third parties
d. Providing for a contractual dollar liability limitation
(R/99, Law, #16, 6867)

25. Under a nonnegotiable bill of lading, a carrier who accepts goods for shipment, must deliver the goods to
a. Any holder of the bill of lading
b. Any party subsequently named by the seller
c. The seller who was issued the bill of lading
d. The consignee of the bill of lading
(11/92, Law, #43, 3125)

26. Bell Co. owned 20 engines which it deposited in a public warehouse on May 5, receiving a negotiable warehouse receipt in its name. Bell sold the engines to Spark Corp. On which of the following dates did the risk of loss transfer from Bell to Spark?
a. June 11—Spark signed a contract to buy the engines from Bell for $19,000. Delivery was to be at the warehouse.
b. June 12—Spark paid for the engines.
c. June 13—Bell negotiated the warehouse receipt to Spark.
d. June 14—Spark received delivery of the engines at the warehouse. (11/85, Law, #45, 8020)

27. Under the Documents of Title Article of the UCC, which of the following terms must be contained in a warehouse receipt?

I. A statement indicating whether the goods received will be delivered to the bearer, to a specified person, or to a specified person or her/his order
II. The location of the warehouse where the goods are stored

a. I only
b. II only
c. Both I and II
d. Neither I nor II (11/96, Law, #5, 6446)

28. Under the Documents of Title Article of the UCC, which of the following statements is (are) correct regarding a common carrier's duty to deliver goods subject to a negotiable, bearer bill of lading?

I. The carrier may deliver the goods to any party designated by the holder of the bill of lading
II. A carrier who, without court order, delivers goods to a party claiming the goods under a missing negotiable bill of lading is liable to any person injured by the misdelivery

a. I only
b. II only
c. Both I and II
d. Neither I nor II (R/01, Law, #20, 7055)

29. Which of the following statements is correct concerning a bill of lading in the possession of Major Corp. that was issued by a common carrier and provides that the goods are to be delivered "to bearer"?
a. The carrier's lien for any unpaid shipping charges does **not** entitle it to sell the goods to enforce the lien.
b. The carrier will **not** be liable for delivering the goods to a person other than Major.
c. The carrier may require Major to endorse the bill of lading prior to delivering the goods.
d. The bill of lading can be negotiated by Major by delivery alone and without endorsement.
(11/93, Law, #47, 4344)

30. Which of the following statements is correct concerning a common carrier that issues a bill of lading stating that the goods are to be delivered "to the order of Ajax"?
a. The carrier's lien on the goods covered by the bill of lading for storage or transportation expenses is ineffective against the bill of lading's purchaser.
b. The carrier may **not,** as a matter of public policy, limit its liability for the goods by the terms of the bill.
c. The carrier must deliver the goods only to Ajax or to a person who presents the bill of lading properly endorsed by Ajax.
d. The carrier would have liability only to Ajax because the bill of lading is nonnegotiable.
(5/91, Law, #47, 0568)

Problem 36-2 ADDITIONAL MULTIPLE CHOICE QUESTIONS (45 to 60 minutes)

31. Under the Negotiable Instruments Article of the UCC, which of the following circumstances would prevent a promissory note from being negotiable?
a. An extension clause that allows the maker to elect to extend the time for payment to a date specified in the note
b. An acceleration clause that allows the holder to move up the maturity date of the note in the event of default
c. A person having a power of attorney signs the note on behalf of the maker
d. A clause that allows the maker to satisfy the note by the performance of services or the payment of money (5/95, Law, #44, 5378)

32. Under the Negotiable Instruments Article of the UCC, which of the following documents would be considered an order to pay?

I. Draft
II. Certificate of deposit

a. I only
b. II only
c. Both I and II
d. Neither I nor II (5/95, Law, #41, amended, 5375)

33. Third Corp. agreed to purchase goods from Silk Corp. Third could not pay for the goods immediately. A draft was then drawn by Silk ordering Third to pay Silk the price of the goods at a specified future date. Third signed the draft and returned it to Silk. Under the Negotiable Instruments Article of the UCC, what type of draft was created?
a. A trade acceptance
b. A letter of credit
c. A bank draft
d. A check (R/03, REG, 1832L, #20, 7662)

34. A check has the following endorsements on the back:

Paul Folk
without recourse

George Hopkins
payment guaranteed

Ann Quarry
collection guaranteed

Rachell Ott

Which of the following conditions occurring subsequent to the endorsements would discharge all of the endorsers?
a. Lack of notice of dishonor
b. Late presentment
c. Insolvency of the maker
d. Certification of the check
(11/92, Law, #41, 3123)

35. In order to negotiate bearer paper, one must
a. Endorse the paper
b. Endorse and transfer possession of the paper with consideration
c. Transfer possession of the paper
d. Transfer possession of and endorse the paper
(11/87, Law, #47, amended, 8022)

36. Under the Negotiable Instruments Article of the UCC, for an instrument other than a check to be negotiable, it must
a. Be payable to order or to bearer
b. Be signed to the payee
c. Contain references to all agreements between the parties
d. Contain necessary conditions of payment
(5/95, Law, #43, amended, 5377)

37. In general, which of the following statements is correct concerning the priority among checks drawn on a particular account and presented to the drawee bank on a particular day?
a. The checks may be charged to the account in any order convenient to the bank.
b. The checks may be charged to the account in any order provided **no** charge creates an overdraft.
c. The checks must be charged to the account in the order in which the checks were dated.
d. The checks must be charged to the account in the order of lowest amount to highest amount to minimize the number of dishonored checks.
(11/88, Law, #39, 8021)

38. The instrument below is a

> To: Middlesex National Bank
> Nassau, N.Y.
>
> September 15, Year 4
>
> Pay to the order of Robert Silver $4,000.00
>
> Four Thousand and xx/100 Dollars
>
> on October 1, Year 4
>
> *Lynn Dexter*
> Lynn Dexter

a. Draft
b. Postdated check
c. Trade acceptance
d. Promissory note
(5/95, Law, #42, amended, 5376)

Items 39 and 40 are based on the following.

> May 19, Year 1
>
> I promise to pay to the order of A. B. Shark $1,000 (One thousand one hundred dollars) with interest thereon at the rate of 12% per annum.
>
> *T. T. Tile*
> T. T. Tile
>
> **Guaranty**
>
> I personally guaranty payment by T. T. Tile.
>
> *N. A. Abner*
> N. A. Abner

39. The instrument is a
a. Promissory demand note
b. Sight draft
c. Check
d. Trade acceptance
(11/91, Law, #46, amended, 2374)

40. The instrument is
a. Nonnegotiable, even though it is payable on demand
b. Nonnegotiable, because the numeric amount differs from the written amount
c. Negotiable, even though a payment date is **not** specified
d. Negotiable, because of Abner's guaranty
(11/91, Law, #47, amended, 2375)

41. Union Co. possesses the following instrument:

> Holt, MT $4,000 April 15, Year 9
>
> Fifty days after date, or sooner, the undersigned promises to pay to the order of
>
> Union Co.
> Four Thousand Dollars
> at Salem Bank, Holt, MT
> Ten percent interest per annum
>
> This instrument is secured by the maker's business inventory.
>
> EASY, INC.
>
> By: *Thomas Foy*
> Thomas Foy, President

Assuming all other requirements of negotiability are satisfied, this instrument is
a. Not negotiable, because of a lack of a definite time for payment
b. Not negotiable, because the amount due is unspecified
c. Negotiable, because it is secured by the maker's inventory
d. Negotiable, because it is payable in a sum certain in money (11/90, Law, #46, amended, 0531)

42. Jane Lane, a sole proprietor, has in her possession several checks which she received from her customers. Lane is concerned about the safety of the checks since she believes that many of them are bearer paper which may be cashed without endorsement. The checks in Lane's possession will be considered order paper rather than bearer paper if they were made payable (in the drawer's handwriting) to the order of

a. Cash
b. Ted Tint, and endorsed by Ted Tint in blank
c. Bearer, and endorsed by Ken Kent making them payable to Jane Lane
d. Bearer, and endorsed by Sam Sole in blank

(11/85, Law, #37, 0564)

43. West Corp. received a check that was originally made payable to the order of one of its customers, Ted Burns. The following endorsement was written on the back of the check:

Ted Burns, without recourse, for collection only

Which of the following describes the endorsement?

	Special	Restrictive
a.	Yes	Yes
b.	No	No
c.	No	Yes
d.	Yes	No

(11/92, Law, #35, 3117)

44. An instrument reads as follows:

> $10,000 Ludlow, Vermont February 1, Year 4
>
> I promise to pay to the order of Custer Corp. $10,000 within 10 days after the sale of my two-carat diamond ring. I pledge the sale proceeds to secure my obligation hereunder.
>
> *R. Harris*
> R. Harris

Which of the following statements correctly describes the above instrument?

a. The instrument is nonnegotiable because it is **not** payable at a definite time.
b. The instrument is nonnegotiable because it is secured by the proceeds of the sale of the ring.
c. The instrument is a negotiable promissory note.
d. The instrument is a negotiable sight draft payable on demand.

(5/93, Law, #40, amended, 4008)

45. Under the Negotiable Instruments Article of the UCC, which of the following statements best describes the effect of a person endorsing a check "without recourse"?

a. The person has **no** liability to prior endorsers.
b. The person makes **no** promise or guarantee of payment on dishonor.
c. The person gives **no** warranty protection to later transferees.
d. The person converts the check into order paper.

(5/95, Law, #48, amended, 5382)

46. The following note was executed by Elizabeth Quinton on April 17, Year 9 and delivered to Ian Wolf:

(Face)

> April 17, Year 9
>
> On demand, the undersigned promises to pay to the order of Ian Wolf
>
> Seven Thousand and 00/100 Dollars
>
> *Elizabeth Quinton*
> Elizabeth Quinton

(Back)

> *Ian Wolf*
> Ian Wolf
>
> Pay: George Vernon
>
> *Samuel Thorn*
> Samuel Thorn
>
> Pay: Alan Yule
>
> *George Vernon*
> George Vernon
>
> *Alan Yule*
> Alan Yule

In sequence, beginning with Wolf's receipt of the note, this note is properly characterized as what type of negotiable instruments?

a. Bearer, bearer, order, order, order
b. Order, bearer, order, order, bearer
c. Order, order, bearer, order, bearer
d. Bearer, order, order, order, bearer

(11/90, Law, #49, amended, 0534)

47. The following endorsements appear on the back of a negotiable promissory note made payable "to bearer." Clark has possession of the note.

Pay to Sam North *Alice Fox* *Sam North* (without recourse)

Which of the following statements is correct?
a. Clark's unqualified endorsement is required to further negotiate the note.
b. To negotiate the note, Clark must have given value for it.
c. Clark is **not** a holder because North's qualified endorsement makes the note nonnegotiable.
d. Clark can negotiate the note by transfer of possession alone. (5/92, Law, #46, amended, 2859)

48. Hunt has in his possession a negotiable instrument which was originally payable to the order of Carr. It was transferred to Hunt by a mere delivery by Drake, who took it from Carr in good faith in satisfaction of an antecedent debt. The back of the instrument read as follows, "Pay to the order of Drake in satisfaction of my prior purchase of a new video calculator, signed Carr." Which of the following is correct?
a. Hunt has the right to assert Drake's rights, including his standing as a holder in due course and also has the right to obtain Drake's signature.
b. Drake's taking the instrument for an antecedent debt prevents him from qualifying as a holder in due course.
c. Carr's endorsement was a special endorsement; thus Drake's signature was **not** required in order to negotiate it.
d. Hunt is a holder in due course.
(11/85, Law, #41, 0565)

49. Under the Negotiable Instruments Article of the UCC, which of the following circumstances would prevent a person from becoming a holder in due course of an instrument?
a. The person was notified that payment was refused.
b. The person was notified that one of the prior endorsers was discharged.
c. The note was collateral for a loan.
d. The note was purchased at a discount.
(5/95, Law, #47, amended, 5381)

50. The value requirement in determining whether a person is a holder in due course with respect to a check will **not** be satisfied by the taking of the check
a. As security for an obligation to the extent of the obligation
b. As payment for an antecedent debt
c. In exchange for another negotiable instrument
d. In exchange for a promise to perform services in the future (5/88, Law, #48, 0549)

51. Bond fraudulently induced Teal to make a note payable to Wilk, to whom Bond was indebted. Bond delivered the note to Wilk. Wilk negotiated the instrument to Monk, who purchased it with knowledge of the fraud and after it was overdue. If Wilk qualifies as a holder in due course, which of the following statements is correct?
a. Monk has the standing of a holder in due course through Wilk.
b. Teal can successfully assert the defense of fraud in the inducement against Monk.
c. Monk personally qualifies as a holder in due course.
d. Teal can successfully assert the defense of fraud in the inducement against Wilk.
(5/90, Law, #38, 0536)

52. Robb, a minor, executed a promissory note payable to bearer and delivered it to Dodsen in payment for a stereo system. Dodsen negotiated the note for value to Mellon by delivery alone and without endorsement. Mellon endorsed the note in blank and negotiated it to Bloom for value. Bloom's demand for payment was refused by Robb because the note was executed when Robb was a minor. Bloom gave prompt notice of Robb's default to Dodsen and Mellon. None of the holders of the note were aware of Robb's minority. Which of the following parties will be liable to Bloom?

	Dodsen	*Mellon*	
a.	Yes	Yes	
b.	Yes	No	
c.	No	No	
d.	No	Yes	(5/93, Law, #42, 4010)

53. Which of the following actions does **not** discharge a prior party to a commercial instrument?
a. Good faith payment or satisfaction of the instrument
b. Cancellation of that prior party's endorsement
c. The holder's oral renunciation of that prior party's liability
d. The holder's intentional destruction of the instrument (5/92, Law, #48, 2861)

54. Vex Corp. executed a negotiable promissory note payable to Tamp, Inc. The note was collateralized by some of Vex's business assets. Tamp negotiated the note to Miller for value. Miller endorsed the note in blank and negotiated it to Bilco for value. Before the note became due, Bilco agreed to release Vex's collateral. Vex refused to pay Bilco when the note became due. Bilco promptly notified Miller and Tamp of Vex's default. Which of the following statements is correct?

a. Bilco will be unable to collect from Miller because Miller's endorsement was in blank.
b. Bilco will be able to collect from either Tamp or Miller because Bilco was a holder in due course.
c. Bilco will be unable to collect from either Tamp or Miller because of Bilco's release of the collateral.
d. Bilco will be able to collect from Tamp because Tamp was the original payee.

(5/93, Law, #43, 4011)

55.

> Pay to Ann Tyler
> *Paul Tyler*
>
> *Ann Tyler*
>
> *Mary Thomas*
>
> ~~*Betty Ash*~~
>
> Pay George Green Only
> *Susan Town*

Susan Town, on receiving the above instrument, struck Betty Ash's endorsement. Under the Negotiable Instruments Article of the UCC, which of the endorsers of the above instrument will be completely discharged from secondary liability to later endorsers of the instrument?

a. Ann Tyler
b. Mary Thomas
c. Betty Ash
d. Susan Town (5/95, Law, #50, amended, 5384)

56. On February 15, Year 2, P. D. Stone obtained the following instrument from Astor Co. for $1,000. Stone was aware that Helco, Inc. disputed liability under the instrument because of an alleged breach by Astor of the referenced computer purchase agreement. On March 1, Year 2, Willard Bank obtained the instrument from Stone for $3,900. Willard had no knowledge that Helco disputed liability under the instrument.

> February 12, Year 2
>
> Helco, Inc. promises to pay to Astor Co. or bearer the sum of $4,900 (four thousand four hundred and 00/100 dollars) on March 12, Year 2, (maker may elect to extend due date to March 31, Year 2) with interest thereon at the rate of 12% per annum.
>
> HELCO, INC.
>
> By: *A. J. Help*
> A. J. Help, President
>
> Reference: Computer purchase agreement dated February 12, Year 2

The reverse side of the instrument is endorsed as follows:

> Pay to the order of Willard Bank, without recourse
>
> *P. D. Stone*
> P. D. Stone

If Willard Bank demands payment from Helco and Helco refuses to pay the instrument because of Astor's breach of the computer purchase agreement, which of the following statements would be correct?

a. Willard Bank is **not** a holder in due course because Stone was **not** a holder in due course.
b. Helco will **not** be liable to Willard Bank because of Astor's breach.
c. Stone will be the only party liable to Willard Bank because he was aware of the dispute between Helco and Astor.
d. Helco will be liable to Willard Bank because Willard Bank is a holder in due course.

(5/93, Law, #39, amended, 4007)

57. Ball borrowed $10,000 from Link. Ball, unable to repay the debt on its due date, fraudulently induced Park to purchase a piece of worthless costume jewelry for $10,000. Ball had Park write a check for that amount naming Link as the payee. Ball gave the check to Link in satisfaction of the debt Ball owed Link. Unaware of Ball's fraud, Link cashed the check. When Park discovered Ball's fraud, Park demanded that Link repay the $10,000. Under the Negotiable Instruments Article of the UCC, will Link be required to repay Park?

a. No, because Link is a holder in due course of the check
b. No, because Link is the payee of the check and had **no** obligation on the check once it is cashed
c. Yes, because Link is subject to Park's defense of fraud in the inducement
d. Yes, because Link, as the payee of the check, takes it subject to all claims

(R/06, REG, 1249L, #26, 8196)

58. Burke stole several negotiable warehouse receipts from Grove Co. The receipts were deliverable to Grove's order. Burke endorsed Grove's name and sold the warehouse receipts to Federated Wholesalers, a bona fide purchaser. In an action by Federated against Grove,

a. Grove will prevail, because Burke **cannot** validly negotiate the warehouse receipts.
b. Grove will prevail, because the warehouser must be notified before any valid negotiation of a warehouse receipt is effective.
c. Federated will prevail, because the warehouse receipts were converted to bearer instruments by Burke's endorsement.
d. Federated will prevail, because it took the negotiable warehouse receipts as a bona fide purchaser for value. (11/92, Law, #42, 3124)

59. Under the UCC, a warehouse receipt

a. Is negotiable if, by its terms, the goods are to be delivered to bearer or to the order of a named person
b. Will **not** be negotiable if it contains a contractual limitation on the warehouser's liability
c. May qualify as both a negotiable warehouse receipt and negotiable commercial paper if the instrument is payable either in cash or by the delivery of goods
d. May be issued only by a bonded and licensed warehouser (5/92, Law, #49, 2862)

60. Under the UCC, a bill of lading

a. Will **never** be enforceable if altered
b. Is issued by a consignee of goods
c. Will **never** be negotiable unless it is endorsed
d. Is negotiable if the goods are to be delivered to bearer (5/93, Law, #44, 4012)

SIMULATION

Problem 36-3 (20 to 30 minutes)

Under the Negotiable Instruments Article of the UCC, a note must conform to certain requirements to be negotiable. Similarly, a note's negotiability may be restricted or prevented. (Editors, 6427)

Items 1 through 5 are examples of terms, conditions, and endorsements that may appear on a note. For each item, select the effect each term, condition, or endorsement would have on the note's negotiability from the list. An answer may be selected once, more than once, or not at all.

Effect on Negotiability

A. Has no effect on negotiability
B. Restricts negotiability
C. Must be negotiated by delivery
D. Must be indorsed to be negotiated
E. Results in nonnegotiability

Terms, Conditions & Endorsements	Answer
1. The note is postdated.	
2. No place of payment is indicated on the note.	
3. The note is payable to the order of a named individual.	
4. The note is indorsed "For Collection."	
5. The note is payable in either money or goods.	

On October 30, Year 4, Dover, CPA, was engaged to audit the financial records of Crane Corp., a tractor manufacturer. During the review of notes receivable, Dover reviewed a promissory note given to Crane by Jones Corp., one of its customers, in payment for a tractor. The note appears below.

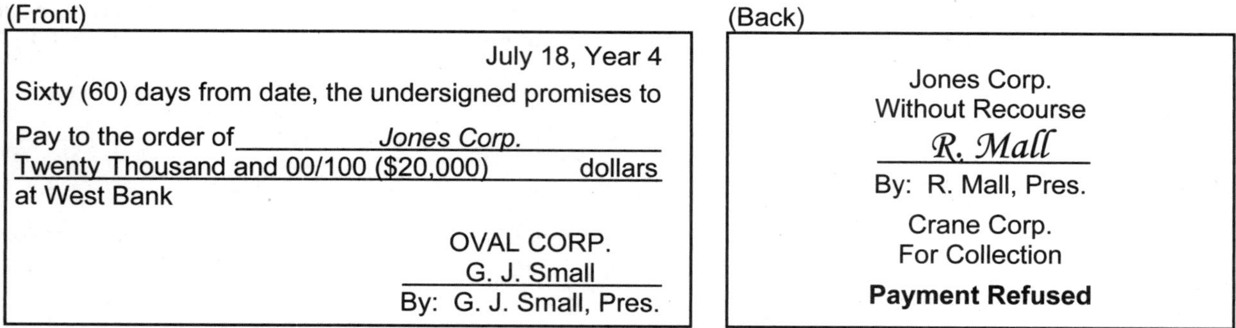
(Front)

July 18, Year 4
Sixty (60) days from date, the undersigned promises to
Pay to the order of *Jones Corp.*
Twenty Thousand and 00/100 ($20,000) dollars
at West Bank

OVAL CORP.
G. J. Small
By: G. J. Small, Pres.

(Back)

Jones Corp.
Without Recourse
R. Mall
By: R. Mall, Pres.

Crane Corp.
For Collection

Payment Refused

On the note's due date, Crane deposited the note for collection and was advised by the bank that Oval had refused payment. After payment was refused, Crane contacted Oval. Oval told Crane that Jones fraudulently induced Oval into executing the note and that Jones knew about Oval's claim before Jones endorsed the note to Crane.

As an audit team member on this engagement, write a memo to the partner-in-charge identifying, explaining, and stating your conclusions about the legal issues pertaining to the Oval Corporation note. The memo should address the following:

a. Whether Crane is a holder in due course

b. Whether Oval will be required to pay the note

c. Whether Jones is liable to pay the note

Research Question: What code section and subsection, if applicable, provides guidance on the rate of the hospital insurance tax imposed on every employee on his or her wages as part of the Federal Insurance Contributions Act (FICA)?

Section & Subsection Answer: §_____ (___)

Solution 36-1 MULTIPLE CHOICE ANSWERS

Negotiable Instrument Types

1. (c) Certificates of deposit are subject to the provisions of Article 3, Negotiable Instruments, of the Uniform Commercial Code (UCC). Bills of lading, warehouse receipts, and investment securities are governed by other articles of the UCC: Article 7, *Warehouse Receipts, Bills of Lading and Other Documents of Title,* and Article 8, *Investment Securities.*

2. (b) Notes can be payable on installment and still be subject to the UCC Negotiable Instruments Article. Warehouse receipts and bills of lading are documents of title governed by Article 7 of the UCC. Investment bonds, such as corporate bearer bonds, are investment securities subject to Article 8 of the UCC.

3. (a) A certificate of deposit is a written acknowledgement by a bank of the receipt of a sum of money with an engagement to repay that sum. A time draft is a written order from one person directing a second person to pay a sum certain of money to a third person or to the bearer at a certain future date. The concept of a banker's acceptance is similar to a trade acceptance, except that the draft is drawn on the buyer's bank instead of on the buyer personally. A cashier's check is a check drawn by a bank on itself, ordering itself to pay a sum of money to a third person.

Negotiability Requirements

4. (b) To be negotiable, an instrument must include an unconditional order or promise to pay a sum certain in money. The place of payment and underlying consideration need not be stated, nor must the instrument be dated.

5. (b) For an instrument to be payable on demand or at a definite time, it must be possible to determine the last possible date that the holder of the instrument will be paid from the face of the instrument. The date of a person's marriage, a reasonable time for an extension, and one month after an undated note are not definite (objectively known) times.

6. (c) An instrument is payable at a definite time if by its terms it is payable at a definite time subject to extension. If the extension is at the option of the maker or acceptor, it must be at a further definite time, or automatically upon the occurrence of a specified event (e.g., maker may elect to extend due date to March 31, Year 4). A reference to the purchase agreement out of which an instrument arose will not prevent it from being negotiable. The instrument would be nonnegotiable if the instrument were subject to the computer purchase agreement. In the case of inconsistencies between words and figures, the words control; negotiability is not affected by a discrepancy. Negotiability was not destroyed when the note was transferred to Willard Bank.

7. (b) Six prerequisites must be met to create a negotiable instrument: 1) the instrument must be in writing and signed by the maker (note) or drawer (draft, check); 2) the instrument must contain an unconditional promise or order to pay; 3) the amount of money must be a fixed amount; 4) the instrument must be made payable to order or to bearer (except for checks); 5) the instrument must be payable on demand or at a definite time; and 6) the promise or order may not have any other promise, order, obligation, or power given by the maker or drawer except as authorized by Article 3 of the UCC.

Issue & Negotiation

8. (d) Due negotiation of a negotiable document of title occurs when the transferee takes in good faith, in the regular course of business of the transferor, and for present (not antecedent) value (UCC 7-501). If it is a bearer document, a negotiable document of title does not need indorsement to be negotiated. If it is an order document, a negotiable document requires indorsement in addition to delivery to be negotiated. A document of title must be for present value, not antecedent value; thus a document of title could not be used in payment of a prior money obligation. Note that this rule is different than for commercial paper; commercial paper may be given for antecedent value.

9. (a) The first indorsement presumes the instrument was negotiable when made. Indorsement, unless "without recourse," will establish the indorser's secondary liability. According to Revised UCC Article 3, if an instrument is dishonored, an indorser is obliged to pay the amount due on the instrument. By indorsing this instrument, Faye Smith becomes liable for payment of the instrument if it is not honored by the maker or drawee. The instrument qualifies as order paper with the words, "Pay to John Doe," in the indorsement; status as order paper does not restrict further negotiation.

10. (d) A "holder" is a person who is in possession of a document of title, an instrument, or a certified investment security drawn, issued, or endorsed to her/him, to her/his order, to bearer, or in

blank. Although there are good faith and value requirements for an HDC, no such requirements apply to a mere holder. A holder could take possession of an order or bearer check.

11. (a) A "without recourse" endorsement on an instrument disclaims the endorser's secondary liability to pay the instrument in the event it is dishonored. It does not impair negotiability or prevent the transferee from becoming a holder in due course and does not change the warranty. An indorser (other than a qualified indorser) engages that upon dishonor and any necessary notice of dishonor and protest, the indorser will pay the instrument according to its tenor at the time of her/his indorsement to the holder or to any subsequent holder who takes up the instrument. In the absence of an effective "without recourse" disclaimer, the indorser is jointly and severally (secondarily) liable with the drawer. Thus, a holder is not required (after presentment and dishonor) to make a demand upon or proceed against the drawer before enforcing the indorser's liability.

12. (d) John Smith endorsed the note in blank (did not specify any endorsee), thus, converting the note to bearer paper. Bearer paper may be negotiated effectively by delivery alone. Therefore, Harris' signature was not required. An instrument does not become nonnegotiable as a result of an endorsement. An instrument is either negotiable or nonnegotiable on its face and endorsements do not affect negotiability. As a representative of the corporation, Parker has express authority to sign the note. Therefore, negotiability was not affected by his endorsement. Harris' conditional endorsement was an effective restrictive endorsement. A restrictive endorsement restricts the rights of the endorsee in some manner, but does not prohibit transfer or negotiation. A qualified endorsement ("without recourse") does not impair negotiability.

13. (c) Words indicating a purpose of deposit or collection make an endorsement restrictive. A blank endorsement is one where the transferor's signature appears alone, without specifying any particular endorsee. A qualified endorsement usually is characterized by writing "without resource" on the instrument. A special endorsement names the person to whose order the instrument is now payable.

Holder in Due Course

14. (b) Under the Negotiable Instruments Article of the UCC, in order for a person to qualify as an HDC of a promissory note, (1) they must qualify as a holder, (2) the note must be negotiable, and (3) they must take the note for value, in good faith, and without notice that it is overdue, dishonored, or there is a defense against it.

15. (b) Although one who finds a bearer instrument is a holder, the finder is not entitled to the rights of a holder in due course (HDC) because the instrument was not transferred. According to UCC 3-203(a), "An instrument is transferred when it is delivered by a person other than its issuer for the purpose of giving to the person receiving delivery the right to enforce the instrument." Under the shelter rule in UCC 3-203(b), a party who receives an instrument from an HDC gets the rights of the HDC, even though the party has knowledge of a defense. A party receiving an instrument as a gift from an HDC is entitled to the rights of an HDC because the instrument was transferred for the purpose of giving the receiver the right to enforce the instrument. A party who, in good faith and without notice of any defect, gave value for an instrument becomes an HDC with enforcement rights of an HDC.

16. (c) If a thief steals a negotiable instrument that has been endorsed in blank so that the instrument can be negotiated by mere delivery alone, a thief can pass good title to an HDC. Ott is an HDC to the extent of $3,333. Once Ott learns of the theft, Ott cannot be an HDC for any further amount. The promised performance (price) is $4,500 and the partial performance while an HDC is $3,000. Therefore, the holder is an HDC for: $3,000/$4,500 × the face of $5,000 = $3,333. UCC Section 3-302, *Holder in Due Course,* paragraph (d) states, "If the promise of performance that is the consideration for an instrument has been partially performed, the holder may assert rights as a holder in due course of the instrument only to the fraction of the amount payable under the instrument is equal to the value of the partial performance divided by the value of the promised performance."

17. (c) In order for a transferee of a negotiable instrument to qualify as a holder, the transferee must take the instrument either by issue or by negotiation. In order to take by negotiation, a transferee of order paper must take by proper endorsement and transfer of possession. A transferee of order paper is entitled to the endorsement of the transferor.

Liabilities, Defenses & Rights

18. (d) An unauthorized completion of an instrument is treated as a material alteration; however, it is not a real defense against an HDC. A party whose substantial contributing negligence invites the material alteration is estopped from raising the alteration as a defense. Thus, Cobb is liable for the entire amount of the check to Josephs.

19. (d) A lack of consideration is a personal defense. A maker of a note may use a real defense against an HDC, but not a personal defense. Answers (a), (b), and (c) represent real defenses.

20. (c) Smith Industries, as drawer of the instrument, is only secondarily liable for it. Upon Clark's acceptance, it then became primarily liable while Smith remained secondarily liable. The instrument meets all the requirements of negotiability.

21. (b) Under the Negotiable Instruments Article of the UCC, real defenses available against an HDC include material alteration of the instrument and discharge of a person with primary or secondary liability in bankruptcy. Breach of contract is a personal defense not available against an HDC.

22. (d) An HDC takes an instrument free of personal defenses but is subject to real defenses—those that pertain to the validity of an instrument. Therefore, the HDC would take the note free of personal defenses such as breach of contract or nonperformance of a condition precedent.

Warehouse Receipt

23. (b) A warehouse person has a duty of care and is liable for loss or injury to goods caused by the failure to exercise such care as a reasonably careful person would exercise under like circumstances. The problem does not specify that liability was limited by a written agreement, so Field would be held liable because he was negligent. A warehouser is not strictly liable for any loss on goods held in a warehouse. The negotiability of the warehouse receipt has no effect on Field's liability or the duty of care he is held to. Hall need only establish that Field was negligent, not grossly negligent.

24. (d) The common carrier is held to a standard of care based on strict liability, rather than a standard of reasonable care, in protecting bailed personal property. This means that the common carrier is absolutely liable, regardless of negligence, for all loss or damage to goods except loss or damage caused by one of the five common law exceptions: an act of God, an act of a public enemy, an order of a public authority, an act of the shipper, or the inherent nature of the goods. Strict liability includes liability for vandalism, power outages, and willful acts of third parties. Contractually limiting the amount of dollar liability would be a way to limit the common carrier's liability.

25. (d) Under a nonnegotiable bill of lading, a carrier who accepts goods for shipment, must deliver the goods to the consignee of the bill of lading. Answers (a), (b), and (c) would be correct if the bill of lading was negotiable.

26. (c) When title is to be transferred by negotiable warehouse receipt without movement of the goods, risk of loss passes to the transferee along with title to the goods at the time of receipt of the document. The risk of loss was transferred at the time Bell negotiated the warehouse receipt to Spark.

27. (c) The UCC Documents of Title Article requires that a warehouse receipt include both (1) a statement indicating whether the goods received will be delivered to the bearer, to a specified person, or to a specified person on that person's order and (2) the location of the warehouse where the goods are stored.

Bill of Lading

28. (c) Carriers must exercise that degree of care that a reasonably careful person would exercise under like circumstances. Although common carriers may limit liability to some extent, the general view is that common carriers are strictly liable for loss or damage to goods.

29. (d) A bill of lading becomes negotiable bearer paper if, by its terms, the goods are to be delivered to "bearer." "Bearer" paper may be negotiated merely by delivery. The carrier's lien entitles it to sell the goods to cover unpaid shipping charges. The carrier will be liable to whoever "bears" the bill of lading. The bill of lading is bearer paper and may be negotiated without endorsement.

30. (c) An "order" instrument must be delivered to the named person or to the representative of the named person so the bill of lading can be properly endorsed. To duly negotiate an order document, the document must be properly endorsed and delivered. The carrier's lien would be effective against the bill of lading's purchaser. The carrier may limit its liability by the terms of the bill. The carrier may have liability to others because the bill of lading is treated, in this case, as being negotiable.

Solution 36-2 ADDITIONAL MULTIPLE CHOICE ANSWERS

Negotiable Instrument Types

31. (d) A clause in a promissory note that allows the maker to satisfy the note by the performance of services or the payment of money defeats the requirement that the instrument be payable in money and will prevent the note from being negotiable. An extension clause that allows the maker to elect to extend the time for payment to a date specified in the note does not defeat the requirement that an instrument be payable at a definite time. Nor does an acceleration clause that allows the holder to move up the maturity date of the note in the event of default. Thus, neither clause will prevent a promissory note from being negotiable. A person having a power of attorney who signs the note on behalf of the maker does not prevent the note from being negotiable.

32. (a) Under the Negotiable Instruments Article of the UCC, drafts (except checks) must contain an *order* to pay. Debt instruments (notes and certificates of deposit) must contain a *promise* to pay. Thus, only the draft would be considered an order to pay.

33. (a) A trade acceptance is a draft drawn by the seller-drawer on the buyer-drawee which is payable to the seller at some certain future date. The seller transmits the draft to the buyer for "acceptance" by the buyer. A letter of credit is a nonnegotiable instrument that is an engagement (usually by a bank) made at the request of a bank customer that states that the bank-issuer will make payments and otherwise honor its customer's obligations. A bank draft is a draft (check) drawn by one bank on another bank. Checks are drafts drawn on a bank or other financial institution (savings and loan, credit union, etc.) and payable on demand.

34. (d) Certification procured by the holder discharges the drawer and any prior endorsers; the bank becomes primarily liable. An endorser still might be held liable for breach of warranty even if the check is presented late. An endorser would have to cause an instrument to be dishonored for the notice of dishonor to be excused. The maker's insolvency does not affect the endorsers' responsibilities.

35. (c) Revised UCC 3-201 only requires transfer of possession to negotiate bearer paper. In contrast, order paper requires both endorsement **and** transfer of possession for negotiation. The negotiability of an instrument, regardless of whether it is order or bearer paper, is not affected by the fact that no consideration is stated in the instrument.

36. (a) Under the Negotiable Instruments Article of the UCC, for an instrument to be negotiable, it must be in writing; signed by the drawer or maker; contain an unconditional promise or order to pay a sum certain in money, on demand, or at an ascertainable time; and be payable to order or to bearer (except checks).

37. (a) A bank may charge checks against an account in any order it deems convenient.

38. (a) The instrument depicted is a draft containing a delayed payment, drawn on a bank. Since the instrument indicates three parties, it must be a draft or a check. Since it is not payable on demand, it must be a draft, not a check. A promissory note would not be drawn on a bank. On a trade acceptance, the drawer and payee are the same person.

39. (a) Promissory notes are two-party instruments where a maker promises to pay a payee a certain sum of money. This instrument meets that definition. Also, the instrument is payable on demand, because no date of payment is specified. Therefore, this instrument is a promissory demand note. Sight drafts, checks, and trade acceptances are *drafts,* not notes.

Negotiability Requirements

40. (c) The lack of a specific payment date will not effect the negotiability of the instrument. When no date is specified, it is considered payable on demand. The note is negotiable, because it is in writing and signed by the maker, it contains an unconditional promise to pay a sum certain in money with no other promise, it is payable on demand, and it is payable to order or to bearer. These are the prerequisites of negotiability. An inconsistency between the amount in words and the amount in numbers does not effect the instrument's negotiability: the written amount will take precedent over the numerical amount. The guaranty by Abner has no bearing on negotiability.

41. (d) This instrument has all the requirements to be negotiable: it is in writing, contains an unconditional promise to pay, payable to the order of, a sum certain, payable at a definite time, signed by the maker, and it represents an unconditional promise to pay. This instrument is payable at a definite time. The amount due is specific. It is permissible to state that the instrument is secured by some asset; had the instrument stated it was subject to some other agreement, the note would be nonnegotiable.

Issue & Negotiation

42. (c) Order paper is payable to a specific person or her/his order. The instrument, although initially payable to bearer, was endorsed by Kent and made payable to a specific person. An instrument payable to cash is bearer paper. Whether payable to a specific person or to bearer, if an instrument is endorsed in blank, no specific endorsee is indicated and the instrument becomes bearer paper.

43. (c) The endorsement is restrictive, since it is "for collection only," and it is **not** special, since it does not specify the person to whose order the instrument is now payable. A special endorsement on bearer paper converts it to order paper.

44. (a) In order to satisfy the requirements of negotiability, an instrument must be payable at a definite time or on demand. Since this instrument is payable 10 days after the maker sells a diamond ring, it is not payable at a definite time and, therefore, is not negotiable. Reference to secured collateral does not prevent it from being negotiable. A sight draft is a three-party instrument requiring a drawee. This instrument is a nonnegotiable note that is not payable at a definite time.

Indorsement

45. (b) Under the Negotiable Instruments Article of the UCC, a person endorsing a check "without recourse" disclaims the endorser's secondary liability to pay the check in the event it is dishonored. This qualified endorsement does not prevent the endorser from being liable for breach of warranty. The "without recourse" endorsement does not convert the check into order paper.

46. (b) When Wolf received the note, it was an "order" instrument. After Wolf signed in blank, the instrument was "bearer" paper. It became an "order" instrument after Thorn gave it a special endorsement, "Pay: Vernon." When Vernon signed it with a special endorsement, "Pay Yule," it continued to be an order instrument. When Yule signed the instrument in blank, it became a "bearer" instrument.

47. (d) Clark may negotiate, by transfer of possession alone, the negotiable promissory note, since the last endorsement did not name a specific endorsee.

Holder in Due Course

48. (a) Taking an instrument in payment of an antecedent debt satisfies the requirement that an HDC take the instrument for value. A special endorsement converts the instrument to order paper, requiring the endorsee's signature in order to be negotiable. An HDC must take by original issue or by negotiation. Order paper is negotiated by proper endorsement plus transfer of possession. In this situation, Drake transferred possession of the instrument, but did not endorse it.

49. (a) Under the Negotiable Instruments Article of the UCC, in order for a person to become an HDC, they must take the instrument for value, in good faith, and without notice that it is overdue, has been dishonored, or that there is any defense or claim against it. Thus, a person notified that payment was refused would have notice of dishonor and could not become an HDC. The fact that the note was collateral for a loan or purchased at a discount would not affect HDC status nor would notice that one of the prior endorsers was discharged.

50. (d) A promise to perform services in the future is not considered "value" for purposes of qualifying as an HDC. Answers (a), (b), and (c) all represent the giving of value.

51. (a) Under the "shelter provision," an instrument's transfer vests in the transferee the same rights as the transferor had. Thus, Monk, although not himself an HDC, enjoys the benefits of such status, since Wilk had been an HDC.

Liabilities, Defenses & Rights

52. (d) Dodsen effectively negotiated the note for value to Mellon by delivery alone and without endorsement. Therefore, he has a warranty liability to Mellon, but not to Bloom. When a person does not endorse an instrument, but negotiates it by delivery alone, her/his warranty extends only to the person to whom it was given. Thus, Dodsen's warranty extends only to Mellon and not to Bloom. Mellon, however, endorsed the note and thus has contractual liability. Under contractual liability, the endorser guarantees payment of the instrument if the appropriate party for payment dishonors the note.

53. (c) A holder may discharge any prior party by renunciation. However, this renunciation cannot be made orally. It may be accomplished only by a signed writing stating that the holder releases the party or by surrendering the instrument to the party to be discharged.

54. (c) An endorser normally has a right of recourse against primary parties, prior endorsers, or the drawer of a note. If any of the rights of an endorser are affected by the actions of the holder, such as early release of the collateral, that endorser

is discharged from liability on the instrument to the extent that the endorser has been injured by the holder's action. It appears that the note was 100% collateralized; thus, releasing the collateral without agreement by the endorsers will release Tamp or Miller from liability. Miller's negotiation in blank merely converted the note to bearer paper and will not affect liability to Bilco.

55. (c) Under the Negotiable Instruments Article of the UCC, all endorsers of an instrument have secondary liability to later endorsers of the instrument. Since Betty Ash's signature has been stricken from the instrument, she no longer appears as an endorser. Ann Tyler's, Mary Thomas', and Susan Town's unqualified endorsements are all present on the instrument; thus, each of them will have secondary liability for payment.

56. (d) The transfer of a negotiable instrument to an HDC cuts off all personal defenses against the HDC. As an HDC, Helco would be liable to Willard Bank. Willard Bank, as an HDC, has the right to collect. Helco will have to seek recourse directly from Astor. Note that Helco cannot collect from Stone because Stone endorsed the instrument "without recourse." Willard Bank qualifies as an HDC in spite of the fact that he received the instrument from someone (Stone) who was not an HDC.

57. (a) A holder in due course (HIDC) takes a negotiable instrument free of personal defenses. Link is a HIDC as Link took the check for value, in good faith, and without notice that there was a defense against it. The situation described is fraud in the inducement; however, this is a personal defense.

Warehouse Receipt

58. (a) A negotiable warehouse receipt "duly negotiated" can give certain good-faith purchasers greater rights than those possessed by the transferor (similar to the rules of a holder in due course). In this question, the warehouse receipt was not duly negotiated since a proper endorsement is required for negotiation, and a forged document is not valid. Grove will prevail since Burke cannot validly negotiate the warehouse receipt. There is no rule that a warehouser must be notified before any valid negotiation of a warehouse receipt is effective. Burke's endorsement is invalid and does not convert the instrument to a bearer instrument.

59. (a) A negotiable warehouse receipt is a document issued as evidence of the receipt of goods by a person engaged in the business of storing goods for hire. The warehouse receipt is negotiable if the face of the document contains the words of negotiability (order or bearer).

Bill of Lading

60. (d) A bill of lading is negotiable if the goods are to be delivered to order or bearer. An immaterial alteration will not necessarily render a bill of lading unenforceable. A bill of lading is issued by the carrier, not the consignee. To be negotiable, a bill of lading will need to be endorsed only if it contains a promise to deliver the goods to a named person.

PERFORMANCE BY SUBTOPICS

Each category below parallels a subtopic covered in Chapter 36. Record the number and percentage of questions you correctly answered in each subtopic area.

Negotiable Instrument Types

Question #	Correct √
1	
2	
3	
# Questions	3
# Correct	
% Correct	

Negotiability Requirements

Question #	Correct √
4	
5	
6	
7	
# Questions	4
# Correct	
% Correct	

Issue & Negotiation

Question #	Correct √
8	
9	
10	
11	
12	
13	
# Questions	6
# Correct	
% Correct	

Holder in Due Course

Question #	Correct √
14	
15	
16	
17	
# Questions	4
# Correct	
% Correct	

Liabilities, Defenses & Rights

Question #	Correct √
18	
19	
20	
21	
22	
# Questions	5
# Correct	
% Correct	

Warehouse Receipt

Question #	Correct √
23	
24	
25	
26	
27	
# Questions	5
# Correct	
% Correct	

Bill of Lading

Question #	Correct √
28	
29	
30	
# Questions	3
# Correct	
% Correct	

SIMULATION SOLUTION

Solution 36-3 Negotiability

Negotiability (4 points)

1. A

An instrument may be undated, antedated, or post-dated without affecting negotiability.

2. A

Negotiability is not affected when a specific place of payment is not indicated in the note.

3. D

When a note is payable to the order of a named individual, it is negotiated by proper indorsement plus delivery.

4. B

When a note is indorsed "For Collection," its negotiability is restricted; however, it does not prevent further negotiation of the instrument.

5. E

When a note is payable in either money or goods, it is not negotiable.

Written Communication (5 points)

To: Dover, CPA
From: A. Junior
Re: Crane Audit: Oval Corporation Note

I have identified and explained the issues and offer my conclusions on the legal issues pertaining to the Oval Corporation note.

a. Crane is a **holder in due course** because Crane took a **negotiable** note for **value**, in **good faith**, and **without knowledge** of any **defenses** by the maker. The later disclosure that Oval has a personal defense against Jones does not affect that status as a holder in due course.

b. Crane **should** be able to **collect** from **Oval** because Oval's defense is **personal** and a holder in due course is not subject to personal defenses.

c. Crane should be able to collect from **Jones** despite Jones' qualified endorsement (without recourse) of the note. Jones was aware of Oval's defense of fraud at the time Jones endorsed the note to Crane. This knowledge is a **breach** of the **implied transfer warranty** against defenses. Accordingly, Jones' **qualified endorsement** does **not prevent** Crane from collecting the note from Jones.

Research (1 point)

IRC Section Answer: §3101(b)

Code §3101(b) states, "HOSPITAL INSURANCE.—In addition to the tax imposed by the preceding subsection, there is hereby imposed on the income of every individual a tax equal to the following percentages of the wages (as defined in section 3121(a)) received by him with respect to employment (as defined in section 3121(b))… 3101(b)(6) with respect to wages received after December 31, 1985, the rate shall be 1.45 percent."

Frequency of Tested Areas

Relatively Heavily Tested

Ch. 32	Accountant's Professional Responsibilities
Ch. 33	Accountant's Legal Responsibilities
Ch. 44	Federal Taxation: Individuals
Ch. 45	Federal Taxation: Estates & Trusts
Ch. 46	Federal Taxation: Corporations
Ch. 47	Federal Taxation: Partnerships

Relatively Moderately Tested

Ch. 35	Sales
Ch. 40	Federal Securities Regulation
Ch. 41	Other Regulations
Ch. 43	Federal Taxation: Property & Other Topics

Relatively Lightly Tested

Ch. 34	Contracts
Ch. 36	Negotiable Instruments & Documents of Title
Ch. 37	Secured Transactions
Ch. 38	Debtor & Creditor Relationships
Ch. 39	Agency
Ch. 42	Property

More helpful exam information is included in the **Practical Advice** appendix of this volume. Please note that the editors intentionally omit pages equivalent to this one from other CPA review volumes. The interrelated concepts in other volumes make assigning such designations reckless.

Updating Supplements

Bisk Education's updating supplements are small publications available from either customer representatives or our CPA Review website (http://www.cpaexam.com/content/support.asp). The editors recommend checking the website for new supplements a month and again a week before your exam. Version 39 (and higher) updating supplements are appropriate for candidates with the 39th edition. Information from earlier supplements (for instance, Version 38.2) are incorporated into this edition. Supplements are issued no more frequently than every three months. Supplements are not necessarily issued every three months; supplements are issued only as information appropriate for supplements becomes available.

CHAPTER 37

SECURED TRANSACTIONS

EXAM COVERAGE: The business law portion of the Regulation section of the CPA exam is designated by the examiners to be 20-25 percent of the section's point value. More information about point distribution and information eligible to be tested is included in the **Practical Advice** section of this volume.

CHAPTER 37

SECURED TRANSACTIONS

I. UCC Article 9

A. Overview

The purpose of a security agreement is to create a validly enforceable security interest between debtor and creditor. The main purpose of Article 9 of the Uniform Commercial Code is to bring most consensual security interests in personal property and fixtures under one uniform codification.

1. **Included Transactions** Article 9 applies to any transaction, regardless of its form, which is intended to create a security interest in tangible or intangible personal property or fixtures.

   a. Types of collateral covered by Article 9 include goods, documents, instruments, general intangibles (pure intangibles and intangibles), chattel paper, and accounts.

   b. Article 9 applies to security interests created by contract including: assignment, chattel mortgage, trust deed, or conditional sales contract or any other lien or title retention contract. It also applies to a lease accounted for as a capital lease under SFAS 13 or consignment intended as security.

2. **Excluded Transactions** The following is a partial summary of transactions that are excluded from Article 9 (UCC 9-109).

   a. Transactions involving interests in real estate. Article 9 does not apply to the creation of a real estate mortgage. However, if a promissory note is executed along with the mortgage and the mortgagee later assigns the promissory note as collateral (e.g., "instrument") for a separate loan, this lending transaction between mortgagee and third party is within Article 9.

   b. Transfers of interests in timber which are **not** to be severed and minerals that have not been removed from the land. Conversely, minerals that have been extracted, timber that is under contract to be cut, and growing crops in their unsevered or severed state are within the scope of Article 9.

   c. Security interests subject to any statute of the United States to the extent that the statute expressly governs priority rights of the parties.

   d. Landlord and artisan liens.

   e. Assignments and sales of accounts and chattel paper are excluded to the extent that they are either a part of the sale of the business in which they arose or a part of an assignment for the purpose of collection.

   f. Transfers of claims by employees for wages, salary, or other compensation.

   g. Transfers of interests in insurance policies as well as transfers of any portion of a tort claim.

   h. Assignments of deposit accounts in consumer transactions, regardless of the financing size.

3. **Attachment** The specific moment in time when a newly created security interest becomes enforceable against the debtor. Attachment occurs when: (1) value is given by the secured party; (2) the debtor obtains rights in the collateral; and (3) the debtor and creditor

acknowledge the creation of a security interest in an agreement signed by the debtor, or the collateral is in the possession of the secured party (UCC 9-203).

4. **Buyer in the Ordinary Course of Business (BOC)** A person who buys in good faith and without knowledge that the sale to her/him is in violation of the ownership rights or security interest of another. The buyer also must purchase in the ordinary course from a person in the business of selling goods of that kind [UCC 1-201(9)].

5. **Collateral** Property subject to a security interest [UCC 9-102(12)].

    a. **Tangibles** All goods (except intangibles, documents and money) which are movable at the time the security attaches or which are fixtures. Tangibles are classified according to their use or intended use by the debtor. Use is determined at the time tangibles are acquired by the debtor who is subject to the security agreement.

        (1) **Consumer Goods** Goods that are used or bought to be used primarily for personal, family, or household purposes [UCC 9-102(23)].

        (2) **Equipment** Goods that are used or bought primarily for use in a business (including farming or a profession). It also describes goods bought or used by a debtor who is an organization, agency, or government subdivision. Equipment also covers all tangible goods which may not be included as consumer goods, farm products, or inventory [UCC 9-102(33)]. Debtor sells collateral for cash and other noncash property. Because the sale is not made pursuant to a specific right to sell in the security agreement, the secured party's perfected interest also generally continues in the cash and noncash proceeds of the sale. Additionally, the secured party's interest would continue in any subsequent proceeds from a subsequent sale of the noncash proceeds.

        (3) **Inventory** Goods that are held for sale or lease. Also, raw materials, work in progress, or materials used or consumed in a business [UCC 9-102(48)].

        (4) **Farm Products** Goods that are used or produced in farming operations as long as they are in their unmanufactured state (such as milk, eggs, crops, or fertilizer). They remain farm products only while they are in the possession of a debtor engaged in farming operations [UCC 9-102(34)].

    b. **Pure Intangibles** Personal property that has no separate physical existence; rather, it is only a right to receive property. Included within this category are accounts, general intangibles, and other property not embodied in a single instrument of title (e.g., patents, literary rights, and rights to performance).

        (1) **Accounts** Any rights to payment for goods sold or leased or for services rendered, that are not evidenced by an instrument or chattel paper. Accounts include earned, as well as unearned, rights to payment [UCC 9-102(2)]. Accounts includes rights to receive payments for general intangibles (such as those arising out of the sale, lease, or license of software); payment streams (such as franchise fees, license fees, credit card receivables, and loans, whether or not evidenced by promissory notes); and security interests in promissory note sales, payment intangibles sales, agricultural liens, commercial tort claims, and deposit accounts.

        (2) **General Intangibles** Any personal property other than goods, accounts, chattel paper (mortgages), documents, and money. General intangibles include goodwill, literary rights, trademarks, copyrights, and patents [UCC 9-102(42)].

    c. **Intangibles** Any personal property, such as instruments or chattel paper, the ownership rights to which are embodied in an indispensable writing. Transfer of the writing is tantamount to transfer of the underlying rights in that instrument.

(1) **Instruments** Include negotiable instruments (as defined in UCC 3-104), investment securities (as defined in UCC 8-102), and any other writing that evidences the right to payment of money and is not itself a security interest or lease [UCC 9-102(47)].

(2) **Documents** Documents of title including warehouse receipts, bills of lading, and dock warrants [UCC 9-102(30)].

(3) **Chattel Paper** Writings that simultaneously embody a monetary obligation and a security interest [UCC 9-102(11)]. (A promissory note with an appended security agreement together constitute chattel paper. However, the promissory note alone would merely be an instrument, not chattel paper, while a security agreement standing alone may be chattel paper.)

(4) **Money**

6. **Debtor-Requested Accounting** Upon request, the creditor must provide the debtor with an accounting of the amount of unpaid indebtedness and a list of the collateral that secures the debt. The secured party must comply with such a request without charge once every six months during the outstanding period of the security interest (UCC 9-210).

7. **Financing Statement** A document containing required information which is filed by a secured party in a particular location and which indicates that a secured party claims a security interest in specific collateral [UCC 9-102(39)]. A security agreement must contain collateral's description and be signed by the debtor.

8. **Fixtures** Goods that are attached to real estate in such a manner that an interest in them arises under real property law. This includes all goods that are integrally incorporated into the real estate, but excludes ordinary building materials incorporated into an improvement on land [UCC 9-102(41)]. Accessions are personal property that by installation become a permanent part of real property or other personal property.

9. **Lien Creditor** Creditor who has acquired a lien on the property involved by attachment, levy, or the like. Included within the definition of a lien creditor are assignees for the benefit of creditors from the time of assignment and trustees in bankruptcy from the date of filing of the petition or from the date of appointment [UCC 9-102(52)].

10. **Mortgage** A consensual lien created by a real estate mortgage, trust deed on real estate, or other like contract [UCC 9-102(55)].

11. **Proceeds** Whatever is received upon the sale, exchange, collection, or other disposition of collateral or proceeds [UCC 9-102(64)].

12. **Secured Party** A lender-seller or other person in whose favor there is a security interest. This may include purchasers of accounts or chattel paper [UCC 9-102(72)].

13. **Security Agreement** An agreement that creates or provides for a security interest [UCC 9-102(73)].

B. Attachment

A security interest is created when the debtor and creditor enter into an agreement giving the creditor rights in the debtor's property as collateral for the debt. However, a security interest is not enforceable against the debtor until it attaches. Attachment does not occur until and unless all three qualifying events occur (UCC 9-203). The events may occur in any order.

Example 1 ▸ Attachment

> Debtor farmer borrows $5,000 from bank in return for signing a written security agreement, which gives creditor a security interest in a tractor as collateral. The security interest attaches when a written security agreement is signed by the debtor, even though the debtor keeps the tractor in his possession.

Example 2 ▸ Attachment

> Debtor orders inventory from seller on February 1 (debtor gets rights in the goods). On February 2, debtor borrows the purchase price from bank giving bank a written and signed security agreement (value and the agreement). The security interest attaches on February 2, the earliest time of occurrence of all three elements of attachment.

1. **Security Interest** A security interest is an interest in personal property or fixtures which secures a payment or the performance of an obligation. A lease or consignment for the purpose of obtaining security creates a security interest [UCC 1-201(37)]. Along with the agreement to give the creditor a security interest in the collateral, the debtor must either (a) give the collateral into the creditor's possession; (b) give the creditor a signed written security agreement, or (c) provide an authenticated security agreement. (Authentication was developed recently to enable electronic transactions and is unlikely to be heavily tested on the CPA exam.) A written security agreement must contain a description reasonably sufficient to identify the collateral.

2. **Value Given by Creditor** Value must be given by the secured party (creditor). Value is deemed to have been given if the creditor has made a binding commitment to extend credit in the future or has an antecedent debt or previously existing claim against the debtor.

3. **Debtor Rights in Collateral** Debtor must have rights in the collateral. Rights in this context is broadly viewed as any type of ownership right.

   a. **Rights** A debtor has rights in any property that s/he either owns or in which s/he has an insurable interest in the case of theft, destruction, or non-delivery. For example, a debtor may have rights in earmarked inventory still in the manufacturer's ownership and possession or is enroute to the debtor via common or contract carrier.

   b. **Title** As between debtor and secured party, title to the collateral is immaterial regarding rights, obligations, and remedies under Article 9.

C. Security Agreement Variations

1. **Purchase Money Security Interest** If the debtor gives the creditor a security interest in the same collateral that the debtor is buying on credit or borrowing money to buy, the security interest is called a purchase money security interest (PMSI). The PMSI is governed by a few extraordinary rules. A PMSI creditor has extraordinary priority in certain situations.

   Example 3 ▸ PMSI

   > A debtor buys a refrigerator on credit from a retailer and gives the retailer a security interest in the refrigerator she is buying. The creditor would have a PMSI. A PMSI also would result if the debtor borrows money from a bank to buy the refrigerator and gives the bank a security interest in the refrigerator she is buying.

2. **After-Acquired Property & Future Advances** A security agreement may provide that any or all obligations covered by the agreement are to be additionally secured by property later acquired by the debtor (UCC 9-204).

Example 4 ▶ After-Acquired Property

> A debtor department store signs a security agreement with a bank which gives the bank an interest in "all accounts receivable and proceeds and all inventory owned and to be acquired." As the debtor obtains rights in future receivables and inventory, the bank's interest will attach and be protected from most third parties.

a. Article 9 also provides limitations on the creditor's power to include after-acquired property as collateral. No after-acquired interest may attach to consumer goods (except accessions) unless the debtor acquires rights in the consumer goods within 10 days after the secured party gives value.

b. In addition to after-acquired property, a security interest may secure value given in the future by the same creditor. Thus, future advances or other extensions of value, which may be provided to the debtor at some later date by the secured party, may be included within a present security agreement and, therefore, secured by the present collateral (UCC 9-204).

D. Debtor in Possession

A security interest can be effected through a financing statement or through possession by the creditor. Regardless of the method used to attach and perfect the secured interest, situations generally will arise when the debtor will retain possession of the collateral (for example, inventory on the debtor's showroom floor, or machinery in the debtor's factory). With collateral in the debtor's possession, the problem becomes one of preventing fraud upon the secured creditor or other (third party) creditors who deal with the debtor, while at the same time permitting the debtor freedom to carry on her/his business activity. The following provisions apply to debtor rights and creditor safeguards in debtor-possession situations.

1. **Transfer Rights** The debtor voluntarily or involuntarily may sell or transfer her/his rights in the collateral, notwithstanding a contrary provision in the security agreement (UCC 9-318).

2. **Secured Party's Interest** The secured party's interest generally continues in collateral notwithstanding the sale or transfer by the debtor (UCC 9-320), except when the sale was authorized specifically by the secured party in the security agreement, or in other specifically enumerated UCC situations (e.g., sale by debtor to a BOC).

Example 5 ▶ Collateral Sale

> Debtor sells nonfarm collateral to purchaser (not in the ordinary course of business); the secured party's perfected interest continues in the collateral in the purchaser's possession. However, the result would favor the purchaser if the sale was made to a buyer in the ordinary course of business or if the secured party's interest was unperfected.

3. **Secured Party's Perfected Interest** Without specific language in the security agreement to the contrary, the secured party has a continuously perfected interest in the proceeds as well as any proceeds that result from the debtor's sale or transfer of the collateral (UCC 9-320).

Example 6 ▶ Interest in Proceeds

> Debtor sells collateral for cash and other noncash property. Because the sale is not made pursuant to a specific right to sell in the security agreement, the secured party's perfected interest also generally continues in the cash and noncash proceeds of the sale. Additionally, the secured party's interest would continue in any subsequent proceeds from a subsequent sale of the noncash proceeds.

E. Secured Party in Possession

A secured party must use reasonable care in the custody and preservation of collateral in the party's possession. In the case of an instrument or chattel paper, reasonable care includes taking the necessary steps to preserve rights against prior parties. A secured party is liable for any loss caused by her/his failure to meet any obligation imposed by this Section, but the party does not lose her/his security interest. Unless otherwise agreed, when collateral is in the secured party's possession, the following apply (UCC 9-207).

1. Reasonable expenses incurred in taking and maintaining custody of the collateral are chargeable to the debtor and secured by the collateral.

2. The risk of accidental loss or damage is on the debtor to the extent of any deficiency in insurance coverage held by the creditor.

3. The secured party may hold any increase or profits realized from the collateral, but must keep the collateral identifiable.

4. The secured party (creditor) may use the debtor's collateral as her/his own collateral to the creditor's creditor upon terms that do not impair the debtor's right to redeem it.

II. Perfection

A. Overview

Although not specifically defined in the UCC, the essence of perfection is the giving of notice to the world that the secured party has an interest in the collateral. The importance of having a perfected security interest cannot be overemphasized. An unperfected secured creditor is subjugated to the interests of perfected secured creditors, lien creditors, (including trustees in bankruptcy), and in some cases mere transferees of the collateral. Perfection generally is tested on the CPA exam in one of three ways: filing, possession, or automatic perfection.

1. **Filing** Filing a valid financing statement

2. **Possession** The creditor taking possession of the collateral

3. **Automatic** Automatically by law (temporary or permanent automatic perfection)

4. **Field Warehousing** A unique financing arrangement that provides the necessary security to the creditor while at the same time permitting the debtor to have access to the collateral securing a loan. In the usual field warehousing situation, collateral that is the subject of the security agreement is set aside and placed under the control of a bonded warehouseman who remains on the debtor's premises. The secured party, therefore, has the alternative of either perfecting the security interest by possession through her/his warehouseman, or by filing. If perfection is obtained by filing, the warehouseman will issue a negotiable warehouse receipt which then becomes the subject of a properly filed financing statement. The advantages of field warehousing are the ease and inexpensiveness with which the debtor may sell the collateral, usually inventory. The disadvantage of field warehousing—especially warehousing that is perfected by possession rather than filing—is that it may result in a fraud upon other creditors. In order to prevent the debtor from misrepresenting the status of the collateral, a field warehousing should be effected with the following safeguards.

   a. Collateral should be clearly segregated from other property of the same type and placed in a secured, limited access portion of the premises.

   b. Warehoused area should be under clear control of warehouseman. Warehouseman must be independent of the debtor.

   c. Temporary relinquishment to debtor for sale is permissible with proper safeguards. (Recall that the creditor still has 20 days for automatic perfection if the field warehouse interest originally was perfected by possession.)

5. **Consignment** A type of sales transaction that may be a secured sale under UCC 9-102(20) or a true consignment or bailment for the purpose of sale under UCC 2-326. In a true consignment the consignor, as title owner, places property in possession of the consignee as her/his agent for the purpose of sale. Upon consummating the sale, the title shifts to the consignee, then to the third-party customer. The consignee then remits the proceeds less commission to the consignor. Until the goods are sold, the risk of loss and decrease in value remains with the consignor.

   a. If the transaction is, in fact, a true sale or return consignment, the consignor can insulate the goods from the consignee's creditors by adhering to the requirements of UCC 2-326. Under this provision, goods delivered to the consignee primarily for resale (sale or return) will not be subject to consignee's creditors if the consignor does any of the following.

      (1) Places signs at the consignee's place of business indicating the consignor's ownership interest in the goods.

      (2) Establishes that the person conducting the consignee's business is generally known by her/his creditors to be substantially engaged in selling the goods of others.

      (3) Complies with the filing provisions of Article 9.

   b. If the consignment is, in fact, a sale of the goods with title retained by the creditor-consignor pending the receipt of the sales price, then the transaction is a secured transaction under Article 9 rather than a bailment for sale under Article 2. If the purpose of the consignment was to provide security for receipt of payment, the consignor must file a financing statement in the appropriate filing place(s) to protect her/his interest from the consignee's creditors.

B. Filing

Perfection by filing a financing statement is the most common method of perfecting security interests (UCC 9-312). Procedurally, perfection by filing is accomplished by depositing a properly completed financing statement with a filing officer (usually a recorder of deeds). Both the place of filing and the time of filing are important in the consideration of the rights and priorities of conflicting creditors. An insufficient financing statement, or one that is filed in an untimely or inappropriate manner, may deprive the secured party of perfected status.

> **Note:** A purchase money secured creditor has an extra 20 days to file the financing statement, at which time the filing is retroactive to the date of purchase.

1. **Collateral Which Must Be Perfected by Filing** Security interests in pure intangibles (accounts and general intangibles, e.g., goodwill, literary rights, patents) must be perfected by filing (UCC 9-312).

2. **Collateral Which May Be Perfected by Filing** Generally, all other types of collateral may be perfected by filing or by possession. Inventory, equipment, chattel paper, and negotiable documents of title can be perfected by filing (UCC 9-312). Some types of collateral can be permanently perfected only by possession. These include money and instruments.

3. **Filing Sufficiency & Duration** Generally, there is a sufficient filing of the financing statement if a proper statement is presented to the proper filing officer and the filing fee has been paid. Once the financing statement is filed, it remains in force for five years from the date of filing. If not renewed by means of a continuation statement, the secured interest will become unperfected at the end of this five-year period. The continuation statement must be filed in the same location as the financing statement during a six-month period ending on the expiration date of the five-year period (UCC 9-502).

4. **Termination Statement** Upon the satisfaction of the obligation, and not having any commitments to make advances, the debtor may, by written demand, order the secured party to remove the financing statement from the public records. The creditor is required to send the debtor and each filing officer a termination statement to the effect that the creditor no longer claims a security interest (UCC 9-513).

5. **Filing Location** The jurisdiction for most filings is determined by the debtor's location, rather than the collateral's location. A natural person's location is at their residence. Corporations' and limited partnerships' locations are in the state of organization. Debtors located in a jurisdiction that does not provide for public filing or registration (for example, outside the U.S.), are deemed to be located in the District of Columbia.

> **Note:** Perfection of a security interest in fixtures is accomplished by filing a financing statement in the office where a mortgage on the same real estate would be filed or by notation on the real estate records (UCC 9-501).

6. **Financing Statement Elements** A financing statement must contain the following information (UCC 9-502).

   a. **Debtor's Name & Mailing Address** Partnership name and address, if debtor is a partnership. Legal name and address, if debtor trades under an assumed name (the assumed name may be added for clarity). Corporate name and address, if debtor is a corporation.

   b. **Creditor's Name & Mailing Address**

   c. **Collateral Description** Such as to assure specific identification of the item.

      (1) Unerring accuracy of identification is not required.

      (2) If collateral is related to real estate (e.g., machinery in a building or growing crops), then the legal description of the land or address of the building is required.

   d. **Debtor's Signature** Signature waived on multiple filings or if the debtor is not available.

C. Possession

Although perfection by filing is the most common method, perfection by possession is equally permissible in certain situations. For perfection by possession, unlike filing, no security agreement is necessary. To clarify the methods for different types of collateral, the following comparison is presented (UCC 9-312-314).

1. **Must Be Perfected by Possession**

   a. **Instruments** Includes both negotiable and nonnegotiable instruments as well as investment securities. Also included are checks, drafts, and certificates of deposit.

   b. **Nonnegotiable Documents of Title** (e.g., straight bill of lading).

   c. **Money**

2. **May Be Perfected by Possession or Filing**

   a. **Goods** (immobile or mobile except as covered by certificate of title under state or federal statutes, e.g., automobile registration).

b. **Chattel Paper** (e.g., lease and negotiable instrument; mortgage and negotiable instrument, if transferred together as a package).

c. **Letters & Advices of Credit**

d. **Negotiable Documents of Title** (e.g., negotiable bill of lading or negotiable warehouse receipt).

3. **Must Be Perfected by Filing**

a. **Accounts**

b. **General Intangibles**

D. **Automatic Perfection**
In a few specialized situations, perfection by filing or possession is preceded or, in some cases, entirely supplanted by temporary or permanent automatic perfection by law (UCC 9-309). Automatic perfection occurs upon attachment.

1. **To Give Creditor Time to Gain Possession—Temporarily for 20 Days** A security interest in instruments and negotiable documents of title is automatically perfected effective upon attachment and without filing or possession for a period of 20 days to allow the creditor to gain possession of the collateral (UCC 9-312).

Example 7 ▸ Give Creditor Time to Gain Possession

Creditor on June 1 gives value to debtor in form of $80,000 loan. Parties agree that creditor will have security interest in a certificate of deposit with a face value of $100,000, currently in possession of debtor. The creditor has a temporary automatically perfected security interest in the CD for 20 days from date of attachment. However, due to the fact that negotiable instruments are a type of collateral that can only be permanently perfected by possession, the creditor must take possession of the CD by June 21, or the security interest will become unperfected.

2. **For Release of Possession—Temporarily for 20 Days** A situation may arise wherein the debtor must take possession of collateral over which the secured party has a perfected security interest. In order to protect the creditor during this period of debtor possession, especially if the UCC requires perfection by possession, UCC 9-312 provides for a 20-day perfected security interest in the collateral from the date of release to the debtor. However, this provision is limited somewhat in its scope, as follows.

a. If the collateral is an instrument, it must have been released to the debtor for sale, presentment for payment (negotiable instrument), or collection.

b. If the collateral is a document of title over bailed goods, the release of the document (negotiable or nonnegotiable) must have been for sale, transshipment, or manufacturing.

3. **Because Collateral Is Proceeds of Perfected Collateral—Temporarily for 20 Days** If the collateral consists of "the proceeds of collateral," a slightly different rule prevails.

a. UCC 9-315 provides that if a security interest in collateral is already perfected but the proceeds of that collateral are not fully protected (e.g., proceeds different in character from the collateral or not identifiable cash proceeds), then the secured party has only 20 days from the date the debtor receives the proceeds to fully protect her/his interest in the proceeds.

b. As a basic rule, the creditor need not specifically include proceeds in the text of the financing statement, since the retention of a secured interest in identifiable proceeds is assumed. However, the creditor is required to file a proceeds financing statement when the proceeds are no longer identifiable or of a different type or require a different filing place than the collateral from which they emanate (UCC 9-315).

Example 8 ▸ Collateral Is Proceeds of Perfected Collateral

Debtor gives creditor a security interest in a drill press used in her machining business. The financing statement does not indicate that proceeds are covered. Debtor sells the press for cash. The cash proceeds are identifiable and are, therefore, covered without any additional filing. If, however, debtor received a portion of a crop to be harvested later that month, creditor would have 20 days to file another security in the county where the crop is located.

4. **Consumer Goods in Purchase Money Secured Transaction—Permanently** Any creditor who acquires a PMSI in consumer goods automatically has such interest permanently perfected (UCC 9-324). No filing or possession is required; the automatic perfection occurs upon attachment. However, there are three qualifications to this provision.

   a. It does not apply to collateral controlled by a title statute (e.g., motor vehicle registration).

   b. If the consumer good is to become a fixture, the secured party must file to perfect her/his interest over collateral after it becomes affixed to real property.

   c. A PMSI in consumer goods is not good against a subsequent *bona fide* purchaser who buys the goods from the original consumer, unless the purchase money secured party has filed a financing statement covering the goods.

Example 9 ▸ PMSI in Consumer Goods

Bank finances debtor's purchase of an air conditioner. Bank has a PMSI to the extent debtor used the loan to purchase the air conditioner. Bank's interest became perfected when the last event for attachment occurred; that is, when debtor purchased the air conditioner. At this point, Bank's interest is superior to all other creditors.

5. **Random, Isolated, Casual Assignment of Account(s) Receivable—Permanently** Security interests in accounts are usually perfected only if effected through a filed financing statement. Thus, any person who regularly takes assignments of debtor's accounts (e.g., accounts receivable) should file to perfect. However, UCC 9-310 provides an exemption from filing requirements for assignments that do not transfer a significant part of the debtor's accounts. Therefore, if assignee-creditor takes an insignificant percentage of debtor's accounts on a casual or isolated basis as collateral, then that casual assignee need not file to perfect her/his security interest.

III. Priority Among Parties

A. Overview

The UCC establishes rules of priority to protect buyers of tangible and intangible property from overreaching by anxious creditors. Article 9 seeks to effect a balance between the secured interests of creditors and the free flow of goods to buyers in the marketplace. The result is a system of priorities based on such criteria as whether the Article 9 secured creditor is perfected or unperfected, and also the status of a competing creditor. The rules differ according to whether the Article 9 secured creditor's security interest is unperfected or perfected. Types of creditors and others with whom the Article 9 creditor must compete for the collateral if the debtor stops paying her/his debts include the following.

1. **Unsecured Creditors** General unsecured creditors of the debtor.

2. **Purchasers of Collateral** Those who have purchased the Article 9 creditor's collateral from the debtor; purchasers of the collateral are divided into two groups.

   a. Buyers in the ordinary course of the seller's business (seller's usual customers).

   b. Buyers not in the ordinary course of the seller's business (not the seller's usual customers).

3. **Secured Creditors** Other Article 9 secured creditors in the same collateral of the same debtor.

4. **Lien Creditors** Lien creditors of the debtor.

5. **Real Property Interest Holders** The owner, mortgagee, or lien holder of real property to which the same personal property collateral has been affixed.

6. **Personal Property Interest Holders** Personal property owner, mortgagee, or lien holder of personal property to which the same personal property collateral has been affixed.

B. General Rules & Exceptions

The debtor may have other general creditors who have lent money to the debtor or sold the debtor something on credit, but did not take a security interest in any specific collateral. Generally, an Article 9 creditor, unperfected or perfected, would defeat general unsecured creditors as to the particular collateral in which the Article 9 creditor has a security interest.

Example 10 ▸ Debtor's General Creditors

> A debtor has a credit card with a department store. The store allows the debtor to buy on credit and does not require any collateral. That store is a general unsecured creditor of the debtor.

1. **Buyers Who Purchased Collateral From Debtor** A debtor in possession of collateral may sell the collateral to a purchaser. The Article 9 creditor may be unperfected or perfected.

   a. **Creditor & BOC** Generally, the unperfected or perfected Article 9 creditor of tangible or intangible collateral loses her/his interest in the collateral to BOC, even if the buyer knows of the Article 9 security interest in the collateral. The Article 9 creditor prevails against the buyer if either: the buyer knows the goods should not be sold at all; or the buyer is a BOC of farm products.

Example 11 ▸ Buyer in the Ordinary Course of Business

> Bank lends money to debtor-retailer to allow her to purchase inventory and immediately files a financing statement covering its purchase money security interest in the inventory. Retailer subsequently sells an item of inventory to X, a BOC. Bank's filed PMSI is subordinate to the rights of X, even if X knows that the bank has a security interest in the inventory.

Example 12 ▸ Bad Faith

> The same facts as in Example 11, except that X knows that the inventory (designer blue jeans) consists entirely of stolen and illegally copied blue jeans. X could not become a BOC due to the fact that X purchased the blue jeans in bad faith and with knowledge that the sale to him was in violation of the ownership rights of a third person (the true owner and designer).

Example 13 ▸ Farm Operation

> The same facts as in Example 11, except that the seller is a person engaged in farming operations who also sells farm products (crops, livestock, and products of crops or livestock). The bank would prevail. UCC 9-320 excludes from BOC status a person who buys farm products from a person engaged in farming operations. Buyer in this situation is relegated to the status of a buyer other than in the ordinary course of business.

b. **Unperfected Creditor & Buyer Not in the Ordinary Course of Business** Generally, an unperfected Article 9 creditor loses her/his interest in tangible or intangible collateral to the buyer not in the ordinary course of business, a transferee in bulk, or a buyer of farm products in the ordinary course of business, if three conditions are met.

(1) The buyer or transferee gives value,

(2) The buyer or transferee takes delivery of the collateral (the buyer of pure intangibles does not have to take delivery), and

(3) The buyer or transferee has no knowledge of the security interest. (UCC 9-320)

Example 14 ▸ Unperfected Creditor & Equipment

> Bank makes a loan to newly opened Stationery Store to allow Store to purchase small desktop computers for use in its office. Bank, therefore, has a PMSI in these goods. Bank, however, does not perfect its security interest by filing. Store subsequently sells several computers to Y who is a buyer not in the ordinary course of business. Y takes free of Bank's security interest, because Bank did not file or perfect before the purchase by Y. Y gave value and took delivery.

c. **Perfected Creditor & Buyer Not in the Ordinary Course of Business** Generally, a perfected Article 9 creditor **defeats** the buyer not in the ordinary course of the seller's business, with the following exceptions.

(1) **Exception #1** If the Article 9 creditor was **automatically** perfected, the perfected Article 9 creditor loses against a buyer not in the ordinary course of business if: (a) the buyer buys without knowledge of the security interest; (b) for value; and (c) for her/his own personal, family, or household purposes; (d) unless prior to the purchase, the secured party has perfected by filing a financing statement covering such goods, in addition to having an automatic perfection (UCC 9-320).

Example 15 ▸ Consumer Goods

> Stereo Showroom gives Bank a security interest on all of its inventory and proceeds in order to borrow money for the purchase of new stereos from the manufacturer. Bank properly files its financing statement. Consumer A buys a stereo system from Stereo Showroom on the installment plan basis. Stereo has an automatically perfected PMSI because A is a buyer in the ordinary course of Stereo's business. Additionally, because A is a BOC, he takes free of the Bank's security interest. If Stereo does not file a financing statement and A subsequently sells the stereo to his neighbor B, a consumer, without telling B of Stereo's security interest, then B will take free of Stereo's interest.

Example 16 ▸ Consumer Goods

X buys a stove for home use from Appliance Store on a revolving charge plan. Store, therefore, has a PMSI in the stove which is automatically perfected. Store also fails to file a financing statement believing that none is required. X later sells the stove to the neighbor next door, who does not know of the store's security interest, for home use as a consumer good. Neighbor takes free of the store's security interest because it was purchased for value, without knowledge of store's unfiled purchase money security interest, and for personal, family, or household purposes.

(2) **Exception #2** If a perfected Article 9 security interest creditor makes future advances to the debtor, the perfected Article 9 creditor loses if either of the following apply.

(a) Such advances are made by the Article 9 creditor **after** the secured party acquires knowledge that the collateral has been sold to a buyer not in the ordinary course of business **or**

(b) Such advances are made by the secured party more than 45 days after the collateral has been sold, whichever occurs first.

- If the advance is made pursuant to an **irrevocable commitment** which was entered into before the creditor knew of the sale of the collateral and before the expiration of the 45-day period subsequent to the purchase, the Article 9 creditor is protected (UCC 9-320).

(3) **Exception #3** If a perfected Article 9 creditor has a security interest in the proceeds of the collateral which are chattel paper or negotiable instruments, the Article 9 creditor loses if either of the following apply.

(a) The negotiable instrument is sold to a Holder in Due Course.

(b) The chattel paper proceeds are sold by the debtor to a purchaser of intangibles who purchases intangibles in the ordinary course of the purchaser's (not the seller's) business.

Example 17 ▸ Holder in Due Course

A purchaser of a large home appliance may give the seller appliance store a security agreement and a promissory note for the purchase price. The security agreement and the note together are chattel paper. The seller appliance store may either subsequently sell the chattel paper or instead use it as collateral for a bank loan to purchase more inventory. (The bank may then sell it or keep it as assignee.)

UCC 9-320 provides that a purchaser of chattel paper or instruments who gives value and receives possession of the intangibles in the ordinary course of business (e.g., a purchaser of mortgages) takes free of any security interest, perfected or unperfected, in those intangibles if the purchaser acts without knowledge that the specific intangibles were subject to a security interest.

Alternatively, UCC 9-320 provides that even if the purchaser knows that the particular intangibles are subject to a security interest, the purchaser takes them free of the perfected security interest if the secured party's claim to the chattel paper or instrument is merely as proceeds of inventory subject to a security interest.

UCC 9-320 completes the priority rules applicable to purchasers of instruments (including investment securities) and documents of title by providing that a holder in due course of a negotiable instrument, or a bona fide purchaser of an investment security, takes free of an earlier security interest (even though perfected). The rationale for this rule can be found in the perfection rules. Security interests in instruments can only be perfected by possession (except for 20-day temporary perfection). Therefore, the UCC in effect holds that if the instrument has legitimately found its way into the stream of commerce, it will stay there free of any interest in it which is no longer perfected by the secured party.

The fact that the secured party has filed a financing statement covering the specific instrument or document in question does not constitute "notice of a security interest" to holders in due course or *bona fide* purchasers (UCC 9-320). Thus, the transferee's status as a holder in due course or *bona fide* purchaser will not be destroyed by a charge of bad faith in that each purchaser had "notice of a claim or defense" to the instrument (see UCC 3-302).

Example 18 ▸ Business of Purchasing Chattel Paper

Appliance Store gives PMSI in inventory to Bank for loan to enable Store to purchase the inventory. Bank properly perfects its interest in the inventory. (Recall that a financing statement automatically claims proceeds emanating from the collateral.) Appliance subsequently sells an appliance to consumer on the installment sale plan. Consumer gives Appliance a security agreement and promissory note for the amount due (agreement and note together are chattel paper). Appliance immediately sells the chattel paper to Z, a person in the business of purchasing chattel paper. Even though Z knows of Bank's security interest in the inventory and impliedly in the proceeds, she takes free of the interest because she gave new value and took possession of the chattel paper. Conversely, the result would be in favor of Bank if Bank had stamped or noted on the chattel paper that Bank was expressly claiming the paper as proceeds. By this act Bank indicates that it has a right to the proceeds, not merely a claim to the proceeds.

2. **Debtor's Other Article 9 Creditors** The debtor may have given another security interest in the same collateral to another Article 9 creditor.

Example 19 ▸ Two Article 9 Creditors

A debtor's inventory is worth $1,000,000. The debtor gives one creditor a secured interest in the inventory for a $600,000 loan and another creditor a secured interest in the inventory for $300,000. If the inventory value drops below $900,000, both Article 9 creditors compete for the same collateral.

a. **General Rule** Generally, a perfected Article 9 creditor defeats an unperfected Article 9 creditor, and, if both are unperfected or both perfected, the first in time wins. **Note:** UCC 9-518 provides that an improperly filed financing statement still will be effective for perfection purposes to the extent of compliance. Furthermore, such an improperly or incompletely filed financing statement is effective against a person who has knowledge of the contents of the financing statement.

(1) If no party's interest is perfected, then by the order of attachment.

(2) If all parties are perfected by filing, then by the order of filing of the financing statement.

Example 20 ▶ Filing Order

> Creditor A gives value on March 1, and debtor obtains rights in collateral on same day. Creditor B gives value on same collateral to same debtor on March 3. Creditor B perfects by filing on March 3, and Creditor A perfects by filing on March 4. Creditor B has priority over Creditor A.

(3) If all parties are perfected, but one has perfected some other way than filing, then by the order of perfection.

Example 21 ▶ Perfection Order

> Creditor C gives value to debtor and takes a security interest in negotiable documents of title on April 1. C attempts to perfect by filing on April 1, but the filing is made in the wrong location. Creditor D also gives value on the same collateral and, after failing to locate Creditor C's financing statement in any of the proper filing locations, perfects his interest by taking possession of the collateral on April 2. Creditor D takes priority over the defectively filed security interest of Creditor C. When neither of the secured creditors perfect by filing, the first to perfect wins.

b. **Exception #1: PMSI in Inventory** A perfected PMSI in inventory has priority over a conflicting security interest in the same inventory or its cash or noncash proceeds (UCC 9-322) if both of the following requirements are met.

Example 22 ▶ Inventory PMSI

> Pursuant to a commitment to make future advances, Bank X gives value to retailer, taking back a security interest. Bank X perfects by filing. Although not a PMSI, Bank X's security agreement covers present and after-acquired inventory. Subsequently, Bank Y gives value to retailer to enable retailer to purchase inventory. Bank Y has a negotiable warehouse receipt for the inventory which it has perfected by possession. Bank Y will prevail over Bank X, if Bank Y: (1) perfects its PMSI at the time retailer takes possession of the inventory, *and* (2) gives written notification to Bank X of Bank Y's PMSI before Bank Y's 20-day perfection period begins to run. Finally, Bank Y will take priority over identifiable cash proceeds received by retailer on the sale of the inventory to the extent that the proceeds are received by the retailer before the inventory is delivered to the buyer.

(1) The PMSI is perfected at the time the debtor receives possession of the inventory.

(2) The purchase money secured party gives notification in writing to the holder of a filed conflicting security interest if the holder had filed a financing statement covering the same types of inventory before the date of the filing made by the purchase money secured party or before the beginning of the 20-day period when the PMSI is temporarily perfected without filing or possession (UCC 9-322).

c. **Exception #2: PMSI in Collateral Other Than Inventory** A PMSI in collateral other than inventory has priority over a security interest in the same collateral or its cash and noncash proceeds if the interest is perfected within 20 days after the time the debtor receives possession of the collateral (UCC 9-322).

Example 23 ▸ Equipment PMSI

> Bank B gives value to debtor Copy Center and properly files a financing statement covering all of debtor's present and after-acquired copying equipment. Bank C gives value to debtor to enable debtor to purchase a new copier. Bank C's interest in the copier will be superior to Bank B's interest if Bank C perfects its interest by filing either before debtor receives the copier or within 20 days thereafter.

3. **Lien Creditors** The debtor may have lien creditors who have an interest in collateral by statute or judicial process (creditors who have resorted to judicial relief against the debtor may have a judgment lien against the debtor.) Examples: If the general unsecured creditor sues the debtor and gets a judgment against the debtor, the creditor may have a judicial lien against the debtor's property, including the collateral. In a bankruptcy, the trustee, representing the interests of all unsecured and general creditors, becomes a lien creditor. An artisan who repairs the collateral and is not paid may have a statutory lien on the collateral.

    a. **Perfection** A perfected Article 9 creditor loses to a lien creditor who obtains a lien on the collateral by attachment, levy, or the like. (UCC 9-308) Remember: A PMSI perfected during the 20-day temporary perfection period is considered perfected retroactively to the date of purchase (UCC 9-312).

    b. **Exception** As between the perfected Article 9 creditor and the lien creditor, first in time usually wins. Note these exceptions.

        (1) **Future Advances** Perfected Article 9 creditors who were first in time lose to a second in time lien creditor, if the Article 9 creditor makes future advances after the lien to the extent that the advance was made with knowledge of the lien or more than 45 days thereafter (UCC 9-323).

        (2) **Artisan's Lien** If state law so allows, a common law artisan's, mechanic's, materialman's, or laborer's lien is superior to a perfected Article 9 creditor. However, for such liens to be superior, the lien holder must be in possession of the collateral (UCC 9-333).

4. **Real Property** An Article 9 security interest creditor versus the owner, mortgagee or lien holder of real property to which the collateral is affixed.

    a. **Unperfected** Generally, an unperfected Article 9 creditor with a security interest in fixtures loses to a conflicting interest of an encumbrancer or owner of the real estate **unless** [UCC 9-334(f)] either of the following apply.

        (1) The encumbrancer or owner has consented in writing to the security interest or has disclaimed an interest in the goods as fixtures.

        (2) The debtor has the right to remove the goods.

    b. **Perfected** Generally, a perfected Article 9 security interest creditor wins over a conflicting interest of an encumbrancer or owner of the real estate where both of the following apply.

        (1) The security interest is perfected by a fixture filing before the interest of the encumbrancer or owner is of record.

        (2) If the security interest is a PMSI perfected by filing **in real estate records** within 20 days after the goods become fixtures.

5. **Personal Property Collateral Affixed to Personal Property** For instance, a debtor gives a creditor an Article 9 security interest in a stereo bought on credit. The debtor then installs

the stereo in a car that s/he does not own, or has mortgaged to the bank, or upon which there is a lien.

a. **Unperfected** Generally, an unperfected Article 9 security interest creditor who has a security interest in the collateral before it becomes affixed takes priority over the claims of a person who **presently has a claim** to the whole.

b. **Perfected** Generally, a perfected Article 9 security interest creditor defeats anyone who **presently or subsequently** has claims to the whole.

IV. Remedies Upon Default & Rights of Parties

A. Default Procedures

1. **Claims** Upon default, the secured party may reduce the claim to judgment, foreclose, or otherwise enforce the security interest by any available judicial procedure. If the collateral is documents, the secured party may proceed either as to the documents or as to the goods covered thereby. Unless otherwise agreed, a secured party has the right to take possession of the collateral. In taking possession, a secured party may proceed without judicial process, if this can be done without breach of the peace. Otherwise, the party must proceed pursuant to judicial process (UCC 9-601).

2. **Real vs. Personal Property** If the security agreement covers both real and personal property, the secured party may proceed under Article 9 as to the personal property. Additionally, the party has the option of proceeding as to both the real and personal property in accordance with her/his rights and remedies in respect to the real property. If this course of action is followed, the provisions of Article 9 do not apply (UCC 9-601).

3. **Later Liens** When a secured party has reduced her/his claim to judgment, any lien a party thereafter acquires by execution relates back to the date of the perfection of the security interest (UCC 9-601).

4. **Secured Party's Collection Rights** When so agreed, and in any event upon default, the secured party is entitled to notify an account debtor or the obligor on an instrument to make payment to her/him. The secured party also may take control of any proceeds to which s/he is entitled (UCC 9-607). A secured party who undertakes to collect from the account debtor or obligor must proceed in a *commercially reasonable manner.* The secured party may deduct her/his reasonable expenses from the money s/he realizes through the collections (UCC 9-607).

5. **Debtor's Right to Redeem Collateral** At any time before the secured party has disposed of the collateral or otherwise discharged her/his obligations under Article 9, the debtor or any other secured party may redeem the collateral. In order to redeem, that person must tender fulfillment of all obligations secured by the collateral as well as reasonable expenses, including reasonable legal expenses (UCC 9-623).

6. **Secured Party's Noncompliance With Article 9** If it is established that the secured party is not proceeding in accordance with the provisions of Article 9, disposition may be ordered or restrained on appropriate terms and conditions. If the disposition has occurred, the debtor or any person whose security interest has been made known to the secured party prior to the disposition has a right to recover from the secured party any loss caused by a failure to comply with the provisions of Article 9 (UCC 9-625).

7. **Commercially Reasonable Manner** The fact that a better price could have been obtained by a sale at a different time or in a different method from that selected by the secured party is not alone sufficient to establish that the sale was not in a commercially reasonable manner. If the secured party sells the collateral in the usual manner and at the current price, the secured party is selling in a commercially reasonable manner (UCC 9-625).

B. Collateral Disposition

1. **Proceeds** A secured party, after default, may sell, lease, or otherwise dispose of any or all of the collateral. When necessary, a secured party may prepare the collateral for sale. The proceeds of disposition are applied in the following order (UCC 9-610).

    a. First, to satisfy the reasonable expenses of retaking and holding the collateral for sale, lease, or disposal.

    b. Second, to satisfy the indebtedness secured by the security interest under which the disposition is made.

    c. Finally, to satisfy the indebtedness secured by any subordinate security interest in the collateral, if written notification of demand is received before distribution of the proceeds is completed.

2. **Accountability** If the security interest secures an indebtedness, the secured party must account to the debtor for any surplus, and, unless otherwise agreed, the debtor is liable for any deficiency. But if the underlying transaction was a sale of accounts or chattel paper, the debtor is entitled to any surplus or is liable for any deficiency only if the security agreement so provides (UCC 9-608).

3. **Terms** Disposition may be made by public or private proceedings and by way of one or more contracts. Sale or other disposition may be made on any terms, but every aspect of the disposition must be commercially reasonable. Except when not practical due to the nature of the collateral, the secured party must notify the debtor of the time and place of a public sale or the time after which any private disposition is to be made. The secured party must also furnish such information to any other secured party from whom s/he has received written notice of a claim. The secured party may buy the collateral at any public sale, and if the collateral is of a type for which a standard market or price exists, the secured party may buy at a private sale (UCC 9-610).

4. **Effect** When collateral is disposed of by a secured party after default, the disposition transfers to a purchaser, for value, all of the debtor's rights therein. Such sale also discharges the security interest under which it is made and any security interest or lien subordinated thereto. The purchaser takes free of all such rights and interest even though the secured party fails to comply with the requirements of this Section or of any judicial proceedings if either of the following applies (UCC 9-610).

    a. **Public Sale** The purchaser, in the case of a public sale, has no knowledge of any defects in the sale and if the purchaser does not buy in collusion with the secured party, other bidders, or the person conducting the sale.

    b. **Private Sale** If the purchaser, in all other cases, acts in good faith.

5. **Transfer of Rights & Duties** A person who is liable to a secured party under a guaranty, endorsement, repurchase agreement, or the like, and who receives a transfer of collateral from the secured party or is subrogated to her/his rights, has thereafter the rights and duties of the secured party. Such a transfer of collateral is not a sale or disposition of the collateral under Article 9 (UCC 9-618).

6. **Time Limit** If the debtor has paid 60% of the cash price, in the case of a PMSI in consumer goods, the secured party in possession of the collateral must dispose of it within 90 days after taking possession. If the secured party fails to do so, the debtor may, at her/his option, recover in conversion or under Article 9 (see A.,6., above). The debtor may renounce or modify these rights by signed statement. The above provisions also apply when a debtor has paid 60% of a loan secured by an interest in consumer goods (UCC 9-620).

7. **Retention of Collateral as Satisfaction** In any other case involving consumer goods or any other collateral, a secured party in possession may, after default, propose to retain the collateral in satisfaction of the obligation. Written notice of such proposal shall be sent to the debtor if s/he has not signed, after default, a statement renouncing or modifying her/his rights under Article 9. In the case of consumer goods, no other notice need be given. In other cases, notice must be sent to any other secured party who has supplied the primary secured party with written notice of her/his claim. If the secured party receives objection in writing from any person entitled to notice, within 20 days after the notice was sent, the secured party must dispose of the collateral (see B., above). In the absence of such written objection, the secured party may retain the collateral in satisfaction of the debtor's obligation (UCC 9-620).

CHAPTER 37—SECURED TRANSACTIONS

Problem 37-1 MULTIPLE CHOICE QUESTIONS (30 to 40 minutes)

1. Under the Secured Transactions Article of the UCC, which of the following requirements is necessary to have a security interest attach?

	Debtor has rights in the collateral	*Proper filing of a security agreement*	*Value given by the creditor*
a.	Yes	Yes	Yes
b.	Yes	Yes	No
c.	Yes	No	Yes
d.	No	Yes	Yes

(11/94, Law, #57, 5234)

2. On March 1, Green went to Easy Car Sales to buy a car. Green spoke to a salesperson and agreed to buy a car that Easy had in its showroom. On March 5, Green made a $500 down payment and signed a security agreement to secure the payment of the balance of the purchase price. On March 10, Green picked up the car. On March 15, Easy filed the security agreement. On what date did Easy's security interest attach?

a. March 1
b. March 5
c. March 10
d. March 15 (5/93, Law, #46, 4014)

3. Winslow Co., which is in the business of selling furniture, borrowed $60,000 from Pine Bank. Winslow executed a promissory note for that amount and used all of its accounts receivable as collateral for the loan. Winslow executed a security agreement that described the collateral. Winslow did not file a financing statement. Which of the following statements best describes this transaction?

a. Perfection of the security interest occurred even though Winslow did not file a financing statement.
b. Perfection of the security interest occurred by Pine having an interest in accounts receivable.
c. Attachment of the security interest did not occur because Winslow failed to file a financing statement.
d. Attachment of the security interest occurred when the loan was made and Winslow executed the security agreement. (11/93, Law, #58, 4355)

4. A secured creditor wants to file a financing statement to perfect its security interest. Under the UCC Secured Transactions Article, which **two** of the following must be included in the financing statement?

a. A listing or description of the collateral
b. An after-acquired property provision
c. The creditor's name and address
d. The creditor's signature
e. The collateral's location

(11/92, Law, #48, amended, 3130)

5. Under the UCC Secured Transactions Article, which of the following after-acquired property may be attached to a security agreement given to a secured lender?

	Inventory	*Equipment*
a.	Yes	Yes
b.	Yes	No
c.	No	Yes
d.	No	No

(5/94, Law, #49, 4804)

6. Grey Corp. sells computers to the public. Grey sold and delivered a computer to West on credit. West executed and delivered to Grey a promissory note for the purchase price and a security agreement covering the computer. West purchased the computer for personal use. Grey did not file a financing statement. Is Grey's security interest perfected?

a. Yes, because Grey retained ownership of the computer
b. Yes, because it was perfected at the time of attachment
c. No, because the computer was a consumer good
d. No, because Grey failed to file a financing statement (11/93, Law, #59, 4356)

7. Under the Secured Transactions Article of the UCC, which of the following statements is(are) correct regarding the filing of a financing statement?

I. A financing statement must be filed before attachment of the security interest can occur.
II. Once filed, a financing statement is effective for an indefinite period of time provided continuation statements are timely filed.

a. I only
b. II only
c. Both I and II
d. Neither I nor II (R/07, REG, 1868L, #31, 8455)

8. Mars, Inc. manufactures and sells VCRs on credit directly to wholesalers, retailers, and consumers. Mars can perfect its security interest in the VCRs it sells without having to file a financing statement or take possession of the VCRs if the sale is made to
a. Retailers
b. Wholesalers that sell to distributors for resale
c. Consumers
d. Wholesalers that sell to buyers in the ordinary course of business (5/93, Law, #47, 4015)

9. On June 15, Harper purchased equipment for $100,000 from Imperial Corp. for use in its manufacturing process. Harper paid for the equipment with funds borrowed from Eastern Bank. Harper gave Eastern a security agreement and financing statement covering Harper's existing and after-acquired equipment. On June 21, Harper was petitioned involuntarily into bankruptcy under Chapter 7 of the Federal Bankruptcy Code. A bankruptcy trustee was appointed. On June 23, Eastern filed the financing statement. Which of the parties will have a superior security interest in the equipment?
a. The trustee in bankruptcy, because the filing of the financing statement after the commencement of the bankruptcy case would be deemed a preferential transfer.
b. The trustee in bankruptcy, because the trustee became a lien creditor before Eastern perfected its security interest.
c. Eastern, because it had a perfected purchase money security interest without having to file a financing statement.
d. Eastern, because it perfected its security interest within the permissible time limits.
(5/91, Law, #59, 0582)

10. Burn Manufacturing borrowed $500,000 from Howard Finance Co., secured by Burn's present and future inventory, accounts receivable, and the proceeds thereof. The parties signed a financing statement that described the collateral and it was filed in the appropriate state office. Burn subsequently defaulted in the repayment of the loan and Howard attempted to enforce its security interest. Burn contended that Howard's security interest was unenforceable. In addition, Green, who subsequently gave credit to Burn without knowledge of Howard's security interest, is also attempting to defeat Howard's alleged security interest. The security interest in question is valid with respect to
a. Both Burn and Green
b. Neither Burn nor Green
c. Burn but not Green
d. Green but **not** Burn (5/89, Law, #60, 0590)

11. Under the UCC Secured Transactions Article, which of the following actions will best perfect a security interest in a negotiable instrument against any other party?
a. Filing a security agreement
b. Taking possession of the instrument
c. Perfecting by attachment
d. Obtaining a duly executed financing statement
(5/94, Law, #50, 4805)

12. Under the UCC Secured Transactions Article, perfection of a security interest by a creditor provides added protection against other parties in the event the debtor does not pay its debts. Which of the following parties is **not** affected by perfection of a security interest?
a. Other prospective creditors of the debtor
b. The trustee in a bankruptcy case
c. A buyer in the ordinary course of business
d. A subsequent personal injury judgment creditor
(5/94, Law, #51, 4806)

13. Wine purchased a computer using the proceeds of a loan from MJC Finance Company. Wine gave MJC a security interest in the computer. Wine executed a security agreement and financing statement, which was filed by MJC. Wine used the computer to monitor Wine's personal investments. Later, Wine sold the computer to Jacobs, for Jacobs' family use. Jacobs was unaware of MJC's security interest. Wine now is in default under the MJC loan. May MJC repossess the computer from Jacobs?
a. No, because Jacobs was unaware of the MJC security interest
b. No, because Jacobs intended to use the computer for family or household purposes
c. Yes, because MJC's security interest was perfected before Jacobs' purchase
d. Yes, because Jacobs' purchase of the computer made Jacobs personally liable to MJC
(5/91, Law, #60, 0583)

14. Under the Secured Transactions Article of the UCC, what would be the order of priority for the following security interests in consumer goods?

I. Financing agreement filed on April 1
II. Possession of the collateral by a creditor on April 10
III. Financing agreement perfected on April 15

a. I, II, III
b. II, I, III
c. II, III, I
d. III, II, I (11/94, Law, #59, 5236)

15. Larkin is a wholesaler of computers. Larkin sold 40 computers to Elk Appliance for $80,000. Elk paid $20,000 down and signed a promissory note for the balance. Elk also executed a security agreement giving Larkin a security interest in Elk's inventory, including the computers. Larkin perfected its security interest by properly filing a financing statement in the state of Whiteacre. Six months later, Elk moved its business to the state of Blackacre, taking the computers. On arriving in Blackacre, Elk secured a loan from Quarry Bank and signed a security agreement putting up all inventory (including the computers) as collateral. Quarry perfected its security interest by properly filing a financing statement in the state of Blackacre. Two months after arriving in Blackacre, Elk went into default on both debts. Which of the following statements is correct?

a. Quarry's security interest is superior because Larkin's time to file a financing statement in Blackacre had expired prior to Quarry's filing.
b. Quarry's security interest is superior because Quarry had no actual notice of Larkin's security interest.
c. Larkin's security interest is superior even though at the time of Elk's default Larkin had not perfected its security interest in the state of Blackacre.
d. Larkin's security interest is superior provided it repossesses the computers before Quarry does. (5/94, Law, #53, 4808)

16. A party who filed a security interest in inventory on April 1, Year 4, would have a superior interest to which of the following parties?

a. A holder of a mechanic's lien whose lien was filed on March 15, Year 4
b. A holder of a purchase money security interest in after-acquired property filed on March 20, Year 4
c. A purchaser in the ordinary course of business who purchased on April 10, Year 4
d. A judgment lien creditor who filed its judgment on April 15, Year 4 (5/93, Law, #49, amended, 4017)

17. In what order are the following obligations paid after a secured creditor rightfully sells the debtor's collateral after repossession?

I. Debt owed to any junior security holder
II. Secured party's reasonable sale expenses
III. Debt owed to the secured party

a. I, II, III
b. II, I, III
c. II, III, I
d. III, II, I (11/93, Law, #53, 4350)

18. Under the UCC Secured Transactions Article, which of the following statements is correct concerning the disposition of collateral by a secured creditor after a debtor's default?

a. A good faith purchaser for value and without knowledge of any defects in the sale takes free of any subordinate liens or security interests.
b. The debtor may not redeem the collateral after the default.
c. Secured creditors with subordinate claims retain the right to redeem the collateral after the collateral is sold to a third party.
d. The collateral may only be disposed of at a public sale. (5/93, Law, #50, 4018)

Items 19 and 20 are based on the following:

Drew bought a computer for personal use from Hale Corp. for $3,000. Drew paid $2,000 in cash and signed a security agreement for the balance. Hale properly filed the security agreement. Drew defaulted in paying the balance of the purchase price. Hale asked Drew to pay the balance. When Drew refused, Hale peacefully repossessed the computer.

19. Under the UCC Secured Transactions Article, which of the following rights will Drew have?

a. Redeem the computer after Hale sells it
b. Recover the sale price from Hale after Hale sells the computer
c. Force Hale to sell the computer
d. Prevent Hale from selling the computer (5/94, Law, #55, 4810)

20. Under the UCC Secured Transactions Article, which of the following remedies will Hale have?

a. Obtain a deficiency judgment against Drew for the amount owed
b. Sell the computer and retain any surplus over the amount owed
c. Retain the computer over Drew's objection
d. Sell the computer without notifying Drew (5/94, Law, #54, 4809)

Problem 37-2 ADDITIONAL MULTIPLE CHOICE QUESTIONS (15 to 20 minutes)

21. Under the Secured Transactions Article of the UCC, a secured party generally must comply with each of the following duties except

a. Filing or sending the debtor a termination statement when the debt is paid
b. Confirming, at the debtor's request, the unpaid amount of the debt
c. Using reasonable care in preserving any collateral in the secured party's possession
d. Assigning the security interest to another party at the debtor's request

(R/05, REG, 0101L, #7, 7853)

22. Under the UCC Secured Transactions Article, which of the following conditions must be satisfied for a security interest to attach?

a. The debtor must have title to the collateral.
b. The debtor must agree to the creation of the security interest.
c. The creditor must be in possession of part of the collateral.
d. The creditor must properly file a financing statement. (11/92, Law, #45, 3127)

23. Under the UCC Secured Transactions Article, which of the following events will always prevent a security interest from attaching?

a. Failure to have a written security agreement
b. Failure of the creditor to have possession of the collateral
c. Failure of the debtor to have rights in the collateral
d. Failure of the creditor to give present consideration for the security interest

(5/94, Law, #48, 4803)

24. Which of the following transactions would illustrate a secured party perfecting its security interest by taking possession of the collateral?

a. A bank receiving a mortgage on real property
b. A wholesaler borrowing to purchase inventory
c. A consumer borrowing to buy a car
d. A pawnbroker lending money

(5/93, Law, #48, 4016)

25. Noninventory goods were purchased and delivered on June 15, Year 4. Several security interests exist in these goods. Which of the following security interests has priority over the others?

a. Security interest in future goods attached June 10, Year 4
b. Security interest attached June 15, Year 4
c. Security interest perfected June 20, Year 4
d. Purchase money security interest perfected June 24, Year 4

(11/93, Law, #60, amended, 4357)

26. Under the Secured Transactions Article of the UCC, which of the following purchasers will own consumer goods free of a perfected security interest in the goods?

a. A merchant who purchases the goods for resale
b. A merchant who purchases the goods for use in its business
c. A consumer who purchases the goods from a consumer purchaser who gave the security interest
d. A consumer who purchases the goods in the ordinary course of business

(11/94, Law, #58, 5235)

27. On July 8, Ace, a refrigerator wholesaler, purchased 50 refrigerators. This comprised Ace's entire inventory and was financed under an agreement with Rome Bank that gave Rome a security interest in all refrigerators on Ace's premises, all future-acquired refrigerators, and the proceeds of sales. On July 12, Rome filed a financing statement that adequately identified the collateral. On August 15, Ace sold one refrigerator to Cray for personal use and four refrigerators to Zone Co. for its business. Which of the following statements is correct?

a. The refrigerators sold to Zone will be subject to Rome's security interest.
b. The refrigerator sold to Cray will not be subject to Rome's security interest.
c. The security interest does not include the proceeds from the sale of the refrigerators to Zone.
d. The security interest may not cover after-acquired property even if the parties agree.

(11/92, Law, #49, 3131)

28. Under the UCC Secured Transactions Article, what is the order of priority for the following security interests in store equipment?

I. Security interest perfected by filing on April 15, Year 4
II. Security interest attached on April 1, Year 4
III. Purchase money security interest attached April 11, Year 4 and perfected by filing on April 20, Year 4

a. I, III, II
b. II, I, III
c. III, I, II
d. III, II, I (5/94, Law, #52, amended, 4807)

29. Under the UCC Secured Transactions Article, if a debtor is in default under a payment obligation secured by goods, the secured party has the right to

	Peacefully repossess the goods without judicial process	*Reduce the claim to a judgment*	*Sell the goods and apply the proceeds toward the debt*
a.	Yes	Yes	Yes
b.	No	Yes	Yes
c.	Yes	Yes	No
d.	Yes	No	Yes

(11/92, Law, #50, 3132)

30. Under the Secured Transactions Article of the UCC, which of the following remedies is available to a secured creditor when a debtor fails to make a payment when due?

	Proceed against the collateral	*Obtain a general judgment against the debtor*
a.	Yes	Yes
b.	Yes	No
c.	No	Yes
d.	No	No

(11/94, Law, #60, 5237)

SIMULATION

Problem 37-3 (20 to 30 minutes)

On January 2, Fab Interiors, a furniture retailer, contracted with Shore Manufacturing Co. to purchase 150 sofas for its inventory. The purchase price was $250,000. Fab paid $50,000 cash and gave Shore a note and security agreement for the balance. On March 1, the sofas were delivered. On March 10, Shore filed a financing statement.

On February 1, Fab negotiated a $1,000,000 line of credit with Ship Bank, pledged its present and future inventory as security, and gave Ship a security agreement. On February 20, Fab borrowed $100,000 from the line of credit. On March 5, Year 4, Ship filed a financing statement.

On April 1, Connor, a consumer purchaser in the ordinary course of business, purchased a sofa from Fab. Connor was aware of both security interests.

All of these transactions occurred within the same calendar year. (Editors, 5413)

For items 1 through 6, determine whether (A), (B), or (C) is correct.

Statements	Answer
1. Shore's security interest in the sofas attached on A. January 2 B. March 1 C. March 10	
2. Shore's security interest in the sofas was perfected on A. January 2 B. March 1 C. March 10	
3. Ship's security interest in Fab's inventory attached on A. February 1 B. March 1 C. March 5	
4. Ship's security interest in Fab's inventory was perfected on A. February 1 B. February 20 C. March 5	
5. A. Shore's security interest has priority because it was a purchase money security interest. B. Ship's security interest has priority because Ship's financing statement was filed before Shore's. C. Ship's security interest has priority because Ship's interest attached before Shore's.	
6. A. Connor purchased the sofa subject to Shore's security interest. B. Connor purchased the sofa subject to both the Shore and Ship security interests. C. Connor purchased the sofa free of either the Shore or Ship security interests.	

On October 30, Year 4, Dover, CPA, was engaged to audit the financial records of Crane Corp., a tractor manufacturer.

Dover reviewed a security agreement signed by Harper, a customer, given to Crane to finance Harper's purchase of a tractor for use in Harper's farming business. On October 1, Year 4, Harper made a down payment and gave Crane a purchase money security interest for the balance of the price of the tractor. Harper executed a financing statement that was filed on October 10, Year 4. The tractor had been delivered to Harper on October 5, Year 4. On October 8, Year 4, Harper gave Acorn Trust a security agreement covering all of Harper's business equipment, including the tractor. Harper executed a financing statement that Acorn filed on October 9, Year 4.

As an audit team member on this engagement, write a memo to the partner-in-charge identifying, explaining, and stating your conclusions about the legal issues pertaining to the security interest. The memo should address when Crane's security interest was perfected and whether it has priority over Acorn's security interest.

Scenario | Priority | Communication | Research

Research Question: What code section and subsection, if applicable, provides guidance on the requirement imposed on every employer to withhold employees' taxes on wages as part of the Federal Insurance Contributions Act (FICA)?

Section & Subsection Answer: §_____ (___)

Solution 37-1 MULTIPLE CHOICE ANSWERS

Attachment

1. (c) UCC 9-203 states that attachment occurs when (1) the creditor has given value, (2) the debtor has rights in the collateral, and (3) when the creditor either obtains a security agreement signed by the debtor or obtains possession of the collateral. Filing a security agreement is not necessary for attachment.

2. (c) Attachment occurs when (1) value is given by the secured party, (2) the debtor attains rights in the collateral, and (3) the debtor and creditor acknowledge the creation of a security interest by a signed security agreement or by collateral in the possession of the secured party. In this situation, attachment occurred on March 10 because the following occurred on or before that date: (1) Green picked up the car, (2) the car had been identified to the contract, therefore, Green had a right in the property, and (3) Green signed a security agreement.

3. (d) The requirements for attachment include: (1) creditor gives value to debtor, (2) debtor has rights in the collateral, and (3) agreement in writing, unless creditor has possession of the collateral. Filing a financing statement has nothing to do with attachment, only perfection. Perfection in accounts receivable generally cannot occur when the financing statement is not filed.

4. (a, c) Both answers required for full point value. Included in the financing statement must be the names of the debtor and the secured party (the creditor), the signature of the debtor, an address of the secured party from which information concerning the security interest may be obtained, a mailing address of the debtor, and a statement indicating the types, or describing the items of collateral. An after-acquired property provision and the location of the collateral are not required to be included in the financing statements. The financing statement must contain the debtor's, not the creditor's, signature.

5. (a) UCC 9-204 permits a creditor to attach to a security agreement both after-acquired inventory and after-acquired equipment.

Perfection

6. (b) Automatic perfection occurs when a purchase money security interest (PMSI) is in *consumer goods* and the requirements of attachment have been met. The facts of the problem indicate that a PMSI does exist and attachment had occurred when the security agreement was delivered. Grey did not retain ownership but it did perfect its security interest since it had an attached PMSI in consumer goods. Grey's PMSI in a consumer good *was* perfected upon attachment without the need for the filing of a financing statement.

7. (b) Attachment is when a security interest becomes enforceable against the debtor; it occurs when value is given by the secured party, the debtor obtains rights in the collateral, and the debtor and creditor acknowledge the creation of a security interest in an agreement signed by the debtor. A financing statement need not be filed for attachment to occur, although one may need to be filed for perfection to occur. Once a financing statement is filed, perfection lapses after five years; unless continuation statements are filed timely.

8. (c) A purchase money security interest in consumer goods is perfected automatically. A filing generally is necessary when goods are sold to wholesalers and other retailers.

9. (d) If a creditor takes a purchase money security interest in equipment and files a financing statement within 20 days of attachment, the creditor will have priority over other secured creditors. In this situation, Eastern filed the financing statement within the 20-day period and, thus, Eastern will have priority over the bankruptcy trustee. In addition, filing the financing statement after commencement of the bankruptcy case is not a preferential transfer. This represents a contemporaneous exchange since present value was given in exchange for the perfected security interest.

10. (a) Under UCC 9-203(1) a security interest attaches against the debtor, Burn, when: (1) the collateral is in the secured party's possession pursuant to a signed security agreement, (2) value has been given to the debtor, and (3) the debtor has rights in the collateral. Howard's security interest is valid with respect to Green because the financing statement was filed prior to Green's extension of credit to Burn. Green's lack of knowledge is immaterial as he is deemed to have knowledge (constructive notice) under the statute due to Howard's prior filing.

11. (b) UCC 9-312 provides that a security interest in negotiable instruments can be perfected only by possession.

Priorities

12. (c) UCC 9-320 provides that a perfected security interest is not enforceable against a buyer in the ordinary course of business, even if the buyer had knowledge of the secured interest. A perfected security interest is enforceable against other prospective

creditors of the debtor, the bankruptcy trustee, and a subsequent personal injury judgment creditor.

13. (c) MJC can repossess since a financing statement was filed prior to the purchase by Jacobs. It does not matter if Jacobs was unaware of the MJC security interest since Jacobs had constructive knowledge (Jacobs is deemed to know what has been filed). MJC can repossess the computer even though Jacobs' purchase was in good faith and for personal use and Jacobs was unaware of MJC's interest. Wine was not a merchant and the purchase was not "in the ordinary course of business." Therefore, under UCC 9-320, MJC's filing of the financing statement gave MJC the priority interest in this case. If MJC had not filed a financing statement, MJC would have lost to Jacobs. Jacobs has no personal liability to MJC when Jacobs purchases the computer.

14. (a) UCC 9-322(a) states that conflicting security interests rank according to priority in time of filing or perfection. UCC 9-312 states that a security interest is perfected by possession from the time possession is taken. Possession is as valid a means of perfection as any other. In this instance, the conflicting interests are all perfected, thus, they would rank in order of perfection, by date.

15. (c) UCC 9-103(1) provides that when collateral such as inventory is perfected properly in one jurisdiction and then is removed to another jurisdiction, the creditor will have a four-month period in which to perfect its interest in the new jurisdiction. The collateral remains perfected during the four-month period, and, thus, is perfected against creditors who perfected their interests before the expiration of the four months.

16. (d) A security interest perfected before a lien has priority. A lien creditor has priority over an unperfected security interest or a security interest perfected after attachment of the lien. In addition, it is the general rule that a mechanic's lien has priority over a prior perfected security interest. A purchase money security interest in after-acquired property has priority over an after-acquired property secured creditor. Buyers in the ordinary course of business take free of any security interest whether perfected or not.

Default

17. (c) Proceeds from the disposition of collateral must be applied in the following order.

1. Reasonable expenses incurred in retaking, holding, and selling the collateral.
2. Satisfaction of the debt owed the secured party.
3. Subordinate security interests in the property.
4. Any surplus goes back to the debtor.

18. (a) A good faith purchaser for value and without knowledge of any defects in the sale takes free of any subordinate liens or security interests, but remains subject to security interests which are senior to that being discharged at the sale. A debtor has a right to redeem collateral before a secured party disposes of it by paying the entire debt and the secured party's reasonable expenses. Disposition may be made by public or private proceedings.

19. (c) UCC 9-620 requires the creditor to sell the collateral where there has been a purchase money security interest (PMSI) in consumer goods and the debtor has paid 60% or more of the purchase price. Both of these elements are satisfied here. UCC 9-623 provides that a debtor may redeem collateral at any time before the collateral is sold, but after its sale the purchaser will have superior rights. The UCC Secured Transactions Article has no provision to permit a debtor to either recover the sales price from the creditor or to prevent the creditor from selling the computer.

20. (a) UCC 9-601 permits a secured party to peacefully repossess the collateral. UCC 9-610 permits the secured party to sell the collateral, and if the proceeds from the sale do not satisfy the obligation, the creditor may obtain a deficiency judgment against the debtor for the balance.

Solution 37-2 ADDITIONAL MULTIPLE CHOICE ANSWERS

Attachment

21. (d) There is no requirement that the security interest be assigned to another party at the debtor's request. Upon satisfaction of the obligation, the debtor may order the secured party to remove the financing statement from the public records, by written demand. Upon request, the creditor must provide the debtor with an accounting of the amount of unpaid indebtedness once every six months without charge. A secured party must use reasonable care in the custody and preservation of collateral in its possession.

22. (b) Attachment occurs when (1) value is given by the secured party, (2) the debtor obtains rights in the collateral, and (3) the debtor and creditor acknowledge the creation of a security interest by a signed security agreement or by collateral in the

possession of the secured party. The debtor must have rights, but need not have title. It is not *always* required that the creditor take possession for the security interest to attach, and filing a financing statement has nothing to do with attachment, only perfection.

23. (c) UCC 9-203 requires that in order for attachment to take place, (1) the creditor must give value, (2) the debtor must have rights in the collateral, and (3) the creditor must either take possession of the collateral or obtain a signed security agreement from the debtor. The creditor may either take possession or obtain a signed security agreement. The Secured Transactions Article does not require that the creditor give present consideration for the security interest, only that the creditor give value.

Perfection

24. (d) Perfection by possession occurs when the secured party takes possession of the collateral, such as when a pawnbroker lends money after taking possession of the debtor's property. A mortgage is a conveyance of an interest in land. A wholesaler borrowing to purchase inventory is a purchase money security interest in inventory. A consumer borrowing to buy a car is an example of a secured transaction where perfection would not occur until a financing statement was filed.

Priorities

25. (d) A purchase money security interest in noninventory collateral takes priority over other perfected interests if the purchase money interest is perfected at the time the debtor takes possession of the collateral or within 20 days of receipt.

26. (d) UCC 9-320 provides that a buyer in the ordinary course of business will own goods free of a perfected security interest, even if the buyer knows of its existence. A merchant who purchases goods, for resale or for use in its business, would not take the goods free of a perfected security interest in the goods, nor would a consumer who purchases the goods from a consumer purchaser (a good faith purchaser for value) take the goods free of a perfected security interest.

27. (b) Under UCC 9-320, a buyer in the ordinary course of business takes free of a security interest created by her/his seller even though the security interest is perfected and even though the buyer knows of its existence. Neither Cray nor Zone is subject to the security interest. A security agreement may provide that any or all obligations covered by the agreement are to be additionally secured by property later acquired by the debtor. Unless otherwise provided in the security agreement, the secured party has a continuously perfected security interest in the proceeds that result from the debtor's sale or transfer of the collateral.

28. (c) UCC 9-324(a) states that where there are conflicting interests in the same collateral, the first to have perfected its interest will prevail. This section also provides that creditors who have perfected their security interests will prevail over those who have merely attached. UCC 9-327 provides that where there is a purchase money security interest (PMSI) in equipment, the creditor has a 20-day period after attachment to perfect its interest. If the creditor properly perfects within the 20-day period, then perfection will be held to have occurred retroactively on the date of attachment. In this instance, a PMSI exists and the security interest was perfected effective April 11, Year 4. This precedes the April 15, Year 4, filing of Creditor I. Creditor II never perfected its interest and thus, would fall behind those creditors who have perfected. Creditor III would prevail over Creditor I, who would in turn prevail over Creditor II.

Default

29. (a) Under Article 9, upon default, the secured party has the right to reduce the claim to a judgment, sell the goods and apply the proceeds toward the debt, or take possession of the goods without judicial process.

30. (a) Article 9 states that when a debtor defaults, a secured creditor may repossess the collateral or reduce the claim to judgment. In the latter case, the creditor can obtain a judgment against the perfected collateral, and, then can obtain a general judgment against the debtor, which would enable a creditor to proceed against any nonexempt property of the debtor.

PERFORMANCE BY SUBTOPICS

Each category below parallels a subtopic covered in Chapter 37. Record the number and percentage of questions you correctly answered in each subtopic area.

Attachment

Question #	Correct √
1	
2	
3	
4	
5	
# Questions	5
# Correct	
% Correct	

Perfection

Question #	Correct √
6	
7	
8	
9	
10	
11	
# Questions	6
# Correct	
% Correct	

Priorities

Question #	Correct √
12	
13	
14	
15	
16	
# Questions	5
# Correct	
% Correct	

Default

Question #	Correct √
17	
18	
19	
20	
# Questions	4
# Correct	
% Correct	

SIMULATION SOLUTIONS

Solution 37-3 Priority

Perfection & Priority (4 points)

1. B

The UCC's Article on Secured Transactions provides that a security interest attachés when the creditor has given value, the debtor has rights in the collateral, and the debtor has signed a security agreement or the collateral is in the possession of the secured party. Since Shore did not give value until March 1, all three elements necessary for attachment were not present until that date.

2. C

Shore's security interest was perfected as of March 10, the date on which Shore filed a financing statement.

3. A

The UCC's Article on Secured Transactions states that attachment occurs when the creditor has given value, when the debtor has rights in the collateral, and when the debtor has signed a security agreement or the collateral is in the creditor's possession. Since Fab could have accessed the line of credit with Ship Bank on February 1, all elements necessary for attachment occurred on that date.

4. C

Ship's security interest in Fab's inventory was perfected on March 5, when the financing statement was filed.

5. B

Shore Furniture Company is a Purchase Money Security Interest (PMSI) inventory creditor of Fab. A PMSI in inventory collateral has priority over a conflicting security interest in the same collateral if (1) it is perfected when the debtor gets possession, and (2) written notice is given to all other secured parties before the debtor takes possession of the inventory. Since Shore did not perfect until after Fab received the inventory and since Shore did not give written notice to Ship, Shore does not have a priority as a result of its PMSI. Where more than one party has perfected their security interest by filing, priority is determined by ascertaining which party filed or otherwise perfected their interest first. When the party's interest is attached, is, at that point, irrelevant.

6. C

The Secured Transactions Article of the UCC provides that a buyer in the ordinary course of business purchases property free of a security interest, even if perfected.

Communication (5 points)

To: Dover, CPA
From: A. Junior
Re: Crane Audit: Harper Security Interest

The perfection of the security interest relates back to the date Harper took **possession** of the tractor (**collateral**) (October 5, Year 4) because the security interest was a **non-inventory purchase money security interest,** and the financing statement was filed on October 10, Year 4, **within** the statutory **filing period.** Accordingly, Crane's **security interest** has **priority** over Acorn's security interest despite Acorn's earlier filing on October 9, Year 4.

Research (1 point)

IRC Section Answer: §3102(a)

Code §3102(a) states, "REQUIREMENT.—The tax imposed by section 3101 shall be collected by the employer of the taxpayer, by deducting the amount of the tax from the wages as and when paid. An employer who in any calendar year pays to an employee cash remuneration to which paragraph (7)(B) of section 3121(a) is applicable may deduct an amount equivalent to such tax from any such payment of remuneration, even though at the time of payment the total amount of such remuneration paid to the employee by the employer in the calendar year is less than the applicable dollar threshold (as defined in section 3121(x)) for such year; and an employer who in any calendar year pays to an employee cash remuneration to which paragraph (7)(C) or (10) of section 3121(a) is applicable may deduct an amount equivalent to such tax from any such payment of remuneration, even though at the time of payment the total amount of such remuneration paid to the employee by the employer in the calendar year is less than $100; and...."

Using Audio Tutor to Study

Actively listen to the audio lectures, taking notes if convenient. In the Audio Tutor product, the lecturers supplement the content in this material with the insight gained from years of CPA review experience.

If you are strong in a topic, your audio review and question drill may be sufficient. If your strength is moderate in a topic, you might find that reading the related text before listening to the audio lectures is helpful. If you are weak in a topic, one successful strategy is to listen to the audio lectures, read the book, and then listen to the audio lectures again.

FYI: The Audio Tutor lectures have similar content as the Hot*Spot, Intensive, and online video lectures, but they are not exactly the same. Audio Tutor and this book have topics arranged in essentially the same chapters, although material might be organized differently within the chapters.

Call a customer service representative for more details about Audio Tutor.

STUDY TIP

Bankruptcy Inflation-Adjusted Amounts

The United States Code bankruptcy amounts are inflation-adjusted by the Judicial Conference of the United States every three years. The next time these are scheduled to change is April, 2010. Assuming no new legislation, the inflation-adjusted amounts in this chapter are eligible to be tested until the October-November 2010 exam window. Candidates should check the Bisk Education web-site (www.cpaexam.com) for series 39 and higher updating supplements a month before their examinations.

CHAPTER 38

DEBTOR & CREDITOR RELATIONSHIPS

EXAM COVERAGE: The business law portion of the Regulation section of the CPA exam is designated by the examiners to be 20-25 percent of the section's point value. More information about point distribution and information eligible to be tested is included in the **Practical Advice** section of this volume.

CHAPTER 38

DEBTOR & CREDITOR RELATIONSHIPS

I. Bankruptcy

A. Overview

Federal bankruptcy law is administered by bankruptcy courts, which constitute adjuncts of the United States District Courts.

1. Definitions

a. **Claim** Any right to payment.

b. **Community Claim** A claim against community property.

c. **Creditor** An entity that has a claim against the debtor that arose before the filing of bankruptcy or is treated by the Bankruptcy Code as arising before such filing, or an entity that has a community claim.

d. **Debt** A liability on a claim.

e. **Debtor** An entity liable to a creditor.

f. **Entity** A person, estate, trust, or governmental unit.

g. **Equity Security** A share in a corporation, an interest in a limited partnership, or a warrant or right to purchase, sell, or subscribe to such share or interest.

h. **Equity Security Holder** Holder of an equity security of the debtor.

i. **Estate** A collective term referring to all of the debtor's legal and equitable interests in property at the time bankruptcy is commenced.

j. **Exempt Property** Property that, under either federal or state exemption laws, is exempt from seizure and sale for the payment of the debtor's debts. In bankruptcy, exempt property does not become part of the bankrupt's estate.

k. **Insolvent** Financial condition of an entity wherein:

(1) **Bankruptcy Sense** The debts exceed the non-exempt assets, at a fair valuation.

(2) **Equity Sense** A debtor is not paying her/his undisputed debts as they come due.

l. **Transfer** Every mode of disposing of property or an interest in property.

2. **Code** The bankruptcy law is federal, consisting primarily of the Federal Bankruptcy Code. Thus, under principles of federal supremacy, state insolvency laws generally have been superseded. The result is one uniform bankruptcy law. However, not all state law is inapplicable in a bankruptcy proceeding; the Bankruptcy Code in many of its provisions specifically incorporates certain aspects of state law (such as contract law, real property law, etc.).

- **Emphasis** Unlike state law, with its emphasis on prompt action by creditors to enforce their rights against the debtor's limited and insufficient assets, federal bankruptcy law emphasizes equality of treatment among creditors within the same class. Once a bankruptcy proceeding is commenced, a creditor cannot improve her/his position vis-à-vis other creditors by resorting to such remedies as attaching the debtor's property, executing on the property, etc.

3. **Privacy Protection** Under previous law, nearly every item of information filed in a bankruptcy case was made available to the public. The Bankruptcy Abuse Prevention & Consumer Protection Act of 2005 (BAPCPA '05) restricts public access to certain personal information contained a bankruptcy case file, to the extent the court finds the disclosure of such information would create undue risk of identity theft or other unlawful injury to the individual or the individual's property.

B. Operative Chapters

There are five principal operative chapters under the Federal Bankruptcy Code. They represent five types of bankruptcy proceedings. Bankruptcy cases are filed under only one chapter at any one time. The material discussed in the rest of the chapter generally applies to Chapter 7, Chapter 11, and Chapter 13 proceedings. The material generally does not apply to a Chapter 9 or 12 proceeding, unless specific reference is made to Chapter 9 or 12.

1. **Chapter 7: Straight Bankruptcy or Liquidation** The typical bankruptcy proceeding is commenced under Chapter 7. This chapter applies equally to business and consumer bankruptcy cases. Such a case is in the nature of a liquidation proceeding. It basically involves the collection of the debtor's nonexempt property, the liquidation or sale of such property, and the distribution of the proceeds to the creditors by the trustee in the manner provided by the Federal Bankruptcy Code.

   - The two other heavily tested bankruptcy proceedings (Chapter 11 and 13) are known as "debtor rehabilitation proceedings." They differ from a Chapter 7 proceeding in that the debtor looks to rehabilitation and reorganization rather than liquidation. Generally, the creditors look to future earnings of the debtor for satisfaction of their claims instead of property held by the debtor at the commencement of the bankruptcy case.

2. **Chapter 9: Adjustment of Debts of Municipality** Chapter 9 provides a procedure so that a municipality that has encountered financial difficulty may work with its creditors to adjust its debts. This is accomplished by having the debtor work out a plan with its creditors for the adjustment, refinancing, and payment of its claims and by having the court confirm the plan. (Chapter 9 tends to be tested lightly on the CPA exam.)

3. **Chapter 11: Reorganizations** Although Chapter 11 is designed primarily for business cases, it may be used by individuals. It is the chapter to be followed for all business reorganizations. The purpose of a Chapter 11 reorganization, unlike a Chapter 7 liquidation, is to restructure a business' finances so that it may continue to operate, pay its creditors, and generate a return for its stockholders. The goal of the Chapter 11 case is to formulate and confirm a plan of reorganization for the debtor. This plan determines the amount and the manner in which the creditors will be paid, in what form the business will continue, and any other necessary details. Businesses with less than $2 million in debts may file a shortened Chapter 11 plan. Creditors of a Chapter 11 debtor may propose a reorganization plan after 18 months if the debtor has not done so already.

4. **Chapter 12: Family Farmers & Fishers** BAPCPA '05 provides heightened protections for family farmers facing financial distress. Under BAPCPA '05, family fishers may qualify for a special form of bankruptcy relief previously available only to family farmers. (Chapter 12 tends not to be tested on the CPA exam.)

5. **Chapter 13: Adjustment of Debts of Individual With Regular Income** The purpose of Chapter 13 is to enable a debtor who is an individual to formulate and perform a plan for the repayment of her/his creditors over an extended period. Such a plan might provide for full repayment or may offer creditors only a percentage of their claims in full settlement. The

benefit of the Chapter 13 repayment plan is that it allows the debtor to retain her/his property, even that which is nonexempt, unless s/he otherwise agrees in the plan.

C. Debtor

The debtor is the person or municipality that is the subject of a bankruptcy. A person includes an individual, partnership, or corporation, but **not** a governmental unit, a decedent's estate, or a trust. A municipality means a political subdivision, public agency, or instrumentality of a state but does not include the District of Columbia or U.S. territories.

1. **General** The general eligibility rule provides that only the following may be a debtor.

   a. A person who either resides in the United States or has a domicile, a place of business, or property in the United States.

   b. A municipality.

2. **Specific** Additionally, specific eligibility rules and exclusions apply in specific chapters of the Bankruptcy Code. For Chapter 7 and 13, the court must appoint a trustee. For Chapter 11, the court may appoint a trustee.

   a. **Chapter 7**

      (1) Debtor may not be a railroad, domestic insurance company, bank, or other specified lending institution.

      (2) Debtor may be a debtor under Chapter 11 reorganization except for railroads (restricted to special provisions of Chapter 11) and stockbrokers and commodity brokers (restricted to special provisions of Chapter 7).

   b. **Chapter 13** Limited to an individual who has: (1) regular income, (2) less than $336,900 of unsecured debts, and (3) less than $1,010,650 of secured debts.

   c. **Chapter 11** Court is required to select a creditors' committee from unsecured creditors, and a trustee may be appointed.

3. **Means Test** Under BAPCPA '05, individuals who file for Chapter 7 relief must fail a "means test." If the debtor does not fail a means test, a Chapter 7 filing will be dismissed, or, with the debtor's permission, converted to a Chapter 13 filing. Disabled veterans who incurred indebtedness during a period of active duty or while performing a homeland security defense activity are exempt from the means test. The means test takes into account the filer's income, debt burden, and various allowable living expenses.

   Example 1 ▸ Means Test

   Heather Smith has $35,000 in unsecured debt and files for bankruptcy under Chapter 7. After deducting allowed expenses, she has $160 of net monthly income.

   Heather's filing for bankruptcy under Chapter 7 would be disallowed because she passed the means test. Heather could repay $9,600 over 5 years ($160 × 60 months), which is more than 25 percent of her $35,000 unsecured debt.

   Note: If Heather had $40,000 in unsecured debt, her bankruptcy filing under Chapter 7 would be allowed, because she would have failed the means test. Heather could afford to pay $9,600 over 5 years, which is less than 25 percent of her $40,000 unsecured debt.

   a. **Living Expenses** A key determinant in whether a debtor passes or fails the means test is the amount by which actual monthly income is reduced by various allowances and living expenses. The allowable living expenses (the IRS Collections Financial Standards) are subject to several variables. The allowances set out monthly living expenses in the following categories. Calculation of the living expense allowance is mostly likely beyond the scope of the CPA exam.

(1) **Food, Clothing & Other Items** Living expenses vary according to the size of the household and gross monthly income.

(2) **Housing & Utilities** Allowance for housing and utilities varies according to household size and geographical location.

(3) **Transportation** The standards provide regional allowances, with variations for persons living in specified metropolitan areas.

(4) **Miscellaneous** Monthly expenses for purposes of the means test also may include: (a) health and disability insurance, health savings accounts, and long-term care costs; (b) a dependent's education expenses; (c) justified unusual home energy costs; (d) average monthly payments on secured debts and on priority claims (e.g., child support, student loans, alimony, etc.); (e) safety expenses; and (f) administrative costs incurred in a Chapter 13 bankruptcy.

b. **Income Available to Repay Debt** The code determines income available to repay debt as income minus allowable living expenses (net monthly income) multiplied by 60. Essentially, this calculates a five-year amount.

(1) If the five-year amount is greater than an **upper** threshold ($10,950), a Chapter 7 filing will be disallowed.

(2) If the five-year amount is less than a **lower** threshold ($6,575), a Chapter 7 filing will be allowed.

(3) If the five-year amount is between the **lower** threshold and the **upper** threshold, a Chapter 7 filing will be disallowed, if net income exceeds 25 percent of unsecured debt.

4. **Mandatory Credit Counseling** Under BAPCPA '05, an individual debtor is prohibited from filing a bankruptcy petition until the debtor receives a briefing from an approved nonprofit budget and credit counseling service unless the U.S. trustee or bankruptcy administrator determines that the service is not reasonably able to provide adequate services for the requirement.

a. Credit counseling must be within 180 days of filing of the bankruptcy petition.

b. An exemption applies to debtors whom the court determines are unable to comply due to incapacity, disability, or active military duty in a military combat zone.

5. **Responsibilities** The debtor must:

a. **File** File (with the bankruptcy court) a list of creditors, a schedule of assets and liabilities, and a statement of financial affairs. BAPCPA '05 also requires copies of tax returns, payroll stubs, and similar documents.

b. **Cooperate** Cooperate with the trustee in the performance of the trustee's duties. If a meeting of creditors is held, the debtor must appear and submit to examination under oath.

c. **Notify** Send effective notices to creditors of the filing. If notice is not received by a creditor, that creditor is not subject to penalties for automatic stay violations.

d. **Attend** Attend the hearing on discharge.

e. **Surrender** Surrender all estate property to the trustee. Within 45 days after the petition filing date, Chapter 7 debtors must either reaffirm loans secured with personal property or surrender the property; the case is dismissed automatically if the debtor does not do so.

D. Commencement

1. **Voluntary Bankruptcy** A voluntary case may be commenced by the filing of a petition in bankruptcy court involving either Chapter 7, 11, or 13. The petitioner must be an eligible entity under the chapter invoked.

    a. **Order for Relief** Filing of the petition constitutes an order for relief under the invoked chapter.

    b. **Debts** The debtor need not be insolvent, just needs to state that s/he has debts.

2. **Joint Bankruptcy** A joint case is commenced by the filing of a single petition for the individual and her/his spouse in bankruptcy court invoking either Chapter 7, 11, or 13, but neither may undertake it without the other's knowledge and consent. The individuals must be eligible under the chapter invoked.

    a. **Order for Relief** Filing of the petition constitutes an order for relief under the invoked chapter.

    b. **Consolidation Extent** In a joint case, the court must consider the consolidation of the two debtors' estates; that is, to what extent, if at all, the assets and liabilities of the debtors will be combined to pay creditors. Factors included in the court's determination are the extent of jointly held property and the amount of jointly owed debts.

3. **Involuntary Bankruptcy** Involuntary proceedings may be commenced under Chapter 7 liquidation or Chapter 11 reorganization against a Chapter 7 or 11 debtor, but not against a farmer (a person who derives more than 80 percent of her/his gross income from farming, ranching, or the raising of poultry or livestock), church, school, or charitable foundation. The minimum involuntary bankruptcy threshold is $13,475.

    a. **Petition** An involuntary case is commenced by the filing of a petition in the bankruptcy court.

        (1) **Many Creditors** Three or more creditors may file the petition if the debtor has 12 or more creditors with claims that are not contingent and, in the aggregate, the claims of the petitioners exceed any security they hold in the debtor's property by the minimum threshold.

        (2) **Few Creditors** One or more creditors may file the petition if the debtor has fewer than 12 such creditors, provided that the unsecured portion of the claims of the petitioner(s) is, in the aggregate, the minimum threshold.

        (3) **Partnership Debtor** Filing of an involuntary petition against a partnership.

            (a) Less than all of the general partners may file the petition notwithstanding a contrary agreement, state law, or local law.

            (b) If relief has been ordered under any chapter of the Bankruptcy Code with respect to all of the general partners in a partnership, but not as to their partnership, then the trustee of the estate of a general partner or a holder of a claim against the partnership may file an involuntary petition against the partnership.

b. **Answer** The debtor, or a general partner in a partnership debtor that did not join in the petition, may file an answer to an involuntary petition that has been filed against the debtor or the partnership (e.g., controverted).

c. **Business & Property** Except to the extent that the bankruptcy court orders otherwise, and until an order for relief is entered in the involuntary case, any business of the debtor may continue to operate. Furthermore, the debtor may continue to use, acquire, or dispose of property as if the involuntary case had not been commenced.

d. **Relief** If the petition is not controverted timely by the debtor (the Rules of Bankruptcy Procedure fix the time limit), the bankruptcy court will enter an order for relief against the debtor under the chapter under which the petition was filed. If the petition is controverted timely, the bankruptcy court will, after trial, enter an order for relief against the debtor, only if it is found that either:

(1) The debtor generally is not paying its undisputed debts as they become due (equity-sense insolvency definition).

(2) Within 120 days before the date of the filing of the petition, a custodian was appointed or took possession of the debtor's property.

e. **Dismissal** If the involuntary petition is timely controverted and neither of the two requisite grounds for entry of an order of relief is established, the petition will be dismissed by the bankruptcy court.

E. Trustee Role

A trustee is appointed or elected to be the representative of the bankruptcy estate. A trustee is required in Chapters 7 and 13 proceedings, but not in Chapters 9 and 11 proceedings. The trustee is charged with the administration of the estate. The trustee can sue and be sued.

1. **Employment** The trustee may, with the bankruptcy court's approval, employ attorneys, accountants, appraisers, or other professional persons to assist the trustee in carrying out its duties.

2. **Meeting of Creditors** In bankruptcy proceedings, a meeting of creditors generally is held in which the trustee presides. The debtor must appear and submit to examination under oath. A creditor, trustee, or examiner may examine the debtor. The examination purpose is to determine if assets have improperly been disposed of, concealed, or if there are grounds for objection to the debtor's discharge. The scope of such examination includes the debtor's acts, conduct, property, or any matter that may affect the estate administration or the debtor's right to a discharge. Under BAPCPA '05, if the debtor files a plan for which the debtor asked for acceptance before the beginning of the bankruptcy petition, then the creditor's meeting may not be necessary.

F. Administrative Powers

1. **Automatic Stay** A fundamental debtor protection is the automatic stay that stops all collection efforts, all harassment, and all foreclosure or other legal proceedings. It also protects creditors in that no one creditor can obtain an advantage to the detriment of the others by expediting nonbankruptcy remedies against the debtor. An automatic stay does not vitiate the rights of creditors. It puts them on hold pending an orderly examination of the debtor's and creditor's rights.

a. **Scope** In general, the filing of a bankruptcy petition operates as a stay, applicable to all entities, of the following.

(1) The commencement or continuation of a judicial, administrative, or other proceeding.

(2) The enforcement, against the debtor or estate property, of an existing judgment.

(3) Any act to obtain possession of property of the estate.

(4) Any act to create, perfect, or enforce any lien against property of the estate.

(5) Any act to create, perfect, or enforce any lien against property of the debtor (property that the debtor acquires after the date of the filing of the petition, property that is exempt, or property that does not pass to the estate) to the extent that the lien secures a claim that arose before the commencement of the bankruptcy case.

(6) Any act to collect, assess, or recover a claim against the debtor that arose before the commencement of the bankruptcy case.

(7) The setoff of any prebankruptcy debt owing to the debtor.

(8) The commencement or continuation of any proceeding concerning the debtor before the United States Tax Court.

b. **Exceptions** The bankruptcy petition filing does not operate as a stay of the following.

(1) The commencement or continuation of a criminal proceeding against the debtor.

(2) The collection of alimony, maintenance, or support payments from property that is not property of the estate.

(3) Any act to perfect an interest in property to the extent that the trustee's rights and powers are subject to such perfection.

(4) The commencement of any action by the Secretary of Housing and Urban Development to foreclose or take possession in a case of a loan insured under the National Housing Act.

(5) The issuance of a notice of tax deficiency.

(6) The initiation or continuation of eviction proceedings pertaining to a residential lease.

c. **Duration** Generally, the stay of an act against property of the estate continues until such property ceases to be estate property, such as by sale, abandonment, or exemption. Generally, the stay of any other act continues until the earliest of the time the case is closed, the case is dismissed, or a discharge is granted or denied.

2. **Estate Property Use, Sale, or Lease**

a. **Ordinary Course of Business** Without notice or hearing, a trustee who has been authorized to operate a business of the debtor generally may use, sell, or lease property in the ordinary course of business.

b. **Notice** Upon notice to interested parties, and a hearing if there are objections, the trustee (debtor or debtor in possession if there is no trustee) may use, sell, or lease, other than in the ordinary course of business, property of the estate.

3. **Executory Contracts & Unexpired Leases** The Bankruptcy Code provides for the assumption or rejection of such contracts and leases by the trustee subject to court approval. An executory contract is unperformed generally to some extent by *both* sides. Thus, a promissory note usually is not an executory contract. Rejection constitutes a breach and gives rise to a claim for damages against the estate.

G. **Filing of Proofs of Claims or Interests**

A creditor presents her/his claim to the bankruptcy court by filing a proof of claim, and an equity security holder does so by filing a proof of interest.

1. **Accountable Persons** A person, such as a surety, co-debtor, or guarantor, who is liable with a debtor to a creditor may file a proof of claim if the creditor does not timely do so.

2. **Eligible Persons** If a creditor does not file a timely proof of claim, the debtor or trustee may do so for such creditor.

H. **Allowance of Claims or Interests**

Generally, only allowed claims may share in the distribution of the property of the estate.

1. **Evidence** A proof of claim or a proof of interest is *prima facie* evidence of the claim or interest and is allowed unless a party in interest objects to its allowance.

2. **Objection** Generally, once an objection to a claim is made, the bankruptcy court must determine the amount of the claim as of the petition filing date and must either allow or disallow the claim in whole or in part.

3. **Estimates** All claims against the debtor must be converted into dollar amounts. Thus, contingent or unliquidated claims must be estimated.

4. **Disallowed Claims** The bankruptcy court must disallow the entire claim of any entity that fails to pay or turn over money or property to the estate that the trustee is entitled to recover. One example of such an entity is the transferee of a voidable transfer.

5. **Co-Debtors, Sureties & Guarantors Claims**

   a. The bankruptcy court must disallow any claim for reimbursement or contribution of a co-debtor, surety, or guarantor that is liable with the debtor on, or that has secured, the claim of a creditor, to the extent that the creditor's claim against the estate is disallowed.

   b. Generally, a co-debtor, surety, or guarantor is permitted a claim for reimbursement or contribution only if s/he has paid the assured creditor in full. The claim for reimbursement or contribution must be disallowed, however, to the extent the co-debtor, surety, or guarantor chooses to be subrogated to the rights of the creditor.

      - The thrust of b. above, is that the co-debtor, surety, or guarantor has a choice since s/he may not be allowed both a claim for contribution or reimbursement and a claim as subrogee to the rights of the creditor whom s/he has paid.

6. **Pre-Petition Claims** In an involuntary bankruptcy case, a claim arising in the ordinary course of the debtor's business or financial affairs *after* the filing of the petition, but *before* the order for relief, must be treated as a pre-petition claim. Holders of these claims are known as middlemen or involuntary gap creditors.

7. **Creditor Penalties** Creditors who unreasonably refuse to negotiate a pre-bankruptcy debt repayment plan with a debtor may be penalized; the bankruptcy judge may reduce such a creditor's allowable claim by 20 percent.

I. **Administrative Expenses**

The distinction between treatment of a claim as a pre-petition claim and treatment as an administrative expense is important because administrative expenses take priority over most other unsecured claims in the distribution of the assets of the estate. An administrative expense claimant must file a request for payment of the expense with the bankruptcy court, not with the trustee. The following are allowed as administrative expenses.

1. **Expenses** The actual, necessary costs and expenses of preserving the estate, including wages, salaries, or commissions for services rendered after the commencement of the case.

2. **Taxes** Generally, most taxes incurred by the estate.

3. **Fines & Penalties** Any fine, penalty, or reduction in credit, relating to any tax that is allowed as an administrative expense.

4. **Compensation** Compensation and reimbursement awarded to trustees, examiners, professional persons hired by the trustee, and the debtor's attorney.

5. **Services** Reasonable compensation for professional services rendered by an attorney or an accountant of an entity whose expense is allowed.

6. **Fees** Witness fees and mileage.

7. **Eligible Persons** The actual and necessary expenses incurred by:

   a. A creditor that files an involuntary bankruptcy petition.

   b. A creditor that, with court approval, recovers for the benefit of the estate any property transferred or concealed by the debtor.

   c. A creditor that acts in connection with the prosecution of a criminal offense relating to the case.

   d. A custodian upon being superseded by the representative of the estate.

J. Secured Claims Determination

An allowed claim of a creditor that is secured by a lien on property in which the estate has an interest is a secured claim to the extent of the value of the creditor's interest in the collateral. It is an unsecured claim to the extent that the value of the creditor's interest in the collateral is less than the amount of the creditor's allowed claim.

1. **Subject to Setoff** An allowed claim of a creditor that is subject to setoff under the Bankruptcy Code is a secured claim to the extent of the amount subject to setoff. It is an unsecured claim to the extent that the amount so subject to setoff is less than the creditor's claim.

2. **Disallowed Liens** Generally, a lien passes through the bankruptcy case unaffected. However, if a claim secured by a lien is disallowed, then the lien is void **unless either:**

   a. There was no objection to the claim by a party in interest, **or**

   b. The only reason the claim was disallowed was because such claim was one for reimbursement or contribution by a co-debtor or surety who chose to be subrogated.

K. Priority of Claims

Although, in bankruptcy, equality of distribution among creditors is the policy, certain claims have priority based on a priority ranking system for distribution. Thus, under a Chapter 7 liquidation, since assets must be utilized to satisfy priority claims until depleted, if the assets are insufficient to satisfy all claims, higher ranking claims may be satisfied in full while lower ranking claims receive nothing. **Note:** Each claim must be paid in full at one priority level before any lower claim is paid anything. If a class of claim cannot be paid in full, the claims in that class will be paid on a *pro rata* basis. The order of priority for claims for Chapter 7 is as follows.

Exhibit 1 ▸ Priority of Claims (Chapter 7)

"SCAM WED TUG"

S	**S**ecured creditors
C	**C**hild support and alimony claims
A	**A**dministrative claims
M	**M**iddleman debts: Debts occurring after filing date but before the order for relief.
W	Unpaid **W**ages (maximum $10,950)
E	Unpaid **E**mployee benefits (maximum $10,950)
D	**D**eposits for consumer goods (maximum $2,425)
T	Unpaid **T**ax (unsecured claims on federal and state income and sales tax)
U	**U**nder-the-influence liability
G	**G**eneral unsecured creditors

Note: This mnemonic doesn't include the claims of farm producers and fishermen against storage facilities, which rarely is tested on the CPA exam. Each letter indicates a separate priority; for instance, there is no reason for the space between "M" and "W" in this mnemonic other than to form words that may be remembered readily.

1. **Secured Claims** A creditor holding an allowed claim secured by a lien on property is entitled to this first priority only in the distribution of the proceeds from the liquidation of its collateral and only to the extent of its secured claim. Collateral must be applied first to satisfy the claim that it secures. BAPCPA '05 requires Chapter 13 debtors to continue making payments on secured loans as obligated originally; these payments are made to the trustee until a payment plan is confirmed or denied.

2. **Child Support & Alimony** Allowed claims for debts to a spouse, former spouse, or child of the debtor for alimony, maintenance, or support of such spouse or child. (BAPCPA '05 gave child support and alimony obligations first priority among unsecured creditors.)

3. **Allowed Administrative Expenses** Allowable administrative claims must be filed with the bankruptcy court, not the trustee.

4. **Middleman or Involuntary Gap Creditor Debts** Unsecured claims for debts incurred after the commencement of an involuntary bankruptcy case but before the order of relief.

5. **Unpaid Wages** Allowed unsecured claims for wages, salaries, or commissions earned by an individual employee of the debtor within 180 days before the date of the filing of the petition or 90 days before the date of cessation of the debtor's business, whichever occurs first, to the extent of $10,950 for each employee. Court approval is required for a corporate debtor's bonus payments, severance payments, and other payments to insiders after the bankruptcy case is filed.

6. **Unpaid Employee Benefits** Certain allowed unsecured claims for contributions to employee benefit plans arising from services rendered by the debtor's employees within 180 days before the date of the filing of the petition or the date of the cessation of the debtor's business, whichever occurs first. The maximum amount allowed is $10,950, less the amount of allowed unsecured claims for wages, salaries, or commissions in the previous priority.

7. **Farmers & Fishers** Farm producers and fishers have a priority claim against debtors who operate grain or fish produce storage facilities up to $5,400 per claim.

8. **Consumer Goods Deposits** Allowed unsecured claims of individuals to the extent of $2,425 for each individual who, prior to the commencement of the case, deposited money

with the debtor in connection with the purchase or rental of property for the personal, family, or household use of the individual, and who never received such goods or property.

9. **Taxes** Allowed unsecured claims of a governmental unit (whether federal, state, or local) for certain taxes.

   a. Such taxes generally include income taxes, property taxes, withholding taxes, excise taxes, employment taxes, and customs duties.

   b. The claims that are given priority here do not include fines or penalties which are not compensation for actual pecuniary loss.

10. **DUI Liability** Liability related to motor vehicle operation under the influence of drugs or alcohol.

L. Distribution Rules
There are general distribution rules in addition to those priority distribution rules discussed above, which are applicable only in a Chapter 7 case. Claims within a particular class are to be paid *pro rata* when there are inadequate funds to pay in full.

1. **Priority** After the property of the estate, which usually has been reduced to money by the trustee in the liquidation case, has been distributed to satisfy all of the priority claims, the remaining property then is distributed in the following order.

   a. In payment of any allowed unsecured claim, proof of which was filed timely

   b. In payment of any allowed unsecured claim, proof of which was filed tardily

   c. In payment of any allowed claim, whether secured or unsecured, for any fine, penalty, or forfeiture or for multiple, exemplary, or punitive damages, which arose before the order for relief and which is not compensation for actual pecuniary loss suffered by the holder of such claim

   d. In payment of any interest, accruing from the date of the filing of the bankruptcy petition, on any paid claim

   e. In payment (of any surplus) to the debtor

2. **Community Property** Community property in the estate must be segregated from noncommunity property. Such community property then is subject to its own distribution rules.

M. Exemptions
To give an individual debtor a fresh start after bankruptcy, certain property may be claimed by the individual as exempt and retained by her/him.

1. **System** An individual debtor may choose between two exemption systems. Under a joint bankruptcy case, each debtor is entitled to her/his own election of exemptions.

   a. **Federal Bankruptcy Code** In lieu of other exemption systems, the debtor may choose the federal bankruptcy code exemptions, but only if these are allowed by the law of the debtor's state of domicile. These exemptions include the following.

      (1) Up to $20,200 of real or personal property of the residence used by the debtor or the debtor's dependent(s).

      (2) Up to a $3,225 interest in one motor vehicle.

(3) Household goods, furnishings, clothing, appliances, books, animals, and crops, that are held primarily for the personal, family, or household use of the debtor or the debtor's dependent(s) but not to exceed $525 in value in any particular item.

(4) Up to $1,350 in jewelry held primarily for the personal, family, or household use of the debtor or the debtor's dependent(s).

(5) Up to $1,075, plus any unused amount of the exemption provided in paragraph (1), above, in any property.

(6) Up to $2,025 in any implements, professional books, or tools of the trade of the debtor or the debtor's dependent(s).

(7) Any unmatured life insurance contract owned by the debtor, other than a credit life insurance contract.

(8) Up to $10,775 in any accrued dividend or interest under, or loan value of, any unmatured life insurance contract owned by the debtor and insuring either the debtor or an individual of whom the debtor is a dependent(s).

(9) Any professionally prescribed health aids for the debtor or the debtor's dependent(s).

(10) The debtor's right to receive social security benefits; unemployment compensation; veterans' benefits; disability or illness benefits; reasonable alimony, support, or separate maintenance; certain stock bonus, pension, profit sharing, or annuity payments; and up to $1,095,000 in tax-exempt retirement accounts (such as IRAs).

(11) The debtor's right to receive certain compensation for losses, such as crime victim's reparation benefits, wrongful death benefits, and payments under a life insurance contract that insured the life of an individual of whom the debtor was a dependent on the date of such individual's death.

(12) Up to $5,475 in pre-purchased tuition or education savings accounts (accounts meeting IRS requirements).

b. **Other Systems** The debtor may exempt from the estate any property that is exempt under federal nonbankruptcy law and the law of the state of domicile and any interest in property that s/he had as a tenant by the entirety or joint tenant before the commencement of bankruptcy proceedings that is exempt under nonbankruptcy law.

(1) **State** State exemption laws generally are those laws that give the debtor a right or privilege to retain a portion of her/his property free from seizure and sale by creditors under judicial process.

(2) **Nonbankruptcy** Examples of federal nonbankruptcy law exemptions are social security payments, veterans' benefits, and certain civil service retirement benefits.

(3) **Homestead Exemption** In states that exempt a debtor's primary residence from inclusion in nonexempt property, the debtor must reside in that state for 1,215 days or more prior to the filing. If the debtor does not meet this requirement, then the debtor may exempt up to only $136,875 of interest in a homestead, regardless of the level of the state exemption.

2. **Claim** The debtor must file a list of property that s/he claims as exempt. Absent an objection by a party in interest, the property claimed as exempt is exempt. If there is an objection, the court will rule on the exemption.

3. **Significance** Unless the bankruptcy case is dismissed, exempt property may not be seized during or after the case for any debt of the debtor that arose, or that is treated as if it had arisen, before the commencement of the case, except for:

   a. Debt for taxes not discharged in bankruptcy;

   b. Debt for alimony, maintenance, or child support; and

   c. Valid liens not avoided by the trustee.

4. **Waiver** To protect the debtor's exemptions, any waiver of exemptions executed in favor of a creditor that holds an unsecured claim against the debtor is unenforceable in the bankruptcy case.

N. **Discharge**
As a general rule, a debtor is entitled to only one Chapter 7 discharge from bankruptcy during an eight-year period running from a prior petition in which debtor was discharged. Furthermore, BAPCPA '05 requires a Chapter 13 case for any debtor who received a discharge in a Chapter 7, 11, or 12 case within the preceding four years or in another Chapter 13 case within the preceding two years.

1. **Ordinary Exceptions** Under Chapters 7, 11, and 13, certain debts of an individual are **not** discharged, as follows.

   a. **Taxes** Federal, state, and local tax debts entitled to priority claim status that were due within 3 years of filing of the bankruptcy petition; and tax debts related to a fraudulent return or which the debtor willfully attempted to evade.

   b. **Unscheduled Debts** Debts that were not included on the schedules required to be filed by the debtor or were not included in time to permit timely action by the creditor unless such creditor had notice or actual knowledge of the case.

   c. **Child Support & Alimony** Debts to a spouse, former spouse, or child of the debtor for alimony, maintenance, or child support.

   d. **Fines** Debts for fines, penalties, or forfeitures payable to and for the benefit of a governmental unit, which are not compensation for actual pecuniary loss, other than certain tax penalties.

   e. **Educational Loan** Debts to a governmental unit, or a nonprofit institution of higher education, for an educational loan, unless the loan first becomes due more than seven years before the date of filing the petition or unless excepting the debt from discharge would impose undue hardship on the debtor.

   f. **Previous Surviving Debts** Debts that survived an earlier bankruptcy proceeding because the debtor was denied a discharge other than on the basis of elapsed time since a prior discharge or because the debtor waived discharge.

   g. **Luxury Goods** A consumer debt owed to a single creditor totaling more than $550 for luxury goods or services, incurred within 90 days of the order for relief.

   h. **Advances** Cash advances totaling more than $825, based on consumer open-end credit, such as a credit card, incurred within 70 days of the order for relief.

   i. **DUI Liability** Judgments against a debtor for liability for injuries caused by driving while intoxicated.

   j. **Car Loans** Automobile loans entered into within 3 years prior to the bankruptcy.

k. **Domestic Support Payments**

l. **Homeowners' Association Fees**

m. **Pension & Profit-Sharing Debts**

2. **Special Exemptions** A creditor who is owed one of the following types of debts must initiate proceedings in the bankruptcy court for a determination of the nondischargeability of such debt. If the creditor does not act, the debt is discharged. However, if the debtor has not listed the creditor, then the creditor does not have to initiate such proceedings, and the debtor is not discharged from such debts.

   a. **Fraud** A debt for obtaining money, property, services, or an extension or renewal of credit, by means of false pretenses, false representations, actual fraud, or by means of a materially false written financial statement, made by the debtor with intent to deceive and reasonably relied upon by the creditor. Includes debts for fraud while the debtor was acting in a fiduciary capacity, and debts for embezzlement or larceny.

   b. **Willful & Malicious Injury** Debts for willful and malicious injury by the debtor to another person or to the property of another person.

3. **Effect**

   a. The following results are not defeated even if the debtor waives the discharge of any particular debt. A discharge in a bankruptcy case under any chapter:

      (1) Voids any existing and future judgments that are determinations of the personal liability of the debtor with respect to any discharged debt.

      (2) Operates as an injunction against the commencement or continuation of an action at law, the employment of legal process, or any act (including telephone calls and letters) to recover, collect, or offset any discharged debt as a personal liability of the debtor or from the property of the debtor.

      (3) Generally operates as an injunction against the commencement or continuation of an action at law. Finally, a discharge is effective against community creditors of the nondebtor spouse as well as the debtor spouse.

   b. Generally, the discharge of a debt does not affect the liability of any co-debtors, sureties, or guarantors for such debt.

4. **Order to Discharge** An order to discharge releases the debtor from all dischargeable debts arising or treated as arising before commencement of bankruptcy whether a proof of claim has been filed or allowed. The court must grant a discharge unless:

   a. **Ineligible Status** The debtor is not an individual.

   b. **Taxes** The discharge is for loans used to pay taxes (including those paid on credit cards).

   c. **Previous Discharge** Generally, the debtor has been granted a discharge in a bankruptcy case commenced within six years preceding the present bankruptcy case. BAPCPA '05 increases this to eight years for Chapter 7 cases.

   d. **Waiver** The bankruptcy court approves a written waiver of discharge executed by the debtor after the order of relief.

   e. **Bankruptcy Offences** The debtor has committed any of the following acts on, or within one year before, the date of the filing of the bankruptcy petition.

(1) The debtor, with intent to hinder, delay, or defraud a creditor or an officer of the estate, has transferred, removed, destroyed, mutilated, or concealed property of the debtor or the estate within a year before or after commencement of bankruptcy, respectively.

(2) The debtor has concealed, falsified, or failed to preserve any books or records from which her/his financial condition might be ascertained, unless the act or failure to act was justified.

(3) The debtor knowingly and fraudulently:

(a) Made a false oath or account;

(b) Presented or used a false claim;

(c) Gave, offered, received, or attempted to obtain money, property, or advantage, or a promise therefore, for acting or forbearing to act; or

(d) Withheld recorded information from an officer of the estate entitled to possession of such information when the information related to the debtor's financial affairs.

(4) The debtor has failed to explain satisfactorily any loss of assets or deficiency of assets to meet the debtor's liabilities.

(5) The debtor has refused, in the case, to obey any lawful order of the court or to testify after having been granted immunity or after having improperly invoked the constitutional privilege against self-incrimination.

5. **Objection** The trustee or a creditor may object to discharge, and upon request of a party in interest, the court may order the trustee to examine the debtor to determine whether grounds exist to deny discharge.

6. **Revocation** The bankruptcy court may revoke an order of discharge, if such order was procured by fraud.

O. Estate Property

The property of the estate consists of the debtor's assets administered in bankruptcy. The estate acquires the same rights as were held by the debtor. For example, if the debtor held a beneficial interest, the estate would hold the debtor's interest.

1. **Inclusions** The debtor's property interests become a part of the estate despite any provisions restricting transfer or despite any forfeiture provisions contingent on bankruptcy filing or appointment of a receiver or trustee. On commencement of bankruptcy, an estate is created of the following.

a. All legal and equitable interests in property and, with certain limitations, in community property.

b. Proceeds, product, offspring, rents, and profits of estate property.

c. Property interests acquired by the estate after commencement.

d. Property interests acquired by the debtor within 180 days after commencement by bequest, devise, inheritance, as a result of a property settlement agreement with a spouse, or as a beneficiary of a life insurance policy or health benefit plan.

e. Any interest in property received by the trustee through the debtor's avoiding power.

f. Any interest in property recovered from a nonbankruptcy receiver, assignee (of an ABC), trustee, agent, or other custodian.

2. **Exclusions** Property that does not become a part of the estate includes the following.

a. Earnings from services of an individual after bankruptcy commencement, except under Chapter 13.

b. Any power, such as a power of appointment, exercisable by the debtor for the benefit of another.

c. Property held in trust by the debtor.

(1) Bare legal title held by the debtor comes into the estate, but not a beneficial interest of another person.

(2) Constructive trust property, such as insurance payments received for an unpaid doctor bill, does not become estate property.

3. **Offset** Generally, the Bankruptcy Code leaves unaffected any right of a creditor to offset a mutual debt it owes to the debtor against a claim it possesses against the debtor, so long as both the claim and the debt arose before the commencement of the bankruptcy case.

P. Trustee's Avoiding Powers

To implement the policy of fair and equitable treatment of creditors, the bankruptcy laws grant the trustee avoiding powers to set aside certain conveyances and liens including the following.

1. **Statutory Liens**

a. Liens that first become effective upon the insolvency or bankruptcy of the debtor.

b. Liens that, on the date of bankruptcy filing, are unperfected or unenforceable against a bona fide purchaser.

c. Liens for rent or of distress for rent, whether statutory or common law.

2. **Preferential Transfers** Several tests must be satisfied to establish a preferential transfer.

Exhibit 2 ▸ Preference Elements

"BAN TIM"	
B	Transfer of property that **B**enefits a creditor
A	**A**ntecedent debt (debt that existed before the transfer)
N	Within **N**inety days before filing
T	Threshold of $5,475
I	Debtor was **I**nsolvent.
M	Creditor received **M**ore than through bankruptcy.

a. **Criteria** A preferential transfer is a transfer of the property of the debtor:

(1) **Benefit** To or for the benefit of a creditor.

(2) **Antecedent Debt** For or on account of an antecedent debt owed by the debtor

(3) **Ninety Days** Made on or within 90 days before the date of bankruptcy filing or between 90 days and 1 year before the filing date, if the creditor at the time of transfer was an insider and had reason to believe the debtor was insolvent. Insiders are relatives, officers, directors, and controlling shareholders of the debtor. If made to an insider and that, in turn, is transferred to a non-insider transferee, it is not subject to recovery by the trustee.

(4) **Threshold** $5,475 minimum

(5) **Insolvent** Made while the debtor was insolvent in the bankruptcy sense (debtor presumed insolvent in the 90-day period immediately preceding the filing of bankruptcy).

(6) **More** That enables the creditor to receive more than it otherwise would receive as a distributive share under a Chapter 7 liquidation

b. **Exceptions** The trustee cannot avoid the following transfers as preferential.

(1) A contemporaneous exchange for new value given to the debtor.

(2) Payment in the ordinary course of business in financial affairs of the debtor and transferee made not later than 45 days after the debt was incurred.

(3) A transfer of a security interest in property acquired by the debtor that enables the debtor to purchase the property (e.g., a purchase money security interest).

(4) Generally, transfers of security interests by the debtor that are offset by new value which the creditor subsequently gave to the debtor. (These transfers usually are found in those settings involving after-acquired property clauses and future advance clauses contained in security agreements.)

(5) Generally, certain transfers by the debtor of security interests in its inventory or accounts receivable.

(6) A transfer that is the fixing of a statutory lien that is not avoidable by the trustee under her/his second avoiding power.

(7) Child support and alimony payments.

3. **Fraudulent Transfers** A fraudulent transfer is the transfer of an interest of the debtor in property, or any obligation incurred by the debtor, that was made or incurred within two years before the date of the filing of the petition and that was made or incurred either:

a. By the debtor with actual intent to hinder, delay, or defraud any present or future creditor.

b. Under circumstances whereby the debtor received less than a reasonably equivalent value in exchange for the transfer or obligation and whereby the debtor:

(1) Was insolvent at the time or became insolvent as a result thereof.

(2) Was engaged in business, or was about to engage in business, for which the debtor's remaining property was unreasonably small capital.

(3) Intended to incur, or believed that s/he would incur, debts that would be beyond the debtor's ability to pay as they matured.

4. **Partnership Debtor** When the debtor is a partnership, a transfer can be avoided by the trustee if it was made to a general partner within a year before bankruptcy filing and at the time the partnership was insolvent or if by the transfer the partnership became insolvent.

II. Consumer Credit Law

A. Truth in Lending Act (TILA) of 1968

The federal Truth in Lending Act superseded state disclosure requirements and requires the uniform disclosure of credit terms, in writing, for consumer credit including consumer loans and credit sales, up to $25,000. This maximum does not apply when a creditor takes a security interest in a debtor's real or personal property. This act applies to consumer credit extended primarily for personal, family, or household purposes and does not apply to business, commercial, or agricultural transactions.

1. **Terms** Disclosure of credit terms is required, including interest, sales charges, finder's fees, mortgage guarantee insurance, and any mandatory credit life insurance. Finance charges and interest rates are required to be quoted in terms of an annual percentage rate (APR).

2. **Revolving or Open-End Credit** Revolving or open-end credit permits the debtor to make a series of credit transactions and pay them in a lump sum or in a series of installments, such as credit cards. A statement of account is required to be given to the debtor each billing period. Disclosure is required of how the finance charge is calculated, when it is charged, what other charges may be imposed, and whether the creditor retains or acquires a security interest.

3. **Closed-End Credit** Closed-end credit is extended for a specified time and the debtor generally makes periodic payments, such as in a real estate mortgage or a car loan. Disclosure is required of information about the total amount financed, the cash price, details of the installment payments, including the number, amount and due date of installments, delinquency charges, and a description of any security involved.

4. **Adjustable Rate Mortgages (ARMs)** Additional disclosures are required in variable or adjustable rate mortgages, known as "ARMs," including providing the creditor with an information handbook on ARMs and a loan program disclosure statement that discloses the terms of each ARM that the creditor offers.

B. Fair Credit Reporting Act

This act requires credit reporting agencies to follow reasonable procedures to assure maximum possible accuracy in reporting consumer credit histories and prohibits the agencies from including inaccurate or obsolete information in consumer reports.

1. **Time** Most information generally is considered obsolete after 7 years. Bankruptcy information after 10 years.

2. **Written Notification** Consumers must be given written notice before consumer reporting agencies can make investigative reports.

3. **Right to Receive** Consumers have the right to receive, upon request, copies of their files from any consumer reporting agency, including information regarding the sources of information contained in their files, and the names of recipients, for the preceding 6 months, of the information contained in their files. If the information released to third parties was for employment purposes, the names of the recipients for the preceding 2 years may be obtained by the individual.

4. **Challenge** This act also provides for an individual to challenge inaccurate or incomplete information. An agency is required to reinvestigate the information challenged and, if inaccurate, promptly delete the inaccurate information. The individual is entitled to submit a brief explanation of any unresolved dispute which is then required to be incorporated into the individual's reports.

C. Equal Credit Opportunity Act of 1974

This Act prohibits all businesses regularly extending credit from discriminating against any applicant on the basis of sex, marital status, race, color, religion, national origin, or age and restricts the type of information that a creditor may ask on a credit application.

1. **Practices** The act prohibits an earlier practice of refusing credit to women of childbearing age under the assumption that such women were apt to quit work to have children and compromise their repayment ability. The Federal Reserve Board issued Regulation B, which, along with the Women's Business Ownership Act of 1988, prohibits asking an applicant's marital status or the likelihood of having children.

2. **Income Source** The act prohibits discrimination because a source of an applicant's income is a public assistance program, or because an applicant exercised in good faith a right under the Consumer Protection Act.

3. **Notification** The creditor is required to notify a credit applicant of the action taken within 30 days of application. A denial must be accompanied by specific reasons for the denial.

4. **Enforcement** The Federal Trade Commission has the enforcement authority for this act, which is administered by several federal agencies.

5. **Remedies** Remedies for violations include actual and punitive damages plus attorneys' fees.

D. Fair Debt Collection Practices Act of 1977

This federal act prohibits abusive, deceptive, and unfair practices by debt collectors attempting to collect from debtors. Note that this act applies only to debt collectors and not to creditors using their own names in collection efforts. Debtors may be protected by state laws or common law against unfair collection practices by the actual creditor. This federal act forbids abusive collection practices, including:

1. **Third-Party Communication** Certain communication with third parties about a consumer's debt. Collectors may contact a third party only to request the whereabouts of the debtor, but the collectors are prohibited from disclosing the purpose of the request.

2. **Time** Contacting the consumer at inconvenient or unusual hours. If the debtor's employer objects, the collector cannot contact the debtor at the debtor's place of employment.

3. **Attorney** Contact with the consumer if the consumer is represented by an attorney.

4. **Communication** Harassing, intimidating, oppressive, or abusive communication with the consumer. Threats of violence and the use of obscene language are forbidden. The debt collector also is prohibited from using false or misleading information such as posing as a police officer.

5. **Means** Any other unfair or unconscionable means to attempt to collect the debt.

6. **Written Notification** A debt collector is required to cease further communication with a consumer who has provided written notification to the debt collector of refusal to pay a debt or a request that the debt collector cease further communication with the consumer. The debt collector may, however, notify the consumer that specified remedies are being taken, such as filing a lawsuit, to collect the debt.

E. Other Statutes

1. **Federal Consumer Credit Protection Act (FCCPA) of 1968** This act requires that creditors disclose finance charges, including interest and other charges. It also requires the disclosure of credit extension charges, and sets limits on garnishment proceedings. Additional titles to this law have been enacted since 1968.

2. **Fair Credit Billing Act of 1975** This act prohibits a creditor, upon proper receipt of a complaint, to report the disputed amount as delinquent, to take action to collect the disputed amount, or to restrict the use of an open-ended credit account because the disputed amount is unpaid until the creditor has properly responded to the complaint. It also established procedures for consumers to make complaints about billing errors and requires the creditor to explain or correct such errors. Billing errors include extensions of credit that were not made or not made in the amount indicated on the billing statement, undelivered or unaccepted goods or services, incorrect reporting of payments or credits, and any accounting or computational errors.

3. **Consumer Leasing Act of 1988** This act extends protection to consumers leasing automobiles and other goods priced up to $25,000, if the lease term exceeds 4 months. Lessors are required to disclose in writing all of the material terms of the lease.

4. **Fair Credit & Charge Card Disclosure Act of 1988** This act requires all credit and charge card applications and solicitations to include extensive disclosures. The required disclosures vary, depending upon the type of card involved and the method of solicitation involved, such as mail or telephone.

5. **Electronic Fund Transfers Act (EFTA)** This act prohibits the use of any counterfeit, stolen, or fraudulently obtained card, code, or other device to obtain money or goods in excess of a specified amount through an electronic fund transfer system, and makes any such activity a federal crime. The act also prohibits shipping in interstate commerce devices or goods, or to knowingly receive goods, that have been obtained by the fraudulent use of the transfer system.

6. **Credit Card Fraud Act of 1984** This act prohibits fraudulent acts associated with credit cards, including possession of unauthorized cards, counterfeiting or altering credit cards, and using account numbers alone. In addition, under the Federal Consumer Credit Protection Act, credit card holders are protected from loss by limiting the card holder's liability to $50 for the unauthorized use of the holder's card by another person prior to the holder timely notifying the issuer that the card has been stolen or lost. This applies only to credit cards that the holder has accepted. Consumers are not liable for any unauthorized use of a card issued in the card holder's name that was unsolicited and unaccepted.

7. **Home Mortgage Disclosure Act (HMDA)** This act prohibits geographic discrimination, known as "redlining." Financial institutions cannot legally refuse to provide reasonable residential financing terms to qualified applicants because the location is in an area of declining value. This act also requires public disclosure of an institution's geographic pattern of mortgage lending.

8. **Community Reinvestment Act (CRA)** This law was enacted by Congress to encourage financial institutions to meet the credit needs of their local communities.

9. **Financial Institutions Reform, Recovery & Enforcement Act of 1989 (FIRREA)** In this banking bailout bill, disclosure and reporting requirements for all mortgage lenders was expanded and federal agencies were mandated to evaluate and rate CRA performance reports.

10. **Home Equity Loan Consumer Protection Act of 1988 (HELCPA)** This act requires that a disclosure statement and consumer pamphlet be provided by the lender along with any application to a potential borrower. It applies to all open-end credit plans for consumer loans secured by the borrower's principal dwelling, which as defined by this act (but not by other Truth-in-Lending statutes) to include second or vacation homes.

11. **Real Estate Settlement Procedures Act of 1974 (RESPA)** This act applies to all federally related mortgage loans, which includes most first mortgage loans, and requires advance disclosure of the nature and cost of all settlement costs. It also prohibits kickbacks and

referral fees and limits the amount that can be required in escrow accounts for real estate taxes and insurance.

12. **Financial Services Modernization Act of 1999** This privacy law prohibits all financial institutions from transmitting private personal information to nonaffiliated third parties without prior notice to the customer and without a customer option to prevent it. In addition, it prohibits the transmission of account numbers or other form of access codes or numbers to non-affiliated third parties for marketing purposes. Note that this act does NOT prohibit the sharing of information between a financial institution and its affiliates.

13. **Telemarketing Sales Rule (TSR)** Prohibits deceptive and abusive telemarketing acts and practices, and requires certain disclosures. The TSR restricts call times and prohibits calls to consumers who have expressed their desire not to be called. It requires telemarketers to promptly identify the seller or charitable organization, the purpose of the call, and to disclose all material information of the sale.

    a. **Do-Not-Call Registry** The registry streamlines the process for consumers to reduce the number of unwanted telemarketing calls.

        (1) **Five Years** Registered telephone numbers remain in the registry for five years, unless disconnected or deleted by the consumer. Consumers may renew their registration after five years.

        (2) **Telemarketers** Requires telemarketers to search the registry every three months and synchronize their call lists. Telemarketers who fail to comply may be fined up to $11,000 for each violation.

        (3) **Exemptions** Political organizations, charities, telephone surveyors, and the insurance businesses, to the extent regulated by state law, are permitted to call. For-profit telemarketers calling on behalf of charitable organizations must honor consumer's request to be on the charity's do-not-call list.

            (a) **Business Relationship** Companies with which the consumer has an established business relationship can call for up to 18 months after the last purchase, payment, or delivery.

            (b) **Inquiries** Organizations to which the consumer made an inquiry or submitted an application can call for three months.

            (c) **Permission** If the consumer asks a company not to call, the company must honor the request. However, consumers may give written permission to particular companies they would like to hear from.

    b. **Unauthorized Billing Restrictions** Telemarketers must get the consumer's express consent before charging their account. This includes goods or services offered on a free trial basis before automatically charging the consumer's account (free-to-pay conversion offers).

    c. **Abandoned Call Reduction** Telemarketers are required to connect calls to sales representatives within two seconds of the consumer's greeting. If telemarketers don't have representatives standing by, a recorded message must state who called and their telephone number. Telemarketers may not hang up before 15 seconds or four rings.

    d. **Caller-ID Transmission** Telemarketers must transmit their telephone number and name, if possible, to consumer caller identification services.

14. **Uniform Consumer Credit Code (UCCC)** The National Conference of Commissioners on Uniform State Laws promulgated the Uniform Consumer Credit Code in 1968. This code

provides for the regulation of all consumer credit transactions; however, it has been adopted in only some states.

F. Right of Rescission

Purchasers have the right of rescission of a contract under certain laws and in certain transactions for a specified amount of time after purchase or entering into a credit transaction.

1. **States** State "cooling-off" laws vary in length from state to state and generally require door-to-door solicitation.

2. **Federal Trade Commission** The FTC trade regulation rescission period is 3 days from signing of the contract, applies to only door-to-door solicitation, and applies to both credit and cash transactions.

3. **Consumer Credit Protection Act** The Consumer Credit Protection Act rescission period is 3 days from signing the contract, applies to any credit obligation secured by a mortgage on the debtor's home, unless the mortgage was obtained to acquire the home. Door-to-door solicitation is not required.

4. **Interstate Land Sales Full Disclosure Act** The Interstate Land Sales Full Disclosure Act rescission period is 7 days from signing the contract, does not require door-to-door solicitation and applies to both credit and cash transactions involving sales or leases of unimproved land.

III. Default

A. Custodian

A nonbankruptcy receiver, trustee, assignee for the benefit of creditors, or other agent appointed to take charge of the debtor's property.

B. Secured & Lien Creditors

A lien is an interest in property securing payment or other performance for an underlying obligation. When debt secured by a lien remains unpaid, the property may be sold and the proceeds applied to the debt. The categories of liens are as follows.

1. **Consensual Liens** Liens created with the debtor's consent are consensual liens. These liens are created when the debtor agrees to give the creditor a right to some personal or real property or a right against a surety in return for a loan or credit sale.

   a. When the debtor gives the creditor a right to foreclose on some personal property that the debtor owns if the debtor defaults on the debt, the consensual lien is called a secured transaction (also see Chapter 37).

   b. When the debtor gives the creditor a right to foreclose on some real property that the debtor owns if the debtor defaults on the debt, the consensual lien is called a mortgage (also see Chapter 42).

   c. When the debtor can get a third person to assure performance upon default, the agreement is called a suretyship contract (see VIII.).

2. **Statutory & Common Law Liens** Liens created by operation of law are statutory liens, and are created when specified circumstances or conditions occur. Common law liens generally allow creditors, including landlords and innkeepers, to retain possession of a debtor's property until the debt is paid.

   a. **Mechanic's Lien** A mechanic's lien is a statutory lien given to a creditor to ensure payment for work performed and materials furnished in the repair or improvement of real property, and is recorded in the real estate records to provide constructive notice of its existence. Unpaid debt secured by a mechanic's lien is paid from the proceeds of the next sale of the real property.

b. **Artisan's Lien** An artisan's lien is a possessory common law lien given to a person who has made improvements and added value to another person's personal property, such as an automobile, as security for payment of services performed. The artisan has the right to retain the property until receiving payment for the work performed. If possession is surrendered voluntarily, the lien is terminated, even if the debt remains unpaid.

c. **Bailee's Lien** Carriers and warehousemen are granted possessory liens that allow them to retain possession of goods entrusted to them until payment for shipment or storage charges are paid.

d. **Landlord's & Innkeeper's Lien** Owners of property may secure payment of rent or hotel charges by a possessory common law lien on the tenant's personal property located on the leased premises.

e. **Tax Lien** A state or the federal government or a government subdivision may obtain a tax lien to secure payment of delinquent taxes.

3. **Judicial Liens** Judicial liens are created by judgment, levy, garnishment, or other legal or equitable process or proceeding.

C. **Unsecured Creditors**

When a debtor defaults on its payments or obligations owed to an unsecured creditor, the unsecured creditor may institute legal action to enforce its rights. These types of legal actions encourage a "race of diligence" among creditors, pitting one against the other in an effort to reach the debtor's usually limited and insufficient assets. The creditor may do any of the following:

1. **Attachment** Obtain a statutory writ of attachment, whereby the debtor's property will be seized to secure payment either prior or subsequent to a judgment being rendered for the creditor.

2. **Garnishment** Obtain an order of garnishment to attach or gain access to assets of the debtor held by a third party to satisfy the unpaid debt, such as attaching a debtor's bank account by having an order of garnishment issued to the debtor's bank, or garnishing the wages of the debtor by having an order of garnishment issued to the debtor's employer.

3. **Execution** Obtain a judgment and enforce it by execution, whereby the debtor's nonexempt property will be levied upon or seized and sold to satisfy the judgment. A statutory supplementary proceeding may be instituted if the judgment is not satisfied by execution and the proceeding may give access to the debtor's nonexempt property that is not subject to execution.

D. **Fraudulent Conveyances**

In most states, a creditor may bring an action to set aside a fraudulent conveyance of a debtor or to levy on and sell fraudulently conveyed property. Generally, a creditor to whom the conveyance is fraudulent needs only a matured, valid claim to challenge the transfer. A judgment is not required.

1. **Definition** A fraudulent conveyance is a conveyance made by a debtor with intent to delay, hinder, or defraud creditors, or one made without fair consideration by a person who is or will thereby become insolvent.

2. **Exempt Property** A transfer of exempt property cannot be a fraudulent conveyance.

E. **Collective Creditor Actions**

1. **Assignment** The debtor may make an assignment for the benefit of creditors (ABC). Generally, creditor consent is not a precondition to the assignment. ABCs affect all general creditors.

a. An ABC is a voluntary transfer of all the debtor's nonexempt assets to another person in trust, the assignee, who liquidates the assets and distributes the proceeds to the creditors. Legal title to the assets, generally subject to valid liens or claims, passes to the assignee and bars the creditors from levying on the assets.

b. If an interest or benefit in the property conveyed is reserved in the debtor, it usually is construed as a fraudulent conveyance.

c. Generally, the debtor is not fully discharged if deficiencies in the debts owed remain after distribution of the proceeds to the creditors.

d. ABCs are regulated by specific statutes in most states. In the absence of a statute, the general legal principles of the law of trusts apply.

2. **Composition Agreement** The debtor and its creditors may enter into a composition or extension agreement. Generally, creditors unwilling to accept the terms of a composition or extension agreement are not required to do so. Creditors who do not agree to the agreement are not affected by it.

a. A **composition agreement** is an agreement between a debtor and its creditors in which the participating creditors agree to accept an immediate or early payment of a lesser sum in full satisfaction of the debt due them.

b. An **extension** is an agreement between a debtor and its creditors in which the participating creditors take full payment of their claims, but extended over a period of time beyond the original due date.

c. Such agreements are contractual. Thus, all essential elements of a contract must be present to make the agreement valid, including the element of consideration.

(1) The consideration given by the participating creditors is their mutual promises to accept less than the full amount or later payment of their claims. A composition or extension agreement requires the participation of at least two or more creditors because there must be such mutual promises among the participating creditors.

(2) The consideration given by the debtor is the immediate or future payments stipulated in the agreement.

d. The participating creditors may void the agreement if either of the following applies:

(1) They are not made aware of any creditors who are not participating in the agreement.

(2) Any participating creditor is given secret preferential treatment by the debtor.

e. The debtor is discharged from all debts that it pays under the agreement. The debtor retains all of its property following the agreement, except as provided in the agreement.

3. **Equity Receivership** Creditors may petition the state court for an *equity receivership.* An equity receivership is a court-supervised liquidation or reorganization that does not discharge the debtor from debts.

a. A receiver is appointed by the court to administer and take charge of the debtor's property. The receiver may liquidate, or hold and preserve property, and continue to operate any business of the debtor.

b. The receiver takes possession of, but not title to, the debtor's property. Existing liens on the property remain valid, but cannot be enforced during receivership. Creditors who petition for receivership do not thereby gain a lien on the debtor's property.

c. Equity receivership as an equitable remedy will not apply if there is an adequate remedy at law (e.g., collection suit).

IV. Suretyship

A. Suretyship Contract

An agreement whereby a person secures the debt of another by assuring performance upon the debtor's default. In a broad sense, contracts of guarantors, indemnitors, and endorsers are forms of suretyship contracts. Generally, suretyship contracts must contain all the elements of a traditional contract.

1. **Offer & Acceptance** All suretyship contracts must have a valid offer and acceptance, but the acceptance need not always be by express notice to the surety. In most jurisdictions, an *absolute guaranty* may be accepted without any formal notice. On the other hand, a *continuing guaranty* may usually be accepted only by an express notice. An express notice is not necessary if circumstances exist whereby the nature of the transaction itself informs the guarantor of the acceptance. Additionally, an express notice of acceptance is not needed when the guarantor waives notice in the letter of guaranty, or when s/he enters into a guaranty agreement in exchange for an extension of time.

2. **Consideration** When the surety contract is contemporaneous with the primary contract, there is no need for any separate consideration beyond that supporting the primary contract. When the surety contract is entered into subsequent to the primary contract, it must be supported by its own consideration.

3. **Statute of Frauds** Generally, suretyship and guaranty contracts are agreements to "answer for" the debt of another and, thus, they are within the Statute of Frauds. They must be in writing to be enforceable. There are two exceptions to this general rule:

   a. **Indemnification Contracts** Indemnification contracts (insurance contracts) are agreements to hold another harmless. They are outside the Statute of Frauds because they are two party contracts (not three party contracts as are surety agreements) and because they operate independently of any default by the principal debtor.

   b. **Primary Suretyship Contracts** Contracts that are entered into primarily for the benefit of the surety, rather than the debtor, are held to be outside the Statute of Frauds. For example, a *del credere agent* (a sales agent who guarantees the payment of her/his purchasers) is the primary beneficiary of her/his guaranty. Her/his guaranty is not a "...promise to answer for the debt of another." Thus, it is not within the Statute.

4. **Capacity** Generally, the rules that govern an individual's capacity to contract also govern the surety's capacity.

   a. **Partnerships** Unless specifically prohibited by the partnership agreement, a partnership has the capacity to enter into a suretyship contract. A partner does not have the power to bind the partnership to a suretyship contract unless that power is expressly authorized in the articles of co-partnership or a separate partnership agreement.

   b. **Corporations** Ordinarily, corporations may not enter into suretyship contracts unless such powers are authorized specifically.

5. **Parties** All suretyship contracts involve three persons: the principal debtor, the creditor, and the surety or guarantor.

a. **Principal Debtor** The principal debtor (principal) is the party who owes the ultimate burden of performing the obligation. The principal debtor owes a duty to both the creditor and surety.

b. **Creditor** The creditor is the party to whom the obligation is owed and to whom the surety is bound.

c. **Surety** The surety is the party who agrees to be answerable for the obligation. The surety is primarily liable (e.g., her/his duty is not conditioned strictly on the default of the principal debtor). The surety is liable if the debtor fails to perform for any reason.

6. **Surety Bond** A surety bond is a written acknowledgment of a duty to make good the performance by another of some obligation or responsibility. Surety bonds usually are issued by companies that, for a stated consideration, assume the risk of performance by the bonded party. Surety bonds usually are classified in the following manner.

a. **Performance or Construction** Performance or construction bonds guarantee the faithful performance of a contract. They are used most often in connection with supply and/or construction contracts. Courts uniformly have held that construction bonds cover the performance of the actual contract work. However, there is a split of authority on whether such bonds also cover payment of the construction workers' wages. For this reason, surety companies today also provide a payment bond.

b. **Fidelity** Fidelity bonds guarantee the faithful performance of duties by an employee. The surety has a right of subrogation if the employee commits any act in violation of the provisions of the bond. Any significant change in the employee's duties may serve to release the surety from her/his obligation.

c. **Official** Official bonds guarantee the faithful performance of duties by a public official. These bonds often are required by law for all public officials who administer public funds.

d. **Judicial** Judicial bonds include all bonds used in judicial proceedings (for example, bail bonds or attachment bonds).

7. **Unavailable Defenses** These situations, which do not discharge the surety's duty to perform, are mentioned throughout the chapter and are summarized here.

a. **Personal Defenses** Any personal defenses of the debtor or co-surety, such as death, insolvency, or incapacity. (However, personal defenses of the surety against the creditor provide the surety with a defense to the suretyship agreement.)

b. **Insolvency** The surety's own insolvency will not discharge her/his estate's liability.

c. **Creditor Failure** Generally, the creditor either failed to proceed against the debtor or failed to notify the surety of the debtor's default.

d. **Collateral** Failure on the part of the creditor to resort to any collateral security that s/he holds.

e. **Fraud** Fraudulent representations by the debtor (without creditor knowledge) to the surety to induce a suretyship agreement.

B. **Similar Relationships**
Suretyship and guaranty often are used interchangeably in law. However, they technically denote different contractual arrangements.

1. **Suretyship** A suretyship contract generally is created simultaneously with the primary contract and is considered part of the same transaction. Therefore, there is no need for separate

consideration to support the suretyship contract. This follows because the consideration supporting the principal contract is deemed also to support the suretyship contract. The surety is primarily liable to the creditor without any demand first being made on the debtor after default.

a. **Proceed Against Debtor** A surety may request the creditor to proceed first against the debtor. The creditor normally is not bound to do so, and the creditor's failure to try to enforce the debt against the debtor will not discharge the surety's obligation. However, when the suretyship contract is conditional, or whenever the surety requests the creditor to proceed against the debtor, the surety is entitled to any damages caused by the creditor's noncompliance.

b. **Resort to Collateral Security** A surety may request the creditor to resort first to any collateral security if s/he can show that the collateral is depreciating seriously in value, or if s/he can show undue hardship otherwise will result.

2. **Guaranty** On the other hand, a guaranty contract generally is created separately from the primary contract; it is considered to be an agreement distinct from the main contract. By virtue of the fact that there are two distinct agreements, there usually is a separate consideration supporting the guaranty. The guarantor's liability is secondary, or conditioned, on the default of the debtor. However, unless otherwise provided (a "collection guaranteed"), no demand need be made on the guarantor to activate her/his liability. Thus, from a mechanical point of view, guaranty liability may at times be activated merely by debtor default.

a. **Conditional vs. Unconditional** A conditional guaranty subjects the creditor's right to proceed against the guarantor to some condition precedent. Usually, this means that the creditor first must exhaust her/his remedies against the principal debtor or must show that the pursuit of any remedies would be futile (e.g., guarantor of collection). An unconditional guaranty places no conditions on the right of the creditor to proceed against the guarantor. An unconditional guarantor is bound to perform when the debtor defaults (e.g., guarantor of payment).

b. **Temporary vs. Continuing** A temporary guaranty is limited by its terms to a specific duration or transaction. A continuing guaranty is not limited to any specific time period or number of transactions.

c. **Special vs. General** A special guaranty is one addressed to a particular person. A general guaranty is extended to anyone who knows and relies on the contract of guaranty.

3. **Indemnification** An indemnification contract is a direct, original, two-party contract in which the indemnitor agrees to keep another harmless from a specific consequence. The indemnitor ordinarily has no right to reimbursement from the protected party. Most insurance contracts are indemnification contracts. Indemnity contracts are not within the Statute of Frauds, whereas suretyship and guaranty contracts are; this is due to the fact that surety and guaranty contracts are promises to answer for the debt or default of another.

4. **Endorsement** An endorsement contract creates only secondary liability on the part of the endorser. The endorser agrees to pay the holder of the instrument only after a demand has been made on the maker and notice of a dishonor is given to the endorser. An endorser is also liable for all warranties s/he makes to subsequent holders.

C. Creditor Rights

If the debtor fully pays, the collateral must be returned.

1. Against Debtor

a. **Proceed Against Debtor** Unless otherwise agreed, the creditor may proceed immediately against the debtor upon her/his default. There is no requirement that the creditor first allow the surety to make good.

b. **Debt Choice** In cases in which the debtor owes more than one debt, the creditor may apply any payment received to the debt of her/his choice. Thus, if two debts are owed and only one is guaranteed, the creditor is free to apply funds solely towards the satisfaction of the unsecured debt.

2. **Against Surety**

a. **Proceed Against Surety** Unless otherwise agreed, the creditor may proceed immediately against the surety upon default. The surety is immediately liable, and there is no duty on the part of the creditor to first ask the debtor for payment or to notify the surety of the debtor's default.

b. **Guarantor** When the surety is a guarantor, a creditor usually must give notice of the debtor's default before proceeding against the guarantor.

3. **Against Collateral Pledged With Creditor**

a. Upon default, the creditor is not bound to resort to the collateral; the creditor may proceed immediately against the surety.

b. If the creditor chooses to resort to the collateral, any amount realized by its disposal, which is in excess of the amount due, must be returned to the debtor. If the collateral is insufficient, the creditor has the right to proceed against the debtor and the surety for the balance due. If the creditor holds collateral pledged by both the debtor and the surety, the creditor must first look to the debtor's collateral for satisfaction of the debt.

c. If the creditor voluntarily surrenders or intentionally destroys the collateral s/he holds, the creditor reduces the surety's obligation by that amount.

d. If the surety satisfies the principal debtor's obligation, the surety becomes subrogated to the creditor's rights in the collateral.

4. **Against Collateral Pledged With Surety**

a. **Before Default** Prior to default, the creditor has an interest in the collateral, even if both the primary debtor and the surety are solvent. Thus, the creditor may, if necessary, seek equitable relief to enjoin the surety from wasting, releasing, or otherwise impairing the collateral. This is true even when the collateral has been pledged with the intent that it only benefit the surety. Generally, the surety maintains possession of the collateral as a trustee for the creditor's benefit.

b. **After Default** Upon default, the creditor may use the collateral to satisfy the debtor's duty, or the creditor may proceed directly against the surety on her/his promise. After the debt is paid in full, the surety may use the collateral to satisfy her/his right to reimbursement.

D. **Co-Suretyship**

1. **Common Law** Where two or more sureties are liable on the same obligation to the same creditor, the obligation is shared by each surety. Generally, the rights and duties as between co-sureties are fixed by the contract. In the absence of any agreement to the contrary, the following rules apply.

a. **Guarantee** Generally, co-sureties are jointly and severally liable to the creditor; however, as between co-sureties, each is individually liable only in the amount that has been guaranteed personally.

b. **Burden** Two or more persons may be co-sureties even if they do not know of each other's existence and even though they are bound for different amounts. They only need share the same burden.

c. **Co-Suretyship vs. Sub-Suretyship** A sub-suretyship usually requires an express agreement. The principal surety is primarily liable and bears the entire burden of performance. The sub-surety is in effect a surety for the principal surety.

2. **Right of Contribution Between Co-Sureties** Each co-surety has a right of contribution from the other co-sureties to the extent s/he has paid more than her/his proportionate share. The difference between the amount actually paid by a co-surety and the amount s/he is required to pay is the amount recoverable from other co-sureties.

Exhibit 3 ▸ Co-Surety Contribution Formula

$$\frac{\textit{Dollar amount of liability assumed by co-surety}}{\textit{Total dollar amount of liability assumed by all co-sureties}} \times \textit{Dollar amount of liability paid upon default of debt} = \textit{Dollar amount of contribution required of co-surety}$$

Example 2 ▸ Co-Surety's Share of Payment

Alice, Bob, and Colin are co-sureties of a $25,000 debt owed by Debra. Alice is liable for $5,000, Bob for $8,000, and Colin for $12,000. After making payments of $5,000, Debra defaults on the debt and Colin pays the remaining $20,000. Colin's proportionate share of the liability paid is $9,600; he is entitled to recover a total of $10,400: $4,000 from Alice and $6,400 from Bob. These amounts are computed as follows.

Alice:	($5,000 / $25,000)	×	$20,000	=	$4,000
Bob:	($8,000 / $25,000)	×	$20,000	=	$6,400
Colin:	($12,000 / $25,000)	×	$20,000	=	$9,600

3. **Rights to Collateral** Each co-surety is entitled to share in any collateral pledged to any of the co-sureties in proportion to her/his liabilities.

Example 3 ▸ Co-Surety's Share of Collateral

The same facts as in Example 2, except that Colin is in possession of collateral pledged by Debra worth $12,000. Since Colin has assumed 48% of the total amount of the debt, he is entitled to $5,760 of the collateral. Alice would be entitled to 20%, or $2,400, and Bob would be entitled to 32%, or $3,840.

4. **Creditor Release of Co-Surety** Unless the creditor specifically reserves her/his rights, a release of a co-surety releases the other co-sureties in the amount of the released surety's share. If rights are reserved, the remaining co-sureties have the right to go after the released co-surety.

E. Surety Rights & Defenses

Exhibit 4 ▸ Surety Remedies

"ICES"

I	**I**ndemnity—from principal debtor
C	**C**ontribution—from co-sureties
E	**E**xoneration—free surety from debt
S	**S**ubrogation—rights of creditor against debtor (collateral)

1. **Right of Indemnity or Reimbursement** This is the right of the surety to recover from the principal debtor for the obligation performed by the surety. The surety's rights under various circumstances are as follows.

   a. Where the principal debtor has consented to the retention of a surety, the surety may recover from the debtor in the amount that the surety actually has paid. The statute of limitations on such actions runs from the date of payment and **not** the date of default.

   b. Where the surety is retained without the consent of the principal debtor, the surety is entitled to recover from the debtor only to the extent that the debtor has been enriched unjustly.

   c. Where the surety's payment is voluntary, the surety is not entitled to reimbursement. This situation may arise when both the surety and the debtor have a legal defense, such as the statute of limitations, and the surety voluntarily performs.

2. **Right of Contribution** A surety has a right of contribution against co-sureties (see surety defenses).

3. **Right of Exoneration** A surety may seek exoneration from the debtor or co-sureties. A surety does this by bringing a suit in equity to require the debtor or co-sureties to pay so that s/he will not be required to satisfy her/his obligation. An exoneration is an action by the surety against the debtor that seeks to force the debtor to pay her/his creditor. The surety must show that the debtor wrongfully is withholding assets sufficient to satisfy the debt.

4. **Right of Subrogation** Subrogation is the surety's right to succeed to the rights of the creditor once the surety has made good on the debtor's obligation. Thus, the surety has the right to enforce any lien, pledge, or mortgage securing the principal debt to the extent that an excess exists after the creditor has been satisfied. A subrogation is the substitution of the surety, who has paid the debt of another, in place of the creditor to whom the debt was paid. Subrogation allows the surety to succeed to all of the creditor's rights against the debtor.

5. **Defenses Derived From Debtor Personal Defenses** The debtor's defenses, except for personal defenses, generally are available to the surety.

   a. **Fraud or Duress** If a creditor obtains the debtor's promise by use of fraud, duress, misrepresentation, concealment, etc., and the debtor elects to rescind, then the surety may assert the defense of fraud. If the debtor affirms the contract, the surety is likewise bound. Additionally, if the creditor uses fraud and the surety knows of the fraud, s/he may not avail her/himself of that defense.

   b. **Consideration** A material failure by the creditor to render the agreed-upon consideration discharges the surety's liability.

   c. **Performance or Tender of Performance** If the debtor properly performs, meeting all requirements of the contract, the surety is discharged. A proper tender of performance by the debtor discharges the surety even though it may not discharge the debtor.

   d. **Impossibility or Illegality** If the debtor's performance is impossible because of illegality or otherwise, the surety's liability is discharged.

6. **Personal Defenses** The surety also has the surety's personal defenses.

   a. **Unenforceable or Void Contract** A surety contract must have all the elements of a normal contract. For instance, if the surety's signature is a forgery, the contract would be void.

   b. **Fraud or Duress** If the creditor obtains the surety's promise through fraud, duress, misrepresentation, etc., the contract is voidable by the surety. If the principal debtor obtains the surety's promise through fraud, the contract is not voidable unless the creditor knew of the fraud.

c. **Undisclosed Material Facts** The creditor must disclose all material facts concerning the debtor and bearing upon her/his ability to perform. If the creditor fails to notify the surety of any material facts in her/his possession material to determining the surety's risk, the surety may avoid liability.

d. **Legal Remedies Render Contract Unenforceable** For instance, if the statute of limitations has run, the surety may avoid liability.

7. **Defenses Arising From Creditor Actions** The surety may have defenses arising from creditor actions.

a. **Release**

(1) **Collateral** Any release of collateral by the creditor before satisfaction of the debtor's obligation, releases the surety to the extent of the collateral released. A creditor's surrender or waste of the collateral may discharge the surety in the amount that the security is depreciated.

(2) **Co-Surety** A release of any co-sureties without the consent of a surety releases that surety.

(3) **Principal Debtor** A release of the principal without the consent of the surety releases the surety, unless the creditor specifically reserves her/his rights against the surety. The surety who pays then has the right to recover from the released debtor. An agreement to release a debtor while retaining rights against a surety is treated as a covenant not to sue rather than a release. When a debtor fraudulently effects her/his release, the surety is excused only to the extent that s/he has been prejudiced.

b. **Principal Contract Alteration** Under old common law, any variance in the suretyship contract, no matter how minor, discharged the surety. The prevailing rule today is that only material changes in the principal contract will discharge the surety.

(1) Material variances include a change in the identity of the debtor; an extension of the time for payment or other change in the amount, rate, or manner of payment; a substantial change in the duties of a bonded employee (for example, from a teller to loan officer); a surrender or impairment of the security.

(2) Consent by the surety to any variation waives the right to release.

(3) The modern trend is to make a distinction between a gratuitous and a compensated surety. Current cases generally hold that only a variation that is injurious to a compensated surety will discharge her/him.

CHAPTER 38—DEBTOR & CREDITOR RELATIONSHIPS

Problem 38-1 MULTIPLE CHOICE QUESTIONS (45 to 60 minutes)

1. Which of the following statements is correct with respect to the reorganization provisions of Chapter 11 of the Federal Bankruptcy Code?
a. A trustee must always be appointed.
b. The debtor must be insolvent if the bankruptcy petition was filed voluntarily.
c. A reorganization plan may be filed by a creditor anytime after the petition date.
d. The commencement of a bankruptcy case may be voluntary or involuntary.
(11/93, Law, #34, 4331)

Items 2 and 3 are based on the following:

Strong Corp. filed a voluntary petition in bankruptcy under the reorganization provisions of Chapter 11 of the Federal Bankruptcy Code. A reorganization plan was filed and agreed to by all necessary parties. The court confirmed the plan and a final decree was entered.

2. Which of the following parties ordinarily must confirm the plan?

	1/2 of the secured creditors	*2/3 of the shareholders*
a.	Yes	Yes
b.	Yes	No
c.	No	Yes
d.	No	No

(5/95, Law, #34, 5368)

3. Which of the following statements best describes the effect of the entry of the court's final decree?
a. Strong Corp. will be discharged from all its debts and liabilities.
b. Strong Corp. will be discharged only from the debts owed creditors who agreed to the reorganization plan.
c. Strong Corp. will be discharged from all its debts and liabilities that arose before the date of confirmation of the plan.
d. Strong Corp. will be discharged from all its debts and liabilities that arose before the confirmation of the plan, except as otherwise provided in the plan, the order of confirmation, or the Bankruptcy Code. (5/95, Law, #35, 5369)

4. Which of the following statements is correct concerning the voluntary filing of a petition in bankruptcy?
a. If the debtor has 12 or more creditors, the unsecured claims must total at least $13,475.
b. The debtor must be insolvent.
c. If the debtor has less than 12 creditors, the unsecured claims must total at least $13,475.
d. The petition may be filed jointly by spouses.
(11/91, Law, #28, amended, 2356)

Items 5 through 10 are based on the following:

Dart, Inc., a closely held corporation, was petitioned involuntarily into bankruptcy under the liquidation provisions of Chapter 7 of the Federal Bankruptcy Code. Dart contested the petition. Dart has not been paying its business debts as they became due, has defaulted on its mortgage loan payments, and owes back taxes to the IRS. The total cash value of Dart's bankruptcy estate after the sale of all assets and payment of administration expenses is $100,000. Dart has the following creditors:

- Fracon Bank is owed $75,000 principal and accrued interest on a mortgage loan secured by Dart's real property. The property was valued at and sold, in bankruptcy, for $70,000.
- The IRS has a $12,000 recorded judgment for unpaid corporate income tax.
- JOG Office Supplies has an unsecured claim of $3,000 that was timely filed.
- Nanstar Electric Co. has an unsecured claim of $1,200 that was not timely filed.
- Decoy Publications has a claim of $19,000, of which $2,000 is secured by Dart's inventory that was valued and sold, in bankruptcy, for $2,000. The claim was timely filed.

5. Which of the following creditors must join in the filing of the involuntary petition?

I. JOG Office Supplies
II. Nanstar Electric Co.
III. Decoy Publications

a. I, II, and III
b. II and III
c. I and II
d. III only (5/95, Law, #28, amended, 5362)

6. Which of the following statements would correctly describe the result of Dart's opposing the petition?
a. Dart will win because the petition should have been filed under Chapter 11.
b. Dart will win because there are **not** more than 12 creditors.
c. Dart will lose because it is **not** paying its debts as they become due.
d. Dart will lose because of its debt to the IRS.
(5/95, Law, #29, amended, 5363)

7. Which of the following events will follow the filing of the Chapter 7 involuntary petition?

	A trustee will be appointed	*A stay against creditor collection proceedings will go into effect*
a.	Yes	Yes
b.	Yes	No
c.	No	Yes
d.	No	No

(5/95, Law, #30, amended, 5364)

For items 8 through 10 assume that the bankruptcy estate was distributed.

8. What dollar amount would Nanstar Electric Co. receive?
a. $0
b. $ 800
c. $1,000
d. $1,200 (5/95, Law, #31, amended, 5365)

9. What total dollar amount would Fracon Bank receive on its secured and unsecured claims?
a. $75,000
b. $73,600
c. $73,200
d. $70,000 (5/95, Law, #32, amended, 5366)

10. What dollar amount would the IRS receive?
a. $0
b. $ 8,000
c. $10,000
d. $12,000 (5/95, Law, #33, amended, 5367)

11. Under the liquidation provisions of Chapter 7 of the Federal Bankruptcy Code, a debtor will be denied a discharge in bankruptcy if the debtor
a. Fails to list a creditor
b. Owes alimony and support payments
c. Cannot pay administration expenses
d. Refuses to satisfactorily explain a loss of assets
(11/97, Law, #12, 6510)

12. Which **two** of the following claims will **not** be discharged in bankruptcy?
a. A claim that arises from alimony or maintenance
b. A claim that arises out of the debtor's breach of a contract
c. A claim brought by a secured creditor that remains unsatisfied after the sale of the collateral
d. A claim brought by a judgment creditor whose judgment resulted from the debtor's negligent operation of a motor vehicle
e. A claim that arises from a tax debt due within three years of filing the bankruptcy petition.
(11/94, Law, #33, amended, 5210)

13. By signing a reaffirmation agreement on April 15, Year 1, a debtor agreed to pay certain debts that would be discharged in bankruptcy. On June 20, Year 1, the debtor's attorney filed the reaffirmation agreement and an affidavit with the court indicating that the debtor understood the consequences of the reaffirmation agreement. The debtor obtained a discharge on August 25, Year 1. The reaffirmation agreement would be enforceable only if it was
a. Made after discharge
b. Approved by the bankruptcy court
c. Not for a household purpose debt
d. Not rescinded before discharge
(11/91, Law, #31, amended, 2359)

14. Which of the following acts by a debtor could result in a bankruptcy court revoking the debtor's discharge?

I. Failure to list one creditor
II. Failure to answer correctly material questions on the bankruptcy petition

a. I only
b. II only
c. Both I and II
d. Neither I nor II (11/93, Law, #31, 4328)

15. Under the liquidation provisions of Chapter 7 of the Federal Bankruptcy Code, certain property acquired by the debtor after the filing of the petition becomes part of the bankruptcy estate. An example of such property is
a. Inheritances received by the debtor within 180 days after the filing of the petition.
b. Child support payments received by the debtor within one year after the filing of the petition.
c. Social Security payments received by the debtor within 180 days after the filing of the petition.
d. Wages earned by the debtor within one year after the filing of the petition. (R/00, Law, #6, 6971)

16. Under the federal Bankruptcy Code, which of the following rights or powers does a trustee in bankruptcy **not** have?
a. The power to prevail against a creditor with an unperfected security interest
b. The power to require persons holding the debtor's property at the time the bankruptcy petition is filed to deliver the property to the trustee
c. The right to use any grounds available to the debtor to obtain the return of the debtor's property
d. The right to avoid any statutory liens against the debtor's property that were effective before the bankruptcy petition was filed
(R/05, REG, 0172L, #11, 7857)

17. Which of the following transfers by a debtor, within ninety days of filing for bankruptcy, could be set aside as a preferential payment?
a. Making a gift to charity
b. Paying a business utility bill
c. Borrowing money from a bank secured by giving a mortgage on business property
d. Prepaying an installment loan on inventory
(11/93, Law, #30, 4327)

18. On June 5, Year 8, Gold rented equipment under a four-year lease. On March 8, Year 9, Gold was petitioned involuntarily into bankruptcy under the Federal Bankruptcy Code's liquidation provisions. A trustee was appointed. The fair market value of the equipment exceeds the balance of the lease payments due. The trustee
a. May **not** reject the equipment lease because the fair market value of the equipment exceeds the balance of the lease payments due
b. May elect **not** to assume the equipment lease
c. Must assume the equipment lease because its term exceeds one year
d. Must assume and subsequently assign the equipment lease (11/90, Law, #27, amended, 0613)

19. Under the liquidation provisions of Chapter 7 of the Federal Bankruptcy Code, certain property acquired by the debtor after the filing of the petition becomes part of the bankruptcy estate. An example of such property is
a. Municipal bond interest received by the debtor within 180 days after the filing of the petition
b. Alimony received by the debtor within one year after the filing of the petition
c. Social Security payments received by the debtor within 180 days after the filing of the petition
d. Gifts received by the debtor within one year after the filing of the petition (R/99, Law, #10, 6861)

20. Which of the following liens generally require(s) the lienholder to give notice of legal action before selling the debtor's property to satisfy the debt?

	Mechanic's lien	*Artisan's lien*
a.	Yes	Yes
b.	Yes	No
c.	No	Yes
d.	No	No

(11/95, Law, #27, 5896)

21. The federal Fair Debt Collection Practices Act prohibits a debt collector from engaging in unfair practices. Under the Act, a debt collector generally can be prevented from
a. Contacting a third party to ascertain a debtor's location
b. Continuing to collect a debt
c. Communicating with a debtor who is represented by an attorney
d. Commencing a lawsuit to collect a debt
(R/05, REG, 0410L, #8, 7874)

22. Which of the following will enable a creditor to collect money from a debtor's wages?
a. An order of receivership
b. An order of garnishment
c. A writ of execution
d. A writ of attachment (11/96, Law, #13, 6424)

23. Which of the following actions between a debtor and its creditors will generally cause the debtor's release from its debts?

	Composition of creditors	*Assignment for the benefit of creditors*
a.	Yes	Yes
b.	Yes	No
c.	No	Yes
d.	No	No

(11/94, Law, #27, 5204)

24. A party contracts to guaranty the collection of the debts of another. As a result of the guaranty, which of the following statements is correct?
a. The creditor may proceed against the guarantor without attempting to collect from the debtor.
b. The guaranty must be in writing.
c. The guarantor may use any defenses available to the debtor.
d. The creditor must be notified of the debtor's default by the guarantor. (5/94, Law, #24, 4779)

25. Sorus and Ace have agreed, in writing, to act as guarantors of collection on a debt owed by Pepper to Towns, Inc. The debt is evidenced by a promissory note. If Pepper defaults, Towns will be entitled to recover from Sorus and Ace unless
a. Sorus and Ace are in the process of exercising their rights against Pepper.
b. Sorus and Ace prove that Pepper was insolvent at the time the note was signed.
c. Pepper dies before the note is due.
d. Towns has **not** attempted to enforce the promissory note against Pepper.
(11/90, Law, #26, 0637)

26. Which of the following events will release a noncompensated surety from liability to the creditor?
a. The principal debtor was involuntarily petitioned into bankruptcy.
b. The creditor failed to notify the surety of a partial surrender of the principal debtor's collateral.
c. The creditor was adjudicated incompetent after the debt arose.
d. The principal debtor exerted duress to obtain the surety agreement. (R/01, Law, #14, 7049)

27. When a principal debtor defaults and a surety pays the creditor the entire obligation, which of the following remedies gives the surety the best method of collecting from the debtor?
a. Exoneration
b. Contribution
c. Subrogation
d. Attachment (11/95, Law, #30, 5899)

28. Which of the following rights does one co-surety generally have against another co-surety?
a. Exoneration
b. Subrogation
c. Reimbursement
d. Contribution (11/95, Law, #28, 5897)

29. Ingot Corp. lent Flange $50,000. At Ingot's request, Flange entered into an agreement with Quill and West for them to act as compensated co-sureties on the loan in the amount of $100,000 each. Ingot released West without Quill's or Flange's consent, and Flange later defaulted on the loan. Which of the following statements is correct?
a. Quill will be liable for 50% of the loan balance.
b. Quill will be liable for the entire loan balance.
c. Ingot's release of West will have **no** effect on Flange's and Quill's liability to Ingot.
d. Flange will be released for 50% of the loan balance. (11/94, Law, #31, 5208)

30. Teller, Kerr, and Ace are co-sureties on a $120,000 loan with maximum liabilities of $20,000, $40,000, and $60,000, respectively. The debtor defaulted on the loan when the loan balance was $60,000. Ace paid the lender $48,000 in full settlement of all claims against Teller, Kerr, and Ace. What amount may Ace collect from Kerr?
a. $0
b. $16,000
c. $20,000
d. $28,000 (R/03, REG, 0413L, #16, 7658)

Problem 38-2 ADDITIONAL MULTIPLE CHOICE QUESTIONS (54 to 72 minutes)

31. Robin Corp. incurred substantial operating losses for the past three years. Unable to meet its current obligations, Robin filed a petition for reorganization under Chapter 11 of the Federal Bankruptcy Code. Which of the following statements is correct?
a. The creditors' committee must select a trustee to manage Robin's affairs.
b. The reorganization plan may only be filed by Robin.
c. A creditors' committee, if appointed, will consist of unsecured creditors.
d. Robin may continue in business only with the approval of a trustee. (11/93, Law, #32, 4329)

32. Under Chapter 11 of the Federal Bankruptcy Code, which of the following would **not** be eligible for reorganization?
a. Retail sole proprietorship
b. Advertising partnership
c. CPA professional corporation
d. Savings and loan corporation
(11/92, Law, #32, 3114)

33. The filing of an involuntary bankruptcy petition under the Federal Bankruptcy Code
a. Terminates liens on exempt property
b. Terminates all security interests in property in the bankruptcy estate
c. Stops the debtor from incurring new debts
d. Stops the enforcement of judgment liens against property in the bankruptcy estate
(11/93, Law, #27, 4324)

34. A party involuntarily petitioned into bankruptcy under Chapter 7 of the Federal Bankruptcy Code who succeeds in having the petition dismissed could recover

	Court costs and attorney's fees	*Compensatory damages*	*Punitive damages*
a.	Yes	Yes	Yes
b.	Yes	Yes	No
c.	No	Yes	Yes
d.	Yes	No	No

(11/92, Law, #30, 3112)

35. Flax, a sole proprietor, has been petitioned involuntarily into bankruptcy under the Federal Bankruptcy Code's liquidation provisions. Simon & Co., CPAs, has been appointed trustee of the bankruptcy estate. If Simon also wishes to act as the tax return preparer for the estate, which of the following statements is correct?

a. Simon is prohibited from serving as both trustee and preparer under any circumstances because serving in that dual capacity would be a conflict of interest.
b. Although Simon may serve as both trustee and preparer, it is entitled to receive a fee only for the services rendered as a preparer.
c. Simon may employ itself to prepare tax returns if authorized by the court and may receive a separate fee for services rendered in each capacity.
d. Although Simon may serve as both trustee and preparer, its fee for services rendered in each capacity will be determined solely by the size of the estate. (11/90, Law, #28, 8023)

36. Hall, CPA, is an unsecured creditor of Tree Co. for $15,000. Tree has a total of 10 creditors, all of whom are unsecured. Tree has not paid any of the creditors for three months. Under Chapter 11 of the federal Bankruptcy Code, which of the following statements is correct?

a. Hall and two other unsecured creditors must join in the involuntary petition in bankruptcy.
b. Hall may file an involuntary petition in bankruptcy against Tree.
c. Tree may **not** be petitioned involuntarily into bankruptcy under the provisions of Chapter 11.
d. Tree may **not** be petitioned involuntarily into bankruptcy because there are less than 12 unsecured creditors. (R/03, REG, 0161L, #15, 7657)

37. A family farmer with regular annual income may file a voluntary petition for bankruptcy under any of the following Chapters of the Federal Bankruptcy Code **except**

a. 7
b. 9
c. 11
d. 13 (R/02, Law, #6, 7116)

38. To file for bankruptcy under Chapter 7 of the Federal Bankruptcy Code, an individual must

a. Have debts of any amount
b. Be insolvent
c. Be indebted to more than three creditors
d. Have debts in excess of $13,475

(11/91, Law, #29, amended, 2357)

39. Which of the following types of claims would be paid first in the distribution of a bankruptcy estate under the liquidation provisions of Chapter 7 of the Federal Bankruptcy Code if the petition was filed July 15, Year 6?

a. A secured debt properly perfected on March 20, Year 6
b. Inventory purchased and delivered August 1, Year 6
c. Employee wages due April 30, Year 6
d. Federal tax lien filed June 30, Year 6

(11/93, Law, #39, amended, 4336)

40. Under Chapter 7 of the Federal Bankruptcy Code, what affect does a bankruptcy discharge have on a judgment creditor when there is **no** bankruptcy estate?

a. The judgment creditor's claim is nondischargeable.
b. The judgment creditor retains a statutory lien against the debtor.
c. The debtor is relieved of any personal liability to the judgment creditor.
d. The debtor is required to pay a liquidated amount to vacate the judgment. (R/02, Law, #5, 7115)

41. In general, which of the following debts will be discharged under the voluntary liquidation provisions of Chapter 7 of the Federal Bankruptcy Code?

a. A debt due to the negligence of the debtor arising before filing the bankruptcy petition
b. Alimony payments owed the debtor's spouse under a separation agreement entered into two years before the filing of the bankruptcy petition
c. A debt incurred more than 90 days before the filing of the bankruptcy petition and **not** disclosed in the petition
d. Income taxes due within two years before the filing of the bankruptcy petition

(5/91, Law, #31, 0608)

42. On April 1, Roe borrowed $100,000 from Jet to pay Roe's business expenses. On June 15, Roe gave Jet a signed security agreement and financing statement covering Roe's inventory. Jet immediately filed the financing statement. On July 1, Roe filed for bankruptcy. Under the federal Bankruptcy Code, can Roe's trustee in bankruptcy set aside Jet's security interest in Roe's inventory?

a. Yes, because a security agreement may only cover goods actually purchased with the borrowed funds
b. Yes, because Roe giving the security interest to Jet created a voidable preference
c. No, because the security interest was perfected before Roe filed for bankruptcy
d. No, because the loan proceeds were used for Roe's business (R/07, REG, 1420L, #27, 8451)

Items 43 and 44 are based on the following:

On May 1, Year 5, two months after becoming insolvent, Quick Corp., an appliance wholesaler, filed a voluntary petition for bankruptcy under the provisions of Chapter 7 of the Federal Bankruptcy Code. On October 15, Year 4, Quick's board of directors had authorized and paid Erly $50,000 to repay Erly's April 1, Year 4, loan to the corporation. Erly is a sibling of Quick's president. On March 15, Year 5, Quick paid Kray $100,000 for inventory delivered that day.

43. Which of the following is **not** relevant in determining whether the repayment of Erly's loan is a voidable preferential transfer?

a. Erly is an insider.
b. Quick's payment to Erly was made on account of an antecedent debt.
c. Quick's solvency when the loan was made by Erly.
d. Quick's payment to Erly was made within one year of the filing of the bankruptcy petition.

(5/91, Law, #33, amended, 0610)

44. Quick's payment to Kray would

a. Not be voidable, because it was a contemporaneous exchange
b. Not be voidable, unless Kray knew about Quick's insolvency
c. Be voidable, because it was made within 90 days of the bankruptcy filing
d. Be voidable, because it enabled Kray to receive more than it otherwise would receive from the bankruptcy estate

(5/91, Law, #34, amended, 0611)

45. On February 28, Master, Inc. had total assets with a fair market value of $1,200,000 and total liabilities of $990,000. On January 15, Master made a monthly installment note payment to Acme Distributors Corp., a creditor holding a properly perfected security interest in equipment having a fair market value greater than the balance due on the note. On March 15, Master voluntarily filed a petition in bankruptcy under the liquidation provisions of Chapter 7 of the Federal Bankruptcy Code. One year later, the equipment was sold for less than the balance due on the note to Acme. Master's payment to Acme could

a. Be set aside as a preferential transfer because the fair market value of the collateral was greater than the installment note balance
b. Be set aside as a preferential transfer unless Acme showed that Master was solvent on January 15
c. Not be set aside as a preferential transfer because Acme was oversecured
d. Not be set aside as a preferential transfer if Acme showed that Master was solvent on March 15

(11/91, Law, #44, amended, 2372)

Items 46 through 48 are based on the following:

On August 1, Year 2, Hall filed a voluntary petition under Chapter 7 of the Federal Bankruptcy Code. Hall's assets are sufficient to pay general creditors 40% of their claims. The following transactions occurred before the filing:

- On May 5, Year 2, Hall gave a mortgage on Hall's home to National Bank to secure payment of a loan National had given Hall two years earlier. When the loan was made, Hall's twin was a National employee.
- On June 1, Year 2, Hall purchased a boat from Olsen for $10,000 cash.
- On July 1, Year 2, Hall paid off an outstanding credit card balance of $500. The original debt had been $6,500.

46. The National mortgage was

a. Preferential, because National would be considered an insider
b. Preferential, because the mortgage was given to secure an antecedent debt
c. Not preferential, because Hall is presumed insolvent when the mortgage was given
d. Not preferential, because the mortgage was a security interest

(11/92, Law, #37, amended, 3119)

47. The payment to Olsen was
a. Preferential, because the payment was made within 90 days of the filing of the petition
b. Preferential, because the payment enabled Olsen to receive more than the other general creditors
c. Not preferential, because Hall is presumed insolvent when the payment was made
d. Not preferential, because the payment was a contemporaneous exchange for new value
(11/92, Law, #38, amended, 3120)

48. The credit card payment was
a. Preferential, because the payment was made within 90 days of the filing of the petition
b. Preferential, because the payment was on account of an antecedent debt
c. Not preferential, because the payment was for a debt of less than $5,475
d. Not preferential, because the payment was less than 40% of the original debt
(11/92, Law, #39, amended, 3121)

49. A debtor may attempt to conceal or transfer property to prevent a creditor from satisfying a judgment. Which of the following actions will be considered an indication of fraudulent conveyance?

	Debtor remaining in possession after conveyance	*Secret conveyance*	*Debtor retains an equitable benefit in the property conveyed*
a.	Yes	Yes	Yes
b.	No	Yes	Yes
c.	Yes	Yes	No
d.	Yes	No	Yes

(5/94, Law, #21, 4776)

50. A homestead exemption ordinarily could exempt a debtor's equity in certain property from post-judgment collection by a creditor. To which of the following creditors will this exemption apply?

	Valid home mortgage lien	*Valid IRS tax lien*
a.	Yes	Yes
b.	Yes	No
c.	No	Yes
d.	No	No

(5/94, Law, #22, 4777)

51. Which of the following statements is(are) correct regarding debtors' rights?

I. State exemption statutes prevent all of a debtor's personal property from being sold to pay a federal tax lien.
II. Federal social security benefits received by a debtor are exempt from garnishment by creditors.

a. I only
b. II only
c. Both I and II
d. Neither I nor II (11/95, Law, #26, 5895)

52. The federal Credit Card Fraud Act protects a credit card holder from loss by
a. Restricting the interest rate charged by the credit card company
b. Limiting the card holder's liability for unauthorized use
c. Requiring credit card companies to issue cards to qualified persons
d. Allowing the card holder to defer payment of the balance due on the card (5/98, Law, #5, 7695)

53. Under the Federal Fair Debt Collection Practices Act, which of the following would a collection service using improper debt collection practices be subject to?
a. Abolishment of the debt
b. Reduction of the debt
c. Civil lawsuit for damages for violating the Act
d. Criminal prosecution for violating the Act
(11/94, Law, #26, 5203)

54. Which of the following prejudgment remedies would be available to a creditor when a debtor owns **no** real property?

	Writ of attachment	Garnishment
a.	Yes	Yes
b.	Yes	No
c.	No	Yes
d.	No	No

(11/94, Law, #28, 5205)

55. Which of the following rights does a surety have?

	Right to compel the creditor to collect from the principal debtor	*Right to compel the creditor to proceed against the principal debtor's collateral*
a.	Yes	Yes
b.	Yes	No
c.	No	Yes
d.	No	No

(11/94, Law, #30, 5207)

56. Which of the following acts always will result in the total release of a compensated surety?
a. The creditor changes the manner of the principal debtor's payment.
b. The creditor extends the principal debtor's time to pay.
c. The principal debtor's obligation is partially released.
d. The principal debtor's performance is tendered.
(11/95, Law, #29, 5898)

57. Green was unable to repay a loan from State Bank when due. State refused to renew the loan unless Green provided an acceptable surety. Green asked Royal, a friend, to act as surety on the loan. To induce Royal to agree to become a surety, Green fraudulently represented Green's financial condition and promised Royal discounts on merchandise sold at Green's store. Royal agreed to act as surety and the loan was renewed. Later, Green's obligation to State was discharged in Green's bankruptcy. State wants to hold Royal liable. Royal may avoid liability
a. If Royal can show that State was aware of the fraudulent representations
b. If Royal was an uncompensated surety
c. Because the discharge in bankruptcy will prevent Royal from having a right of reimbursement
d. Because the arrangement was void at the inception (5/95, Law, #26, 5360)

58. Which of the following events will release a noncompensated surety from liability?
a. Release of the principal debtor's obligation by the creditor but with the reservation of the creditor's rights against the surety
b. Modification by the principal debtor and creditor of their contract that materially increases the surety's risk of loss
c. Filing of an involuntary petition in bankruptcy against the principal debtor
d. Insanity of the principal debtor at the time the contract was entered into with the creditor
(5/94, Law, #25, 4780)

59. Ivor borrowed $420,000 from Lear Bank. At Lear's request, Ivor entered into an agreement with Ash, Kane, and Queen for them to act as co-sureties on the loan. The agreement between Ivor and the co-sureties provided that the maximum liability of each co-surety was: Ash, $84,000; Kane, $126,000; and Queen, $210,000. After making several payments, Ivor defaulted on the loan. The balance was $280,000. If Queen pays $210,000 and Ivor subsequently pays $70,000, what amounts may Queen recover from Ash and Kane?
a. $0 from Ash and $0 from Kane
b. $42,000 from Ash and $63,000 from Kane
c. $70,000 from Ash and $70,000 from Kane
d. $56,000 from Ash and $84,000 from Kane
(11/92, Law, #26, 3108)

60. Queen paid Pax & Co. to become the surety on a loan which Queen obtained from Squire. The loan is due and Pax wishes to compel Queen to pay Squire. Pax has not made any payments to Squire in its capacity as Queen's surety. Pax will be most successful if it exercises its right to
a. Reimbursement (Indemnification)
b. Contribution
c. Exoneration
d. Subrogation (11/86, Law, #28, 0642)

61. Which of the following defenses by a surety will be effective to avoid liability?
a. Lack of consideration to support the surety undertaking
b. Insolvency in the bankruptcy sense by the debtor
c. Incompetency of the debtor to make the contract in question
d. Fraudulent statements by the principal debtor which induced the surety to assume the obligation and which were unknown to the creditor
(5/82, Law, #23, 8024)

62. Nash, Owen, and Polk are co-sureties with maximum liabilities of $40,000, $60,000 and $80,000, respectively. The amount of the loan on which they have agreed to act as co-sureties is $180,000. The debtor defaulted at a time when the loan balance was $180,000. Nash paid the lender $36,000 in full settlement of all claims against Nash, Owen, and Polk. The total amount that Nash may recover from Owen and Polk is
a. $0
b. $ 24,000
c. $ 28,000
d. $140,000 (11/93, Law, #25, 4322)

63. Which of the following defenses would a surety be able to assert successfully to limit the surety's liability to a creditor?

a. A discharge in bankruptcy of the principal debtor
b. A personal defense the principal debtor has against the creditor
c. The incapacity of the surety
d. The incapacity of the principal debtor

(11/94, Law, #29, 5206)

64. Wright cosigned King's loan from Ace Bank. Which of the following events would release Wright from the obligation to pay the loan?

a. Ace seeking payment of the loan only from Wright.
b. King is granted a discharge in bankruptcy.
c. Ace is paid in full by King's spouse.
d. King is adjudicated mentally incompetent.

(5/95, Law, #27, 5361)

SIMULATION

Problem 38-3 (20 to 30 minutes)

On March 15, 2010, Wren Corp., an appliance wholesaler, was petitioned involuntarily into bankruptcy under the liquidation provisions of Chapter 7 of the Federal Bankruptcy Code. The following transactions occurred before the bankruptcy petition was filed.

- On December 31, 2009, Wren paid off a $10,000 loan from Mary Lake, the sister of one of Wren's directors.
- On January 30, 2010, Wren donated $2,000 to Universal Charities.
- On February 1, 2010, Wren gave Young Finance Co. a security agreement covering Wren's office fixtures to secure a loan previously made by Young.
- On March 1, 2010, Wren made the final $1,000 monthly payment to Integral Appliance Corp. on a two-year note.
- On April 1, 2010, Wren purchased from Safety Co., a new burglar alarm system for its factory, for $10,000 cash.

When the petition was filed, Wren's creditors included the following.

Secured creditors	Amount owed
Fifth Bank—1st mortgage on warehouse owned by Wren	$50,000
Hart Manufacturing Corp.—perfected purchase money security interest in inventory	30,000
TVN Computers, Inc.—perfected security interest in office computers	15,000

Unsecured creditors	Amount owed
IRS—2007 federal income taxes	$20,000
Acme Office Cleaners—services for January, February, and March 2010	750
Joan Sims (employee)—March 2010 commissions	1,500
Power Electric Co.—electricity charges for January, February, and March 2010	600
Soft Office Supplies—supplies purchased in 2009	2,000

All of Wren's assets were liquidated. The warehouse was sold for $75,000, the computers were sold for $12,000, and the inventory was sold for $25,000. After paying the bankruptcy administration expenses of $8,000, secured creditors, and priority general creditors, there was enough cash to pay each non-priority general creditor 50 cents on the dollar. (4029)

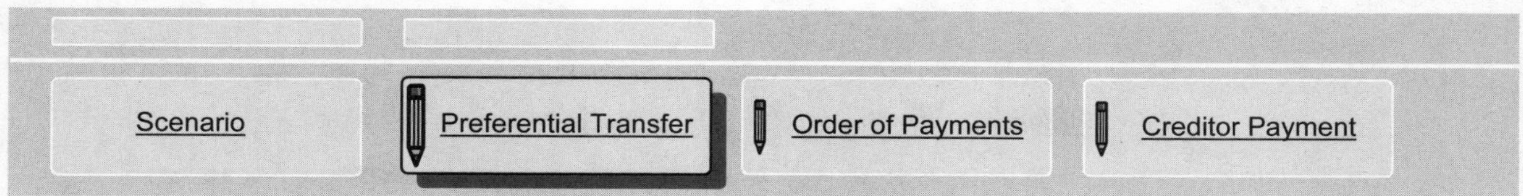

For Items 1 through 5, determine whether or not the transaction that occurred before the filing of the bankruptcy petition would be set aside as a preferential transfer by the bankruptcy court. Answer "Yes" if the transaction would be set aside or "No" if the transaction would **not** be set aside.

Transaction	Answer
1. On December 31, 2009, Wren paid off a $10,000 loan from Mary Lake, the sister of one of Wren's directors.	
2. On January 30, 2010, Wren donated $2,000 to Universal Charities.	
3. On February 1, 2010, Wren gave Young Finance Co. a security agreement covering Wren's office fixtures to secure a loan previously made by Young.	
4. On March 1, 2010, Wren made the final $1,000 monthly payment to Integral Appliance Corp. on a two-year note.	
5. On April 1, 2010, Wren purchased from Safety Co., a new burglar alarm system for its factory, for $10,000 cash.	

Items 6 through 10 represent creditors claims against the bankruptcy estate. Indicate each creditor's order of payment in relation to the other named creditors using the letters (A) through (E), with (A) being the highest priority and (E) being the lowest priority.

Claim	Answer
6. Bankruptcy administration expense	
7. Acme Office Cleaners	
8. Fifth Bank	
9. IRS	
10. Joan Sims	

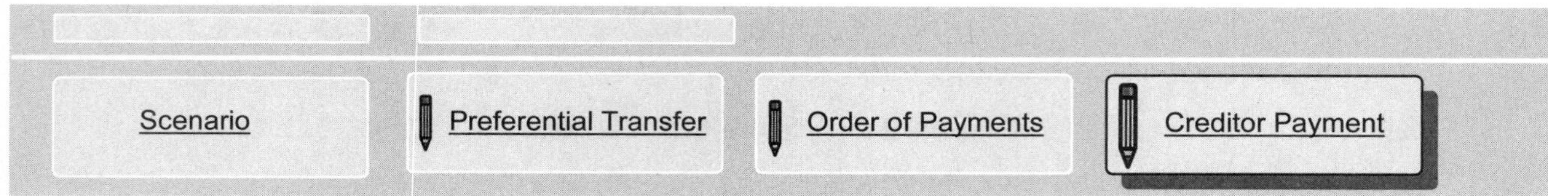

Items 11 through 13 also represent creditor claims against the bankruptcy estate. For each creditor listed, indicate the amount that creditor will receive.

Creditor	Answer
11. TVN Computers, Inc.	
12. Hart Manufacturing Corp.	
13. Soft Office Supplies	

Techno, Inc. is a computer equipment dealer. On March 9, 2010, Allied Building Maintenance, Cleen Janitorial Services, and Jones, CPA, filed an involuntary petition in bankruptcy against Techno under the provisions of Chapter 7 of the Federal Bankruptcy Code. At the time of the filing, Techno had liabilities of $229,000 (owed to 23 creditors) and assets with a fair market value of $191,000. During the entire year before the bankruptcy filing, Techno's liabilities exceeded the fair market value of its assets.

The bankruptcy court approved the involuntary petition.

During the course of the bankruptcy proceeding, the following transactions were disclosed:

- On October 6, 2009, Techno paid its president $9,900 as repayment of an unsecured loan made to the corporation on September 18, 2007.
- On February 19, 2010, Techno paid $10,150 to Alexis Computers, Inc. for eight computer monitors. These monitors were delivered to Techno on February 9, 2010, and placed in inventory.
- On January 12, 2010, Techno bought a new delivery truck from Maple Motors for $17,900 cash. On the date of the bankruptcy filing, the truck was worth $10,000.

Write a memo to your supervisor, the partner in charge of an audit of one of Techno's general creditors, outlining whether the payments to Techno's president, Alexis, and Maple are likely to be ruled preferential transfers.

Research Question: What code section and subsection, if applicable, provides guidance on the denial of foreign tax credit to any income from a foreign country with respect to which the United States has severed diplomatic relations?

Section & Subsection Answer: §_____(___)

Solution 38-1 MULTIPLE CHOICE ANSWERS

Operative Chapters

1. (d) Like a liquidation proceeding, a reorganization may be either voluntary or involuntary. The appointment of a trustee is not required under Chapter 11. A debtor is not precluded from filing for bankruptcy if the debtor is solvent. During the first 120 days after the order of relief, *only* the debtor may file a plan of reorganization.

2. (d) Under the provisions of Chapter 11 of the Federal Bankruptcy Code, a reorganization plan always must be confirmed by the court. Prior to court confirmation, *approval* of the plan is generally required by creditors holding two-thirds in amount and one-half in number of each class of claims. It is not necessary that any creditors or any shareholders *confirm* the reorganization plan.

3. (d) Under Chapter 11 of the Federal Bankruptcy Code, a corporation will be discharged from all its debts and liabilities that arose before the confirmation of the plan, except as otherwise provided in the plan, the order of confirmation, or the bankruptcy code. If there are exceptions, Strong Corp. will not be discharged from all its debts and liabilities. Creditor approval of the reorganization plan is not a prerequisite to the discharge of debts.

Bankruptcy Commencement

4. (d) A joint voluntary bankruptcy petition can be filed by a husband and wife. The threshold pertains to an involuntary petition. There is no rule that a debtor be insolvent to file a petition in bankruptcy.

5. (d) An involuntary bankruptcy case is commenced by the filing of a petition with the bankruptcy court. One creditor may file the petition if the debtor has fewer than 12 such creditors, provided that the unsecured portion of the petitioner's claims is equal to a minimum threshold ($13,475, through April 1, 2010). Since Dart has fewer than 12 creditors, any one creditor owed at least the threshold amount may file the petition. Since Decoy has an unsecured claim for $17,000, Decoy may file the petition alone.

6. (c) When an involuntary petition is filed, the debtor may oppose/controvert the petition upon proof that the debtor is paying its debts as they become due. Dart will lose because it is **not** paying its debts as they become due. There is no reason that the petition should have been filed under Chapter 11, nor is there a requirement that there be more than 12 creditors. Dart's debt to the IRS has no effect on Dart's ability to contest the petition.

7. (a) Following the filing of a Chapter 7 involuntary petition, the court issues a stay against creditor collection proceedings and, in most cases, a trustee will be appointed.

Creditors & Claims

8. (a) The distribution rules for a Chapter 7 case require that **all** priority claims be satisfied first. Any remaining property is then distributed as follows: (1) in payment of any unsecured claim, proof of which was timely filed; (2) in payment of any unsecured claim, proof of which was not timely filed. Since there is insufficient property to satisfy the unsecured claims which were filed timely, Nanstar, whose claim was not timely filed, would receive nothing.

9. (c) After payments to secured creditors (Fracon, $70,000; Decoy, $2,000) and after payment of $12,000 to the IRS, there is only $16,000 remaining in the bankruptcy estate. The claims of unsecured creditors whose claims were filed timely is $25,000 ($5,000 + $3,000 + $17,000). Each unsecured creditor would receive 64% ($16,000 / $25,000) of their claim. Fracon would, thus, receive $70,000 as a secured creditor and $3,200 ($5,000 × 64%) as an unsecured creditor.

10. (d) After payments to secured creditors (Fracon, $70,000; Decoy, $2,000), $28,000 remains in the bankruptcy estate. Of Dart's creditors, the IRS has the next highest priority after payment of administration expenses; its claim is paid in full.

Debtor's Benefits

11. (d) If the debtor refuses to satisfactorily explain a loss of assets, it is considered a bankruptcy offense and the bankruptcy court will not grant a bankruptcy discharge. Failure to list a creditor results in an exception to discharge for the debt owed to that creditor, but does not cause the entire petition to be denied discharge. Alimony and support payment debts are not discharged in bankruptcy, but do not prevent a debtor from being given a bankruptcy discharge. Administrative expenses are paid after secured creditors and before most other priorities, but any deficiencies may be discharged.

12. (a, e) Both answers are required for full point value. Under Chapters 7, 11, and 13 of the Bankruptcy Code, certain debts are excepted from discharge. These include claims that arise from alimony or maintenance and claims arising from tax debts due within three years of filing the bankruptcy petition. Claims arising from a breach of contract,

from an unsecured creditor, or from an action in negligence are all dischargeable.

13. (d) The reaffirmation of a debt is a commitment to pay a debt that can be discharged in bankruptcy. To be enforceable, a reaffirmation must be implemented under state law and the debtor must have received adequate notice on the effects of signing the reaffirmation. If the reaffirmation is rescinded before discharge, or within 60 days after filing the reaffirmation agreement, then it is not enforceable. In this case, the reaffirmation agreement would be enforceable if it was not rescinded before discharge because the time period of 60 days from the date of filing the agreement lapsed prior to discharge.

14. (b) Revocation of the discharge may be granted by the court if it was obtained through fraud. Failure to answer material questions correctly on the bankruptcy petition most probably would be considered a fraudulent act. However, the failure to list one creditor may be considered unintentional and thus non-fraudulent. While this failure to list one creditor will not, in general, disqualify the debtor from filing for bankruptcy, that one debt will not be discharged in bankruptcy since it was "unscheduled."

Bankruptcy Estate

15. (a) The estate's property consists of the debtor's assets administered in bankruptcy. At bankruptcy commencement, an estate is created of (in part): property interests acquired by the debtor within 180 days after commencement by bequest, devise, inheritance, as a result of a property settlement agreement with a spouse, or as a beneficiary of a life insurance policy or health benefit plan. Child support payments, social security payments, and wages earned after the filing of the petition are excluded from a Chapter 7 bankruptcy estate.

16. (d) Liens that are effective against the debtor's property before the bankruptcy petition was filed represent property that is not part of the bankruptcy estate; therefore, the trustee may not avoid these liens. An unperfected secured creditor is subjugated to the interest of perfected secured creditors, lien creditors, and trustees in bankruptcy. Generally, the trustee may use, sell, or lease the property of the bankruptcy estate. The bankruptcy estate acquires the same rights as were held by the debtor; the trustee has the power to exercise these rights.

17. (d) A "preferential transfer" is any payment or transfer of property from an insolvent debtor to a creditor for a *preexisting* debt within 90 days of filing a petition in bankruptcy court. There was no preexisting debt in answer (a). The courts generally assume that payments for services rendered within ten to fifteen days prior to the payment represent current consideration and are not a preference. There was a contemporaneous exchange (mortgage in exchange for money) in answer (c). A debtor making a payment to one creditor on a preexisting debt meets the criteria of a preferential transfer.

18. (b) In the administration of the bankrupt's estate, the trustee can assume or reject executory contracts and unexpired leases subject to the approval of the court or judge. A trustee may elect not to assume the equipment lease. The lease may be rejected even if it is for more than one year.

19. (a) Municipal bond interest received by the debtor within 180 days after the filing of the Chapter 7 bankruptcy petition becomes part of the bankruptcy estate. Alimony and social security payments received by the debtor are excluded from the bankruptcy estate under the Federal Bankruptcy Code exemptions. Inheritances received by the debtor within 180 days after commencement would become part of the bankruptcy estate; however, gifts are excluded.

Liens & Non-Bankruptcy Resolution

20. (a) Both a mechanic's lien and an artisan's lien require the lienholder to give notice of legal action before selling the debtor's property to satisfy a debt.

21. (c) The federal Fair Debt Collection Practices Act basically prohibits a debt collector from harassing a debtor. If a debtor is represented by an attorney, the debt collector may not contact the debtor directly. A debt collector generally may ascertain a debtor's location, continue to collect a debt, and commence a lawsuit to collect a debt.

22. (b) An order of garnishment will enable a creditor to collect money from a debtor's wages. The other options apply to assets of a debtor, but not wages. An order of receivership would allow a receiver appointed by the court to take possession but not title to the debtor's property. A writ of execution allows the debtor's property to be seized and sold to satisfy a judgment. A writ of attachment allows the debtor's property to be seized to secure payment of a judgment.

23. (b) A composition agreement involves a modification of the original credit agreement/contract whereby the creditors agree to accept an immediate payment of a lesser amount in satisfaction of the debt. If the debtor makes the payments due, then the debtor will be released from the debt. An Assignment for the Benefit of Creditors (ABC) involves a voluntary transfer of the debtor's nonexempt assets

to an assignee who liquidates the assets and distributes the proceeds to the creditors. All of the debtor's general creditors participate; however, the debtor is not released from its debts if these are not satisfied as a result of the distribution.

Guaranty of Collection

24. (b) The Statute of Frauds requires that all promises to be liable for the debt of another be in writing; thus, in order for the guarantor to be liable the agreement must be in writing and signed by the guarantor. A guarantor has secondary liability and, thus, the creditor must attempt to collect from the debtor first. Although a guarantor may use some defenses available to the debtor, the debtor's lack of capacity, or bankruptcy, are defenses personal to the debtor and, thus, not available to a guarantor. It is not necessary that the guarantor notify the creditor of the debtor's default.

25. (d) If a "guarantor of collection" is involved, the creditor is required to proceed against the debtor first, and only when the creditor is unable to collect from the debtor, is the creditor allowed to go after the surety. In this problem, the surety is a "guarantor of collection." Thus, the creditor (Towns) must proceed against the debtor (Pepper) prior to proceeding against Sorus and/or Ace.

Suretyship

26. (b) Any release of collateral by the creditor before satisfaction of the debtor's obligation, releases the surety to the extent of the collateral released. Personal defenses of the principal debtor are not available to the surety. If the principal debtor obtains the surety's promise through duress or fraud, the contract is not voidable unless the creditor knew of the duress or fraud.

27. (c) When a principal debtor defaults and the surety pays the entire obligation, the surety inherits from the creditor all of the creditor's rights against the debtor. This is called subrogation.

28. (d) A co-surety who pays more than their *pro rata* share of a liability is entitled to contribution from any other co-sureties. Exoneration, subrogation, and reimbursement represent rights a surety has against a debtor.

29. (a) Unless a creditor specifically preserves her/his/its rights, a release of a co-surety releases the other co-sureties in the amount of the released surety's share. Thus, Quill will only be liable for 50% of the loan balance. Release of a co-surety will have no effect on the debtor's liability.

30. (b) When there are two or more sureties (co-sureties), the right of contribution requires that a surety who pays more than her/his proportionate share on a debtor's default, may recover from the other co-sureties the amount paid above her/his obligation. Ace paid $48,000 in full settlement of the claims against the co-sureties. Each co-surety's proportionate share of the $48,000 liability is determined by their maximum liabilities under the surety contract. The liability is divided among the co-sureties according to their respective *pro rata* share in the surety contract. Kerr had a maximum liability of $40,000 on a surety contract with total liability of $120,000. Kerr's share of the liability is $16,000 [($40,000 / $120,000) × $48,000 = $16,000]. Therefore, Ace may recover $16,000 from Kerr.

Solution 38-2 ADDITIONAL MULTIPLE CHOICE ANSWERS

Operative Chapters

31. (c) Chapter 11 of the Federal Bankruptcy Code specifies that the court is required to appoint a committee of creditors holding *unsecured* claims. A trustee does not have to be appointed under a Chapter 11 filing. Any interested party may propose a plan after the first 120 days following the order for relief. Robin may continue in business without the approval of a trustee and a trustee may not even have been appointed.

32. (d) A savings and loan is not eligible for reorganization under Chapter 11. A retail sole proprietorship, an advertising partnership, and a CPA professional corporation are permitted to file for reorganization under Chapter 11.

Bankruptcy Commencement

33. (d) The filing of a petition of bankruptcy, either voluntary or involuntary, stops the enforcement of judgment liens against property in the bankruptcy estate, and it, in general, stops all other legal actions against the debtor except for legal actions involving alimony, child support, and criminal actions. Bankruptcy proceedings act to protect the assets of the debtor until an equitable distribution of those assets among all creditors can be achieved. A discharge of debt under the Federal Bankruptcy Code has no effect on exempt property. The Federal Bankruptcy Code considers security interests in property in the bankruptcy estate when it assigns priority to creditors for the distribution of assets. The Federal

Bankruptcy Code has no power to limit the debtor's actions regarding new debt.

34. (a) Judgment may be granted against the petitioning creditors for court costs and attorney's fees incurred by the debtor in defending against an involuntary petition which is dismissed by the court. Also, if the petition is filed in bad faith, both compensatory and punitive damages can be awarded for injury to the debtor's reputation.

35. (c) A CPA may serve as both a trustee of an estate and act as its tax return preparer if authorized by the bankruptcy court. A separate fee may be obtained for each service. The fee is determined by the type of work performed and not by the size of the estate (although the size of the estate may be a factor in the type of work performed).

36. (b) An involuntary bankruptcy case is commenced by the filing of a petition with the bankruptcy court. One creditor may file the petition if the debtor has fewer than 12 such creditors, provided that the unsecured portion of the petitioner's claims is equal to at least $13,475. Since Tree has fewer than 12 creditors and Hall has an unsecured claim for $15,000, Hall may file the petition alone. The involuntary bankruptcy requirement of 3 more creditors involves a debtor who has 12 or more creditors. Involuntary bankruptcy proceedings are permitted only under Chapters 7 and 11.

37. (b) Chapter 9 provides a procedure so that a municipality that has encountered financial difficulty may work with its creditors to adjust its debts. Chapter 9 is reserved for municipalities; individuals may file under Chapters 7, 11, and 13. Family farmers and fishers also may file under Chapter 12.

38. (a) To file for bankruptcy under Chapter 7 voluntarily, an individual must have debt, the amount of which is irrelevant. The debtor need not be insolvent, be indebted to a minimum number of creditors, or have debt above a specified amount, in order to file under Chapter 7.

Creditors & Claims

39. (a) Creditor's claims are ranked according to guidelines established by the Federal Bankruptcy Code. Secured creditors are highest in priority and are paid on their security interests before those with junior claims.

Debtor's Benefits

40. (c) A discharge in a bankruptcy case under any chapter voids any existing and future judgments that are determinations of the personal liability of the debtor with respect to any discharged debt, and operates as an injunction against the commencement or continuation of an action at law, the employment of legal process, or any act (including telephone calls and letters) to recover, collect, or offset any discharged debt as a personal liability of the debtor or from the property of the debtor.

41. (a) Debts due to negligence arising before the petition was filed are dischargeable in bankruptcy as long as the debtor lists the debt on the bankruptcy petition. Alimony payments are not dischargeable in bankruptcy. Unscheduled debts (debts not listed in the bankruptcy petition) are not dischargeable in bankruptcy. Income taxes due within three years before the filing of the bankruptcy petition are not dischargeable in bankruptcy.

Bankruptcy Estate

42. (b) The Jet transaction meets all six criteria of a preferential transfer: (1) a transfer of property or interest in property that benefits a creditor; (2) for or on account of an antecedent debt; (3) made within 90 days of the bankruptcy filing; (4) a minimum threshold ($5,475, through April 1, 2010); (5) made while the debtor was insolvent; and (6) that enables the creditor to receive more in the bankruptcy distribution than it would have without the transfer. A bankruptcy trustee may set aside a preferential transfer. A security agreement need not cover only goods purchased with the borrowed funds. Perfection of a preferential transfer does not overcome the claims of the bankruptcy estate. The use of the loan proceeds is irrelevant to the trustee's ability to set aside a preferential transfer.

43. (c) Quick's solvency when the loan was made by Erly is not a relevant factor in determining whether the repayment of Erly's loan is a voidable transfer. Quick's solvency when the loan is repaid is a relevant factor. The fact that Erly is an insider, Quick's payment to Erly was for an antecedent debt, and Quick's payment to Erly was made within one year of the filing of the petition, are all relevant in determining if a voidable preferential transfer was made.

44. (a) Quick's payment to Kray is considered a contemporaneous exchange and not a voidable preferential transfer. When Quick paid Kray $100,000, Quick received $100,000 of inventory. Thus, a contemporaneous exchange took place; value for value. This transaction is not voidable even if Kray knew about Quick's insolvency since this transaction is a contemporaneous exchange. It does not matter that the transaction took place within 90 days of filing of the petition, nor that Kray

received more than it would have received in bankruptcy.

45. (c) The bankruptcy laws grant the trustee avoiding powers to set aside certain conveyances, including preferential transfers. A preferential transfer is a property transfer that meets all six of the following: (1) a transfer of property to or for the benefit of a creditor; (2) for or on account of an antecedent debt owed by the debtor; (3) generally, on or within 90 days before the date of bankruptcy filing; (4) a minimum threshold ($5,475, through April 1, 2010); (5) made while the debtor was insolvent; and (6) that enables the creditor to receive more than it would receive as a distributive share under a Chapter 7 liquidation. All six tests must be met to establish a preferential transfer. The sixth test in this case is not met because secured creditors have priority over other creditors, and Acme was oversecured at the time of the monthly installment payment.

46. (b) To constitute a preference that may be recovered, an insolvent debtor must have transferred property, for a preexisting, or antecedent debt, within 90 days of the filing of the petition. Hall gave the mortgage to National Bank 75 days before he filed his petition, so he was insolvent at the time. A preferential transfer may be made to an insider (National) if the transfer did not occur within 12 months prior to the filing of the petition and because secured creditors are not considered insiders for purposes of a preferential transfer. Answer (d) is incorrect because National was an unsecured creditor.

47. (d) Hall's purchase of the boat from Olsen is a contemporaneous exchange for new value given and no antecedent debt was involved; therefore, a preference is not present. The payment was not preferential. Hall's insolvency is not a factor in a contemporaneous exchange.

48. (c) The credit card payment was not preferential. There is a $5,475 minimum on preference items, through April 1, 2010. The amount of a payment relative to the amount of an original debt is not the deciding factor as to whether a payment is preferential.

Bankruptcy Estate

49. (a) A debtor's remaining in possession of property transferred, a debtor's retention of an equitable benefit in property conveyed, and the fact that a conveyance occurred in secret are all indicators of a fraudulent conveyance.

50. (d) Homestead exemption legislation protects a debtor's property from seizure by unsecured creditors, such as the IRS, but the IRS debt would not be discharged. A secured creditor with a valid home mortgage lien could seize the property.

51. (b) State exemption statutes do not prevent all of a debtor's personal property from being sold to pay any creditor since only property exempt by statute may be retained by the debtor. They may protect *some* of a debtor's property from being sold. Federal social security benefits are exempt from garnishment by creditors.

Non-Bankruptcy Resolution

52. (b) A credit card holder is protected from loss by limiting the card holder's liability for unauthorized use, to a maximum of $50 if the card involved was accepted by the card holder. A card holder, however, has no liability for unauthorized use of cards mailed on an unsolicited basis. Although some states have usury laws, there is currently no federal law that restricts the interest rate allowed to be charged by a credit card company. The Equal Credit Opportunity Act, an amendment of the Truth in Lending Act, prohibits the denial of credit solely on the basis of race, religion, national origin, color, sex, marital status, or age. Thus, credit card companies may not refuse to issue cards to qualified persons. Allowing the card holder to defer payment of the balance due on the card is a standard credit card practice not specifically addressed by the federal Credit Card Fraud Act.

53. (c) The Fair Debt Collection Practices Act, which is largely enforced by the Federal Trade Commission, permits debtors to recover civil damages, including attorney's fees, from a collection service for violations of the Act. There are no provisions for criminal liability for violating the Act, nor does the Act provide that reduction or abolishment of the debt are appropriate remedies.

54. (a) Attachment involves a prejudgment, court-ordered seizure of property (including personal property) that is in controversy because of a debt. Garnishment is also a prejudgment remedy that permits a creditor to proceed against property or property rights held by a third person. Garnishments and writs of attachment are *both* prejudgment remedies available to a creditor where the debtor owns no real property.

Suretyship

55. (d) A surety (as opposed to a guarantor) has primary liability to the creditor and, thus, does not have the right to either compel the creditor to collect from the principal debtor or to proceed against the principal debtor's collateral.

56. (d) If the principal debtor offers to satisfy the obligation (i.e., tenders performance), then the surety is released of any further liability. A principal debtor's partial release also would partially release a surety from liability. A change in the manner or time for repayment has no impact on a surety's liability.

57. (a) If a creditor obtains a surety's promise through fraud, the contract is voidable by the surety. If the principal debtor obtains the surety's promise through fraud, the contract is not voidable unless the creditor knew of the fraud. Thus, if Royal can show that State was aware of the fraud, Royal will have a defense against liability. The fact that Royal was an uncompensated surety will not relieve her/him of liability. The debtor's discharge in bankruptcy is a risk the surety assumes and will have no affect on the surety's liability. There is nothing to indicate that the arrangement was void at its inception.

58. (b) The general rule of law is that a material change in the suretyship contract will release a noncompensated surety from liability. The release of the principal debtor by the creditor will release the surety as well, unless the creditor specifically reserves her/his rights against the surety. The bankruptcy of the principal debtor is not a defense available to a surety. The principal debtor's lack of capacity is not a defense available to a surety.

59. (b) The right of contribution arises when one co-surety, in performance of the principal debtor's obligation, pays more than her/his proportionate share of the total liability. This allows the performing co-surety to receive reimbursement from the other co-sureties for their *pro rata* shares of the liability. Queen paid his maximum liability of $210,000, or 50% of the debt; then Ivor paid $70,000, reducing the balance to $210,000. Ash's liability of $84,000 represents 20%, so Queen may collect 20% of the remainder, or $42,000, from Ash. Kane's liability of $126,000 represents 30%, so Queen may collect $63,000 from Kane.

60. (c) The right of exoneration allows a surety to bring a suit in equity against the debtor in order to force the debtor to pay the matured debt so that the surety will not be required to satisfy the obligation. Reimbursement or indemnification refers to the surety's right to recover from the debtor after the surety has paid the debt. Contribution describes the surety's right to recover from any co-surety to the extent the surety has paid more than her/his proportionate share. Subrogation is the surety's right to succeed to the rights of the creditor once the surety has satisfied the debtor's obligation.

61. (a) A suretyship agreement is a contract which must be supported by consideration. When the suretyship agreement is contemporaneous with the primary contract, there is no need for separate consideration. The surety may exercise any real defenses on the contract which are available to the debtor. Thus, fraud, duress, illegality, forgery, etc., will discharge both surety and debtor. However, the surety may not rely on the debtor's personal defenses (e.g., incapacity, insolvency, or death) to avoid the suretyship obligation. The surety also is discharged from liability if the surety agreement was procured by duress or fraudulent misrepresentation by the *creditor.* Thus, if the creditor fraudulently contracts with the debtor or fraudulently procures the suretyship agreement itself, the agreement is voidable. However, if the debtor procures the suretyship agreement by fraudulent misrepresentation, the surety remains liable to the creditor.

62. (c) The right of contribution provides that a surety who pays more than her/his proportionate share on a debtor's default may recover from the co-sureties the amount paid above her/his obligation. Nash paid $36,000 in full settlement of the claims against the co-sureties. Each co-surety's proportionate share of the $36,000 liability is determined by their maximum liabilities under the surety contract. The liability is divided among the co-sureties according to their respective *pro rata* share in the surety contract. Nash had a maximum liability of $40,000 on a surety contract with total liability of $180,000. Nash's share of the liability is $8,000 ($40,000 / $180,000 × $36,000 = $8,000). Therefore, Nash may recover from Owen and Polk, the co-sureties, the amount by which he overpaid his obligation, $28,000 ($36,000 – $8,000 = $28,000).

63. (c) The surety's incapacity is a personal defense of the surety against the creditor and can be asserted successfully to limit the surety's liability to the creditor. A surety may not avail her/himself of any personal defenses of the debtor against the creditor, such as the debtor's incapacity or bankruptcy.

64. (c) If the debtor, or someone acting on behalf of the debtor, fully performs all requirements of the contract, the surety is discharged. If King's spouse satisfies the debt to Ace, Wright will be released from liability. A surety has primary liability upon the debtor's default; the creditor may seek payment exclusively from the surety. The debtor's discharge in bankruptcy is a risk the surety assumes, as is the debtor's adjudication of mental incompetence; neither releases the surety from liability.

PERFORMANCE BY SUBTOPICS

Each category below parallels a subtopic covered in Chapter 38. Record the number and percentage of questions you correctly answered in each subtopic area.

Operative Chapters

Question #	Correct √
1	
2	
3	
# Questions	3
# Correct	
% Correct	

Bankruptcy Commencement

Question #	Correct √
4	
5	
6	
7	
# Questions	4
# Correct	
% Correct	

Creditors & Claims

Question #	Correct √
8	
9	
10	
# Questions	3
# Correct	
% Correct	

Debtor's Benefits

Question #	Correct √
11	
12	
13	
14	
# Questions	4
# Correct	
% Correct	

Bankruptcy Estate

Question #	Correct √
15	
16	
17	
18	
19	
# Questions	5
# Correct	
% Correct	

Liens & Non-Bankruptcy Resolution

Question #	Correct √
20	
21	
22	
23	
# Questions	4
# Correct	
% Correct	

Guaranty of Collection

Question #	Correct √
24	
25	
# Questions	2
# Correct	
% Correct	

Suretyship

Question #	Correct √
26	
27	
28	
29	
30	
# Questions	5
# Correct	
% Correct	

SIMULATION SOLUTION

Solution 38-3 Preferential Transfers & Creditor Claims

Preferential Transfer (1.5 points)

1. Y

A transfer is considered preferential if made between 90 days and 1 year before the filing date if the creditor at the time was an insider. Insiders are relatives, officers, directors, and controlling shareholders of the debtor. Mary Lake, the sister of one of Wren's directors, is considered an insider, and the transaction occurred on December 31, 2009, within a year of the petition date of March 15, 2010.

2. N

A preferential transfer is a property transfer that meets all six of the following: (1) to or for the benefit of a creditor; (2) for or on account of an antecedent debt owed by the debtor; (3) generally, on or within 90 days before the date of bankruptcy filing; (4) a minimum threshold ($5,475, through April 1, 2010); (5) made while the debtor was insolvent; and (6) that enables the creditor to receive more than it would receive as a distributive share under a Chapter 7 liquidation. A donation to charity does not meet the six characteristics of a preferential transfer. Therefore, it would not be set aside.

3. Y

A preferential transfer is a property transfer that meets all six of the following: (1) to or for the benefit of a creditor; (2) for or on account of an antecedent debt owed by the debtor; (3) generally, on or within 90 days before the date of bankruptcy filing; (4) a minimum threshold ($5,475, through April 1, 2010); (5) made while the debtor was insolvent; and (6) that enables the creditor to receive more than it would receive as a distributive share under a Chapter 7 liquidation. The security agreement to Young covering Wren's office fixtures to secure a loan previously made by Young meets all six of these requirements and would be set aside.

4. N

A preferential transfer is a property transfer that meets all six of the following: (1) to or for the benefit of a creditor; (2) for or on account of an antecedent debt owed by the debtor; (3) generally, on or within 90 days before the date of bankruptcy filing; (4) a minimum threshold ($5,475, through April 1, 2010); (5) made while the debtor was insolvent; and (6) that enables the creditor to receive more than it would receive as a distributive share under a Chapter 7 liquidation. The payment to Integral Appliance Corp. made on March 1, 2010, on a two-year note is considered a normal payment that did not have the intent of favoring one creditor over another.

5. N

Wren's purchase from Safety would be considered a contemporaneous exchange for new value and not a preferential transfer. A preferential transfer is voidable. When Wren paid $10,000 cash, Wren received a new alarm system. Thus, a contemporaneous exchange took place.

Order of Payments (1 point)

6. B

As there are no child support or alimony claims, bankruptcy administrative expenses are second in the order of payment behind secured claims.

7. E

The payment to Acme Office Cleaners for services for January, February, and March would be last in the order of payment because it represents a payment to a general unsecured creditor.

8. A

The payment to Fifth Bank represents a secured claim; therefore, it would be first in the order of payment.

9. D

The payment to the IRS represents federal income taxes and would be fourth in the order of payment.

10. C

The payment to Joan Sims for March commissions represents wages of the bankrupt's employees ($10,950 maximum each, through April 1, 2010) accrued within 180 days before the petition is filed, and would be third of the listed items in the order of payment.

Creditor Payment (1.5 points)

11. $13,500

As a secured creditor, TVN Computers, Inc. would be entitled to the proceeds from the sale of the collateral of $12,000. The remainder is considered as part of the nonpriority general creditors. There was enough to pay 50 cents on the dollar; therefore, TVN would get an additional $1,500, [($15,000 – $12,000) × 50%] for a total of $13,500.

12. $27,500

As a secured creditor, Hart Manufacturing Corp. would be entitled to the proceeds from the sale of the inventory of $25,000. The remainder is considered as part of the nonpriority general creditors. There was enough to pay 50 cents on the dollar; therefore, Hart would get an additional $2,500 ($30,000 – $25,000 = $5,000 × 50%) for a total of $27,500.

13. $1,000

Payment to Soft Office Supplies for supplies purchased in the previous year represents an amount owed to a general unsecured creditor. Therefore, Soft would receive $1,000 ($2,000 × 50%).

Communication (5 points)

To: D. Boss
From: Candidate
Re: Techno—Possible Preferential Transfers

A preferential transfer is a property transfer that meets **all** of six criteria. First, the payment is to or for the **benefit** of a creditor. Second, the payment is for or on account of an **antecedent** debt owed by the debtor. Third, the payment is generally on or within 90 days before the **date** of bankruptcy filing. This 90-day limit is extended to one year for payments to insiders. Fourth, the payment amount surpasses a minimum **threshold** ($5,475). Fifth, the payment is made while the debtor was **insolvent.** Finally, the payment is such that it enables the creditor to receive **more** than it would receive as a distributive share under a Chapter 7 liquidation.

The payment to Techno's president would be regarded as a **preferential transfer.** Because the president is an "**insider,**" payments made on the **unsecured** loan during the **year** preceding the bankruptcy filing would be considered a preferential transfer.

The payment to Alexis was not a preferential transfer because it was made in the **ordinary course of business** and under ordinary business terms.

The payment to Maple for the truck was not a preferential transfer because it was not made on account of an antecedent debt, but as a **contemporaneous exchange** for **new value.**

Research (1 point)

IRC Section Answer: §901(j)

IRC §901(j) states, "DENIAL OF FOREIGN TAX CREDIT, ETC., WITH RESPECT TO CERTAIN FOREIGN COUNTRIES.—901(j)(1) IN GENERAL.—Notwithstanding any other provision of this part—901(j)(1)(A) no credit shall be allowed under subsection (a) for any income, war profits, or excess profits taxes paid or accrued (or deemed paid under section 902 or 960) to any country if such taxes are with respect to income attributable to a period during which this subsection applies to such country, and 901(j)(1)(B) subsections (a), (b), and (c) of section 904 and sections 902 and 960 shall be applied separately with respect to income attributable to such a period from sources within such country. 901(j)(2) COUNTRIES TO WHICH SUBSECTION APPLIES.—901(j)(2)(A) IN GENERAL.—This subsection shall apply to any foreign country... 901(j)(2)(A)(ii) with respect to which the United States has severed diplomatic relations...."

Adaptive Testing

Each testlet is designed to cover all of the topics for an exam section. After the first testlet is finished, the software selects a second testlet based on the candidate's performance on the first testlet. If a candidate did well on the first testlet, the second testlet will be a little more difficult than average. Conversely, if a candidate did poorly on the first testlet, the second testlet will be a little less difficult than average. The examiners plan on adaptive testing eventually allowing for less questions, resulting in more time for testing skills.

Initially, testlets with different levels of difficulty will have the same number of questions; however, the point value of a question from an "easy" testlet will be less than a question from a "difficult" testlet. Thus, some candidates may think that they are not doing well because they are finding the questions difficult; when in reality, they are getting difficult questions because of exceptional performance on previous testlets. Other candidates may think that they are doing well because they are finding the questions easy; when in reality, they are getting easy questions because of poor performance on previous testlets.

More helpful exam information is included in the **Practical Advice** appendix in this volume.

CHAPTER 39

AGENCY

EXAM COVERAGE: The business law portion of the Regulation section of the CPA exam is designated by the examiners to be 20-25 percent of the section's point value. More information about point distribution and information eligible to be tested is included in the **Practical Advice** section of this volume.

CHAPTER 39

AGENCY

I. Nature

A. Relationship

Agency is a consensual relationship whereby one person, the agent, agrees to act on behalf and under the control of another, the principal. An agent has the authority to represent the principal in contractual matters so as to affect the legal relationships between the principal and third parties.

1. **Contractual Arrangement** When an agency arises from a contractual arrangement, as it normally does, the law of contracts applies. However, agency may arise solely from the consent of the principal to have the agent represent her/him.

2. **Fiduciary Relationship** Agency is a fiduciary relationship. An agent acting for the benefit of the principal is distinguished from a servant and an independent contractor.

3. **Principal** A principal must have sufficient legal capacity to consent to the agency. Corporations must act through agents; partnerships, on the other hand, may act through partners or through outside agents. Unincorporated associations are not legal entities and, thus, cannot appoint agents, only their individual members, as principals, may appoint agents.

    a. **Capacity** Infants may appoint agents in most jurisdictions and may void the appointment of an agent, unless that agent acts as an agent for securing necessities (food, clothing, shelter, education). Insane persons' appointments of agents are voidable if made prior to judicial determination of insanity and are void if made after such judicial determination.

    b. **Spouse** Marriage does not prevent spouses from acting as principal and agent for each other.

4. **Agent** Anyone who has the ability to carry out instructions may be an agent. The agent need not possess the legal capacity to contract, because contracts properly negotiated as an agent will not personally bind the agent.

5. **Notice** Notice by a third person to an agent is considered notice to the principal if the agent has actual or apparent authority to receive the notice. However, if the third person has knowledge that the agent's personal interest is adverse to the principal's interest, then notice to the agent is not notice to the principal.

6. **Knowledge** Similarly, the agent's knowledge is imputed to the principal if the agent has the authority to represent the principal in the matter, unless the agent's personal interest is adverse to the principal's interest.

7. **Admissions** Out-of-court statements by an agent to a third person, which are within the scope of her/his employment, may be treated as admissions of the principal and introduced into evidence against the principal.

B. Principal's Duties to Agent

The principal owes the agent the following duties.

1. **Compensation for Services** To compensate the agent for services rendered, either according to their agreement or, if there is no agreement, in an amount that reasonably reflects the value of the services.

2. **Reimbursement of Expenses** To reimburse the agent for reasonable expenses incurred in the course of the agency.

3. **Indemnification** To indemnify the agent against loss or liability for acts performed at the principal's direction, unless they are unlawful.

4. **Compensation for Injury** To compensate the agent for physical injury (for example, workers' compensation).

C. Agent's Duties to Principal

1. **Loyalty** An agent has a fiduciary duty to be loyal to her/his principal. An agent who violates the duty of loyalty is subject to liability for any losses caused thereby and is not entitled to compensation, reimbursement, or indemnification.

   a. The agent cannot act for two principals with conflicting interests unless both principals consent.

   b. The agent cannot deal for her/his own interest (for example, to make a profit at the principal's expense), and if the agent does, s/he is a constructive trustee for the principal of whatever should have been acquired for the principal.

   c. The agent cannot compete with her/his principal without the principal's consent.

   d. The agent cannot disclose to others any confidential information learned during the agency relationship.

2. **Follow Instructions** An agent must follow the principal's lawful instructions, using reasonable care and skill.

   a. The agent cannot delegate duties involving discretion, except with the principal's permission.

   b. The agent is liable to the principal for losses resulting from her/his own negligence.

3. **Communicate Material Facts** An agent has the duty to communicate notice of any material facts that come to the agent's attention while s/he is acting in her/his agency capacity.

4. **Account for Property or Money** An agent must account for any property or money s/he receives through the agency. The agent may not commingle her/his own funds with those of the principal. If the agent does, s/he is liable for any resulting loss.

D. Agent's Authority to Bind Principal

1. **Actual** An agent's actual authority is that power consented to by the principal that affects the principal's legal relations.

2. **Express or Implied** This authority may be express or implied from the principal's conduct. Implied authority includes the authority to do acts reasonably necessary to accomplish an authorized act. Implied authority also may arise from customary practices in the business community.

3. **Apparent or Ostensible** If the conduct of the principal leads a third party to believe that an agent has authority beyond that to which the principal actually has consented, the agent is said to have apparent authority. For example, if a principal places an agent with limited authority in a position usually held by an agent with greater authority, the principal may lead others to believe the agent has greater authority than actually is the case.

a. Between the principal and the third party, it is as if the agent's authority were actual and neither can deny it.

b. If losses to the principal result, the principal can hold the agent liable for exceeding her/his actual authority.

E. **Agent Types**

1. **General Agent** Has broad authority to act for the principal in a variety of transactions.

2. **Special Agent** Has authority that is limited to a single transaction or series of related transactions (e.g., attorneys, auctioneers, brokers, etc.). **Note:** A principal is less likely to be liable for a special agent's unauthorized acts than s/he would be for a general agent's unauthorized acts.

3. **Sub-Agent** An agent appointed by another agent who is authorized to appoint sub-agents in connection with her/his performance of the principal's business. A sub-agent has a duty of loyalty to both the principal and agent. Sub-agency is distinguished from the following.

   a. **Co-Agent** An agent hired by another agent to act as an ancillary agent for the principal. The co-agent is subject to the principal's control; the co-agent is not subject to the employing agent's control.

   b. **Agent of an Agent** An agent appointed by another agent who has not been given the authority by the principal to appoint other agents. S/he is an agent for the appointing agent, not a sub-agent for the principal.

4. **Gratuitous Agent** One who agrees to act as agent without compensation. The gratuitous agent is not bound to perform, but if the agent begins to perform s/he must not act negligently.

5. **Agency Coupled With an Interest** An **irrevocable** agency in which the principal gives the agent a property (or security) interest in the thing subject to the power of the agency.

Example 1 ▸ Agency Coupled With an Interest

> P agrees with A that if A will lend P $5,000, A shall have a one-half interest in P's property, and A shall have exclusive authority to sell the property, with A's loan to be repaid out of the proceeds. A's agency power is irrevocable.
>
> However, agency coupled with an interest is to be distinguished from a situation in which an agent merely is entitled to receive some of the proceeds or profits from the sale of property. For example, a real estate agent who merely receives a commission from the sale of property does not have an agency coupled with an interest.

6. **Del Credere Agent** A sales agent who promises to pay the principal if the principal's customer fails to pay. If the debt is not paid when due, the principal's action is against the agent. Though the agent guarantees to pay the debt of another, the agent's promise does not come within the Statute of Frauds because the promise is made for her/his own benefit (usually, a higher commission from the principal).

7. **Exclusive Agent** An agent is an exclusive agent if s/he is the only agent a principal will deal with for a particular purpose. For example, a principal who appoints an exclusive real estate agent for the purpose of procuring a buyer for her/his property may not sell to a buyer procured by another agent; however, the principal may sell to a buyer s/he procures without any broker assistance.

8. **Factor** A commercial agent for the sale or other disposition of goods for a commission ("factorage"). The factor is a bailee in possession of goods whose title remains in the principal. Because the factor has the appearance of ownership, the factor may sell the goods in her/

his own name. Furthermore, the factor has the power to convey title to a good faith purchaser for value, and this title transfer is valid as against the principal, even if the conveyance exceeds the factor's authority.

II. Creation

A. Appointment

A principal may appoint an agent. An express agency is created by written or oral agreement between the parties that one shall act for and be subject to the control of the other. An implied agency is created by conduct of the principal that manifests the intention that the agency relationship should exist.

1. **Consideration** Consideration is not necessary.

2. **Writing** The principal may create an agency by a written instrument called a *power of attorney,* authorizing another, the "attorney in fact," to act as her/his agent. Most agency relationships need not be in writing to be valid; however, some are required by statute to be evidenced by a written memorandum. For example, if the agent's duties involve the making of a contract governed by the Statute of Frauds, such as a sale of real property, the agent's authority usually must be in writing. Also, the agreement must be in writing if the agency contract cannot be completed within one year.

3. **Exceptions** One may not appoint an agent to perform certain duties.

    a. Those that the principal is bound to perform personally (nondelegable duties).

    b. Those precluded by statute (for example, the execution of a will).

    c. Those that the principal cannot perform (for example, a minor cannot appoint an agent to convey real estate since s/he can void the conveyance).

B. Ratification (Approval)

Acts performed by one who is not an agent, or unauthorized acts performed by an agent, may be ratified by the principal. A single transaction must be ratified in its entirety or not at all. Ratification may be either express or implied, depending on the circumstances.

1. **Requirements** Ratification requires the following.

    a. An act capable of ratification (for example, a tort may be ratified, but a crime may not be ratified) that is performed on behalf of the principal.

    b. A principal who:

        (1) Has the capacity to appoint the agent.

        (2) Has knowledge of the material facts of the transaction.

        (3) Was in existence at the time the act was done (for example, a corporation cannot ratify the acts of its promoters done before it came into existence; however, it may later adopt those acts).

        (4) Was either a fully or partially disclosed principal. A fully undisclosed principal cannot ratify.

    c. Any formalities that would be required for an appointment.

2. **Timing** If the purported agent contracts with a third party on the principal's behalf, the third party can withdraw at any time prior to ratification. Her/his withdrawal cuts off the principal's

power to ratify. Alternatively, if the principal impairs the third party's rights by waiting too long, the principal also may lose her/his power to ratify.

3. **Effect** After ratification, the parties stand in the same position as if the agent had authority to do the act at the time it was done. The ratification "relates back" to the time the act was performed; thus, it is as if the act were authorized when performed.

    a. The principal cannot charge the agent with exceeding her/his authority nor can the third party hold the agent liable for breach of warranty of authority.

    b. The principal cannot retract her/his ratification.

C. **Operation of Law**
The law may operate so as to create an agency relationship.

1. **Estoppel** Where no actual agency relationship in fact exists, but because the acts of the principal cause a third party to reasonably believe in the existence of the agency, and to reasonably rely on the existence of the agency, the principal is estopped from denying its existence.

2. **Representation, Appearance, or Apparent Authority** A person who represents to a third party that another is her/his agent may be bound to that party by her/his "agent's" actions, whether or not the third party acted in reliance.

3. **Necessity** The law implies an agency in certain situations, such as emergencies.

III. Principal's Liability

A. ***Respondeat Superior***
A maxim that means that a master is liable in certain cases for the wrongful acts of her/his servant, and a principal is liable for the wrongs of her/his agent. Under this doctrine, the master is responsible for want of care on the servant's part toward those to whom the master owes a duty of care, provided the servant's failure to exercise due care occurred during the course of that servant's employment. In other words, the principal is vicariously liable (e.g., liable regardless of whether s/he is at fault) for the torts of an employee agent if they are committed within the scope (actual or apparent) of the agent's employment.

1. **Master & Servant** A servant is one who is in the employ of another (the master). A servant's physical conduct in the performance of her/his work is controlled or is subject to the right of control by the master. The servant has no authority to legally bind the master. *Respondeat superior* is the same for master and servant.

2. **Independent Contractor** An independent contractor is one who contracts to do a particular job for another. An independent contractor is subject to the control or supervision of her/his employer only as to the result; that is, the independent contractor works according to her/his own methods. An independent contractor is not a servant.

3. **Question of Fact** The question of whether the employee committing the tortious act is the principal's agent (or servant) is a question of fact.

4. **Scope of Agent's Employment** The act falls within the scope of the agent's employment if it is the type of act the agent is authorized to perform, if it takes place substantially within the time and place that is authorized, and if it is intended to serve the principal in some way.

    a. Even if the agent violated the principal's instructions in committing the tort, the rule of respondeat superior applies.

    b. However, if the agent or servant departs from the performance of her/his duties and acts on her/his own ("independent journey," "frolic and detour"), the principal is not liable. **Note:** An intentionally tortious act is not likely to be performed within the scope of employment. It usually is for the agent's own benefit.

5. **Liability & Recovery** The agent remains liable for her/his own tort and the injured third person can choose to hold the agent or the agent's principal liable. However, the injured party is entitled to only one recovery.

B. Agent's Crimes

Ordinarily, a principal is not liable for her/his agent's crimes even when they are committed in the course of the agent's employment. A principal cannot ratify crimes of an agent after their commission. A principal is liable if either of the following occurs.

1. **Participation** The principal participated in the crime in some way (e.g., the principal planned, directed, ordered, or acquiesced in its commission).

2. **Statute** If a statute makes the principal liable (e.g., the sale of liquor to minors).

C. Contracts

A material misrepresentation of the facts inducing the third party to enter into the contract may be grounds for her/his rescission.

1. **Disclosed** If the third party dealing with the agent knows of the existence of the agency and the identity of the principal, then contracts made by the agent in the exercise of her/his actual or apparent authority will bind the principal only.

2. **Partially Disclosed** If the third party dealing with the agent knows of the existence of the agency but not the identity of the principal, then contracts made by the agent bind both the agent and the principal.

3. **Undisclosed** If the third party dealing with the agent has no knowledge of either the existence of the agency or the identity of the principal, then contracts made by the agent bind the **agent** only. The undisclosed principal has the right to enforce the contract against the third party, so long as it does not involve personal service, trust, or confidence. Defenses the agent has against the third party that arose from the transaction and are not personal to the agent are available to the principal. The principal takes the contract subject to the following.

    a. Any defenses the third party has arising from the transaction,

    b. Any personal defenses or set-offs the third party has against the principal, and

    c. In cases where it is authorized implicitly, any set-offs the third party has against the agent.

4. **Discovery of Principal** After discovering the identity of the principal, the third party may choose to hold her/him liable for acts either actually or apparently authorized unless:

    a. The contract is a negotiable or sealed instrument.

    b. The agent already has performed.

    c. The third party already has elected to hold the agent liable after discovering the principal's identity.

    d. The contract provides that no undisclosed principal shall be liable.

IV. Agent's Liability to Third Parties

A. Torts

Torts (civil wrongs) conventionally are classified as intentional torts, negligence, or strict liability. One action may be both a crime and a tort, but not all torts involve crimes. An agent is liable to third parties for her/his own torts, even if the agent's principal is also vicariously liable for them. However, the third party is entitled to only one recovery. **Note:** Unless varied by statute, the agent is solely liable for her/his own crimes.

- **Compared to Crime** A crime (offence against society) differs from a tort (offence against a person). Criminal law primarily is concerned with punishment and rehabilitation of criminals; tort remedies focus on compensating the injured person. Most crimes also involve torts. The state prosecutes criminal cases; crimes involve jail sentences and fines. Private persons bring civil actions; torts involve damages.

B. Contracts

1. **Act for Disclosed Principal** An agent who is authorized to act by a disclosed principal is personally liable to third parties if:

    a. The agent contracts in her/his own name (for example, by carelessly signing her/his name to a written contract without indicating her/his representative capacity).

    b. The agent makes her/himself a party to the contract between the principal and the third party.

    c. The agent personally guarantees the principal's performance and the principal does not perform.

    d. The agent signs a negotiable or sealed instrument on which the principal's name does not appear.

2. **Act for Partially Disclosed Principal** When an agent is representing a partially disclosed principal, the agent is liable on contracts for that principal unless both:

    a. The agent and third party agree that the agent is not to be bound.

    b. The identity of the principal is indicated so that it can become known.

3. **Unauthorized Acts** An agent who fails to bind her/his principal because her/his act is unauthorized is generally liable on the contract unless the third party knew of the "agent's" lack of authority.

    a. The agent is liable to a third party for breaching her/his implied warranty of authority. Damages are limited to those that the third party could have recovered from the principal had the agent been bound (for example, if the principal is insolvent, damages obtainable from the agent are nominal).

    b. The agent also may be liable in tort for fraud and deceit.

4. **Act for Nonexistent Principal** A person who purports to contract as an agent for a principal the person knows to be nonexistent or incompetent is liable on the contract so long as the person either:

    a. Knows the third party is ignorant of the nonexistence or incompetence.

    b. Represents to the third party that the principal exists or is competent.

V. Termination

A. Methods

1. Agreement

a. The agency agreement may specify that it will terminate at a particular date, that it will end when an objective is accomplished, or that either party may terminate the relationship at will.

b. The parties mutually may consent to terminate their relationship at any time.

2. **Renunciation** The agent always has the power to renounce the agency; however, the agent may be liable to the principal for breach, unless the principal violated her/his duties or the agency was gratuitous. In most cases, the principal has the power to revoke the agency.

   a. If the principal has given an "agency coupled with an interest," it is irrevocable, (e.g., s/he has neither the right nor the power to revoke).

   b. In all other cases, the principal has the power to revoke, but if the principal has no right to revoke (for example, the principal has contracted not to revoke) the principal will be subject to liability for breach of the agency contract.

   c. If the agent violates her/his duties to the principal, the principal has the right to revoke the agency.

3. **Operation of Law** On the occurrence of certain events, most agencies will terminate by operation of law. A partial list of these events includes the following.

   a. Death or insanity of either party.

   b. Bankruptcy or insolvency of the principal.

   c. Bankruptcy of the agent if it affects the agency relationship.

   d. Illegality or impossibility.

B. Notice

No notice is required if the agency terminates by operation of law. In all other cases, notice must be given. If the principal revokes or the agent renounces, each must notify the other.

1. **Actual** Third parties who have dealt with the agent must be given actual notice; otherwise, if they have no knowledge of the termination, their transactions with the agent still will bind the principal.

2. **Constructive** Third parties who have not previously dealt with the agent may be given constructive notice (for example, by publication).

Boards of Accountancy

Certified Public Accountants are licensed to practice by Boards of Accountancy in 54 jurisdictions. Application forms and requirements to sit for the CPA exam should be requested from your particular board. IT IS EXTREMELY IMPORTANT THAT YOU COMPLETE THE APPLICATION FORM CORRECTLY AND RETURN IT TO YOUR STATE BOARD BEFORE THE SPECIFIED DEADLINE. Errors or delays may result in the rejection of your application. Be extremely careful in filling out the application and be sure to enclose all required materials. In many jurisdictions, applications must be received by the board at least **ninety** days before the examination date. Requirements as to education, experience, internship, and other matters vary. If you have not already done so, take a moment to contact the appropriate board for specific current requirements. Complete the application in a timely manner.

It may be possible to sit for the exam in another state as an out-of-state candidate. Candidates wishing to do so should contact the Board of Accountancy in their home jurisdiction as well as the other jurisdiction.

Approximately one month before the exam, check to see that your application to sit for the exam has been processed. DON'T ASSUME THAT YOU ARE PROPERLY REGISTERED UNLESS YOU HAVE RECEIVED YOUR NOTICE TO SCHEDULE.

The AICPA publishes a booklet entitled, *The Uniform CPA Examination Candidate Bulletin: Information for Applicants,* is usually distributed by Boards of Accountancy to candidates upon receipt of their applications. You may download a copy from the AICPA's exam website, www.cpa-exam.org.

Addresses of State Boards are in the **Practical Advice** section of this volume and on the site of the National Association of the State Boards of Accountancy (http://www.nasba.org).

CHAPTER 39—AGENCY

Problem 39-1 MULTIPLE CHOICE QUESTIONS (30 to 40 minutes)

1. A principal and agent relationship requires a
a. Written agreement
b. Power of attorney
c. Meeting of the minds and consent to act
d. Specified consideration (5/92, Law, #6, 2819)

2. Which of the following statements represent(s) a principal's duty to an agent who works on a commission basis?

I. The principal is required to maintain pertinent records, account to the agent, and pay the agent according to the terms of their agreement.
II. The principal is required to reimburse the agent for all authorized expenses incurred unless the agreement calls for the agent to pay expenses out of the commission.

a. I only
b. II only
c. Both I and II
d. Neither I nor II (5/96, Law, #3, 6259)

3. Under the agent's duty to account, which of the following acts must a gratuitous agent perform?

	Commingle funds	*Account for the principal's property*
a.	Yes	Yes
b.	Yes	No
c.	No	Yes
d.	No	No

(R/05, REG, 0034L, #4, 7850)

4. Blue, a used car dealer, appointed Gage as an agent to sell Blue's cars. Gage was authorized by Blue to appoint subagents to assist in the sale of the cars. Vond was appointed as a sub-agent. To whom does Vond owe a fiduciary duty?
a. Gage only
b. Blue only
c. Both Blue and Gage
d. Neither Blue nor Gage (R/01, Law, #6, 7041)

5. Frost's accountant and business manager has the authority to
a. Mortgage Frost's business property
b. Obtain bank loans for Frost
c. Insure Frost's property against fire loss
d. Sell Frost's business (5/91, Law, #3, 0649)

6. North, Inc. hired Sutter as a purchasing agent. North gave Sutter written authorization to purchase, without limit, electronic appliances. Later, Sutter was told not to purchase more than 300 of each appliance. Sutter contracted with Orr Corp. to purchase 500 tape recorders. Orr had been shown Sutter's written authorization. Which of the following statements is correct?
a. Sutter will be liable to Orr because Sutter's actual authority was exceeded.
b. Sutter will not be liable to reimburse North if North is liable to Orr.
c. North will be liable to Orr because of Sutter's actual and apparent authority.
d. North will not be liable to Orr because Sutter's actual authority was exceeded.
(11/93, Law, #15, 4312)

7. Trent was retained, in writing, to act as Post's agent for the sale of Post's memorabilia collection. Which of the following statements is correct?

I. To be an agent, Trent must be at least 21 years of age.
II. Post would be liable to Trent if the collection was destroyed before Trent found a purchaser.

a. I only
b. II only
c. Both I and II
d. Neither I nor II (5/95, Law, #6, 5340)

8. Noll gives Carr a written power of attorney. Which of the following statements is correct regarding this power of attorney?
a. It must be signed by both Noll and Carr.
b. It must be for a definite period of time.
c. It may continue in existence after Noll's death.
d. It may limit Carr's authority to specific transactions. (11/93, Law, #11, 4308)

9. Which **two** of the following actions requires an agent for a corporation to have a written agency agreement?
a. Purchasing office supplies for the principal's business
b. Purchasing an interest in undeveloped land for the principal
c. Hiring an independent general contractor to renovate the principal's office building
d. Hiring a consultant for an eleven-month contract, with the work to begin three months later
e. Retaining an attorney to collect a business debt owed the principal
(11/94, Law, #16, amended, 5193)

10. Which of the following acts, if committed by an agent, will cause a principal to be liable to a third party?

a. A negligent act committed by an independent contractor, in performance of the contract, which results in injury to a third party
b. An intentional tort committed by an employee outside the scope of employment, which results in injury to a third party
c. An employee's failure to notify the employer of a dangerous condition that results in injury to a third party
d. A negligent act committed by an employee outside the scope of employment that results in injury to a third party

(R/05, REG, 0039L, #2, 7868)

11. Generally, a disclosed principal will be liable to third parties for its agent's unauthorized misrepresentations if the agent is an

	Employee	*Independent Contractor*
a.	Yes	Yes
b.	Yes	No
c.	No	Yes
d.	No	No

(11/93, Law, #13, 4310)

12. An agent will usually be liable under a contract made with a third party when the agent is acting on behalf of a(an)

	Disclosed principal	*Undisclosed principal*
a.	Yes	Yes
b.	Yes	No
c.	No	Yes
d.	No	No

(11/94, Law, #19, 5196)

13. Which of the following statements is(are) correct regarding the relationship between an agent and a nondisclosed principal?

I. The principal is required to indemnify the agent for any contract entered into by the agent within the scope of the agency agreement.
II. The agent has the same actual authority as if the principal had been disclosed.

a. I only
b. II only
c. Both I and II
d. Neither I nor II

(R/99, Law, #4, 6855)

14. Which of the following rights will a third party be entitled to after validly contracting with an agent representing an undisclosed principal?

a. Disclosure of the principal by the agent
b. Ratification of the contract by the principal
c. Performance of the contract by the agent
d. Election to void the contract after disclosure of the principal

(11/93, Law, #14, 4311)

15. When an agent acts for an undisclosed principal, the principal will **not** be liable to third parties if the

a. Principal ratifies a contract entered into by the agent.
b. Agent acts within an implied grant of authority.
c. Agent acts outside the grant of actual authority.
d. Principal seeks to conceal the agency relationship.

(11/91, Law, #12, 2340)

16. When a valid contract is entered into by an agent on the principal's behalf, in a nondisclosed principal situation, which of the following statements concerning the principal's liability is correct?

	The principal may be held liable once disclosed	*The principal must ratify the contract to be held liable*
a.	Yes	Yes
b.	Yes	No
c.	No	Yes
d.	No	No

(5/95, Law, #8, 5342)

17. Which of the following is(are) available to a principal when an agent fraudulently breaches a fiduciary duty?

	Termination of the agency	*Constructive trust*
a.	Yes	Yes
b.	Yes	No
c.	No	Yes
d.	No	No

(R/00, Law, #3, 6968)

18. Pell is the principal and Astor is the agent in an agency coupled with an interest. In the absence of a contractual provision relating to the duration of the agency, who has the right to terminate the agency before the interest has expired?

	Pell	*Astor*
a.	Yes	Yes
b.	No	Yes
c.	No	No
d.	Yes	No

(5/89, Law, #11, 0657)

19. Thorp was a purchasing agent for Ogden, a sole proprietor, and had the express authority to place purchase orders with Ogden's suppliers. Thorp placed an order with Datz, Inc. on Ogden's behalf after Ogden was declared incompetent in a judicial proceeding. Thorp was aware of Ogden's incapacity. Which of the following statements is correct concerning Ogden's liability to Datz?

a. Ogden will be liable because Datz was not informed of Ogden's incapacity.
b. Ogden will be liable because Thorp acted with express authority.
c. Ogden will not be liable because Thorp's agency ended when Ogden was declared incompetent.
d. Ogden will **not** be liable because Ogden was a nondisclosed principal. (5/95, Law, #7, 5341)

20. Bolt Corp. dismissed Ace as its general sales agent and notified all of Ace's known customers by letter. Young Corp., a retail outlet located outside of Ace's previously assigned sales territory, had never dealt with Ace. Young knew of Ace as a result of various business contacts. After his dismissal, Ace sold Young goods, to be delivered by Bolt, and received from Young a cash deposit for 20% of the purchase price. It was not unusual for an agent in Ace's previous position to receive cash deposits. In an action by Young against Bolt on the sales contract, Young will

a. Lose, because Ace lacked any implied authority to make the contract
b. Lose, because Ace lacked any express authority to make the contract
c. Win, because Bolt's notice was inadequate to terminate Ace's apparent authority
d. Win, because a principal is an insurer of an agent's acts (11/94, Law, #17, 5194)

Problem 39-2 ADDITIONAL MULTIPLE CHOICE QUESTIONS (9 to 12 minutes)

21. Young Corp. hired Wilson as a sales representative for six months at a salary of $5,000 per month plus 6% of sales. Which of the following statements is correct?
a. Young does **not** have the power to dismiss Wilson during the six-month period without cause.
b. Wilson is obligated to act solely in Young's interest in matters concerning Young's business.
c. The agreement between Young and Wilson is not enforceable unless it is in writing and signed by Wilson.
d. The agreement between Young and Wilson formed an agency coupled with an interest.
(5/95, Law, #9, 5343)

22. Pine, an employee of Global Messenger Co., was hired to deliver highly secret corporate documents for Global's clients throughout the world. Unknown to Global, Pine carried a concealed pistol. While Pine was making a delivery, he suspected an attempt was being made to steal the package, drew his gun and shot Kent, an innocent passerby. Kent will **not** recover damages from Global if
a. Global discovered that Pine carried a weapon and did nothing about it.
b. Global instructed its messengers not to carry weapons.
c. Pine was correct and an attempt was being made to steal the package.
d. Pine's weapon was unlicensed and illegal.
(5/90, Law, #2, 0651)

23. A principal will **not** be liable to a third party for a tort committed by an agent
a. Unless the principal instructed the agent to commit the tort
b. Unless the tort was committed within the scope of the agency relationship
c. If the agency agreement limits the principal's liability for the agent's tort
d. If the tort is also regarded as a criminal act
(11/89, Law, #2, 0655)

24. Part agreed to act as Young's agent to sell Young's land. Part was instructed to disclose that Part was acting as an agent but not to disclose Young's identity. Part contracted with Rice for Rice to purchase the land. After Rice discovered Young's identity, Young refused to fulfill the contract. Who does Rice have a cause of action against?

	Part	*Young*
a.	Yes	Yes
b.	Yes	No
c.	No	Yes
d.	No	No

(R/06, REG, 0927L, #24, 8194)

25. Able, as agent for Baker, an undisclosed principal, contracted with Safe to purchase an antique car. In payment, Able issued his personal check to Safe. Able could not cover the check but expected Baker to give him cash to deposit before the check was presented for payment. Baker did not do so and the check was dishonored. Baker's identity became known to Safe. Safe may **not** recover from
a. Baker individually on the contract
b. Able individually on the contract
c. Baker individually on the check
d. Able individually on the check
(5/90, Law, #4, 0653)

26. Generally, an agency relationship is terminated by operation of law in all of the following situations **except** the
a. Principal's death
b. Principal's incapacity
c. Agent's renunciation of the agency
d. Agent's failure to acquire a necessary business license
(5/90, Law, #1, 0650)

SIMULATION

Problem 39-3 (20 to 30 minutes)

Place Corporation orally contracted with Alto, an independent consultant, for Alto to work part-time as Place's agent to perform Place's customers' service calls. Alto, a computer programmer and software designer, was authorized to customize Place's software to the customers' needs, on a commission basis, but was specifically told not to sell Place's computers.

On September 15, Alto made a service call on Teal Co. to repair Teal's computer. Alto previously had called on Teal, customized Place's software for Teal, and collected cash payments for the work performed. During the call, Alto convinced Teal to buy an upgraded Place computer for a price much lower than Place normally would charge. Teal previously had purchased computers from other Place agents and had made substantial cash down payments to the agents. Teal had no knowledge that the price was lower than normal. Alto received a $1,000 cash down payment and promised to deliver the computer the next week. Alto never turned in the down payment and left town. When Teal called the following week to have the computer delivered, Place refused to honor Teal's order.

(Editors, 5930)

For items 1 through 10, indicate whether the statements are true (T) or false (F).

Statements		Answer
1.	Place's agreement with Alto had to be in writing for it to be a valid agency agreement.	
2.	Place's agreement with Alto empowered Alto to act as Place's agent.	
3.	Teal was entitled to rely on Alto's implied authority to customize Place's software.	
4.	Teal was entitled to rely on Alto's express authority when buying the computer.	
5.	Place's agreement with Alto was automatically terminated by Alto's sale of the computer.	
6.	Place must notify Teal before Alto's apparent authority to bind Place will cease.	
7.	Place is not bound by the agreement made by Alto with Teal.	
8.	Place may unilaterally amend the agreement made by Alto to prevent a loss on the sale of the computer to Teal.	
9.	Place, as a disclosed principal, is solely contractually liable to Teal.	
10.	Both Place and Alto are contractually liable to Teal.	

Peep & Prior Partnership appointed Ed Gingko as its agent to market its various product lines. Gingko entered into a two-year written agency contract with the partnership which provided that Gingko would receive a 10% sales commission. The agency contract was signed by Gingko and, on behalf of the partnership, by Peep and Prior.

After six months, Gingko was terminated without cause. Gingko asserts that:

- He is an agent coupled with an interest.
- The agency relationship may not be terminated without cause prior to the expiration of its term.
- He is entitled to damages because of the termination of the agency relationship.

Write a memo to your supervisor discussing the merits of Gingko's assertions, setting forth reasons for your conclusions.

Research Question: What code section and subsection, if applicable, provides guidance as to the classification of payments made to a partner for services determined without regard to partnership income as made to one who is not a member of the partnership for determining trade or business expenses?

Section & Subsection Answer: §_____ (___)

Solution 39-1 MULTIPLE CHOICE ANSWERS

Nature

1. (c) Agency is a consensual relationship whereby one person, the agent, agrees to act on behalf of another, the principal. Generally, the agency need not be in writing (exceptions are the sale of real property or the appointment of an agent for more than one year). A power of attorney (a written authorization to act) is not necessary. A specified consideration is not always necessary (for example, in the case of a gratuitous agent).

2. (c) Included in the duties that the principal owes the agent are to compensate the agent for services rendered, either according to their agreement or, if there is no agreement, in an amount that reasonably reflects the value of the services; and to reimburse the agent for reasonable expenses incurred in the course of the agency.

3. (c) An agent must account for any property the agent receives through the agency. An agent may not commingle the agent's own funds with those of the principal.

4. (c) An agent owes a duty to her/his principal. The appointing agent is a like a "sub-principal" to a sub agent.

5. (c) The accountant and business manager has authority to do "normal" or "reasonable" business activities. Insuring property against fire loss is the activity that would be the most "reasonable" for a business manager to perform. The others all involve activities that would not generally happen within "normal" business activities. An agent would not have the apparent authority to mortgage the business property, obtain bank loans, or sell the business. In those situations, he would need specific authorization.

6. (c) Sutter had actual authority to purchase 300 of the tape recorders. Sutter also had apparent authority due to the fact that the third party, Orr, was aware of the written authorization giving Sutter unlimited power to purchase electronic appliances.

However, Orr was not informed that this authority had been revoked by North. Therefore, the apparent authority of Sutter existed with respect to Orr. This combination of actual and apparent authority effectively bound North to the contract and makes North liable to Orr. Sutter would be liable for breaching the implied warranty of authority. An agent with apparent authority can bind a principal and third party to a contract even though s/he has exceeded her/his actual authority. Therefore, both North and Sutter would be liable to the third party on the contract, but the best answer is (c) because the third party would be more likely to pursue the party with more assets, usually the principal. If losses to the principal result, the principal can hold the agent liable for exceeding her/his actual authority. North will be held liable to Orr due to the fact that Sutter's apparent authority does bind North to contract.

Creation & Capacity

7. (d) In order to be an agent, a person need not possess legal capacity to contract because contracts properly negotiated as an agent will not personally bind the agent. Impossibility of performance would terminate the agency relationship by operation of law and releases Post from any liability to Kent. Thus, neither of the statements is correct.

8. (d) A power of attorney may be either "special" or "general" in nature. A "special" power of attorney permits the agent to do specified acts only. Therefore, a power of attorney can be written in such a way as to limit Carr's authority to specific transactions. A power of attorney is effective when signed by the person transferring power. A power of attorney may be established for a period of indefinite duration. A power of attorney expires upon the death of the person transferring power.

9. (b, d) Both answers are required for full point value. It is generally not necessary for an agent to have a written agency agreement. An exception to the general rule exists if the agent's duties will involve the buying and selling of real property or if the agency agreement is to last more than one year.

Liability

10. (c) Under the respondeat superior doctrine, a principal is liable for the wrongs of the agent. An employee acting within the scope of employment is an agent of the employer. An independent contractor is not an agent. If an employee commits an action outside of the scope of employment, then the employer generally is not liable.

11. (b) As a general rule, an independent contractor is hired to accomplish a specific task and is not subject to the supervision and control of the principal. Thus, generally, a principal is not liable for the misrepresentations of the independent contractor. On the other hand, the employee is subject to the supervision and control of the employer. In general, principals are liable for the misrepresentations of their employees.

Undisclosed Principal

12. (c) An agent will not usually be liable under a contract made with a third party if the principal is disclosed and if the agent acts within the scope of her/his agency. Agents for undisclosed principals always have contract liability.

13. (c) The relationship between the principal and the agent is the same disclosed or undisclosed. The principal has the duty to indemnify the agent for acts performed at the principal's direction. The agent has the same actual authority as if the principal had been disclosed.

14. (c) When neither the agency relationship nor the identity of the principal is disclosed, a third party is deemed to be dealing with the agent personally, and the agent is liable as a party to the contract. A third party is not entitled to disclosure of the principal or ratification by the principal. A third party may not elect to void the contract after disclosure of the principal.

15. (c) Actual authority is that power consented to by the principal which affects the principal's legal relations. If a third party dealing with an agent has no knowledge of either the existence of the agency or the identity of an undisclosed principal, then contracts made by the agent bind the agent only, and the principal will not be liable.

16. (b) When an agent enters into a contract on behalf of a nondisclosed principal, the agent may be held liable on the contract. If the agent acted with authority, the principal may also be held liable upon disclosure. It is not necessary for a principal to ratify a contract in order to be held liable.

Termination

17. (a) If the agent violates her/his fiduciary duties to the principal, the principal has the right and the power to revoke (terminate) the agency. In addition, the courts will impose a constructive trust treating any property held by the agent to be held as a trustee for the principal. A constructive trust in this case is a remedy in the form of a trust created by operation of law to prevent unjust enrichment. A constructive trust is imposed whenever the court establishes that the agent who acquired title to property is obligated to transfer it back to the principal

because the acquisition was by breach of a fiduciary duty.

18. (b) The general rule is that a principal always has the power to terminate an agency but not necessarily the right. The only exception is where the agency is coupled with an interest. In this situation the principal has neither the power nor the right to terminate the agency. The agent, however, can terminate the agency as it is the agent's interest that the law seeks to protect. If the agent wishes to waive such interest, the agent is free to do so.

19. (c) A declaration of incompetency terminates the agency relationship by operation of law. Notice to third parties is not required when the agency terminates by operation of law. Odgen will not be liable because Thorp's authority ended upon the declaration of incompetency. The agent would be liable on the contract since an agent guarantees the principal's capacity to enter into the contract.

20. (c) Where an agency relationship terminates for any reason other than by operation of law, the principal must give actual notice of the termination to all third parties who have previously dealt with the agent and constructive notice to all other parties to terminate the agent's apparent authority. Since Bolt did not give constructive notice, and since Young had no knowledge of the termination, Young will be able to hold Bolt liable for the Ace contract. It is irrelevant that Ace lacked any express or implied authority since apparent authority to act was still present.

Solution 39-2 ADDITIONAL MULTIPLE CHOICE ANSWERS

Nature

21. (b) An agent's duties to a principal include an obligation to act solely in the principal's interest in matters concerning the principal's business. Unless there is an agency coupled with an interest, the principal has the power to terminate the agency relationship, although the principal may not have the right to do so. The Statute of Frauds does not apply to the agreement between Young and Wilson, since the contract was for less than one year. Thus, their oral agreement is enforceable. An agency coupled with an interest results when the principal gives the agent a property or security interest in the subject matter of the agency. The paying of a commission does not create a property or security interest.

Liability

22. (d) Tort liability under respondeat superior arises when the agent is acting within the scope of her/his employment. Conduct was motivated by service to the principal. Thus, only if Pine's weapon was unlicensed and illegal is Global not liable.

23. (b) The general rule is that the principal is vicariously liable for the torts of her/his agent if the tort is committed within the scope of the employment (the doctrine of respondeat superior). The principal is generally liable whether the principal instructed the agent to commit the tort or not. A limitation of liability in an agency agreement has no bearing on the right of the third party to sue the principal. It is possible for a principal to be liable for a tort that is also a criminal act (for example, where the principal instructs the agent to injure a customer if the customer does not pay).

Undisclosed Principal

24. (a) When an agent is representing a partially disclosed principal, the contract generally binds both the principal and agent. After discovering the identify of the principal, the third party may choose to hold the principal liable.

25. (c) Not being a signatory to the check, Baker cannot be held liable on it. As the check's drawer, Able can be held liable on the check. The third party can elect to hold either the agent or the principal liable when the agent makes a contract.

Termination

26. (c) The agent's renunciation of the agency does not automatically terminate by operation of law. The other answers listed do terminate an agency.

PERFORMANCE BY SUBTOPICS

Each category below parallels a subtopic covered in Chapter 39. Record the number and percentage of questions you correctly answered in each subtopic area.

Nature

Question #	Correct √
1	
2	
3	
4	
5	
6	
# Questions	6
# Correct	______
% Correct	______

Creation & Capacity

Question #	Correct √
7	
8	
9	
# Questions	3
# Correct	______
% Correct	______

Liability

Question #	Correct √
10	
11	
# Questions	2
# Correct	______
% Correct	______

Undisclosed Principal

Question #	Correct √
12	
13	
14	
15	
16	
# Questions	5
# Correct	______
% Correct	______

Termination

Question #	Correct √
17	
18	
19	
20	
# Questions	4
# Correct	______
% Correct	______

SIMULATION SOLUTION

Solution 39-3 Agency

Statements (4 points)

1. F

The only element necessary to create a valid agency relationship is mutual consent. A writing is necessary only if the Statute of Frauds applies. As the Statute of Frauds does not apply in this situation, the oral agreement is valid.

2. T

The agreement empowered Alto to act as Place's agent.

3. T

Teal was entitled to rely on Alto's implied authority to customize Place's software since Alto previously performed such services on Place's behalf for Teal.

4. F

Teal was not entitled to rely on Alto's express authority to sell computers, as it did not exist.

5. F

An agent's relationship with the principal is not terminated automatically by the agent's violation of her/his express authority. The principal must take action to terminate the agency relationship.

6. T

To terminate an agent's apparent authority, the principal must give actual notice to all third parties who have dealt with the agent previously and constructive notice to others. Thus, Place must notify Teal to terminate Alto's apparent authority.

7. F

Alto had apparent authority to sell Place's computers because of Alto's similarity to Place's other agents. Place is bound by the contract.

8. F

Although a principal may ratify an agent's unauthorized acts, ratification requires that the principal accept the contract as negotiated. A principal cannot amend an agreement unilaterally.

9. T

Place, a disclosed principal, is liable to Teal since Alto had apparent authority to sell the computer. Alto is not contractually liable to Teal, as Alto was the apparent agent for a disclosed principal.

10. F

Alto is not contractually liable to Teal, as Alto was the apparent agent for a disclosed principal.

Written Communication (5 points)

To: A. Supervisor
From: A. Junior
Re: Gingko's Assertions Against Peep & Prior Partnership

Gingko's first assertion that he is an agent coupled with an interest is incorrect. An agency coupled with an interest in the subject matter arises when the **agent** has an **interest** in the **property** that is the **subject** of the agency. The fact that Gingko entered into a two-year written agency agreement with the partnership that would pay Gingko a commission clearly will not establish an interest in the subject matter of the agency. The mere **expectation of profits to be realized** or proceeds to be derived from the sale of the partnership's products is **not sufficient** to create an agency coupled with an interest. As a result, the principal-agency relationship may be terminated at any time.

Gingko's second assertion that the principal-agency relationship may not be terminated without cause prior to the expiration of its term is incorrect. When a principal-agency relationship is **based** upon a **contract** to engage the agent for a **specified period** of time, the principal may **discharge** the agent despite the fact such discharge is **wrongful**. Although the principal does not have the **right** to discharge the agent, he does have the **power** to do so. Thus, Gingko may be discharged without cause.

Gingko's third assertion that he is entitled to damages because of the termination of the agency relationship is correct. When a principal **wrongfully discharges** its agent, the principal is **liable** for **damages** based on **breach of contract**. Under the facts, Gingko's discharge by the partnership without cause constitutes a breach of contract for which Gingko may **recover** damages.

Research (1 point)

IRC Section Answer: §707(c)

The Internal Revenue Code §707(c) states, "GUARANTEED PAYMENTS.—To the extent determined without regard to the income of the partnership, payments to a partner for services or the use of capital shall be considered as made to one who is not a member of the partnership, but only for the purposes of section 61(a) (relating to gross income) and, subject to section 263, for purposes of section 162(a) (relating to trade or business expenses)."

Question Reference Numbers

This page is included due to questions editors have received from some candidates using previous editions; however, it is not essential for your review.

In the lower right-hand corner of a multiple choice question, you may note a question reference. This reference is included primarily so that editors may trace a question to its source and readily track it from one edition to another and from one media to another.

The reference indicates the source of the question and, possibly, a similar question in the software. For instance, a question with reference 11/93, Aud., #4, 4241, was question number 4 from the November 1993 AICPA Auditing & Attestation examination. When the reference has an "R" instead of 5 or 11, the AICPA released the question from a "nondisclosed" exam without specifying the exam month. Questions marked "Editors" are questions that are modeled after AICPA questions, but are not actually from the examiners. The examiners occasionally move topics from one exam section to another. You may see a question from a former AUD exam, for instance, in the REG or BEC volume. The following abbreviations indicate former exam section titles.

BLPR	Business Law & Professional Responsibilities	AR	Accounting & Reporting
BL	Business Law	PI	Accounting Practice, Part I
T	Accounting Theory	PII	Accounting Practice, Part II

At first glance, candidates may assume that very early questions are irrelevant for preparation for upcoming exams. Provided that they are updated appropriately, many early questions are excellent choices for review questions. When the exam was fully disclosed, editors noted that it was **more** likely that questions from early exams would reappear than questions from relatively recent exams. For instance, on a 1994 exam, it was more likely than an updated question from a 1988 exam would appear than an updated question from a 1993 exam. Second-guessing what questions the examiners will ask typically is more difficult and less reliable than merely learning the content eligible to be tested on the exam.

The four-digit number in these references often corresponds to a four-digit ID number in our software and online courses. Sometimes questions are removed from the software but not the book (and *vice versa*), so a question in the book is not necessarily in the software. Also, questions may vary slightly between the book and software. The four-digit number has no significance for a candidate who is not using our software. If you need help finding a question from the book in the software using this four-digit ID number, please contact our technical support staff at support@cpaexam.com or 1-800-742-1309 and ask them to explain using the "jump" feature for questions.

More helpful exam information is included in the **Practical Advice** appendix in this volume.

CHAPTER 40

FEDERAL SECURITIES REGULATION

EXAM COVERAGE: The business law portion of the Regulation section of the CPA exam is designated by the examiners to be 20-25 percent of the section's point value. More information about point distribution and information eligible to be tested is included in the **Practical Advice** section of this volume.

CHAPTER 40

FEDERAL SECURITIES REGULATION

I. Overview

A. Definitions

1. **Security** The statutory definition includes conventional securities such as stocks, bonds, or notes and any interest or instrument commonly known as a "security." It also includes any certificate or interest or participation in, temporary or interim certificate for, receipt for, guarantee of, or warrant or right to subscribe to or purchase, any of the foregoing. Courts have defined a security as requiring (1) an investment in (2) a common enterprise (3) premised on a reasonable expectation of profits (4) to be derived from the managerial efforts of others. A limited partnership interest generally is treated as a security because limited partners are not involved in management. A general partnership interest usually is not treated as a security because of management involvement. Whether a limited liability company (LLC) interest is treated as a security is dependent upon the management rights of the members. If all members are not given the opportunity to be involved in management, the LLC interest is more likely to be treated as a security.

2. **Equity Security** Any stock or similar security, or any security convertible into such a security, or carrying any warrant or right to subscribe to or purchase such warrant or right, or any security that the SEC shall prescribe to treat as an equity security.

3. **Sale or Sell** Includes every contract of sale or disposition of a security for value. The terms offer to sell or offer to buy shall include every offer to dispose of or purchase, or any solicitation of an offer to buy or sell, a security or interest in a security. These terms do not include preliminary negotiations or agreements between an issuer and any underwriter or among underwriters who are to be in privity of contract with an issuer.

4. **Person** An individual, a corporation, a partnership, an association, etc.

5. **Dealer** Any person who engages either for all or part of her/his time, directly or indirectly, as agent, broker, or principal in the business of offering, buying, selling, or otherwise dealing or trading in securities issued by another.

6. **Underwriter** Any person who has purchased from an issuer with a view to, or offers or sells for an issuer in connection with, the distribution of any security, or who participates in such undertaking. An underwriter does not include a person whose interest is limited to a commission from an underwriter or a dealer not in excess of the usual and customary distributor's or seller's commission.

7. **Issuer** Every person who issues or proposes to issue any security. For the purposes of registration, controlling persons are considered to be issuers. Thus, controlling persons who make secondary offerings are issuers.

8. **Controlling Person** Any person directly or indirectly controlling the issuer or under direct or indirect common control with the issuer. Factors indicating control are the following: stock ownership and actual or practical control ("control" is construed broadly and includes any person capable of influencing the management or policies of the issuer). Thus, a 5%-or-less owner who is an officer or director could be a controlling person.

9. **Insider** Directors and officers of the issuer and every person who is directly or indirectly the beneficial owner of more than 10% of any class of an equity security that is registered pursuant to the 1934 Act.

10. **Beneficial Ownership** A holder of securities, in the name of her/his spouse and minor children; in a trust in which the insider or any member of her/his family has an interest in either the corpus or income; or in a trust created by an insider and over which s/he has retained a power to revoke, when that trust contains 20% or more of a security subject to reporting requirements.

11. **Interstate Commerce** Trade or commerce in securities or any transportation or communication relating thereto among or between the states and territories of the United States, or between those states and territories and foreign countries.

12. **Prospectus** Any notice, circular, advertisement, letter, or any communication written or broadcast, which offers any security for sale or confirms the sale of any security. Note the following exceptions.

    a. A communication sent after the effective date of the registration statement shall not be deemed a prospectus if a written prospectus has been previously or is being contemporaneously provided to the person to whom the communication was made.

    b. A notice, circular, advertisement, letter, or communication shall not be deemed a prospectus if it states from whom a written prospectus may be obtained and, in addition, does no more than identify the security, state the price thereof, state by whom offers will be executed, and contain other information deemed appropriate by the SEC.

13. **Registration Statement** The disclosure document required to be filed by the 1933 Act in connection with a registered offering. It includes any amendment thereto and any report, document, or memorandum filed as part of such statement or incorporated therein by reference.

14. **Shelf Registration** An established issuer may file a registration statement and hold the securities until an opportune time to offer them arises. The statement must be updated continuously.

B. Securities & Exchange Commission (SEC)

The SEC was created by the 1934 Act to administer all federal security law, which includes those provided in both the 1933 and 1934 Acts as well as the Public Utility Holding Company Act of 1935, the Trust Indenture Act of 1939, the Investment Company Act of 1940, and the Investment Advisor Act of 1940. The SEC is composed of five commissioners appointed by the President. No more than three of the commissioners may be of the same political party. The SEC is an independent agency.

1. **Rulemaking** Under the 1933 and 1934 Acts, Congress has vested the SEC with the power to enact rules to construe and implement the law contained in those Acts. The SEC must publish these proposed rules, solicit comments, and in rare instances conduct public hearings before finalizing these rules. However, once finalized, the rules have the force and effect of law.

2. **Administrative Interpretations** The SEC may issue formal and informal opinions construing and interpreting the Acts as applied to proposed actions by natural persons and entities.

3. **Investigations** The SEC has broad subpoena powers that enable it to investigate practices within the securities market. In order to investigate potential violations, the SEC holds quasi-judicial proceedings to determine compliance with the Acts and the rules that it administers. All such rulings are subject to judicial review.

a. The SEC may suspend or revoke the registration of persons, exchanges, or securities, as required by the 1933 and 1934 Acts.

b. The SEC may seek preliminary and final injunctions in order to prevent violations of the Acts or rules.

c. In appropriate circumstances, the SEC may institute criminal proceedings against violators of the Acts. These proceedings are tried in the Federal District Court and may result in imprisonment and/or fines.

C. Independence Standards Board

After the SEC revised independence rules that apply to auditors of SEC-registered companies in 2001, the ISB was dissolved. Three ISB pronouncements remain in effect; however, only two are within the scope of the CPA exam.

D. State "Blue Sky" Laws

In addition to federal securities regulation, most states have their own laws regulating the offer and sale of securities in their state. These laws are often called "blue sky" laws. These laws typically regulate the offer and sale of securities within the geographical borders of the state and/or to residents of the state. Issuers must comply with both the state and the SEC. Furthermore, exemptions from federal laws are not exemptions from state laws.

II. Securities Act of 1933

A. Purpose

The 1933 Act is intended to provide the interested public with the information necessary to evaluate the merits of various securities being offered and to protect the potential investor from fraudulent acts, misleading statements, or omissions by the selling party. The 1933 Act is concerned with the original issuance of securities intended for sale to the public, provided the transaction or any communication relating thereto involves interstate commerce.

1. **Prohibitions** The 1933 Act makes it unlawful for any person, directly or indirectly, to make use of any means or instruments of interstate commerce or the mails to do the following.

   a. **Registration** Sell, carry, or transmit for the purpose of sale any security, unless a registration statement is *in effect* as to such security. It is unlawful to offer to sell or buy any security, unless a registration statement has been *filed* as to such security, or while the registration statement is subject to a refusal order or stop order.

   b. **Prospectus** Carry or transmit for the purpose of sale any security, unless such security is accompanied or preceded by a prospectus that meets the requirements of the Act.

   c. **Fraud** Employ any fraudulent schemes or devices, make any misstatement of a material fact, or omit any material facts so as to defraud a purchaser. This provision covers all securities, whether or not registration of such securities is required.

2. **Violations** The 1933 Act provides for civil liabilities for failure to meet the registration and/or prospectus requirements of the Act. The Act also provides for a variety of administrative proceedings for violations of any rule or regulation promulgated by the SEC. Included in these administrative proceedings are stop orders, injunctions, and criminal sanctions for violation of any rule or regulation promulgated by the SEC. Liability extends to the underwriters, issuers, directors, partners, and all experts (including accountants) who have prepared or certified any part of the registration statement.

3. **Compliance** Under the 1933 Act, the SEC is empowered to seek writs of mandamus commanding any person to comply with the provisions of the Act or any rules promulgated under the Act.

B. Fraudulent Conveyances

The 1933 Act generally prohibits the use of fraud by any person who offers or sells a security in interstate commerce. This prohibition applies to all securities, whether or not those securities must be registered. The Act specifically prohibits (1) the use of any device, scheme, or artifice to defraud; (2) the obtaining of money or property by means of an untrue statement of material fact or by an omission of a material fact; and (3) the engaging in any transaction or practice that would operate as a fraud or deceit on the purchaser.

C. Exempt Securities

The 1933 Act exempts certain types of securities from its registration requirements. Such securities may be sold and resold any number of times and never be subject to the registration and/or prospectus requirements of the Act. These exemptions are granted because (1) it is felt that registration is not necessary to protect the public interest, (2) the securities are regulated by another government agency, or (3) the nature of the security (for example, commercial paper) necessitates that it be exempt. So-called "exempt" securities still are subject to the anti-fraud provisions of the Act. The following are exempt securities.

1. **Governmental Purposes** Securities issued for governmental purposes by federal, state, territorial, and local governments or by any entities acting as instrumentalities of the government, such as banks, carriers, building and loan associations, and farm cooperatives. (Securities of public utilities are not exempt.)

2. **Not for Profit** Securities of nonprofit, religious, educational, or charitable organizations.

3. **Intrastate Offering Exemption** Any security that is part of an issue offered and sold only to persons within a single state by an issuer resident (or incorporated) and doing business within that same state. A violation of these rules voids the intrastate exemption for the entire issue.

   a. The issuer of the security must be organized and "doing business" (e.g., 80% of its gross revenue must be derived from operations in that state, and 80% of the sale proceeds must be used in connection with its business operations in that state) in the same state of residence as all offerees and purchasers.

   b. All offers and sales must be limited to residents of the state in which the issuer is organized and doing business.

   c. Resales of the issue may be made only to residents of the issuer's state of residence for nine months following the last sale by the issuer.

4. **Insurance Products** Insurance policies or conventional variable annuity contracts subject to other governmental supervision.

5. **No-Sale Transactions** Any security exchanged by the issuer with its existing security holders exclusively where no commission or other remuneration is given. For example, stock splits or any security offered partly in exchange and partly for cash where such transaction is approved by the appropriate government agency.

6. **Short-Term Paper** Commercial paper, such as checks, notes, and bills of exchange, arising out of current transactions or the proceeds of which have been or are to be used for current transactions, which have a maturity date not exceeding 9 months.

7. **Small Issues (Regulation A)** Securities that are part of an issue not exceeding $5 million when registration is not necessary to protect the public interest. These securities must be issued in accordance with SEC Regulation A. "Reg. A," promulgated pursuant to Section 3 of the 1933 Act, is a less restrictive method of registration than is a full registration under Section 5 of the 1933 Act. Under "Reg. A," sales must be made using an "offering circular" rather than a prospectus. "Reg. A" permits an issuer to offer up to $5 million of securities in any 12-month period without Section 5 registration if the issuer files a notification and offering circular with the SEC regional office. Each purchaser must be supplied with an offering

circular. Securities issued under "Reg. A" are not "restricted." Thus, they may be traded freely after sale.

8. **Court Controlled** Securities offered in any reorganization subject to court control (e.g., bankruptcy).

9. **SBI Act** Securities issued by an investment company under the Small Business Investment Act of 1958 when it finds that registration is not necessary to protect the public interest.

10. **Grandfather Clause** Any security sold prior to or within 60 days after May 27, 1933, the date of enactment of the 1933 Act.

D. Exempt Transactions

The Act exempts certain transactions from its registration requirements. When only the particular transaction is exempt, a resale of the same security may not be exempt from the Act's registration and prospectus requirements. This is in contrast to exempt securities which are exempt for all transactions. The scope of the transaction exemptions is very broad, allowing the vast majority of security sales by investors to take place without any registration. It is important to keep in mind that the anti-fraud provisions of the 1933 and 1934 Acts are applicable in every case. The following is a list of the major exempted transactions.

1. **Certain Transactions by Any Person Other Than an Issuer, Underwriter, or Dealer Under Section 4(1) of the 1933 Act** The term "underwriter" includes (a) a controlling person who sells on behalf of the issuer, (b) in many instances lenders who sell securities that have been pledged by a control person, and (c) persons who purchase from a controlling person for the purpose of distribution or who sell or offer for sale securities in connection with a distribution.

2. **Regulation D, Private Offerings** Public and nonpublic companies issuing certain private offerings are exempt from registration. The SEC must be notified within 15 days of the first sale of securities in an offering.

   a. **Rule 504** Rule 504 permits nonpublic companies not registered under the 1934 Act (usually closely held companies) to offer securities for sale without fulfilling the Section 5 (1933 Act) registration and disclosure requirements.

      (1) **Limit** The exemption extends to offerings of securities up to $1 million in a 12-month period.

      (2) **Notice** General solicitations and advertising are permitted only under certain conditions. In state(s) that allow solicitation, the offering may be made only to accredited investors unless the state requires substantive disclosure and such disclosure is made to all purchasers.

      (3) **Resale** Resale within the first two years is permitted only under certain conditions. In states that allow such resale, the offering may be made only to accredited investors unless the state requires substantive disclosure.

   b. **Rule 505** Rule 505 permits nonpublic and public companies to offer, without fulfilling the Section 5 (1933 Act) registration requirements, up to $5 million in a 12-month period.

      (1) **Purchasers** Sales can be made to up to 35 "nonaccredited purchasers" and an unlimited number of "accredited investors." The issuer must "reasonably believe" that there are no more than 35 nonaccredited purchasers. (In counting this number, related persons are excluded.) "Accredited investors" include institutional investors, any executive of the issuer, and an individual with a net worth or annual income figure in excess of certain levels.

(2) **Information** Rule 505 requires that certain information be provided to offerees if there are any nonaccredited purchases within the offering group. Included among the required information are a set of audited financial statements for the most recent year or, if a public issuer, its most recent shareholder's annual report or the most recent Form 10-K or Form S-1.

(3) **Notice** No general advertising or solicitation may be used to offer or sell the securities involved in Rule 505. "General advertising or solicitation" is defined to include any advertisement or notice by any medium.

(4) **Motive** The issuer must exercise reasonable care to ensure that purchasers are not underwriters under Rules 505 and 506. Thus, there must be reasonable inquiry into the motive for purchase (e.g., must not be for resale), and there must be a disclosure made to each purchaser to the effect that the securities have not been registered for public sale as required by Section 5 of the 1933 Act.

(5) **Resale** The issuer must place a legend on each certificate indicating the restrictions on transferability and resale.

c. **Rule 506** Rule 506 permits nonpublic and public companies to raise, without full Section 5 (1933 Act) registration, an **unlimited amount** of money from an unlimited number of "accredited purchasers" and 35 "nonaccredited investors."

(1) **Purchasers** Under Rule 506, there are no specific net worth requirements beyond the "accredited purchaser" tests; accredited purchasers are assumed to be sophisticated. The issuer must reasonably believe that each nonaccredited purchaser "has such knowledge and...financial experience as to be capable of evaluating the offering's merits and risks..."

(2) **Information** The nonpublic and public issuer must provide offerees with the same information as is required in Rule 505.

(3) **Notice** No general advertising or solicitation may be used to offer or sell the securities involved in Rule 506.

(4) **Resale** The securities may not be purchased for immediate resale and a legend must be placed on each certificate indicating the restrictions on transferability and resale.

Exhibit 1 ▸ Regulation D Exemptions

	Rule 504	Rule 505	Rule 506
Amount	Up to $1 million	Up to $5 million	Unlimited
Time	Within 12 months	Within 12 months	No time limit
Investors:			
Accredited	Any number	Unlimited	Unlimited
Unaccredited	Any number	35 or less	35 or less (sophisticated)
Disclosure	None required, unless general solicitation is used	If unaccredited, then must disclose to include *audited financial statements*	Same as Rule 505
General Solicitation	Permitted with limitations	Not permitted	Same as Rule 505
Resale Within First 2 years	Under certain conditions	Must hold 2 or more years (long-term investment)	Same as Rule 505

3. **Private Offerings Under Section 4(2) of the 1933 Act** The issuer must demonstrate that the potential offerees and purchasers are sufficiently sophisticated so that they do not need the protection of the Act. Pursuant to showing that the offerees are sophisticated, the issuer must demonstrate that information sufficient to allow for an intelligent appraisal is readily available to the offerees. Certain courts have required that this information actually be placed into the hands of the purchasers. Other important factors that have been considered by the courts include the following.

   a. The number and diversity of the potential investors.

   b. The amount of the offering and the extent to which the securities are readily marketable (for example, when a large number of securities are offered in small denominations, it is more likely that the intent is to distribute to the public at large).

   c. The manner of the offering and whether or not advertising was used.

   d. The purpose for which the securities are purchased. When they are resold quickly rather than retained as an investment, the presumption is that the original sale was public.

4. **Certain Post-Distribution Transactions by Dealer** When the dealer is not participating in the original distribution and the issuing company is filing periodic reports with the SEC pursuant to the 1934 Act, the prospectus requirements do not apply to the dealer. This exemption for dealers is available only after the distribution period has ended.

   a. **Distribution Period**

      (1) **Old Companies** When the securities being offered are by a company that has previously issued securities to the public, the distribution period commences with either the effective date of the registration statement or the start of the offering, whichever date occurs later, and continues for a period of 40 days.

      (2) **New Companies** When the securities are being offered by a company that is issuing securities to the public for the first time, the distribution period runs for 90 days.

   b. **Post-Distribution Period** Once the distribution period has run, dealers need not deliver a prospectus to an offeree or purchaser. The exemption applies to dealers transacting in securities in the post-distribution period even though a registration statement never was filed. This prevents innocent dealers selling illegally unregistered securities from being found in violation of the Act. The exemption does not apply to dealers who are participating in the original distribution and have not yet sold their original allotment.

5. **Rule 144** When a person meets the requirements of Rule 144, s/he may resell restricted securities.

   a. **Restricted Securities** Restricted securities are securities received in a private offering (e.g., securities sold pursuant to Reg. D). Restricted securities may not be resold unless they are registered or they are exempted from registration (e.g., under Section 4 or Rule 144).

   b. **Controlled Securities** Controlled securities are securities sold by controlling persons. A controlling person can sell either restricted securities or nonrestricted securities acquired as part of a registered public distribution. If the latter is the case, the controlling person need not conform with Rule 144's two-year holding period.

   c. **Safe Harbor** Rule 144 establishes the following safe harbor criteria that must be met by persons claiming this exemption.

(1) **Information** Adequate information concerning the issuer must be made publicly available. **Note:** When a company is required to report and has been reporting, under the 1934 Act, such adequate information is presumed available.

(2) **Ownership Risk** A person must have been the beneficial owner and have borne the risk of ownership in the securities for a period of at least two years prior to sale and have fully paid for the securities by the date of sale. This rule attempts to make certain that the person purchased the securities for the purpose of investment rather than for resale to the public. **Note:** Controlling persons who sell nonrestricted securities need not comply with this requirement.

(3) **Limits** During a three-month period, only the following amounts of securities may be sold. **Note:** This applies to both "listed" and "unlisted" securities.

(a) 1% of all outstanding shares of that class, or

(b) The average weekly reported volume of trading in such securities for all security exchanges through which the securities are traded for the four calendar weeks preceding the sale.

(4) **Notice** The seller must file a notice with the SEC of her/his intention to sell the restricted securities.

(5) **Brokers' Transactions** Generally, all sales must take place in brokers' transactions, the requirements of which are as follows. Besides brokers' transactions, the sale also may take place directly with a market maker.

(a) **Commission** The broker must receive only the ordinary brokerage commission.

(b) **Publish** The broker may not solicit any offers to buy, but may publish a bid and ask prices if s/he regularly has been dealing in the security to be sold.

(c) **Inquiry** The broker must inquire reasonably into whether the seller is entitled to the Rule 144 exception.

(d) **General Requirement Exceptions** Estates and beneficiaries are exempt from the brokers' transaction requirement.

(6) **Rule 237** When there is no public market for securities, Rule 144 is of little benefit. In these situations, Rule 237 provides an exemption for sales of restricted securities. However, the Rule 237 resale safe harbor applies only to noncontrolling persons and only to the lesser of $50,000 or 1% of the outstanding securities in a one-year period. Securities resold pursuant to Rule 237 must have been held for 5 years.

E. Registration Process

Prior to the initial issuance of any security, the Act requires that a registration statement be filed with the SEC. The registration statement contains all the information necessary to enable the potential investors to determine the desirability of the offered securities. This information, condensed to the essentials, also is used to make up the prospectus which must be provided to all offerees.

1. **Registration Statement Information** All experts, including accountants, who are listed as having prepared or certified any of the information contained in the registration statement must consent to their listing in writing. The registration statement must contain all information specified in Schedule A of the Act, unless abrogated by the SEC. A summary of Schedule A requirements is as follows.

a. **Basic Information** Such as names and addresses of the issuer, directors, controlling persons, and underwriters. The statement also must disclose the percentage amount of securities under the control of individual directors or controlling persons.

b. **Financial Information** The statement must include detailed information of the securities to be issued and securities previously issued, a balance sheet of the issuer not more than 90 days old at the time of filing, a profit and loss statement for the last fiscal year and at least two preceding years, unless the issuer has been in business less than three years, then for such time as the issuer has been in business, and a statement of all material contracts entered into by the issuer during the two years before the filing.

c. **Material Facts** Other facts deemed material by the SEC, such as any difference in value that may exist between the offering price and actual book value of the securities, any information concerning directors or top executives tending to demonstrate lack of integrity or potential conflicts of interest, and any information that would serve to put a person on notice that the securities being offered may be "high risk" securities.

2. **Prospectus** The prospectus must contain most of the basic information concerning the issuer, directors, executives, controlling persons, underwriters, and all financial information required under Schedule A. However, any information that the SEC designates as not being necessary to protect the public may be omitted from the prospectus.

3. **Red Herring Prospectuses** Once the registration statement and prospectus are filed with the SEC, persons may, through use of "red herring" prospectuses or other limited preliminary prospectuses, announce proposed offerings. Persons also may make offers to sell or buy securities during this "waiting period" (the period after filing and before the effective date of the registration statement).

a. All written offers must be accompanied by a "red herring" or other preliminary prospectus. A preliminary prospectus must contain most of the information required in a final prospectus, but may exclude such items as the price of the securities, which usually is not decided until just before the effective date. Such a prospectus may be used only during the waiting period.

b. No prospectus is needed for verbal offers and agreements to sell or buy entered into during the waiting period.

4. **Registration Statement Processing** Unless it is subjected to an SEC refusal or stop order, a registration statement becomes effective 20 days after filing. The SEC may issue an acceleration order to advance the effective date. Once filed, a registration statement is reviewed by the SEC.

a. **Letters of Deficiency** The SEC may issue letters of deficiency to the issuer. The issuer then is allowed to cure such deficiencies by making amendments to the registration statement.

b. **Refusal Order** The SEC may issue a refusal order, which will delay the effective date in order to allow the SEC to further review the security. However, the SEC must issue such an order within 10 days after the filing.

c. **Stop Order** The SEC may issue a stop order, which has the same effect as a refusal, at any time. However, the SEC may issue such an order only when there are material deficiencies in the registration statement and only after a hearing with notice.

F. Criminal Penalties

The Act establishes criminal penalties of a fine of not more than $10,000 and/or imprisonment of up to 5 years for anyone who willfully (1) violates any provision of the Act or the rules and regulations promulgated by the SEC, or (2) makes any untrue statement of a material fact or omits to state any material fact.

G. Civil Liability

1. **Plaintiff** A person who sues under the anti-fraud provisions (e.g., schemes to defraud, material omissions, and false or misleading statements) must prove the following.

   a. The registration statement contained false or misleading information or material omissions.

   b. The securities purchased were covered by the defective statement.

2. **Reliance, Negligence, or Fraud** The injured purchaser need not prove reliance on the statement. Furthermore, the injured person need not prove negligence or fraud. Rather, the burden of persuasion shifts away from the person injured to the experts (attorneys, accountants, officers, directors) who must prove that they exercised due diligence in dealing with the defective statement.

3. **Due Diligence Defense** No person, other than the issuer, shall be liable when s/he can prove the following.

   a. Before the effective date of the statement s/he resigned, or advised the SEC and the issuer that s/he planned to resign, and would not be responsible for such a statement, or, if the statement became effective without her/his knowledge, the SEC was contacted and given reasonable public notice of the fact upon becoming aware of the issuance.

   b. In regard to any part of the statement not purporting to be made on the authority of an expert, s/he had, after reasonable investigation, reasonable grounds to believe and did believe the statement to be true and without material omissions.

   c. In regard to any part of the statement made upon her/his authority as an expert, s/he had, after reasonable investigation, reasonable grounds to believe the statement to be true and without material omissions.

   d. In regard to any part of the statement purporting to be made upon the authority of an expert other than her/himself, there were no reasonable grounds to believe and s/he did not believe that the statement was untrue or contained material omissions. The standard of reasonableness is that of a prudent person in the management of her/his own property.

4. **Issuer's Defense** The issuer's only defense is that the injured person knew of the misleading or omitted information before the purchase of the securities.

5. **Joint & Several Liability** All or any of the persons specified as being liable are jointly and severally liable. Generally, they have the right of contribution.

6. **Recoverable Amount Limit** In no case may the amount recoverable under this section exceed the price at which the security was offered to the public.

7. **Liability** In addition to the previously mentioned liabilities arising from an improper registration statement, the 1933 Act provides that any person who sells or offers to sell a security in violation of the Act's registration requirement, or who offers or sells a security in interstate commerce by use of any communication that makes an untrue statement or omits to state a material fact, shall be liable to the purchaser. This liability can take the form of either the consideration paid for the security with interest, less the amount of any income received thereon, or damages if s/he no longer owns the security. The defendant may escape liability by showing that s/he did not know and in the exercise of reasonable care could not have known of such untruth or omission.

8. **Statute of Limitations** The following limitations pertain to civil liability.

   a. In most instances, an action must be brought within one year of the discovery of an untruth or omission or one year after the discovery should have been made by the exercise of due diligence. Actions based on a violation of the Act's registration requirements must be brought within one year of the violation.

   b. In no event may an action be brought later than three years after a security was offered in good faith to the public.

III. Securities Exchange Act of 1934

A. Overview

The purpose of the 1934 Act is to regulate and control security transactions in order to protect interstate commerce; the national credit, banking systems, and the Federal Reserve System; and to ensure the maintenance of fair and honest markets. The 1934 Act takes over where the 1933 Act leaves off, focusing on secondary offerings of securities.

1. **Registration Scope** The following are required to register under the 1934 Act.

   a. National securities exchanges

   b. Brokers and dealers transacting business in interstate commerce

   c. Corporations whose securities are traded on a national security exchange or whose assets are in excess of $10 million, and which have a class of equity security held on record by 500 or more persons

2. **Registration Statement Content** The following are required disclosures in the registration.

   a. The nature of the business

   b. The names of officers and directors

   c. The financial structure of the firm

   d. Any bonus and profit-sharing arrangements

3. **Manipulative & Deceptive Practices** The 1934 Act regulates practices intended to manipulate the price of securities and prohibits deceptive practices.

4. **Regulation of Certain Practices**

   a. **Tender Offers** The 1934 Act regulates stock purchases and tender offers by persons acquiring 5% or more of a company's equity securities.

   b. **Proxy Solicitations** The 1934 Act regulates the manner by which proxy votes may be solicited from company shareholders.

   c. **Margin Requirements** The SEC regulates the amount of credit that may be extended initially or maintained subsequently on any security.

B. Reporting Requirements

1. **Corporations** A company registering under the 1934 Act must supply information similar to, but less extensive than, the information required in a 1933 Act registration statement. Reporting deadlines are dependent on the company's size.

Exhibit 2 ▸ SEC Reporting Deadlines

Issuer Category	Public Float	10-K	10-Q
Large Accelerated Filer	$700 million or more	60 days	40 days
Accelerated Filer	Between $75 and $700 million	75 days	40 days
Non-Accelerated Filer	Less than $75 million	90 days	45 days

a. **Annually (Form 10-K)** Every issuer registered under the 1934 Act must file annual reports with the SEC for each fiscal year within 90 days of the close of that fiscal year. These reports must contain financial statements certified by CEO/CFOs and audited by independent public accountants.

b. **Quarterly (Form 10-Q)** Unaudited reports must be filed quarterly within 45 days of the close of that quarter. These reports must contain financial information certified by CEO/CFOs and reviewed by independent public accountants.

c. **Occasionally (Form 8-K)** Certain specified events must be reported to the SEC. Current reports must be filed after certain specific events have occurred. The deadline is four days after the event or, if the event occurs on a weekend, four business days afterwards. These events include a change in auditor, newly appointed officers, the resignation of a director, bankruptcy, default of a debt instrument, or a sale of assets not in the ordinary course of business.

2. **National Securities Exchanges** National securities exchanges must file reports with the SEC advising of any changes in their rules or regulations.

3. **Insiders** Directors, officers, and 10% security holders either must disclose significant information or refrain from trading the corporation's stock.

C. **Anti-Fraud Provisions**
Section 10(b) of the 1934 Act makes it unlawful for any person to use interstate commerce or any facility of any national security exchange to directly or indirectly effect a short sale (less than six months). It also makes it unlawful for any person to use or employ in connection with the purchase or sale of any security any deceptive or manipulative practice in contrary to the rules or regulations prescribed by the SEC as necessary to protect the public interest.

1. **Coverage** Section 10(b) was written broadly so as to give the SEC power to regulate substantially all securities transactions over which the federal government may exercise control.

a. **Securities** This provision covers transactions in both registered and unregistered securities.

b. **Persons** This provision covers all persons transacting in securities (not just insiders, issuers, or dealers).

c. **Transactions** This provision covers both sales and purchases, thus protection is extended to defrauded sellers. Additionally, the wording "in connection with any sale or purchase" has been held to cover not only situations in which the person engaged in "fraud" is buying or selling, but also situations in which reasonable investors would rely on the "fraud" in making investment decisions. For example, a corporation may not release false information that may influence the decision of a reasonable investor to buy or sell.

2. **Rule 10b-5** Pursuant to its rulemaking authority, the SEC promulgated Rule 10b-5 in an attempt to clarify the meaning of Section 10(b). Rule 10b-5 makes it unlawful for any person (in connection with the purchase or sale of any security) to use interstate commerce, the mails, or any facility of any national securities exchange to do the following:

a. Employ any device, scheme, or artifice to defraud.

b. Make any untrue statement of a material fact or to omit to state a material fact.

c. Engage in any act, practice, or course of business that operates or would operate as a fraud or deceit upon any person.

3. **Material Fact** Courts will balance both the indicated probability that an event will occur and the anticipated magnitude of the event in light of the totality of the company's activity. Courts may look to the importance attached to the event by those who knew about it and were in a position to evaluate it. For instance, a substantial mineral find and a pending merger have been held to be material facts. A material fact has been defined by the court as follows.

   a. The basic test of materiality is whether a reasonable person would attach importance to that fact in determining a choice of action in the transaction in question.

   b. Material facts include not only the information disclosing the earnings and distributions of a company, but also those facts that affect the future of the company and those that may affect the desire of investors to buy, sell, or hold the company's securities.

4. **Disclosure Requirements** There is no direct requirement that corporations or their directors or officers disclose important developments within the corporation. However, insiders in possession of such information either must disclose that information or refrain from trading the corporation's stock. For purposes of this prohibition, insiders include directors and officers of the issuer and every person who is directly or indirectly the beneficial owner of more than 10% of any class of an equity security registered pursuant to the 1934 Act. Insiders also include anyone in possession of material inside information; that is, anyone privy to a (secret) "tip."

5. **Liability** Persons found to be in violation of Section 10 of the 1934 Act or Rule 10b-5 may be liable to private parties and/or the SEC as follows.

   a. **SEC** The SEC may bring an action in any United States District Court to enjoin any activity in violation of the anti-fraud provisions, or to compel, by a writ of mandamus, any person to comply with these provisions or any order issued by the SEC. Pursuant to this power, the SEC may subpoena witnesses, compel their attendance, and require the production of relevant material.

      (1) The SEC may base actions under Section 10(b) on a showing of reckless disregard of the truth; it has no duty to establish specific fraudulent intent. In an enforcement action brought by the SEC to enjoin future violations of Section 10(b), the conduct complained of can be judged under a *negligence* standard.

      (2) Persons who willfully violate any provision of Section 10(b) may be held criminally liable and subject to a fine of up to $100,000 or imprisonment of not more than 5 years or both.

   b. **Private Parties** Any person who, in reliance on any statement in violation of Section 10(b) of the 1934 Act and with no knowledge of the falsity of such statement, buys or sells a security and thereby suffers a loss, may bring an action in law or equity.

      (1) Only purchasers or sellers may bring an action. Persons who hold or refrain from buying have no cause of action.

      (2) Persons suing under this section must allege *fraud* on the part of the persons in violation of the Act. Scienter must be proven. However, there is no requirement to establish privity between those defrauded and the violating parties.

D. Proxy Solicitation

A proxy is an authorization from a shareholder to vote her/his shares. It is unlawful for any person, by use of interstate commerce, the mails, or any facility of a national security exchange, to solicit from holders of securities required to be registered under the 1934 Act a proxy in violation of SEC rules.

1. **Written Proxy Statement** Subject to several exemptions, before any proxy may be solicited, each person contacted must be furnished with a written proxy statement. This statement must contain the following.

   a. A statement as to whether or not the proxy is revocable.

   b. The identity of the person (or persons) making the solicitation and a statement by her/him as to her/his interest in any matter to be acted upon.

   c. Information relevant to voting for new directors.

   d. A list of matters to be acted upon and whether they are proposed by the management or a security holder.

2. **Form** The form of proxy presented to the security holders must include whether or not the proxy is solicited on behalf of the management, a specially designated blank space for dating the proxy, a list of each matter intended to be acted upon, and a means to express a view on each matter.

3. **Annual Report** If the solicitation is made on behalf of the management of the issuer and relates to an annual meeting of security holders at which directors are to be elected, an annual report must accompany the proxy statement. This report shall contain a financial statement for the last two fiscal years audited by an independent accountant.

4. **File With SEC** The proxy statement, form of proxy, and annual reports shall be filed with the SEC at least 10 days before such information is sent to the holders.

5. **Rule 14a-9** Rule 14a-9 prohibits false or misleading statements in any material required to be filed with the SEC. Violation of this rule gives rise to a private cause of action. In some instances, a mere showing of negligence is sufficient to establish liability. In the majority of cases, intent or reckless disregard must be shown.

E. Tender Offers & Other Significant Acquisitions

The 1934 Act was amended so as to make it unlawful for anyone, directly or indirectly, by use of interstate commerce, the mails, or any facility of a national securities exchange, to acquire (Section 13) or to make a tender offer (Section 14) of any class of equity security (required to be registered under the 1934 Act) if, after acquisition of those securities, s/he would become the beneficial owner of 5% or more of such class of security without filing a report with the SEC, with the pertinent security exchange, and with the issuer; and if a tender offer is made, to holders of that class of security.

1. **Report Filed With SEC** The report generally must include information about the purchaser, the source and amount of funds or other consideration used in making the purchases, and the purpose for the purchase (for example, to take over control of the business or to liquidate the business). It also must include the number of shares actually owned (by the offeror) and any related activity (tender offers) planned.

2. **Tender Offer** A tender offer is a general offer to all shareholders of a class of securities to purchase their shares for cash at a specified price, which ordinarily is higher than the prevailing market price. The offer usually is contingent on the tender of sufficient shares to ensure takeover. If more shares are tendered than the offeror is willing to purchase, the offeror must purchase shares from each shareholder on a *pro rata* basis.

IV. Other Federal Securities Regulation

A. Private Securities Litigation Reform Act of 1995

The Private Securities Litigation Reform Act of 1995 amends the Securities Acts of 1933 and 1934. This Act establishes guidelines for CPAs to disclose corporate fraud.

1. **Audit Procedures** Under Title III of this Act, *Auditor Disclosure of Corporate Fraud,* independent public accountants must include procedures to (1) detect illegal acts that would have a direct and material effect on the financial statements, (2) identify related party transactions that would have a material effect on the financial statements, and (3) evaluate an issuer's ability to continue as a going concern.

2. **Illegal Activities Discovered** An independent public accountant who, during the course of an audit, becomes aware of possible illegal activities shall inform the entity's management and assure that the audit committee or the board of directors is adequately informed. If the auditor concludes that the illegal act has a material effect on the financial statements and management has not taken appropriate remedial actions, and this failure reasonably warrants departure from a standard report, the auditor shall report this directly to the board of directors. The entity is required to notify the SEC no later than 1 business day after receipt of such report.

3. **CPAs' Further Obligation** If the entity fails to notify the SEC within 1 business day, the independent public accountant must resign from the engagement and/or report to the SEC within 1 business day.

4. **Liability** An auditor shall not be liable in a private action for complying with the guidelines of this act. An auditor may face civil penalties for noncompliance with this Act.

B. Securities Litigation Uniform Standards Act of 1998

Most federal securities class-action lawsuits involving 50 or more parties must be filed in federal courts, rather than in state courts under state law. This legislation was passed to stop evasion of the 1995 Private Securities Litigation Reform Act.

C. Regulation FD (Fair Disclosure)

Regulation FD (Fair Disclosure) addresses selective disclosure. An issuer or a person acting on the issuer's behalf that discloses material nonpublic information to certain enumerated persons must make public disclosure of that information. In general, the enumerated persons include securities market professionals and holders of the issuer's securities who may trade on the basis of the information.

1. **Intentional** If the selective disclosure was intentional, the issuer must make public disclosure simultaneously.

2. **Non-Intentional** If the disclosure was non-intentional, the public disclosure must be made promptly, by filing or furnishing a Form 8-K, or by another method or combination of methods reasonably designed to effect broad, non-exclusionary distribution of the information to the public.

CHAPTER 40—FEDERAL SECURITIES REGULATION

Problem 40-1 MULTIPLE CHOICE QUESTIONS (60 to 80 minutes)

1. Under the registration requirements of the Securities Act of 1933, which of the following items is(are) considered securities?

	Investment contracts	*Collateral-trust certificates*
a.	Yes	Yes
b.	Yes	No
c.	No	Yes
d.	No	No

(5/96, Law, #6, 6262)

2. Under the Securities Act of 1933, which of the following statements is(are) correct regarding the purpose of registration?

I. The purpose of registration is to allow for the detection of management fraud and prevent a public offering of securities when management fraud is suspected.
II. The purpose of registration is to adequately and accurately disclose financial and other information upon which investors may determine the merits of securities.

a. I only
b. II only
c. Both I and II
d. Neither I nor II (R/05, REG, 0086L, #6, 7852)

3. The prospectus for the sale of securities of a not-for-profit corporation contained material misrepresentations due to the negligence of the person who prepared the financial statements. As a result of the misrepresentations, purchasers of the shares lost their investment. Do the anti-fraud provisions of the Securities Act of 1933 apply in this situation?

a. Yes, because the securities are required to be registered
b. Yes, because the misrepresentations were material
c. No, because the securities are exempt from registration
d. No, because only the issuer was negligent

(R/02, Law, #8, 7118)

4. One of the elements necessary to recover damages if there has been a material misstatement in a registration statement filed under the Securities Act of 1933 is that the

a. Issuer and plaintiff were in privity of contract with each other.
b. Issuer failed to exercise due care in connection with the sale of the securities.
c. Plaintiff gave value for the security.
d. Plaintiff suffered a loss. (11/93, Law, #37, 4334)

5. The Securities Act of 1933 provides an exemption from registration for

	Bonds issued by a municipality for governmental purposes	*Securities issued by a not-for-profit charitable organization*
a.	Yes	Yes
b.	Yes	No
c.	No	Yes
d.	No	No

(R/07, REG, 0327L, #1, 8425)

6. Which of the following securities would be regulated by the provisions of the Securities Act of 1933?

a. Securities issued by not-for-profit, charitable organizations
b. Securities guaranteed by domestic governmental organizations
c. Securities issued by savings and loan associations
d. Securities issued by insurance companies

(11/94, Law, #42, 5219)

7. Which of the following statements concerning an initial intrastate securities offering made by an issuer residing in and doing business in that state is correct?

a. The offering would be exempt from the registration requirements of the Securities Act of 1933.
b. The offering would be subject to the registration requirements of the Securities Exchange Act of 1934.
c. The offering would be regulated by the SEC.
d. The shares of the offering could **not** be resold to investors outside the state for at least one year.

(11/94, Law, #52, 5229)

8. Which of the following facts will result in an offering of securities being exempt from registration under the Securities Act of 1933?
a. The securities are nonvoting preferred stock.
b. The issuing corporation was closely held prior to the offering.
c. The sale or offer to sell the securities is made by a person other than an issuer, underwriter, or dealer.
d. The securities are AAA-rated debentures that are collateralized by first mortgages on property that has a market value of 200% of the offering price. (11/94, Law, #48, 5225)

9. An offering made under the provisions of Regulation A of the Securities Act of 1933 requires that the issuer
a. File an offering circular with the SEC
b. Sell only to accredited investors
c. Provide investors with the prior four years' audited financial statements
d. Provide investors with a proxy registration statement (11/93, Law, #40, 4337)

10. Which of the following transactions will be exempt from the full registration requirements of the Securities Act of 1933?
a. All intrastate offerings
b. All offerings made under Regulation A
c. Any resale of a security purchased under a Regulation D offering
d. Any stockbroker transaction (5/94, Law, #37, 4792)

11. Tork purchased restricted securities that were issued pursuant to Regulation D of the Securities Act of 1933. Which of the following statements is correct regarding Tork's ability to resell the securities?
a. Tork may resell the securities so long as the sale does involve interstate commerce.
b. Tork may resell the securities as part of another transaction exempt from registration.
c. Tork may **not** resell the securities if the certificates contain a legend indicating that they are unregistered securities.
d. Tork may **not** resell the securities unless Tork obtains a written SEC exemption. (R/02, Law, #7, 7117)

12. Regulation D of the Securities Act of 1933
a. Restricts the number of purchasers of an offering to 35
b. Permits an exempt offering to be sold to both accredited and nonaccredited investors
c. Is limited to offers and sales of common stock that do **not** exceed $5 million
d. Is exclusively available to small business corporations as defined by Regulation D (5/93, Law, #35, amended, 4003)

13. Lux Limited Partnership intends to offer $600,000 of its limited partnership interests under Rule 504 of Regulation D of the Securities Act of 1933. Which of the following statements is correct?
a. The resale of the limited partnership interests by a purchaser may be restricted.
b. The limited partnership interests may be sold only to accredited investors.
c. The exemption under Rule 504 is **not** available to an issuer of limited partnership interests.
d. The limited partnership interests may **not** be sold to more than 35 investors. (11/93, Law, #38, amended, 4335)

14. Under Regulation D of the Securities Act of 1933, which of the following conditions apply to private placement offerings? The securities
a. Cannot be sold for longer than a six month period
b. Cannot be the subject of an immediate unregistered reoffering to the public, under Rules 505 and 506
c. Must be sold to accredited institutional investors
d. Must be sold to fewer than 20 nonaccredited investors (5/94, Law, #40, amended, 4795)

15. Data, Inc. intends to make a $750,000 common stock offering under Rule 504 of Regulation D of the Securities Act of 1933. Data
a. May sell the stock to an unlimited number of investors
b. Must make the offering through a general advertising
c. Must offer the stock for a period of more than 12 months
d. Must provide all investors with a prospectus (5/92, Law, #44, amended, 2857)

16. Imperial Corp. is offering $450,000 of its securities under Rule 504 of Regulation D of the Securities Act of 1933. Under Rule 504, Imperial is required to
a. Provide full financial information to all nonaccredited purchasers
b. Make the offering through general solicitation
c. Register the offering under the provisions of the Securities Exchange Act of 1934
d. Notify the SEC within 15 days after the first sale of the securities (11/90, Law, #43, 0747)

17. Miner Corp. wants to make a $5 million public stock offering under the exempt transaction limited offering provisions of the Securities Act of 1933. What must Miner do to comply with the Act?
a. File a registration statement
b. Advertise the offering
c. Issue a "red herring" prospectus
d. Limit sales of the offering to **no** more than 35 unaccredited investors (R/03, REG, 1798L, #19, 7661)

18. For an offering to be exempt under Regulation D of the Securities Act of 1933, Rule 505 and Rule 506 each require which **two** of the following?
a. The SEC be notified within 10 days of the first sale.
b. The offering be made without general advertising.
c. All accredited investors receive the issuer's financial information.
d. The investment be held for two or more years.
e. There be a maximum of 35 investors.
(11/94, Law, #49, amended, 5226)

19. Kamp is offering $10 million of its securities. Under Rule 506 of Regulation D of the Securities Act of 1933,
a. The securities may be debentures.
b. Kamp must be a corporation.
c. There must be more than 35 purchasers.
d. Kamp may make a general solicitation in connection with the offering. (11/91, Law, #40, 2368)

Items 20 and 21 are based on the following:

Pix Corp. is making a $6,000,000 stock offering. Pix wants the offering exempt from registration under the Securities Act of 1933.

20. Which of the following provisions of the Act would Pix have to comply with for the offering to be exempt?
a. Regulation A
b. Regulation D, Rule 504
c. Regulation D, Rule 505
d. Regulation D, Rule 506 (11/93 Law, #43, 4340)

21. Which of the following requirements would Pix have to comply with when selling the securities?
a. No more than 35 investors
b. No more than 35 nonaccredited investors
c. Accredited investors only
d. Nonaccredited investors only
(11/93, Law, #44, 4341)

22. A tombstone advertisement
a. May be substituted for the prospectus under certain circumstances
b. May contain an offer to sell securities
c. Notifies prospective investors that a previously-offered security has been withdrawn from the market and is, therefore, effectively "dead"
d. Makes known the availability of a prospectus
(5/94, Law, #33, 4788)

23. Under the Securities Act of 1933, which of the following statements is correct concerning a public issuer of securities who has made a registered offering?
a. The issuer is required to distribute an annual report to its stockholders.
b. The issuer is subject to the proxy rules of the SEC.
c. The issuer must file an annual report (Form 10-K) with the SEC.
d. The issuer is **not** required to file a quarterly report (Form 10-Q) with the SEC, unless a material event occurs. (5/94, Law, #36, 4791)

Items 24 and 25 are based on the following:

World Corp. wanted to make a public offering of its common stock. On May 10, World prepared and filed a registration statement with the SEC. On May 20, World placed a "tombstone ad" announcing that it was making a public offering. On May 25, World issued a preliminary prospectus and the registration statement became effective on May 30.

24. On what date may World first make oral offers to sell the shares?
a. May 10
b. May 20
c. May 25
d. May 30 (5/92, Law, #39, 2852)

25. On what date may World first sell the shares?
a. May 10
b. May 20
c. May 25
d. May 30 (5/92, Law, #40, 2853)

26. Which of the following requirements must be met by an issuer of securities who wants to make an offering by using shelf registration?

	Original registration statement must be kept updated	*The offeror must be a first-time issuer of securities*
a.	Yes	Yes
b.	Yes	No
c.	No	Yes
d.	No	No

(11/94, Law, #43, 5220)

27. Universal Corp. intends to sell its common stock to the public in an interstate offering that will be registered under the Securities Act of 1933. Under the Act,

a. Universal can make offers to sell its stock before filing a registration statement, provided that it does **not** actually issue stock certificates until after the registration is effective.
b. Universal's registration statement becomes effective at the time it is filed, assuming the SEC does **not** object within 20 days thereafter.
c. A prospectus must be delivered to each purchaser of Universal's common stock unless the purchaser qualifies as an accredited investor.
d. Universal's filing of a registration statement with the SEC does **not** automatically result in compliance with the "blue-sky" laws of the states in which the offering will be made.

(5/91, Law, #40, 0737)

28. Under the liability provisions of Section 18 of the Securities Exchange Act of 1934, for which of the following actions would an accountant generally be liable?

a. Negligently approving a reporting corporation's incorrect internal financial forecasts
b. Negligently filing a reporting corporation's tax return with the IRS
c. Intentionally preparing and filing with the SEC a reporting corporation's incorrect quarterly report
d. Intentionally failing to notify a reporting corporation's audit committee of defects in the verification of accounts receivable

(R/05, REG, 0023L, #3, 7849)

29. Under the Securities Exchange Act of 1934, which of the following conditions generally will allow an issuer of securities to terminate the registration of a class of securities and suspend the duty to file periodic reports?

	The corporation has fewer than 300 shareholders	*The securities are listed on a national securities exchange*
a.	Yes	Yes
b.	Yes	No
c.	No	Yes
d.	No	No

(R/99, Law, #11, 6862)

30. Adler, Inc. is a reporting company under the Securities Exchange Act of 1934. The only security it has issued is voting common stock. Which of the following statements is correct?

a. Because Adler is a reporting company, it is **not** required to file a registration statement under the Securities Act of 1933 for any future offerings of its common stock.
b. Adler need **not** file its proxy statements with the SEC because it has only one class of stock outstanding.
c. Any person who owns more than 10% of Adler's common stock must file a report with the SEC.
d. It is unnecessary for the required annual report (Form 10K) to include audited financial statements.

(11/93, Law, #41, 4338)

31. Which of the following situations would require Link Corporation to be subject to the reporting provisions of the 1934 Act?

	Share listed on a national securities exchange	*More than one class of stock*
a.	Yes	Yes
b.	Yes	No
c.	No	Yes
d.	No	No

(11/94, Law, #45, amended, 5222)

Items 32 through 33 are based on the following:

Link Corp. is subject to the reporting provisions of the Securities Exchange Act of 1934.

32. Which of the following documents must Link file with the SEC?

	Quarterly reports (Form 10-Q)	*Proxy statements*
a.	Yes	Yes
b.	Yes	No
c.	No	Yes
d.	No	No

(11/94, Law, #46, 5223)

33. Which of the following reports must also be submitted to the SEC?

	Report by any party making a tender offer to purchase Link's stock	*Report of proxy solicitations by Link stockholders*
a.	Yes	Yes
b.	Yes	No
c.	No	Yes
d.	No	No

(11/94, Law, #47, 5224)

34. Under the Securities Exchange Act of 1934, the SEC is responsible for all of the following activities **except**

a. Requiring disclosure of facts concerning offerings of securities listed on national securities exchanges
b. Prosecuting criminal violations of federal securities laws
c. Regulating the activities of securities brokers
d. Investigating securities fraud

(5/96, Law, #5, 6261)

35. Under the Securities Exchange Act of 1934, a corporation with common stock listed on a national stock exchange

a. Is prohibited from making private placement offerings
b. Is subject to having the registration of its securities suspended or revoked
c. Must submit Form 10-K to the SEC except in those years in which the corporation has made a public offering
d. Must distribute copies of Form 10-K to its stockholders (5/93, Law, #32, 4000)

36. Which of the following persons is **not** an insider of a corporation subject to the Securities Exchange Act of 1934 registration and reporting requirements?

a. An attorney for the corporation
b. An owner of 5% of the corporation's outstanding debentures
c. A member of the board of directors
d. A stockholder who owns 10% of the outstanding common stock (11/93, Law, #42, 4339)

37. The antifraud provisions of Rule 10b-5 of the Securities Exchange Act of 1934

a. Apply only if the securities involved were registered under either the Securities Act of 1933 or the Securities Exchange Act of 1934
b. Require that the plaintiff show negligence on the part of the defendant in misstating facts
c. Require that the wrongful act must be accomplished through the mail, any other use of interstate commerce, or through a national securities exchange
d. Apply only if the defendant acted with intent to defraud (5/91, Law, #44, 0740)

38. Corporations that are exempt from registration under the Securities Exchange Act of 1934 are subject to the Act's

a. Antifraud provisions
b. Proxy solicitation provisions
c. Provisions dealing with the filing of annual reports
d. Provisions imposing periodic audits

(5/93, Law, #31, 3999)

39. Dean, Inc., a publicly traded corporation, paid a $10,000 bribe to a local zoning official. The bribe was recorded in Dean's financial statements as a consulting fee. Dean's unaudited financial statements were submitted to the SEC as part of a quarterly filing. Which of the following federal statutes did Dean violate?

a. Federal Trade Commission Act
b. Securities Act of 1933
c. Securities Exchange Act of 1934
d. North American Free Trade Act

(R/01, Law, #15, 7050)

40. An original issue of transaction exempt securities was sold to the public based on a prospectus containing intentional omissions of material facts. Under which of the following federal securities laws would the issuer be liable to a purchaser of the securities?

I. The anti-fraud provisions of the Securities Act of 1933
II. The anti-fraud provisions of the Securities Exchange Act of 1934

a. I only
b. II only
c. Both I and II
d. Neither I nor II (R/02, Law, #9, 7119)

Problem 40-2 ADDITIONAL MULTIPLE CHOICE QUESTIONS (20 to 26 minutes)

41. Which of the following statements concerning the prospectus required by the Securities Act of 1933 is correct?
a. The prospectus is a part of the registration statement.
b. The prospectus should enable the SEC to pass on the merits of the securities.
c. The prospectus must be filed after an offer to sell.
d. The prospectus is prohibited from being distributed to the public until the SEC approves the accuracy of the facts embodied therein.
(5/94, Law, #31, 4786)

42. When a common stock offering requires registration under the Securities Act of 1933,
a. The registration statement is automatically effective when filed with the SEC
b. The issuer would act unlawfully if it were to sell the common stock without providing the investor with a prospectus
c. The SEC will determine the investment value of the common stock before approving the offering
d. The issuer may make sales 10 days after filing the registration statement
(11/91, Law, #36, 2364)

43. Under the Securities Act of 1933, which of the following statements most accurately reflects how securities registration affects an investor?
a. The investor is provided with information on the stockholders of the offering corporation.
b. The investor is provided with information on the principal purposes for which the offering's proceeds will be used.
c. The investor is guaranteed by the SEC that the facts contained in the registration statement are accurate.
d. The investor is assured by the SEC against loss resulting from purchasing the security.
(11/94, Law, #41, 5218)

44. A preliminary prospectus, permitted under SEC Regulations, is known as the
a. Unaudited prospectus
b. Qualified prospectus
c. "Blue-sky" prospectus
d. "Red-herring" prospectus (5/94, Law, #32, 4787)

45. Frey, Inc. intends to make a $2,000,000 common stock offering under Rule 505 of Regulation D of the Securities Act of 1933. Frey
a. May sell the stock to an unlimited number of investors
b. May make the offering through a general advertising
c. Must notify the SEC within 15 days after the first sale of the offering
d. Must provide all inspectors with a prospectus
(11/93, Law, #45, 4342)

46. A $10,000,000 offering of corporate stock intended to be made pursuant to the provisions of Rule 506 of Regulation D of the Securities Act of 1933 would **not** be exempt under Rule 506 if
a. The offering was made through a general solicitation or advertising.
b. Some of the investors are nonaccredited.
c. There are more than 35 accredited investors.
d. The SEC was notified 14 days after the first sale of the securities. (11/90, Law, #45, 0749)

47. Which of the following is **least** likely to be considered a security under the Securities Act of 1933?
a. Stock options
b. Warrants
c. General partnership interests
d. Limited partnership interests
(5/93, Law, #30, 3998)

48. Which of the following securities is exempt from registration under the Securities Act of 1933?
a. Shares of nonvoting common stock, provided their par value is less than $1.00
b. A class of stock given in exchange for another class by the issuer to its existing stockholders without the issuer paying a commission
c. Limited partnership interests sold for the purpose of acquiring funds to invest in bonds issued by the United States
d. Corporate debentures that were previously subject to an effective registration statement, provided they are convertible into shares of common stock (5/93, Law, #34, 4002)

49. If securities are exempt from the registration provisions of the Securities Act of 1933, any fraud committed in the course of selling such securities can be challenged by

	SEC	*Person defrauded*
a.	Yes	Yes
b.	Yes	No
c.	No	Yes
d.	No	No

(5/94, Law, #39, 4794)

50. Exemption from registration under the Securities Act of 1933 would be available for
a. Promissory notes maturing in 12 months
b. Securities of a bank
c. Limited partnership interests
d. Corporate bonds (11/91, Law, #35, 2363)

51. Under the Securities Exchange Act of 1934, which of the following types of instruments is excluded from the definition of "securities?"
a. Investment contracts
b. Convertible debentures
c. Nonconvertible debentures
d. Certificates of deposit (5/94, Law, #38, 4793)

52. Under the Securities Exchange Act of 1934, which of the following penalties could be assessed against a CPA who intentionally violated the provisions of Section 10(b), Rule 10b-5 of the Act?

	Civil liability of monetary damages	*Criminal liability of a fine*
a.	Yes	Yes
b.	Yes	No
c.	No	Yes
d.	No	No

(R/06, REG, 1707L, #6, 8176)

53. Under Section 12 of the Securities Exchange Act of 1934, in addition to companies whose securities are traded on a national exchange, what class of companies is subject to the SEC's continuous disclosure system?
a. Companies with annual revenues in excess of $5 million and 300 or more shareholders
b. Companies with annual revenues in excess of $10 million and 500 or more shareholders
c. Companies with assets in excess of $5 million and 300 or more shareholders
d. Companies with assets in excess of $10 million and 500 or more shareholders

(R/07, REG, 1935L, #32, 8456)

SIMULATION

Problem 40-3 (20 to 30 minutes)

Butler Manufacturing Corp. planned to raise capital for a plant expansion by making several stock offerings. Butler, a privately held company, engaged Weaver, CPA, to audit its December 31, Year 2, financial statements. Butler told Weaver that the financial statements would be included in the prospectuses for the stock offerings.

In performing the audit, Weaver was aware of a pending class action product liability lawsuit that was not disclosed in Butler's financial statements. Despite being advised by Butler's legal counsel that Butler's potential liability under the lawsuit would result in material losses, Weaver issued an unqualified opinion on Butler's financial statements. These audited financial statements were distributed to investors in each stock offering.

In Year 3, Butler raised an additional $16,450,000 through the following stock offerings, which were sold completely:

- June—Butler made a $450,000 unregistered offering of Class B nonvoting common stock under Rule 504 of Regulation D of the Securities Act of 1933. This offering was sold over two years to 30 non-accredited investors and 20 accredited investors with no general solicitation. The SEC was notified eight days after the first sale of this offering.
- August—Butler made a $6,000,000 unregistered offering of preferred stock under Rule 505 of Regulation D of the Securities Act of 1933. This offering was sold during a one-year period to 40 nonaccredited investors by private placement. The SEC was notified 18 days after the first sale of this offering.
- November—Butler made a $10,000,000 unregistered offering of Class A voting common stock under Rule 506 of Regulation D of the Securities Act of 1933. This offering was sold over two years to 200 accredited investors and 30 nonaccredited investors through a private placement. The SEC was notified 14 days after the first sale of this offering.

Shortly after obtaining the offering, Butler was found liable in the product liability suit. This resulted in a judgment Butler could not pay. Butler was petitioned into bankruptcy involuntarily. This caused Butler's stockholders to lose their investments.

As a result:

- The SEC claimed that all three of Butler's offerings were made improperly and were not exempt from registration.
- The stockholders who purchased Butler's stock through the offerings sued Weaver, alleging fraud under Section 10(b) and Rule 10b-5 of the Securities Exchange Act of 1934.

These transactions took place in a jurisdiction providing for accountant's liability for negligence to known and intended users of financial statements. (Editors, 3143)

Items 1 through 6 relate to the June offering made under Rule 504 of Regulation D of the Securities Act of 1933.

Question	Answer
1. Did the offering comply with the dollar limitation?	
2. Did the offering comply with the method of sale restrictions?	
3. Was the offering sold during the applicable time limit?	
4. Was the offering sold to the correct number and type of investors?	
5. Was the SEC notified timely of the first sale of the securities?	
6. Was the SEC correct in claiming that this offering was not exempt from registration?	

Items 7 through 13 relate to the August offering made under Rule 505 of Regulation D of the Securities Act of 1933.

Question	Answer
7. Did the offering comply with the dollar limitation?	
8. Did the offering comply with the method of sale restrictions?	
9. Was the offering sold during the applicable time limit?	
10. Was the offering sold to the correct number and type of investors?	
11. Was the SEC notified timely of the first sale of the securities?	
12. Was the SEC correct in claiming that this offering was not exempt from registration?	
13. Did the offering comply with the requirements for disclosure to investors?	

Items 14 through 20 relate to the November offering made under Rule 506 of Regulation D of the Securities Act of 1933.

Question	Answer
14. Did the offering comply with the dollar limitation?	
15. Did the offering comply with the method of sale restrictions?	
16. Was the offering sold during the applicable time limit?	
17. Was the offering sold to the correct number and type of investors?	
18. Was the SEC notified timely of the first sale of the securities?	
19. Was the SEC correct in claiming that this offering was not exempt from registration?	
20. Will there be any restrictions on when the purchasers may re-sell the stock?	

Write a memo to your supervisor explaining whether the investors who purchased Butler's stock though the Year 3 offerings likely would succeed in a suit against Weaver under the anti-fraud provisions of Section 10(b) and Rule 10b-5 of the Securities Exchange Act of 1934.

Scenario | Regulation D | Communication | **Research**

Research Question: What code section and subsection, if applicable, provides guidance on the assumption, for tax purposes, that a gift is made when property is transferred for less than adequate consideration?

Section & Subsection Answer: §_____ (___)

Solution 40-1 MULTIPLE CHOICE ANSWERS

Securities Act of 1933

1. (a) Under the Securities Act of 1933, both investment contracts and collateral-trust certificates are considered securities. They are cited as examples of securities in 15 USC Section 2(1).

2. (b) The registration statement contains information necessary to enable the potential investors to determine the desirability of the offered securities. Registration is rarely sufficient to detect management fraud, as management generally performs most of the preparation of the registration statements.

3. (b) The 1933 Act generally prohibits the use of fraud by any person who offers or sells a security in interstate commerce. This prohibition applies to all securities, whether or not those securities must be registered. The Act specifically prohibits (1) use of any device, scheme, or artifice to defraud; (2) obtaining money or property by means of an untrue statement of material fact or by an omission of a material fact; and (3) engaging in any transaction or practice that would operate as a fraud or deceit on the purchaser. Material misrepresentation is gross negligence; gross negligence is fraud.

4. (d) An action brought under the 1933 Securities Act does not require that the injured party prove that s/he relied on the misleading information, but s/he is required to prove s/he actually incurred a loss. Privity of contract is not a requirement as the 1933 Act is designed to protect the "investing public." The plaintiff does not have to prove negligence in the issuance of the securities, only that the misleading information was material. Any person acquiring securities covered by the registration statement is covered by the Act. There is no requirement that value be given for the security.

Exempt Securities

5. (a) The Securities Act of 1933 exempts certain securities from its registration requirements. These exempted securities include those issued by not-for-profit charitable organizations and governments.

6. (d) The Securities Act of 1933 exempts certain securities from its registration requirements. These exempted securities include those issued by not-for-profit charitable organizations, savings and loan associations, and banks, as well as those guaranteed by domestic governmental organizations. Although the Act exempts insurance policies and annuity contracts, securities issued by insurance companies are not exempt.

7. (a) The Securities Act of 1933 provides an exemption from its registration requirements for intrastate offerings. In order to qualify for this exemption, all securities that are part of the issue must be sold to persons residing within the same state as the issuer. Also, resales of the offering may only be made to residents of the issuer's state of residence for a period of at least nine months.

Exempt Transactions

8. (c) The Securities Act of 1933 exempts transactions made by any person other than an issuer, underwriter, or dealer. There are no provisions in the Act to exempt securities that are nonvoting preferred stock, nor to exempt securities of a closely held corporation, nor AAA-rated debentures.

9. (a) Reg. A is a less restrictive method of registration than is a full registration under §5 of the 1933 Act. Under Reg. A, sales must be made using an "offering circular" rather than a prospectus. Each purchaser must be provided with an "offering circular." There are no restrictions placed on the purchasers of the securities. Reg. A does not require that audited financial statements be provided to the purchasers. The only information required to be distributed to the purchaser is the offering circular.

10. (b) Offerings made under Regulation A are exempt from the *full* registration requirement of the 1933 act; sales must be made using an "offering circular" rather than a prospectus and the issuer must file a notification and offering circular with the SEC. Intrastate offerings are exempted securities, however, any resales of an issue made to a resident of another state within nine months following the last sale will void the intrastate exemption for the entire issue. Resales of securities purchased under a Regulation D offering subject to Rule 505 or 506 are restricted and subject to a full registration requirements. Stockbroker transactions may or may not be subject to the full registration requirements.

11. (b) Restricted securities may not be resold unless the transaction is registered or the securities are exempted from registration.

12. (b) Regulation D of the Securities Act of 1933 permits an exempt offering to be sold to both accredited and nonaccredited investors. Rule 504 of Regulation D does not restrict the number of purchasers. Rule 505 restricts the sale to up to

35 "nonaccredited investors" and an unlimited number of "accredited investors" within 12 months. Rule 506 restricts the sale to an unlimited number of "accredited investors" and up to 35 sophisticated "unaccredited investors." While Rule 504 of Regulation D restricts the sale to $1 million and Rule 505 restricts the sale to $5 million, Rule 506 has no dollar limitation. Regulation D is not restricted to small business corporations.

13. (a) Rule 504 allows resale within the first two years only within certain restrictions. Rule 504 does not disallow the sale of securities to any class of investors. The Rule 504 exemption is available to the issuers of limited partnership interests. Rule 504 does not place restrictions on the class or number of investors to whom the securities may be sold.

14. (b) Resale of securities purchased pursuant to Rule 505 and 506 of Regulation D is restricted and, thus, cannot be the subject of an immediate unregistered public offering. To qualify for exemption from registration under Regulation D, Rule 504 and 505, the private placement offerings cannot be sold for longer than a twelve month (not six month) period. Rule 506 has no such limitation. Under Rule 504, the private placement offerings can be sold to any type and number of investors. Under Rule 505 and 506, the offerings can be sold to an unlimited number of accredited investors, which includes, but is not limited to, institutional investors. Under Rule 505, the offerings can be sold to 35 or less unaccredited investors. This condition applies also to Rule 506, with the added condition that the unaccredited investors must be *sophisticated* investors.

15. (a) Rule 504 of the Securities Act of 1933 permits the sale of up to $1 million of securities to an unlimited number of investors within a 12 month period, without fulfilling the registration and disclosure requirements of the Act. A prospectus is not required. The offering may be publicly promoted only under certain circumstances.

16. (d) Under Rule 504 of Regulation D, Imperial is required to notify the SEC within 15 days after the first sale of the securities. No specific disclosure is required under Rule 504. Under Rule 504 of Regulation D, a general solicitation may be allowed with certain restrictions, but is not required. The purpose of meeting the requirements of Regulation D is to avoid the general registration requirements of the 1934 Act.

17. (d) Rule 505 of Regulation D permits nonpublic and public companies to offer, without fulfilling the SEC Act of 1933 registration requirements, up to $5 million in a 12-month period. These sales can be made to up to 35 "nonaccredited purchasers" and an unlimited number of "accredited investors." The SEC Act of 1933 exempts certain transactions from its registration requirements, thus a registration statement need not be filed to comply with the Act. No general advertising or solicitation may be used to offer or sell securities involved in Rule 505. A "red herring" prospectus is used to announce proposed offerings during the "waiting period" after the registration statement and prospectus are filed with the SEC.

18. (b, d) Both answers are required for full point value. Rule 505 and 506 require that the offering be made without general advertising. The investment must be held for two or more years. The SEC must be notified within 15 days of the first sale. No disclosure is required to accredited investors. Although Rule 505 and 506 limit the number of unaccredited investors to 35, there is no limit on the number of accredited investors.

19. (a) There is no restriction concerning debentures being offered under Rule 506 of Regulation D of the Securities Act of 1933. There is no requirement that the issuing company be incorporated. Rule 506 permits an unlimited amount of money from an unlimited number of "accredited purchasers" and 35 "nonaccredited sophisticated investors." A general solicitation is not permitted under Rule 506.

20. (d) The amount of the stock offering eliminates all possibilities except for Rule 506, which has no limit. Any offering exceeding $5 million will be required to use Rule 506. Regulation A is limited to $5 million. Regulation D, Rule 504 is limited to $1 million. Regulation D, Rule 505 is limited to $5 million.

21. (b) Rule 506 places a limit on the number of nonaccredited investors eligible to purchase securities in the stock offering. The 35 nonaccredited investors must also "have such knowledge and... financial experience as to be capable of evaluating the offering's merits and risks...."

Registration Process

22. (d) A tombstone advertisement is a written advertisement that informs potential investors where and how they may obtain a prospectus. Normally, this is the only type of post-waiting period advertising permitted under the 1933 Federal Securities Act. A tombstone advertisement does not substitute for a prospectus nor may it contain an offer to sell.

23. (c) Under the Securities Act of 1933, an issuer of securities who has made a registered offering is required to meet the reporting requirements of

the 1934 Act for the year following the registration, which include filing an annual report with the SEC. The 1933 Act does not require the issuance of an annual report to the stockholders. The requirements for filing form 10-Q as well as rules pertaining to pr oxy solicitation are governed by the Securities Exchange Act of 1934, not the 1933 Act.

24. (a) Once the registration statement and prospectus are filed with the SEC, oral offers and/or written offers (note, however, that written offers can only be made through a statutory prospectus) may be made to sell the shares. These offers may be extended throughout the "waiting period," which in this question begins on May 10th (the filing date) and ends on May 30th (the effective date).

25. (d) Securities subject to the Securities Act of 1933 may only be sold after the effective date, provided that the buyer has received a final prospectus. The effective date is that date on which the SEC declares the registration effective. In this question it was stated that the registration became effective on May 30.

26. (b) Securities and Exchange Commission (SEC) Rule 415 permits shelf registration of securities. A shelf registration is only available to established (as opposed to first-time) issuers and enables the issuer to file a registration statement and then put the securities "on the shelf" until an opportune time to offer the securities arises. Rule 415 requires that the original registration statement be continuously updated.

27. (d) The filing of a registration statement with the SEC does not automatically result in compliance with the "blue-sky" laws of the states in which the offering will be made. Each state will have their own securities laws ("blue-sky" laws) and compliance is necessary with both the state and with the SEC. There is no automatic state exemption just because the SEC has approved the offering. There can be no offers to sell until the registration statement is filed with the SEC. Once the registration is filed with the SEC, offers to sell may be made during the 20-day "waiting period." The registration does not become effective until the end of the 20-day period, assuming the SEC does not object. A prospectus must be delivered to each purchaser regardless if they are accredited or not.

Securities Act of 1934

28 (c) Generally, anyone filing an intentionally incorrect report with the SEC may be liable. Typically, approval of internal financial forecasts and preparation of tax returns filed with the IRS do not come under the jurisdiction of the SEC. The Sarbanes-Oxley Act of 2002, not the Securities Exchange Act of 1934, requires the auditor to notify the audit committee of the methods, practices, and policies behind the audit work.

29. (b) Corporations whose securities are traded on a national securities exchange or whose assets are in excess of $10 million, and which have a class of equity security held on record by 500 or more persons, are required to register under the 1934 Act and meet the reporting requirements of the Act. A corporation that has fewer than 300 shareholders generally would be allowed to terminate the registration of this class of securities, as long as it is not traded on a national exchange.

30. (c) The Securities Exchange Act of 1934 regulates stock purchases and tender offers by persons acquiring more than 5% of a company's equity securities. Hence, any person who owns more than 5% of a reporting company's common stock must file a report with the SEC. A reporting company under the 1934 Act is not exempt from the filing requirements of the 1933 Act. Adler is required to file its proxy statements with the SEC at least 10 days before such information is sent to the stockholders. The required annual report (Form 10-K) must contain financial statements audited by independent public accountants.

31. (b) The Securities Exchange Act of 1934 requires corporations whose securities are traded on a national exchange to comply with the reporting provisions of the Act. The Act's reporting requirements are not based on the number of classes of stock.

32. (a) An issuer registered under the 1934 Securities Exchange Act must file quarterly reports (Form 10-Q). The 1934 Act also requires that before any proxy may be solicited, each person solicited must be provided with a proxy statement. The proxy statement also must be filed with the SEC at least 10 days prior to being sent to the shareholders.

33. (a) Rule 13 of the 1934 Securities Exchange Act requires any party making a tender offer to file a report (Schedule 13D) with the SEC. The Act also requires that, prior to soliciting a proxy from any shareholder, a proxy statement, form of proxy, and annual reports be filed with the SEC.

34. (b) The SEC is responsible for requiring disclosure of facts concerning offerings of securities listed on national exchanges, for regulating the activities of securities brokers, and for investigating securities fraud. The SEC, however, is not responsible for prosecuting criminal violations of federal securities

laws. The SEC may report such violations to proper authorities, who then may prosecute.

35. (b) A corporation with stock listed on a national stock exchange is required to register under the 1934 Act. The Securities Exchange Commission may suspend or revoke the registration of persons, exchanges, or securities, as required by the 1933 and 1934 Acts. Rule 505 and 506 of Regulation D allow publicly listed companies to make private placements if they meet certain requirements. An issuer of securities under the 1934 Act must file Form 10-K annually, regardless of whether it has made a public offering in a certain year. Form 10-K should not be confused with reports to shareholders. Companies are not required under the 1934 Act to distribute Form 10-K to their stockholders.

36. (b) Insiders are directors, officers, employees, and agents of the issuer, as well as others privy to information that is not available to the general public. An owner of debenture bonds does not gain access to corporate information which is unavailable to the general public. Therefore, the owner of debenture bonds is not an insider with respect to the corporation. An attorney is an agent of the corporation and is privy to corporate information not available to the general public so s/he qualifies as an insider. A director is specifically designated an insider due to the position s/he holds and information s/he has access to. Those stockholders owning 10% of equity securities registered under Section 12 of the 1934 Act are designated insiders by the SEC.

37. (c) The Securities Exchange Act of 1934 applies (including the antifraud provisions) if "interstate" commerce is involved, such as where transactions use the mail, or any other use of interstate commerce, or through the use of a national securities exchange. The antifraud provisions of the 1934 Act will apply even if the securities were not required to be registered under the 1933 or 1934 Securities Act. There is no requirement that the plaintiff must show negligence on the part of the defendant in misstating facts. It is not necessary to show that the defendant acted with intent to defraud. Gross negligence would be enough for the antifraud provisions to apply. However, in order to recover a loss, a seller or purchaser of securities must prove the defendant acted with the intent to defraud (scienter).

38 (a) Even if a corporation is exempt from registration under the Securities Exchange Act of 1934, it still is subject to the Act's antifraud provisions. Provisions dealing with proxy solicitation, filing of annual reports, and imposing periodic audits do not apply if the corporation is exempt from registration under the 1934 Act.

39 (c) Corporations must file quarterly reports (Form 10-Q). Rule 10b-5 makes it unlawful to make any untrue statement of a material fact or to omit to state a material fact. A material fact is one where a reasonable person would attach importance to the fact in determining a choice of action.

40. (c) The 1933 Act generally prohibits the use of fraud by any person who offers or sells a security in interstate commerce. This prohibition applies to all securities, whether or not those securities must be registered. The Act specifically prohibits (1) use of any device, scheme, or artifice to defraud; (2) obtaining money or property by means of an untrue statement of material fact or by an omission of a material fact; and (3) engaging in any transaction or practice that would operate as a fraud or deceit on the purchaser. Section 10(b) of the 1934 Act makes it unlawful for any person to use interstate commerce or any facility of any national security exchange to directly or indirectly affect a short sale. It also makes it unlawful for any person to use or employ in connection with the purchase or sale of any security any deceptive or manipulative practice in contrary to the rules or regulations prescribed by the SEC as necessary to protect the public interest.

Solution 40-2 ADDITIONAL MULTIPLE CHOICE ANSWERS

Securities Act of 1933

41. (a) Under the Federal Securities Act of 1933, a prospectus is part of the registration statement and must be filed with the Securities and Exchange Commission (SEC). The SEC does not pass on the merits of securities offered for sale. The SEC merely requires that certain information be provided to security purchasers to enable them to make knowledgeable investment decisions. The prospectus and registration statement must be filed with the SEC before any offer to sell can be made. A preliminary prospectus may be distributed during the 20-day waiting period. Furthermore, although the SEC looks for material deficiencies in the financial statement, it does not approve the accuracy of the facts contained therein.

42. (b) The 1933 Act makes it unlawful for any person, directly or indirectly, to make use of any means or instruments of interstate commerce to carry or transmit for the purpose of sale, any security, including common stock, unless such security is

accompanied or preceded by a prospectus that meets the requirements of the Act.

43. (b) Under the Securities Act of 1933, registration of certain securities is required to provide investors with information material to making an investment decision. The registration statement will generally include a description of the issuer's business and property, a description of management, a description of the security to be issued and its relationship to the issuer's other securities, and the issuer's most recent audited financial statement. The investor is generally not provided information on the stockholders of the offering corporation. The SEC does not guarantee the accuracy of the information in registration statements, nor does it assure against loss.

44. (d) A "red herring" prospectus is a limited preliminary prospectus that must accompany any written offers to sell an initial issue of a security after the filing of the registration period and during the 20-day waiting period. Although the financial statement which is part of the registration statement must be audited, and the audit should be unqualified, there is no such thing as an unaudited, qualified, or "blue sky" prospectus.

45. (c) Rule 505 of Regulation D requires that the offering be reported to the SEC within 15 days after the first sale of the offering. The number of nonaccredited purchasers is limited to 35. Rule 505 specifically prohibits general advertisement. The required information includes audited financial statements and not a prospectus.

46. (a) Rule 506 (also Rule 505) does not allow a general solicitation. Rule 506 allows sales to up to 35 nonaccredited investors who are "sophisticated investors" and to an unlimited number of accredited investors. Under Rule 506, the SEC must be notified within 15 days after the first sale of the securities. Thus, notifying the SEC 14 days after the first sale would not cause the securities to lose their exemption.

47. (c) Under the Securities Act of 1933, securities are defined broadly as any security that allows an investor to make a profit on an investment through the efforts of others rather than through her/his own efforts. Therefore, a general partnership interest would not likely be considered a security under the 1933 Act since partners in a general partnership have a right to manage and are considered active in the management of the business. Under the 1933 Act, securities are broadly defined to include stock options, warrants, and limited partnership interests.

48. (b) Among those securities that are exempt from registration under the 1933 Act is a class of stock given in exchange for another class by the issuer to its existing stockholders without the issuer paying a commission. Answers (a), (c), and (d) are not among the specified exempt securities.

49. (a) Securities exempt from the registration requirements of the Securities Act of 1933 are not exempt from the Act's fraud provisions. The 1933 Act provides that both the SEC and persons defrauded may challenge fraudulent activities.

50. (b) Securities of a bank are specifically listed as being exempt from registration under the Securities Act of 1933. Exempt securities may be sold and resold any number of times and never be subject to the registration and/or prospectus requirements of the Act. These exemptions are granted because (1) it is felt that registration is not necessary to protect the public interest, (2) the securities are regulated by another government agency, or (3) the nature of the security, for example commercial paper, necessitates that it be exempt. Answers (a), (c), and (d) are all securities or offerings that are not specifically listed as exempt, and must be registered under the 1933 Act.

Securities Act of 1934

51. (d) The statutory definition of a security includes conventional securities, such as stocks, bonds, or notes and any interest or instrument commonly known as a "security." It also includes any certificate or interest or participation in, temporary or interim certificate for, receipt for, guarantee of, or warrant or right to subscribe to or purchase, any of the foregoing. A certificate of deposit is a written acknowledgment by a bank of the receipt of a stated sum of money with an engagement to repay that sum. A certificate of deposit does not represent an interest in or participation in a company and, therefore, does not meet the definition of a security.

52. (a) A person who successfully sues under the anti-fraud provisions may recover damages. Persons who willfully violate any provision of Section 10(b) may be held criminally liable and are subject to a fine or imprisonment.

53. (d) Corporations whose securities are traded on a national security exchange or whose assets are in excess of $10 million and have a class of equity security held on record by 500 or more persons must register under the 1934 Act.

PERFORMANCE BY SUBTOPICS

Each category below parallels a subtopic covered in Chapter 40. Record the number and percentage of questions you correctly answered in each subtopic area.

Securities Act of 1933

Question #	Correct √
1	
2	
3	
4	
# Questions	4
# Correct	______
% Correct	______

Exempt Securities

Question #	Correct √
5	
6	
7	
# Questions	3
# Correct	______
% Correct	______

Exempt Transactions

Question #	Correct √
8	
9	
10	
11	
12	
13	
14	
15	
16	
17	
18	
19	
20	
21	
# Questions	14
# Correct	______
% Correct	______

Registration Process

Question #	Correct √
22	
23	
24	
25	
26	
27	
# Questions	6
# Correct	______
% Correct	______

Securities Act of 1934

Question #	Correct √
28	
29	
30	
31	
32	
33	
34	
35	
36	
37	
38	
39	
40	
# Questions	13
# Correct	______
% Correct	______

SIMULATION SOLUTION

Solution 40-3 Issuance of Securities

Regulation D (4 points)

1. Yes

Rule 504 allows up to $1 million in interstate sales. In this case, the offering was for $450,000—well within the limit.

2. Yes

Rule 504 allows an offering by general solicitation if certain restrictions are in place.

3. No

Rule 504 specifies that the sale must be completed within 12 months. In this case, the sale took place over two years—well outside the limit.

4. Yes

Rule 504 does not limit the number of investors.

5. Yes

Under Rule 504 the issuer must notify the SEC within 15 days of the sale. In this case, the notification was made eight days after the first sale—well within the limit.

6. Yes

This offering was not exempt because it was not sold during the applicable time limit.

7. No

Rule 505 sets a dollar limit of $5 million for a sale. In this case, the sale was for $6 million—well outside the limit.

8. Yes

Rule 505 prohibits general solicitation; it does not prohibit a sale made by private placement.

9. Yes

Rule 505 specifies that the sale must take place within twelve months. In this case, it was stated that the sale took place during a one-year time period—within the limit.

10. No

Rule 505 limits the sale to 35 non-accredited investors. In this case, the sale was made to 40 non-accredited investors—outside the limit.

11. No

Under Rule 505 the issuer must notify the SEC within 15 days of the sale. In this case, the notification was made 18 days after the sale—outside the limit.

12. Yes

This offering was not exempt because it did not comply with the dollar limit of the sale, the limits on the number of non-accredited investors, or with the requirement governing notification of the SEC.

13. Yes

Under Rule 505, if there are any non-accredited investors, disclosures must include audited financial statements. The Year 2 audited financial statements were distributed to investors in each stock offering.

14. Yes

Rule 506 does not set a dollar limit on the amount of the sale.

15. Yes

Rule 506 prohibits general solicitation; it does not prohibit a sale made by private placement.

16. Yes

Rule 506 does not limit the time in which the sale must take place.

17. Yes

Rule 506 limits the sale to 35 nonaccredited investors and an unlimited number of accredited investors. In this case, the offering was sold to 30 nonaccredited investors and 200 accredited investors—well within the limit.

18. Yes

Under Rule 506, the issuer must notify the SEC within 15 days of the sale. In this case, the notification was made 14 days after the sale—within the limit.

19. No

This offering would be permitted under Rule 506, since it did not violate any of the applicable requirements.

20. Yes

Under Rule 506, purchasers must hold the stock 2 or more years before resale.

Communication (5 points)

To: D. Boss
From: A. Candidate
Re: Weaver's Possible Liability—Butler Audit

Butler's stockholders who purchased stock under the Year 3 offerings likely will be successful in their suit against Weaver under Section 10(b) and Rule 10b-5 of the Securities Exchange Act of 1934. Under the Act, stock purchaser must show:

- **intentional material** misstatement or omission (scienter)
- **reliance**
- **loss**

Weaver's failure to qualify its opinion for Butler's potential legal liability was **material** and done intentionally (**scienter**). Weaver will be liable for losses sustained by the purchasers who **relied** on Weaver's opinion.

Research (1 point)

IRC Section Answer: §2512(b)

Code §2512(b) states, "Where property is transferred for less than an adequate and full consideration in money or money's worth, then the amount by which the value of the property exceeded the value of the consideration shall be deemed a gift, and shall be included in computing the amount of gifts made during the calendar year."

Hot•Spot™ Video Descriptions

(Selected subjects only; subject to change without notice.)

CPA 2165, Commercial Paper & Documents of Title
John Norman provides coverage of commercial paper, including the types of commercial paper, elements of negotiability, types of endorsements, liabilities of parties, and holders in due course. The documents of title discussion includes the form, content, negotiability, and effects of documents of title.

CPA 2296, Secured Transactions
In this video program, John Norman provides detailed coverage of the UCC rules for secured transactions.

CPA 3190, Bankruptcy & Suretyship
During this program, John Norman explains the different chapters of the federal bankruptcy code, including the means test and the credit counseling requirement. He contrasts voluntary and involuntary bankruptcy and outlines the disposition of a bankrupt's property. Jack explains preferential transfers, fraudulent conveyances, the priority of debts, and limitations on discharge. He outlines the roles of creditors, debtors, and trustees. Jack compares suretyship and guaranty contracts, highlighting the differences and similarities. He explains the obligations, rights, defenses, and remedies of sureties and guarantors.

CPA 3450, Fiduciary Relationships
John Norman discusses the types of estates and common distribution terms. He examines trust elements, types, allocations and terminations. Jack considers agency relationships, including different types of authority, duties, liabilities, and termination.

CPA 2135, Government Regulation of Business
During this program, John Norman reviews securities law, payroll tax issues, the regulation of human resources, and antitrust statutes. Jack explains the purpose and provisions of the Securities Act of 1933 and of the Securities Exchange Act of 1934, including filing and reporting requirements and proxy rules. He discusses the anti-fraud provisions. Jack reviews the major areas of employment-related regulation of business, including Social Security, unemployment tax acts, and workers' compensation. He explains how antitrust laws prohibit anticompetitive behavior.

CPA 3480, Property & Insurance
Ivan Fox discusses the differences among real property and fixtures, types of deeds, the recording statutes for both mortgages and deeds, as well as assuming a mortgage and taking subject to a mortgage. Landlord and tenant law is explained. Insurance topics also are covered.

STUDY TIP

Environmental Regulation

Although the AICPA's Content Specifications Outline (CSO) dated June 2002 does not specifically list environmental regulations under Other Government Regulation (CSO location of II.D.2), there is a slight possibility of it being tested on the CPA exam. The editors suggest candidates review this material only after mastery of other exam topics is complete. See the Practical Advice appendix for the complete CSO.

CHAPTER 41

OTHER REGULATIONS

EXAM COVERAGE: The business law portion of the Regulation section of the CPA exam is designated by the examiners to be 20-25 percent of the section's point value. More information about point distribution and information eligible to be tested is included in the **Practical Advice** section of this volume.

CHAPTER 41

OTHER REGULATIONS

I. Federal Social Security Act

A. Social Insurance Programs

The Social Security Act contains provisions for several social insurance programs that affect employer-employee relationships. The availability of benefits under these programs depends upon the attainment by the individual of insured status. Certain lengths of working time are required to attain insured status.

1. **Old-Age, Survivors & Disability Insurance Benefits** An individual who is insured fully is eligible for the following benefits: survivors' benefits for dependents; benefits for dependents of retired disabled workers; lump-sum death benefits; and old age retirement benefits. Divorced spouses may receive benefits under some circumstances.

   a. The amount of benefits paid under these programs generally depends on the following: the average monthly earnings of the insured before retirement; the relationship of the beneficiary to the retired, deceased, or disabled worker; increased benefits based on the cost of living; and increased benefits for delayed retirement.

   b. A reduction of social security benefits can occur in the following situations. Early retirement results in reduced benefits. Returning to work after retirement can reduce social security benefits. Social security retirement benefits are reduced $1 for every $2 of earned income above a base amount that varies from year to year. Receipt of payments under a private pension plan will not limit the payment of social security benefits to an otherwise qualifying individual.

2. **Unemployment Insurance Benefits** Benefits received as unemployment compensation are fully includible in gross (taxable) income.

   a. **State Laws** State laws govern eligibility for unemployment benefits and the amount of such benefits. All states require substantial past employment. Generally, unemployment benefits are provided to workers who are discharged through no fault of their own. The amount of benefits varies from state to state. Unemployment benefits are **not** available to the self-employed.

   b. **Employer Funding** Unemployment benefits are funded by contributions from employers only and are considered to be deductible as a business expense for federal income tax purposes.

B. Financing

1. **Old-Age, Survivors, Disability & Hospital Insurance Programs** The old-age, survivors, disability, and hospital insurance programs are financed through payments made under the provisions of the Federal Insurance Contributions Act (FICA) and the Self-Employment Contributions Act. The tax consists of a component for Social Security and a component for Medicare. For both employees' and self-employed people's contributions, there is a maximum wage base subject to social security tax; however, there is no limit on the Medicare portion of the tax.

   a. **FICA** Both the employer and employee are taxed at the same percentage rate. FICA requires the employer to withhold the employee's share from the employee's wages as they are paid.

(1) **Notice** The employer is required to furnish the employee with a written statement of wages paid and contributions withheld during the calendar year.

(2) **Penalty** The employer's failure to withhold the employee's contribution may cause the employer to be responsible for both the employee's and employer's share of taxes (e.g., a double tax liability).

(3) **Business Related** FICA contributions made by the employer for employee services are generally deductible as a business expense.

(4) **Non-Business Related** If the services rendered by the employee are not business oriented (e.g., household help), then no deduction by the employer is allowed.

(5) **Employee Contributions** The share of contributions paid by the employee is not deductible by the employer.

(6) **Partially Excludable Benefits** For the employee, social security benefits are excludable from gross income, subject to certain limitations.

b. **Self-Employment** The self-employed rate is twice what employees pay; essentially a self-employed person pays both the employee's and employer's share. Individuals may deduct one-half of their self-employment taxes for income tax purposes as an adjustment to gross income. Effectively, this deduction is equivalent to the employer's deduction for the employer's share.

2. **Unemployment Insurance** The unemployment insurance program is financed through payments made by employers under federal and state unemployment insurance laws.

a. **Federal Unemployment Tax Act (FUTA)** An employer must pay the federal unemployment tax if s/he pays $1,500 or more in wages during any calendar quarter or if s/he employs one or more persons at least one day per week for 20 weeks during a calendar year. FUTA is paid only on the first $7,000 in wages paid to each covered employee in a calendar year, and is a deductible as a business expense for federal tax purposes.

b. **State Unemployment Tax Act (SUTA)** Employers are required to contribute to the Social Security Act's unemployment insurance program through the payment of state unemployment taxes.

(1) **Adjustment for Claims** The state unemployment tax may be adjusted according to the number and frequency of claims filed against the employer.

(2) **Credit Against FUTA** Employers, in states with acceptable claims levels, may credit their state unemployment tax payments against the federal unemployment tax for up to 90% of the federal unemployment tax liability.

C. **Coverage**

To be under the Social Security Act, a person must be an "employee," the services the person performs must be "employment," and the compensation the person receives must be "wages." Self-employed persons also are covered.

1. **Employee** An "employee" is a person whose performance is subject to the control of an employer. This control extends not only to the result, but to the details and means by which the result is accomplished.

a. Part-time as well as full-time employees are included under the coverage of the Act.

b. Partners, independent contractors, and self-employed persons are not covered by the unemployment compensation provisions since they are not "employees." They are treated as self-employed persons for purposes of coverage under the old-age, survivors, and disability programs.

c. Corporate officers and directors may qualify as "employees" depending upon the services they perform and the remuneration they receive.

2. **Employment** Employment includes all services performed by an employee for the person employing her/him.

a. Certain services are expressly exempted from the Act's definition of "employment." For example, services performed by ministers, student nurses, nonresident aliens, and certain public employees are not considered "employment" for purposes of coverage under the Social Security Act.

b. In order to constitute "employment," the services provided must be of a continuing or recurring nature.

3. **Wages** "Wages" generally include all remuneration for employment, including remuneration paid in a medium other than cash.

a. Such items as vacation and severance pay, bonuses, commissions, and tips (if amounting to $20 per month or more) are included in wages. Wages do not include the following: (1) insurance premiums paid by the employer; (2) employer-paid retirement benefits; (3) tips, if not in cash or if less than $20 per month; (4) compensation exceeding the maximum wage base; and (5) reimbursed travel expenses.

b. For purposes of the employer's share of FICA taxes, wages includes all cash tips subject to the employee FICA tax. Thus an employer must pay FICA taxes on the total amount of cash tips and other remuneration (up to the amount of compensation included as wages).

4. **Mandatory Coverage** Coverage under the Social Security Act is mandatory. Employees qualifying for coverage are not permitted to exchange their coverage for other benefits. Employees cannot elect not to be covered.

5. **Self-Employed** A person is self-employed if s/he carries on a trade or business either as an individual or in a partnership.

a. Carrying on a trade or business means engaging in extensive or repeated business activity for profit.

b. Self-employment income generally means the net compensation from self-employment and does not include earnings in excess of the maximum wage base.

II. Workers' Compensation

A. Purpose

Workers' compensation statutes were enacted to enable employees to recover for injuries regardless of negligence. Every state in the country has some form of workers' compensation law; federal employees are covered by a federal statute. These laws have four generally recognized objectives.

1. **Prompt Benefits** To provide prompt, reasonable benefits and compensation to work-related accident victims or their dependents.

2. **Single Remedy** To provide a single, relatively simple remedy for victims of work-related accidents. The remedy generally provided by workers' compensation laws does **not** require a finding of fault.

3. **Burden on Industry** To shift the financial burden of industrial accidents from public and private charities to the industry itself.

4. **Encourage Safety** To encourage employer interest in safety.

B. **Scope**
The workers' compensation laws in the various states are fairly uniform in the scope of their coverage. None of the state workers' compensation laws extend coverage to all employees. Some of the more common exceptions include domestic workers, agricultural workers, casual employees, and employees of common carriers. Most workers' compensation laws extend coverage to minors. The laws of most states permit employers to purchase insurance from either a private insurance company or a competitive state fund. However, several states require employers to purchase insurance from a state fund. Virtually all states permit employers to assume liability for workers' compensation claims. However, these self-insurers are required to demonstrate financial responsibility before they are permitted to forego the purchase of insurance. There are two general types of workers' compensation statutes. The current trend among the states is toward compulsory workers' compensation laws and away from elective laws.

1. **Employers** When an employee accepts the benefits of the workers' compensation laws, s/he is generally barred from suing the employer for damages.

2. **Third Parties** The employee's acceptance of benefits does not bar a suit against a third party whose negligence caused the injury. However, if the employee recovers from the third party, the employer is entitled to compensation for the benefits paid to the employee. If the employee's recovery exceeds the benefits paid to her/him by the employer, the employee may keep the excess.

3. **Elective** Elective workers' compensation statutes permit the employer to either accept or reject the provisions of the statute. An employer who rejects the elective statute loses the three common law defenses—**assumption of risk, negligence of fellow employees, and contributory negligence.** As a practical matter, this means that all workers' compensation laws are compulsory, since the loss of these defenses seriously impairs an employer's overall legal defense when an employee sues for damages.

4. **Compulsory** Compulsory workers' compensation laws require employers to accept the laws' provisions and provide the specified benefits.

C. **Benefits**
Benefits under workers' compensation laws usually fall into four categories: cash benefits, medical benefits, death benefits, and rehabilitation benefits. Amounts received under state workers' compensation acts are fully excludable from taxable income. Similarly, amounts received as a result of suit for injury or from employee paid health or accident insurance plans are also excludable from taxable income. However, amounts received from employer paid health and accident insurance plans, to the extent they are not reimbursements for expenses paid, are includible in the employees' gross income.

1. **Cash Benefits** Cash benefits are based on a percentage of the employee's regular weekly wage. They are limited with regard to the amount and number of payments. They include the following:

   a. Impairment benefits that are paid whenever the injury results in physical impairment.

   b. Disability benefits that are paid whenever there is physical impairment and wage loss.

2. **Medical Benefits** Medical benefits furnish the employee with medical care for job-related injuries or disease. There is usually no dollar or time limitation on medical benefits.

3. **Death Benefits** Death benefits generally include a burial allowance plus the payment of a percentage of the worker's former weekly wage. Payments are generally directed to the

deceased worker's spouse and minor children; however, payments normally cease upon the spouse's remarriage.

4. **Rehabilitation Benefits** Rehabilitation benefits include the following.

   a. Medical rehabilitation to facilitate a more complete recovery.

   b. Vocational rehabilitation, when the nature or severity of the injury necessitates retraining.

5. **Additional Benefits** In addition, some workers' compensation plans provide payment schedules for the loss of a limb or an eye.

D. **Administration**
Workers' compensation claims normally are handled by a state compensation board or commission. However, a few states delegate the administration of claims to the state judicial system. The time periods for reporting injuries and filing claims generally begin to run from the time the injury is first noticed, rather than from the time of the accident.

1. **Employer Reporting** Employers are required, under the penalty of law, to report all injuries.

2. **Employee Reporting to Employer** Employees are required to notify their employer promptly (usually within 30 days) of any injury.

3. **Employee Filing Claims** Employees are also required to file their claims with the appropriate state authority within a specified period (usually 60 days to two years).

   a. In some states, the failure of the employee to file the claim on time bars her/his recovery.

   b. In other states, the failure to file on time will bar the claim only if the delay has been prejudicial to the employer.

4. **Claims** Workers' compensation laws provide coverage for injuries that occur on the job or in the course of employment. Unless the workers' compensation coverage is inadequate, an employer who is covered by the workers' compensation laws may **not** be sued by her/his employees for unintentional job-related injuries. Employers may be sued for damages in excess of, or in lieu of, workers' compensation recoveries, if the employer intentionally injured the employee.

   a. The fact that the injury was caused by the injured employee's own negligence is **not** a bar to recovery.

   b. Employees usually are **not** covered during transit to and from the job. Coverage generally begins when the employee arrives on the employer's premises.

   c. Under most programs, coverage is not extended to injuries that are intentionally self-inflicted and injuries resulting from the employee's intoxication.

III. Other Employment-Related Laws

A. **Equal Employment Opportunity Commission (EEOC)**
The following employment laws come under the jurisdiction of the EEOC.

1. **Title VII of Civil Rights Act of 1964 (amended by Civil Rights Act of 1991)** Prohibits sexual harassment and employment discrimination on the basis of race, color, religion, sex, or national origin. Title VII applies to: employers and labor organizations whose businesses affect interstate commerce and who employ at least 15 people for at least 20 weeks a year; employment agencies; and federal, state, and local governments.

a. **Illegal Discrimination** Illegal discrimination, as described under Title VII, includes the following.

(1) Employer uses prescribed rules, which affect a protected class, in making an employment decision (hiring, firing, promoting, etc.)

(2) Employer engages in conduct that perpetuates past discriminatory practices.

(3) Employer adopts rules that adversely affect a protected class and are not necessary for business.

b. **Defenses** Defenses to alleged Title VII violations are limited to the following.

(1) Bona fide occupational qualification (This may be a defense to allegations of discrimination involving religion, sex, and national origin, but not race.)

(2) National security

(3) Seniority or merit system

(4) Professionally developed ability test

2. **Age Discrimination in Employment Act** Protects workers, age 40 or older, from discrimination in hiring, firing, compensating, and other employment-related processes, on the basis of age. This Act also prohibits the mandatory retirement of most employees, no matter what their age. Exception is provided for in the case of bona fide executives and high policy-making employees. Remedies include back pay, injunctive relief, affirmative action, and liquidated damages equal to the amount of the award for "willful" violations.

3. **Rehabilitation Act of 1973** Directs federal contractors and agencies to take affirmative action with respect to hiring "otherwise qualified" handicapped individuals and prohibits discrimination on the basis of handicap in federal and federally assisted programs.

4. **Equal Pay Act** Prohibits wage discrimination on the basis of sex.

5. **Americans With Disabilities Act of 1990** Protects disabled individuals from discrimination and guarantees equal access to services.

6. **Civil Rights Act of 1991** Reaffirms the rights of complainants alleging employment discrimination.

7. **Reverse Discrimination** There has been a growing number of challenges to employer's affirmative action plans that remedy the under-representation of a protected class by considering a person's race or gender as hiring criteria.

a. **Private Employers** Challenges to private employer's affirmative action plans are brought under Title VII.

b. **Government Employers** Challenges to affirmative action plans imposed by government agencies are brought under the Equal Protection Clause in the fourteenth amendment of the United States Constitution.

B. **Occupational Safety & Health Act (OSHA)**
OSHA was enacted by Congress in 1970 in order to ensure a safe working environment for employees.

1. **Coverage** OSHA applies to all employees of businesses that affect interstate commerce.

a. **Temporary Exemptions** Employers may obtain temporary exemptions from some OSHA standards when an inability to comply within required time can be demonstrated.

b. **Permanent Exemptions** Permanent exemptions from some OSHA standards may sometimes be given to employers if they can show that their safety methods comply with the safety standards of OSHA.

2. **Enforcement** The Occupational Safety and Health Administration is in charge of administering the act. OSHA allows inspectors to enter the workplace.

a. **Warrant** OSHA regulations require that an inspector have a warrant in order to inspect a business. The legal standard, "probable cause," is necessary to obtain a warrant. Probable cause is not a high standard. Employee complaints may be sufficient for probable cause. Employees making complaints may have names withheld upon request.

b. **Employer Records** OSHA requires that employers keep records of accidents and report serious accidents to the Occupational Safety and Health Administration.

3. **Penalties** The Occupational Safety and Health Administration can issue citations, impose fines, and assess civil penalties for violations to the act. Willful violations that lead to an employee's death may result in criminal prosecution. Employers can be forced to correct violations. Penalties and citations may be appealed to the Occupational Safety and Health Review Commission.

C. **Federal Fair Labor Standards Act (Wage-Hour Law)**
The Fair Labor Standards Act of 1938 is applicable to all employers engaged in interstate commerce.

1. **Maximum Hours** Any employee who works more than 40 hours per week must be paid no less than one and one half times her/his regular pay for those hours exceeding 40 hours. An exception exists for certain employees whose duties necessitate irregular working hours and who also meet other criteria.

2. **Minimum Wage** Congress specifies the minimum wage per hour for employees in covered industries. This amount is periodically revised by Congress.

3. **Opportunity Wage** Employees under the age of 20 years may be hired at a wage of less than minimum wage but no less than a specified wage, for the first 90 consecutive calendar days of employment.

4. **Child Labor** Children under the age of sixteen cannot be employed full-time, except by a parent under certain circumstances. Also, children between the ages of sixteen and eighteen cannot be employed in hazardous jobs or perform tasks detrimental to their health and well-being.

D. **Employee Retirement Income Security Act (ERISA)**
This 1974 act does not require employers to set up a pension plan for their employees, but it does set standards that employers must follow if they choose to implement a plan. Employee contributions to the pension plan must vest immediately. Employee's rights to employer's contributions must vest after five years of employment. Investment of pension funds is subject to certain standards in order to avoid mismanagement.

E. **Federal Consolidated Budget Reconciliation Act (COBRA)**
The Federal Consolidated Budget Reconciliation Act (COBRA) provides that former employees, whether they quit, are fired, or laid-off, may retain their health insurance coverage for a period of up to 18 months (or up to 36 months in certain circumstances), at their own expense. Under the American Recovery & Reinvestment Act of 2009 (ARRA '09), people involuntarily separated from employment from September 1, 2008, through December 31, 2009, may elect for payments of 35% of COBRA coverage treated as full payment. The former employer is reimbursed for the difference by crediting it against income taxes.

IV. Antitrust Regulation

A. Overview

Aims to prevent unreasonable restraints on trade or commerce that would weaken or halt competition by prohibiting anticompetitive practices. The Federal Trade Commission (FTC) is charged with the prevention of unfair methods of competition and unfair or deceptive practices.

B. Sherman Antitrust Act

Prohibits contracts, combinations, and conspiracies that restrain trade and monopolization (including attempts and conspiracies to monopolize). Violations can result in criminal and civil penalties. There are two standards used by courts.

1. **Rule of Reason** The rule of reason is a standard used by the courts to determine whether a practice unreasonably restricts trade by analyzing the anticompetitive and procompetition effects of the restraint. Price fixing is an agreement among producers or sellers to raise or maintain the price at a certain level as to impede free enterprise. Price fixing agreements can be either horizontal or vertical. Horizontal price fixing agreements are agreements between sellers at the same level who determine the price of goods or services. Vertical price fixing agreements are agreements between distributors and retailers in the same distribution chain who determine the price of goods and services.

   a. **Vertical Price Fixing** Vertical maximum price fixing agreements (agreements between distributors and retailers who determine the *maximum* price of goods and services) are judged under the rule of reason. Effective June 28, 2007, vertical minimum price fixing agreements (agreements between distributors and retailers who determine the *minimum* price of goods and services) also are judged under the rule of reason.

   b. **Horizontal Price Fixing** All horizontal price fixing agreements are *per se* unlawful.

2. ***Per se* Violations** Activities determined by the courts to be detrimental to competition (by their nature are deemed unreasonable).

   a. **Horizontal Restraints** Agreements among competitors at the same level in the distribution chain.

   b. **Market Allocation** Market separation by customer type, geographic area, or product whereby competitors agree not to compete. Horizontal agreements are *per se* unlawful, whereas vertical agreements are judged under the rule of reason.

   c. **Group Boycotts** Agreements among competitors who refuse to deal with a third party to eliminate competition or force group standards on a competitor.

   d. **Tying Arrangements** Seller conditions the sale of a desired product (tying product) on the buyer's purchasing a second product (tied product). If the seller has substantial economic power in the tying product and affects a "not insubstantial" amount of sales in the tied product, then the tying arrangement is considered *per se* unlawful.

3. **Monopolies** Monopolization requires market power (ability to control price or exclude competition) plus either the unfair attainment of or abuse of such power. Attempts (specific intent plus a dangerous probability of success) to and conspiracies (plan) to monopolize are also prohibited. Monopolization includes both monopoly power and "willful acquisition or maintenance of monopoly power in a relevant market as opposed to growth as a consequence of superior product, business acumen, or historical accident" indicates monopolization. A relevant market includes both the geographic and the product market.

   - **Patents** There is a contradiction between antitrust and patent objectives of promoting competition and innovation, respectively. A patent is a legal monopoly. The right to license others to manufacture the patented item essentially would be negated if the patent holder could not set prices for the patented goods sold by its licensees;

however, the patent holder can not set the prices that purchasers of the patented goods charge their customers. Generally, patent rights would be exploited unjustifiably by activities such as price fixing, price discrimination, or tying arrangements.

C. Clayton Act

The Clayton Act prohibits arrangements that tend to create a monopoly or may substantially lessen competition. Only civil penalties can result from these violations. In addition to tying arrangements, the Clayton Act prohibits the following.

1. **Exclusive Dealing Arrangements** The seller has absolute right to all requirements for a product.

2. **Horizontal Merger** A company's acquisition of a company at the same distribution level (competitor). Horizontal mergers generally raise the market share and reduce the number of competitors.

3. **Vertical Merger** A company's acquisition of a company at different levels of the distribution chain (supplier or customer). Vertical mergers generally raise entry barriers in the industry or deprive other business of substantial number of customers or suppliers to be competitive.

4. **Conglomerate Merger** An acquisition of a company that is not competitor, customer, or supplier (unrelated businesses). Conglomerate mergers generally raise the market share and may potentially reduce the number of competitors.

D. Robinson-Patman Act

Further prohibits price discrimination by prohibiting buyers from inducing or sellers from giving different prices to buyers of commodities of similar grade and quality. Violations can result in criminal and civil penalties. The plaintiff may prove injury to competitors of the seller (primary-line injury), to competitors of other buyers (second-line injury), or to purchasers from other secondary-line injury seller (tertiary-line injury). Cost justification and meeting competition are defenses.

V. Appendix: Environmental Regulation

A. National Environmental Policy Act (NEPA)

This act established the Council on Environmental Quality (CEQ) which helps insure that various environmental laws are followed. NEPA also requires an environmental impact statement before any federal laws can be adopted or activities undertaken that might affect the environment.

B. Environmental Protection Agency (EPA)

Established by presidential executive order, the EPA is authorized to enforce all laws whose design is to protect the environment. The EPA may use both civil and criminal prosecution.

1. **Safe Drinking Water Act** This act empowers the EPA to set standards for drinking water.

2. **Resource Conservation & Recovery Act (RCRA)** This act empowers the EPA to set standards related to the generation, transporting and disposal of hazardous wastes. The EPA has the power to seek injunctions against violators.

3. **Toxic Substances Control Act (TSCA)** This act requires the EPA to control the manufacture, processing, and distribution of all chemicals in the United States. TSCA gives the EPA authority to review all new chemicals before they are introduced in the marketplace and to regulate chemicals where they present reasonable risks. The EPA may require companies to conduct certain health effects and environmental testing. TSCA also contains requirements for the reporting and retention of information on the risks of TSCA-regulated substances.

C. Clean Air Act (CAA)

This act covers stationary emission sources, mobile emission sources, acid rain, and toxic industrial emissions. Industrial facilities that emit toxic air pollutants are required by CAA to reduce emissions by installing the best available emission control technology. Environmental impact and costs are considered in the enforcement of CAA.

D. Federal Water Pollution Control Act (Clean Water Act)
This act is designed to improve the quality of our nation's waterways by making the water safe for recreational use and protecting wildlife associated with the waterways. Activities regulated under the Clean Water Act include the discharge of heated water by nuclear power plants and the dredging of wetlands. Industrial sources of pollution are required by this Act to install the best available technology for control and treatment of the pollution, taking into account costs and other factors.

E. Comprehensive Environmental Response, Compensation & Liability Act (CERCLA)
Congress passed CERCLA in 1980 and amended it in 1986 by the Superfund Amendments & Reauthorization Act (SARA). CERCLA provides for the establishment of a national inventory of inactive hazardous waste sites, and the creation of a multimillion dollar Hazardous Waste Fund (commonly called Superfund) to pay the cost of eliminating or containing the condemned waste sites. It also provides for severe penalties.

1. **Strict Liability** The courts have interpreted CERCLA to impose **strict liability;** responsible parties are liable regardless of fault. The following are **jointly and severally liable** for the cleanup costs.

   a. The person who created the waste

   b. The person who transported the waste to the site

   c. The owner or operator of the site at disposal time

   d. The **current** owner or operator

2. **Unusual Results** Liability under CERCLA leads to some unusual results.

   a. A person who created only a fraction of the waste at a site may be held liable for all cleanup costs at that site.

   b. A corporation's officers, shareholders, and secured creditors, who had the authority to exercise control over the financial management of the facility to a degree indicating influence on the corporation's handling of hazardous waste, have been included in the definition of owners or operators and have been found liable.

F. Emergency Planning & Community Right to Know Act (EPCRA)
Enacted as part of the Federal Superfund Amendments and Reauthorization Act (SARA), this act is based on the principle that citizens have a right to know about hazardous and toxic chemicals in their communities. Entities that have certain quantities of extremely hazardous substances are required to notify state and local authoritative agencies and annually report releases of certain toxic chemicals that occur as a result of normal business operations. This information is made available to the general public.

"On-Demand" Exam

There are four windows annually; the first one starts in January. A candidate may sit for any particular exam section only once during a window. Between windows there is a dark period of about a month when the exam is not administered. Once a candidate has a passing score for one section, that candidate has a certain length of time (typically 18 months) to pass the other three exam sections, or lose the credit for passing that first exam section. Candidates should check with the appropriate Board of Accountancy concerning details on the length of time to pass all four sections. Exam sites typically are open on Monday through Friday; some are open on Saturday as well.

January	February	March
April	May	June
July	August	September
October	November	December

More helpful exam information is included in the **Practical Advice** appendix in this volume.

CHAPTER 41—OTHER REGULATIONS

Problem 41-1 MULTIPLE CHOICE QUESTIONS (60 to 80 minutes)

1. Under the Federal Insurance Contributions Act (FICA), which of the following acts will cause an employer to be liable for penalties?

	Failure to supply taxpayer identification numbers	*Failure to make timely FICA deposits*
a.	Yes	Yes
b.	Yes	No
c.	No	Yes
d.	No	No

(11/95, Law, #31, 5900)

2. Lee repairs high-speed looms for Sew Corp., a clothing manufacturer. Which of the following circumstances best indicates that Lee is an employee of Sew and **not** an independent contractor?
a. Lee's work is not supervised by Sew personnel.
b. Lee's tools are owned by Lee.
c. Lee is paid weekly by Sew.
d. Lee's work requires a high degree of technical skill. (R/01, Law, #5, 7040)

3. An employer who fails to withhold Federal Insurance Contributions Act (FICA) taxes from covered employees' wages, but who pays both the employer and employee shares would
a. Be entitled to a refund from the IRS for the employees' share
b. Be allowed **no** federal tax deduction for any payments
c. Have a right to be reimbursed by the employees for the employees' share
d. Owe penalties and interest for failure to collect the tax (5/92, Law, #36, 2849)

4. Under the Federal Insurance Contributions Act (FICA) and the Social Security Act (SSA),
a. Persons who are self-employed are **not** required to make FICA contributions.
b. Employees who participate in private retirement plans are **not** required to make FICA contributions.
c. Death benefits are payable to an employee's survivors only if the employee dies before reaching the age of retirement.
d. The receipt of earned income by a person who is also receiving social security retirement benefits may result in a reduction of such benefits.
(5/89, Law, #37, 0725)

5. Social security benefits may include all of the following **except**
a. Payments to divorced spouses
b. Payments to disabled children
c. Medicare payments
d. Medicaid payments (5/91, Law, #36, 0716)

6. Which of the following forms of income, if in excess of the annual exempt amount, will cause a reduction in a retired person's social security benefits?
a. Annual proceeds from an annuity
b. Director's fees
c. Pension payments
d. Closely held corporation stock dividends
(5/93, Law, #26, 3994)

7. Social security may be obtained by
a. Qualifying individuals who are also receiving benefits from a private pension plan
b. Qualifying individuals or their families only upon such individual's disability or retirement
c. Children of a deceased worker who was entitled to benefits until such children reach age 25 or complete their education, whichever occurs first
d. Only those individuals who have made payments while employed (11/86, Law, #39, 0731)

8. Syl Corp. does **not** withhold FICA taxes from its employees' compensation. Syl voluntarily pays the entire FICA tax for its share and the amounts that it could have withheld from the employees. The employees' share of FICA taxes paid by Syl to the IRS is
a. Deductible by Syl as additional compensation that is includible in the employees' taxable income
b. Not deductible by Syl because it does **not** meet the deductibility requirement as an ordinary and necessary business expense
c. A nontaxable gift to each employee, provided that the amount is less than $1,000 annually to each employee
d. Subject to prescribed penalties imposed on Syl for its failure to withhold required payroll taxes
(5/94, Law, #26, 4781)

9. Taxes payable under the Federal Unemployment Tax Act (FUTA) are
a. Calculated as a fixed percentage of all compensation paid to an employee
b. Deductible by the employer as a business expense for federal income tax purposes
c. Payable by employers for all employees
d. Withheld from the wages of all covered employees (11/95, Law, #32, 5901)

10. An employer having an experience unemployment tax rate of 3.2% in a state having a standard unemployment tax rate of 5.4% may take a credit against a 6.2% federal unemployment tax rate of
a. 3.0%
b. 3.2%
c. 5.4%
d. 6.2% (5/91, Law, #37, 0717)

11. For the entire year, Ral Supermarket, Inc. conducted its business operations without any permanent or full-time employees. Ral employed temporary and part-time workers during each of the 52 weeks in the year. Under the provisions of the Federal Unemployment Tax Act (FUTA), which of the following statements is correct regarding Ral's obligation to file a federal unemployment tax return?
a. Ral must file a FUTA return only if aggregate wages exceeded $100,000.
b. Ral must file a FUTA return because it had at least one employee during at least 20 weeks.
c. Ral is obligated to file a FUTA return only if at least one worker earned $50 or more in any calendar quarter.
d. Ral does not have to file a FUTA return because it had **no** permanent or full-time employees. (11/94, Law, #35, amended, 5212)

12. Which of the following payments are deducted from an employee's salary?

	Unemployment compensation insurance	*Workers' compensation insurance*
a.	Yes	Yes
b.	Yes	No
c.	No	Yes
d.	No	No

(5/95, Law, #36, 5370)

13. Which of the following parties generally is ineligible to collect workers' compensation benefits?
a. Minors
b. Truck drivers
c. Union employees
d. Temporary office workers (R/01, Law, #16, 7051)

14. Which of the following claims is(are) generally covered under workers' compensation statutes?

	Occupational disease	*Employment aggravated pre-existing disease*
a.	Yes	Yes
b.	Yes	No
c.	No	Yes
d.	No	No

(11/95, Law, #33, 5902)

15. Generally, which of the following statements concerning workers' compensation laws is correct?
a. The amount of damages recoverable is based on comparative negligence.
b. Employers are strictly liable without regard to whether or **not** they are at fault.
c. Workers' compensation benefits are **not** available if the employee is negligent.
d. Workers' compensation awards are payable for life. (11/95, Law, #34, 5903)

16. Kroll, an employee of Acorn, Inc., was injured in the course of employment while operating a forklift manufactured and sold to Acorn by Trell Corp. The forklift was defectively designed by Trell. Under the state's mandatory workers' compensation statute, Kroll will be successful in

	Obtaining workers' compensation benefits	*A negligence action against Acorn*
a.	Yes	Yes
b.	Yes	No
c.	No	Yes
d.	No	No

(5/93, Law, #28, 3996)

17. If an employee is injured, full workers' compensation benefits are **not** payable if the employee
a. Was injured because of failing to abide by written safety procedures
b. Was injured because of the acts of fellow employees
c. Intentionally caused self-inflicted injury
d. Brought a civil action suit against a third party who caused the injury (11/90, Law, #38, 0721)

18. Under the Federal Age Discrimination in Employment Act, which of the following practices is prohibited?
a. Termination of employees between the ages of 65 and 70 for cause
b. Mandatory retirement of any employee
c. Unintentional age discrimination
d. Termination of employees as part of a rational business decision (11/96, Law, #14, 6425)

19. Under the Age Discrimination in Employment Act, which of the following remedies is(are) available to a covered employee?

	Early retirement	*Back pay*
a.	Yes	Yes
b.	Yes	No
c.	No	Yes
d.	No	No

(11/95, Law, #35, 5904)

20. Under the Federal Age Discrimination in Employment Act, which of the following practices would be prohibited?

	Compulsory retirement of employees below the age of 65	*Termination of employees between the ages of 65 and 70 for cause*
a.	Yes	Yes
b.	Yes	No
c.	No	Yes
d.	No	No

(11/94, Law, #38, 5215)

21. Which of the following Acts prohibit(s) an employer from discriminating among employees based on sex?

	Equal Pay Act	*Title VII of the Civil Rights Act*
a.	Yes	Yes
b.	Yes	No
c.	No	Yes
d.	No	No

(11/95, Law, #36, 5905)

22. Under Title VII of the 1964 Civil Rights Act, which of the following forms of discrimination is **not** prohibited?

a. Sex
b. Age
c. Race
d. Religion (5/94, Law, #28, 4783)

23. Under the provisions of the Americans With Disabilities Act of 1990, in which of the following areas is a disabled person protected from discrimination?

	Public transportation	*Privately operated public accommodations*
a.	Yes	Yes
b.	Yes	No
c.	No	Yes
d.	No	No

(5/95, Law, #38, 5372)

24. Which of the following employee benefits is(are) exempt from the provisions of the National Labor Relations Act?

	Sick pay	*Vacation pay*
a.	Yes	Yes
b.	Yes	No
c.	No	Yes
d.	No	No

(11/95, Law, #40, 5909)

25. Which of the following statements is(are) correct regarding the authority of the Occupational Safety and Health Administration (OSHA)?

I. OSHA is authorized to establish standards that protect employees from exposure to substances that may be harmful to their health.
II. OSHA is authorized to develop safety equipment and require employers to instruct employees in its use.

a. I only
b. II only
c. Both I and II
d. Neither I nor II (5/97, Law, #4, 6445)

26. Under which of the following conditions is an on-site inspection of a workplace by an investigator from the Occupational Safety and Health Administration (OSHA) permissible?

a. Only if OSHA obtains a search warrant after showing probable cause
b. Only if the inspection is conducted after working hours
c. At the request of employees
d. After OSHA provides the employer with at least 24 hours notice of the prospective inspection

(5/95, Law, #37, 5371)

27. Which of the following statements is correct regarding the scope and provisions of the Occupational Safety and Health Act (OSHA)?

a. OSHA requires employers to provide employees a workplace free from risk.
b. OSHA prohibits an employer from discharging an employee for revealing OSHA violations.
c. OSHA may inspect a workplace at any time regardless of employer objection.
d. OSHA preempts state regulation of workplace safety. (5/94, Law, #27, 4782)

28. When verifying a client's compliance with statutes governing employees' wages and hours, an auditor should check the client's personnel records against relevant provisions of which of the following statutes?

a. National Labor Relations Act
b. Fair Labor Standards Act
c. Taft-Hartley Act
d. Americans With Disabilities Act

(5/95, Law, #39, 5373)

29. Under the Fair Labor Standards Act, which of the following pay bases may be used to pay covered, nonexempt employees who earn, on average, the minimum hourly wage?

	Hourly	*Weekly*	*Monthly*
a.	Yes	Yes	Yes
b.	Yes	Yes	No
c.	Yes	No	Yes
d.	No	Yes	Yes

(11/95, Law, #37, 5906)

30. Under the Federal Fair Labor Standards Act, which of the following would be regulated?

	Minimum wage	*Overtime*	*Number of hours in the work week*
a.	Yes	Yes	Yes
b.	Yes	No	Yes
c.	Yes	Yes	No
d.	No	Yes	Yes

(11/94, Law, #39, 5216)

31. Under the Employee Retirement Income Security Act of 1974 (ERISA), which of the following areas of private employer pension plans is(are) regulated?

	Employee vesting	*Plan funding*
a.	Yes	Yes
b.	Yes	No
c.	No	Yes
d.	No	No

(11/95, Law, #39, 5908)

32. Under the provisions of the Employee Retirement Income Security Act of 1974 (ERISA), which of the following statements is(are) correct regarding employee rights?

I. Employers are required to establish either a contributory or noncontributory employee pension plan.
II. Employers are required to include employees as pension-plan managers.

a. I only
b. II only
c. Both I and II
d. Neither I nor II (R/06, REG, 0337L, #1, 8171)

33. Under the Federal Consolidated Budget Reconciliation Act of 1985 (COBRA), when an employee voluntarily resigns from a job, the former employee's group health insurance coverage that was in effect during the period of employment with the company

a. Automatically ceases for the former employee and spouse, if the resignation occurred before normal retirement age
b. Automatically ceases for the former employee's spouse, but continues for the former employee for an 18-month period at the former employer's expense
c. May be retained by the former employee at the former employee's expense for at least 18 months after leaving the company, but must be terminated for the former employee's spouse
d. May be retained for the former employee and spouse at the former employee's expense for at least 18 months after leaving the company

(5/94, Law, #30, 4785)

34. Which of the following statements is (are) correct regarding the methods a target corporation may use to ward off a takeover attempt?

I. The target corporation may make an offer ("self-tender") to acquire stock from its own shareholders.
II. The target corporation may seek an injunction against the acquiring corporation on the grounds that the attempted takeover violates federal antitrust law.

a. I only
b. II only
c. Both I and II
d. Neither I nor II (R/01, Law, #10, 7584)

35. Royal Jewelry, a retailer, entered into agreements with other retail merchants whereby they agreed not to sell below Royal's minimum "suggested" retail price of $250 in exchange for Royal's agreeing not to sell its watches at retail in their respective territories. The agreement does not preclude the retail merchants from selling competitors' watches. It is illegal

a. Even though the price fixed is reasonable
b. If the product is a brand name or trademarked item
c. If the power to fix maximum prices is *not* surrendered
d. Unless it can be shown that the parties to the agreement were preventing ruthless competition (Editors, 7482)

36. Elle Corporation has made a major breakthrough in the development of a web-surfing "pen." Elle has patented the product and is seeking to maximize the profits from it. Elle legally may

a. Require its retailers to sell only Elle's products, including the web-surfing pen, and not sell similar competing products
b. Require its retailers to purchase, in addition to the pen, stipulated quantities of other products that are not required to use the web-surfing pen
c. Sell the product at whatever price the traffic will bear even though Elle has a monopoly
d. Sell the product to its retailers upon condition that they do not sell the web-surfing pen below a minimum price (Editors, 8525)

37. Due to recent significant cost increases, several competing road construction businesses decided to allocate construction projects among themselves based upon historic market share. Under the arrangement, a company would be designated to submit a low bid for each project, ensuring that the designated company would be awarded that contract. Such an arrangement is

a. Illegal *per se*
b. Illegal as judged under the rule of reason
c. Legally justifiable due to economic conditions in the marketplace
d. Legal under antitrust law since it does not fix prices (Editors, 8526)

38. Grounder Company, a price-cutting retail appliance dealer, is disliked by other retail appliance dealers and appliance manufacturers. Grounder's sales constitute less than 0.001% of the retail appliance market. The marketplace has an abundance of retailers and vigorous competition. In January 2008, appliance manufacturers and retailers jointly decide to boycott Grounder, limiting availability of inventory to it. Grounder has commenced legal action against these manufacturers and retailers based on a violation of the Sherman Antitrust Act.

a. Grounder is entitled to injunctive relief since the facts indicate a *per se* violation.
b. Grounder is entitled to injunctive relief against the interstate parties, but not intrastate parties.
c. Grounder's complaint would be dismissed since it alleges only a private wrong as opposed to a public wrong.
d. Grounder is entitled to injunctive relief against the other retail appliance dealers, but not the appliance manufacturers. (Editors, 8527)

39. Which of the following remedies is available against a real property owner to enforce the provisions of federal acts regulating air and water pollution?

	Citizen suits against the Environmental Protection Agency to enforce compliance with the laws	*State suits against violators*	*Citizen suits against violators*
a.	Yes	Yes	Yes
b.	Yes	Yes	No
c.	No	Yes	Yes
d.	Yes	No	Yes

(5/94, Law, #59, 4814)

40. Under the Comprehensive Environmental Response, Compensation, and Liability Act (CERCLA) if land is found to be contaminated, which of the following parties would be **least** likely to be liable for cleanup costs?

a. A bank that foreclosed a mortgage on the land and purchased the land at the foreclosure sale
b. A parent corporation of the corporation that owned the land
c. A minority stockholder of the public corporation that owned the land
d. A trustee appointed by the owner of the land to manage the land (R/05, REG, 0092L, #4, 7870)

Problem 41-2 ADDITIONAL MULTIPLE CHOICE QUESTIONS (30 to 40 minutes)

41. Tower drives a truck for Musgrove Produce Inc. The truck is owned by Musgrove. Tower is paid on the basis of a formula that takes into consideration the length of the trip, cargo, and fuel consumed. Tower is responsible for repairing or replacing all flat tires. Musgrove is responsible for all other truck maintenance. Tower drives only for Musgrove. If Tower is a common law employee and **not** an independent contractor, which of the following statements is correct?

a. All social security retirement benefits are fully includible in the determination of Tower's federal taxable income if certain gross income limitations are exceeded.
b. Musgrove remains primarily liable for Tower's share of FICA taxes if it fails to withhold and pay the taxes on Tower's wages.
c. Musgrove would **not** have to withhold FICA taxes if Tower elected to make FICA contributions as a self-employed person.
d. Bonuses or vacation pay that are paid to Tower by Musgrove are **not** subject to FICA taxes because they are **not** regarded as regular compensation. (5/90, Law, #26, 8026)

42. Under the Federal Insurance Contributions Act (FICA), all of the following are considered wages **except**

a. Contingent fees
b. Reimbursed travel expenses
c. Bonuses
d. Commissions (11/90, Law, #36, 0719)

43. An unemployed CPA generally would receive unemployment compensation benefits if the CPA

a. Was fired as a result of the employer's business reversals
b. Refused to accept a job as an accountant while receiving extended benefits
c. Was fired for embezzling from a client
d. Left work voluntarily without good cause (11/91, Law, #33, 2361)

44. The primary purpose for enacting workers' compensation statutes was to

a. Eliminate all employer-employee negligence lawsuits
b. Enable employees to recover for injuries regardless of negligence
c. Prevent employee negligence suits against third parties
d. Allow employees to recover additional compensation for employer negligence (5/91, Law, #38, 0718)

45. Under the Fair Labor Standards Act, if a covered, nonexempt employee works consecutive weeks of 45, 42, 38, and 33 hours, how many hours of overtime must be paid to the employee?

a. 0
b. 7
c. 18
d. 20 (11/95, Law, #38, 5907)

46. Which of the following statements correctly describes the funding of noncontributory pension plans?

a. All of the funds are provided by the employees.
b. All of the funds are provided by the employer.
c. The employer and employee each provide 50% of the funds.
d. The employer provides 90% of the funds, and each employee contributes 10%. (11/94, Law, #40, 5217)

47. Marvel Company manufacturers and sells distinctive clocks. Tinker Company purchased 100 of these clocks from Marvel at $99 each. One of Tinker's competitors, Soldier Company, also purchased 100 of the same model of clock from Marvel at $94 per clock. Marvel gives such discounts to all customers who, like Soldier, have done business with it continuously for ten years or more. In the event that Tinker litigates the issue,

a. Tinker must either show that Marvel has engaged in predatory pricing with intent to harm competition or present a detailed market analysis that demonstrates how the defendant's price discrimination actually harmed competition.
b. Marvel will prevail if Tinker cannot show that Marvel has engaged in predatory pricing with intent to harm competition.
c. Marvel will prevail if it can show that it sold clocks at the lower price to all customers that had done business with it continuously for ten years or more.
d. Marvel will prevail if it can establish that there were several other clock companies with which Tinker could deal if dissatisfied with Marvel. (Editors, 8528)

48. Which of the following types of penalties is(are) available against an individual who has violated the federal antitrust laws?

	Civil	*Criminal*
a.	Yes	Yes
b.	Yes	No
c.	No	Yes
d.	No	No

(Editors, 8533)

49. Masterpiece Reproductions, Inc., makes high quality lithographs of famous artists' works and sells them to art wholesalers nationwide. It requires its wholesalers not to purchase lithographs of competing companies during the three-year duration of the contract. The wholesalers may sell all other types of artwork, including oil, watercolor, and charcoal pictures. This exclusive dealing arrangement
a. Could be found to be illegal under the Clayton Act
b. Is legal *per se* since its duration is less than five years
c. Is legal since the wholesalers may sell all other types of artwork
d. Will be tested under the rule of reason and, only if found to be unreasonable, will be declared illegal (Editors, 8529)

50. Which of the following is a *per se* violation of federal antitrust laws?
a. Exclusive territorial rights to sell and corresponding limitations on selling outside the allocated territory by a manufacturer and its distributors
b. Sale of a patented product at an unreasonably high price
c. Tacit agreement with several leading competitors to respect each others' established relationships with customers
d. Unilateral refusal to deal with a troublesome wholesaler (Editors, 8530)

51. Alpine Corporation manufactures and sells a high-end line of featherweight luggage. In order to realize the full profit potential of its products, Alpine decides to enter into a franchising arrangement with selected outlets throughout the country. Its basic arrangement was to grant each outlet the exclusive right to sell in a designated geographic area and for each outlet not to sell outside its designated area. This arrangement
a. Is illegal *per se*
b. Is not illegal provided each outlet has the right to sell other manufacturers' featherweight luggage
c. Must be a consignment arrangement in order to avoid illegality under antitrust laws
d. Will be tested under the rule of reason and is legal if found to be reasonable (Editors, 8531)

52. TruServ Corporation makes a line of travel clothing from patented, wrinkle-resistant, drip-dry, and breathable cloth. TruServ discovered a discount store regularly using products from this line as loss leaders. In order to protect its product line, TruServ insisted on adherence to its minimum retail prices or a halt to deliveries to the discount store. TruServ
a. Engaged in price discrimination that is illegal *per se*
b. Engaged in price fixing, the legality of which will be judged under the rule of reason
c. Is not in violation of federal antitrust law as retail price maintenance is legal
d. Is not in violation of federal antitrust law as the product is under patent (Editors, 8532)

53. The phrase "illegal *per se*" as it is used in antitrust law
a. Applies exclusively to market allocation and tying arrangements
b. Applies exclusively to market allocation and group boycotts
c. Indicates conduct or agreements that are inherently illegal and without legal justification
d. Must be established in order to impose criminal penalties (Editors, 8534)

54. Under the federal statutes governing water pollution, which of the following areas is(are) regulated?

	Dredging of coastal or freshwater wetlands	*Drinking water standards*
a.	Yes	Yes
b.	Yes	No
c.	No	Yes
d.	No	No

(R/00, Law, #7, 6972)

55. Under the Clean Air Act, which of the following statements is(are) correct regarding actions that may be taken against parties who violate emission standards?

I. The federal government may require an automobile manufacturer to recall vehicles that violate emission standards.
II. A citizens' group may sue to force a coal-burning power plant to comply with emission standards.

a. I only
b. II only
c. Both I and II
d. Neither I nor II (11/98, Law, #9, 6754)

56. Which of the following actions should a business take to qualify for leniency if an environmental violation has been committed?

	Conduct environmental audits	*Report environmental violations to the government*
a.	Yes	Yes
b.	Yes	No
c.	No	Yes
d.	No	No

(R/99, Law, #12, 6863)

57. Under the Comprehensive Environmental Response, Compensation, and Liability Act (CERCLA), commonly known as Superfund, which of the following parties would be liable to the Environmental Protection Agency (EPA) for the expense of cleaning up a hazardous waste disposal site?

I. The current owner or operator of the site
II. The person who transported the wastes to the site
III. The person who owned or operated the site at the time of the disposal

a. I and II
b. I and III
c. II and III
d. I, II, and III (5/95, Law, #56, 5390)

58. Under the Federal Clean Air Act, which of the following statements is correct?

a. Power plants are required to eliminate all air polluting emissions.
b. Factories that emit toxic air pollutants are required to reduce emissions by installing the best available emission control technology.
c. Automobile manufacturers are required to have emission control equipment installed on previously manufactured vehicles.
d. Homeowners are required to remove all pollutants from their residences.

(5/96, Law, #7, 6263)

59. Which of the following activities is(are) regulated under the Federal Water Pollution Control Act (Clean Water Act)?

	Discharge of heated water by nuclear power plants	*Dredging of wetlands*
a.	Yes	Yes
b.	Yes	No
c.	No	Yes
d.	No	No

(11/95, Law, #57, 5926)

60. Which of the following parties is(are) responsible for enforcing federal air and water quality standards?

	Industry associations	*Political action groups*
a.	Yes	Yes
b.	Yes	No
c.	No	Yes
d.	No	No

(R/99, Law, #13, 6864)

SIMULATION

Problem 41-3 (20 to 30 minutes)

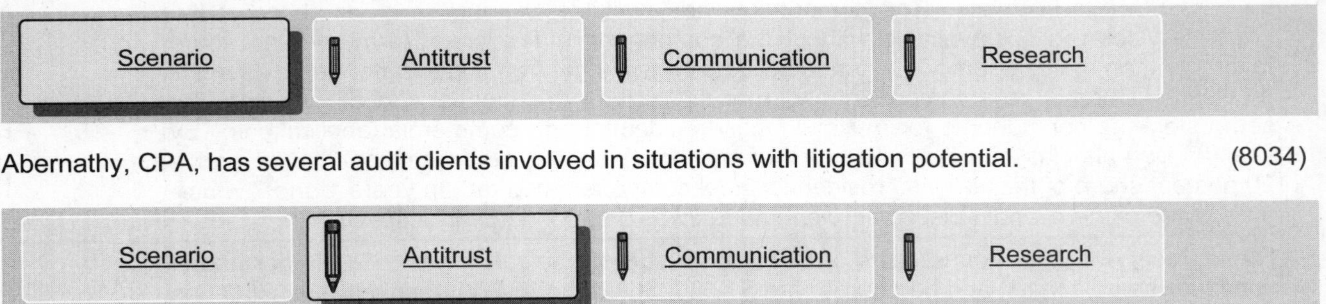

Abernathy, CPA, has several audit clients involved in situations with litigation potential. (8034)

For items 1 through 16 indicate if the actions of the business first named in each situation are (A) illegal price discrimination, (B) illegal monopolization or attempted monopolization, (C) an illegal tying arrangement, or (D) permissible under antitrust law.

	Situation	Answer
1.	Luxor Company, a car manufacturer, accounts for 5 percent of national car sales. Luxor maintains an exceptional reputation for reliable vehicles, with 75 percent of owners being repeat purchasers. Luxor considers it crucial that its dealers offer standardized products to protect customer confidence. Luxor requires franchised Luxor dealerships nationwide to agree to use only genuine Luxor parts in the repair or servicing of Luxor cars for quality assurance and protection of its trademark's reputation. Luxor makes approximately half of its parts and acquires the rest from other manufacturers producing parts in accordance with Luxor's specifications. Each shipment or lot is tested stringently by Luxor, after being tested at the plant. Any deficient parts discovered in testing cause the entire shipment or lot to be rejected. Michaels Wholesaling, a automotive parts distributor, filed an antitrust suit against Luxor, alleging that the sale of replacement parts is tied to the sale of Luxor cars illegally. Michaels Wholesaling claims furnishing manufacturing specifications for replacement parts to independent producers would eliminate any need for a tying arrangement.	
2.	In year 1, Laser Company started manufacturing fax machines, printers, and copiers. It sold this equipment nationwide. Laser furnishes service after an initial warranty period either through annual service contacts or on a per-call basis. Some service calls involve only service and some involve replacement parts. Laser also supplies parts and repair manuals to customers who prefer to service their own machines. Other manufacturer's parts are not interchangeable with Laser parts. Some parts are produced by Laser and others are made to Laser's specifications by original equipment manufacturers (OEMs). Several independent service provider (ISPs) repair and service equipment made by Laser and its competitors. In year 5, Laser started selling replacement parts only to Laser equipment buyers who use Laser service or repair their own machines and include clauses in contracts with OEMs to sell Laser parts only to Laser. Most ISPs discontinued service of Laser equipment, being unable to obtain parts reliably. Laser provided approximately 35 and 95 percent of the service for its machines in years 4 and 5, respectively. Several ISPs brought suit against Laser, claiming that Laser illegally tied the sale of service to replacement parts and attempted monopolization of the sale of service for Laser machines. Laser contends that even if it has a monopoly share of the replacement parts market, it doesn't have the economic power to impose significant restrictions in the service market as any increase in prices of service and parts above a level charged in a competitive market would be offset by a corresponding loss from lower equipment sales as consumers switched to equipment with cheaper lifecycle costs.	

3.	In year 1, steel use in single-family homes was minimal. In year 2, Durable Steel Corporation provided attractive credit services to single-family residential builders purchasing Durable's steel building components (beams, studs, and connectors) in the seven states where it has 95 percent of its business. The components are available without the credit services; the credit services are not available without the components. The credit terms are not more favorable than multiple-family residence builders typically get from independent credit service providers. Durable sells components sold for single-family residential applications from the same stock as components for multiple-family residential and commercial applications. By year 3, Durable has a 3 percent share of the home builder credit service market and a 20 percent share of the fledgling residential steel component market. In years 1 and 2, Durable's share of the overall steel component market was 5 and 7 percent, respectively.	
4.	P&Q Grocery has per pound costs of $3.50 for a side of beef. Normally, P&Q's per pound prices for steak, roasts, and hamburger are $12.00, $6.00, and $4.00, respectively. P&Q has branches in three states.	
5.	P&Q Grocery normally sells a half gallon of ice cream for $6.00. During a wide-spread power outage, P&Q did not know how long the blackout would last and decreased its price for a half gallon of ice cream to $1.00 in affected stores. P&Q has branches in three states.	
6.	Ali Baba, Inc., imported 1,000 rugs of similar quality and pattern for $1,500 each and sold them at $3,000 to most retail outlets and $2,750 to retail outlets that had done business with it for five years or more. The retail outlets were in seven states.	
7.	In September, Alpine Outfitters purchased 1,000 sets of skis at $100/set and started selling them at $150/set. With an unusually warm winter predicated to continue, Alpine sold sets of skis in January at $120, in February at $110, and in March at $100. Alpine is planning to resume selling the same brands of skis again in the autumn. Alpine has branches in seven states.	
8.	In year 1, Iowa Outfitters purchased 500 sets of scuba tanks at $100/set and started selling them at $150/set. In year 3, Iowa's decided to discontinue selling scuba equipment, figuring that its estimate of the sales due to a new local tourist attraction proved overly optimistic. Iowa sold the remaining 250 sets at cost. A third of Iowa's customers are from out of state.	
9.	Gold Coast Outfitters makes fiberglass sailboats. The towns of Grande Haven, Bootlegger's Cove, and Newport—in three states—have comparable marine facilities and are the same distance from Gold Coast's manufacturing facility. Gold Coast sells its 45-foot boats to retailers in Grande Haven and Bootlegger's Cove for $75,000. In Newport, Gold Coast sells to retailers at a $1,500 discount to lure buyers from a competitor selling comparable boats for its list price of $74,000.	
10.	Spider Talk Corporation has its Wilbur and Charlotte model mobile phones on sale on the day after Thanksgiving for $50 and $100, respectively All individuals who are present in its stores at some time between 8 and 9 that morning may get one non-transferable coupon for an additional $25 discount on either of these models, even if they purchase the phone later that day. Spider Talk has stores nationwide.	
11.	Solti Roof Products makes ceramic and concrete roof tiles of the same raw materials in two styles: Spanish and American. Individual orders for tiles are roughly the same quantities for both styles. As they are 20 percent the price of the American-style tiles, there is 40 times the demand for the Spanish-style tiles as for the American-style tiles. The Spanish-style tiles are formed with a modern automatic machine. The American-style tiles are formed with an old machine that requires three times the labor for the same amount of tiles as the Spanish-style machine. This results in significantly higher costs for the American-style tiles. An automatic machine could be made to form American-style tiles, but Solti does not want to invest the significant capital as demand currently is low for American-style tiles. The Scottsdale Preservation Institute & Trust supports the use of the American-style tiles in renovations in Scottsdale and alleges that Solti practices illegal price discrimination.	

12.	Phoenix Company sells photovoltaic systems, including solar panels, inverters, and batteries. The salaried sales staff typically spend considerable time with first-time retail customers to educate them about optimal configurations. Sales staff typically spend considerably less time with repeat retail customers and distributors. A typical home system has 16 to 24 panels and 1 inverter. Phoenix gives a 10 percent discount to customers who purchase either 20 to 30 panels or 2 inverters and a 15 percent discount to customers who purchase more than either 30 panels or 2 inverters. Customers who place a second order within six months of a previous order get an additional 5 percent discount. Phoenix ships nationwide.	
13.	In year 2, Phoenix Company held a 5 percent share of the photovoltaic roof shingle market. In year 3, Phoenix Company introduced a patented photovoltaic shingle 30 percent more durable and 5 percent more efficient than any similar product on the market. Despite a price 25 percent higher than the highest priced competing product, Phoenix increased its market share to 85 percent in year 3. Phoenix ships nationwide.	
14.	Speedy Chef was a pioneer in assembling and selling packaged mixes for bread and cake. It rarely advertises on radio or television and never offers coupons. The only free samples Speedy ever distributed was in the packaged mix market's infancy—decades ago. Speedy consistently delivers a reliable product, in one convenient size, in popular varieties, at prices that fluctuate only with raw material and conversion costs. Its overhead costs are among the lowest of national brands. Speedy's prices are toward the low end of the market's range, but typically are above private-label brands and sometimes above some other national brands after deducting their coupons' amounts. Despite having fewer varieties that its brand-name competitors, Speedy Chef has shelf space in 90 percent of grocery stores and sells 65 percent of the packaged baking mixes to retail consumers in the United States.	
15.	Tocsin manufactures fire and intruder alarms, with about 10 percent of the market share. When regional service stations accredited by major insurance underwriters were becoming established, Tocsin started six different wholly owned subsidiaries that offer fire, intruder, and combination fire and intruder services through both non-accredited and accredited regional station services in 48 states. These services involve hazard alarms installed on subscribers' sites connected to a regional service station. Tocsin since expanded by opening facilities in localities previously without other services and by acquisition of 30 other services. Insurance underwriters discount premiums significantly for subscribers to regional station services accredited by the underwriters. Insurance discounts for non-accredited services are similar to the minimal discounts for non-service product installation. In most regions, Tocsin regularly reduces rates to meet competition or potential competition. In regions where Tocsin was the sole provider of a service, it renews contracts for that service at rates 20 percent higher, on average, than its rates in other cities, adjusted for regional price differences. With 20 and 75 percent market share in the nationwide non-accredited and accredited regional station industry, respectively, Tocsin has offers outstanding to four of the five next-largest firms offering accredited regional station services. Tocsin claims that fire alarm services and intruder alarm services are too diverse to be considered the same relevant market; they are not interchangeable. Further, Tocsin claims that non-accredited and accredited regional station services as well as non-service products all comprise the relevant markets of fire alarm products and services and intruder alarm products and services.	
16.	Tin Solder, LLC, manufactures aluminum foil, but no other flexible wrapping material, for food storage. Tin Solder sells some foil under its national brand and some under private label brands. Tin Solder has a 75 percent share of the nationwide aluminum foil market, which equates to a 12 percent share of the nationwide flexible wrapping material market.	

Maple owns 75 percent of the common stock of Salam Exterminating, Inc. Maple is not an officer or employee of the corporation, and does not serve on its board of directors. Salam is in the business of providing exterminating services to residential and commercial customers.

Dodd performed exterminating services on behalf of Salam. Dodd suffered permanent injuries as a result of inhaling one of the chemicals used by Salam. This occurred after Dodd sprayed the chemical in a restaurant that Salam regularly services. Dodd was under the supervision of one of Salam's district managers and was trained by Salam to perform exterminating services following certain procedures, which he did. Later that day several patrons who ate at the restaurant also suffered permanent injuries as a result of inhaling the chemical. The chemical was manufactured by Ace Chemical Corp. and sold and delivered to Salam in a closed container. It was not altered by Salam. It has now been determined that the chemical was defectively manufactured and the injuries suffered by Dodd and the restaurant patrons were a direct result of the defect.

Salam has complied with an applicable compulsory workers' compensation statute by obtaining an insurance policy from Spear Insurance Co.

As a result of the foregoing, the following actions have been commenced:

- Dodd sued Spear to recover workers' compensation benefits.
- Dodd sued Salam based on negligence in training him.

As a team member on an engagement to audit Salam Exterminating, write a memo to Abernathy, CPA, discussing the merits of the actions commenced by Dodd, indicating the likely outcomes and your reasons therefore.

Research Question: What code section and subsection, if applicable, provides authorization to the Secretary of the Treasury to enter into an agreement with any state to collect, as its agent, such state's unemployment taxes imposed on wages paid to a nanny in the private home of a employer?

Section & Subsection Answer: §_____ (___)

Solution 41-1 MULTIPLE CHOICE ANSWERS

FICA

1. (a) Under the Federal Insurance Contributions Act (FICA) an employer may incur penalties for failing to supply taxpayer identification numbers and to make timely FICA deposits.

2. (c) In order to constitute employment, service provided must be of a continuing or recurring nature. Weekly payments suggest this relationship. Lack of supervision, Lee's tool ownership, and a high degree of technical skill all tend to support an independent contractor status.

3. (c) Employers are required to withhold FICA taxes on covered employees' taxable wages, and file quarterly FICA tax returns. The liability to make the tax deposits begins when the wages are paid. In this case, since the employer paid both its share and the employees' share, the employer's obligation to pay the FICA taxes has been fulfilled. The employer then is entitled to reimbursement of the employee FICA taxes for the employees' share.

4. (d) Social Security retirement benefits are reduced $1 for every $2 of *earned income* above a base amount which varies from year to year. Self-employed individuals are taxed on their *net income* if over $400. Participation in the Social Security retirement system is mandatory even though the employee also participates in a private retirement plan. Death benefits are payable if death occurs after retirement in certain situations.

5. (d) Social Security benefits may include payments to divorced spouses, payments to disabled children, and Medicare payments, but not Medicaid payments.

6. (b) Earned income (such as director's fees) which exceeds an annual limitation results in reduced benefits of $1 for each $2 of earnings above a specified amount of annual earned income. Annual proceeds from an annuity, pension payments, and closely held corporation stock dividends all are unearned income and do not affect benefits.

7. (a) Receipt of payments under a private pension plan will not limit the payment of Social Security benefits to an otherwise qualifying individual. An individual (or her/his family) may also qualify for benefits if the individual reaches age 62, whether or not s/he is disabled or retired, so long as her/his earned income is below the qualifying level. Normally, the benefits paid to a deceased worker's child cease when the child reaches age 18. If the child is a full-time high school student, s/he may continue to receive benefits until three months after reaching age 19 or until s/he stops full-time school attendance, whichever occurs first. Benefit payments may be made to the spouse or dependents of an otherwise qualifying individual in certain situations.

8. (a) Where an employer pays an employee's share of FICA taxes, the amount of FICA taxes paid on behalf of that employee qualifies as taxable income to the employee and as an ordinary and necessary business expense to the employer. The FICA requires an employer to withhold and pay both the employer's and the employee's share of FICA taxes. An employer who fails to withhold the employee's share will be liable for payment of both the employer's and employee's share. There are no additional penalties imposed on an employer who voluntarily pays its employee's share.

FUTA

9. (b) Taxes paid under the Federal Unemployment Tax Act (FUTA) are deductible by the employer as a business expense for federal income tax purposes. The tax rate is 6.2% for the first $7,000 in wages paid to each covered employee. Employers must pay the FUTA tax if they pay $1,500 or more in wages in any calendar quarter or employ more than one person at least one day a week for 20 weeks during a calendar year. FUTA taxes are paid by the employer and are not withheld from employees.

10. (c) The employer is allowed a credit on FUTA for taxes paid into a state unemployment program, up to a maximum rate of 5.4%. Because the state unemployment tax rate is 5.4%, the entire state unemployment rate would qualify as a credit. The fact that the employer pays less than the full rate to the state because of good unemployment history is irrelevant. The credit in this case is based on the state's standard rate.

11. (b) The Federal Unemployment Tax Act (FUTA) requires an employer to file a federal unemployment tax return if the employer pays wages of $1,500 or more in any calendar quarter or employs one or more persons at least one day per week for 20 weeks during a calendar year. Ral Supermarket clearly meets the latter requirement and must file.

12. (d) Unemployment compensation insurance is financed through payments made by employers under federal and state unemployment insurance laws. Workers' compensation insurance also is financed by payments made by employers under state workers' compensation laws. No payments are

deducted from an employee's salary for either type of insurance.

Workers' Compensation

13. (d) Most state workers' compensation laws exempt some employees. The most common exemptions include casual (temporary) employees. Although employees of common carriers also are commonly exempted, not all truck drivers work for common carriers.

14. (a) Worker's compensation statutes cover occupational diseases, even providing coverage for pre-existing conditions if aggravated by current working conditions.

15. (b) Under worker's compensation statutes, employers are held strictly liable without regard to whether or not they are at fault. The amount of damages recoverable is based on state statute. Generally, payments are not payable for life. An employee's own negligence will not prevent the employee from receiving such benefits.

16. (b) The workers' compensation statutes enable employees to recover for job-related injuries or diseases whether the employer is negligent or not. When an employee accepts the benefits of the workers' compensation laws, s/he generally is barred from suing the employer for damages. The employee's acceptance of benefits does not bar suit against a third party whose negligence caused the injury. Thus, Kroll will be successful in obtaining workers' compensation benefits but not in a negligence action against Acorn. However, Kroll would be able to sue Trell, the third party whose negligence caused the accident.

17. (c) Workers' compensation benefits are allowed to employees who are injured "on the job" even if the employee is negligent. However, an employee intentionally causing self-inflicted injury cannot collect. Failing to abide by safety procedures will not preclude the injured worker from collecting workers' compensation. An injured employee can collect even if the injury was caused by a fellow employee. An injured worker can collect workers' compensation and still maintain a civil suit against a third party who caused the injury.

EEOC

18. (c) The Federal Age Discrimination in Employment Act prohibits unintentional age discrimination and protects workers age 40 or older from discrimination on the basis of age. Any employee may be terminated for cause or as part of a rational business decision. Employees working in managerial positions may be subject to mandatory retirement.

19. (c) Under the Age Discrimination in Employment Act, back pay is a remedy available to a covered employee, but early retirement is not.

20. (b) The Federal Age Discrimination in Employment Act prohibits employment discrimination on the basis of age against persons 40 years of age and older; thus, compulsory retirement of employees below the age of 65 would violate the Act. Terminating employees for cause is not age-based discrimination and does not violate the Act.

21. (a) Sexual discrimination among employees is prohibited under both the Equal Pay Act and Title VII of the Civil Rights Act.

22. (b) Title VII of the Civil Rights Act of 1964 prohibits discrimination in employment on the bases of race, sex, religion, color, and national origin. The Age Discrimination in Employment Act protects workers age 40 or older from discrimination.

23. (a) Under the provisions of the Americans With Disabilities Act, a disabled person is protected from discrimination by providers of public transportation, as well as privately operated public accommodations. Thus, the Act protects a disabled person in both areas.

24. (d) Neither sick pay nor vacation pay are exempt from the provisions of the National Labor Relations Act.

OSHA

25. (a) OSHA is authorized to establish standards that protect employees from exposure to substances that may be harmful to their health in order to ensure a safe working environment for employees. The development of safety equipment is beyond the scope of OSHA.

26. (c) An on-site inspection of a workplace by an investigator from the Occupational Safety and Health Administration (OSHA) is permissible after a request by employees. Employee requests provide OSHA with the probable cause necessary to obtain a warrant. Since OSHA may conduct an on-site inspection without a warrant if the owner consents, it is not true that OSHA can *only* inspect the premises with a search warrant. It is not necessary that an on-site inspection be conducted after working hours, nor that the employer be given any prior notice of the inspection.

27. (b) OSHA prohibits an employer from firing an employee for reporting OSHA violations. OSHA requires an employer to maintain a work environment free from recognized hazards. It does not require that the employer provide a completely risk-free

environment. An agency such as OSHA must obtain an administrative warrant to inspect the premises if the employer does not give permission for the site search. OSHA is a federal law and, thus, is only applicable when the employer is engaged in interstate commerce or an activity affecting interstate commerce. States are not prohibited from also enacting legislation to protect worker health and safety.

Wage-Hour Law

28. (b) The Fair Labor Standards Act is the Federal Statute that governs employees' wages and hours. The National Labor Relations and Taft-Hartley Act govern employees' rights to bargain collectively. The Americans With Disabilities Act protects persons with disabilities from discrimination.

29. (a) Under the Fair Labor Standards Act (FLSA) hourly, weekly, and monthly pay bases may be used to pay covered, nonexempt employees who earn, on average, the minimum hourly wage.

30. (a) The Fair Labor Standards Act (FLSA) requires covered employers to pay a legally specified minimum wage. The FLSA does not establish the number of hours to be worked in a work week; however, it does regulate the compensation rate of hours worked in excess of 40, which is a regulation of the number of hours.

ERISA

31. (a) ERISA regulates both employee vesting and plan funding of private employer pension plans.

32. (d) ERISA does not require employers to have pension plans, but does set standards that employers must follow if they have a plan. These standards do not include employees as pension-plan managers.

COBRA

33. (d) The Federal Consolidated Budget Reconciliation Act of 1985 (COBRA) provides that when an employee voluntarily resigns from a job, the former employee's group health insurance coverage may be retained for the former employee and spouse at the employee's expense for at least 18 months.

Antitrust

34. (c) Most courts hold that a corporation may purchase its own shares, provided such action promotes the corporate business. A corporation has express power to perform any act authorized by state law, its articles of incorporation, or its bylaws. A takeover attempt doesn't restrict these actions.

35. (a) The Sherman Antitrust Act prohibits contracts, combinations, and conspiracies that restrain trade and monopolize. Price fixing is an agreement among producers or sellers to raise or maintain the price level as to impede free enterprise. All horizontal price fixing arrangements (between sellers at the same level) are *per se* unlawful.

36. (c) A monopoly granted by a patent is legal. An exclusive dealing arrangement requires retailers to sell only one supplier's product. A tying arrangement requires retailers to purchase other products from a supplier. The Clayton Act prohibits arrangements that tend to create a monopoly or may substantially lessen competition, such as exclusive dealing and tying arrangements. Vertical price fixing involves a supplier requiring retailers to sell its products at or above a minimum price. The Sherman Antitrust Act prohibits price fixing and tying arrangements.

37. (a) Market allocation is a *per se* violation of the Sherman Antitrust Act.

38. (a) The Sherman Antitrust Act prohibits agreements among competitors who refuse to deal with a third party to eliminate competition or force groups standards on a competitor and agreements among parties at different levels of the distribution chain; these are deemed *per se* violations. Even if a business buys and sells within one state only, it influences competition by businesses that have interstate sales. Wrong is done to purchasers who might have purchased lower-priced appliances from Grounder, as well as Grounder.

Environment

39. (a) The federal acts regulating air and water pollution permit citizens or states to enforce the provisions of these acts either by bringing private suits against violators or by suing the Environmental Protection Agency to enforce compliance with the laws.

40. (c) Under CERCLA, almost any past or current owner of land found to be contaminated may be held responsible for cleanup costs. A minority stockholder of a public corporation generally is protected from personal liability.

Solution 41-2 ADDITIONAL MULTIPLE CHOICE ANSWERS

FICA

41. (b) Under the provisions of FICA, the employer's failure to withhold the employee's contribution may cause the employer to be responsible for both the employee's and employer's share of taxes. Musgrove can be made to pay because it failed to withhold and pay FICA taxes on Tower's wages.

42. (b) Under the Federal Insurance Contributions Act (FICA), wages generally include all remuneration for employment including bonuses, commissions, and contingent fees. "Wages" does not include reimbursed travel expenses.

FUTA

43. (a) Generally, unemployment compensation is provided to workers who are discharged through no fault of their own. As a result, a CPA who is fired as a result of an employer's business reversals qualifies to receive benefits. The accountant could not continue to receive unemployment compensation if s/he refused a job that s/he was qualified to perform. Being fired for embezzlement is the fault of the worker. Voluntarily leaving work, without adequate cause, does not qualify one for unemployment benefits.

Workers' Compensation

44. (b) The primary purpose for enacting workers' compensation statutes was to enable employees to recover for injuries regardless of negligence. The primary purpose for enacting workers' compensation statutes was not to eliminate *all* employer-employee negligence lawsuits. Workers' compensation statutes do not prevent lawsuits against third parties. The purpose of workers' compensation statutes is not to allow employees to recover *additional* compensation for employer negligence.

Wage-Hour Law

45. (b) The Fair Labor Standards Act (FLSA) requires that covered, nonexempt employees be paid overtime for any hours in excess of 40 worked in a week. In two of the listed weeks, the employee worked in excess of 40 hours and is entitled to overtime pay. It is irrelevant that the employee worked less than 40 hours in the following weeks.

ERISA

46. (b) A noncontributory pension fund is one to which only the employer contributes. Employees make no contributions.

Antitrust

47. (a) The Robinson-Patman Act prohibits price discrimination by prohibiting sellers from charging different prices to buyers for commodities of similar grade and quality. A plaintiff must either show that the defendant has engaged in predatory pricing with intent to harm competition or present a detailed market analysis that demonstrates how the defendant's price discrimination actually harmed competition. Permissible price differentials are justified by proof of either a cost savings to the seller or a good-faith price reduction to meet the lawful price of a competitor, but not the length of time of a business relationship. The existence of other inventory sources are immaterial.

48. (a) Violations of federal antitrust laws can result in both civil and criminal penalties.

49. (a) The Clayton Act prohibits arrangements that tend to create a monopoly or may substantially lessen competition, including exclusive dealing arrangements. There is no minimum exempt time limit in antitrust law.

50. (c) Market allocation among competitors by customer type, geographic area, or product whereby competitors agree not to compete are *per se* violations of the Sherman Antitrust Act. Both explicit and implicit agreements to respect each others' established relationships with customers are forms of market allocation by customer type. An arrangement involving exclusive territorial rights to sell within and corresponding limitations on selling outside a designated territory by a manufacturer and its distributors—unlike an agreement among competitors—would be judged based on the rule of reason. Sale of a patented product at an unreasonably high price and refusal to deal with a troublesome entity are legal.

51. (d) An arrangement involving exclusive territorial rights to sell within and corresponding limitations on selling outside a designated territory by a manufacturer and its distributors would be judged based on the rule of reason. Note that this is different than market allocation by competitors. The retention by each outlet of the right to sell other manufacturers' featherweight luggage is not necessarily sufficient to ensure legality. The existence of a consignment arrangement would not ensure legality.

52. (b) Horizontal price fixing involves a competitors' agreement not to reduce prices below a minimum. Vertical price fixing involves a supplier requiring retailers to sell its products at or above a

minimum price. Vertical price fixing is judged under the rule of reason. Price discrimination involves charging different prices to buyers for commodities of similar grade and quality. Retail price maintenance is not a justification for the restriction of trade. The existence of a patent, by itself, does not exempt the federal antitrust law from application.

53. (c) The phrase "illegal *per se*" indicates conduct or agreements that are inherently illegal and without legal justification. Group boycotts, market allocation, tying arrangements, and other situations are deemed illegal *per se* under antitrust law. An "illegal *per se*" status is not a prerequisite to imposing criminal penalties.

Environment

54. (a) The Federal Water Pollution Control Act (Clean Water Act) is designed to improve waterway quality by making the water safe for recreational use and protecting wildlife associated with the waterways. Activities regulated under the Clean Water Act include the discharge of heated water by nuclear power plants and the dredging of wetlands. The Safe Drinking Water Act of 1986 empowers the EPA to set standards for drinking water.

55. (c) Under the Clean Air Act, the federal government may require an automobile manufacturer to recall vehicles that violate emission standards and a citizens' group may sue to force a coal burning power plant to comply with emission standards.

56. (a) Conducting an environmental audit and reporting the violation to the governmental authority shows good faith on the part of the violating company and may qualify the business for leniency.

57. (d) Under the Comprehensive Environmental Response, Compensation, and Liability Act (CERCLA), known as Superfund, current and prior owners or operators of a site, as well as any person who transported waste to the site, would be liable to the Environmental Protection Agency for the expense of cleaning up a hazardous waste disposal site.

58. (b) Under the Federal Clean Air Act, factories that emit toxic air pollutants are required to reduce emissions by installing the best available emission control technology, taking into consideration the cost of compliance. The act does not require power plants to eliminate all air polluting emissions, or automobile manufacturers to have emission control equipment installed on previously manufactured vehicles, or for homeowners to remove all pollutants from their residences, which would be virtually impossible.

59. (a) The Federal Water Pollution Control Act (Clean Water Act) regulates both the discharge of heated water by nuclear power plants and the dredging of wetlands.

60. (d) Enforcement of federal air and water quality standards is the responsibility of the governmental entities making the standards. The Environmental Protection Agency (EPA) is authorized to enforce all laws designed to protect the environment. Although industry associations may play an important part in helping businesses comply with environmental standards, they are not responsible for enforcement. Political action groups may bring suits on behalf of individual citizens to enforce federal air and water quality standards, but they are not responsible for doing so.

PERFORMANCE BY SUBTOPICS

Each category below parallels a subtopic covered in Chapter 41. Record the number and percentage of questions you correctly answered in each subtopic area.

FICA

Question #	Correct √
1	
2	
3	
4	
5	
6	
7	
8	
# Questions	8
# Correct	______
% Correct	______

FUTA

Question #	Correct √
9	
10	
11	
12	
# Questions	4
# Correct	______
% Correct	______

Workers' Compensation

Question #	Correct √
13	
14	
15	
16	
17	
# Questions	5
# Correct	______
% Correct	______

EEOC

Question #	Correct √
18	
19	
20	
21	
22	
23	
24	
# Questions	7
# Correct	______
% Correct	______

OSHA

Question #	Correct √
25	
26	
27	
# Questions	3
# Correct	______
% Correct	______

Wage-Hour Law

Question #	Correct √
28	
29	
30	
# Questions	3
# Correct	______
% Correct	______

ERISA

Question #	Correct √
31	
32	
# Questions	2
# Correct	______
% Correct	______

COBRA

Question #	Correct √
33	
# Questions	1
# Correct	______
% Correct	______

Antitrust

Question #	Correct √
34	
35	
36	
37	
38	
# Questions	5
# Correct	______
% Correct	______

Environment

Question #	Correct √
39	
40	
# Questions	2
# Correct	______
% Correct	______

SIMULATION SOLUTION

Solution 41-3 Antitrust & Workers' Compensation

Antitrust (4 points)

The following partial explanation applies to **items 1 through 3:** To establish an illegal tying arrangement generally requires: (1) a link of two distinct goods or services; (2) sufficient economic (market) power in the tying product market to impose significant restrictions in the tied product market; and (3) an effect on a non-insubstantial volume of commerce in the tied product market. Economic power ensues (1) from patent or similar monopoly, (2) a high market share, or (3) a unique product that rivals can not supply.

1. D

While Luxor has a line of unique cars, it does not possess the market power to force dealers to purchase the tied product rather than acquire a franchise to sell a different car brand if they do not wish to do so. A tying arrangement justified by business necessity does not violate antitrust law if implemented for a valid purpose and if a less restrictive alternative is not available. As Luxor's quality assurance program is unlikely to be replaced adequately by dealerships or distributors, furnishing manufacturing specifications for replacement parts to independent producers would not eliminate the need for a tying arrangement.

2. C

Laser's contention does not account for the facts that: (1) there could be an optimum price at which increased revenues from higher-priced sales of service and replacement parts would more than offset lower revenues from lost equipment sales, (2) determining the lifecycle costs is problematic and expensive for buyers, nor (3) the cost to current owners of switching to different products is considerable. Evidence of two distinct products exists, as not all service calls required parts and not all parts were sold with service calls. As the service could be done by customers, Laser's service apparently was not required to protect the quality of the product. The inference is that Laser had market power to eliminate competition in the service market as the ISPs were driven from the market.

3. D

Durable does not possess market power in either the home builder credit services market (the tied product) or the steel component market.

The following partial explanation applies to **items 4 through 12:** Price discrimination is prohibited between buyers of like commodities where the effect of this discrimination may be to substantially lessen competition or create a monopoly in any line of commerce. Price discrimination is permitted when it can be justified on the basis of (1) a difference in grade, quality, or quantity; (2) transportations costs involved in contract performance; (3) a good-faith effort to meet (not beat) competition; (4) differences in methods or quantities; (5) deterioration of goods; or (5) a close-out sale of a particular line of goods.

4. D

Price discrimination is permitted when it can be justified on the basis of a difference in grade, quality, or quantity.

5. D

Section 2(a) of the Sherman Act explicitly exempts price discrimination that reflects changing conditions in the marketability of goods—such as the deterioration of goods.

6. A

In this situation, none of the exceptions to prohibited price discrimination are met; there is no exception for established business relationships.

7. D

Section 2(a) of the Sherman Act explicitly exempts price discrimination that reflects changing conditions in the market for or the marketability of the goods—such as a declining market for seasonal goods.

8. D

Section 2(a) of the Sherman Act explicitly exempts price discrimination that reflects changing conditions in the market for or the marketability of the goods. Price discrimination is permitted for close-out sales of a particular line of goods.

9. A

Section 2(a) of the Robinson-Patman Act explicitly exempts price discrimination that if the lower price is charged "in good faith to meet [not beat] an equally low price of a competitor." Gold Coast undercut the competitor's price, rather than met it. As the towns are the same distance from Gold Coast's manufacturing facility and have comparable marine facilities, it is unlikely that Gold Coast's transportation costs or methods are appreciably different.

10. D

A supplier's pricing plan is not deemed to be discriminatory when the supplier offers to sell to anyone at a reduced price if specific conditions are met even if not all buyers can meet the conditions.

11. D

Price discrimination is permitted when it can be justified on the basis of differences in methods. Solti is not required to have the same capital investment in similar product lines. Indeed, if the effect of this discrimination is to leave a demand in the market that may be filled profitably by a competitor, Solti's actions may increase the likelihood of competition.

12. D

Price discrimination is permitted when it can be justified on the basis of differences in methods or quantities. The significant time differences that the sales staff spends with different types of customers indicates a difference in methods.

The following partial explanation applies to **items 13 through 16:** Monopolization includes both monopoly power and "willful acquisition or maintenance of monopoly power in a relevant market as opposed to growth as a consequence of superior product, business acumen, or historical accident" indicates monopolization. A relevant market includes both the geographic market and the product market.

13. D

A patent is a legal monopoly, as long as it is not unjustifiably exploited, created to reward innovation.

14. D

Speedy's high market share is due to a no-frill business model rather than to an intent to monopolize.

15. B

Tocsin's behavior indicates both monopoly power and willful acquisition and maintenance of monopoly power in the relevant market. Property protection (both fire alarm service and intruder alarm service) is the same basic service, efficiently provided by a combination regional station. The significant difference in insurance discounts for accredited and non-accredited services contradicts the claim that accredited and other protection services or non-service products are interchangeable.

16. D

Products that are "reasonably interchangeable by consumers for the same purposes" determine the relevant product market (also called the functional interchangeability test). An entity's ability to fix prices is limited by the availability of other products that consumers accept as substitutes. Tin Solder's share of the flexible wrapping material market is too small to amount to monopoly power.

Communication (5 points)

To: Abernathy, CPA
From: A. Junior
Re: Salam Audit: Dodd Actions

Dodd is entitled to recover workers' compensation benefits from Spear because Dodd was an **employee** of Salam, the injury was **accidental**, and the **injury occurred** out of and in the **course** of his **employment** with Salam. Based on the facts of this case, Dodd would be considered an employee and **not** an **independent contractor** because Salam had **control** over the **details** of Dodd's work by training Dodd to perform the services in a specified manner and Dodd was **subject** to Salam's **supervision**.

Dodd will be unsuccessful in his action against Salam based on **negligence** in training him because Dodd is an **employee** of Salam, and Salam has complied with the applicable compulsory workers' compensation statute by obtaining workers' compensation insurance. An employee who **receives workers' compensation benefits** may **not** maintain an action for negligence **against the employer** seeking **additional** compensation. Therefore, whether Salam was negligent in training Dodd is irrelevant.

Research (1 point)

IRC Section Answer: §3510(f)

Code §3510(f) states, "AUTHORITY TO ENTER INTO AGREEMENTS TO COLLECT STATE UNEMPLOYMENT TAXES.—3510(f)(1) IN GENERAL.—The Secretary is hereby authorized to enter into an agreement with any State to collect, as the agent of such State, such State's unemployment taxes imposed on remuneration paid for domestic service in a private home of the employer. Any taxes to be collected by the Secretary pursuant to such an agreement shall be treated as domestic service employment taxes for purposes of this section…."

CHAPTER 42

PROPERTY

EXAM COVERAGE: The business law portion of the Regulation section of the CPA exam is designated by the examiners to be 20-25 percent of the section's point value. More information about point distribution and information eligible to be tested is included in the **Practical Advice** section of this volume.

CHAPTER 42

PROPERTY

I. Estates

A. Definitions

In the strict legal sense, property is an aggregate of rights that are guaranteed and protected by law. The essence of property is exclusive ownership, (e.g., the right to dispose of a thing in every legal way: to possess it, use it, and exclude everyone else from interfering with it). The term extends to every species of valuable right and interest. It includes both tangibles (land, goods, documents, and instruments) and intangibles (accounts, contract rights, and generally any rights to payment).

1. **Alienable** An alienable right or interest may be properly transferred from the holder to another person.

2. **Condition Precedent** A condition that must be fulfilled before the agreement's promises or covenants are binding on the other party. Generally, a condition precedent is a future and uncertain event, the happening of which depends on the existence of an obligation.

3. **Condition Subsequent** A condition, the performance or happening of which causes the agreement's currently enforceable promises or covenants to cease being binding on one or both parties.

4. **Convey** To pass or transmit the title to property from one to another.

5. **Devest (Divest)** To deprive, take away, or withdraw. Usually it is spoken of as an authority or power. Property subject to such a power is said to be subject to devestment (divestment).

6. **Devise** A testamentary (pertaining to a will) disposition of land or realty.

7. **Encumbrance (Incumbrance)** Any right to, or interest in, land that subsists in another. This includes any claim, lien, or liability which binds an estate.

8. **Subsequent *Bona Fide* Purchaser** A purchaser who, without actual or constructive notice of any prior interest in a piece of property, pays value for an interest in such property.

9. **Real Property** Land and generally whatever is erected, growing upon, or affixed in a permanent or semipermanent manner to the land, and includes the air above the land.

10. **Personal Property** In the broadest sense, everything that is the subject of ownership and not real property.

11. **Fixtures** A chattel or item of personal property which is affixed to the land. This is a hybrid term which encompasses both personal and real property. The Uniform Commercial Code defines a fixture as a good so related to particular real estate that an interest in it arises under real estate law. On the other hand, the so-called trade fixtures doctrine classifies several types of fixtures as personal property and allows the tenant to remove any fixtures that s/he has attached for the purpose of conducting business. The tenant's right is limited to the extent that her/his action in removing the fixture may not materially damage the realty. This doctrine has been extended to include easily removable agricultural (farming equipment) and consumer or domestic (large appliances) fixtures. The basic test used by the courts to determine whether a fixture is real or personal property is the *objective intent test.* The test is phrased as a question asking the following: "Would the ordinary reasonable person be justified in assuming that the person attaching the chattel intended it to become a part of the real estate?" This question usually is answered by examining the chattel's method of

annexation, the degree to which the chattel is adapted to the use of the realty, and the prevailing custom of the time, place, and business.

a. By definition, there must be at least some annexation. The general rule is that a chattel becomes part of the realty when it cannot be removed without causing material injury to the realty.

b. A chattel's appropriateness to the use or purpose of the realty is particularly important in trade or business cases. The test may become two-fold in these situations. First, a chattel generally is considered a part of the realty when it is necessary to the commonly accepted use of the realty. Second, a chattel that is necessary to the business which happens to be conducted on the premises, but which could be as easily or profitably used at another location, usually is considered personal property.

c. Considerations bearing on whether or not a fixture has become a part of the realty also depend on the custom at the place of affixing, the length of time of affixation, and the particular industry involved in the affixation.

12. Freehold Estates A freehold estate (ownership right for an indefinite time or the life of a person) is the highest form of estate. A freeholder possesses and owns her/his estate. A nonfreeholder, or a leaseholder, only has possession. Additionally, freehold estates are different from future interests. Freehold estates are classified according to their potential duration, and may be held singly or jointly.

B. Fee Simple Estates

1. Fee Simple Absolute An estate of potentially infinite duration. There are no limitations on its inheritability, and it is not subject to a power of divestment. Under common law, it was necessary to use the words "to A and his heirs" to create a fee simple estate. Under modern law, a deed is presumed to convey a fee simple absolute or the largest estate that can be owned by the grantor. Thus, any words of conveyance, not expressly limited, will pass the grantor's entire estate.

2. Fee Simple Defeasible A fee simple may be created so that it is defeasible upon the occurrence of a particular event. There are three classifications of defeasible estates.

a. Fee Simple Determinable An estate which automatically terminates upon the occurrence of a particular event. If and when the specified event occurs, the land automatically reverts to the grantor.

(1) A fee simple determinable is freely transferable, but the transferred estate remains subject to the condition.

(2) A fee simple determinable may be created by words such as "so long as," "until," or "while." Example: "A to B, so long as she shall continue to farm Blackacre."

b. Fee Simple Subject to a Condition Subsequent An estate which does not automatically terminate, but may terminate at the election of the grantor. If and when the specified event occurs, the grantor has the right to reenter the land and terminate the estate.

(1) A fee simple subject to a condition subsequent is freely transferable, but the transferred estate remains subject to the condition.

(2) A fee simple subject to a condition subsequent is created by words such as "but if," "upon the condition that," or "provided, however." Example: "A to B, but if B shall ever use Blackacre other than as a farm…"

c. **Fee Simple Subject to an Executory Interest** An estate which automatically terminates upon the occurrence of a particular event. However, the estate transfers to a third person and not to the grantor or the heirs.

(1) A fee simple subject to an executory interest is freely transferable, but the transferred estate remains subject to the condition.

(2) A fee simple subject to an executory interest is created by using the same words as those used to create a fee simple determinable. The only difference is that upon the occurrence of the event, the property transfers to a third party.

C. Life Estate

An estate limited in duration to the life of some particular person specified in the deed. This person may be referred to as the measuring life.

1. **Types** A life estate may be either for the life of the grantee or "pour autre vie" (e.g., for the life of another). Under the modern view, if A is the grantee and B is the measuring life of the estate, and if A predeceases B, then A's estate descends to her/his heirs. A's heirs own the estate until B's death.

2. **Defeasible Life Estates** These estates may be defeasible in the same manner as a defeasible fee simple estate.

3. **Alienability** A life estate is freely transferable. However, the transferred estate still is limited in duration by the original measuring life.

4. **Rights & Duties of Life Tenant** Generally, a life tenant has all the rights and duties of a fee simple owner. However, the life tenant's rights and duties are limited by the concept of waste.

   a. **Use** A life tenant has the right to use and enjoy the land and to exclude others from the land. A life tenant also has the duties of a fee simple holder, such as the duty to pay taxes and assessments for public improvements. However, if the public improvement is of a permanent nature so that the holder of the future interest also will benefit from it, then the life tenant and future interest holders must apportion the assessment.

   b. **Waste** A life tenant's rights and duties are limited by the concept of waste. Waste is conduct by the life tenant who impairs the value of the land and, therefore, the interest of the future interest holder.

5. **Created by Operation of Law** Under common law, certain estates were created to protect the survivors or heirs of a decedent. State statutes have altered or almost wholly abolished these estates as they existed under common law.

   a. **Dower** The right a wife has in her husband's property. Dower is either inchoate (while the husband is alive) or choate (upon his death).

   b. **Statutory Forced Share** The right of a surviving spouse (sometimes limited to a surviving wife) to an absolute share of all the decedent's property owned by the decedent at her/his death. Usually, this share applies to real and personal property.

   c. **Community Property** The one-half interest each spouse has in all property acquired during their relationship from earnings or investment of community property.

D. Future Interests

A future interest is an interest in property where the right to possession is postponed until some future time. There are five classifications of future interests: reversion, possibility of reverter, right of reentry, remainder, and executory interest.

1. **Reversion** The interest left in the grantor when s/he conveys away less than the entire estate is a reversion. For example, if O (the owner of Blackacre in fee simple) conveys Blackacre to A for life, A has a life estate, and O has a reversion. A reversion interest is freely alienable.

2. **Possibility of Reverter** The conditional reversionary interest which is left in the grantor after her/his conveyance of *a fee simple* determinable is a possibility of reverter. For example, O dedicates land "to be used as a public park." If several years later, the land ceases to be used as a park, then O's heirs would be entitled to the land.

3. **Right of Reentry** A right of reentry is the future interest left to the grantor when s/he conveys a fee simple subject to a condition subsequent.

4. **Remainder** The future interest created in a third-person transferee which otherwise would be a reversion is a remainder. For example, if O (owner of Blackacre in fee simple) conveys Blackacre to A for life, remainder to B, B's future interest is a vested remainder. Remainders may be either vested or contingent.

    a. **Vested** A vested remainder is similar to a reversion in that it is not subject to a condition precedent. It must also be in the possession of an ascertained person.

    b. **Contingent** A remainder is contingent if it is either subject to a condition precedent (not subsequent) or limited to an unascertained person.

        (1) **Condition Precedent** A condition precedent is an event which must occur before the interest vests. For example, O conveys to A for life, then to B if B attains age 30. B has a contingent remainder which vests when he becomes 30.

        (2) **Unascertained Person** For example, O conveys to A for life, then to the children of B (B now has no children). There is a contingent remainder which will vest as soon as B has her first child.

5. **Executory Interest** An executory interest is the future interest created in a third-person transferee which corresponds to a grantor's possibility of reverter.

E. **Concurrent Estates in Land**

1. **Joint Tenancy** A concurrent estate with the *right of survivorship* is a joint tenancy. The most important characteristic of a joint tenancy is the right of survivorship. On the death of any joint tenant, her/his interest in the estate terminates, and the estate is held by the surviving joint tenants. There may be any number of co-tenants, so long as there are at least two. Each co-tenant has a share in the whole, subject to each other tenant's share.

    a. **Creation** Under modern law, a person seeking to convey a joint tenancy must use specific words of conveyance such as "O to A and B as joint tenants with right of survivorship." If the language is in any way ambiguous, the courts will construe it so as to create the legally preferred tenancy *in common.* Additionally, a joint tenancy may not be created in the absence of the four unities. The four unities are as follows.

        (1) Unity of **time,** which means each joint tenant's interest must arise at the same time;

        (2) Unity of **title,** which means each joint tenant must acquire her/his interest by the same instrument;

        (3) Unity of **interest,** which means each joint tenant's interest must be of the same type and duration; and

        (4) Unity of **possession,** which means that each joint tenant must have an undivided right to use the whole property.

b. **Termination** A joint tenancy may be terminated by the unilateral action of any joint tenant, during her/his lifetime, which destroys one of the required unities.

(1) An *inter vivos* conveyance (transferred during life) by one joint tenant terminates the joint tenancy, because it affects the grantee. The grantee's interest is a tenancy in common with the remaining joint tenants. However, the remaining joint tenants' interests still represent a joint tenancy.

(2) Termination also may be accomplished by the co-tenants' agreeing to revoke their rights of survivorship or by a judicial severance proceeding.

2. **Tenancy in Common** A concurrent estate with no right of survivorship. Therefore, each co-tenant's interest is inheritable. A tenancy in common may be shared by any number of co-tenants, so long as there is more than one. Each co-tenant has an undivided interest in the whole property.

a. **Creation** Under modern statutes, a tenancy in common is the preferred type of co-tenancy. The only required unity is the unity of interest.

b. **Termination** A tenancy in common may be terminated by agreement of all the co-tenants or by a court-ordered partition.

3. **Tenancy by the Entirety** A tenancy by the entirety's characteristics are generally similar to those of a joint tenancy except that it may be created only by a husband and wife.

a. **Creation** All the requirements that need to be met to create a joint tenancy must be met to create a tenancy by the entirety; plus, it may only be created by a husband and wife. **Note:** Some states have relaxed the requirements of the four unities.

b. **Termination** A tenancy by the entirety may not be terminated by the unilateral action of one spouse. It may be terminated only by death, divorce, or agreement.

4. **Rights & Duties Among Co-Tenants** Each tenant is bound to pay her/his share of the taxes and her/his share of the interest on any outstanding mortgage. A co-tenant has no duty to make repairs or improvements. Generally, each co-tenant may occupy or use the whole of a joint estate, so long as her/his use does not act to exclude the other co-tenants. A tenant in possession has no duty to account to or reimburse co-tenants not in possession. Exceptions to this generalization include:

a. **Ouster** The action of one co-tenant that denies another co-tenant's title or right to use or possess the land, or action that denies another the rightful share of any proceeds. This is a tortious or wrongful act. The ousted tenant may maintain an action for the value of the reasonable use of the land or for her/his share of the profits.

b. **Realized Profits** A co-tenant is accountable for any profit realized by her/him from activity which reduces the value of the land. Thus, for example, that co-tenant must reimburse each co-tenant a proportionate share of all profits realized from the exploitation of minerals.

c. **Voluntary Waste** A co-tenant is liable for any voluntary waste (see II.,C.,4.,b., above). Voluntary, destructive waste is a tortious act and the co-tenant may be liable for double or treble damages.

II. Real Property Acquisition

A. Overview

The most common method of acquiring title to real property is by deed of conveyance. The grantor, or previous owner, conveys the estate or other interest in the land to the grantee. This transaction is represented by a deed. The deed is filed in a land records office, which is open to the public, in order to put all persons on notice of the owner's interest in the property. Normally, the sale of real property is a two-step process. The parties first contract for the sale of the land and, second, at some later date, "close." At the "closing," the deed is exchanged for the agreed consideration.

B. Executory Contract for Sale of Land
This is the first step in most real property transactions.

1. **Statute of Frauds** The Statute of Frauds requires that all contracts for the sale of real property must be in writing and signed by the party to be charged (the grantor). The writing may be a memorandum or some other informal writing and need not be a formal document.

   a. **Terms** The writing must contain the following essential terms: identification of the parties, a description of the property sufficient to identify it, and the terms and conditions such as price or consideration and manner of payment.

   b. **Oral Contract** In rare instances, the courts will enforce an oral contract. The usual situation involves a part performance or activity that occurs as a result of a party's detrimental reliance on the terms of an oral contract. For example, if O orally contracts to sell Blackacre to A, and A, in reliance, erects substantial improvements on Blackacre, the courts may (in an equity proceeding) enforce specific performance.

   c. **Oral Agreement** A written contract for the sale of land may be revoked or modified by an oral agreement between the parties.

   d. **Time** Unless the contract states that "time is of the essence," the parties have a reasonable time in which to perform.

2. **Marketable Title** Unless the contract specifies otherwise, it is implied that the seller will furnish a marketable title. A marketable title is one that is free from plausible or reasonable objections; it need not be perfect. It must be free from private encumbrances not otherwise specified in the title, such as easements or mortgages. However, zoning laws or subdivision restrictions generally will not render a title unmarketable. Unless so stated, marketable title does not have to be record title; therefore, a title based on adverse possession (see D., below) may be marketable. Finally, the seller usually contracts to furnish title at closing. The seller is not required to have title when s/he contracts.

3. **Title Insurance** Covers losses resulting from defects or failure of title to real property. Any exceptions not insured must be shown on the face of the policy. This type of insurance is usually issued to the purchaser or mortgagor. Most state statutes require that the policy indicate on its face the extent of the risk assumed. Many statutes also establish specific premium schedules. Unlike other types of insurance, no title insurance policy or guarantee of title may be issued on a casualty basis (issued without regard to the possible extent of adverse matters or defects of title). Thus, the issuer of a title insurance policy must first examine the title abstract which summarizes the conveyances, mortgages, and known encumbrances and liabilities affecting the property. Only if the title examiner believes that there are no material defects of title may the insurer issue a policy. In this respect, title insurance resembles a guaranty in which the insurer warrants the validity of the title. As a practical matter, most title insurance policies exclude coverage of any defect which is not of record.

4. **Payment & Delivery of Deed** Payment of the purchase price and delivery of the deed are concurrent conditions. Neither party may hold the other in breach unless s/he is capable of tendering performance.

5. **Remedies Upon Breach of Contract for Sale**

   a. **Buyer's Remedies**

      (1) **Specific Performance** The buyer is entitled to specific performance, because land is considered to be "unique" property.

(2) **Abatement in Price** In situations where the estate is less than what the seller contracted to sell, the buyer may complete the sale and seek an abatement in price.

(3) **Damages** If the seller is unable to deliver the land, the buyer may seek monetary damages.

b. **Seller's Remedies**

(1) **Specific Performance** The seller is allowed to sue for specific performance of the sales contract.

(2) **Damages** If the seller chooses to sue for damages, s/he is entitled to the difference between the contract price and the current market price.

(3) **Liquidated Damages** The contract may call for liquidated damages, usually forfeiture of the down payment. These clauses are enforceable only when the seller can show some connection between the liquidated damages and the actual damages.

6. **Equitable Conversion and Risk of Loss** After the contract for sale has been executed and before the closing, the majority of courts place the risk of loss on the buyer. This is based on the doctrine of equitable conversion. The seller's right to the real estate is converted into a right to receive the purchase price for the real estate (equitable conversion).

C. **Deed**
Instrument by which the grantor conveys or transfers title of property to a grantee.

1. **Requirements** The formal requirements of a deed differ from those of a sales contract. It is important to understand these differences.

a. **Writing** The Statute of Frauds requires a writing signed by the grantor for the transfer of an interest in real property. Usually, this writing takes the form of a deed. There is no requirement that a transfer of land be supported by consideration; therefore, a deed need not contain a statement of the consideration. If the deed fails to state clearly what interest it purports to convey, it will be presumed to convey the grantor's entire interest.

b. **Name** The deed must name a grantee and sufficiently describe her/him.

c. **Description** The land must be described sufficiently to furnish some means of identification. The description is usually by bounds, reference to a government survey, or by reference to a plat or street name and number. Parol evidence is generally admissible to clarify any ambiguities. Parol evidence is extraneous evidence which is not furnished by the deed or other document itself. Rather, it originates from other sources, such as witnesses or outside documents.

2. **Delivery** There is no effective transfer of an interest in land until the grantor has delivered the deed or other writing.

a. "Delivery" means more than simply the physical transfer of the deed out of the hands of the grantor. The grantor must intend to transfer an immediate interest in the property. Actual intent rather than physical action controls. Any type of evidence is admissible to prove this intent, including parol evidence and evidence of the grantor's conduct or statements before and after delivery of the deed.

b. The grantor need not deliver the deed to the grantee; the grantor may deliver it to a third party so long as the third party is not wholly under her/his control.

c. A delivery of a deed, valid on its face, but which is subject to an oral condition, effectively transfers the interest to the grantee, whether or not s/he fulfills the condition. Parol evidence is inadmissible to establish the existence of the condition.

3. **Covenants of Title** The following covenants may be expressed or implied in a deed.

a. **Covenant of Seizen** The grantor warrants that s/he owns the property and has a right to convey it.

b. **Covenant of Quiet Enjoyment** The grantee will not be disturbed in her/his possession of the property by the grantor or some third party's lawful claim of ownership.

c. **Covenant Against Encumbrances** The grantor promises that there are no existing encumbrances on the title to the property.

d. **Covenant of Further Assurance** The grantor will execute or obtain any further documents or assurances necessary to perfect the title.

e. **Covenant of Warranty Forever** The grantor will forever warrant title to the property.

4. **Deed Types**

a. **General Warranty Deed** A deed that contains all five of the usual covenants (see 3., above) is a general warranty deed. This deed warrants the title good against all encumbrances arising prior to the transfer.

b. **Special Warranty Deed** A deed that contains all five of the usual covenants, but limits its coverage to defects arising while the grantor owned the property.

c. **Quitclaim Deed** A transfer by the grantor of all her/his interest in the land, whatever it might be. However, a quitclaim deed makes no warranties.

5. **Contents** Generally, real property deeds contain the following clauses. **Note:** All of these provisions are not required.

a. **Premise Clause** Includes the date of delivery, names of the parties, purpose of the conveyance, and a statement of the consideration.

b. **Granting Clause** Includes a description of the land and the words of conveyance.

c. **Habendum or "to have" Clause** Sets forth the estate conveyed.

d. **Reddendum Clause** Contains any conditions or reservations.

e. **Covenants Clause** Contains the seller's title warranties.

f. **Conclusion** Contains the signatures of the parties and any witnesses and the seal.

6. **Recording Statutes** In order to protect her/his title against subsequent conflicting interests, the grantee must record her/his deed in the appropriate land records office. Recording or lack of recording only affects the rights of the grantee as against subsequent recorded parties in interest. The only purpose of recording is to put subsequent purchasers on notice. Thus, recording protects the rights of the grantee from interference by subsequent purchasers. It does not validate an invalid deed or protect the grantee from conflicting interests which arise by operation of law.

a. **Race-Notice** Once s/he records, a subsequent *bona fide* purchaser is protected against any prior unrecorded parties in interest.

b. **Notice** A subsequent *bona fide* purchaser is protected, whether or not s/he records against prior unrecorded parties in interest. Regardless of who files first, a person who knows that someone else already has bought a property cannot claim priority on that property.

c. **Race** The first party to record prevails.

D. **Adverse Possession**
Mere possession of property alone tends to raise an inference that the possessor has legal title. Therefore, the law has developed in such a manner that proof of long continued possession will establish title. This method of acquiring legal title is termed adverse possession. Most states have established a statute of limitations which bars others from ousting the possessor after a certain period of time. Once this statute of limitations has run, the possessor has valid title by adverse possession, and, if so desired, the possessor may bring a quiet title action and obtain title of record. In order for possession to ripen into title, it must be open, notorious, continuous, exclusive, adverse, and with claim of right for the statutory period (usually 20 years).

1. **Open & Notorious** For possession to be open and notorious, it must be visible and in the usual manner that such property would be possessed, so as to put the real owner and the community at large on notice.

2. **Continuous & Exclusive** The possession must be continuous for the entire statutory period; short, disconnected periods of use may not be added together to establish the required number of years. The possession must be to the exclusion of all other persons.

3. **Adverse** The possession must be adverse to the interests of the real owner (e.g., without permission or acquiescence).

4. **Claim of Right** Normally, this requirement demands only that the possessor hold her/himself out, by words and actions, as the true owner of the land. Some states require that an adverse possessor have some instrument purporting to be a title or that the adverse possessor pay taxes on the land for the statutory period.

III. Leasehold Estate

A. **Overview**
Landlord and tenant law recently has undergone more development than any other area of real property law. Courts and state legislatures have changed not only much of the common law concerning the rights and duties of landlords and tenants, they also have added whole new bodies of law to expand the recognized rights of the various parties. There are four recognized tenancies.

1. **For Years** A tenancy for years is a tenancy for a specified duration, even if the period is less than a year. There is usually a specific termination date. However, a tenancy for years also may run until a certain event occurs. For example, a tenancy for years may run until a construction contract is completed.

a. **Writing** Generally, the Statute of Frauds requires that a tenancy for years which will run for more than one year must be in writing to be enforceable.

b. **Limitation** A tenancy for years may be limited by conditions or covenants. However, remember that, traditionally, covenants associated with leases are assumed to be independent of the lease.

2. **From Period to Period** A tenancy that continues from year to year, month to month, or any other fraction of a year, is a tenancy from period to period. Usually, the measuring period is the same as the rent period. **Note:** Every tenancy from period to period must originate as a tenancy for a fixed term. For example, if L and T agree to a month-to-month tenancy, with T paying each month's rent on the first, then the first month's tenancy is a fixed term (e.g., neither party may terminate within the first month).

a. **Creation** A tenancy from period to period may be created by an express agreement or by operation of law.

(1) **Express Agreement** The parties may agree on a lease from month to month or for any other period. If the parties agree to a rent period but do not set a lease termination date, they have created a tenancy from period to period.

(2) **Operation of Law** In some jurisdictions, if the tenant holds over after the end of the term, the landlord may elect to hold her/him liable for rent for an additional rent period. In addition, if the purported lease agreement is invalid (for example, because it violates the Statute of Frauds) and the tenant pays rent periodically, the courts will imply a tenancy from period to period.

b. **Termination** A distinctive feature of a tenancy from period to period is that it continues until termination by proper notice. Under common law, notice must be given in the same amount of time as the rent period or tenancy period. For example, if tenancy is from month to month, then the tenant or landlord must give at least one month's notice. In addition, the terminating party may terminate a lease only at the end of a period. Finally, it is important to note that many states have enacted statutory modifications to these common law rules.

3. **At Will** A tenancy at will is one that continues until either party terminates. It is distinguished from a tenancy from period to period because there is no requirement that the terminating party give notice. However, most states have enacted statutes that require some notice. This in effect transforms a tenancy at will into a tenancy from period to period.

a. **Action** The parties may terminate a tenancy at will by any action that manifests intent to terminate. Thus, if the tenant abandons or assigns, s/he has terminated the lease.

b. **Operation of Law** A tenancy at will is considered to be a personal relationship and thus, terminates by operation of law whenever the personal relationship ceases. Consequently, if the landlord dies or sells the rental property, the tenancy at will terminates.

4. **At Sufferance** If the tenant holds over after the expiration of the tenancy term without the consent of the landlord, there is a tenancy at sufferance. This tenancy continues until the landlord terminates it by an action for eviction, by reentering the premises and treating the holdover tenant as a trespasser, or by creating a new lease.

5. **Lessor's Right to Terminate** Under common law and most statutes, the lessor has a right to terminate the lease if the tenant fails to pay rent. Generally, the lessor may not terminate if the tenant breaches other covenants. In response to this, most leases today contain express clauses giving the lessor the right to terminate upon breach of any enumerated covenant. These clauses are enforceable.

a. **Surrender** If the tenant voluntarily gives up possession to the landlord and the landlord accepts with the intent that the estate be terminated, a surrender has occurred. **Note:** The lessor's acceptance of an assignment or sublease does not connote a surrender.

b. **Abandonment** If the tenant abandons the property without the consent of the landlord, the landlord has two options. The landlord may keep the property unoccupied and sue for the rent as it becomes due, or the landlord may relet the premises and sue for damages. There is no general duty on the part of the landlord to relet the premises and thereby mitigate her/his damages.

c. **Illegal Use** A landlord may terminate a lease if the tenant uses the leased property for a purpose that is illegal.

6. **Tenant's Right to Terminate** The landlord's breach of most covenants does not entitle the tenant to terminate the lease. However, the breach of the following covenants entitle the tenant to terminate.

   a. **Covenants**

      (1) **Material Value** Generally, the landlord's breach of any covenant that materially supports the value of the estate entitles the tenant to terminate.

      (2) **Quiet Enjoyment** The landlord's breach of the covenant of quiet enjoyment, by actual or constructive eviction, terminates the lease as a matter of law.

      (3) **Habitability** The modern trend is that the landlord's breach of the covenant of habitability entitles the tenant to terminate.

   b. **Third-Party Eviction by Title Paramount** If the lessee is evicted by a third party who has superior title, the lessee may terminate the lease and hold the lessor liable for damages.

   c. **Destruction** If the premises are destroyed in any manner other than by the tenant's negligence, the tenant may surrender possession and terminate the lease. Under the old common law and in situations where the tenant has agreed to bear the risk, s/he may not terminate upon destruction.

   d. **Frustration of Purpose** If the premises are leased for a particular purpose recognized by both the landlord and tenant and that purpose later is frustrated (e.g., it becomes illegal or impossible to perform), the tenant usually has the power to terminate. For example, if the premises are rented as a brewery and the manufacture of alcoholic beverages is later outlawed, the tenant would have the power to terminate.

7. **Eminent Domain Condemnation** If the estate is taken in an eminent domain proceeding entirely and permanently, the leasehold is extinguished. Less than a total taking creates only a right for damages in favor of both the tenant and landlord.

B. Landlord's Rights, Duties & Liabilities

Substantial statutory modification in recent years is in response to the change from a rural, agrarian society to an urban, industrial society. Under early common law, the landlord's only duty was to grant an interest in the land. Most tenants were farmers and all-around handymen; it was their responsibility to put and maintain the premises in a habitable condition.

1. **Possession** The majority rule at modern common law is that the landlord has the duty to transfer to the tenant both the legal right to enter the premises and actual possession of the premises. This change results from the legal concept that the tenant bargains for use of the property, not the legal right to evict a prior tenant.

2. **Quiet Enjoyment** A covenant of quiet enjoyment is implied in all leases.

   a. **Entire** If the tenant is physically evicted from the entire premises, the duty to pay rent ceases.

   b. **Partial** If the tenant is physically evicted from any part of the premises through the fault of the landlord, the duty to pay rent also ceases entirely. However, if the tenant is evicted from a part of the premises by a third party, the duty to pay rent abates in proportion to the extent of the eviction.

   c. **Interference** If the tenant's use and enjoyment of the premises is substantially interfered with through the fault of the landlord, the duty to pay rent ceases. The interference must be such that a reasonable person would feel compelled to vacate the premises.

3. **Entrance** Under old common law, the landlord had no right to enter the premises. However, under modern law the landlord may enter the premises to inspect, repair, or exhibit them to potential renters or purchasers. The landlord must give the tenant notice of intent to enter, and the landlord may enter only during reasonable hours.

4. **Habitable Premises**

   a. **Common Law** Under common law, there is no general duty on the part of the landlord to deliver the premises in a habitable condition. Exceptions to this general principle include the following.

      (1) If the lease is a short-term lease for furnished premises, there is an implied covenant of habitability.

      (2) If there are hidden defects known to the landlord, s/he must either repair those defects or disclose them to the tenant.

      (3) If a building is being constructed for a particular use and the tenant enters into a lease agreement before construction is finished, there is an implied covenant of habitability.

   b. **Implied Covenant** Recently, many jurisdictions have held that there is an implied covenant of habitability for urban dwellings and commercial buildings. If the premises are not habitable, the tenant may terminate the lease. In the case of a dwelling, the tenant also has the contract remedy for damages. If the tenant knows of the defect, and freely bargains for a special rent rate, s/he is estopped from asserting the covenant of habitability.

   c. **Statute** Most states have enacted statutes that require the premises to be delivered in a habitable condition. Usually, habitable is defined as complying with the relevant housing code.

5. **Duty to Repair After Entry by Tenant** Under old common law, there is no implied duty to repair. The duty to maintain is placed on the tenant. The tenant's failure to maintain is known as permissive waste.

   a. **Implied Covenant** Recently, many jurisdictions have implied a continuing covenant of habitability. Modern courts hold that the duty to pay rent is dependent on the landlord's duty to repair. Thus, where the landlord fails to repair, the tenant may either terminate the lease or repair and deduct the costs from the rent due.

   b. **Statute** Several states have enacted landlord and tenant acts which require the landlord to maintain dwellings in a habitable condition. These acts usually state what constitutes habitable. Upon breach, the tenant has the duty to terminate, repair, and subtract the cost from the rent due, or pay the rent into escrow until the repairs are made. The law is split as to whether or not the lease may include an exculpatory clause which shifts the duty to repair back to the tenant. Some jurisdictions hold such clauses absolutely void; others require that the lessee freely bargain away her/his right in a separately signed clause.

6. **Tort Liability** As a general rule, the landlord is not liable for injuries caused by the negligent acts of the tenant. However, the landlord may be liable when the tenant's use of the premises is inherently dangerous. For example, if the tenant mines the property, the landlord may be vicariously liable for nuisance actions against the tenant.

   a. **Common Law** Under old common law, there is generally no liability on the landlord for injuries to the tenant or her/his guest which occurred on the leased premises. Exceptions to this general premise include the following.

(1) **Defect** The landlord may be held liable when the injury is caused by a hidden defect of which the landlord had knowledge or had reason to know.

(2) **Negligence** When the lessor negligently makes repairs which cause an injury to the tenant or her/his guest, the landlord may be held liable, even if s/he had no duty to repair, but did so voluntarily.

(3) **Duty** A landlord has the duty to inspect and repair common areas (hallways, stairways, etc.). Any injuries which result from a breach of this duty may result in the landlord being held liable.

b. **Modern Trend** The modern trend is to impose liability on the landlord for all injuries resulting from any unsafe conditions on the premises. This follows from the concurrent trend requiring the landlord to maintain the premises in a habitable condition. Some cases have gone so far as to hold a lessor strictly liable for any injuries occurring on the leased premises.

C. **Tenant's Rights, Duties & Liabilities**

1. **Duty to Repair** Under old common law, the tenant is accountable for waste.

a. **Permissive Waste** In the past, the tenant was bound to maintain the premises in the same condition as they were at the commencement of the lease. The tenant was under a duty not only to repair defects caused by use, but the tenant also had the affirmative duty to protect the property from damages caused by the elements. The tenant's failure to meet this duty was termed permissive waste.

b. **Affirmative Waste** The tenant still is liable for any affirmative or voluntary waste. Affirmative waste consists of any activity that either damages the premises or substantially changes the leased premises. However, many modern long-term leases do give the tenant the right to alter the premises.

2. **Duty to Pay Rent** Rent payment is an inherent obligation of the landlord and tenant relationship. Practically speaking, the landlord's prime remedy for nonpayment is eviction. Under common law, eviction terminates the lease and excuses the tenant from any further liability. In recent years, several additional remedies have been fashioned to further protect the landlord in the event the tenant defaults.

a. **Landlord Liens** Several states have enacted statutes which create a lien in favor of the landlord on all the tenant's personal property. Other states allow the landlord to peaceably enter the premises and seize the tenant's personal property, except her/his life's necessities, as security for the unpaid rent.

b. **Lease Deposits & Damage Clause** Many leases now require some sort of advance payment which provides security for the landlord. The most common forms these prepayments take are as follows:

(1) **Advance Rent** Many leases require that the tenant prepay a certain period's rent. For example, the lease may require 1 month's rent be paid in advance. If the lease is terminated prematurely, the landlord may retain this fee.

(2) **Security Deposit** Other leases require an advance as a security deposit. Should the lease be terminated prematurely, the deposit may be retained only to cover the landlord's actual expenses or damages; any excess must be returned to the tenant.

(3) **Liquidated Damages** Commercial leases often contain a clause requiring a deposit for liquidated damages. Courts will uphold these clauses if the sum deposited is related reasonably to the actual damages.

3. **Right to Assign or Sublet** If there is no restrictive clause, the tenant has the right to assign her/his leasehold or to sublet any portion of the estate. Most jurisdictions consider covenants against assignment and/or sublease enforceable; however, these covenants are strictly construed. A covenant against assignment does not prohibit a sublease and vice versa.

   a. **Assignment** If the tenant transfers the entire interest in the estate and retains no reversionary interest, s/he has assigned the estate. The majority view is that the primary tenant may retain a right of reentry, in the event the assignee-tenant fails to pay the rent, without transforming the assignment into a sublease. Other jurisdictions hold that the retention of any interest, including a right of reentry, creates a sublease and not an assignment.

      (1) **Assignee** An assignment establishes privity of estate between the lessor and assignee; therefore, the assignee becomes personally liable for the rent.

      (2) **Lessee** The original lessee remains in privity of contract with the lessor, unless released by the lessor. Therefore, s/he remains personally liable for all covenants.

   b. **Sublease** If the tenant retains a reversionary interest (for example, the tenant leases less than the entire premises or leases all the property for less than the full term of the lease), the tenant has subleased the estate.

      (1) **Sublessee** The sublessee does not come into privity of estate with the lessor; therefore, s/he is not personally liable for the rent. If the rent is not paid, the lessor may terminate the lease and oust the sublessee, but the lessor may not proceed against the sublessee for back rent.

      (2) **Lessee** The original lessee remains personally liable for the rent and all the covenants contained in the lease agreement.

IV. Mortgages

A. Overview

Under the common law, any estate created by a conveyance absolute in its form, but intended to secure a debt or obligation, is a mortgage. It is a conditional estate, however, in that it becomes absolutely void once the obligation is performed in accordance with the terms of the mortgage agreement. The modern trend, which is in force in many states, is to treat a mortgage as a mere lien and not as an estate. Under the title theory of mortgage, termination extinguishes the mortgage estate. Under the lien theory, termination frees the property from the mortgage lien. Termination may occur in the following ways.

1. **Performance** Once the mortgagor has performed her/his obligation according to the provisions of the agreement, the mortgage is extinguished.

2. **Merger** If the mortgagee acquires the mortgagor's interest or *vice versa*, the mortgage is extinguished by merger.

3. **Tender** If the mortgagor tenders proper performance and the mortgagee refuses, the mortgage is extinguished. The debt or obligation remains outstanding.

B. Formalities in Execution of Mortgage Agreements

Even in those jurisdictions that do not treat a mortgage as an estate, it is considered to be an interest in real property. Therefore, it is required by the Statute of Frauds to be in writing and signed by the party to be charged (mortgagor). Generally, a mortgage must meet the requirements of a deed; it is unenforceable against subsequent *bona fide* parties at interest unless it is recorded or unless it is noted on the property's deed or title which is recorded in the land records office. Usually the agreement contains the following.

1. **Names** The names of the parties.

2. **Amount** The amount of the principal secured by the mortgage, the date it is due, the payment schedule, and the interest rate.

3. **Description** A complete legal description of the mortgaged property.

4. **Right** A statement to the effect that the mortgagor has the sole possessory right to the property.

5. **Covenants** A list of the mortgagor's covenants.

    a. **Pay Debt** A promise to pay the debt under the agreed to conditions,

    b. **Insure Property** A promise to insure the property and to not "waste" the property without the mortgagee's consent, and

    c. **Acceleration Clause** This last clause allows the mortgagee to demand full payment in the event the mortgagor defaults.

C. **Recording Statutes**
A mortgage may be recorded to give constructive notice of the mortgage and protect against subsequent mortgages. Recording or lack of recording only affects the rights of the grantee as against subsequent recorded parties in interest. It does not validate an invalid mortgage or protect the lender from conflicting interest which arises by operation of law. A recorded mortgage takes priority over any subsequent interests which may be acquired in the mortgaged property. There are three types of recording statutes.

1. **Notice** A subsequent *bona fide* mortgagee is protected, whether or not s/he records, as against prior unrecorded mortgagees. Regardless of who files first, a person who knows that someone already has bought a property cannot claim priority on that property.

2. **Race-Notice** Once s/he records, a subsequent *bona fide* mortgagee is protected as against any prior unrecorded mortgagees.

3. **Race** The first party to record a mortgage prevails.

D. **Parties' Rights**
The parties to a mortgage are the mortgagee, the person to whom the obligation is owed; and the mortgagor, who owes the obligation.

1. **Mortgagee's Rights**

    a. **Lien** The mortgagee has either a lien on the land or actual title subject to defeasance (e.g., the title terminates upon satisfactory completion of the obligation).

    b. **Assignment** The mortgagee may freely assign her/his right to a third party.

    c. **Foreclosure** The mortgagee may foreclose her/his mortgage upon the mortgagor's default. If the foreclosure is successful, the court will direct that the property be sold at a foreclosure sale. A foreclosure sale serves to extinguish the mortgagee's interest in the property, and the mortgagee must return any amount realized which is in excess of that necessary to cover the obligation and expenses. If the proceeds from the sale are insufficient to satisfy the debt in full, the mortgagor remains liable for any deficiency. If there is more than one mortgage on the property, the mortgage that has priority (as determined under the state's recording statute) will be satisfied in full first before any proceeds may go towards satisfying the second mortgage.

2. **Mortgagor's Rights**

   a. **Possess** The mortgagor has the right to possess the premises and make any reasonable use of them.

   b. **Lease** The mortgagor may lease the land.

   c. **Sell** The mortgagor may sell the land; however, a sale does not extinguish the mortgage unless the mortgagee releases her/him.

   d. **Redemption** The mortgagor has the right of redemption. This right entitles her/him to retain the property even after foreclosure, but before the foreclosure sale, by paying the amount due plus interest and any other costs.

E. **Sale of Mortgaged Property**
The mortgagor has the right to sell the mortgaged property. This sale does not extinguish her/his personal liability nor does it affect the status of the mortgaged property. The grantee of the property may take in two ways. Generally, a grantee is better off buying subject to the mortgage because s/he, thereby, avoids personal liability.

1. **Subject to the Mortgage** A grantee who takes subject to the mortgage does not assume any personal liability for the mortgage. However, the grantee's interest in the property is "subject to" the outstanding mortgage for which the mortgagor remains liable. The property continues to secure a debt, and the mortgagee retains the power to foreclose.

2. **Assume the Mortgage** If a grantee expressly "assumes" the mortgage, s/he, thereby, becomes personally liable for it. The grantee's interest in the land also is subject to the outstanding mortgage. The grantor/mortgagor remains personally liable, unless the mortgagee releases her/him. S/he is treated as a surety.

V. Insurance Contracts

A. Definitions

1. **Assured** The party for whose benefit the contract was made. Often, the terms "assured" and "insured" are used synonymously.

2. **Hazard** A condition or situation that causes or increases the risk or chance of loss.

3. **Insured** The party who is protected by insurance from certain risks.

4. **Insurer** The party (such as an insurance company) who, in return for a premium, agrees to undertake the risk of loss from certain specified perils.

5. **Legal Interests** Legal interests include ownership and possessory interests (including equitable interests), future interests, and the interests of secured creditors, including mortgagees. For example, tenants have an insurable interest in their leaseholds, stockholders have an interest in their corporation's property, and bailees have an interest in bailed property.

6. **Representations** Representations are statements made by the applicant to the prospective insurer concerning facts and conditions, and on the basis of which the insurance policy is written. These statements may be made orally or in writing. Representations are inducements to enter into the contract.

7. **Pecuniary Interests** An insured must have a pecuniary interest (e.g., the insured must stand to suffer an economic or financial loss if the property is damaged or destroyed). Insurance provides only monetary protection; therefore, only those with a pecuniary interest are protected.

8. **Peril** The particular active harm that may cause the economic damage that insurance seeks to protect against (for example, fire, wind, or water).

9. **Policy** The written insurance contract.

10. **Premium** The consideration (money) paid by the assured in return for insurance.

11. **Warranties** Warranties are statements (conditions precedent) that must be true before the insurer will be liable. They appear in, and are considered a part of, the insurance contract. As in general contract law, a breach of a warranty by one party excuses the other party from performing. For example, if a warranty made by the insured is not true, or is "breached," the insurer is excused from paying the claim. However, the falsity of an immaterial representation will not excuse the insurer's performance.

B. **Fire & Property Insurance**
Generally, fire and property insurance covers losses arising from accidental damage to property caused by certain stipulated perils. Fire insurance minimally covers all damage directly or indirectly resulting from a fire (including smoke and water). Fire insurance policies often cover losses resulting from other named perils such as wind, flooding, and lightning.

1. **Types**

a. **Open vs. Valued Policy** An open policy is one that does not stipulate the value of the property; instead, only a maximum liability is specified. The value of the property and the extent of damages must be proved at the time a claim is filed. A valued policy is one that stipulates the value of the insured property. Upon total destruction, this value is conclusive unless the insurer can show fraud.

b. **Blanket Policy** A blanket policy is one under which several items are insured and a maximum overall liability is stipulated. The value and liability for each item is not specified.

c. **Floating vs. Specific Policy** A floating policy is one that covers constantly changing property such as inventory or stock. A specific policy specifies the insurer's maximum liability for the destruction of each individual item.

2. **Standard Provisions** The most important provisions will be covered under separate headings elsewhere in the outline. Below are some less important, but commonly found provisions.

a. **Friendly Fire Exemptions** Precludes recovery for damages resulting from "friendly" or planned fires that occur during normal operation. For example, if fireplace masonry cracks from excessive heat developing in the fireplace, repairs would not be covered. However, losses arising from friendly fires that have become hostile are covered. Thus, for example, a fireplace fire that spreads to the carpet, etc., eventually causing extensive room damage is a hostile fire and repairs are covered.

b. **Increase of Hazard Clause** Relieves the insurer from liability if the insured has done something that increases the risk of loss. For example, if the insured, in an effort to provide adequate fuel for the family vehicle during an energy shortage, begins storing drums of gasoline in her/his garage, the resultant increase in the risk of loss may cause her/his insurance policy to be voidable by the insurer.

c. **Proof of Loss** Usually, a policy will require "satisfactory" proof of loss within a reasonable time (60 to 90 days) after the occurrence of the damages or the date of notification. To comply, an insured must file a written and verified statement containing all of the information required by the policy.

d. **Cancellation** Most policies allow either the insured or the insurer to cancel after giving notice.

3. **Payment of Proceeds** In cases where only one party has an interest, the insurer merely pays the proceeds due that party. Often, however, more than one party has an insurable interest in the insured property.

   a. **Mortgagor vs. Mortgagee** Most mortgage agreements require the mortgagor to insure the property for the benefit of both parties. (The mortgagor is the party who borrows funds from the mortgagee, who is the lender.) The mortgagor and mortgagee each have a separate insurable interest (see 4. and 5. below) and may insure for their own benefit.

   b. **Creditors vs. Possessor/Insured** Generally, a creditor has no rights in the possessor's insurance before the property is destroyed or damaged.

      (1) Article 9 of the Uniform Commercial Code provides that secured creditors automatically have a security interest in proceeds. Proceeds is defined so as to include insurance proceeds.

      (2) As was the case for mortgagees, secured creditors have an insurable interest in collateral; thus, they may procure their own insurance.

      (3) General creditors have no special rights to any of the debtor's insurance, nor do they have an insurable interest in any of the debtor's property.

   c. **Seller vs. Buyer** Some jurisdictions follow the rule that the risk of loss is on the buyer from the moment the contract is entered into. In these jurisdictions, the buyer has a right to any insurance proceeds the seller has realized for damaged or destroyed property during the time the buyer bore the risk of loss.

   d. **Life Tenant vs. Remainderman** The law of insurance in this area is very similar to that covering mortgagees and mortgagors.

      (1) When a policy is purchased for the benefit of both parties, the proceeds usually go first to rebuilding principal, to protect the interest of each party.

      (2) Each party has an insurable interest and may purchase insurance for her/his own benefit.

4. **Legal & Pecuniary Interests** The rule with respect to insurable interests in fire or property insurance contracts requires that there be both a legally recognized interest and the possibility of a pecuniary (financial or economic) loss in the event the property is damaged or destroyed.

5. **Insurable Interest at Time of Loss** Under the broad common law rule, the insured is required to have insurable interests (legal and pecuniary) both at the time of issuance and at the time the loss is incurred. However, under a substantial body of minority opinion, an insurable interest under a fire or property insurance policy must exist only at the time of loss. For CPA exam purposes, an insurable interest must exist only at the time of loss.

C. **Liability Insurance**
Covers the liability of the insured for damages to other persons or property caused by unintentional acts of the insured or the insured's agents.

1. **Automobile Liability Insurance** Provides coverage for damages to other persons and their property caused either by the insured or those for whom the insured is held liable.

Example 1 ▸ Automobile Liability Insurance

A is negligently driving his car and accidentally injures B. Although A is at "fault," because the accident was unintentional, A's liability insurance will pay for the damages to B and B's property.

- **"No-Fault" Insurance** Certain states have adopted forms of no-fault insurance. Basically, each vehicle owner's insurer pays her/his insured's own expenses that result from an automobile accident, whether or not the insured was at fault. Generally, the party who is not at fault cannot sue the party at fault for damages unless the accident causes certain specified serious physical injuries.

2. **Personal Liability** Various kinds of personal liability insurance are available to protect against losses associated with injuries to other persons for which the insured is liable.

   a. **Homeowner's Insurance** Most homeowner's policies cover liability for accidents to others that occur in the insured's home. If A is visiting B in B's home, and while walking up the steps slips and falls, B's liability insurance will pay for A's injuries.

   b. **Malpractice Insurance** Malpractice insurance is another type of liability insurance which protects against liability for errors and omissions in connection with professional work.

Example 2 ▸ Malpractice Insurance

A is a stockholder in Company X, which B audits. If B negligently makes a material error in connection with the audit of X's financial statements, B's malpractice insurance will pay A's damages if A sues.

D. Formation

1. **Elements** Essentially the same elements are required for an insurance contract as are necessary for any other enforceable agreement.

   a. **Agreement** For an insurance contract to be binding, there must be an agreement between the parties (e.g., a meeting of the minds). The components of an agreement are typically phrased as "offer" and "acceptance."

      (1) The "offer" generally is made by the applicant in the application for insurance.

      (2) The "acceptance" of the offer is made by the insurer when it acknowledges that it agrees to insure the applicant. This generally is accomplished by the issuance of a policy. The policy contains all the terms, conditions, and exclusions of the insurance contract.

   b. **Consideration** Consideration is that money paid by the insured in return for the insurer's promises to cover certain risks. Recall that this consideration is called a "premium." The insurer's consideration is her/his promise to make payment in the event of a loss.

   c. **Capacity** Both parties to the insurance contract must have the legal capacity to enter into a contract (sanity, age, authority).

   d. **Legality of Subject Matter** A policy is void if the subject matter is either illegal or not in existence at the time the policy is issued, and if this fact is known by one of the parties. For example, insurance that covers losses associated with criminal activities is void. In addition, a policy that insures property not in existence usually will be issued only pursuant to a misrepresentation or a fraud. It is thus an illegal contract and, therefore, would be void.

e. **Writing** Although insurance contracts are not required by the Statute of Frauds to be in writing, most states have enacted statutes that require such. However, some property insurance contracts may be consummated by verbal agreement.

f. **Delivery** In insurance law, delivery of the policy is primarily a matter of intent. That is, actual physical delivery of the policy is not necessary to the creation of a valid contract. However, there must be an intention to deliver the policy to the applicant or her/his agents.

(1) **Constructive Delivery** Constructive delivery occurs when the insurance company unconditionally accepts the application of the insured and takes steps to communicate this to the insured. For example, there is constructive delivery when the insurance company executes and mails the policy to the insured. Additionally, when the insurer mails and/or delivers the policy to the local agent of the insurer, courts generally have held that constructive delivery has occurred. The insurance policy is held to be effective as of the date of the mailing or delivery to the agent.

(2) **Oral** Property insurance contracts generally are held to be effective even without delivery. For example, oral contracts, such as those made over the telephone, are valid and effective when the agreement is reached or at the time otherwise agreed to by the parties.

(3) **Binder** A "binder" or "binding slip" is a written memorandum that an insurer's agent often will issue to signify that the contract is to become effective prior to the actual physical delivery of a policy.

2. **Voidable** The insurance contract is voidable by the insurer if the applicant has concealed information or misrepresented a material fact. "Voidable" means that the policy is valid, but may be invalidated by the insurer, at her/his option, upon discovery of the misrepresentation or concealment. Because the breach of a warranty excuses the insurer from paying, it is important that any false statement be classified properly as either a "warranty" or a "representation." The chief distinction between representations and warranties is that representations are inducements to enter into a contract, while warranties are part of the contract. Many insurance contracts specifically make all statements "warranties."

a. **State Statutes** Most states have statutes that provide that all statements made by an applicant are to be deemed representations, not warranties.

b. **Materiality of Statement** Most statutes provide that those misstatements made in good faith and without fraud do not void the policy unless the misstatement relates to a matter that is material to the risk of the insured. In addition, only omissions that materially increase the risk borne by the insurer are grounds for excused performance.

c. **Fraud** Even immaterial statements that are made fraudulently void the policy and excuse performance by the insurer. The same is true for fraudulent omissions.

3. **Ambiguities** Because most insurance contracts are written by the insurer and generally include certain standardized language, any ambiguities in the contract (or policy) are construed against the insurer. That is, any question about the meaning of any terms or conditions used in the policy will be resolved in favor of the insured.

4. **Agents** Because insurance companies generally act through agents, the rules of agency law apply to this aspect of the law of insurance.

5. **Waiver, Estoppel & Election** If the insurer has knowledge that the insured has made a misrepresentation or breached a warranty, but, nevertheless, elects to issue the policy or allow the policy to remain in effect in spite of the misrepresentation, the insurer then has waived the fraud defense. Thereafter, the insurer is estopped from asserting that defense; s/he must perform her/his obligations under the contract.

   a. **Waiver** The voluntary relinquishment of a known right. For example, an agent of the insurer may properly waive certain requirements of the policy, such as the requirement that a claim be submitted in writing within 30 days of the loss.

   b. **Estoppel** A barrier raised by the law that prevents the insurer from asserting or denying certain facts that are inconsistent with its previous acts or allegations. For example, the insurer may be estopped from asserting the fact that the claim was not submitted in writing within 30 days if the insurer waived this requirement.

   c. **Election** The voluntary exercise of a right to choose one alternative over another. An election has the same effect as a waiver in that the party, once it has made its choice, forever loses its rights under the other alternative. For example, an insured failed to report several car accidents in breach of one of the policy provisions. Once the insurer discovers the breach, it may choose to cancel the policy or excuse the breach and continue to accept premiums. If it chooses the latter, the insurer subsequently cannot assert the breach to avoid liability.

E. Assignment

An insurance contract is considered to be "personal" in nature between the insured and the insurer. Therefore, the assignment of an insurance contract is subject to certain rules and restrictions.

1. **Fire or Property Insurance** Historically, property insurance contracts are not assignable without the consent of the insurer because the risk assumed by the insurer varies with the person protected. However, exceptions to this are as follows.

   a. **Assignment as Collateral** An insured may assign a fire policy as collateral. For example, an insured may assign her policy to a person who has acquired the mortgage on the insured property. In this circumstance, the insured retains an interest in the property insured (because she is still the owner).

   b. **Assignment of Loss Proceeds** The prohibition against the assignment of a fire policy without the permission of the insurer does not preclude the assignment of proceeds due or payable following a loss. Just as any other claim for money is assignable, so is the claim for the proceeds of an insurance policy. Moreover, provisions in policies that prohibit the assignment of these claims are not enforceable.

2. **Marine Insurance** Marine insurance generally is assignable unless the policy specifically requires the consent of the insurer.

F. Subrogation

The right of the insurer, upon paying the loss, to recover from some third person who actually caused the loss is known as subrogation. In essence, the insurance company "stands in the shoes" of the insured in order to recover from the person who is legally liable for the loss.

1. **Applicability** In fire or property insurance policies, there is generally a right of subrogation.

2. **Release** If the damaged insured party releases the party causing the injury prior to the payment of the loss by the insured, s/he also releases the insurer from any duty to pay on the policy. In addition, if the insured releases the party causing the loss subsequent to the payment by the insurer, s/he forfeits the right to retain the insurance proceeds. The reason for these two rules is that the insured, by releasing the party causing the loss, has terminated the insurer's right to subrogation.

G. Coinsurance

A coinsurance clause provides that if the insured fails to carry an amount of insurance equal to a stated percentage (usually 80%) of the value of the property insured, then the insured becomes a coinsurer and must proportionally bear the loss. The share of the loss borne by the insurer will be the lower of (1) the face value of the policy, (2) fair market value of property at date of loss, or (3) the coinsurance amount.

1. **Total Loss** If there is a total loss, the insured will collect the full amount of the insurance if it is the lowest of the three measures of recovery.

2. **Partial Loss** The amount of recovery for a partial loss is equal to (1) the face value of the insurance policy, divided by the coinsurance percent times the actual fair value of the property, times (2) the actual loss. Mathematically, this formula appears as follows:

$$\textit{Recovery} = \frac{\textit{Face value of insurance}}{\textit{Coinsurance \% × FV of property}} \times \textit{Actual loss}$$

Example 3 ▸ Partial Loss of Underinsured Property

A carries only $35,000 of insurance on property worth $100,000, and the policy contains a coinsurance clause that requires that the property must be insured at 80% of its fair market value. A fire inflicts actual damages in the amount of $25,000.

A's recovery will be $35,000 / (80% × $100,000) × $25,000 = $10,937.50

Thus, A will be liable, as the co-insurer, for $14,062.50. If A had been insured in the amount of $80,000 or more, A would have recovered the full $25,000 and not been personally liable for any damages.

H. *Pro Rata* Recovery

Where the insured has several policies with different insurance companies all covering the same property and the aggregate insurance exceeds the actual loss, s/he may collect from each company only its proportionate or *pro rata* share. A proportionate share is that percentage of an insured's total insurance that is carried with an individual company.

Example 4 ▸ Partial Loss of Property Insured by Multiple Companies

A has two fire insurance policies covering the same property, one for $10,000 and the other for $15,000. The property is damaged in the amount of $20,000. A will collect $8,000 from the first insurer and $12,000 from the second insurer.

First: $10,000 / ($10,000 + $15,000) × $20,000 = $8,000

Second: $15,000 / ($10,000 + $15,000) × $20,000 = $12,000

1. **Over-Insurance Clause** Serves the same general purpose as do the rules governing *pro rata* or proportionate recovery (e.g., they prohibit a double or excessive recovery). This clause prohibits an insured from procuring other or additional insurance to cover losses for which the insured is insured completely. If the insured violates such a clause, the policy is voidable by the insurer.

2. **Other Party** An over-insurance clause does not prohibit another party who has the requisite insurable interest from insuring her/his interest. For example, both a mortgagor and mortgagee may insure their individual interests separately.

Don't forget the helpful hints in the material at the front and back of this text!

Now that you have had a chance to become familiar with the text format, you may want to skim the **Getting Started, Practical Advice,** and **Writing Skills** sections of the book again. These provide:

- Information on how to integrate materials so they work best for you
- Helpful information on answering all question types
- Information on the heavily tested topics on exams
- Information on how to use your time wisely
- Exam-taking techniques that will earn extra points on the exam

Remember, with the techniques and information in your material,

A passing score is well within reach!

CHAPTER 42—PROPERTY

Problem 42-1 MULTIPLE CHOICE QUESTIONS (45 to 60 minutes)

1. Which of the following would change if an asset is treated as personal property rather than as real property?

	Requirements for transfer	*Creditor's rights*
a.	Yes	No
b.	No	Yes
c.	Yes	Yes
d.	No	No

(11/92, Law, #51, 3133)

2. Trees were cut down and made into lumber. The lumber was used to build a house. Which of the following statements best describes the property aspect of these events?

a. The trees were and remained tangible personal property.
b. The trees were and remained real property.
c. The trees were real property, then became and remained personal property.
d. The trees were real property, became personal property, then reverted to being real property.

(R/05, REG, 0114L, #5, 7871)

3. Tower, Nolan, and Oak were deeded a piece of land as tenants in common. The deed provided that Tower owned 1/2 the property and Nolan and Oak owned 1/4 each. If Oak dies, the property will be owned as follows:

a. Tower 1/2, Nolan 1/4, Oak's heirs 1/4
b. Tower 1/3, Nolan 1/3, Oak's heirs 1/3
c. Tower 5/8, Nolan 3/8
d. Tower 1/2, Nolan 1/2

(5/95, Law, #51, amended, 5385)

4. Court, Fell, and Miles own a parcel of land as joint tenants with right of survivorship. Court's interest was sold to Plank. As a result of the sale from Court to Plank,

a. Fell, Miles, and Plank each own one-third of the land as joint tenants.
b. Fell and Miles each own one-third of the land as tenants in common.
c. Plank owns one-third of the land as a tenant in common.
d. Plank owns one-third of the land as a joint tenant.

(5/94, Law, #56, 4811)

5. What interest in real property generally gives the holder of that interest the right to sell the property?

a. Easement
b. Leasehold
c. License
d. Fee simple (11/98, Law, #14, 6759)

6. Which of the following is a defect in marketable title to real property?

a. Recorded zoning restrictions
b. Recorded easements referred to in the contract of sale
c. Unrecorded lawsuit for negligence against the seller
d. Unrecorded easement (5/94, Law, #57, 4812)

7. A standard title insurance policy will generally insure that

a. There are **no** other deeds to the property.
b. The purchaser has good record title as of the policy's date.
c. All taxes and assessments are paid.
d. The insurance protection will be transferable to a subsequent purchaser. (5/93, Law, #54, 4022)

8. On February 2, Mazo deeded a warehouse to Parko for $450,000. Parko did not record the deed. On February 12, Mazo deeded the same warehouse to Nexis for $430,000. Nexis was aware of the prior conveyance to Parko. Nexis recorded its deed before Parko recorded. Who would prevail under the following recording statutes?

	Notice statute	*Race statute*	*Notice-race statute*
a.	Nexis	Parko	Parko
b.	Parko	Nexis	Parko
c.	Parko	Nexis	Nexis
d.	Parko	Parko	Nexis

(5/90, Law, #55, 8027)

9. Which of the following elements must be contained in a valid deed?

	Purchase price	*Description of the land*
a.	Yes	Yes
b.	Yes	No
c.	No	Yes
d.	No	No

(11/95, Law, #54, 5923)

10. Delta Corp. leased 60,000 square feet in an office building from Tanner under a written 25-year lease. Which of the following statements is correct?
a. Tanner's death will terminate the lease and Delta will be able to recover any resulting damages from Tanner's estate.
b. Tanner's sale of the office building will terminate the lease unless both Delta and the buyer consented to the assumption of the lease by the buyer.
c. In the absence of a provision in the lease to the contrary, Delta does **not** need Tanner's consent to assign the lease to another party.
d. In the absence of a provision in the lease to the contrary, Delta would need Tanner's consent to enter into a sublease with another party.
(5/90, Law, #54, 8028)

11. A tenant renting an apartment under a three-year written lease that does **not** contain any specific restrictions may be evicted for
a. Counterfeiting money in the apartment
b. Keeping a dog in the apartment
c. Failing to maintain a liability insurance policy on the apartment
d. Making structural repairs to the apartment
(5/90, Law, #53, 8029)

12. In general, which of the following statements is correct with respect to a real estate mortgage?
a. The mortgage may **not** be given to secure an antecedent debt.
b. The mortgage must contain the actual amount of the underlying debt.
c. The mortgage must be signed by both the mortgagor (borrower) and mortgagee (lender).
d. The mortgagee may assign the mortgage to a third party without the mortgagor's consent.
(5/93, Law, #55, 4023)

13. Rich purchased property from Sklar for $200,000. Rich obtained a $150,000 loan from Marsh Bank to finance the purchase, executing a promissory note and a mortgage. By recording the mortgage, Marsh protects its
a. Rights against Rich under the promissory note
b. Rights against the claims of subsequent bona fide purchasers for value
c. Priority against a previously filed real estate tax lien on the property
d. Priority against all parties having earlier claims to the property (11/95, Law, #55, 5924)

Items 14 through 16 are based on the following:

On February 1, Frost bought a building from Elgin, Inc. for $250,000. To complete the purchase, Frost borrowed $200,000 from Independent Bank and gave Independent a mortgage for that amount; gave Elgin a second mortgage for $25,000; and paid $25,000 in cash. Independent recorded its mortgage on February 2, and Elgin recorded its mortgage on March 12.

The following transactions also took place:

- On March 1, Frost gave Scott a $20,000 mortgage on the building to secure a personal loan Scott had previously made to Frost.
- On March 10, Scott recorded this mortgage.
- On March 15, Scott learned about both prior mortgages.
- On June 1, Frost stopped making payments on all the mortgages.
- On August 1, the mortgages were foreclosed. Frost, on that date, owed Independent $195,000; Elgin $24,000; and Scott $19,000.

A judicial sale of the building resulted in proceeds of $220,000 after expenses were deducted. The above transactions took place in a notice-race jurisdiction.

14. What amount of the proceeds will Scott receive?
a. $0
b. $ 1,000
c. $12,500
d. $19,000 (11/92, Law, #58, 3140)

15. Why would Scott receive this amount?
a. Scott knew of the Elgin mortgage.
b. Scott's mortgage was recorded before Elgin's and before Scott knew of Elgin's mortgage.
c. Elgin's mortgage was first in time.
d. After Independent is fully paid, Elgin and Scott share the remaining proceeds equally.
(11/92, Law, #59, 3141)

16. Frost may redeem the property before the judicial sale only if
a. There is a statutory right of redemption.
b. It is probable that the sale price will result in a deficiency.
c. All mortgages are paid in full.
d. All mortgagees are paid a penalty fee.
(11/92, Law, #60, 3142)

17. Wilk bought an apartment building from Dix Corp. There was a mortgage on the building securing Dix's promissory note to Xeon Finance Co. Wilk took title subject to Xeon's mortgage. Wilk did not make the payments on the note due Xeon and the building was sold at a foreclosure sale. If the proceeds of the foreclosure sale are less than the balance due on the note, which of the following statements is correct regarding the deficiency?

a. Xeon must attempt to collect the deficiency from Wilk before suing Dix.
b. Dix will **not** be liable for any of the deficiency because Wilk assumed the note and mortgage.
c. Xeon may collect the deficiency from either Dix or Wilk.
d. Dix will be liable for the entire deficiency.

(5/91, Law, #19, 0810)

18. Jerry's House of Jewelry, Inc., took out an insurance policy with the Old Time Insurance Company which covered the stock of jewelry displayed in the store's windows. Old Time agreed to indemnify Jerry's House for losses due to window smashing and theft of the jewels displayed. The application contained the following provision: "It is hereby warranted that the maximum value of the jewelry displayed shall not exceed $10,000." The insurance policy's coverage was for $8,000. The application was initialed alongside the warranty and attached to the policy. Subsequently, thieves smashed the store window and stole $4,000 worth of jewels. The total value of the display during that week, including the day of the robbery, was $12,000. Which of the following is correct?

a. Jerry's House will recover nothing.
b. Jerry's House will recover $2,000, the loss less the amount in excess of the $10,000 display limitation.
c. Jerry's House will recover the full $4,000 since the warranty will be construed as a mere representation.
d. Jerry's House will recover the full $4,000 since attaching the application to the policy is insufficient to make it a part thereof.

(11/81, Law, #55, 8030)

19. Which of the following losses, resulting from a fire, generally may be recovered under a standard fire insurance policy?

	Water damage resulting from extinguishing the fire	*Loss of income due to business interruption*
a.	Yes	Yes
b.	Yes	No
c.	No	Yes
d.	No	No

(5/96, Law, #10, 6266)

20. Daly tried to collect on a property insurance policy covering a house that was damaged by fire. The insurer denied recovery, alleging that Daly had no insurable interest in the house. In which of the following situations will the insurer prevail?

a. The house belongs to a corporation of which Daly is a 50% stockholder.
b. Daly is **not** the owner of the house but a long-term lessee.
c. The house is held in trust for Daly's mother and, on her death, will pass to Daly.
d. Daly gave an unsecured loan to the owner of the house to improve the house.

(11/92, Law, #57, 3139)

21. On February 1, Papco Corp. entered into a contract to purchase an office building from Merit Company for $500,000 with closing scheduled for March 20. On February 2, Papco obtained a $400,000 standard fire insurance policy from Abex Insurance Company. On March 15, the office building sustained a $90,000 fire loss. On March 15, which of the following is correct?

I. Papco has an insurable interest in the building.
II. Merit has an insurable interest in the building.

a. I only
b. II only
c. Both I and II
d. Neither I **nor** II

(11/90, Law, #60, 0848)

22. Beal occupies an office building as a tenant under a 25-year lease. Beal also has a mortgagee's (lender's) interest in an office building owned by Hill Corp. In which capacity does Beal have an insurable interest?

	Tenant	*Mortgagee*
a.	Yes	Yes
b.	Yes	No
c.	No	Yes
d.	No	No

(5/88, Law, #60, 8031)

23. Which of the following statements correctly describes the requirement of insurable interest relating to property insurance? An insurable interest
a. Must exist when any loss occurs
b. Must exist when the policy is issued and when any loss occurs
c. Is created only when the property is owned in fee simple
d. Is created only when the property is owned by an individual (11/95, Law, #60, 5929)

24. One of the primary purposes of including a coinsurance clause in a property insurance policy is to
a. Encourage the policyholder to insure the property for an amount close to its full value
b. Make the policyholder responsible for the entire loss caused by some covered perils
c. Cause the policyholder to maintain a minimum amount of liability insurance that will increase with inflation
d. Require the policyholder to insure the property with only one insurance company (11/90, Law, #57, 0847)

25. A building was purchased for $350,000 and insured under a $300,000 fire insurance policy containing an 80% coinsurance clause. Several years later, the building, having a fair market value of $500,000, sustained fire damage of $40,000. What is the amount recoverable from the insurance company?
a. $28,000
b. $30,000
c. $32,000
d. $40,000 (R/00, Law, #10, 6975)

26. MNC Corp. bought a building for $300,000. At the same time, MNC purchased a $200,000 fire insurance policy from Building Insurance Co. and a $100,000 fire insurance policy from Property Insurance Co. Each policy contained a standard 80% coinsurance clause. Three years later, when the building had a fair market value of $400,000, the building was totally destroyed in a fire. What amount would MNC recover from the two insurance companies?
a. $240,000
b. $300,000
c. $320,000
d. $400,000 (R/03, REG, A0117L, #4, 7646)

Items 27 and 28 are based on the following:

In Year 3, Pod bought a building for $220,000. At that time, Pod purchased a $150,000 fire insurance policy with Owners Insurance Co. and a $50,000 fire insurance policy with Group Insurance Corp. Each policy contained a standard 80% coinsurance clause. In Year 8, when the building had a fair market value of $250,000, it was damaged in a fire.

27. How much would Pod recover from Owners and Group if the fire totally destroyed the building?
a. $160,000
b. $200,000
c. $220,000
d. $250,000 (5/93, Law, #60, amended, 4028)

28. How much would Pod recover from Owners if the fire caused $180,000 in damage?
a. $ 90,000
b. $120,000
c. $135,000
d. $150,000 (5/93, Law, #59, amended, 4027)

29. Mason Co. maintained two standard fire insurance policies on one of its warehouses. Both policies included an 80% coinsurance clause and a typical "other insurance" clause. One policy was with Ace Fire Insurance, Inc., for $24,000, and the other was with Thrifty Casualty Insurance Co., for $16,000. At a time when the warehouse was worth $100,000, a fire in the warehouse caused a $40,000 loss. What amounts can Mason recover from Ace and Thrifty, respectively?
a. $0 and $0
b. $10,000 and $10,000
c. $12,000 and $8,000
d. $24,000 and $16,000 (11/91, Law, #60, 2388)

30. In Year 1, King bought a building for $250,000. At that time, King took out a $200,000 fire insurance policy with Omni Insurance Co. and a $50,000 fire insurance policy with Safe Insurance Corp. Each policy contained a standard 80% coinsurance clause. In Year 6, when the building had a fair market value of $300,000, a fire caused $200,000 in damage. What dollar amount would King recover from Omni?
a. $100,000
b. $150,000
c. $160,000
d. $200,000 (R/99, Law, #17, amended, 6868)

Problem 42-2 ADDITIONAL MULTIPLE CHOICE QUESTIONS (45 to 60 minutes)

31. What is an example of property that can be considered either personal property or real property?
a. Air rights
b. Mineral rights
c. Harvested crops
d. Growing crops (11/98, Law, #15, 6760)

32. Which of the following factors help determine whether an item of personal property has become a fixture?

	Manner of affixation	*Value of the item*	*Intent of the annexor*
a.	Yes	Yes	Yes
b.	Yes	Yes	No
c.	Yes	No	Yes
d.	No	Yes	Yes

(5/95, Law, #55, 5389)

33. Which of the following statements is the best definition of real property?
a. Real property is only land.
b. Real property is all tangible property including land.
c. Real property is land and intangible property in realized form.
d. Real property is land and everything permanently attached to it. (R/06, REG, 1583L, #29, 8199)

34. Long, Fall, and Pear own a building as joint tenants with the right of survivorship. Long gave Long's interest in the building to Green by executing and delivering a deed to Green. Neither Fall nor Pear consented to this transfer. Fall and Pear subsequently died. After their deaths, Green's interest in the building would consist of
a. A 1/3 interest as a joint tenant
b. A 1/3 interest as a tenant in common
c. No interest because Fall and Pear did **not** consent to the transfer
d. Total ownership due to the deaths of Fall and Pear (11/95, Law, #51, 5920)

35. Which of the following unities (elements) are required to establish a joint tenancy?

	Time	*Title*	*Interest*	*Possession*
a.	Yes	Yes	Yes	Yes
b.	Yes	Yes	No	No
c.	No	No	Yes	Yes
d.	Yes	No	Yes	No

(5/93, Law, #52, 4020)

36. A person may own property as a joint tenant with the right of survivorship with any of the following **except** a(an)
a. Divorced spouse
b. Related minor child
c. Unaffiliated corporation
d. Unrelated adult (5/90, Law, #50, 8032)

37. A method of transferring ownership of real property that most likely would be considered an arm's-length transaction is transfer by
a. Inheritance
b. Eminent domain
c. Adverse possession
d. Sale (11/95, Law, #52, 5921)

38. For a deed to be effective between a purchaser and seller of real estate, **two** of the conditions is that the deed must
a. Be recorded within the permissible statutory time limits
b. Be delivered by the seller with an intent to transfer title
c. Contain the actual sales price
d. Contain the signatures of the seller and purchaser
e. Contain a sufficient description to identify the real property (5/95, Law, #53, amended, 5387)

39. Which of the following warranties is(are) contained in a general warranty deed?

I. The grantor has the right to convey the property.
II. The grantee will **not** be disturbed in possession of the property by the grantor or some third party's lawful claim of ownership.

a. I only
b. II only
c. I and II
d. Neither I **nor** II (5/93, Law, #53, 4021)

40. Which of the following deeds will give a real property purchaser the greatest protection?
a. Quitclaim
b. Bargain and sale
c. Special warranty
d. General warranty (11/90, Law, #56, 0817)

41. A purchaser who obtains real estate title insurance will

a. Have coverage for the title exceptions listed in the policy
b. Be insured against all defects of record other than those excepted in the policy
c. Have coverage for title defects that result from events that happen after the effective date of the policy
d. Be entitled to transfer the policy to subsequent owners (11/91, Law, #54, 2382)

42. Which of the following requirements must be met, by any type of deed, in order for title to real property to be transferred?

a. The deed must be delivered to the purchaser of the property.
b. The deed must be recorded by the seller of the property.
c. The deed must include a statement of the property's value.
d. The deed must include a general warranty of title. (R/07, REG, 1054L, #3, 8427)

43. Which of the following rights is(are) generally given to a lessee of residential property?

I. A covenant of quiet enjoyment
II. An implied warranty of habitability

a. I only
b. II only
c. Both I and II
d. Neither I nor II (11/98, Law, #13, 6758)

44. Which of the following provisions must be included to have an enforceable written residential lease?

	A description of the leased premises	*A due date for the payment of rent*
a.	Yes	Yes
b.	Yes	No
c.	No	Yes
d.	No	No

(11/95, Law, #53, 5922)

45. Which of the following forms of tenancy will be created if a tenant stays in possession of the leased premises without the landlord's consent, after the tenant's one-year written lease expires?

a. Tenancy at will
b. Tenancy for years
c. Tenancy from period to period
d. Tenancy at sufferance (11/92, Law, #53, 3135)

46. Bronson is a residential tenant with a 10-year written lease. In the absence of specific provisions in the lease to the contrary, which of the following statements is correct?

a. The premises may **not** be sublet for less than the full remaining lease term.
b. Bronson may **not** assign the lease.
c. The landlord's death will automatically terminate the lease.
d. Bronson's purchase of the property will terminate the lease. (11/90, Law, #52, 0813)

47. When the original tenant of real property subleases the property to a third party (sublessee), who is responsible for the payment of the rent to the owner of the property?

a. The sublessee only
b. The original tenant only
c. Either the original tenant or the sublessee
d. Both the sublessee and the original tenant (R/02, Law, #18, 7128)

48. On January 1, Chance bought a piece of property by taking subject to an existing unrecorded mortgage held by Hay Bank. On April 1, Chance borrowed money from Link Finance and gave Link a mortgage on the property. Link did not know about the Hay mortgage and did not record its mortgage until July 1. On June 1, Chance borrowed money from Zone Bank and gave Zone a mortgage on the same property. Zone knew about the Link mortgage but did not know about the Hay mortgage. Zone recorded its mortgage on June 15. Which mortgage would have priority if these transactions took place in a notice-race jurisdiction?

a. The Hay mortgage, because it was first in time
b. The Link mortgage, because Zone had notice of the Link mortgage
c. The Zone mortgage, because it was the first recorded mortgage
d. The Zone and Link mortgages share priority because neither had notice of the Hay mortgage (5/93, Law, #57, amended, 4025)

49. Ritz owned a building on which there was a duly recorded first mortgage held by Lyn and a recorded second mortgage held by Jay. Ritz sold the building to Nunn. Nunn assumed the Jay mortgage and had no actual knowledge of the Lyn mortgage. Nunn defaulted on the payments to Jay. If both Lyn and Jay foreclosed, and the proceeds of the sale were insufficient to pay both Lyn and Jay,

a. Jay would be paid after Lyn was fully paid.
b. Jay and Lyn would be paid proportionately.
c. Nunn would be personally liable to Lyn but not to Jay.
d. Nunn would be personally liable to Lyn and Jay. (11/90, Law, #58, 0818)

50. Gilmore borrowed $60,000 from Dix Bank. The loan was used to remodel a building owned by Gilmore as investment property and was secured by a second mortgage that Dix did not record. FCA Loan Company has a recorded first mortgage on the building. If Gilmore defaults on both mortgages, Dix
a. Will **not** be entitled to any mortgage foreclosure sale proceeds, even if such proceeds are in excess of the amount owed to FCA
b. Will be unable to successfully claim any security interest in the building
c. Will be entitled to share in any foreclosure sale proceeds *pro rata* with FCA
d. Will be able to successfully claim a security interest that is subordinate to FCA's security interest
(11/90, Law, #59, 0819)

51. Generally, which of the following federal acts regulate mortgage lenders?

	Real Estate Settlement Procedures Act (RESPA)	*Federal Trade Commission Act*
a.	Yes	Yes
b.	Yes	No
c.	No	Yes
d.	No	No

(5/95, Law, #54, 5388)

52. Which of the following conditions must be met to have an enforceable mortgage?
a. An accurate description of the property must be included in the mortgage
b. A negotiable promissory note must accompany the mortgage
c. Present consideration must be given in exchange for the mortgage
d. The amount of the debt and the interest rate must be stated in the mortgage
(5/94, Law, #58, 4813)

53. Wyn bought real estate from Duke and gave Duke a purchase money mortgage. Duke forgot to record the mortgage. Two months later, Wyn gave a mortgage on the same property to Goode to secure a property improvement loan. Goode recorded this mortgage nine days later. Goode knew about the Duke mortgage. If these events took place in a notice-race statute jurisdiction, which mortgage would have priority?
a. Duke's, because it was the first mortgage given
b. Duke's, because Goode knew of the Duke mortgage
c. Goode's, because it was the first mortgage recorded
d. Goode's, because it was recorded within ten days
(11/91, Law, #58, 2386)

54. A mortgage on real property must
a. Be acknowledged by the mortgagee
b. State the exact amount of the debt
c. State the consideration given for the mortgage
d. Be delivered to the mortgagee
(11/91, Law, #55, 2383)

55. A mortgagor's right of redemption will be terminated by a judicial foreclosure sale unless
a. The proceeds from the sale are **not** sufficient to fully satisfy the mortgage debt.
b. The mortgage instrument does **not** provide for a default sale.
c. The mortgagee purchases the property for market value.
d. The jurisdiction has enacted a statutory right of redemption. (5/93, Law, #58, 4026)

56. Which of the following is correct regarding foreclosure of a purchase money mortgage by judicial sale of the property?
a. The mortgagor has the right to any remaining sale proceeds after the mortgagee is paid.
b. The purchaser at the sale is liable for any deficiency owed the mortgagee.
c. The court must confirm any price received at the sale.
d. The mortgagor can never be liable for a deficiency owed the mortgagee.
(11/91, Law, #57, 2385)

57. Omega Corp. owned a factory that was encumbered by a mortgage securing Omega's note to Eagle Bank. Omega sold the factory to Spear, Inc., which assumed the mortgage note. Later, Spear defaulted on the note, which had an outstanding balance of $15,000. To recover the outstanding balance, Eagle
a. May sue Spear only after suing Omega
b. May sue either Spear or Omega
c. Must sue both Spear and Omega
d. Must sue Spear first and then proceed against Omega for any deficiency
(11/90, Law, #24, 0811)

58. Which of the following parties has an insurable interest?

I. A corporate retailer in its inventory
II. A partner in the partnership property

a. I only
b. II only
c. Both I and II
d. Neither I nor II (5/95, Law, #60, 5394)

59. The earliest time a purchaser of existing goods will acquire an insurable interest in those goods is when

a. The purchaser obtains possession.
b. Title passes to the purchaser.
c. Performance of the contract has been completed or substantially completed.
d. The goods are identified to the contract.

(11/86, Law, #59, 0853)

60. Clark Corp. owns a warehouse purchased for \$150,000 several years ago. The current market value is \$200,000. Clark has the warehouse insured for fire loss with Fair Insurance Corp. and Zone Insurance Co. Fair's policy is for \$150,000 and Zone's policy is for \$75,000. Both policies contain the standard 80% coinsurance clause. If a fire totally destroyed the warehouse, what total dollar amount would Clark receive from Fair and Zone?

a. \$225,000
b. \$200,000
c. \$160,000
d. \$150,000

(5/95, Law, #59, amended, 5393)

SIMULATION

Problem 42-3 (20 to 30 minutes)

On February 1, Year 4, Tower and Perry, as tenants in common, purchased a two-unit apartment building for $250,000. They made a down payment of $100,000, and gave a $100,000 first mortgage to Midway Bank and a $50,000 second mortgage to New Bank. These events took place in a "notice-race" statute jurisdiction.

New was aware of Midway's mortgage but, as a result of clerical error, Midway did not record its mortgage until after New's mortgage was recorded.

At the time of purchase, a $200,000 fire insurance policy was issued by Acme Insurance Co. to Tower and Perry. The policy contained an 80% coinsurance clause and a standard mortgagee provision.

Tower and Perry rented an apartment to Young under a month-to-month oral lease. They rented the other apartment to Zimmer under a three-year written lease.

On December 8, Year 5, Perry died leaving a will naming the Dodd Foundation as the sole beneficiary of Perry's estate. The estate was distributed on January 15, Year 6. That same date, the ownership of the fire insurance policy was assigned to Tower and Dodd with Acme's consent. On January 21, Year 6, a fire caused $180,000 in structural damage to the building. At that time, its market value was $300,000 and the Midway mortgage balance was $80,000 including accrued interest. The New mortgage balance was $40,000 including accrued interest.

The fire made Young's apartment uninhabitable and caused extensive damage to the kitchen, bathrooms, and one bedroom of Zimmer's apartment. On February 1, Year 6, Young and Zimmer moved out. The resulting loss of income caused a default on both mortgages.

On April 1, Year 6, Acme refused to pay the fire loss claiming that the required insurable interest did not exist at the time of the loss and that the amount of the insurance was insufficient to provide full coverage for the loss. Tower and Dodd are involved in a lawsuit contesting the ownership of the building and the claims they have both made for any fire insurance proceeds.

On June 1, Year 6, Midway and New foreclosed their mortgages and also are claiming any fire insurance proceeds that may be paid by Acme.

On July 1, Year 6, Tower sued Zimmer for breach of the lease and is seeking to collect the balance of the lease term rent. (Editors, 6524)

Wolf purchased a factory building for $800,000. At the time of the purchase, Wolf obtained a fire insurance policy with a face value of $400,000 from Acme Insurance Co. At the same time, Wolf obtained another fire insurance policy with a face value of $200,000 from Prevent Fire Insurance Corp. Each policy contained a standard 80% coinsurance clause and a *pro rata* clause. Two years later, when the building had a fair market value of $1,000,000, a fire caused $600,000 damage.

For Items 1 through 8, enter the appropriate dollar amount. Items 6 through 8 relate to the two-unit apartment building discussed on the "Scenario" tab.

Question	Answer
1. What dollar amount of fire insurance coverage should Wolf have obtained when purchasing the building to avoid being considered a coinsurer?	
2. What dollar amount of fire insurance coverage should Wolf have at the time of the fire to avoid being considered a coinsurer?	
3. What dollar amount should Wolf recover from Acme and Prevent under the insurance policies?	
4. What dollar amount should Wolf recover under the Acme insurance policy?	
5. What dollar amount should Wolf recover under the Prevent Fire insurance policy?	
6. What dollar amount would Zimmer owe to the owner of the two-unit apartment building?	
7. What maximum dollar amount of any insurance proceeds paid by Acme would Midway get?	
8. What dollar amount would Acme be required to pay in total?	

Your employer is Acme's auditor. Write a memo to the your supervisor answering the following questions and giving the reasons for your conclusions.

1. Who had title to the two-unit apartment building on January 21, Year 6?

2. Did Tower or Dodd have an insurable interest in the two-unit apartment building when the fire occurred? If so, when would such an interest have arisen?

Research Question: What code section and subsection, if applicable, provides guidance on the calculation of the exemption from taxable gifts, as adjusted for inflation?

Section & Subsection Answer: §_____ (___)

Solution 42-1 MULTIPLE CHOICE ANSWERS

Realty vs. Personalty

1. (c) Requirements for transfer and creditor's rights would differ based on whether an asset was treated as personal property or real property. Requirements for transfer would differ because transfer of real property would require the transfer of the related deed for the property, whereas, transfer of personal property would not require a deed. Creditor's rights would differ in that rules for foreclosure on real property differ from those for repossession of personal property.

2. (d) Real property includes generally whatever is built or growing upon land. Personal property is everything that may be owned that is not real property. While growing, the trees were real property. They became personal property when cut into lumber. The lumber became real property when incorporated into a building.

Ownership

3. (a) A distinguishing feature of a tenancy in common is that there is no right of survivorship; therefore, each co-tenant's interest is inheritable. Oak's death will not affect the shares of the other co-tenants and Oak's heirs will inherit Oak's share.

4. (c) If one joint tenant in a joint tenancy with rights of survivorship makes an *inter vivos* conveyance of his share, the grantee of that share would be a tenant in common with the remaining joint tenants. The joint tenants who do not make such an *inter vivos* transfer continue to hold their interests as joint tenants.

5. (d) Fee simple is a freehold estate in which the holder possesses and owns the estate, with the right to sell the property. A leasehold interest only entitles the holder to possession of the property, not ownership. An easement is a nonpossessory right to use the land of another for a special purpose, by either express or implied agreement. The holder of an easement does not own the property and may not sell the property. A license is a revocable right or privilege to go on a property for a certain purpose, but does not give any title or estate in such property.

Real Property Transfers

6. (d) A marketable title is one which is free from reasonable objections. It must be free from private encumbrances not otherwise specified in the title, such as easements or mortgages. Zoning laws generally will not render a title unmarketable. The easements are recorded on the title. A recorded lawsuit against the seller would not qualify as a lien, mortgage or other encumbrance to the property.

7. (b) Title insurance generally insures that the purchaser has good title as of the policy's date, covering losses that result from defects or failure of title to real property. Title insurance covers only defects of record, does not ensure that all taxes and assessments are paid, and does not pass to subsequent purchasers.

8. (b) Nexis knew about the prior conveyance and thus was not a *bona fide* (good faith) purchaser. Nexis' lack of good faith prevents his prevailing under a notice statute or a notice-race statute. However, under a purely race statute, where good faith is not an issue (simply a question of who recorded first), Nexis would prevail.

9. (c) A valid deed must contain a description of the land but need not state the purchase price.

Landlords & Tenants

10. (c) Unless there is a clause restricting or prohibiting assignments and/or subleases, a tenant has the right to assign or sublease to another party. Therefore, Delta does not need Tanner's consent to assign the lease to another party.

11. (a) A landlord may terminate the lease (and of course, evict the tenant) if the tenant uses the leased property for a purpose that is illegal and the landlord is not a party to that illegal use. Even if the landlord were a party to the illegal use, and intended for the property to be so used, the enforceability of the lease is quite doubtful and, thus, the tenant most likely could be evicted. Since counterfeiting money is illegal, that would be cause for eviction.

Mortgages

12. (d) A mortgage is generally freely transferable and, in the absence of any restrictions in the document, the mortgagee may assign the mortgage to a third party without the mortgagor's consent. A mortgage may be given to secure an antecedent debt. It is not mandatory for the mortgage to contain the amount of the debt and the rate of interest in order to be valid. The mortgage is required to be signed only by the mortgagor and not the mortgagee.

13. (b) By recording a mortgage a creditor protects its priority against all parties having subsequent (not earlier) claims to the property. Previously filed

tax liens still would have priority over the mortgage lien. A creditor's rights against a debtor already are protected under the promissory note, and recording of the mortgage is not necessary.

14. (d) In a notice-race jurisdiction, the recording of the mortgages would determine the priority of the creditors unless a mortgagee had knowledge of a preexisting unrecorded interest. Here, Independent recorded on February 2, Scott recorded on March 10, while Elgin recorded on March 12. Therefore, the $220,000 would be divided as follows: Independent $195,000, Scott $19,000, and Elgin the remaining $6,000. Scott would get the full amount Frost owed him.

15. (b) In a notice-race jurisdiction the recording of the mortgages would determine the priority of the creditors. Here, Independent recorded on February 2, Scott recorded on March 10, while Elgin recorded on March 12. Therefore, the $220,000 would be divided as follows: Independent $195,000, Scott $19,000, and Elgin the remaining $6,000. Answer (a) is incorrect because Scott was not aware of the prior mortgages until after he had recorded his own mortgage. Thus, this had no effect on the priority of the mortgages. Although Elgin's mortgage was the first in time, it would have priority only if it had been recorded before Scott's. The mortgages are paid in the order of their priority. The proceeds are not split equally.

16. (c) Frost's right of redemption entitles him to retain the property even after foreclosure, but before the foreclosure sale, by paying the amount due plus interest and any other costs. A statutory right of redemption occurs after a judicial sale. This right entitles the mortgagor a period of time, usually one year, to reinstate the debt and mortgage by paying to the purchaser at the judicial sale the amount of the purchase price plus the statutory rate of interest. Frost may redeem the property before the judicial sale by paying all mortgages in full. The probable sales price of the property is irrelevant. Frost would not have to pay any penalty fees to the mortgagees.

17. (d) Wilk, the buyer, purchased the property "subject to the mortgage." Since the buyer never assumed the liability of the mortgage, only the mortgagor, Dix, will be liable.

Insurance Contracts

18. (a) The written clause limiting the value of displayed jewelry to $10,000 was a statement of fact which became a basis for the insurance company's risk in writing this theft policy. As such, it was a warranty rather than a mere representation. More importantly, the continued compliance with this warranty was a condition precedent to the insurer's liability for any theft loss. At the time of loss the warranty was not being complied with; therefore, Jerry's house will recover nothing.

19. (b) A standard fire insurance policy covers losses arising from accidental damage to property caused directly or indirectly from a fire, including smoke and water damage. Loss of income due to business interruption, however, is not part of a standard fire insurance policy.

Insurable Interests

20. (d) Generally, there must be a relationship between the insured and the risk covered such that, if specified events occur, the insured will suffer substantial loss or injury. With regard to property insurance, there must be a legally recognized interest and the possibility of financial or economic loss, which would not occur in this case, when the only interest Daly had in the property was having given an unsecured loan to the owner of the house. Stockholders have a legally insurable interest in corporation property. Possessory interests, such as leaseholds, are legally insurable interests.

21. (c) To recover under a property insurance contract, the insured must have an insurable interest in the property at the time of the loss. An insurable interest exists when an entity has both a legal interest in the property and the possibility of a monetary loss if the property is damaged. In this question, the seller of the building has an insurable interest in the building until the seller receives the entire purchase price. The buyer has an insurable interest in the building as soon as the buyer enters into a contract to purchase the building.

22. (a) For an insurable interest to arise, there must exist such an interest between the insured and the risk covered, so that if specified events occur, the insured will suffer some substantial loss or injury. Such an interest includes the possessory interest of a tenant of property and the interests of secured creditors, including mortgagees.

23. (a) An insurable interest must be present at the time of loss, even if it is not present at the time of issuance. Under what type of fee the property is owned and whether the owner is an individual or a corporation are irrelevant as to whether an insurable interest exists.

Coinsurance

24. (a) One of the primary purposes of the coinsurance clause is to encourage the insured to maintain a certain amount of insurance on the property in relation to the fair market value of the property. For example, if there is an 80% coinsurance clause, the insurance company encourages the insured to maintain insurance on the property equal to at least 80% of the fair market value of the property. In the event the policy holder does not maintain sufficient insurance, the insured will not receive 100% of the partial losses. The coinsurance clause has nothing to do with excluding certain types of perils. The coinsurance clause encourages the policyholder to maintain a certain amount of property insurance, not liability insurance. The insured can insure with more than one insurance company; however, the insured can collect only once (e.g., one cannot profit from insurance).

25. (b) A coinsurance clause provides that if the insured fails to carry an amount of insurance equal to a stated percentage of the value of the property insured, then the insured becomes a coinsurer and must proportionally bear the loss. The coinsurance clause does not apply if there is a total loss. The amount of recovery for a partial loss is equal to (1) the face value of the insurance policy, divided by the coinsurance percent times the actual fair value of the property, times (2) the actual loss. In this example: $300,000 / (80% × $500,000) × $40,000 = $30,000.

Multiple Insurers

26. (b) The coinsurance rules only apply to partial losses. Since this was a total loss, the insured is paid the total amount of the insurance policies, up to the fair market value of the property. (One cannot profit by insurance, only recover an actual loss.)

27. (b) Under a fire insurance policy with an 80% coinsurance clause, when there is a *total loss,* the insured will collect the full amount of the insurance, if it is the *lowest* of the three measures of recovery: (1) the $200,000 face value of the policies; (2) the $250,000 fair market value of the property at date of loss; or (3) the coinsurance amount of $200,000 ($250,000 × 80% = $209,000). Thus, Pod can collect a total of $200,000. This amount will be prorated between the two insurance companies.

28. (c) Pod's recoverable loss is calculated using the coinsurance formula.

$$\text{Recovery} = \text{Actual loss} \times \frac{\text{Amount of insurance}}{\text{Coinsurance \%} \times \text{FV of property}}$$

$$= \$180{,}000 \times \frac{\$200{,}000}{80\% \times \$250{,}000} = \$180{,}000$$

The amount recoverable from Owners is $180,000 × $150,000 / $200,000 = $135,000.

29. (c) A coinsurance clause provides that if the insured fails to carry an amount of insurance equal to the stated percentage (80% in this case) of the value of the property insured, then the insured becomes a coinsurer and must proportionally bear the loss. The *total* amount of loss borne by the insurers is the lower of (1) the $40,000 face value of the policies, (2) the $100,000 fair market value of property at date of loss, or (3) the coinsurance amount of $20,000 [($40,000/$80,000) × $40,000]. Thus, the loss borne by the insurers is $20,000. Ace is responsible for 60% of the loss ($12,000) because it provided 60% of the total insurance ($24,000/ $40,000). Thrifty is responsible for 40% of the loss ($8,000) because it provided 40% of the total insurance ($16,000/$40,000).

30. (c) King meets the requirements of the coinsurance clause. King has a total of $250,000 insurance coverage on the building with a fair market value of $300,000, which is more than the 80% required in the coinsurance clause. The $250,000 insurance coverage exceeds the loss of $200,000; thus King will recover the full amount of the loss from Omni and Safe. Omni is responsible for 80% of the loss because it provided 80% of the total insurance (80% × $200,000 = $160,000).

Solution 42-2 ADDITIONAL MULTIPLE CHOICE ANSWERS

Realty vs. Personalty

31. (d) The definition of real property includes land, air rights and mineral rights, plant life and vegetation, and fixtures. Harvested crops are considered personal property and the sale of such crops is a sale of goods governed by the Uniform Commercial Code rather than by real property laws. Under UCC 2-107(2), crops sold while they are growing usually are considered to be goods whether they are to be severed by the buyer or the seller. However, if the real property on which a crop is growing is sold, the crop is considered real property and the new owner of the real property also would become the owner of the growing crops.

32. (c) In order to determine whether an item of personal property has become a fixture, it is necessary to determine the degree and/or manner of affixation/attachment and/or whether the owner/annexor intended for the item to be a fixture. The value of an item is irrelevant in determining whether it is a fixture.

33. (d) The definition of real property includes land, air and mineral rights, plant life and vegetation, and fixtures. Not all tangible or intangible property is real property.

Ownership

34. (b) An *inter vivos* (during life) conveyance terminates a joint tenancy. The grantee's (Green's) interest is a tenancy in common with the remaining joint tenants. The remaining joint tenants' interests still represent a joint tenancy. Thus Green has a 1/3 interest as a tenant in common. Green is not a joint tenant because the right of survivorship as to his share was extinguished upon the transfer from Long. The consent of other joint tenants is not necessary for an *inter vivos* conveyance by a joint tenant. Fall's and Pear's shares would not fall to Green upon their deaths. Rather, whichever joint tenant (Fall or Pear) survived the other became the sole owner of the remaining 2/3 share and a tenant in common with Green.

35. (a) A joint tenancy requires the following four unities: (1) time, (2) title, (3) interest, and (4) possession.

36. (c) Rights of survivorship involve natural persons. A corporation is not such a person. (Indeed, corporations generally opt for "perpetual existence" in the corporate documents.) Therefore, a joint tenant with the right of survivorship cannot involve an unaffiliated corporation.

Real Property Transfers

37. (d) A sale is a method of transferring ownership of real property in what would be considered an arm's-length transaction. Inheritance, eminent domain, and adverse possession are not considered arm's-length transactions.

38. (b, e) Both answers are required for full point value. In order for a deed to be effective between a purchaser and seller of real estate, the deed must be delivered by the seller with the intent to transfer title. The deed must be in writing and signed by the seller/grantor, must name the grantee and describe her/him, and must contain a description of the land. It is not necessary for the deed to contain the sales price or the signature of the purchaser/grantee. The recording of the deed is effective between the purchaser and third parties and not between the purchaser and the seller of real estate.

39. (c) A general warranty deed contains the following covenants: (1) the grantor warrants that s/he owns the property and has a right to convey it, (2) the grantee will not be disturbed in possession of the property by the grantor or some third party's lawful claim of ownership, (3) the grantor promises that there are no existing encumbrances on the title to the property, (4) the grantor will execute or obtain further documents or assurances necessary to perfect title, and (5) the grantor will forever warrant title to the property.

40. (d) A general warranty deed gives the purchaser the greatest protection when purchasing property, and a quitclaim deed gives the buyer the least amount of protection.

41. (b) Title insurance covers losses resulting from defects or failure of title to real property. As a practical matter, most title insurance policies *exclude* coverage of any defect which is not of record. Title exceptions listed in the policy are *not* covered. Coverage is only for defects of record that exist as of the effective date of the policy. Title insurance is not transferable.

42. (a) Generally, there is no effective transfer of an interest in land until the grantor has delivered the deed or other writing. Recording the deed protects the seller from subsequent claims by third parties. The deed must include the grantee's name and a land description sufficient for identification.

The deed need not state the property's value or general warranty of title; a quitclaim deed, for instance, makes no such warranty.

Landlords & Tenants

43. (c) A covenant of quiet enjoyment is implied in all leases. Although at common law there is no general duty on the part of the landlord to deliver the premises in a habitable condition, many jurisdictions have held that there is an implied covenant of habitability and most states have enacted statutes which require the premises to be delivered in a habitable condition.

44. (b) An enforceable written residential lease would have to include a description of the leased premises, but would not have to specify a due date for the payment of rent.

45. (d) If the tenant holds over after the expiration of the tenancy term without the consent of the landlord, there is a tenancy at sufferance. A tenancy at will is one that continues until either party terminates. A tenancy for years is a tenancy for a specified duration, even if the period is less than a year. A tenancy from period to period is one which continues from year to year, month to month, or any other fraction of a year.

46. (d) A tenant has a possessory interest in property according to the lease, and the landlord has a reversionary interest (e.g., once the lease expires, the possession of the property "reverts" to the landlord). If a tenant purchases the building so that the tenant and the landlord are the same party, the lease is terminated since the tenant and landlord are the same. If a lease does not prohibit assigning or subletting, the tenant is free to assign or sublet without the permission of the landlord. The landlord's death does not terminate the lease.

47. (b) The sublessee does not come into privity of estate with the lessor; therefore, s/he is not personally liable for the rent. If the rent is not paid, the lessor may terminate the lease and oust the sublessee, but the lessor may not proceed against the sublessee for back rent. The original lessee remains personally liable for the rent and all the covenants contained in the lease agreement.

Mortgages

48. (b) A mortgage is recorded to give constructive notice of the mortgage and protect against subsequent mortgagees. Under a notice-race statute, if the first mortgage is not recorded, a subsequent mortgagee who has no knowledge of the first mortgage will have priority once s/he records. However, if the subsequent mortgagee did have notice of the first mortgage, s/he can't get priority. Thus, the Link mortgage has priority because Zone had notice of the Link mortgage. The first mortgage in time has priority only if it is recorded first. The Zone mortgage can't have priority since Zone knew about the Link mortgage. Although neither Zone nor Link had notice of the Hay mortgage, Link has priority because Zone had notice of the Link mortgage.

49. (a) Since both mortgages were recorded, the purchaser (Nunn) of the property constructively is aware of the first mortgage held by Lyn. While Nunn assumed the second mortgage, Nunn purchases the property subject to the first mortgage. If Nunn defaults, proceeds from the sale of the property will go toward paying the first mortgage held by Lyn, and if any money remains, the money will be paid to Jay, the second mortgage holder. A first mortgage is paid in full before a second mortgage receives anything. Nunn has no personal liability to Lyn since the first mortgage was never assumed.

50. (d) If a mortgage is not recorded, the owner of the mortgage still can bring a claim for payment when the debtor defaults. In this question, Dix is entitled to payment after the first mortgage has been satisfied. Dix's second priority status would be lost if a subsequent lender in good faith loaned money and recorded another mortgage. Dix can claim a security interest in the property even if the mortgage was not recorded. There is no *pro rata* sharing of proceeds if the debtor defaults. Money is distributed to the first recorded mortgage and when this interest is paid in full, the second mortgage is entitled to payment.

51. (b) The Real Estate Settlement Procedures Act (RESPA) regulates the activities of mortgage lenders. The Federal Trade Commission Act generally regulates nonreal estate consumer credit transactions.

52. (a) In order for a mortgage to be enforceable, there must be a description of the property sufficiently accurate to furnish some means of identification. It is not necessary that a negotiable promissory note accompany the mortgage, or that present consideration be given in exchange for the mortgage, or that the amount of the debt and the interest rate be stated.

53. (b) In states with notice-race recording statutes, the first mortgagee to file prevails. In order to have a superior security interest, however, the mortgagee must not have knowledge of a prior mortgage. Because Goode knew of the Duke mortgage, Duke's mortgage has priority.

54. (d) Generally, a mortgage must meet the requirements of a deed, including its delivery to the mortgagee. Since a mortgage is considered an interest in real property, it must be in writing and signed by the *mortgagor.* There is no requirement of acknowledgment by the *mortgagee.* It is not mandatory for a mortgage to contain the amount of the debt or consideration given to be valid.

55. (d) Right of redemption is a statutory right that occurs after the judicial sale. States that have enacted a right of redemption allow a mortgagor a period of time, usually one year after the foreclosure sale, to reinstate the debt and mortgage by paying to the purchaser at the judicial sale the amount of the purchase price plus the statutory interest rate. The mortgagor has the right to redeem the property prior to the judicial sale by paying the mortgage in full plus interest and other costs. Foreclosure requires a judicial action; the mortgage instrument does not need to provide for a default sale. The mortgagor, not the mortgagee, can redeem the property by paying interest, outstanding debt, and expenses.

56. (a) In a judicial sale of property, proceeds first are applied to the foreclosure costs (such as court filing fees and advertising) and then toward payment of the debt. Any surplus after the sale goes to the mortgagor. When the proceeds from the sale do not cover the debt, the mortgagor (not the subsequent purchaser) is responsible for the deficiency. It is only the foreclosure sale *proceedings* that are court approved; the sales *price* need not be approved or "confirmed" by the court.

57. (b) When a mortgagor sells her/his property and the buyer assumes the mortgage debt, unless otherwise agreed, the mortgagor remains liable to the mortgagee (the bank), and the bank becomes the creditor beneficiary of the buyer's agreement to assume the mortgage. Thus, in the event of default, the bank can proceed against either the original mortgagor or the buyer who assumed the mortgage. The bank can go after either the mortgagor (Omega) or after the individual who assumed the mortgage (Spear). There is no requirement that the bank proceed against one or the other first since no order or priority is necessary. There is no need to sue both.

Insurance

58. (c) The rule with respect to fire or property insurance contracts requires that there be both a legally recognized interest and the possibility of economic loss if the property is damaged or destroyed. Both the corporate retailer and the partner have an ownership interest in their respective property and would suffer possible economic loss if the property were damaged or destroyed. Thus, each has an insurable interest.

59. (d) UCC 2-501(1) provides that the earliest time that a purchaser of existing goods may acquire an insurable interest in those goods is when the goods are identified to the contract.

60. (b) The coinsurance rules only apply to partial losses, and since this was a total loss, the insured is paid the total amount of the insurance policies, up to the fair market value of the property. (One cannot profit by insurance, only recover one's actual loss.)

PERFORMANCE BY SUBTOPICS

Each category below parallels a subtopic covered in Chapter 42. Record the number and percentage of questions you correctly answered in each subtopic area.

Realty vs. Personalty

Question #	Correct √
1	
2	
# Questions	2
# Correct	
% Correct	

Ownership

Question #	Correct √
3	
4	
5	
# Questions	3
# Correct	
% Correct	

Real Property Transfers

Question #	Correct √
6	
7	
8	
9	
# Questions	4
# Correct	
% Correct	

Landlords & Tenants

Question #	Correct √
10	
11	
# Questions	2
# Correct	
% Correct	

Mortgages

Question #	Correct √
12	
13	
14	
15	
16	
17	
# Questions	6
# Correct	
% Correct	

Insurance Contracts

Question #	Correct √
18	
19	
# Questions	2
# Correct	
% Correct	

Insurable Interests

Question #	Correct √
20	
21	
22	
23	
# Questions	4
# Correct	
% Correct	

Coinsurance

Question #	Correct √
24	
25	
# Questions	2
# Correct	
% Correct	

Multiple Insurers

Question #	Correct √
26	
27	
28	
29	
30	
# Questions	5
# Correct	
% Correct	

SIMULATION SOLUTION

Solution 42-3 Insurance & Tenancies

Insurance (4 points)

1. $640,000

A coinsurance clause provides that if the insured fails to carry an amount of insurance equal to a stated percentage of the value of the property insured, then the insured becomes a coinsurer and must proportionally bear the loss. At the time of purchasing the building, Wolf should have obtained fire insurance coverage for at least $640,000, 80% of the $800,000 purchase price, to have avoided being considered a coinsurer.

2. $800,000

A coinsurance clause provides that if the insured fails to carry an amount of insurance equal to a stated percentage of the value of the property insured, then the insured becomes a coinsurer and must proportionally bear the loss. At the time of the fire, Wolf needed insurance coverage of at least $800,000, 80% of the fair market value of $1,000,000, to avoid being considered a coinsurer.

3. $450,000

Wolf should recover from Acme and Prevent based on the coinsurance formula in the case of a partial loss.

$$\text{Recovery} = \frac{\text{Face value of insurance}}{\text{Coinsurance \% × FV of property}} \times \text{Actual loss}$$

$$= \frac{\$400{,}000 + \$200{,}000}{80\% \times \$1{,}000{,}000} \times \$600{,}000 = \$450{,}000$$

4. $300,000

Wolf should recover $300,000 under the Acme fire insurance policy.

$$\text{Recovery} = \frac{\text{Face value of insurance}}{\text{Coinsurance \% × FV of property}} \times \text{Actual loss}$$

$$= \frac{\$400{,}000}{80\% \times \$1{,}000{,}000} \times \$600{,}000 = \$300{,}000$$

5. $150,000

Wolf should recover $150,000 under the Prevent fire insurance policy.

$$\text{Recovery} = \frac{\text{Face value of insurance}}{\text{Coinsurance \% × FV of property}} \times \text{Actual loss}$$

$$= \frac{\$200{,}000}{80\% \times \$1{,}000{,}000} \times \$600{,}000 = \$150{,}000$$

6. $0

Tower would not be able to collect rent from Zimmer for the balance of the term of the lease because Zimmer moved as a result of the extensive fire damage to the apartment. The implied warranty of habitability would be considered breached by the landlord and a constructive eviction of Zimmer would be deemed to have taken place because the premises could no longer be used for their intended purpose. Constructive eviction releases both the landlord and the tenant from their obligations under the lease.

7. $80,000

The conflict between Midway and New would be resolved in favor of Midway. In a notice-race statute jurisdiction, New's knowledge of Midway's first mortgage would give Midway priority despite New's earlier filing. Midway gets $80,000 representing the balance due on the mortgage including accrued interest, because Midway as a mortgagee is included as a contingent beneficiary in the policy. New gets $40,000 for the same reasons, but is not paid until after Midway is paid fully. Tower and Dodd get $30,000 divided equally as tenants in common.

8. $150,000

a. Acme would have to honor the insurance contract and pay part of the loss. Despite Tower and Perry not maintaining insurance coverage of 80% of the property's market value, the coinsurance clause allows for a percentage of recovery, as follows.

$$\text{Recovery} = \frac{\text{Face value of insurance}}{\text{Coinsurance \% × FV of property}} \times \text{Actual loss}$$

$$= \frac{\$200{,}000}{80\% \times \$300{,}000} \times \$180{,}000 = \$150{,}000$$

Communication (5 points)

To: D. Boss
From: A. Candidate
Re: Tower—Property Ownership & Insurance

1. The **tenants in common** form of ownership allows either party to dispose of its undivided interest by sale or on death. **Any** person **purchasing** or **inheriting** Perry's interest would become a tenant in common with Tower. Thus, on January 21, Year 6, Tower and Dodd are tenants in common, each owning a one-half **undivided** interest in the house.

2. **Both** Tower and Dodd have an **insurable interest** in the house. Tower's interest arose when the **property** was **purchased**, continued when the insurance policy was purchased, and still existed at the **time** of the fire **loss**. Dodd's interest arose when Dodd **inherited** Perry's interest in the house. Acme's **consent** to the **assignment** of the policy to Tower and Dodd entitled Dodd to a **share** of the **proceeds** of the policy.

Research (1 point)

IRC Section Answer: §2503(b)

IRC §2503(b) states, "EXCLUSIONS FROM GIFTS.—2503(b)(1) IN GENERAL.— In the case of gifts (other than gifts of future interests in property) made to any person by the donor during the calendar year, the first $10,000 of such gifts to such person shall not, for purposes of subsection (a), be included in the total amount of gifts made during such year. Where there has been a transfer to any person of a present interest in property, the possibility that such interest may be diminished by the exercise of a power shall be disregarded in applying this subsection, if no part of such interest will at any time pass to any other person. 2503(b)(2) INFLATION ADJUSTMENT.—In the case of gifts made in a calendar year after 1998, the $10,000 amount contained in paragraph (1) shall be increased by an amount equal to—2503(b)(2)(A) $10,000, multiplied by2503(b)(2)(B) the cost-of-living adjustment determined under section 1(f)(3) for such calendar year by substituting "calendar year 1997" for "calendar year 1992" in subparagraph (B) thereof. If any amount as adjusted under the preceding sentence is not a multiple of $1,000, such amount shall be rounded to the next lowest multiple of $1,000."

CHANGE ALERT

The *American Recovery & Reinvestment Act of 2009* (ARRA '09) became law on February 17, 2009, which made it first eligible to be tested in the **October-November 2009** exam window.

The *Emergency Economic Stabilization Act of 2008* (EESA '08) became law on October 3, 2008, which made it first eligible to be tested in the **July-August 2009** exam window.

These changes are integrated into this chapter to the extent they are within the scope of the CPA exam.

WHICH YEAR WILL BE TESTED?

The examiners tend to focus on fundamentals, rather than on changes from one year to the next. The amounts of inflation-adjusted figures, in particular, usually are given in questions; candidates must demonstrate that they understand when and how to apply these figures.

Accounting and auditing pronouncements are eligible to be tested on the Uniform CPA Examination in the window beginning six months after a pronouncement's effective date, unless early application is permitted. When early application is permitted, the new pronouncement is eligible to be tested in the window beginning six months after the issuance date. In this case, both the old and new pronouncements may be tested until the old pronouncement is superseded.

For the federal taxation area, the Internal Revenue Code and federal tax regulations in effect six months before the beginning of the current window may be tested on the Uniform CPA Examination.

For all other materials covered in the Regulation and Business Environment and Concepts sections, material eligible to be tested includes federal laws in the window beginning six months after their effective date and uniform acts in the window beginning one year after their adoption by a simple majority of the jurisdictions.

The above three paragraphs from the AICPA's *Uniform CPA Examination Candidate Bulletin: Information For Applicants* indicates that the later 2009 exams will ask questions about situations in the 2010 tax year, with the exception of those tax laws passed within six months of the examination date. However, note that questions asked in November 1997 (for instance) had 1996 dates in them. The examiners repeatedly have asked questions on the November exam for the previous calendar year, but there is no assurance that they will continue to do so. The editors recommend that candidates study the laws applicable to both years. If candidates feel they must limit their studies to one tax year, the editors suggest that it be the previous calendar year.

CHAPTER 43

FEDERAL TAXATION: PROPERTY & OTHER TAX TOPICS

EXAM COVERAGE: The property taxation portion of the Regulation section of the CPA exam are designated by the examiners to be 8-12 percent of the section's point value. Federal tax procedures and accounting issues account for another 8-12 percent. More information about point distribution and information eligible to be tested is included in the **Practical Advice** section of this volume.

CHAPTER 43

FEDERAL TAXATION: PROPERTY & OTHER TAX TOPICS

I. Basis

A. Definition

A taxpayer's basis in property acquired in a taxable transaction (as opposed to gifts or inheritances) is generally equal to the cost or the purchase price of the property. The cost is equal to the cash or fair market value of any property paid, plus any expenses associated with the purchase and any liabilities assumed in connection with the property.

Example 1 ▸ Basis

> Anna purchases an automobile for use in her business for $1,000 cash plus a promissory note of $14,000. Anna takes an initial cost basis in the automobile of $15,000.
>
> The basis is *not* altered as the debt is paid off, but is altered by depreciation charges allowed over the asset's life.
>
> **Note:** No depreciation is permitted without a business purpose.

1. **Income** Where property is acquired such that the property itself is an item of gross income (e.g., a salesman receives a new car as commission), the cost basis is the amount included in gross income—the fair market value of the property received.

2. **Written Off** If property is acquired and written off as a current expense in the year it is acquired, its cost basis equals zero.

B. Adjusted Basis

The original cost basis of property is increased by any capital expenditures made to the property and decreased by any depreciation, amortization, or depletion deductions allowed or allowable. Amounts excluded from income due to mortgage debt relief under the *Mortgage Forgiveness Debt Relief Act of 2007* (MFDRA '07) reduce the basis of the related home. Exclusions under MFDRA '07 are discussed in greater detail in Chapter 44.

Example 2 ▸ Adjusted Basis

> Gerald owns a piece of real estate. Gerald's basis is $10,000, the cash price he paid several years ago. The property is now worth $100,000. Gerald arranges for a bank to lend him $20,000, using the property as collateral. Gerald has no income, and his basis in the property remains $10,000. If Gerald uses that $20,000 to improve the land (e.g., by clearing it), then his basis is increased by $20,000. It is not the borrowing that increases basis; it is the expenditure of funds to improve the land.

C. Property Acquired by Gift

If the property is acquired by gift and the donor's basis is greater than the fair market value at the time of the gift, then the basis to the donee is determined at the time of disposal. Otherwise, the donor's basis becomes the basis to the donee.

1. **Disposal** When the property is later disposed of in a taxable transaction:

   a. At a loss, then the basis used to compute the loss is the lower of the property's fair market value at the date of the gift or the adjusted basis to the donor.

b. At a gain, then the basis used to determine the gain is the property's adjusted basis in the hands of the donor.

c. At a price between the fair market value at the date of the gift and the adjusted basis of the property in the hands of the donor, and the fair market value of the property at the date of the gift was less than the adjusted basis to the donor, then no gain or loss is recognized on the disposition.

2. Holding Period When the basis in the hands of the donor is the basis of the property to the donee, then the donee's holding period includes the holding period of the donor. If, however, the fair market value at the time of the gift is the basis to the donee, then the holding period begins on the date of the gift.

D. Property Acquired From Decedent (Inheritance)

The holding period for inherited property always is deemed to be long term. Inherited property has a basis equal to the property's fair market value on the date of the decedent's death or the alternate valuation date, which is six months after death.

1. If the alternate valuation date is elected and the property is distributed or otherwise disposed of before this date, then the basis is the fair market value on the date of disposition.

2. The alternate valuation date may be selected only if it decreases both the value of the gross estate and the estate tax liability.

II. Cost Recovery

A. General

A deduction is allowed for the exhaustion of property used in a business or held for production of income. Cost recovery deductions impact the basis of property. The original basis of the property is decreased by any depreciation, §179 expense, amortization, or depletion.

1. Amortization Certain *acquired* intangible assets have a uniform 15-year straight-line amortization period. Taxpayers may use 15-year amortization for certain intangibles either acquired after July 25, 1991, or just for property acquired after August 10, 1993.

a. Eligible Purchased intangibles that are eligible for this write off include: goodwill, going-concern value, work force in place, information bases, know-how, customer-based intangibles, supplier-based intangibles, licenses, permits and other rights granted by governmental units, covenants not to compete, franchises, trademarks, and trade names.

b. Non-Eligible Assets that are not eligible include: self-created intangibles; interests in a corporation, partnership, trust or estate; interests in a futures (or similar) contract; any interest in land; and interests in films, sound recordings, video tapes, books and similar property if not acquired with the assets of a trade or business.

c. Computer Software Although off-the-shelf computer software is not eligible for 15-year amortization, it generally can be written off straight-line over 36 months, beginning with the month placed into service. Software bought with computer hardware generally is depreciated along with the hardware.

2. Depletion Depletion is allowed for exhaustible natural resources.

a. Cost Depletion Under this method, the basis of the property is divided by the number of recoverable units, resulting in the cost depletion per unit. The depletion per unit is then multiplied by the number of units extracted and sold during the year. The result is the amount of the cost depletion deduction allowed for the year.

b. **Percentage Depletion** Under this method, a set percentage (not exceeding 50%) of gross income from the property is taken as the depletion deduction. The allowable percentage depends on the type of property being extracted. Generally, for oil and gas properties, the deduction cannot exceed net income. The *Emergency Economic Stabilization Act of 2008* (EESA '08) suspends the taxable income limit for any tax year beginning in calendar year 2009 for oil and gas properties.

B. Depreciation

Most assets placed in service after 1986 are depreciated using the Modified Accelerated Cost Recovery System (MACRS). Alternatively, taxpayers may use the straight-line method. Depreciation is reported on Form 4562, *Depreciation and Amortization.*

1. **Depreciable Property** Depreciation is available for personal or real (but not land) property used in a trade or business or for the production of income. Depreciation is not allowed on land or inventory. Personal-use property (residence, sailboat, car, etc.) is not depreciable.

2. **Class Lives** MACRS personal property is divided into six classes based on Asset Depreciation Range (ADR) midpoint life, while real property has two main classifications.

   a. **3-year** Includes breeding hogs, race horses that are more than 2 years old, and tractor units for use over the road.

   b. **5-year** Includes automobiles, light trucks, research and experimentation property, and certain technological equipment such as computers. EESA '08 classifies most farm machinery and equipment originally placed in service by the taxpayer in 2009 in a farming business as five-year property.

   c. **7-year** Includes office furniture and office equipment. It also includes property that is not classified elsewhere.

   d. **10-year** Includes vessels, barges, tugs, and similar water transportation equipment.

   e. **15-year** Includes municipal wastewater treatment plants and assets used in the production of cement.

   f. **20-year** Includes municipal sewers and farm buildings.

   g. **27½-year** Includes residential rental property, such as duplexes and apartment buildings.

   h. **39-year** Includes nonresidential real property placed in service after May 1993, such as warehouses and office buildings. (Such property purchased before May 1993 uses a 31½-year life.)

3. **Rates** The property classes determine the MACRS rates. 3-, 5-, 7- and 10-year property is depreciated using the 200% declining-balance method, switching to the straight-line method when it results in a greater deduction. 15- and 20-year property is depreciated using the 150% declining-balance method, switching to the straight-line method when it results in a greater deduction. 27½- and 39-year real property is depreciated using the straight-line method. Salvage value is disregarded for purposes of MACRS deductions.

4. **Section 179 Expense** An election is available to treat the cost of qualifying business-use personal property (including off-the-shelf computer software) as an expense rather than a capital expenditure. The *American Recovery & Reinvestment Act of 2009* (ARRA '09) sets the maximum amount that may be expensed at $250,000 for 2009. This is reduced dollar-for-dollar by the cost of qualifying property that exceeds $800,000 that was placed into service during 2009. Any amount disallowed under this rule may be carried forward indefinitely. In addition, the expense cannot exceed taxable income derived from active conduct of a trade or business during the year, nor can it be purchased from a related party.

Example 3 ▸ Section 179 Deduction

On June 1, 2009, Eagle Corporation bought and placed in service laptop computers at a total of $405,000 and office furniture for $472,000. Eagle has 2009 taxable income before depreciation of $930,000. Eagle takes the full 2009 §179 election available to it, but elected out of bonus depreciation.

Required: What is Eagle Corporation's basis for determining MACRS depreciation?

Solution:

Assets purchased and placed in service	$ 877,000	$877,000
Limitation threshold	(800,000)	
Reduction from maximum Section 179 election	$ 77,000	
Maximum Section 179 election amount	$ 250,000	
Reduction from maximum Section 179 election	(77,000)	
Section 179 election deduction (less than taxable income)	$ 173,000	173,000
Basis for MACRS depreciation		$704,000

5. **Conventions** The determination of whether to use the mid-year or the mid-quarter convention for personal property is made *after* the §179 election is assigned to specific assets.

Exhibit 1 ▸ Conventions & Section 179

In 2009, Growing Corporation placed the following assets into service and elected out of bonus depreciation.

Asset	Date	Asset Life	Cost
Furniture	March 13	7 years	$ 10,000
Computer	July 30	5 years	10,000
Trucks	October 21	5 years	260,000
Total			$180,000

Analysis: Without the §179 deduction, Growing Corp. has more than 40% of its assets placed into service in the last quarter of the year and, therefore, must use the mid-quarter convention. However, if Growing uses the §179 deduction on the trucks purchased in the fourth quarter, Growing may use the half-year convention.

Without Section 179:

Asset	Cost	Depreciable Basis	DDB Factor	Mid-Quarter Factor	Depreciation
Furniture	$ 10,000	$ 10,000	0.285	0.875	$ 2,494
Computer	10,000	10,000	0.400	0.375	1,500
Trucks	260,000	260,000	0.400	0.125	13,000
Total	$280,000	$280,000			$ 16,994

With Section 179:

Asset	Cost	§179	Depreciable Basis	DDB Factor	Half-Year Factor	Depreciation
Furniture	$ 10,000		$ 10,000	0.285	0.50	$ 1,425
Computer	10,000		10,000	0.400	0.50	2,000
Trucks	260,000	$250,000	10,000	0.400	0.50	2,000
Total	$280,000	$250,000	$ 30,000			$ 5,425
Section 179 deduction						250,000
Total cost recovery deductions for the year						$255,425

a. **Half-Year Convention** The half-year convention applies to personal MACRS property. Under this convention, property is treated as placed in service in the middle of the year. Thus, regardless of when the property is placed in service, one-half of the first year's depreciation deduction is allowed in the first year. In addition, one-half a year of depreciation expense is allowed in the year of disposal.

b. **Mid-Quarter Convention** The mid-quarter convention is an exception to the half-year convention. It also applies to personal property. If more than 40% of the aggregate cost of the property placed in service during the year is placed in service in the last quarter of the year, then *all* personal property placed in service during the year is subject to the mid-quarter convention. The MACRS deduction is computed by first determining the deduction for a full year and then multiplying it by a percentage based on what quarter the property was placed in service. These percentages are 87.5% for property placed in service in the first quarter, 62.5% for property placed in service in the second quarter, 37.5% for property placed in service in the third quarter, and 12.5% for property placed in service in the fourth quarter.

c. **Mid-Month Convention** The mid-month convention applies to real property. Under this convention, property is deemed to be placed in service in the middle of the month regardless of the day that it actually is placed in service.

6. **MACRS Tables** IRS established percentage tables that incorporate the applicable method (switching to straight-line when it becomes more advantageous) and convention to assist in the depreciation deduction calculation under MACRS. The percentage table rates are applied to the property's unadjusted basis. The percentage tables cannot be used for property placed in service in a short tax year. For a short tax year, the applicable rate is multiplied by a fraction based on the number of months the property is deemed to be in service. (See Appendix D for selected MACRS tables.)

7. **Bonus Depreciation** ARRA '09 provides qualifying taxpayers 50% first-year bonus depreciation of the adjusted basis of qualifying property placed in service in 2009. To be eligible, property must be new and (1) eligible for MACRS with a depreciation period of 20 years or less; (2) water utility property; (3) computer software (off-the-shelf); (4) qualified leasehold property; or (5) new real property. Bonus depreciation is allowed in full for AMT purposes. A taxpayer may elect out of bonus depreciation; there is an option to accelerate research and AMT credits instead of taking bonus depreciation. Bonus depreciation is determined after the Section 179 deduction and before regular depreciation.

8. **Automobiles** The first year's depreciation deduction on cars generally is limited to a ceiling of $10,960 for 2009. If the taxpayer does not qualify for bonus depreciation or elects out of bonus depreciation, then the first year's depreciation is $8,000 less. For trucks and vans, these amounts are $11,060 and $3,060 for 2009.

a. **Nonbusiness Use** These limits assume 100% business usage. If an automobile is used less than 100% for business, these limits must be further reduced. If an automobile is used less than 50% for business, the alternative depreciation system (ADS), which essentially is straight-line with longer recovery periods, must be used.

b. **Higher Limitation** Special rules and higher limits apply to hybrid vehicles. The limits for "clean fuels" and electric cars also are higher.

9. **Environmental Remediation Costs** EESA '08 allows an election to expense environmental remediation costs for expenses or expenditures paid or incurred during 2009 as a current expense. A qualified environmental remediation expenditure is paid or incurred in connection with the abatement or control of hazardous substances at a qualified contaminated site (e.g., property held for use in trade or business, for the production of income, or as inventory that is certified by the appropriate state environmental agency and contains hazardous

substance). Any deduction allowed under this provision is treated as a depreciation deduction in the event of sale or other disposition (e.g., recapture rules apply).

III. Property Dispositions

A. General

The sale or other disposition of property generally results in the recognition of gain or loss. Depending on the type of property, the gain or loss may be ordinary or capital. Losses on property purchased for personal use usually are not recognized.

1. **Taxable Exchange** In a taxable exchange, the gain or loss on the disposal of property is generally equal to the difference between the amount realized in the transaction and the adjusted basis of the property relinquished. The amount realized is the sum of money received, the fair value of property received, and the amount of liability relieved.

2. **Nontaxable Exchange** In a nontaxable exchange, no gain or loss realized is recognized currently. It usually is deferred until the property subsequently is disposed of in a taxable transaction. (The gain or loss is realized, but not recognized.) Some nontaxable exchanges qualify for a permanent exclusion of income recognition.

B. Capital Gain or Loss

A capital gain or loss can result only from the sale or exchange of a *capital* asset. Certain gains are *treated* as if they were capital gains.

1. **Definition** Capital assets are all assets *except* the following.

   a. Inventory and other property held primarily for sale to customers in the ordinary course of business

   b. Depreciable personal property, or real property, used in business (This property is sometimes treated as if it was a capital asset.)

   c. Certain copyrights, artistic compositions, letters, etc., in the hands of the creator.

   d. Accounts or notes receivable acquired in the ordinary course of business for services rendered or sales of inventory

   e. Any U.S. government publication received free of charge by the taxpayer

2. **Holding Period** There are significant differences between "long-term" and "short-term" capital gains and losses for non-corporate taxpayers. Long-term is defined as more than 12 months. Short-term is defined as 12 months or less and is taxed as ordinary income.

   a. Property received in a tax-free exchange, or by gift, "tacks on" the holding period of the prior transferor when the donee's basis is the same as the donor's basis. If the donor's basis is the FMV at the time of the gift, the donee's holding period begins on the date of the gift.

   b. Property acquired from a decedent automatically is considered held for more than the requisite long-term holding period.

3. **Treatment** A taxpayer nets capital gains and losses to arrive at either a net capital gain or a net capital loss.

   a. The net long-term capital gains of non-corporate taxpayers are taxed at a maximum rate that is lower than the maximum rate for ordinary income. The reduced rate of 15% (5% for low-income taxpayers) applies to gains from stocks and bonds (except qualified small business stock) as well as real property for certain entities. Individuals (not corporations) are among these entities. These reduced rates do not apply to most collectibles (artwork, antiques, stamps, coins, metals, and gems), which are taxed at a maximum rate of 28%.

Exhibit 2 ▸ Non-Corporate Capital Gain Tax Rates (Except Collectibles)

Tax Bracket	Holding Period	Maximum Capital Gain Tax Rate
At 15%	Short-term (ordinary income)	15%
	Long-term	5%
Above 15%	Short-term (ordinary income)	35%
	Long-term	15%

Note: Taxpayers receive an annual tax benefit via the deduction for depreciation on depreciable real property. If the property is held *long-term* and is later sold at a gain, the taxpayer is entitled to taxation at the lower capital gains rate. However, the tax law requires the taxpayer to *recapture* the previously taken depreciation benefit. This is accomplished by taxing a *portion* of the capital gain at a higher rate. For long-term real property sold after May 6, 1997, the recapture amount is all depreciation claimed, and the recapture rate is 25%.

b. Individuals may deduct net capital losses only to the extent of the lesser of (1) $3,000 per year or (2) taxable income. Individuals cannot carry back unused capital losses; however, they can carry the losses forward indefinitely.

c. Corporate taxpayers may deduct capital losses only to the extent of capital gains. Corporations can carry capital losses back three years and forward five years. The corporate rates for capital gains currently equal the rates for ordinary income.

C. Installment Sales

The installment method of reporting gains may be elected when at least one payment is received in a tax year after the year of the sale. The amount of gain that is taxable each year is computed by multiplying the payments received that year by the gross profit percentage. The gross profit percentage is equal to the anticipated total gross profit to be received divided by the total contract price. The installment sale method generally may not be used by dealers in property.

Example 4 ▸ Installment Sales

In Year 1, Ed sells Steve some personal use property for $10,000 to be paid in equal installments over a 5-year period. Ed's basis in the property is $7,000. In Year 1, Steve pays Ed $2,000. Ed must recognize gain as follows.

$10,000 – $7,000	=	$3,000 total profit
$3,000 / $10,000	=	30% gross profit percentage
$2,000 × 30%	=	$600 profit recognized in Year 1

D. Section 1231 Property

Section 1231 property is depreciable property or land that is used in a trade or business. If the losses from sale or disposition of §1231 property exceed the gains, then the net loss is treated as an *ordinary* loss. However, if the gains exceed losses, then the net gain is treated as a *capital* gain. When property is disposed of, resulting in a §1231 gain, then some of the gain may have to be recaptured as ordinary income because of depreciation deductions that were previously taken. Property subject to recapture provisions include:

1. **Section 1245 Property** This is primarily depreciable personalty. Any depreciation recaptured must be treated as ordinary income.

2. **Section 1250 Property** This is depreciable realty. All "excess" depreciation recaptured is treated as ordinary income. Unrecaptured §1250 gain (gain otherwise treated as ordinary income) is taxed at a maximum rate of 25%.

E. Long-Term Contracts

The percentage of completion method is used by a corporation to recognize income on long-term contracts. Determining income under the percentage of completion method requires a comparison of estimates of total costs incurred during the current year to the total estimated costs of the project. Because the final income recognized usually differs from that estimated during the project's life, a look-back calculation is required. However, a taxpayer may elect not to make (or reapply in the case of completed contracts) a look-back calculation if, for each year prior to completion, the cumulative estimated taxable income or loss is within 10% (*de minimis*) of the actual income or loss recognized on the project.

F. Transactions Between Related Parties

No loss is allowed to be recognized with respect to sales or exchanges between related parties. A related party is defined as the following.

1. **Family Members** An individual's brothers, sisters, spouse, ancestors, and lineal descendents.

2. **Entities** A pass-through entity or a corporation owned more than 50%, either directly or indirectly, by an individual. Stock in a corporation may be owned indirectly because of the constructive ownership rules that state that an individual shall be considered to own the stock owned directly by her/his spouse, children, grandchildren, and parents.

3. **Controlled Corporations** Two corporations that are members of the same controlled group.

4. **Trust** Most relationships between a trust and its grantor, fiduciary trustee, beneficiary, or a corporation owned 50% or more by the trust grantor.

G. Like-Kind Exchanges

A like-kind exchange is an exchange of property of the same nature or character. (Real property must be exchanged for real property and personal property for personal property.) No gain or loss is recognized on a like-kind exchange of property held for productive use in a trade or business or for investment, if the property received is either held for productive use in a trade or business or for investment. Property held for investment may be exchanged for property to be used in a trade or business and vice versa. The like-kind exchange rules do not apply to property held for personal use, such as stocks, bonds, notes, certificates of trust, beneficial interests, or partnership interests. Trade-in allowances are covered by the like-kind exchange rules.

Example 5 ▸ Like-Kind Exchange

Harry's Hardware gives Sally's Shells a computer with a fair market value of $3,000 and an adjusted basis of $1,900. In return, Sally gives Harry an old computer with a fair market value of $2,000 and an adjusted basis of $600. Sally also gives Harry $900 in cash. How much gain must each recognize?

Solution:

		Harry		Sally
Amount realized [FMV]	($2,000 + $900)	$ 2,900		$ 3,000
Amount relinquished [Adjusted basis]		(1,900)	($600 + $900)	(1,500)
Realized gain		$ 1,000		$ 1,500
Amount of boot received		$ 900		$ 0
Recognized gain (lesser of gain realized or boot received)		$ 900		$ 0

1. **Basis** When no gain is recognized from the exchange, the basis of the property received is the adjusted basis of the property given up.

2. **Boot** If boot (money or other non-like-kind property) is received as part of the like-kind exchange, then gain is recognized to the extent of the lesser of the gain realized or the boot received. However, a loss is not recognized.

   a. The basis of property received is equal to the basis of the property given up, plus gain recognized, plus boot given, less the fair market value of boot received.

   b. Liabilities assumed by one party in the exchange are treated as boot. If the liability was assumed by the other party, it is treated as boot received. Likewise, if the tax-payer assumes the liability, it is treated as boot given.

H. Sale of Principal Residence

An individual taxpayer may exclude the gain from gross income in some situations. An exclusion of gain ($500,000 married filing jointly or $250,000 for a single individual or head of household) is available to a taxpayer who owned and occupied the home as a principal residence in two of the five years immediately preceding the sale after May 6, 1997. This exclusion may be claimed as frequently as once every two years.

1. ***Pro Rata* Exclusion** Taxpayers may claim a ratable portion of the exclusion, if they do not meet the two-year requirement due to health problems, employment relocation, or other unforeseen circumstances.

   Example 6 ▸ *Pro Rata* Exclusion

   > Fred sold his principal residence in Year 1, after living there 1 year, due to an employment relocation. His gain on the sale of the home is $20,000. As a single taxpayer, he would be eligible for a $250,000 exclusion of gain, had he lived there 2 years. Fred may exclude $20,000 of gain, because it is less than the *pro rata* exclusion. ($250,000 × 50% = $125,000)

2. **Marriage of Taxpayers** A $250,000 exclusion may be used by a spouse whose residence is sold if a married couple did not share a principal residence. The marriage of a taxpayer, to someone who recently used a $250,000 exclusion, does not preclude the use of another $250,000 exclusion for that taxpayer.

3. **Death of Spouse** A taxpayer may exclude $500,000 from the sale of a residence jointly owned and occupied by the taxpayer and the taxpayer's deceased spouse, provided the sale occurs no later than two years from the spouse's death.

4. **Mortgage Forgiveness Relief** The basis of the home is reduced by the amount of debt relief excluded from income under MFDRA '07.

5. **Non-Qualifying Use** For home sales after December 31, 2008, involving non-qualifying use periods, the *Housing Assistance Tax Act of 2008* (HATA '08) reduces the exclusion of gain from a sale of a home by the amount of appreciation attributable to non-qualified use. HATA '08 determines excluded appreciation on a *pro rata* basis rather than requiring a valuation when use changes. A qualifying use period includes the time that the property is used as a principal residence plus a subsequent period in which it is empty. Any period after December 31, 2008, in which the property is a vacation home or rental property counts as a non-qualifying use period.

Example 7 ▸ Non-Qualifying Use

On January 2, 2008, Wilma bought a house for $200,000 and used it as her vacation home until June 30, 2009, when she converted it to her principal residence. On October 2, 2012, Wilma moved out of the house and listed it for sale. Wilma sold the home for $250,000 on January 2, 2013.

Period	Use	Qualifying?	Duration
January 2, 2008, to December 31, 2008	vacation home	yes	12 months
January 1, 2009, to June 30, 2009	vacation home	no	6 months
July 1, 2009, to October 1, 2012	principal residence	yes	39 months
October 2, 2012, to January 2, 2013	empty	yes	3 months

Wilma's exclusion for the sale of a principal residence is reduced by the appreciation attributed to the 6 months of vacation home use after December 31, 2008. As Wilma used the property for a non-qualifying purpose for half a year of the 5 years of ownership, 10% (0.5 year / 5 years) of the appreciation is not eligible to be excluded from gain. Wilma must include 10% of the $50,000 gain, or $5,000, in taxable income.

I. Involuntary Conversions

An involuntary conversion takes place when money, similar, or dissimilar property is received for property that has been damaged, stolen, or condemned.

1. **Gain (Loss) Recognition** No gain is recognized if the property is converted directly into similar-use property. (Similar-use is a stricter standard than like-kind.) In addition, the taxpayer may elect to not recognize gain on an involuntary conversion, if the taxpayer replaces the property with property that is similar or related in service or use to the property converted. Alternatively, the taxpayer may purchase an 80% controlling interest in a corporation owning or, within a specified time, acquiring replacement property. Gain is then recognized only to the extent that gain realized on the conversion exceeds the cost of the replacement property. C corporations (and certain partnerships with corporate partners) are not entitled to defer gain, if the replacement property is purchased from a related party. This denial applies to any other taxpayer (including individuals) with an aggregate realized gain over $100,000 for the taxable year. The recognition or nonrecognition of loss is not affected by the involuntary conversion rules.

2. **Replacement Period** The property must be replaced within a period beginning with the date the property was (1) damaged, stolen, condemned, etc., or (2) the earlier of the date the condemnation first was threatened or became imminent, and ending two years after the close of the first tax year in which any part of the gain is realized. This two-year period is extended to three years when real property is condemned or threatened to be condemned. Condemnations are held only to the standard of like-kind, not similar-use.

3. **Special Disaster Relief** Special relief is available for people whose qualified property is involuntarily converted as a result of a disaster for which a presidential declaration is made. The provision applies to main homes and/or contents, trade, business, and investment property. There are three special breaks.

   a. **Exclusion** Taxpayers may exclude insurance proceeds received for unscheduled personal property.

   b. **Pool of Funds** The insurance proceeds for a home or its contents are treated as a common pool of funds received for a single item of property. A taxpayer may elect not to recognize gain currently on this pool of funds to the extent it is timely reinvested in another home (or contents).

c. **Period of Time** The period of time for the replacement of property involuntarily converted due to a disaster ends 4 years after the close of the first tax year in which any part of the gain upon conversion is realized.

IV. Securities

A. Transactions

The trade date is the date of sale.

1. **Wash Sales** A loss from the sale or other disposition of stock or security is disallowed if substantially the same stock or security is purchased during a time period beginning 30 days prior to the sale and ending 30 days after that date. In the case where a loss is not allowed, the basis of the disposed stock is carried over to the newly acquired stock.

2. **Stock Dividends** Generally, when stock dividends are received, it is a nontaxable transaction and, thus, are not included in gross income. The basis of the original stock is allocated proportionally between the original stock and the dividends received based on their fair market values as of the dates of distribution. If there is an option to receive cash instead of the stock dividend, the transaction is taxable, even if the stock dividend is received.

3. **Stock Splits** Increase the number of shares outstanding and proportionally decrease the par or stated value of the stock. There is no change in the dollar amount of the stock.

B. Worthless Stock

The basis of the stock is deductible in the year that it becomes completely worthless. If the stock was a capital asset to the taxpayer, then generally the loss is a capital loss. However, there is an exception (known as §1244 stock) for investment in a small business company, which is limited to the first million of stock issue. The *original* investor is allowed an ordinary loss rather than a capital loss for such stock. The ordinary loss is limited to $50,000 ($100,000 for joint filers).

C. Small Business Stock

A non-corporate taxpayer who holds qualified small-business stock for more than 5 years is allowed to exclude 50% of any gain on the sale or exchange of the stock. For stock acquired from February 18, 2009, to December 31, 2010, ARRA '09 increased the exclusion of gain from the sale of qualified small business stock to 75%. The amount of gain eligible for the exclusion is limited to the greater of (1) 10 times the taxpayer's basis in the stock, or (2) a $10 million gain from the stock. The $10 million limit is applied on a shareholder-by-shareholder basis.

1. **Eligible Stock** The stock must be acquired by the taxpayer after August 10, 1993, at the original issuance in exchange for money, other property (not including stock), or as compensation for services provided to the corporation (other than services performed as an underwriter of the stock).

2. **Qualified Corporations** The small business must be a C corporation, have less than $50 million of aggregated capital as of the date of stock issuance, and at least 80%, by value, of corporate assets must be used in the active conduct of one or more trades or businesses. The corporation cannot be involved in the performance of personal services (e.g., health, law, accounting, etc.) or in the finance, banking, leasing, real estate, farming, mineral extraction, or hospitality industries.

V. Preparer Responsibilities

A. Preparer Penalties

A preparer is one who is paid to prepare a substantial portion of a return or claim for refund.

1. **Disclosure** The IRC provides penalties for disclosures of confidential information to persons unnecessary to the preparation or filing of a taxpayer's return. Preparers may disclose information in a peer or quality review, for processing, or pursuant to an administrative order from a state agency that registers tax return preparers.

2. **Unrealistic Position** A return preparer may be liable for a penalty of $1,000 or half the income derived by the preparer if the return or refund claim reflects an understatement of tax liability that is based on an unrealistic position. EESA '08 established three categories of unrealistic positions to which the preparer penalty will apply. The reasonable cause/good faith defense still is available.

   a. **General (Undisclosed) Positions** Avoid penalty by having substantial authority for the position.

   b. **Disclosed Positions** Avoid penalty by having reasonable basis and disclosure.

   c. **Tax Shelters & Reportable Transactions** Avoid penalty by meeting a more-likely-than-not standard.

3. **Due Diligence** There is a $100 penalty for a tax return preparer who does not comply with due diligence requirements of claiming the earned income credit.

4. **Willful or Reckless Disregard** The preparer may be liable for a $5,000 penalty if the understatement is willful or due to the preparer's intentional disregard of a rule or regulation. To avoid the penalty, the preparer must disclose the position to the IRS and include support indicating that the position represents a good faith challenge to the regulation's validity.

B. Practicing Before the IRS (Circular 230)

Code of Federal Regulations, Title 31, Subtitle A, Part 10, contains rules governing the recognition of attorneys, certified public accountants, enrolled agents, and other persons representing taxpayers before the Internal Revenue Service.

1. **Knowledge of Omission** A tax practitioner who knows the client has not complied with the revenue rules or made an error or omission from any return or document with which the client submitted under the laws must advise the client of the consequences of non-compliance.

2. **Diligence as to Accuracy**

   a. **Work of Preparer** Generally, a tax practitioner must exercise due diligence: (1) in the preparation or assistance in the preparation of, approval, and filing of tax returns, documents, affidavits, and other papers relating to IRS matters; and (2) in the determination of correctness of oral or written representations made by the practitioner to clients with reference to any matter administered by the IRS.

   b. **Work of Others** A tax practitioner will be presumed to have exercised due diligence if the practitioner relies on the work product of another person and used reasonable care in the engagement, supervision, training, and evaluation of that person, taking the nature of the relationship between the practitioner and that person into proper account.

3. **Contingent Fees** Any fee based, in whole or in part, on whether a position taken on a tax return or other filing avoids challenge by the IRS or is sustained either by the IRS or in litigation. Contingent fees include any fee arrangement in which the practitioner will reimburse the client for all or a portion of the client's fee in the event a position taken on a tax return or other filing is challenged by the IRS or is not sustained, whether pursuant to an indemnity agreement, guarantee, rescission rights, or any other arrangement with a similar effect.

   a. **Original Returns** A contingent fee may not be charged for preparing an original tax return or for any advice rendered in connection with a position taken or to be taken on an original tax return.

   b. **Amended Returns** A contingent fee may be charged for preparation of or advice in connection with an amended tax return or a claim for refund (other than on an original tax return), but only if the practitioner reasonably anticipates at the time the fee arrangement is entered into that the amended tax return or refund claim will receive substantive review by the IRS.

4. **Return of Records** Generally, a practitioner must promptly return any and all records of the client that are necessary for the client to comply with her/his Federal tax obligations. The practitioner may retain copies of the records returned to a client.

5. **Advertisements** A practitioner may not in any way use or participate in the use of any form of public communication or private solicitation containing: a false, fraudulent, or coercive statement or claim; or a misleading or deceptive statement or claim.

6. **Solicitation** A practitioner may not make, directly or indirectly, an uninvited written or oral solicitation of employment in matters related to the IRS if the solicitation violates federal or state law or other applicable rule. Any lawful solicitation made by or on behalf of a practitioner eligible to practice before the IRS must, nevertheless, clearly identify the solicitation as such and, if applicable, identify the source of the information used in choosing the recipient.

7. **Standards for Advice on Tax Return Positions**

   a. **Reasonable Belief Standard** A practitioner may not sign a tax return as a preparer if the practitioner does not have a reasonable belief that the tax treatment of the position was more likely than not the proper treatment. A practitioner may not advise a client to take a position on a tax return, or prepare the portion of a tax return on which a position is taken, unless either of the following.

      (1) The practitioner determines that the position satisfies the reasonable belief standard.

      (2) The position is non-frivolous and the practitioner advises the client of any opportunity to avoid the accuracy-related penalty under §6662 by adequately disclosing the position and of the requirements for adequate disclosure.

   b. **Potential Penalties** A practitioner advising a client to take a position on a tax return, or preparing or signing a tax return as a preparer, must inform the client of the penalties that are reasonably likely to apply to the client with respect to the position advised, prepared, or reported. The practitioner also must inform the client of any opportunity to avoid any such penalty by disclosure, if relevant, and of the requirements for adequate disclosure.

8. **Sanctions** The Secretary of the Treasury, or her/his delegate, after notice and an opportunity for a proceeding, may censure, suspend or disbar any practitioner from practice before the IRS if the practitioner is shown to be incompetent or disreputable, fails to comply with any of the regulations, or with intent to defraud, willfully and knowingly misleads or threatens a client or prospective client. Censure is a public reprimand.

VI. Tax Procedures

A. Burden of Proof

If the taxpayer introduces credible evidence and satisfies four conditions, the IRS has the burden of proof in any court proceeding with respect to a factual issue regarding a taxpayer's tax liability. These conditions are (1) the taxpayer must substantiate items, (2) the taxpayer must maintain adequate records, (3) the taxpayer must comply with reasonable requests for interviews and information, and (4) the taxpayer must have a net worth of less than $7 million. The net worth condition is inapplicable to individuals.

B. Accounting Issues

1. **Accounting Periods** A tax year can be either calendar or fiscal year. A fiscal year (12-month period ending on the last day of a month other than December) may be elected by a taxpayer who keeps accurate books and records; otherwise, a calendar year must be used. Married filing joint taxpayers must use the same tax year, but they may have different accounting methods. C corporations may choose either a calendar or a fiscal year. Generally, S corporations and personal service corporations (PSC) must use a calendar year, unless there is a valid business purpose for electing a fiscal year. Once a tax year is established, a taxpayer may change that annual accounting period only with the consent of the IRS.

2. **Accounting Methods** A taxpayer who has average annual gross receipts of less than $1 million generally may use the cash method of accounting. If a taxpayer must account for inventory, then the taxpayer is required to use the accrual method of accounting for sales and cost of goods sold. Corporations generally are barred from using the cash method of accounting; however, a non tax-shelter entity that is a qualified personal service corporation or meets the less than $5 million of gross receipts test may use the cash method.

3. **Inventory Methods** If a taxpayer elects to use the LIFO method for tax accounting purposes, that method also must be used for all financial accounting reports. The Uniform Capitalization Rules (UNICAP) provides uniform rules requiring the capitalization of direct as well as most indirect costs of producing certain property. These rules generally apply to real and tangible personal property produced by the taxpayer for use in a trade or business or for investment purposes and to personal and real property purchased for resale to customers. In the case of property purchased for resale, a taxpayer is exempt if its average gross receipts for the preceding three years are $10 million or less.

4. **Due Date** If the due date of a return or payment falls on a weekend or a legal holiday, the return or payment is due on the next business day. An extension extends the time for filing the return, not for paying the tax

C. Authoritative Hierarchy

1. **Legislative Sources of Tax Law** Generally, tax legislation is considered first by the House Ways and Means Committee. If acceptable to this committee, a proposed bill is approved or disapproved as is by the entire House of Representatives. Bills approved by the House of Representatives are considered by the Senate Finance Committee. If acceptable to this committee, it is considered by the entire Senate. As senators may readily make amendments to tax bills, the Senate may pass a different version than the House did. A joint committee (composed of members of the House Ways and Means Committee and the Senate Finance Committee) resolves any divergence between the House and Senate versions of the bill. Then, both bodies of Congress vote on this compromise version. If passed by Congress, the bill goes to the President. If the President signs the bill or the President's veto is overruled by Congress, the bill becomes law and is incorporated into the Internal Revenue Code.

   a. **IRC References** As section numbers do not re-initialize with each new subtitle, chapter, subchapter, or part, the code may be referenced by section number (for example, Section 1 or §1) or in greater detail, starting with the section number [for example, §1(a)].

   b. **Committee Reports** Each of the three committees (the House Ways and Means Committee, the Senate Finance Committee, and the Joint Conference Committee) issues reports. As these reports document Congress' intent, the courts (and others) use them to interpret legislation.

   c. **Senate Origin** The Senate may originate tax bills as amendments to other legislative proposals. These bills then re-enter the process at the point where bills are considered by the House Ways and Means Committee.

d. **Tax Treaties** Tax treaties are agreements with foreign countries relating to taxation. If there is direct conflict between tax law and a tax treaty, the most recent item prevails.

Exhibit 3: Internal Revenue Code (IRC) Organization

Title 26, Internal Revenue Code
- Subtitle A, Income Taxes
  - Chapter 1, Normal Taxes and Surtaxes
    - Subchapter A, Determination of Tax Liability
      - Part I, Tax on Individuals
        - Section I, Tax imposed
          - (a) Married individuals filing joint returns and surviving spouses
          - (b) Heads of households
          - <detail omitted>
        - Section 2, Definitions and special rules
        - <detail omitted>
      - Part II, Tax on Corporations
        - Section 11, Tax imposed
        - <detail omitted>
      - Part IV, Credits Against Tax
        - Subpart A, Nonrefundable Personal Credits
          - Section 21, Expenses for household and dependent care services necessary for gainful employment
          - Section 22, Credit for the elderly and the permanently disabled
          - Section 23, Adoption expenses
          - Section 24, Child tax credit
          - Section 25, Interest on certain home mortgages
          - Section 25A, Hope and Lifetime Learning credits
          - Section 25B, Elective deferrals and IRA Contributions by certain individuals
          - Section 25C, Nonbusiness energy property
          - Section 25D, Residential energy efficient property
          - Section 26, Limitation based on tax liability, definition of tax liability
        - Subpart B, Other Credits
        - <continued>

2. **Administrative Sources of Tax Law**

a. **Treasury Regulations** Under authority granted by Congress, the U.S. Treasury issues regulations in proposed, temporary, or final form. Regulations interpret the code. Typically, new regulations or revisions to regulations are issued in proposed form. Proposed regulations have little force; finalized regulations have the effect of law. Temporary regulations generally are issued when there is some urgency; they have the effect of law until they automatically expire. The regulations' numbering system incorporates the related code section number. The burden of proof is on taxpayers to show that final regulations vary from the statute or lack support in committee reports. The **legislative reenactment doctrine** presumes that a long-standing finalized regulation has congressional approval if Congress has not amended the relevant IRC. Final regulations may be classified as follows.

Exhibit 4: Regulation Numbering System

Reg. §§1.41-1 through 1.41-7 interpret IRC §41

(1) **Procedural Regulations** Procedural regulations neither establish nor clarify tax law. They outline internal IRS conduct and the information that taxpayers must report.

(2) **Interpretive Regulations** Essentially, interpretive regulations are elaborations on, and clarifications of, committee reports. While these rarely are overturned, the U.S. Supreme Court instructs lower courts to examine regulations before honoring them.

(3) **Legislative Regulations** Some laws practically delegate legislative authority to the Treasury Department to complete details of specified issues. Legislative regulations carry greater weight than interpretive regulations.

b. **Revenue Rulings** The IRS national office issues revenue rulings, typically to deal with narrow situations, for the guidance of taxpayers, tax preparers, and IRS personnel. Revenue rulings are interpretations of law that have less force than Regulations. They often provide examples of how the IRS applies a law. Technical advice given to IRS district offices, court decisions, and suggestions from tax practitioner groups may prompt the IRS to issue a revenue ruling.

c. **Revenue Procedures** Issued in a manner similar to revenue rulings, revenue procedures are administrative in nature.

d. **Letter Rulings** For a fee, a taxpayer may request a letter ruling—a description of how the IRS will treat a proposed transaction. The national IRS office issues letter rulings only in certain tax areas. While letter rulings are applicable only to the requesting taxpayer, they are substantial authority for purposes of the accuracy-related penalty. Letter rulings with identifying details removed are available for public inspection. The IRS may convert letter rulings to revenue rulings.

e. **Determination Letters** Regional IRS offices may issue (unpublished) determination letters at taxpayers' requests. These outline how the IRS will treat a given transaction, typically a completed transaction.

3. **Judicial Sources of Tax Law** If remedies available within the IRS are exhausted, a taxpayer may take a dispute to the courts.

a. **Court of Original Jurisdiction** A court of original jurisdiction first considers the dispute. The Small Cases Division of the U.S. Tax Court considers cases involving amounts of $50,000 or less. Cases tried in the Small Cases Division have no appeal and do not set precedent for other court decisions. Cases in other courts may set precedent and, thus, create judicial law. The three other courts of original jurisdiction are as follows.

(1) **Federal District Court** The payment of any deficiency is made before the trial. There is the option to have a jury trial (the jury may decide questions of fact, not law). Decisions made in these courts set precedent within that district only.

(2) **U.S. Court of Federal Claims** The payment of any deficiency is made before the trial. There is no option to have a jury trial.

(3) **U.S. Tax Court** The payment of any deficiency need not be made before the trial, but there is no option to have a jury trial. This court hears cases involving tax issues only.

b. **Appellate Courts** Courts of original jurisdiction must follow the precedents set by the court of appeals of jurisdiction which, in turn, follow precedents set by the U.S. Supreme Court. A party losing in the U.S. Court of Federal Claims or U.S. Tax Court may appeal in the U.S. Court of Appeals which is divided into geographical districts. A party losing in Federal District Court may appeal in the U.S. Court of Appeals for the Federal Circuit.

(1) **Precedent** A precedent set in one geographical district need not be followed in another, sometimes influencing the taxpayer's choice of court of original

jurisdiction. When researching tax issues, greater weight must be given to precedent set by the applicable district appellate court than those set by other district appellate courts. One court of appeals need not follow a precedent set by another court of appeals of equivalent standing.

Example 8: Selecting a Court of Original Jurisdiction

> The U.S. Court of Appeals is divided into geographical districts. Bill lives in a district where cases similar to his own has been decided in favor of the IRS by the district's appellate court. In other districts, cases similar to Bill's case have been decided in favor of the taxpayer. By selecting the Federal District Court, the taxpayer avoids the precedent set by his district's appellate court.

(2) **Actions on Decisions** The IRS may indicate agreement (acquiescence) or disagreement (nonacquiescence) with a court decision. These positions may be changed retroactively. The lack of an appeal by the IRS does not necessarily indicate that the IRS will not litigate similar cases. A heavy litigation load, a particular taxpayer's sympathetic position, or a greater likelihood of success in another court of appeals may cause the IRS to wait to appeal in a similar unsuccessful case.

D. Tax Planning

The purpose of tax planning is to maximize the taxpayer's after-tax return. Tax planning must be balanced with other considerations. A course of action producing the lowest tax bill while undermining sound business judgment or neglecting personal needs is undesirable.

Exhibit 5: Sample Actions to Reduce or Defer Tax

Strategy	Example
Eliminate tax	Exclusion of income from the sale of a principal residence
	Contribute to a Roth IRA; earnings are nontaxable for qualified withdrawals
Eliminate taxable income	Rent home during a special event for an extraordinary sum, but restrict the rental duration below the maximum where income need be declared (and where related expenses are not deducted)
	Purchase bonds that earn tax-exempt interest instead of purchasing bonds that earn interest subject to tax
Defer tax	Defer the receipt of income
	Contribute to a traditional IRA; contributions and earnings are taxable when withdrawn
Reduce tax rate	Convert ordinary income into capital gains by holding property expected to appreciate instead of holding interest-earning property
	Give gifts of income-producing property to family members (except children) in lower tax brackets
Accelerate deductions	Elect accelerated depreciation to reduce current income
Time deductions	Schedule major medical expenses within one calendar year, taking an itemized deduction in that year and a standard deduction in the next when there are reduced expenses
Offset taxable income	Convert passive income into ordinary income by becoming involved in rental property management
	Sell stock at loss to offset some ordinary income
Eliminate double taxation	Elect a limited liability company structure instead of a corporate structure

1. **Current Year** Reducing or deferring the current-year tax often is an intermediate goal toward the goal of maximizing long-term after-tax returns. Bear in mind, an action that reduces tax in one year may burden future years with an unfavorable position, negating the initial favorable action.

2. **Eligibility** Some provisions are applicable to certain types of entities only; selection of an entity type may be the tax planning decision that has the biggest impact on after-tax return.

Tax Research

The AICPA has not specified the exact contents of the taxation database; however, the AICPA has stated that the database provided during a Regulation (REG) simulation will:

- Be used by candidates in answering the research element
- Include certain portions of the Internal Revenue Code (IRC)
- Include all necessary information to complete the research element

CPA exam candidates can get a free six-month subscription to professional literature used in the computerized CPA examination; however, this online package only includes accounting and auditing literature. The AICPA does not provide exam candidates with access to the IRC or any portion thereof to be included in the taxation database used for the CPA exam. Nor have the examiners specified a commercially available database as the one it will use. Therefore, candidates have no way of learning, before sitting for the REG exam section, the exact organization or features of the database. This makes preparing for the research element of a REG simulation slightly more challenging, but there still are ways that candidates can and should prepare.

Ideally, candidates should try to obtain access to an electronic copy of a database containing the IRC (preferably a searchable database); possibly through a university or law library. The search engine functionality of the taxation database used on the CPA examination is likely to resemble the functionality in the fee-based subscription databases used most widely by tax professionals.

However, if you cannot gain access to a fee-based subscription database, you also can access and search the IRC as part of the United States Code from good, free Internet editions. A good one to use is the electronic edition of the United States Code prepared and published by the Office of the Law Revision Counsel of the U.S. House of Representatives. It is available for free on the Internet by selecting SEARCH at: http://uscode.house.gov. The Internal Revenue Code is Title 26 of the United States Code, so use this information in the Title field to limit your search to the IRC.

Whatever resource you end up using, the important thing is that you become comfortable with finding tax citations using appropriate search terms. It is not important that you have the most cutting edge tax research software to practice this basic skill.

CHAPTER 43—FEDERAL TAXATION: PROPERTY & OTHER TAX TOPICS

Problem 43-1 MULTIPLE CHOICE QUESTIONS (45 to 60 minutes)

1. Fred Berk bought a plot of land with a cash payment of $40,000 and a purchase money mortgage of $50,000. In addition, Berk paid $200 for a title insurance policy. Berk's basis in this land is
a. $40,000
b. $40,200
c. $90,000
d. $90,200 (11/90, PII, #29, 1613)

Items 2 and 3 are based on the following:

In Year 1, Flora Ring bought a diamond necklace for her own use, at a cost of $10,000. In Year 4, when the fair market value was $12,000, Flora and her husband gave this necklace to her daughter, Ruth. No gift tax was due.

2. Ruth's holding period for this gift
a. Starts in Year 4
b. Starts in Year 1
c. Depends on whether the necklace is sold by Ruth at a gain or at a loss
d. Is irrelevant because Ruth received the necklace for no consideration of money or money's worth (Editors, 1625)

3. If Ruth sells this diamond necklace in Year 4 for $13,000, Ruth's recognized gain would be
a. $3,000
b. $2,000
c. $1,000
d. $0 (Editors, 1627)

4. Carter purchased 100 shares of stock for $50 per share. Ten years later, Carter died on February 1 and bequeathed the 100 shares of stock to a relative, Boone, when the stock had a market price of $100 per share. One year later, on April 1, the stock split 2 for 1. Boone gave 100 shares of the stock to another of Carter's relatives, Dixon, on June 1 that same year, when the market value of the stock was $150 per share. What was Dixon's basis in the 100 shares of stock when acquired on June 1?
a. $ 5,000
b. $ 5,100
c. $10,000
d. $15,000 (R/06, REG, A0164T, #11, 8181)

Items 5 and 6 are based on the following:

On March 1, Year 7, Lois Wheat was bequeathed 1,000 shares of Lane Corp. common stock under the will of her uncle, Pat Prisy. Pat had paid $5,000 for the Lane stock in Year 2. Fair market value of the Lane stock on March 1, Year 7, the date of Pat's death, was $8,000 and had increased to $11,000 six months later. The executor of Pat's estate elected the alternate valuation date for estate tax purposes. Lois sold the Lane stock for $9,000 on May 1, Year 7, the date that the executor distributed the stock to her.

5. How much should Lois include in her individual income tax return for the inheritance of the 1,000 shares of Lane stock which she received from Pat's estate?
a. $0
b. $ 5,000
c. $ 8,000
d. $11,000 (Editors, 1635)

6. Lois' basis for gain or loss on sale of the 1,000 shares of Lane stock is
a. $ 5,000
b. $ 8,000
c. $ 9,000
d. $11,000 (Editors, 8035)

7. Daven inherited property from a parent. The property had an adjusted basis to the parent of $1,600,000. It was valued at $2,000,000 at the date of death and valued at $1,800,000 six months after the date of death. The executor elected the alternative valuation date. What is Daven's basis in the property?
a. $0
b. $1,600,000
c. $1,800,000
d. $2,000,000 (R/03, REG, 1318T, #12, 7654)

8. Fuller was the owner and beneficiary of a $200,000 life insurance policy on a parent. Fuller sold the policy to Decker, for $25,000. Decker paid a total of $40,000 in premiums. Upon the death of the parent, what amount must Decker include in gross income?
a. $0
b. $135,000
c. $160,000
d. $200,000 (R/02, AR, #18, 7083)

9. A taxpayer purchased and placed in service a $530,000 piece of equipment in a year with a maximum allowable Section 179 amount of $250,000 and a ceiling of $800,000 of qualifying property. The equipment is 7-year property. The first-year depreciation for 7-year property is 14.29%. Before considering any depreciation deduction, the taxpayer had $700,000 of taxable income. The taxpayer did not elect out of bonus depreciation. What amount is the maximum allowable depreciation deduction?

a. $252,144
b. $265,000
c. $410,006
d. $517,144

(R/03, REG, A0014T, #6, amended, 7648)

10. Which of the following conditions must be satisfied for a taxpayer to expense, in the year of purchase, under Internal Revenue Code Section 179, the cost of new or used tangible depreciable personal property?

I. The property must be purchased for use in the taxpayer's active trade or business.
II. The property must be purchased from an unrelated party.

a. I only
b. II only
c. Both I and II
d. Neither I nor II (R/01, AR, #23, 7008)

11. Data Corp., a calendar year corporation, purchased and placed into service office equipment during November, Year 4. No other equipment was placed into service during the year. Data qualifies to use the general MACRS depreciation system. Data wants to take the largest deduction possible. What convention will Data use?

a. Full-year
b. Half-year
c. Mid-quarter
d. Mid-month (11/95, AR, #5, amended, 5749)

12. On August 1, Graham purchased and placed into service an office building costing $264,000 including $30,000 for the land. What was Graham's MACRS deduction for the office building in that year?

a. $9,600
b. $6,000
c. $3,600
d. $2,250 (5/95, AR, #5, amended, 5423)

13. Baker Corp., a calendar year C corporation, realized taxable income of $36,000 from its regular business operations for calendar Year 1. In addition, Baker had the following capital gains and losses:

Short-term capital gain	$ 8,500
Short-term capital loss	(4,000)
Long-term capital gain	1,500
Long-term capital loss	(3,500)

Baker did not realize any other capital gains or losses since it began operations. What is Baker's total taxable income for Year 1?

a. $46,000
b. $42,000
c. $40,500
d. $38,500 (11/95, AR, #7, amended, 5751)

14. Which of the following sales should be reported as a capital gain?

a. Sale of equipment
b. Real property subdivided and sold by a dealer
c. Sale of inventory
d. Government bonds sold by an individual investor

(R/06, REG, A0561T, #12, 8182)

15. Lee qualified as head of a household for tax purposes. Lee's Year 1 taxable income was $100,000, exclusive of capital gains and losses. Lee had a net long-term loss of $8,000 in Year 1. What amount of this capital loss can Lee offset against Year 1 ordinary income?

a. $0
b. $3,000
c. $4,000
d. $8,000 (11/92, PII, #15, amended, 3349)

16. Capital assets include which **two** of the following?

a. A corporation's accounts receivable from the sale of its inventory
b. Seven-year MACRS property used in a corporation's trade or business
c. A manufacturing company's investment in U.S. Treasury bonds
d. An individual's corporate securities held for investment
e. A corporate real estate developer's unimproved land that is to be subdivided to build homes, which will be sold to customers

(11/95, AR, #6, amended, 5750)

17. In Year 4, Bach sold a painting for $50,000 purchased for his personal use in Year 1 at a cost of $20,000. In Bach's Year 4 income tax return, the sale of the painting should be treated as a transaction resulting in
a. No taxable gain
b. Section 1231 (capital gain–ordinary loss rule) gain
c. Long-term capital gain
d. Ordinary income
(R/03, REG, 0051T, #1, amended, 7643)

18. On January 2, Year 3, Bates Corp. purchased and placed into service 7-year MACRS tangible property costing $100,000. On December 31, Year 5, Bates sold the property for $102,000, after having taken $47,525 in MACRS depreciation deductions. What amount of the gain should Bates recapture as ordinary income?
a. $0
b. $ 2,000
c. $47,525
d. $49,525 (11/94, AR, #34, amended, 5011)

19. The following information pertains to installment sales of personal-use property made by Carl Woode in his retail furniture store.

Year of sale	Installment sales	Gross profit	Collections in Year 3
1	$100,000	$ 30,000	$20,000
2	150,000	60,000	60,000
3	200,000	100,000	80,000

These sales were **not** under a revolving credit plan. Under the installment method, Woode should report a gross profit for Year 3 of
a. $ 70,000
b. $100,000
c. $160,000
d. $260,000 (Editors, 1624)

20. Among which of the following related parties are losses from sales and exchanges **not** recognized for tax purposes?
a. Father-in-law and son-in-law
b. Brother-in-law and sister-in-law
c. Grandfather and granddaughter
d. Ancestors, lineal descendants, and all in-laws
(11/92, PII, #18, 3352)

Items 21 and 22 are based on the following:

Conner purchased 300 shares of Zinco stock for $30,000 in Year 3. On May 23, Year 5, Conner sold all the stock to his daughter Alice for $20,000, its then fair market value. Conner realized no other gain or loss during Year 3. On July 26, Year 5, Alice sold the 300 shares of Zinco for $25,000.

21. What amount of the loss from the sale of Zinco stock can Conner deduct in Year 3?
a. $0
b. $ 3,000
c. $ 5,000
d. $10,000 (5/95, AR, #3, amended, 5421)

22. What was Alice's recognized gain or loss on her sale?
a. $5,000 long-term loss
b. $5,000 long-term gain
c. $5,000 short-term loss
d. $0 (5/95, AR, #4, amended, 5422)

23. Wright exchanged investment real property, with an adjusted basis of $80,000 and subject to a mortgage of $35,000, and received from Lloyd $15,000 cash and other investment real property having a fair market value of $125,000. Lloyd assumed the mortgage. What is Wright's recognized gain in the year of exchange on the exchange?
a. $15,000
b. $35,000
c. $45,000
d. $50,000 (Editors, 8038)

24. Kelly is single with no dependents. In Year 4, Kelly's principal residence was sold for the net amount of $400,000 after all selling expenses. Kelly bought the house in Year 1 and occupied it until sold. On the date of sale, the house had a basis of $80,000. What is the maximum exclusion of gain on the sale of the residence that may be claimed on Kelly's Year 4 income tax return?
a. $320,000
b. $250,000
c. $125,000
d. $0 (Editors, 3342)

25. An office building owned by Bob Elin was condemned by the state on January 2, Year 0. Bob received the condemnation award on March 1, Year 1. In order to qualify for nonrecognition of gain on this involuntary conversion, what is the last date for Bob to acquire qualified replacement property?
a. August 1, Year 2
b. January 2, Year 3
c. March 1, Year 4
d. December 31, Year 4 (Editors, 8036)

26. Smith, an individual calendar-year taxpayer, purchased 100 shares of Core Co. common stock for $15,000 on December 15, Year 1, and an additional 100 shares for $13,000 on December 30, Year 1. On January 3, Year 2, Smith sold the shares purchased on December 15, Year 1, for $13,000. What amount of loss from the sale of Core's stock is deductible on Smith's Year 1 and Year 2 income tax returns?

	Year 1	*Year 2*
a.	$0	$0
b.	$0	$2,000
c.	$1,000	$1,000
d.	$2,000	$0

(11/93, PII, #25, amended, 4454)

27. Jackson, a single individual, inherited Bean Corp. common stock from Jackson's parents. Bean is a qualified small business corporation under Code Sec. 1244. The stock cost Jackson's parents $20,000 and had a fair market value of $25,000 at the parents' date of death. During the year, Bean declared bankruptcy and Jackson was informed that the stock was worthless. What amount may Jackson deduct as an ordinary loss in the current year?

a. $0
b. $ 3,000
c. $20,000
d. $25,000 (R/02, AR, #16, 7081)

28. Which of the following acts constitute(s) grounds for a tax preparer penalty?

I. Without the taxpayer's consent, the tax preparer disclosed taxpayer income tax return information under an order from a state court.
II. At the taxpayer's suggestion, the tax preparer deducted the expenses of the taxpayer's personal domestic help as a business expense on the taxpayer's individual tax return.

a. I only
b. II only
c. Both I and II
d. Neither I nor II (R/00, AR, #10, 6915)

29. In evaluating the hierarchy of authority in tax law, which of the following carries the greatest authoritative value for tax planning of transactions?

a. Internal Revenue Code
b. IRS regulations
c. Tax court decisions
d. IRS agents' reports

(R/06, REG, C00315R, #15, 8185)

30. Which one of the following will result in an accruable expense for an accrual-basis taxpayer?

a. An invoice dated prior to year end but the repair completed after year end
b. A repair completed prior to year end but **not** invoiced
c. A repair completed prior to year end and paid upon completion
d. A signed contract for repair work to be done and the work is to be completed at a later date

(R/06, REG, C01393R, #18, 8188)

Problem 43-2 ADDITIONAL MULTIPLE CHOICE QUESTIONS (47 to 62 minutes)

31. Smith made a gift of property to Thompson. Smith's basis in the property was $1,200. The fair market value at the time of the gift was $1,400. Thompson sold the property for $2,500. What was the amount of Thompson's gain on the disposition?
a. $0
b. $1,100
c. $1,300
d. $2,500 (R/02, AR, #22, 7087)

32. Farr made a gift of stock to her child, Pat. At the date of gift, Farr's stock basis was $10,000 and the stock's fair market value was $15,000. No gift taxes were paid. What is Pat's basis in the stock for computing gain?
a. $0
b. $ 5,000
c. $10,000
d. $15,000 (R/05, REG, 1075T, #19, 7865)

33. Hall was bequeathed 500 shares of common stock under his father's will. Hall's father had paid $2,500 for the stock ten years ago. Fair market value of the stock on February 1, Year 1, the date of his father's death, was $4,000 and had increased to $5,500 six months later. The executor of the estate elected the alternate valuation date for estate tax purposes. Hall sold the stock for $4,500 on June 1, Year 1, the date that the executor distributed the stock to him. How much income should Hall include in his individual income tax return for the inheritance of the 500 shares of stock which he received from his father's estate?
a. $5,500
b. $4,000
c. $2,500
d. $0 (5/94, AR, #32, amended, 4637)

34. On June 1, Year 1, Ben Rork sold 500 shares of Kul Corp. stock. Rork had received this stock on May 1 as a bequest from the estate of his uncle, who died on March 1, Year 1. Rork's basis was determined by reference to the stock's fair market value on March 1, Year 1. Rork's holding period for this stock was
a. Short-term
b. Long-term
c. Short-term if sold at a gain; long-term if sold at a loss
d. Long-term if sold at a gain; short-term if sold at a loss (5/89, PII, #52, amended, 1618)

35. In October, Browne, a self-employed taxpayer, had business net income of $900,000 prior to any expense deduction for equipment purchases. Browne purchased and placed into service, for business use, office machinery costing $600,000. This was Browne's only capital expenditure during this year—a year with a maximum allowable Section 179 amount of $250,000 and a ceiling of $800,000 of qualifying property. Browne's business establishment was not in an economically distressed area. Browne elected out of bonus depreciation. Browne made a proper and timely expense election to deduct the maximum amount. Browne was not a member of any pass-through entity. What is Browne's deduction under the Section 179 election?
a. $ 25,000
b. $250,000
c. $300,000
d. $600,000 (5/95, AR, #2, amended, 5420)

36. Dove Corp. began operating a hardware store in the current year after constructing a building at a total cost of $100,000 on land previously acquired for $50,000. In the current year, the land had a fair market value of $60,000. Dove paid real estate taxes of $5,000 in the current year. What is the total depreciable basis of Dove's business property?
a. $100,000
b. $150,000
c. $155,000
d. $160,000 (R/05, REG, 1169T, #14, 7880)

37. Starr, a self-employed individual, purchased a piece of equipment for use in Starr's business. The costs associated with the acquisition of the equipment were:

Purchase price	$55,000
Delivery charges	725
Installation fees	300
Sales tax	3,400

What is the depreciable basis of the equipment?
a. $55,000
b. $58,400
c. $59,125
d. $59,425 (R/06, REG, 1264T, #27, 8197)

38. Rock Crab, Inc. purchases the following assets during the year:

Computer	$ 3,000
Computer desk	1,000
Office furniture	4,000
Delivery van	25,000

What should be reported as the cost basis for MACRS five-year property?
a. $ 3,000
b. $25,000
c. $28,000
d. $33,000 (R/07, REG, C03310R, #36, 8460)

39. Platt owns land that is operated as a parking lot. A shed was erected on the lot for the related transactions with customers. With regard to capital assets and Section 1231 assets, how should these assets be classified?

	Land	*Shed*
a.	Capital	Capital
b.	Section 1231	Capital
c.	Capital	Section 1231
d.	Section 1231	Section 1231

(11/92, PII, #17, 3351)

Items 40 and 41 are based on the following:

Martin, an unmarried physical therapist, had the following capital gains and losses in Year 3 and Year 4.

	Year 3	Year 4
Net short-term gain (loss)	($4,500)	$500
Net long-term gain (loss)	$ 500	($900)

40. What is the capital loss amount that can be carried over to Year 4?
a. $ 900
b. $1,000
c. $3,000
d. $4,500 (Editors, 7709)

41. What amount of capital loss can Martin deduct against ordinary income on his Year 4 income tax return?
a. $ 500
b. $ 900
c. $1,400
d. $3,000 (Editors, 7600)

42. An individual had the following capital gains and losses for the year:

Short-term capital loss	$70,000
Long-term gain (unrecaptured §1250 at 25%)	56,000
Collectibles gain (28% rate)	10,000
Long-term gain (15% rate)	20,000

What will be the net gain(loss) reported by the individual and at what applicable tax rate(s)?
a. Long-term gain of $16,000 at the 15% rate
b. Short-term loss of $3,000 at the ordinary rate and long-term capital gain of $86,000 at the 15% rate
c. Long-term capital gain of $3,000 at the 15% rate, collectibles gain of $10,000 at the 28% rate, and Section 1250 gain of $56,000 at the 25% rate
d. Short-term loss of $3,000 at the ordinary rate, long-term capital gain of $10,000 at the 15% rate, collectibles gain of $10,000 at the 28% rate, and Section 1250 gain of $56,000 at the 25% rate (R/07, REG, C03328R, #37, 8461)

43. Archer Corp. sold machinery for $40,000 on December 31, Year 4. This machinery was purchased on January 2, Year 1, for $34,000, and had an adjusted basis of $20,000 at the date of sale. For Year 4, Archer should report
a. Ordinary income of $6,000 and §1231 gain of $14,000
b. Ordinary income of $14,000 and §1231 gain of $6,000
c. Ordinary income of $20,000
d. §1231 gain of $20,000 (Editors, 8037)

44. Gibson purchased stock with a fair market value of $14,000 from Gibson's adult child for $12,000. The child's cost basis in the stock at the date of sale was $16,000. Gibson sold the same stock to an unrelated party for $18,000. What is Gibson's recognized gain from the sale?
a. $0
b. $2,000
c. $4,000
d. $6,000 (R/07, REG, 1291T, #9, 8433)

45. Leker exchanged a truck that was used exclusively for business and had an adjusted tax basis of $20,000 for a new truck. The new truck had a fair market value of $10,000, and Leker also received $3,000 in cash. What was Leker's tax basis in the acquired truck?
a. $20,000
b. $17,000
c. $13,000
d. $ 7,000 (5/98, AR, #1, amended, 6638)

46. Patty Leave owned an apartment house for ten years. Depreciation was taken on a straight-line basis. When Patty's adjusted basis for this property was $300,000, she traded it for an office building having a fair market value of $700,000. The apartment house has 100 dwelling units, while the office building has 40 units rented to business enterprises. The properties are not located in the same city. What is Patty's reportable gain on this exchange?

a. $400,000 Section 1250 gain
b. $400,000 Section 1231 gain
c. $400,000 long-term capital gain
d. $0 (Editors, 1630)

47. The following information pertains to the sale of the Bran's former principal residence:

Year of sale	Year 17
Year of purchase	Year 7
Net sales price	$750,000
Adjusted basis	$ 70,000

John and Marcy Bran (both age 70) are married. The Brans purchased and occupied the home until it was sold. What is the maximum exclusion of gain on the sale of the residence that may be claimed on Bran's income tax return?

a. $125,000
b. $250,000
c. $500,000
d. $680,000 (Editors, 1617)

48. Taylor owns 1,000 shares of Media Corporation common stock with a basis of $22,000 and a fair market value of $33,000. Media paid a nontaxable 10% common stock dividend. What is the basis for each share of Media common stock owned by Taylor after receipt of the dividend?

a. $20
b. $22
c. $30
d. $33 (R/07, REG, 1191T, #7, 8431)

49. Allen owns 100 shares of Prime Corp., a publicly-traded company, which Allen purchased on January 1, Year 1, for $10,000. On January 1, Year 3 Prime declared a 2-for-1 stock split when the fair market value (FMV) of the stock was $120 per share. Immediately following the split, the FMV of Prime stock was $62 per share. On February 1, Year 3 Allen had his broker specifically sell the 100 shares of Prime stock received in the split when the FMV of the stock was $65 per share. What amount should Allen recognize as long-term capital gain income on his Form 1040, *U.S. Individual Income Tax Return,* for Year 3?

a. $ 300
b. $ 750
c. $1,500
d. $2,000 (R/05, REG, 0803T, #11, amended, 7877)

50. For a cash basis taxpayer, gain or loss on a year-end sale of listed stock arises on the

a. Date of delivery of stock certificate
b. Settlement date
c. Date of receipt of cash proceeds
d. Trade date (5/91, PII, #21, amended, 1610)

51. Wallace purchased 500 shares of Kingpin, Inc., 15 years ago for $25,000. Wallace has worked as an owner/employee and owned 40% of the company throughout this time. This year, Kingpin, which is not an S corporation, redeemed 100% of Wallace's stock for $200,000. What is the treatment and amount of income or gain that Wallace should report?

a. $0
b. $175,000 long-term capital gain
c. $175,000 ordinary income
d. $200,000 long-term capital gain (R/06, REG, A0073T, #10, 8180)

52. Which one of the following statements is correct with regard to an individual taxpayer who has elected to amortize the premium on a bond that yields taxable interest?

a. The amortization is treated as an itemized deduction.
b. The amortization is **not** treated as a reduction of taxable income.
c. The bond's basis is reduced by the amortization.
d. The bond's basis is increased by the amortization. (11/90, PII, #34, 1615)

53. A tax return preparer is subject to a penalty for knowingly or recklessly disclosing corporate tax return information, if the disclosure is made

a. To enable a third party to solicit business from the taxpayer
b. To enable the tax processor to electronically compute the taxpayer's liability
c. For peer review
d. Under an administrative order by a state agency that registers tax return preparers (11/94, AR, #55, 5031)

54. Which, if any, of the following could result in penalties against an income tax return preparer?

I. Knowing or reckless disclosure or use of tax information obtained in preparing a return
II. A willful attempt to understate any client's tax liability on a return or claim for refund

a. Neither I nor II
b. I only
c. II only
d. Both I and II (5/94, AR, #20, 4625)

55. Morgan, a sole practitioner CPA, prepares individual and corporate income tax returns. What documentation is Morgan required to retain concerning each return prepared?

a. An unrelated party compliance statement
b. Taxpayer's name and identification number or a copy of the tax return
c. Workpapers associated with the preparation of each tax return
d. A power of attorney (11/97, AR, #11, 6539)

56. To avoid tax return preparer penalties for a return's understated tax liability due to an intentional disregard of the regulations, which of the following actions must a tax preparer take?

a. Audit the taxpayer's corresponding business operations
b. Review the accuracy of the taxpayer's books and records
c. Make reasonable inquiries if the taxpayer's information is incomplete
d. Examine the taxpayer's supporting documents (11/98, AR, #20, 6686)

57. Vee Corp. retained Water, CPA, to prepare its Year 8 income tax return. During the engagement, Water discovered that Vee had failed to file its Year 4 income tax return. What is Water's professional responsibility regarding Vee's unfiled Year 4 income tax return?

a. Prepare Vee's Year 4 income tax return and submit it to the IRS
b. Advise Vee that the Year 4 income tax return has not been filed and recommend that Vee ignore filing its Year 4 return since the statute of limitations has passed
c. Advise the IRS that Vee's Year 4 income tax return has not been filed
d. Consider withdrawing from preparation of Vee's Year 8 income tax return until the error is corrected (R/99, AR, #15, amended, 6804)

58. A husband and wife can file a joint return even if

a. The spouses have different tax years, provided that both spouses are alive at the end of the year.
b. The spouses have different accounting methods.
c. Either spouse was a nonresident alien at any time during the tax year, provided that at least one spouse makes the proper election.
d. They were divorced before the end of the tax year. (5/91, PII, #33, 1560)

59. Which of the following is correct concerning the LIFO method (as compared to the FIFO method) in a period when prices are rising?

a. Deferred tax and cost of goods sold are lower.
b. Current tax liability and ending inventory are higher.
c. Current tax liability is lower and ending inventory is higher.
d. Current tax liability is lower and cost of goods sold is higher. (R/06, REG, 1746T, #30, 8200)

60. Which of the following entities may adopt any tax year end?

a. C corporation
b. S corporation
c. Limited liability company
d. Trust (R/06, REG, A1120T, #36, 8206)

61. Under the uniform capitalization rules applicable to taxpayers with property acquired for resale, which of the following costs should be capitalized with respect to inventory if no exceptions have been met?

	Repackaging costs	*Off-site storage costs*
a.	Yes	Yes
b.	Yes	No
c.	No	Yes
d.	No	No

(R/07, REG, 0361T, #39, 8463)

SIMULATIONS

Problem 43-3 (20 to 30 minutes)

Harrison was involved in several transactions during the year relating to the sale or exchange of property throughout the year. She asked her CPA to review the transactions to determine any tax deductions, gain recognition, or gain deferment that would result from them.

In Year 5, Harrison sold a painting to an unrelated party for $60,000, with three equal payments to be received over a three-year period. The painting had an adjusted basis of $6,000. Harrison used the painting in her home; she is not a dealer in paintings. (Editors, 8549)

1. In Year 5, Harrison sold land used in her business for $10,000 cash and the buyer assumed a $25,000 mortgage on the land. Harrison purchased the land in Year 0 for $18,000.

2. In January, Year 3, Harrison purchase and placed into service a painting costing $1,000. In December, Year 5, Harrison sold the painting for $10,000 after having taken $475 in MACRS depreciation deductions.

3. Harrison received a gift of property during the year. The donor's basis in the property on the date of the gift was $12,000. The fair market value at the time of the gift was $14,000. Harrison subsequently sold the property for $25,000.

4. Harrison's land with a fair market value of $50,000 and a basis of $30,000 has a mortgage of $12,000 against it. Mayfair will assume Harrison's mortgage of $12,000 and give her land with a fair market value of $38,000.

Question	Amount
1. What is the amount of the gain realized from the sale of land used in the business?	
2. What amount of gain from the painting sale is treated as ordinary gain?	
3. What amount of gain from the painting sale is treated as long-term capital gain?	
4. What is the amount of Harrison's gain on the disposition of the gift?	
5. What is the deferred gain from the sale of land with a fair market value of $50,000?	

Write a memo to Harrison regarding the use of the installment method to report the gain on the sale of the painting.

Scenario	Transactions	Communication	Research

Research Question: What code section and subsection, if applicable, provides guidance on a loss that resulted from the sale of stock, where it appears the taxpayer purchased substantially identical stock beginning 30 days before and ending 30 days after the date of the sale, that would be deductible if the taxpayer were a dealer in stock and the loss resulted from a transaction made in the ordinary course of business?

Section & Subsection Answer: §_____ (___)

Problem 43-4 (20 to 30 minutes)

Dixon, CPA, is a sole practitioner who prepares tax returns for clients.

John and Ellen Wright are married and file a joint return. As John is terminally ill, he is interested in selling their home before he dies so that the most gain may be excluded from taxable income. With the sale proceeds, the Wrights plan to buy a similar house in the same area. House prices and liquidity in the region are not expected to change significantly in the next four years. (11/96, AR, #2, amended, 6309)

Items 1 through 8 each represent an independent factual situation in which Dixon, CPA, has prepared and signed the taxpayer's income tax return. For each item, select from the following list the correct response regarding Dixon's responsibilities. A response may be selected once, more than once, or not at all.

Result of Action Taken

P. Dixon's action constitutes an act of tax preparer misconduct subject to the Internal Revenue Code penalty.

E. The Internal Revenue Service will examine the facts and circumstances to determine whether the reasonable cause exception applies; the good faith exception applies; or both exceptions apply.

N. Dixon's action does not constitute an act of tax preparer misconduct.

Situation	Answer
1. Dixon disclosed taxpayer income tax return information under an order from a state court, without the taxpayer's consent.	
2. Dixon relied on the advice of an advisory preparer to calculate the taxpayer's tax liability. Dixon believed that the advisory preparer was competent and that the advice was reasonable. Based on the advice, the taxpayer had understated income tax liability.	
3. Dixon did not charge a separate fee for the tax return preparation and paid the taxpayer the refund shown on the tax return less a discount. Dixon negotiated the actual refund check for the tax preparer's own account after receiving power of attorney from the taxpayer.	
4. Dixon relied on information provided by the taxpayer regarding deductible travel expenses. Dixon believed that the taxpayer's information was correct but inquired about the existence of the travel expense records. Dixon was satisfied by the taxpayer's representations that the taxpayer had adequate records for the deduction. Based on this information, the income tax liability was understated.	
5. The taxpayer provided Dixon with a detailed check register to compute business expenses. Dixon knowingly overstated the expenses on the income tax return.	
6. Dixon disclosed taxpayer income tax return information during a quality review conducted by CPAs. Dixon maintained a record of the review.	
7. Dixon relied on incorrect instructions on an IRS tax form that were contrary to the regulations. Dixon was not aware of the regulations nor the IRS announcement pointing out the error. The understatement was immaterial as a result of the isolated error.	
8. Dixon used income tax return information without the taxpayer's consent to solicit additional business.	

John and Ellen Wright are considering selling their residence with an adjusted basis of $125,000 for a sale price of $650,000. John and Ellen Wright have lived in the house for the last fifteen years. All of the Wright's three children are adults and are living in their own homes. As a member of Dixon, CPA's staff, prepare a memo to John and Ellen Wright explaining the tax treatment of the sale before John's death, two years after John's death, and three years after John's death.

Scenario | Transactions | Communication | Research

Research Question: What code section and subsection, if applicable, provides guidance on the penalty assessed when an understatement of the income tax liability resulted from a willful attempt to understate the tax liability by an income tax return preparer?

Section & Subsection Answer: §______ (___)

Solution 43-1 MULTIPLE CHOICE ANSWERS

Adjusted Basis

1. (d) When mortgaged property is purchased, its basis is the cash paid, or FMV of other property given, the amount of any mortgage assumed, plus any other costs connected with the purchase.

Gift

2. (b) Since the fair market value of the gift on the date of the gift exceeds the donor's adjusted basis for the property on this date, the donor's adjusted basis will be used in all gain or loss situations. Since the donee's basis for the gift property is determined with reference to the adjusted basis of the property in the hands of the donor, the donee's holding period includes the donor's holding period [§1223(2)].

3. (a) Since the FMV of the gift on the date of the gift exceeds the donor's adjusted basis for the property on this date, the donor's adjusted basis of $10,000 will be used in all gain or loss situations. Ruth' s recognized gain is determined as follows.

Cash proceeds received	$ 13,000
Less: Adjusted basis of necklace to Ruth	(10,000)
Capital gain	$ 3,000

4. (a) The basis of inherited property is the value of the property on the date of death (or the alternate valuation date, if selected). The basis of a gift to the donee is the basis in the hands of the donor, adjusted for any gift tax paid. Boone's basis in the inherited stock was $100/share × 100 shares = $10,000. After the 2-for-1 split, Boone's basis was $10,000 / 200 shares = $50/share. When Boone gave half of the stock to Dixon, Dixon's basis in the 100 shares on June 1 was half of Boone's total basis, or 100 shares × $50/share = $5,000.

Inheritance

5. (a) Section 102(a) provides that gross income does not include the value of property acquired by gift, bequest, devise, or inheritance.

6. (c) Section 1014 provides that when the alternate valuation date is elected, the basis of property inherited by the decedent is equal to the value of the property as it is determined under §2032. Under §2032, the value of property distributed from the estate after the date of death, but before the alternate valuation date, is equal to the FMV on the date of distribution. Thus, Lois' basis in the stock is $9,000 (e.g., the stock's FMV on the date of distribution).

7. (c) Inherited property has a basis of the property's fair market value on the date of the decedent's death or, if elected, the alternate valuation date, which is six months after death.

8. (b) Generally, life insurance proceeds (face value of the policy) paid by reason of death of the insured are excluded from gross income. When the life insurance policy subsequently is transferred in exchange for consideration, it is purchased asset. The sale or disposition of property generally results in the recognition of gain or loss. Thus, payments by reason of death of the insured are income to the assignee to the extent they exceed the consideration and premiums paid. In a taxable exchange, the gain or loss on the disposal of property generally is equal to the difference between the amount realized in the transaction and the adjusted basis of the property relinquished.

Insurance proceeds of transferred policy	$200,000
Less: Cost	(25,000)
Premiums paid	(40,000)
Included in gross income	$135,000

Cost Recovery

9. (c) In 2009, 7-year property is eligible for 50% bonus depreciation; bonus depreciation is calculated after the §179 deduction. The equipment constitutes §179 property under §179(d)(1) and §1245(a)(3). Section 179 property is tangible, depreciable personal property that is purchased for use in a trade or business. Section 179 authorizes a deduction for §179 property placed in service during the year, but limits this deduction to the maximum expense threshold. Additionally, §179(b)(3) limits this deduction to the net income from the active conduct of any trade or business before the §179 deduction. This taxpayer's deduction is not affected by this limit. Under §179(b)(2), this maximum is reduced by $1 for each $1 of §179 property placed in service during the year that exceeds the placed-in-service ceiling. This reduction does not apply in this case. [Editor's Note: In recently disclosed questions involving §179 calculations, the examiners provided the §179 amount.]

Equipment cost	$ 530,000	
Section 179 deduction	(250,000)	$250,000
Basis for bonus depreciation	$ 280,000	
Bonus depreciation ($280K x ½)	(140,000)	140,000
Basis for MACRS depreciation	$ 140,000	
First-year depreciation rate	14.29%	
MACRS depreciation		20,006
Maximum allowable deduction		$410,006

10. (c) In order to qualify for the Section 179 expense deduction, the property must be purchased for use in the taxpayer's active trade or business and it must be purchased from an unrelated party.

11. (c) Under §168(d)(3), if the aggregate basis of depreciable personal property placed in service during the last 3 months of the taxable year exceeds 40% of the aggregate basis of such property placed in service during the taxable year, then the taxpayer must use the mid-quarter convention for all such property placed in service during the year. In this case, the taxpayer purchased and placed into service 100% of depreciable personal property in the last 3 months of the taxable year. Because this percentage is greater than 40%, Data Corp. must use the mid-quarter convention in determining MACRS deductions with respect to the office equipment.

12. (d) Only the $234,000 allocated to the cost of the building ($264,000 – $30,000) is subject to cost recovery. The office building is nonresidential real property and is subject to a recovery period of 39 years under §168. Salvage value is disregarded. The mid-month convention must be used in determining the cost recovery deduction of real estate. Thus, the property is deemed to have been placed in service in the middle of August, leaving 4.5 months of cost recovery for the first tax year. The straight-line method of cost recovery must be used for nonresidential real property, as provided by §168(b)(3)(A). Therefore, the cost recovery deduction for the office building for the first tax year is $2,250 = [($234,000 / 39) × (4.5 / 12)].

Section 1231 & Capital Assets

13. (d) Section 1211(a) allows a corporation to deduct capital losses only against capital gains. However, corporations may offset a net long-term capital loss against a net short-term capital gain. Baker Corp. does not have a net capital loss, but rather has capital gain net income of $2,500 under §1222(9). The capital gains are included in gross income under §61(a)(3) and the capital losses are deducted from gross income under §165(f) up to the amount of capital gains under §1211(a).

Taxable income from regular operations			$36,000
Short-term capital gain	$ 8,500		
Short-term capital loss	(4,000)		
Net short-term capital gain		$4,500	
Long-term capital gain	$ 1,500		
Long-term capital loss	(3,500)		
Net long-term capital loss		(2,000)	
Net capital gain income			2,500
Taxable income			$38,500

14. (d) Section 1221 defines capital assets as property held by the taxpayer except for a number of items listed. Government bonds are not so listed. Section 1221(4) excludes accounts receivable from the sale of inventory from being treated as capital assets. Section 1221 excludes depreciable property used in a business and excludes inventory or property held primarily for sale to customers in the ordinary course of business from the definition of capital assets. Subdivided land sold by a dealer is inventory to the dealer.

15. (b) Individuals may use up to $3,000 of net capital losses per year to offset ordinary income. Any additional amounts may be carried forward for an unlimited amount of time until they are fully utilized.

16. (c, d) Both answers are required for full point value. Section 1221 defines capital assets as property held by the taxpayer except for a number of items listed. Section 1221(4) excludes accounts receivable from the sale of inventory from being treated as capital assets. Section 1221 excludes depreciable property used in a business and excludes inventory or property held primarily for sale to customers in the ordinary course of business from the definition of capital assets. Section 1237(a) provides that real property in the hands of a taxpayer other than a corporation shall not be treated as held primarily for sale to customers in the ordinary course of business, if certain conditions are met. The real estate developer holds the unimproved land to be subdivided to build homes to be sold to customers. Therefore, the unimproved land does not qualify for the exception provided by §1237(a) and is not a capital asset under §1221(1). Investments in stock or bonds are not excluded from the definition of capital assets in §1221.

17. (c) The painting is considered a capital asset because it does not fall within one of the five categories that would exclude it from being a capital asset under §1221. The sale of the painting is taxable as it was sold for an amount that was greater than its basis. The painting is not §1231 property because it was not depreciable property used in the taxpayer's trade or business. Nor is the painting ordinary income property because it was not held primarily for sale to customers in the ordinary course of the business.

18. (c) On a sale of depreciable personal property, ordinary income under §1245 is generally equal to the lesser of (1) the total gain realized or (2) the accumulated depreciation. Section 1231 treats any remaining gain as a §1231 gain, which is not ordinary income under §64. The §1245 gain and the remaining §1231 gain are computed as follows.

Amount realized		$102,000
Cost	$100,000	
Less: Accum. depreciation	(47,525)	
Less: Adjusted basis		(52,475)
Gain realized		$ 49,525
Sec. 1245 (ordinary) gain (lesser of $49,525 or $47,525)		$ 47,525
Sec. 1231 (capital) gain		2,000
Total gain realized		$ 49,525

Installment Sales

19. (b) A dealer in real estate or a merchant selling personal property can no longer use the installment sales method for tax purposes. Woode is a merchant selling personal property; therefore, he must report the full amount of gross profit, $100,000.

Related Party Transactions

20. (c) In-laws are not related parties. Ancestors and lineal descendants are related parties.

21. (a) Conner realizes a $10,000 loss ($20,000 – $30,000) under §1001(a). Because the sale was to a related party, none of the loss is recognized. Section 267(a)(1) disallows the deduction of any loss on the sale or exchange of property between certain related parties, as defined in §267(b). Section 267(b)(1) includes members of a family, as defined in §267(c)(4), as related parties. Section 267(c)(4) includes brothers, sisters, spouse, ancestors and lineal descendants as family members who are related parties under §267. None of Conner's loss may be recognized, notwithstanding the fact that the sale was for the stock's fair market value.

22. (d) Alice acquired a cost basis of $20,000 in the stock under §1012. When Alice sells the stock for $25,000, she realizes a $5,000 gain ($25,000 – $20,000) under §1001(a). Usually, all of this gain would be recognized under §1001(c). However, §267(d) provides any loss not recognized under the provision of §267(a)(1) because it was a related party loss, may be used to offset gain recognized on a subsequent sale by the related party purchaser. The previously disallowed loss may not be used to create or add to a loss on a subsequent sale by the related party purchaser. Therefore, Alice may use $5,000 of the $10,000 previously disallowed loss to Conner when Alice bought the stock to completely eliminate her recognized gain. The $5,000 remainder of the previously disallowed loss is lost forever.

Exchanges

23. (d) In a like-kind exchange under §1031, the taxpayer is required to recognize gain in an amount equal to the lesser of (1) the realized gain or (2) the amount of money and/or other property (e.g., boot) received in the exchange. Liabilities assumed by the other party are treated as boot received by the taxpayer. Therefore, the net reduction in the taxpayer's mortgage indebtedness is treated as money or other property received [Reg. §1.1031(d)-2]. In this problem, Wright realized a gain of $95,000 ($15,000 cash + $125,000 FMV of property received + $35,000 reduction in indebtedness – $80,000 adjusted basis of property exchanged). However, only $50,000 of gain is recognized because of the receipt of money or other property ($15,000 cash + $35,000 reduction in mortgage indebtedness).

Sale of Home

24. (b) A single taxpayer may exclude up to $250,000 of gain from the sale of a principal residence provided the taxpayer occupied the home in two of the five preceding years. The exclusion may be applied once every two years.

Involuntary Conversions

25. (d) Section 1033(a)(2) provides that in order to qualify for nonrecognition of gain, a taxpayer, in the case of an involuntary conversion into money, has to acquire qualified replacement property within 2 years after the close of the first taxable year in which any part of the gain upon conversion is realized. Section 1033(g)(4) extends this period another year in the case of a condemnation of real property held for productive use in a trade or business or for investment. Part of the gain was first realized on March 31, Year 1. Thus, the taxpayer has until 3 years from the close of Year 1 (e.g., until December 31, Year 4), to replace the condemned office building.

Securities

26. (a) Smith realized a loss of $2,000 ($13,000 – $15,000) under §1001(a) on the sale of the 100 shares bought on December 15. However, none of this loss is recognized in Year 1 because no loss was realized in Year 1. The loss is not recognized in Year 2, either, under the wash sale provisions (§1091). Smith bought 100 identical shares on December 30, Year 1, which is within 30 days on either side of the date of sale. The unrecognized loss adds to the basis of the 100 shares bought on December 30, Year 1. The basis of the 100 shares bought on December 30, Year 1, is $15,000 ($13,000 + $2,000).

27. (a) When investments in a small business investment company become worthless, §1244

allows for an ordinary rather than a capital loss deduction. Qualified small business stock must be acquired by the taxpayer at the original issuance in exchange for money, other property (not stock), or as compensation for services provided to the corporation. Thus, Jackson cannot take an ordinary deduction for the worthless stock, but would be entitled to a long-term capital loss of $25,000 (his basis in the stock at the time of the inheritance).

Preparer Responsibilities

28. (b) A preparer properly discloses information without the taxpayer's consent under a court order, for a peer review, for processing purposes, or under an order from a state agency that registers tax return preparers. A preparer may be liable for a penalty if the return reflects an understatement of tax liability based on a position that does not have a realistic chance of being sustained on its merits.

29. (a) IRS regulation and agents get their authority from the internal revenue code (IRC). While court decisions may overturn the IRC, they generally are issued too late for planning purposes.

Tax Procedures

30. (b) The accrual basis of accounting recognizes expenses in the period incurred. If the work is not done, the expense is not incurred yet. Expenses are not accrued after they already are paid. Candidates with concerns regarding the placement of this question in the REG, rather than the FAR, exam section should contact the AICPA.

Solution 43-2 ADDITIONAL MULTIPLE CHOICE ANSWERS

Gift

31. (c) If the property is acquired by gift, then the basis to the donee is determined at the time of disposal. When the property is later disposed of in a taxable transaction at a loss, then the basis used to compute the loss is the lower of the property's fair market value at the date of the gift or the adjusted basis to the donor. When the property is later disposed of in a taxable transaction at a gain, then the basis used to determine the gain is the property's adjusted basis in the hands of the donor. When the property is later disposed of in a taxable transaction at a price between the fair market value at the date of the gift and the adjusted basis of the property in the hands of the donor, and the fair market value of the property at the date of the gift was less than the adjusted basis to the donor, then no gain or loss is recognized on the disposition. Since the fair market value of the gift on the date of the gift exceeds the donor's adjusted basis for the property on this date, the donor's adjusted basis of $1,200 will be used in all gain or loss situations. Thompson's recognized gain is determined as follows.

Cash proceeds received	$ 2,500
Less: Adjusted basis to Thompson	(1,200)
Capital gain	$ 1,300

32. (c) The stock basis for computing gain of property received as a gift is the property's adjusted basis in the hands of the donor.

Inheritance

33. (d) Inheritances are excluded from taxable income. For Hall to have taxable income, the stock must be sold at a gain. In general, §1014 provides that the basis of property acquired from a decedent shall be its fair market value as of the date of the decedent's death. However, §1014 provides an exception if the executor elects under §2032 to use the alternative valuation date. In such a case, §1014 provides that the basis of property acquired from a decedent shall be its value at the applicable valuation date under §2032. Section 2032 provides that if the executor elects the alternative valuation date, the basis of property distributed within 6 months of the decedent's death shall be its value as of the date of distribution. Section 2032 states that under the alternative valuation date, the value of property not distributed within 6 months of the decedent's death shall be its value as of the date 6 months after the decedent's death. In this case, Hall received the property within 6 months of the decedent's death. Thus, Hall's basis is the $4,500 value of the property as of the date of distribution. He sold the property immediately for $4,500. The amount realized of $4,500 less his basis of $4,500 results in zero recognized gain under §1001.

34. (b) Property acquired from a decedent is automatically considered to have been held for more than the requisite long-term holding period under §1223. Thus, Rork's holding period will be long-term.

Cost Recovery

35. (b) The equipment constitutes §179 property under §179(d)(1) and §1245(a)(3). Section 179 property is tangible, depreciable personal property that is purchased for use in a trade or business. Section 179 authorizes a deduction for §179 property placed in service during the year, but limits the deduction to a maximum expense threshold. Section 179(b)(3) limits this deduction to the net income from the active conduct of any trade or business before the §179 deduction. Browne's deduction is not affected by this limit. Under §179(b)(2), the maximum deduction is reduced by $1 for each $1 of §179 property placed in service during the year that exceeds the placed in-service ceiling. As the maximum threshold is $250,000 and the ceiling is $800,000, this reduction does not apply in this case. The basis for the §179 deduction is $250,000.

36. (a) A depreciation deduction is allowed for the exhaustion of property used in a business or held for production of income. The basis of property in a taxable transaction is generally equal to the cost or purchase price of the property. Only the $100,000 cost of the building is subject to cost recovery, because depreciation is not allowed on the land.

37. (d) The depreciable basis of property includes the costs necessary to put the equipment in a condition and location for use.

38. (c) MACRS divides personal property into six classes. The 5-year class includes automobiles, light trucks, and computers. The 7-year class includes office furniture and office equipment. $3,000 + $25,000 = $28,000

Section 1231 & Capital Assets

39. (d) Section 1231 assets are land or depreciable assets that are used in a trade or business. Both the parking lot and the shed qualify as §1231 assets.

40. (b) Martin's net capital loss carryover for Year 4 is determined as follows.

Net short-term loss for Year 3	$ (4,500)
Net long-term gain for Year 3	500
Capital loss for Year 3	$ (4,000)
Maximum amount of ordinary income that may be offset by capital losses	3,000
Net short-term capital loss carried over to Year 4	$ (1,000)

41. (c) Martin's total amount deductible from ordinary income in Year 4 is determined as follows.

Year 4 net short-term gain	$ 500
Year 3 net short-term capital loss carryover	(1,000)
Net short-term capital loss	$ (500)
Year 4 net long-term capital loss	(900)
Amount deductible from ordinary income Year 4	$ (1,400)

42. (a) Losses offset all of the unrecaptured Section 1250 gain and the collectibles gain as well as part of the 15%-rate long-term gain. $56,000 + $10,000 + $20,000 – $70,000 = $16,000

43. (b) Section 1245(a)(1) provides that upon the sale of depreciable business property (other than depreciable real property), the seller must recapture as ordinary income an amount equal to the lesser of (1) the realized gain on the sale or (2) the depreciation claimed over the life of the property, *notwithstanding any other income tax provision.* Section 1231 governs the tax treatment of gains and losses from the sale or exchange of property used in a trade or business. The machinery was sold for a realized gain of $20,000 ($40,000 sales price less $20,000 adjusted basis). Up to the time of sale, $14,000 of depreciation had been claimed on the machinery. Thus, $14,000 is recognized as ordinary income under §1245. The remaining $6,000 of gain is treated as §1231 gain.

Related Party Transactions

44. (b) Gibson's $6,000 gain ($18,000 – $12,000) on the sale is partially offset by the $4,000 loss ($16,000 – $12,000) incurred by Gibson's child. $6,000 – $4,000 = $2,000

Exchanges

45. (b) The basis in the new truck is the basis in the assets surrendered less the fair market value of the boot. ($20,000 – $3,000)

46. (d) Under §1031, no gain or loss is recognized on like-kind exchanges of property. To qualify as a like-kind exchange, the properties must be of "a similar nature or character"; the grade or quality of the properties is not important in this determination. Since both properties involved realty that was held for investment, the exchange would come within §1031, and Patty would report no gain.

Sale of Home

47. (c) Married taxpayers may exclude up to $500,000 of gain from the sale of a personal residence provided they occupied the home in two of the five preceding years. This exclusion may be applied once every two years. As $750,000 – $70,000 = $680,000, the Brans may take the full exclusion.

Securities

48. (a) Generally, stock dividends are tax free to the shareholder; however, tax-free distributions reduce the shareholder's per-share basis in the stock, as the basis is spread over more shares. $22,000 / (1,000 shares + 100 shares) = $20

49. (c) Stock splits are issued mainly to reduce the unit market price per share of the stock, in order to obtain a wider distribution (ARB 43). Stock splits increase the number of shares outstanding and proportionately decrease the par or stated value of the stock. Before the stock split, Dole had 100 shares of stock valued at $10,000 ($100 / share). After the stock split, Dole has 200 shares of stock valued at $10,000 ($50 / share). Therefore, the basis of the 100 shares of stock sold is $5,000 (100 shares × $50 / share).

Sale proceeds (100 shares × $65 / share)	$ 6,500
Basis of stock (100 shares × $50 / share)	(5,000)
Gain recognized	$ 1,500

50. (d) The trade date (e.g., the date the broker completes the transaction on the stock exchange) is the date of sale. The holding period for the stock sold ends with the trade date. The settlement date—the date the cash or other property is paid to the seller of the stock—is not relevant in determining the date of sale. The date of delivery of the stock certificate is also not relevant in determining the date of sale.

51. (b) A capital gain results from the sale or exchange of a capital asset. As the asset was held for more than 12 months, the gain is long term. The purchase price is subtracted from the selling price to determine the amount of the gain. $200,000 – $25,000 = $175,000.

52. (c) Amortization of the bond premium reduces the basis of that bond. The amount of the amortized premium on taxable bonds is permitted as an interest deduction and is considered a recovery of the cost or basis of the bond. For bonds purchased after 1987, the premium amortization is an offset to the interest income.

Preparer Responsibilities

53. (a) Section 6713 authorizes a civil penalty and §7216 authorizes a criminal penalty for the unauthorized disclosure by a tax preparer of information furnished to the preparer by a taxpayer. Reg. §301.7216-2(o) allows disclosure for the purpose of a quality or peer review. Reg. §301.7216-2(c) allows disclosure pursuant to an administrative order by a state agency that registers tax return preparers. Reg. §301.7216-2(h) allows disclosure for the purpose of processing the tax return, including electronic filing. Disclosure for the purpose of enabling a third party to solicit from the taxpayer is not an exception to the general prohibition.

54. (d) Section 7216(a) prohibits a tax preparer from disclosing or using, for a purpose unrelated to the preparation of the taxpayer's tax return, information provided to him in connection with the preparation of any such return. A preparer who is guilty of such a violation is subject to a penalty of $1,000 and/or 1 year imprisonment, plus the costs of prosecution. Section 6694(b) provides a penalty of $1,000 for any tax preparer who willfully attempts to understate any client's tax liability.

55. (b) The tax return preparer must keep a copy of the return or a list of taxpayer names, identification numbers, and tax years for three years following the close of the return period.

56. (c) A preparer generally may rely in good faith without verification upon information furnished by a taxpayer. The preparer is not required to audit, examine, or review the taxpayer's records or operations. The preparer must make reasonable inquiries if the furnished information appears to be incorrect or incomplete.

57. (d) Section 7216(a) prohibits a tax preparer from disclosing, for a purpose unrelated to the preparation of the taxpayer's tax return, information provided in connection with the preparation of such return.

Tax Procedures

58. (b) The same accounting method does not have to be used by both husband and wife. For example, if the husband regularly uses the accrual method, and the wife the cash basis, each one computes her/his own income according to the appropriate accounting method, and the amounts so determined are aggregated for the purposes of the joint return. In order to file a joint return, the taxable years of both spouses must begin and end on the same day. As indicated in §6013(g), one spouse may be a nonresident alien, but *both* must make the election which subjects their worldwide income to U.S. taxation. Only married couples may file joint returns, and marital status is determined as of the last day of the taxable year.

59. (d) LIFO expenses the most recently purchased inventory; FIFO expenses the oldest inventory. In a period of rising prices, the cost of goods sold will be higher with LIFO than with FIFO, resulting in lower ending inventory, current income, and current income tax liability. Candidates with concerns regarding the placement of this question in the REG, rather than the FAR, exam section should contact the AICPA.

60. (a) A corporation has the most flexibility with regard to its tax year end. An S corporation must adopt a calendar year or a fiscal year that is the same as the fiscal year used by shareholders owning more than 50% of the stock. A limited liability company (LLC) with more than one member generally is treated as a partnership for federal tax purposes; a partnership generally has the same tax year as that of its partners owning a majority interest. Most trusts must adopt a calendar year.

61. (a) The costs to purchase, assemble, produce, and store inventory are included among the costs to capitalize. In the case of property purchased for resale, a taxpayer is exempt from the uniform capitalization rules (UNICAP), if its average gross receipts for the preceding three years are $10 million or less.

PERFORMANCE BY SUBTOPICS

Each category below parallels a subtopic covered in Chapter 43. Record the number and percentage of questions you correctly answered in each subtopic area.

Adjusted Basis

Question #	Correct √
1	
# Questions	1
# Correct	______
% Correct	______

Gift

Question #	Correct √
2	
3	
4	
# Questions	3
# Correct	______
% Correct	______

Inheritance

Question #	Correct √
5	
6	
7	
8	
# Questions	4
# Correct	______
% Correct	______

Cost Recovery

Question #	Correct √
9	
10	
11	
12	
# Questions	4
# Correct	______
% Correct	______

Section 1231 & Capital Assets

Question #	Correct √
13	
14	
15	
16	
17	
18	
# Questions	6
# Correct	______
% Correct	______

Installment Sales

Question #	Correct √
19	
# Questions	1
# Correct	______
% Correct	______

Related Party Transactions

Question #	Correct √
20	
21	
22	
# Questions	3
# Correct	______
% Correct	______

Exchanges

Question #	Correct √
23	
# Questions	1
# Correct	______
% Correct	______

Sale of Home

Question #	Correct √
24	
# Questions	1
# Correct	______
% Correct	______

Involuntary Conversions

Question #	Correct √
25	
# Questions	1
# Correct	______
% Correct	______

Securities

Question #	Correct √
26	
27	
# Questions	2
# Correct	______
% Correct	______

Preparer Responsibilities

Question #	Correct √
28	
29	
# Questions	2
# Correct	______
% Correct	______

Tax Procedures

Question #	Correct √
30	
# Questions	1
# Correct	______
% Correct	______

SIMULATION SOLUTIONS

Solution 43-3 Sale or Exchange of Property

Transactions (4 points)

1. $17,000

In a taxable exchange, the gain or loss on the disposal of property is equal to the difference between the amount realized in the transaction and the adjusted basis of the property relinquished. The amount realized is the sum of money received, the fair value of property received, and the amount of liability relieved.

Cash received	$ 10,000
Debt relieved	25,000
Amount realized	$ 35,000
Less: Adjusted basis	(18,000)
Harrison's realized gain	$ 17,000

2. $475

On a sale of depreciable personal property, ordinary income under §1245 is generally equal to the lesser of (1) the total gain realized or (2) the accumulated depreciation. Section 1231 treats any remaining gain as a §1231 gain, which is not ordinary income under §64. The §1245 gain and the remaining §1231 gain are computed as follows.

Amount realized		$ 10,000
Cost	$ 1,000	
Less: Accum. depreciation	(475)	
Less: Adjusted basis		(525)
Total gain realized		$ 9,475
Sec. 1245 (ordinary) gain (lesser of $9,475 or $475)		$ 475
Sec. 1231 (capital) gain		9,000
Total gain realized		$ 9,475

3. $9,000

See the explanation to item #2.

4. $13,000

If the property is acquired by gift, then the basis to the donee is determined at the time of disposal. When the property is later disposed of in a taxable transaction at a loss, then the basis used to compute the loss is the lower of the property's fair market value at the date of the gift or the adjusted basis to the donor. When the property is later disposed of in a taxable transaction at a gain, then the basis used to determine the gain is the property's adjusted basis in the hands of the donor. When the property is later disposed of in a taxable transaction at a price between the fair market value at the date of the gift and the adjusted basis of the property in the hands of the donor, and the fair market value of the property at the date of the gift was less than the adjusted basis to the donor, then no gain or loss is recognized on the disposition. Since the fair market value of the gift on the date of the gift exceeds the donor's adjusted basis for the property on this date, the donor's adjusted basis of $12,000 will be used in all gain or loss situations. Harrison's recognized gain is determined as follows.

Cash proceeds received	$ 25,000
Less: Adjusted basis to Harrison	(12,000)
Capital gain	$ 13,000

5. $8,000

A like-kind exchange is an exchange of property of the same nature or character. No gain or loss is recognized on a like-kind exchange of property held for productive use in a trade or business or for investment, if the property received is either held for productive use in a trade or business or for investment. If boot (money or other non-like-kind property) is received as part of the like-kind exchange, gain is recognized to the extent of the lesser of the gain realized or the boot received. The deferred gain on the sale of the land is calculated as follows.

FMV of new land received	$ 38,000
Debt relief	12,000
Amount realized	$ 50,000
Less: Basis of old land	(30,000)
Gain realized	$ 20,000
Gain recognized (capital gain)	(12,000)
Gain deferred	$ 8,000

Communication (5 points)

April 10, Year 6

To: Ms. Harrison
From: Irma Preparer
Re: Installment Sale of Painting

The installment method of recognizing gain may be used when payments are received in **more than one tax year** by a seller who is **not a dealer** in the type of property being sold.

The amount of gain recognized in a particular year is computed by multiplying the **payments received** in that year by the **gross profit percentage.** The gross profit percentage is the anticipated **total gross profit** divided by the **total contract price.**

The sale of your painting **meets these criteria:** you do not deal in paintings and the contract provides for three equal payments over a three-year period. If collections proceed according to the contract, you will recognize **gain** of **$18,000** in each of the **three years.**

Research (1 point)

Code Section Answer: §1091(a)

Code §1091(a) states, "In the case of any loss claimed to have been sustained from any sale or other disposition of shares of stock or securities where it appears that, within a period beginning 30 days before the date of such sale or disposition and ending 30 days after such date, the taxpayer has acquired (by purchase or by an exchange on which the entire amount of gain or loss was recognized by law), or has entered into a contract or option so to acquire, substantially identical stock or securities, then no deduction shall be allowed under section 165 unless the taxpayer is a dealer in stock or securities and the loss is sustained in a transaction made in the ordinary course of such business."

Solution 43-4 Preparer Responsibility

Situations (4 points)

1. N

A court order is an appropriate exception to the confidentially provisions per §6103(d).

2. E

A return preparer may be liable for a $250 penalty if the return reflects an understatement of tax liability based on a position that does not have a realistic chance of being sustained. Other preparers are not generally considered substantial authorities. This situation probably would call for more investigation.

3. P

A tax return preparer may not negotiate a client's refund check.

4. N

Section 6604 imposes a penalty on any income tax return preparer who willfully attempts to understate a taxpayer's liability for tax. However, a preparer may generally rely in good faith without verification upon information furnished by the taxpayer.

5. P

Section 6604 imposes a penalty on any income tax return preparer who willfully attempts to understate a taxpayer's liability for tax.

6. N

Reg. §301.7216-20 allows disclosure for the purpose of a quality or peer review.

7. E

The preparer is responsible for preparing the return correctly, regardless of instructions on the form. The preparer may be liable for a $1,000 penalty if the understatement is willful or due to the preparer's intentional disregard of a rule or regulation.

8. P

Section 7216(a) prohibits a tax preparer from disclosing or using, for a purpose unrelated to the preparation of the taxpayer's return, information provides in connection with tax return preparation.

Communication (5 points)

To: John and Ellen Wright
From: Dixon, CPA
Re: Sale of Home

As you expect to sell your home for $650,000 and the adjusted basis of this home at the time of sale would be $125,000, you would have a **gain** of $525,000.

Exclusion of gain is available provided the taxpayer(s) owned and occupied the home as a **principal residence** in **two** of the **five** years **immediately preceding** the sale. Your outlined plans meet these criteria. The rest of this memo assumes these ownership and occupancy criteria for exclusion are met.

Married taxpayers are able to exclude up to **$500,000** of this gain. That is, if the home is sold before John's death, only $25,000 of the projected gain would be taxable. Even if the house is sold after John's death but in the same tax year as John's death, the full $500,000 exclusion is available.

Starting in 2008, a **widow**ed taxpayer may exclude up to $500,000 in the **two years** following the deceased spouse's death. Thus, as long as the home is sold within two years of the last day of the tax year after John's death, assuming the same gain, the same amount of gain would be taxed.

If the home is sold three years after John's death, the tax treatment is less favorable. Generally, an **unmarried** taxpayer may exclude up to **$250,000** of the gain from the sale of a home. In this case, $250,000 of the $525,000 expected gain would be excluded from gross income and $275,000 would be included in gross (taxable) income.

This exclusion may be claimed as **frequently as once every two years.** Use of this exclusion now does **not preclude** the use of **another** $250,000 exclusion, provided that taxpayer meets the criteria for that other residence.

Bear in mind, this memo assumes that the law and the circumstances do not change. This memo is provided only with the understanding that there is no obligation to communicate subsequent developments.

Research (1 point)

Code Section Answer: §6694(b)

Code §6694(b) states, "If any part of any understatement of liability with respect to any return or claim for refund is due to a willful attempt in any manner to understate the liability for tax by a person who is an income tax return preparer with respect to such return or claim, or to any reckless or intentional disregard of rules or regulations by any such person, such person shall pay a penalty of $1,000 with respect to such return or claim."

CHANGE ALERT

The *American Recovery & Reinvestment Act of 2009* (ARRA '09) became law on February 17, 2009, which made it first eligible to be tested in the **October-November 2009** exam window.

The *Emergency Economic Stabilization Act of 2008* (EESA '08) became law on law on October 3, 2008, which made it first eligible to be tested in the **July-August 2009** exam window.

These changes are integrated into this and other chapters, to the extent they are within the scope of the CPA exam.

STUDY TIP: MEMORIZING TAX AMOUNTS

Specific tax numbers candidates may want to commit to memory from the first two tax chapters are the residence gain exclusion amount, the amount of capital loss deductible on an individual's return, the tax-exempt employer-provided life insurance benefit amount, and the maximum amount of IRA contributions. A feel for the approximate amounts of most other numbers is more than adequate for the exam. Formerly, the Section 179 expense amount was tested; however, this was before it started being changed frequently.

Many tax amounts are included in the tax chapters more to forestall candidate curiosity than to provide information necessary for the upcoming exams. These amounts, particularly the inflation-adjusted ones, have been tested lightly on past exams and likely will remain so in the future. For exam purposes, it usually is not important to know the exact amount of standard deductions, the personal exemption amount, and phase-out ranges, for example. The examiners are more interested in testing whether candidates know that these items exist and how to apply them.

If you question this, review the questions in these chapters, which are from—or modeled after—previous exams. You will perceive the relative absence of the necessity to know specific amounts to answer most questions.

EXAM COVERAGE

Keep in mind that, per AICPA guidelines, candidates are responsible for knowledge of the Internal Revenue Code (IRC) and the Federal Tax Regulations in effect six months before the exam. In the past, the examiners have tested prior year amounts on the last half of the current year's exams, which deviates from their stated six-month policy. Generally, if the examiners ask questions involving inflation-adjusted amounts, these amounts are given in the questions. (As we go to press, many 2010 amounts are unknown. Updating supplements, if needed, will be available with applicable changes.)

CHAPTER 44

FEDERAL TAXATION: INDIVIDUALS

EXAM COVERAGE: The individual taxation portion of the Regulation section of the CPA exam is designated by the examiners to be 12-18 percent of the section's point value. More information about point distribution is included in the **Practical Advice** section of this volume.

CHAPTER 44

FEDERAL TAXATION: INDIVIDUALS

I. Introduction

A. Flow of Form 1040

To help you understand how an individual's tax liability is determined, presented below is a summary of the flow of the Individual Income Tax Return, Form 1040.

Step One: Determine Gross Income

1. Wages, salaries, tips
2. Interest (Schedule B)
3. Dividends (Schedule B)
4. Taxable refunds of state and local taxes
5. Alimony received
6. Business income (Schedule C)
7. Capital gain or loss (Schedule D)
8. Other gains or losses (Form 4797)
9. IRA distributions, pensions, and annuities
10. Rents, royalties, partnerships, S corporations, trusts, etc. (Schedule E)
11. Farm income (Schedule F)
12. Unemployment compensation
13. Social Security benefits
14. Other income (includes gambling winnings)

Step Two: Less Adjustments for Gross Income (Above-the-Line Deductions)

1. IRA deduction
2. Student loan interest deduction
3. Health savings account deduction
4. Moving expenses
5. One-half of self-employment tax
6. Self-employed health insurance
7. Self-employed SEP, SIMPLE, and qualified plans
8. Penalty for early withdrawal of savings
9. Alimony paid

Step Three: Equals Adjusted Gross Income (AGI)

Step Four: Less the Greater of the Standard Deduction Or Itemized Deductions (Schedule A)

1. Medical and dental expenses
2. Taxes paid
3. Interest paid
4. Charitable contributions
5. Casualty and theft losses
6. Miscellaneous expenses (includes unreimbursed employee expenses)

Step Five: Less Exemptions

Step Six: Equals Taxable Income

Step Seven: Determine Tentative Tax Liability

Step Eight: Less Credits

1. Child and dependent care
2. Credit for the elderly or the disabled
3. Foreign tax credit
4. Other credits (includes education, child, adoption, etc.)

Step Nine: Plus Additional Taxes

1. Self-employment tax
2. Alternative minimum tax
3. Recapture taxes
4. Social Security tax on tip income
5. Tax on qualified retirement plans

Step Ten: Less Payments

1. Federal income tax withheld
2. Estimated tax payments
3. Overpayment applied to current year liability
4. Earned income credit
5. Amount paid with extension (Form 4868)
6. Excess FICA
7. Other payments

Step Eleven: Equals Amount Overpaid Or Balance Due

B. Exemptions

Each taxpayer may be entitled to an exemption for her/himself, her/his spouse, and for each dependent. For 2009, each exemption is $3,650.

1. Personal Exemption Each taxpayer is entitled to an exemption for her/himself, unless s/he can be claimed as a dependent on another taxpayer's return.

- If a husband and wife file a joint return, neither one may be claimed as a dependent on another taxpayer's return unless they are filing a return only to obtain a recovery of all federal tax withheld or paid in.

2. Spousal Exemption The spousal exemption is **not** a dependency exemption. It is a personal exemption based on the marital relationship. Therefore, it is not subject to the support test for a dependency exemption.

a. If the taxpayer's spouse dies during the year, the taxpayer may still claim the spousal exemption for that year if s/he has not remarried.

b. If the taxpayers are divorced or legally separated at the end of the year, neither one may claim the other as an exemption.

c. A married spouse filing separately may take only one personal exemption, unless the other spouse is the filing spouse's dependent and has no gross income for the tax year.

3. Dependency Exemptions A taxpayer is allowed an exemption for each dependent [§151(c)]. A dependent cannot claim any dependents. Dependents are either qualifying children or qualifying relatives; these two classifications have separate eligibility standards. A child who is not a qualifying child may nevertheless be a qualifying relative.

a. **Uniform Definition of a Qualifying Child** The *Working Families Tax Relief Act of 2004* established a uniform definition for a qualifying child for several purposes, most notably the dependency exemption and filing status. In order to claim a person as a qualifying child, six tests must be satisfied.

(1) **Relationship** The child must be the taxpayer's child, step child, sibling, step sibling, half sibling, or a descendant of any such individual. A child of the taxpayer also includes an individual who is legally adopted or lawfully placed with the taxpayer for legal adoption as well as a foster child who is a member of the taxpayer's household for the entire year.

(2) **Residency** The child must have the same principal residence as the taxpayer for more than one-half of the tax year. Exceptions apply for children of divorced or separated parents and temporary absences due to illness, education, business, vacation, or military service.

(3) **Age** Generally a qualifying child must be (a) younger than the taxpayer and (b) under age 19, a full-time student under age 24, or a totally and permanently disabled person of any age. A student is enrolled full-time at an educational institution during five calendar months.

(4) **Support** The child does not provide more than one-half of her/his own support for the year. Scholarships are not included as support for this test.

(5) **Return Status** The child must not have filed a joint return. Spouses may be dependents of a third person and still file a joint return if neither spouse is required to file a return, there would be no gross tax liability if the couple filed separate returns, and the joint return was filed solely for a full refund (not for the payment of taxes).

(6) **Citizenship or Residence** The child must be a U.S. citizen or national, or a resident of the U.S., Canada or Mexico.

(7) **Tiebreaker Rules** If a child meets these tests for two or more taxpayers, the child will be a qualifying child of: (a) the parent; (b) if more than one taxpayer is the child's parent, then the parent with whom the child lived for the longest time during the year or, if the time is equal, the parent with the highest adjusted gross income; and (c) if no taxpayer is the child's parent, then the taxpayer with the highest adjusted gross income. The *Emergency Economic Stabilization Act of 2008* (EESA '08) permits a taxpayer to claim a child as a qualifying child, if that taxpayer's AGI is higher than the highest AGI of the child's parents and the parents can claim the child, but neither does.

b. **Uniform Definition of a Qualifying Relative** In order for a taxpayer to claim another person as a qualifying relative, five tests must be satisfied.

(1) **Gross Income** The person's (taxable) gross income must be less than the personal exemption amount for that tax year.

(2) **Support** The taxpayer provides over one-half of the person's total annual support.

(3) **Relationship or Household** The person is either a lineal descendant (child or grandchild), ancestor (parent or grandparent), or sibling of the taxpayer by whole or half blood, including father-, mother-, sisters- and brothers-in-law or the person is an unrelated individual who lives in the taxpayer's home for the entire taxable year. A person can be a member of the taxpayer's household and not live with her/him. For example, a person living in a nursing home for the entire year still may be a member of the taxpayer's household.

(4) **Return Status** The person must not have filed a joint return. However, spouses may be dependents of a third person and still file a joint return if neither spouse is required to file a return, there would be no gross tax liability if the couple filed separate returns, and the joint return was filed solely for a refund (not for the payment of taxes).

(5) **Citizenship or Residence** The person must be a U.S. citizen or national, or a resident of the U.S., Canada or Mexico.

4. **Phase-out** The exemption amounts are phased out by 2% for each $2,500, or portion thereof, by which the taxpayer's adjusted gross income exceeds the threshold amounts. The maximum reduction is at most 1/3 of the amount calculated before the reduction.

Exhibit 1 ▸ 2009 Exemption Phase-out Thresholds

Filing Status	Phase-out
Married Filing Jointly	$250,200
Single Individual	166,800
Head of Household	208,500
Married Filing Separately	125,100

5. **Multiple Support Agreement** A multiple support agreement is used when more than one taxpayer contributes to the support of someone who otherwise would be a *qualifying relative,* but no one person contributes more than 50% of the support. A taxpayer who meets all tests for the exemption except for the support test may claim an exemption if the others agree, as long as s/he contributes more than 10% of the individual's support and, collectively, the contributors provide more than 50% of the support. The agreement must be signed by all of the contributors and attached to the return of the taxpayer claiming the exemption.

C. **Filing Status**

The tax rate applicable to a taxpayer's taxable income depends on her/his filing status. The amount of a taxpayer's standard deduction also is influenced by filing status.

1. **Single (S)** Taxpayers who are not married or heads of households. Legally separated spouses who are living apart also are considered single, unless they qualify as head of household.

2. **Married Filing Jointly (MFJ)** This status is available to taxpayers who meet all of the following conditions:

   a. Married and not legally separated on the last day of the tax year. If the taxpayer's spouse died during the tax year, the surviving spouse may file a joint return with the deceased spouse for that year unless s/he remarries before the end of the year. If a marriage is annulled, the annulment is retroactive and, thus, both individuals must file amended returns as single taxpayers or head of household.

   b. Neither spouse was a nonresident alien at any time during the year. If one spouse was a nonresident alien, the couple can elect to file jointly by agreeing to be taxed on combined worldwide income.

   c. Both spouses' tax years begin on the same date. (They may have separate accounting methods (e.g., cash basis vs. accrual basis)

   d. Both spouses sign the return.

3. **Married Filing Separately (MFS)** Married individuals may elect to file separate returns. In a separate property state, each spouse must report her/his own income, deductions,

exemptions, and credits. In a community property state, each spouse is allocated 50% of the income, deductions, exemptions, and credits.

4. **Surviving Spouse (SS)** (Also known as Qualifying Widow[er].) If the surviving spouse remains unmarried and pays more than 50% to maintain a household that is the principal place of residence for the entire year of the taxpayer's child who qualifies as her/his dependent, s/he may use the joint return rates for two years after the death of her/his spouse.

5. **Head of Household (HH)** A person cannot qualify more than one taxpayer as HH for the same year. To qualify, all of the following must be met.

   a. The taxpayer must not be married at the end of the year or a surviving spouse.

   b. The taxpayer must pay more than 50% to maintain, as her/his home, a household that is the principal place of residence for more than 50% of the year for a qualifying child or qualifying relative for whom the taxpayer may claim a dependency exemption. A qualifying child is determined without regard to the exception for children of divorced or separated parents. Also, a qualifying child who is married at the end of the year must meet the nationality and marital status tests for the dependency exemption. Additionally, a taxpayer cannot claim the head of household status for a person who is a dependent only because s/he lived with the taxpayer for the whole year nor because the taxpayer can claim her/him as a dependent under a multiple support agreement.

      (1) A married taxpayer who files a separate return, has lived separately from her/his spouse, and does not claim an unmarried qualifying child as a dependent, but otherwise meets the qualifications for head of household may claim the head of household status.

      (2) The head of household status may be claimed with respect to a parent who does not live with the taxpayer, but for whom the taxpayer may claim a dependency exemption.

D. Filing Requirements

1. **General** Generally, an individual must file a tax return if her/his income is greater than the sum of her/his personal exemption plus the standard deduction for her/his filing status. The following individuals also are required to file.

   a. An individual who has net earnings from self-employment of $400 or more;

   b. An individual who can be claimed as a dependent on another taxpayer's return and has unearned income of $1 or more and gross income of $800 or more;

   c. Individuals who receive advance payments of the earned income credit; or

   d. Married individuals who file separately must file if their income is greater than their personal exemption.

2. **Due Date** An individual's tax return is due on or before the 15th day of the fourth month following the close of the year. For a calendar year taxpayer, the return is due on or before April 15th of the following year.

3. **Extension** An automatic six-month extension will be granted for a taxpayer who is unable to file her/his return by the due date. Any extension extends only the time to file. Therefore, to avoid penalty, the taxpayer must pay all taxes due by the 15th day of the fourth month following the close of the year.

4. **Assessment** Generally, all taxes must be assessed within three years after the later of the due date or the filing date. If the taxpayer omitted more than 25% when reporting her/his

gross income, this three-year period is extended to six years. In the case of fraud, there is no statute of limitations. A taxpayer must file to claim a refund by the later of three years from the time the return was filed or two years after the payment of tax. A return that is filed before the due date is treated as if it were filed on the due date. Individuals have the same deadlines when amending returns (Form 1040X).

II. Gross Income

A. Realization & Recognition

Gross income includes all income from whatever source derived, unless there is a specific exclusion provided by law. Gross income includes money, property, or services. Property and services received are included in gross income at their fair market values. Income is taxable when it is both realized and recognized by the taxpayer.

Example 1 ▸ Gross Income

> Sally, a real estate agent, closes a big deal and her employer compensates her by giving her a new BMW. The fair market value of that BMW is gross income to Sally, and it is a deductible trade or business expense for the employer.

1. **Constructive Receipt** A cash basis taxpayer is taxed on income once it is **constructively** received even though it may not be **actually** received. Constructive receipt occurs when the income is credited to the taxpayer or made available to her/him without any restrictions or substantial limitations.

2. **Income in Respect of a Decedent (IRD)** This income is included in either the decedent's final income tax return or the heir's return. Common examples are accrued salary (earned before death) and tax-deferred pension plans paid to heirs or beneficiaries.

B. Specific Exclusions From Gross Income

Income items that are not included in gross income and are not subject to income tax. Do not confuse an exclusion with a deduction. Generally, exclusions are not required to be shown on the tax return while deductions must be shown.

1. **Life Insurance** Generally, life insurance proceeds (the face amount of the policy) paid by reason of death of the insured are excluded from gross income.

   a. **Installment Options** If the beneficiary elects to receive the benefits in installments, the interest portion is includible in income.

   b. **Dividends** Dividends received that are considered a return of premiums paid are not included in income.

2. **Annuities** Annuities are excluded from gross income to the extent that they are a return of capital. Once the total amount of the investment has been recovered, all remaining payments are included in income. Additionally, if the recipient dies before completely recovering her/his investment, the unrecovered portion may be deducted on her/his final tax return as an itemized deduction. After 1996, taxpayers must use the "simplified" method to determine the excludable portion. The excludable portion under the "simplified" method is the investment in the annuity divided by the expected number of payments. The number of payments is set by Treasury Regulations based on age at time the annuity payments begin.

3. **Gifts, Bequests & Inheritances** Gifts, bequests, and inheritances are excluded from income. However, neither the income from nor gain on disposal of such property is excluded.

4. **Certain Prizes & Awards** Prizes and awards generally are included in gross income, unless the prize or award is received for religious, charitable, scientific, educational, artistic, literary, or civic achievement, and each of the following conditions are met.

a. The recipient is selected without any action on her/his part to enter the contest or proceeding.

b. The recipient is not required to render substantial future services as a condition for receiving the prize or award.

c. The prize or award is transferred by the payor to a governmental unit or charitable organization pursuant to the recipient's request.

5. **Scholarships & Fellowships** Gross income does not include amounts received as a qualified scholarship by an individual who is a candidate for a degree at an approved educational institution.

   a. A qualified scholarship is any amount that is used to pay for tuition, fees, books, supplies, and equipment. Amounts used for other purposes are included in gross income.

   b. Amounts that represent payment for teaching, research, or other services are not excludable from gross income.

6. **Gain on Sale of Principal Residence** A taxpayer may exclude a portion of the gain from gross income. (Additional details are in Chapter 43.)

7. **Personal Injury Awards** Amounts received for personal injury are not included in gross income. This rule applies to workers' compensation payments, damages received (except for punitive damages), accident and health insurance claims (except those attributable to employer contributions that were not income to the employee), and disability benefits. Holocaust restitution payments received are excluded from income as well as not taken into account for any calculation that picks up otherwise excludable gross income, such as Social Security benefits.

8. **Interest on Tax-Exempt Government Obligations** Gross income does not include interest on bonds issued by a state or any of its political subdivisions, the District of Columbia, and U.S. possessions. This exclusion does not apply to arbitrage bonds, hedge bonds, private activity bonds that are not qualified, pre-August 16, 1986 industrial development bonds, or U.S. Treasury Bonds.

9. **Social Security Benefits** Social Security benefits and other types of welfare payments are generally excluded from gross income. However, high-income taxpayers are subject to a two-tiered system that may result in 50% or 85% of the Social Security benefits being taxed.

   a. Provisional income is modified adjusted gross income (MAGI) plus one-half of the Social Security benefits. Modified adjusted gross income, for this purpose, equals adjusted gross income computed without regard to the foreign earned income, Social Security benefits, or deductions for student loan interest and qualified tuition expenses, and increased by tax-exempt interest income and any employer's adoption assistance.

   b. In years when provisional income exceeds the first base amount, the taxpayer must include in income, the lesser of one-half of the Social Security benefits or one-half of the amount, if any, by which the sum of the taxpayer's provisional income exceeds the base amount.

   c. In years when the provisional income exceeds a second base amount, gross income includes the lesser of (a) 85% of the Social Security benefit or (b) the sum of 85% of the excess of provisional income over the new threshold and the smaller of the amount that would otherwise be included under IRC §86(a)(1) or $4,500 for single taxpayers or $6,000 for married taxpayers filing jointly.

Exhibit 2 ▸ Taxable Social Security Benefits

Provisional Income MFJ	Provisional Income Single	MFS	Percentage of Benefits Taxed
$1 to $31,999	$1 to $24,999	None	0%
$32,000 to $43,999	$25,000 to $33,999	None	50%
$44,000 and above	$34,000 and above	$1 and above	85%

Example 2 ▸ Taxable Social Security Benefits

FYI: Example 2B is likely more in-depth than will be tested on the CPA exam.

A. Doug and Barbara are both 66 years old. Together they receive $8,100 of Social Security benefits for the calendar year. They have an adjusted gross income of $28,000 from employment, net rents, royalties, interest, and dividends. Additionally, they receive $4,200 of tax-exempt income from municipal bonds. They file jointly.

B. Steve and Nancy are both 66 years old. Together they receive $8,100 of Social Security benefits for the calendar year. They have an adjusted gross income of $46,000 from employment, net rents, royalties, interest, and dividends. Additionally, they receive $4,200 of tax-exempt income from municipal bonds. They file jointly.

	Example 2A	Example 2B
Adjusted Gross Income (AGI)	$ 28,000	$ 46,000
Tax-exempt income	4,200	4,200
Modified Adjusted Gross Income (MAGI)	$ 32,200	$ 50,200
50% of Soc. Sec. benefits ($8,100 × 50%)	4,050	4,050
Provisional income	$ 36,250	$ 54,250
Provisional income	$ 36,250	
Less: First base amount (MFJ)	(32,000)	
Excess over first base amount	$ 4,250	
First base rate (50%)	× 50%	
50% of excess over first base amount	$ 2,125	
Include in AGI (lower of two: $4,050 vs. $2,125)	$ 2,125	
Provisional income		$ 54,250
Less: Second base amount (MFJ)		(44,000)
Excess over second base amount		$ 10,250
Second base rate (85%)		× 85%
85% of excess over second base amount		$ 8,713
Lesser of 50% of Soc. Sec. benefits or $6,000 (MFJ)		4,050
Adjusted 85% of excess over second base amount		$ 12,763
Soc. Sec. benefits		8,100
Second base rate (85%)		× 85%
Include in AGI (lesser of two: $6,885 vs. $12,763)		$ 6,885

10. **Property Settlements** Property transfers from an individual to a spouse or a former spouse incidental to a divorce are nontaxable transactions. A transfer is incident to a divorce if it occurs within one year after the marriage ends or is related to the ending of the marriage.

11. **Child Support** Payments made that are specifically designated as child support by the terms of the divorce instrument are not included as income by the recipient and are nondeductible by the payor. Additionally, any reductions in alimony that are related to a **contingency** involving the child (such as age 18 or marriage) will cause the amount of the reduction to be treated as child support for tax purposes. Furthermore, if the divorce decree specifies that a fixed amount of the payment is for child support, and the payor pays less than the total amount of the payment, then the payment is treated as child support to the extent of this designated amount.

Example 3 ▸ Child Support

Harold pays Winnona $400 in alimony per month under the terms of a divorce decree. The terms of the decree also provide that the amount is to be reduced to $300 in the event that David, the child of Harold and Winnona, marries, reaches age 21, or dies.

Alimony payments received by a taxpayer are includible in the gross income of the recipient and deductible by the payor. Winnona must include $300 (while she is receiving the entire $400) in her gross income, and Harold is entitled to a $300 deduction. The remaining $100 is deemed child support and it is not deductible by Harold nor is it considered income to Winnona (or to David).

Example 4 ▸ Child Support

Per the terms of a divorce agreement, Howard is required to pay $200 a month for the full year to his former wife Wilma, $100 of which is for the support of their minor children. If Howard only pays Wilma $200 a month for 9 months ($1,800), then $1,200 ($100 × 12 months) is considered to be child support. The remaining $600 is treated as alimony.

12. **Employee Benefits** Certain fringe benefits are excluded from an employee's income.

a. **Fringe Benefits** Fringe benefits are excluded from gross income if

(1) No additional cost service (e.g., free stand-by flights to airline employees)

(2) Qualified employee discounts (e.g., employee discounts on employer goods or services)

(3) Working condition fringe benefit (e.g., use of company car for employer business)

(4) *De minimis* (minimal) fringe benefit (e.g., use of the employer's copy machine for personal business)

b **Group Term Life Insurance** Premiums paid by the employer for up to $50,000 worth of insurance coverage is excluded.

c. **Accident & Health Plans** Premiums paid by an employer are excluded if they compensate the employee for the following:

(1) Loss of earnings due to personal injuries and illness (benefits are includible); however, if the employer contributions to the plan are included in the employee's income, then the benefits would be excluded.

(2) Reimbursement of medical care expenses for employee, spouse, or dependents. (The employee cannot take an itemized deduction for these expenses.)

(3) Permanent injury or loss of bodily function.

d. **Meals or Lodging** Meals or lodging furnished for the convenience of the employer on the employer's premises are excluded.

e. **Dependent Care Services** Employer-provided dependent care services are excluded if they are pursuant to a written, nondiscriminatory plan. The amount excludable is limited to $5,000 per year ($2,500 for married individuals filing separate tax returns).

f. **Educational Assistance Programs** Payments of up to $5,250 per year for undergraduate and graduate-level tuition, fees, books, etc., may be excluded.

g. **Workers' Compensation** Workers' compensation is excluded if received for an occupational sickness or injury and paid under a workers' compensation act or statute. The American Recovery & Reinvestment Act of 2009 (ARRA '09) excludes $2,400 of unemployment benefits received in 2009 from taxable income. Editor's Note: This temporary exclusion is scheduled to lapse after 2009.

h. **Qualified Adoption Expenses** The limitations, restrictions, and phase-out amounts for the credit are equally applicable to the exclusion of expenses paid by employers.

i. **Parking Fringe Benefit** A taxpayer may exclude up to $230 (for 2009) for employer-provided parking from taxable compensation, even if a cash option is offered. If the taxpayer elects to take the cash, it is taxable compensation. Alternatively, the same amount of employer-provided transit benefits (transit passes and pooling) may be excluded.

j. **Qualified Retirement Planning Services** Qualified retirement planning services are excluded from taxable compensation.

k. **Retirement Plans** A taxpayer excludes retirement benefits for both defined benefit and defined contribution plans from income in the year of service, because benefits are taxable when paid. Employers often match or partially match employee contributions. For defined benefit plans, employees may defer up to the lesser of $195,000 (for 2009) or 100% of average high three years' compensation [§415(b)]. For defined contribution plans, employees may defer up to the lesser of 25% of annual compensation or $49,000 (for 2009) for all annual additions (everything except earnings and gains) to all plans of the same employer [§415(c)].

(1) **Cash or Deferred Arrangements (CODA)** Under a §401(k), §403(b), §457, or SEP plan in 2009, employees may defer up to the lesser of 100% of annual compensation or $16,500 under any combination of deferred arrangement plans for all employers. Employees are allowed to make contributions to a separate account through the employer plan that are deemed Traditional IRAs or Roth IRAs (discussed later in this chapter) and not considered deferred compensation.

(2) **SIMPLE Plans (401(k) & IRAs)** All funds in SIMPLE plans are vested fully. Under a SIMPLE plan in 2009, employees may defer up to the lesser of $11,500 of elective contributions or 25% of annual compensation. Employers may match up to $11,500 or 3% of annual compensation.

(3) **Catch-Up Contributions** In 2009, participants of §401(k), §403(b), or §457 plans who are age 50 or older before the end of the plan year may defer up to an additional $5,500. Participants in SIMPLE plans may defer up to an additional $2,500. A special formula is used to ascertain the catch-up contributions are allowed in the last three years before retirement for participants in §457 plans.

(4) **Rollover Provisions** Participants or their surviving spouses with §401(k), §403(b), or §457 plans are allowed to rollover funds among these plans as well as IRAs. There are no provisions for tax-free rollover of after-tax amounts from an IRA.

13. **Savings Bonds** The interest income from qualified U.S. savings bonds, such as series EE, redeemed to finance qualified higher education costs for the taxpayer, spouse, or dependents is excluded. Qualified higher education costs include tuition and fees. To qualify, the taxpayer must be the sole owner of the bonds or a joint owner with her/his spouse. This exclusion is subject to a phase-out range above which no exclusion is allowed. For 2009, the phase-out ranges begin at $104,900 for married individuals filing a joint tax return and $69,950 for single individuals and heads of households.

14. **Survivor Annuity** The survivor annuity of a public safety officer killed on duty is tax-exempt to the deceased officer's spouse, ex-spouse, or child.

15. **Adoption Assistance** Amounts received by an adoptive parent under an adoption assistance agreement with a state pursuant to the *Adoption Assistance and Child Welfare Act of 1980* are not taxable income.

C. **Inclusions in Gross Income**
Gross income includes all items from whatever source derived except those items specifically excluded. This section discusses some of the more common income items included in gross income.

1. **Compensation** Including wages, salaries, fees, bonuses, commissions, tips, death benefits, and fringe benefits that do not qualify for statutory exclusions. If compensation is received in the form of property, then the amount included in gross income is the fair market value of the property received.

   a. **Jury Duty Pay** If an employee surrenders jury duty pay to her/his employer in exchange for receiving her/his salary during the time of jury service, then the payment for jury duty is deductible for adjusted gross income (AGI).

   b. **Reimbursed Employee Business Expenses** Employee business expenses that are reimbursed are deductible **for** AGI if the employer includes these reimbursements in the employee's gross income. Reimbursed employee expenses that are not included in the employee's gross income are not deductible from AGI. Any excess reimbursement by the employer must be included in gross income by the employee. Unreimbursed employee business expenses are only deductible from AGI as miscellaneous itemized deductions subject to the 2% floor and a 50% limitation on meal and entertainment expenses. Also, no deduction is allowed for any type of club dues.

Example 5 ▶ Reimbursed Travel Expenses

ABC Co. fully reimburses its employees for travel expenses, including transportation and accommodations and, in addition, provides a $20 daily allowance for meals and entertainment. In a recent 10-day trip, Joe, an ABC Co. employee, incurred the following expenses:

Airfare	$ 400
Hotel rooms	550
Rental car	150
Meals and entertainment	350
Total cost incurred	$1,450

ABC reimbursed Joe for $1,300 (the cost of the airfare, hotel, and car rental as detailed by Joe plus the maximum $20-per-day meal and entertainment allowance for 10 days). On his return, Joe will neither include in income nor deduct the $1,300 in reimbursed expenses subject to a detailed accounting. Of the remaining $150 ($350 – $200), Joe may deduct $75 ($150 × 50%), but only as a miscellaneous deduction subject to a 2% of AGI floor.

2. **Interest** Unless specifically exempt from tax, interest is taxable gross income. Examples of taxable interest include amounts received for certificates of deposit, corporate and U.S. government bonds, and imputed interest from below-market-rate and interest-free loans.

3. **Dividends** A distribution of money, securities, or other property by the corporation to its shareholders out of accumulated or current earnings and profits. Generally, dividends paid by most domestic or qualified foreign corporations are taxed at capital gain rates.

4. **Refunds** If a taxpayer obtains a refund for which s/he received a prior tax benefit (e.g., deduction), then this refund is included in gross income. A typical example would be a refund of state or local taxes paid by the taxpayer. Under the *Mortgage Forgiveness Debt Relief Act of 2007,* volunteer firefighter and emergency medical responders who receive a state and

local tax reduction or rebate due to their volunteer services may exclude up to $360 of such amount each year.

5. **Alimony** Alimony received is included in gross income.

   a. **Qualified Payments** To qualify as alimony, the payment must: (1) be made pursuant to a divorce or separate maintenance agreement, (2) consist of cash payments, (3) not be made to someone who lives in the same household at the time of the payment, (4) not continue after the death of the payee-spouse (e.g., to the payee's estate), and (5) not be designated as anything other than alimony (e.g., child support).

   b. **Recapture Rule** A three-year recapture rule applies to excess alimony payments to prevent property settlement payments from qualifying as alimony. Excess alimony is defined as the sum of the excess payments made in both the first and second post-separation year, and must be recaptured in the third post-separation year. The excess payments in the first year equal the amount that exceeds the average of the second year payments (minus any excess payments) and third year payments by more than $15,000. Similarly, the excess payments in the third year equal the amount that exceeds the average payments in the third year by more than $15,000. The recapture rules do not apply if the payments were terminated due to the death or remarriage of the payee-spouse.

Example 6 ▸ Recapture of Alimony

Henry and June were divorced in Year 1. Per the terms of the divorce agreement, Henry paid June $50,000 in Year 1, $30,000 in Year 2, and $10,000 in Year 3. How much does Henry need to recapture in Year 3?

Solution:

(1) Amount to recapture from Year 2 equals the amount paid in Year 2 ($30,000), that is in excess of the sum of the amount paid in Year 3 ($10,000) plus $15,000.

Recapture = $30,000 – ($10,000 + $15,000) = $5,000

(2) Amount to recapture from Year 3 equals the amount paid in Year 1 ($50,000) that exceeds the sum of the average amount paid in Year 2 ($30,000) less any recapture from Year 2 ($5,000) and the average amount paid in Year 3 ($10,000) plus $15,000.

$$\text{Recapture} = \$50{,}000 - \left(\frac{(\$30{,}000 - \$5{,}000 + \$10{,}000)}{2} + \$15{,}000\right)$$

$$= \$50{,}000 - \$32{,}500 = \$17{,}500$$

(3) Total recapture = $5,000 + $17,500 = $22,500

6. **Net Self-Employment Income** The gross income from an individual's trade or business less allowable deductions equals net self-employment income. These net earnings are included in the taxpayer's gross income and are subject to the self-employment tax. An unincorporated business jointly operated by a married couple exclusively may elect not to be treated as a partnership. Instead, each spouse reports her/his share of income, gain, expense, loss, etc. as a sole proprietor on Schedule C.

   a. Director's fees are self-employment income to the recipient.

   b. Some otherwise allowable deductions are not allowed because of the taxpayer's method of accounting. For example, a cash basis taxpayer is not allowed a bad debt expense from uncollectible account receivables because these receivables were not previously included in income.

7. **Capital Gains & Losses** A capital gain or loss occurs when a capital asset is sold or exchanged. Capital assets include all assets *except* the following: (a) inventory or other property held primarily for the sale to customers in the ordinary course of the taxpayer's trade or business, (b) a trade note or account receivable, (c) depreciable business property or real property used in the taxpayer's trade or business, and (d) a copyright; a literary, musical, or artistic composition; a letter, memorandum, or similar property held by the creator or one whose basis in the property is determined from the creator. (Capital gains and losses are covered more thoroughly in Chapter 43.)

   a. **Deductibility** Individuals may deduct capital losses to the extent of capital gains plus $3,000 per year. Any excess losses may be carried forward indefinitely. Personal gains (gains resulting from the disposal of assets acquired for personal use) are taxable, but personal losses are not deductible.

   b. **Taxation** Schedule D is used to ensure that the amount of income taxes paid on net capital gains does not exceed one of several capital gain rates that are lower than regular tax rates. (Generally, net capital gains realized are taxed at a maximum rate of 15%.)

8. **Unemployment Compensation** Unemployment compensation historically has been fully taxable. ARRA '09 excludes $2,400 of unemployment benefits received in 2009 from taxable income. Editor's Note: This temporary exclusion is scheduled to lapse after 2009.

9. **Gambling Winnings** Winnings from gambling are taxable. Gambling losses are deductible as an itemized deduction, but only to the extent of gambling winnings.

10. **Distributive Share of Partnership or S Corporation Income** Share of distributed income includes income that has not yet been distributed to the partner or shareholder.

11. **Income From the Discharge of Indebtedness** Income from the discharge of indebtedness is taxable **unless** the debt is discharged due to insolvency (and then only to the extent of forgiveness results in solvency) in a bankruptcy proceeding, the discharge is a gift, or a student loan is discharged because the individual fulfilled a service obligation. The *Mortgage Forgiveness Debt Relief Act of 2007* (MFDRA '07) excludes up to $2 million of discharge of indebtedness income from January 1, 2007, through December 31, 2009, related to debt incurred in the acquisition, construction, or substantial improvement of the principal residence that secured the debt. Qualified mortgage insurance premiums are allowed as qualified residential interest from January 1, 2007, to December 31, 2010, for contracts entered into during that period. EESA '08 extends the exclusion initiated by MFDRA '07 through 2012.

12. **Passive Activity Losses** A passive activity is a trade or business activity in which the taxpayer does not materially participate. In addition, all rental activities are deemed to be passive activities (except some real estate professionals). Generally, passive activity losses may be used only to offset passive activity income. In other words, they may not be deducted against ordinary (active) or portfolio (interest, dividends, etc.) income. Any passive activity losses that cannot be used in the current year are suspended and carried forward indefinitely until there is sufficient income from passive activities to absorb them. Any losses that remain suspended when the activity is sold in a taxable transaction may be deducted against both ordinary and portfolio income.

   a. **Rental Activity Exception** Up to $25,000 of losses from rental activities may be deducted against ordinary and portfolio income if the taxpayer actively participates in the activity. The individual must own at least a 10% interest in the activity to be considered an active participant for purposes of this exception. This exception is phased out for taxpayers whose AGI exceeds $100,000. The deduction is reduced by 50% of the AGI over the phase-out amount. Therefore, the deduction is zero when AGI reaches $150,000.

b. **Real Estate Professional Exception** Real estate professionals are able to offset nonpassive income with their rental real estate losses. A taxpayer is considered a real estate professional if more than one-half of the personal services performed by the taxpayer during the year are performed in real property businesses in which the taxpayer materially participates and the taxpayer also performs more than 750 hours of service during the tax year in the same real property business.

13. **Net Rents & Royalties** Rent and royalty income and expenses are reported on Schedule E. Rental and royalty payments, including nonrefundable deposits, premiums, and lease breaking payments are taxable in the period received, regardless of the taxpayer's basis of accounting.

- **Rental of Vacation Home** The deductibility of vacation home rental expenses depends on the allocation between the rental and personal use of the property.

  (1) If the property is rented for less than 15 days, no expenses are deductible except for those ordinarily deductible from AGI (mortgage interest, real estate taxes, and casualty loss expenses), and no rental income is includable in gross income.

  (2) If the property is rented for 15 or more days and is not used for personal purposes for (a) more than 14 days or (b) more than 10% of the number of days it was rented at a fair market value price, whichever is greater, then the property is treated as a rental and the expenses are deductible subject to the passive activity loss rules.

  (3) If the property is rented for 15 or more days but use exceeds the personal use test, then rental expenses are limited to the amount that gross income exceeds the deductions otherwise allowable such as mortgage interest and taxes.

III. Adjusted Gross Income (AGI)

A. Adjustment Overview

Adjustments are certain deductions taken from gross income to arrive at adjusted gross income (AGI). Therefore, these deductions are considered to be above-the-line deductions and AGI is "the line." Any one adjustment may be claimed without regard for the others. In addition, many limitations on below-the-line or itemized deductions and other phase-out amounts that reduce specified tax benefits are based on AGI.

1. **Self-Employed Health Insurance** A self-employed individual may deduct 100% of medical insurance for the taxpayer, spouse, and dependents. This deduction cannot be greater than the net self-employment earnings (self-employment earnings less one-half of the self-employment earnings tax). This deduction is not allowed for any individual who is eligible to participate in any subsidized health plan of an employer of either the individual or spouse.

2. **Educational Loan Interest** Interest on qualified educational loans is deductible, but subject to modified adjusted gross income (MAGI) thresholds. EESA '08 allows up to a $4,000 deduction for single taxpayers with AGI of $65,000 or less ($130,000 MFJ). EESA '08 allows up to a $2,000 deduction for single taxpayers with AGI of $80,000 or less ($160,000 MFJ). This temporary increase is scheduled to lapse after 2009.

   a. **Modified Adjusted Gross Income (MAGI)** Adjusted gross income increased by the following exclusions: foreign earned income, Social Security income, adoption assistance, and U.S. Savings Bonds used for education; as well as increased by the following adjustments: IRA contributions, passive losses, and educational loan interest.

   b. **Requirements** Married couples must file a joint return in order to claim the deduction. No deduction is allowed under this provision if a deduction is allowed under another provision (for instance, a home equity interest deduction). A dependent may not claim a deduction for educational loan interest.

c. **Qualified Education Loan** A loan incurred to pay qualified educational expenses (tuition, fees, books, room, and board reduced by scholarships, U.S. Savings Bond provisions, or state qualified tuition programs) for at least half-time attendance for the taxpayer, spouse, or dependents when the debt was incurred.

d. **AGI Impact** This adjustment does not impact the calculation of AGI for purposes of determining exclusions from income for Social Security, U.S. Savings Bond interest used to pay for education, adoption expenses, IRA contributions, and passive activity loss limitations.

3. **New Vehicle Sales Tax** ARRA '09 allow most buyers to deduct the state and local sales and excise taxes attributable to the first $49,500 of the purchase of new cars, motorcycles, and light trucks purchased between February 17, 2009, and December 31, 2009, as an above-the-line deduction. The deduction is phased out for single taxpayers with adjusted gross income of $125,000 ($250,000 for MFJ). This temporary increase is scheduled to lapse after 2009.

4. **Educator Expenses** EESA '08 allows educators to deduct up to $250 of eligible educator expenses. This temporary increase is scheduled to lapse after 2009.

B. **Individual Retirement Account (IRA)**
Taxpayers may contribute money to an IRA to defer income tax on IRA earnings. Individuals who are ineligible to deduct IRA contributions still may have the opportunity to defer income tax on IRA earnings.

1. **Contributions** Annual contributions can be split between all types of IRAs. Individuals who are 50 by the end of the tax year have the contribution limit increased by $1,000.

a. **Self** Any employee (not a self-employed individual) may contribute the lesser of the individual's earned income or $5,000 in 2009 to an IRA. If both spouses work, each may contribute the lesser of total earned income or the individual limit to an IRA. Alimony payments received are treated as earned income for purposes of determining how much an individual is allowed to contribute to an IRA.

b. **Spouse** A taxpayer with a nonworking spouse may set up a spousal IRA, with a combined contribution limit of the lesser of double the individual limit or earned income for the year. The total contribution may be allocated in any way between the two IRAs as long as no more than the individual limit is allocated to either one. Roth spousal IRAs may be established under the same rules as a traditional spousal IRA.

2. **Traditional IRA** Traditional IRAs are personal tax-advantaged retirement savings arrangements.

a. **Deductions** Contributions may be deductible for AGI depending on AGI before deductions for IRA contributions and participation in an employer-sponsored retirement plan. The term active participant generally includes individuals who are eligible to participate in an employer-sponsored plan, even if no amounts currently are being credited to the employee's account.

(1) **Non-Active Participant** If the taxpayer (and her/his spouse, if filing jointly) is not an active participant, contributions are deductible to the extent of the aforementioned limits.

(2) **Active Participants** Individuals who are active participants in a retirement plan still are able to deduct their contributions if their AGI (before deducting IRA contributions) is less than the phase-out amount. If they are in the phase-out range, they may deduct at least $400 of their contributions.

Exhibit 3 ▸ 2009 Active Participant IRA Phase-out Thresholds

Filing Status	AGI Before Deduction
Married Filing Jointly	$89,000 to $109,000
Single or Head of Household	$55,000 to $ 65,000
Married Filing Separately	$0 to $ 10,000

(3) **Spouse of an Active Participant** Spouses of active participants are able to deduct contributions if their AGI (before deducting IRA contributions) is less than a spousal phase-out range of $166,000 to $176,000, in 2009.

Example 7 ▸ Individual Retirement Accounts—Traditional

In 2008, Thomas earned $125,000 at Tall Corporation, where he is an active participant in the pension plan. Isabelle earned $1,500 from a part-time job at Fresh Florist where there is no pension plan. Thomas and Isabelle are each 45 years old.

Required: What is the maximum amount that may be contributed to Thomas' and Isabelle's individual retirement accounts and deducted from gross income?

Solution: As Thomas is an active participant in his employer's plan and Thomas and Isabelle have AGI greater than the phase-out range, none of his contribution is deductible. However, $5,000 may be contributed to an IRA for each person: $5,000 for Thomas based on his earned income and $5,000 for Isabelle under the non-working spouse provisions. As the AGI is less than $150,000, Isabelle's $5,000 contribution is fully deductible.

b. **Penalty** Early withdrawals (before age 59½) are subject to a 10% penalty tax, in addition to regular income tax, unless the withdrawal is due to participant's death, disability, or other special conditions. These special conditions include: (1) medical expenses in excess of 7.5% of AGI; (2) medical insurance by individuals who have received 12 consecutive weeks of unemployment compensation under federal or state law (including eligible self-employed individuals); (3) college tuition, fees, books, supplies, and equipment (plus room and board, if the student attends school on at least a half-time basis) for the taxpayer, spouse, or their child or grandchild; and (4) up to $10,000 used within 120 days to acquire a **first** home as the principal residence for the taxpayer, spouse, or any child, grandchild or ancestor of the taxpayer or spouse.

3. **Roth IRA** All Roth IRA contributions are nondeductible. Earnings of a Roth IRA are tax deferred and all qualified distributions are exempt from income tax. There is no age limit for contributions.

a. **Contribution Phase-out** The maximum Roth IRA contribution is phased out for taxpayers whose AGI exceeds a threshold (for 2009, single: $105,000; MFJ: $166,000; MFS: $0).

b. **Distributions** Qualified distributions are made at least **five** years after the first year an original contribution is made and the distribution is made on account of the participant reaching age 59½, participant's death or disability, or qualified first-time homebuyer expenses. The holding period begins with the related tax year, not the actual date of the contribution. Unqualified distributions are subject to a 10% excise tax in addition to the regular income tax.

c. **Conversions** A taxpayer with AGI of less than $100,000 (computed without regard to any amount that must be included in income as a result of the rollover) may roll over a traditional IRA (deductible or nondeductible) into a Roth IRA. The five-year holding period begins at the date of conversion.

C. **Health Savings Accounts (HSA)**
Tax-exempt trusts or custodial accounts that allow taxpayers to pay for or be reimbursed for certain medical expenses that occurred after the account has been established. Qualified medical expenses are those that qualify for the itemized medical expense deduction (discussed later in this chapter); however, taxpayers cannot take qualified medical expenses as an itemized deduction equal to the tax-free distribution from a HSA. The accrued interest and distributions for qualified medical expenses are not subject to tax; however, withdrawals made for other reasons are subject to tax and possibly 10% penalty.

1. **Eligibility** HSAs must be used in conjunction with a high-deductible health plan (HDHP). A HDHP has a higher annual deductible than typical health plans and a maximum limit on the sum of the annual deductible and out-of-pocket medical expenses. Eligible individuals cannot have other medical insurance coverage, be entitled to Medicare benefits, or be claimed as a dependent on another taxpayer's return. Other medical insurance does not include coverage for accidents, disability, dental care, vision care, long-term care, specific disease or illness, fixed amount per day of hospitalization, and benefits related to workers' compensation.

2. **Contributions** HSA contributions must be made in cash or through an employer cafeteria plan, and remain in the account until used. The allowable annual contribution depends on the type of HDHP coverage and the taxpayer's age. For 2008, taxpayers can contribute up to the amount of the health plan's annual deductible, but not more than $2,900 for individual coverage and $5,800 for family coverage. Current year contributions may be made up until April 15th of the following year. Excess contributions may be includible in gross income and subject to 6% excise tax.

   a. **Limitations** Eligible contributions to HSA established during the year are computed on a *pro rata* basis (reduced by one-twelfth for each full month the taxpayer did not have a HDHP). Eligible contributions also are reduced by the amount contributed to an Archer MSA (including employer contributions) and employer contributions to the HSA that were excluded from income.

   b. **Rollover** Contributions may be made from Archer MSAs and other HSAs. However, rollovers are not allowed from an IRA, health reimbursement arrangement, or flexible spending account.

3. **Archer Medical Savings Accounts (MSA)** Trust accounts (similar to IRAs) that may be established by a limited number of taxpayers. The details concerning MSAs are more complex than discussed here. (The editors expect exam coverage to be minimal because of the limited number of eligible participants.)

   a. **Eligibility** A self-employed individual or an employee of a small employer is eligible to establish an MSA. An individual must be covered under a high-deductible medical plan before s/he can establish an MSA, but may not be covered under another medical plan except: Medicare supplemental insurance; insurance for a specific disease; insurance that provides a fixed payment for hospitalization; or insurance under which the coverage relates primarily to worker's compensation, tort liability, or property liability (e.g., auto insurance).

   b. **Treatment** Within limits, amounts contributed to an MSA are deductible by an eligible individual and excludable from the employee's income if the contribution is made by the employer. Contributions are limited to 65% of the deductible of the taxpayer's high-deductible plan for single coverage and 75% for family coverage. Earnings of MSAs are nontaxable. Distributions from MSAs are not taxable, if made for medical expenses of an eligible individual. If not made for eligible medical expenses, a 15% excise tax is imposed, unless the payment is made after age 65 or on account of death or disability.

D. Moving Expenses
An employee or a self-employed individual may deduct moving expenses paid or incurred in connection with the commencement of work at a new principal place of employment.

1. **Distance Rule** The new place of work must be at least 50 miles farther from the old residence than the old place of work was from the old residence.

2. **Time Rules** The time rules are waived if the taxpayer dies, becomes disabled, is transferred by the employer, or is laid-off by the employer for other than willful misconduct.

   a. **Employee** The individual must be employed at the new place of employment for at least 39 weeks out of the 12 months following the move.

   b. **Self-Employed** If the individual is self-employed, s/he must be self-employed 78 weeks during the 24 months following the move. In addition, at least 39 of those weeks must fall in the 12-month period that immediately follows the individual's arrival at the new place of work.

3. **Allowable Expenses** Allowable expenses include (1) the cost of moving goods and (2) costs of travel including lodging (not meals) to the new residence. Actual automobile expenses or an inflation-adjusted mileage rate may be deducted.

4. **Disallowed Expenses** Disallowed expenses include (1) costs of house-hunting trips; (2) temporary living expenses; (3) expenses incurred in selling the old residence, buying the new residence, or settling an unexpired lease; and (4) meal expenses.

5. **Reimbursements** Reimbursements received from an employer for qualified moving expenses are excluded from the employee's income. However, the same expense cannot be reimbursed (and thus excluded from income) and deducted from income.

E. Self-Employment Tax
A self-employed individual can deduct one-half of the self-employment tax paid for the year.

F. Keogh Plan
Generally, a self-employed individual subject to the self-employment tax may set up a Keogh plan. The maximum deduction for a defined contribution plan is limited to the lesser of

1. $49,000 (for 2009), or

2. 20% of net self-employment earnings (net earned income minus the Keogh deduction minus one-half of the self-employment tax) which is mathematically equivalent to 25% of gross self-employment earnings

G. Penalties for Premature Withdrawals of Time Deposits
All the interest is included in gross income and then the penalty amount is subtracted for AGI.

H. Alimony Paid
Amounts paid pursuant to a divorce or separate maintenance agreement are deductible for AGI by the payer.

IV. Deductions From AGI

A. Standard Deduction
The standard deduction depends on the taxpayer's filing status. Either the standard deduction or itemized deductions are used on any one return, not both.

Exhibit 5 ▸ 2009 Standard Deductions

Filing Status	Standard Deduction
Married filing joint (MFJ) and surviving spouses	$11,400
Single	5,700
Head of household (HH)	8,350
Married filing separate (MFS)	5,700
MFS, spouse itemizes	-0-

1. **Increased Standard Deduction**

   a. **Age or Blindness** Taxpayers who are age 65 (or older) or blind are entitled to an increased standard deduction. The standard deduction is increased by $1,100 for 2009 for a married person (filing jointly or separately) or for a surviving spouse. For an unmarried individual, (filing as single or head of household) the standard deduction is increased by $1,400 for 2009. The standard deduction increase is doubled if the taxpayer is both blind and 65 or older.

   b. **Property Tax (Temporary)** EESA '08 allows those homeowners who do not itemize a limited deduction for property taxes by increasing the amount of their standard deduction by the lesser of the amount of state or local real property taxes paid or $500 ($1,000 for MFJ). This temporary increase is scheduled to lapse after 2009.

2. **Reduced Standard Deduction** Taxpayers claimed as another taxpayer's dependent have a standard deduction that is the lesser of the standard deduction for single taxpayers or the greater of $950 (for 2009) or the dependent taxpayer's earned income plus $300.

B. Itemized Deductions

Itemized deductions are taken only if, in aggregate, they are greater than the standard deduction. A taxpayer's itemized deduction is determined on Schedule A.

1. **Phase-out** Itemized deductions are subject to phase-out when the taxpayer's AGI exceeds certain thresholds. An individual whose AGI in 2009 exceeds $166,800 ($83,400 for MFS) is required to reduce the amount of allowable itemized deductions by 1% of the excess over the threshold amount. This limitation is applied after taking other limitations into account.

2. **Cap** The reduction cannot exceed 80% of the individual's allowable deductions (all deductions except those in 3., below) that are subject to the phase-out.

3. **Exceptions** No reduction is required for medical expenses, investment interest, casualty and theft losses, or gambling losses.

C. Medical Expenses

Taxpayers are allowed a deduction for expenses paid during the taxable year for medical care for themselves, their spouses and dependents, and those who would otherwise qualify as dependents except that they did not pass the income test.

1. **Limitation** Medical expenses are deductible only to the extent that they exceed 7.5% of AGI.

2. **Cash Basis** The deduction is allowable only for medical expenses actually paid during the taxable year, regardless of when the expense was incurred or the taxpayer's method of accounting. Medical expenses charged on a credit card are considered paid when charged, not when paid to the credit card company. The deduction is the amount actually paid, less any insurance reimbursement. If the taxpayer is reimbursed in a later year for medical expenses deducted in an earlier year, the reimbursement is includible in gross income to the extent that the prior year's medical expense deduction decreased the income subject to taxes.

3. **Qualified Expenses** Medical care expenses include amounts paid for (a) the diagnosis, cure, mitigation, treatment, or prevention of disease, (b) the purpose of affecting any structure or function of the body, or for transportation primarily for and essential to medical care, (c) prescription drugs and insulin, (d) premiums for medical care insurance, and (e) lodging (not exceeding $50 per night, per individual) incurred while away from home in seeking medical care provided by a physician in a hospital or facility related to, or the equivalent of, a hospital (e.g., the Mayo Clinic). The deduction for lodging expenses also encompasses the amounts incurred for those persons accompanying the patient. School tuition is deductible when the primary reason for enrollment is the availability of medical care.

4. **Home Alterations** A medical expense deduction is also allowed for the cost of making a home more amenable to the needs of the handicapped. These medically related costs include (a) building entrance ramps, (b) widening of interior and exterior doors and hallways, (c) installing railings or support bars in bathrooms, (d) modifying kitchen cabinetry and equipment to make them accessible to the handicapped, and (e) relocating electrical fixtures and outlets. Only those costs in excess of an increase in the value of the residence are deductible.

5. **Nonqualified Expenses** Expenses paid for cosmetic surgery not necessary to treat a deformity, a congenital abnormality, a personal injury trauma, or a disfiguring disease are not deductible.

D. Taxes

A deduction is allowed for the following taxes: (1) state, local, and foreign real property taxes paid by the owner, (2) state and local personal property taxes paid by the owner, and (3) state, local, and foreign income taxes. A deduction is not allowed for the following taxes: (1) federal income taxes, (2) federal excess profits taxes, (3) federal, state, and local inheritance, legacy, and gift taxes, (4) social security taxes, (5) taxes on real property that are apportioned to another taxpayer due to the sale of the property, and (6) special assessments paid for local benefits such as sidewalks, streets, and sewer systems, except if the assessment is made for maintenance or repair purposes. For 2009, EESA '08 allows taxpayers the option to substitute state and local sales taxes paid for state and local income taxes paid. This temporary measure is scheduled to lapse after 2009.

Example 8 ▶ Local Tax Refund

During Year 5, Basil (a single cash basis taxpayer) had $3,300 withheld from his wages for state income taxes and paid local property taxes of $2,000. Basil elected to itemize. In Year 6, he received a refund of $850 on his Year 5 state income taxes.

Analysis: Basil's total itemized deductions were $5,300 on the Year 5 return. The refund of state income taxes usually would be included in gross income on the Year 5 federal tax return. Because Basil could have elected the Year 5 standard deduction of $5,000 instead of the revised itemized deductions of $4,450 ($5,300 – $850), only $300 ($5,300 – $5,000) of the refund is recognized as taxable income in Year 6.

1. **Cash-Method Taxpayers** Taxes generally are deductible in the year they are paid. Buyers and sellers of real estate allocate the tax liability and deduction based on the proportion of which each party was in possession during the real property taxable year. The party in possession on the due date actually pays the entire tax liability.

2. **Accrual-Method Taxpayers** Taxes generally are deductible only in the year in which they accrue.

3. **Observations** (1) Tax surcharges paid by a tenant as additional rent on a rented residence are not deductible as real property tax payments. (2) Refunds of state, local, and foreign income taxes are includible in the year of receipt if the taxpayer itemized the deduction for the taxes paid in the prior year and received a tax benefit from the prior year's deduction.

Conversely, refunds may be excluded in whole or part to the extent they exceed the portion of the refund that provided a tax benefit in the prior year of deduction.

E. Interest

Interest expense is deductible for mortgages for home acquisition, home equity indebtedness, and investment interest expense. Personal or consumer interest is no longer deductible.

1. **Acquisition Indebtedness** Interest on up to $1,000,000 of debt incurred to buy, construct, or substantially improve a first or second home is deductible as qualified residence interest.

2. **Home Equity Indebtedness** Debt that is secured by the taxpayer's first or second home but is not acquisition indebtedness. Interest on up to $100,000 of debt is deductible as home equity interest expense. The proceeds from a home equity loan do not have to be used for home improvements—if they are, the debt is acquisition indebtedness.

Example 9 ▸ Home Equity Interest

Mr. and Mrs. McKee purchased a home for $80,000 ten years ago, paying 20% down and financing the balance. The outstanding balance on their home mortgage is $55,000. The house has been currently appraised at $250,000. In the current year, the McKees borrowed $125,000 against a second mortgage on the house to buy a boat.

Analysis: The $55,000 balance on the first mortgage is acquisition indebtedness. The $125,000 is home equity indebtedness and is limited to the lesser of the current appraised value of the residence minus any acquisition indebtedness ($250,000 – $55,000 = $195,000). However, only interest on up to $100,000 of home equity debt is tax deductible. Thus, the $125,000 qualifies as home equity indebtedness, but only interest expense on $100,000 of this $125,000 debt is deductible.

3. **Investment Interest** Interest paid or accrued on indebtedness incurred to purchase or carry property held for investment is deductible to the extent of net investment income. Any excess may be carried over indefinitely. Investment interest does not include interest earned from or paid on a loan to secure an interest in a passive activity.

   a. Net investment income is the excess of investment income over investment expenses.

   b. Investment income includes the following.

      (1) Gross income from interest, dividends, rents, and royalties

      (2) Portfolio income generated by a passive activity

      (3) Gain from sale or other disposition of investment property (subject to restrictions in paragraph c., below)

   c. Net capital gain is excluded from investment income for purposes of computing the investment income limitation unless the taxpayer makes a special election. A taxpayer may elect to include an unlimited amount of the net capital gain in investment income, if the taxpayer also reduces the amount of net capital gain eligible for the maximum capital gains rate by the same amount. (This prevents a high-income taxpayer from deducting investment interest against the top rate of 35% while simultaneously taking advantage of the lower rates on long-term capital gains.)

   d. Investment expenses are generally those ordinary and necessary expenses directly connected with the production of investment income. Investment expenses are a tier 2 miscellaneous deduction (subject to the 2% of AGI floor limitation). Expenses incurred for the production of tax-exempt interest income are not deductible.

F. Charitable Contributions

Contributions actually paid to a qualified donee during the year are deductible, but are subject to a percentage of AGI limitation. Contributions may be in cash or property. If the contribution is made using a credit card, it is considered paid when the charge is made, regardless of when the charge is actually paid. Political contributions are not deductible.

Example 10 ▸ Charitable Contributions

Mr. and Mrs. Fellow had adjusted gross income of $50,000 and cash contributions of $1,000 to the Carlsbad Community Hospital and $18,000 to the Fraternal Order of Swamp Rats.

Analysis: The contributions are deductible, but subject to limitations.

Public charity donations (hospital)			$ 1,000
Plus the lesser of:			
(1) 30% × $50,000		$15,000 or	
(2) 50% × $50,000	$ 25,000		
Reduced by public charity donations	(1,000)		
Qualified private charity donations		$24,000	15,000
Current year contribution deduction			$16,000
Carry-forward contributions ($19,000 – $16,000)			$ 3,000

Example 11 ▸ Charitable Contributions

Mr. and Mrs. Maladroit had adjusted gross income of $100,000 and made the following cash contributions. For the contribution to the operatic society, the Maladroits received four free tickets valued at $300.

Recipient	Amount
Carlsbad Community Hospital	$25,000
Committee to Re-elect Commissioner Huff	1,000
Carlsbad Operatic Society	20,000
Fraternal Order of Swamp Rats	6,000

Analysis: The political contribution is not a charitable contribution and is not deductible. The other contributions are deductible, subject to limitations.

Hospital	$ 25,000		
Operatic society ($20,000 – $300)	19,700		
Public charity donations			$44,700
Plus the lesser of:			
(1) 30% × $100,000		$30,000 or	
(2) 50% × $100,000	$ 50,000		
Reduced by public charity donations	(44,700)		
Private charity donations		$ 5,300	5,300
Current year contribution deduction			$50,000
Carry-forward contributions ($6,000 – $5,300)			$ 700

1. **Qualified Donees** Include (1) federal, state, or local governments, if the gift is made exclusively for public purposes and (2) domestic organizations and foundations operated exclusively for religious, charitable, scientific, literary, or educational purposes.

2. **Contribution Base** The taxpayer's adjusted gross income computed without regard to any net operating loss carryback. Contributions made in excess of the limits may be carried forward for five years.

   a. **Organization Type** The annual deduction cannot exceed 50% of the taxpayer's contribution base for donations to (1) churches, (2) educational organizations, (3) hospitals, (4) governmental units, (5) private operating foundations, (6) certain organizations holding property for state and local colleges and universities, and (7) an organization organized and operated for religious, charitable, educational, scientific, or literary purposes. A contribution cannot exceed 30% of the taxpayer's contribution base to a qualifying organization that is not a 50% organization, such as a war veterans organization or a fraternal order.

b. **LTCG Property** If the individual makes a contribution of appreciated long-term capital gain property, the amount of the contribution is equal to the fair market value of the property contributed, but if the contribution is to a 50% charity, the 50% limitation is reduced to 30% unless the taxpayer elects to use her/his basis in the property as the amount contributed. If the contribution is made to a 30% charity, the 30% limitation is reduced to 20% and there is no special election available.

3. **Premium** If the taxpayer receives something of value for the contribution, the allowable deduction is reduced by that amount. For example, if a taxpayer makes a charitable contribution by purchasing a ticket to a dinner that costs $100 and the actual cost of the dinner is $40, only $60 is allowed as a charitable deduction.

4. **Valuation** Appreciated property that would realize long-term capital gain if sold instead of donated is valued at fair market value. Other property is valued at the lesser of basis or fair market value.

5. **Expenses** A taxpayer may deduct unreimbursed out-of-pocket expenses incurred as a result of donating services to a qualified charitable organization including actual automobile expenses or a mileage rate. However, there is no deduction for the value of the services contributed.

6. **Documentation** No deductions are allowed for any charitable contributions of $250 or more unless the taxpayer has written substantiation from the donee organization.

7. **Foreign Students** Amounts paid to maintain a domestic or foreign student in one's home are deductible if (1) the student is not a relative or dependent of the taxpayer, (2) the student is in the 12th grade or lower, (3) there is a written agreement with a qualified charitable organization, and (4) no reimbursement is received. The deduction is limited to $50 per month.

G. Casualty & Theft Losses

Casualty and theft losses attributable to property not connected with a trade or business or with a transaction entered into for profit (e.g., personal casualties and thefts) are allowable as a deduction to the extent such losses exceed the gains from other personal casualties and thefts, and to the extent the total excess losses exceed 10% of the taxpayer's adjusted gross income. In addition, there is a $100 floor per casualty event. Furthermore, if the casualty is covered by insurance, the loss is deductible only if the taxpayer files a timely insurance claim. The loss must be reduced by any amount recovered through insurance. EESA '08 increases the $100 limitation for each casualty or theft to $500 for tax years beginning in 2009. EESA '08 also permits personal casualty losses arising from a federally declared disaster to be deducted without regard to the 10% of AGI limitation in 2009. Other personal casualty losses remain subject to the 10% limit. The EESA '08 changes are scheduled to lapse after 2009.

1. **Conditions** A casualty loss must be due to some sudden, unexpected, or unusual cause. The gradual erosion of a private beach is not a casualty loss. However, the loss of a beach due to a hurricane, tornado, etc., is a casualty loss.

2. **Theft** A loss arising from theft is deductible in the year in which the taxpayer discovers the loss.

3. **Loss Year** A casualty loss is allowed as a deduction only for the taxable year in which the loss occurred. A loss sustained in a federal declared disaster area may be deducted in the preceding year by filing an amended tax return for that year.

Example 12 ▸ Casualty & Theft Losses

In 2009, Scott had adjusted gross income of $15,000 and incurred the following gains and losses:

- A stereo component system with a fair market value of $1,200 was stolen from his house. The system, which originally cost him $2,000, was not insured.
- A flood washed away and totally destroyed his car, which he purchased for $5,000. The insurance proceeds for the car amounted to $6,000.
- In another burglary, $4,500 worth of collector's plates were stolen. The plates cost $4,000 and were uninsured.

Analysis: The theft of the stereo results in a $700 theft loss for tax purposes [e.g., $1,200 (lesser of basis or decrease in FMV) – $500]. The theft of the plates resulted in a loss of $3,500 ($4,000 – $500). Thus, Scott's total losses for tax purposes amounted to $4,200. The destruction of the car in the flood yielded a gain of $1,000 [e.g., $6,000 (proceeds) – $5,000 (basis)]. The $1,000 gain is offset by $1,000 of the losses. The excess $2,500 ($3,500 – $1,000) loss for tax purposes is deductible as an itemized deduction to the extent it exceeds 10% of Scott's AGI. 10% of $15,000 equals $1,500. Scott may deduct $1,000 ($2,500 – $1,500) in losses if he itemizes.

H. Miscellaneous Deductions

There are two broad types of miscellaneous deductions, *first-tier* and *second-tier* deductions.

1. **First-Tier Deductions** First-tier deductions are not subject to 2% of AGI floor.

   a. Impairment-related work expenses for handicapped employees

   b. Estate tax related to income in respect of a decedent

   c. Deductions allowable in connection with personal property used in a short sale

   d. Certain deductions related to computation of tax where the taxpayer restores a substantial amount held under a claim of right

   e. Unrecovered investment in an annuity when payments cease

   f. Amortization of premium on bonds purchased before October 23, 1986

   g. Deductions relating to certain cooperative housing corporations

   h. Gambling losses to the extent of gambling winnings

2. **Second-Tier Deductions** Second-tier deductions are allowable only to the extent they, in aggregate, exceed 2% of AGI.

   a. Home office expenses

   b. Continuing educational expenses

   c. Unreimbursed employee expenses such as uniforms, safety equipment, small tools, supplies, dues to professional organizations, union dues, subscriptions to professional journals, expense of looking for a job in the taxpayer's present occupation, travel, transportation, and 50% of business entertainment expenses

   d. Expenses of producing income including certain legal and accounting fees, safe deposit box rental (to the extent used to protect income-producing property), custodial fees, investment counsel fees, etc.

   e. Tax return preparation fees

f. Appraisals to determine casualty losses

g. Legal fees to procure alimony

V. Income Tax Computation

A. Tax Rates

Income tax is levied on an individual's taxable income. Capital gains generally are taxed at 15% (maximum rate of 28% on collectibles). Therefore, taxpayers with net capital gains probably will need to use Schedule D to compute the income tax liability correctly.

Exhibit 6 ▸ 2009 Tax Rate Schedule

Rate	MFJ*	Head of Household	Single	MFS
10%	0-$ 16,700	0-$ 11,950	0-$ 8,350	0-$ 8,350
15%	$ 16,701-$ 67,900	$ 11,951-$ 45,500	$ 8,351-$ 33,950	$ 8,351-$ 33,950
25%	$ 67,901-$137,050	$ 45,501-$117,450	$ 33,951-$ 82,250	$ 33,951-$ 68,525
28%	$137,051-$208,850	$117,451-$190,200	$ 82,251-$171,550	$ 68,526-$104,425
33%	$208,851-$372,950	$190,201-$372,950	$171,551-$372,950	$104,426-$186,475
35%	Over $372,950	Over $372,950	Over $372,950	Over $186,475

* Also surviving spouse.

B. Earnings Taxes

The maximum earnings or wages subject to the full tax is $106,800 for 2009, with no maximum for the 1.45% Medicare tax.

1. **Social Security Tax (FICA)** Social security is imposed on both employers and employees. The employees' share is 7.65%, of which 1.45% is for Medicare. If an individual works for more than one employer, the FICA withheld may exceed the maximum amount required. If this happens, the individual is allowed to take a credit on her/his income tax return to offset the amount of income tax liability due.

2. **Self-Employment Tax** The combined self-employment tax rate is 15.3%, of which 2.9% is the Medicare portion.

C. Tax on Children's Unearned Income

The net **unearned** income of children who have not reached age **14** by the end of the tax year is taxed at the parent's top rate instead of at the child's rate. The amount taxed at the parent's rate for 2009 is the child's unearned income less the sum of $950 and either (1) $950 or (2) itemized deductions related to the production of the unearned income.

D. Alternative Minimum Tax (AMT)

The purpose of the alternative minimum tax (AMT) is to ensure that all taxpayers who have realized gains or income during the year pay at least a minimum amount of tax. The AMT only applies if a taxpayer's AMT liability is greater than her/his regular tax liability. AMT paid in a taxable year may be carried over as a credit to subsequent taxable years. The credit is allowed to reduce future regular tax liability but not future alternative minimum tax liability. It may be carried forward indefinitely. The following is a simplified version of the calculation of AMT liability.

1. **Regular Taxable Income**

2. **Plus (Add Back) NOL Deduction**

3. **Plus or Minus AMT Adjustments** These are: (a) standard deduction; (b) medical expenses must be computed using a 10% floor instead of 7.5%; (c) miscellaneous itemized deductions from Schedule A subject to the 2% threshold; (d) taxes from Schedule A; (e) refund of taxes (always a subtraction); (f) home mortgage interest not due to acquisition; (g) investment interest expense; (h) depreciation on tangible property placed in service after 1986;

(i) circulation and research and experimental expenditures paid or incurred after 1986; (j) mining exploration and development costs paid or incurred after 1986; (k) long-term contracts entered into after February 28, 1986; (l) pollution control facilities placed in service after 1986; (m) installment sales of certain property; (n) adjusted gain or loss; (o) incentive stock options; (p) certain loss limitations; (q) tax shelter farm activities; (r) passive activity loss; and (s) beneficiaries of estates and trusts.

4. **Plus Tax Preferences** These are: (a) private activity bonds tax-exempt interest; (b) percentage depletion; (c) pre-1987 real property accelerated depreciation; (d) pre-1987 leased personal property accelerated depreciation; and (e) intangible drilling costs. The interest on private activity bonds issued in 2009 and 2010 is excluded from AMT.

5. **Equals Alternative Minimum Taxable Income (AMTI)**

Example 13 ▸ Alternative Minimum Taxable Income

Anne and Mike Temple are married, file jointly, have no dependents, and have regular taxable income before personal exemptions of $171,000. Tax-exempt municipal bond interest of $2,000 and private activity bond (issued in March 1992) interest of $900 are not included in this figure. Included in the calculation of their regular taxable income are the following itemized deductions:

Property taxes on primary residence	$3,000
State and local income taxes	6,500
Interest on acquisition indebtedness for the primary residence	7,000
Interest on a home equity loan used to buy a personal-use boat (secured by the primary residence)	4,600

Required: What is the Temple's alternative minimum taxable income?

Solution:

Regular taxable income	$171,000
Adjustments:	
Taxes ($3,000 + $6,500)	9,500
Home equity loan interest	4,600
Preferences—Private activity bond interest	900
Alternative minimum taxable income	$186,000

6. **Less Exemption** The exemption is reduced by 25% of the amount by which AMTI exceeds a phase-out amount. The AMT amounts are not adjusted for inflation. While the phase-out threshold amounts are likely to remain the same, the 2009 and 2010 personal AMT exemption amounts are particularly subject to change by legislation similar to the way that the 2008 amounts were changed. The phase-out ceiling amounts each are four times the exemption amount plus the related phase-out threshold amount.

Exhibit 7 ▸ AMT Exemption & Phase-out Threshold Amounts

Filing Status	2009 Exemption	Phase-out Threshold
Married filing jointly or Surviving spouse	$70,950	$150,000
Single or Head of household	46,700	112,500
Married filing separately	35,475	75,000

7. **Multiplied by the AMT Rate** A 26% rate applies to the first $175,000 of a taxpayer's AMTI over the exemption amount. A 28% rate is applied to AMTI in excess of $175,000 over the exemption amount ($87,500 for MFS).

8. **Less Select Credits** The foreign tax credit, retirement savings credit, and the refundable child tax credit are the only tax credits allowed when computing the AMT liability.

9. Equals Alternative Minimum Tax

Example 14 ▶ Alternative Minimum Tax

Anne and Mike Temple are married, file jointly, and have alternative minimum taxable income of $186,000 (See Example 13).

Required:

a. What is the Temple's AMT exemption?

b. What is the Temple's alternative minimum tax?

Solution:

a.	Base exemption (2009)		$ 70,950
	AMT income	$ 186,000	
	Threshold	(150,000)	
	Excess	$ 36,000	
	Exemption Rate	25%	
	Reduction		(9,000)
	AMT exemption		$ 61,950
b.	AMT income		$186,000
	AMT exemption		(61,950)
	Nonexempt AMT income		$124,050
	First AMT rate		26%
	Alternative minimum tax		$ 32,253

VI. Tax Payments

A. Tax Credits

Tax credits directly reduce taxes payable on a dollar-for-dollar basis.

1. **Child Care Credit** A credit of between 20% and 35% of eligible expenses is available up to a maximum of $3,000 for one qualifying dependent and $6,000 for two or more. The taxpayer may claim the child and dependent care credit (if all other applicable requirements are met) for a child who lives with the taxpayer for more than one-half of the year, even if the taxpayer does not provide more than one-half of the cost of maintaining the household. Additionally, the eligibility requirement that an individual who is physically or mentally incapable of caring for her/himself has been modified to include the requirement that the taxpayer and the dependent have the same principal residence for more than one-half of the tax year. Lastly, a qualifying child is determined without regard to the exception for children of divorced or separated parents.

   a. The full 35% is available if the taxpayer's AGI is $15,000 or less. The credit is reduced 1% for each $2,000, or portion thereof, of the AGI in excess of $15,000. However, the credit is not reduced below 20%.

   b. The credit is limited to the taxpayer's earned income (or the spouse's earned income, if less).

   c. To qualify for the credit, generally, at least one spouse must be working. However, if a non-working spouse is physically or mentally incapable of self care, or is a full-time student, then that spouse is treated as being gainfully employed. The non-working spouse is deemed to earn $250 per month if there is one, and $500 a month if there are two or more, qualifying dependent(s).

   d. Married taxpayers must file a joint return to claim the credit. For divorced or separated parents, the credit is available to the parent who had custody for the majority of the year.

e. Payments to a relative qualify for the credit unless the taxpayer claims a dependency exemption for the relative, or if the relative is the taxpayer's child and is less than 19 years old.

2. **Credit for Elderly & Permanently Disabled** A credit of 15% of eligible income is available to individuals who are either 65 or older, or permanently disabled.

   a. The initial amount of the credit depends on the taxpayer's filing status.

   b. These initial amounts are reduced by annuities, pensions, Social Security, or disability income that are excluded from gross income and further reduced by 50% of AGI in excess of a ceiling that depends on filing status.

Exhibit 8 ▸ Credit for Elderly or Permanently Disabled Schedule

Filing Status	Initial Amount	AGI Ceiling
Single	$5,000	$ 7,500
Married filing jointly, one spouse qualifies	5,000	10,000
Married filing jointly, both spouses qualify	7,500	10,000
Married filing separately	3,750	5,000

3. **Foreign Tax Credit** A taxpayer may take either a deduction or a tax credit for amounts paid or accrued for foreign income taxes. A separate limitation is calculated for certain categories of income, such as earned and passive income. The credit limitation is

$$\text{Tentative U.S. tax (before credit)} \times \frac{\text{Taxable income from foreign sources}}{\text{Total taxable income}}$$

4. **Child Credit** In 2009 and 2010, a credit of up to $1,000 may be claimed against income taxes due for each qualifying child under the age of 17 at the end of the year. After 2010, this credit is scheduled to revert to $500 and to have no portion refundable. Qualifying children are those who meet the dependency criteria. The names and Social Security numbers of the qualifying children must be included on the tax return. The phase-out ranges start at $110,000 of modified AGI for MFJ, $55,000 for MFS, and $75,000 for singles. For each $1,000, or portion of $1,000, of modified AGI above these ceilings, the credit reduction is $50.

   a. The child credit is refundable to the extent of 15% of the taxpayer's earned income in excess of a threshold (set at $3,000 for 2009 and 2010 by ARRA '09) or for taxpayers with three or more children, the amount of Social Security taxes that exceed the earned income credit. The refundable portion of the child credit is excluded from the definition of income and may not be considered as resources for purposes of determining eligibility or the amount or nature of benefits or assistance under a federal program or any state or local program financed with federal funds.

   b. Taxpayers with three or more qualifying children may be able to claim a refund with an *additional* credit, for the amount of the employee's share of withheld Social Security taxes that exceed the earned income credit, if that amount is greater than the refundable credit based on the taxpayer's earned income in excess of the threshold. (The editors do not expect this calculation to be tested on the CPA exam and, thus, details are not presented here.)

5. **Earned Income Credit** The earned income credit (EIC) is a refundable credit. This means that if the credit is greater than the taxpayer's tax liability, then the taxpayer will receive a refund. To qualify, the taxpayer must have earned income, must be eligible to work in the U.S. and, if married, must file a joint return. Any income earned under a *Workfare* program, to the extent subsidized under a state program, will not constitute earned income for this credit.

Editor's Note: The examiners have not required candidates to compute the credit on any disclosed exam questions.

a. **Child** A qualifying child shares the taxpayer's principal place of abode for over one-half of the year and is less than 19 years old, a full-time student less than 24 years old, or permanently disabled. The qualifying child also must be: (1) the taxpayer's child, stepchild, sibling, or any of their descendants; or (2) the taxpayer's foster child. Additional requirements include the following.

   (1) A qualifying child does not have to meet the support test.

   (2) A qualifying child must have lived with the taxpayer in the United States for more than one-half of the year and have a social security number that is valid for employment in the United States.

   (3) A qualifying child is determined without regard to the exception for children of divorced or separated parents. Also, a qualifying child who is married also must meet the nationality and marital status tests for the dependency exemption.

b. **No Child** A reduced credit is available to low-income workers age 25-65 who do not have any qualifying children and who cannot be claimed as a dependent on another return.

c. **Phase-out** The credit is reduced if the taxpayer has earned income (or greater AGI) in excess of a ceiling or investment income greater than $3,100 (for 2009). Nontaxable employee compensation is not included in earned income for EIC purposes.

d. **Penalty** Taxpayers making fraudulent EIC claims (later determined to be ineligible) are barred from claiming the credit for the next 10 years. For taxpayers making claims with reckless or intentional disregard for the tax law, the disallowance period is two years.

Exhibit 9 ▸ 2009 Earned Income Credit Schedule

Qualifying Children	Credit Rate	Computed on Earned Income of	Maximum Credit	Start of Phase-out	Complete Phase-out
0	7.65%	$ 5,970	$ 457	$ 7,470*	$13,440*
1	34.00%	8,950	3,043	16,420*	35,463*
2	40.00%	12,570	5,028	16,420*	40,295*
3	45.00%	12,570	5,657	16,420*	43,281*

*For MFJ taxpayers, these amounts are increased by $5,000.

6. **General Business Credit** The general business credit is comprised of the investment tax credit that includes the rehabilitation, energy, and reforestation credits, the targeted jobs credit, the alcohol fuel credit, the research credit, the low-income housing credit, the enhanced oil recovery credit, the disabled access credit, the renewable electricity production credit, the welfare-to-work credit, and the small business pension plan startup costs credit.

   a. The general business credit may not exceed net income tax less the greater of the tentative minimum tax or 25% of net regular tax liability greater than $25,000.

   b. Any portion of the credit that cannot be used in the current tax year may be carried back 1 year and forward 20 years.

7. **Adoption Expenses Credit** A $12,150 (for 2009) credit is permitted for qualified adoption expenses (adoption, attorney, and court fees). The credit is a flat amount equal to the ceiling for special needs child adoption regardless of adoption expenses; otherwise, it is the amount

spent for adoption expenses up to the ceiling. No credit is allowed for reimbursed expenses. Fees from the adoption of a step-child are ineligible for this credit.

a. The credit is claimed in the year that the adoption becomes final, or that payment occurs, whichever is later. Married couples must file a joint return to claim this credit.

b. The phase-out range starts at $182,180 modified AGI for 2009. Phased-out credits can be carried forward for 5 years.

c. A special needs child is a U.S. citizen or resident who a state determines cannot or should not be returned to her/his parents' residence and who is unlikely to be adopted without assistance. A special needs child's adoption has no requirement for qualified adoption expenses. No credit with respect to a special needs child's adoption is allowed if the adoption is not finalized.

8. **Education Credits** Many of the education provisions have phase-out ranges based on different definitions of modified AGI (MAGI). Different provisions also consider different types of expenses; some consider only tuition and fees, while others also consider books or room and board. For the following two credits, any expenses for tuition and fees must be reduced by excludable scholarships and other excludable assistance (but not gifts, bequests, or loans) before the credit is calculated. A dependent may not claim a credit; however, any qualifying expenses paid by the dependent student may be attributed to the parent and may be used in calculating the credit claimed on the parent's return. A tax credit may not be claimed for any amount that any other provision of the tax law provides for a deduction. The credits are phased-out starting at MAGI of $100,000 for MFJ, and $50,000 for a single filer or HH for 2009. MAGI is AGI plus any income earned outside the U.S. and not subject to U.S. tax.

a. **American Opportunity Tax Credit** ARRA '09 renamed the Hope Education credit as the American Opportunity credit. For 2009 and 2010, this credit is increased, expanded, and made 40% refundable. It increases the maximum credit per student to $2,500 (figured as 100% of the first $2,000 and 25% of the second $2,000). ARRA '09 extends eligibility to four years of postsecondary education as well as course materials, such as textbooks. Phase-out ranges are $80,000 to $90,000 for single taxpayers ($160,000 to $180,000 for MFJ).

b. **Lifetime Learning Tax Credit** A taxpayer may claim a nonrefundable 20% credit for tuition and fees of up to $10,000 for the same people who qualify for the American Opportunity credit. This credit is limited to $2,000 per year per taxpayer (not per student). There is no need for the student to be at least a half-time student, nor is there a limit to the number of years the credit may be claimed. This credit may be used for undergraduate and graduate courses, but not course materials.

c. **Credit Interaction** The American Opportunity and Lifetime Learning credits are not available for the same student in the same year. These credits may be claimed in the same year that amounts are distributed from a qualified state tuition program, but not in the same year that the taxpayer receives a nontaxable distribution from a Coverdell Education Savings Account.

9. **Retirement Savings Credit** Eligible individuals are able to claim from 10% to 50% of annual retirement savings contribution to IRAs, 401(k), and similar plans as a credit. The maximum credit is $1,000. Eligible individuals must be age 18 or older, other than full-time students, and cannot be claimed as a dependent on another person's tax return. The applicable percentage is determined by the individual's filing status and adjusted gross income. A credit may be taken if adjusted gross income is less than the thresholds of $50,000 for married filing jointly, $37,500 for head of household, and $25,000 for single.

10. **Economic Recovery Payment** For 2009 only, ARRA '09 provides a person on a fixed income (social security recipient, disabled veteran, government retiree, etc.) eligibility for a $250 payment. While named a payment, this essentially is a refundable credit.

11. **Making Work Pay (MWP) Credit** ARRA '09 permits a credit for 2009 and 2010 for 6.2% of earned income up to a total of $400 for individuals ($800 for MFJ). This credit phases out at 2% of MAGI above $75,000 for individuals ($150,000 for MFJ). Economic recovery payments received reduce any MWP credit.

12. **First-Time Homebuyer Tax Credit** The *Housing Assistance Tax Act of 2008* allows first-time homebuyers a refundable tax credit up to the lesser of 10% of the home's purchase price or $7,500 ($3,750 for MFS). Under HATA '08, homes purchased from unrelated parties on or after April 9, 3008, and before July 1, 2009, are eligible. Under ARRA '09, the amount is increased to $8,000 and the eligible title closing date is extended at that level to November 30, 2009. For this credit, a first-time homebuyer had no ownership interest in a principal residence during the 3-year period before the purchase; thus, those who rent a principal residence while owning a vacation home are eligible for this credit.

    a. **Timing** Buyers may claim the credit on a 2008 or 2009 return. Qualified buyers who purchase a principal residence in 2009 may claim the credit on an amended 2008 return.

    b. **Repayment** A unique feature of this credit is that generally it must be repaid in equal installments over 15 years. ARRA '09 eliminates the repayment provisions for houses purchased in 2009. Repayments start two years after the year of purchase. If the taxpayer dies, the balance of the credit need not be repaid. Special rules (beyond the scope of the exam) apply to a home transferred in a divorce or involved in an involuntary conversion. Any unpaid balance becomes due in the year in which the property no longer is used as a principal residence or is sold to the extent that the balance exceeds the amount of gain from the sale of the property to an unrelated person.

    c. **Phase-out** The credit phases out for modified AGI between $75,000 and $95,000 for single taxpayers ($150,000 and $170,000 for MFJ).

    d. **Eligibility** The following are ineligible for the credit: buyers who resell the property or convert the property to other than a principal residence before the end of the tax year in which the credit is claimed; buyers who are nonresident aliens; buyers who take the District of Columbia first-time homebuyer tax credit; and buyers who have financing from tax-exempt mortgage revenue bonds. (State and local government housing finance agencies sell mortgage revenue bonds and use the proceeds to finance below-market rate mortgages for qualifying first-time homebuyers.)

13. **Qualified Plug-in Electric Drive Motor Vehicle Credit:** This credit runs from 2009 through 2014 for both individuals and businesses, under ESSA '08. When the vehicle is used by a tax-exempt organization or government unit, the seller may claim the credit.

    a. **Qualified Plug-in Electric Drive Vehicle:** Has a high-power battery for vehicle traction with at least four kilowatt hours of capacity; has an off-board source of energy to recharge the battery; and meets specified clean air act provisions.

    b. **Calculation:** The credit is $2,500 plus $417 for each kilowatt hour of traction battery capacity in excess of four kilowatt hours. The maximum credit, dependent on gross vehicle weight, ranges from $7,500 for a vehicle under 10,000 pounds to $15,000 for a vehicle of 26,000 pounds.

B. Estimated Payments

If an individual does not pay enough taxes during the year through withholding, s/he must make quarterly estimated tax payments in order to avoid a penalty for underpayment of tax. However, there is an exception when the underpayment is less than $1,000.

1. **Required Payments** To avoid a penalty, an individual must pay, through withholding and estimated payments, the lesser of either of the following.

   a. 90% of the current year's tax

   b. A safe harbor percentage of the prior year's tax.

      (1) The safe harbor percentage for a taxpayer with AGI of $150,000 or less is 100%.

      (2) Most taxpayers with a return with an AGI of more than $150,000 ($75,000 for MFS) must have paid 110% of the preceding year's tax liability.

      (3) Taxpayers with more than 50% of their gross income from a small business (averaging fewer than 500 employees) and have adjusted gross income of less than $500,000 may make estimated tax payments that equal 90% of the prior year's tax liability.

2. **Annualized Method** A taxpayer whose income is much higher in one part of the year may use the annualized method under §6654(d). The annualized method allows taxpayers to lower or eliminate the amount of one or more required quarterly estimated tax payments.

3. **Due Dates** These quarterly payments are due on the 15th day of the 4th, 6th, and 9th month of the year, and the 15th day of the 1st month of the following year. For a calendar year taxpayer, this would mean April 15, June 15, September 15, and January 15 of the following year.

Frequently Asked Questions: Federal Taxation

FAQ are not necessarily tested heavily by the examiners, merely frequently asked by candidates. They are not intended to summarize, or identify highlights of, the tax chapters. For more complete discussions, see the related material in the text and explanations to questions.

FAQ: *Why is alimony included in gross income and then deducted to arrive at AGI?*

A: Alimony **received** is included in gross income. Alimony **paid** is deducted from gross income to arrive at adjusted gross income (AGI). Usually alimony received and alimony paid are **not** on the same return. For example, if a former husband pays alimony to a former wife, the former husband deducts the alimony on his return to calculate his AGI and the former wife includes it in her gross income.

FAQ: *What is the purpose of the alimony recapture rules?*

A: Alimony recapture rules preclude a divorced person from deducting an in-substance property settlement to a former spouse [non-deductible by the paying former spouse (PFS)] that is spread over a two year period as alimony payments (deductible by the PFS). In essence, if the alimony payments in the first and second years of a divorce exceed the alimony payments of the third year (plus a cushion of $15,000), the IRS will reclassify the excess payments as a property settlement. (The PFS will have to recapture this as income.)

FAQ: *How does the discharge of debt create taxable income?*

A: **Gross income includes all income unless there is a specific exclusion provided by law.** The loan proceeds are not income at the time of receipt. If the loan is not repaid, the taxpayer effectively has received income. Although exceptions apply in the case of bankruptcy, insolvency, and certain mortgage forgiveness, there is no general exclusion for this situation.

FAQ: *Why is the loss on the sale of a personal-use sailboat not deductible from income?*

A: **No expenditures are tax deductible unless there is a specific provision allowing their deduction.** There are very few provisions for personal expenses or losses.

CHAPTER 44—FEDERAL TAXATION: INDIVIDUALS

Problem 44-1 MULTIPLE CHOICE QUESTIONS (120 to 160 minutes)

1. Smith, a divorced person, provided over one half the support for his widowed mother, Ruth, and his son, Clay, both of whom are U.S. citizens. Ruth did not live with Smith. She received $9,000 in social security benefits. Clay, a full-time graduate student, and his wife lived with Smith. Clay had no income but filed a joint return for the year, owing an additional $500 in taxes on his wife's income. How many exemptions was Smith entitled to claim on his tax return?
a. 4
b. 3
c. 2
d. 1 (5/95, AR, #14, amended, 5432)

2. Al and Mary Lew are married and filed a joint 2009 income tax return in which they validly claimed the $3,650 personal exemption for their dependent 17-year-old daughter, Doris. Since Doris earned $6,400 from a part-time job at the college she attended full-time, Doris also was required to file an income tax return. What amount was Doris entitled to claim as a personal exemption in her individual income tax return?
a. $0
b. $2,500
c. $3,650
d. $5,700 (11/90, PII, #24, amended, 4597)

3. Sarah Hance, who is single and lives alone in Idaho, has no income of her own and is supported in full by the following persons:

	Amount of support	Percent of total
Alan (an unrelated friend)	$ 7,200	48
Barbara (Sarah's sister)	6,450	43
Chris (Sarah's son)	1,350	9
	$15,000	100

Under a multiple support agreement, Sarah's dependency exemption can be claimed by
a. No one
b. Alan
c. Barbara
d. Chris (Editors, 8041)

4. In Year 1, Alan Cox provided more than half the support for his following relatives, none of whom qualified as a member of Alan's household:

Cousin
Nephew
Foster parent

None of these relatives had any income, nor did any of these relatives file an individual or a joint return. All of these relatives are U.S. citizens. Which of these relatives could be claimed as a dependent on Alan's Year 1 return?
a. No one
b. Nephew
c. Cousin
d. Foster parent (Editors, 8040)

5. Jim and Kay Ross contributed to the support of their two children, Dale and Kim, and Jim's widowed parent, Grant. Dale, a 19-year-old full-time college student, earned $4,500 as a baby-sitter. Kim, a 23-year-old bank teller, earned $12,000. Grant received $5,000 in dividend income and $4,000 in nontaxable social security benefits. Grant, Dale, and Kim are U.S. citizens and were over one-half supported by Jim and Kay. How many exemptions can Jim and Kay claim on their joint income tax return?
a. Two
b. Three
c. Four
d. Five (5/94, AR, #14, amended, 4619)

6. While Emma and John were married, John died on July 1, Year 3. With regard to John's and Emma's filing status for Year 3, Emma should file
a. As a single individual, and a separate return should be filed for John as unmarried head of household
b. As a qualifying widow, and a separate return should be filed for John as married head of household
c. As a qualifying widow, and a separate return should be filed for John as a single deceased individual
d. A joint return, including John, as married taxpayers (Editors, 8039)

7. For head of household filing status, which of the following costs are considered in determining whether the taxpayer has contributed more than one half the cost of maintaining the household?

	Food consumed in the home	*Value of services rendered in the home by the taxpayer*
a.	Yes	Yes
b.	No	No
c.	Yes	No
d.	No	Yes

(11/92, PII, #10, 3344)

8. Sam Gow's wife died in Year 1. Sam did not remarry, and he contributed more than 50% of maintaining the home for his dependent infant child during Year 2 and Year 3, providing full support for himself and his child during these years. For Year 1, Sam properly filed a joint return. For Year 3, Sam's filing status is

a. Single
b. Head of household
c. Qualifying widower with dependent child
d. Married filing joint return (Editors, 1581)

9. Which of the following is(are) among the requirements to enable a taxpayer to be classified as a "qualifying widow(er)"?

I. A dependent has lived with the taxpayer for six months.
II. The taxpayer has maintained the cost of the principal residence for six months.

a. I only
b. II only
c. Both I and II
d. Neither I nor II (5/95, AR, #13, 5431)

10. Joe and Barb are married, but Barb refuses to sign a joint return. On Joe's separate return, an exemption may be claimed for Barb if

a. Barb was a full-time student for the entire school year.
b. Barb attaches a written statement to Joe's income tax return, agreeing to be claimed as an exemption by Joe.
c. Barb was under the age of 19.
d. Barb had **no** gross income and is **not** claimed as another person's dependent.

(11/93, PII, #30, amended, 4465)

11. On April 15, Year 2, a married couple filed their joint Year 1 calendar-year return showing gross income of $120,000. Their return had been prepared by a professional tax preparer who mistakenly omitted $45,000 of income, which the preparer in good faith considered to be nontaxable. No information with regard to this omitted income was disclosed on the return or attached statements. By what date must the Internal Revenue Service assert a notice of deficiency before the statute of limitations expires?

a. April 15, Year 8
b. December 31, Year 7
c. April 15, Year 5
d. December 31, Year 4

(11/92, PII, #6, amended, 3340)

12. A taxpayer filed his income tax return after the due date but neglected to file an extension form. The return indicated a tax liability of $50,000 and taxes withheld of $45,000. On what amount would the penalties for late filing and late payment be computed?

a. $0
b. $ 5,000
c. $45,000
d. $50,000 (R/01, AR, #25, 7010)

13. A claim for refund of erroneously paid income taxes, filed by an individual before the statute of limitations expires, must be submitted on Form

a. 1139
b. 1045
c. 1040X
d. 843 (5/95, AR, #20, 5438)

14. Martinsen, a calendar-year individual, files a year 1 tax return on March 31, year 2. Martinsen reports $20,000 of gross income. Martinsen inadvertently omits $500 interest income. The IRS may assess additional tax up until which of the following dates?

a. March 31, year 5
b. April 15, year 5
c. March 31, year 8
d. April 15, year 8

(R/07, REG, C00821R, #20, 8444)

15. If an individual paid income tax in Year 1 but did **not** file a Year 1 return because his income was insufficient to require the filing of a return, the deadline for filing a refund claim is

a. Two years from the date the tax was paid
b. Two years from the date a return would have been due
c. Three years from the date the tax was paid
d. Three years from the date a return would have been due (11/90, PII, #22, amended, 1562)

16. A cash basis taxpayer should report gross income
a. Only for the year in which income is actually received in cash
b. Only for the year in which income is actually received whether in cash or in property
c. For the year in which income is either actually or constructively received in cash only
d. For the year in which income is either actually or constructively received, whether in cash or in property (5/95, AR, #15, 5433)

17. Perle, a dentist, billed Wood $600 for dental services. Wood paid Perle $200 cash and built a bookcase for Perle's office in full settlement of the bill. Wood sells comparable bookcases for $350. What amount should Perle include in taxable income as a result of this transaction?
a. $0
b. $200
c. $550
d. $600 (11/93, PII, #21, 4450)

18. Unless the Internal Revenue Service consents to a change of method, the accrual method of tax reporting is mandatory for a sole proprietor when there are

	Accounts receivable for services rendered	*Year-end merchandise inventories*
a.	Yes	Yes
b.	Yes	No
c.	No	No
d.	No	Yes

(11/92, PII, #13, 3347)

19. DAC Foundation awarded Kent $75,000 in recognition of lifelong literary achievement. Kent was not required to render future services as a condition to receive the $75,000. What condition(s) must have been met for the award to be excluded from Kent's gross income?

I. Kent was selected for the award by DAC without any action on Kent's part.
II. Pursuant to Kent's designation, DAC paid the amount of the award either to a governmental unit or to a charitable organization.

a. I only
b. II only
c. Both I and II
d. Neither I nor II (R/05, REG, 0007T, #1, 7867)

20. In Year 1, Emily Judd received the following dividends from:

Grainte Life Insurance Co., on Emily's life insurance policy (total dividends received have not yet exceeded accumulated premiums paid)	$100
National Bank, on bank's common stock	300
Roe Mfg. Corp., a Delaware corporation, on preferred stock	500

What amount of dividend income should Emily report in her Year 1 income tax return?
a. $900
b. $800
c. $500
d. $300 (Editors, 1598)

21. With regard to the inclusion of social security benefits in gross income, which of the following statements is correct?
a. The social security benefits in excess of modified adjusted gross income are included in gross income.
b. The social security benefits in excess of 85% the modified adjusted gross income are included in gross income.
c. 85% of the social security benefits is the maximum amount of benefits to be included in gross income.
d. The social security benefits in excess of the modified adjusted gross income over $34,000 are included in gross income.
(5/94, AR, #4, amended, 4609)

22. In a tax year where the taxpayer pays qualified education expenses, interest income on the redemption of qualified U.S. Series EE Bonds may be excluded from gross income. The exclusion is subject to a modified gross income limitation and a limit of aggregate bond proceeds in excess of qualified higher education expenses. Which of the following is (are) true?

I. The exclusion applies for education expenses incurred by the taxpayer, the taxpayer's spouse, or any person whom the taxpayer may claim as a dependent for the year.
II. "Otherwise qualified higher education expenses" must be reduced by qualified scholarships not includible in gross income.

a. I only
b. II only
c. Both I and II
d. Neither I nor II (5/94, AR, #2, 4607)

23. Klein, a master's degree candidate at Briar University, was awarded a $12,000 scholarship from Briar in 1996. The scholarship was used to pay Klein's 1996 university tuition and fees. Also in 1996, Klein received $5,000 for teaching two courses at a nearby college. What amount is includible in Klein's 1996 gross income?
a. $0
b. $ 5,000
c. $12,000
d. $17,000 (11/97, AR, #1, 6529)

24. Darr, an employee of Sorce C corporation, is not a shareholder. Which of the following would be included in a taxpayer's gross income?
a. Employer-provided medical insurance coverage under a health plan.
b. An $11,000 gift from the taxpayer's grandparents.
c. The fair market value of land that the taxpayer inherited from an uncle.
d. The dividend income on shares of stock that the taxpayer received for services rendered. (R/01, AR, #30, 7015)

25. Harold sustained a serious injury in the course of his employment. As a result of this injury, Harold received the following payments during the current year:

Workers' compensation	$ 6,500
Reimbursement from his employer's insurance plan for medical expenses paid by Harold and not deducted by him	4,000
Damages for personal physical injuries	16,000

The amount to be included in Harold's gross income for the current year should be
a. $26,500
b. $16,000
c. $ 4,000
d. $0 (Editors, 1601)

26. Ash had the following cash receipts:

Wages	$13,000
Interest income from U.S. Treasury bonds	350
Workers' compensation following a job-related injury	8,500

What is the total amount that must be included in gross income on Ash's income tax return?
a. $13,000
b. $13,350
c. $21,500
d. $21,850 (R/99, AR, #1, amended, 6790)

27. Walt's employer pays 100% of the cost of all employees' group term life insurance under a qualified plan. Under this plan, the maximum amount of tax-free coverage that may be provided for Walt by his employer is
a. $100,000
b. $ 50,000
c. $ 10,000
d. $ 5,000 (Editors, 1593)

28. Cassidy, an individual, reported the following items of income and expense during the current year:

Salary	$50,000
Alimony paid to a former spouse	10,000
Inheritance from a grandparent	25,000
Proceeds of a lawsuit for physical injuries	50,000

What is the amount of Cassidy's adjusted gross income?
a. $ 40,000
b. $ 50,000
c. $115,000
d. $125,000 (R/07, REG, 1168T, #6, 8430)

29. Mosh, a sole proprietor, uses the cash basis of accounting. At the beginning of the current year, accounts receivable were $25,000. During the year, Mosh collected $100,000 from customers. At the end of the year, accounts receivable were $15,000. What was Mosh's gross taxable income for the current year?
a. $ 75,000
b. $ 90,000
c. $100,000
d. $110,000 (R/05, REG, 1056T, #12, 7878)

30. Don Wolf became a general partner in Gata Associates on January 1, Year 1, with a 5% interest in Gata's profits, losses, and capital. Gata is a distributor of auto parts. Wolf does not materially participate in the partnership business. For Year 1, Gata had an operating loss of $100,000. In addition, Gata earned interest of $20,000 on a temporary investment. Gata has kept the principal temporarily invested while awaiting delivery of equipment that is presently on order. The principal will be used to pay for this equipment. Wolf's passive loss for Year 1 is
a. $0
b. $4,000
c. $5,000
d. $6,000 (11/90, PII, #27, amended, 1566)

31. Mock operates a retail business selling illegal narcotic substances. Which of the following item(s) may Mock deduct in calculating business income?

I. Cost of merchandise
II. Business expenses other than the cost of merchandise

a. I only
b. II only
c. Both I and II
d. Neither I nor II (R/01, AR, #24, 7009)

32. Billings, a retired corporate executive, earned consulting fees of $9,000 and director's fees of $4,000 in the current year. Billings' gross income from self-employment in the current year was
a. $0
b. $ 4,000
c. $ 9,000
d. $13,000 (Editors, 1573)

33. On December 1, Year 1, Krest, a self-employed cash basis taxpayer, borrowed $200,000 to use in her business. The loan was to be repaid on November 30, Year 2. Krest paid the entire interest amount of $24,000 on December 1, Year 1. What amount of interest was deductible on Krest's Year 1 income tax return?
a. $0
b. $ 2,000
c. $22,000
d. $24,000 (5/98, AR, #3, amended, 6640)

34. Porter was unemployed for part of 2009. Porter received $35,000 of wages, $4,000 from a state unemployment compensation plan, and $2,000 from his former employer's company-paid supplemental unemployment benefit plan. What is the amount of Porter's 2009 gross income?
a. $37,000
b. $38,600
c. $39,000
d. $41,000
(R/06, REG, 1000T, #4, amended, 8174)

35. In the current year, Jane won $6,000 in a state lottery. Jane also spent $300 for the purchase of lottery tickets. Jane elected the standard deduction on her current year income tax return. The amount of lottery winnings that should be included in Jane's current year taxable income is
a. $0
b. $2,000
c. $5,700
d. $6,000 (Editors, 1583)

36. Kent received the following interest income:

On Veterans Administration insurance dividends left on deposit with the VA	$20
On U.S. Treasury certificates	30
On state income tax refund	40

What amount should Kent include for interest income in his tax return?
a. $90
b. $70
c. $50
d. $20 (Editors, 1575)

37. Baum, an unmarried optometrist and sole proprietor of Optics, buys and maintains a supply of eyeglasses and frames to sell in the ordinary course of business. In Year 1, Optics had $350,000 in gross business receipts and its year-end inventory was not subject to the uniform capitalization rules. Baum's Year 1 adjusted gross income was $90,000 and Baum qualified to itemize deductions. During Year 1, Baum recorded the following information:

Business expenses:	
Optics cost of goods sold	$35,000
Optics rent expense	28,000
Liability insurance premium on Optics	5,250
Other expenditures:	
Baum's self-employment tax	$29,750
Baum's self-employment health insurance	8,750
Estimated payments of Year 1 federal income taxes	13,500

What amount should Baum report as Year 1 net earnings from self-employment?
a. $243,250
b. $252,000
c. $273,000
d. $281,750 (R/99, AR, #2, amended, 6791)

38. Which of the following conditions must be present in a post-1984 divorce agreement for a payment to qualify as deductible alimony?

I. Payments must be in cash.
II. The payments must end at the recipient's death.

a. I only
b. II only
c. Both I and II
d. Neither I nor II (R/01, AR, #27, 7012)

39. Easel Co. elected to reimburse employees for business expenses under a nonaccountable plan. Easel does not require employees to provide proof of expenses and allows employees to keep any amount not spent. Under the plan, Mel, an Easel employee for a full year, gets $500 per month for business automobile expenses. At the end of the year Mel informs Easel that the only business expense incurred was for business mileage of 12,000 at a rate of 40 cents per mile, the IRS standard mileage rate at the time. Mel encloses a check for $1,200 to refund the overpayment to Easel. What amount should be reported in Mel's gross income for the year?
a. $0
b. $1,200
c. $4,800
d. $6,000 (R/99, AR, #3, amended, 6792)

40. Destry, a single taxpayer, reported the following on his U.S. Individual Income Tax Return Form 1040:

Income:	
Wages	$ 5,000
Interest on savings account	1,000
Net rental income	4,000
Deductions:	
Personal exemption	$ 3,650
Standard deduction	5,700
Net business loss	20,000
Net short-term capital loss	2,000

What is Destry's net operating loss that is available for carryback or carryforward?
a. $11,000
b. $13,000
c. $20,000
d. $20,350 (R/99, AR, #7, amended, 6796)

41. Adams owns a second residence that is used for both personal and rental purposes. During Year 1, Jackson used the second residence for 50 days and rented the residence for 200 days. Which of the following statements is correct?
a. Depreciation may not be deducted on the property under any circumstances.
b. A rental loss may be deducted if rental-related expenses exceed rental income.
c. Utilities and maintenance on the property must be divided between personal and rental use.
d. All mortgage interest and taxes on the property will be deducted to determine the property's net income or loss. (R/01, AR, #22, amended, 7007)

42. Nare, an accrual basis taxpayer, owns a building which was rented to Mott under a ten-year lease expiring August 31, Year 8. On January 2, Year 5, Mott paid $30,000 as consideration for canceling the lease. On November 1, Year 5, Nare leased the building to Pine under a five-year lease. Pine paid Nare $10,000 rent for the two months of November and December, and an additional $5,000 for the last month's rent. What amount of rental income should Nare report in its Year 5 income tax return?
a. $10,000
b. $15,000
c. $40,000
d. $45,000 (11/93, PII, #23, amended, 4452)

43. Dale received $1,000 in the current year for jury duty. In exchange for regular compensation from her employer during the period of jury service, Dale was required to remit the entire $1,000 to her employer. In Dale's income tax return, the $1,000 jury duty fee should be
a. Claimed in full as an itemized deduction
b. Claimed as an itemized deduction to the extent exceeding 2% of adjusted gross income
c. Deducted from gross income in arriving at adjusted gross income
d. Included in taxable income without a corresponding offset against other income (5/91, PII, #26, amended, 1552)

44. An unmarried individual with modified adjusted gross income of $25,000 paid $1,000 interest on a qualified education loan entered into on July 1. How may the individual treat the interest for income tax purposes?
a. As a $500 deduction to arrive at AGI for the year
b. As a $1,000 deduction to arrive at AGI for the year
c. As a $1,000 itemized deduction
d. As a nondeductible item of personal interest (R/06, REG, 0873T, #22, 8192)

45. For calendar Year 1, Ralph earned $1,000 interest at Ridge Savings Bank on a certificate of deposit scheduled to mature in Year 3. In January Year 2, before filing his Year 1 income tax return, Ralph incurred a forfeiture penalty of $500 for premature withdrawal of the funds. Ralph should treat this $500 forfeiture penalty as a
a. Reduction of interest earned in Year 1, so that only $500 of such interest is taxable on Ralph's Year 1 return
b. Deduction from Year 2 adjusted gross income, deductible only if Ralph itemizes his deductions for Year 2
c. Penalty **not** deductible for tax purposes
d. Deduction from gross income in arriving at Year 2 adjusted gross income (Editors, 1595)

46. Grey, a calendar year taxpayer, was employed and resided in New York. On February 2, Grey was permanently transferred to Florida by his employer. Grey worked full-time for the entire year. Grey incurred and paid the following unreimbursed expenses in relocating:

Lodging and travel expenses while moving	$1,000
Pre-move househunting costs	1,200
Costs of moving household furnishings and personal effects	1,800

What amount was deductible as moving expense on Grey's tax return?
a. $4,000
b. $2,800
c. $1,800
d. $1,000 (5/95, AR, #6, amended, 5424)

47. Which allowable deduction can be claimed in arriving at an individual's adjusted gross income?
a. Alimony payment
b. Charitable contribution
c. Personal casualty loss
d. Unreimbursed business expense of an outside salesperson (11/93, PII, #27, 4456)

48. Val and Pat White, both age 45, filed a joint return for 2009. Val earned $36,000 in wages and was covered by his employer's qualified pension plan. Pat was unemployed and received $4,000 in alimony payments for the first 4 months of the year before remarrying. The couple had no other income. Each contributed $5,000 to an IRA account. The allowable IRA deduction on their joint 2009 tax return is
a. $10,000
b. $ 9,000
c. $ 5,000
d. $0 (5/94, AR, #7, amended, 4612)

49. Mike and Julia Crane are married, age 35, and filed a joint return for 2009. Mike earned a salary of $100,000 in 2009 from his job at Troy Corp., where Mike is covered by his employer's pension plan. In addition, Mike and Julia earned interest of $3,000 on their joint savings account. Julia is not employed, and the couple had no other income. On January 15, 2010, Mike contributed $5,000 to a traditional IRA for himself, and $5,000 to an IRA for his spouse. The allowable IRA deduction in the Cranes' 2009 joint return is
a. $0
b. $ 3,000
c. $ 5,000
d. $10,000 (Editors, 1580)

50. Davis, a sole proprietor with no employees, has a Keogh profit-sharing plan to which he may contribute 20% of his annual earned income. For this purpose, "earned income" is defined as net self-employment earnings reduced by the
a. Deductible Keogh contribution
b. Self-employment tax
c. Self-employment tax and one-half of the deductible Keogh contribution
d. Deductible Keogh contribution and one-half of the self-employment tax (11/93, PII, #28, amended, 4457)

51. Which of the following requirements must be met in order for a single individual to qualify for the additional standard deduction amount?

	Must be age 65 or older or blind	*Must support dependent child or aged parent*
a.	Yes	Yes
b.	No	No
c.	Yes	No
d.	No	Yes

(11/91, PII, #21, amended, 2469)

52. In 2009, Poole, a carpenter, is 45 years old and unmarried. He has adjusted gross income of $29,000. The following information applies to Poole:

Medical expenses	$8,600
Standard deduction	5,700
Personal exemption	3,650

Poole wishes to minimize his income tax. What is Poole's taxable income?
a. $25,350
b. $19,650
c. $18,925
d. $16,750 (11/93, PII, #38, amended, 4467)

53. In the current year, Drake, a disabled taxpayer, made the following home improvements:

	Cost
Pool installation, which qualified as a medical expense and increased the value of the home by $25,000	$100,000
Widening doorways to accommodate Drake's wheelchair. The improvement did not increase the value of his home	10,000

For regular income tax purposes and without regard to the adjusted gross income percentage threshold limitation, what maximum amount would be allowable as a medical expense deduction in the current year?
a. $110,000
b. $ 85,000
c. $ 75,000
d. $ 10,000 (R/05, REG, 0018T, #2, 7848)

54. During Year 2, Scott charged $4,000 on his credit card for his dependent son's medical expenses. Payment to the credit card company had not been made by the time Scott filed his income tax return in Year 3. However, in Year 2, Scott paid a physician $2,800 for medical expenses of his wife, who died in Year 1. Disregarding the adjusted gross income percentage threshold, what amount could Scott claim in his Year 2 income tax return for medical expenses?
a. $0
b. $2,800
c. $4,000
d. $6,800 (5/91, PII, #31, amended, 1557)

55. Carroll, an unmarried taxpayer with an adjusted gross income of $100,000, incurred and paid the following unreimbursed medical expenses for the year:

Doctor bills resulting from a serious fall	$ 5,000
Cosmetic surgery that was necessary to correct a congenital deformity	15,000

Carroll had no medical insurance. For regular income tax purposes, what was Carroll's maximum allowable medical expense deduction, after the applicable threshold limitation, for the year?
a. $0
b. $12,500
c. $15,000
d. $20,000 (R/01, AR, #21, 7006)

56. Tom and Sally White, married and filing joint income tax returns, derive their entire income from the operation of their retail stationery shop. Their adjusted gross income was $100,000. The Whites itemized their deductions on Schedule A. The following unreimbursed cash expenditures were among those made by the Whites during the current year:

Repair and maintenance of motorized wheelchair for physically handicapped dependent child	$ 600
Tuition, meals, and lodging at special school for physically handicapped dependent child in an institution primarily for the availability of medical care, with meals and lodging furnished as necessary incidents to that care	8,000

Without regard to the adjusted gross income percentage threshold, what amount may the Whites claim as qualifying medical expenses?
a. $8,600
b. $8,000
c. $ 600
d. $0 (5/95, AR, #12, amended, 5430)

57. In Year 1, Wells paid the following expenses:

Premiums on an insurance policy against loss of earnings due to sickness or accident	$3,000
Physical therapy after spinal surgery	2,000
Premium on an insurance policy that covers reimbursement for the cost of prescription drugs	500

In Year 1, Wells recovered $1,500 of the $2,000 that she paid for physical therapy through insurance reimbursement from a group medical policy paid for by her employer. Disregarding the adjusted gross income percentage threshold, what amount could be claimed on Wells' Year 1 income tax return for medical expenses?
a. $4,000
b. $3,500
c. $1,000
d. $ 500 (5/94, AR, #13, amended, 4618)

58. In Year 1, Farb, a cash basis individual taxpayer, received an $8,000 invoice for personal property taxes. Believing the amount to be overstated by $5,000, Farb paid the invoiced amount under protest and immediately started legal action to recover the overstatement. In November, Year 2, the matter was resolved in Farb's favor, and he received a $5,000 refund. Farb itemizes his deductions on his tax returns. Which of the following statements is correct regarding the deductibility of the property taxes?
a. Farb should deduct $8,000 in his Year 1 income tax return and should report the $5,000 refund as income in his Year 2 income tax return.
b. Farb should **not** deduct any amount in his Year 1 income tax return and should deduct $3,000 in his Year 2 income tax return.
c. Farb should deduct $3,000 in his Year 1 income tax return.
d. Farb should **not** deduct any amount in his Year 1 income tax return when originally filed, and should file an amended Year 1 income tax return in Year 2. (11/93, PII, #33, amended, 4462)

59. The Browns borrowed $20,000, secured by their home, to pay their son's college tuition. At the time of the loan, the fair market value of their home was $400,000, and it was unencumbered by other debt. The interest on the loan qualifies as
a. Deductible personal interest
b. Deductible qualified residence interest
c. Nondeductible interest
d. Investment interest expense (5/94, AR, #10, 4615)

60. Jackson owns two residences. The second residence, which has never been used for rental purposes, is the only residence that is subject to a mortgage. The following expenses were incurred for the second residence:

Mortgage interest	$5,000
Utilities	1,200
Insurance	6,000

For regular income tax purposes, what is the maximum amount allowable as a deduction for Jackson's second residence?
a. $6,200 in determining adjusted gross income
b. $11,000 in determining adjusted gross income
c. $5,000 as an itemized deduction
d. $12,200 as an itemized deduction
(5/98, AR, #2, amended, 6639)

61. Wilson, CPA, uses a commercial tax software package to prepare clients' individual income tax returns. Upon reviewing a client's computer-generated year 1 itemized deductions, Wilson discovers that the schedule's deductible investment interest expense is less than the amount paid by the taxpayer and the amount that Wilson entered into the computer. After analyzing the entire tax return, Wilson determines that the computer-generated investment interest expense deduction is correct. Why is the computer-generated investment interest expense deduction correct?

I. The client's investment interest expense exceeds net investment income.
II. The client's qualified residence interest expense reduces the deductible amount of investment interest expense.

a. I only
b. II only
c. Both I and II
d. Neither I nor II (R/07, REG, 0577T, #2, 8426)

62. In 2009, Wood's residence had an adjusted basis of $150,000 when it was destroyed by a tornado. An appraiser valued the decline in market value at $175,000. The tornado was not a federally declared disaster. Wood received $130,000 from his insurance company for the property loss and did not elect to deduct the casualty loss in an earlier year. Wood's adjusted gross income was $60,000 and he did not have any casualty gains. What total amount can Wood deduct as an itemized deduction for the casualty loss, after the application of the threshold limitations?
a. $39,000
b. $38,500
c. $19,500
d. $13,500 (11/97, AR, #3, amended, 6531)

63. Moore, a single taxpayer, had $50,000 in adjusted gross income for the current year. During the current year, she contributed $18,000 to her church. She had a $10,000 charitable contribution carryover from her prior year church contribution. What was the maximum amount of properly substantiated charitable contributions that Moore could claim as an itemized deduction for the current year?
a. $10,000
b. $18,000
c. $25,000
d. $28,000 (5/95, AR, #7, amended, 5425)

64. On January 2, Year 1, the Philips paid $50,000 cash and obtained a $200,000 mortgage to purchase a home. In Year 3, they borrowed $15,000 secured by their home, and used the cash to add a new room to their residence. That same year they took out a $5,000 auto loan. The following information pertains to interest paid in Year 7:

Mortgage interest	$17,000
Interest on room construction loan	1,500
Auto loan interest	500

For Year 7, how much interest is deductible, prior to any itemized deduction limitations?
a. $17,000
b. $17,500
c. $18,500
d. $19,000 (5/94, AR, #11, amended, 4616)

65. Matthews was a cash basis taxpayer whose records showed the following:

Year 1 state and local income taxes withheld	$1,500
Year 1 state estimated income taxes paid December 30, Year 1	400
Year 1 federal income taxes withheld	2,500
Year 1 state and local income taxes paid April 17, Year 2	300

What total amount was Matthews entitled to claim for taxes on her Year 1 Schedule A of Form 1040?
a. $4,700
b. $2,200
c. $1,900
d. $1,500 (5/95, AR, #8, amended, 5426)

66 How may taxes paid by an individual to a foreign country be treated?
a. As an itemized deduction subject to the 2% floor
b. As a credit against federal income taxes due
c. As an adjustment to gross income
d. As nondeductible
(R/07, REG, A0498T, #15, amended, 8439)

67. An individual's losses on transactions entered into for personal purposes are deductible only if

a. The losses qualify as casualty or theft losses.
b. The losses can be characterized as hobby losses.
c. The losses do not exceed $3,000 ($6,000 on a joint return).
d. No part of the transactions was entered into for profit. (5/91, PII, #29, 1555)

68. Which items are subject to the phase out of the amount of certain itemized deductions that may be claimed by high-income individuals?

a. Charitable contributions
b. Medical costs
c. Nonbusiness casualty losses
d. Investment interest deductions

(5/95, AR, #11, 5429)

69. Which of the following is **not** a miscellaneous itemized deduction?

a. An individual's tax return preparation fee
b. Education expense to meet minimum entry level education requirements at an individual's place of employment
c. Custodial fees for a brokerage account
d. An individual's subscription to professional journals (5/94, AR, #9, amended, 4614)

70. Baker, a sole proprietor CPA, has several clients that do business in Spain. While on a four-week vacation in Spain, Baker took a five-day seminar on Spanish business practices that cost $700. Baker's round-trip airfare to Spain was $600. While in Spain, Baker spent an average of $100 per day on accommodations, local travel, and other incidental expenses, for total expenses of $2,800. What amount of educational expense can Baker deduct on Form 1040 Schedule C, "Profit or Loss From Business?"

a. $ 700
b. $1,200
c. $1,800
d. $4,100 (R/99, AR, #6, 6795)

71. The credit for prior year alternative minimum tax liability may be carried

a. Forward for a maximum of 5 years
b. Back to the 3 preceding years or carried forward for a maximum of 5 years
c. Back to the 3 preceding years
d. Forward indefinitely (5/94, AR, #16, 4621)

72. Alternative minimum tax preferences include

	Tax exempt interest from private activity bonds issued during 1994	*Charitable contributions of appreciated capital gain property*
a.	Yes	Yes
b.	Yes	No
c.	No	Yes
d.	No	No

(5/95, AR, #18, 5436)

73. Robert had current-year adjusted gross income of $100,000 and potential itemized deductions as follows:

Medical expenses (before percentage limitations)	$12,000
State income taxes	4,000
Real estate taxes	3,500
Qualified housing and residence mortgage interest	10,000
Home equity mortgage interest (used to consolidate personal debts)	4,500
Charitable contributions (cash)	5,000

What are Robert's itemized deductions for alternative minimum tax?

a. $17,000
b. $19,500
c. $21,500
d. $25,500 (R/07, REG, 0821T, #23, 8447)

74. To qualify for the child care credit on a joint return, at least one spouse must

	Have an adjusted gross income of $15,000 or less	*Be gainfully employed when related expenses are incurred*
a.	Yes	Yes
b.	No	No
c.	Yes	No
d.	No	Yes

(11/92, PII, #11, amended, 3345)

75. Sunex Co., an accrual basis, calendar-year domestic C corporation, is taxed on its worldwide income. In the current year, Sunex's U.S. tax liability on its domestic and foreign source income is $60,000 and no prior-year foreign income taxes have been carried forward. Which factor(s) may affect the amount of Sunex's foreign tax credit available in its current-year corporate income tax return?

	Income source	*The foreign tax rate*
a.	Yes	Yes
b.	Yes	No
c.	No	Yes
d.	No	No

(R/99, AR, #11, 6800)

76. Which of the following credits is a combination of several tax credits to provide uniform rules for the current and carryback-carryover years?
a. General business credit
b. Foreign tax credit
c. Minimum tax credit
d. Enhanced oil recovery credit
(11/94, AR, #49, 5025)

77. Which of the following credits can result in a refund even if the individual had **no** income tax liability?
a. Credit for prior year minimum tax
b. Elderly and permanently and totally disabled credit
c. Earned income credit
d. Child and dependent care credit
(5/94, AR, #17, 4622)

78. An accuracy-related penalty applies to the portion of tax underpayment attributable to

I. Negligence or a disregard of the tax rules or regulations.
II. Any substantial understatement of income tax.

a. I only
b. II only
c. Both I and II
d. Neither I nor II (5/95, AR, #16, 5434)

79. A CPA's adjusted gross income (AGI) for the preceding 12-month tax year exceeds $150,000. Which of the following methods is(are) available to the CPA to compute the required annual payment of estimated tax for the current year in order to make timely estimated tax payments and avoid the underpayment of estimated tax penalty?

I. The annualization method
II. The seasonal method

a. I only
b. II only
c. both I and II
d. Neither I nor II (R/05, REG, 0355T, #13, 7859)

80. Krete, an unmarried taxpayer with income exclusively from wages, filed her initial income tax return for the Year 1 calendar year. By December 31, Year 1, Krete's employer had withheld $16,000 in federal income taxes and Krete had made no estimated tax payments. On Monday, April 17, Year 2, Krete timely filed an extension request to file her individual tax return and paid $300 of additional taxes. Krete's Year 1 income tax liability was $16,500 when she timely filed her return on April 30, Year 2, and paid the remaining income tax liability balance. What amount would be subject to the penalty for the underpayment of estimated taxes?
a. $0
b. $ 200
c. $ 500
d. $16,500
(5/98, AR, #4, 6641)

Problem 44-2 ADDITIONAL MULTIPLE CHOICE QUESTIONS (62 to 82 minutes)

81. Parker, whose spouse died during the preceding year, has not remarried. Parker maintains a home for a dependent child. What is Parker's most advantageous filing status?
a. Single
b. Head of household
c. Married filing separately
d. Qualifying widow(er) with dependent child
(R/05, REG, C01409R, #20, 7886)

82. In which of the following situations may taxpayers file as married filing jointly?
a. Taxpayers who were married but lived apart during the year
b. Taxpayers who were married but lived under a legal separation agreement at the end of the year
c. Taxpayers who were divorced during the year
d. Taxpayers who were legally separated but lived together for the entire year
(R/06, REG, C00801R, #17, 8187)

83. A calendar-year taxpayer files an individual tax return for Year 1 on March 20, Year 2. The taxpayer neither committed fraud nor omitted amounts in excess of 25% of gross income on the tax return. What is the latest date that the Internal Revenue Service can assess tax and assert a notice of deficiency?
a. March 20, Year 5
b. March 20, Year 4
c. April 15, Year 5
d. April 15, Year 4 (5/94, AR, #18, amended, 4623)

84. In April 2009, Chrisp, an unmarried taxpayer, renegotiated his mortgage with the lender. The mortgage is secured by Chrisp's principal residence. Due to the renegotiation, the outstanding loan balance was reduced by $600,000. Under which of the following circumstances would the debt forgiveness not be excluded from income?
a. The indebtedness was for more than $1 million at the time of the renegotiation.
b. The indebtedness was used to renovate, rather than to construct or acquire, Chrisp's home.
c. The home remained in Chrisp's possession after the renegotiation.
d. Chrisp received the discharge due to legal services performed for the lender. (Editors, 7647)

85. In the current year Jensen had the following items:

Salary	$50,000
Inheritance	25,000
Alimony from ex-spouse	12,000
Child support from ex-spouse	9,000
Capital loss on investment stock sale	(6,000)

What is Jensen's AGI for the current year?
a. $44,000
b. $59,000
c. $62,000
d. $84,000 (R/07, REG, 0892T, #24, 8448)

86. Clark bought Series EE U.S. Savings Bonds after 1989. Redemption proceeds will be used for payment of college tuition for Clark's dependent child. One of the conditions that must be met for tax exemption of accumulated interest on these bonds is that the
a. Purchaser of the bonds must be the sole owner of the bonds (or joint owner with her or his spouse).
b. Bonds must be bought by a parent (or both parents) and put in the name of the dependent child.
c. Bonds must be bought by the owner of the bonds before the owner reaches the age of 24.
d. Bonds must be transferred to the college for redemption by the college rather than by the owner of the bonds. (5/91, PII, #28, 1554)

87. Which payment(s) is (are) included in a recipient's gross income?

I. Payment to a graduate assistant for a part-time teaching assignment at a university. Teaching is not a requirement toward obtaining the degree
II. A grant to a Ph.D. candidate for his participation in a university-sponsored research project for the benefit of the university

a. I only
b. II only
c. Both I and II
d. Neither I nor II (5/95, AR, #1, 5419)

88. Charles and Marcia are married cash basis taxpayers. They had interest income as follows:

- $500 interest on federal income tax refund.
- $600 interest on state income tax refund.
- $800 interest on federal government obligations.
- $1,000 interest on state government obligations.

What amount of interest income is taxable on Charles and Marcia's joint income tax return?
a. $ 500
b. $1,100
c. $1,900
d. $2,900 (11/93, PII, #22, amended, 4451)

89. Rich is a cash basis self-employed air-conditioning repairman with gross business receipts of $20,000. Rich's cash disbursements were as follows:

Air conditioning parts	$2,500
Yellow Pages listing	2,000
Estimated federal income taxes on self-employment income	1,000
Business long-distance telephone calls	400
Charitable contributions	200

What amount should Rich report as net self-employment income?
a. $15,100
b. $14,900
c. $14,100
d. $13,900 (5/94, AR, #5, amended, 4610)

90. Lee, an attorney, uses the cash receipts and disbursements method of reporting. In December of the current year, a client gave Lee 500 shares of a listed corporation's stock in full satisfaction of a $10,000 legal fee the client owed to Lee. This stock had a fair market value of $8,000 on the date it was given to Lee. The client's basis for this stock was $6,000. Lee sold the stock for cash in January. In Lee's current year income tax return, what amount of income should be reported in connection with the receipt of the stock?
a. $10,000
b. $ 8,000
c. $ 6,000
d. $0 (5/91, PII, #24, amended, 1550)

91. If an individual taxpayer's passive losses and credits relating to rental real estate activities cannot be used in the current year, then they may be carried
a. Forward up to a maximum period of 15 years, but they cannot be carried back.
b. Forward indefinitely or until the property is disposed of in a taxable transaction.
c. Back three years or forward up to 15 years, at the taxpayer's election.
d. Back three years, but they cannot be carried forward. (Editors, 1576)

92. With regard to the passive loss rules involving rental real estate activities, which one of the following statements is correct?
a. The term "passive activity" includes any rental activity without regard as to whether or not the taxpayer materially participates in the activity.
b. Passive rental activity losses may be deducted only against passive income, but passive rental activity credits may be used against tax attributable to nonpassive activities.
c. Gross investment income from interest and dividends **not** derived in the ordinary course of a trade or business is treated as passive activity income that can be offset by passive rental activity losses when the "active participation" requirement is **not** met.
d. The passive activity rules do **not** apply to taxpayers whose adjusted gross income is $300,000 or less. (Editors, 4596)

93. Jim owns a two-family house which has two identical apartments. Jim lives in one apartment and rents out the other. In Year 1, the rental apartment was fully occupied and Jim received $7,200 in rent. During Year 1, Jim paid the following:

Real estate taxes	$6,400
Painting of rental apartment	$ 800
Annual fire insurance premium	$ 600

In Year 1, depreciation for the entire house was determined to be $5,000. What amount should Jim include in his adjusted gross income for Year 1?
a. $2,900
b. $ 800
c. $ 400
d. $ 100 (Editors, 1594)

94. Barkley owns a vacation cabin that was rented to unrelated parties for 10 days during the year for $2,500. The cabin was used personally by Barkley for three months and left vacant for the rest of the year. Expenses for the cabin were as follows.

Real estate taxes	$1,000
Maintenance and utilities	2,000

How much rental income(loss) is included in Barkley's adjusted gross income?
a. $0
b. $ 500
c. $ (500)
d. $(1,500) (R/06, REG, 1829T, #32, 8202)

95. Ed and Ann Ross were divorced on January 2, Year 9. In accordance with the divorce decree, Ed transferred the title in their home to Ann. The home, which had a fair market value of $150,000, was subject to a $50,000 mortgage that had 20 more years to run. Monthly mortgage payments amounted to $1,000. Under the terms of settlement, Ed is obligated to make the mortgage payments on the home for the full remaining 20-year term of the indebtedness, regardless of how long Ann lives. Ed made 12 mortgage payments in Year 9. What amount is taxable as alimony in Ann's Year 9 return?
a. $0
b. $ 12,000
c. $100,000
d. $112,000 (11/90, PII, #25, amended, 1565)

96. Tana's divorce decree requires Tana to make the following transfers to Tana's former spouse during the current year:

Alimony payments of $3,000
Child support of $2,000
Property division of stock with a basis of $4,000 and a fair market value of $6,500

What is the amount of Tana's alimony deduction?
a. $ 3,000
b. $ 7,000
c. $ 9,500
d. $11,500 (R/06, REG, 1171T, #25, 8195)

97. John and Mary were divorced in Year 1. The divorce decree provides that John pay alimony of $10,000 per year, to be reduced by 20% on their child's 18th birthday. During Year 5, John paid $7,000 directly to Mary and $3,000 to Spring College for Mary's tuition. What amount of these payments should be reported as income in Mary's Year 5 income tax return?
a. $ 5,600
b. $ 8,000
c. $ 8,600
d. $10,000 (11/93, PII, #24, amended, 4453)

98. Paul and Sally Lee, both age 48, are married and filed a joint return for 2009. Their adjusted gross income was $180,000, including Paul's $89,000 salary and Sally's $90,000 investment income. Neither spouse was covered by an employer-sponsored pension plan. What amount could the Lee's contribute to IRAs for 2009 to take advantage of their maximum allowable IRA deduction in their 2009 return?
a. $0
b. $ 5,000
c. $10,000
d. $12,000 (Editors, 1589)

99. In 2009, Matilda had her 50th birthday and received taxable alimony of $25,000. In addition, she received $900 earnings from a part-time job. Her employer did not provide a retirement plan for part-time employees. What was the maximum IRA contribution that Matilda could have made for 2009, that she could have deducted on her 2009 individual tax return, assuming that everything was done on a timely basis?
a. $ 900
b. $3,000
c. $5,000
d. $6,000 (Editors, 1602)

100. A calendar-year individual is eligible to contribute to a deductible IRA. The taxpayer obtained a four-month extension to file until August 15 but did not file the return until November 1. What is the latest date that an IRA contribution can be made in order to qualify as a deduction on the prior year's return?
a. October 15
b. April 15
c. August 15
d. November 1 (R/06, REG, 1810T, #31, 8201)

101. The self-employment tax is
a. Fully deductible as an itemized deduction
b. Fully deductible in determining net income from self-employment
c. One-half deductible from gross income in arriving at adjusted gross income
d. Not deductible (5/94, AR, #6, 4611)

102. Health savings accounts (HSA) are tax-exempt trusts or custodial accounts that allow taxpayers to pay for or be reimbursed for certain medical expenses. Which statement about HSAs is **not** correct?
a A HSA must be used in conjunction with a high-deductible health plan.
b. Eligible individuals for HSA purposes are entitled to receive Medicare benefits.
c. Qualified medical expenses for HSA purposes are those that qualify for the itemized medical expense deduction.
d. Distributions from a HSA for qualified medical expenses are not subject to tax. (Editors, 7601)

103. Smith paid the following unreimbursed medical expenses:

Dentist and eye doctor fees	$ 5,000
Contact lenses	500
Facial cosmetic surgery to improve Smith's personal appearance (surgery is unrelated to personal injury or congenital deformity)	10,000
Premium on disability insurance policy to pay him if he is injured and unable to work	2,000

What is the total amount of Smith's tax-deductible medical expenses before the adjusted gross income limitation?
a. $17,500
b. $15,500
c. $ 7,500
d. $ 5,500 (R/05, REG, 0457T, #9, 7875)

104. Which one of the following expenditures qualifies as a deductible medical expense for tax purposes?
a. Vitamins for general health **not** prescribed by a physician
b. Health club dues
c. Transportation to physician's office for required medical care
d. Mandatory employment taxes for basic coverage under Medicare A (11/90, PII, #33, 1569)

105. Bell, a cash basis calendar year taxpayer, died on June 1, Year 1. Prior to her death, Bell incurred $2,000 in medical expenses. The executor of the estate paid the medical expenses, which were a claim against the estate, on July 1, Year 1. If the executor files the appropriate waiver, the medical expenses are deductible on
a. The estate tax return
b. Bell's final income tax return
c. The estate income tax return
d. The executor's income tax return
(11/94, AR, #56, amended, 5032)

106. In Year 9, Smith paid $6,000 to the tax collector of Wek City for realty taxes on a two-family house owned by Smith's mother. Of this amount, $2,800 covered back taxes for Year 8, and $3,200 covered Year 9 taxes. Smith resides on the second floor of the house, and his mother resides on the first floor. In Smith's itemized deductions on his Year 9 return, what amount was Smith entitled to claim for realty taxes?
a. $6,000
b. $3,200
c. $3,000
d. $0 (11/90, PII, #32, amended, 1568)

107. William did not itemize his deductions on his Year 7 and Year 8 federal income tax returns. However, William plans to itemize his deductions for Year 9. The following information relating to his state income taxes is available:

Taxes withheld in Year 9	$2,000
Refund received in Year 9 of Year 8 tax	300
Assessment paid in Year 9 of Year 7 tax	200

What amount should William utilize as state and local income taxes in calculating itemized deductions for his Year 9 federal income tax return?
a. $1,700
b. $1,900
c. $2,000
d. $2,200 (Editors, 8042)

108. The Rites are married, file a joint income tax return, and qualify to itemize their deductions in the current year. Their adjusted gross income for the year was $55,000, and during the year they paid the following taxes:

Real estate tax on personal residence	$2,000
Ad valorem tax on personal automobile	500
Current-year state and city income taxes withheld from paycheck	1,000

What total amount of the expense should the Rites claim as an itemized deduction on their current-year joint income tax return?
a. $1,000
b. $2,500
c. $3,000
d. $3,500 (R/06, REG, 0531T, #2, 8172)

109. The Year 3 deduction by an individual taxpayer for interest on investment indebtedness is
a. Limited to the investment interest paid in Year 3
b. Limited to the taxpayer's Year 3 interest income
c. Limited to the taxpayer's Year 3 net investment income
d. Not limited (5/94, AR, #8, amended, 4613)

110. For regular tax purposes, with regard to the itemized deduction for qualified residence interest, home equity indebtedness incurred
a. Includes acquisition indebtedness secured by a qualified residence.
b. May exceed the fair market value of the residence.
c. Must exceed the taxpayer's net equity in the residence.
d. Is limited to $100,000 on a joint income tax return. (5/91, PII, #27, amended, 1553)

111. Stein, an unmarried taxpayer, had adjusted gross income of $80,000 for the year, and qualified to itemize deductions. Stein had no charitable contribution carryovers and only made one contribution during the year. Stein donated stock, purchased seven years earlier for $17,000, to a tax-exempt educational organization. The stock was valued at $25,000 when it was contributed. What is the amount of charitable contributions deductible on Stein's current year income tax return?
a. $17,000
b. $21,000
c. $24,000
d. $25,000 (R/99, AR, #8, 6797)

112. Taylor, an unmarried taxpayer, had $90,000 in adjusted gross income for the year. Taylor donated land to a church and made no other contributions. Taylor purchased the land ten years ago as an investment for $14,000. The land's fair market value was $25,000 on the day of the donation. What is the maximum amount of charitable contribution that Taylor may deduct as an itemized deduction for the land donation for the current year?
a. $25,000
b. $14,000
c. $11,000
d. $0 (R/00, AR, #6, amended, 6911)

113. Which expense, both incurred and paid in the current year, can be claimed as an itemized deduction subject to the two-percent-of-adjusted-gross-income floor?
a. Self-employed health insurance
b. One-half of the self-employment tax
c. Employee's unreimbursed moving expense
d. Employee's unreimbursed business car expense (5/95, AR, #9, amended, 5427)

114. Smith, a single individual, made the following charitable contributions during the current year. Smith's adjusted gross income is $60,000.

Donation to Smith's church	$5,000
Art work donated to the local art museum. Smith purchased it for $2,000 four months ago. A local art dealer appraised it for	3,000
Contribution to a needy family	1,000

What amount should Smith deduct as a charitable contribution?
a. $5,000
b. $7,000
c. $8,000
d. $9,000 (R/02, AR, #17, 7082)

115. Spencer, who itemizes deductions, had adjusted gross income of $60,000 in Year 1. The following additional information is available:

Cash contribution to church	$4,000
Purchase of art object at church bazaar (with a fair market value of $800 on the date of purchase)	1,200
Donation of used clothing to Salvation Army (fair value evidenced by receipt received)	600

What is the maximum amount Spencer can claim as a deduction for charitable contributions in Year 1?
a. $5,400
b. $5,200
c. $5,000
d. $4,400 (11/93, PII, #31, amended, 4460)

116. Which one of the following types of itemized deductions is included in the category of unreimbursed expenses deductible only if the aggregate of such expenses exceeds 2% of the taxpayer's adjusted gross income?
a. Interest expense
b. Medical expenses
c. Employee moving
d. Tax return preparation fees (5/91, PII, #32, 8043)

117. Dole's adjusted gross income exceeds $500,000. After the application of any other limitation, itemized deductions are reduced by
a. The *lesser* of 3% of the excess of adjusted gross income over the applicable amount or 80% of *certain* itemized deductions.
b. The *lesser* of 3% of the excess of adjusted gross income over the applicable amount or 80% of *all* itemized deductions.
c. The *greater* of 3% of the excess of adjusted gross income over the applicable amount or 80% of *certain* itemized deductions.
d. The *greater* of 3% of the excess of adjusted gross income over the applicable amount or 80% of *all* itemized deductions.
(5/94, AR, #12, amended, 4617)

118. Don Mills, a single taxpayer, had $70,000 in taxable income before personal exemptions. Mills had no tax preferences. His itemized deductions were as follows:

State and local income taxes	$5,000
Home mortgage interest on loan to acquire residence	6,000
Miscellaneous deductions that exceed 2% of adjusted gross income	2,000

What amount did Mills report as alternative minimum taxable income before the AMT exemption?
a. $72,000
b. $75,000
c. $77,000
d. $83,000 (5/95, AR, #17, amended, 5435)

119. Mr. and Mrs. Sloan paid the following expenses on December 15, 2009, when they adopted a child:

Child's medical expenses	$7,000
Legal expenses	9,000
Agency fee	5,000

What amount of the above expenses may the Sloans claim as an adoption credit on their 2009 joint income tax return?
a. $21,000
b. $16,000
c. $14,000
d. $12,150 (Editors, 4463)

120. An employee who has had social security tax withheld in an amount greater than the maximum for a particular year, may claim
a. Such excess as either a credit or an itemized deduction, at the election of the employee, if that excess resulted from correct withholding by two or more employers.
b. Reimbursement of such excess from her/his employers, if that excess resulted from correct withholding by two or more employers.
c. The excess as a credit against income tax, if that excess resulted from correct withholding by two or more employers.
d. The excess as a credit against income tax, if that excess was withheld by one employer.
(5/91, PII, #34, 1559)

121. Chris Baker's adjusted gross income on her Year 3 tax return was $160,000, $85,000 of this was due to wages. The amount covered a 12-month period. For Year 4, Baker may avoid the penalty for the underpayment of estimated tax if the timely estimated tax payments equal the required annual amount of

I. 90% of the tax on the return for the current year, paid in four equal installments.
II. 100% of prior year's tax liability, paid in four equal installments.

a. I only
b. II only
c. Both I and II
d. Neither I nor II (5/95, AR, #19, amended, 5437)

SIMULATIONS

Editor's Note: Forms for additional practice may be downloaded from http://www.irs.gov/formspubs/index.html.

Problem 44-3 (40 to 60 minutes)

Mark and Christie Sagan were married with two children, George, age 13, and Helen, age 20. On July 7, 2009, Mark died. Helen is a full-time student at the state university. The Sagans own their home at 123 Spruce Street, Anytown, USA. They have lived there for the past 7 years. Mark had been disabled since 2003. Christie is an insurance adjuster and sings in her church choir. Mark's social security number is 149-99-9999. Christie's social security number is 299-99-9999. George's social security number is 149-82-9999. Helen's social security number is 149-79-9999. (R/05, REG, #41, amended, 8553)

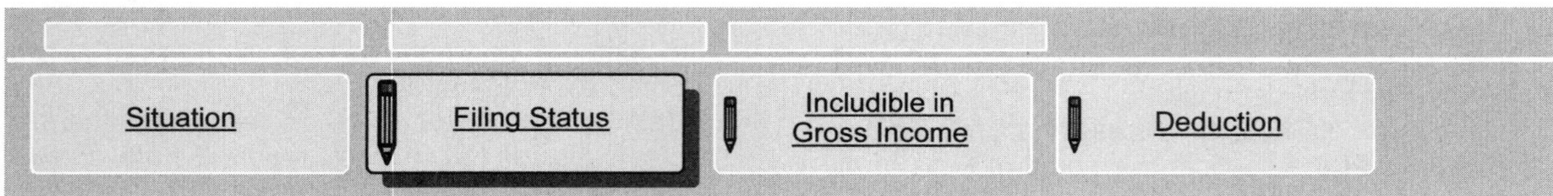

1. Indicate the filing status that is most appropriate for Christie Sagan for the 2009 tax year.

A. Married filing jointly		D. Single	
B. Married filing separately		E. Head of household	
C. Qualifying Widow(er)			

Christie and Mark Sagan filed a joint income tax return for 2008. For each of the items or events listed below, indicate which are (I) includible and (N) not includible in gross income.

	Answer
2. Christie received a payment of $60,000 as the beneficiary of her father's life insurance policy.	
3. In 2008, the State of California issued an income tax refund of $900 for the tax year 2007. Mark and Christie did not itemize for 2007, but did itemize for 2008.	
4. Mark received a $650 dividend from a mutual fund that listed its source as 100% various European companies.	
5. George received a $600 dividend from a fund he owned under the state's Gifts to Minors Act. He will not file separately, and this is his only income for the year.	
6. Mark sold 20 shares of common stock at a gain of $4,000.	
7. Christie won a raffle and collected $2,000 in cash.	
8. Christie received $200 for serving as a juror in a state court proceeding.	

Using the following table, characterize each of the following items or events as (A) Deductible for Adjusted Gross Income (AGI), (B) Deductible from AGI, or (C) Nondeductible for tax year 2009 by checking the appropriate box next to each item. Disregard any AGI limitations. Be sure a box is selected for each of the items or events.

	Answer
9. Christie made a $1,800 Roth IRA contribution.	
10. Repair costs of $1,500 to replace part of the bathroom floor that had rotted due to moisture.	
11. Medical insurance premiums of $820 deducted from Mark's disability checks.	
12. Over-the-counter cold remedies totaling $450 used by the family.	
13. Homeowner's insurance of $540 paid on the family home.	
14. Life insurance premiums of $750 for Mark.	
15. Alimony payments made by Mark to a former spouse.	
16. Interest expense of $600 paid on Christie's margin balance in her brokerage account.	

For the 2008 tax year, the Sagan family had various items of income and expenditures, as listed below. Determine either the amount of income, or the adjustment to income, that should be included or deducted on the Sagans' Form 1040—Individual Income Tax Return, to arrive at adjusted gross income. Insert the appropriate items of income in the shaded cells (lines 7 through 21) and the appropriate adjustments to income in the shaded cells (lines 23 through 32a). The total of items of income and adjustments to income will calculate automatically on lines 22 and 33, respectively. Adjusted gross income will also calculate automatically on line 34.

- The Sagans received a $200 state income tax refund of the prior year's tax. The Sagans had deducted $2,000 of state income taxes in the prior year, all of which resulted in federal tax savings.
- The Sagans received a $1,000 federal tax refund of the prior year's tax. The Sagans had paid $4,000 of federal income tax in the prior year.
- Mark received $5,000 of qualified cash dividends from a corporation listed on the New York stock exchange; and received $500 of interest from a bank savings account.
- Christie received $4,000 of tax-exempt interest.
- Christie's federal taxable wages reported on Form W-2 amounted to $50,000.
- Christie contributed $3,000 to a traditional IRA account.
- Mark paid a $25 penalty on a premature withdrawal of a certificate of deposit.
- In 2008, Christie paid $500 of self-employment tax on her 2007 net self-employment income.
- Christie is the sole owner of rental real estate on which current-year income exceeded expenses by $6,000 as reported on Schedule E. The Sagans had no other income on losses from passive activities. Christie actively participates in managing the property.
- The Sagans paid $6,500 of real estate taxes on their personal residence.
- George and Helen each received a $5,000 gift from their wealthy uncle.

Form **1040** Department of the Treasury—Internal Revenue Service
U.S. Individual Income Tax Return 2008 (99) IRS Use Only—Do not write or staple in this space.

For the year Jan. 1–Dec. 31, 2008, or other tax year beginning , 2008, ending , 20 OMB No. 1545-0074

Label (See instructions on page 14.) Use the IRS label. Otherwise, please print or type.

LABEL HERE

Your first name and initial	Last name	Your social security number
If a joint return, spouse's first name and initial	Last name	Spouse's social security number
Home address (number and street). If you have a P.O. box, see page 14.	Apt. no.	▲ You must enter your SSN(s) above. ▲
City, town or post office, state, and ZIP code. If you have a foreign address, see page 14.		Checking a box below will not change your tax or refund.

Presidential Election Campaign ▶ Check here if you, or your spouse if filing jointly, want $3 to go to this fund (see page 14) ▶ ☐ You ☐ Spouse

Filing Status

Check only one box.

1 ☐ Single
2 ☐ Married filing jointly (even if only one had income)
3 ☐ Married filing separately. Enter spouse's SSN above and full name here. ▶
4 ☐ Head of household (with qualifying person). (See page 15.) If the qualifying person is a child but not your dependent, enter this child's name here. ▶
5 ☐ Qualifying widow(er) with dependent child (see page 16)

Exemptions

6a ☐ Yourself. If someone can claim you as a dependent, do not check box 6a
b ☐ Spouse

Boxes checked on 6a and 6b
No. of children on 6c who:
• lived with you
• did not live with you due to divorce or separation (see page 18)
Dependents on 6c not entered above
Add numbers on lines above ▶

c Dependents:

(1) First name Last name	(2) Dependent's social security number	(3) Dependent's relationship to you	(4) ✓ if qualifying child for child tax credit (see page 17)
			☐
			☐
			☐
			☐

If more than four dependents, see page 17.

d Total number of exemptions claimed

Income

Attach Form(s) W-2 here. Also attach Forms W-2G and 1099-R if tax was withheld.

If you did not get a W-2, see page 21.

Enclose, but do not attach, any payment. Also, please use Form 1040-V.

7	Wages, salaries, tips, etc. Attach Form(s) W-2		7	
8a	Taxable interest. Attach Schedule B if required		8a	
b	Tax-exempt interest. Do not include on line 8a	8b		
9a	Ordinary dividends. Attach Schedule B if required		9a	
b	Qualified dividends (see page 21)	9b		
10	Taxable refunds, credits, or offsets of state and local income taxes (see page 22)		10	
11	Alimony received		11	
12	Business income or (loss). Attach Schedule C or C-EZ		12	
13	Capital gain or (loss). Attach Schedule D if required. If not required, check here ▶ ☐		13	
14	Other gains or (losses). Attach Form 4797		14	
15a	IRA distributions 15a	b Taxable amount (see page 23)	15b	
16a	Pensions and annuities 16a	b Taxable amount (see page 24)	16b	
17	Rental real estate, royalties, partnerships, S corporations, trusts, etc. Attach Schedule E		17	
18	Farm income or (loss). Attach Schedule F		18	
19	Unemployment compensation		19	
20a	Social security benefits 20a	b Taxable amount (see page 26)	20b	
21	Other income. List type and amount (see page 28)		21	
22	Add the amounts in the far right column for lines 7 through 21. This is your total income ▶		22	

Adjusted Gross Income

Line	Description	Line	Amount	Line	Amount
23	Educator expenses (see page 28)	23			
24	Certain business expenses of reservists, performing artists, and fee-basis government officials. Attach Form 2106 or 2106-EZ	24			
25	Health savings account deduction. Attach Form 8889	25			
26	Moving expenses. Attach Form 3903	26			
27	One-half of self-employment tax. Attach Schedule SE	27			
28	Self-employed SEP, SIMPLE, and qualified plans	28			
29	Self-employed health insurance deduction (see page 29)	29			
30	Penalty on early withdrawal of savings	30			
31a	Alimony paid b Recipient's SSN ▶	31a			
32	IRA deduction (see page 30)	32			
33	Student loan interest deduction (see page 33)	33			
34	Tuition and fees deduction. Attach Form 8917	34			
35	Domestic production activities deduction. Attach Form 8903	35			
36	Add lines 23 through 31a and 32 through 35			36	
37	Subtract line 36 from line 22. This is your adjusted gross income ▶			37	

For Disclosure, Privacy Act, and Paperwork Reduction Act Notice, see page 88. Cat. No. 11320B Form **1040** (2008)

Your client received the following notice from the Internal Revenue Service and sent it to you, asking for your assistance. As your client's CPA, write a letter to your client explaining the significance of the notice and telling them what information you need to respond to the IRS.

> Department of the Treasury — Date of Notice: September 9, 2008
> Internal Revenue Service — Form: 1040 Tax Period: December 31, 2007
>
> Mark and Christie Sagan
> 123 Spruce Street
> Anytown, USA
>
> NOTICE OF LATE FILING AND PAYMENT OF TAXES
> YOU HAVE AN AMOUNT DUE
>
> Our records indicate that your 2007 return and the accompanying income tax payment were received late. As a result, we have assessed late filing and late payment of tax penalties in the amount of $1,000. Payment is due October 15, 2008. Additional interest and penalties will accrue if payment is not received by this date. If you think we made a mistake, please reply to this letter no later than September 30, 2008.

Research Question: Christie received a gift of stock valued at $2,000 from a friend. Which code section and subsection provides whether or not the gift is includible in gross income?

Section & Subsection Answer: §______ (___)

Problem 44-4 (20 to 30 minutes)

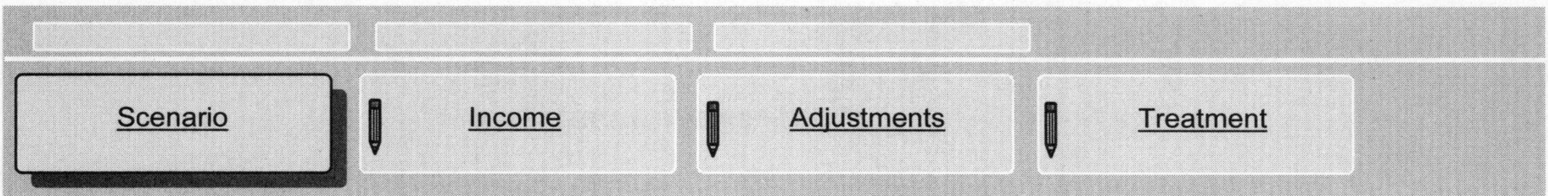

William and Ainsley McGurn, both CPAs, filed a joint Year 2 federal income tax return showing $70,000 in taxable income. William's daughter Laura, age 17, resided with William's former spouse. Laura had no income of her own and was not William's dependent. The McGurns' total medical expenses were less than 7.5% of adjusted gross income. (11/95, AR, #3, amended, 5827)

Determine the amount of income or loss, if any, that should be included on page one of the McGurns' Form 1040.

Income	Answer
1. The McGurns had no capital loss carryovers from prior years. The McGurns had the following stock transactions which resulted in a net capital loss. | | Date acquired | Date sold | Sales price | Cost | Revco | 2-1-1 | 3-17-2 | $15,000 | $25,000 Abbco | 2-18-2 | 4-1-2 | 8,000 | 4,000	
2. In Year 0, Ainsley received an acre of land as an *inter vivos* gift from her grandfather. At the time of the gift, the land had a fair market value of $50,000. The grandfather's adjusted basis was $60,000. Ainsley sold the land in Year 2 to an unrelated third party for $56,000.	
3. The McGurns received a $500 security deposit on their rental property in Year 2. They are required to return the amount to the tenant.	
4. William's wages were $53,000. In addition, William's employer provided group-term life insurance on William's life in excess of $50,000. The value of such excess coverage was $2,000.	
5. The McGurns received a $2,500 federal tax refund and a $1,250 state tax refund for Year 1 overpayments. In Year 1, the McGurns were not subject to the alternative minimum tax and were not entitled to any credit against income tax. The McGurns' Year 1 adjusted gross income was $80,000 and itemized deductions were $1,450 in excess of the standard deduction. The state tax deduction for Year 1 was $2,000.	

For Item 6, determine the amount of the adjustment, if any, to arrive at adjusted gross income.

Transaction	Answer
6. As required by a Year 0 divorce agreement, William paid an annual amount of $8,000 in alimony and $10,000 in child support during Year 2.	

For Items 7 through 12, select the appropriate tax treatment from the list for transactions that took place during Year 2. A tax treatment may be selected once, more than once, or not at all.

Tax Treatment

A. Not deductible on Form 1040.

B. Deductible in full in Schedule A—Itemized Deductions.

C. Deductible in Schedule A—Itemized Deductions, subject to a threshold of 7.5% of adjusted gross income.

D. Deductible in Schedule A—Itemized Deductions, subject to a limitation of 50% of adjusted gross income.

E. Deductible in Schedule A—Itemized Deductions, subject to a $100 floor and a threshold of 10% of adjusted gross income.

F. Deductible in Schedule A—Itemized Deductions, subject to a threshold of 2% of adjusted gross income.

Transaction	Answer
7. On March 23, William sold 50 shares of Zip stock at a $1,200 loss. He repurchased 50 shares of Zip on April 15.	
8. Payment of a personal property tax based on the value of the McGurns' car.	
9. Used furniture was donated to church organizations.	
10. William paid for subscriptions to accounting journals.	
11. Interest was paid on a $10,000 home-equity line of credit secured by the McGurns' residence. The fair market value of the home exceeded the mortgage by $50,000. William used the proceeds to purchase a sailboat.	

For Items 13 through 15, determine whether the statement is true (T) or false (F) regarding the McGurns' tax return.

Statement	Answer
12. The McGurns were subject to the phase-out of half their personal exemptions for regular tax because their adjusted gross income was $75,000.	
13. The McGurns' unreimbursed medical expenses for AMT had to exceed 10% of adjusted gross income.	
14. The McGurns' personal exemption amount for regular tax was not permitted for determining AMT.	

Write a memo to the McGurns' explaining why premiums paid covering insurance against William's loss of earnings are nondeductible.

Research Question: What code section and subsection, if applicable, provides guidance on the amount of the credit for which the taxpayer may claim with respect to the payment of foreign taxes?

Section & Subsection Answer: §_____ (___)

Problem 44-5 (20 to 30 minutes)

Jason and Daphne Soffit are married and filing a joint 2008 income tax return. Jason, 65, was retired from government service and Daphne, 55, was employed as a university instructor. The Soffits contributed all of the support to Daphne's father, Andre Dupont, an unmarried French citizen and French resident who had no gross income. Jason and Daphne Soffit's social security numbers are 987-65-4321 and 123-54-6789, respectively.

Complete the "Filing Status," "Exemptions," "Income," and "Adjusted Gross Income" sections of the Form 1040 for the Soffits based on the information on the "Scenario" tab.

1. Daphne received a $30,000 cash gift from her aunt.
2. Daphne contributed $5,500 to her Individual Retirement Account (IRA) on January 15, 2009. She also contributed $500 to her Roth IRA on January 20, 2009. In 2008, she earned $60,000 as a university instructor. The Soffits were not active participants in an employer's qualified pension or annuity plan.
3. The Soffits received a $1,000 federal income tax refund.
4. Jason, a 50% partner in Diske General Partnership, received a $4,000 guaranteed payment from Diske for services that he rendered to the partnership that year.
5. Jason received $10,000 as beneficiary of his deceased brother's life insurance policy.
6. Daphne's employer pays 100% of the cost of all employees' group term life insurance under a qualified plan. Policy cost is $5 per $1,000 of coverage. Daphne's group term life insurance coverage equals $450,000.
7. Jason won $5,000 at a casino and had $2,000 in gambling losses.
8. The Soffits received $1,000 interest income associated with a refund of their prior years' federal income tax.
9. The Soffits sold their first and only residence for $200,000. They purchased their home five years ago for $50,000 and have lived there since then. There were no other capital gains, losses, or capital loss carryovers. The Soffits do not intend to buy another residence. (11/97, AR #2, amended, 6562)

Scenario | Form 1040 | Communication | Research

Form **1040** Department of the Treasury—Internal Revenue Service
U.S. Individual Income Tax Return 2008 (99) IRS Use Only—Do not write or staple in this space.

For the year Jan. 1–Dec. 31, 2008, or other tax year beginning , 2008, ending , 20 OMB No. 1545-0074

Label (See instructions on page 14.) Use the IRS label. Otherwise, please print or type.

LABEL HERE

Your first name and initial | Last name | Your social security number

If a joint return, spouse's first name and initial | Last name | Spouse's social security number

Home address (number and street). If you have a P.O. box, see page 14. | Apt. no. | ▲ You must enter your SSN(s) above. ▲

City, town or post office, state, and ZIP code. If you have a foreign address, see page 14.

Checking a box below will not change your tax or refund.

Presidential Election Campaign ▶ Check here if you, or your spouse if filing jointly, want $3 to go to this fund (see page 14) ▶ ☐ You ☐ Spouse

Filing Status

Check only one box.

1 ☐ Single
2 ☐ Married filing jointly (even if only one had income)
3 ☐ Married filing separately. Enter spouse's SSN above and full name here. ▶
4 ☐ Head of household (with qualifying person). (See page 15.) If the qualifying person is a child but not your dependent, enter this child's name here. ▶
5 ☐ Qualifying widow(er) with dependent child (see page 16)

Exemptions

6a ☐ Yourself. If someone can claim you as a dependent, do not check box 6a

b ☐ Spouse

Boxes checked on 6a and 6b ____

c Dependents:

(1) First name Last name	(2) Dependent's social security number	(3) Dependent's relationship to you	(4) ✓ if qualifying child for child tax credit (see page 17)
			☐
			☐
			☐
			☐

If more than four dependents, see page 17.

No. of children on 6c who:
- lived with you ____
- did not live with you due to divorce or separation (see page 18) ____

Dependents on 6c not entered above ____

d Total number of exemptions claimed

Add numbers on lines above ▶

Income

Attach Form(s) W-2 here. Also attach Forms W-2G and 1099-R if tax was withheld.

If you did not get a W-2, see page 21.

Enclose, but do not attach, any payment. Also, please use Form 1040-V.

7	Wages, salaries, tips, etc. Attach Form(s) W-2	7
8a	Taxable interest. Attach Schedule B if required	8a
b	Tax-exempt interest. Do not include on line 8a — 8b	
9a	Ordinary dividends. Attach Schedule B if required	9a
b	Qualified dividends (see page 21) — 9b	
10	Taxable refunds, credits, or offsets of state and local income taxes (see page 22)	10
11	Alimony received	11
12	Business income or (loss). Attach Schedule C or C-EZ	12
13	Capital gain or (loss). Attach Schedule D if required. If not required, check here ▶ ☐	13
14	Other gains or (losses). Attach Form 4797	14
15a	IRA distributions — 15a — b Taxable amount (see page 23)	15b
16a	Pensions and annuities — 16a — b Taxable amount (see page 24)	16b
17	Rental real estate, royalties, partnerships, S corporations, trusts, etc. Attach Schedule E	17
18	Farm income or (loss). Attach Schedule F	18
19	Unemployment compensation	19
20a	Social security benefits — 20a — b Taxable amount (see page 26)	20b
21	Other income. List type and amount (see page 28)	21
22	Add the amounts in the far right column for lines 7 through 21. This is your total income ▶	22

Adjusted Gross Income

23	Educator expenses (see page 28)	23
24	Certain business expenses of reservists, performing artists, and fee-basis government officials. Attach Form 2106 or 2106-EZ	24
25	Health savings account deduction. Attach Form 8889	25
26	Moving expenses. Attach Form 3903	26
27	One-half of self-employment tax. Attach Schedule SE	27
28	Self-employed SEP, SIMPLE, and qualified plans	28
29	Self-employed health insurance deduction (see page 29)	29
30	Penalty on early withdrawal of savings	30
31a	Alimony paid b Recipient's SSN ▶	31a
32	IRA deduction (see page 30)	32
33	Student loan interest deduction (see page 33)	33
34	Tuition and fees deduction. Attach Form 8917	34
35	Domestic production activities deduction. Attach Form 8903	35
36	Add lines 23 through 31a and 32 through 35	36
37	Subtract line 36 from line 22. This is your adjusted gross income ▶	37

For Disclosure, Privacy Act, and Paperwork Reduction Act Notice, see page 88. Cat. No. 11320B Form **1040** (2008)

You prepare the Soffits' personal taxes. Write a memo to the client explaining the treatment of a stock dividend declared by Zeno Corporation. Zeno Corp. declared a stock dividend and Daphne received one additional share of Zeno common stock for three shares of Zeno common stock that she held. The stock that Daphne received had a fair market value of $9,000. There were no provisions to receive cash instead of stock.

Scenario | Form 1040 | Communication | Research

Research Question: What code section and subsection, if applicable, provides guidance on the accounting methods that may be used when the taxpayer engages in more than one business?

Section & Subsection Answer: §_____ (___)

Problem 44-6 (20 to 30 minutes)

Maple, an unmarried custodial parent, had one dependent three-year-old child and worked in a CPA firm. Maple, who had adjusted gross income of $40,000, qualified to itemize deductions and was subject to federal income tax liability. Maple's social security number is 123-45-6789.

1. Maple paid $900 toward continuing education courses and was not reimbursed by her employer.
2. Maple had a $30,000 cash charitable contribution carryover from her 2007 cash donation to the American Red Cross. Maple made no additional charitable contributions during 2008.
3. Maple had $1,200 investment interest expense and $1,500 net investment income.
4. Maple's lottery ticket losses were $450. She had no gambling winnings.
5. Maple paid $2,500 in real property taxes on her vacation home, which she used exclusively for personal use.
6. Maple paid a $500 premium for a homeowner's insurance policy on her principal residence.
7. Maple paid a $2,800 health insurance premium for hospitalization coverage through her employer.
8. Maple paid $4,000 interest on the $60,000 acquisition mortgage of her principal residence. The mortgage is secured by Maple's home.
9. Maple paid $3,600 real property taxes on residential rental property at 927 Mulberry Street, My Town, FL in which she actively participates. Maple received $12,000 in rental income. There was no personal use of the rental property.

Prepare IRS Schedule A and Schedule E for Maple. (11/97, AR #2, amended, 6553)

SCHEDULES A&B (Form 1040)
Department of the Treasury Internal Revenue Service (99)

Schedule A—Itemized Deductions

(Schedule B is on back)

► Attach to Form 1040. ► See Instructions for Schedules A&B (Form 1040).

OMB No. 1545-0074
2008
Attachment Sequence No. 07

Name(s) shown on Form 1040 | Your social security number

Section	Line	Description	Box	Amount	Box	Amount
Medical and Dental Expenses		Caution. Do not include expenses reimbursed or paid by others.				
	1	Medical and dental expenses (see page A-1)	1			
	2	Enter amount from Form 1040, line 38 [2]				
	3	Multiply line 2 by 7.5% (.075)	3			
	4	Subtract line 3 from line 1. If line 3 is more than line 1, enter -0-			4	
Taxes You Paid (See page A-2.)	5	State and local (check only one box): a ☐ Income taxes, or b ☐ General sales taxes	5			
	6	Real estate taxes (see page A-5)	6			
	7	Personal property taxes	7			
	8	Other taxes. List type and amount ►	8			
	9	Add lines 5 through 8			9	
Interest You Paid (See page A-5.)	10	Home mortgage interest and points reported to you on Form 1098	10			
	11	Home mortgage interest not reported to you on Form 1098. If paid to the person from whom you bought the home, see page A-6 and show that person's name, identifying no., and address ►	11			
Note. Personal interest is not deductible.	12	Points not reported to you on Form 1098. See page A-6 for special rules	12			
	13	Qualified mortgage insurance premiums (see page A-6)	13			
	14	Investment interest. Attach Form 4952 if required. (See page A-6.)	14			
	15	Add lines 10 through 14			15	
Gifts to Charity	16	Gifts by cash or check. If you made any gift of $250 or more, see page A-7	16			
If you made a gift and got a benefit for it, see page A-7.	17	Other than by cash or check. If any gift of $250 or more, see page A-8. You must attach Form 8283 if over $500	17			
	18	Carryover from prior year	18			
	19	Add lines 16 through 18			19	
Casualty and Theft Losses	20	Casualty or theft loss(es). Attach Form 4684. (See page A-8.)			20	
Job Expenses and Certain Miscellaneous Deductions (See page A-9.)	21	Unreimbursed employee expenses—job travel, union dues, job education, etc. Attach Form 2106 or 2106-EZ if required. (See page A-9.) ►	21			
	22	Tax preparation fees	22			
	23	Other expenses—investment, safe deposit box, etc. List type and amount ►	23			
	24	Add lines 21 through 23	24			
	25	Enter amount from Form 1040, line 38 [25]				
	26	Multiply line 25 by 2% (.02)	26			
	27	Subtract line 26 from line 24. If line 26 is more than line 24, enter -0-			27	
Other Miscellaneous Deductions	28	Other—from list on page A-10. List type and amount ►			28	
Total Itemized Deductions	29	Is Form 1040, line 38, over $159,950 (over $79,975 if married filing separately)? ☐ No. Your deduction is not limited. Add the amounts in the far right column for lines 4 through 28. Also, enter this amount on Form 1040, line 40. ☐ Yes. Your deduction may be limited. See page A-10 for the amount to enter. ►			29	
	30	If you elect to itemize deductions even though they are less than your standard deduction, check here ► ☐				

For Paperwork Reduction Act Notice, see Form 1040 instructions. Cat. No. 11330X Schedule A (Form 1040) 2008

SCHEDULE E (Form 1040)

Department of the Treasury Internal Revenue Service (99)

Supplemental Income and Loss

(From rental real estate, royalties, partnerships, S corporations, estates, trusts, REMICs, etc.)

▶ Attach to Form 1040, 1040NR, or Form 1041. ▶ See Instructions for Schedule E (Form 1040).

OMB No. 1545-0074

2008

Attachment Sequence No. 13

Name(s) shown on return | Your social security number

Part I **Income or Loss From Rental Real Estate and Royalties** Note. If you are in the business of renting personal property, use Schedule C or C-EZ (see page E-3). If you are an individual, report farm rental income or loss from Form 4835 on page 2, line 40.

1	List the type and address of each rental real estate property:
A	
B	
C	

2 For each rental real estate property listed on line 1, did you or your family use it during the tax year for personal purposes for more than the greater of:
- 14 days or
- 10% of the total days rented at fair rental value?

(See page E-3)

	Yes	No
A		
B		
C		

		Properties A	Properties B	Properties C	Totals (Add columns A, B, and C.)
Income:					
3 Rents received	3				3
4 Royalties received	4				4
Expenses:					
5 Advertising	5				
6 Auto and travel (see page E-4)	6				
7 Cleaning and maintenance	7				
8 Commissions	8				
9 Insurance	9				
10 Legal and other professional fees	10				
11 Management fees	11				
12 Mortgage interest paid to banks, etc. (see page E-5)	12				12
13 Other interest	13				
14 Repairs	14				
15 Supplies	15				
16 Taxes	16				
17 Utilities	17				
18 Other (list) ▶	18				
19 Add lines 5 through 18	19				19
20 Depreciation expense or depletion (see page E-5)	20				20
21 Total expenses. Add lines 19 and 20	21				
22 Income or (loss) from rental real estate or royalty properties. Subtract line 21 from line 3 (rents) or line 4 (royalties). If the result is a (loss), see page E-5 to find out if you must file Form 6198	22				
23 Deductible rental real estate loss. **Caution.** Your rental real estate loss on line 22 may be limited. See page E-5 to find out if you must file Form 8582. Real estate professionals must complete line 43 on page 2	23	( )	( )	( )	

24	**Income.** Add positive amounts shown on line 22. Do not include any losses	24
25	**Losses.** Add royalty losses from line 22 and rental real estate losses from line 23. Enter total losses here.	25 ( )
26	**Total rental real estate and royalty income or (loss).** Combine lines 24 and 25. Enter the result here. If Parts II, III, IV, and line 40 on page 2 do not apply to you, also enter this amount on Form 1040, line 17, or Form 1040NR, line 18. Otherwise, include this amount in the total on line 41 on page 2	26

For Paperwork Reduction Act Notice, see page E-8 of the Instructions. Cat. No. 11344L **Schedule E (Form 1040) 2008**

You prepare Maple's personal taxes. Write a memo to Maple explaining why her gambling losses are nondeductible.

Research Question: What code section and subsection, if applicable, provides guidance on the time requirement for which a taxpayer, who is required to file an income tax return, may claim a refund of an overpayment of tax?

Section & Subsection Answer: §_____ (___)

Problem 44-7 (20 to 30 minutes)

Rogue is self-employed as a human resources consultant and reports on the cash basis for income tax purposes. (5/93, PII, #4, amended, 4167)

For Items 1 through 11, select the appropriate tax treatment from the following list.

Tax Treatments

A. Taxable as other income on Form 1040

B. Reported in Schedule B—*Interest and Dividend Income*

C. Reported in Schedule C as trade or business income

D. Reported in Schedule E—*Supplemental Income and Loss*

E. Not taxable

Transaction	Answer
1. Retainer fees received from clients.	
2. Oil royalties received.	
3. Interest on refund of federal taxes.	
4. Death benefits from term life insurance policy on parent.	
5. Share of ordinary income from an investment in a limited partnership reported in Form 1065, Schedule K-1.	
6. Taxable income from rental of a townhouse owned by Rogue.	
7. Prize won as a contestant on a TV quiz show.	
8. Payment received for jury service.	

You prepare Rogue's personal taxes. Write a memo to the client explaining why the interest on general obligation state and local government bonds is not taxable, even though the interest on the refunds of their state and local taxes and their U.S. Treasury bonds is taxable. Also, explain how dividends from mutual funds investing in tax-free government obligations are treated.

Scenario | Tax Treatment | Communication | Research

Research Question: What code section and subsection, if applicable, provides guidance on the deductibility of charitable contributions as a business expense?

Section & Subsection Answer: §_____ (___)

Problem 44-8 (20 to 30 minutes)

Mrs. Guild, a 40-year-old cash basis taxpayer, earned $45,000 as a teacher and $5,000 as a part-time real estate agent in Year 1. Mr. Guild, who died on July 1, Year 1, had been permanently disabled on his job and collected state disability benefits until his death. For all of Year 1 and Year 2, the Guild's residence was the principal home of both their 11-year-old daughter, Joan, and Mrs. Guild's unmarried cousin, Fran Phillips, who had no income in either year. During Year 1, Joan received $200 a month in survivor social security benefits that began on August 1, and will continue at least until her 18th birthday. In Year 1 and Year 2, Mrs. Guild provided over one-half the support for Joan and Fran, both of whom were U.S. citizens. Mrs. Guild did not remarry. Mr. and Mrs. Guild received the following in Year 1:

Earned income	$50,000
State disability benefits	1,500
Interest on:	
Refund from amended tax return	50
Savings account and certificates of deposit	350
Municipal bonds	100
Gift	3,000
Pension benefits	900
Jury duty pay	200
Gambling winnings	450
Life insurance proceeds	5,000

- Mrs. Guild received the $3,000 cash gift from her uncle.
- Mrs. Guild received the pension distributions from a qualified pension plan, paid for exclusively by her husband's employer.
- Mrs. Guild had $100 in gambling losses.
- Mrs. Guild was the beneficiary of the life insurance policy on her husband's life. She received a lump-sum distribution. The Guilds had paid $500 in premiums.
- Mrs. Guild received Mr. Guild's accrued vacation pay of $500 in Year 2. (11/94, AR, #3, amended, 5046)

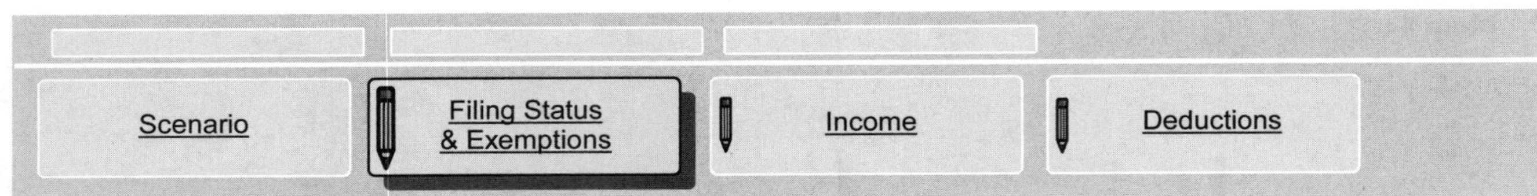

For Items 1 and 2, determine **both** the filing status and number of exemptions for each item.

Filing Status

S. Single

M. Married filing joint

H. Head of household

Q. Qualifying widow with dependent child

Item	Filing Status	Number of Exemptions
1. Determine the filing status and the number of exemptions that Mrs. Guild can claim on the Year 1 federal income tax return, to get the most favorable tax results.		
2. Determine the filing status and the number of exemptions that Mrs. Guild can claim on the Year 2 federal income tax return to get the most favorable tax results, if she solely maintains the costs of her home.		

For Items 3 through 9, determine the taxable amount, if any, that should be included in Adjusted Gross Income (AGI) on the Year 1 federal income tax return.

Income	Answer
3. State disability benefits	
4. Interest income	
5. Pension benefits	
6. Gift	
7. Life insurance proceeds	
8. Jury duty pay	
9. Gambling winnings	

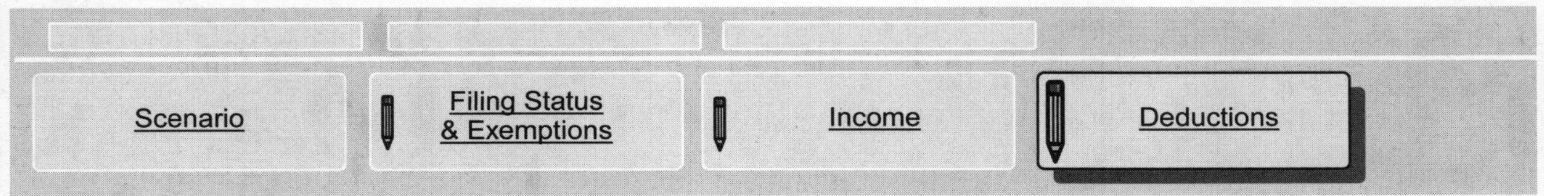

For Items 10 through 23, select the appropriate tax treatment from the list for payments or losses that incurred during Year 1. A tax treatment may be selected once, more than once, or not at all.

Tax Treatments

A. Not deductible

B. Deductible in Schedule A—*Itemized Deductions,* subject to threshold of 7.5% of adjusted gross income

C. Deductible in Schedule A—*Itemized Deductions,* subject to threshold of 2% of adjusted gross income

D. Deductible on page 1 of Form 1040 to arrive at adjusted gross income

E. Deductible in full in Schedule A—*Itemized Deductions*

F. Deductible in Schedule A—*Itemized Deductions,* subject to threshold of 50% of adjusted gross income

Payment & Loss	Answer
10. Premiums on Mr. Guild's personal life insurance policy	
11. Penalty on Mrs. Guild's early withdrawal of funds from a certificate of deposit	
12. Mrs. Guild's substantiated cash donation to the American Red Cross	
13. Payment of estimated state income taxes	
14. Payment of real estate taxes on the Guild home	
15. Loss on the sale of the family car	
16. Cost in excess of the increase in value of residence, for the installation of a stairlift in January, related directly to the medical care of Mr. Guild	
17. The Guilds' health insurance premiums for hospitalization coverage through Mrs. Guild's employer	
18. CPA fees to prepare the tax return for the previous year	
19. Amortization over the life of the loan of points paid to refinance the mortgage at a lower rate on the Guild home	
20. One-half the self-employment tax paid by Mrs. Guild	
21. Mrs. Guild's $100 in gambling losses	
22. Mrs. Guild's union dues	
23. Year 0 federal income tax paid with the Guild's tax return on April 15, Year 1	

For Items 24 through 31, determine whether the statement is true (T) or false (F) regarding the Guilds' Year 1 income tax return.

Statement	Answer
24. The funeral expenses paid by Mr. Guild's estate is a Year 1 itemized deduction.	
25. Any federal estate tax on the income in respect of decedent, to be distributed to Mrs. Guild, may be taken as a miscellaneous itemized deduction not subject to the 2% of adjusted gross income floor.	
26. A casualty loss deduction on property used in Mrs. Guild's part-time real estate business is reported as an itemized deduction.	
27. The Guilds' income tax liability will be reduced by the credit for the elderly or disabled.	
28. The CPA preparer is required to furnish a completed copy of the income tax return to Mrs. Guild.	
29. Since Mr. Guild died during the year, the income limitation for the earned income credit does not apply.	
30. Mr. Guild's accrued vacation pay, at the time of his death, is to be distributed to Mrs. Guild in Year 2. This income should be included in the Year 1 Federal income tax return.	
31. The Guilds paid alternative minimum tax in Year 0. The amount of alternative minimum tax that is attributable to "deferral adjustments and preferences" can be used to offset the alternative minimum tax in following years.	

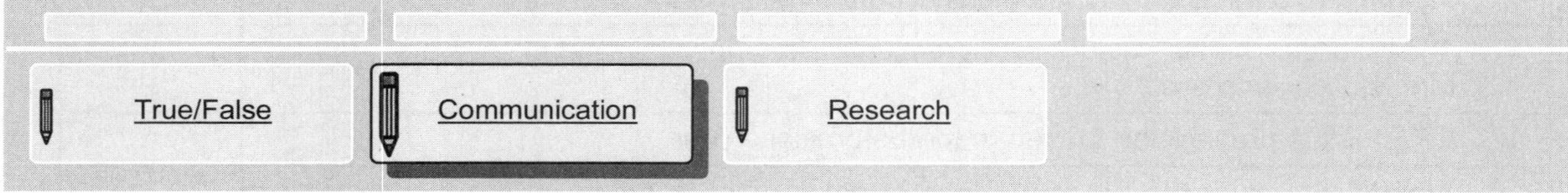

Write a memo to the Guilds' explaining why the personal life insurance premiums paid are nondeductible.

Research Question: What code section and subsection, if applicable, provides guidance on the amount of the deduction for a debt that becomes uncollectible during the tax year?

Section & Subsection Answer: §_____ (___)

Problem 44-9 (40 to 60 minutes)

In the following simulation, you will be asked various questions regarding business income or loss generated by a farm operated as a sole proprietorship and reported on Schedule F, Farm Income and Expenses, of Form 1040, *U.S. Individual Income Tax Return.* You will use the content in the **Information Tabs** to complete the tasks in the **Work Tabs.** (The following pictures are for illustration only; the actual tabs in your simulation may differ from these.)

Information Tabs

Beginning with the Directions tab at the left side of the screen, go through each of the **Information Tabs** to familiarize yourself with the simulation content. Note that the **Resources** tab will contain useful information, including formulas and definitions, to help you complete the tasks. You may want to refer to this information while you are working.

Work Tabs:

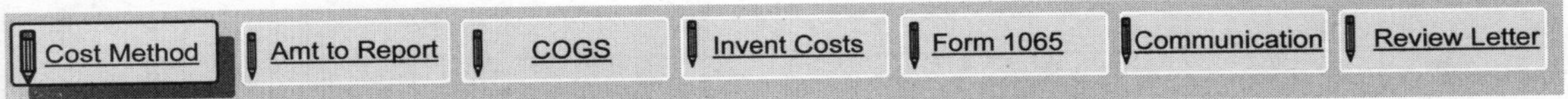

The **Work Tabs,** on the right side of the screen, contain the tasks for you to complete.

Once you complete any part of a task, the pencil for that tab will be shaded. Note that a shaded pencil does NOT indicate that you have completed the entire task.

You must complete all of the tasks in the **Work Tabs** to receive full credit.

If you have difficulty answering a **Work Tab,** read the tab directions carefully.

Note: If you believe you have encountered a software malfunction, report it to the test center staff immediately.

Cameron Sullivan recently purchased a farm. The farm is being operated as a sole proprietorship. Farm operations began on January 1, year 1, and became profitable in year 2. Cameron uses the cash basis of accounting for book and tax purposes.

During year 2, Cameron employed as many as 20 part-time workers, including Cameron's spouse, Elinor, and children, Edward and Darla, ages 19 and 14, respectively. Elinor was unemployed during year 1, and Cameron had no other earned income for year 1, except from the farm. Cameron and Elinor filed a joint income tax return for year 2 and year 1.

Cameron is not yet providing the farm employees with life insurance, medical and dental coverage, or retirement benefits. Cameron is paying the life and medical insurance premiums for the family from personal funds.

(R/07, REG, #41, amended, 8554)

The following table includes a partial listing of the income and expense items that Cameron recorded on the farm's books for year 2. For each item of income and expense, select the appropriate cell to indicate whether the item should be reported on Cameron's Schedule F, shown elsewhere on the joint income tax return, or not included or deducted anywhere on the joint income tax return. Cameron and Elinor Sullivan have consistently itemized deductions on their joint income tax return.

		A	B	C	
		Reported on Cameron's Schedule F	Shown elsewhere on the joint return	Not included or deducted on the joint return	1
Revenue and Receipts					2
1. Cash receipts from the sale of cattle bought for resale	$201,300				3
2. Proceeds from farm line of credit	31,100				4
3. Bank interest on Edward's personal bank account	300				5
4. Bank interest on Cameron's farm account	600				6
					7
Expenses and Disbursements					8
5. Cost of cattle sold this year	113,800				9
6. Interest on farm line of credit loan	8,600				10
7. Principal repayments on farm line of credit	1,200				11
8. Chemicals and pesticides	8,100				12
9. Contribution to Cameron's Roth IRA account	2,000				13
10. State estimated tax payments on farm earnings	2,300				14
11. Property taxes on the Sullivan home	1,700				15
12. Fertilizer costs	2,300				16
13. Farm travel expenses	1,200				17
14. Late payment penalties on farm payroll taxes	200				18
15. Livestock feed expenses	1,400				19
16. Repairs and maintenance on farm equipment	900				20

Cameron Sullivan had a net loss before MACRS depreciation and Section 179 deduction on the farm operations for 2008. Cameron elected out of all applicable bonus depreciation allowances, if any, and did not elect the straight-line method of depreciation. Calculate the depreciation on Cameron's farm assets for 2008 using the information in the table below and the 150% MACRS tables found by clicking the tab marked RESOURCES. Note that any property used in a farming business cannot be depreciated using the 200% declining balance method under MACRS for tax purposes.

- In cells F2 and F3, enter the appropriate MACRS basis for each of the assets listed.
- In cells G2 and G3, calculate and enter the year 1 MACRS depreciation for each asset.
- The total year 1 MACRS depreciation will automatically calculate in cell G4.

Note: To use a formula in the spreadsheet, it must be preceded by an equal sign, e.g., =B1+B2.

A	B	C	D	E	F	G	
Date placed in service	**Asset**	**Cost**	**Life**	**Section 179 elected**	**MACRS basis**	**Year 1 MACRS depreciation**	1
17. January 1, year 1	Truck	44,000	5 years	—			2
18. January 1, year 1	Combine	60,000	7 years	25,000			3
Total year 1 MACRS depreciation							4

On November 1, 2009, Cameron purchased a new truck, and on November 30, 2009, Cameron sold an old truck. The new truck was the only asset purchased during the year. Cameron did not elect any Section 179 deduction for 2009. Calculate the depreciation on Cameron's farm assets shown below for 2009 using the information provided and the 150% MACRS tables found by clicking the tab marked RESOURCES. Enter your answers in the shaded spaces provided. The total 2009 MACRS depreciation will automatically calculate in cell G5.

For purposes of this tab (Depreciation) only, assume that Cameron had net farm income for 2009 of $200,000 before MACRS depreciation and Section 179 deduction.

A	B	C	D	E	F	G	
Date placed in service	**Asset**	**Cost**	**Life**	**Section 179 elected in year 1**	**Section 179 elected in year 2**	**Year 2 MACRS depreciation**	1
19. January 1, year 1	Old truck	44,000	5 years	0	0		2
20. January 1, year 1	Combine	60,000	7 years	25,000	0		3
21. November 1, year 2	New truck	65,000	5 years	0	0		4
Total year 2 MACRS depreciation							5

In the shaded cells below, answer the following questions related to the $25,000 Section 179 deduction elected in 2008.

A	G	
22. How much is allowed in 2008 for tax purposes?		1
23. How much is allowed in 2009 for tax purposes?		2

Cameron Sullivan is required to pay a self-employment tax based on the net profits of the farm business. For purposes of this tab (Self-Employment Tax), assume that Cameron had a net profit of $105,000 from the farm business for year 3 and $10,000 of Section 1231 gain.

Complete Section A of the Form 1040, Schedule SE, for year 3 below by entering the appropriate values in the shaded cells. Round values to the nearest dollar. If a cell should be left empty, enter a zero.

H7 | 12.3

Section A--Short Schedule SE. Caution. Read above to see if you can use Short Schedule SE.

1	Net farm profit or (loss) from Schedule F, line 36, and farm partnerships, Schedule K-1 (Form 1065), line 15a	1	
2	Net profit or (loss) from Schedule C, line 31; Schedule C-EZ, line 3; Schedule K-1 (Form 1065), line 15a (other than farming); and Schedule K-1 (Form 1065-B), box 9. Ministers and members of religious orders, see SE-1 for amounts to report on this line. See page SE-2 for other income to report	2	
3	Combine lines 1 and 2	3	
4	Net earnings from self-employment. Multiply line 3 by 92.35% (.9235). If less than $400, do not file this schedule; you do not owe self-employment tax ▶	4	
5	Self-employment tax. If the amount on line 4 is: • $87,000 or less, multiply line 4 by 15.3% (.153). Enter the result here and on Form 1040, line 55. • More than $87,000, multiply line 4 by 2.9% (.029). Then, add $10,788.00 to the result. Enter the total here and on Form 1040, line 55.	5	
6	Deduction for one-half of self-employment tax. Multiply line 5 by 50% (.5). Enter the result here and on Form 1040, line 28.	6	

For Paperwork Reduction Act Notice, see Form 1040 instructions. Cat. No. 11358Z Schedule SE (Form 1040)

Climpson, another of your clients, plans to start a farming business as a sole proprietor. Write Climpson a letter identifying and explaining specific types of expenses that can be included on Climpson's Schedule F. In your letter, you should discuss at least two of the following topics:

- Cash or accrual method of accounting
- Personal income and deductions reported elsewhere on the return
- Payroll tax return filings necessary for businesses with employees
- Self-employment tax for Climpson

REMINDER: Your response will be graded for both technical content and writing skills. Technical content will be evaluated for information that is helpful to the intended reader and clearly relevant to the issue. Writing skills will be evaluated for development, organization, and the appropriate expression of ideas in professional correspondence. Use a standard business memo or letter format with a clear beginning, middle, and end. Do not convey information in the form of a table, bullet point list, or other abbreviated presentation.

Research Question: Cameron expects income for the first four years of farm operations to be very volatile and is interested in income averaging on his tax return. Which code section and subsection provides the authority for Cameron to elect averaging of farm income for purposes of computing his tax liability?

Section & Subsection Answer: §_____ (___)

MACRS Table (half-year convention
150 percent declining-balance method)

Depreciation rate for recovery period				
Year	3 years	5 years	7 years	10 years
1	25.00%	15.00%	10.71%	7.50%
2	37.50%	25.50%	19.13%	13.88%
3	25.00%	17.85%	15.03%	11.79%
4	12.50%	16.66%	25.25%	10.02%
5		16.66%	25.25%	8.74%
6		8.33%	25.25%	8.74%
7			25.25%	8.74%
8			6.13%	8.74%
9				8.74%
10				8.74%
11				4.37%

MACRS Table (mid-quarter convention
150 percent declining-balance method)
Property placed in service in First Quarter

Depreciation rate for recovery period				
Year	3 years	5 years	7 years	10 years
1	43.75%	26.25%	18.75%	13.13%
2	28.13%	22.13%	17.41%	13.03%
3	25.00%	16.52%	13.68%	11.08%
4	3.12%	16.52%	12.16%	9.41%
5		16.52%	12.16%	8.71%
6		2.06%	12.16%	8.71%
7			12.16%	8.71%
8			1.52%	8.71%
9				8.71%
10				8.71%
11				1.09%

MACRS Table (mid-quarter convention
150 percent declining-balance method)
Property placed in service in Second Quarter

Depreciation rate for recovery period				
Year	3 years	5 years	7 years	10 years
1	31.25%	18.75%	13.39%	9.38%
2	34.38%	24.38%	18.56%	13.59%
3	25.00%	17.06%	14.58%	11.55%
4	9.37%	16.76%	12.22%	9.82%
5		16.76%	12.22%	8.73%
6		6.29%	12.22%	8.73%
7			12.23%	8.73%
8			4.58%	8.73%
9				8.73%
10				8.73%
11				3.28%

MACRS Table (mid-quarter convention
150 percent declining-balance method)
Property placed in service in Third Quarter

Depreciation rate for recovery period				
Year	3 years	5 years	7 years	10 years
1	18.75%	11.25%	8.04%	5.63%
2	40.63%	28.63%	19.71%	14.16%
3	25.00%	18.64%	15.48%	12.03%
4	15.62%	16.56%	12.27%	10.23%
5		16.57%	12.28%	8.75%
6		10.35%	12.27%	8.75%
7			12.28%	8.75%
8			7.67%	8.74%
9				8.75%
10				8.74%
11				5.47%

MACRS Table (mid-quarter convention
150 percent declining-balance method)
Property placed in service in Fourth Quarter

Depreciation rate for recovery period				
Year	3 years	5 years	7 years	10 years
1	6.25%	3.75%	2.68%	1.88%
2	46.88%	28.88%	20.85%	14.72%
3	25.00%	20.21%	16.39%	12.51%
4	21.87%	16.40%	12.87%	10.63%
5		16.41%	12.18%	9.04%
6		14.35%	12.18%	8.72%
7			12.19%	8.72%
8			10.66%	8.72%
9				8.72%
10				8.71%
11				7.63%

Problem 44-10 (20 to 30 minutes)

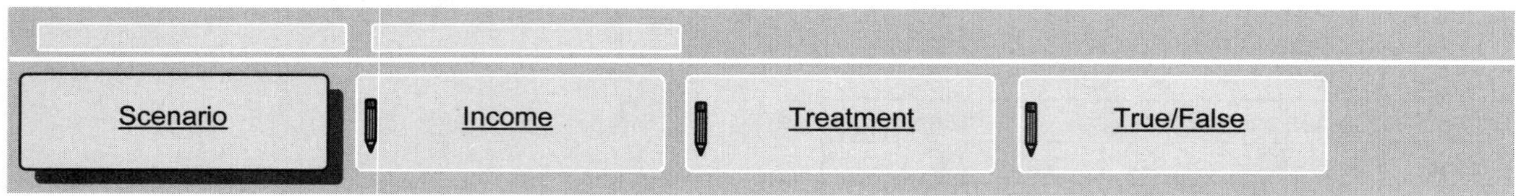

David and Kalila Ryan, both CPAs, filed a joint 2009 federal income tax return showing $70,000 in taxable income. David's daughter Laura, age 17, resided with David's former spouse. Laura had no income of her own and was not David's dependent. The Ryans' total medical expenses were less than 7.5% of adjusted gross income. (11/95, AR, #3, amended, 5828)

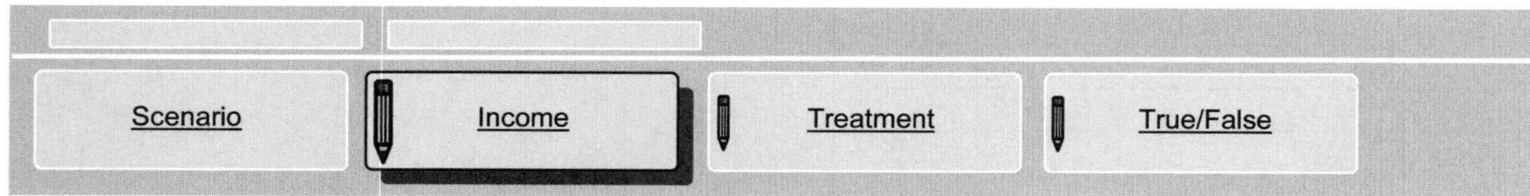

Determine the amount of income or loss, if any, that should be included on page one of the Ryans' Form 1040.

Income	Answer
1. Kalila received $1,300 in unemployment compensation benefits. Her employer made a $100 contribution to the unemployment insurance fund on her behalf.	
2. The Ryans received $8,400 in gross receipts from their rental property. The expenses for the residential rental property were: Bank mortgage interest $1,200 Real estate taxes 700 Insurance 500 MACRS depreciation 3,500	
3. The Ryans received a stock dividend from Ace Corp. They had the option to receive either cash or Ace stock with a fair market value of $900 as of the date of distribution. The par value of the stock was $500.	
4. Kalila received $3,500 as beneficiary of the death benefit provided by her brother's employer. Kalila's brother did not have a nonforfeitable right to receive the money while living.	
5. David received $10,000, consisting of $5,000 each of principal and interest, when he redeemed a Series EE savings bond in 2009. The bond was issued in his name in 1990 and the proceeds were used to pay for Laura's college tuition. David had not elected to report the yearly increases in the value of the bond.	

For Items 6 through 11, select the appropriate tax treatment from the list for transactions that took place during 2009. A tax treatment may be selected once, more than once, or not at all.

Tax Treatment

A. Not deductible on Form 1040.

B. Deductible in full in Schedule A—Itemized Deductions.

C. Deductible in Schedule A—Itemized Deductions, subject to a threshold of 7.5% of adjusted gross income.

D. Deductible in Schedule A—Itemized Deductions, subject to a limitation of 50% of adjusted gross income.

E. Deductible in Schedule A—Itemized Deductions, subject to a $100 floor and a threshold of 10% of adjusted gross income.

F. Deductible in Schedule A—Itemized Deductions, subject to a threshold of 2% of adjusted gross income.

Transaction	Answer
6. Amounts were paid in excess of insurance reimbursement for prescription drugs.	
7. Funeral expenses were paid by the Ryans for Kalila's brother.	
8. Theft loss was incurred on Kalila's jewelry in excess of insurance reimbursement. There were no personal casualty gains.	
9. Loss on the sale of the family's sailboat.	
10. Interest was paid on the $300,000 acquisition mortgage on the Ryans' home. The mortgage is secured by their home.	
11. Kalila performed free accounting services for the Red Cross. The estimated value of the services was $500.	

For Items 12 through 14, determine whether the statement is true (T) or false (F) regarding the Ryans' tax return.

Statement	Answer
12. The Ryans paid $1,200 in additional taxes when they filed their return on April 14, 2010. Their 2009 federal tax withholdings equaled 100% of Year 1 tax liability. Therefore, they were not subject to the underpayment of tax penalty.	
13. The Ryans, both being under age 50, were subject to an early withdrawal penalty on their IRA withdrawals used for medical expenses.	
14. The Ryans were allowed an earned income credit against their tax liability equal to a percentage of their wages.	

Write a memo to the Ryans explaining the basis of land that Kalila received as a gift from her uncle. The fair market value at the date of the gift was $50,000. Her uncle's basis in the land was $60,000. Kalila sold the land for $56,000.

Research Question: What code section and subsection, if applicable, provides general guidance on the exclusion of scholarships from gross income?

Section & Subsection Answer: §_____ (___)

Problem 44-11 (20 to 30 minutes)

Vermillion is self-employed as a human resources consultant and reports on the cash basis for income tax purposes. (5/93, PII, #4, amended, 4168)

For Items 1 through 14, select the appropriate tax treatment from the following list.

A. Fully deductible on Form 1040 to arrive at adjusted gross income
B. Fifty percent deductible on Form 1040 to arrive at adjusted gross income
C. Reported in Schedule A—*Itemized Deductions* (deductibility subject to threshold of 7.5% of adjusted gross income)
D. Reported in Schedule A—*Itemized Deductions* (deductibility subject to threshold of 2% of adjusted gross income)
E. Reported in Form 4562—*Depreciation and Amortization* and deductible in Schedule A—*Itemized Deductions* (deductibility subject to threshold of 2% of adjusted gross income)
F. Reported in Form 4562—*Depreciation and Amortization*, and deductible in Schedule C—*Profit or Loss from Business*
G. Fully deductible in Schedule C—*Profit or Loss from Business*
H. Partially deductible in Schedule C—*Profit or Loss from Business*
I. Reported in Form 2119—*Sale of Your Home*, and deductible in Schedule D—*Capital Gains and Losses*
J. Not deductible

Transaction	Answer
1. Qualifying medical expenses not reimbursed by insurance.	
2. Personal life insurance premiums paid by Vermillion.	
3. Expenses for business-related meals where clients were present.	
4. Depreciation on personal computer used for business.	
5. Business lodging expenses, while out of town.	
6. Subscriptions to professional journals used for business.	
7. Self-employment taxes paid.	
8. Qualifying contributions to a simplified employee pension plan.	
9. Election to expense business equipment purchased in the current year.	
10. Qualifying alimony payments made by Vermillion.	
11. Subscriptions for investment-related publications.	
12. Interest expense on a home-equity line of credit for an amount borrowed to finance Vermillion's business.	
13. Interest expense on a loan for an auto used 75% for business.	
14. Loss on sale of residence.	

You prepare Vermillion's personal taxes. Write a memo to the client explaining why the loss on the sale of Vermillion's sailboat is nondeductible and outlining any deductible personal losses.

Scenario | Tax Treatment | Communication | Research

Research Question: What code section and subsection, if applicable, provides guidance on the allowance of deductions for personal exemption(s) for an individual taxpayer and the taxpayer's spouse, if any?

Section & Subsection Answer: §_____ (___)

Problem 44-12 (20 to 30 minutes)

Cecilia Ross is a single taxpayer. Her social security number is 123-45-6789. Cecilia does not have a separate business name or employer ID number; she has no employees. Cecilia neither purchased nor disposed of fixed assets for her business in 2008. All of Cecilia's investment is at risk.

As an independent sales representative, Cecilia demonstrates and sells Blinking Cosmetics Company's cosmetics in customers' homes. She has no other employment. She has an office in her home at 39 Pleasant Avenue, Celebration, FL, 34747, which she uses exclusively for her business: storing inventory, keeping records, ordering inventory, and managing appointments. She uses the accrual method of accounting for the business, values closing inventory at cost, and had no change in determining quantities, costs, or valuation between opening and closing inventory.

Cecilia Ross keeps written logs for the use of her car and computer. She placed the car in business service on January 15, 2007. During 2008, she drove 7,300 miles for business, 0 miles for commuting, and 8,100 miles for other personal uses. She does not have another vehicle available for personal use. Cecilia has two phones—she uses one exclusively for business. The amount listed for sales includes the 7% amount collected from customers and remitted to the state for sales tax. The expenses in the following list are that portion of expenditures that apply only to the business. The amount listed for business use of home is from her properly completed Form 8829.

	Amount		Amount
Sales	$75,000	Legal services	$ 200
Returns and allowances	1,500	Office supplies & postage	150
Advertising	750	Repairs & maintenance (for car)	130
Charitable contribution	100	Taxes & licenses	5,500
Depreciation (including car)	3,550	Utilities—phone & Internet	350
Gasoline (for car)	1,080	Business use of home	160
Health insurance	2,400	Beginning inventory	1,000
Car insurance	1,242	Purchases	38,000
Other insurance	600	Ending inventory	1,500

On the "Schedule C" tab, prepare Cecilia Ross' Schedule C. (Editors, 5829)

Editor's Note: On the actual exam, there likely would be a link to 2008 *Instructions for Schedule C and* 2008 *Instructions for Form 8829* on a "Resources" tab or menu item. These may be downloaded in full at www.irs.gov under Forms and Instructions.

Scenario | Schedule C | Communication | Research

SCHEDULE C (Form 1040)
Department of the Treasury Internal Revenue Service (99)

Profit or Loss From Business

(Sole Proprietorship)

▶ Partnerships, joint ventures, etc., generally must file Form 1065 or 1065-B.
▶ Attach to Form 1040, 1040NR, or 1041. ▶ See Instructions for Schedule C (Form 1040).

OMB No. 1545-0074
2008
Attachment Sequence No. 09

Name of proprietor | Social security number (SSN)

A Principal business or profession, including product or service (see page C-3 of the instructions) | B Enter code from pages C-9, 10, & 11 ▶

C Business name. If no separate business name, leave blank. | D Employer ID number (EIN), if any

E Business address (including suite or room no.) ▶
City, town or post office, state, and ZIP code

F Accounting method: (1) ☐ Cash (2) ☐ Accrual (3) ☐ Other (specify) ▶

G Did you "materially participate" in the operation of this business during 2008? If "No," see page C-4 for limit on losses ☐ Yes ☐ No

H If you started or acquired this business during 2008, check here ▶ ☐

Part I Income

1	Gross receipts or sales. Caution. See page C-4 and check the box if: • This income was reported to you on Form W-2 and the "Statutory employee" box on that form was checked, or • You are a member of a qualified joint venture reporting only rental real estate income not subject to self-employment tax. Also see page C-4 for limit on losses. ▶ ☐	1	
2	Returns and allowances	2	
3	Subtract line 2 from line 1	3	
4	Cost of goods sold (from line 42 on page 2)	4	
5	Gross profit. Subtract line 4 from line 3	5	
6	Other income, including federal and state gasoline or fuel tax credit or refund (see page C-4)	6	
7	Gross income. Add lines 5 and 6 ▶	7	

Part II Expenses. Enter expenses for business use of your home only on line 30.

8	Advertising	8		18	Office expense	18	
9	Car and truck expenses (see page C-5)	9		19	Pension and profit-sharing plans	19	
10	Commissions and fees	10		20	Rent or lease (see page C-6):		
11	Contract labor (see page C-5)	11		a	Vehicles, machinery, and equipment	20a	
12	Depletion	12		b	Other business property	20b	
13	Depreciation and section 179 expense deduction (not included in Part III) (see page C-5)	13		21	Repairs and maintenance	21	
				22	Supplies (not included in Part III)	22	
				23	Taxes and licenses	23	
				24	Travel, meals, and entertainment:		
				a	Travel	24a	
14	Employee benefit programs (other than on line 19)	14		b	Deductible meals and entertainment (see page C-7)	24b	
15	Insurance (other than health)	15		25	Utilities	25	
16	Interest:			26	Wages (less employment credits)	26	
a	Mortgage (paid to banks, etc.)	16a		27	Other expenses (from line 48 on page 2)	27	
b	Other	16b					
17	Legal and professional services	17					

28	Total expenses before expenses for business use of home. Add lines 8 through 27 ▶	28	
29	Tentative profit or (loss). Subtract line 28 from line 7	29	
30	Expenses for business use of your home. Attach Form 8829	30	
31	Net profit or (loss). Subtract line 30 from line 29. • If a profit, enter on both Form 1040, line 12, and Schedule SE, line 2, or on Form 1040NR, line 13 (if you checked the box on line 1, see page C-7). Estates and trusts, enter on Form 1041, line 3. • If a loss, you must go to line 32.	31	

32 If you have a loss, check the box that describes your investment in this activity (see page C-8).
• If you checked 32a, enter the loss on both Form 1040, line 12, and Schedule SE, line 2, or on Form 1040NR, line 13 (if you checked the box on line 1, see the line 31 instructions on page C-7). Estates and trusts, enter on Form 1041, line 3.
• If you checked 32b, you must attach Form 6198. Your loss may be limited.

32a ☐ All investment is at risk.
32b ☐ Some investment is not at risk.

For Paperwork Reduction Act Notice, see page C-9 of the instructions. Cat. No. 11334P Schedule C (Form 1040) 2008

Schedule C (Form 1040) 2008 Page 2

Part III Cost of Goods Sold (see page C-8)

33 Method(s) used to value closing inventory: a ☐ Cost b ☐ Lower of cost or market c ☐ Other (attach explanation)

34 Was there any change in determining quantities, costs, or valuations between opening and closing inventory? If "Yes," attach explanation . . . ☐ Yes ☐ No

35	Inventory at beginning of year. If different from last year's closing inventory, attach explanation	35	
36	Purchases less cost of items withdrawn for personal use	36	
37	Cost of labor. Do not include any amounts paid to yourself	37	
38	Materials and supplies	38	
39	Other costs	39	
40	Add lines 35 through 39	40	
41	Inventory at end of year	41	
42	Cost of goods sold. Subtract line 41 from line 40. Enter the result here and on page 1, line 4	42	

Part IV **Information on Your Vehicle.** Complete this part **only** if you are claiming car or truck expenses on line 9 and are not required to file Form 4562 for this business. See the instructions for line 13 on page C-5 to find out if you must file Form 4562.

43 When did you place your vehicle in service for business purposes? (month, day, year) ► ____/____/____

44 Of the total number of miles you drove your vehicle during 2008, enter the number of miles you used your vehicle for:

a Business ____________ b Commuting (see instructions) ____________ c Other ____________

45 Was your vehicle available for personal use during off-duty hours? . . . ☐ Yes ☐ No

46 Do you (or your spouse) have another vehicle available for personal use? . . . ☐ Yes ☐ No

47a Do you have evidence to support your deduction? . . . ☐ Yes ☐ No

b If "Yes," is the evidence written? . . . ☐ Yes ☐ No

Part V **Other Expenses.** List below business expenses not included on lines 8–26 or line 30.

48 Total other expenses. Enter here and on page 1, line 27	48	

Schedule C (Form 1040) 2008

Write a memo to Cecilia Ross explaining why the self-employment taxes she pays are not on Schedule C.

Research Question: What code section and subsection, if applicable, defines alimony?

Section & Subsection Answer: §_____ (___)

Principal Business or Professional Activity Codes (partial listing)

Health & Personal Care Services	
446120	Cosmetics, beauty supplies, & perfume stores
446130	Optical goods stores
446110	Pharmacies & drugstores
446190	Other health & personal care stores
999999	Unclassified establishments (unable to classify)

Nonstore Retailers	
454112	Electronic auctions
454111	Electronic shopping
454310	Fuel dealers
454113	Mail-order houses
454210	Vending machine operators
454390	Other direct selling establishments (including door-to-door retailing, frozen food plan providers, party plan merchandisers, & coffee-break service providers)

Solution 44-1 MULTIPLE CHOICE ANSWERS

Exemptions

1. (c) Smith is entitled to claim an exemption deduction for himself under §151. Section 151(c)(1) allows an exemption deduction for each dependent. Smith is entitled to an exemption for his widowed mother, Ruth. Although §151(c)(1) states that the dependent must have gross income that is less than the personal exemption amount, Ruth's social security benefits are excluded from her gross income under §86 because of her income level. Ruth meets the tests for a dependent of §152(a) because she is his mother and Smith provided over half of her support. There is no requirement that a relative live with the taxpayer to qualify as a dependent. Section 151(c)(2) disallows a dependency exemption for a married person who would otherwise qualify as a dependent if such person files a joint return. There is an exception if neither spouse is required to file a return, there would be no gross tax liability if the couple filed separate returns, and the joint return is filed solely to receive a refund.

2. (a) No personal exemption is allowed on the return of an individual who is claimed as a dependent on another taxpayer's return.

3. (c) Alan fails the relationship or member of household test. Chris provides less than 10% of Sarah's support. Barbara passes both the relationship and the 10% test. In order for her to claim the exemption, Alan would have to sign the multiple support agreement.

4. (b) In order to be a qualified relative and be claimed as a dependent, an individual must pass five tests. The first four: gross income, support, joint return, and citizenship or residence tests are passed by all of the relatives. However, the fifth test an individual must pass is the relationship or member of household test. Since none of the relatives qualified as a member of Alan's household, only the ones which pass the relationship test may be claimed as a dependent. Per §152, the following pass the relationship test: child or dependent of child; stepchild; brother or sister (including half-blood); stepbrother or stepsister; father, mother, or ancestor of either; stepfather or stepmother; nephew or niece; uncle or aunt; and brother-, sister-, father-, mother-, son-, or daughter-in-law.

5. (b) Jim and Kay each may claim an exemption for themselves under §151(a) and §151(b). Dale passes all four tests (relationship, residence, age and support) and the two additional general tests (martial status and citizenship) under the uniform definition, allowing Jim and Kay to claim a dependency exemption for him. No exemption is allowed on Jim and Kay's joint return for Kim. Kim fails the gross income test of §151(d)(1)(B). Kim is neither a qualifying child (age test) nor a qualifying relative (gross income test). Neither is an exemption allowed for Grant because he fails the gross income test of §151(d)(1)(B). Thus, Jim and Kay may claim three exemptions on their joint return.

Filing Status

6. (d) A joint return may be filed when one or both spouses died during the tax year. A joint return may not be filed with the deceased spouse if the surviving spouse remarries before the end of the year in which the deceased spouse died.

7. (c) The cost of maintaining the household must be an actual cash expenditure. Therefore, the cost of food is included, but the value of the services rendered is not included for purposes of determining whether the taxpayer has contributed more than one-half of the cost of maintaining the household.

8. (c) Because Sam did not remarry, he was able to file a joint return in the year his wife died, and contributed more than 50% of maintaining a home for a dependent child, he meets the definition of a qualifying widower under §2(a). This status allows Sam to use the married filing joint tax rates for two years after the year of death.

9. (d) Section 2(a)(1) defines a surviving spouse as a taxpayer whose spouse died during either of the two preceding tax years and who maintains as her/his home a household which is the principal place of abode for the taxable year of a dependent son, stepson, daughter, or stepdaughter. A taxpayer is deemed to maintain the household if over half the cost of maintaining the household is furnished by the taxpayer. Not all dependents will qualify the taxpayer as a qualifying widow(er). The dependent must be a child or stepchild. In addition, except for allowable temporary absences, the child or stepchild must live with the taxpayer for the entire taxable year, not just for six months. In this case, if the cost of maintaining the household is the same for each month, the taxpayer would have provided exactly half the cost of maintaining the household. Section 2(a)(1) requires that the taxpayer provide over half the cost of maintaining the household. Therefore, neither statement is a requirement for the taxpayer to qualify as a qualifying widow(er).

10. (d) Section 151(b) provides that a taxpayer may claim an exemption for a spouse if no joint return is filed and the spouse has no gross income and is not a dependent of another taxpayer.

Filing Requirements

11. (a) The general rule is that all income taxes must be assessed within three years after the later of the due date or the filing date of the original return. However, if income is understated by more than 25% of the amount stated on the return, then there is a 6-year statute of limitations period. The Burgs omitted $45,000 which is equal to 37.5% of the gross income stated on their return. Therefore, the statute of limitations expires on April 15, Year 8.

12. (b) The tax liability at the due date is the tax on the return less tax payments withheld ($50,000 – $45,000 = $5,000). This is the unpaid tax liability on which the penalties for late filing and late payment would be computed.

13. (c) Form 1040X is an amended income tax return for individuals. Form 1139 is a claim for tentative refund of a corporation's income taxes for, among other things, a carryback of net operating losses. Form 1045 is a tentative claim for refund for an individual's income taxes for, among other things, a carryback of net operating losses. Form 843 is a claim for refund that is used for other types of taxes.

14. (b) Generally, all taxes must be assessed within three years after the later of the due date or the filing date. If the taxpayer omitted more than 25% of gross income when reporting, this period is extended to six years; $500 is substantially less than 25% of Martinsen's gross income. The due date was April 15, year 2; April 15, year 5, is three years later.

15. (a) In a case where the taxpayer had income tax withheld, but did not file a return due to insufficient income, a claim for refund must be filed within *two years* from the date the income tax was *paid* [§6511(a)].

Realization & Recognition

16. (d) Section 451(a) provides that any amount of income is to be included in the taxpayer's gross income for the taxable year in which such amount is received by the taxpayer, unless the taxpayer's method of accounting requires the amount to be included in gross income for a different year. Reg. §1.451-2(a) provides that income, although actually received, is constructively received by a taxpayer when the income is made available to her/him and is not subject to any substantial restrictions or limitations. Section 61(a) states that gross income includes all income from whatever source, unless the item of income is excluded from gross income by other sections of the Internal Revenue Code or other applicable law. Reg. §1.61-1(a) states that income may be realized in any form including cash, services, or property.

17. (c) Perle must include $550 in taxable income. The $200 cash is included and the $350 fair market value of the bookcase must also be included [§61(a)(2)]. Reg. §1.61-2(d)(1) states "...if services are paid for in property, the fair market value of the property taken in payment must be included in income as compensation." Therefore, Perle must include the fair market value of what he received, not what he billed.

18. (d) Generally, if a taxpayer carries merchandise inventories, the accrual method of accounting must be used. However, if a taxpayer has accounts receivable for services rendered, the taxpayer is not precluded from using the cash method.

Exclusions From Gross Income

19. (c) In order for a prize or award to be excludable from income, the recipients must: (1) be selected without any action on their part; (2) not be required, as a condition of receipt, to render substantial future services; and (3) assign the award to a charitable or governmental organization.

20. (b) The term "dividend" means any distribution of property made by a corporation to its shareholders out of accumulated or current earnings and profits [§316(b)(1)]. This definition does *not* apply to the term "dividend" as used in reference to dividends of insurance companies paid to policyholders as such [§316(b)(1)].

21. (c) Section 86(a) provides that the amount of Social Security benefits included in gross income is the lesser of one-half of the Social Security benefits or one-half of the excess described in §86(b)(1). Section 86(b) provides that this amount is the amount by which the sum of modified adjusted gross income plus one-half of the Social Security benefits exceeds a base amount. The base amount depends upon filing status as described in §86(c). This is altered for taxpayers whose modified adjusted gross income plus one-half of the Social Security benefits is equal to $44,000 for married taxpayers filing jointly or $34,000 for all other taxpayers. In these situations, up to 85% of Social Security benefits are taxable. Thus, 85% of Social Security benefits received is the maximum amount that is includible in gross income.

22. (c) Section 135 states that qualified higher education expenses include tuition and fees for the enrollment or attendance of the taxpayer, the taxpayer's spouse, or any dependent of the taxpayer at an eligible institution. Section 135 states that the higher education expenses are to be reduced by any qualified scholarship that is excluded from gross income under §117. Thus, both statements are true.

23. (b) Section 117(a) excludes from gross income amounts received as qualified scholarships by individuals who are degree candidates at a qualified educational organization. Section 117(b) defines qualified scholarships as payments for tuition, fees, books, supplies, and equipment related to the courses of instruction. The payments received for teaching are compensation for services. [**Note:** This question is unchanged from the Nov. 1997 exam. The examiners asked about tax year 1996, even though they specify that candidates should know the law in effect six months before the exam. In this case, the law is the same in 2009 and 2010 as in 1996.]

24. (d) Dividends are included in gross income and taxed as ordinary income to shareholders. Employer-provided health coverage, gifts, and inheritances are generally excluded from a taxpayer's gross income.

25. (d) Section 104 provides for the exclusion from gross income of certain types of compensation received for injury or sickness. The types of compensation which are excluded include amounts received under workers' compensation acts as compensation for personal injury or sickness, and the amount of any damages received on account of personal physical injuries or physical sickness. Furthermore, §105(b) generally states "gross income does not include... (amounts that are received by an employee through accident or health insurance plans that are attributable to employer contributions which were not includible in the gross income of the employee)...if such amounts are paid, directly or indirectly, to the taxpayer to reimburse the taxpayer for expenses incurred by him for...medical care..." and for which no deduction was taken under §213. Therefore, none of the amounts received by Harold are includible in his gross income.

26. (b) All income is taxable, unless it is specifically exempt. Compensation for injuries is exempt, but U.S. Treasury bond interest and wage income are not exempt.

27. (b) Section 79(a) provides that up to $50,000 of group term life insurance provided by an employer is excludable from gross income for an employee. Any amounts expended by the employer for additional life insurance coverage will be included in the employee's gross income.

28. (a) Salaries are included in gross income. Alimony paid is deducted from gross income in arriving at adjusted gross income. Both inheritances and personal injury awards are excluded from gross income. $50,000 – $10,000 = $40,000

Inclusions in Gross Income

29. (c) Section 451(a) provides that any amount of income is to be included in the taxpayer's gross income for the taxable year in which such amount is received by the taxpayer, unless the taxpayer's method of accounting requires the amount to be included in gross income for a different year. In cash basis of accounting, the income is generally reported in the year it is actually or constructively received. Regulation §1.451-2(a) provides that income, although actually received, is constructively received by a taxpayer when the income is made available to her/him and is not subject to any substantial restrictions or limitations.

30. (c) A passive loss is any loss from activities involving the conduct of a trade or business in which the taxpayer does not materially participate. With respect to this partner, any loss generated from operations will be considered a passive loss since he is not a material participant. Passive loss is calculated as 5% (partnership percentage) × $100,000 = $5,000. This passive loss may generally be used only to offset income from passive activities.

31. (a) Mock may deduct the cost of merchandise, but may not deduct other amounts paid or incurred as business expenses of her/his illegal drug sales.

32. (d) Self-employment income, under Reg. §1.1402(b)-1 includes both earnings as a self-employed consultant and as a director of a corporation.

33. (b) Interest expense is deductible in the period that it accrues, regardless of the taxpayer's basis of accounting. The total interest Krest may deduct is $2,000 [($24,000 / 12) × 1 month].

34. (d) All income is taxable unless specifically exempt. Whether from the state or from a supplemental benefit plan, unemployment compensation generally is not exempt. AARA '09 excludes up to $2,400 of unemployment benefits received in 2009 from taxable income. This temporary exclusion is expected to lapse after 2009.

35. (d) Jane must include the entire state lottery winnings in gross income. If Jane is a nonprofessional gambler (one who does not continuously and regularly engage in the trade or business of gambling to make a profit), she may take her gambling losses as an itemized deduction on Schedule A. As Jane decided to take the standard deduction, she cannot itemize the $300 of gambling losses.

36. (b) All interest income, unless specifically excluded by law, is includible in taxable income, regardless of the source. Interest is exempt on certain bonds of state governments, but this does not include interest earned on state income tax refunds. There is no provision for excluding interest income from most federal debt. Interest earned on dividends left on deposit with the V.A. is not included in taxable income (Rev. Rul. 91-14, 1991-1, C.B. 18).

37. (d) Net earnings (reported on Schedule C) include the gross business receipts less cost of goods sold, rent expense, and business liability insurance. Self-employment tax and health employment insurance premiums are adjustments to gross income, and are not involved in the calculation of net earnings.

38. (c) To qualify as alimony, payments must be: made pursuant to a divorce or separate maintenance agreement, made in cash, not made to someone in the same household, stopped upon the death of the payee-spouse, and not designated as anything other than alimony.

39. (d) All income is taxable, unless specifically exempt. There is no exemption for employee expense reimbursements under a nonaccountable plan. Mel can deduct the supportable business expenses as miscellaneous itemized deductions subject to 2% of AGI.

40. (a) The net business loss may only offset business income. Wages and rental income are considered business income. Interest income is deemed non-business income. Destry's net operating loss is $11,000 ($5,000 + $4,000 – $20,000).

41. (c) The deductibility of a vacation home's expenses depends on the allocation of personal and rental use of the property. Depreciation may be allowed, but losses are not.

42. (d) Cancellation payments are rent to the landlord in the year received, so Nare must include the $30,000 received in cancellation of Mott's lease. Although Nare is an accrual basis taxpayer he must include $5,000 for the last month's rent when received rather than when earned under the claim of right doctrine. Nare also must include the $10,000 for November and December. Thus, Nare must include a total of $45,000 as rental income for the current year.

Deductions for AGI

43. (c) Employees who remit jury duty pay to employers in exchange for their regular compensation during the jury service period may deduct the jury duty pay from gross income in arriving at AGI.

44. (b) Interest on qualified educational loans is deductible to arrive at adjusted gross income (AGI), subject to modified AGI thresholds. This individual is well under the threshold for single taxpayers.

45. (d) The forfeited interest penalty for premature withdrawal of time deposits is a deduction from gross income in arriving at adjusted gross income. [§62(a)(9)].

46. (b) Section 217 allows an adjustment for moving expenses, but imposes tests that must be met before any deduction for moving expenses is allowed. The taxpayer's new place of work must be more than 50 miles further from the former residence than was the former place of work. The taxpayer must be employed full time for 39 weeks of the 12-month period following the move. The move from New York to Florida meets the 50-mile test. The taxpayer was employed from February 2 to December 31, meeting the time test. Section 217(b)(1) defines moving expenses as the reasonable expenses of moving household goods and the expense of traveling, including lodging, to the new residence. Grey may not deduct the pre-move househunting costs. Therefore, Grey can deduct $2,800 ($1,000 + $1,800) as moving expense.

47. (a) Alimony paid is deductible in arriving at AGI under §62(a)(10). The other items are deductible **from** AGI as itemized deductions.

48. (a) Under §219(b), an individual may take a deduction for a qualified retirement contribution up to the lesser of $5,000 or the individual's compensation in 2009. Val and Pat each would be entitled to deduct $5,000. The amount deductible is disallowed when an employee is covered by an employer pension plan and their AGI before the IRA deduction is greater than the active participant phase-out limit. Compensation for purposes of a qualified retirement contribution includes alimony. The AGI for this purpose is $40,000 ($36,000 + $4,000), which is below the limit. Therefore, there is no reduction in the deduction for their contributions to their IRAs.

49. (c) Generally, under §219, an employee and her/his nonworking spouse may each contribute (and deduct) up to $5,000 of earnings to an IRA in 2009. If one spouse is covered by an employer pension plan, and their AGI is greater than the active participant phase-out limit, then the participating spouse's deduction is disallowed. Mike is covered by his employer's plan and the AGI of Mike and Julia is $103,000, so Mike's contribution is not deductible. Because their AGI is less than $150,000, Julia's contribution is fully deductible. Contributions to an IRA may be made up to April 15 of the year after the taxable year. Thus, a contribution may be made in January of the next year.

50. (d) Section 401(c)(2)(A) defines earned income as the net earnings from self-employment after certain deductions allowed by §404. Section 404(a)(8) allows a deduction for the Keogh contribution and 50% of the self-employment tax.

Deductions From AGI

51. (c) A taxpayer 65 years old (or older) or blind is entitled to an increased standard deduction amount. The support of a dependent is **not** an eligibility requirement for the increased standard deduction amount.

52. (c) Poole's deductible medical expenses must be reduced by a 7.5% of AGI floor. Thus, Poole's deductible medical expenses are $6,425 [$8,600 – ($29,000 × 0.075)]. The deductible medical expenses exceed the standard deduction amount, so Poole itemizes.

AGI	$29,000
Less: Itemized deductions	(6,425)
Less: Personal exemption	(3,650)
Taxable income	$18,925

53. (b) A medical expense deduction is allowed for the total cost of making a residence more amenable to the needs of the handicapped, if the costs do not increase the value of the home. However, if the medical expense increases the value of the residence, then only those costs in excess of an increase in the value of the residence are deductible. Therefore, the maximum allowable medical deduction is $85,000 [($100,000 – $25,000) + $10,000)].

54. (d) The use of bank credit cards is deemed to be payment for purposes of timing the deductibility of charitable and medical expenses. Therefore, the $4,000 Scott charged on his credit card for his dependent son's medical expenses can be claimed by Scott as a medical expense in the year charged. Scott can also claim the $2,800 of medical expenses Scott paid in Year 2 on his Year 2 tax return because medical expenses are deductible in the year paid and the medical expenses were for his spouse at the time the expenses were incurred.

55. (b) Cosmetic surgery expenses are only deductible for deformity, congenital abnormality, personal injury trauma, or disfiguring disease. The medical expenses in this question are deductible to the extent they exceed 7.5% of Carroll's AGI (7.5% × $100,000). Total deductible medical expenses of $20,000, less $7,500, equal $12,500.

56. (a) Section 213(a) authorizes a deduction for medical care expenses incurred on behalf of a dependent to the extent such expenses exceed 7.5% of AGI. Reg. §1.213-1(e)(1)(iii) provides that expenditures for the maintenance or operation of a capital asset are deductible medical expenses if such expenditures have medical care as their primary purpose. Reg. §1.213-1(e)(1)(v)(a) provides that the cost of medical care includes the cost of special schooling for handicapped individuals. The individual's condition must be such that the resources of the school for alleviating the handicap are a principal reason that the person is enrolled in the special school. This regulation further provides that the cost of meals and lodging is deductible as a medical expense if the meals and lodging are necessary incidents to the medical care. Thus, the tuition, meals, and lodging at the special school qualify. The total amount that may be deducted as a medical expense before the 7.5% AGI floor is $8,600 ($600 + $8,000).

57. (c) Section 213 allows a deduction for medical care that is not compensated for by insurance or otherwise. Wells must reduce the $2,000 cost of physical therapy by the $1,500 insurance reimbursement. The remaining $500 is deductible. Wells may also deduct the $500 for an insurance policy that covers the cost of prescription drugs. Wells may not deduct the cost of the insurance policy that covers loss of earnings due to sickness or accident. Section 213 provides that the cost of insurance for medical care including transportation is deductible. Thus, Wells is entitled to a deduction for medical care before the 7.5% AGI floor of $1,000.

58. (a) Section 461(f) provides that a deduction will be allowed in the year that money or other property is transferred to provide for satisfaction of an asserted liability that the taxpayer is contesting. Reg. §1.461-2(a)(3) provides that refunds of any portion of a contested liability for which a deduction has been allowed are included in gross income under the tax benefit rule of §111 and the regulations thereunder. Therefore, Farb should deduct $8,000 in Year 1 under §164(a) and recognize $5,000 gross

income in Year 2 to the extent it created a tax benefit in the year deducted.

59. (b) Section 163 allows a deduction for all interest paid or accrued within the taxable year on indebtedness. However, §163 denies deductions for personal interest expense. Section 163 excludes any qualified residence interest from the term personal interest. Section 163 includes interest on home equity indebtedness with respect to any qualified residence as qualified residence interest. Section 163 defines home equity indebtedness as any indebtedness other than acquisition indebtedness secured by a qualified residence to the extent that the fair market value of such residence does not exceed the acquisition indebtedness. However, §163 limits the amount of home equity indebtedness to $100,000. Section 163 defines a qualified residence as the taxpayer's principal residence and one other residence that the taxpayer uses as a residence. Thus, the Browns meet the definition and limitations of §163 and are entitled to deduct the interest on this loan as qualified residence interest.

60. (c) Home mortgage interest is deductible as an itemized deduction. Personal utility and insurance expenses are not deductible.

61. (a) Interest paid or accrued on indebtedness incurred to purchase or carry property held for investment is deductible as an itemized deduction to the extent of net investment income. The amount of qualified residential interest expense is irrelevant to the deductibility of investment interest expense.

62. (d) Section 165(a) allows a deduction for any loss that is not compensated for by insurance or from any other source. Although §165(c) places limitations on the deductibility of losses by individuals, §165(c)(3) allows deductions for an individual's casualty losses. In 2009, Section 165(h)(1) reduces the casualty loss by $500 for each casualty. Section 165(h)(2)(A) then places a limit on the deductibility of casualty losses. If casualty losses exceed casualty gains, the excess is subject to a 10% of AGI floor. Section 165(b) limits the amount of the loss before insurance reimbursement to the adjusted basis of the property. Reg. §1.165-7(b)(1) provides that the amount of the casualty loss before insurance reimbursement for personal use property is the lesser of the property's adjusted basis or the decline in the fair market value (FMV) of the property because of the casualty. In this case, the decline in the property's FMV equals the property's adjusted basis.

Adjusted basis or decline in FMV, the lesser	$ 150,000
Less: Insurance reimbursement	(130,000)
Casualty loss before the floors	$ 20,000
Less: $500 floor	(500)
Casualty loss before the 10% AGI floor	$ 19,500
10% AGI floor ($60,000 × 10%)	(6,000)
Deductible casualty loss	$ 13,500

63. (c) Section 170(a)(1) authorizes a deduction for charitable contributions that are paid during the taxable year. Section 170(f)(8) requires that contributions of $250 or more be substantiated by a contemporaneous receipt from the charitable organization. Moore's contributions are properly substantiated. Section 170(b)(1) limits an individual's deduction for charitable contributions to 50% of the taxpayer's contribution base and defines contribution base as AGI computed without regard to the deduction for net operating loss carrybacks. Section 170(d)(1)(A) provides that the charitable contributions in excess of 50% of the contribution base are to be carried over for five years, with contributions made for the current year deducted first. Moore deducts the $18,000 of charitable contributions made in the current year. Moore also deducts $7,000 of the charitable contribution carryover from the prior year for a total deduction of $25,000, which equals 50% of Moore's AGI for the current year. Moore has a charitable contribution carryover of $3,000 ($10,000 – $7,000) from the prior year to future years.

64. (c) Section 163 allows a deduction for all interest paid or accrued within the taxable year on indebtedness. However, the interest on the auto loan is not deductible because no deduction is allowed for personal interest. An auto loan is not mentioned in the exceptions to personal interest listed in §163. However, §163 excludes any qualified residence interest from the term personal interest and includes interest on acquisition indebtedness as qualified residence interest. Section 163 states that acquisition indebtedness includes any indebtedness incurred in acquiring, constructing, or substantially improving any qualified residence of the taxpayer, and is secured by such residence. Section 163 limits the aggregate amount of acquisition indebtedness to $1,000,000. Section 163 defines a qualified residence as the taxpayer's principal residence and one other residence that the taxpayer uses as a residence. The mortgage interest and the interest on the room construction loan meet the definition and are within the limit to qualify as interest on acquisition indebtedness. Thus, the mortgage interest and the interest on the room construction loan are qualified residence interest.

65. (c) Section 164(a)(3) allows a deduction for state and local income taxes that are paid or accrued during the year. Section 275(a)(1) disallows

any deduction for federal income taxes. Because Matthews is on the cash basis of accounting, she may deduct state and local income taxes in the year paid. The $1,500 in state and local income tax withheld is deemed paid when withheld by the employer. Matthews is also allowed to deduct the $400 state estimated income taxes paid on December 30. To deduct this $400 payment, Matthews must have a good faith belief that this payment represents payment for taxes due and owing over and above the $1,500 withheld. The fact that Matthews owes an additional $300 in state and local income taxes for Year 1 is indicative of such a good faith belief. Because the additional $300 in state and local income taxes for tax year Year 1 were not paid until Year 2, Matthews may not deduct this $300 in Year 1. Taxes are deductible on Schedule A as an itemized deduction from adjusted gross income ($1,500 + $400 = $1,900).

66. (b) Foreign income taxes may be treated as a credit against federal income taxes or deducted as an itemized deduction. If treated as an itemized deduction, they are not subject to the 2% floor. They are not adjustments to gross income.

67. (a) An individual may deduct a loss under §165(c) in the following circumstances: (1) the loss is incurred in a trade of business, (2) the loss is incurred in a transaction entered into for profit, or (3) the loss is caused by casualty or by theft. Thus, an individual's losses on transactions entered into for personal purposes are deductible only if the losses qualify as casualty or theft losses.

68. (a) Section 68(a) places an overall limitation on itemized deductions for taxpayers whose adjusted gross income exceed amounts stated in §68(b). However, §68(c)(1) states that the deduction allowed for medical expenses under §213 is not included in the term itemized deductions solely for purposes of the overall limitation on itemized deductions imposed by §68(a). Likewise, §68(c)(2) provides that the deduction for investment interest allowed by §163 is not subject to the overall limitation. Also, §68(c)(3) provides that the deduction for casualty losses of individuals allowed under §165 is not subject to the overall limitation.

69. (b) Reg. §1.162-5(b)(2)(i) states that an individual's educational expenses that are required to meet the minimum educational requirements for qualification in his employment are not deductible. Thus, the education expense to meet the minimum entry level education requirements at an individual's place of employment is not deductible as any type of deduction. Section 67(b) defines miscellaneous itemized deductions as itemized deductions other than those listed therein. Tax return preparation fees, subscriptions to professional journals, and custodial fees for a brokerage account are not listed in §67(b). Thus, they are itemized deductions. The tax return preparation fees and the custodial fees for a brokerage account would be deductible under §212. The subscriptions to professional journals would be deductible under §162(a) as an itemized deduction if incurred by an employee under §62(a)(1).

70. (b) The cost of the seminar and daily living expenses are a direct result of education that maintains or improves skills connected to the current business. The primary purpose of the trip is not education-related (as evidenced by the percentage of time for the seminar), so the airfare is not an education expense.

Cost of seminar	$ 700
Five days at $100 per day	500
Total educational costs	$ 1,200

AMT

71. (d) Section 53(a) allows a credit against the alternative minimum tax (AMT). Section 53(b) provides that the AMT credit for the taxable year is the excess, if any, of the adjusted minimum tax imposed over the amount allowable as a credit for such prior taxable years. Thus, the AMT credit may be carried forward indefinitely.

72. (b) Section 57(a)(5)(A) treats interest on specified private activity bonds as a tax preference for purposes of the alternative minimum tax. Section 57(a)(5)(C) defines these bonds as any private activity bonds issued after August 7, 1986, the interest on which is excluded from gross income under §103. Charitable contributions of capital gain property are not included in the list of tax preferences in §57.

73. (a) For alternative minimum tax (AMT), the medical expense deduction must be computed used a 10% floor instead of 7.5%. For AMT purposes, the state income taxes, mortgage interest unrelated to acquisition, and real estate taxes are not itemized deductions. Thus, the itemized deductions for AMT are medical expenses using a 10% floor [$12,000 – ($100,000 × 10%)], the residence mortgage interest, and charitable contributions: $2,000 + $10,000 + $5,000 = $17,000.

Tax Credits

74. (d) The child care credit is available in full if the taxpayer's AGI is $15,000 or less. A reduced credit is still available if the taxpayer's AGI is greater

than $15,000. Generally, *both* spouses must work in order to qualify for the credit. However, if one spouse does not work but is a full-time student, or is physically or mentally incapable of taking care of him or herself, the credit is still available.

75. (a) A taxpayer may take either a deduction or a tax credit for amounts paid for foreign income taxes. A separate calculation is involved for certain categories of income, such as passive income.

76. (a) Section 38(b) provides that the general business credit is the sum of several credits listed therein. The enhanced oil recovery credit is one of those credits so listed. Section 38(a) allows the general business credit against the tax, including carrybacks and carryforwards of such credit. The foreign tax credit and the minimum tax credit are single credits.

77. (c) Section 26 limits the amount of any credits allowed in Subpart A of Part IV of Subchapter A of Chapter 1 to the excess of the taxpayer's regular tax liability over the tentative minimum tax. The child and dependent care credit is allowed by §21 (in Subpart A). The credit for the elderly and totally disabled is allowed by §22 (in Subpart A). Section 53(c) limits the amount of the credit for prior year minimum tax to the excess of the regular tax liability reduced by certain other credits over the tentative minimum tax for the year. The earned income credit (EIC) is allowed by §32 which is in Subpart C "Refundable Credits" of Part IV of Subchapter A of Chapter 1. Thus, the EIC is refundable and the other credits listed are not refundable.

Estimated Tax Payments

78. (c) Section 6662(a) imposes a 20% accuracy-related penalty for underpayment of tax for reasons specified in §6662. Section 6662(b) states that the penalty will apply to underpayment of tax for negligence or disregard of rules and regulations and for any substantial underpayment of income tax.

79. (a) It is not clearly understood where the examiners are going with this question, because the required estimated tax payment safe harbor percentage for taxpayers whose adjusted gross income exceeds $150,000 ($75,000 for MFS) is 110% of the preceding year's tax liability, which is not addressed by either the annualization or seasonal method. It appears that candidates are supposed to infer that the CPA's income is not distributed evenly throughout the year, such as in a tax only practice. With that assumption being made, then the annualization method is the only available method, since it is appropriate for taxpayers whose income is much higher in one part of the year under §6654(d). On the other hand, the annualization and seasonal methods are available to corporations.

80. (a) The extension of the time to file does not include an extension of the time to pay. The full amount of liability is due on April 15. Taxpayers are permitted an underpayment of *estimated* taxes up to $1,000 without a penalty if taxes are paid on time.

Solution 44-2 ADDITIONAL MULTIPLE CHOICE ANSWERS

Filing Status

81. (d) Section 2(a)(1) defines a surviving spouse as a taxpayer whose spouse died during either of the two preceding tax years and who maintains, as her/his home, a household which is the principal place of abode for the taxable year of a dependent son, stepson, daughter, or stepdaughter. A taxpayer is deemed to maintain the household if over half the cost of maintaining the household is furnished by the taxpayer. In addition, except for allowable temporary absences, the child or stepchild must live with the taxpayer for the entire taxable year, not just for six months. Since Parker did not remarry and maintained a home during the year for his dependent child, s/he meets the definition of a qualifying widower under §2(a) and, therefore, may use the joint return rates for two years after the death of her/his spouse.

82. (a) Married filing jointly status is available to taxpayers who meet all of the following conditions: (1) married and not legally separated on the last day of the year, (2) neither spouse was a nonresident alien during the tax year, (3) both spouses' tax years begin on the same date, and (4) both spouses sign the return.

Filing Requirements

83. (c) Section 6072(a) requires that the individual who uses a calendar year file his federal income tax return by April 15 of the following year unless the taxpayer receives an extension under §6081(a). Section 6501(a) provides that, in general, no assessment of additional taxes may be made after 3 years from the time the tax return was filed. However, §6501(b)(1) provides that a return that is filed early will be deemed to have been filed on its due

date. Thus, the return filed on March 20, Year 2, is deemed to have been filed on April 15, Year 2, for purposes of §6501. Section 6501(a) then gives the IRS until April 15, Year 5, to assess additional taxes and assert a notice of deficiency.

Exclusions From Gross Income

84. (d) Normally, cancelled debt is taxable income. The Mortgage Forgiveness Debt Relief Act of 2007 allows for exclusion of income due to certain mortgage relief, with a corresponding reduction in the basis of the home. Debt cancellation on up to $2 million of qualified principal residence indebtedness may be excluded from taxable income from January 1, 2007, through December 31, 2009. A renegotiation that results in a lower monthly payment or delay of adjustable rate resets result in forgiveness of qualified principal residential indebtedness may be excluded from taxable income for the same period. If the loan is discharged due to services performed for the lender or the taxpayer is in Chapter 11 bankruptcy, the exclusion is not available. Indebtedness secured by a principal residence and incurred in the acquisition, construction, or substantial improvement of the principal residence.

85. (b) Salaries and alimony received are included in gross income. Up to $3,000 of a net capital loss may offset other gross income for an individual taxpayer annually; excess losses may be carried forward indefinitely. Inheritances and child support are excluded from gross income. $50,000 + $12,000 – $3,000 = $59,000

86. (a) Section 3105 indicates that Series EE savings bonds, bought after 1989, can be redeemed tax-free if the proceeds of the bonds are used to pay tuition and fees for higher education for the taxpayer, her/his spouse or dependents. To qualify, the taxpayer must be the sole owner or a joint owner with her/his spouse. There is no requirement that says a purchaser must be a parent. The bonds must be issued to an individual who is at least 24 years of age. There is no requirement that the bonds be transferred to, and redeemed by, the college.

87. (c) Section 117(a) excludes from gross income amounts received as qualified scholarships by individuals who are degree candidates at a qualified educational organization. Section 117(b) defines qualified scholarships as payments for tuition, fees, books, supplies, and equipment related to the courses of instruction. However, §117(c) states that the exclusion provided by §117(a) shall not apply to payments received for teaching, research, and other services as a condition for receiving the scholarship. In substance, these payments are compensation for services, rather than bona fide scholarships.

Inclusions in Gross Income

88. (c) The $1,000 interest on state government obligations is excluded from gross income under §103(a). The remaining items are included in gross income under §61(a)(4). Thus, the amount included in gross income is $1,900 ($500 + $600 + $800).

89. (a) Under §1402(a) net self-employment income includes the gross income from a trade or business less trade or business expenses allowable under §162. Estimated tax payments are treated as a prepayment of income taxes rather than as a deductible business expense. Charitable contributions are deductible as an itemized deduction on Schedule A rather than as a business expense on Schedule C. The other expenses are deductible as business expenses.

Gross business receipts		$20,000
Less: Air conditioning parts	$(2,500)	
Yellow Pages listing	(2,000)	
Business long-distance telephone calls	(400)	
Total business expenses		(4,900)
Net self-employment income		$15,100

90. (b) A taxpayer who receives property in exchange for her/his services must, under §83, report the fair market value of the property or services as income in the year the property is received, free of any restrictions. If services are rendered at a stipulated price, that price, in absence of contrary evidence, is presumed to be the fair market value of the property. As Lee accepted property with a known fair market value of $8,000 in full payment of his legal services, he must report this amount as income on his tax return. There is contrary evidence ($8,000 known fair market value) that overrules the stipulated original price of $10,000. In other words, Lee's services must really be worth $8,000 as he accepted this amount in full satisfaction of his services. The client's basis in the property before the exchange will be used in computing gain on the client's return, not Lee's return. The cash method of accounting recognizes property, as well as cash, in the year it is received.

91. (b) If passive losses and credits cannot be used in the current year, they are carried forward indefinitely or until the property is disposed of under §469(b).

92. (a) Section 469(c)(2) defines a passive activity to include *any* rental activity. However, a taxpayer is allowed to deduct a certain amount of a rental property's losses if he materially participates in the rental activity. Interest and dividends are *never* treated as passive activity income. Passive activity credits *are* subject to the same rules as passive activity losses (e.g., the credits have to be used against tax that is attributable to passive activity income). The passive activity rules apply to *everyone*. (Section 469(c)(2) provides an exception for qualified real estate professionals.)

93. (c)

Rental payments received		$7,200
Real estate taxes paid ($6,400 / 2)	$3,200	
Payment for painting of rental apartment	800	
Fire insurance premium paid ($600 / 2)	300	
Depreciation ($5,000 / 2)	2,500	
Deductible expenses		(6,800)
Net rental income		$ 400

94. (a) Rental income and expense recognition depends on the allocation between the rental and personal use of the property. If the property is rented for less than 15 days, no expenses are deductible except for those ordinarily deductible from AGI (mortgage interest, etc.) and no rental income is includable in gross income.

95. (a) A transfer of property other than cash to a former spouse under a decree of divorce is not a taxable event. Cash payments are not taxable if under the decree the payor spouse is liable for payment after the death of the payee spouse. Therefore, none of the transferred property or payments is taxable on Ann's return.

96. (a) To qualify as alimony, payments must be: made pursuant to a divorce or separate maintenance agreement, made in cash, not made to someone in the same household, stopped upon the death of the payee-spouse, and not designated as anything other than alimony. Child support and property settlements are not alimony.

97. (b) Section 71(a) states that gross income includes alimony, and that alimony is any payment made in cash and required by the divorce decree. It also states that alimony does not include payments made to support minor children. Furthermore, if any amount specified in the divorce decree will be reduced on the happening of a contingency relating to a child (such as attaining a specified age or at a time which can clearly be associated with such a contingency), then an amount equal to such reduction will be considered as payments made to support minor children. Thus, the $10,000 alimony must be reduced by the 20% by which it will be reduced on their child's 18th birthday, and the alimony is considered to be $8,000. Child support payments received are not included in the gross income of the recipient. Section 71(b)(1)(A) states that payments made in cash to third parties on behalf of the payee spouse under the terms of the divorce or separation instrument can be alimony. The fact that $3,000 of the $10,000 payment is paid to Spring College on behalf of Mary does not disqualify the $3,000 payment as alimony. Total alimony payments are the tuition payments plus the cash payments less the child support. $3,000 + $7,000 − $2,000 = $8,000

Deductions for AGI

98. (c) Since neither Paul nor Sally was covered by an employer-sponsored pension plan, the Lees could take a total IRA deduction of $10,000 in 2009 regardless of who had earned the income. As they are both under age 50 of the end of the year, neither is eligible for catch-up contributions.

99. (d) Section 219 provides a qualifying individual with a deduction up to the lesser of $5,000 in 2009 or an amount equal to the compensation includible in the individual's gross income for the taxable year. This limit is increased by $1,000 for taxpayers who are at least age 50 at the end of the year. For purposes of determining an individual's maximum contribution to an IRA, alimony payments are considered compensation.

100. (b) Contributions to an IRA may be made up to April 15 of the year after the tax year. An extension to file doesn't extend the IRA contribution deadline.

101. (c) Section 164 provides that one-half of the self-employment tax imposed for the year is deductible and provides that this deduction is to be attributed to a trade or business activity that does not consist of the performance of services as an employee. Section 62(a)(1) states that business expenses are deductible from gross income in arriving at AGI if the trade or business does not consist of the performance of services as an employee.

102. (b) For Health Savings Accounts (HSA) purposes, eligible individuals cannot have other medical coverage, be entitled to Medicare benefits, or be claimed as a dependent on another taxpayer's return. A HSA must be used in conjunction with a high-deductible health plan. Qualified HSA medical expenses are those that qualify for the itemized medical expense deduction. Accrued interest and distributions from a HSA for qualified medical expenses are not subject to tax.

Deductions From AGI

103. (d) Section 213 allows a deduction for medical care expenses that is not compensated for by insurance or otherwise. Medical care expenses include amount paid for the diagnosis, cure, mitigation, treatment, or prevention of disease as well as premiums for medical care insurance. Only cosmetic surgery expenses for deformity, congenital abnormality, personal injury trauma, or disfiguring disease are only deductible. Therefore, the cost of the facial surgery to improve the personal appearance is not deductible. Premiums on disability insurance policy that covers loss of earnings due to sickness or accident are also not deductible.

104. (c) Transportation expenses incurred for medical care are deductible as a medical expense subject to 7.5% of AGI. This includes transportation to and from a point of treatment, as well as for a parent accompanying a child who is receiving medical care. A person giving assistance to someone traveling to receive medical care is also allowed this deduction. The other answers are specifically included in the Code as being nondeductible medical expenses.

105. (b) The $2,000 in unpaid medical expenses could be deducted from the gross estate in arriving at the taxable estate on the estate tax return as a claim against the estate under §2053. The executor may elect, under §642(g), to deduct certain expenses on the estate's income tax return, rather than taking them as a deduction on the estate tax return. However, Reg. §1.642(g)-2 states that medical expenses of the decedent that are paid by the estate of the decedent are not among those expenses. Section 213 and Reg. §1.213-1 provides that for purposes of §213, medical expenses paid by a decedent's estate within one year of the date of the decedent's death shall be treated as paid by the decedent at the time the medical services were rendered. Section 213 and Reg. §1.213-1 requires that the executor of the decedent's estate file a waiver of the right to claim the medical expenses as a deduction from the gross estate under §2053. The medical expenses may be deducted on Bell's final income tax return as an itemized deduction subject to the 7.5% AGI floor.

106. (d) To be deductible, real estate taxes must be paid by the person on whom the tax is imposed. Smith is not eligible to deduct the real estate taxes since he does not own the house. Had Smith owned the house, all the real estate taxes paid during that year would have been deductible because cash basis taxpayers deduct real estate taxes when paid and not in the year assessed.

107. (d) Section 164(a) states that a deduction will be allowed for the taxable year within which state income taxes are paid or accrued. The refund of tax is not included in income, nor does the refund reduce the current deduction for taxes, because William never claimed a deduction for the payment of the Year 8 tax (§111).

108. (d) An itemized deduction is allowed for state, local, and foreign real property taxes paid by the owner; state and local personal property taxes paid by the owner; and state, local, and foreign income taxes.

109. (c) Section 163(d)(1) limits the deduction of an individual's investment interest to the individual's net investment income for the taxable year.

110. (d) Home equity indebtedness is limited to $100,000 on a joint income tax return ($50,000 if MFS). Home equity indebtedness does *not* include acquisition indebtedness (e.g., indebtedness incurred in acquiring, constructing, or substantially improving a qualified residence of the taxpayer). Home equity indebtedness may **not** exceed the taxpayer's net equity in the qualified residence.

111. (c) Generally, in-kind charitable contributions are limited to 30% of a taxpayer's adjusted gross income. $80,000 × 30% = $24,000

112. (a) Generally, the fair market value of appreciated property donated to a qualified charity may be deducted if it doesn't exceed 30% of the donor's AGI. $25,000 < (30% × $90,000)

113. (d) An employee's unreimbursed business car expenses are deductible as an itemized deduction from AGI. Section 67(a) states that miscellaneous itemized deductions are allowed only to the extent they exceed 2% of AGI. Section 67(b) states that miscellaneous itemized deductions are those itemized deductions not listed in §67(b). Unreimbursed employee business expenses are not listed in §67(b). Moving expenses allowed by §217 are deductible in arriving at AGI under §62(a)(15). One half of the self-employment tax is deductible in arriving at AGI under §62(a)(1). The self-employed health insurance deduction allowed by §162(1) is deductible in arriving at AGI under §62(a)(1).

114. (b) Amounts actually paid to a qualified donee during the year are deductible subject to a percentage of AGI limitation. Smith can deduct the $5,000 cash contribution to the church under §170. The deduction of a charitable contribution of appreciated property depends on the status of the property. Appreciated property that would realize long-term

capital gain if sold instead of donated is valued at fair market value. Other property (including short-term capital gain property) is valued at the lesser of basis or fair market value. Art work owned for four months would not realize a long-term gain. Qualified donees include domestic organizations and foundations operated exclusively for religious, charitable, scientific, literary, or educational purposes. Individuals are not qualified donees; therefore, gifts to individuals, such as a gift to a needy family, are not deductible.

115. (c) Spencer can deduct the cash contribution under §170. The used clothing is likewise deductible. Spencer can also deduct $400 for the purchase of the art object which is the difference between what he paid and the fair market value of the art object ($1,200 – $800 = $400).

116. (d) Tax return preparation fees are a second tier miscellaneous deduction. Interest expense is specifically exempted from the 2% of AGI floor. Medical expenses are subject to a 7.5% of AGI floor. Employee moving expenses are fully deductible *for* AGI.

117. (a) Section 68(a) provides that the amount of itemized deductions otherwise allowable shall be reduced by the lesser of 3% of the excess of AGI over the applicable amount or 80% of the itemized deductions otherwise allowable. However, §68(c) states that certain itemized deductions are excluded from the definition of itemized deductions for purposes of §68. Thus, the itemized deductions are reduced by the lesser of 3% of the excess of AGI over the applicable amount or 80% of certain itemized deductions.

AMT

118. (c) Section 56(b)(1)(A)(i) disallows any deduction for an individual's miscellaneous itemized deductions in computing alternative minimum taxable (AMT) income. Section 56(b)(1)(A)(ii) disallows any deduction for taxes described in §164(a). Section 164(a)(3) includes state and local income taxes. Hence, state and local income taxes are not deductible in arriving at AMT income. Section 56(b)(1)(C)(i) disallows the deduction for qualified residence interest in arriving at AMT income. Instead §56(e) allows a deduction for qualified housing interest which includes interest on acquisition indebtedness but not other home equity loans, unless the taxpayer used the loan proceeds to improve the residence. Thus, the home mortgage interest on a loan to acquire a residence is deductible in arriving at AMT income and accordingly does not have to be added back to taxable income. Section 55(b)(2) defines AMT income as the taxable income of the taxpayer, determined with regard to the adjustments required by §§56 and 58 and increased by the preferences described in §57. Taxable income, as defined in §63(a), is gross income minus deductions. Section 56(b)(1)(E) disallows the standard deduction and deduction for personal exemptions in arriving at AMT income. Don Mills' AMT income before the AMT exemption is determined as follows:

Taxable income before personal exemption		$70,000
Add back:	Miscellaneous itemized deductions	2,000
	State and local income taxes	5,000
AMT income before the AMT exemption		$77,000

Tax Credits

119. (d) Generally, an adoption credit of up to $12,150 is available to the extent of adoption expenses ($9,000 + $5,000 = $14,000) in 2009. Section 213(a) authorizes an itemized deduction, not a credit, for a dependent's medical expenses.

120. (c) Any employee who has worked for two or more employers in any one taxable year and has been subjected to excessive FICA withholding may correct the over withholding by taking the excess amount as a credit against her or his income tax on Form 1040.

Estimated Tax Payments

121. (a) Section 6654 allows an individual to avoid the penalty for underpayment of estimated tax by paying in 90% of the tax shown on the return in timely installments. In general, §6654 provides that an individual may avoid the penalty for underpayment of estimated tax by paying 100% of the tax shown on the return for the preceding tax year. However, if an individual's AGI exceeds $150,000, the individual may avoid the penalty for underpayment of estimated tax by paying a safe harbor percentage of 110%, rather than 100%, of the tax shown on the return for the prior year.

PERFORMANCE BY SUBTOPICS

Each category below parallels a subtopic covered in Chapter 44. Record the number and percentage of questions you correctly answered in each subtopic area.

Exemptions

Question #	Correct √
1	
2	
3	
4	
5	
# Questions	5
# Correct	______
% Correct	______

Filing Status

Question #	Correct √
6	
7	
8	
9	
10	
# Questions	5
# Correct	______
% Correct	______

Filing Requirements

Question #	Correct √
11	
12	
13	
14	
15	
# Questions	5
# Correct	______
% Correct	______

Realization & Recognition

Question #	Correct √
16	
17	
18	
# Questions	3
# Correct	______
% Correct	______

Exclusions From Gross Income

Question #	Correct √
19	
20	
21	
22	
23	
24	
25	
26	
27	
28	
# Questions	10
# Correct	______
% Correct	______

Inclusions in Gross Income

Question #	Correct √
29	
30	
31	
32	
33	
34	
35	
36	
37	
38	
39	
40	
41	
42	
# Questions	14
# Correct	______
% Correct	______

Deductions for AGI

Question #	Correct √
43	
44	
45	
46	
47	
48	
49	
50	
# Questions	8
# Correct	______
% Correct	______

Deductions From AGI

Question #	Correct √
51	
52	
53	
54	
55	
56	
57	
58	
59	
60	
61	
62	
63	
64	
65	
66	
67	
68	
69	
70	
# Questions	20
# Correct	______
% Correct	______

AMT

Question #	Correct √
71	
72	
73	
# Questions	3
# Correct	______
% Correct	______

Tax Credits

Question #	Correct √
74	
75	
76	
77	
# Questions	4
# Correct	______
% Correct	______

Estimated Tax Payments

Question #	Correct √
78	
79	
80	
# Questions	3
# Correct	______
% Correct	______

SIMULATION SOLUTIONS

Solution 44-3 Tax Treatments

Filing Status (0.25 points)

1. A

A joint return may be filed if one or both spouses dies during the year.

Includible in Gross Income (0.75 points)

2. N

Generally, life insurance proceeds paid by reason of death of the insured are excluded from gross income. (IRC §101)

3. N

If a taxpayer obtains a refund for which he or she received a prior tax benefit (e.g., deduction), then this refund is included in income. (IRC §111) That is not the case in this instance.

4. I

Gross income includes all items from whatever source derived except those items specifically excluded. (IRC §61)

5. N

The net unearned income of children who have not reached age 14 by the end of the tax year is taxed at the parent's top rate. For 2008, the amount taxed at the parent's rate is the child's unearned income less the sum of $900 and either $900 or itemized deductions related to the production of the unearned income ($950 in 2009).

6. I

Gross income included all items from whatever source derived except those items specifically excluded. (IRC §61)

7. I

Gross income included all items from whatever source derived except those items specifically excluded. (IRC §61)

8. I

Gross income included all items from whatever source derived except those items specifically excluded. (IRC §61)

Deductions (2 points)

9. C

All Roth IRA contributions are nondeductible. (IRC §408A)

10. C

A casualty loss must be due to some sudden, unexpected, or unusual cause. Rotting due to moisture is not a casualty loss.

11. B

Medical care expenses include amounts paid for premiums for medical care insurance. (IRC §213)

12. C

Legally procured prescription drugs and insulin are deductible medical expense. Other over-the-counter drugs are not deductible. (IRC §213)

13. C

No expenditures are deductible unless there is a specific provision allowing their deduction. There is no provision allowing the deduction of homeowner's insurance.

14. C

No expenditures are deductible unless there is a specific provision allowing their deduction. There is no provision allowing the deduction of life insurance.

15. A

Alimony paid is deductible in arriving at AGI under IRC §62(a)(10).

16. B

IRC §163 allows a deduction for interest paid on investment indebtedness, although it is limited to the individual's net investment income for the taxable year.

Form 1040 (1 point)

Form 1040 Department of the Treasury—Internal Revenue Service
U.S. Individual Income Tax Return 2008 (99) IRS Use Only—Do not write or staple in this space.

For the year Jan. 1–Dec. 31, 2008, or other tax year beginning , 2008, ending , 20 OMB No. 1545-0074

Label (See instructions on page 14.) Use the IRS label. Otherwise, please print or type.

Your first name and initial	Last name	Your social security number
Mark	Sagan	149 : 99 : 9999
If a joint return, spouse's first name and initial	Last name	Spouse's social security number
Christie	Sagan	299 : 99 : 9999
Home address (number and street). If you have a P.O. box, see page 14.	Apt. no.	▲ You must enter your SSN(s) above. ▲
123 Spruce Street		
City, town or post office, state, and ZIP code. If you have a foreign address, see page 14.		Checking a box below will not change your tax or refund.
Anytown, USA		

Presidential Election Campaign ▶ Check here if you, or your spouse if filing jointly, want $3 to go to this fund (see page 14) ▶ ☐ You ☐ Spouse

Filing Status

Check only one box.

1 ☐ Single
2 ☑ Married filing jointly (even if only one had income)
3 ☐ Married filing separately. Enter spouse's SSN above and full name here. ▶
4 ☐ Head of household (with qualifying person). (See page 15.) If the qualifying person is a child but not your dependent, enter this child's name here. ▶
5 ☐ Qualifying widow(er) with dependent child (see page 16)

Exemptions

6a ☐ Yourself. If someone can claim you as a dependent, do not check box 6a
b ☐ Spouse

Boxes checked on 6a and 6b: 2

c Dependents:

(1) First name Last name	(2) Dependent's social security number	(3) Dependent's relationship to you	(4) ✓ if qualifying child for child tax credit (see page 17)
George Sagan	149 : 82 : 9999	son	☑
Helen Sagan	149 : 79 : 9999	daughter	☐
			☐
			☐

If more than four dependents, see page 17.

No. of children on 6c who: • lived with you: 2
• did not live with you due to divorce or separation (see page 18)
Dependents on 6c not entered above

d Total number of exemptions claimed — Add numbers on lines above ▶ 4

Income

Attach Form(s) W-2 here. Also attach Forms W-2G and 1099-R if tax was withheld.

If you did not get a W-2, see page 21.

Enclose, but do not attach, any payment. Also, please use Form 1040-V.

Line	Description	Line	Amount
7	Wages, salaries, tips, etc. Attach Form(s) W-2	7	50,000
8a	Taxable interest. Attach Schedule B if required	8a	500
b	Tax-exempt interest. Do not include on line 8a — 8b 4,000		
9a	Ordinary dividends. Attach Schedule B if required	9a	5,000
b	Qualified dividends (see page 21) — 9b 5,000		
10	Taxable refunds, credits, or offsets of state and local income taxes (see page 22)	10	200
11	Alimony received	11	
12	Business income or (loss). Attach Schedule C or C-EZ	12	
13	Capital gain or (loss). Attach Schedule D if required. If not required, check here ▶ ☐	13	
14	Other gains or (losses). Attach Form 4797	14	
15a	IRA distributions 15a — b Taxable amount (see page 23)	15b	
16a	Pensions and annuities 16a — b Taxable amount (see page 24)	16b	
17	Rental real estate, royalties, partnerships, S corporations, trusts, etc. Attach Schedule E	17	6,000
18	Farm income or (loss). Attach Schedule F	18	
19	Unemployment compensation	19	
20a	Social security benefits 20a — b Taxable amount (see page 26)	20b	
21	Other income. List type and amount (see page 28)	21	
22	Add the amounts in the far right column for lines 7 through 21. This is your total income ▶	22	61,700

Adjusted Gross Income

Line	Description	Line	Amount	Line	Amount
23	Educator expenses (see page 28)	23			
24	Certain business expenses of reservists, performing artists, and fee-basis government officials. Attach Form 2106 or 2106-EZ	24			
25	Health savings account deduction. Attach Form 8889	25			
26	Moving expenses. Attach Form 3903	26			
27	One-half of self-employment tax. Attach Schedule SE	27	250		
28	Self-employed SEP, SIMPLE, and qualified plans	28			
29	Self-employed health insurance deduction (see page 29)	29			
30	Penalty on early withdrawal of savings	30	25		
31a	Alimony paid b Recipient's SSN ▶	31a			
32	IRA deduction (see page 30)	32	3,000		
33	Student loan interest deduction (see page 33)	33			
34	Tuition and fees deduction. Attach Form 8917	34			
35	Domestic production activities deduction. Attach Form 8903	35			
36	Add lines 23 through 31a and 32 through 35			36	3,275
37	Subtract line 36 from line 22. This is your adjusted gross income ▶			37	58,425

For Disclosure, Privacy Act, and Paperwork Reduction Act Notice, see page 88. Cat. No. 11320B Form **1040** (2008)

Communication (5 points)

Editor's Note: The AICPA did not provide a solution for the contents of the Communication tab. This solution was developed by Bisk Education.

September 11, 2008

Mark and Christie **Sagan**
123 Spruce Street
Anytown, USA

Dear Mr. & Mrs. Sagan:

The Notice of Late Filing & Payment of Taxes states that your 2007 return and accompanying income tax payment were received late. I believe the Internal Revenue Service is incorrect, but it is necessary to **verify** the accuracy of the facts as presented in the Notice of Late Filing & Payment of Taxes. I need from you copies of any supporting documentation that you have that your income tax **return** was indeed mailed prior to April 16, 2008. If you sent your income tax return by **certified mail,** as suggested in the filing instructions I provided with your return, you should have a certified mail **receipt** with a postmark date on it.

I also need copies of the supporting documentation that the **payment** was made timely. If your payment was by check or money order, please provide a photocopy of the front and back of the cancelled check or money order. You may need to contact your financial institution to obtain the photocopy, since some financial institutions do not provide cancelled checks with the monthly statements. If your payment was made by credit card, please provide the confirmation number that you were given at the end of the transaction and the tax payment amount.

Please deliver the items described above to my office no later than September 25, so I can resolve this matter as soon as possible. It is imperative that this issue be addressed by September 30, to avoid the **additional** interest and penalties that will begin to accrue if payment is not received by October 15.

Sincerely,

J. Smith, C.P.A.

Research (1 point)

Code Section Answer: §102(a)

Code §102(a) states, "GENERAL RULE.—Gross income does not include the value of property acquired by gift bequest, devise, or inheritance." search term: gift received

Solution 44-4 Tax Treatments

Income (1.25 points)

1. ($3,000)

Under §1222(4) the McGurns realized a long-term capital loss of $10,000 ($15,000 – $25,000) on the sale of Revco. Under §1222(1) the McGurns realized a short-term capital gain of $4,000 ($8,000 – $4,000) on the sale of Abbco. The McGurns have a net capital loss of $6,000 ($4,000 – $10,000) under §1222(10). Section 165(f) and §1211(b)(1) limit the amount of a net capital loss that may be deducted by taxpayers other than corporations to $3,000 a year. Thus, the McGurns would show a loss of $3,000 on Form 1040 and have a $3,000 long-term capital loss carryforward under §1212(b)(1).

2. $0

Under §1015(a) Ainsley's basis for determining gain is $60,000. The donor's basis and Ainsley's basis, for determining loss, is $50,000, the fair market value of the property at the time of the gift. Under Reg. §1.1015-1(a)(2), if the donee sells the property for an amount in between the basis for loss and the basis for gain, there is no gain or loss. Since Ainsley sold the property for $56,000, she realizes no gain or loss.

3. $0

The security deposit represents a liability, not income, because the McGurns must refund the deposit to the tenant when the tenant moves.

4. $55,000

The $53,000 in wages is included in gross income under §61(a)(1). The $2,000 value of the group term life insurance in excess of $50,000 is included in gross income under §79(a). The taxable amount is based on IRS rates rather than actual premiums paid.

5. $1,250

The $1,250 state income tax refund is included in gross income under the tax benefit rule of §111(a). The amount included is the lesser of the $1,250 refund received or the $1,450 amount by which their itemized deductions exceeded the standard deduction in the previous tax year. The $1,250 is listed on a separate line on Form 1040, page 1.

Adjustments (0.50 points)

6. $8,000

Section 215(a) allows a deduction for alimony. Section 215(b) provides that alimony means any alimony that is includible in the gross income of the recipient under §71. Section 71(a) includes alimony in the gross income of the recipient. However, §71(c)(1) excludes child support from being included in the gross income of the recipient. Temporary Reg. 1.71-1T(c) states clearly that child support is not included in the gross income of the payee and not deductible by the payor. Section 62(a) defines adjusted gross income as gross income less certain specified deductions. Alimony is listed in §62(a)(10). Thus, the $8,000 in alimony, but not the $10,000 in child support, is allowed as an adjustment to gross income in arriving at AGI.

Treatment (1.50 points)

7. A

Although William realized a $1,200 loss, §1091(a) disallows the recognition of any loss because he acquired the same shares within 30 days of the sale of the shares that resulted in a loss. This is referred to as a wash sale.

8. B

To be deductible, personal property taxes must be based on the value of the property (ad valorem taxes) under §164(b)(1). Section 164(a) allows a deduction for such personal property taxes. Section 62(a) defines AGI as gross income less certain specified deductions. Taxes are not listed therein. Thus, taxes are deductible as an itemized deduction. Section 67(a) allows a deduction for miscellaneous itemized deductions only to the extent that they exceed 2% of AGI. Section 67(b) defines miscellaneous itemized deductions as those itemized deductions other than those listed therein. Taxes are listed in §67(b)(2). Thus, taxes are fully deductible as an itemized deduction.

9. D

Section 170 allows a deduction for contributions to qualified charitable organizations. A church is a qualified charitable organization under §170. Reg. §1.170 provides that if a contribution is made in property other than money, the amount that may be deducted is limited to the property's fair market value. Section 62(a) defines adjusted gross income (AGI) as gross income less certain specified deductions. Charitable contributions are not listed therein. Thus, charitable contributions are deductible as an itemized deduction. Section 67(a) allows a deduction for miscellaneous itemized deductions only to the extent that they exceed 2% of AGI. Section 67(b) defines miscellaneous itemized deductions as those itemized deductions other than those listed therein. Charitable contributions are listed in Section 67(b)(4). However, §170(b)(1)(A) limits an individual's deduction for charitable contributions to 50% of AGI. Thus, the used furniture is a deductible charitable contribution as an itemized deduction up to 50% of AGI.

10. F

Since William is an accountant, the amount he paid for subscriptions to accounting journals qualifies as a deductible business expense under §162(a). Employee business expenses are deductible as a miscellaneous itemized deduction subject to the 2% of AGI threshold.

11. B

Section 163 allows a deduction for interest on home equity indebtedness with respect to any qualified residence of the taxpayer. Section 163 defines home equity indebtedness as any indebtedness secured by a qualified residence. The amount is limited to the extent that such indebtedness does not exceed the fair market value of such residence reduced by any acquisition indebtedness with respect to such residence. Section 163 limits the amount of qualifying home equity indebtedness to $100,000. Section 163 defines a qualified residence as the taxpayer's principal residence and one other residence selected and used by the taxpayer. The interest on this loan meets the requirements for deductibility. The interest is deductible in full as an itemized deduction on Schedule A.

True/False (0.75 points)

12. F

The phase out of personal exemptions for regular tax starts when adjusted gross income for a married couple filing jointly is much higher than $75,000.

13. T

In the calculation of alternative minimum tax (AMT), adjustments are made for several items, including standard deductions, medical expenses, and post-1986 depreciation on tangible property. For AMT, unreimbursed medical expenses have to exceed 10% of AGI to be deductible.

14. T

The personal exemption amount for regular tax is not permitted for determining alternative minimum tax (AMT). AMT exemptions are different from the personal exemptions of regular tax calculations.

Communication (5 points)

To: Mr. & Ms. **McGurn**
From: Candidate
Re: **Loss-of-Wages Insurance Premiums**

Premiums paid for disability insurance are considered personal expenses. Tax law disallows deductions for personal expenses unless expressly allowed. However, premiums paid for medical care insurance would be an allowable itemized deduction. Medical expenses exceeding 7.5% of the taxpayer's adjusted gross income are deductible.

There is no provision allowing a deduction for disability income insurance premiums paid by an individual; however, benefits from such a policy, if paid, are not taxed.

Research (1 point)

Code Section Answer: §904(a)

Code §904(a) states, "The total amount of [foreign tax] credit taken…shall not exceed the same proportion of the tax against which such credit is taken which the taxpayer's taxable income from sources without the United States (but not in excess of the taxpayer's entire taxable income) bears to his entire taxable income for the same taxable year."

Solution 44-5 Income For AGI

Form 1040 (4 points)

(Form 1040 shown on a subsequent page.)

1. Gifts are tax-exempt to the recipient.

2. $60,000 on Form 1040, Line 7; $5,500 on Form 1040, Line 32

If neither married taxpayer is an active participant in an employer-sponsored plan, both are eligible to deduct the full amount of their regular IRA contributions, regardless of income levels. Total IRA contributions for 2008 may be up to $5,000 for most taxpayers (also in 2009). Taxpayers who are at least age 50 by the end of the year may contribute an additional $1,000. All Roth IRA contributions are nondeductible. (The candidate must make the assumption that the 2009 contributions are for 2008.)

3. Only refunds for which a taxpayer received prior tax benefits are includible in income. There is no deduction from income on a federal return for federal income taxes paid.

4. $4,000 on Form 1040, Line 17

Payments made to a partner for services or for the use of capital (guaranteed payments) are treated as made to one who is not a partner. These payments are deductible by the partnership and are income to the recipient.

5. Life insurance proceeds paid by reason of death of the insured are excluded from gross income. If the beneficiary elects to receive the benefits in installments, the interest portion is includible in income.

6. Additional $2,000 on Form 1040, Line 7

Premiums paid by the employer for up to $50,000 worth of insurance coverage are excluded from income. $5/$1,000 × ($450,000 – $50,000) = $2,000

7. "Gambling winnings" and $5,000 on Form 1040, Line 21

Gambling winnings must be included in income. Gambling losses may be deducted from income to the extent of gambling winnings only if the taxpayer itemizes deductions.

8. $1,000 on Form 1040, Line 8a

All interest income is included in taxable income, unless there is a specific exclusion. There is no exclusion for interest income due to a federal income tax refund.

9. Married taxpayers may exclude up to $500,000 of gain from the sale of a personal residence provided they occupied the home in two of the five previous years.

10. Andre Dupont is not an eligible dependent. Dependents must be citizens or residents of the U.S., or a citizen of Canada, or Mexico.

Communication (5 points)

To: Mr. and Mrs. **Soffit**
From: Candidate
Re: **Stock Dividend**

The $9,000 **stock dividend** is tax-free, unless a **cash option** is available. In this case, no cash option was available. The **basis** of the individual shares is **reduced**.

A copy of the income tax return is enclosed. Please keep the copy for your records.

Research (1 point)

Code Section Answer: §446(d)

Code §446(d) states, "A taxpayer engaged in more than one trade or business may, in computing taxable income, use a different method of accounting for each trade or business."

Form **1040** Department of the Treasury—Internal Revenue Service
U.S. Individual Income Tax Return 2008 (99) IRS Use Only—Do not write or staple in this space.

For the year Jan. 1-Dec. 31, 2008, or other tax year beginning , 2008, ending , 20 OMB No. 1545-0074

Label		
(See instructions on page 14.)	Your first name and initial: Jason	Last name: Soffit	Your social security number: 987 65 4321
Use the IRS label.	If a joint return, spouse's first name and initial: Daphne	Last name: Soffit	Spouse's social security number: 123 54 6789
Otherwise, please print or type.	Home address (number and street). If you have a P.O. box, see page 14.: Any Street	Apt. no.	▲ You must enter your SSN(s) above. ▲
	City, town or post office, state, and ZIP code. If you have a foreign address, see page 14.: Any City		Checking a box below will not change your tax or refund.

Presidential Election Campaign ▶ Check here if you, or your spouse if filing jointly, want $3 to go to this fund (see page 14) ▶ ☐ You ☐ Spouse

Filing Status

Check only one box.

1 ☐ Single
2 ☑ Married filing jointly (even if only one had income)
3 ☐ Married filing separately. Enter spouse's SSN above and full name here. ▶
4 ☐ Head of household (with qualifying person). (See page 15.) If the qualifying person is a child but not your dependent, enter this child's name here. ▶
5 ☐ Qualifying widow(er) with dependent child (see page 16)

Exemptions

6a ☑ Yourself. If someone can claim you as a dependent, do not check box 6a — Boxes checked on 6a and 6b: 2
b ☑ Spouse

c Dependents:

(1) First name Last name	(2) Dependent's social security number	(3) Dependent's relationship to you	(4) ✓ if qualifying child for child tax credit (see page 17)
			☐
			☐
			☐
			☐

No. of children on 6c who:
• lived with you
• did not live with you due to divorce or separation (see page 18)
Dependents on 6c not entered above

If more than four dependents, see page 17.

d Total number of exemptions claimed — Add numbers on lines above ▶ 2

Income

Attach Form(s) W-2 here. Also attach Forms W-2G and 1099-R if tax was withheld.

If you did not get a W-2, see page 21.

Enclose, but do not attach, any payment. Also, please use Form 1040-V.

7	Wages, salaries, tips, etc. Attach Form(s) W-2	7	62,000
8a	Taxable interest. Attach Schedule B if required	8a	1,000
b	Tax-exempt interest. Do not include on line 8a — 8b		
9a	Ordinary dividends. Attach Schedule B if required	9a	
b	Qualified dividends (see page 21) — 9b		
10	Taxable refunds, credits, or offsets of state and local income taxes (see page 22)	10	
11	Alimony received	11	
12	Business income or (loss). Attach Schedule C or C-EZ	12	
13	Capital gain or (loss). Attach Schedule D if required. If not required, check here ▶ ☐	13	
14	Other gains or (losses). Attach Form 4797	14	
15a	IRA distributions 15a — b Taxable amount (see page 23)	15b	
16a	Pensions and annuities 16a — b Taxable amount (see page 24)	16b	
17	Rental real estate, royalties, partnerships, S corporations, trusts, etc. Attach Schedule E	17	4,000
18	Farm income or (loss). Attach Schedule F	18	
19	Unemployment compensation	19	
20a	Social security benefits 20a — b Taxable amount (see page 26)	20b	
21	Other income. List type and amount (see page 28)	21	5,000
22	Add the amounts in the far right column for lines 7 through 21. This is your total income ▶	22	72,000

Adjusted Gross Income

23	Educator expenses (see page 28)	23			
24	Certain business expenses of reservists, performing artists, and fee-basis government officials. Attach Form 2106 or 2106-EZ	24			
25	Health savings account deduction. Attach Form 8889	25			
26	Moving expenses. Attach Form 3903	26			
27	One-half of self-employment tax. Attach Schedule SE	27			
28	Self-employed SEP, SIMPLE, and qualified plans	28			
29	Self-employed health insurance deduction (see page 29)	29			
30	Penalty on early withdrawal of savings	30			
31a	Alimony paid b Recipient's SSN ▶	31a			
32	IRA deduction (see page 30)	32			
33	Student loan interest deduction (see page 33)	33			
34	Tuition and fees deduction. Attach Form 8917	34			
35	Domestic production activities deduction. Attach Form 8903	35			
36	Add lines 23 through 31a and 32 through 35			36	4,500
37	Subtract line 36 from line 22. This is your adjusted gross income ▶			37	67,500

For Disclosure, Privacy Act, and Paperwork Reduction Act Notice, see page 88. Cat. No. 11320B Form **1040** (2008)

Solution 44-6 Schedules A & E

Schedule A (3.5 points)

(Schedule A shown on next page.)

1. "Continuing education expenses" and $900 on Schedule A, Line 21

Employees are allowed to treat unreimbursed education expenses as a miscellaneous itemized deduction subject to the 2% of AGI limitation. The education must be to maintain or improve a skill required in the individual's employment or meets the express requirements of the employer or laws or regulations.

2. $20,000 on Schedule A, Line 18

Contributions made that exceed the 50% limit in one year may be carried forward for five years.

3. $1,200 on Schedule A, Line 14

Investment interest is deductible to the extent of net investment income.

4. Not deductible

Gambling losses are first-tier miscellaneous deductions (not subject to the 2% of AGI limitation) that are limited to the extent of gambling winnings. As Maple had no gambling winnings, the losses are not deductible.

5. $2,500 on Schedule A, Line 6

Local, state, and foreign real property taxes are deductible by the cash-basis taxpayer upon whom they are imposed in the year in which they were paid.

6. Not deductible

Premiums for property insurance are not deductible.

7. $2,800 on Schedule A, Line 1

Qualified medical expenses are deductible on Schedule A subject to a 7.5% of AGI floor. Health insurance premiums are a qualified medical expense.

8. $4,000 on Schedule A, Line 10

Interest on up to $1,000,000 of debt incurred to buy, construct, or substantially improve a first or second home is deductible as qualified residential interest.

Schedule E (0.5 points)

(Schedule E shown on a subsequent page.)

9. $3,600 on Schedule E, Line 16

The amount of rental income to be included in gross income is determined on Schedule E, *Supplemental Income and Loss,* by subtracting deductible expenses from rental payments received. Real property taxes are deductible expenses. (The schedule cannot be completed in full as insufficient information is provided.)

Communication (5 points)

To: Mr./Ms. Maple
From: Candidate
Re: Gambling Losses

The **$450** of **gambling losses** would be a first tier (**not** subject to the 2% of adjusted gross income limitation) miscellaneous deduction that is limited to the extent of gambling winnings. In order to deduct gambling losses, gambling **winnings** must be included in income. Since you did not have any gambling winnings, these losses are not deductible.

Research (1 point)

Code Section Answer: §6511(a)

Code §6511(a) states, "Claim for credit or refund of an overpayment of any tax imposed by this title in respect of which tax the taxpayer is required to file a return shall be filed by the taxpayer within 3 years from the time the return was filed or 2 years from the time the tax was paid, whichever of such periods expires the later, or if no return was filed by the taxpayer, within 2 years from the time the tax was paid."

SCHEDULES A&B (Form 1040)
Department of the Treasury Internal Revenue Service (99)

Schedule A—Itemized Deductions

(Schedule B is on back)

► Attach to Form 1040. ► See Instructions for Schedules A&B (Form 1040).

OMB No. 1545-0074 | 2008 | Attachment Sequence No. 07

Name(s) shown on Form 1040: Maple | Your social security number: 123 ¦ 45 ¦ 6789

Section	Line	Description	Box	Amount	Line	Total
Medical and Dental Expenses		Caution. Do not include expenses reimbursed or paid by others.				
	1	Medical and dental expenses (see page A-1)	1	2,800		
	2	Enter amount from Form 1040, line 38 [2: 40,000]				
	3	Multiply line 2 by 7.5% (.075)	3	3,200		
	4	Subtract line 3 from line 1. If line 3 is more than line 1, enter -0-			4	0
Taxes You Paid (See page A-2.)	5	State and local (check only one box): a ☐ Income taxes, or b ☐ General sales taxes	5			
	6	Real estate taxes (see page A-5)	6	2,500		
	7	Personal property taxes	7			
	8	Other taxes. List type and amount ►	8			
	9	Add lines 5 through 8			9	2,500
Interest You Paid (See page A-5.)	10	Home mortgage interest and points reported to you on Form 1098	10	4,000		
	11	Home mortgage interest not reported to you on Form 1098. If paid to the person from whom you bought the home, see page A-6 and show that person's name, identifying no., and address ►	11			
Note. Personal interest is not deductible.	12	Points not reported to you on Form 1098. See page A-6 for special rules	12			
	13	Qualified mortgage insurance premiums (see page A-6)	13			
	14	Investment interest. Attach Form 4952 if required. (See page A-6.)	14	1,200		
	15	Add lines 10 through 14			15	5,200
Gifts to Charity	16	Gifts by cash or check. If you made any gift of $250 or more, see page A-7	16			
If you made a gift and got a benefit for it, see page A-7.	17	Other than by cash or check. If any gift of $250 or more, see page A-8. You must attach Form 8283 if over $500	17			
	18	Carryover from prior year	18	20,000		
	19	Add lines 16 through 18			19	20,000
Casualty and Theft Losses	20	Casualty or theft loss(es). Attach Form 4684. (See page A-8.)			20	
Job Expenses and Certain Miscellaneous Deductions (See page A-9.)	21	Unreimbursed employee expenses—job travel, union dues, job education, etc. Attach Form 2106 or 2106-EZ if required. (See page A-9.) ►	21	900		
	22	Tax preparation fees	22			
	23	Other expenses—investment, safe deposit box, etc. List type and amount ►	23			
	24	Add lines 21 through 23	24	900		
	25	Enter amount from Form 1040, line 38 [25:]				
	26	Multiply line 25 by 2% (.02)	26	800		
	27	Subtract line 26 from line 24. If line 26 is more than line 24, enter -0-			27	100
Other Miscellaneous Deductions	28	Other—from list on page A-10. List type and amount ►			28	
Total Itemized Deductions	29	Is Form 1040, line 38, over $159,950 (over $79,975 if married filing separately)? ☐ No. Your deduction is not limited. Add the amounts in the far right column for lines 4 through 28. Also, enter this amount on Form 1040, line 40. ☐ Yes. Your deduction may be limited. See page A-10 for the amount to enter. ►			29	27,800
	30	If you elect to itemize deductions even though they are less than your standard deduction, check here ► ☐				

For Paperwork Reduction Act Notice, see Form 1040 instructions. Cat. No. 11330X Schedule A (Form 1040) 2008

SCHEDULE E (Form 1040)

Department of the Treasury Internal Revenue Service (99)

Supplemental Income and Loss

(From rental real estate, royalties, partnerships, S corporations, estates, trusts, REMICs, etc.)

► Attach to Form 1040, 1040NR, or Form 1041. ► See Instructions for Schedule E (Form 1040).

OMB No. 1545-0074

2008

Attachment Sequence No. 13

Name(s) shown on return: Maple

Your social security number: 123 45 6789

Part I **Income or Loss From Rental Real Estate and Royalties** **Note.** If you are in the business of renting personal property, use **Schedule C** or **C-EZ** (see page E-3). If you are an individual, report farm rental income or loss from **Form 4835** on page 2, line 40.

1 List the type and address of each **rental real estate property:**

A Residential rental property 927 Mulberry Street, My Town, FL

B

C

2 For each rental real estate property listed on line 1, did you or your family use it during the tax year for personal purposes for more than the greater of:
- 14 days **or**
- 10% of the total days rented at fair rental value?

(See page E-3)

	Yes	No
A		✔
B		
C		

	Line	Properties A	Properties B	Properties C	Line	Totals (Add columns A, B, and C.)
Income:						
3 Rents received	3	12,000			3	12,000
4 Royalties received	4				4	
Expenses:						
5 Advertising	5					
6 Auto and travel (see page E-4)	6					
7 Cleaning and maintenance	7					
8 Commissions	8					
9 Insurance	9					
10 Legal and other professional fees	10					
11 Management fees	11					
12 Mortgage interest paid to banks, etc. (see page E-5)	12				12	
13 Other interest	13					
14 Repairs	14					
15 Supplies	15					
16 Taxes	16	3,600				
17 Utilities	17					
18 Other (list) ►	18					
19 Add lines 5 through 18	19	3,600			19	3,600
20 Depreciation expense or depletion (see page E-5)	20				20	
21 Total expenses. Add lines 19 and 20	21	3,600				
22 Income or (loss) from rental real estate or royalty properties. Subtract line 21 from line 3 (rents) or line 4 (royalties). If the result is a (loss), see page E-5 to find out if you must file **Form 6198**	22	8,400				
23 Deductible rental real estate loss. **Caution.** Your rental real estate loss on line 22 may be limited. See page E-5 to find out if you must file **Form 8582.** Real estate professionals **must** complete line 43 on page 2	23	( )	( )	( )		

24 **Income.** Add positive amounts shown on line 22. **Do not** include any losses	24	8,400
25 **Losses.** Add royalty losses from line 22 and rental real estate losses from line 23. Enter total losses here.	25	( )
26 **Total rental real estate and royalty income or (loss).** Combine lines 24 and 25. Enter the result here. If Parts II, III, IV, and line 40 on page 2 do not apply to you, also enter this amount on Form 1040, line 17, or Form 1040NR, line 18. Otherwise, include this amount in the total on line 41 on page 2	26	8,400

For Paperwork Reduction Act Notice, see page E-8 of the instructions. Cat. No. 11344L **Schedule E (Form 1040) 2008**

Solution 44-7 Tax Treatments

Tax Treatment (4 points)

1. C

Schedule C is used to report trade or business income and expenses. Retainer fees from clients are an example of trade or business income.

2. D

Schedule E is used to report income or loss from rental real estate, royalties, partnerships, S corporations, estates, and trusts.

3. B

The interest income from a refund of federal taxes is an example of interest income which is taxable on Schedule B.

4. E

Death benefits from a life insurance policy are not taxable income.

5. D

Schedule E is used to report income or loss from rental real estate, royalties, partnerships, S corporations, estates, and trusts. Income from a limited partnership is an example of Schedule E partnership income.

6. D

Schedule E is used to report income or loss from rental real estate, royalties, partnerships, S corporations, estates, and trusts. Income from the rental of a townhouse is an example of taxable rental real estate income.

7. A

Prize money is an example of other income reported on Form 1040.

8. A

Payment received for jury service is taxable as other income on Form 1040.

Communication (5 points)

To: Mr./Ms. **Rogue**
From: Candidate
Re: Tax-Exempt & Taxable Interest

Interest income on **general obligation state** and **local government** bonds generally is not taxable. This exemption does not extend to federal government obligations nor to interest on state or local tax refunds.

Interest on U.S. Treasury bonds is taxable income. U.S. Treasury bonds are obligations of the federal government.

Dividend income from mutual funds that invest in **tax-free** government obligations is not taxable. Essentially, the mutual fund passess the tax exempt income through to the shareholder without changing its nature.

Research (1 point)

Code Section Answer: §162(b)

Code §162(b) states, "No deduction shall be allowed for any contribution or gift which would be allowable as a deduction...were it not for the percentage limitations, the dollar limitations, or the requirements as to the time of payment, set forth in such section."

Solution 44-8 Tax Treatments

Filing Status & Exemptions (0.50 points)

1. M, 4

Section 6013(a)(3) allows a spouse to file a joint return in the year of the other spouse's death, provided that the decedent did not file her/his own return before death, no executor or administrator has been appointed, and no executor or administrator is appointed before the due date of the return. If an executor or administrator is appointed after the joint return is filed, the executor or administrator may disaffirm the joint return until one year from its due date. Thus, Mrs. Guild is entitled to one personal exemption for herself and one personal exemption for the late Mr. Guild. Mrs. Guild may claim one dependency exemption each for her daughter, Joan, because she passes all four tests (relationship, residence, age and support) and the two additional general tests (martial status and citizenship) under the uniform definition. Mrs. Guild may also claim a dependency exemption for her unmarried cousin, Fran Phillips. Although Fran is not considered a relative, Fran qualifies as a dependent because she lived with the Guilds for all of the taxable year. Fran also meets the gross income test since her gross income of zero is less than the personal exemption amount. Both Joan and Fran meet the citizenship test and received over half of their support from the Guilds, as required.

2. Q, 3

For the year after Mr. Guild's death, Mrs. Guild will file as a qualifying widow with dependent child. This filing status is known in the Internal Revenue Code as "surviving spouse." This filing status is available for the two tax years following a spouse's death if the surviving spouse does not remarry and maintains a household for a dependent child. Mrs. Guild is entitled to one personal exemption for herself. Mrs. Guild may claim one dependency exemption each for her daughter, Joan, and for her unmarried cousin, Fran Phillips. See the answer to question #1, above, for an explanation of Joan's and Fran's eligibility as dependents.

Income (1 point)

3. $0

The disability benefits are fully excluded from gross income under §104(a)(1) and Reg. §1.104-1(b). The benefits are specifically job related, so they qualify for exclusion as workers' compensation.

4. $400

The interest from a refund from an amended tax return and interest on a savings account are included in gross income under §61(a)(4). The $100 interest on the municipal bonds is excluded from gross income under §103(a).

5. $900

Because the pension plan was a qualified plan and the contributions made entirely by Mr. Guild's employer, Mr. Guild had never included these amounts in gross income. Mrs. Guild must include all $900 in gross income as income in respect of a decedent.

6. $0

Gifts are excluded from gross income as long as the gift is not from the taxpayer's employer.

7. $0

The life insurance proceeds are excluded from gross income because they were paid to Mrs. Guild on account of the death of her insured husband.

8. $200

The jury duty pay is included in gross income. Gross income includes all income unless specifically excluded. If jury duty pay is paid to the taxpayer's employer because the employer compensated the employee during the period of jury service, the taxpayer is entitled to deduct such amount from gross income in arriving at AGI under §62(a)(13).

9. $450

The gambling winnings are included in gross income under §61(a) and Reg. §1.61-14(a).

Deductions (2.5 points)

10. A

No deduction is allowed for personal expenses under §262(a). Premiums on personal life insurance premiums are considered a personal expense under Reg. §1.262-1(b)(1).

11. D

Penalties on early withdrawal of a certificate of deposit are deductible for AGI.

12. F

A cash donation to the American Red Cross is deductible under §170(a). Charitable contributions are an itemized deduction that are not subject to the 2% of AGI threshold. Under §170(b)(1)(A), there is a 50% of AGI limit on the amount of charitable contributions that an individual may deduct in any one tax year. (Candidates must assume that the examiners meant response (F) to read "ceiling" instead of "threshold.")

13. E

State income taxes are deductible as an itemized deduction not subject to the 2% of AGI threshold in the year paid or accrued, depending upon the taxpayer's accounting method.

14. E

Real property taxes are deductible as an itemized deduction not subject to the 2% of AGI threshold in the year paid or accrued, depending upon the taxpayer's accounting method.

15. A

The loss on the sale of the family car is a loss on the sale of a personal-use asset, and therefore is not deductible. Individuals may deduct losses from a trade or business, for a transaction entered into for the production of income, and casualty and theft losses.

16. B

A capital expenditure that is directly related to the medical care of the taxpayer may be deducted to the extent that the expenditure exceeds the increase in the value of the residence. Medical expenses are an itemized deduction, deductible to the extent that they exceed 7.5% of AGI.

17. B

Health insurance is included in the definition of medical expenses deductible as an itemized deduction to the extent that they exceed 7.5% of AGI.

18. C

The CPA fees to prepare a tax return are deductible in the year paid, for a cash basis taxpayer. Tax preparation fees are not listed as a deduction in arriving at AGI unless they qualify as a trade or business expense or as a deduction attributable to rents or royalties; thus, these fees are an itemized deduction. These fees are subject to the threshold of 2% of AGI.

19. E

Points paid to refinance a mortgage on a home represent prepaid interest. Interest on a home is deductible and prepaid interest is deductible in the period to which it is allocable. Points paid to refinance the taxpayer's principal residence must be capitalized and amortized over the life of the loan. Interest is deductible as an itemized deduction that is not subject to the 2% of AGI threshold.

20. D

Half of the self-employment taxes paid are deductible from gross income in arriving at AGI.

21. E

Under §165(d), gambling losses are allowed only to the extent of gains from gambling. Since Mrs. Guild had at least $100 in gains from gambling, she may deduct the $100 in gambling losses in full. Allowable gambling losses are deductible as an itemized deduction not subject to the 2% of AGI threshold.

22. C

Union dues are an employee business expense deductible as an itemized deduction, subject to the 2% of AGI threshold.

23. A

Section 275(a) disallows any deduction for federal income taxes paid.

True/False (1 point)

24. F

Funeral expenses are considered a personal expense. Generally, no deduction is allowed for personal expenses. Section 641(b) provides that the taxable income of an estate is to be determined in the same manner as that of an individual, with certain noted exceptions. Thus, the funeral expenses are not deductible on the estate's income tax return. Funeral expenses may be deducted only from the gross estate in determining the taxable estate for estate tax purposes.

25. T

Section 691(c) allows a deduction for the estate tax attributable to the income in respect of a decedent included in the recipient's gross income. Such estate tax is deductible as an itemized deduction, not subject to the 2% of AGI threshold.

26. F

The loss on property used in a real estate business is a business loss, not a casualty loss. Losses on the involuntary conversion of business property are deductible in arriving at AGI.

27. F

Section 22(a) allows the credit for the elderly and the permanently and totally disabled to be taken against the tax liability. The credit is determined by multiplying a flat 15% rate by the base for the credit. However, for a married couple filing a joint return in which neither spouse has attained age 65 by the close of the tax year, the base amount is limited to the sum of the spouses' disability income. Assuming the Guilds have not attained age 65, the base amount for the credit is limited to the $1,500 in state disability benefits. There is a phase out of this base amount for taxpayers with AGI over a specified amount, based upon filing status. Under this phase out, the base amount is reduced by one half of the excess of AGI over the specified amount. For a married couple filing a joint return, the specified amount is $10,000. The Guilds would lose all of the credit if their AGI is $13,000 or greater: ($13,000 – $10,000) × 50% = $1,500. Clearly, the Guilds have AGI much higher than $13,000.

28. T

Section 6695(a) requires an income tax return preparer to furnish a copy of the return to the taxpayer. The $50 penalty may be waived if the preparer can prove that the failure was due to reasonable cause and not willful neglect.

29. F

The earned income credit is allowed under the provisions of §32. There is no provision under this section that makes the income limitation for the earned income credit inapplicable for the year in which the taxpayer died. The only provision concerning death in §32 is §32(e), which provides that the taxable year must be a full taxable year except in the case of the death of the taxpayer.

30. F

The accrued vacation pay at the time of Mr. Guild's death represents income in respect of a decedent to Mrs. Guild. Income in respect of a decedent is included in the gross income of the recipient in the taxable year when received. Mrs. Guild would report the accrued vacation pay when received.

31. F

Per §53 (a) and (c), the credit can only be used against the "regular" tax in future years, not the alternative minimum tax.

Communication (4 points)

To: Mr. & Ms. Guild
From: Candidate
Re: Life Insurance

The personal life insurance premium paid is not deductible. No deduction is allowed for **personal** expenses unless expressly allowed. However, premiums paid for **medical care** insurance would be an **allowable itemized deduction**. Medical expenses are subject to a 7.5% of adjusted gross income limitation.

Correspondingly, the proceeds paid to beneficiaries are not included in taxable income.

Research (1 point)

Code Section Answer: §166(b)

Code §166(b) states, "...The basis for determining the amount of the deduction for any bad debt shall be the adjusted basis...for determining the loss from the sale or other disposition of property."

Solution 44-9 Farm Income

Income & Expense (2 points)

1. A

The cost or other basis of livestock and other items bought for resale is reported in Part I of Schedule F, where it is subtracted from sales of livestock and other times bought for resale. Note that this is similar to how cost of sales is handled on Schedule C.

2. C

Loan proceeds are not income.

3. C

The income of an adult child doesn't appear on his parents' income tax return.

4. B

A sole proprietorship is not a separate entity for tax purposes. Interest on a checking account used for a trade or business that is a sole proprietorship is reported on page 1 of Form 1040 as personal income.

5. A

See item #1.

6. A

Interest expense on a loan relating to the farm is reported in Part II of Schedule F. Note that this is similar to how expenses are handled on Schedule C.

7. C

Repayments of loan principal are not expenses. Also see item #6.

8. A

Chemicals and pesticides costs are farm expenses reported in Part II of Schedule F. Also see item #6.

9. C

Contributions to a Roth IRA are not deductible.

10. B

As Cameron and Elinor Sullivan itemize their deductions, state estimated tax payments are deducted on Schedule A.

11. B

Property taxes on a farmer's home are a personal expense eligible to be deducted on Schedule A.

12. A

Fertilizer costs are farm expenses reported in Part II of Schedule F. Also see item #6.

13. A

Farm travel expenses are farm expenses reported in Part II of Schedule F. Also see item #6.

14. C

No deductions for penalties are allowed. Also see item #6.

15. A

Livestock feed costs are farm expenses reported in Part II of Schedule F. Also see item #6.

16. A

Repairs and maintenance on farm equipment are farm expenses reported in Part II of Schedule F. Also see item #6.

Depreciation (1.75 points)

17. $44,000, $6,600

A depreciation deduction is allowed for the exhaustion of property used in a business or held for production of income. MACRS depreciation is calculated on the basis of property—generally equal to the cost or purchase price of the property, increased by costs necessary to get the asset ready for use and reduced by any depreciation previously taken. From the MACRS tables provided, the depreciation factor for a 5-year asset using the half-year convention and the 150% declining balance method in the first year is 15.00%. The first year's depreciation is $44,000 × 15.00% = $6,600.

18. $35,000, $3,749

Section 179 property is tangible, depreciable personal property that is purchased for use in a trade or business. Section 179 authorizes a deduction for §179 property placed in service during the year. This deduction reduces the amount available for the MACRS basis. $60,000 – $25,000 = $35,000. From the MACRS tables provided, the depreciation factor for a 7-year asset using the half-year convention and the 150% declining balance method in the first year is 10.71%. The first year's depreciation is $35,000 × 10.71% = $3,749. Also see item #17.

19. $5,610

From the MACRS tables provided, the depreciation factor for a 5-year asset using the half-year convention and the 150% declining balance method in the second year is 25.50%. The second year's full depreciation is $44,000 × 25.50% = $11,220. Presumably, this is the truck that was sold on November 1, year 2; therefore, only half a year's depreciation is incurred in year 2. As this is not included in the factor provided by the table, the depreciation amount must be adjusted accordingly. $11,220 / 2 = $5,610. Also see item #17.

20. $6,696

EESA '08 classifies most farm machinery and equipment originally placed in service by a taxpayer in 2009 in a farming business as 5-year property; however, the combine was purchased and placed in service in 2008. From the MACRS tables provided, the depreciation factor for a 7-year asset using the half-year convention and the 150% declining balance method in the second year is 19.13%. The second year's depreciation is $35,000 × 19.13% = $6,696. Also see item #18.

21. $2,438

Under §168(d)(3), if the aggregate basis of depreciable personal property placed in service during the last 3 months of the taxable year exceeds 40% of the aggregate basis of such property placed in service during the taxable year, then the taxpayer must use the mid-quarter convention for all such property placed in service during the year. In this case, the taxpayer purchased and placed into service 100% of depreciable personal property in the last 3 months of the taxable year. From the MACRS tables provided, the depreciation factor for a 5-year asset using the mid-quarter convention for an asset placed in service in the fourth quarter and the 150% declining balance method in the first year is 3.75%. The first year's depreciation is $65,000 × 3.75% = $2,438. Also see item #17.

22. $0

As the farm had a net loss in year 1, a Section 179 election cannot be deducted in year 1.

23. $25,000

Any Section 179 deduction disallowed due to insufficient taxable income derived from the trade or business may be carried forward indefinitely [Section 179(b)(3)(B)].

Self-Employment Tax (0.75 points)

24. $105,000

Cameron's net farm profits in year 3 are $105,000.

25. $0

Cameron has no Schedule C or K-1 income in year 3.

26. $13,600

($105,000 × 0.9235) × 0.029 + $10,788 = $13,600

Communication (5 points)

Editor's Note: The AICPA declined to present an unofficial solution for this portion of the simulation. The solution presented here was composed by the Bisk editors.

April 17, year 2

John Climpson
123 Rural Route 1
Anyton, IA

Dear Mr. Climpson:

Pursuant to our conversation regarding your plans to start a farm as a sole proprietor, here are some preliminary items for you to consider regarding specific types of expenses that would be included on your Schedule F.

As a sole proprietor, you would have the option to use either the **cash** or **accrual** method of accounting for tax purposes. As a cash basis taxpayer, you would not be allowed to deduct an **uncollectible account receivable** because the receivable would not have been included in income previously. As an accrual basis taxpayer, you must pay tax on accrued income, even if the related payment has not been received. If the cash method is selected, there are some income items that may be reported for tax purposes other than the year in which payment is received or made. If the accrual method is selected, there are some income items that may be reported for tax purposes other than the year in which revenue is accrued or expenses are incurred. These exceptions include the purchase and depreciation of **capital assets, interest, rents,** and crop disaster payments.

Personal income and personal expenses may not be reported on Schedule F; however, personal income is reported elsewhere on your return and select personal expenses may be deductible on your return. As examples of personal income, **investment income** and **jury duty pay** both are reported on Form 1040 as personal income. As examples of personal expenses, **mortgage interest** and **property taxes** paid on your **home** both are deductible as itemized deductions on Schedule A.

If you have employees, the **wages** and **benefits** you pay them and the taxes incurred related to their employment would be deductible on Schedule F. You also would have to make timely payments of **employment taxes** that you incur (such as unemployment and the employer's portion of social security) and all taxes **withheld** on your employees' behalf. These are not annual payments; typically, these payments are made at least quarterly, often more frequently.

The **self-employment tax** is comparable to an employee's social security tax, but it is double in amount, as a sole proprietor essentially pays both the employee's and employer's share. As a sole proprietor, you do not have an employer withholding taxes on your behalf, so you would have to make estimated tax payments throughout the year, based on estimates of your income tax and self-employment tax combined.

I. Ma Preparer, CPA

Research (1 point)

Code Section Answer: §1301(a)

Code §1301(a) states, "IN GENERAL.—At the election of an individual engaged in a farming business or fishing business, the tax imposed by section 1 for such taxable year shall be equal to the sum of—1301(a)(1) a tax computed under such section on taxable income reduced by elected farm income, plus 1301(a)(2) the increase in tax imposed by section 1 which would result if taxable income for each of the 3 prior taxable years were increased by an amount equal to one-third of the elected farm income. Any adjustment under this section for any taxable year shall be taken into account in applying this section for any subsequent taxable year." Search term: "farm income averaging"

Solution 44-10 Tax Treatments

Income (1.25 points)

1. $0

Section 85(a) provides that unemployment compensation is included in gross income; however, ARRA '09 excludes up to $2,400 of unemployment benefits received in 2009. This amount is shown on a separate line on page 1 of Form 1040. The employer's payment to an unemployment insurance fund is not unemployment compensation.

2. $2,500

The $8,400 in rental receipts is included in gross income under §61(a)(5). Expenses of rental income are deductible under §162(a) as business expenses or under §212 as expenses for the production of income depending on whether the rental activity is considered a business. Sec. 62(a) defines AGI as gross income less certain specified deductions, including those attributable to rents and royalties. Thus, expenses attributable to rental income are deductible from gross income in arriving at AGI. Rental income and expenses are reported on Schedule E and the $2,500 net rental income is transferred to Form 1040, page 1.

3. $900

Section 305(a) generally excludes the value of a distribution of stock with respect to stock in the same corporation. However, §305(b)(1) states that the exclusion will not apply to distributions made in lieu of money. Dividends are included in gross income under §61(a)(7). Section 301(b)(1) states that the amount of a dividend paid in property shall be the fair market value of the property. Thus, the Ryans must include $900 in gross income. This amount will be reported on Schedule B and then transferred to Form 1040, page 1. They will also have a $900 basis in the shares received under §301(d).

4. $3,500

Old §101(b) death benefit exclusion for amounts paid by an employer and received by beneficiaries or the employee's estate on account of the death of the employee no longer exists.

5. $5,000

Interest generally is included in gross income under §61(a)(4). Section 135(a) allows an exclusion from gross income for interest realized from a redemption of any qualified U.S. Savings Bond used to pay for a dependent's higher education tuition and fees. The Ryans' AGI is below the phase-out threshold. Section 135(c)(1) states to be a qualified U.S. Savings Bond, the bond must have been issued after 1989. However, as Laura is not David's dependent, the interest is included in gross income.

Treatment (2 points)

6. C

Section 62(a) defines AGI as gross income less certain specified deductions. Medical expenses are not listed in §62(a). Thus, medical expenses are not deductible in arriving at AGI. Payments for prescription drugs are a medical expense under §213(b). Section 213(a) allows a deduction for medical expenses to the extent that such expenses exceed 7.5% of AGI. Thus, the medical expenses are allowed as an itemized deduction subject to a threshold of 7.5% of AGI.

7. A

Funeral expenses are considered a personal expense. Section 262(a) disallows deductions for personal expense unless expressly allowed. There is no provision allowing a deduction for funeral expenses for income tax purposes.

8. E

Section 165(c) allows an individual to deduct losses from casualty or theft. The loss is deductible as an itemized deduction because §165(h)(4)(A) allows a deduction for personal casualty losses to the extent of personal casualty gains in computing AGI. Section 165(h)(1) imposes a $100 floor on each casualty or theft. Additionally, Sec. 165(h)(2) imposes a 10% of AGI floor on all casualties and thefts combined.

9. A

Section 165(c) allows an individual to deduct losses only on business property, investment property, and losses on personal use property from casualty or theft.

10. B

Section 163 defines a qualified residence as the taxpayer's principal residence and one other residence selected and used by the taxpayer. Because the loan is under $1 million, was incurred in the acquisition of the Ryans' home, and is secured by their home, the interest is deductible in full as an itemized deduction on Schedule A.

11. A

A taxpayer may deduct contributions of cash, property to a qualified charity and expenses incurred on behalf of a qualified charity. However, a taxpayer may not deduct the value of labor donated to a charity under Regs. §1.170-2(a)(2) and §1.170A-1(g).

True/False (0.75 points)

12. T

In order to avoid a penalty, taxpayers must pay the lesser of either 90% of the current year's tax, or 100% of the prior year's tax, unless AGI is more than $150,000. The Ryans' AGI is less than $150,000 and they paid 100% of the prior year's tax.

13. T

Generally, withdrawals from IRA's before the owners meet the age requirements are subject to regular income tax plus an early withdrawal penalty of 10%, without regard for the use of the money. There is an exception when the life expectancy of the owner is short or the money is used to pay for medical expenses in excess of 7.5% of AGI, or for medical insurance while unemployed. The Ryans do not appear to meet the exceptions.

14. F

Earned income credit is a refundable credit for low-income taxpayers who meet certain conditions. The Ryans' earned income is so far above these limits that the credit is eliminated entirely.

Communication (5 points)

To: Mr. & Ms. **Ryan**
From: Candidate
Re: Basis of Gift Property

Your basis for determining gain on the **gift** of **land** is $60,000, your uncle's **basis**. For determining loss, your basis is $50,000, the **fair market value** of the property at the **time** of the **gift**. If a donee sells gifted property for an amount in between the basis for loss and the basis for gain, there is no gain or loss. Since Kalila sold the property for $56,000, she realizes **no** taxable **gain** or **loss** on this transaction.

Research (1 point)

Code Section Answer: §117(a)

Code §117(a) states, "GENERAL RULE. -- Gross income does not include any amount received as a qualified scholarship by an individual who is a candidate for a degree at an educational organization described in section 170(b)(1)(A)(ii)." Search terms: exclude AND scholarship

Solution 44-11 Tax Treatments

Tax Treatment (4 points)

1. C

Qualifying medical expenses are deductible on Schedule A subject to a 7.5% of AGI floor.

2. J

Life insurance premiums are not deductible.

3. H

50% of business meals are deductible as a business expense on Schedule C.

4. F

The computer is used for business so the depreciation expense is reported on Form 4562 and is deductible on Schedule C.

5. G

Business lodging expenses while out of town are fully deductible on Schedule C.

6. G

Subscriptions to professional journals used for business are fully deductible on Schedule C.

7. B

50% of the self-employment taxes paid by an individual are deducted on Form 1040 for AGI.

8. A

Qualifying contributions to a simplified employee pension plan are fully deductible on Form 1040 to arrive at AGI.

9. F

This election is made under §179. It is reported on Form 4562 and is deductible on Schedule C.

10. A

Qualifying alimony payments are deductible on Form 1040 to arrive at AGI.

11. D

Subscriptions for investment-related publications are reported on Schedule A and are deductible subject to a 2% of AGI floor.

12. G

The money was used to finance Green's business. Therefore, the interest expense is deductible on Schedule C.

13. H

The automobile is partially used for business. Therefore, the interest expense is partially deductible on Schedule C.

14. J

The loss on the sale of a residence is a nondeductible personal loss.

Communication (5 points)

To: Mr./Ms. **Vermillion**
From: Candidate
Re: **Nondeductible Transactions**

The loss on the sale of your sailboat is a nondeductible **personal** loss. Personal **casualties** and **thefts** are allowable as a deduction to the extent such losses exceed gains and the total excess loss exceeds 10% of your adjusted gross income, plus a threshold. These losses are calculated after factoring in any insurance reimbursement.

Research (1 point)

Code Section Answer: §151

Code §151 states, "ALLOWANCES OF DEDUCTIONS FOR PERSONAL EXEMPTIONS. 151(a) ALLOWANCE OF DEDUCTIONS.—In the case of an individual, the exemptions provided by this section shall be allowed…." search term: personal exemption

Solution 44-12 Schedule C

Schedule C (4 points)

SCHEDULE C (Form 1040) — **Profit or Loss From Business** (Sole Proprietorship) — OMB No. 1545-0074 — **2008**

Department of the Treasury Internal Revenue Service (99)

▶ Partnerships, joint ventures, etc., generally must file Form 1065 or 1065-B.
▶ Attach to Form 1040, 1040NR, or 1041. ▶ See Instructions for Schedule C (Form 1040).

Attachment Sequence No. 09

Name of proprietor: Cecilia Ross — Social security number (SSN): 123 45 6789

A Principal business or profession, including product or service (see page C-3 of the instructions): retail sale of cosmetics

B Enter code from pages C-9, 10, & 11 ▶ 4 5 1 3 9 0

C Business name. If no separate business name, leave blank.

D Employer ID number (EIN), if any

E Business address (including suite or room no.) ▶ 39 Pleasant Avenue
City, town or post office, state, and ZIP code: Celebration, FL 34747

F Accounting method: (1) ☐ Cash (2) ☑ Accrual (3) ☐ Other (specify) ▶

G Did you "materially participate" in the operation of this business during 2008? If "No," see page C-4 for limit on losses ☑ Yes ☐ No

H If you started or acquired this business during 2008, check here ▶ ☐

Part I Income

		Line	Amount
1	Gross receipts or sales. **Caution.** See page C-4 and check the box if: • This income was reported to you on Form W-2 and the "Statutory employee" box on that form was checked, or • You are a member of a qualified joint venture reporting only rental real estate income not subject to self-employment tax. Also see page C-4 for limit on losses. ▶ ☐	1	75,000
2	Returns and allowances	2	1,500
3	Subtract line 2 from line 1	3	73,500
4	Cost of goods sold (from line 42 on page 2)	4	37,500
5	**Gross profit.** Subtract line 4 from line 3	5	36,000
6	Other income, including federal and state gasoline or fuel tax credit or refund (see page C-4)	6	
7	**Gross income.** Add lines 5 and 6 ▶	7	36,000

Part II Expenses. Enter expenses for business use of your home **only** on line 30.

		Line	Amount			Line	Amount
8	Advertising	8	750	18	Office expense	18	150
9	Car and truck expenses (see page C-5)	9	2,452	19	Pension and profit-sharing plans	19	
10	Commissions and fees	10		20	Rent or lease (see page C-6): a Vehicles, machinery, and equipment	20a	
11	Contract labor (see page C-5)	11			b Other business property	20b	
12	Depletion	12		21	Repairs and maintenance	21	
13	Depreciation and section 179 expense deduction (not included in Part III) (see page C-5)	13	3,550	22	Supplies (not included in Part III)	22	
				23	Taxes and licenses	23	5,500
				24	Travel, meals, and entertainment: a Travel	24a	
14	Employee benefit programs (other than on line 19)	14			b Deductible meals and entertainment (see page C-7)	24b	
15	Insurance (other than health)	15	600	25	Utilities	25	350
16	Interest:			26	Wages (less employment credits)	26	
a	Mortgage (paid to banks, etc.)	16a		27	Other expenses (from line 48 on page 2)	27	
b	Other	16b					
17	Legal and professional services	17	200				

		Line	Amount
28	**Total expenses** before expenses for business use of home. Add lines 8 through 27 ▶	28	13,552
29	Tentative profit or (loss). Subtract line 28 from line 7	29	22,448
30	Expenses for business use of your home. Attach **Form 8829**	30	160
31	**Net profit or (loss).** Subtract line 30 from line 29. • If a profit, enter on both **Form 1040, line 12,** and **Schedule SE, line 2,** or on **Form 1040NR, line 13** (if you checked the box on line 1, see page C-7). Estates and trusts, enter on **Form 1041, line 3.** • If a loss, you **must** go to line 32.	31	22,288

32 If you have a loss, check the box that describes your investment in this activity (see page C-8).
• If you checked 32a, enter the loss on both **Form 1040, line 12,** and **Schedule SE, line 2,** or on **Form 1040NR, line 13** (if you checked the box on line 1, see the line 31 instructions on page C-7). Estates and trusts, enter on **Form 1041, line 3.**
• If you checked 32b, you **must** attach **Form 6198.** Your loss may be limited.

32a ☑ All investment is at risk.
32b ☐ Some investment is not at risk.

For Paperwork Reduction Act Notice, see page C-9 of the instructions. Cat. No. 11334P **Schedule C (Form 1040) 2008**

Schedule C (Form 1040) 2008 — Page 2

Part III — Cost of Goods Sold (see page C-8)

33 Method(s) used to value closing inventory: a ☑ Cost b ☐ Lower of cost or market c ☐ Other (attach explanation)

34 Was there any change in determining quantities, costs, or valuations between opening and closing inventory? If "Yes," attach explanation . . . ☐ Yes ☑ No

35	Inventory at beginning of year. If different from last year's closing inventory, attach explanation	35	1,000
36	Purchases less cost of items withdrawn for personal use	36	38,000
37	Cost of labor. Do not include any amounts paid to yourself	37	
38	Materials and supplies	38	
39	Other costs	39	
40	Add lines 35 through 39	40	39,000
41	Inventory at end of year	41	1,500
42	**Cost of goods sold.** Subtract line 41 from line 40. Enter the result here and on page 1, line 4	42	37,500

Part IV — Information on Your Vehicle. Complete this part **only** if you are claiming car or truck expenses on line 9 and are not required to file Form 4562 for this business. See the instructions for line 13 on page C-5 to find out if you must file Form 4562.

43 When did you place your vehicle in service for business purposes? (month, day, year) ▶ ____/____/____

44 Of the total number of miles you drove your vehicle during 2008, enter the number of miles you used your vehicle for:

a Business ____________ b Commuting (see instructions) ____________ c Other ____________

45 Was your vehicle available for personal use during off-duty hours? . . . ☐ Yes ☐ No

46 Do you (or your spouse) have another vehicle available for personal use? . . . ☐ Yes ☐ No

47a Do you have evidence to support your deduction? . . . ☐ Yes ☐ No

b If "Yes," is the evidence written? . . . ☐ Yes ☐ No

Part V — Other Expenses. List below business expenses not included on lines 8–26 or line 30.

48 Total other expenses. Enter here and on page 1, line 27 — 48	

Schedule C (Form 1040) 2008

Communication (5 points)

To: Cecilia Ross
From: Ima Preparer
Re: Self-Employment Taxes

Self-employment taxes of are not deductible on Schedule C. Half of them are not deductible at all—this half is equivalent to the social security taxes that employees pay. **Half** of self-employment taxes are deductible on page 1 of From 1040 as an **adjustment to gross income.** This half is equivalent to the social security taxes that employers pay and then deduct on their income tax returns.

Research (1 point)

Code Section Answer: §71(b)

Code §71(b) states, "Alimony or separate maintenance payments defined. For purposes of this section—(1) In general the term "alimony or separate maintenance payment" means any payment in cash if—(A) such payment is received by (or on behalf of) a spouse under a divorce or separation instrument, (B) the divorce or separation instrument does not designate such payment as a payment which is not includible in gross income under this section and not allowable as a deduction under section 215, (C) in the case of an individual legally separated from his spouse under a decree of divorce or of separate maintenance, the payee spouse and the payor spouse are not members of the same household at the time such payment is made, and (D) there is no liability to make any such payment for any period after the death of the payee spouse…."
Search terms: alimony defined

Editor's Note: This copy of Form 1040, page 2 is here merely for your information. It is unconnected to any particular question or simulation.

Form 1040 (2008) Page 2

Tax and Credits

38 Amount from line 37 (adjusted gross income) 38

39a Check if: { ☐ You were born before January 2, 1944, ☐ Blind. } Total boxes
{ ☐ Spouse was born before January 2, 1944, ☐ Blind. } checked ▶ 39a

b If your spouse itemizes on a separate return or you were a dual-status alien, see page 34 and check here ▶ 39b ☐

c Check if standard deduction includes real estate taxes or disaster loss (see page 34) ▶ 39c ☐

40 Itemized deductions (from Schedule A) or your standard deduction (see left margin) . 40

41 Subtract line 40 from line 38 41

42 If line 38 is over $119,975, or you provided housing to a Midwestern displaced individual, see page 36. Otherwise, multiply $3,500 by the total number of exemptions claimed on line 6d . 42

43 Taxable income. Subtract line 42 from line 41. If line 42 is more than line 41, enter -0- . 43

44 Tax (see page 36). Check if any tax is from: a ☐ Form(s) 8814 b ☐ Form 4972 . 44

45 Alternative minimum tax (see page 39). Attach Form 6251 45

46 Add lines 44 and 45 . . . . ▶ 46

47 Foreign tax credit. Attach Form 1116 if required 47

48 Credit for child and dependent care expenses. Attach Form 2441 48

49 Credit for the elderly or the disabled. Attach Schedule R . . 49

50 Education credits. Attach Form 8863 50

51 Retirement savings contributions credit. Attach Form 8880 . 51

52 Child tax credit (see page 42). Attach Form 8901 if required . 52

53 Credits from Form: a ☐ 8396 b ☐ 8839 c ☐ 5695 . 53

54 Other credits from Form: a ☐ 3800 b ☐ 8801 c ☐ ______ 54

55 Add lines 47 through 54. These are your total credits 55

56 Subtract line 55 from line 46. If line 55 is more than line 46, enter -0- . . . . ▶ 56

Standard Deduction for—
- People who checked any box on line 39a, 39b, or 39c or who can be claimed as a dependent, see page 34.
- All others:

Single or Married filing separately, $5,450

Married filing jointly or Qualifying widow(er), $10,900

Head of household, $8,000

Other Taxes

57 Self-employment tax. Attach Schedule SE 57

58 Unreported social security and Medicare tax from Form: a ☐ 4137 b ☐ 8919 . . 58

59 Additional tax on IRAs, other qualified retirement plans, etc. Attach Form 5329 if required . . 59

60 Additional taxes: a ☐ AEIC payments b ☐ Household employment taxes. Attach Schedule H 60

61 Add lines 56 through 60. This is your total tax . . . . ▶ 61

Payments

62 Federal income tax withheld from Forms W-2 and 1099 . . 62

63 2008 estimated tax payments and amount applied from 2007 return 63

64a Earned income credit (EIC) 64a

b Nontaxable combat pay election 64b

65 Excess social security and tier 1 RRTA tax withheld (see page 61) 65

66 Additional child tax credit. Attach Form 8812 66

67 Amount paid with request for extension to file (see page 61) 67

68 Credits from Form: a ☐ 2439 b ☐ 4136 c ☐ 8801 d ☐ 8885 68

69 First-time homebuyer credit. Attach Form 5405 69

70 Recovery rebate credit (see worksheet on pages 62 and 63) . 70

71 Add lines 62 through 70. These are your total payments . . . . ▶ 71

If you have a qualifying child, attach Schedule EIC.

Refund

Direct deposit? See page 63 and fill in 73b, 73c, and 73d, or Form 8888.

72 If line 71 is more than line 61, subtract line 61 from line 71. This is the amount you overpaid 72

73a Amount of line 72 you want refunded to you. If Form 8888 is attached, check here ▶ ☐ 73a

▶ b Routing number ▶ c Type: ☐ Checking ☐ Savings

▶ d Account number

74 Amount of line 72 you want applied to your 2009 estimated tax ▶ 74

Amount You Owe

75 Amount you owe. Subtract line 71 from line 61. For details on how to pay, see page 65 ▶ 75

76 Estimated tax penalty (see page 65) 76

Third Party Designee

Do you want to allow another person to discuss this return with the IRS (see page 66)? ☐ Yes. Complete the following. ☐ No

Designee's name ▶ Phone no. ▶ ( ) Personal identification number (PIN) ▶

Sign Here

Joint return? See page 15. Keep a copy for your records.

Under penalties of perjury, I declare that I have examined this return and accompanying schedules and statements, and to the best of my knowledge and belief, they are true, correct, and complete. Declaration of preparer (other than taxpayer) is based on all information of which preparer has any knowledge.

Your signature | Date | Your occupation | Daytime phone number ( )

Spouse's signature. If a joint return, both must sign. | Date | Spouse's occupation

Paid Preparer's Use Only

Preparer's signature ▶ | Date | Check if self-employed ☐ | Preparer's SSN or PTIN

Firm's name (or yours if self-employed), address, and ZIP code ▶ | EIN | Phone no. ( )

Form **1040** (2008)

Printed on recycled paper

CHAPTER 45

FEDERAL TAXATION: ESTATES & TRUSTS

EXAM COVERAGE: The individual taxation portion of the Regulation section of the CPA exam is designated by the examiners to be 12-18 percent of the section's point value. The taxation of estates is included in this category. The entities taxation portion of the Regulation section of the CPA exam is designated by the examiners to be 22-28 percent of the section's point value. The taxation of trusts is included in this category. The material in this chapter's appendix is unlikely to be tested explicitly, but many candidates may need to review this information to be prepared to answer questions on the taxation of estates and trusts. More information about point distribution is included in the **Practical Advice** section of this volume.

CHAPTER 45

FEDERAL TAXATION: ESTATES & TRUSTS

I. Estate & Trust Income Taxation

A. Overview

Estates and trusts are separate income tax-paying entities. Beneficiaries also may be taxed, but there is no double taxation. Either the estate or trust or the beneficiaries are taxed on the income, but not both entities. In any discussion of estates and trusts, it is important to keep in mind the distinction between the assets of the estate or trust, known as the principal or the corpus, and the income earned from those assets.

1. **Conduit** The estate or trust is said to be a conduit. A double tax is prevented by virtue of a distribution deduction [IRC §§651 and 661]. Basically, the estate or trust reports all income earned but then gets a deduction for distributions (actual or constructive) to the beneficiaries (but only to the extent the beneficiaries must include the distribution in income).

2. **Estate Formation** An estate is created when an individual dies. On that date, all the decedent's income-producing assets begin generating income for a new taxpayer, the estate.

3. **Trust Formation & Termination** A trust is an arrangement whereby a trustee takes legal title to property and manages the property for beneficiaries. A trust may be created by will (a testamentary trust) or during life (an *inter vivos* trust). **Note:** So-called "short-term trusts" are not considered to be trusts subject to taxation.

    a. **Transfers of Appreciated Property to Trust** If a settlor transfers appreciated property to a trust and the property is sold by the trust within two years, the trust is taxed on the gain based on the settlor's tax rates. This is to avoid the transfer of appreciated property by high-bracket taxpayers to lower-bracket trusts so as to tax the gain upon sale at a lower rate.

    b. **Unused Losses & Deductions in Year of Trust Termination** If the trust or estate has unused loss carryovers, capital loss carryovers, or current year deductions in the year of termination, these unused items may be passed on to the beneficiaries.

4. **Trust Classification** Trusts are classified as simple or complex. A simple trust is a trust that requires all income to be distributed each year, that does not make any charitable contributions, and that actually does not make any distributions, except out of current income. All other trusts are complex.

    a. Estates and complex trusts are subject to the same rules.

    b. A trust may be a simple trust one year and a complex trust another year.

    c. Complex trusts may accumulate income and, consequently, they accrue income tax liability each year. If, on some future date, the accumulated income is distributed, a throwback rule comes into play. Generally, the accumulated income is carried back to the year it was earned, and the beneficiary is taxed as if it were received in that year. The beneficiary then gets credit for the taxes actually paid by the trust.

5. **Income Calculation** The taxable income of an estate or trust is basically computed the same as that of an individual [IRC §641(b)]. The estate or trust gets a distribution deduction for income distributed to beneficiaries. Because of the "conduit" theory at work, income may be split between estate or trust and beneficiary. If this occurs, most deductions and credits also must be allocated. Estates and trusts are entitled to a personal exemption, as follows [IRC §642(b)]:

a. Estates—$600

b. Simple trusts—$300

c. Complex trusts—$100

6. **Timing** A simple trust's income is taxed to the beneficiary in the year the income is required to be distributed, whether or not it actually is distributed [IRC §652(a)]. The income is taxable to the beneficiary for her/his taxable year in which the estate or trust taxable year ends.

7. **Taxable Year** An estate has the option of choosing a fiscal or calendar year. For taxable years after 1986, most trusts must adopt a calendar year. However, a trust that qualifies as an IRC §501(a) tax-exempt organization or a charitable trust described in IRC §4947(a) can elect to use a fiscal year.

8. **Filing Requirements** A trust or an estate must file an income tax return (Form 1041) if it has gross income of $600 or more and pay the tax by the 15th day of the fourth month after the end of its taxable year.

9. **Estimated Payments** All trusts are required to make estimated quarterly tax payments. Estates are required to make estimated tax payments with regard to any taxable year ending two years after the date of the decedent's death.

B. Distributable Net Income (DNI)

Distributable net income has application only in the context of the income taxation of estates and trusts. DNI determines the amount of the distribution deduction to the estate or trust and the amount of the corresponding inclusion in the beneficiary's gross income. The character of the income is preserved as it passes through to the beneficiary. For example, tax-exempt interest and long-term capital gains retain their character to the beneficiary.

1. **Determination** The taxable income of the estate or trust is modified by the following [IRC §643(a)].

   a. Distribution deduction is excluded.

   b. Personal exemption is excluded.

   c. Capital gains and losses normally are excluded, as they usually are allocated to principal rather than income.

   d. Tax-exempt interest income is included.

2. **Effect** Any distribution of money or property to a beneficiary is taken out of DNI for the current year and thereby requires the beneficiary to take that amount of the distribution into income to the extent that the distributed items are taxable.

C. Distributions of Property

Distributions of property are subject to several different rules.

1. **Specific Bequests** Specific bequests of property found in a will or trust instrument produce no income to the beneficiary, regardless of DNI. Furthermore, no gain or loss is recognized by the estate or trust on the transfer of the property.

Example 1 ▸ Specific Bequest

A will provides that the decedent's automobile, worth $5,000, specifically is given to Sam. Since the auto is being distributed by a specific bequest, Sam has no income. In the absence of this specific bequest, if the estate had earned $5,000 of income related to the auto, then a distribution of the auto to Sam would carry out that distributable net income (DNI) of $5,000 to Sam.

2. **Specific Bequest Replacement** If a specific bequest is satisfied by other property, the distribution is a taxable transfer to the estate or trust.

   Example 2 ▸ Other Property

   A will specifically leaves Chris $5,000 cash. In satisfaction of this bequest, Chris accepts an auto with a value of $5,000 and an adjusted basis to the estate of $4,000. The estate has $1,000 of gross income on the distribution.

D. **Real Estate Investment Trust (REIT)**
A REIT is authorized by the provisions of the Real Estate Investment Trust Act of 1960. It is created by a transfer of the legal title to real estate to a trustee. The trustee manages the trust property for the benefit of specified beneficiaries. A qualifying trust need not pay corporate taxes, preventing double taxation of trust income. Failure to meet the qualifying provisions results in the trust being taxed as a corporation.

1. **Qualification** To qualify as a REIT, the following provisions must be met.

   a. The certificates of ownership must be freely transferable.

   b. There must be 100 or more certificate holders during each year and no fewer than 6 may own 50 percent of all outstanding certificates.

   c. The trust's primary business cannot be to buy and sell real estate.

   d. The major portion of the trust's income must be derived from real estate (e.g., rent, interest on mortgages, and gains on sale of real property).

   e. The trustee must have centralized control.

   f. The trust must distribute at least 90 percent of taxable income to certificate holders each year.

2. **Statute of Frauds** A REIT falls within the provisions of the Statute of Frauds and must be in writing to be enforceable.

3. **Limited Liability** Certificate holders (beneficiaries) are not personally liable for debts and other obligations of the trust. Their liability is limited to their investment in the trust.

4. **Tax Treatment** Ordinary income and capital gains distributed by the trust are taxable only to the beneficiaries. Depreciation and other losses do not pass through to the beneficiaries.

E. **Funeral Trust**
A pre-need funeral trust is an arrangement where an individual purchases funeral services or merchandise from a funeral home for the benefit of a specified person in advance of that person's death. Part or all of the price is held in trust during the beneficiary's lifetime and is paid to the seller upon the beneficiary's death. The beneficiary may be either the purchaser or another person.

1. **General Rule** Pre-need funeral trusts generally are treated as grantor trusts, and the annual income earned by those trusts is taxable income to the purchaser/grantor of the trust. A grantor trust is any trust to the extent the assets of the trust are treated as owed by a person other than the trust.

2. **Election** If the proper election is made, a qualified funeral trust is not treated as a grantor trust and the amount of tax paid with respect to each purchaser's trust is determined in accordance with the income tax rate schedule generally applicable to estates and trusts, but no personal exemption deduction is allowed under IRC §642(b). The tax on the annual earnings of the trust is payable by the trustee.

a. **Qualified Funeral Trust** A qualified funeral trust is any domestic trust if (1) the trust arises as a result of a contract with a business engaged in providing funeral or burial services or related property; (2) the purpose of the trust is to hold, invest, and use funds solely to make payments for funeral or burial services or property for the trust beneficiary; (3) the only trust beneficiaries are individuals who have entered into contracts to have funeral or burial services or merchandise provided upon their death; (4) the only contributions to the trust are by or for the benefit of the trust beneficiary; and (5) the trustee makes the proper election (for each purchaser's trust).

b. **Contribution Limitation** A limitation is placed on the aggregate contributions that may be made to all qualified funeral trusts for one beneficiary. For contracts entered into in 2008, the limit is $9,000.

c. **Cancellation** The beneficiary doesn't recognize gain or loss for payments from the trust upon cancellation of the contract. The beneficiary takes a carryover basis in any assets received from the trust upon cancellation.

F. Coverdell Education Savings Account (CESA)

A CESA is a trust established with an approved trustee to pay qualifying education expenses of a beneficiary. A CESA operates in a manner similar to a Roth IRA.

1. **Qualifying Expenses** Qualifying expenses include tuition, fees, room and board, reduced by scholarships and other nontaxable educational assistance. Elementary and secondary school expenses connected with enrollment or attendance at a public, private, or religious school are allowed as qualified expenses. Special needs services are also included as qualified expenses. Room and board expenses qualify only if the student attends school at least half-time.

2. **Contributions** Subject to an income phase-out rule, any taxpayer can contribute up to $2,000 in cash annually to a CESA for a beneficiary under the age of 18. Any number of individuals can contribute to CESAs for any number of beneficiaries, but the total annual contributions for any one beneficiary cannot exceed the ceiling. Contributions are not deductible from income. Contributions may be deemed to be made on the last day of the preceding year if made before April 15.

   a. The maximum contribution is reduced on a *pro rata* basis for a taxpayer with MAGI in the following ranges: single, $95,000 to $110,000; and married filing jointly, $190,000 to $220,000, exactly twice the range for single taxpayers. MAGI is AGI increased by exempt foreign income. Corporations and other entities (including tax-exempt organizations) may contribute to education IRAs, regardless of income.

   b. Contributions to a CESA and a qualified tuition payment program (discussed later in this chapter) may be in the same year for the same beneficiary.

3. **Distributions** Distributions from the trust are nontaxable, if they do not exceed the total qualifying education expenses for the year. Funds distributed in excess of the qualifying expenses are subject to income tax and a 10% penalty tax. As long as the CESA distribution is not used for the same educational expenses for the same student for which a credit is claimed, a taxpayer can claim a Hope or Lifetime Learning credit and exclude CESA distributions from gross income in the same year.

   a. The penalty is waived if the distribution is due to the beneficiary's death or disability, or to the extent that the beneficiary receives nontaxable scholarships or other allowances.

   b. Funds in the CESA not used by the beneficiary's 30th birthday are deemed distributed, subject to regular income taxes and 10% penalty taxes.

   c. Prior to the beneficiary's 30th birthday, any unused balance may be transferred to another family member (while still remaining in the trust), including a former spouse under a divorce agreement. A cousin is deemed to be a family member for this purpose.

4. **Gift** A CESA contribution is considered a completed gift of a present interest and qualifies for the annual gift tax exemption, but not the additional educational gift tax exclusion of IRC §2503(e). The contribution also is exempt from the generation-skipping tax.

   a. A transfer from one beneficiary to another is not subject to gift tax if both beneficiaries are members of the same family and generation. If these two criteria are not met, the transfer may give rise to gift tax liability if it exceeds the annual exclusion amount.

   b. The value of a CESA is included in the estate of a beneficiary, never a contributor.

5. **Special Need Beneficiaries** A special needs beneficiary (SNB) is exempt from certain CESA requirements. For a SNB, contributions may continue to be made to a CESA after the beneficiary attains age 18. No deemed distribution occurs when a SNB reaches age 30. The age 30 limit does not apply to a rollover contribution for the benefit of a SNB or a change in beneficiaries to a SNB.

G. **Qualified Tuition Programs (QTP)**
Several states have qualified tuition payment programs (also known as Section 529 plans) with tax-exempt status. Most tuition plans commonly are prepaid plans under which future tuition is locked in at current rates. Some plans are savings plan trusts that are operated like a mutual fund.

1. **Qualified Plans** The program must be established and maintained by a state (or one of its agencies) or an eligible educational institution under which a person may either purchase tuition credits, that constitute a waiver or payment of qualified higher education costs, or contribute to an account designed to meet the education costs. A private institution may be treated as qualified if it has received a ruling or determination from the IRS that it satisfies applicable requirements and it holds the program assets in a trust organized in the U.S. for the exclusive benefit of plan beneficiaries, with a independent responsible party as its trustee.

   a. Qualified higher education costs include tuition, fees, books, room and board costs, and equipment for attendance at college, university or certain vocational schools. For 2009 and 2010, ARRA '09 permits tax-free distributions to pay for computers and computer technology, including internet access.

   b. Contributions must be cash. A contributor is prohibiting from directly or indirectly directing the investment of any contribution.

   c. Investment account earnings may be refunded to the contributor or beneficiary, but the program must impose a more than *de minimis* refund penalty, unless the refund is

      (1) Used for beneficiary's qualified higher education expenses;

      (2) Made on account of the beneficiary's death or disability; or

      (3) Made on account of a scholarship received by the student to the extent that the refund does not exceed the scholarship amount used for qualified expenses.

2. **Transfers** Contributions to a QTP are completed gifts of a present interest and qualify for the annual gift tax exemption. The contribution is also exempt from the generation-skipping transfer tax. However, the amount does not qualify for the additional educational gift tax exclusion of IRC §2503(e). Contributions are exempt from the generation-skipping transfer tax.

   a. A transfer from one beneficiary to another is not subject to the gift tax if both beneficiaries are members of the same family and generation. (The original beneficiary's spouse and first cousin are deemed a member of the same family.) If these two criteria are not met, the transfer may give rise to gift tax liability if it exceeds the annual exclusion amount.

b. The value of a QTP account is included in the estate of a beneficiary. (In no event is the value to be included in the estate of a contributor.)

3. **Distributions** The deferred income is taxable income to the beneficiary unless it can be excluded under another provision of the tax law. If amounts are distributed to a contributor, the amount is taxed to the extent it exceeds the amounts originally contributed.

   a. Distributions are treated as *pro rata* shares of principal and income. The distributee, or a taxpayer claiming the distributee as a dependent, can use the distribution as a basis for claiming either the Hope or Lifetime Learning credits, assuming requirements for these credits are met.

   b. Distributions are excluded from gross income, to the extent such distributions are used to pay for qualified higher education expenses. A taxpayer is allowed to claim a Hope or Lifetime Learning credit and exclude from gross income amounts distributed from a qualified program on behalf of the same student in the same year as long as the distribution is not used for expenses for which a credit is claimed.

4. **Incomplete Gift** Pre-1998 contributions to the program are incomplete gifts, deferring any potential gift tax implications until program distributions are made. Waivers (or payments) of qualified expenses are treated as qualified transfers, excluding them from gift tax. Contributions to a program (and earnings thereon) are included in the estate of a contributor if the contributor dies before the funds are distributed.

II. Transfer Taxes

A. Estate Tax

The estate tax is a transfer tax (not an income tax), imposed on the value of property "transferred" by a decedent at death. The gift tax is also a transfer tax based on the same tax rate schedule as the estate tax. However, the gift tax is imposed on inter vivos (lifetime) transfers of property. Thus, a transfer tax cannot be avoided simply by giving property away before death. (EGTRRA '01 repeals the estate tax, but not the gift tax, effective in 2010. After 2010, the estate and generation-skipping transfer taxes will revert to their status prior to EGTRRA '01, except for provisions made permanent by subsequent legislation.)

1. **Gross Estate** The first step in determining the estate tax due is to obtain the value of the gross estate (see schematic, below). The value of the gross estate can be placed at the time of death or at an alternative valuation date, which is six months after the date of death. To be able to use the alternative valuation date, the election must decrease the value of the gross estate and it must reduce any estate tax liability [IRC §2032]. The gross estate includes not only property actually owned by the decedent, but also property constructively owned by her/him. In addition, certain gifts, such as life insurance policies, made within three years of death may be includable in the gross estate.

2. **Deductions** The gross estate is reduced by nondiscretionary deductions to arrive at the adjusted gross estate. The adjusted gross estate is reduced further by discretionary deductions to obtain the taxable estate.

3. **Adjusted Taxable Gifts** To the taxable estate we must add post-1976 adjusted taxable gifts other than gifts that were included in the gross estate. This equals the tentative tax base, on which a tentative estate tax is determined based on the table in IRC §2001(c). The next step is to subtract from this tentative tax the amount of taxes that would have been payable (at the IRC §2001(c) rates in effect at date of death) on gifts included in the tentative tax base. The objective of this whole scheme is to increase the marginal rates at which the estate is taxed (e.g., by increasing the tax base by the amount of gifts made); however, double taxation of gifts is prevented by providing for the reduction of the tentative estate tax by the amount of gift taxes that would have been payable on the gifts themselves.

4. **Credits** The last two items in the tax computation are credits against the estate tax: the unified tax credit and other miscellaneous tax credits. These adjustments taken together produce the estate tax due. The effective unified credit exemption amount is $3,500,000 for 2009.

Example 3 ▸ Taxable Estate

Jennifer Bohl died on March 3, 2009. She and her husband, Mark, owned a home in joint tenancy subject to a $30,000 mortgage with annual principal payments due on December 31. She had four specific bequests. The remainder of the estate is left 1/3 to Mark and 2/3 to Susan. The executor selected the alternate valuation date. The car was given to Carol on April 3. Funeral expenses were $22,000.

Specific Bequests:

Carol, a niece	car
Susan, a daughter	necklace
Mark	home
United Charities	$12,000

Asset Valuation:

Assets	March 3	April 3	September 3
Home	$ 240,000	$ 240,000	$ 240,000
Car	30,000	29,500	29,000
Necklace	12,000	10,000	11,000
Investments	3,010,000	2,990,000	3,009,000

Required: What is the taxable estate?

Solution:

Value of home	$240,000	
Less: Indebtedness on home	(30,000)	
Net value of home	$210,000	
Estate's portion of home (which goes to Mark) [$210,000 × 50%]		$ 105,000
Mark's portion of investments [$3,009,000 – $12,000) / 3]		999,000
Marital deduction		$ 1,104,000
Value of car on distribution date		$ 29,500
Estate's portion of home		105,000
Value of necklace		11,000
Value of investments		3,009,000
Gross estate		$ 3,154,500
Less: Funeral expenses		(22,000)
Adjusted gross estate		$ 3,132,500
Less: Charitable deduction		(12,000)
Less: Marital deduction		(1,104,000)
Taxable estate		$ 2,016,500

Note: The $3,500,000 of 2009 exclusion amount still is in the taxable estate. There is no deduction of $3,500,000. Instead, a tax credit shelters $3,500,000 of the estate.

B. **Gift Tax**

Gift tax is an excise tax imposed on the transfer of property during the life of the donor. Property, for gift tax purposes, is defined broadly to include real and personal as well as tangible and intangible property. Gifts are defined similarly to include any transfer of property, outright or in trust, to the extent it is made without full and adequate consideration.

1. **Similar to Estate Tax** Although the estate tax is an excise tax on transfers made at death, while the gift tax is an excise on transfers made during life, essentially the same concepts apply. The only aspect that is different is the timing of the gift. Thus, if it is made during life, it is subject to the gift tax; if at death, it is subject to the estate tax. Transfers at death and lifetime taxable gifts are taxed on a cumulative basis.

2. **Computation** The gift tax schematic illustrates the computation of the tax, beginning with the total gross amount of gifts for the calendar year. This amount includes the total amount of cash and the FMV of other property gifted. Included are gifts created by transfer to a trust by the donor (e.g., donor-grantor transfers an apartment building to a trust, with the income to her/himself, and the remainder fee-simple interest in the building to the donee); by creation of joint interests (the donor with the donee); and by purchase of an insurance policy (the donor purchases an insurance policy and transfers all rights in the policy to the donee).

3. **Total Gifts** The statutory total amount of gifts made during the calendar year equals the total gross amount of gifts for the year made by the donor, reduced by the gift-splitting provisions under IRC §2513 and the inflation-adjusted annual per-donee exclusion ($13,000 for 2009) under IRC §2503. Total taxable gifts for the calendar year is the residual amount remaining after the statutory total amount of gifts made during the calendar year is reduced by the unlimited marital and charitable deductions. (See below for further explanation on these exclusions and deductions.) Note that certain qualified transfers are excluded when determining total taxable gifts. Qualified transfers include the amount paid directly to the institution on behalf of another individual (regardless of the relationship to the donor) for tuition at an accredited educational institution or for medical care. The exclusion for tuition does not include payment for dormitory fees, supplies, or textbooks.

4. **Cumulative** The gift tax is a cumulative tax, which causes the most recently made gifts to be taxed at a higher marginal transfer tax rate than gifts made in prior years. Mechanically, this is accomplished by adding all taxable gifts made in the current calendar year (Schedule A, Form 709) to all taxable gifts from prior years (Schedule B, Form 709). This total equals total taxable gifts.

5. **Tentative Tax** The actual computation of the gift tax due requires a "with and without" type of calculation. Using the unified transfer tax schedule of IRC §2001(c), a tentative tax is computed on total taxable gifts. A tentative tax is computed separately on the amount of taxable gifts from prior years (Schedule B). The difference between the two tentative taxes produces the tentative tax for the current calendar year before the unified credit. This tentative tax is reduced by the amount of the unified credit remaining to the donor and is reduced further by any foreign tax credits. For 2009, the credit effectively exempts $3,500,000 of gifts from taxation. The tax remaining equals the gift tax due.

C. Generation-Skipping Transfer Tax

This is a separate tax that is imposed in addition to the gift tax and the estate tax. It applies to transfers to beneficiaries who are more than one generation below the transferor's generation and is taxed at a rate of 45% for 2009. This tax is inapplicable if the transfer is to a grandchild if the child's parent (the decedent's child) predeceases the transferor. This exception extends to other generation-skipping transfers, if the decedent has no living descendants in the intervening generation at the time of the transfer. For example, a decedent may make a transfer to a grandniece, if the grandniece's parent (the decedent's niece or nephew) also is dead, without incurring the generation-skipping tax. A lifetime exemption from the generation-skipping transfer tax is available to all taxpayers.

D. Schematic of Estate Tax Computation

In the following schematic, we expound upon the overview by summarizing each block in the flow chart with textual material to the right of the chart. As you read down the chart, keep in mind the main objective of the estate tax—to identify, value, and levy an appropriate tax on the transfer of all of a decedent's property.

Gross Estate

The gross estate of a decedent who is a U.S. citizen or resident includes the value at the date of death (or alternate valuation date six months after date of death) of all of the decedent's worldwide property, both real and personal, tangible and intangible [IRC §2031]. This all-inclusive definition of property identified to the gross estate includes the following.

- Certain gifts, such as life insurance policies, made within three years of death may be includable in the gross estate.
- The value of all property to the extent of the decedent's beneficial interest, including income due the decedent at the time of her/his death in the form of salary, rents, royalties, dividends, insurance proceeds payable to the estate's executor as the estate's representative, and business interests [IRC §2033]. This income also is included in the estate's fiduciary income tax return, since it is considered income in respect of the decedent (IRD).
- The value of any interest in property gratuitously transferred by the decedent during life but over which the decedent retained control during her/his life. Thus, if the decedent transferred securities, real rental property, or other income-producing property but retained the right to control the property and/or its income stream, the entire value of the property is included in the gross estate [IRC §2036]. Similarly included are gratuitous transfers conditioned on the transferee's surviving the decedent [IRC §2037].
- The value of property gratuitously transferred during life to the extent of the portion of the property over which the decedent had a right to revoke. Thus, if the decedent during life gifted securities to her/his son with income to her/his daughter and with a right to revoke the income gift, the discounted value of the income, but not the value of the security, is included [IRC §2038].
- The value of a joint and survivor annuity purchased by the decedent for her/him and another is included [IRC §2039].
- One-half the fair market value of community property, and one-half the fair market value of property held by spouses in joint tenancy or tenancy in the entirety.

(Less)

The gross estate, as identified and valued above, is reduced by the following deductions.

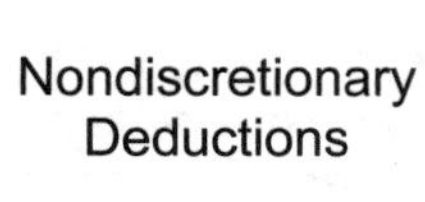

- Funeral expenses
- Administration expenses
- Claims against the estate
- Casualty and theft losses
- Indebtedness of property included in gross estate
- Certain taxes (income taxes accrued after death are not deductible)

Observation: Ordinary and necessary administration expenses, including commissions and other selling expenses, can either be taken as a deduction in computing the Estate Tax (Form 706) or the Fiduciary Income Tax (Form 1041). In order for these administrative expenses to be deducted for income tax purposes, the executor must waive the right to take the deduction for estate tax purposes.

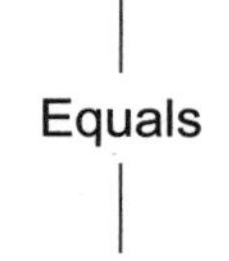

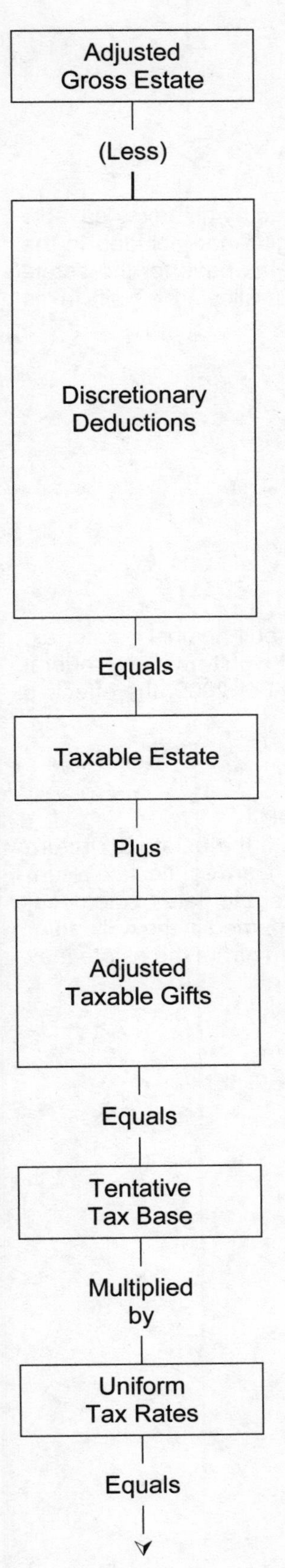

The adjusted gross estate is diminished by the discretionary deductions. The most common discretionary deductions are the following.

- Contributions to a charitable organization if the decedent's will specifically provides for the contribution and the recipient is a qualified charitable organization. The amount of the transfer is limited only by the value of the gross estate [IRC §2055].
- The marital deduction generally is unlimited. Thus, as with the charitable deduction, the decedent could give the entire net estate after expenses to her/his surviving spouse. The only limitation on the marital deduction is that the marital deduction interest consist of a non-terminable interest in property included in the gross estate. A terminable interest is an interest in property given to the surviving spouse that will lapse after a certain time (e.g., life estate or term of years), or upon the occurrence of an event or contingency or its failure to occur (e.g., until wife's remarriage) [IRC §2056].

The unified transfer tax system was introduced in 1976. Under this system, one transfer tax schedule [IRC §2001(c)] is used to compute gift tax as well as estate tax. The system also requires the inclusion of all lifetime gifts in the determination of the tentative tax base. The adjusted taxable gifts inclusion brings into the computation all taxable gifts (net of both the annual exclusion and gifts made within three years of death that are included in the gross estate already).

The tentative tax base is applied against the appropriate rates set forth in IRC §2001(c).

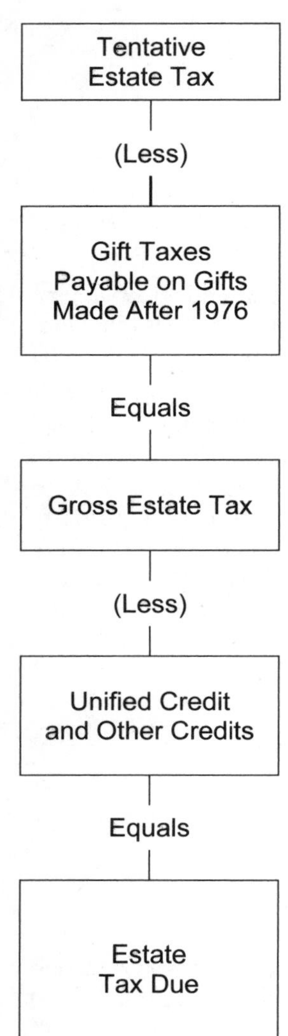

The tentative estate tax, as computed above, then is reduced by gift taxes payable on gifts made after 1976. Since adjusted taxable gifts (gifts not included in the gross estate by [IRC §2035] were pulled into the tentative tax base for the estate tax computation using the uniform tax rates, a reduction is allowed for gift taxes payable on those gifts to avoid double taxation.

The tentative estate tax is reduced further by the unified credit against estate tax. Therefore, if an estate is valued at the threshold or less, it won't owe any federal estate tax, nor will it be required to file an estate tax return. For 2009, the effective exclusion amount is $3,500,000.

The executor or administrator of the estate is required to file the estate tax return [IRC §6018] and pay any estate tax due [IRC §2002]. If an estate tax return (Form 706) is required, then it must be filed nine months after the date of the decedent's death. Where no executor or administrator has been named in the will and/or appointed by the court, property transferees receiving property from the estate may be liable for the return and any tax due.

E. Schematic of Gift Tax Computation

1. Computation of Total Taxable Gifts

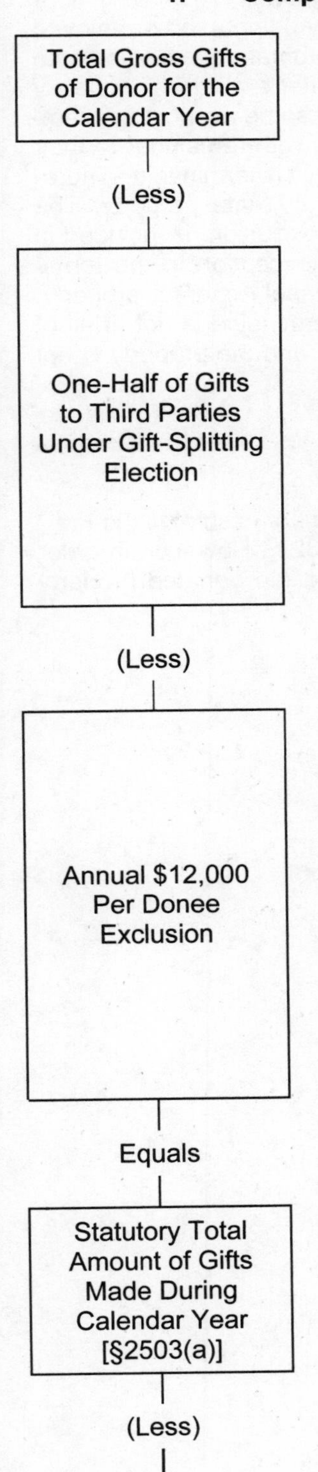

This section allows a husband and wife to elect to treat gifts made by either of them to a third party as having been made one-half by each spouse. This election has the effect of doubling the annual per donee exclusion, because each spouse is treated as having made a gift. For example, the husband wishes to give $30,000 worth of securities to each of his two sons in 2009. If the wife does not elect to split the husband's gift, $26,000 ($13,000 × 2 sons) is excluded by IRC §2503 (see below), and $34,000 ($60,000 – $26,000) is included in the amount of taxable gifts for the year (Schedule A). However, if the wife elects to split the gift [IRC §2513], both she and her husband each are treated as making a $15,000 gift to each son. Both spouses can utilize two $13,000 per donee exclusions, and each will include $4,000 ($30,000 – $26,000) as their statutory total amount of gifts made during the calendar year.

Each donor is entitled to exclude up to $13,000 (for 2009) of gifts of a present interest in property to any person during a calendar year from the amount of total gross gifts under IRC §2503(b). A gift of a present interest in property is a gift in which the donee obtains an unrestricted right to the immediate use, possession, or enjoyment of the property or the income from the property. For example, donor transfers rental property to a trust, with income payable to his son. However, the rental revenue generated must be used to pay off the mortgage indebtedness before any revenue accrues to the donee. The donor is not entitled to the gift tax exclusion because the donee does not have a present interest in the gift of the income from rental property. An exception to the present interest requirement applies to gifts to minors. A gift to a person under 21 years of age is considered to be a gift of present interest, as long as all of the property and its income is made available to the donee upon obtaining age 21.

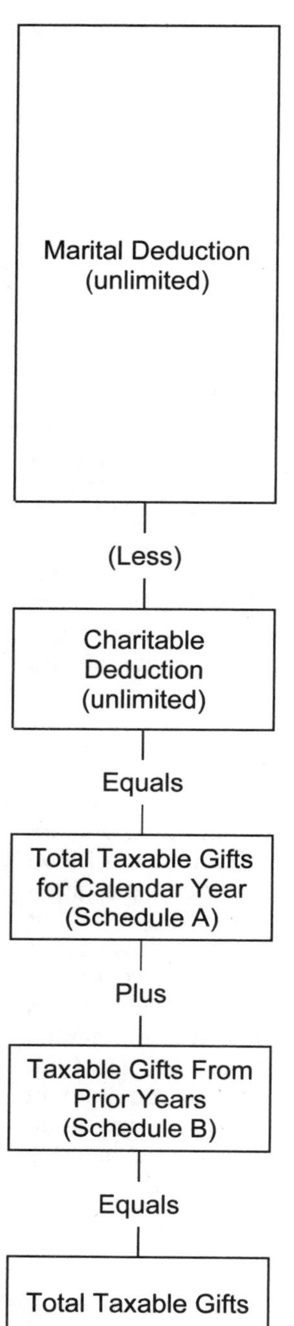

Spouses are entitled to deduct from the statutory total amount of gifts made during the calendar year an unlimited amount of gifts to each other if these gifts are of a present non-terminable interest in property under IRC §2523. A present non-terminable interest is one that must be capable of instantly being used or enjoyed upon completion of the gift and which must not end and automatically vest in some third party upon (a) the death of the donee spouse, (b) after a certain number of years, or (c) upon the occurrence or failure of occurrence of some event. For example, donor gives a rental property to his wife for 15 years, with remainder to their son after the fifteenth year. The gift is a present interest, but it is terminable. Therefore, the husband has no marital deduction for the value of the rental property. The entire amount of the property, less the annual per-donee exclusion, is included in the donor's taxable gifts for the year (Schedule A). An exception to the terminable-interest rule is provided for a gift of qualified terminable interest property. Under this exception, property that would otherwise be terminable is not, if all of the income from the property is paid to the spouse-donee and the property is not subject to transfer during the spouse-donee's lifetime.

Donors are entitled to an unlimited deduction for the amount of cash plus the FMV of other property given to qualified charities under IRC §2322. However, in order to qualify for the deduction, the qualified charity must use the donated property within the United States.

2. Computation of Gift Tax Due

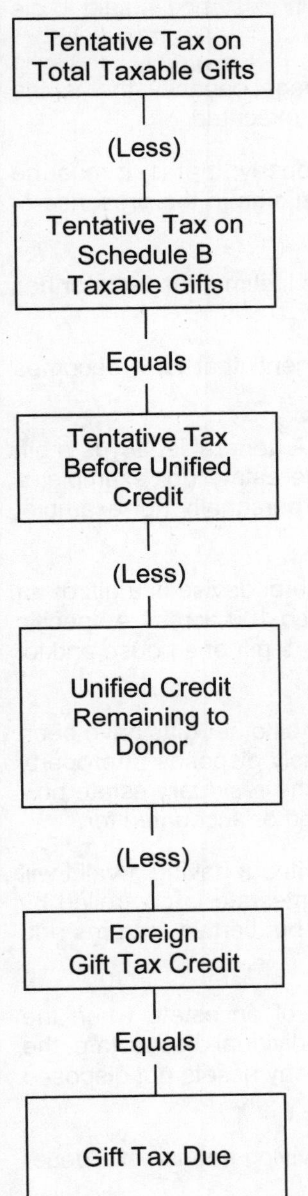

In order to exclude smaller estates from the estate tax and gifts from the gift tax, the unified tax credit under IRC §2505 was installed for gifts made after 1976. This is equivalent to exempting the first $3,500,000 of taxable estate from the unified transfer tax for 2009. The amount of transfer tax credit remaining to a donor for gifts is equal to the credit less the amounts allowed as credits to that donor in prior calendar years.

A gift tax return must be filed on a calendar-year basis, with the return due on or before April 15 of the following year. If the donor subsequently dies, the gift tax return is due no later than the date for filing the federal estate tax return (9 months after the date of death).

III. Appendix: Estate & Trust Overview

A. Estates

An estate is a legal entity that comes into existence upon the death of an individual and succeeds to the title of property owned by the individual at the time of death. The estate also assumes liability for all debts owed by the decedent at the time of death. The administration of the estate includes the entire process of assembling the assets of the estate, paying off claims against the estate (including taxes), and distributing the assets of the estate according to the testator's intentions or the law of intestate succession.

1. **Testate** An individual may control the distribution of the assets of the estate by means of a valid will. A will is a legal declaration of an individual's intentions and desires with respect to the distribution of property after her/his death. A valid will has the effect, upon the testator's death, of distributing the decedent's assets to those beneficiaries who are named in the will.

a. **Testator** The person who makes a will and whose intentions are reflected in the will is called a "testator." An individual who dies with a valid will in existence is said to die "testate."

b. **Capacity** In order to make a valid will, a testator must have legal capacity; that is, the testator must be of legal age and sound mind when the will is executed.

c. **Execution** In order to be valid, a will must be executed properly; that is, it must be signed by the testator in the presence of witnesses who then sign in the presence of each other.

d. **Ambulatory** A will is ambulatory; that is, during the testator's lifetime, the testator has the power to alter, amend, or revoke the will.

e. **Testamentary Instrument** A will is a testamentary instrument; that is, it becomes effective only upon the death of the testator.

f. **Legacy** A legacy is a gift of personal property under a will. A general legacy is a gift of personal property payable out of the general assets of the estate (for example, a gift of $500). A specific legacy is a gift of a specified item or personalty (for example, a particular painting).

g. **Devise** A devise is a gift of real property under a will. A general devise is a gift of an unspecified piece of realty; for example, a gift of an unidentified 100 acres. A specific devise is a gift of a particular piece of real estate; for example, a gift of a house and lot at a specified address.

h. **Residuary Estate** The residuary estate is what remains after all other gifts have been distributed. Most wills include a residuary clause that expressly disposes of property not distributed as general and specific gifts. The content of the residuary estate normally is not determined until all other gifts have been distributed or accounted for.

2. **Intestate** An individual is said to die "intestate" if the person dies without having a valid will in existence. Distribution of the assets of an individual who dies intestate is controlled by state law. Statutes of intestate succession vary from state to state, but certain features and provisions are common to virtually all intestate succession statutes.

a. **Succession** The disposition and distribution of the assets of an estate when the assets are not disposed of or distributed by a valid will. If an individual dies testate, the laws of intestate succession still will govern the distribution of any assets not disposed of by the will.

b. **Spouse** Most state statutes give first consideration to the surviving spouse of a decedent who dies intestate.

(1) The surviving spouse is generally the recipient of a stated percentage (often one-half) of the decedent's estate.

(2) Additionally, in many states the surviving spouse of an individual who dies testate may elect to receive a stated percentage (often one-third) of the decedent's estate instead of taking under the will.

c. **Others** After the surviving spouse has been provided for, the usual order of distribution of the remaining assets of the estate is as follows.

(1) Descendants (children and grandchildren) of the deceased; or if none survive,

(2) Ascendants (parents and grandparents) of the deceased; or if none survive,

(3) Collaterals (such as brothers and sisters) of the deceased.

3. ***Per Capita*** The manner of distribution of property in which the heirs to an intestate's estate share and share alike.

4. ***Per Stirpes*** The manner of distribution of property in which a class or group of distributees take the share that their deceased percent would have been entitled to. For example: A dies leaving one son, B, and two grandchildren of deceased daughter, C. B takes one-half and the two grandchildren each take one-quarter. (They share equally in what their deceased parent would have taken, if living.)

5. **Probate Court** The probate court has jurisdiction to determine and approve the validity of a will and to supervise the administration of the estate. Probating a will involves proving that an instrument that purports to be a will was in fact signed, witnessed, and otherwise executed in accordance with the requirements of the law.

   a. **Probate** Probate is the process of proving the validity of a will by demonstrating that an instrument purporting to be a will was executed in accordance with legal requirements. Probate generally is initiated by filing the will in the proper court along with a petition for probate.

      (1) The petition normally includes an estimate of the value of the estate and a list of the names of the beneficiaries.

      (2) The petition usually is accompanied by the sworn statements of the original witnesses attesting to their belief that the will is valid.

   b. **Executor** Admission of the will to probate is accompanied by the execution of letters testamentary in which the court empowers the executor to administer the estate.

6. **Administrator or Executor** The administration of the estate is carried out by the executor or the administrator of the estate.

   a. **Representative** The executor or administrator acts as the representative of the estate. The executor is a person who is appointed by the testator to carry out the testator's directions concerning the disposition of property under her/his will. The administrator is a person who is appointed by the court to administer the estate of an individual who died intestate. An executor named in the decedent's will need not serve if s/he does not wish to do so. In such a case, the court will appoint an administrator who will have the same powers and duties as an executor.

   b. **Due Diligence** The general duty of an executor or administrator is to use reasonable diligence and to act in good faith on behalf of the estate and in accordance with the terms of the will (if one exists). In fulfilling this general duty, the executor or administrator usually possesses the following powers.

      (1) S/he may contract on behalf of the estate (with the approval of the court).

      (2) S/he may engage attorneys, accountants, appraisers, etc., to perform services necessary to the administration of the estate.

      (3) S/he may sell the assets of the estate to pay debts.

         (a) Generally, s/he must sell personalty first; realty may be sold only with court approval if all debts cannot be satisfied by selling personalty.

         (b) The testator may in her/his will empower the executor to sell realty for any and all purposes.

c. **Duties** The following additional duties are imposed on the executor or administrator.

(1) S/he must use reasonable care and diligence in promptly collecting and preserving the assets of the estate.

(a) Personal liability may be imposed on the executor or administrator for negligent failure to discover and collect assets.

(b) Personal liability also may be imposed for any shrinkage of the assets of the estate caused by the negligence of the executor or administrator.

(2) S/he must refrain from commingling the assets of the estate with her/his own funds or property. Personal liability may result from any shrinkage of the assets of the estate due to commingling. In addition, such commingling is punishable in some states as a misdemeanor.

(3) S/he must represent the estate in lawsuits brought against it. The executor is generally not personally liable on any contracts entered into in her/his capacity as such, unless the executor fails to reveal her/his representative capacity and identify the estate.

7. **Procedure** Once an executor or administrator has been appointed, the general steps in the administration of an estate are as follows.

a. **Preserve Assets** The executor must collect and preserve all of the assets of the estate and file with the court an inventory of the property.

b. **Publish Notice** The executor will publish a notice of the administration of the decedent's estate that will require all claims against the estate to be filed within a certain period of time. If a creditor does not file the claim on time, s/he will be barred from collecting on the debt.

c. **Payments** Once the claims have been filed and proved, the executor will pay the debts in accordance with their statutory priority.

(1) **Abatement** is the process of determining the distribution of the estate when the total available assets in the estate are insufficient to satisfy the provisions of the will.

(2) **Ademption** occurs when a specific bequest or devise becomes impossible to perform due to circumstances or events occurring after the execution of the will.

d. **Final Accounting** At the conclusion of her/his duties, the executor must file a final accounting of the administration of the estate with the court.

e. **Discharged** The final step in the administration of a decedent's estate is for the executor to be discharged by the court and the estate closed.

B. Trusts

A trust is a fiduciary relationship with respect to property in which one person (a trustee) holds legal title to the property for the benefit of another (a beneficiary). Thus, a trust involves two forms of ownership—one legal, the other equitable—in the same property at the same time. Trusts are classified according to the duties imposed upon the trustees, the purpose of the trust, and the manner in which the trust was created.

1. **Elements** There are four elements that are essential to the existence of a valid trust: a settlor, a trustee, trust property, and a beneficiary. The legal relationship between the trustee and beneficiary is that the trustee holds legal title to the trust property for the benefit and use of the beneficiary.

a. **Settlor** A settlor (or trustor) is the person who causes the trust to come into existence. The settlor may also be a trustee or beneficiary, but may not be both the sole trustee and the sole beneficiary. Even though the settlor creates the trust, the settlor generally may terminate the trust only if s/he is empowered to do so by the trust instrument.

b. **Trustee** A trustee holds the legal title to the trust property for the benefit of the beneficiaries.

(1) Trustees stand in a fiduciary relationship to beneficiaries. As a fiduciary, a trustee may not use her/his position for personal advantage.

(2) A trustee manages the trust property and distributes the trust income to the beneficiaries as directed by the trust instrument.

(a) In addition to the powers expressly conferred upon the trustee by the trust instrument, a trustee possesses those powers that are necessary and appropriate to carry out the trust purposes.

(b) A trustee may not delegate her/his control over the administration of the trust. However, the trustee may seek advice from such professionals as lawyers, accountants, and appraisers, and contract for their services.

(c) Generally, a trust that satisfies all other requirements will not fail due to the refusal or incapacity of the trustee to serve. In such cases, the court will appoint a trustee.

(3) In administering a trust, the trustee must exercise that degree of care and skill that a reasonably prudent businessperson would exercise in dealing with her/his own property.

(a) A trustee has a duty to the beneficiaries to preserve the assets of the trust and to make the trust property productive.

(b) A trustee may not invest trust assets in speculative ventures, and s/he must rid the trust of assets that are nonproductive.

(c) A trustee must strive for diversity in investing the assets of the trust.

(d) A trustee has a duty to enforce all rights and claims belonging to the trust, and is required to defend suits brought against the trust.

(e) A trustee must keep trust assets separate from her/his personal assets and from the assets of any other trust that s/he is administering.

c. **Trust Property** The trust property (or *trust res*) is the property interest that the trustee holds for the benefit of the beneficiaries. The trust property must be an existing interest in identifiable property that is capable of being owned and conveyed.

(1) An interest that has not yet come into existence (e.g., an expectancy) cannot be held in trust. For example, property that the settlor later may inherit cannot be the subject of a present trust, since the settlor has only an expectancy, not an existing interest, in the trust res. However, a future interest in property may be held in trust so long as it is a presently-existing and transferable interest.

(2) The *trust res* must be identified or at least described with sufficient specificity so that it can be identified with certainty. For example, a declaration that "a large part of my assets shall be held in trust" is too indefinite to establish a trust. However, a declaration that "all of my real property except my current residence shall be held in trust" is probably sufficiently specific to adequately identify the *trust res*.

(3) Since a trust is created by a transfer of ownership from the settlor, the trust res must be capable of being owned and sold.

(4) The rule against perpetuities limits the duration of a trust to a life in being plus 21 years.

d. **Beneficiary** A beneficiary is the person for whose benefit the trust property is held by the trustee. The beneficiary holds the equitable interest in the trust property, and is empowered to enforce the terms of the trust.

(1) Any ascertainable person or group of persons may be beneficiaries.

(2) Corporations, clubs, churches, and other entities may be beneficiaries so long as they are sufficiently identifiable to permit a determination of who is empowered to enforce the terms of the trust.

2. **Intent** In order to create a trust, the settlor must indicate her/his present intention to establish the separation of legal and equitable title.

a. This intention usually is expressed in writing (a trust instrument); however, the requisite intent to create a trust may be manifested orally or by conduct.

(1) When the *trust res* is real property, the trust must be evidenced by a writing to satisfy the statute of frauds.

(2) The writing need be signed only by the settlor in order to create a valid trust of real property.

b. The beneficiaries of the trust and the trust property must be identified adequately.

c. No consideration is necessary for the present creation of a trust. However, an agreement to create a trust in the future is subject to the same requirements of consideration as any other contract.

d. A trust must be created for a lawful purpose. Any trust that is created for an illegal purpose is invalid. For example, a trust is invalid if it is created for the purpose of fraudulently avoiding payment of the settlor's creditors.

3. **Termination** Generally, a validly created trust may be terminated either by those methods provided in the trust instrument or by operation of law.

a. Under certain limited circumstances, the parties to a trust may terminate the trust.

(1) The settlor may unilaterally terminate the trust only if the trust instrument expressly reserves to the settlor the right of termination.

(2) Similarly, the trustee has only such powers of termination as are conferred upon her/him by the trust instrument.

(3) If all of the beneficiaries (including potential future beneficiaries) join in a suit to terminate a trust, the trust may be terminated if termination would not defeat a material trust purpose.

b. A trust terminates by its own effect when the instrument specifies a definite period of duration or a termination date.

c. A trust may terminate when the purposes for which the trust was created are fulfilled completely or upon complete failure of the trust purpose.

(1) A trust created exclusively for the purpose of sending the settlor's daughter through college would terminate upon her completion of college.

(2) A trust established for the purpose of sending the settlor's daughter through college also would terminate if the daughter died or became mentally incompetent before she completed college.

d. The merger doctrine states that if the sole trustee and the sole beneficiary are the same person, the trust will go out of existence because the legal title (held by the trustee) and the equitable title (held by the beneficiary) have "merged."

4. **Active & Passive Trusts** An active trust imposes affirmative duties of management and administration on the trustees. A passive trust imposes no real duties on the trustees; they are mere holders of the legal title to the trust property until ownership passes to the beneficiaries.

5. **Charitable & Private Trusts** A trust that is intended to confer a benefit on the public at large or on a large segment of the public is a charitable trust. All other trusts are private trusts.

a. **Charitable Trusts** Charitable trusts are created for the purpose of benefiting the public at large or some particular class of the public indefinite in number. In order for a trust to be classified as charitable, the trust purpose must be exclusively charitable. Special rules apply to charitable trusts. These rules are designed to give the most liberal effect to the settlor's intentions.

(1) The *doctrine of cy pres* is applied by the courts when the stated purpose of a charitable trust is impossible or impractical to carry out. Under this doctrine, a court will apply the trust assets to a purpose as nearly like the stated purpose as possible.

(2) Charitable trusts are valid even though they may be indefinite in identifying specific beneficiaries.

(3) Charitable trusts are not subject to the rule against perpetuities.

b. **Private Trusts** Private trusts are subject to more rigid substantive rules. They will be allowed to fail for indefiniteness in some situations, while a similarly vague charitable trust would be upheld.

6. **Express & Implied Trusts** An express trust is created by the settlor's expression of her/his intention to establish a division of legal and equitable title in property. In an implied trust, the intention to create the trust is inferred or presumed by law. There are two types of implied trusts: (1) a resulting trust and (2) a constructive trust.

a. **Resulting Trust** A resulting trust arises due to the presumed intention of a settlor to create a trust when the intent to do otherwise is not expressed adequately. A resulting trust may be implied in law under the following circumstances.

(1) Failure of an express trust for any reason.

(2) Fulfillment of the trust purpose and trust property still remains.

(3) The title to property is taken in the name of one who did not furnish consideration.

Example 4 ▶ Resulting Trust

A politician pays the purchase price of a parcel of land, but the title is taken in the name of her/his associate without the intention of making it a gift. The presumption here is that the parties intended the associate to hold the property for the politician's benefit, and the associate will be treated as a trustee upon a resulting trust.

b. **Constructive Trust** A constructive trust is a remedy in the form of a trust created by operation of law to prevent unjust enrichment. The court converts the legal owner into a trustee for the party who is entitled to beneficial enjoyment. A constructive trust is imposed whenever the court establishes that the one who acquired title to property is obligated to transfer it because acquisition was by breach of fiduciary duty, wrongful killing, fraud, duress, or undue influence.

7. ***Inter Vivos* Trust** An *inter vivos* trust is created by the settlor while s/he is living and comes into existence during her/his lifetime.

8. **Testamentary Trust** A testamentary trust is generally created in a testamentary instrument (usually a will) and comes into existence only upon the settlor's death.

9. **Spendthrift Trust** A spendthrift trust may be either *inter vivos* or testamentary. This type of trust prohibits any transfer of a beneficiary's rights by assignment or otherwise. It is often created to protect a beneficiary from creditors or from her/his squandering of the trust's assets. If the trust is irrevocable, it may not be terminated by the settlor during the term of the trust. A spendthrift trust is terminated at the end of the term of trust or when all beneficiaries die.

10. **Tentative or Totten Trust** A "tentative" or "Totten" trust is created when the settlor opens a bank account in her/his own name "as trustee" for another. Such a trust may be revoked by the settlor simply by withdrawing the funds from the account. The trust becomes irrevocable upon the settlor's death. If the beneficiary dies before the settlor, the trust terminates.

C. **Uniform Principal & Income Act**
The allocation of principal and income generally is governed by the provisions of the Uniform Principal & Income Act. The provisions of the Uniform Act are applicable to both estates and trusts. The following rules and principles generally are applicable to the administration of estates as well as trusts.

1. **Allocation Decisions** Problems involving the allocation of principal and income frequently occur when a will or trust instrument provides for the income to be distributed to one or several beneficiaries and for the principal to be distributed to others. For example, problems of principal and income allocation might arise when a trust instrument creates a life estate in one beneficiary and a remainder interest in another. (A remainder is a future interest created in a third person that takes effect at the end of the prior possessory interest, the life estate.) In such a situation, the trustee must make decisions bearing on the allocation of the benefits (receipts) and burdens (expenses) between the income beneficiary and the remainderman.

   a. If the trust instrument expressly empowers the trustee to determine what is principal and what is income, her/his determination is usually conclusive.

   b. When the instrument is silent, the trustee's decisions generally are governed by the Uniform Act.

2. **Trustee Liability** The trustee may be held personally liable to the income beneficiary and/or remainderman for commingling or misallocating costs and benefits.

3. **Equitable Proration** Some types of receipts and expenses are apportioned equitably between income and principal, such as annuities and administrative expenses, including trustees' fees.

4. **Income Allocation** In allocating benefits between the income beneficiary and the remainderman, the general rule is that ordinary receipts are treated as income, while extraordinary receipts are treated as additions to principal.

   a. **Ordinary** Ordinary receipts include the following.

      (1) Net rents received from property owned by the estate or trust, as well as the net income from a partnership or proprietorship managed by the executor or trustee (Operating losses from such an enterprise are allocated solely to principal.)

      (2) Cash dividends (regular or extraordinary)

      (3) Rights to subscribe to shares of another corporation, as well as distributions of stock in another corporation

      (4) Interest on notes and bonds held by the estate or trust (including discount portion of treasury bills)

      (5) Royalties from property subject to depletion (depletion allowance chargeable to principal)

   b. **Extraordinary** Extraordinary receipts include the following.

      (1) Stock dividends and stock splits (not cash dividends)

      (2) Proceeds from the sale or exchange of trust assets

      (3) Sums received in settlement of claims for injury to trust property

      (4) Income earned on property prior to the formation of the trust

5. **Expense Allocation** In allocating the burdens (expenses) between the income account and the principal account, the general rule is that current administration expenses incurred to keep the trust property productive should be paid out of trust income, while extraordinary expenses and those that primarily benefit the remainderman should be borne by the principal account.

   a. **Ordinary** Examples of ordinary expenses incurred in the production or collection of income, and chargeable to the income account, include the following.

      (1) Cost of insuring trust property

      (2) Interest on loans and mortgages secured by trust assets

      (3) Ordinary income taxes and real estate taxes

      (4) Cost of repairing and preserving trust property

      (5) Depreciation allowance

   b. **Extraordinary** Examples of extraordinary expenses and expenses incurred in the improvement of trust principal chargeable to principal include the following.

      (1) Cost of permanent (capital) improvements

      (2) Losses sustained in the operation of businesses owned by the trust

(3) Mortgage and loan principal payments

(4) Costs incurred in the purchase or sale of trust property

(5) Real estate taxes on improvements

CHAPTER 45—FEDERAL TAXATION: ESTATES & TRUSTS

Problem 45-1 MULTIPLE CHOICE QUESTIONS (45 to 60 minutes)

1. Which of the following is an attribute of a complex trust?
a. It distributes income to more than one beneficiary.
b. It has a grantor that is not an individual.
c. It has a beneficiary that is not an individual.
d. It distributes corpus.
(R/07, REG, 1799T, #10, 8434)

2. The standard deduction for a trust or an estate in the fiduciary income tax return is
a. $0
b. $100
c. $300
d. $600 (11/91, PII, #24, amended, 2472)

3. An executor of a decedent's estate that has only U.S. citizens as beneficiaries is required to file a fiduciary income tax return, if the estate's gross income for the year is at least
a. $ 400
b. $ 500
c. $ 600
d. $1,000 (5/91, PII, #37, 1697)

4. For income tax purposes, the estate's initial taxable period for a decedent who died on October 24
a. May be either a calendar year, or a fiscal year beginning on the date of the decedent's death
b. Must be a fiscal year beginning on the date of the decedent's death
c. May be either a calendar year, or a fiscal year beginning on October 1 of the year of the decedent's death
d. Must be a calendar year beginning on January 1 of the year of the decedent's death
(R/00, AR, #9, 6914)

5. With regard to estimated income tax, estates
a. Must make quarterly estimated tax payments starting no later than the second quarter following the one in which the estate was established
b. Are exempt from paying estimated tax during the estate's first two taxable years
c. Are **not** required to make payments of estimated tax
d. Must make quarterly estimated tax payments only if the estate's income is required to be distributed currently (Editors, 1740)

Items 6 and 7 are based on the following:

Astor, a cash-basis taxpayer, died on February 3, Year 1. During Year 1, the estate's executor made a distribution of $12,000 from estate income to Astor's sole heir and adopted a calendar year to determine the estate's taxable income. The following additional information pertains to the estate's income and disbursements in Year 1:

Estate income	
Taxable interest	$65,000
Net long-term capital gains allocable to corpus	5,000
Estate disbursements	
Administrative expenses attributable to taxable income	14,000
Charitable contributions from gross income to a public charity, made under the terms of the will	9,000

6. For the calendar year, what was the estate's distributable net income (DNI)?
a. $39,000
b. $42,000
c. $58,000
d. $65,000 (R/99, AR, #13, amended, 6802)

7. Astor's executor does not intend to file an extension request for the estate fiduciary income tax return. By what date must the executor file the Form 1041, U.S. Fiduciary Income Tax Return, for the estate's Year 1 calendar year?
a. Wednesday, March 15, Year 2
b. Monday, April 17, Year 2
c. Thursday, June 15, Year 2
d. Friday, September 15, Year 2
(5/95, AR, #32, amended, 5450)

8. On January 1, Year 7, Carlt created a $300,000 trust that provided his mother with a lifetime income interest starting on January 1, Year 7, with the remainder interest to go to his son. Carlt expressly retained the power to revoke both the income interest and the remainder interest at any time. Who will be taxed on the trust's Year 7 income?
a. Carlt's mother
b. Carlt's son
c. Carlt
d. The trust (11/98, AR, #19, 6685)

9. A distribution to an estate's sole beneficiary for the Year 1 calendar year equaled $15,000, the amount currently required to be distributed by the will. The estate's Year 1 records were as follows:

Estate income
$40,000 Taxable interest

Estate disbursements
$34,000 Expenses attributable to taxable interest

What amount of the distribution was taxable to the beneficiary?
a. $40,000
b. $15,000
c. $ 6,000
d. $0 (11/95, AR, #35, amended, 5779)

10. The charitable contribution deduction on an estate's fiduciary income tax return is allowable
a. If the decedent died intestate
b. To the extent of the same adjusted gross income limitation as that on an individual income tax return
c. Only if the decedent's will specifically provides for the contribution
d. Subject to the 2% threshold on miscellaneous itemized deductions (5/91, PII, #38, 1698)

11. Income in respect of a cash basis decedent
a. Covers income earned before the taxpayer's death but **not** collected until after death
b. Receives a stepped-up basis in the decedent's estate
c. Must be included in the decedent's final income tax return
d. Cannot receive capital gain treatment (11/90, PII, #39, 1709)

12. Rose, a calendar-year, cash-basis taxpayer who died in June was entitled to receive a $10,000 fee that had not been collected before the date of death. The executor of Rose's estate collected the full $10,000 in July. This $10,000 should appear in
a. Only the decedent's final individual income tax return
b. Only the estate's fiduciary income tax return
c. Only the estate tax return
d. Both the fiduciary income tax return and the estate tax return (Editors, 1733)

13. Which of the following credits may be offset against the gross estate tax to determine the net estate tax of a U.S. Citizen?

	Unified credit	*Credit for gift taxes paid on gifts made after 1976*	
a.	Yes	Yes	
b.	No	No	
c.	No	Yes	
d.	Yes	No	(11/92, PII, #20, 3354)

14. What amount of a decedent's taxable estate is effectively tax-free in 2009 if the maximum unified estate and gift credit is taken?
a. $ 13,000
b. $ 675,000
c. $1,000,000
d. $3,500,000 (11/93, PII, #39, amended, 4468)

15. Under the provisions of a decedent's will, the following cash disbursements were made by the estate's executor:

I. A charitable bequest to the American Red Cross
II. Payment of the decedent's funeral expenses

What deduction(s) is(are) allowable in determining the decedent's taxable estate?
a. I only
b. II only
c. Both I and II
d. Neither I nor II (11/97, AR, #9, 6537)

16. If the executor of a decedent's estate elects the alternate valuation date and none of the property included in the gross estate has been sold or distributed, the estate assets must be valued as of how many months after the decedent's death?
a. 12
b. 9
c. 6
d. 3 (11/94, AR, #58, 5034)

17. Fred and Amy Kehl, both U.S. citizens, are married. All of their real and personal property is owned by them as tenants by the entirety or as joint tenants with right of survivorship. The gross estate of the first spouse to die
a. Includes 50% of the value of all property owned by the couple, regardless of which spouse furnished the original consideration
b. Includes only the property that had been acquired with the funds of the deceased spouse
c. Is governed by the federal statutory provisions relating to jointly held property, rather than by the decedent's interest in community property vested by state law, if the Kehls reside in a community property state
d. Includes one-third of the value of all real estate owned by the Kehls, as the dower right in the case of the wife or curtesy right in the case of the husband (5/91, PII, #35, 1695)

18. Within how many months after the date of a decedent's death is the federal estate tax return (Form 706) due if **no** extension of time for filing is granted?
a. 9
b. 6
c. 4½
d. 3½ (11/91, PII, #27, 2475)

19. Proceeds of a life insurance policy payable to the estate's executor, as the estate's representative, are
a. Includible in the decedent's gross estate only if the premiums had been paid by the insured
b. Includible in the decedent's gross estate only if the policy was taken out within three years of the insured's death under the "contemplation of death" rule
c. Never includable in the decedent's gross estate
d. Always includable in the decedent's gross estate (Editors, 8048)

20. Following are the fair market values of Wald's assets at the date of death:

Personal effects and jewelry	$ 150,000
Land bought by Wald with Wald's funds five years prior to death and held with Wald's sister as joint tenants with right of survivorship	1,800,000

The executor of Wald's estate did not elect the alternate valuation date. The amount includible as Wald's gross estate in the federal estate tax return is
a. $ 150,000
b. $1,150,000
c. $1,800,000
d. $1,950,000 (11/90, PII, #37, amended, 1707)

21. Alan Maade, a U.S. citizen, died on March 1, leaving an adjusted gross estate with a fair market value of $1,600,000 at the date of death. Under the terms of Alan's will, $475,000 was bequeathed outright to his widow, free of all estate and inheritance taxes. The remainder of Alan's estate was left to his mother. Alan made no taxable gifts during his lifetime. In computing the taxable estate, the executor of Alan's estate should claim a marital deduction of
a. $ 250,000
b. $ 475,000
c. $ 600,000
d. $1,125,000 (Editors, 1746)

22. During 2009, Blake transferred a corporate bond with a face amount and fair market value of $20,000 to a trust for the benefit of her 16-year old child. Annual interest on this bond is $2,000, which is to be accumulated in the trust and distributed to the child on reaching the age of 21. The bond is then to be distributed to the donor or her successor-in-interest in liquidation of the trust. Present value of the total interest to be received by the child is $8,710. The amount of the gift that is excludable from taxable gifts is
a. $26,000
b. $13,000
c. $ 8,710
d. $0 (11/91, PII, #26, amended, 2474)

23. In 2009, Sayers, who is single, gave an outright gift of $50,000 to a friend, Johnson, who needed the money to pay medical expenses. In filing the gift tax return, Sayers was entitled to a maximum exclusion of
a. $0
b. $13,000
c. $26,000
d. $50,000 (5/94, AR, #33, amended, 4638)

24. Don and Linda Grant, U.S. citizens, were married for the entire 2009 calendar year. In 2009, Don gave a $60,000 cash gift to his sister. The Grants made no other gifts in 2009. They each signed a timely election to treat the $60,000 gift as one made by each spouse. Disregarding the unified credit and estate tax consequences, what amount of the 2009 gift is taxable to the Grants for gift tax purposes?
a. $0
b. $34,000
c. $47,000
d. $60,000
(R/05, REG, 0168T, #10, amended, 7856)

25. Under the unified rate schedule,
a. Lifetime taxable gifts are taxed on a noncumulative basis.
b. Transfers at death are taxed on a noncumulative basis.
c. Lifetime taxable gifts and transfers at death are taxed on a cumulative basis.
d. The gift tax rates are 5% higher than the estate tax rates. (11/91, PII, #37, 2485)

26. The generation-skipping transfer tax is imposed
a. Instead of the gift tax
b. Instead of the estate tax
c. As a separate tax in addition to the gift and estate taxes
d. On transfers of future interest to beneficiaries who are more than one generation above the donor's generation (11/91, PII, #38, 2486)

27. A will provided that an estate was to be distributed "*per stirpes*" to the deceased's heirs. The only possible heirs are two daughters, who each have three children, and two children of a predeceased son. What fraction of the estate will each child of the predeceased son receive?
a. 0
b. 1/10
c. 1/6
d. 1/4 (R/99, Law, #7, 6858)

28. Gardner, a U.S. citizen and the sole income beneficiary of a simple trust, is entitled to receive current distributions of the trust income. During the year, the trust reported:

Interest income from corporate bonds	$5,000
Fiduciary fees allocable to income	750
Net long-term capital gain allocable to corpus	2,000

What amount of the trust income is includible in Gardner's gross income?
a. $7,000
b. $5,000
c. $4,250
d. $0 (R/03, REG, 0570T, #9, 7651)

29. Dart created an irrevocable trust naming Larson as trustee. The trust provided that the trust income would be paid to Frost for 15 years, with the principal then reverting to Dart. Larson died after 10 years, Frost died after 20 years, and Dart died after 22 years. When does the trust terminate?
a. After 10 years
b. After 15 years
c. After 20 years
d. After 22 years (R/00, Law, #4, 6969)

30. Cox transferred assets into a trust under which Smart is entitled to receive the income for life. After Smart's death, the remaining assets are to be given to Mix. In Year 1, the trust received rent of $1,000, stock dividends of $6,000, interest on certificates of deposit of $3,000, municipal bond interest of $4,000, and proceeds of $7,000 from the sale of bonds. Both Smart and Mix are still alive. What amount of the Year 1 receipts should be allocated to trust principal?
a. $ 7,000
b. $ 8,000
c. $13,000
d. $15,000 (11/92, Law, #6, amended, 3088)

Problem 45-2 ADDITIONAL MULTIPLE CHOICE QUESTIONS (23 to 30 minutes)

31. Which of the following types of entities is entitled to the net operating loss deduction?
a. Partnerships
b. S corporations
c. Trusts and estates
d. Not-for-profit organizations
(R/06, REG, C04238R, #20, 8190)

32. Ordinary and necessary administration expenses paid by the fiduciary of an estate are deductible
a. Only on the fiduciary income tax return (Form 1041) and never on the federal estate tax return (Form 706)
b. Only on the federal estate tax return and never on the fiduciary income tax return
c. On the fiduciary income tax return only if the estate tax deduction is waived for these expenses
d. On both the fiduciary income tax return and on the estate tax return by adding a tax computed on the proportionate rates attributable to both returns (11/91, PII, #39, 2487)

33. Which of the following fiduciary entities are required to use the calendar year as their taxable period for income tax purposes?

	Estates	Trusts (except those that are tax exempt)
a.	Yes	Yes
b.	No	No
c.	Yes	No
d.	No	Yes

(11/91, PII, #25, 2473)

34. A distribution from estate income, that was *currently* required, was made to the estate's sole beneficiary during its calendar year. The maximum amount of the distribution to be included in the beneficiary's gross income is limited to the estate's
a. Capital gain income
b. Ordinary gross income
c. Distributable net income
d. Net investment income (5/95, AR, #33, 5451)

35. Andi Corp. issued $1,000,000 face amount of bonds in Year 1 and established a sinking fund to pay the debt at maturity. The bondholders appointed an independent trustee to invest the sinking fund contributions and to administer the trust. In Year 6, the sinking fund earned $60,000 in interest on bank deposits and $8,000 in net long-term capital gains. All of the trust income is accumulated with Andi's periodic contributions so that the aggregate amount will be sufficient to pay the bonds when they mature. What amount of trust income was taxable to Andi in Year 6?
a. $0
b. $ 8,000
c. $60,000
d. $68,000 (11/91, PII, #44, amended, 2492)

36. Raff died in Year 5 leaving her entire estate to her only child. Raff's will gave full discretion to the estate's executor with regard to distributions of income. For Year 6, the estate's distributable net income was $15,000, of which $9,000 was paid to the beneficiary. None of the income was tax exempt. What amount can be claimed on the estate's Year 6 fiduciary income tax return for the distributions deduction?
a. $0
b. $ 6,000
c. $ 9,000
d. $15,000 (5/91, PII, #39, amended, 1699)

37. End and Law, both U.S. citizens, died in 2009. End made taxable lifetime gifts of $150,000 that are **not** included in End's gross estate. Law made no lifetime gifts. At the dates of death, End's gross estate was $1,000,000, and Law's gross estate was $1,400,000. A federal tax return must be filed for

	End	Law
a.	No	No
b.	No	Yes
c.	Yes	No
d.	Yes	Yes

(Editors, 1730)

38. For federal estate taxation, the alternate valuation date

a. If elected on the first return filed for the estate, may be revoked in an amended return provided that the first return was filed on time
b. Is required to be used if the fair market value of the estate's assets has increased since the decedent's date of death
c. Must be used for valuation of the estate's liabilities if such date is used for valuation of the estate's assets
d. Can be elected only if its use decreases both the value of the gross estate and the estate tax liability (Editors, 1731)

39. Which of the following is (are) deductible from a decedent's gross estate?

I. Expenses of administering and settling the estate
II. State inheritance or estate tax

a. I only
b. II only
c. Both I and II
d. Neither I nor II (11/93, PII, #40, 4469)

40. Jan, an unmarried individual, gave the following outright gifts in 2009:

Donee	Amount	Use by Donee
Jones	$20,000	Down payment on house
Craig	20,000	College tuition
Kande	5,000	Vacation trip

Jan's 2009 exclusions for gift tax purposes total

a. $39,000
b. $31,000
c. $20,000
d. $13,000 (11/90, PII, #35, amended, 1705)

41. Which of the following requires filing a gift tax return, if the transfer exceeds the available annual gift tax exclusion?

a. Medical expenses paid directly to a physician on behalf of an individual unrelated to the donor
b. Tuition paid directly to an accredited university on behalf of an individual unrelated to the donor
c. Payments for college books, supplies, and dormitory fees on behalf of an individual unrelated to the donor
d. Campaign expenses paid to a political organization (11/91, PII, #40, 2488)

42. On July 1, Year 5, Vega made a transfer by gift in an amount sufficient to require the filing of a gift tax return. Vega was still alive in Year 6. If Vega did **not** request an extension of time for filing the Year 5 gift tax return, the due date for filing was

a. March 15, Year 6
b. April 15, Year 6
c. June 15, Year 6
d. June 30, Year 6 (5/91, PII, #40, amended, 1700)

43. When Jim and Nina became engaged in April of Year 1, Jim gave Nina a ring that had a fair market value of $50,000. After their wedding in July of Year 2, Jim gave Nina $75,000 in cash so that Nina could have her own bank account. Both Jim and Nina are U.S. citizens. What was the amount of Jim's marital deduction?

a. $0
b. $ 75,000
c. $115,000
d. $125,000 (11/90, PII, #36, amended, 1706)

44. A distinguishing feature between the making of an *inter vivos* gift and the creation of a trust is that

a. A gift may be made orally whereas a trust must be in a signed writing.
b. Generally, a gift is irrevocable whereas a trust may be revoked in certain cases.
c. In order to create a valid trust, the creator must receive some form of consideration.
d. The beneficiary of a trust must be notified of the trust's creation. (11/88, Law, #58, 8045)

45. Brown transfers property to a trust. A local bank was named trustee. Brown retained no powers over the trust. The trust instrument provides that current income and $6,000 of principal must be distributed annually to the beneficiary. What type of trust was created?

a. Simple
b. Grantor
c. Complex
d. Revocable (R/07, REG, 1797T, #30, 8454)

Problem 45-3 EXTRA MULTIPLE CHOICE QUESTIONS (43 to 58 minutes)

46. Generally, which of the following parties would have the first priority to receive the estate of a person who dies without a will?
a. The state
b. A child of the deceased
c. A parent of the deceased
d. A sibling of the deceased (11/97, Law, #9, 6507)

47. A personal representative of an estate would breach fiduciary duties if the personal representative
a. Combined personal funds with funds of the estate so that both could purchase treasury bills
b. Represented the estate in a lawsuit brought against it by a disgruntled relative of the decedent
c. Distributed property in satisfaction of the decedent's debts
d. Engaged a non-CPA to prepare the records for the estate's final accounting

(5/89, Law, #19, 8044)

48. Which of the following assets generally will be distributed outside of the probate estate and regardless of intestacy laws, provided the estate is **not** the named beneficiary?

	Totten trusts	*Proceeds from insurance policies*
a.	Yes	Yes
b.	Yes	No
c.	No	Yes
d.	No	No

(11/97, Law, #8, 6506)

49. A decedent's will provided that the estate was to be divided among the decedent's issue, *per capita* and not *per stirpes*. If there are two surviving children and three grandchildren who are children of a predeceased child at the time the will is probated, how will the estate be divided?
a. 1/2 to each surviving child
b. 1/3 to each surviving child and 1/9 to each grandchild
c. 1/4 to each surviving child and 1/6 to each grandchild
d. 1/5 to each surviving child and grandchild

(11/92, Law, #9, 3091)

50. Generally, an estate is liable for which debts owed by the decedent at the time of death?
a. All of the decedent's debts
b. Only debts secured by the decedent's property
c. Only debts covered by the Statute of Frauds
d. None of the decedent's debts

(5/89, Law, #17, 0862)

51. Rita Ryan died leaving a will naming her children, John and Dale, as the sole beneficiaries. In her will, Rita designated John as the executor of her estate and excused John from posting a bond as executor. At the time of Rita's death, she owned a parcel of land with her sister, Ann, as joint tenants with right of survivorship. In general, John as executor, must
a. Post a bond despite the provision to the contrary in Rita's will
b. Serve without compensation because John is also a named beneficiary in the will
c. File a final account of the administration of the estate
d. Relinquish the duties because of the conflict of interest as executor and beneficiary

(11/87, Law, #18, 0866)

52 Which of the following parties is necessary to create an express trust?

	A remainderman	*A successor trustee*
a.	Yes	Yes
b.	Yes	No
c.	No	Yes
d.	No	No

(11/97, Law, #6, 6504)

53. If **not** expressly granted, which of the following implied powers would a trustee have?

I. Power to sell trust property
II. Power to borrow from the trust
III. Power to pay trust expenses

a. I and II
b. I and III
c. II and III
d. I, II, and III (11/92, Law, #7, 3089)

Items 54 and 55 are based on the following:

Arno plans to establish a spendthrift trust naming Ford and Sims as life income beneficiaries, Trip residuary beneficiary, and Bing as trustee. Arno plans to fund the trust with an office building.

54. Assume an enforceable trust was formed. Sims has the following personal creditors:

I. Bank holding a home mortgage note deficiency judgment
II. Judgment creditor as a result of an automobile accident

To which of these creditors can Bing pay Sims' share of trust income?
a. I only
b. II only
c. Both I and II
d. Neither I **nor** II (5/93, Law, #17, 3985)

55. For the trust to be enforceable, Arno must
a. Execute a written trust instrument
b. Provide for Bing's trustee fees
c. Designate a successor trustee
d. Deed the property to Bing as trustee
(5/93, Law, #16, 8046)

56. On the death of the grantor, which of the following testamentary trusts would fail?
a. A trust created to promote the public welfare
b. A trust created to provide for a spouse's health care
c. A trust created to benefit a charity
d. A trust created to benefit a childless person's grandchildren (5/95, Law, #10, 5344)

57. To properly create an *inter vivos* trust funded with cash, the grantor must
a. Execute a written trust instrument
b. Transfer the cash to the trustee
c. Provide for payment of fees to the trustee
d. Designate an alternate trust beneficiary
(5/91, Law, #8, 0856)

58. In a written trust containing **no** specific powers, the trustee will have all of the following implied powers **except**
a. Sell trust property
b. Pay management expenses
c. Accumulate income
d. Employ a CPA to prepare trust tax returns
(5/94, Law, #17, 4772)

59. When a trust instrument is silent regarding a trustee's powers, which of the following implied powers does a trustee generally have?

	The power to make distributions of principal to income beneficiaries	*The power to lease trust property to third parties*
a.	Yes	Yes
b.	Yes	No
c.	No	Yes
d.	No	No

(11/97, Law, #7, 6505)

60. Which of the following investments generally will be a violation of a trustee's fiduciary duty to the trust?
a. Secured first mortgages on land
b. High interest unsecured loans
c. Tax-exempt municipal bonds
d. Guaranteed savings certificates
(5/96, Law, #4, 6260)

61. Mason's will created a testamentary trust for the benefit of Mason's spouse. Mason's sister and Mason's spouse were named as co-trustees of the trust. The trust provided for discretionary principal distributions to Mason's spouse. It also provided that, on the death of Mason's spouse, any remaining trust property was to be distributed to Mason's children. Part of the trust property consisted of a very valuable coin collection. After Mason's death, which of the following statements would be correct?
a. Mason's spouse may **not** be a co-trustee because the spouse is also a beneficiary of the trust.
b. Mason's sister may delegate her duties as co-trustee to the spouse and thereby **not** be liable for the administration of the trust.
c. Under **no** circumstances could the spouse purchase the coin collection from the trust without breaching fiduciary duties owed to the trust and Mason's children.
d. The co-trustees must use the same degree of skill, judgment, and care in managing the trust assets as reasonably prudent persons would exercise in managing their own affairs.
(5/91, Law, #10, 0858)

62. Which of the following fiduciary duties may be violated by the trustee if the trustee, without express direction in the trust instrument, invests trust assets in unsecured loans to a co-trustee?

I. Duty to invest prudently
II. Duty of loyalty to the trust

a. I only
b. II only
c. Both I and II
d. Neither I nor II (5/95, Law, #13, 5347)

63. An irrevocable trust that contains no provision for change or termination can be changed or terminated only by the
a. Courts
b. Income beneficiaries
c. Remaindermen
d. Grantor (5/95, Law, #11, 5345)

64. An irrevocable testamentary trust was created by Park, with Gordon named as trustee. The trust provided that the income will be paid to Hardy for life with the principal then reverting to Park's estate to be paid to King. The trust will automatically end on the death of
a. Park
b. Gordon
c. Hardy
d. King (5/94, Law, #19, 4774)

65. Which of the following situations would cause a resulting trust to be created?

I. Failure of an express trust
II. Application of the *cy pres* doctrine
III. Fulfillment of the trust purpose

a. I and II
b. I and III
c. II and III
d. I, II, and III (11/92, Law, #5, 3087)

66. To which of the following trusts would the rule against perpetuities **not** apply?
a. Charitable
b. Spendthrift
c. Totten
d. Constructive (11/92, Law, #8, 3090)

67. Cord's will created a trust to take effect on Cord's death. The will named Cord's spouse as both the trustee and personal representative (executor) of the estate. The will provided that all of Cord's securities were to be transferred to the trust and named Cord's child as the beneficiary of the trust. Under the circumstances,
a. Cord has created an inter vivos trust.
b. Cord has created a testamentary trust.
c. The trust is invalid because it will **not** become effective until Cord's death.
d. Cord's spouse may **not** serve as both the trustee and personal representative because of the inherent conflict of interest. (5/95, Law, #15, 5349)

68. Which **two** of the following expenditures resulting from a trust's ownership of commercial real estate should be allocated to the trust's principal?
a. Building management fees
b. Depreciation
c. Insurance premiums
d. Mortgage principal payments
e. Sidewalk assessments (5/94, Law, #16, 4771)

69. On January 1, Year 3, Dix transferred certain assets into a trust. The assets consisted of Lux Corp. bonds with a face amount of $500,000 and an interest rate of 12%. The trust instrument named Dix as trustee, Dix's child as life beneficiary, and Dix's grandchild as remainderman. Interest on the bonds is payable semiannually on May 1 and November 1. Dix had purchased the bonds at their face amount. As of January 1, Year 3, the bonds had a fair market value of $600,000. The accounting period selected for the trust is a calendar year. The trust instrument is silent as to whether Dix may revoke the trust. Assuming the trust is valid, how should the amount of interest received in Year 3 be allocated between principal and income if the trust instrument is otherwise silent?

	Principal	Income
a.	$0	$60,000
b.	$0	$72,000
c.	$10,000	$50,000
d.	$12,000	$60,000

(11/89, Law, #9, amended, 8047)

70. Absent specific directions, which of the following parties will ordinarily receive the assets of a terminated trust?
a. Income beneficiaries
b. Remaindermen
c. Grantor
d. Trustee (5/95, Law, #14, 5348)

71. Frost's will created a testamentary trust naming Hill as life income beneficiary, with the principal to Brown when Hill dies. The trust was silent on allocation of principal and income. The trust's sole asset was a commercial office building originally valued at $100,000 and having a current market value of $200,000. If the building was sold, which of the following statements would be correct concerning the allocation of the proceeds?

a. The entire proceeds would be allocated to principal and retained.
b. The entire proceeds would be allocated to income and distributed to Hill.
c. One half of the proceeds would be allocated to principal and one half to income.
d. One half of the proceeds would be allocated to principal and one half distributed to Brown.

(5/95, Law, #12, 5346)

72. Arno plans to establish a spendthrift trust naming Ford and Sims life income beneficiaries, Trip residuary beneficiary, and Bing as trustee. Arno plans to fund the trust with an office building. Assume an enforceable trust was formed. Which of the following will be allocated to trust principal?

	Annual property tax	*Monthly mortgage principal payment*
a.	Yes	Yes
b.	Yes	No
c.	No	Yes
d.	No	No

(5/93, Law, #18, 3986)

73. Which of the following would ordinarily be distributed to a trust income beneficiary?

I. Royalties
II. Stock received in a stock split
III. Cash dividends
IV. Settlements of claims for damages to trust property

a. I and II
b. I and III
c. II and III
d. II and IV

(11/92, Law, #10, 3092)

74. Jay properly created an inter vivos trust naming Kroll as trustee. The trust's sole asset is a fully rented office building. Rental receipts exceed expenditures. The trust instrument is silent about the allocation of items between principal and income. Among the items to be allocated by Kroll during the year are insurance proceeds received as a result of fire damage to the building and the mortgage interest payments made during the year. Which of the following items is(are) properly allocable to principal?

	Insurance proceeds on building	*Current mortgage interest payments*
a.	No	No
b.	No	Yes
c.	Yes	No
d.	Yes	Yes

(5/90, Law, #10, 8049)

SIMULATIONS

Problem 45-4 (20 to 30 minutes)

Before his death, Douglas, a U.S. citizen, made cash gifts of $7,000 each to his three brothers. In Year 1, Douglas also paid $2,000 in tuition directly to his grandchild's university on the grandchild's behalf. Douglas made no other lifetime transfers. Douglas died on January 9, Year 1, and was survived by his wife and only child, both of whom were U.S. citizens. The Douglas' did not live in a community property state.

At his death, Douglas owned:

Cash	$650,000
Marketable securities (Fair market value)	900,000
Life insurance policy with Douglas' wife named as the beneficiary (fair market value)	500,000

Under the provisions of Douglas' will, the net cash, after payment of executor's fees and medical and funeral expenses, was bequeathed to Douglas' son. The marketable securities were bequeathed to Douglas' spouse. During Year 1, Douglas' estate paid:

Executor's fees to distribute the decedent's property (deducted on the fiduciary tax return)	$15,000
Decedent's funeral expenses	25,000

The estate's executor extended the time to file the estate tax return.

On January 3, Year 2, the estate's executor paid the decedent's outstanding $10,000 Year 1 medical expense and filed the extended estate tax return. (5/98, AR, #2, amended, 6647)

For Items 1 through 5, identify the federal estate tax treatment for each item. An answer may be selected once, more than once, or not at all.

Estate Tax Treatments

F. Fully includible in Douglas' gross estate
P. Partially includible in Douglas' gross estate
N. Not includible in Douglas' gross estate

Transaction	Answer
1. What is the estate tax treatment of the $7,000 cash gift to each brother?	
2. What is the estate tax treatment of the life insurance proceeds?	
3. What is the estate tax treatment of the marketable securities?	
4. What is the estate tax treatment of the $2,000 tuition payment?	
5. What is the estate tax treatment of the $650,000 cash?	

For Items 6 through 10, identify the federal estate tax treatment for each item. An answer may be selected once, more than once, or not at all.

Estate Tax Treatments

G. Deductible from Douglas' gross estate to arrive at Douglas' taxable income
I. Deductible on Douglas' Year 1 individual income tax return
E. Deductible on either Douglas' Year 1 estate tax return or Douglas' Year 1 individual income tax return
N. Not deductible on either Douglas' estate tax return or Douglas' Year 1 individual income tax return

Transaction	Answer
6. What is the estate tax treatment of the executor's fees?	
7. What is the estate tax treatment of the cash bequest to Douglas' son?	
8. What is the estate tax treatment of the life insurance proceeds paid to Douglas' spouse?	
9. What is the estate tax treatment of the funeral expenses?	
10. What is the estate tax treatment of the $10,000 Year 1 medical expense incurred before the decedent's death and paid by the executor on January 3, Year 2?	

As the preparer of Douglas' personal and estate tax returns, write a memo to the executor of the estate explaining the transaction(s) that are not included on tax return. Include the amount and a description of each nondeductible transaction.

Research Question: What code section and subsection, if applicable, provides guidance on the value of property included in a decedent's gross estate?

Section & Subsection Answer: §_____ (___)

Problem 45-5 (20 to 30 minutes)

Various clients went to Cologne, CPA, for tax advice concerning possible gift tax liability on transfers they made throughout the year. (5/96, AR, #7-16, amended, 6205)

For items 1 through 9, indicate whether the transfer of cash, the income interest, or the remainder interest is a gift of present interest (P), gift of a future interest (F), or not a completed gift (N).

Pipe created a $500,000 trust that provided his mother with an income interest for her life and the remainder interest to go to his sister at the death of his mother. Pipe expressly retained the power to revoke both the income interest and the remainder interest at any time.

Interest	Answer
1. The income interest at the trust's creation	
2. The remainder interest at the trust's creation	

Able created a $100,000 trust that provided her nephew with the income interest until he reached 45 years of age. When the trust was created, Able's nephew was 25. The income distribution is to start when Able's nephew is 29. After Able's nephew reaches the age of 45, the remainder interest is to go to Able's niece

Interest	Answer
3. The income interest	

Isle, an unmarried taxpayer, made a $10,000 cash gift to her son in May and a further $12,000 cash gift to him in August.

Transfer	Answer
4. The cash transfers	

During the current year, Yeats transferred property worth $20,000 to a trust with the income to be paid to her 22-year-old niece Anna. After Anna reaches the age of 30, the remainder interest is to be distributed to Yeats' brother. The income interest is valued at $9,700 and the remainder interest at $10,300

Interest	Answer
5. The income interest	
6. The remainder interest	

Tom and Ann Thorn, U.S. citizens, were married for the entire calendar year. Tom gave a $40,000 cash gift to his uncle, Ellis. The Thorns made no other gifts to Ellis in the current year. Tom and Ann each signed a timely election stating that each made one half of the $40,000 gift.

Transfer	Answer
7. The cash transfer	

Adams created a $1,000,000 trust that provided his brother with an income interest for ten years, after which the remainder interest passes to Adams' sister. Adams retained the power to revoke the remainder interest at any time. The income interest was valued at $600,000.

Interest	Answer
8. The income interest	
9. The remainder interest	

Adrian's daughter, Kim, has one child, Dale. In 2009, Adrian made an outright $5,000,000 gift to Dale.

Write a memo to your employer, Cologne, CPA, discussing whether Adrian's transfer is subject to the generation-skipping tax, the gift tax, or both taxes. Disregard the use of any exclusions and the unified credit.

Research Question: What code section and subsection, if applicable, provides guidance on a gift made to a third party by a spouse when both spouses are citizens of the United States at the time of the gift?

Section & Subsection Answer: §_____ (___)

Problem 45-6 (10 to 15 minutes)

Karen Dell, an unmarried U.S. citizen, made no lifetime transfers prior to the current year. During 2009, Dell made the following transfers:

- Gave a $10,000 cash gift to Cedric, a close friend.
- Made two separate $10,000 cash gifts to her only child.
- Created an irrevocable trust that provided her aunt with an income interest to be paid for the next five years. The remainder interest is to pass to Dell's sole cousin. The income interest is valued at $26,000 and the remainder interest is valued at $74,000.
- Paid $25,000 tuition directly to her grandchild's university on her grandchild's behalf.
- Created an irrevocable trust that provided her brother with a lifetime income interest beginning in two years, after which a remainder interest passes to their sister.
- Created a revocable trust with her niece as the sole beneficiary. During 2009, the niece received $15,000 interest income from the trust. (11/98, AR, #3, amended, 6692)

For Items 1 through 7, determine whether the transactions are fully taxable, partially taxable, or not taxable to Dell in the current year for gift tax purposes after considering the gift tax annual exclusion. Ignore the unified credit when answering the items. An answer may be selected once, more than once, or not at all.

Gift Tax Treatments

F. Fully taxable to Dell for gift tax purposes
P. Partially taxable to Dell for gift tax purposes
N. Not taxable to Dell for gift tax purposes

Transactions	Answer
1 What is the gift tax treatment of Dell's gift to Cedric?	
2 What is the gift tax treatment of Dell's cash gifts to her child?	
3 What is the gift tax treatment of the trust's income interest to Dell's aunt?	
4 What is the gift tax treatment of the trust's remainder interest to Dell's cousin?	
5 What is the gift tax treatment of the tuition payment to Dell's grandchild's university?	
6 What is the gift tax treatment of the trust's income interest to Dell's brother?	
7. What is the gift tax treatment of the $15,000 interest income that Dell's niece received from the revocable trust?	

You prepare Karen Dell's personal taxes. Write a memo to the client explaining the transaction(s) that are not taxable on the gift tax return. Include the description and amount of each nontaxable transaction.

Scenario	Gift Tax	Communication	Research

Research Question: What code section and subsection, if applicable, provides guidance on the personal exemption deduction allowed by estates and trusts?

Section & Subsection Answer: §______ (___)

Solution 45-1 MULTIPLE CHOICE ANSWERS

Fiduciary Income Return

1. (d) A simple trust is a trust that requires all income to be distributed each year, that does not make any charitable contributions, and that does not make any distributions, except from current income. All other trusts are complex. The number or types of beneficiaries or grantors are not relevant to this characterization.

2. (a) The standard deduction is not available to estates, trusts, corporations, or partnerships. Estates and trusts may have a personal exemption.

3. (c) An executor of a decedent's estate that has only U.S. citizens as beneficiaries is required to file a fiduciary income tax return if the estate's gross income for the year is $600 or more.

4. (a) Estates have the option of choosing a calendar year or a fiscal year based on the date of the decedent's death. Most trusts established after 1986 must use a calendar year.

5. (b) Estates are required to make estimated tax payments with respect to any taxable year ending two or more years after the date of the decedent's death.

6. (b) Capital gains and losses normally are excluded from DNI, as they usually are allocated to principal rather than income. Deductions are allowed for charitable contributions to a qualified organization, if made pursuant to the will. Deductions are allowed for administrative expenses. Distributions of money or property to beneficiaries are not included in the calculation because they are removed from DNI for the current year. Thus, the DNI is $42,000 ($65,000 – $14,000 – $9,000).

7. (b) Section 6072(a) states that returns required to be filed by §6012 are to be filed on or before the 15th day of April following the close of the taxable year if the taxpayer is a calendar year taxpayer. Section 7503 provides that if the last day for filing is on a Saturday, Sunday, or legal holiday, the return will be considered filed in a timely manner if it is filed by the succeeding day after the due date that is not a Saturday, Sunday, or legal holiday.

8. (c) The lifetime income interest and the remainder interest are both incomplete transfers, as Carlt retained the power to revoke them. Thus, the assets remain Carlt's, and Carlt is taxed on the income from the assets.

9. (c) Section 652(a) provides that beneficiaries of estates and trusts must include in their gross income the amount of income required to be distributed to them. However, the income to be included may not exceed the distributable net income (DNI) of the estate or trust. Section 643(a) defines DNI as the taxable income of the estate or trust computed with certain modifications. Section 643(a)(2) provides that the estate may not take an exemption deduction in computing DNI. Thus, the DNI is $6,000 ($40,000 – $34,000). Because this amount is less than the $15,000 distributed, the beneficiary must include $6,000 in gross income from the estate under §61(a)(15).

10. (c) The charitable contribution deduction on an estate's fiduciary income tax return is allowable only if the charitable bequest is specified by a

provision in the decedent's will. Generally speaking, a deduction does not materialize when an individual dies intestate (without a will). Estates are not subject to a limitation on the extent of their deductible charitable contributions for the year (e.g., to a percentage of taxable or AGI).

Decedent's Income

11. (a) Income in respect to a cash basis decedent is income that has been earned by the decedent up to the point of death, but is not reported on the final income tax return because it has not been received. It will be included in the estate tax return at its fair market value.

12. (d) As a cash basis taxpayer, Rose would not recognize the $10,000 fee until she actually or constructively received it. Because this receipt occurs after Rose's death, the $10,000 is called "income in respect of the decedent" (IRD). IRD must be reported on *both* the estate's fiduciary income tax return under §691(a) and the estate tax return under §2033.

Estate Tax

13. (d) The amount of gift tax paid on post-1976 gifts is subtracted to arrive at the gross estate tax. Once the amount of gross estate tax is determined, the unified credit is taken from the gross estate tax to get the net estate tax due.

14. (d) In 2009, the effect of the unified credit is to exempt up to $3.5 million of a decedent's estate from estate taxation.

15. (c) The gross estate is reduced by non-discretionary deductions to arrive at the adjusted gross estate, which is further reduced by discretionary deductions to obtain the taxable estate. Funeral expenses are non-discretionary deductions. Charitable deductions are discretionary deductions.

16. (c) If the executor elects and the assets were not sold or distributed within 6 months after the date of the decedent's death, the assets in the decedent's gross estate are to be valued 6 months after the date of the decedent's death.

17. (a) The decedent's fractional share of property is included in the gross estate [Reg. §20.20401(a)(1)]. In this case, two individuals are involved; therefore 50% of the value of property owned is included. The question of who furnished the original consideration is not considered.

18. (a) If an estate tax return is required, then it must be filed nine months after the date of the decedent's death. Six months after the date of the decedent's death is the time frame for the "alternate valuation date" of the gross estate.

19. (d) Proceeds of insurance on the life of the decedent, payable to the executor as the estate's representative are always includible in the gross estate under §2042(1).

20. (d) All property owned by the decedent at the time of death is included in the gross estate by §2033. No distinction is made between personal effects and those belonging to a business interest. Wald's gross estate includes the personal items and jewelry as well as the jointly held land.

21. (b) The marital deduction is allowed for property included in the deceased spouse's gross estate that passes or has passed to the surviving spouse. The marital deduction is unlimited in amount.

Gift Tax

22. (d) No part of the value of a gift of *future interest* may be excluded in determining the total amount of taxable gifts. However, no part of a transfer for the benefit of a minor will be considered a gift of future interest *if:* (1) the property *and* its income may be expended by or for the benefit of the minor before he reaches 21; and (2) any portion of the property and its income not so expended will pass to the minor upon reaching 21, or will go either to his estate or as he may appoint under the general powers of appointment. Because the property (the bond) is to be distributed to the donor or successor-in-interest instead of the minor upon his reaching the age of 21, the transfer to the trust is considered a gift of future interest. Therefore, a gift tax exclusion is not permitted.

23. (b) Section 2503(b) provides for an exclusion from taxable gifts of $13,000 per donee in 2009. Section 2503(e)(2)(B) provides that all of the gift is excluded from taxable gifts if the gift was made on behalf of an individual to any person who provides medical care. Sayers is not entitled to exclude the entire gift because the amount was paid directly to Johnson and not to a person who provided Johnson with medical care. Sayers could exclude $26,000 if Sayers and Sayers' spouse consented under §2513 to have the gift treated as made one half by each. However, Sayers is single and therefore is entitled to only one annual exclusion under §2503(b).

24. (b) The election to treat a gift to a third party as made equally by husband and wife is allowed by §2513. For 2009, Section 2503(b) allows a $13,000 exclusion from taxable gifts for each gift to each donee of a present interest in property. Don and Linda are each considered to have made a $30,000 ($60,000 / 2) gift for which each is entitled to this $13,000 exclusion. Thus, Don and Linda each have made a taxable gift of $17,000 ($30,000 – $13,000). Therefore, their total taxable gifts for the year are $34,000 ($17,000 + $17,000) before the unified credit.

25. (c) Under the unified transfer tax system, one transfer tax schedule is used to compute the gift tax as well as the estate tax. Transfers at death and lifetime taxable gifts are taxed on a cumulative basis.

Generation-Skipping Tax

26. (c) The generation-skipping transfer tax is a separate tax imposed in addition to the gift tax and the estate tax. The generation-skipping transfer tax applies to transfers to beneficiaries who are more than one generation *below* the transferor's generation.

Estate & Trust Overview

27. (c) "*Per stirpes*" is the manner of distribution of property in which a class or group of distributees take the share that their predeceased would have been entitled to. In this case, the deceased had three children, two of which were living. The third child was survived by two of his own children. Each living child would receive one-third and the two children of the predeceased son would receive one-sixth each. This manner of distribution is distinguished from "*per capita*" where each heir would receive an equal share.

28. (c) In allocating benefits between the income beneficiary and the remainderman, the general rule is that ordinary receipts and current administration expenses are allocated to trust income, while extraordinary receipts and expenses are allocated to trust principal. Interest income from corporate bonds and fiduciary fees allocable to income are allocated to trust income, whereas net long-term capital gains allocable to corpus are allocated to trust principal. Therefore, $4,250 ($5,000 – $750) would be included in Gardner's (the income beneficiary) gross income.

29. (b) A trust terminates by its own effect when the instrument specifies a definite period of duration or a termination date. In this question, Dart established a 15-year duration. Since Frost, the income beneficiary, died after the termination date, the duration was in fact 15 years. Larson, the trustee, died before the termination date. Generally, however, a trust that satisfies all other requirements will not fail due to the refusal or incapacity of the trustee to serve. In such cases, the court will appoint a successor trustee. Dart, the grantor, died after the termination date. On the termination date, the property reverted to Dart.

30. (c) In allocating benefits between the income beneficiary (Smart) and the remainderman (Mix), the general rule is that *ordinary* receipts, such as rents, interest on certificates of deposit, and municipal bond interests, are treated as income, and *extraordinary* receipts, such as stock dividends and the proceeds from the sale of bonds, are treated as additions to principal. Therefore, the amount of Year 1 receipts that should be allocated to trust principal is $13,000 ($6,000 from stock dividends plus $7,000 from the sale of bonds).

Solution 45-2 ADDITIONAL MULTIPLE CHOICE ANSWERS

Fiduciary Income Return

31. (c) Individuals, estates, and trusts may take a deduction for net operating losses (NOL). As pass-through entities, partnerships and S corporations generally cannot take deductions; however, partners or S corporation shareholder use their distributive share of partnerships' and S corporations' business income and deductions to figure their individual NOL. Editor's Note: It is unclear why the examiners included not-for-profit organizations as an option to this question when exempt organizations are not listed in the content specification outline. Unfamiliar terms in answer options generally are incorrect.

32. (c) Ordinary and necessary administration expenses, including commissions and other selling expenses, can *either* be taken as a deduction in computing the estate tax (Form 706) *or* the fiduciary income tax return (Form 1041). Administration expenses cannot be taken on *both* Form 706 and Form 1041. In order for administration expenses to be deducted for income tax purposes the executor must waive the right to take the deduction for estate tax purposes and file a statement that the amount

involved has not already been allowed as a deduction for estate tax purposes.

33. (d) Most trusts must adopt a calendar year. Only a trust which qualifies as a §501(a) tax-exempt organization or a charitable trust described in §4947(a) can elect to use a fiscal year. An estate has the option of choosing a fiscal or calendar year.

34. (c) Under §652(a), the income required to be distributed currently from an estate or trust is included in the gross income of the beneficiaries to whom the income is required to be distributed. However, §652(a) limits the amount to be included in the gross income of the beneficiary to the beneficiary's share of distributable net income.

35. (d) The money in a sinking fund or trust is an asset of the corporation, even if a trustee is authorized to invest and reinvest the trust funds. Any income (including capital gains) generated from the sinking fund assets, is included in the gross income of the corporation by Reg. §1.61-13. Therefore, both the interest income of $60,000 and the $8,000 of net long-term capital gains are taxable to the corporation.

36. (c) As long as a distribution to a beneficiary does not exceed the distributable net income of the estate, the estate is allowed a deduction for the amount of the distribution that is subject to income tax on the beneficiary's return. Thus, the estate may claim a distribution deduction of $9,000 (e.g., $9,000 < $15,000) on its fiduciary income tax return.

Estate Tax

37. (a) An estate tax return is required to be filed in 2009 for any estate where the value at the date of death exceeds $3,500,000 under §6018. Since End's estate and Law's estate each are worth less than this minimum (e.g., $1,150,000 for End and $1,400,000 for Law), no estate tax return is required to be filed for either of their estates. End's estate is valued at $1,150,000 because any taxable gifts that are made during a decedent's lifetime are added back to the estate in determining if an estate tax return has to be filed by the executor of the estate.

38. (d) Under §2032, the alternative valuation date can be used only to value a decedent's estate if the election will decrease the value of the estate and if it will reduce any estate tax liability. The election can be used only if the election will decrease the value of the estate. The election once made is irrevocable and cannot be changed by filing an amended return. The election applies only to the gross estate and not to the net value of the estate (e.g., after liabilities and allowable deductions).

39. (c) The expenses of administering an estate are deductible under §2053(a)(2). The state inheritance or estate tax is also deductible. EGTRRA '01 replaced the former state death credit with the state death tax deduction for estates of individuals dying after 2004.

Gift Tax

40. (b) Section 2503(b) allows the first $13,000 of a gift to any person to be excluded from the total amount of gifts made during 2009. Therefore, Jan may exclude up to $13,000 on each of the gifts made to Jones and Craig, and all of the $5,000 made to Kande. ($13,000 + $13,000 + $5,000 = $31,000). Section 2503(e)(2)(B) provides that a transfer is excluded from taxable gifts if made on behalf of an individual for tuition at an accredited educational institution. Jan may not exclude the entire gift to Craig because the amount was not paid directly to the educational institution.

41. (c) Certain qualified transfers are excluded when determining total taxable gifts. Qualified transfers include amounts paid on the behalf of another individual (regardless of their relationship to the donor) for tuition at an accredited educational institution or for medical care. The exclusion for tuition does not include payment for dormitory fees, supplies, or textbooks.

42. (b) Pursuant to §6075(b), when a gift tax return is due, it must be filed on or before April 15 following the year of gift, regardless of whether the taxpayer uses a calendar year or a fiscal year, unless an extension of time for filing is requested. Section 7503 provides that if the last day for filing is on a Saturday, Sunday, or legal holiday, the return will be considered filed in a timely manner if it is filed by the succeeding day after the due date that is not a Saturday, Sunday, or legal holiday.

43. (b) Section 2523 indicates that where a donor transfers by gift an interest in property to his spouse, a deduction will be allowed in computing taxable gifts for the calendar year equal to the amount of the gift. The ring was given prior to the marriage, thus only the $75,000 is a marital deduction.

Estate & Trust Overview

44. (b) Once the necessary elements of a gift are present, the gift may not be revoked. A trust may be revoked if the settlor has reserved the power to revoke the trust or if the settlor and beneficiaries

of an irrevocable trust mutually agree to terminate the trust. The requisite intent to create a trust may be manifested orally or in writing. No consideration is necessary for the present creation of a valid trust; however, an agreement to create a trust in the future would require consideration. Though there must be identifiable beneficiaries of a private trust, they need not be notified of the trust or of its creation.

45. (c) A simple trust is a trust that requires all income to be distributed each year, that does not make any charitable contributions, and that does not make any distributions, except from current income; all other trusts are complex. A grantor trust holds collateral for mortgage-backed securities. A revocable trust is one that may be revoked by the settlor.

Solution 45-3 EXTRA MULTIPLE CHOICE ANSWERS

Estates

46. (b) After the surviving spouse has been provided for, the usual order of distribution of the remaining assets is the descendants (such as children and grandchildren) of the deceased; or if none survive, the ascendants (such as parents and grandparents); or if none survive, the collaterals (such as brothers and sisters). The state would receive the estate if the descendant has no living descendants, ascendants, or collaterals.

47. (a) The personal representative of an estate would breach fiduciary duties by commingling the assets of the estate with her/his own property. Personal liability may result from any shrinkage of estate assets due to commingling. The personal representative of an estate could be involved in the activities in answers (b), (c), and (d) without violating the fiduciary duties required of all personal representatives.

48. (a) Both Totten trusts and insurance policies have named beneficiaries and unless the estate is named as one of the beneficiaries, the proceeds would be distributed outside of the probate estate and regardless of intestacy laws.

49. (d) For a *per capita* distribution of an estate, each person takes an equal share of the estate. Since, in this case, there are a total of five issues (two surviving children and three grandchildren of a predeceased child), the estate would be divided into five equal parts. Answers (b) would be correct if the distribution were to be made on a *per stirpes* basis.

50. (a) An estate is a legal entity which comes into existence upon the death of an individual and succeeds to the title of all property owned by the individual. It also assumes liability for all debts owed by the decedent at the time of his death.

51. (c) An executor must file a final account of the administration of an estate. Generally, the terms of a valid will control its administration. Thus, John need not post bond. Whether the named executor is a beneficiary does not affect her/his potential right to reasonable compensation, nor does it require her/him to relinquish the duties of the appointment.

Trusts

52. (d) An express trust may be created without a remainderman or a successor trustee. The four elements of a valid trust are a settlor, a trustee, trust property, and a beneficiary.

53. (b) A trustee has express powers conferred upon her/him by the trust instrument and has implied powers which are reasonably necessary to enable the trustee to carry out the purpose of the trust. If not expressly granted, the power to sell trust property (I) and the power to pay trust expenses (III) would be considered reasonably necessary, but implied powers would not extend to mortgaging the trust property or to borrowing money from the trust (II).

54. (d) A spendthrift trust often is created to protect a beneficiary from creditors or from her/his squandering of the trusts' assets. This type of trust prohibits any transfer of beneficiary's rights by assignment or otherwise, and prevents creditors of the beneficiary from obtaining trust principal or its income until it actually is paid to the beneficiary.

55. (d) The AICPA's unofficial answer is (d). The trustee holds legal title to property in a trust for the benefit of the beneficiaries and is a requirement for the trust to be valid. However, our editorial board feels (a) also is correct. A trust may be created orally or in writing. However, for an express trust of real property to be enforceable, it must be in writing under the Statute of Frauds. Because this trust is funded by an office building (real property), it must be in writing. There is no rule that for a trust to be enforceable, there must be a provision for trustee fees. A trust will never fail for lack of a successor trustee.

56. (d) The rule against perpetuities limits the duration of a trust to a life in being plus 21 years; thus, a trust created to benefit a childless person's

grandchildren would fail. Trusts created to promote the public welfare, to provide for a spouse's health care, and/or to benefit a charity are valid and would not fail.

57. (b) Trust property must exist at the time of the creation of the trust and must be transferred to the trustee during the grantor's lifetime. An *inter vivos* trust is not required to be in writing. It is not necessary to provide for payment of fees to the trustee since it is implied that a trustee can collect a reasonable fee for her/his services. There is no requirement that an alternate trust beneficiary be designated.

58. (c) A written trust containing no specific powers does not grant the trustee the implied power to accumulate income. The most common implied powers are the power to sell assets, the power to lease assets and the power to incur reasonable expenses.

59. (c) When a trust instrument is silent regarding a trustee's powers, the trustee has the implied power to lease trust property to third parties. Leasing of trust property falls within the trustee's duty to beneficiaries to preserve the trust assets and to make the trust property productive. Making distributions of principal to income beneficiaries would be in violation of the Uniform Principal & Income Act.

60. (b) In administering a trust, the trustee must exercise that degree of care and skill which a reasonably prudent businessperson would exercise in dealing with her/his own property. A trustee may not invest trust assets in speculative ventures, which includes unsecured loans. Secured first mortgages on land, tax-exempt municipal bonds, and guaranteed savings certificates generally are considered prudent investments.

61. (d) A trustee has a fiduciary duty. As a result, a trustee or co-trustees must use the same degree of skill, judgment, and care in managing the trust assets as reasonably prudent persons would exercise in managing their own affairs. A spouse can be a co-trustee even if the spouse is a beneficiary. The "merger doctrine" states that if the sole trustee and the sole beneficiary are the same person, the trust will go out of existence because the legal title (held by the trustee) and the equitable title (held by the beneficiary) have "merged." Since the wife is not the sole trustee, there is no problem presented. A trustee will not escape liability by delegating duties to someone else. A trustee could purchase trust property under certain circumstances, such as when the trust document does not prevent it, there is full disclosure, and the fair market value is paid. Also, the court would have to grant its approval.

62. (c) A trustee must act with honesty, good faith, and prudence in administering the trust. A trustee is held to the standard of care that a prudent person would exercise in conducting her/his personal affairs. A trustee also is charged with a duty of loyalty that requires the trustee to act in the exclusive interest of the beneficiary. A trustee who invests trust assets in unsecured loans to a co-trustee violates both duties.

63. (a) An irrevocable trust that contains no provision for change or termination can be changed or terminated only by the courts. The grantor, income beneficiaries, and remaindermen have no power to change or terminate the trust.

64. (c) A trust will terminate by operation of law when there are no longer any income beneficiaries. Since Hardy is the only beneficiary, the trust will terminate upon his death. Hardy's life is the measuring life of the trust, and he is the trust's only income beneficiary. The timing of the deaths of Park, Gordon and King are irrelevant to the trust's termination.

65. (b) A resulting trust may arise where an express trust has been created gratuitously and it fails (I) because it is impossible to carry out. Also, the fulfillment of a trust purpose (III) could result in the creation of a resulting trust if trust property still remained. The application of the *cy pres* doctrine (II) would not cause a resulting trust to be created. It is applied in those situations in which a gift to a charitable trust cannot be carried out in the manner specified by the donor. In that case, the doctrine would allow that the trust be carried out as closely as possible to the intent of the donor.

66. (a) Charitable trusts are **not** subject to the rule against perpetuities. The rule against perpetuities limits the duration of a private trust to a life in being plus 21 years. This rule does apply to spendthrift trusts, totten trusts, and constructive trusts.

67. (b) A testamentary trust generally is created in an instrument such as a will and comes into existence only upon the settlor's death. The fact that a trust will not become effective until the settlor's death does not render the trust invalid. An *inter vivos* trust comes into existence during the settlor's lifetime. There is nothing to preclude a person from serving as both the trustee of a trust and the personal representative of an estate.

Principal & Income Allocation

68. (d, e) Both answers are required for full point value. The Uniform Principal & Income Act allocates extraordinary expenses to trust principal. Extraordinary expenses are those which are not ordinary and

include the cost of capital improvements such as the principal portion of mortgage payments and sidewalk assessments. The Act provides that ordinary and current operating expenses are chargeable to income. Current and ordinary operating expenses would include building management fees, insurance premiums, and depreciation.

69. (c) Generally, in the absence of contrary directions in the trust instrument, income generated from trust assets is allocated to income and not principal. Thus, income accruing after the assets were transferred to the trust is allocated to trust income, [$500,000 × 12% × (10 months / 12 months) = $50,000] while interest accruing prior to the transfer is allocated to principal [$500,000 × 12% × (2 months / 12 months) = $10,000].

70. (b) Trust income is distributed to, or held for the benefit of, the income beneficiaries during the lifetime of the trust. Upon termination of a trust, any remaining assets/principal will go to the remaindermen.

71. (a) In allocating benefits between principal and income, the general rule is that ordinary receipts are treated as income, while extraordinary receipts are treated as additions to principal. Extraordinary receipts include proceeds from the sale of trust assets. If the building, a trust asset, was sold, the entire proceeds would be allocated to principal.

72. (c) In general, current administration expenses incurred to keep the trust property productive, such as annual property tax, should be paid out of trust income. Extraordinary expenses and expenses incurred in the improvement of trust principal, such as mortgage principal payments, should be allocated to trust principal.

73. (b) A trust income beneficiary would receive the ordinary receipts, or income, of the trust. Royalties (I) and cash dividends (III) are considered income; stock received in a stock split (II) and settlements of claims for damages to trust property (IV) are considered extraordinary receipts, or allocation of principal.

74. (c) The insurance proceeds constitute sums received in settlement of claims for injury to the trust property (e.g., an extraordinary receipt). It should be allocated to principal. On the other hand, mortgage *interest* payments (as opposed to mortgage principal payments) are an ordinary expense, properly allocated to trust income.

PERFORMANCE BY SUBTOPICS

Each category below parallels a subtopic covered in Chapter 45. Record the number and percentage of questions you correctly answered in each subtopic area.

Fiduciary Income Return

Question #	Correct √
1	
2	
3	
4	
5	
6	
7	
8	
9	
10	
# Questions	10
# Correct	________
% Correct	________

Decedent's Income

Question #	Correct √
11	
12	
# Questions	2
# Correct	________
% Correct	________

Estate Tax

Question #	Correct √
13	
14	
15	
16	
17	
18	
19	
20	
21	
# Questions	9
# Correct	________
% Correct	________

Gift Tax

Question #	Correct √
22	
23	
24	
25	
# Questions	4
# Correct	________
% Correct	________

Generation-Skipping Tax

Question #	Correct √
26	
# Questions	1
# Correct	________
% Correct	________

Estate & Trust Overview

Question #	Correct √
27	
28	
29	
30	
# Questions	4
# Correct	________
% Correct	________

SIMULATION SOLUTIONS

Solution 45-4 Estate & Gift Tax

Gross Estate (2.5 points)

1. N

Gifts made within three years of the donor's death usually are not included in the gross estate, unless the donor retained powers to amend or revoke the gift.

2. F

The gross estate includes the value of all property to the extent of the decedent's beneficial interest, including insurance proceeds in which the decedent retained a beneficial interest. (Note that the fact pattern states, "At his death, Douglas owned: ...Life insurance policy....") The policy would not be included in the gross estate if an employer, for example, owned it without the employee having any beneficial interest.

3. F

The gross estate includes the value of all property to the extent of the decedent's beneficial interest, including marketable securities.

4. N

The 2009 annual per-donee exclusion of §2503 is $32,000. Gifts meeting this exclusion are not taxed. In addition, tuition (or medical bills) paid directly to an accredited institution or medical care provider is exempt from gift tax even if it exceeds this limit.

5. F

The gross estate includes the value of all property to the extent of the decedent's beneficial interest, including cash.

Deductibility (2.5 points)

6. N

The executor's fees to distribute property were deducted on the fiduciary tax return, so they may not be deducted on the estate tax return as well. (In order to be deducted for income tax purposes, the executor must waive the right to take the deduction for estate tax purposes.)

7. N

There is no exemption or deduction for bequests to a son or daughter.

8. G

There is an unlimited martial deduction for bequests to a spouse.

9. G

Funeral expenses are a nondiscretionary deduction that reduces the gross estate.

10. E

Medical expenses are either an itemized deduction on the decedent's income tax return or a nondiscretionary deduction that reduces the gross estate.

Communication (1.5 points)

To: **Estate Executor**
From: CPA Firm
Re: **Non-inclusive Transactions for Estate Tax Purposes**

During the preparation of the Douglas estate tax return, we came across a few transactions that do not appear on the estate tax return. The non-includible transactions are as follows.

The **$7,000 cash gift** to each brother was made within 3 years of the donor's death. Usually gifts made within 3 years of the donor's death are not included in the gross estate, unless the donor retained powers to amend or revoke the gift.

The **$2,000 tuition payment** paid directly to the grandchild's university is not taxed. The annual per-donee gift exclusion is $13,000 for 2009. Gifts less than this exclusion are not taxed. In addition, tuition and medical bills paid directly to an accredited institution or medical care provider are exempt from gift tax even if they exceed this limit.

The **executor's fees of $15,000** to distribute property were deducted on the fiduciary tax return, so they may not be deducted on the estate tax return as well. In order for them to be deducted for income tax purposes, the executor must waive the right to take the deduction for estate tax purposes.

There is no exemption or deduction for bequests to a son or daughter.

A copy of the Douglas estate tax return is enclosed. Please keep the copy for your records.

Research (1 point)

Code Section Answer: §2033

Code section §2033 states, "The value of the gross estate shall include the value of all property to the extent of the interest therein of the decedent at the time of his death."

Solution 45-5 Gifts & Transfers

Nature of Gift (4 points)

1. N

Because Pipe may revoke the income interest at any time, this is not a completed gift.

2. N

Because Pipe may revoke the remainder interest at any time, this is not a completed gift.

3. F

Because the income distribution will not start for four years, this is a gift of future interest.

4. P

The gift cannot be revoked and is in control of the recipient.

5. P

The gift cannot be revoked and is in control of the recipient.

6. F

Because the income distribution will not start for 8 years, this is a gift of future interest.

7. P

The gift cannot be revoked and is in control of the recipient.

8. P

The gift cannot be revoked and is in control of the recipient.

9. N

Because Adams may revoke the remainder interest at any time, this is not a completed gift.

Communication (5 points)

To: Cologne, CPA
From: Ima Junior
Re: Adrian's Transfer

Transfers generally are subject to the generation-skipping tax if a taxpayer gives gifts to a **grandchild**. For 2009, there is a $3.5 million exemption to the generation-skipping tax. If the donor's son or daughter who is the recipient's **parent** is **deceased**, special rules apply; however, that is not the case in this situation.

Transfers are subject to the gift tax if a taxpayer gives a gift **larger** than the **annual per-donor** exclusion. For 2009, this limit is $13,000.

Both of these conditions are met in Adrian's transfer to Dale.

Research (1 point)

Code Section Answer: §2513(a)

Code section §2513(a) states, "A gift made by one spouse to any person other than his spouse shall, for the purposes of this chapter, be considered as made one-half by him and one-half by his spouse, but only if at the time of the gift each spouse is a citizen or resident of the United States."

Solution 45-6 Gifts & Transfers

Gift Tax (6 points)

1. N

Section 2503(b) indicates that the first $13,000 of a gift to any person may be excluded from the total amount of gifts made during 2009.

2. P

Section 2503(b) indicates that the first $13,000 of a gift to any person may be excluded from the total amount of gifts made during 2009. The gifts during the year that exceed this amount are taxable.

3. P

Section 2503(b) indicates that the first $13,000 of a gift to any person may be excluded from the total amount of gifts made during 2009.

4. F

No part of the value of a gift of future interest may be excluded in determining the total amount of taxable gifts.

5. N

Certain qualified transfers are excluded when determining total taxable gifts. Qualified transfers include amounts paid on the behalf of another individual for tuition at an accredited educational institution or for medical care. (The payment must be made directly to the institution or care provider.)

6. F

No part of the value of a gift of future interest may be excluded in determining the total amount of taxable gifts.

7. P

Section 2503(b) indicates that the first $13,000 of a gift to any person may be excluded from the total amount of gifts made during 2009.

Communication (3 points)

To: **Karen Dell**
From: CPA Firm
Re: **Nontaxable Transaction for Gift Tax Purposes**

During the preparation of your gift tax return, we discovered a transaction that does not appear on the gift tax return.

The **$25,000 tuition payment** to your grandchild's university is not a taxable gift. There are certain transfers that are excluded when determining total taxable gifts. These qualified transfers include amounts paid on the **behalf** of another individual for tuition at an accredited educational institution or for medical care, provided they are made **directly** to the educational institution or care provider.

A copy of your gift tax return is enclosed. Please keep the copy for your records.

Research (1 point)

Code Section Answer: §642(b)

Code section §642(b) states, "An estate shall be allowed a deduction of $600. A trust which, under its governing instrument, is required to distribute all of its income currently shall be allowed a deduction of $300. All other trusts shall be allowed a deduction of $100. The deductions allowed by this subsection shall be in lieu of the deductions… relating to deduction for personal exemption."

STUDY TIP

Bisk Education CPA review materials are designed to help you pass the current exam. Provisions that are not yet effective are not tested; thus, you unnecessarily add time to your review by studying them. We do not discourage your interest in these provisions, but we caution you not to delude yourself that this study is exam preparation. Generally, provisions that are not effective until 2011 or later are not in this edition. Some future changes to current provisions are discussed when the additional space to do so is not significant. Future editions and updating supplements will provide information about provisions as they become eligible for testing. Study those provisions that are applicable to your exam.

CHAPTER 46

FEDERAL TAXATION: CORPORATIONS

EXAM COVERAGE: The entities taxation portion of the Regulation section of the CPA exam is designated by the examiners to be 22-28 percent of the section's point value. More information about the point value of different topics is included in the **Practical Advice** section of this volume.

CHAPTER 46

FEDERAL TAXATION: CORPORATIONS

I. Overview

A. Flow of Form 1120

Many of the concepts that apply to individuals also apply to corporations. Therefore, this chapter concentrates on explaining and highlighting how the tax rules for a corporation are different from those for individuals. As an overview, we begin by outlining Form 1120, *U.S. Corporation Income Tax Return.*

Step One: Determine Income

	Gross receipts
Less:	Cost of goods sold (Schedule A)
Equals:	Gross profit
Plus:	1. Dividends (Schedule C) 2. Interest 3. Rent 4. Royalties 5. Capital gains (Schedule D) 6. Other gains and losses (Form 4797) 7. Other income

Step Two: Less Deductions

1. Compensation of officers (Schedule E)
2. Salaries and wages
3. Repairs and maintenance
4. Bad debts
5. Rents
6. Taxes and licenses
7. Interest
8. Charitable contributions
9. Depreciation (Form 4562)
10. Depletion
11. Advertising
12. Pension, profit sharing plans
13. Employee benefit programs
14. Other deductions
15. Net operating loss
16. Special deductions (Schedule C)

Step Three: Equals Taxable Income

Step Four: Compute Tax (Schedule J)

Step Five: Less Payments

1. Prior year overpayment applied to current year
2. Estimated payments
3. Payment with extension

Step Six: Less Credits

1. Credit from regulated investment companies
2. Credit for federal tax on fuels

Step Seven: Equals Overpayment or Amount Due

B. Characteristics
A corporation is an entity formed by associates to conduct a business venture and divide the profits among the investors. A corporation files a charter and articles of incorporation with a state government. It also prepares bylaws, has a board of directors, and issues shares of stock.

- Treasury regulations set forth the definition of a corporation for federal tax purposes. An entity satisfying the definition is taxed as a corporation. Those same regulations also provide for the federal tax treatment of entities not meeting the corporate definition. Some entities may elect to be treated as either corporations or partnerships for federal tax purposes.

C. Transfers in Exchange for Stock
No gain or loss is recognized if property is transferred to a corporation solely in exchange for stock if, immediately after the transfer, the transferor(s) are in control of the corporation.

1. **Property** Includes everything except services.

2. **Control** Defined for purposes of these rules as owning 80% of the voting power and 80% of the nonvoting stock.

3. **Boot** Receipt of boot (property other than stock) triggers gain recognition. However, no loss is recognized. *Non-qualified preferred stock* is treated as boot.

   a. **Property Subject to Liability** If property that is subject to a liability is transferred, gain is recognized if the liabilities exceed the basis of the property transferred.

   b. **Non-Qualified Preferred Stock** Non-qualified preferred stock has one of the following characteristics.

      (1) The issuer is required to redeem or purchase the stock.

      (2) The holder has the right to require the issuer (or a related person) to redeem or purchase the stock.

      (3) The issuer has the right to redeem or purchase the stock and, as of the issue date, it is more likely than not that this right will be exercised.

      (4) The dividend rate on the stock varies according to interest rates, commodity price, or similar indices, in form or substance.

   c. **Exclusions** The following exchanges are excluded from this gain recognition.

      (1) Certain exchanges of preferred stock for comparable preferred stock of the same or lesser value.

      (2) Exchange of preferred stock for common stock.

      (3) Certain exchanges of debt securities for preferred stock of the same or lesser value.

      (4) Exchanges of stock in certain recapitalizations of family-owned corporations.

4. **Basis**

a. The shareholder's basis in the stock is equal to the adjusted basis of the property transferred plus any gain recognized less any boot received.

b. The basis of the property to the corporation is the transferor's adjusted basis plus any gain recognized by the transferor on the transfer.

D. **Filing Requirements**
A C corporation must file Form 1120 with the IRS on or before the 15th day of the third month after the close of its tax year. For a calendar year corporation, the return is due March 15. An automatic six-month extension is available by filing Form 7004. However, this extends the time for filing the return, not for paying the tax.

E. **Estimated Payments**
If a corporation's tax liability is $500 or more, it must make quarterly estimated tax payments. The installments are due on the 15th day of the fourth, sixth, ninth, and twelfth month of the tax year. For a calendar year corporation, the installments are due April 15, June 15, September 15, and December 15. Corporations may use either the annualized or seasonal methods to lower one or more of the quarterly estimated tax payments.

1. **Annualized Method** Quarterly estimated tax payments are computed by multiplying the taxable income for the applicable period by 12, and then dividing by the number of months in the period.

2. **Seasonal Method** May be used if taxable income for the same six-month period averages 70% or more of annual taxable income.

F. **Tax Rates**

Exhibit 1 ▸ Tax Rate Schedule

Taxable Income	Tax Rate	Taxable Income	Tax Rate
$0 - $ 50,000	15%	$ 335,001 - $10,000,000	34%
$ 50,001 - $ 75,000	25%	$10,000,001 - $15,000,000	35%
$ 75,001 - $100,000	34%	$15,000,001 - $18,333,333	38%
$100,001 - $335,000	39%	Over $18,333,333	35%

1. **Personal Service Corporations** Certain personal service corporations must pay a flat rate of tax of 35%, regardless of their taxable income.

2. **Surtax** The 5% surtax on corporate income between $100,000 and $335,000 is imposed to phase out the benefit of the 15% and 25% bracket for high income corporations. The 3% surtax on corporate income between $15 million and $18,333,333 also is imposed to phase out the benefit of the 34% rate.

II. Corporate Income Tax

A. **Gross Income**
All deductible corporate expenses are assumed to be incurred in the furtherance of trade or business, and are subtracted directly from gross income. The concepts of adjusted gross income, itemized deductions, standard deduction, and personal exemptions that apply to the taxation of individuals do not apply to corporations.

B. **Organizational & Startup Expenses**
A corporation may elect to deduct up to $5,000 of organizational expenses (additional $5,000 for startup costs) incurred in the tax year its business begins. The $5,000 deduction is reduced on a

dollar-for-dollar basis for those expenses in excess of $50,000. Any remaining balance must be amortized over 15 years.

1. **Organizational Costs** Organizational costs are costs incurred incident to the creation of the corporation and are chargeable to a capital account [§248]; however, if the corporation has a limited life, the organizational costs are amortizable over that life. To qualify for this election, the organizational expenses must be incurred before the end of the first tax year in which the corporation is in business.

   a. **Include** Organizational expenses that qualify for the election include the costs of temporary directors, organizational meetings, state incorporation fees, and legal and accounting expenses incidental to the organization.

   b. **Exclude** Costs related to the issuance of stock are not organizational expenses. (Stock issuance costs are netted against the proceeds in the tax year in which they are incurred.)

2. **Startup Costs** Startup costs are costs of active trade or business creation (including investigation) or acquisition [§195]. Examples of startup costs include amounts incurred in connection with an activity engaged in for profit or for the production of income in anticipation of the activity becoming an active trade or business. To qualify for this election, the startup costs must have incurred before the day the active trade or business begins.

   a. **Include** Startup costs that qualify for this election include analysis or survey of potential markets, products, etc., advertisements of opening, salaries and fees for executives and consultants, salaries and wages for training employees, and cost necessary to secure prospective distributors, suppliers, or customers.

   b. **Exclude** Startup costs do not include deductible interest, taxes, or research and experimental costs.

C. Dividend-Received Deduction

C corporations are entitled to a special deduction for dividends received from domestic corporations. The deduction by the recipient corporation is limited to a percentage of the dividends received based on the percentage ownership of the distributing corporation.

Exhibit 2 ▸ Dividend-Received Deduction Percentages

Percentage of Ownership by Corporate Shareholder	Deduction Percentage
Less than 20%	70%
20% or more to less than 80%	80%
80% or more (affiliated groups)	100%

1. **Holding Period** No deduction is allowed for stock that is held for short periods of time. For purposes of this rule, the holding period is measured from the dividend date to the disposition date. Generally, stock must be held for more than 45 days during a 90-day period beginning 45 days before the taxpayer becomes entitled to receive the dividend. For preferred stock, the holding period is more than 90 days during a 180-day period beginning 90 days before the taxpayer becomes entitled to receive the dividend. (This provision was aimed at preventing hedging or short sales by the taxpayer to protect itself against the risk of loss.)

2. **Calculation** Generally, the deduction is limited to 80% (70% if less than 20% ownership) of taxable income computed without regard to the dividend-received deduction. However, if taking the full dividend-received deduction creates a net operating loss, or a net operating loss exists before the dividend-received deduction, then the taxable income limitation is not applicable.

Example 1 ▶ Dividend-Received Deduction

For Year 1, Tree Sap Corporation had $500,000 of income from logging operations, $550,000 in expenses, and $100,000 of dividend income from a 40% owned corporation. Based on this information, Tree Sap is able to deduct 80% of the dividends it received, resulting in a $30,000 net operating loss.

Income from logging operations	$ 500,000
Plus: Dividend income	100,000
Equals: Total income	$ 600,000
Less: Expenses	(550,000)
Equals: Tentative taxable income (computed without regard to the 80% dividend-received deduction)	$ 50,000
Less: 80% dividend-received deduction	(80,000)
Equals: Net operating loss for Year 1	$ (30,000)*

* Taking the 80% dividend-received deduction from tentative taxable income results in a net operating loss. The 80% of taxable income limitation does **not** apply whenever use of the dividend-received deduction results in a net operating loss; therefore, the deduction is allowed for $80,000 (the full 80% of the dividends).

D. Key-Person Life Insurance

Premiums on key-person life insurance policies are not deductible by the corporation. The proceeds from these policies are not included in taxable corporate income.

E. Charitable Contributions

A corporation's deduction for charitable contributions generally is limited to 10% of taxable income without regard to (1) the deduction for charitable contributions, (2) the dividend-received deduction, (3) any net operating loss carryback to that year, and (4) any capital loss carryback to that year. The current and carried-forward deduction is limited each year to 10% of taxable income. Any contributions that are not deductible currently because of the 10% rule may be carried forward for five years.

F. Capital Gains & Losses

Corporate capital losses are deductible only against capital gains. In other words, unlike individuals, corporations are not allowed to deduct any net capital losses.

1. **Excess Losses** Excess capital losses may be carried back three years and carried forward five years.

2. **Carryover Treatment** Capital losses that are carried forward or back are treated as short-term capital losses.

G. Net Operating Loss (NOL)

When deductions exceed income, the result is a net operating loss. This loss may be carried back two years and forward twenty. Carrybacks and carryforwards are not included in the computation of a current year NOL. An AMT NOL may offset up to 90% of AMTI calculated without regard to this deduction. The allowance previously only for casualty and theft type of losses has been extended to almost any business NOL. It does not apply to certain interest expense relating to equity reduction transactions and similar items beyond the scope of the exam.

- ARRA '09 allows a small business (average gross receipts of $15 million or less) to carry back a 2008 NOL for up to five years. For a 2009 NOL, the regular two-year carry back period is in effect.

III. Alternative Minimum Tax (AMT)

A. General

The purpose of the alternative minimum tax rules is to ensure that corporations pay a minimum amount of tax. If a corporation's tentative alternative tax exceeds its regular tax liability, the excess is paid in addition to the regular tax due. The starting point for computing a corporation's alternative minimum taxable income (AMTI) is regular taxable income.

1. **Exempt Corporations** Qualifying small corporations are exempt from AMT. A corporation with gross receipts of less than $5 million in its first year is a small corporation. A corporation with average gross receipts of less than $7.5 million for the 3-year period before the current tax year is a small corporation.

2. **Formerly Exempt Corporations** Once a corporation loses its small corporation status, it may not be regained. A former small corporation is subject to corporate AMT only with respect to preferences and adjustments relating to transactions entered into after losing its small corporation status.

B. **Adjustments**
Corporate adjustments for AMT are very similar to individual adjustments for AMT. Adjustments can be either positive or negative. Examples include the following.

1. **Long-Term Contracts** Percentage of completion methods used after February 28, 1986.

2. **Installment Sales** Installment sales does not apply to any nondealer disposition of property after August 16, 1986, but before January 1, 1987.

3. **Excess Depreciation** Depreciation must be recalculated for AMT purposes. Excess depreciation of post-1986 real property over straight-line. Excess depreciation of post-1986 personal property over 150% MACRS. This provision is modified by bonus depreciation (discussed in Chapter 43). Taxpayers may elect to use the 150% rate for regular income tax purpose, eliminating the difference between regular income tax depreciation and AMT depreciation.

4. **Basis Adjustments** Basis adjustments in determining gain or loss from the sale or exchange of property, resulting from different methods used to calculate depreciation.

5. **Passive Activities** Passive activity of certain closely held corporations and personal service corporations.

6. **Certain Loss Limitations**

C. **Preferences**
Corporate preferences for AMT are very similar to individual preferences for AMT. Preferences are always positive. Examples of preferences include the following.

1. **Percentage Depletion** Percentage depletion in excess of adjusted basis of the property.

2. **Tax-Exempt Interest** Tax-exempt interest from private activity bonds issued after August 7, 1986.

3. **Appreciated Property** Appreciated property given to charity.

4. **Intangible Drilling Costs** Intangible drilling costs in excess of 65% of net oil/gas income, which is applicable to integrated oil companies, but not independent producers.

5. **Accelerated Depreciation** Accelerated depreciation on pre-1987 real property.

D. **Adjusted Current Earnings (ACE)**
The most distinctive difference between individual and corporate AMT calculations is the adjustment for ACE. Certain adjustments are made to AMTI to arrive at ACE. If ACE exceeds AMTI, 75% of this difference becomes a positive adjustment to AMTI. The ACE adjustment can be negative; however, any negative adjustments are limited to prior positive adjustments. Municipal interest

income and the dividend-received deduction (under 20% ownership) are examples of adjustments to arrive at ACE.

E. **Exemption**
Corporations are allowed a $40,000 exemption when computing AMT. This exemption is phased out by 25% of AMTI that exceeds $150,000. Therefore, the exemption is zero when corporate AMTI is $310,000 or more.

Example 2 ▸ AMT

Max Corporation has minimum taxable income of $250,000 and a foreign tax credit of $10,000. Max is ineligible for the small business exception.

Required: Compute Max's AMT exemption and liability.

Solution:

Standard exemption		$ 40,000
Minimum taxable income (MTI)	$ 250,000	
Phase-out threshold	(150,000)	
Excess MTI over threshold	$ 100,000	
Reduction percentage	× 25%	
Reduction		(25,000)
Maximum AMT exemption		$ 15,000
Minimum taxable income		$250,000
Less: AMT exemption		(15,000)
AMT taxable income		$235,000
AMT rate		× 20%
Alternative minimum tax		$ 47,000
Less: Foreign tax credit		(10,000)
Alternative tax liability		$ 37,000

F. **AMT Credit**
To the extent AMT exceeds the regular tax liability, the corporation is entitled to a credit for the excess AMT. This credit may be carried over indefinitely, but can be used only to offset the corporation's regular tax.

Example 3 ▸ AMT Credit

In Year 1, Alpha Corporation's regular tax liability was $30,000, and its AMT liability was $45,000. Thus, Alpha was entitled to a $15,000 AMT credit. For Year 2, the regular tax is $60,000 and the AMT only $50,000. Alpha is entitled to reduce its Year 2 regular tax liability by the AMT credit carryover, but not below the Year 2 alternative tax amount. Thus, Alpha will reduce its regular tax by $10,000 (from $60,000 to $50,000) and carry over the unused $5,000 ($15,000 – $10,000) portion of the credit to Year 3 and subsequent years.

IV. Reconciliation of Book Income to Taxable Income

A. **Schedule M-1**
Book income may not equal taxable income due to temporary and permanent differences between financial accounting and the Internal Revenue Code. Schedule M-1 of Form 1120 is used to reconcile book income to taxable income. The net book income is adjusted until it reconciles with the taxable income. Unlike in financial accounting, Schedule M-1 does not require permanent and temporary differences to be distinguished.

1. **Additions to Book Income**

   a. **Federal Income Tax Expense**

   b. **Excess Capital Losses** The excess of capital losses over capital gains.

   c. **Income** Income items for tax purposes that are not included in book income, (e.g., prepaid rents, royalties, interest, and service fees).

   d. **Expenses** Expenses deducted for book purposes that are not deductible for tax purposes, (e.g., accrued contingent liabilities, premiums on key-person life insurance policies, business gifts to the extent that they exceed $25, charitable contributions in excess of the 10% of taxable income limitation, expenses incurred in connection with tax-exempt income, and different methods used for computing depreciation).

2. **Subtractions From Book Income**

   a. **Income** Income reported on the books but not for tax, (e.g., interest on municipal bonds and life insurance proceeds on key-person life insurance).

   b. **Expenses** Deductions reported on the tax return but not charged against book income, (e.g., the dividend-received deduction, charitable contribution carryovers, and different methods used for computing depreciation).

B. **Schedule M-3**
Generally, Schedule M-3 is filed in lieu of Schedule M-1 for corporations with $10 million or more in total assets. The purpose of Schedule M-3 is to make the difference between financial accounting net income and taxable income more transparent for large and mid-size business.

1. **Reconciliation** Schedule M-3 requires high-level detail reporting of book-tax differences, which includes comprehensive lists of income or loss and expense items. Unlike Schedule M-1, Schedule M-3 requires temporary and permanent differences between financial and tax income and expense to be reported separately. Schedule M-3 also reconciles worldwide consolidated net income (loss) per the income statement to the net income (loss) per income statement of includible corporations (consolidated tax groups).

2. **Reportable Transactions** Taxpayers who are not required to file Schedule M-3 may file the schedule as an alternative to the disclosure procedures which requires the disclosure of "reportable transactions" [Reg. §1.6011-4]. Reportable transactions include: listed transactions; confidential transactions (limitation on disclosure); transactions with contractual protection (right to full or partial refund of fees); loss transactions (under §165); and transactions of interest (as identified by the IRS).

V. Earnings & Profits

A. **Overview**
Understanding the concept of earnings and profits (E&P) is key to determining the taxability of corporate distributions to shareholders, since distributions are taxable as dividends to the extent of E&P. The term "earnings and profits" is not defined explicitly in the IRC. E&P is similar to, but not the same as, retained earnings and has been defined as a corporation's "economic ability to pay dividends." There are two types of earnings and profits: current and accumulated. Accumulated E&P is the sum of all previous years' current E&P as computed on the first day of each taxable year. Even though distributions are taxable to the extent of total E&P, it is necessary to distinguish between current E&P and accumulated E&P for the following reasons.

1. **Positive Current E&P** If current E&P is positive and accumulated E&P is negative, then distributions are treated as dividends to the extent of current E&P.

2. **Negative Current E&P** If current E&P is negative and accumulated E&P is positive, then the two accounts are netted at the date of the distribution. If the net result is positive, the distribution is a dividend to the extent of net E&P. If the net result is less than or equal to zero, the distribution is a return of capital.

3. **Allocation** Current E&P is allocated on a *pro rata* basis to the distributions made during the year. On the other hand, accumulated E&P is applied to the distributions in the order that they are made.

Example 4 ▸ Earnings & Profits Allocation

X Corp. had $30,000 in accumulated E&P. During the current year, X Corp. reported earnings and profits of $20,000 and paid $50,000 in cash distributions to its shareholders in both May and October.

The current E&P balance allocated to each of the $50,000 distributions is $10,000 [$50,000 × ($20,000 / $100,000)]. Thus, only $40,000 of the $50,000 May distribution would be taxable as a dividend. For the October distribution, $10,000 would be taxable as a dividend.

4. **Computation** E&P is computed in a similar manner as taxable income, however, there are several adjustments that must be made to taxable income to arrive at E&P.

   a. **Additions to Taxable Income**

      (1) Tax-exempt income

      (2) Key-person life insurance proceeds

      (3) Charitable contributions deduction carried over from a previous year

      (4) Percentage depletion

      (5) Accelerated depreciation greater than straight-line amount

      (6) Deferred gain on an installment sale

      (7) Intangible drilling costs deducted currently

      (8) Mine exploration and development costs

   b. **Subtractions From Taxable Income**

      (1) Federal income taxes

      (2) Loss on sale between related parties

      (3) Key-person life insurance premiums

      (4) Charitable contributions made in excess of the 10% taxable income limitation

B. Distributions

Distributions can be made in cash, property, or stock. Generally, stock dividends are tax-free to the shareholder.

Example 5 ▸ Property Distributions

> Service Corporation distributed property with a basis of $50,000 and a fair market value of $100,000 to its two shareholders. Shareholder A is a 50% owner of Service Corporation and has a basis in her stock of $50,000. Shareholder B also is a 50% owner in Service Corporation and has a basis in his stock of $30,000. Service Corporation has a balance in its current E&P account of $20,000 and $40,000 in its accumulated E&P account, before considering the effect of the distribution.
>
> Service Corporation recognizes a gain of $50,000 on the distribution ($100,000 FMV – $50,000 adj. basis). Thus, current E&P increases to $70,000 ($20,000 + $50,000), while accumulated E&P remains at $40,000. E&P then is reduced by the fair market value of the distribution, which is $100,000. Thus, current E&P is reduced to $0 ($70,000 – $70,000) and accumulated E&P is reduced to $10,000 [$40,000 – ($100,000 – $70,000)]. Therefore, each shareholder receives a $50,000 taxable dividend and has a basis in the property equal to its fair market value.

1. **Effect of Property Dividend to Shareholder** When the corporation distributes property to a shareholder, the distribution is equal to the fair market value (FMV) of the property on the date of the distribution. First, the distribution is treated as a dividend to the extent of E&P. Distributions in excess of E&P are treated as a tax-free return of capital to the extent of the shareholder's basis in the corporation's stock. Distributions in excess of a shareholder's basis are treated as capital gains.

2. **Effect of Property Dividend to Corporation** When the corporation distributes property, it is treated as if it sold the property to its shareholders for the property's FMV. The corporation recognizes gain, but not loss, on the distribution. Generally the gain recognized equals the fair market less the adjusted basis. However, if the property distributed is subject to a liability, then the fair market value of the property cannot be less than the liability for gain determination purposes.

3. **Effect of Distributions on E&P** When the corporation makes a distribution, E&P is reduced by the amount of cash distributed and by the greater of the FMV or adjusted basis of any property distributed, less the amount of any liability on the property. E&P is increased by the gain recognized on any property distributed.

VI. Redemptions & Liquidations

A. Stock Redemption

If a corporation buys back its own stock from its shareholders, the transaction is treated like a sale for tax purposes. If one of the following five tests is met, the shareholder generally will recognize a capital gain or loss on the redemption. Otherwise, the redemption proceeds will be taxable as a dividend.

1. **Non-Equivalent** The redemption is not essentially equivalent to a dividend. This has been interpreted to mean that there has been a meaningful reduction in the shareholder's voting rights, share in the earnings, and share of the assets upon liquidation.

2. **Disproportionate** The redemption is substantially disproportionate. This test is met if, after the redemption, the shareholder owns less than 50% of the total number of voting shares outstanding and less than 80% of the percentage s/he owned immediately before the redemption.

3. **Entirety** All of the shareholder's stock is redeemed.

4. **Shareholder** The redemption is from a noncorporate shareholder in a partial liquidation.

5. **Death Taxes** The redemption is effected to pay death taxes.

B. Complete Liquidation

A complete liquidation is a distribution by a corporation in a single or series of transactions that redeem all of the corporation's stock.

1. **Consequences to Shareholders** Shareholders recognize gain or loss on the distribution to the extent that the money and FMV of property received (less liabilities subject to or assumed) differ from their bases in the stock.

   a. If the stock is a capital asset in the hands of the shareholder, then the distribution equals a capital gain or loss.

   b. The basis of the property received is its FMV at the date of distribution.

2. **Consequences to Corporation** Generally, the corporation recognizes gain or loss on the distribution of its assets in a complete liquidation.

   a. The gain or loss is computed as if the corporation had sold the property to the distributee at FMV.

   b. If the distributed property is subject to a liability or the shareholder assumes a liability in excess of the basis of the distributed property, FMV is deemed to be at least the amount of the liability.

   c. A corporation does not recognize gain or loss on a liquidating distribution to a controlling corporate shareholder that takes a carryover basis in the distributed property (e.g., a subsidiary is liquidated into its parent).

VII. Penalty Taxes

A. Accumulated Earnings Tax

The purpose of the accumulated earnings tax is to penalize corporations that accumulate earnings beyond the reasonable needs of the business to avoid the taxation of their shareholders. Reasonable needs for accumulation of earnings include expansion, retirement of debt, and working capital needs. The number of shareholders has no effect on whether or not the tax is imposed.

1. **Exempt** The following corporations are exempt from the tax: S Corporations, personal holding companies, foreign personal holding companies, tax-exempt organizations, and passive foreign investment companies.

2. **Credit** Corporations are allowed a credit equal to $250,000 ($150,000 for certain service corporations) plus dividends paid during the first 2½ months of the following tax year, minus accumulated E&P at the close of the preceding tax year. In other words, a corporation is allowed to accumulate up to the credit amount before it has to prove that there is a reasonable need for the accumulation.

3. **Tax Rate** The accumulated earnings tax is 15% of accumulated taxable income.

B. Personal Holding Company Tax

The purpose of the personal holding company (PHC) tax is to discourage the sheltering of certain types of passive income in corporations. Similar to the accumulated earnings tax, the personal holding company tax is designed to encourage the distribution of corporate earnings to the shareholders. If a corporation passes a gross income test and a stock ownership test, it is considered a personal holding company.

1. **Gross Income Test** This test is met if 60% or more of the corporation's adjusted ordinary gross income (AOGI) consists of certain passive income. Examples of passive PHC income include dividends, interest, rents, royalties, and personal service contracts.

2. **Stock Ownership Test** This test is met if more than 50% of the value of the outstanding stock is owned either directly or indirectly by five or fewer individuals at any time during the last half of the tax year.

3. **Penalty Tax** A corporation that is classified as a PHC must pay a penalty tax in addition to the regular corporate income tax. The PHC tax rate is 15%. The PHC tax is self-assessed by filing Form PH with the Form 1120.

4. **Consent Dividends** A corporation that meets the definition of a PHC may avoid this tax if the shareholders agree to receive consent dividends. These are hypothetical dividends on which the shareholders pay tax, even though nothing actually is received.

VIII. Corporate Reorganizations

A. Types of Reorganizations

There are seven types of corporate reorganizations.

1. **Type "A"** A statutory merger or consolidation. A merger occurs when one corporation absorbs another. A consolidation occurs when two corporations form a new corporation and the former corporations dissolve. Up to 50% of the consideration paid by the acquiring corporation can be in cash or other property, but at least 50% must be in stock to comply with the continuity of interest concept.

2. **Type "B"** The acquisition of at least 80% of the voting power of all classes of stock and at least 80% of the total number of shares of nonvoting stock in exchange for all or part of the acquiring company's voting stock. No boot may be exchanged.

3. **Type "C"** The acquisition of substantially all of the assets of a corporation in exchange for voting stock. The acquired corporation must distribute all of the consideration that it receives, as well as all of its property. "Substantially all of the assets" means at least 90% of the FMV of net assets and at least 70% of the FMV of the gross assets.

4. **Type "D"** A transfer by a corporation of all or part of its assets to another corporation if, immediately after the transfer, the transferor or at least one of its shareholders owns at least 80% of the voting power of all classes of stock and at least 80% of the nonvoting stock.

5. **Type "E"** A recapitalization where there is a major change in the character and amount of the capital structure.

6. **Type "F"** A mere change in identity, form, or place of organization.

7. **Type "G"** A bankruptcy reorganization.

B. Tax Consequences of Reorganization

A corporate reorganization is considered a mere restructuring of the form of business and is a tax-free event, except to the extent of any boot received.

1. **Gain or Loss Recognition** In a tax-free reorganization, the acquiring corporation does not recognize gain or loss, unless it transfers appreciated property to the transferor corporation. The transferor corporation does not recognize gain or loss, unless it fails to distribute other property received in the exchange or it distributes appreciated property to its shareholders.

2. **Basis** The basis of property received by the acquiring corporation from the transferor corporation is equal to the transferor's basis plus any gain recognized by the transferor on the transfer.

Example 6 ▸ Basis

Transferor Corporation transfers assets with a FMV of $75,000 and a basis of $20,000 to Acquiring Corporation for $75,000 worth of stock in Acquiring Corporation. This qualifies as a type "D" reorganization. Neither corporation recognizes a gain on the exchange. Transferor Corporation's basis in the Acquiring Corporation's stock is $20,000.

Example 7 ▸ Gain or Loss Recognition

The same facts as in Example 6 except that Acquiring Corporation transfers stock worth $50,000 and property with a FMV of $25,000 and a basis of $10,000. In this case, Acquiring Corporation will recognize a gain of $15,000. If Transferor Corporation does not distribute the property, it will have to recognize a gain equal to the lesser of the gain realized or $25,000.

IX. Affiliated & Controlled Corporations

A. Comparison

A controlled group refers to both parent-subsidiary and brother-sister corporations, while an affiliated group includes only parent-subsidiary corporations.

1. **Parent-Subsidiary Relationship** A parent-subsidiary relationship exists within an affiliated group when one corporation (the parent) owns 80% of the total voting power of all classes of stock **and** 80% of the value of nonvoting stock of another corporation (the subsidiary). This relationship exists within a controlled group when one corporation (the parent) owns 80% of the total voting power of all classes of stock **or** 80% of the total value of all classes of stock.

2. **Brother-Sister Relationship** A brother-sister relationship exists within a controlled group. A controlled group contains two or more corporations with five or fewer persons who are individuals, estates, or trusts owning either more than 50% of the total combined voting power of all classes of voting stock or more than 50% of the total value of all stock.

B. Controlled Group Characteristics

1. **Treatment** The members are treated as one corporation for purposes of the first $75,000 of taxable income being taxed at less than 34%, the accumulated earnings credit, the AMTI exemption, the Section 179 expense deduction, etc.

2. **Loss** Losses realized on intercompany sales are disallowed; however, if property subsequently is sold to an unrelated third party at a gain, the gain is reduced by the amount of any previously disallowed loss.

3. **Gain** Any gain recognized on an intercompany sale of depreciable property must be recognized as ordinary income.

C. Affiliated Group Characteristics

The members may elect to file a consolidated tax return. Advantages of filing a consolidated return include using the losses from one entity to offset income from another entity in the consolidated group, as well as income elimination and gain deferral. Once the election is made, it is binding on all future returns.

1. **Eliminations** If a consolidated return is filed, intercompany dividends are eliminated. If separate returns are filed, dividends from affiliated corporations are eligible for the 100% dividend-received deduction.

2. **Gain Deferral** The filing of a consolidated return enables the members of the affiliated group to defer any gains on intercompany profits.

X. S Corporations

A. S Status Election

An S corporation has the advantage of being classified as a corporation while generally being taxed at the shareholder level instead of at the corporate level. All current shareholders, plus any shareholders who held stock during the taxable year before the date of the election, must consent to the election.

1. **Due Date** To be valid for the current year, the election may be made on Form 2553 either (a) during the preceding year, or (b) on or before the 15th day of the third month of the current taxable year. A late election is considered an election for the subsequent year. Small businesses that missed filing Form 2553 before filing their first Form 1120S, *U.S. Income Tax Return for an S Corporation*, may file both forms simultaneously.

2. **Ineffective Election** If the election is ineffective at the time it is made (e.g., a shareholder failed to consent or the corporation had too many shareholders) but the situation is corrected after the election date, it is considered an election for the subsequent year.

B. Eligibility

1. **Number of Shareholders** No more than 100 shareholders. Family members (spouses, ancestors, or lineal descendents) may elect to be treated as one shareholder. Each beneficiary of a voting trust is considered a shareholder.

2. **Class of Stock** Only one class of stock is allowed. A corporation with shares of stock that differ solely in voting rights will not be treated as having more than one class of stock. All stockholders must share in all distributions and liquidations proportionately.

3. **Eligible Shareholders** Shareholders may be individuals, estates (testamentary and bankruptcy), and trusts including the following: (a) grantor trusts during the life of the grantor plus 60 days, or plus 2 years if the trust is includable in the grantor's gross estate, (b) testamentary trusts for 60 days after the stock is transferred to the trust, (c) stock voting trusts, (d) qualified Subchapter S trusts, or (e) electing small business trusts. Tax-exempt entities may be S corporation shareholders. Nonresident aliens, corporations, and foreign trusts may not be shareholders.

4. **Ineligible Corporations** Ineligible corporations generally include members of affiliated groups, some corporations owning 80% subsidiaries, financial institutions, insurance companies, companies electing the possessions tax credit, and Domestic International Sales Corporations (DISCs). Certain banks that do not use the reserve method of accounting for bad debts may elect S status. S corporations may own certain 80% subsidiaries.

C. Taxable Year

An S corporation generally is required to adopt a December 31 year end or a fiscal year that is the same as the fiscal year used by shareholders owning more than 50% of the corporation's stock.

1. **Fiscal Year** If a valid business purpose exists, an S corporation may ask for IRS approval to adopt a different fiscal year. A valid business purpose exists if for three consecutive years at least 25% of the S corporation's gross receipts are received in the last two months of the selected fiscal year.

2. **Payment** An S corporation may elect under Section 444 to use a fiscal year as long as the fiscal year does not result in a deferral period that is greater than 3 months. If an S corporation elects to use a fiscal year under Section 444, then it must make required payments to the IRS every year. In essence, this required payment is a refundable, noninterest-bearing deposit that is intended to compensate the government for the revenue lost as a result of the tax deferral. The payment is determined by a formula and is due on May 15 each year. This payment must be recomputed each year. Note that if for any year the required payment is $500 or less, the S corporation is exempted from making the payment for that year.

D. **Computation of Taxable Income**

In general, S corporations pass items of income, loss, deductions, and credits through to their shareholders. Consequently, taxes on S corporation income generally are paid at the shareholder level instead of at the corporate level. S corporations file Form 1120S instead of Form 1120. Form 1120S is due on the 15th day of the third month following the end of the tax year. For a calendar year S corporation, the due date is March 15th. The return is an informational return that reports total corporate income and each shareholder's *pro rata* share of this income. Shareholders then pay tax on their *pro rata* share of S corporation income regardless of whether or not any income actually was distributed to them. There are two types of income that are passed through to shareholders: nonseparately stated income and separately stated income.

1. **Nonseparately Stated** This type of income is netted with expenses at the corporate level and then passed through to shareholders. It consists of ordinary income such as income derived from the active conduct of business and depreciation deductions recaptured as ordinary income. This income is reported on page 1 of Form 1120S.

2. **Separately Stated** This income retains its original character as it passes through to the shareholders. Any limitations are computed at the shareholder level instead of at the corporate level.

   a. This income is reported in total on Schedule K and each shareholder receives a Schedule K-1 which denotes her/his *pro rata* share of S corporation income.

   b. Examples of separately stated income include: capital gains and losses; Section 1231 gains and losses; tax-exempt interest income; foreign income, losses, and taxes; passive gains, losses, and credits; interest and dividend income; royalty income; Section 179 expense deduction; tax preferences; depletion; investment income and expenses; charitable contributions; net income or loss from real estate activity; and net income or loss from rental activity.

3. ***Pro Rata* Share** A shareholder's *pro rata* share of each corporate item is computed on a daily basis according to the number of shares of stock held by the shareholder on each day of the corporation's taxable year.

   a. If stock changes hands on a particular day, it is considered owned by the transferee on that day. If the relative interests of the shareholders do not change during the year, a daily calculation is not necessary.

   b. If a shareholder terminates her/his interest, there is an election available to allocate S corporation income as if the taxable year ended on the date the shareholder's interest was terminated.

4. **Corporate Level Taxation** There are some instances in which the S corporation is required to pay taxes at the corporate level. Examples include excess passive investment income, LIFO recapture, and built-in gains (the excess of the FMV of assets over their bases at the beginning of the first year in which the S corporation is effective).

E. **Deduction of Losses**

A shareholder may not be able to deduct her/his entire share of corporate losses currently because there are basis, at-risk, and passive loss limitations.

1. **Basis Limitations** A shareholder is not allowed to deduct losses in excess of her/his basis in the S corporation's stock and debt. Losses first reduce a shareholder's basis in the stock of the S corporation. Once this basis is reduced to zero, any additional losses reduce the shareholder's basis in S corporation debt. Any losses that are not currently deductible are carried over until the shareholder has sufficient basis to absorb the losses. A shareholder's initial basis in the corporation's stock is increased by the shareholder's *pro rata* share of nonseparately stated income, separately stated income, and depletion in excess of basis in the

property. In addition to the shareholder's *pro rata* share of losses, basis in stock is reduced by separately stated deduction items, distributions not reported as income by the shareholder (AAA distributions), and nondeductible expenses of the corporation. Debt basis is restored (up to the original amount) before basis is restored in stock.

2. **At-Risk Rules** Generally, a shareholder is considered at risk with respect to an activity to the extent of cash and the adjusted basis of other property contributed to the activity plus amounts borrowed with respect to the activity, to the extent the taxpayer is personally liable for the repayment or has pledged property not used in the activity that is used as security for the borrowed amount.

3. **Passive Loss Rules** A shareholder can deduct passive losses only to the extent of passive income. Any losses that are not currently deductible are carried forward until there is sufficient passive income to absorb them or the ultimate disposal of the passive activity. The basis and at-risk limitations are applied before the passive loss limitations.

F. **Accumulated Adjustments Account (AAA)**

This account is the cumulative total of undistributed net income items for S corporation taxable years beginning after 1982. Prior to 1982, S corporations had earnings and profits similar to C corporations. The adjustments made to AAA are similar to those made to the shareholders' stock bases, except that there is no adjustment for tax-exempt income and related expenses or for federal taxes paid attributable to a C corporation tax year. Tax-exempt income and related expenses are reported in the Other Adjustments Account (OAA). For shareholder contributions made after December 31, 2005, an AAA adjustment is required to reflect the shareholder's adjusted basis in contributed property (instead of FMV). Unlike a shareholder's stock basis, AAA can have a negative balance. In addition, any decreases in stock basis have no impact on AAA when AAA is negative. The AAA balance is computed at the end of the taxable year.

G. **Distributions to Shareholder**

The amount of any distribution to a shareholder is equal to the cash plus the FMV of any property received. Distributions are deemed to occur on the last day of the year. There are two sets of rules that apply to distributions depending on whether or not the S corporation has accumulated E&P.

1. **S Corporation Without Accumulated E&P** The distributions are tax-free to the extent of the shareholder's basis in the stock of the S corporation. Any excess distributions are treated as gain from the sale of stock.

2. **S Corporation With Accumulated E&P** The tax consequences of the distributions follow a layered approach. First distributions are made out of AAA. These are tax-free to the extent of AAA (limited to the shareholder's basis in the stock). The distribution reduces both AAA and the shareholders' bases in their stock. The AAA balance is computed at the end of the tax year, not when the distribution is made. If more than one distribution is made during the year, a *pro rata* portion of each distribution is treated as made from AAA. After AAA is exhausted, the distribution is tax-free to the extent of any previously taxed income (PTI) from pre-1983 tax years if the distribution is made in cash. Once PTI is exhausted, the distribution is a dividend to the extent of accumulated E&P. Once accumulated E&P is used up, any remaining amounts are treated as a tax-free return of capital. Any distributions in excess of the shareholder's basis in the stock are treated as gains from the sale of stock.

H. **Fringe Benefits**

Fringe benefits provided to a more than 2% shareholder-employee must be included in that shareholder's gross income and are deductible by the S corporation. Accident and health premiums paid by the S corporation for a more than 2% shareholder are deductible by the corporation and included in the income of the shareholder, but they are not treated as wages for FICA purposes.

I. S Status Termination

Termination of S corporation status may be by the failure to satisfy the eligibility requirements, by the receipt of excess passive investment income, or by voluntary termination.

1. **Revocation** Revocation may be made by the consent of shareholders collectively owning a majority of the stock. The revocation may specify any prospective revocation date. If no date is specified, the revocation is retroactive to the first day of the taxable year if made on or before the 15th day of the third month of the year; otherwise, it is effective the first day of the subsequent year.

2. **Effective Date** If S status is terminated due to failure to satisfy an eligibility requirement, the termination is effective as of the date the eligibility requirement was violated.

3. **Passive Investment Income** Termination will occur if the S corporation has passive investment income exceeding 25% of its gross receipts for each of three consecutive years **and,** if during these three years, the corporation was a corporation with accumulated earnings and profits attributable to prior C corporation status. Passive investment income includes receipts from rents, royalties, dividends, interest, annuities, and the gain from sales or exchanges of stock or securities. The termination is effective as of the first day of the fourth taxable year.

4. **Re-Election** Once S status has been terminated, it cannot be re-elected for five years unless permission for an earlier re-election is granted by the IRS. If S status is terminated inadvertently, and the situation is corrected, the IRS may treat the event as if it had never occurred.

CPA Exam Week Checklist

Pack for exam week:

1. CPA exam registration material, Notice to Schedule, and two eligible forms of matching identification.
2. An inexpensive watch that may be left in the testing site locker.
3. Cash and/or a major credit card.
4. Alarm clock—Don't rely on a hotel wake-up call.
5. Comfortable clothing that can be loosened to suit varying temperatures.
6. Healthy snack foods.
7. Hotel confirmation, if traveling.

Evening before exam:

1. Read through your Bisk Education chapter outlines for the next day's section(s).
2. Eat lightly and monitor your intake of alcohol and caffeine. Get a good night's rest.
3. Do **not** try to cram. A brief review of your notes will help to focus your attention on important points and remind you that you are well prepared, but too much cramming can shatter your self-confidence. If you have reviewed conscientiously, you already are well-prepared for the CPA exam.

Day of exam:

1. Eat a satisfying breakfast or lunch. It will be several hours before your next meal. Eat enough to ward off hunger, but not so much that you feel sleepy or uncomfortable.
2. Dress appropriately. Wear layers you can loosen to suit varying temperatures in the room.
3. Arrive at the exam center at least 30 minutes early. Check in as soon as you are allowed to do so.

More helpful exam information is included in the **Practical Advice** appendix in this volume.

CHAPTER 46—FEDERAL TAXATION: CORPORATIONS

Problem 46-1 MULTIPLE CHOICE QUESTIONS (120 to 160 minutes)

Items 1 through 3 are based on the following:

Lind and Post organized Ace Corp., which issued voting common stock with a fair market value of $120,000. They each transferred property in exchange for stock as follows:

	Property	Adjusted basis	Fair market value	Percentage of Ace stock acquired
Lind	Building	$40,000	$82,000	60%
Post	Land	$ 5,000	$48,000	40%

The building was subject to a $10,000 mortgage that was assumed by Ace.

1. What amount of gain did Lind recognize on the exchange?
a. $0
b. $10,000
c. $42,000
d. $52,000 (11/96, AR, #8, amended, 6301)

2. What was Ace's basis in the building?
a. $30,000
b. $40,000
c. $72,000
d. $82,000 (11/96, AR, #9, amended, 6302)

3. What was Lind's basis in Ace stock?
a. $82,000
b. $40,000
c. $30,000
d. $0 (11/96, AR, #10, amended, 6303)

4. Jones incorporated a sole proprietorship by exchanging all the proprietorship's assets for the stock of Nu Co., a new corporation. To qualify for tax-free incorporation, Jones must be in control of Nu immediately after the exchange. What percentage of Nu's stock must Jones own to qualify as "control" for this purpose?
a. 50.00%
b. 51.00%
c. 66.67%
d. 80.00% (11/93, PII, #45, 4474)

5. Feld, the sole stockholder of Maki Corp., paid $50,000 for Maki's stock in Year 1. In Year 2, Feld contributed a parcel of land to Maki but was not given any additional stock for this contribution. Feld's basis for the land was $10,000, and its fair market value was $18,000 on the date of the transfer of title. What is Feld's adjusted basis for the Maki stock?
a. $50,000
b. $52,000
c. $60,000
d. $68,000 (11/92, PII, #19, amended, 3353)

6. Adams, Beck, and Carr organized Flexo Corp. with authorized voting common stock of $100,000. Adams received 10% of the capital stock in payment for the organizational services that he rendered for the benefit of the newly formed corporation. Adams did not contribute property to Flexo and was under no obligation to be paid by Beck or Carr. Beck and Carr transferred property in exchange for stock as follows:

	Adjusted basis	Fair market value	Percentage of Flexo stock acquired
Beck	5,000	20,000	20%
Carr	60,000	70,000	70%

What amount of gain did Carr recognize from this transaction?
a. $40,000
b. $15,000
c. $10,000
d. $0 (11/94, AR, #52, 5028)

7. Jackson Corp., a calendar year corporation, mailed its Year 1 tax return to the Internal Revenue Service by certified mail on Friday, March 10, Year 2. The return, postmarked March 10, Year 2, was delivered to the Internal Revenue Service on March 20, Year 2. The statute of limitations on Jackson's corporate tax return begins on
a. December 31, Year 1
b. March 10, Year 2
c. March 16, Year 2
d. March 20, Year 2 (11/94, AR, #54, amended, 5030)

8. A civil fraud penalty can be imposed on a corporation that underpays tax by
a. Omitting income as a result of inadequate recordkeeping
b. Failing to report income it erroneously considered **not** to be part of corporate profits
c. Maintaining false records and reporting fictitious transactions to minimize corporate tax liability
d. Filing an incomplete return with an appended statement, making clear that the return is incomplete (11/95, AR, #16, amended, 5760)

9. A corporation's tax year can be reopened after all statutes of limitations have expired if

I. The tax return has a 50% nonfraudulent omission from gross income.
II. The corporation prevails in a determination allowing a deduction in an open tax year that was taken erroneously in a closed tax year.

a. I only
b. II only
c. Both I and II
d. Neither I nor II (11/95, AR, #25, 5769)

10. Edge Corp., a calendar year C corporation, had a net operating loss and zero tax liability for its Year 0 tax year. To avoid the penalty for underpayment of estimated taxes, Edge could compute its first quarter Year 1 estimated income tax payment using the

	Annualized income method	*Preceding year method*
a.	Yes	Yes
b.	Yes	No
c.	No	Yes
d.	No	No

(11/95, AR, #24, amended, 5768)

11. When computing a corporation's income tax expense for estimated income tax purposes, which of the following should be taken into account?

	Corporate tax credits	*Alternative minimum tax*
a.	No	No
b.	No	Yes
c.	Yes	No
d.	Yes	Yes

(11/93, PII, #43, 4472)

12. Bass Corp., a calendar year C corporation, made qualifying Year 1 estimated tax deposits based on its actual Year 0 tax liability. On March 15, Year 2, Bass filed a timely automatic extension request for its Year 1 corporate income tax return. Estimated tax deposits and the extension payment totaled $7,600. This amount was 95% of the total tax shown on Bass' final Year 1 corporate income tax return. Bass paid $400 additional tax on the final Year 1 corporate income tax return filed before the extended due date. For calendar Year 1, Bass was subject to pay

I. Interest on the $400 tax payment made in Year 2
II. A tax delinquency penalty

a. I only
b. II only
c. Both I and II
d. Neither I nor II (11/95, AR, #23, amended, 5767)

13. Which of the following is subject to the Uniform Capitalization Rules of Code §263A?
a. Editorial costs incurred by a freelance writer
b. Research and experimental expenditures
c. Mine development and exploration costs
d. Warehousing costs incurred by a manufacturing company with $12 million in annual gross receipts (R/07, REG, C03295R, #35, 8459)

14. Micro Corp., a calendar year, accrual basis corporation, purchased a 5-year, 8%, $100,000 taxable corporate bond for $108,530, on July 1, Year 1, the date the bond was issued. The bond paid interest semiannually. For Micro's tax return, the bond premium amortization for Year 1 should be

I. Computed under the constant yield to maturity method
II. Treated as an offset to the interest income on the bond

a. Neither I nor II
b. Both I and II
c. I only
d. II only (11/94, AR, #35, amended, 5012)

15. Axis Corp. is an accrual basis calendar year corporation. On December 13, Year 1, the Board of Directors declared a two percent of profits bonus to all employees for services rendered during Year 1 and notified them in writing. None of the employees own stock in Axis. The amount represents reasonable compensation for services rendered and was paid on March 10, Year 2. Axis' bonus expense may

a. Not be deducted on Axis' tax return because payment is a disguised dividend
b. Be deducted on Axis' Year 1 tax return
c. Be deducted on Axis' Year 2 tax return
d. Not be deducted on Axis' Year 1 tax return because the per share employee amount **cannot** be determined with reasonable accuracy at the time of the declaration of the bonus

(11/94, AR, #36, amended, 5013)

16. In Year 1, Stewart Corp. properly accrued $5,000 for an income item on the basis of a reasonable estimate. In Year 2, after filing its Year 1 federal income tax return, Stewart determined that the exact amount was $6,000. Which of the following statements is correct?

a. No further inclusion of income is required as the difference is less than 25% of the original amount reported and the estimate had been made in good faith.
b. The $1,000 difference is includible in Stewart's Year 2 income tax return.
c. Stewart is required to file an amended return to report the additional $1,000 of income.
d. Stewart is required to notify the IRS within 30 days of the determination of the exact amount of the item. (11/95, AR, #10, amended, 5754)

17. In the case of a corporation that is **not** a financial institution, which of the following statements is correct with regard to the deduction for bad debts?

a. Either the reserve method or the direct charge-off method may be used, if the election is made in the corporation's first taxable year.
b. On approval from the IRS, a corporation may change its method from direct charge-off to reserve.
c. If the reserve method was consistently used in prior years, the corporation may take a deduction for a reasonable addition to the reserve for bad debts.
d. A corporation is required to use the direct charge-off method rather than the reserve method.

(11/91, PII, #47, 2495)

18. Rame Corp.'s operating income for Year 1 amounted to $100,000. In Year 1, a machine owned by Rame was completely destroyed in an accident. This machine's adjusted basis immediately before the casualty was $30,000. The machine was not insured and had no salvage value. In Rame's Year 1 tax return, what amount should be deducted for the casualty loss?

a. $ 5,000
b. $ 5,400
c. $29,900
d. $30,000 (Editors, 1688)

19. For the first tax year in which a corporation has qualifying research and experimental expenditures, the corporation

a. Has a choice of either deducting such expenditures as current business expenses, or capitalizing these expenditures
b. Has to treat such expenditures in the same manner as they are accounted for in the corporation's financial statements
c. Is required to deduct such expenditures currently as business expenses or lose the deductions
d. Is required to capitalize such expenditures and amortize them ratably over a period of not less than 60 months (Editors, 1689)

20. Pierce Corp., an accrual-basis, calendar-year C corporation, had the following Year 1 receipts:

Year 2 advance rental payments for a lease ending in Year 3	$250,000
Lease cancellation payment from a five year lease tenant	100,000

Pierce had no restrictions on the use of the advance rental payments and renders no services in connection with the rental income. What amount of gross income should Pierce report on its Year 1 tax return?

a. $350,000
b. $250,000
c. $100,000
d. $0 (11/98, AR, #11, amended, 6677)

21. Which of the following taxpayers may use the cash method of accounting?

a. A tax shelter
b. A qualified personal service corporation
c. A C corporation with annual gross receipts of $50,000,000
d. A manufacturer (R/01, AR, #29, 7014)

22. Banks Corp., a calendar year corporation, provides meals for employees for its own convenience. The employees are present at the meals, which are neither lavish nor extravagant, and the reimbursement is not treated as wages subject to withholdings. For the current year, what percentage of the meal expense may Banks deduct?
a. 0%
b. 50%
c. 80%
d. 100% (11/94, AR, #31, 5008)

23. Haze Corp., an accrual-basis, calendar-year C corporation, began business on January 1, Year 5 and incurred the following costs:

Underwriting fees to issue corporate stock	$ 2,000
Legal fees to draft the corporate charter	16,000

Haze elected to amortize its organization costs. What was the maximum amount of the costs that Haze could deduct for tax purposes on its first calendar year income tax return?
a. $0
b. $3,200
c. $3,600
d. $5,000 (11/98, AR, #10, amended, 6676)

24. A corporation may reduce its regular income tax by taking a tax credit for
a. Dividends-received exclusion
b. Foreign income taxes
c. State income taxes
d. Accelerated depreciation (11/95, AR, #17, 5761)

25. In Year 1, Best Corp., an accrual-basis calendar year C corporation, received $100,000 in dividend income from the common stock that it held in an unrelated domestic corporation. The stock was not debt-financed, and was held for over a year. Best recorded the following information for Year 1:

Loss from Best's operations	$ (10,000)
Dividends received	100,000
Taxable income (before dividends-received deduction)	$ 90,000

Best's dividends-received deduction on its Year 1 tax return was
a. $100,000
b. $ 80,000
c. $ 70,000
d. $ 63,000 (11/95, AR, #4, amended, 5748)

26. In the current year, Acorn Inc. had the following items of income and expense:

Sales	$500,000
Cost of sales	250,000
Dividends received	25,000

The dividends were received from a corporation of which Acorn owns 30%. In Acorn's corporate income tax return, what amount should be reported as income before special deductions?
a. $525,000
b. $505,000
c. $275,000
d. $250,000 (5/93, PII, #41, amended, 4147)

27. Kisco Corp.'s taxable income before taking the dividends received deduction was $70,000. This includes $10,000 in dividends from an unrelated taxable domestic corporation. Given the following tax rates, what would Kisco's income tax be before any credits?

Partial rate table	Tax rate
Up to $50,000	15%
Over $50,000 but not over $75,000	25%

a. $10,000
b. $10,750
c. $12,500
d. $15,750 (5/94, AR, #24, amended, 4629)

28. Mell Corporation's $55,000 income before income taxes includes $10,000 of life insurance policy proceeds. The life insurance policy proceeds represent a lump-sum payment in full as a result of the death of Mell's controller. Mell was the owner and beneficiary of this policy. In its income tax return, Mell should report taxable life insurance proceeds of
a. $10,000
b. $ 8,000
c. $ 5,000
d. $0 (Editors, 8050)

29. In a C corporation's computation of the maximum allowable deduction for contributions, what percentage limitation should be applied to the applicable base amount?
a. 5%
b. 10%
c. 30%
d. 50% (11/91, PII, #46, 2494)

30. Tapper Corp., an accrual-basis calendar-year corporation, was organized on January 2, Year 1. During Year 1, revenue was exclusively from sales proceeds and interest income. The following information pertains to Tapper:

Taxable income before charitable contributions for Year 1	$500,000
Tapper's matching contribution to employee-designated qualified universities made during Year 1	10,000
Board of Directors' authorized contribution to a qualified charity (authorized December 1, Year 1, made February 1, Year 2)	30,000

What is the maximum allowable deduction that Tapper may take as a charitable contribution on its tax return for the year ended December 31, Year 1?

a. $0
b. $10,000
c. $30,000
d. $40,000 (11/94, AR, #37, amended, 5014)

31. If a corporation's charitable contributions exceed the limitation for deductibility in a particular year, the excess

a. Is **not** deductible in any future or prior year
b. May be carried back or forward for one year at the corporation's election
c. May be carried forward to a maximum of five succeeding years
d. May be carried back to the third preceding year (11/95, AR, #9, 5753)

32. In Year 1, Cable Corp., a calendar year C corporation, contributed $80,000 to a qualified charitable organization. Cable's Year 1 taxable income before the deduction for charitable contributions was $820,000 after a $40,000 dividends-received deduction. Cable also had carryover contributions of $10,000 from Year 0. In Year 1, what amount can Cable deduct as charitable contributions?

a. $90,000
b. $86,000
c. $82,000
d. $80,000 (11/95, AR, #8, amended, 5752)

33. Batik is a C corporation with average gross receipts of $20 million. How are Batik's net capital losses used?

a. Deducted from the corporation's ordinary income only to the extent of $3,000
b. Carried back three years and forward five years
c. Carried forward 20 years
d. Deductible in full from the corporation's ordinary income (11/97, AR, #5, amended, 6533)

34. Taylor Corporation has existed since Year 1. For the calendar Year 6, Taylor Corp. had a net operating loss of $200,000. Taylor's average gross receipts for the last three years are $30 million. Taxable income for the earlier years of corporate existence, computed without reference to the net operating loss, was as follows:

	Taxable income
Year 1	$ 5,000
Year 2	$10,000
Year 3	$20,000
Year 4	$30,000
Year 5	$40,000

If Taylor makes **no** special election to waive the net operating loss carryback, what amount of net operating loss will be available to Taylor for Year 7?

a. $200,000
b. $130,000
c. $ 95,000
d. $ 5,000 (11/94, AR, #33, amended, 5010)

35. A corporation's capital loss carryback or carryover is

a. Not allowable under current law
b. Limited to $3,000
c. Always treated as a long-term capital loss
d. Always treated as a short-term capital loss (11/91, PII, #41, 2489)

36. Tan Corp. calculated the following taxes for the current year:

Regular tax liability	$210,000
Tentative minimum tax	240,000
Personal holding company tax	65,000

What is Tan's total tax liability for the year?

a. $210,000
b. $240,000
c. $275,000
d. $305,000 (R/05, REG, 1080T, #20, 7866)

37. Bent Corp., a calendar-year C corporation, purchased and placed into service residential real property during February. No other property was placed into service during the year. What convention must Bent use to determine the depreciation deduction for the alternative minimum tax?

a. Full-year
b. Half-year
c. Mid-quarter
d. Mid-month (R/00, AR, #7, amended, 6912)

38. Rona Corp.'s alternative minimum taxable income was $200,000. The exempt portion of Rona's alternative minimum taxable income was
a. $0
b. $12,500
c. $27,500
d. $52,500 (5/91, PII, #55, amended, 1647)

39. Eastern Corp., a calendar year corporation, was formed January 3, Year 0, and on that date placed five-year property in service. The property was depreciated under the general MACRS system. Eastern did not elect to use the straight-line method. In Year 0, Eastern had gross receipts of $6,000,000 and taxable income of $300,000. The following information pertains to Eastern:

Adjustment for the accelerated depreciation taken on Year 0 five-year property	1,000
Year 0 tax-exempt interest from specified private activity bonds issued after August 7, 1986	5,000

What was Eastern's alternative minimum taxable income before the adjusted current earnings (ACE) adjustment?
a. $306,000
b. $305,000
c. $304,000
d. $301,000 (11/95, AR, #15, amended, 5759)

40. On January 2, Year 1, Shaw Corp., an accrual-basis, calendar-year C corporation, purchased all the assets of a sole proprietorship, including $300,000 in goodwill. Federal income tax expense of $110,100 and $7,500 for impairment of goodwill were deducted to arrive at Shaw's reported book income of $239,200. What should be the amount of Shaw's Year 1 taxable income, as reconciled on Shaw's Schedule M-1 of Form 1120, U.S. Corporation Income Tax Return?
a. $239,200
b. $329,300
c. $336,800
d. $349,300 (R/99, AR, #5, amended, 6794)

41. In Year 1, Cape Co. reported book income of $140,000. Included in that amount was $50,000 for meals and entertainment expense and $40,000 for federal income tax expense. In Cape's Schedule M-1 of Form 1120, which reconciles book income and taxable income, what amount should be reported as Year 1 taxable income?
a. $205,000
b. $180,000
c. $165,000
d. $140,000 (11/93, PII, #42, amended, 4471)

42. Media Corp. is an accrual-basis, calendar-year C corporation. Its reported book income included $6,000 in municipal bond interest income. Its expenses included $1,500 of interest incurred on indebtedness used to carry municipal bonds and $8,000 in advertising expense. What is Media's net M-1 adjustment on its Form 1120, U.S. Corporation Income Tax Return, to reconcile to its taxable income?
a. $(4,500)
b. $ 1,500
c. $ 3,500
d. $ 9,500 (11/98, AR, #9, amended, 6675)

43. The following information pertains to Dahl Corp.:

Accumulated earnings and profits at January 1, Year 0	$120,000
Earnings and profits for the year ended December 31, Year 0	160,000
Cash distributions to individual stock holders during Year 0	360,000

What is the total amount of distributions taxable as dividend income to Dahl's stockholders in Year 0?
a. $0
b. $160,000
c. $280,000
d. $360,000 (11/95, AR, #19, amended, 5763)

44. Kent Corp. is a calendar year, accrual basis C corporation. In Year 1, Kent made a nonliquidating distribution of property with an adjusted basis of $150,000 and a fair market value of $200,000 to Reed, its sole shareholder. The following information pertains to Kent:

Reed's basis in Kent stock at January 1, Year 1	$500,000
Accumulated earnings and profits at January 1, Year 1	125,000
Current earnings and profits for Year 1	60,000

What was taxable as dividend income to Reed for Year 1?
a. $ 60,000
b. $150,000
c. $185,000
d. $200,000 (5/95, AR, #24, amended, 5442)

45. A corporation that has both preferred and common stock has a deficit in accumulated earnings and profits at the beginning of the year. The current earnings and profits are $25,000. The corporation makes a dividend distribution of $20,000 to the preferred shareholders and $10,000 to the common shareholders. How will the preferred and common shareholders report these distributions?

a. Preferred - $20,000 dividend income; common - $10,000 dividend income
b. Preferred - $20,000 dividend income; common - $5,000 dividend income, $5,000 return of capital
c. Preferred - $15,000 dividend income; common - $10,000 dividend income
d. Preferred - $20,000 return of capital; common - $10,000 return of capital (R/07, REG, A1256T, #17, 8441)

46. How does a noncorporate shareholder treat the gain on a redemption of stock that qualifies as a partial liquidation of the distributing corporation?

a. Entirely as capital gain
b. Entirely as a dividend
c. Partly as capital gain and partly as a dividend
d. As a tax-free transaction (11/89, PII, #52, 1665)

47. A corporation was completely liquidated and dissolved during the current year. The filing fees, professional fees, and other expenditures incurred in connection with the liquidation and dissolution are

a. Deductible in full by the dissolved corporation
b. Deductible by the shareholders and **not** by the corporation
c. Treated as capital losses by the corporation
d. Not deductible by either the corporation or the shareholders (R/03, REG, 0794T, #11, 7653)

48. Mintee Corp., an accrual-basis calendar-year C corporation, had no corporate shareholders when it liquidated in Year 0. In cancellation of all their Mintee stock, each Mintee shareholder received in Year 0, a liquidating distribution of $2,000 cash and land with a tax basis of $5,000 and a fair market value of $10,500. Before the distribution, each shareholder's tax basis in Mintee stock was $6,500. What amount of gain should each Mintee shareholder recognize on the liquidating distribution?

a. $0
b. $ 500
c. $4,000
d. $6,000 (11/97, AR, #7, amended, 6535)

49. Par Corp. acquired the assets of its wholly owned subsidiary, Sub Corp., under a plan that qualified as a tax-free complete liquidation of Sub. Which of the following of Sub's unused carryovers may be transferred to Par?

	Excess charitable contributions	*Net operating loss*
a.	No	Yes
b.	Yes	No
c.	No	No
d.	Yes	Yes

(11/91, PII, #45, 2493)

50. Krol Corp. distributed marketable securities in redemption of its stock in a complete liquidation. On the date of distribution, these securities had a basis of $100,000 and a fair market value of $150,000. What gain does Krol have as a result of the distribution?

a. $0
b. $50,000 capital gain
c. $50,000 Section 1231 gain
d. $50,000 ordinary gain (5/90, PII, #28, 1652)

51. Dart Corp., a calendar year domestic C corporation, is not a personal holding company. For purposes of the accumulated earnings tax, Dart has accumulated taxable income for Year 0. Which step(s) can Dart take to eliminate or reduce any Year 0 accumulated earnings tax?

I. Demonstrate that the "reasonable needs" of its business require the retention of all or part of the Year 0 accumulated taxable income
II. Pay dividends by March 15, Year 1

a. I only
b. II only
c. Both I and II
d. Neither I nor II (11/95, AR, #14, amended, 5758)

52. The accumulated earnings tax can be imposed

a. On both partnerships and corporations
b. On companies that make distributions in excess of accumulated earnings
c. On personal holding companies
d. Regardless of the number of stockholders in a corporation (11/95, AR, #18, 5762)

53. Kari Corp., a manufacturing company, was organized on January 2, Year 0. Its Year 0 federal taxable income was $400,000 and its federal income tax was $100,000. What is the maximum amount of accumulated taxable income that may be subject to the accumulated earnings tax for Year 0 if Kari takes only the minimum accumulated earnings credit?
a. $300,000
b. $150,000
c. $ 50,000
d. $0 (5/93, PII, #55, amended, 4160)

54. Kane Corp. is a calendar year domestic personal holding company. Which deduction(s) must Kane make from Year 0 taxable income to determine undistributed personal holding company income prior to the dividend-paid deduction?

	Federal income taxes	*Net long-term capital gain less related federal income taxes*
a.	Yes	Yes
b.	Yes	No
c.	No	Yes
d.	No	No

(11/95, AR, #12, amended, 5756)

55. The following information pertains to Hull, Inc., a personal holding company, for the year ended December 31, Year 0:

Undistributed personal holding company income	$100,000
Dividends paid during Year 0	20,000
Consent dividends reported in the Year 0 individual income tax returns of the holders of Hull's common stock, but not paid by Hull to its stockholders	10,000

In computing its Year 0 personal holding company tax, what amount should Hull deduct for dividends paid?
a. $0
b. $10,000
c. $20,000
d. $30,000 (5/91, PII, #54, amended, 1646)

56. Edge Corp. met the stock ownership requirements of a personal holding company. What sources of income must Edge consider to determine if the income requirements for a personal holding company has been met?

I. Interest earned on tax-exempt obligations
II. Dividends received from an unrelated domestic corporation

a. I only
b. II only
c. Both I and II
d. Neither I nor II (5/95, AR, #23, 5441)

57. Zero Corp. is an investment company authorized to issue only common stock. During the last half of the current year, Edwards owned 450 of the 1,000 outstanding shares of stock in Zero. Another 350 shares of stock outstanding were owned, 10 shares each, by 35 shareholders who are neither related to each other nor to Edwards. Zero could be a personal holding company if the remaining 200 shares of common stock were owned by
a. An estate where Edwards is the beneficiary
b. Edwards' brother-in-law
c. A partnership where Edwards is **not** a partner
d. Edwards' cousin
(11/94, AR, #45, amended, 8052)

58. Keen Holding Corp. has 80 unrelated equal stockholders. For the year ended December 31, Keen's income comprised the following:

Net rental income	$1,000
Commissions earned on sales of franchises	2,000
Dividends from taxable domestic corporations	9,000

Deductible expenses for the year totaled $10,000. Keen paid no dividends for the past three years. Keen's liability for personal holding company tax will be based on
a. $12,000
b. $11,000
c. $ 9,000
d. $0 (Editors, 1686)

59. Sky Corp. was a wholly-owned subsidiary of Jet Corp. Both corporations were domestic C corporations. Jet received a liquidating distribution of property in cancellation of its Sky stock when Jet's tax basis in Sky stock was $100,000. The distributed property had an adjusted basis of $135,000 and a fair market value of $250,000. What amount of taxable gain did Jet, the parent corporation, recognize on the receipt of the property?

a. $250,000
b. $150,000
c. $ 35,000
d. $0 (11/98, AR, #14, 6680)

60. Ace Corp. and Bate Corp. combine in a qualifying reorganization and form Carr Corp., the only surviving corporation. This reorganization is tax-free to the

	Shareholders	*Corporation*
a.	Yes	Yes
b.	Yes	No
c.	No	Yes
d.	No	No

(11/95, AR, #22, 5766)

61. Pursuant to a plan of corporate reorganization adopted in July Year 1, Gow exchanged 500 shares of Lad Corp. common stock that he had bought in January Year 1 at a cost of $5,000 for 100 shares of Rook Corp. common stock having a fair market value of $6,000. Gow's recognized gain on this exchange was

a. $1,000 long-term capital gain
b. $1,000 short-term capital gain
c. $1,000 ordinary income
d. $0 (5/91, PII, #43, amended, 1637)

62. In a type B reorganization, as defined by the Internal Revenue Code, the

I. Stock of the target corporation is acquired solely for the voting stock of either the acquiring corporation or its parent
II. Acquiring corporation must have control of the target corporation immediately after the acquisition

a. I only
b. II only
c. Both I and II
d. Neither I nor II (11/94, AR, #53, 5029)

63. Bank Corp. owns 80% of Shore Corp.'s outstanding capital stock. Shore's capital stock consists of 50,000 shares of common stock issued and outstanding. Shore's Year 0 net income was $140,000. During Year 0, Shore declared and paid dividends of $60,000. In conformity with generally accepted accounting principles, Bank recorded the following entries in Year 0:

	Debit	Credit
Investment in Shore Corp. common stock	$112,000	
Equity in earnings of subsidiary		$112,000
Cash	48,000	
Investment in Shore Corp. common stock		48,000

In its Year 0 consolidated tax return, Bank should report dividend revenue of

a. $48,000
b. $14,400
c. $ 9,600
d. $0 (11/95, AR, #13, amended, 5757)

64. Potter Corp. and Sly Corp. file consolidated tax returns. In January Year 1, Potter sold land with a basis of $60,000 and a fair value of $75,000 to Sly for $100,000. Sly sold the land in December Year 2 for $125,000. In its Year 2 and Year 1 tax returns, what amount of gain should be reported for these transactions in the consolidated return?

	Year 2	*Year 1*
a.	$25,000	$40,000
b.	$50,000	$0
c.	$50,000	$25,000
d.	$65,000	$0

(5/93, PII, #49, amended, 4154)

65. Dane Corp. owns stock in Seaco Corp. For Dane and Seaco to qualify for the filing of consolidated returns, at least what percentage of Seaco's total voting power and total value of stock must be directly owned by Dane?

	Total voting power	*Total value of stock*
a.	51%	51%
b.	51%	80%
c.	80%	51%
d.	80%	80%

(Editors, 1666)

66. Prin Corp., the parent corporation, and Strel Corp., both accrual-basis, calendar-year C corporations, file a consolidated return. During the current year, Strel made dividend distributions to Prin as follows:

	Adjusted tax basis	Fair market value
Cash	$4,000	$4,000
Land	2,000	9,000

What amount of dividend income should be reported on Prin and Strel's consolidated income tax return for the current year?

a. $13,000
b. $11,000
c. $ 6,000
d. $0 (R/03, REG, 0637T, #10, 7652)

67. In the filing of a consolidated tax return for a corporation and its wholly owned subsidiaries, intercompany dividends between the parent and subsidiary corporations are

a. Not taxable
b. Included in taxable income to the extent of 20%
c. Included in taxable income to the extent of 80%
d. Fully taxable (11/94, AR, #47, 5023)

68. Which **two** of the following conditions will prevent a corporation from qualifying as an S corporation?

a. The corporation has both common and preferred stock.
b. The corporation has one class of stock with different voting rights.
c. The corporation has 150 shareholders.
d. One shareholder is an estate.
e. One shareholder is a grantor trust.

(5/93, PII, #51, amended, 4156)

69. Dart Corp., a calendar-year S corporation, had 60,000 shares of voting common stock and 40,000 shares of nonvoting common stock issued and outstanding. On February 23, Year 5, Dart filed a revocation statement with the consent of shareholders holding 30,000 shares of its voting common stock and 5,000 shares of its nonvoting common stock. Dart's S corporation election

a. Did **not** terminate
b. Terminated as of January 1, Year 5
c. Terminated on February 24, Year 5
d. Terminated as of January 1, Year 6

(11/98, AR, #13, amended, 6679)

70. Bristol Corp. was formed as a C corporation on January 1, Year 0, and elected S corporation status on January 1, Year 3. At the time of the election, Bristol had accumulated C corporation earnings and profits which have not been distributed. Bristol has had the same 25 shareholders throughout its existence. In Year 6, Bristol's S election will terminate if it

a. Increases the number of shareholders to 100
b. Adds a decedent's estate as a shareholder to the existing shareholders
c. Takes a charitable contribution deduction
d. Has passive investment income exceeding 90% of gross receipts in each of the three consecutive years ending December 31, Year 6

(11/94, AR, #42, amended, 5019)

71. Village Corp., a calendar year corporation, began business in Year 1. Village made a valid S Corporation election on December 5, Year 6, with the unanimous consent of its shareholders. The eligibility requirements for S status continued to be met throughout Year 7. On what date did Village's S status become effective?

a. January 1, Year 6
b. January 1, Year 7
c. December 5, Year 6
d. December 5, Year 7

(5/95, AR, #21, amended, 5439)

72. After a corporation's status as an S corporation is revoked or terminated, how many years is the corporation required to wait before making a new S election, in the absence of IRS consent to an earlier election?

a. 1
b. 3
c. 5
d. 10 (5/91, PII, #57, 1649)

73. Zinco Corp. was a calendar year S corporation. Zinco's S status terminated on April 1, Year 1, when Case Corp. became a shareholder. During Year 1 (365-day calendar year), Zinco had nonseparately computed income of $310,250. If no election was made by Zinco, what amount of the income, if any, was allocated to the S short year for Year 1?

a. $233,750
b. $155,125
c. $ 76,500
d. $0 (11/94, AR, #41, amended, 5018)

74. Boles Corp., an accrual-basis, calendar-year S corporation, has been an S corporation since its inception and is not subject to the uniform capitalization rules. In Year 3, Boles recorded the following:

Gross receipts	$50,000
Dividends income from investments	5,000
Supplies expense	2,000
Utilities expense	1,500

On Boles's Year 3 S corporation Form Schedule K, *Shareholders' Shares of Income, Credits, Deductions, etc.*, what amount of income should be separately stated from business income?

a. $50,000
b. $48,000
c. $ 5,000
d. $0 (R/05, REG, 0137T, #6, amended, 7872)

75. Bern Corp., an S corporation, had an ordinary loss of $36,500 for the year ended December 31, Year 0. At January 1, Year 0, Meyer owned 50% of Bern's stock. Meyer held the stock for 40 days in Year 0 before selling the entire 50% interest to an unrelated third party. Meyer's basis for the stock was $10,000. Meyer was a full-time employee of Bern until the stock was sold. Meyer's share of Bern's Year 0 loss was

a. $0
b. $ 2,000
c. $10,000
d. $18,250 (5/91, PII, #56, amended, 1648)

76. Baker, an individual, owned 100% of Alpha, an S corporation. At the beginning of the year, Baker's basis in Alpha Corp. was $25,000. Alpha realized ordinary income during the year in the amount of $1,000 and a long-term capital loss in the amount of $3,000 for this year. Alpha distributed $30,000 in cash to Baker during the year. What amount of the $30,000 cash distribution is taxable to Baker?

a. $0
b. $ 5,000
c. $ 7,000
d. $30,000 (R/02, AR, #23, 7088)

77. Magic Corp., a regular C corporation, elected S corporation status at the beginning of the current calendar year. It had an asset with a basis of $40,000 and a fair market value (FMV) of $85,000 on January 1. The asset was sold during the year for $95,000. Magic's corporate tax rate was 35%. What was Magic's tax liability as a result of the sale?

a. $0
b. $ 3,500
c. $15,750
d. $19,250 (R/07, REG, A0277T, #33, 8457)

78. Packer Corp., an accrual-basis, calendar-year S corporation, has been an S corporation since its inception. Starr was a 50% shareholder in Packer throughout the current year and had a $10,000 tax basis in Packer stock on January 1. During the current year, Packer had a $1,000 net business loss and made an $8,000 cash distribution to each shareholder. What amount of the distribution was includible in Starr's gross income?

a. $8,000
b. $7,500
c. $4,000
d. $0 (R/03, REG, 0404T, #8, 7650)

79. An S corporation is **not** permitted to take a deduction for

a. Compensation of officers
b. Charitable contributions
c. Interest paid to individuals who are **not** stockholders of the S corporation
d. Employee benefit programs established for individuals who are **not** stockholders of the S corporation (Editors, 8053)

80. With regard to S corporations and their stockholders, the "at risk" rules applicable to losses

a. Apply at the shareholder level rather than at the corporate level
b. Are subject to the elections made by the S corporation's stockholders
c. Take into consideration the S corporation's ratio of debt to equity
d. Depend on the type of income reported by the S corporation (Editors, 1663)

Problem 46-2 ADDITIONAL MULTIPLE CHOICE QUESTIONS (68 to 90 minutes)

81. Dole, the sole owner of Enson Corp., transferred a building to Enson. The building had an adjusted tax basis of $35,000 and a fair market value of $100,000. In exchange for the building, Dole received $40,000 cash and Enson common stock with a fair market value of $60,000. What amount of gain did Dole recognize?
a. $0
b. $ 5,000
c. $40,000
d. $65,000 (R/05, REG, 0660T, #10, 7876)

82. A corporation's penalty for underpaying federal estimated taxes is
a. Not deductible
b. Fully deductible in the year paid
c. Fully deductible if reasonable cause can be established for the underpayment
d. Partially deductible (11/94, AR, #48, 5024)

83. Which of the following costs are amortizable organizational expenditures?
a. Professional fees to issue the corporate stock
b. Printing costs to issue the corporate stock
c. Legal fees for drafting the corporate charter
d. Commissions paid by the corporation to an underwriter (11/94, AR, #38, 5015)

84. The following information pertains to treasury stock sold by Ram Corp. to an unrelated broker:

Proceeds received	$100,000
Cost	60,000
Par value	18,000

What amount of capital gain should Ram recognize on the sale of this treasury stock?
a. $0
b. $16,000
c. $40,000
d. $61,000 (Editors, 8054)

85. The corporate dividends-received deduction
a. Must exceed the applicable percentage of the recipient shareholder's taxable income
b. Is affected by a requirement that the investor corporation must own the investee's stock for a specified minimum holding period
c. Is unaffected by the percentage of the investee's stock owned by the investor corporation
d. May be claimed by S corporations (5/91, PII, #47, 1641)

86. Beta, a C corporation, reported the following items of income and expenses for the year:

Gross income	$600,000
Dividend income from a 30% owned domestic corporation	100,000
Operating expenses	400,000

What is Beta's taxable income for the year?
a. $200,000
b. $220,000
c. $230,000
d. $300,000 (R/07, REG, 1233T, #8, 8432)

87. For Year 1, Kelly Corp. had net income per books of $300,000 before the provision for Federal income taxes. Included in the net income were the following items:

Dividend income from an unaffiliated domestic taxable corporation (taxable income limitation does not apply and there is no portfolio indebtedness)	$50,000
Bad debt expense (represents the increase in the allowance for doubtful accounts)	80,000

Assuming no bad debt was written off, what is Kelly's taxable income for Year 1?
a. $250,000
b. $330,000
c. $345,000
d. $380,000 (11/94, AR, #32, amended, 5009)

88. A C corporation must use the accrual method of accounting in which of the following circumstances?
a. The business had average sales for the past three years of less than $1 million.
b. The business is a service company and has over $1 million in sales.
c. The business is a personal service business with over $15 million in sales.
d. The business has more than $10 million in average sales. (R/07, REG, A1248T, #16, 8440)

89. The rule limiting the allowability of passive activity losses and credits applies to
a. Partnerships
b. Personal service corporations
c. Widely held C corporations
d. S corporations (5/91, PII, #44, 1638)

Items 90 and 91 are based on the following:

John Budd is the sole stockholder of Ral Corp., an accrual basis taxpayer engaged in wholesaling operations. Ral's retained earnings at January 1, Year 1, amounted to $1,000,000. For the year ended December 31, Year 1, Ral's book income, before federal income tax, was $300,000. Included in the computation of this $300,000 were the following:

Keyman insurance premiums paid on Budd's life (Ral is the beneficiary of this policy)	3,000
Group term insurance premiums paid on $10,000 life insurance policies for each of Ral's four employees (the employees' spouses are the beneficiaries)	4,000
Contribution to a recognized, qualified charity (this contribution was authorized by Ral's board of directors in December Year 1, to be paid on January 31, Year 2)	75,000

90. What amount should Ral deduct for keyman and group life insurance premiums in computing taxable income for Year 1?
a. $0
b. $3,000
c. $4,000
d. $7,000 (5/90, PII, #32, amended, 4584)

91. With regard to Ral's contribution to the recognized, qualified charity, Ral
a. Can elect to deduct in its Year 1 return any portion of the $75,000 that does **not** exceed the deduction ceiling for Year 1
b. Can elect to carry forward indefinitely any portion of the $75,000 **not** deducted in Year 1 or Year 2
c. Can deduct the entire $75,000 in its Year 1 return because Ral reports on the accrual basis
d. Cannot deduct any portion of the $75,000 in Year 1 because the contribution was **not** paid in Year 1 (5/90, PII, #34, amended, 4586)

92. Lyle Corp. is a distributor of pharmaceuticals and sells only to retail drug stores. Lyle received unsolicited samples of nonprescription drugs from a manufacturer. Lyle donated these drugs to a qualified exempt organization and deducted their fair market value as a charitable contribution. What should be included as gross income in Lyle's return for receipt of these samples?
a. Fair market value
b. Net discounted wholesale price
c. $25 nominal value assigned to gifts
d. $0 (11/91, PII, #42, amended, 2490)

93. John Budd is the sole stockholder of Ral Corp., an accrual basis taxpayer engaged in wholesaling operations. Ral's retained earnings at January 1, Year 1 amounted to $1,000,000. For the year ended December 31, Year 1, Ral's book income, before federal income tax, was $300,000. Included in the computation of this $300,000 was a $5,000 loss on sale of investment in stock of an unaffiliated corporation (this stock had been held for two years; Ral had no other capital gains or losses). In computing taxable income for Year 1, Ral should deduct a capital loss of
a. $0
b. $2,500
c. $3,000
d. $5,000 (5/90, PII, #30, amended, 8051)

94. When a corporation has an unused net capital loss that is carried back or carried forward to another tax year,
a. It can be used to offset ordinary income up to the amount of the carryback or carryover.
b. It is treated as a short-term capital loss whether or not it was short-term when sustained.
c. It is treated as a long-term capital loss whether or not it was long-term when sustained.
d. It retains its original identity as short-term or long-term. (5/93, PII, #47, amended, 4153)

95. In the current year, Brown, a C corporation has gross income (before dividends) of $900,000 and deductions of $1,100,000 (excluding the dividends-received deduction). Brown received dividends of $100,000 from a Fortune 500 corporation during the current year. What is Brown's net operating loss?
a. $100,000
b. $130,000
c. $170,000
d. $200,000 (R/06, REG, 1934T, #33, 8203)

96. If a corporation's tentative minimum tax exceeds the regular tax, the excess amount is
a. Carried back to the first preceding taxable year
b. Carried back to the third preceding taxable year
c. Payable in addition to the regular tax
d. Subtracted from the regular tax (5/93, PII, #57, 4162)

97. A corporation's tax preference items that must be taken into account for alternative minimum tax purposes include
a. Use of the percentage of completion method of accounting for long-term contracts
b. Capital gains
c. Accelerated depreciation on pre-1987 real property to the extent of the excess over straight-line depreciation
d. Casualty losses (Editors, 8055)

98. Which of the following items should be included on the Schedule M-1, *Reconciliation of Income (Loss) per Books With Income per Return,* of Form 1120, *U.S. Corporation Income Tax Return,* to reconcile book income to taxable income?
a. Cash distributions to shareholders
b. Premiums paid on key-person life insurance policy
c. Corporate bond interest
d. Ending balance of retained earnings
(R/06, REG, C00361R, #16, 8186)

99. Dahl Corp. was organized and commenced operations in Year 0. At December 31, Year 5, Dahl had accumulated earnings and profits of $9,000 before dividend declaration and distribution. On December 31, Year 5, Dahl distributed cash of $9,000 and a vacant parcel of land to Green, Dahl's only stockholder. At the date of distribution, the land had a basis of $5,000 and a fair market value of $40,000. What was Green's taxable dividend income in Year 5 from these distributions?
a. $ 9,000
b. $14,000
c. $44,000
d. $49,000 (11/90, PII, #26, amended, 1650)

100. Bridge, a C corporation, had $15,000 in accumulated earnings and profits at the beginning of the current year. During the current year, Bridge reported earnings and profits of $10,000 and paid $20,000 in cash distributions to its shareholders in both March and July. What amount of the July distribution should be classified as dividend income to Bridge's shareholders?
a. $20,000
b. $15,000
c. $10,000
d. $ 5,000 (R/05, REG, 0150T, #9, 7855)

101. At the beginning of the year, Cable, a C corporation, had accumulated earnings and profits of $100,000. Cable reported the following items on its current-year tax return:

Taxable income	$50,000
Federal income taxes paid	5,000
Charitable contributions carry forward	1,000
Capital loss carry forward	2,000

What is Cable's accumulated earnings and profits at the end of the year?
a. $145,000
b. $146,000
c. $148,000
d. $150,000 (R/02, AR, #24, 7089)

102. On January 1, Year 1, Locke Corp., an accrual-basis, calendar-year C corporation, had $30,000 in accumulated earnings and profits. For Year 1, Locke had current earnings and profits of $20,000, and made two $40,000 cash distributions to its shareholders, one in April and one in September. What amount of these distributions is classified as dividend income to Locke's shareholders?
a. $0
b. $20,000
c. $50,000
d. $80,000 (R/00, AR, #8, amended, 6913)

103. On January 1, Year 0, Kee Corp., a C corporation, had a $50,000 deficit in earnings and profits. For Year 0, Kee had current earnings and profits of $10,000 and made a $30,000 cash distribution to its stockholders. What amount of the distribution is taxable as dividend income to Kee's stockholders?
a. $30,000
b. $20,000
c. $10,000
d. $0 (5/94, AR, #25, amended, 4630)

104. Tank Corp., which had earnings and profits of $500,000, made a nonliquidating distribution of property to its shareholders in the current year as a dividend in kind. This property, which had an adjusted basis of $20,000 and a fair market value of $30,000 at the date of distribution, did not constitute assets used in the active conduct of Tank's business. How much gain did Tank recognize on this distribution?
a. $30,000
b. $20,000
c. $10,000
d. $0 (11/94, AR, #51, amended, 5027)

105. Aztec, a C corporation, distributed an asset to Burn, a shareholder. The asset had a fair market value of $30,000 and was subject to a $40,000 liability, assumed by Burn. The asset had an adjusted basis of $25,000. What amount of gain must Aztec recognize?
a. $0
b. $ 5,000
c. $10,000
d. $15,000 (R/05, REG, 1234T, #15, 7881)

106. Lincoln Corp., a calendar-year C corporation, made a nonliquidating cash distribution of $1,500,000 to its shareholders with respect to its stock. At that time, Lincoln's current and accumulated earnings and profits totaled $825,000 and its total paid in capital for tax purposes was $10,000,000. Lincoln had no corporate shareholders. Which of the following statements is(are) correct regarding Lincoln's cash distribution?

I. The distribution was taxable as $1,500,000 in ordinary income to its shareholders.
II. The distribution reduced its shareholders' adjusted bases in Lincoln stock by $675,000.

a. I only
b. II only
c. Both I and II
d. Neither I nor II (11/98, AR, #15, 6681)

107. For the collapsible corporation provisions to be imposed, the holding period of the corporation's stock
a. Must be a minimum of six months
b. Must be a minimum of twelve months
c. Is irrelevant
d. Depends on the stockholder's basis for gain or loss (Editors, 1670)

108. Elm Corp. is an accrual-basis calendar-year C corporation with 100,000 shares of voting common stock issued and outstanding as of December 28, 1996. On Friday, December 29, 1996, Hall surrendered 2,000 shares of Elm stock to Elm in exchange for $33,000 cash. Hall had no direct or indirect interest in Elm after the stock surrender. Additional information follows:

Hall's adjusted basis in 2,000 shares of Elm on December 29, 1996 ($8 per share)	$16,000
Elm's accumulated earnings and profits at January 1, 1996	25,000
Elm's 1996 net operating loss	(7,000)

What amount of income did Hall recognize from the stock surrender?
a. $33,000 dividend
b. $25,000 dividend
c. $18,000 capital gain
d. $17,000 capital gain (11/97, AR, #6, 6534)

109. Acme Corp. has two common stockholders. Acme derives all of its income from investments in stocks and securities, and it regularly distributes 51% of its taxable income as dividends to its stockholders. Acme is a
a. Corporation subject to tax only on income **not** distributed to stockholders
b. Corporation subject to the accumulated earnings tax
c. Regulated investment company
d. Personal holding company (5/93, PII, #52, 4157)

110. Jaxson Corp. has 200,000 shares of voting common stock issued and outstanding. King Corp. has decided to acquire 90 percent of Jaxson's voting common stock solely in exchange for 50 percent of its voting common stock and retain Jaxson as a subsidiary after the transaction. Which of the following statements is true?
a. King must acquire 100 percent of Jaxson stock for the transaction to be a tax-free reorganization.
b. The transaction will qualify as a tax-free reorganization.
c. King must issue at least 60 percent of its voting common stock for the transaction to qualify as a tax-free reorganization.
d. Jaxson must surrender assets for the transaction to qualify as a tax-free reorganization. (5/95, AR, #25, 5443)

111. Plant Corp. and Stem Corp. file consolidated returns on a calendar-year basis. In January Year 1, Stem sold land, which it had used in its operations, to Plant for $150,000. Immediately before this sale, Stem's basis for the land was $90,000. Plant held the land primarily for sale to customers in the ordinary course of business. In July Year 2, Plant sold the land to Dubin, an unrelated individual, for $180,000. In determining the consolidated Section 1231 net gain for Year 2, how much should Stem take into account as a result of the Year 1 sale of the land from Stem to Plant?
a. $90,000
b. $60,000
c. $45,000
d. $30,000 (Editors, 8056)

112. ParentCo, SubOne, and SubTwo have filed consolidated returns since their inception. The members reported the following taxable incomes (losses) for the year.

ParentCo	$50,000
SubOne	($60,000)
SubTwo	($40,000)

No member reported a capital gain or loss or charitable contributions. What is the amount of the consolidated net operating loss?

a. $0
b. $ 30,000
c. $ 50,000
d. $100,000 (R/06, REG, 1783T, #8, 8178)

113. With regard to consolidated tax returns, which of the following statements is correct?

a. Operating losses of one group member may be used to offset operating profits of the other members included in the consolidated return.
b. Only corporations that issue their audited financial statements on a consolidated basis may file consolidated returns.
c. Of all intercompany dividends paid by the subsidiaries to the parent, 70% are excludable from taxable income on the consolidated return.
d. The common parent must directly own 51% or more of the total voting power of all corporations included in the consolidated return.

(11/94, AR, #46, 5022)

114. Portal Corp. received $100,000 in dividends from Sal Corp., its 80%-owned subsidiary. What net amount of dividend income should Portal include in its consolidated tax return?

a. $100,000
b. $ 80,000
c. $ 70,000
d. $0 (5/93, PII, #43, amended, 4149)

115. Tech Corp. files a consolidated return with its wholly owned subsidiary, Dow Corp. During Year 1, Dow paid a cash dividend of $20,000 to Tech. What amount of this dividend is taxable on the Year 1 consolidated return?

a. $20,000
b. $14,000
c. $ 6,000
d. $0 (5/94, AR, #23, amended, 4628)

116. Jans, an individual, owns 80% and 100% of the total value and voting power of A and B Corps., respectively, which in turn own the following (both value and voting power):

	Ownership	
Property	A Corp.	B Corp.
C Corp.	80%	-
D Corp.	-	100%

All companies are C corporations except B Corp., which had elected S status since inception. Which of the following statements is correct with respect to the companies' ability to file a consolidated return?

a. A, C, and D may file as a group.
b. A and C may **not** file as a group, and B and D may **not** file as a group.
c. A and C may file as a group, and B and D may file as a group.
d. A and C may file as a group, but B and D may **not** file as a group.

(R/06, REG, 0771T, #21, 8191)

117. If a calendar-year S corporation does **not** request an automatic six-month extension of time to file its income tax return, the return is due by

a. June 30
b. April 15
c. March 15
d. January 31 (Editors, 8057)

118. On January 1, Year 0, Kane owned all 100 issued shares of Manning Corp., a calendar year S corporation. On the 41st day of Year 0, Kane sold 25 of the Manning shares to Rodgers. For the year ended December 31, Year 0 (a 366-day calendar year), Manning had $73,200 in non-separately stated income and made no distributions to its shareholders. What amount of non-separately stated income from Manning should be reported on Kane's Year 0 tax return?

a. $56,900
b. $54,900
c. $16,300
d. $0 (11/94, AR, #43, amended, 5020)

119. Boles Corp., an accrual-basis, calendar-year S corporation, has been an S corporation since its inception and is not subject to the uniform capitalization rules. In the current year, Boles recorded the following:

Gross receipts	$50,000
Dividend income from investments	5,000
Supplies expense	2,000
Utilities expense	1,500

What amount of net business income should Boles report on its Form 1120S, *U.S. Income Tax Return for an S corporation, Schedule K?*

a. $53,500
b. $53,000
c. $48,000
d. $46,500

(R/05, REG, 0136T, #8, amended, 7854)

120. Evan, an individual, has a 40% interest in EF, an S corporation. At the beginning of the year, Evan's basis in EF was $2,000. During the year, EF distributed $100,000 and reported operating income of $200,000. What amount should Evan include in gross income?

a. $ 38,000
b. $ 40,000
c. $ 80,000
d. $118,000 (R/07, REG, 1513T, #29, 8453)

121. A shareholder's basis in the stock of an S corporation is increased by the shareholder's pro rata share of income from

	Tax-exempt interest	Taxable interest
a.	No	No
b.	No	Yes
c.	Yes	No
d.	Yes	Yes

(5/95, AR, #22, 5440)

122. Beck Corp. has been a calendar-year S corporation since its inception on January 2, Year 0. On January 1, Year 3, Lazur and Lyle each owned 50% of the Beck stock, in which their respective tax bases were $12,000 and $9,000. For the year ended December 31, Year 3, Beck had $81,000 in ordinary business income and $10,000 in tax-exempt income. Beck made a $51,000 cash distribution to each shareholder on December 31, Year 3. What was Lazur's tax basis in Beck after the distribution?

a. $ 1,500
b. $ 6,500
c. $52,500
d. $57,500 (R/99, AR, #10, 6799)

123. If an S corporation has **no** accumulated earnings and profits, the amount distributed to a shareholder

a. Must be returned to the S corporation
b. Increases the shareholder's basis for the stock
c. Decreases the shareholder's basis for the stock
d. Has **no** effect on the shareholder's basis for the stock (11/93, PII, #44, 4473)

124. Lane Inc., an S corporation, pays single coverage health insurance premiums of $4,800 per year and family coverage premiums of $7,200 per year. Mill is a ten percent shareholder-employee in Lane. On Mill's behalf, Lane pays Mill's family coverage under the health insurance plan. What amount of insurance premiums is includible in Mill's gross income?

a. $0
b. $ 720
c. $4,800
d. $7,200 (R/99, AR, #4, 6793)

125. An S Corporation has 30,000 shares of voting common stock and 20,000 shares of non-voting common stock issued and outstanding. The S election can be revoked voluntarily with the consent of the shareholders holding, on the day of the revocation,

	Shares of voting stock	Shares of nonvoting stock
a.	0	20,000
b.	7,500	5,000
c.	10,000	16,000
d.	20,000	0

(5/94, AR, #21, 4626)

SIMULATIONS

Problem 46-3 (20 to 30 minutes)

Anvil Corp., an accrual-basis calendar year C corporation, filed its Year 3 federal income tax return on March 15, Year 4. Anvil does not meet the definition of a small corporation for AMT purposes. Anvil elected out of bonus depreciation. (5/95, AR, #3, amended, 5504)

Items 1 through 6 each require two responses. Determine the amount of Anvil's Year 3 Schedule M-1 adjustment. Indicate if the adjustment (I) increase, (D) decrease, or (N) has no effect on Anvil's taxable income.

Transaction	Amount	Effect
1. Anvil's disbursements included reimbursed employees' expenses for travel of $100,000, and business meals of $30,000. The reimbursed expenses met the conditions of deductibility and were properly substantiated under an accountable plan. The reimbursement was not treated as employee compensation.		
2. Anvil's books expensed $7,000 for the term life insurance premiums on the corporate officers. Anvil was the policy owner and beneficiary.		
3. Anvil's books indicated an $18,000 state franchise tax expense for Year 3. Estimated state tax payments for Year 3 were $15,000.		
4. Book depreciation on computers for Year 3 was $10,000. These computers, costing $50,000, were placed in service on January 2, Year 2. Tax depreciation used MACRS with the half-year convention. No election was made to expense part of the computer cost or to use a straight-line method or the alternative depreciation system.		
5. Anvil's books showed a $4,000 short-term capital gain distribution from a mutual fund corporation and a $5,000 loss on the sale of Retro stock that was purchased in Year 0. The stock was an investment in an unrelated corporation. There were no other Year 3 gains or losses and no loss carryovers from prior years.		
6. Anvil's taxable income before the charitable contribution and the dividends received deductions was $500,000. Anvil's books expensed $15,000 in board-of-director authorized charitable contributions that were paid on January 5, Year 4. Charitable contributions paid and expense during Year 3 were $35,000. All charitable contributions were properly substantiated. There were no net operating losses or charitable contributions that were carried forward.		

For Items 7 through 10, indicate if the income is (F) fully taxable, (P) partially taxable, or (N) nontaxable for regular tax purposes on Anvil's federal income tax return. All transactions occurred during Year 3. Anvil filed an amended federal income tax return for Year 2 and received a refund that included both the overpayment of the federal taxes and interest.

Transaction	Answer
7. The portion of Anvil's refund that represented the overpayment of the Year 2 federal taxes.	
8. The portion of Anvil's refund that is attributable to the interest on the overpayment of federal taxes.	
9. Anvil received dividend income from a mutual fund that solely invests in municipal bonds.	
10. Anvil, the lessor, benefited from the capital improvements made to its property by the lessee in Year 3. The lease agreement is for one year ending December 31, Year 3, and provides for a reduction in rental payments by the lessee in exchange for the improvements.	

Write a memo to Anvil Corporation explaining whether the following items are deductible or not. Include a description for each item.

1. Anvil purchased theater tickets for its out-of-town clients. The performances took place after Anvil's substantial and *bona fide* business negotiations with its clients.
2. Anvil accrued advertising expenses to promote a new product line. Ten percent of the new product line remained in ending inventory.
3. Anvil incurred interest expense on a loan to purchase municipal bonds.
4. Anvil paid a penalty for the underpayment of Year 2 estimated taxes.

Research Question: What code section and subsection, if applicable, provides guidance on the allowable deduction for a net operating loss (NOL)?

Section & Subsection Answer: §_____ (___)

Problem 46-4 (20 to 30 minutes)

Capital Corp., an accrual-basis calendar-year C corporation, began operations on January 2, Year 1. Capital timely filed its Year 2 federal income tax return on Wednesday, March 15, Year 3.

(5/97, AR, #1, amended, 6340)

Items 1 through 4 each require two responses. Determine the amount of Capital's Year 2 Schedule M-1 adjustment necessary to reconcile book income to taxable income. In addition, determine if the Schedule M-1 adjustment necessary to reconcile book income to taxable income (I) increases, (D) decreases, or (N) has no effect on Capital's Year 2 taxable income.

Transaction	Amount	Effect
1. At its corporate inception in Year 1, Capital incurred and paid $35,000 in organizational costs for legal fees to draft the corporate charter. In Year 1, Capital correctly elected, for book purposes, to amortize the organizational expenditures over 40 years. For Year 2, Capital amortized $1,000 of the organizational costs on its books.		
2. Capital's Year 2 disbursements included $10,000 for reimbursed employees' expenses for business and entertainment. The reimbursed expenses met the conditions of deductibility and were properly substantiated under an accountable plan. The disbursement was not treated as employee compensation.		
3. Capital's Year 2 disbursements included $15,000 life insurance premium expense paid for its executives as part of their taxable compensation. Capital is neither the direct nor the indirect beneficiary of the policy, and the amount of the compensation is reasonable.		
4. In Year 2, Capital increased its allowance for uncollectible accounts by $10,000. No bad debt was written off in Year 1.		

Write a memo to Capital Corporation explaining whether the following Year 2 items are fully deductible, partially deductible, or, nondeductible for regular income tax purposes on Capital's Year 2 federal income tax return. Include a description for each item.

1. Capital's Year 2 taxable income before charitable contributions and dividends-received deduction was $200,000. Capital's Board of Directors authorized a $38,000 contribution to a qualified charity on December 1, Year 2. The payment was made on February 1, Year 3. All charitable contributions were properly substantiated.

2. During Year 2, Capital was assessed and paid a $300 uncontested penalty for failure to pay its Year 1 federal income taxes on time.

Scenario | Adjustments | Communication | Research

Research Question: What code section and subsection, if applicable, provides guidance on the recognition of a gain or loss with respect to a nonliquidating distribution of unappreciated corporate property?

Section & Subsection Answer: §_____ (___)

Problem 46-5 (20 to 30 minutes)

Pronto Corp., an accrual-basis calendar year repair-service corporation, began business on January 1, Year 1. Pronto's valid S corporation election took effect retroactively on January 1, Year 1. (Editors, 5820)

For Items 1 through 4, determine the amount using the fact pattern for each item.

Calculation	Answer
1. Pronto's Year 1 books recorded the following: Gross receipts $7,260 Interest-income on investments 50 Charitable contributions 1,000 Supplies 1,120 What amount of net business income should Pronto report on its Year 1 Form 1120S, *U.S. Income Tax Return for an S Corporation, Schedule K*?	
2. As of January 1, Year 1, Singer and Serger each owned 100 shares of the 200 issued shares of Pronto stock. On January 31, Year 1, Singer and Serger each sold 20 shares to Newcomb. No election was made to terminate the tax year. Pronto had net business income of $14,520 for the year ended December 31, Year 1, and made no distributions to its shareholders. (The calendar Year 1 had 365 days.) What amount of net business income should have been reported on Newcomb's Year 1 Schedule K-1 from Pronto? Round the answer to the nearest hundred.	
3. Newcomb purchased 40 Pronto shares on January 31, Year 1, for $4,000. Pronto made no distributions to shareholders, and Newcomb's Year 1 Schedule K-1 from Pronto reported an ordinary business loss of $1,000 and municipal bond interest income of $150. What was Newcomb's basis in his Pronto stock at December 31, Year 1?	
4. On January 1, Year 1, Singer and Serger each owned 100 shares of the 200 issued shares of Pronto stock. Singer's basis in Pronto shares on that date was $10,000. Singer sold all of his Pronto shares to Newcomb on January 31, Year 1, and Pronto made a valid election to terminate its tax year. Singer's share of ordinary income from Pronto prior to the sale was $2,000. Pronto made a cash distribution of $3,000 to Singer on January 30, Year 1. What was Singer's basis in Pronto shares for determining gain or loss from the sale to Newcomb?	

Write a memo to your supervisor outlining the following proposed independent actions by Pronto Corporation, your employer's client, and how those actions each could affect Pronto's S Corporation eligibility.

1. Pronto issues shares of both preferred and common stock to shareholders at inception on January 1, Year 1.

2. Pronto, an S corporation since inception, expects passive investment income for a third consecutive year following the year a valid S corporation election takes effect.

Scenario | Calculations | Communication | Research

Research Question: What code section and subsection, if applicable, limits the deductibility of organizational expenditures?

Section & Subsection Answer: §_____ (___)

Problem 46-6 (20 to 30 minutes)

Clipper Corp., an accrual-basis calendar year C corporation, filed its Year 3 federal income tax return on March 15, Year 4. Clipper does not meet the definition of a small corporation for AMT purposes. Clipper elected out of bonus depreciation. (5/95, AR, #3, amended, 5505)

For Items 1 through 5, indicate if the expenses are (F) fully deductible, (P) partially deductible, or (N) non deductible for regular tax purposes on Clipper's federal income tax return.

Transaction	Answer
1. Clipper purchased theater tickets for its out of town clients. The performances took place after Clipper's substantial and bona fide business negotiations with its clients.	
2. Clipper accrued advertising expenses to promote a new product line. Ten percent of the new product line remained in ending inventory.	
3. Clipper incurred interest expense on a loan to purchase municipal bonds.	
4. Clipper paid a penalty for the underpayment of Year 2 estimated taxes.	
5. On December 9, Year 3, Clipper's board of directors voted to pay a $500 bonus to each non-stockholder employee for Year 3. The bonuses were paid on February 3, Year 4.	

For Items 6 through 8, indicate if the statement is true (T) or false (F) regarding Clipper's compliance with tax procedures, tax credits and the alternative minimum tax.

Statement	Answer
6. Clipper's exemption for alternative minimum tax is reduced by 20% of the excess of the alternative minimum taxable income over $150,000.	
7. The statute of limitations on Clipper's fraudulent Year 0 federal income tax return expires six years after the filing date of the return.	
8. The statute of limitations on Clipper's Year 1 federal income tax return, which omitted 30% of gross receipts, expires 2 years after the filing date of the return.	

Write a memo to Clipper Corporation explaining whether the following items are included in taxable income or not. Include a description for each item.

1. Clipper received dividend income from a mutual fund that solely invests in municipal bonds.
2. Clipper benefited from the capital improvements made to its property by a lessee in Year 3. The lease agreement is for one year ending December 31, Year 3, and provides for a reduction in rental payments by the lessee in exchange for the improvements.
3. Clipper collected the proceeds on the term life insurance policy on the life of a debtor who was not a shareholder. The policy was assigned to Clipper as collateral security for the debt. The proceeds exceeded the amount of the debt.

Research Question: What code section and subsection, if applicable, provides guidance on the deductibility of amounts paid to purchase life insurance on the life of a corporate officer when the corporate taxpayer is the beneficiary of the policy?

Section & Subsection Answer: §_____ (___)

Problem 46-7 (20 to 30 minutes)

Raffles Corp., an accrual-basis calendar year C corporation, filed its Year 3 federal income tax return on March 15, Year 4. Raffles does not meet the definition of a small corporation for AMT purposes. Raffles elected out of bonus depreciation. (5/95, AR, #3, amended, 5506)

For items 1 through 5, indicate if the facts (I) increase, (D) decrease, or (N) has no effect on Raffles's alternative minimum taxable income (AMTI) *prior to* the adjusted current earnings adjustment (ACE).

Fact	Answer
1. Raffles used the 70% dividends-received deduction for regular tax purposes.	
2. Raffles received interest from a state's general obligation bonds.	
3. Raffles used MACRS depreciation on seven-year personal property placed into service January 3, Year 3, for regular tax purposes. No expense or depreciation election was made.	
4. Depreciation on nonresidential real property placed into service on January 3, 1995, was under the general MACRS depreciation system for regular tax purposes.	
5. Raffles had only cash charitable contributions for Year 3.	

For Items 6 through 8, indicate if the statement is true (T) or false (F) regarding Raffles's compliance with tax procedures, tax credits and the alternative minimum tax.

Statement	Answer
6. The targeted job tax credit may be combined with other business credits to form part of Raffles' general business credit.	
7. Raffles' tax preparer, a CPA firm, may use the Year 3 corporate tax return information to prepare corporate officers' tax returns without the consent of the corporation.	
8. Raffles must file an amended return for Year 3 within one year of the filing date.	

Write a memo to Raffles Corporation explaining why the following items are included on or omitted from Schedule M-1. Include a description for each item.

1. Raffles' disbursements included reimbursed employees' expenses for travel of $100,000, and business meals of $30,000. The reimbursed expenses met the conditions of deductibility and were properly substantiated under an accountable plan. The reimbursement was not treated as employee compensation.

2. Raffles' books expensed $7,000 for the term life insurance premiums on the corporate officers. Raffles was the policy owner and beneficiary.

3. Raffles' books indicated an $18,000 state franchise tax expense for Year 3. Estimated state tax payments for Year 3 were $15,000.

Research Question: What code section and subsection, if applicable, provides guidance on the deductibility of amounts paid to purchase theater tickets for out-of-town clients when the performances take place after substantial and *bona fide* business negotiations with the clients?

Section & Subsection Answer: §_____ (___)

Problem 46-8 (20 to 30 minutes)

Szabo Corporation, an accrual-basis calendar-year C corporation, began operations on January 2, Year 1. Szabo timely filed its Year 2 federal income tax return on Wednesday, March 15, Year 3.

(5/97, AR, #1, amended, 6342)

For Items 1 through 4, determine if each Year 2 item, taken separately, contributes to (O) overstating, (U) understating, or (C) correctly stating Szabo's Year 2 alternative minimum taxable income (AMTI) prior to the adjusted current earnings adjustment (ACE). Szabo Corp. reported the same amounts for regular income tax and alternative minimum tax purposes.

Transaction	Answer
1. For regular tax purposes, Szabo deducted the maximum MACRS depreciation on seven-year personal property placed in service on January 1, Year 2. Szabo made no Internal Revenue Code Section 179 election to expense the property in Year 2.	
2. For regular income tax purposes, Szabo depreciated nonresidential real property placed in service on January 1, Year 2, under the general MACRS depreciation system for a 39-year depreciable life.	
3. Szabo excluded state highway construction general obligation bond interest income earned in Year 2 for regular income tax and alternative minimum tax (AMT) purposes.	
4. For regular income tax purposes, Szabo deducted a percentage of gross income from its copper mine in excess of its basis in the mine.	

Write a memo to Szabo Corporation explaining why the following Year 2 items are fully taxable, partially taxable, or nontaxable for regular income tax purposes on Szabo's Year 2 federal income tax return.

1. Szabo received dividend income from a 35%-owned domestic corporation. The dividends were not from debt-financed portfolio stock, and the taxable income limitation did not apply.
2. Szabo received a $2,800 lease cancellation payment from a three-year lease tenant.
3. Szabo collected the proceeds on the term life insurance policy on the life of a debtor who was not a shareholder. The policy was assigned to Szabo as collateral security for the debt. The proceeds exceeded the amount of the debt.

Research Question: What code section and subsection, if applicable, provides guidance on the deductibility of amounts paid for on-site meals for employees for the corporate employer's convenience?

Section & Subsection Answer: §_____ (___)

Solution 46-1 MULTIPLE CHOICE ANSWERS

Formation

1. (a) No gain or loss is recognized if property is transferred to a corporation solely in exchange for stock if, immediately after the transfer, the transferors are in control of the corporation.

2. (b) As no gain or loss was recognized, Ace Corporation's basis is the same as Lind's basis.

3. (c) Lind's basis in Ace's stock was the adjusted basis of the building that Lind exchanged for stock less the mortgage that Ace assumed.

4. (d) Under §351(a) and 368(c), the transferors of property to a corporation for its stock must be in control of at least 80% of the stock of the corporation in order for the transfer to be tax deferred.

5. (c) Feld's adjusted basis in the stock is the $50,000 originally paid for it plus Feld's adjusted basis in the land contributed, which is $10,000, for a total basis of $60,000.

6. (d) Section 351(a) provides that no gain or loss will be recognized to the transferors of property to a corporation, solely in exchange for its stock if the transferors are in control of the corporation immediately after the transfer. Control is defined in §368(c) as ownership of at least 80% of the voting stock and at least 80% of all other classes of stock. Beck and Carr are transferors of property and own 90% of Flexo Corp. immediately after the exchange. They received solely stock in exchange for their property and thereby meet the requirements of §351(a). Neither Beck nor Carr would recognize any gain. Adams would recognize ordinary income equal to the fair market value of the stock that was received in exchange for the services rendered.

Filing Requirements

7. (c) Under §6072, the due date for a calendar year corporation's income tax return is March 15 following the close of the tax year. Under §7502, the return is deemed to have been filed when it is postmarked. Thus, Jackson's return is deemed to have been filed on March 10. Section 6501 states that for purposes of determining the statute of limitations, an early return is treated as if filed on its due date. Thus, for determining the statute of limitations on assessment, Jackson's return is deemed to have been filed on March 15. The statute of limitations begins to run the day after the due date, which is March 16.

8. (c) Section 6663 imposes a penalty of 75% of a tax underpayment attributable to fraud. Section 7454(a) places the burden of proof for fraud on the Secretary of the Treasury. Tax Court Rule 142(b) states that such burden is to be carried by clear and convincing evidence. Fraud implies that the taxpayer had bad faith, intentionally understated his tax liability, or had a sinister motive. To be guilty of fraud the taxpayer must have engaged intentionally in wrongful activities to avoid the payment of taxes. Maintaining false records and reporting fictitious transactions to minimize the tax liability would be evidence of fraud. Omitting income as a result of inadequate recordkeeping would be indicative of negligence under §6662(b) and §6662(c), not fraud. Under Reg. §1.6662-3(b)(1) negligence includes any failure by the taxpayer to keep adequate books and records or to substantiate items properly. The penalty for negligence is 20% of the tax underpayment attributable to negligence under §6662(a). Failing to report income that the taxpayer did not consider to be included in gross income is not fraud because there is no bad faith. Whether this action constitutes negligence depends on whether the taxpayer intentionally or recklessly disregarded rules and regulations. Likewise, filing an incomplete return with adequate disclosure is not fraud because there is no evidence of bad faith.

9. (b) Section 6501(e)(1)(A) extends the statute of limitations on assessment to 6 years from the later of the date due or the date filed for a nonfraudulent substantial omission of income. Once this period has expired, the statute of limitations cannot be reopened unless the omission was fraudulent. The statute of limitations can be reopened under the mitigation provisions under §1311(a) if the taxpayer is able to take a deduction in an open year that the taxpayer deducted previously in a year that is now closed as provided in §1312(2).

10. (b) Section 6655(d)(1)(B) provides that a corporation may avoid the penalty for underpayment of estimated tax by making a payment equal to 100% of the tax for the preceding year. However, this rule does not apply if the corporation did not file a return for the previous tax year showing a liability for tax. Since Edge Corp. had a net operating loss and a zero tax liability for Year 0, Edge Corp. may not use the preceding year method to avoid penalty for underpayment of its Year 1 estimated tax. Section 6655(e) allows a corporation to use the annualized income method to determine its estimated tax for the first quarter of Year 1.

11. (d) Under §6655(g), a corporation's "tax" for estimated tax purposes is the excess of: the sum of its regular corporate tax, the alternative minimum tax, the environmental tax, and the tax on gross transportation income, over the sum of its tax credits.

12. (a) Section 6601(a) imposes interest as an addition to tax when the tax is not paid on or before the last date prescribed for payment. Section 6601(b)(1) states that the last date prescribed for payment is to be determined without regard to extensions of time for payment. Under §6651(a)(2), there is a penalty for failure to pay tax when due equal to 0.5% of the net tax due for each month or fraction thereof that the tax is not paid. This penalty in the aggregate may not exceed 25% of the net tax due. However, this provision states that the penalty will not apply if the taxpayer shows reasonable cause for not paying the tax on time. Reg. §301.6651-1(c)(4) provides that reasonable cause will be presumed if a corporation files a timely request for extension to file its return, pays in at least 90% of the tax due by the due date without regard to the extension, and pays the balance due on or before the extended due date. Thus, Bass Corp. must pay interest on the $400 balance due. However, Bass Corp. demonstrated reasonable cause for late payment and thereby avoids the tax delinquency penalty of §6651(a)(2).

13. (d) In the case of property purchased for resale, a taxpayer is exempt from the uniform capitalization rules (UNICAP), if its average gross receipts for the preceding three years are $10 million or less. UNICAP rules generally apply to real and tangible personal property produced by the taxpayer for use in a trade or business or for investment purposes and to personal and real property purchased for resale to customers.

Income & Deductions

14. (b) Section 171(a) states that the amortizable bond premium on a taxable bond may be taken as a deduction. However, §171(c) provides that in the case of a bond on which the interest is not excludable from gross income, §171 shall apply only if the taxpayer so elects. Section 171 provides that the bond is to be amortized using the constant yield to maturity method and in the case of any taxable bond in lieu of any deduction, the amortization of the bond premium may be taken as an offset to the interest payment on such bond.

15. (b) Section 162(a) authorizes a deduction for all ordinary and necessary business expenses paid or accrued during the taxable year. Section 461(h) limits the deduction for accrued expenses until economic performance has occurred and provides that if services are to be performed for the taxpayer by another person, economic performance occurs as such person provides the services. Reg. §1.461-1(a)(2) provides that, for a taxpayer using the accrual method of accounting, no deduction may be taken until all events have occurred that establish the fact of the liability, and the amount of the liability can be determined with reasonable accuracy. In this case, the liability meets both the all-events test and the economic-performance test.

16. (b) Section 451(a) provides that any item of gross income is to be included in the year received unless the amount is properly included in a different period under the taxpayer's method of accounting. Reg. §1.451-1(a) states that under the accrual method of accounting, income is includible when all the events have occurred that fix the right to receive the income and the amount can be determined with reasonable accuracy. This regulation further provides that if an amount is accrued properly on the basis of a reasonable estimate and the exact amount subsequently is determined, the difference is to be taken into account for the taxable year in which the taxpayer makes the subsequent determination. Thus, the $1,000 difference is included properly in Stewart's Year 2 income tax return.

17. (d) For businesses other than financial institutions, bad debts *must* be deducted under the direct charge-off method rather than the reserve method.

18. (d) All activities of a corporation are considered to be business activities. Therefore, corporations may deduct their losses fully because all losses are considered business losses. Unlike individuals, corporations do not have to reduce casualty losses by either a statutory floor or by 10% of AGI. (The concept of AGI is not applicable to corporations.)

19. (a) Section 174 sets forth the treatment accorded to research and experimentation (R&D) expenditures. The law permits three alternatives for the handling of research and experimentation expenditures. These expenditures may be expensed in the year paid or incurred, or they may be deferred and amortized. If neither of these two methods is elected, R&D costs must be capitalized. If the costs are capitalized, a deduction may not be available until the research project is abandoned or is deemed worthless.

20. (a) Rent is income when received, regardless of the taxpayer's basis of accounting.

21. (b) A qualified personal service corporation may use the cash method of accounting as long as it clearly reflects income. Tax shelters, C corporations, and taxpayers with inventories (e.g., manufacturers) must use the accrual method.

22. (d) Banks Corp. may deduct the cost of the reimbursed meals as an ordinary and necessary business expense under §162(a). Generally the deduction limit for business meals is 50% of the amount of the expense. Banks meets the requirements that the cost of the meals is not extravagant and that the taxpayer or the taxpayer's employee be present at the meals. The full deduction is allowed for meals provided to employees for the convenience of the employer.

23. (d) A corporation may elect to deduct up to $5,000 of organization costs incurred in the tax year its business begins under §248. However, the $5,000 deduction is reduced on a dollar-for-dollar basis for those costs in excess of $50,000. Haze's deduction is not affected by this limit. Any remainder may be amortized over 15 years. Underwriting fees to issue corporate stock are not organization costs.

24. (b) Section 27(a) allows a tax credit for foreign income taxes paid. The other answers are allowed as deductions, not credits.

Dividend-Received Deduction

25. (d) Section 243(a)(1) allows a corporation to deduct 70% of the dividends received from a taxable domestic corporation. The phrase "unrelated domestic corporation" indicates that ownership by Best is less than 20%. If no indication of ownership percentage is given in a similar exam question, assume less than 20% ownership. Thus, the tentative dividends received deduction (DRD) is $70,000 ($100,000 × 70%). However, §246(b)(1) limits this deduction to 70% of taxable income before the DRD and certain other deductions. Hence, the DRD limit is $63,000 ($90,000 × 70%). Section 246(b)(2) waives this limitation for any year in which the taxpayer has a net operating loss. The tentative dividend-received deduction does not result in a net operating loss ($90,000 – $70,000 = $20,000).

26. (c) The dividend-received deduction is a special deduction. The question asks for income before special deductions, $500,000 sales plus $25,000 dividends received minus $250,000 cost of sales equals $275,000 income before special deductions. Cost of sales needs to be subtracted because it is not a special deduction. The dividends need to be included in income in total and then the appropriate percentage is subtracted as a special deduction.

27. (b) Section 243(a)(1) provides for a 70% dividend-received deduction for corporations that received dividends from taxable domestic corporations. This deduction is limited to 70% of taxable income determined without regard to the DRD and other specified deductions. In this case, the taxable income limitation of §246(b)(1) is greater than the tentative DRD: $70,000 × 70% = $49,000. Thus, the DRD is $7,000.

Taxable income before DRD	$70,000
Dividends received deduction ($10,000 × 70%)	(7,000)
Taxable Income [Sec. 63(a)]	$63,000
First tier ($50,000 × 15%)	$ 7,500
($63,000 – $50,000 = $13,000; $13,000 × 25%)	3,250
Income Tax [Sec. 11(b)]	$10,750

Key-Person Life Insurance

28. (d) Life insurance proceeds which are payable upon the death of an individual are generally tax-free upon receipt [§101(a)]. Therefore, Mell would not recognize any of the proceeds as taxable income.

Charitable Contributions

29. (b) For corporate taxpayers, the deduction for charitable contributions made to qualified donees is limited to 10% of taxable income computed without regard to the following: (1) deductions for charitable contributions, (2) deductions for dividends received, (3) net operating loss carryback, and (4) capital loss carryback. (The 30% and 50% deduction limits apply to individuals.)

30. (d) Section 170(a) allows a deduction for a charitable contribution made during the year and allows a corporation on the accrual basis of accounting to elect to take a deduction for a charitable contribution in the year that such contribution was authorized by its board of directors, if the corporation makes the contribution on or before the 15th day of the third month following the close of such tax year. Therefore, the corporation may deduct the $10,000 contribution and the payment authorized in Year 1, but paid in Year 2. Section 170(b)(2) limits a corporation's charitable contributions to 10% of taxable income, determined without regard to the deduction for charitable contributions. The charitable contributions are less than this limit ($500,000 × 10% = $50,000) and thus are allowed in full.

31. (c) Section 170(d)(2)(A) provides that a corporation's charitable contributions in excess of the 10% limit of §170(b)(2) shall be carried over for up to 5 years.

32. (b) Section 170(a) allows a deduction for charitable contributions. However, §170(b)(2) limits a corporation's deduction for charitable contributions to 10% of taxable income determined without regard to the charitable contributions deduction, without regard to Part VIII (except §248), net operating loss carrybacks, and capital loss carrybacks. Part VIII includes §243 that authorizes the dividend-received deduction for corporations. Section 170(d)(2)(A) provides that a corporation's charitable contributions in excess of the 10% limit of §170(b)(2) shall be carried over for up to 5 years. However, charitable contributions made in the current year are to be deducted first. Cable Corp.'s tentative charitable contributions deduction for Year 1 includes the carryover of $10,000 from Year 0. The dividend-received deduction must be added back to taxable income before the charitable contributions deduction to determine the limit imposed by §170(b)(2).

Charitable contributions made in Year 1	$ 80,000
Charitable contributions carryover from Year 0	10,000
Tentative charitable contributions deduction	$ 90,000
Taxable income before charitable contributions	$820,000
Add: Dividend-received deduction	40,000
Taxable income for purposes of the limit	$860,000
	× 10%
Limit on charitable contributions deductions	$ 86,000

Gains & Losses

33. (b) Unlike individuals, corporations are not allowed to deduct net capital losses. Excess capital losses may be carried back three years and carried forward five years. Generally, NOLs may be carried back 2 years and forward 20 years. ARRA '09 allows a small business (average gross receipts of $15 million or less) to carry back a 2008 NOL for up to five years. For a 2009 NOL, the regular two-year carry back period is in effect.

34. (b) Section 172(a) allows a deduction for net operating loss (NOL) carryovers and NOL carrybacks. Generally, NOLs have 2-year carryback and 20-year carryforward periods, except for NOLs of farmers and small businesses attributable to losses incurred in presidentially declared disaster areas and small businesses (average gross receipts of $15 million or less). $200,000 – $40,000 – $30,000 = $130,000

35. (d) Corporations only use capital losses to offset capital gains. A corporation's carryback and carryforward capital losses always are treated as short-term capital losses in the year to which they are carried. Excess capital losses of a corporation can be carried back three years and forward five. (The $3,000 limit for offsetting capital losses against ordinary income applies only to individuals.)

Alternative Minimum Tax

36. (d) The purpose of the alternative minimum tax (AMT) is to ensure that all taxpayers who have realized gains or income during the year pay at least a minimum amount of tax. The AMT applies only if a taxpayer's AMT liability is greater than her/his regular tax liability. In addition, a corporation that is classified as a personal holding company must pay a self-assessed penalty tax in addition to the regular corporate income tax. Thus, Tan's total tax liability for the year is $305,000 ($240,000 + $65,000).

37. (d) Both residential and nonresidential real property are depreciated using the mid-month convention for both AMT and regular tax.

38. (c) The alternative minimum tax (AMT) applicable to corporations is 20% of alternative minimum taxable income (AMTI) that exceeds the exemption amount. The exemption amount for a corporation is $40,000 reduced by 25% of the amount that AMTI exceeds $150,000. Thus, the exempt portion of Rona's AMTI is $27,500 (e.g., $40,000 – [($200,000 – $150,000) × 25%]).

39. (a) Section 55(b)(2) defines alternative minimum taxable income (AMTI) as the taxable income determined with regard to adjustments provided in §56 and §58 and increased by the amount of tax preference items as described in §57. Section 56(a)(1)(A)(ii) requires that the taxpayer use 150% declining balance method switching to the straight line method when the straight line method results in a larger deduction in computing AMTI. Section 168(b)(1) provides that for MACRS the taxpayer use the 200% declining balance method switching to straight line method when the straight line method results in a larger deduction. Thus, Eastern Corp. must add back the adjustment for depreciation since the depreciation under MACRS would result in a large r deduction than is allowed in computing AMTI. Section 57(a)(5)(A) states that interest on specified private activity bonds is a tax preference item. Section 57(a)(5)(C)(i) defines specified private-activity bonds as any private-activity bond as defined in §141 that was issued after August 7, 1986, and the interest thereon is excluded from gross income under §103. Eastern Corp. must add back the interest on the specified private activity bonds; such interest is a tax preference item.

Schedule M-1

40. (c) For tax purposes, goodwill is amortized straight-line for 15 years. Federal income taxes are not deductible. $239,200 + $110,100 + $7,500 – ($300,000 / 15) = $336,800

41. (a)

Book income	$140,000
Add: Nondeductible federal income tax	40,000
Add: Nondeductible 50% portion of meals and entertainment expense	25,000
Taxable income	$205,000

42. (a) The $6,000 in municipal bond interest income must be removed from book income to reconcile to taxable income, as it is not taxable income. The $1,500 of interest incurred to carry a tax-exempt investment is not an expense deductible for taxes and thus must be included in book income to reconcile to taxable income. The advertising expense is deductible for both tax and book purposes; no adjustment need be made for it.

Distributions

43. (c) Section 301(c)(1) provides that a distribution with respect to a corporation's stock is treated as a dividend as defined in §316 and included in gross income. Section 316(a) defines a dividend as a distribution of property made by a corporation to its shareholders from accumulated earnings and profits (E&P) and from current E&P. Section 317(a) includes money in the definition of property. Thus, the taxable dividend income to Dahl Corp.'s shareholders is $280,000 ($120,000 + $160,000). The $80,000 ($360,000 – $280,000) of the distribution that is not a dividend reduces the basis of the shareholder's stock, but not below zero, under §301(c)(2). Any remaining distribution is treated as a gain on the sale of the stock under §301(c)(3).

44. (c) Kent Corp. must recognize a gain of $50,000 ($200,000 – $150,000) on the distribution of the property under §311(b)(1). Section 312(b)(1) requires that the corporation's earnings and profits (E&P) be increased by the amount of the gain. However, because the $60,000 current E&P for Year 1 is given, the gain on the distribution has already been included in current E&P. This is true because §316(a) states that current E&P are determined at the close of the taxable year without any reduction for distributions made during the year. The amount of the distribution is the $200,000 fair market value of the property under §301(b)(1). Section 301(c)(1) states that the portion which is a dividend under §316 must be included in the shareholder's gross income. Section 316(a) provides that a distribution is a dividend, first, to the extent of the corporation's current E&P, and second, out of the corporation's accumulated E&P. Because the amount of the distribution exceeds the sum of the current E&P and the accumulated E&P, the distribution is a dividend in the amount of $185,000 ($60,000 + $125,000). The $15,000 remainder of the distribution reduces the shareholder's basis in the stock, and any amount in excess of the basis of the stock is treated as a gain on the deemed sale of the stock under §301(c). The shareholder has a $200,000 basis in the property under §301(d).

45. (b) If current earnings and profits (E&P) is positive and accumulated E&P is negative, then distributions are treated as dividends to the extent of current E&P. Dividends on preferred stock are paid before dividends on common stock.

Redemptions & Liquidations

46. (a) Gain which is incurred by a noncorporate shareholder on the redemption of stock that qualifies as a partial liquidation of the distributing company is treated as a capital gain under §302.

47. (a) These are deductible as business expenses under §162(a).

48. (d) Shareholders recognize gain or loss on a liquidating distribution to the extent that the FMV of property received is greater than their stock bases.

49. (d) Gain or loss generally is not recognized upon the complete liquidation of a subsidiary. Instead, the basis of the subsidiary's assets and other tax attributes, such as the net operating loss deduction and excess charitable contributions, are carried over by the parent.

50. (b) A corporation recognizes gain or loss on the distribution of property in complete liquidation as if such property had been sold to the distributee at fair market value. The type of gain which is recognized depends on the type of property sold. Krol recognizes $50,000 (e.g., $150,000 – $100,000) of capital gain since it is assumed that the securities were a capital asset in the hands of Krol.

Accumulated Earnings Tax

51. (c) Section 535(a) states that accumulated taxable income is taxable income adjusted by the items noted in §535(b) and less the sum of the accumulated earnings credit and the dividends paid deduction. Section 535(c)(1) states that (the general rule) accumulated earnings credit is equal to the

earnings and profits for the taxable year that are retained for the reasonable needs of the business less the net capital gains adjustment. Section 561(a) allows a deduction for dividends paid during the taxable year. Section 563(a) states that a dividend paid after the taxable year and on or before the 15th day of the third month following the close of the taxable year shall be considered as paid during such taxable year.

52. (d) Section 532(c) provides that the accumulated earnings tax (AET) can be imposed on a corporation without regard to the number of shareholders of such corporations. Partnerships are not subject to the AET as §531 states that the tax is imposed on the accumulated taxable income of every corporation. Section 532(b)(1) states that the AET does not apply to personal holding companies. Section 535(a) states that the dividends paid deduction is allowed in computing the accumulated taxable income. Section 561(a) allows a deduction for dividends paid during the taxable year. Thus, if distributions exceed the accumulated earnings there would be no accumulated taxable income and therefore no AET.

53. (c) Starting with its federal taxable income of $400,000, Kari is allowed a deduction for the federal income tax of $100,000. The minimum credit is $250,000. Therefore, the maximum amount that may be subject to the accumulated earnings tax is $400,000 – $100,000 – $250,000 = $50,000.

Personal Holding Company Tax

54. (a) Section 545(b)(1) allows a deduction for federal income taxes in computing undistributed personal holding company (PHC) income. Section 545(b)(5) allows a deduction for net capital gains less the taxes thereon in computing personal holding company income. Section 1222(11) defines a net capital gain as the excess of a net long-term capital gain over any net short term capital loss. Thus, §545(b)(5) allows a deduction for a net long-term capital gain less the related federal income tax in determining undistributed PHC income.

55. (d) The tax base upon which a personal holding company (PHC) is taxed is undistributed PHC income. Basically, this amount is taxable income, subject to certain adjustments, minus the deduction for dividends paid. Dividends actually paid during the tax year ordinarily qualify for the deduction for dividends paid, however, such distributions must be *pro rata.* They must exhibit no preference to any shares of stock over shares of the same class or to any other class of stock over other classes outstanding. The consent dividend procedure involves a hypothetical distribution of corporate income taxed to the shareholders. Since the consent dividend is taxable to the shareholders, a deduction is allowed for the corporation. Therefore, the amount that Hull should deduct for dividends paid is $30,000, the sum of the $20,000 of dividends paid and the $10,000 of consent dividends reported in the individual income tax returns of the shareholders.

56. (b) Dividends are included in personal holding company (PHC) income under §543(a)(1). Interest earned on tax-exempt obligations is not included in PHC income because §542(a)(1) states that for the income test to be met for the corporation to be a personal holding company at least 60% of the corporation's ordinary gross income must be PHC income. Section 543(b)(2) defines ordinary gross income as gross income less the sum of capital gains and §1231 gains. Section 103(a) excludes interest on state and local bonds from gross income. Thus, interest on tax exempt obligations cannot be a part of ordinary gross income and is, therefore, not PHC income.

57. (a) A corporation is a personal holding company (PHC) if two conditions are met. First, under §541(a), at least 60% of the corporation's adjusted ordinary gross income is PHC income. In general, PHC income consists of investment type income such as dividends and interest. Since Zero Corp. is an investment company, one can assume that Zero Corp. meets this income test. The second condition provided by §541(a)(2) is that at any time during the last half of the taxable year, more than 50% in value of the outstanding stock of the corporation be owned directly or indirectly by 5 or fewer individuals. There is no requirement that these 5 individuals be related. The best answer is (a) because under §544(a)(1), stock owned by an estate is deemed to be owned proportionately by its beneficiaries. Thus, Edwards, would be deemed to own the 200 shares owned by the estate, since he is the beneficiary of the estate. Edwards would then be deemed to own 650 shares of the 1,000 shares outstanding. **Note:** Answers (b) and (d) are also correct because 2 individuals would own 65% (650 / 1000) of the stock of Zero Corp. during the last half of the taxable year. One cannot determine if answer (c) is correct or not. Under §544(a)(1), stock owned by a partnership is deemed to be owned proportionately by its partners. Answer (a) seems best because the question implies that it is testing the candidate's knowledge of the attribution rules of §544.

58. (d) Keen has no personal holding company tax liability as it does not meet both tests for a personal holding company [§542(a)]. A substantial portion (60% or more) of corporate income (adjusted

ordinary gross income) must be comprised of passive types of income such as dividends, interest, rents, royalties, or certain personal service income. This test is met. However, more than 50% of the value of the outstanding stock must be owned by five or fewer individuals at any time during the last half of the taxable year. This test is not met.

Reorganizations

59. (d) This event is a tax-free liquidation of a subsidiary.

60. (a) This business combination is a statutory consolidation and is a reorganization under §368(a)(1)(A). Section 354(a)(1) provides that no gain or loss shall be recognized if stock or securities in a corporation that is a party to the reorganization are exchanged, pursuant to a plan of reorganization, solely for stock or securities in such corporation or in another corporation that is a party to the reorganization. Thus, under this reorganization, neither shareholders nor any corporation recognizes gain or loss.

61. (d) Section 354 provides for the nonrecognition of any gain or loss on property transferred to a corporation pursuant to a corporate reorganization in exchange solely for stock or securities of such corporation or in another corporation that is party to the reorganization. Because the taxpayer received only stock in the exchange, no gain or loss is recognized.

62. (c) Section 368(a)(1)(B) provides that a reorganization, known as a Type B reorganization, is the acquisition of the stock of one corporation by another corporation, solely in exchange for the acquiring corporation's voting stock or of the voting stock of a corporation that is in control of the acquiring corporation. Immediately after the acquisition, the acquiring corporation must be in control of the target corporation, as defined in §368(c).

Consolidated Returns

63. (d) Section 61(a)(7) provides that dividends are included in gross income. However, §243(a)(3) allows a deduction for 100% of dividends received from a taxable domestic corporation that are qualifying dividends. Qualifying dividends are any dividends received from a member of the same affiliated group and paid out of the earnings and profits of a taxable year of the distributing corporation. Section 243(b)(2) states that the term affiliated group has the same meaning as in §1504(a). Section 1504(a) provides that an affiliated group consists of corporations with a common parent, if the parent owns at least 80% of the voting power and value of the stock of an affiliated corporation. Thus, on a consolidated tax return, the dividend income would be eliminated.

64. (d) The gain on the sale from Potter to Sly is not recognized at the time of the sale because Porter and Sly file a consolidated tax return. Instead, it is recognized when Sly sells the land to an unrelated third party in a fully taxable transaction.

65. (d) Under §1504(a)(2), at least 80% of the total voting power and 80% of the total value of the stock of the subsidiary must be owned directly by the parent to be eligible to file a consolidated return.

66. (d) Prin must include the dividends in its gross income under §61(a)(7). However, under §243(a)(3) and §243(b) Prin is allowed a deduction for 100% of the dividends received from a corporation that is a member of the same affiliated group. The net result is that the dividends are not taxed on the consolidated return.

67. (a) Under §243, there is a 100% dividend-received deduction (DRD) for dividends received from a member of an affiliated group. Thus, the dividends received are effectively not taxable, because their inclusion in gross income under §61 is offset by the 100% DRD.

S Corporation Status

68. (a, c) Both answers are required for full point value. An S corporation may only have one class of stock and no more than 100 shareholders. Stock may have different voting rights and still be classified as one class of stock. An estate may be an S corporation shareholder. A grantor trust may be an S corporation shareholder.

69. (a) Voluntary revocation of S corporation status is made by shareholders collectively holding a majority of stock.

70. (d) Section 1362(d)(3)(A) states that the S election terminates when an S corporation has subchapter C earnings and profits and more than 25% of its gross receipts for each of 3 consecutive years are passive investment income. An S corporation may have up to 100 shareholders. An S corporation may have an estate as a shareholder. S corporations are allowed to deduct charitable contributions. The charitable contributions are passed down to the shareholders as a separately stated item.

71. (b) Section 1362(b)(3) states that if a corporation makes the S election after the first 2½ months of the tax year, the election becomes effective at the beginning of the following tax year.

Because the election was made in December Year 6 and Village Corp. is a calendar year corporation, the S election becomes effective on January 1, Year 7.

72. (c) After a corporation's status as an S corporation is revoked or terminated, §1362(g) enforces a five-year waiting period before a new election can be made. The Code does, however, allow the IRS to make exceptions to this rule to permit an earlier reelection by the corporation. The IRS may allow an early reelection if (1) there is a more than 50% change in ownership after the first year for which the termination is applicable or (2) the event causing the termination was not reasonably within the control of the S corporation or its majority shareholders.

S Corporation Income & Basis

73. (c) Since no election was made to use an interim closing of the books, §1362(e)(2) requires that the nonseparately computed income must be allocated on a daily basis between the short S year and the short C year. Zinco Corp.'s income allocated to the short S year is $76,500 [(90 / 365) × $310,250]. The days in the short S year are computed as follows: January days 31 + February days 28 + March days 31 = 90 days.

74. (c) Section 1566(a)(2) requires that the S corporation take into account the shareholder's *pro rata* share of non-separately computed income or loss. Section 1366(a)(1) requires that an S corporation take into account the shareholder's pro rata share of items of income, deduction, loss, or credit that could affect the liability for tax of any shareholder. The $5,000 of dividend income is stated separately because it is necessary to determine those dividends that qualify to be taxed at capital gain rates under §1(h)(11).

75. (b) One major advantage of an S election is the ability to pass through any net operating loss (NOL) of the corporation directly to the shareholders. The NOL is allocated on a daily basis to all shareholders. Meyer's share of Bern's loss is computed by multiplying Bern's NOL for the year by the percentage of Bern's stock owned by Meyer and the proportion of days that Meyer owned the stock (e.g., $36,500 × 50% × 40 / 365 = $2,000).

76. (c) The distributions are nontaxable return of capital to the extent of the shareholder's basis in the stock. Any excess distributions are treated as gain from the sale of stock. Shareholder basis is increased by nonseparately and separately stated income and reduced by losses, deductions, and distributions. Baker's basis is increased by ordinary income and reduced by the long-term capital loss.

Baker's basis at beginning of the year	$ 25,000
Add: Ordinary income	1,000
Less: Long-term capital loss	(3,000)
Adjusted basis	$ 23,000
Cash distribution	$ 30,000
Adjusted basis	(23,000)
Taxable portion of the cash distribution	$ 7,000

77. (c) In general, S corporations pass items of income, loss, deductions, and credits through to their shareholders; however, an S corporation pays taxes at the corporate level for built-in gains (the excess of the fair market value of assets over their bases at the beginning of the first year in which the S corporation status is effective). ($85,000 – $40,000) × 35% = $15,750

78. (d) Generally, a corporation that has been an S corporation since its inception would not have Earnings & Profits (E&P). Therefore, the distributions from the S corporation are tax-free to the extent of the shareholder's basis in the stock of the S corporation. Any excess distributions are treated as gain from the sale of stock.

79. (b) An S corporation passes through those items of income, loss, deduction, or credit which could affect the tax liability of its shareholders differently. This includes charitable contributions, dividends, and foreign taxes. Answers (a), (c), and (d) are all items that are deductible by an S corporation.

80. (a) The at-risk rules allow a shareholder of an S corporation to deduct only the losses which are passed to her/him from the S corporation to the extent he has amounts which are considered at-risk. Since the S corporation is not a tax paying entity in general, and all of its income and losses are passed through to its shareholders, the at-risk rules would apply only to the shareholders.

Solution 46-2 ADDITIONAL MULTIPLE CHOICE ANSWERS

Formation

81. (c) No gain or loss is recognized if property is transferred to a corporation solely in exchange for stock if, immediately after the transfer, the transferor(s) are in control of the corporation. However, the receipt of boot (property other than stock) triggers the recognition of gain.

Filing Requirements

82. (a) Section 162(f) disallows any deduction for fines or penalties paid to a government for violation of any law. Therefore, the penalty is not deductible.

Income & Deductions

83. (c) Corporations may elect to deduct up to $5,000 of organization costs incurred in the tax year its business begins under §248. However, the $5,000 deduction is reduced on a dollar-for-dollar basis for those costs in excess of $50,000. Any remainder must be amortized over 15 years. Section 248(b) defines organization costs as costs incident to the creation of the corporation and chargeable to a capital account. Reg. 1.248-1(b) includes costs of drafting the corporate charter as eligible costs and includes professional fees, printing costs, and commissions incurred in the issuing or selling of stock as costs that are **not** eligible costs. These costs are treated as a reduction of the corporation's capital.

84. (a) Under §1032, when a corporation exchanges its own stock (e.g., treasury stock) for property or money, no gain or loss is recognized on the exchange.

85. (b) Section 243 indicates that no DRD is allowed if stock is held less than 46 days or if the taxpayer must make related payments on other property. In addition, §243 states that the deduction is equal to 100% for members of an affiliated group. An 80% deduction is permitted if the recipient owns between 20% and 80%, and 70% can be claimed when holdings are less than 20%. The DRD is limited to a percentage of a corporation's taxable income. Per §243(a), the amount of the DRD depends upon the ownership percentage the corporate shareholder holds in the domestic corporation making the distribution (e.g., a 10% level of ownership results in a 70% deduction, while a 40% level results in an 80% deduction). Certain provisions of the Code governing the computation of taxable income applicable only to corporations, such as the DRD, do not apply to S corporations.

86. (b) If the corporate shareholder owns 20% or more (up to 80%) of another domestic corporation's stock, the corporate shareholder gets an 80% dividend-received deduction. $600,000 – $400,000 + $100,000 – (80% × $100,000) = $220,000

87. (c) Section 243(a) allows corporations to deduct 70% of the amount of dividends received from taxable domestic corporations. The phrase "unaffiliated domestic corporation" indicates that ownership by Kelly is less than 20%. If no indication of ownership percentage is given in a similar exam question, assume less than 20% ownership. The allowance method of accounting for bad debts is not allowed for tax purposes. Section §166(a) provides that bad debts are deductible when wholly worthless or when the taxpayer can prove that a debt is recoverable only in part (the specific charge off method of accounting for bad debts). An increased allowance for doubtful accounts represents an increase in bad debts expense for book purposes.

Book income	$300,000
Less: DRD ($50,000 × 70%)	(35,000)
Add: Addition to allowance for doubtful accounts	80,000
Taxable income	$345,000

88. (d) Corporations generally are barred from using the cash method of accounting; however, a non tax-shelter entity that is a qualified personal service corporation or meets the less-than-$5,000,000-of-gross-receipts test may use the cash method.

89. (b) The passive activity loss rules apply to (1) noncorporate taxpayers, (2) *closely* held C corporations, and (3) personal service corporations. For S corporations and partnerships, passive income or loss flows through to the owners, and the passive activity loss rules are applied at the owner level. The passive activity loss rules apply to *closely* held C corporations—not to *widely* held C corporations.

Key-Person Life Insurance

90. (c) A corporation can deduct premiums paid for group term life insurance for its employees as long as it is not the beneficiary. Premiums on key-person life insurance policies are not deductible by the corporation because the proceeds from these policies are not included in taxable corporate income.

Charitable Contributions

91. (a) An accrual basis corporation can elect to deduct amounts paid to a charitable organization if the board of directors authorizes a charitable contribution during the year and the payment of such

contribution is made on or before the 15th day of the third month following the close of such year. Since Ral Corp.'s board of directors authorized the contribution and the payment was made before March 15, Year 2, it can deduct any amounts which do not exceed the 10% income limitation in Year 1.

92. (a) A taxpayer that deducts the fair market value of unsolicited sample merchandise donated to charity must take into income the fair market value of such property upon contribution.

Gains & Losses

93. (a) A corporation can deduct capital losses only against capital gains. Since Ral Corp. has no capital gains, the entire capital loss is disallowed.

94. (b) Capital losses that a corporation carries back or forward are deemed to be short-term regardless of whether they were short-term or long-term losses when sustained. A corporation can not use capital losses to offset ordinary income.

95. (c) Brown's net operating loss (NOL) before the dividend-received deduction (DRD) is $900,000 – $1,100,000 = $200,000. As the dividends are from a Fortune 500 corporation and no ownership percentage is indicated otherwise in the given information, assume that Brown owns less than 20% of the other company's stock. At less than 20% ownership, the DRD deduction percentage is 70%, so 30% of the dividend is included in the income or NOL, ($200,000) + $30,000 = ($170,000). As the NOL exists before the DRD, the taxable income limitation is inapplicable.

Alternative Minimum Tax

96. (c) The alternative minimum tax is imposed to insure that corporations pay a minimum amount of tax. The portion of the tentative minimum tax which exceeds the regular tax liability is added to the regular tax liability so that the corporation is paying the minimum tax amount.

97. (c) Tax preference items for alternative minimum tax purposes are listed under §57 and include the accelerated depreciation taken on pre-1987 real property that exceeds the depreciation that would have been allowed under the straight-line method. Using the percentage-of-completion method is an adjustment not a tax preference. The Code distinguishes between adjustments and preferences. Casualty losses are a deduction.

Schedule M-1

98. (b) Schedule M-1 reconciles the financial statements and the tax return. Items appearing on Schedule M-1 are those that differ in treatment between financial reporting purposes and tax return purposes. Premiums paid on key-person life insurance policy are deducted to determine financial income, but not taxable income. Neither cash distributions to shareholders nor the ending balance of retained earnings are deducted from either financial or taxable income. Corporate bond interest paid or received is deducted or included, respectively, in arriving at both financial and taxable income.

Distributions

99. (c) Corporate distributions to shareholders on their stock are taxed as dividends to the extent of the corporation's current and/or accumulated earnings and profits (E&P). Also, the distributing corporation recognizes gain on any distribution of appreciated property as if such property were sold at its FMV. Here, the distribution of the vacant land was considered to have been sold at its FMV of $40,000, resulting in a gain of $35,000 (e.g., $40,000 – $5,000) to the corporation. This gain brought the total of accumulated E&P up to $44,000 (e.g., $9,000 + $35,000), all considered to be taxable dividends. The $5,000 [($9,000 + $40,000) – $44,000] of the distribution in excess of existing accumulated E&P is treated as a return of capital.

100. (d) Section 301(c)(1) provides that a distribution with respect to a corporation's stock is treated as a dividend as defined in §316 and included in gross income. Section 316(a) defines a dividend as a distribution of property made by a corporation to its shareholders out of out of earnings and profits (E&P) of the taxable year and accumulated E&P. Section 317(a) includes money in the definition of property. The classification of the March distribution must be determined before the classification of the July distribution can be made because there is not enough current E&P to cover both distributions. Remember, current E&P is allocated on a ***pro rata*** basis to the distributions made during the year, while accumulated E&P, on the other hand, is applied to the distributions in the order that they are made. Thus, the current earnings and profits balance allocated to each of the $20,000 distributions is $5,000 [$20,000 × ($10,000 / $40,000)]. The $20,000 March distribution is classified as dividend income because there was enough E&P to cover the entire distribution ($5,000 + $15,000 – $20,000 = $0). After the March distribution, current E&P (prior to allocation of the July distribution) and accumulated E&P are reduced to zero. Therefore, the only portion of the July

distribution that would be taxable dividend income to Bridge's shareholders the $5,000 allocated to current E&P. The remaining $15,000 ($20,000 – $5,000) of the July distribution that is not a dividend reduces the basis of the shareholder's stock, but not below zero, under §301(c)(2). Any remaining distribution is treated as a gain on the sale of the stock under §301(c)(3).

101. (c) Earnings and profits (E&P) is computed in a similar manner as taxable income. Once taxable income is computed, adjustments must be made to arrive at E&P. E&P is increased by taxable income and charitable contributions carryforward and decreased by federal income taxes paid.

Accumulated E&P, beginning balance	$100,000
Add: Taxable income	50,000
Charitable contribution carryforward	1,000
Capital loss carry forwards	2,000
Less: Federal income taxes paid	(5,000)
Accumulated E&P, ending balance	$148,000

102. (c) Dividends paid from earnings and profits (E&P) are income ($20,000 + $30,000 = $50,000). Dividends paid beyond E&P are a return of capital.

103. (c) Section 301(c)(1) provides that when a distribution of property is from a corporation to a shareholder with respect to its stock, it will be a taxable dividend as defined in §316. Section 316(a) provides that a dividend is any distribution made to shareholders from accumulated earnings and profits (E&P) or from current E&P. Reg. 1.316-2(a) provides that consideration should be given to current E&P first and then to accumulated E&P. In this case, the $30,000 distribution is a dividend to the extent of the $10,000 current E&P. The $50,000 deficit in accumulated E&P is not netted against the current E&P.

104. (c) Section 311(b)(1) provides that if a corporation distributes property to a shareholder, the corporation must recognize gain as if the property were sold for its fair market value. Section 1001(a) states that the gain on the sale of property is the amount realized less the property's adjusted basis.

105. (d) When a corporation distributes property, it is treated as if it sold the property to its shareholders for the property's fair market value. The corporation recognizes gain, but not loss, on the distribution of property. Generally the gain recognized equals the FMV less the adjusted basis. However, if the property distributed is subject to a liability, then the FMV of the property can not be less than the liability for gain determination purposes.

Asset liability (not less than FMV)	$40,000
Adjusted basis of asset	25,000
Gain recognized by Aztec	$15,000

106. (b) Distributions over the current and accumulated earnings and profits are a return of capital. A return of capital is not taxable.

Redemptions & Liquidations

107. (c) When a corporation is liquidated or sold before three years pass after the manufacture, construction, or purchase of certain types of property is completed, and before the corporation realizes two-thirds of the income to be derived from that property, the corporation is collapsible. The stockholder's holding period is irrelevant.

108. (d) Hall's gain is the sale price less the basis in the stock ($33,000 – $16,000 = $17,000). Usually amounts distributed in complete liquidation of a corporation are treated as full payment in exchange for the stock and are a capital gain or loss. Dividends are distributions from a corporation that result in the same ownership percentage by the shareholders. Hall has no ownership interest in the corporation after the transaction, so this is not a dividend. [This question is unchanged from the Nov. 1997 exam. Note that the examiners asked about tax year 1996, even though they specify that candidates should know the law in effect six months before the exam. In this case, the law is the same in 2009 and 2010 as in 1996.]

Personal Holding Company Tax

109. (d) If, at any time during the last half of the tax year, more than 50% of the value of the outstanding stock of a corporation is owned directly or indirectly by five or fewer individuals and at least 60% of the corporation's adjusted ordinary gross income is personal holding company income, then the corporation is a personal holding company.

Reorganizations

110. (b) Under §368(a)(1)(B), this transaction will qualify as a Type B reorganization and, therefore, will be tax free under §354(a)(1). King Corp. acquires control of Jaxson Corp. by exchanging King's voting stock for Jaxson's voting stock. King acquires 90% of Jaxson's voting stock, which means meeting the 80% or more requirement to be in control of Jaxson.

Consolidated Returns

111. (b) The transaction represents the sale of property between a parent and a subsidiary filing a

consolidated tax return, and, thus, it is referred to as a deferred intercompany transaction and receives special treatment. Stem realizes a gain of $60,000 ($150,000 – $90,000) on the sale of the land to Plant. The gain realized is deferred in a suspense account until the restoration event, the sale of the land by Plant to Dubin. In Year 2, Stem recognizes the $60,000 gain realized in Year 1. Plant recognizes a gain of $30,000 ($180,000 – $150,000) as its basis in the land includes the deferred gain of Stem ($90,000 + $60,000 = $150,000).

112. (c) In a consolidated return, the income and operating losses of each of the components are netted, allowing for any intercompany profits or losses. $50,000 – $60,000 – $40,000 = ($50,000)

113. (a) There is no requirement in the IRC that only corporations that issue audited financial statements on a consolidated basis are eligible to file a consolidated return. Under §243, 100% (not 70%) of the dividends paid by a subsidiary to a parent are deductible from gross income. Section 1501 allows an affiliated group of corporations to file a consolidated return. Under §1504(a), an affiliated group consists of corporations connected through a common parent, if the common parent owns at least 80% of the total voting power and at least 80% of the total value of the stock of at least one corporation. Also, one or more of the other corporations must own directly at least 80% of the stock of the remaining corporations. Reg. §1.1502-11(a)(1) provides that the consolidated taxable income shall take into account the separate taxable income of each member of the group.

114. (d) Portal prepares a consolidated return, therefore dividends received from Sal are eliminated at the consolidated level and no dividend income is reported on the consolidated tax return.

115. (d) Dow must include the $20,000 dividend in its gross income under §61(a)(7). However, under §243(a)(3) and §243(b) Dow is allowed a deduction for 100% of the dividends received from a corporation that is a member of the same affiliated group. Thus, Dow is entitled to a dividends received deduction of $20,000. The net result is this $20,000 dividend is not taxed on the consolidated return.

116. (d) S corporations may not be members of affiliated groups. D corporation may not file as a group with A and C corporations as B corporation (an S corporation) owns all of D corporation's stock.

S Corporations

117. (c) Returns of corporations, made on the basis of the calendar year, are to be filed on or before the 15th day of March following the close of the calendar year [§6072(b)].

118. (a) Section 1366(a)(1) requires that the shareholders of an S corporation must report their *pro rata* share of the S corporation's income.

$73,200 × (40 / 366) × (100 / 100)	$ 8,000
$73,200 × (326 / 366) × (75 / 100)	48,900
Kane's *pro rata* share	$56,900

119. (d) Section 1566(a)(2) requires that the S corporation take into account the shareholder's *pro rata* share of non-separately computed income or loss. Section 1366(a)(1) requires that an S corporation take into account the shareholder's *pro rata* share of items of income, deduction, loss, or credit that could affect the liability for tax of any shareholder. The $5,000 of dividend income is stated separately because it is necessary to determine those dividends that qualify to be taxed at the capital gain rates under §1(h)(11).

Gross receipts	$50,000
Less: Supplies	(2,000)
Utilities	(1,500)
Net business income	$46,500

120. (c) In general, S corporations pass items of income, loss, deductions, and credits through to their shareholders. Shareholders then pay tax on their *pro rata* share of income, regardless of whether or not any income actually was distributed to them. $200,000 × 40% = $80,000

121. (d) Section 1367(a)(1)(A) requires an increase in the shareholder's basis of stock in an S corporation for items of income separately stated in §1366(a)(1)(A). Section 1366(a)(1)(A) specifically includes tax-exempt income. Thus, the shareholder's basis in her/his stock of an S corporation is increased for her/his share of tax-exempt interest. Section 1367(a)(1)(B) also requires an increase in a shareholder's basis of stock in an S corporation for nonseparately computed income. Taxable interest would be included in nonseparately computed income. Thus, the shareholder's basis in her/his stock of an S corporation is increased for her/his share of taxable interest.

122. (b) Without debt transactions, a shareholder's adjusted basis in an S corporation interest is the beginning basis plus income minus distributions.

$12,000 + 50% × ($81,000 + $10,000) – $51,000 = $6,500

123. (c) Under §1368(b) a distribution to a shareholder in an S corporation that has no accumulated earnings and profits, in respect of the shareholder's stock in the S corporation, shall not be included in the shareholder's gross income except to the extent that the amount of the distribution exceeds the adjusted basis of the stock. Section 1367(a)(2)(A) provides that distributions by the S corporation that were not includible in income under §1368 shall decrease the basis of the shareholder's stock in the S corporation.

124. (d) Fringe benefits provided to a more than 2% shareholder-employee must be included in the shareholder's gross income.

125. (c) Under §1362(d)(1)(B), an election to be an S corporation may be revoked voluntarily only if shareholders holding more than one-half of the shares of stock of the corporation on the day the revocation is made consent to the revocation. Reg. 18.1362-3 states that such shares include nonvoting shares. With 50,000 shares outstanding, shareholders holding more than 25,000 shares must consent to the revocation. The 10,000 voting shares and 16,000 nonvoting shares total 26,000 shares, which is greater than 25,000 shares.

PERFORMANCE BY SUBTOPICS

Each category below parallels a subtopic covered in Chapter 46. Record the number and percentage of questions you correctly answered in each subtopic area.

Formation

Question #	Correct √
1	
2	
3	
4	
5	
6	
# Questions	6
# Correct	_____
% Correct	_____

Filing Requirements

Question #	Correct √
7	
8	
9	
10	
11	
12	
13	
# Questions	7
# Correct	_____
% Correct	_____

Income & Deductions

Question #	Correct √
14	
15	
16	
17	
18	
19	
20	
21	
22	
23	
24	
# Questions	11
# Correct	_____
% Correct	_____

Dividend-Received Deduction

Question #	Correct √
25	
26	
27	
# Questions	3
# Correct	_____
% Correct	_____

Key-Person Life Insurance

Question #	Correct √
28	
# Questions	1
# Correct	_____
% Correct	_____

Charitable Contributions

Question #	Correct √
29	
30	
31	
32	
# Questions	4
# Correct	_____
% Correct	_____

Gains & Losses

Question #	Correct √
33	
34	
35	
# Questions	3
# Correct	_____
% Correct	_____

Alternative Minimum Tax

Question #	Correct √
36	
37	
38	
39	
# Questions	4
# Correct	_____
% Correct	_____

Schedule M-1

Question #	Correct √
40	
41	
42	
# Questions	3
# Correct	_____
% Correct	_____

Distributions

Question #	Correct √
43	
44	
45	
# Questions	3
# Correct	_____
% Correct	_____

Redemptions & Liquidations

Question #	Correct √
46	
47	
48	
49	
50	
# Questions	5
# Correct	_____
% Correct	_____

Accumulated Earnings Tax

Question #	Correct √
51	
52	
53	
# Questions	3
# Correct	_____
% Correct	_____

Personal Holding Company Tax

Question #	Correct √
54	
55	
56	
57	
58	
# Questions	5
# Correct	_____
% Correct	_____

Reorganizations

Question #	Correct √
59	
60	
61	
62	
# Questions	4
# Correct	_____
% Correct	_____

Consolidated Returns

Question #	Correct √
63	
64	
65	
66	
67	
# Questions	5
# Correct	_____
% Correct	_____

S Corporation Status

Question #	Correct √
68	
69	
70	
71	
72	
# Questions	5
# Correct	_____
% Correct	_____

S Corporation Income & Basis

Question #	Correct √
73	
74	
75	
76	
77	
78	
79	
80	
# Questions	8
# Correct	_____
% Correct	_____

SIMULATION SOLUTIONS

Solution 46-3 C Corporation

Adjustments (3 points)

1. $15,000, I

Section 162(a)(2) allows a deduction for traveling expenses, including meals, incurred in a trade or business. Section 274(n)(1) limits the deduction for business meals to 50% of the cost of such meals. All of the travel cost and the cost of meals were deducted on Anvil's financial accounting books. Because 50% of the cost of business meals may **not** be deducted for tax purposes, such amount must be added back to the financial accounting income in arriving at taxable income ($30,000 × 50%).

2. $7,000, I

The $7,000 in life insurance premiums was deducted in arriving at financial accounting income. However, §264(a)(1) disallows any deduction for life insurance premiums paid on the life of a corporate officer when the taxpayer is the beneficiary of the policy.

3. $0, N

Under §461(a), the amount of any deduction is to be taken in the proper taxable year under the method of accounting used in computing taxable income. Because Anvil is an accrual basis taxpayer, the franchise tax expense is generally deducted in the year accrued. However, §461(h)(4) requires that all events have occurred that fix the fact of the liability and that the amount can be determined with reasonable accuracy. Also, §461(h)(1) states that the all-events test is not deemed to be satisfied until economic performance has occurred. Under Reg. 1.461-4(g)(6), economic performance occurs for a tax liability when the tax liability is paid. However, §461(h)(3)(A) provides an exception for recurring items. For recurring items, the economic performance test is waived if (1) the all-events test is satisfied, (2) economic performance occurs within the shorter of a reasonable time after the close of the tax year or 8½ months after the close of the tax year, (3) the item is recurring in nature and is consistently treated by the taxpayer, and (4) the item is not material or results in a better matching of income and deductions. The accrual of the franchise tax liability should meet the recurring item exception. Therefore, $18,000 should be deducted in arriving at Anvil's taxable income.

4. $6,000, D

Section 168(e)(3)(B)(iv) provides that any qualified technological equipment is 5-year property. Section 168(i)(2) includes computers in the definition of qualified technological equipment; thus, computers are 5-year MACRS property. Section 168(b)(1) requires the double-declining balance method, with a switch to the straight-line method when the straight-line method provides a greater deduction. Section 168(b)(4) states that salvage value is to be ignored. The straight-line depreciation rate would be 20% a year (100% / 5 years). Therefore, the double-declining balance rate is 40% (20% × 2). Section 168(d)(1) requires the use of the half-year convention. Section 168(d)(4)(A) states that the half-year convention treats all property placed in service during the year as placed in service at the mid-point of the year. Therefore, the MACRS deductions for these computers are determined as follows.

For tax Year 2: $50,000 × 40% × 1/2 = $10,000
For tax Year 3: ($50,000 – $10,000) × 40% = $16,000

The MACRS deduction is $6,000 ($16,000 – $10,000) more than the book depreciation.

5. $1,000, I

The $4,000 capital gain distribution was included and the $5,000 loss on the sale of the Retro stock was deducted in arriving at Anvil's financial accounting income. For tax purposes, §§165(f) and 1211(a) limit the deduction of a corporation's capital losses only to the extent of the corporation's capital gains. The $4,000 capital gain distribution is included in Anvil's gross income under §61(a). However, only $4,000 of the $5,000 capital loss is deductible in arriving at taxable income.

6. $0, N

Anvil would have deducted the $35,000 in charitable contributions made during Year 3 and the $15,000 in charitable contributions accrued in Year 3 and paid in Year 4 on its financial accounting books for Year 3. Section 170(a)(1) authorizes a deduction for charitable contributions paid during the taxable year. Also, §170(a)(2) authorizes a deduction for a corporation on the accrual basis of accounting for charitable contributions, authorized by its board of directors during the taxable year, if payment is made by the 15th day of the third month following the taxable year. Thus, Anvil has a potential deduction for charitable contributions of $50,000 ($35,000 + $15,000) for Year 3. However, §170(b)(2) limits a corporation's deduction for charitable contributions to 10% of its taxable income, determined without regard to charitable contributions, the DRD, any NOL carryback, and any net capital loss carryback. Since Anvil's taxable income before the charitable contributions and DRD was $500,000, Anvil's charitable contributions deduction is limited to $50,000 ($500,000 × 10%). The limit equals the potential deduction, and Anvil may deduct all $50,000 in charitable contributions for Year 3.

Income (1 point)

7. N

Section 275(a)(1) disallows any deduction for federal income taxes. When Anvil receives a refund of federal income tax that Anvil previously paid, the refund is excluded from gross income because Anvil received no tax benefit from paying the federal income taxes. Although not directly applicable because Anvil's payment of the federal income taxes was not deductible, see §111 relating to the tax benefit rule. Under this rule, an amount received as a refund of an item previously deducted is included in gross income only to the extent that the deduction provided a tax benefit in a previous tax year.

8. F

Interest income from the Internal Revenue Service is fully included in gross income under §61(a)(4).

9. N

Section 103(a) excludes from gross income the interest on any state or local bond. The income from the mutual fund retains its character under §852(b)(5).

10. F

In general, under §109 a lessor's gross income does not include any improvements made by the lessee on the lessor's property. However, the lessor will recognize gross income to the extent that the rental payments are reduced as a result of the improvements under Regs. §1.109-1(a), §61(a)(5), and §1.61-1(a). The lessor will also receive a basis in the improvements equal to the gross income recognized as a result of the reduction in rental payments.

Communication (5 points)

To: **Anvil** Corporation
From: Ima Preparer
Re: Deductibility of Selected Items

During the preparation of Anvil's income tax return, we received questions from you regarding several items. The following is a short discussion of these items.

The **theater tickets** are deductible as an **ordinary** and **necessary** business expense. Anvil meets the requirement that the entertainment is **associated** with its business. However, the internal revenue code allows only **fifty percent** of the cost of **entertainment** (that is otherwise deductible) as a deduction.

Advertising expenses are fully deductible as an ordinary and necessary business expense in the year paid or incurred. The amount of any deduction is to be taken in the proper taxable year under the **method of accounting** used in computing taxable income. The fact that ten percent of the new product line remains in inventory is **irrelevant**.

The internal revenue code disallows any deduction for **interest** on indebtedness incurred to purchase or to carry **tax-exempt** obligations. Interest on municipal bonds is tax exempt.

The internal revenue code disallows any deduction for business expense for any **fine** or similar **penalty** paid to a government for the **violation** of any law. Such penalties include **civil** penalties that are additions to taxes.

If you have further questions regarding these issues, please contact us for greater detail.

Research (1 point)

Code Section Answer: §172(a)

Code §172(a) states, "There shall be allowed as a deduction for the taxable year an amount equal to the aggregate of (1) the net operating loss carryovers to such year, plus (2) the net operating loss carrybacks to such year."

Solution 46-4 Schedule M-1

Adjustments (4 points)

1. $1,000, D

A corporation may elect to deduct up to $5,000 of organization costs incurred in the tax year its business begins under §248. However, the $5,000 deduction is reduced on a dollar-for-dollar basis for those expense in excess of $50,000. Capital Corp's deduction is not affect by the limit. Any remaining balance must be amortized of 15 years. The increase of an expense decreases taxable income. ($35,000 – $5,000) / 15 – $1,000 = $1,000).

2. $5,000, I

Only 50% of meal and entertainment expenses are deductible. The reduction of an expense increases taxable income.

3. $0, N

Premiums on employee life insurance policies are deductible if the corporation is not the beneficiary.

4. $10,000, I

Only the direct write-off method of recognizing bad debt is allowed for tax purposes. The reduction of an expense increases taxable income.

Communication (5 points)

To: Capital Corporation
From: A. Candidate
Re Eligible Expenses

A corporation's deduction for charitable contributions is **limited** to **10%** of **taxable income** without regard to the deduction for charitable contributions, the DRD, any NOL carry-back to that year, and any capital loss carry-back to that year. As Capital's Year 2 taxable income before charitable contributions was $200,000, the deduction is limited to **$20,000**. A corporation on the **accrual** basis of accounting may elect to deduct a charitable contribution in the year **authorized** by its board of directors, provided the payment is made **before** the return due date. Capital meets this criteria.

Penalties are **not** deductible.

Research (1 point)

Code Section Answer: §311(a)

Code §311(a) states, "Except [for distributions of appreciated property], no gain or loss shall be recognized to a corporation on the distribution (not in complete liquidation) with respect to its stock of (1) its stock (or rights to acquire its stock), or (2) property."

Solution 46-5 S Corporation

Calculations (4 points)

1. $6,140

Section 1366(a)(1) requires that an S corporation take into account the shareholder's *pro rata* share of items of income, deduction, loss, or credit that could affect the liability for tax of any shareholder. Section 1566(a)(2) requires that the S corporation take into account the shareholder's *pro rata* share of nonseparately computed income or loss. The interest income is stated separately because it is necessary in determining the deduction for investment interest expense under §163(d). Charitable contributions are separately stated because they are treated as an itemized deduction under §170 up to 50% of AGI on an individual's return. The net business income (non-separately computed income) is determined as follows.

Gross receipts	$7,260
Less: Supplies	(1,120)
Net business income	$6,140

2. $2,700

335 days are used since Newcomb did not own shares for 30 days out of the 365-day year that began on January 1. Newcomb's share of the S corporation's income (to the nearest hundred) under §1366(a) is determined as follows.

$$\frac{40 \text{ shares}}{200 \text{ shares}} \times \frac{335 \text{ days}}{365 \text{ days}} \times \$14{,}520 = \$2{,}665$$
$$= \text{approx. } \$2{,}700$$

3. $3,150

Newcomb obtains a cost basis of $4,000 on the purchase of the shares under §1012. His basis is increased for his share of the tax-exempt municipal bond interest income under §§1367(a)(1)(A) and 1366(a)(1)(A). His basis is reduced by his share of the $1,000 ordinary business loss under and §1366(a)(1)(B) and §1367(a)(2)(C).

Cost basis for shares purchased	$ 4,000
Add: Municipal bond interest income	150
Less: Ordinary business loss	(1,000)
Newcomb's basis at December 31	$ 3,150

4. $9,000

Singer's basis is increased by his share of the ordinary income under §1367(a)(1)(B) and §1366(a)(1)(B). Singer's basis is decreased by the distribution under §1367(a)(2)(A).

Singer's basis on January 1	$10,000
Add: Ordinary income	2,000
Less: Distribution	(3,000)
Singer's basis at January 31	$ 9,000

Communication (5 points)

To: D. Boss
From: A. Candidate
Re: Pronto S Corporation Status

An S corporation must be a **small** business corporation with only **one class** of **stock**. The Internal

Revenue Code provides that the S election will terminate whenever the corporation ceases to be a small business corporation.

An S corporation election will terminate if the corporation has gross receipts from **passive** sources of **25%** or more of its receipts for **three consecutive years**. An additional requirement before termination is effective is that the S corporation must have **C corporation** earnings and profits at the end of those three consecutive years. In this case, the S election would **not** be terminated since Pronto has never been a C corporation.

Research (1 point)

Code Section Answer: §248(a)

Code §248(a) states, "If a corporation elects the application of this subsection (in accordance with regulations prescribed by the Secretary) with respect to any organizational expenditures, (1) the corporation shall be allowed a deduction for the taxable year in which the corporation begins business in a an amount equal to the lesser of (A) the amount of organizational expenditures with respect to the taxpayer, or (B) $5,000, reduced (but not below zero) by the amount by which such organizational expenditures exceed $50,000, and (2) the remainder of such organizational expenditures shall be allowed as a deduction ratably over the 180-month period beginning with the month in which the corporation begins business."

Solution 46-6 C Corporation

Expenses (2.5 points)

1. P

The theater tickets are deductible under §162(a) as an ordinary and necessary business expense. Clipper meets the requirement of §274(a)(1)(A) that the entertainment is associated with its business. However, §274(n)(1)(B) allows only 50% of the cost of entertainment (that is otherwise deductible) as a deduction.

2. F

Advertising expenses are fully deductible as an ordinary and necessary business expense in the year paid or incurred under §162(a). Under §461(a), the amount of any deduction is to be taken in the proper taxable year under the method of accounting used in computing taxable income. The fact that 10% of the new product line remains in inventory is irrelevant.

3. N

Section 265(a)(2) disallows any deduction for interest on indebtedness incurred to purchase or to carry tax-exempt obligations. According to §103(a) interest on municipal bonds is tax exempt.

4. N

Section 162(f) disallows any deduction for business expense for any fine or similar penalty paid to a government for the violation of any law. Reg. 1.162-21(b)(1) states that such a penalty includes civil penalties that are additions to taxes.

5. F

The bonus is deductible as an ordinary and necessary business expense under §162(a). Under §461(a), the amount of any deduction is to be taken in the proper taxable year under the method of accounting used in computing taxable income. Clipper is an accrual basis taxpayer. However, §461(h)(4) requires that all events have occurred that fix the fact of the liability and that the amount can be determined with reasonable accuracy. Also, §461(h)(1) states that the all-events test is not deemed to be satisfied until economic performance has occurred. Section 461(h)(2)(A)(i) states that if the liability arises out of the performance of services by another person for the taxpayer, economic performance occurs when the other person performs such services. The all-events test is satisfied because the bonus to be paid is a legal liability of the corporation and the amount of the liability is fixed. Economic performance occurred when the employee performed the services. Thus, the bonus is fully deductible in the year accrued. Section 267(a)(2) would delay the deduction until the year paid if the recipients were related parties within the meaning of §267. In this case, the bonus is to be paid to nonstockholders only. Thus, they are not related parties within the meaning of §267 and Clipper is entitled to deduct the bonus in Year 3.

True/False (1.5 points)

6. F

Section 55(d)(3)(A) states that the exemption for the alternative minimum tax (AMT) is reduced by 25% of the amount by which the AMT income exceeds $150,000.

7. F

Section 6501(c)(1) states that in the case of a fraudulent return, the tax may be assessed or a proceeding in court for collection of such tax may be begun without assessment at any time. There is no statute of limitations if a fraudulent return is filed.

8. F

Section 6501(e)(1)(A) provides that if the taxpayer omits gross income on a return greater than 25% of the gross income shown on the return, the tax may be assessed within 6 years after the return was filed. Because §6501(b)(1) states that a return filed early will, for purposes of §6501, be considered as filed on the due date, the statute of limitations in this case is 6 years from the later of the date due or the date filed.

Communication (5 points)

To: **Clipper** Corporation
From: Candidate
Re: Items Included in Taxable Income

During the preparation of Clipper's income tax return, we received questions from you regarding several items. The following is a short discussion of these items.

The **interest** on any **state** or **local** government bond is **excluded** from taxable income. The income from a mutual fund **retains** its character.

In general, a lessor's gross income does not include any **improvements** made by the lessee on the lessor's property. However, the lessor will recognize gross income to the extent that the rental **payments are reduced** as a result of the improvements. The lessor also will receive a **basis** in the improvements equal to the gross income recognized as a result of the reduction in rental payments.

When a **life insurance policy** is **transferred** for valuable consideration, the life insurance proceeds received may be excluded from gross income only to the extent of the taxpayer's **basis** in the consideration and subsequent premiums paid by the taxpayer. Thus, the amount of the proceeds in excess of the debt will be included in Clipper's gross income.

If you have further questions regarding these issues, please contact us for greater detail.

Research (1 point)

Code Section Answer: §264(a)

Code §264(a) states, "GENERAL RULE. – No deduction shall be allowed for – (1) Premiums on any life insurance policy, or endowment or annuity contract, if the taxpayer is directly or indirectly a beneficiary under the policy or contract. (2) Any amount paid or accrued on indebtedness incurred or continued to purchase or carry a single premium life insurance, endowment, or annuity contract...." Search terms: "life insurance" AND beneficiary

Solution 46-7 Corporate AMT

AMTI (2.5 points)

1. N

Under §56(g)(4)(C)(i), the 70% dividends received deduction is added back in computing adjusted current earnings (ACE). Therefore, it is a part of the ACE adjustment and has no effect on Raffle's alternative minimum taxable income prior to the ACE adjustment.

2. N

Under §57(a)(5), interest on specified private activity bonds is a tax preference for purposes of the alternative minimum tax. However, interest on a state's general obligation bonds has no effect on alternative minimum taxable income.

3. I

While the same recovery periods are used for regular taxes and AMT, the AMT rules require the 150%, rather than 200%, declining balance method for personal property. Thus, the adjustment will increase AMTI. This adjustment comes prior to the adjusted current earnings (ACE) adjustment.

4. I

Under §56(a)(1)(A), taxpayers must use the alternative depreciation system (ADS) in computing alternative minimum taxable income (AMTI). In the year of acquisition, the depreciation under the ADS will be less than it is under MACRS. This is true even though for MACRS the nonresidential real property must be depreciated straight-line over 39 years under §§168(b)(3)(A) and 168(c)(1). The reason is that, under §168(g)(2), the ADS uses a 40-year straight-line method. Thus, the adjustment will increase AMTI. This adjustment comes prior to the adjusted current earnings (ACE) adjustment. The Taxpayer Relief Act of 1997 eliminated this adjustment for real property placed in service after 1997.

5. N

There is no adjustment listed in §56 for cash charitable contributions. Cash charitable contributions are also not listed as a tax preference in §57.

True/False (1.5 points)

6. T

Section 38(b) lists the targeted jobs credit as one of a number of tax credits that must be added together to determine the current year business credit. The title of §38 is general business credit. Section 38(a)(2) lists the current year business credit as one of three items that must be added together to arrive at the general business credit.

7. T

Section 6713(a) imposes a civil penalty on tax return preparers for the unauthorized use or disclosure of information obtained while preparing a tax return. However, Reg. §301.7216-2(e)(2) allows a tax return preparer who is lawfully engaged in the practice of law or accountancy to take tax return information into account and act on it in the course of performing legal or accounting services for a client other than the taxpayer. The tax return information may not be disclosed to a person who is not an employee or member of the law or accounting firm unless allowed by another provision. Because a CPA firm is lawfully engaged in the practice of accounting, the CPA firm should be able to use the information obtained in preparing the corporate return to assist in preparing the corporate officers' returns without the consent of the corporation.

8. F

Section 6511(a) states that a claim for refund must be made within 3 years from the time a return was filed or 2 years from the time the tax was paid, whichever is later. The statute of limitations on assessment is generally 3 years from the later of the date due or the date filed under §§6501(a) and 6501(b)(1). Under §6501(c)(7), if an amended return is filed within 60 days of the termination of the statute of limitations on assessment, the statute of limitations on assessment will not expire until 60 days after the IRS receives the amended return.

Communication (5 points)

To: **Raffles** Corporation
From: Candidate
Re: Select Schedule M-1 Items

During the preparation of Raffles' income tax return, we received questions from you regarding several items associated with Schedule M-1. The following is a short discussion of these items.

Schedule M-1 **reconciles** financial accounting income and taxable income. Several items are treated **differently** for financial accounting purposes and tax purposes. **Financial** accounting income is determined in a effort to **report** the operations and financial condition of an entity. **Taxable** income is determined to **comply** with tax laws.

The internal revenue code allows a deduction for **travel** expenses, including meals, incurred in a **trade or business**; however, the business **meal** deduction is limited for to **fifty percent** of the cost of such meals. All of the transportation cost and the cost of meals are deducted on Raffles's financial accounting books. Because fifty percent of the cost of business meals may not be deducted for tax purposes, such amount must be added back to the financial accounting income in arriving at taxable income.

The $7,000 in **life insurance premiums** was deducted in arriving at financial accounting income. However, the internal revenue code disallows any deduction for life insurance premiums paid on the life of a **corporate officer** when the **taxpayer** is the **beneficiary** of the policy. Therefore, the full amount of the premiums must be added back to the financial accounting income in arriving at Raffles's taxable income.

The amount of any deduction is to be taken in the proper taxable year under the method of accounting used in computing taxable income. Because Raffles is an **accrual**-basis taxpayer, the $18,000 **franchise tax** expense generally is deducted in the year accrued. However, the internal revenue code requires that all events have occurred that fix the fact of the liability and that the amount can be determined with reasonable accuracy. Also, the all-events test is not deemed to be satisfied until **economic performance** has occurred. Economic performance occurs for a tax liability when the tax liability is paid. The economic performance test is waived if (1) the **all-events test** is satisfied, (2) economic performance occurs within the **shorter** of a reasonable time after the close of the tax year or 8½ months after the close of the tax year, (3) the item is **recurring** in nature and is consistently treated by the taxpayer, and (4) the item is **not material** or results in a **better matching** of income and deductions. The accrual of the franchise tax liability meets the recurring item exception. Therefore, the full amount of the franchise tax expense is deducted in arriving at Raffles's taxable income. Thus, no adjustment need be made.

If you have further questions regarding these issues, please contact us for greater detail.

Research (1 point)

Code Section Answer: §274(a)

Code §274(a) states, "ENTERTAINMENT, AMUSEMENT, OR RECREATION. -- (1) IN GENERAL. -- No deduction otherwise allowable under this chapter shall be allowed for any item -- (A) ACTIVITY. -- With respect to an activity which is of a type generally considered to constitute entertainment, amusement, or recreation, unless the taxpayer establishes that the item was directly related to, or, in the case of an item directly preceding or following a substantial and *bona fide* business discussion (including business meetings at a convention or otherwise), that such item was associated with, the active conduct of the taxpayer's trade or business...." Search term: entertainment.

Solution 46-8 Corporate AMT

AMTI (4 points)

1. U

MACRS depreciation (200%) is higher in the first year of service than the 150% that is allowed for personal property under AMT. Because this overstates deductions, income is understated.

2. U

Straight-line depreciation over 40, not 39, years is appropriate for AMT purposes for real property. Because the deduction is overstated, income is understated.

3. C

Tax-exempt interest from private activity bonds issued after August 7, 1986 is a preference. However, state highway construction is not a private activity.

4. U

Under the percentage depletion method, a set percentage of gross income from the property is taken as a depletion deduction. Percentage depletion in excess of the adjusted basis of the property is an AMT preference. An overstated deduction results in understated income.

Communication (5 points)

To: **Szabo** Corporation
From: A. Candidate
Re: Taxable Items

1. A dividend-received deduction **shields** part of the **dividend income** from a 35% owned corporation.

2. For tax purposes, rental income is **recognized** when **received**, **regardless** of the taxpayer's **basis** of **accounting**.

3. When a life insurance policy is **transferred** for valuable **consideration**, the Internal Revenue Code provides that the **life insurance** proceeds received may be excluded from gross income **only** to the extent of the taxpayer's **basis** in the consideration and **subsequent premiums** paid by the taxpayer. The amount of the proceeds in **excess** of the debt will be included in taxable income.

Research (1 point)

Code Section Answer: §119(a)

Code §119(a) states, "MEALS AND LODGING FURNISHED TO EMPLOYEE, HIS SPOUSE, AND HIS DEPENDENTS, PURSUANT TO EMPLOYMENT—There shall be excluded from gross income of an employee the value of any meals or lodging furnished to him, his spouse, or any of his dependents by or on behalf of his employer for the convenience of the employer, but only if—119(a)(1) in the case of meals, the meals are furnished on the business premises of the employer...." Search term: "employee meals"

Hot•Spot™ Video Descriptions

(Taxation subjects only; subject to change without notice.)

CPA 3205 Property Taxation
In this program, Robert Monette covers the adjusted basis of property (purchases, gifts, and inheritances), depreciation, depreciation recapture, amortization, capital assets, holding periods, calculation of gain or loss, like-kind exchanges, related party transactions, involuntary conversions, stock sales and losses, and the sale of a principal residence. Bob outlines the provisions of Sections 179, 1231, 1245, 1250, and 1244.

CPA 3277 Gross Income, Tax Liabilities & Credits
Learn the federal income tax treatment of gross income inclusions and exclusions. In this program, Leslie Robinson illustrates computing tax liability, including the alternative minimum tax, the self-employment tax, and various tax credits. The impacts of passive activity losses, statutes of limitations, and certain business expenses are explained. Leslie also discusses preparing for the research element of simulations.

CPA 3400 Individual Taxation
In this program, Leslie Robinson covers filing status, exemptions, dependants, deductions allowed in computing adjusted gross income, standard deductions, itemized deductions, and a brief overview of personal tax credits. Leslie highlights recurring exam topics in her lecture as well as her discussion of questions. Additionally, she includes an introduction to tax research for purposes of the CPA exam. Leslie discusses problem-solving techniques, alerts candidates to common exam tricks, and includes suggestions on how to approach studying tax material.

CPA 3402 Corporate Taxation
In this program, Robert Monette covers both C and S corporations. The tax effects of corporate formation, basis calculations, income, deductions, capital gains and losses, dividends, stock redemptions, and corporate reorganizations are clarified. Administrative items, selected tax forms, consolidated tax returns, accumulated earnings tax, and alternative minimum tax also are discussed.

CPA 3404 Partnerships & Other Tax Topics
Robert Monette guides viewers through the federal income tax treatment of partnerships, including a partner's initial and adjusted basis, related party transactions, contribution basis, and filing requirements, as well as nonliquidating and liquidating distributions. He explains the process of estate taxation, including gross estate valuation, deductions, and credits. Bob illustrates estate and trust income taxation and clarifies the gift tax and the generation-skipping tax.

In order to ensure current materials, Bisk Education leases (rather than sells) videos to candidates. At lease completion (after your exam), contact your customer service representative (either info@cpaexam.com or customerservice@cpaexam.com) regarding the return of videos. If needed, extensions on leases are available—but with material this effective, it's a rare occurrence.

Call a customer representative toll-free at 1 (800) 874-7877 for more details about videos.

CHAPTER 47

FEDERAL TAXATION: PARTNERSHIPS

EXAM COVERAGE: The entities taxation portion of the Regulation section of the CPA exam is designated by the examiners to be 22-28 percent of the section's point value. More information about point distribution is included in the **Practical Advice** section of this volume.

CHAPTER 47

FEDERAL TAXATION: PARTNERSHIPS

I. Partnership Taxation

A. Overview

Generally, partnerships are non-tax-paying entities. Rather, they are conduits through which several types of income, loss, deductions, and credits are passed to the partners [IRC §701].

1. **Entity Classification** Under the *check-the-box* regulations, an eligible entity may elect its classification for federal tax purposes. An eligible entity is an entity that does not meet the definition of a corporation under the regulations, and is not a single owner entity, trust, or otherwise subject to special treatment under the IRC. If the entity fails to elect a classification, the regulations provide a default classification. The use is broader than the common law meaning and may include groups not commonly called partnerships.

   a. A partnership is a syndicate, group, pool, joint venture, or other unincorporated entity through which a business is carried on, and which is not a corporation, trust, or estate.

   b. Mere co-ownership of property is not a partnership. However, if the entity provides services in conjunction with the use of the property by the lessee or licensee, the entity may be characterized as a partnership.

   c. Limited partnerships are subject to the same rules as general partnerships.

   d. Limited liability entities may be classified for federal tax purposes as either corporations or as partnerships. Limited liability companies (LLC), limited liability partnerships (LLP), professional limited liability companies, etc. are frequently designed to take advantage of the pass-through tax status of partnerships and the limited legal liability of corporations, but the partnership tax status is not automatic. Unless a limited liability entity meets conditions that require it to be taxed as a corporation or it elects to be so treated, it is treated as a partnership for tax purposes.

2. **Information Return** Partnerships must file an information tax return (Form 1065) showing partnership income and deductions with each partner's share (Schedule K-1). Failure to file a return can result in a penalty being assessed against the partnership, the amount based on the number of partners. In general, partnerships with more than 100 partners must provide Form 1065 and copies of each partner's Schedule K-1 to the IRS on magnetic media. Returns are due March 15 for calendar-year partnerships.

3. **Tax Year** The partnership's taxable year is generally the same as that of its partners owning a majority interest in the partnership, unless a business purpose can be established for designating a different taxable year [IRC §706(b)(1)]. The taxable year of a partnership generally is not affected by the entry of new partners or the death or retirement of old partners.

   a. **Principal Partners** If partners owning a majority interest do not have the same taxable year, the partnership must adopt the taxable year of its principal partners. Principal partners are partners having an interest of 5% or more in the partnership's profits or capital.

   b. **Calendar Year** If neither partners owning a majority interest nor principal partners have the same taxable year, the partnership must adopt a calendar year as its taxable year.

c. **Fiscal Year** A partnership can elect to use a fiscal year instead of a calendar year as long as the fiscal year does not result in a deferral period that is greater than 3 months [IRC §444]. Therefore, a partnership that normally is required to have a calendar year under IRC §706 can elect to have a fiscal year if the fiscal year ends on September 30, October 31, or November 30. For more information, see the coverage of S Corporations.

d. **Termination** The taxable year closes upon termination of the partnership.

e. **With Respect to One Partner** The taxable year of a partnership closes *with respect to a partner* whose entire interest in the partnership terminates, whether by death, liquidation, sale, exchange, or otherwise. The taxable year of a partnership does not close with respect to a partner who disposes of less than her/his entire interest in the partnership, but that partner's distributive share must reflect her/his varying interests during the year.

4. **Partner Level** Each partner reports her/his distributive share of income, loss, deduction, and credit for the partnership's taxable year that ends within or with the partner's taxable year [IRC §706(a)].

Example 1 ▸ Timing of Income Recognition

A. Both the partnership's and the individual partners' taxable years end on December 31, Year 5. The partners report their shares of Year 5 partnership income, etc., on their Year 5 returns.

B. An individual partner is on a calendar-year basis, while the partnership is on a fiscal-year basis ending January 31. The partner's share of partnership income, etc., for the partnership year ending January 31, Year 5, is reported on her/his Year 5 return, (e.g., the return filed in Year 6.)

B. Distributive Share

Each partner must account for her/his share of partnership items. The partner is taxed on the distributive share regardless of actual distributions. The actual distributions rarely are taxable events, but merely a return of previous investment or previously taxed partnership income.

1. **Partnership Agreement** Generally, the distributive share is determined by the partnership agreement, unless the allocation in the agreement does not have substantial economic effect [IRC §704]. An allocation has substantial economic effect if it actually may affect the dollar amount of the partners' shares of the total partnership income or loss independently of tax consequences. If the allocation does not have substantial economic effect, the partnership agreement concerning the distribution is ignored, and the distribution is made according to the partners' interests in the partnership.

2. **Profits & Losses** If the partnership agreement makes no provision for the distributive share, it is determined in the same manner that the partnership agreement provides for the division of the general profits and losses.

3. **Limitations** A partner's distributive share of partnership loss cannot exceed the partner's adjusted basis in her/his partnership interest. A partner's loss deduction also is limited by the "at-risk" and passive loss rules. Any unused loss is carried forward.

4. **Separately Reported Items** Separately reported items, also accounted for by distributive share, include the following [IRC §702].

   a. Long-term capital gain (loss)

   b. Short-term capital gain (loss)

c. Gain (loss) from sales of certain business property and certain involuntary conversions [IRC §1231(b) property]

d. Charitable contributions

e. Dividend income

f. Foreign taxes paid

g. Taxable income (loss) other than items already separately stated

Example 2 ▸ Income Recognition

The partnership of Bond and Felton has a fiscal year ending March 31. John Bond files his tax return on a calendar-year basis. The partnership paid Bond what the partnership calls a guaranteed salary of $1,000 per month during calendar year Year 1 and $1,500 per month during calendar Year 2. (The IRC calls this a guaranteed payment.) After deducting this salary, the partnership realized ordinary income of $80,000 for the year ended March 31, Year 2, and $90,000 for the year ended March 31, Year 3. Bond's share of the profits is the salary paid him plus 40% of the ordinary income after deducting this salary. For Year 2, Bond should report taxable income from the partnership of $45,500.

Computations:

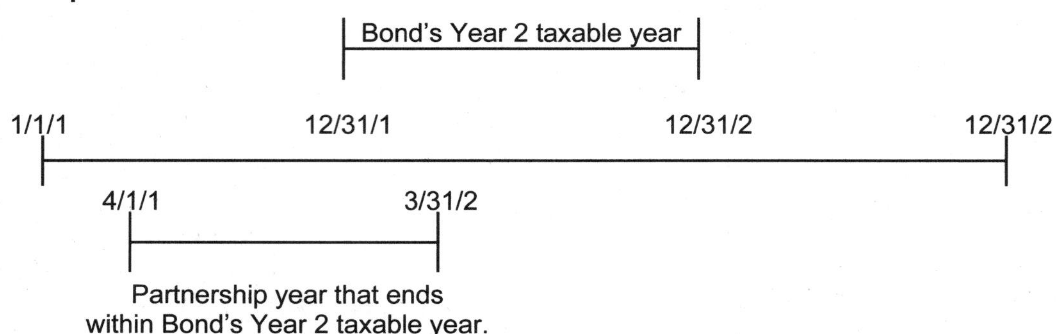

Bond includes in his personal gross income only his pro rata share of partnership income (distributed or undistributed) for his taxable year ending with or within the taxable year of the partnership. Bond's Year 2 taxable year ends on December 31, Year 2. However, the partnership's taxable year begins on April 1, Year 1, and ends on March 31, Year 2. Therefore, Bond's share of partnership income for calendar Year 2 is:

$1,000/month × 9 months of Year 1	$9,000	
$1,500/month × 3 months of Year 2	4,500	
Salary received from April 1, Year 1, to March 31, Year 2		$13,500
Add Bond's share of partnership income realized during April 1, Year 1 to March 31, Year 2 (80,000 × 40%)		32,000
Bond's Year 2 taxable income from the partnership		$45,500

The $13,500 salary that Bond received during the last nine months of Year 2 must be considered in determining his taxable income from the partnership for Year 3. The same applies to his pro rata share of the $90,000 partnership income realized during the partnership's fiscal year, beginning on April 1, Year 2, and ending on March 31, Year 3. This is because it relates to the partnership year that ends with or within Bond's Year 3 taxable year.

Example 3 ▶ Income Flow-Through From Partnership

	XY Partnership Items	Trial Balance	Partnership	Partners
(A)	Sales	$100,000	$100,000	
(B)	Cost of goods sold	(50,000)	(50,000)	
(C)	Salaries	(20,000)	(20,000)	
(D)	Other operating expenses	(10,000)	(10,000)	
(E)	Guaranteed payments	(5,000)	(5,000)	
(F)	Dividends	1,000		$ 1,000
(G)	Short-term capital gains	2,000		2,000
(H)	Short-term capital losses	(4,000)		(4,000)
(I)	Long-term capital gains	10,000		10,000
(J)	Section 1231 casualty loss	(3,000)		(3,000)
(K)	Section 1231 gain	5,000		5,000
(L)	Charitable contributions	(1,000)		(1,000)
(M)	Section 1245 gain	3,000	3,000	
Net income from operations (A, B, C, D, E and M)			$ 18,000	

(1) Items F through L pass through the partnership's return and are not considered in arriving at the partnership's net income from operations. These items are treated individually by the two partners, X and Y, based on special allocations (if having substantial economic effect) or profit-and-loss sharing ratios, and are dealt with in the tax returns of the individual partners. Note that items F through L are items of income and expense that are generally subject to individual taxpayer limitations. Such limitations apply to each individual partner of the partnership. For example, item F, Dividends, is not considered at the partnership level but is passed through and dealt with on the returns of the partners. Thus, in the case of a corporate partner, the dividends are eligible for the 80% deduction of IRC §243.

(2) The partnership's net income from operations, $18,000, is computed on the basis of items A, B, C, D, E, and M. This net taxable income is divided among the partners according to their profit-and-loss sharing ratios.

C. Transactions Between Partner & Partnership

Generally, a partner can engage in a transaction with her/his partnership, and the transaction will be considered as occurring between two completely independent entities. Payments made to a partner for services or for the use of capital (guaranteed payments) are treated as made to one who is not a member of the partnership [IRC §707l]. The partnership deducts the guaranteed payments and the recipients must report such payments as income. Furthermore, certain transactions between a partner and the partnership will be recharacterized as arm's-length transactions. These transactions involve the performance of services or property transfers in exchange for direct or indirect allocations or distributions to one of the partners [IRC §707(a)(2)]. Exceptions (also applicable to sales of property between two commonly controlled partnerships) are:

1. Losses from sales of property between a controlling partner (over 50% interest) and her/his partnership are not allowed [IRC §707(b)(1)].

2. Gains from the sale of property between a controlling partner (over 50% interest) and her/his partnership are characterized as ordinary income [IRC §707(b)(2)].

II. Partnership Formation & Operation

A. Contributions

No gain or loss is recognized by the partnership or any partner when property is contributed to the partnership in exchange for an interest in the partnership [IRC §721(a)].

1. **Exclusions** Note that this provision excludes both (a) a contribution of services for an interest, and (b) a contribution of property for anything other than a partnership interest. Where a partnership interest is received in exchange for the contribution of services, the contributing partner includes in ordinary income an amount equal to the excess of the FMV of the

partnership interest received for the services performed over the amount paid for the partnership interest [IRC §83(a)].

- Note also that, unlike IRC §351 transfers to a corporation, there is no control requirement on transfers to a partnership.

2. **Partner's Basis** The basis of the partner's interest resulting from this contribution of property is the sum of the following [IRC §722]:

   a. Amount of money contributed

   b. Adjusted basis of property contributed

   c. Gain, if any, recognized to the partner under IRC §721(b) on the transfer

3. **Holding Period** A partner's holding period for a partnership interest acquired through contribution of a capital asset or an asset used in the partner's trade or business includes the holding period for the contributed property. If the contributed property is not a capital asset or used in the partner's trade or business, her/his holding period in the partnership interest begins on the date that the interest is acquired.

4. **Partnership's Basis in Assets** The partnership's basis in the assets that are contributed to it by the partners is equal to the partners' bases, increased by the amount of gain recognized by such partners. The holding period of the contributed property includes the period during which the property was held by the contributing partner.

B. Basis of Distributed Property

1. **Nonliquidating** The basis of property (other than money) distributed to a partner in a nonliquidating distribution is equal to the basis of such property in the partnership's hands immediately before the distribution [IRC §732(a)(1)]. However, the basis of the property distributed may not exceed the basis of the partner's interest in the partnership (as reduced by any money distributed in the same transaction) [IRC §732(a)(2)].

Example 4 ▸ Nonliquidating Distribution

Partnership CD distributes to partner D $3,000 cash and equipment with a FMV of $10,000 and a basis of $5,000. D's basis in his partnership interest was $7,000 immediately prior to the distribution. His basis in the equipment is $4,000, computed as follows.

D's basis in partnership interest prior to distribution	$ 7,000
Less cash distributed to D	(3,000)
IRC §732(a)(2) limitation on the basis of noncash assets distributed	$ 4,000
Basis of equipment:	
Lesser of the asset's basis in the partnership's hands immediately before the distribution ($5,000) or the IRC §732(a)(2) limitation ($4,000)	$ 4,000

2. **Liquidating** The basis of property (other than money) distributed to a partner in a liquidating distribution is equal to the adjusted basis of the partner's interest in the partnership (as reduced by any cash received by the partner in the liquidation) [IRC §732(b)].

Example 5 ▸ Liquidating Distribution

> Partnership XYZ distributes $12,000 cash and a computer, with a FMV of $7,000 and a basis of $3,000, to Y in liquidation of Y's interest in the partnership. If Y's basis in his partnership interest immediately before the distribution is equal to $25,000, his basis in the computer (assuming that XYZ has no liabilities) is equal to $13,000, (e.g., $25,000 basis in Y's partnership interest less $12,000 cash received in the distribution.)

3. **Excessive** In the case of liquidating distributions and nonliquidating distributions to which the IRC §732(a)(2) limitation applies, the basis of the partner's interest in the partnership (as reduced by cash received) is allocated first to any unrealized receivables and inventory items in an amount equal to the adjusted basis of such receivables and inventory.

   a. Any remaining basis adjustment, if an increase, is allocated among properties with an unrealized appreciation in proportion to their respective amounts of unrealized appreciation, to the extent of each property's appreciation, and then in proportion to their respective fair market values.

   b. Any remaining basis adjustment, if a decrease, is allocated among properties with unrealized depreciation in proportion to their respective amounts of unrealized depreciation, to the extent of each property's depreciation, and then in proportion to their respective adjusted bases, taking into account the adjustments already made. A remaining basis adjustment that is a decrease arises when the partnership's total adjusted basis in the distributed properties exceeds the amount of the basis in the distributed properties, the partner's basis in its partnership interest, and the latter amount is the basis to be allocated among the distributed properties.

C. Adjusted Basis of Partnership Interest

If a partner acquires a partnership interest from another partner, the basis of the acquired interest is equal to the sum of the cash and the FMV of the other consideration paid for the interest. A partner's adjusted basis in her/his partnership interest frequently changes.

Example 6 ▸ Partner's Adjusted Basis

> Partner X contributes property worth $20,000 with a basis to her of $14,000, subject to liabilities of $16,000, to a new partnership in exchange for a 50% interest in partnership profit, loss, and capital. Y contributes $4,000 of cash to the partnership. The bases for X's and Y's partnership interests are computed as follows.

X's basis in the contributed property [IRC §722]	$ 14,000
Plus X's 50% share of partnership liabilities [IRC §752(a)]	8,000
Less liability subject to which the partnership acquires the property [IRC §752(b)]	(16,000)
Initial basis of X's partnership interest	$ 6,000
Y's basis in the contributed property [IRC §722]	$ 4,000
Plus Y's 50% share of partnership liabilities	8,000
Initial basis of Y's partnership interest	$ 12,000

1. **Distributive Share** The adjusted basis is increased by the partner's share of income and reduced by her/his share of losses (e.g., her/his distributive share) [IRC §705(a)].

2. **Distributions** The adjusted basis is reduced by actual distributions to the partner. The amount of the distribution is generally the amount of money distributed and the adjusted basis to the partnership of any other property distributed [IRC §733].

3. **Liabilities** The partner's share of liabilities affects her/his adjusted basis.

a. An increase in a partner's share of liabilities of the partnership, or an increase in the partner's liabilities by reason of the partner's assumption of the partnership's liabilities, is considered a contribution of money by the partner and thus will increase her/his basis in her/his partnership interest [IRC §752(a)].

b. A decrease in a partner's share of liabilities of the partnership, or a decrease in the partner's liabilities by reason of the partnership's assumption of the partner's individual liabilities, is considered a distribution of money to the partner by the partnership, and thus will result in a decrease in the basis of her/his partnership interest (but not below zero) [IRC §752(b)].

D. Distributions

No gain or loss is recognized by a partner on the distribution of money or other property by the partnership to the partner, except the following [IRC §731].

1. **Excessive** Gain is recognized to the extent that money distributed exceeds the partner's adjusted basis in her/his partnership interest (see I., C., above).

2. **Losses** Loss is recognized only in liquidating distributions where the property received consists solely of money, unrealized receivables (see III., B., below), and inventory items.

3. **Built-in Gain** "Built-in" gain to be recognized by a contributing partner on the distribution of property to another partner within the five-year period (seven years for most property contributed after June 8, 1997) after the property is contributed to the partnership.

E. Electing Large Partnerships

Generally, an electing large partnership (ELP) is a partnership with 100 or more partners in the preceding taxable year that elects the simplified flow-through provisions. The election applies to all subsequent years and may only be revoked with IRS consent. For tax purposes, an ELP will not terminate merely due to the sale or exchange of 50% of its interests within a 12-month period. If substantially all of the partners perform services or the partnership's principal business is commodity trading, the partnership is ineligible for the simplified flow-through provisions.

1. **Simplified Flow-Through Rules** The taxable income of an ELP is computed in the same manner as that of an individual, except that certain items are stated separately and certain modifications are made. These modifications include disallowing the deduction for personal exemptions, the net operating loss deduction and certain itemized deductions.

   a. All limitations and other provisions affecting the computation of taxable income or any credit (except for the at-risk, passive loss and itemized deduction limitations, and any other provision specified in regulations) are applied at the partnership (and not the partner) level.

   b. The provision provides that each partner takes into account separately the partner's distributive share of the following items, which are determined at the partnership level: (1) taxable income or loss from passive loss limitation activities; (2) taxable income or loss from other activities, such as portfolio income or loss; (3) net capital gain or loss to the extent allocable to passive loss limitation activities and other activities; (4) tax-exempt interest; (5) net alternative minimum tax adjustment separately computed for passive loss limitation activities and other activities; (6) general credits; (7) low-income housing credit; (8) rehabilitation credit; (9) credit for producing fuel from a nonconventional source; (10) creditable foreign taxes and foreign source items; and (11) any other items as determined by the IRS.

2. **Due Date** An ELP must furnish information returns to partners by the first March 15th following the close of the partnership's taxable year.

3. **Simplified Audit** ELPs and their partners continue to be subject to unified audit rules. Unlike non-electing partnerships, ELP adjustments generally flow through to the partners for the

year in which the adjustment takes effect. Consequently, the current-year partners' share of current-year ELP items of income, gains, losses, deductions, or credits will be adjusted to reflect ELP adjustments that take effect in that year. The adjustments generally will not affect prior-year returns of any partners, except for changes to distributive shares.

a. Instead of flowing an adjustment through to its partners, the partnership may elect to pay an imputed underpayment. The imputed underpayment generally is calculated by netting the adjustments to the income and loss items of the partnership, multiplied by the highest individual or corporate tax rate. A partner may not file a claim for credit or refund of her/his allocable share of the payment.

b. Regardless of whether a partnership adjustment flows through to the partners, an adjustment must be offset if it requires another adjustment in a year after the adjusted year and before the year the offset adjustment takes effect. In addition, the ELP generally is liable for any interest and penalties that result from a partnership adjustment.

c. Any payment (for federal income taxes, interest, or penalties) that an ELP is required to make is not deductible. All accuracy penalty criteria and waiver criteria are determined on the basis that the ELP is a taxable individual. Accuracy and fraud penalties are assessed and accrue interest as if asserted against a taxable individual.

d. If a petition for readjustment of partnership items is filed by the ELP, the court in which the petition is filed will have jurisdiction to determine the tax treatment of all partnership items of the ELP for the partnership taxable year to which the notice of partnership adjustment relates, and the proper allocation of such items among the partners. (The court's jurisdiction is not limited to the items adjusted in the notice.)

e. Without an agreement to extend the statute of limitations, the IRS generally cannot adjust a partnership item of an ELP more than three years after the later of the filing of the ELP return or the last day for the filing of the ELP return. Special rules apply to false or fraudulent returns, a substantial omission of income, or the failure to file a return. The IRS would assess and collect any deficiency of a partner that arises from any adjustment to a partnership item subject to the limitations period on assessments and collection applicable to the year the adjustment takes effect.

4. **Partners Separate From ELP** Each ELP must designate a partner or other person to act on its behalf. Only the ELP can petition for a readjustment of partnership items. If a partnership ceases to exist before a partnership adjustment takes effect, the former partners are required to take the adjustment into account.

a. A partner is not permitted to report any partnership items inconsistently with the partnership return, even if the partner notifies the IRS of the inconsistency.

b. The IRS may challenge the reporting position of an ELP by conducting a single administrative proceeding to resolve the issue with respect to all partners. Individually, partners have no right to participate in settlement conferences or to request a refund.

c. The IRS may send notice of a partnership adjustment to the ELP and is not required to give notice to individual partners of an administrative proceeding or a final adjustment.

III. Partnership Dissolution

A. Termination

If within a 12-month period, **no** part of the partnership's business is carried on or 50% or more of the total interests in the partnership are sold [IRC §708(b)], it terminates on the terminating event day.

1. **Merger** In a merger, the resulting partnership is a continuation of the merging partnership whose partners have a more than 50% interest in the resulting partnership.

2. **Division** In a division, a resulting partnership is a continuation of the prior partnership if the resulting partnership's partners had a more than 50% interest in the prior partnership.

3. **Electing Large Partnership** An *electing large partnership* does not terminate merely due to the sale or exchange of 50% of its interests within a 12-month period.

B. **Transfer of Partnership Interest**
The gains or losses from the sale or exchange of partnership interests, and gains or losses recognized on partnership distributions or liquidation, generally are characterized as capital gains or losses. Any gain or loss attributable to unrealized receivables or inventory items is ordinary in character [IRC §751(a)].

1. **Calculation** The amount that a partner realizes on the sale of a partnership interest includes any cash received, plus any partnership liabilities that are assumed by the buyer.

2. **Distributive Share** Distributions must bear a *pro rata* share of these ordinary income items. If not, the transaction is recast as if there were such a *pro rata* distribution followed by a taxable exchange of properties, to achieve the result of the actual distribution [IRC §751(b)].

3. **Unrealized Receivables** Unrealized receivables are primarily those amounts due for property or services previously provided, but not yet included in income. A typical example is the accounts receivable of a cash basis partnership. Unrealized receivables also include any potential depreciation recapture in the partnership assets [IRC §751(c)].

4. **Inventory** Inventory items are those items that, if sold by the partnership, would produce ordinary income. A typical example is inventory. For sales before August 6, 1997, there is a further requirement for items to be classified as inventory items: the item must be substantially appreciated (fair market value exceeds 120% of basis) [IRC §751(d)].

CHAPTER 47—FEDERAL TAXATION: PARTNERSHIPS

Problem 47-1 MULTIPLE CHOICE QUESTIONS (45 to 60 minutes)

1. Which one of the following statements regarding a partnership's tax year is correct?
a. A partnership formed on July 1 is required to adopt a tax year ending on June 30.
b. A partnership may elect to have a tax year other than the generally required tax year if the deferral period for the tax year elected does **not** exceed three months.
c. A "valid business purpose" can **no** longer be claimed as a reason for adoption of a tax year other than the generally required tax year.
d. Within 30 days after a partnership has established a tax year, a form must be filed with the IRS as notification of the tax year adopted.
(5/90, PII, #25, 1715)

2. The method used to depreciate partnership property is an election made by
a. The partnership and must be the same method used by the "principal partner"
b. The partnership and may be any method approved by the IRS
c. The "principal partner"
d. Each individual partner (11/93, PII, #51, 4480)

3. Basic Partnership, a cash basis calendar year entity, began business on February 1, Year 1. Basic incurred and paid the following in Year 1.

Filing fees incident to the creation of the partnership	$ 3,600
Accounting fees to prepare the representations in offering materials	12,000

Basic elected to amortize costs. What was the maximum amount that Basic could deduct on the Year 1 partnership return?
a. $ 660
b. $ 3,600
c. $ 5,000
d. $15,600 (5/96, AR, #3, amended, 6200)

4. Which of the following limitations will apply in determining a partner's deduction for that partner's share of partnership losses?

	At-risk	*Passive loss*
a.	Yes	No
b.	No	Yes
c.	Yes	Yes
d.	No	No

(11/91, PII, #55, 2503)

5. The partnership of Marks & Sparks sustained an ordinary loss of $42,000 in Year 1. The partnership, as well as the two partners, are on a calendar-year basis. The partners share profits and losses equally. At December 31, Year 1, Marks had an adjusted basis of $18,000 for his partnership interest, before consideration of the loss. On his Year 1 individual tax return, Marks should deduct an(a)
a. Ordinary loss of $18,000
b. Ordinary loss of $21,000
c. Ordinary loss of $18,000 and a capital loss of $3,000
d. Capital loss of $21,000 (Editors, 8058)

6. Peters has a one-third interest in the Spano Partnership. Peters received a $16,000 guaranteed payment, which was deductible by the partnership, for services rendered to Spano. Spano reported an operating loss of $70,000 before the guaranteed payment. What is(are) the net effect(s) of the guaranteed payment?

I. The guaranteed payment increases Peters' tax basis in Spano by $16,000.
II. The guaranteed payment increases Peters' ordinary income by $16,000.

a. I only
b. II only
c. Both I and II
d. Neither I nor II (R/99, AR, #12, amended, 6801)

7. Freeman, a single individual, reported the following income in the current year:

Guaranteed payment from services rendered to a partnership	$50,000
Ordinary income from an S corporation	20,000

What amount of Freeman's income is subject to self-employment tax?
a. $0
b. $20,000
c. $50,000
d. $70,000 (R/01, AR, #26, 7011)

8. Which **two** are allowed as deductions in computing the ordinary income of a partnership?
a. Contributions to recognized charities
b. Depreciation expense
c. The first $100 of dividends received from qualifying domestic corporations
d. Guaranteed payments to partners
e. Short-term capital losses
(11/93, PII, #53, amended, 4482)

9. A guaranteed payment by a partnership to a partner for services rendered, may include an agreement to pay

I. A salary of $5,000 monthly without regard to partnership income
II. A 25% interest in partnership profits

a. I only
b. II only
c. Both I and II
d. Neither I nor II (5/95, AR, #29, 5447)

10. Don and Lisa are equal partners in the capital and profits of Sabal & Noel, but are otherwise unrelated. The following information pertains to 300 shares of Mast Corporation stock sold by Lisa to Sabal & Noel:

Year of purchase	Year 1
Year of sale	Year 4
Basis (cost)	$8,000
Sales price (equal to fair market value)	$3,000

The amount of long-term capital loss that Lisa realized on the sale of this stock was
a. $5,000
b. $3,000
c. $2,500
d. $0 (Editors, 1723)

11. Kaye owns an 85% interest in the capital and profits of Amor Antiques, a partnership. In Year 2, Kaye sold an oriental lamp to Amor for $6,000. Kaye bought this lamp in Year 1 for her personal use at a cost of $2,000 and had used the lamp continuously in her home until the lamp was sold to Amor. Amor purchased the lamp as inventory for sale to customers in the ordinary course of business. What is Kaye's reportable gain in Year 3 on the sale of the lamp to Amor?
a. $4,000 ordinary income
b. $4,000 capital gain
c. $3,400 ordinary income
d. $3,400 capital gain (Editors, 8059)

12. At partnership inception, Black acquires a 50% interest in Decorators Partnership by contributing property with an adjusted basis of $250,000. Black recognizes a gain if

I. The fair market value of the contributed property exceeds its adjusted basis.
II. The property is encumbered by a mortgage with a balance of $100,000.

a. I only
b. II only
c. Both I and II
d. Neither I nor II (11/95, AR, #28, 5772)

13. On June 1, Kelly received a 10% interest in Rock Co., a partnership, for services contributed to the partnership. Rock's net assets at that date had a basis of $70,000 and a fair market value of $100,000. In Kelly's income tax return, what amount must Kelly include as income from transfer of partnership interest?
a. $ 7,000 ordinary income
b. $ 7,000 capital gain
c. $10,000 ordinary income
d. $10,000 capital gain
(11/93, PII, #49, amended, 4478)

14. The holding period of a partnership interest acquired in exchange for a contributed capital asset begins on the date
a. The partner is admitted to the partnership.
b. The partner transfers the asset to the partnership.
c. The partner's holding period of the capital asset began.
d. The partner is first credited with the proportionate share of partnership capital.
(11/91, PII, #60, 2508)

15. Dean is a 25% partner in Target Partnership. Dean's tax basis in Target on January 1, Year 1, was $20,000. At the end of Year 1, Dean received a nonliquidating cash distribution of $8,000 from Target. Target's accounts recorded municipal bond interest income of $12,000 and ordinary income of $40,000 for the year. What was Dean's tax basis in Target on December 31, Year 1?
a. $15,000
b. $23,000
c. $25,000
d. $30,000 (5/95, AR, #26, amended, 5444)

16. When a partner's share of partnership liabilities increases, that partner's basis in the partnership
a. Increases by the partner's share of the increase
b. Decreases by the partner's share of the increase
c. Decreases, but **not** to less than zero
d. Is **not** affected (11/93, PII, #54, 4483)

17. Bailey contributed land with a fair market value of $75,000 and an adjusted basis of $25,000 to the ABC Partnership in exchange for a 30% interest. The partnership assumed Bailey's $10,000 recourse mortgage on the land. What is Bailey's basis for his partnership interest?
a. $15,000
b. $18,000
c. $65,000
d. $75,000 (R/05, REG, 1119T, #13, 7879)

18. At January 1, this year, Paul owned a 25% interest in Associates partnership. During the year, a new partner was admitted and Paul's interest was reduced to 20%. The partnership liabilities at January 1 were $150,000, but decreased to $100,000 at December 31. Paul's and the other partners' capital accounts are in proportion to their respective interests. Disregarding any income, loss or drawings for the year, the basis of Paul's partnership interest at December 31, compared to the basis of his interest at January 1, was
a. Decreased by $37,500
b. Increased by $20,000
c. Decreased by $17,500
d. Decreased by $5,000
(5/94, AR, #30, amended, 4635)

19. Thompson's basis in Starlight Partnership was $60,000 at the beginning of the year. Thompson materially participates in the partnership's business. Thompson received $20,000 in cash distributions during the year. Thompson's share of Starlight's current operations was a $65,000 ordinary loss and a $15,000 net long-term capital gain. What is the amount of Thompson's deductible loss for the period?
a. $15,000
b. $40,000
c. $55,000
d. $65,000 (R/02, AR, #21, 7086)

20. Anderson's basis in the SBF Partnership is $80,000. Anderson received a nonliquidating distribution of $50,000 cash, and land with an adjusted basis of $40,000 and a fair market value of $50,000. What is Anderson's basis in the land?
a. $50,000
b. $40,000
c. $30,000
d. $20,000 (R/03, REG, 1337T, #13, 7655)

21. Stone's basis in Ace Partnership was $70,000 at the time he received a nonliquidating distribution of partnership capital assets. These capital assets had an adjusted basis of $65,000 to Ace, and a fair market value of $83,000. Ace had no unrealized receivables, appreciated inventory, or properties which had been contributed by its partners. What was Stone's recognized gain or loss on the distribution?
a. $18,000 ordinary income
b. $13,000 capital gain
c. $ 5,000 capital loss
d. $0 (11/95, AR, #32, 5776)

22. Owen's tax basis in Regal Partnership was $18,000 at the time Owen received a *nonliquidating* distribution of $3,000 cash and land with an adjusted basis of $7,000 to Regal and a fair market value of $9,000. Regal did not have unrealized receivables, appreciated inventory, or properties that had been contributed by its partners. Disregarding any income, loss, or any other partnership distribution for the year, what was Owen's tax basis in Regal after the distribution?
a. $9,000
b. $8,000
c. $7,000
d. $6,000 (R/05, REG, 0283T, #12, 7858)

23. Stone and Frazier decided to terminate the Woodwest Partnership as of December 31. On that date, Woodwest's balance sheet was as follows:

Cash	$2,000
Equipment (adjusted basis)	2,000
Capital—Stone	3,000
Capital—Frazier	1,000

The fair market value of the equipment was $3,000. Frazier's outside basis in the partnership was $1,200. Upon liquidation, Frazier received $1,500 in cash. What gain should Frazier recognize?
a. $0
b. $250
c. $300
d. $500 (R/02, AR, #25, 7090)

24. Olson, Wayne, and Hogan are equal partners in the OWH partnership. Olson's basis in the partnership interest is $70,000. Olson receives a liquidating distribution of $10,000 cash and land with a fair market value of $63,000, and a basis of $58,000. What is Olson's basis in the land?
a. $58,000
b. $60,000
c. $63,000
d. $70,000 (R/07, REG, 1133T, #5, 8429)

25. Partnership Abel, Benz, Clark & Day is in the real estate and insurance business. Abel owns a 40% interest in the capital and profits of the partnership, while Benz, Clark, and Day each owns a 20% interest. All use a calendar year. At November 1, the real estate and insurance business is separated, and two partnerships are formed: Partnership Abel & Benz takes over the real estate business, and Partnership Clark & Day takes over the insurance business. Which one of the following statements is correct for tax purposes?

a. Partnership Abel & Benz is considered to be a continuation of Partnership Abel, Benz, Clark & Day.
b. In forming Partnership Clark & Day, partners Clark and Day are subject to a penalty surtax if they contribute their entire distributions from Partnership Abel, Benz, Clark & Day.
c. Before separating the two businesses into two distinct entities, the partners must obtain approval from the IRS.
d. Before separating the two businesses into two distinct entities, Partnership Abel, Benz, Clark & Day must file a formal dissolution with the IRS on the prescribed form.

(5/90, PII, #21, amended, 1711)

26. Under which of the following circumstances is a partnership that is not an electing large partnership considered terminated for income tax purposes?

I. Fifty-five percent of the total interest in partnership capital and profits is sold within a 12-month period.
II. The partnership's business and financial operations are discontinued.

a. I only
b. II only
c. Both I and II
d. Neither I nor II (11/97, AR, #8, 6536)

27. Curry's sale of her partnership interest causes a partnership termination. The partnership's business and financial operations are continued by the other members. What is(are) the effect(s) of the termination?

I. There is a deemed distribution of assets to the remaining partners and the purchaser.
II. There is a hypothetical recontribution of assets to a new partnership.

a. I only
b. II only
c. Both I and II
d. Neither I nor II (11/95, AR, #34, 5778)

Items 28 and 29 are based on the following:

The personal service partnership of Allen, Baker & Carr had the following cash basis balance sheet at December 31, Year 1:

Assets	Adjusted basis per books	Market value
Cash	$102,000	$102,000
Unrealized accounts receivable	—	420,000
Totals	$102,000	$522,000
Liability and Capital		
Note payable	$ 60,000	$ 60,000
Allen, capital	14,000	154,000
Baker, capital	14,000	154,000
Carr, capital	14,000	154,000
Totals	$102,000	$522,000

Carr, an equal partner, sold his partnership interest to Dole, an outsider, for $154,000 cash on January 1, Year 2. In addition Dole assumed Carr's share of the partnership's liability.

28. What was the total amount realized by Carr on the sale of his partnership interest?

a. $174,000
b. $154,000
c. $140,000
d. $134,000 (5/90, PII, #22, amended, 1712)

29. What amount of ordinary income should Carr report in his Year 2 income tax return on the sale of his partnership interest?

a. $0
b. $ 20,000
c. $ 34,000
d. $140,000 (5/90, PII, #23, amended, 1713)

30. On December 31, after receipt of his share of partnership income, Clark sold his interest in a limited partnership for $30,000 cash and relief of all liabilities. On that date, the adjusted basis of Clark's partnership interest was $40,000, consisting of his capital account of $15,000 and his share of the partnership liabilities of $25,000. The partnership has no unrealized receivables or substantially appreciated inventory. What is Clark's gain or loss on the sale of his partnership interest?

a. Ordinary loss of $10,000
b. Ordinary gain of $15,000
c. Capital loss of $10,000
d. Capital gain of $15,000

(R/07, REG, 0801T, #22, 8446)

Problem 47-2 ADDITIONAL MULTIPLE CHOICE QUESTIONS (23 to 30 minutes)

31. Which of the following is an advantage of forming a limited liability company (LLC) as opposed to a partnership?
a. The entity may avoid taxation.
b. The entity may have any number of owners.
c. The owner may participate in management while limiting personal liability.
d. The entity may make disproportionate allocations and distributions to members.
(R/06, REG, C04242R, #40, 8210)

Items 32 and 33 are based on the following:

Flagg and Miles are each 50% partners in Decor Partnership. Each partner had a $200,000 tax basis in the partnership on January 1. Decor's net business income before guaranteed payments was $45,000. During the year, Decor made a $7,500 guaranteed payment to Miles for deductible services rendered.

32. What total amount from Decor is includible in Flagg's tax return?
a. $15,000
b. $18,750
c. $22,500
d. $37,500 (11/98, AR, #16, amended, 6682)

33. What is Miles' tax basis in Decor on December 31?
a. $211,250
b. $215,000
c. $218,750
d. $222,500 (11/98, AR, #17, amended, 6683)

34. Guaranteed payments made by a partnership to partners for services rendered to the partnership, that are deductible business expenses under the Internal Revenue Code, are

I. Deductible expenses on the U.S. Partnership Return of Income, Form 1065, in order to arrive at partnership income (loss)
II. Included on schedules K-1 to be taxed as ordinary income to the partners

a. I only
b II only
c. Both I and II
d. Neither I nor II (5/94, AR, #29, 4634)

35. Walker transferred property used in a sole proprietorship to the WXYZ partnership in exchange for a one-fourth interest. The property had an original cost of $75,000, an adjusted tax basis to Walker of $20,000, and fair market value of $50,000. The partnership has no liabilities. What is Walker's basis in the partnership interest?
a. $0
b. $20,000
c. $50,000
d. $75,000 (R/07, REG, 1102T, #4, 8428)

36. Kerr and Marcus form KM Partnership with a cash contribution of $80,000 from Kerr and a property contribution of land from Marcus. The land has a fair market value of $80,000 and an adjusted basis of $50,000 at the date of the contribution. Kerr and Marcus are equal partners. What is Marcus's basis immediately after formation?
a. $0
b. $50,000
c. $65,000
d. $80,000 (R/06, REG, 2003T, #34, 8204)

37. Smith received a one-third interest of a partnership by contributing $3,000 in cash, stock with a fair market value of $5,000 and a basis of $2,000, and a new computer that cost Smith $2,500. Which of the following amounts represents Smith's basis in the partnership?
a. $10,500
b. $ 7,500
c. $ 5,500
d. $ 3,000 (R/06, REG, A1127T, #37, 8207)

38. Ola Associates is a limited partnership engaged in real estate development. Hoff, a civil engineer, billed Ola $40,000 for consulting services rendered. In full settlement of this invoice, Hoff accepted a $15,000 cash payment plus the following:

	Fair market value	Carrying amount on Ola's books
3% limited partnership interest in Ola	$10,000	N/A
Surveying equipment	7,000	$3,000

What amount should Hoff, a cash basis taxpayer, report in his income tax return as income for the services rendered to Ola?
a. $15,000
b. $28,000
c. $32,000
d. $40,000 (11/91, PII, #56, amended, 2504)

39. Acme and Buck are equal members in Dear, an LLC. Dear has not elected to be taxed as a corporation. Acme contributed $7,000 cash and Buck contributed a machine with an adjusted basis of $5,000 and a fair market value of $10,000, subject to a liability of $3,000. What is Acme's basis in Dear?
a. $ 4,000
b. $ 7,000
c. $ 8,500
d. $10,000
(R/03, REG, 1364T, #14, amended, 7656)

40. Which of the following should be used in computing the basis of a partner's interest acquired from another partner?

	Cash paid by transferee to transferor	*Transferee's share of partnership liabilities*
a.	No	Yes
b.	Yes	No
c.	No	No
d.	Yes	Yes

(11/91, PII, #59, 2507)

41. A partnership had four partners. Each partner contributed $100,000 cash. The partnership reported income for the year of $80,000 and distributed $10,000 to each partner. What was each partner's basis in the partnership at the end of the current year?
a. $170,000
b. $120,000
c. $117,500
d. $110,000 (R/06, REG, A0679T, #13, 8183)

42. Ryan's adjusted basis in his Lux Partnership interest was $18,000 at the time Ryan received the following nonliquidating distributions of partnership property:

Cash	$10,000
Land—Adjusted basis	14,000
Land—Fair market value	20,000

What is Ryan's tax basis in the land received from the partnership?
a. $0
b. $ 8,000
c. $14,000
d. $20,000 (11/98, AR, #18, 6684)

43. Smith, a partner in Ridge Partnership, had a basis in the partnership interest of $100,000 at the time Smith received a nonliquidating distribution of land with an adjusted basis of $75,000 to Ridge and a fair market value of $135,000. Ridge had no unrealized receivables, appreciated inventory, or properties that had been contributed by its partners. Which of the following statements is(are) correct regarding the distribution?

I. Ridge recognized a $60,000 capital gain from the distribution.
II. Smith's holding period for the land includes the time it was owned by Ridge.

a. I only
b. II only
c. Both I and II
d. Neither I nor II (R/03, REG, 0346T, #7, 7649)

44. Reid, Welsh, and May are equal partners in the RWM partnership. Reid's basis in the partnership interest is $60,000. Reid receives a liquidating distribution of $61,000 cash and land with a fair market value of $14,000 and an adjusted basis of $12,000. What gain must Reid recognize upon the liquidation of his partnership interest?
a. $0
b. $ 1,000
c. $13,000
d. $15,000 (R/07, REG, 1135T, #26, 8450)

45. On January 3, the partners' percentage interest in the capital, profits, and losses of Able Partnership were:

Dean	25%
Poe	30%
Ritt	45%

On February 4, Poe sold her entire interest to an unrelated party. Dean sold his 25% interest in Able to another unrelated party on December 20. No other transactions took place during the year. For tax purposes, which of the following statements is correct with respect to Able?
a. Able terminated as of February 4.
b. Able terminated as of December 20.
c. Able terminated as of December 31.
d. Able did **not** terminate.
(11/95, AR, #33, amended, 5777)

Problem 47-3 EXTRA MULTIPLE CHOICE QUESTIONS (11 to 14 minutes)

46. The at-risk limitation provisions of the Internal Revenue Code may limit

I. A partner's deduction for his or her distributive share of partnership losses
II. A partnership's net operating loss carryover

a. I only
b. II only
c. Both I and II
d. Neither I nor II (R/07, REG, 0340T, #21, 8445)

Items 47 and 48 are based on the following:

Jones and Curry formed Major Partnership as equal partners by contributing the assets below:

	Asset	Adjusted basis	Fair market value
Jones	Cash	$45,000	$45,000
Curry	Land	30,000	57,000

The land was held by Curry as a capital asset, subject to a $12,000 mortgage, that was assumed by Major.

47. What was Curry's initial basis in the partnership interest?
a. $45,000
b. $30,000
c. $24,000
d. $18,000 (5/96, AR #1, 6198)

48. What was Jones' initial basis in the partnership interest?
a. $51,000
b. $45,000
c. $39,000
d. $33,000 (5/96, AR, #2, 6199)

49. Smith and White contributed $4,000 and $6,000 in cash, respectively, and formed the Macro General Partnership. The partnership agreement allocated profits and losses 40% to Smith and 60% to White. Macro purchased property from an unrelated seller for $10,000 cash and a $40,000 mortgage note that was the general liability of the partnership. Macro's liability
a. Increases Smith's partnership basis by $16,000
b. Increases Smith's partnership basis by $20,000
c. Increases Smith's partnership basis by $24,000
d. Has **no** effect on Smith's partnership basis (11/95, AR, #30, amended, 5774)

Items 50 and 51 are based on the following:

The adjusted basis of Jody's partnership interest was $50,000 immediately before Jody received a current distribution of $20,000 cash and property with an adjusted basis to the partnership of $40,000 and a fair market value of $35,000.

50. What amount of taxable gain must Jody report as a result of this distribution?
a. $0
b. $ 5,000
c. $10,000
d. $20,000 (11/93, PII, #55, 4484)

51. What is Jody's basis in the distributed property?
a. $0
b. $30,000
c. $35,000
d. $40,000 (11/93, PII, #56, 4485)

52. The basis to a partner of property distributed "in kind" in complete liquidation of the partner's interest is the
a. Adjusted basis of the partner's interest increased by any cash distributed to the partner in the same transaction
b. Adjusted basis of the partner's interest reduced by any cash distributed to the partner in the same transaction
c. Adjusted basis of the property to the partnership
d. Fair market value of the property (11/91, PII, #54, 2502)

SIMULATIONS

Problem 47-4 (20 to 30 minutes)

Melvin, Otto, and Patricia formed the MOP Disaster Recovery Partnership on January 2, Year 2. Melvin contributed $50,000 in cash for a 50% share in capital and profits. Otto contributed land with an adjusted basis of $15,000 and a fair market value of $26,250 for a 20% share. The land was a capital asset to Otto, subject to a $6,250 mortgage, which was assumed by the partnership. Patricia contributed equipment with an adjusted basis of $30,000 and a fair market value of $32,000 for a 30% share.

The partners are unrelated outside of the general partnership.

In Year 2, the partnership had a $20,000 loss.

In Year 3, Melvin sold several pieces of antique furniture that he previously used in his home to the partnership at fair market value, $18,750. Melvin had an adjusted basis in the furniture of $6,250. The antiques subsequently were used as office furniture. The partners are concerned about tax issues due to transactions with a related party. (Editors, 5038)

For items 1 through 3, determine the amount.

Partner	Amount
1. Determine Otto's initial basis in MOP.	
2. Determine Patricia's initial basis in MOP.	
3. Determine Melvin's basis in MOP at the end of Year 2.	

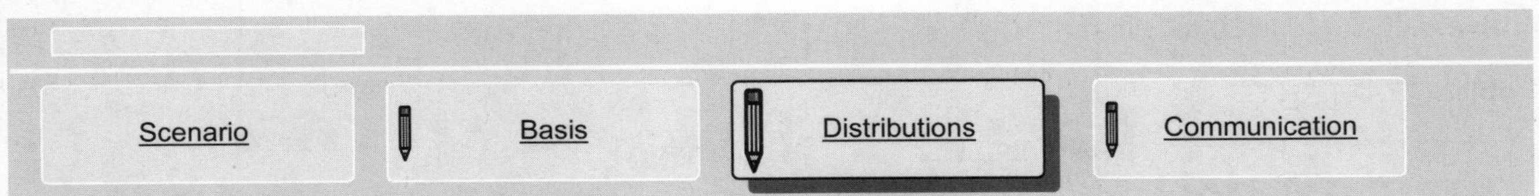

During Year 3, the MOP Partnership breaks even but decides to make distributions to each partner.

For items 4 through 8, determine whether the statement is true (T) or false (F).

Statement	Answer
4. A nonliquidating cash distribution may reduce the recipient partner's basis in her/his partnership interest below zero.	
5. A nonliquidating distribution of unappreciated inventory reduces the recipient partner's basis in her/his partnership interest.	
6. In a liquidating distribution of property other than money, where the partnership's basis of the distributed property exceeds the basis of the partner's interest, the partner's basis in the distributed property is limited to her/his predistribution basis in the partnership interest.	
7. Gain is recognized by the partner who receives a nonliquidating distribution of property, where the adjusted basis of the property exceeds her/his basis in the partnership interest before the distribution.	
8. In a nonliquidating distribution of inventory, where the partnership has no unrealized receivables or appreciated inventory, the basis of inventory that is distributed to a partner cannot exceed the inventory's adjusted basis to the partnership.	

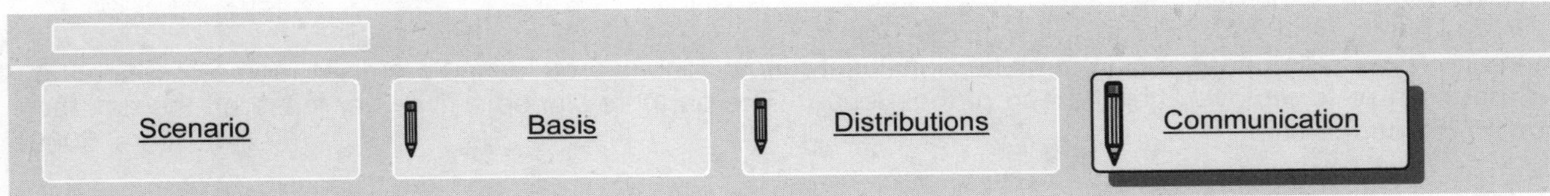

Write a memo to the partnership explaining how Melvin's sale of furniture to the partnership is handled for tax purposes for both the partnership and Melvin.

Research Question: What code section and subsection, if applicable, provides guidance regarding the affect on the other partners' bases in their partnership interests when the partnership makes a nonliquidating distribution of encumbered property to a partner who assumes the mortgage.

Section & Subsection Answer: §_____ (__)

Problem 47-5 (20 to 30 minutes)

On March 1, Year 1, Tonia, a lawyer, joined Alex and Xavier, both accountants, to form the TAX Partnership by contributing the assets below:

	Asset	Adjusted basis	Fair market value	% of partner share in capital, profits & losses
Tonia	Cash	$20,000	$20,000	50%
Alex	Equipment	$6,000	$10,500	20%
Xavier	Supplies	$7,000	$7,000	30%

The equipment was a capital asset to Alex, subject to a $2,500 secured loan, which was assumed by the partnership.

The partners are unrelated outside of the general partnership. Each partner gets a $4,000 guaranteed payment for each month they were active in the business; they all have met this criteria since the partnership was formed. The TAX General Partnership provides services, but does not sell any product.

In addition to the $1,700 depreciation deduction, figured using MACRS, the following is a list of receipts and expenditures relating to Year 1.

Gross receipts	$675,750	Rent	$120,000
Allowances	1,000	Taxes and licenses	23,000
Wages	200,000	Supplies	14,050
Repairs and maintenance	500	Utilities	9,950

In the next year, the partners plan to make significant renovations to their leased premises, some of which they will not be able to remove after the end of their lease. The partners signed a five-year lease on the day they started the partnership. (Editors, 5039)

Scenario | Partial Form 1065 | Communication | Research

Prepare lines 1 through 22 of Form 1065 for the TAX General Partnership.

Form **1065** Department of the Treasury Internal Revenue Service

U.S. Return of Partnership Income

For calendar year 2008, or tax year beginning __________, 2008, ending __________, 20____.
▶ See separate instructions.

OMB No. 1545-0099

2008

A Principal business activity	Use the IRS label. Otherwise, print or type.	Name of partnership	D Employer identification number
B Principal product or service		Number, street, and room or suite no. If a P.O. box, see the instructions.	E Date business started
C Business code number		City or town, state, and ZIP code	F Total assets (see the instructions) $

G Check applicable boxes: (1) ☐ Initial return (2) ☐ Final return (3) ☐ Name change (4) ☐ Address change (5) ☐ Amended return (6) ☐ Technical termination - also check (1) or (2)

H Check accounting method: (1) ☐ Cash (2) ☐ Accrual (3) ☐ Other (specify) ▶

I Number of Schedules K-1. Attach one for each person who was a partner at any time during the tax year ▶

J Check if Schedule M-3 attached ☐

Caution. *Include **only** trade or business income and expenses on lines 1a through 22 below. See the instructions for more information.*

Income	1a	Gross receipts or sales	1a			
	b	Less returns and allowances	1b		1c	
	2	Cost of goods sold (Schedule A, line 8)			2	
	3	Gross profit. Subtract line 2 from line 1c			3	
	4	Ordinary income (loss) from other partnerships, estates, and trusts *(attach statement)*			4	
	5	Net farm profit (loss) *(attach Schedule F (Form 1040))*			5	
	6	Net gain (loss) from Form 4797, Part II, line 17 *(attach Form 4797)*			6	
	7	Other income (loss) *(attach statement)*			7	
	8	**Total income (loss).** Combine lines 3 through 7			8	
Deductions (see the instructions for limitations)	9	Salaries and wages (other than to partners) (less employment credits)			9	
	10	Guaranteed payments to partners			10	
	11	Repairs and maintenance			11	
	12	Bad debts			12	
	13	Rent			13	
	14	Taxes and licenses			14	
	15	Interest			15	
	16a	Depreciation *(if required, attach Form 4562)*	16a			
	b	Less depreciation reported on Schedule A and elsewhere on return	16b		16c	
	17	Depletion **(Do not deduct oil and gas depletion.)**			17	
	18	Retirement plans, etc.			18	
	19	Employee benefit programs			19	
	20	Other deductions *(attach statement)*			20	
	21	**Total deductions.** Add the amounts shown in the far right column for lines 9 through 20			21	
	22	**Ordinary business income (loss).** Subtract line 21 from line 8			22	

Sign Here

Under penalties of perjury, I declare that I have examined this return, including accompanying schedules and statements, and to the best of my knowledge and belief, it is true, correct, and complete. Declaration of preparer (other than general partner or limited liability company member manager) is based on all information of which preparer has any knowledge.

▶ Signature of general partner or limited liability company member manager ▶ Date

May the IRS discuss this return with the preparer shown below (see instructions)? ☐ Yes ☐ No

Paid Preparer's Use Only

Preparer's signature	Date	Check if self-employed ▶ ☐	Preparer's SSN or PTIN
Firm's name (or yours if self-employed), address, and ZIP code ▶		EIN ▶	
		Phone no. ( )	

For Privacy Act and Paperwork Reduction Act Notice, see separate instructions. Cat. No. 11390Z Form **1065** (2008)

Write a memo to the partners explaining how the cost of the planned renovations to the partnership's leased premises will be handled for tax purposes.

Scenario	Partial Form 1065	Communication	Research

Enter the code section and subsection, if applicable, citation from the reference material that addresses the research question in the space provided. On the AICPA's exam, candidates may be instructed to TRANSFER TO ANSWER from a database location rather than enter the citation.

Example §102(a)

Research Question: What code section and subsection, if applicable, provides guidance regarding the basis of a contributing partners interest in the partnership.

Section & Subsection Answer: §_____ (___)

Solution 47-1 MULTIPLE CHOICE ANSWERS

Overview

1. (b) Section 444 requires a partnership to use a calendar year or a year that does not create a deferral period which exceeds three months. A partnership formed during the year must elect to have a taxable year that ends in September, October, November, or December. A partnership can elect to have a taxable year other than a required taxable year as long as the deferral period does not exceed three months. The only form which must be filed with the IRS to adopt its tax year is Form 1065, *U.S. Partnership Return of Income,* which is due three and a half months after the end of its tax year.

Distributive Share

2. (b) Section 703(b) provides that any election affecting the taxable income of a partnership shall be made by the partnership with three noted exceptions. None of the exceptions applies to the depreciation method.

3. (b) Section 709(b)(1)(A) allows a partnership to elect to deduct up to $5,000 of organization costs incurred in the tax year its business begins. However, the $5,000 deduction is reduced on a dollar-for-dollar basis for those expenses in excess of $50,000. Basic's deduction is not affected by this limit. Any remaining balance must be amortized of 15 years under §709(b)(1)(B). Legal fees to prepare the partnership agreement are considered an organization cost eligible under Reg. 1.709-2(a). Reg. 1.709-2(b) specifically disallows accounting fees to prepare the representations in offering materials as an eligible organization cost. These costs must be capitalized and not amortized. (Prior to AJCA '04, an entity could elect to amortize organizational expenses incurred before the end of the first tax year in which the entity was in business over a period of at least 60 months.)

4. (c) A partner's loss deduction generally cannot exceed the amount "at risk" in the activity at the end of the year. Once the amount of loss that is unrestricted by the basis limitation and at-risk rules is determined, pass through losses may be further restricted by the passive activity rules. The partnership provides all partners with a breakdown of income, credit and deduction items from each of its passive activities, because passive activity losses can generally only offset passive activity income.

5. (a) Because Marks and Sparks share profits and losses equally, Marks is allocated $21,000 of the ordinary loss (e.g., 50% of $42,000). Section 704(d) provides that a partner's distributive share of partnership loss is allowed only to the extent of the adjusted basis in that partner's partnership interest. Any loss disallowed under §704(d) will be allowed as a deduction at the end of the first succeeding taxable year to the extent that the partner's adjusted basis at the end of such year exceeds zero [Reg. §1.704-1(d)(1)]. Thus, Marks should deduct an ordinary loss of $18,000. The remaining $3,000 is carried forward and may be deducted in succeeding tax years.

Partners' Transactions With Partnership

6. (b) Generally, a guaranteed payment to a partner is treated as if the partner were unrelated, and thus is a deduction from partnership income and ordinary income to the partner. As there is no indication that the payment was credited to Peters' ownership account as opposed to being paid outright, Peters' partnership basis doesn't increase.

7. (c) Guaranteed payments from a partnership for services rendered are income from self-employment. Ordinary income received from an S corporation was earned by the S corporation, not the shareholder, and retains its character as it passes through to the shareholder.

8. (b, d) Both answers are required for full point value. Section 707(c) provides that payments to a partner for services or the use of capital made without regard to the partnership's income shall be considered as payments made to one who is not a partner for purposes of §162(a), which allows a deduction for all ordinary and necessary business expenses, including depreciation. Charitable contributions and short-term capital losses must be separately stated for deduction on the partner's return. There has not been any $100 exclusion for dividends in many years.

9. (a) Section 707(c) states that guaranteed payments are payments to a partner for services or for the use of capital to the extent determined without regard to the income of the partnership. The $5,000 monthly salary is guaranteed because it is not determined by any reference to the income of the partnership. The payment of 25% of the partnership's profits is not a guaranteed payment because it is determined by taking into account the income of the partnership.

10. (a) If a partner enters into a sale of an asset with such partnership and if the partner owns *more* than 50% of the partnership, no loss is

recognized. Since Lisa owns *only* 50% of the partnership, the entire loss on the sale of the stock (e.g., \$8,000 – \$3,000) is recognized by Lisa as a long-term capital loss.

11. (a) While a partner may engage in a transaction with her/his partnership in a capacity other than as a member of such partnership [§707(a)], if the partner owns, directly or indirectly, more than 50% of the capital or profits interests in such partnership, then the gain upon the sale or exchange of property between them which, in the hands of the *transferee,* is not a capital asset as defined in §1221, shall be considered as ordinary income [§707(b)]. Since Kaye owned 85% of the capital and profits interest of the partnership, her \$4,000 (e.g., \$6,000 – \$2,000) gain is characterized as *ordinary income.*

Contributions

12. (d) Section 721(a) provides that no gain or loss is recognized by the partnership or by any partner on the contribution of property to the partnership in exchange for a partnership interest. The net debt relief is less than the adjusted basis of the property.

13. (c) Kelly has ordinary gross income from services rendered in an amount equal to the fair value of the property received as compensation under §§61 and 83. Reg. 1.61-2(d)(1) states "...if services are paid for in property, the fair market value of the property taken in payment must be included in income as compensation." Thus, Kelly has \$10,000 gross income (\$100,000 × 10%). Although the partnership interest obtained will be a capital asset, the income for services performed to obtain such partnership interest is ordinary under §64.

14. (c) A partner's holding period for a partnership interest acquired through contribution of a *capital asset,* or an asset used in the partner's trade or business, includes the holding period for the contributed property. The holding period begins on the date the partnership interest is acquired only if the contributed property is *not* a capital asset or was not used in the partner's trade or business.

Basis

15. (c) Dean's basis in his partnership interest is increased by his distributive share of the partnership's ordinary income. His basis in the partnership interest is increased by his distributive share of the partnership's tax-exempt income. His basis in the partnership interest is reduced, but not below zero, by cash distributions.

Basis, January 1	\$20,000
Share of municipal bond interest (\$12,000 × 25%)	3,000
Share of ordinary income (\$40,000 × 25%)	10,000
Basis before distribution	\$33,000
Less: Distribution	(8,000)
Basis, December 31	\$25,000

16. (a) The partner's share of an increase in partnership liabilities is treated as a contribution of money from the partner to the partnership under §752(a). The partner then gets to increase her/his basis in the partnership for this deemed contribution of money under §722.

17. (b) Bailey's basis in the partnership interest includes the \$25,000 adjusted basis of property contributed in exchange for such interest under §722. The \$10,000 recourse mortgage assumed by the partnership on the land contributed by Bailey reduces Bailey's basis in the partnership interest by \$10,000 under §733. Bailey's 30% share of the mortgage assumed by the partnership is a deemed contribution of money to the partnership by Bailey. Bailey's basis in his partnership interest is calculated as follows.

Adjusted basis of property transferred	\$ 25,000
Less: Debt assumed by partnership	(10,000)
Add: Share of partnership's debt (\$10,000 × 30%)	3,000
Bailey's initial basis in partnership interest	\$ 18,000

18. (c) Under §752(a), a partner's share of the debts of the partnership is treated as a contribution of money to the partnership for which the partner obtains basis under §722. Under §752(b), a decrease in a partner's share of the debts of the partnership is treated as a distribution of money from the partnership to the partner. This deemed distribution reduces the partner's basis in her/his partnership interest under §733.

Paul's share of debts, Jan. 1 (\$150,000 × 25%)	\$ 37,500
Paul's share of debts, Dec. 31 (\$100,000 × 20%)	(20,000)
Decrease in basis in Paul's partnership interest	\$ 17,500

19. (c) Thompson's basis in the partnership interest is increased by the long-term capital gain under §705. Thompson's basis in the partnership interest is reduced, but not below zero, by cash distributions under §1367.

Thompson's basis at beginning of the year	\$ 60,000
Less: Cash distribution	(20,000)
Add: Long-term capital gain	15,000
Basis before loss	\$ 55,000
Ordinary loss	\$ 65,000
Deductible loss for the period (Smaller of basis or ordinary loss)	\$ 55,000

Nonliquidating Distribution

20. (c) The basis of property distributed to a partner is generally its adjusted basis to the partnership immediately before the distribution. Section 732(a)(2) limits the adjusted basis to the adjusted basis of the partner's interest in the partnership reduced by any money distributed in the same transaction. ($80,000 – $50,000 = $30,000)

21. (d) Section 731(a)(1) provides that a partner does not recognize gain on receiving a distribution from a partnership except to the extent that any money distributed exceeds the adjusted basis of her/his partnership interest immediately before the distribution. Section 731(a)(2) provides that a partner does not recognize loss on a distribution of property from the partnership except in certain liquidating distributions. Section 731(b) also provides that the partnership does not recognize any gain or loss on a distribution to a partner. Since the distribution was a nonliquidating distribution, Stone recognizes no gain or loss.

22. (b) Under §732(a)(1), the basis of property other than money distributed to a partner in a nonliquidating distribution is equal to the basis of such property in the partnership's hands immediately before the distribution. However, if the basis of the property distributed may not exceed the basis of the partner's interest in the partnership (as reduced by any money distributed in the same transaction) under §732(a)(2). Owen's tax basis in Regal after the distribution is computed as follows.

Owen's basis before distribution	$18,000
Less: Cash distribution	(3,000)
Limit on basis of land	$15,000
Basis of land (lesser of partnership's land basis or limit on basis of land)	(7,000)
Owen's tax basis after distribution	$ 8,000

Liquidating Distribution

23. (c) The $1,500 cash distribution received by Frazier is comprised of his portion of the partnership cash ($2,000 × 50%) and his portion of the gain from the sale of equipment ($3,000 – $2,000) × 50%. Gain is recognized to the extent that money distributed exceeds the partner's adjusted basis in the partnership interest.

Cash distribution	$ 1,500
Less: Basis in partnership	(1,200)
Gain recognized	$ 300

24. (b) As this is a liquidating distribution, the adjusted basis in the land is the basis of the partnership interest after deducting the cash. $70K – $10K = $60K

Termination

25. (a) Since more than 50% ownership of the prior partnership continues as the Abel & Benz Partnership, that partnership is considered to be a continuation of Partnership Abel, Benz, Clark & Day. Generally, no tax is imposed on contributions of property to a partnership. A partnership does not need IRS approval to separate a business nor does a partnership have to file its formal dissolution on a prescribed form with the IRS.

26. (c) Except for electing large partnerships, a partnership terminates if no part of its business is carried on within a 12-month period, or if within a 12-month period, 50% or more of the total interest in the partnership are sold [IRC §708(b)].

27. (c) Reg. 1.708-1(b)(1)(iv) provides that if a partnership is terminated by a sale or exchange of an interest that (1) the partnership is deemed to have distributed its properties to the purchaser and the remaining partners in proportion to their respective interests in the partnership properties and (2) immediately thereafter, the purchaser and the other remaining partners are deemed to contribute such properties to the partnership.

Transfer of Partnership Interest

28. (a) The amount which a partner realizes on the sale of a partnership interest includes any cash received, plus any partnership liabilities which are assumed by the buyer. The total amount realized by Carr on the sale of his partnership interest is $174,000 (cash plus partnership liabilities).

29. (d) If a partner sells her/his partnership interest and the partnership has unrealized receivables which have not been recognized as income by the partnership, then the partner has to recognize the proceeds which s/he received for the unrealized receivables as ordinary income. Since Carr's share of the partnership's unrealized receivables is $140,000 (e.g., $420,000 / 3), he has to recognize this amount as ordinary income.

30. (d) The amount that a partner realizes on the sale of a partnership interest includes any cash received, plus any partnership liabilities that are assumed by the buyer. $30,000 cash plus $25,000 liability relief equals $55,000 amount realized. $55,000 amount realized less $40,000 basis equals $15,000 gain. Gains from the sale of partnership interests generally are characterized as capital gains, unless attributable to unrealized receivables or inventory items.

Solution 47-2 ADDITIONAL MULTIPLE CHOICE ANSWERS

Overview

31. (c) Each state statute creating the limited liability company (LLC) business form is extremely flexible. Characteristically, the owners may participate in management while limiting personal liability. Every state allows both single member and multimember LLC's. A partnership generally may have as many partners as wanted, as long as it has at least two. A single-member LLC is disregarded as a separate entity by the IRS. Accordingly, if the single member is an individual, the LLC is taxed as a proprietorship. If the single member is a corporation, the LLC is treated as a division of a corporation. An LLC with multiple members is treated as a partnership for federal tax purposes. Candidates with concerns regarding the placement of this question in the REG, rather than the BEC, exam section should contact the AICPA.

Distributive Share

32. (b) ($45,000 – $7,500) × 0.50 = $18,750

33. (c) As Miles' guaranteed payment was paid, it did not increase Miles' basis. ($45,000 – 7,500) × 0.50 + $200,000 = $218,750

Partners' Transactions With Partnership

34. (c) Section 707(c) provides that payments made to a partner for services or the use of capital determined without reference to the income of the partnership are to be considered as made to a person that is not a member of the partnership only for the purposes of (1) §61(a) relating to gross income and (2) §162(a) relating to the deductibility of ordinary and necessary business expenses, subject to the requirements of §263 to capitalize costs that are properly chargeable to a capital account. Thus, the guaranteed payments are includible as ordinary gross income on the recipient partners' respective income tax returns. The guaranteed payments are also deductible by the partnership as an ordinary and necessary business expense.

Contributions

35. (b) Generally, no gain or loss is recognized by the partnership or any partner when property is contributed to the partnership in exchange for an interest in the partnership. The partner's basis in the partnership interest is the partner's adjusted basis in the contributed property.

36. (b) Generally, no gain or loss is recognized when a partner contributes assets to a partnership in exchange for a partnership interest. The partner's basis in the partnership interest is the partner's basis in the contributed assets, adjusted for any debt relief or debt assumed. Marcus's basis in the partnership interest is the land's adjusted basis of $50,000.

37. (b) Generally, no gain or loss is recognized when a partner contributes assets to a partnership in exchange for a partnership interest. The partner's basis in the partnership interest is the partner's basis in the contributed assets, adjusted for any debt relief or debt assumed. Smith's basis in the partnership interest is Smith's basis in the cash, stock, and computer: $3,000 + $2,000 + $2,500 = $7,500.

38. (c) Gross income can be received in different forms, such as money, property, or services. The fair market value of property or services received must be included in gross income. Thus, Hoff must include the fair market value of the surveying equipment in gross income. Additionally, where a partnership interest is received in exchange for the contribution of services, the contributing partner includes in ordinary income an amount equal to the excess of fair market value of the partnership interest received for the services performed less the amount paid for the partnership interest. Thus, the amount included in gross income for services rendered equals the cash received, the fair market value of the partnership interest, and the surveying equipment (e.g., $15,000 + $10,000 + $7,000).

39. (c) Acme's initial basis in the partnership interest is Acme's adjusted basis in the cash plus Acme's portion of the debt assumed by the partnership. [$7,000 + (50% × $3,000) = $8,500]

40. (d) If a partner acquires a partnership interest from another partner, the basis of the acquired interest is equal to the sum of the cash and the fair market value of the other consideration paid for the interest. An assumption of partnership liabilities is considered a contribution of money by the partner and increases the basis of a partner's interest. The partnership's assumption of a partner's liabilities is considered a distribution of money from the partnership resulting in a decrease in the basis of a partner's interest.

Basis

41. (d) A partner's basis is increased by the partner's share of income as well as reduced by the partner's share of losses and actual distributions to the partner. The question states the income in total and the distributions in a per-partner manner. $100,000 + ($80,000 / 4) – $10,000 = $110,000

Nonliquidating Distribution

42. (b) The basis of property distributed to a partner is generally its adjusted basis to the partnership immediately before the distribution. Section 732(a)(2) limits the adjusted basis to the adjusted basis in the partner's interest in the partnership reduced by any money distributed in the same transaction. ($18,000 – $10,000 = $8,000)

43. (b) Section 731(a)(1) provides that a partner does not recognize gain on receiving a distribution from a partnership, except to the extent that any money distributed exceeds the adjusted basis of her/his partnership interest immediately before the distribution. Generally, partner's holding period for property received in a distribution from a partnership includes the holding period of the partnership respect to such property [Section 735(b)].

Liquidating Distribution

44. (b) Reid recognizes a gain by the amount that the cash exceeds Reid's adjusted basis in the partnership interest: $61,000 – $60,000 = $1,000.

Termination

45. (b) Section 708(b)(1) provides that a partnership is considered as terminated if within a 12-month period there is a sale or exchange of 50% or more of the total interest in partnership capital and profits. Poe sold a 30% interest on February 4, and Dean sold his 25% interest on December 20. Thus, on December 20, 55% of the interest in the partnership's capital and profits had been sold within a 12-month period.

Solution 47-3 EXTRA MULTIPLE CHOICE ANSWERS

Distributive Share

46. (a) A partner's distribution share of partnership loss cannot exceed the partner's adjusted basis in the partnership interest; the partners loss deduction also is limited by the "at-risk" and passive loss rules. Any unused loss is carried forward.

Contributions

47. (c) Curry's initial basis in the partnership interest is Curry's adjusted basis in the land less the debt assumed by the partnership plus Curry's portion of the debt assumed by the partnership. [$30,000 – $12,000 + $6,000 = $24,000]

48. (a) Jones' initial basis in the partnership interest is Jones' adjusted basis in the cash plus Jones' portion of the debt assumed by the partnership. [$45,000 + $6,000 = $51,000]

Basis

49. (a) Smith's share of the partnership's liability is $16,000 ($40,000 × 40%). An increase in a partner's share of the partnership's liabilities is treated as a contribution of money by the partner to the partnership. This deemed contribution of money increases the partner's basis in the partnership interest under §722. Thus, Macro's liability increases Smith's basis in the partnership interest by $16,000.

Nonliquidating Distribution

50. (a) Section 731(a)(1) provides that no gain shall be recognized on a distribution from a partnership to a partner except to the extent that any money distributed exceeds the adjusted basis of such partner's interest in the partnership. The adjusted basis in Jody's partnership interest was $50,000. The money distributed of $20,000 is less than the adjusted basis in Jody's partnership interest.

51. (b) Section 733 provides that the adjusted basis in the partnership interest shall be reduced by the amount of money distributed. Thus, Jody's adjusted basis in the partnership interest is reduced by $20,000 to $30,000. Section 732(a)(1) provides that the adjusted basis of property distributed in a current distribution to a partner is generally equal to the adjusted basis of the property in the hands of the partnership. This would give Jody a $40,000 basis in the property. However, §732(a)(2) provides a limitation on this amount. The limit is the adjusted basis of the partnership interest. Thus, Jody's adjusted basis in the partnership of $30,000 is less than the $40,000 adjusted basis of the property in the hands of the partnership. Therefore, Jody's basis in the property is $30,000. Jody's basis in the partnership interest is reduced by this $30,000 under §733. This leaves Jody with a zero basis in the partnership interest.

Liquidating Distribution

52. (b) The basis of property (other than money) distributed to a partner in a liquidating distribution is equal to the adjusted basis of the partner's interest in the partnership, *reduced* by any cash received by the partner in the liquidation. The partnership's adjusted basis in the property becomes the partner's basis in a *nonliquidating* distribution. It is a *shareholder* that takes the fair market value of property distributed by a *corporation* as her/his basis in the distributed property.

PERFORMANCE BY SUBTOPICS

Each category below parallels a subtopic covered in Chapter 47. Record the number and percentage of questions you correctly answered in each subtopic area.

Overview

Question #	Correct √
1	
# Questions	1
# Correct	______
% Correct	______

Distributive Share

Question #	Correct √
2	
3	
4	
5	
# Questions	4
# Correct	______
% Correct	______

Partners' Transactions With Partnership

Question #	Correct √
6	
7	
8	
9	
10	
11	
# Questions	6
# Correct	______
% Correct	______

Contributions

Question #	Correct √
12	
13	
14	
# Questions	3
# Correct	______
% Correct	______

Basis

Question #	Correct √
15	
16	
17	
18	
19	
# Questions	5
# Correct	______
% Correct	______

Nonliquidating Distribution

Question #	Correct √
20	
21	
22	
# Questions	3
# Correct	______
% Correct	______

Liquidating Distribution

Question #	Correct √
23	
24	
# Questions	2
# Correct	______
% Correct	______

Termination

Question #	Correct √
25	
26	
27	
# Questions	3
# Correct	______
% Correct	______

Transfer of Partnership Interest

Question #	Correct √
28	
29	
30	
# Questions	3
# Correct	______
% Correct	______

SIMULATION SOLUTIONS

Solution 47-4 Basis

Basis (1.5 points)

1. $10,000

Otto's basis in the partnership interest includes the $15,000 adjusted basis of property contributed in exchange for such interest under §722. The $6,250 mortgage assumed by the partnership on the land contributed by Otto reduces Otto's basis in the partnership interest by $6,250 under §733. Otto's 20% share of the mortgage assumed by the partnership is a deemed contribution of money to the partnership by Otto.

Adjusted basis of property transferred	$15,000
Less: Debt assumed by partnership	(6,250)
Add: Share of partnership's debt ($6,250 × 20%)	1,250
Initial basis in MOP partnership interest	$10,000

2. $31,875

Patricia obtains a basis in the partnership interest equal to the $30,000 adjusted basis of the equipment contributed under §722. In addition, Patricia is deemed to have contributed money to the partnership equal to Patricia's share of the partnership's debts. Thus, Patricia is deemed to have contributed $1,875 ($6,250 × 30%) in money for which Patricia obtains additional basis. Therefore, Patricia's initial basis in the MOP partnership interest is $31,875 ($30,000 + $1,875).

3. $43,125

Melvin's initial basis in the partnership interest is his $50,000 initial cash investment plus his share of the debt assumed (50% × $6,250). A partner's basis is increased by the partner's share of income as well as reduced by the partner's share of losses and actual distributions to the partner. In the absence of an agreement to the contrary, losses are allocated on the same basis as profits: $53,125 – 0.50 × $20,000 = $43,125.

Distributions (2.5 points)

4. F

Section 733 states that a partner's basis in her/his partnership interest is to be reduced—but not below zero—by money distributed to the partner in a nonliquidating distribution.

5. T

Section 733 states that a partner's basis in her/his partnership interest is to be reduced—but not below zero—by a nonliquidating distribution of property other than money by the amount of the basis to such partner of distributed property, as determined under §732. Section 732(a)(1) provides that in the case of a nonliquidating distribution, the partner's basis in distributed property is the adjusted basis of the distributed property in the hands of the partnership. However, §732(a)(2) limits the partner's basis in the distributed property to the adjusted basis in the partnership interest.

6. T

Section 732(b) provides that in a liquidating distribution, the partner's basis in distributed property is equal to the adjusted basis in her/his partnership interest reduced by any money distributed in the same transaction.

7. F

Section 731(a)(1) provides that gain will not be recognized on a distribution to a partner, except to the extent that money distributed exceeds the adjusted basis of the partnership interest immediately before the distribution. If the adjusted basis of the property distributed exceeds the adjusted basis in the partnership interest, no gain is recognized, and the adjusted basis in the partnership interest becomes the partner's adjusted basis in the distributed property. The partner's adjusted basis in the partnership interest would then be reduced to zero.

8. T

The basis of inventory distributed to a partner in a nonliquidating distribution is the partnership's adjusted basis in the inventory, not to exceed the partner's adjusted basis in the partnership interest under §732(a). The partnership's adjusted basis in the inventory cannot exceed itself.

Communication (5 points)

October 10, Year 3

To: MOP Partnership
From: Jean Preparer
Re: Related-Party Transactions

Generally, a partner may engage in a transaction with his or her partnership and it will be deemed as occurring between two **independent entities.**

Exceptions include gains and losses from the sale of property between related parties, such as between a **controlling partner** and her partnership. For this purpose, a controlling partner is defined as a partner with a **more than 50%** ownership interest in his partnership. Such gains are **re-characterized** as **ordinary income.** Such losses are **not recognized.**

As Melvin held a 50% ownership interest at the time of the furniture transaction, he is not a controlling partner. Hence, the furniture transaction is not considered to be a related-party transaction. Accordingly, MOP Partnership recognizes this transaction as a **fixed asset** purchase and Melvin recognizes this transaction as a **capital gain.**

Research (1 point)

Code Section Answer: §752(b)

Code §752(b) states, "Any decrease in a partner's share of the liabilities of a partnership, or any decrease in a partner's individual liabilities by reason of the assumption by the partnership of such individual liabilities, shall be considered as a distribution of money to the partner by the partnership." [§733 "In the case of a distribution by a partnership to a partner other than in liquidation of a partner's interest, the adjusted basis to such partner of his interest in the partnership shall be reduced (but not below zero) by (1) the amount of any money distributed to such partner, and (2) the amount of the basis to such partner of distributed property other than money…."]

Solution 47-5 Form 1065

Partial Form 1065 (4 points)

1. 675,750

Line 1a: The gross receipts of $675,750 is provided in the scenario.

2. 1,000

Line 1b: The allowances of $1,000 is provided in the scenario. The software calculates the amount on Line 1c based on the information on lines 1a and 1b.

3. 0

Line 2: The partnership provides services, but does not sell any product; therefore, there is no cost of goods sold. The software calculates the amount on Line 3 based on the information on lines 1c and 2.

4. 0

Line 4: The partnership has no income or loss from other partnerships, estates, or trusts.

5. 0

Line 5: The partnership has no farm income or loss.

6. 0

Line 6: The partnership has no income or loss from Form 4797.

7. 0

Line 7: The partnership has no other income or loss. The software calculates the amount on Line 8 (674,750) based on the information on lines 3 through 7.

8. 200,000

Line 9: The wages of $200,000 is provided in the scenario.

9. 120,000

Line 10: Ten months (March through December) of guaranteed payments to three partners @ $4,000 / month = $120,000.

10. 500

Line 11: The repairs and maintenance expense of $500 is provided in the scenario.

11. 0

Line 12: There is no bad debt expense mentioned in the scenario.

12. 120,000

Line 13: The rent expense of $120,000 is provided in the scenario.

13. 23,000

Line 14: The tax and license expenses of $23,000 are provided in the scenario.

14. 0

Line 15: There is no interest expense mentioned in the scenario.

Partial Form 1065 (continued)

Form **1065** Department of the Treasury Internal Revenue Service

U.S. Return of Partnership Income

For calendar year 2008, or tax year beginning ...., 2008, ending ...., 20.....
▶ See separate instructions.

OMB No. 1545-0099

2008

A Principal business activity	Use the IRS label. Otherwise, print or type.	Name of partnership	D Employer identification number
B Principal product or service		Number, street, and room or suite no. If a P.O. box, see the instructions.	E Date business started
C Business code number		City or town, state, and ZIP code	F Total assets (see the instructions) $

G Check applicable boxes: (1) ☐ Initial return (2) ☐ Final return (3) ☐ Name change (4) ☐ Address change (5) ☐ Amended return
(6) ☐ Technical termination - also check (1) or (2)

H Check accounting method: (1) ☐ Cash (2) ☐ Accrual (3) ☐ Other (specify) ▶

I Number of Schedules K-1. Attach one for each person who was a partner at any time during the tax year ▶

J Check if Schedule M-3 attached ☐

Caution. *Include **only** trade or business income and expenses on lines 1a through 22 below. See the instructions for more information.*

Income	**1a** Gross receipts or sales	1a	675,750		
	b Less returns and allowances	1b		1c	675,750
	2 Cost of goods sold (Schedule A, line 8)			2	1,000
	3 Gross profit. Subtract line 2 from line 1c			3	674,750
	4 Ordinary income (loss) from other partnerships, estates, and trusts *(attach statement)*			4	
	5 Net farm profit (loss) *(attach Schedule F (Form 1040))*			5	
	6 Net gain (loss) from Form 4797, Part II, line 17 *(attach Form 4797)*			6	
	7 Other income (loss) *(attach statement)*			7	
	8 **Total income (loss).** Combine lines 3 through 7			8	674,750
Deductions (see the instructions for limitations)	**9** Salaries and wages (other than to partners) (less employment credits)			9	200,000
	10 Guaranteed payments to partners			10	120,000
	11 Repairs and maintenance			11	500
	12 Bad debts			12	
	13 Rent			13	120,000
	14 Taxes and licenses			14	23,000
	15 Interest			15	
	16a Depreciation *(if required, attach Form 4562)*	16a	1,700		
	b Less depreciation reported on Schedule A and elsewhere on return	16b		16c	1,700
	17 Depletion **(Do not deduct oil and gas depletion.)**			17	
	18 Retirement plans, etc.			18	
	19 Employee benefit programs			19	
	20 Other deductions *(attach statement)*			20	24,000
	21 **Total deductions.** Add the amounts shown in the far right column for lines 9 through 20			21	489,200
	22 **Ordinary business income (loss).** Subtract line 21 from line 8			22	185,550

Sign Here

Under penalties of perjury, I declare that I have examined this return, including accompanying schedules and statements, and to the best of my knowledge and belief, it is true, correct, and complete. Declaration of preparer (other than general partner or limited liability company member manager) is based on all information of which preparer has any knowledge.

▶ Signature of general partner or limited liability company member manager ▶ Date

May the IRS discuss this return with the preparer shown below (see instructions)? ☐ Yes ☐ No

Paid Preparer's Use Only

Preparer's signature	Date	Check if self-employed ▶ ☐	Preparer's SSN or PTIN
Firm's name (or yours if self-employed), address, and ZIP code ▶		EIN ▶	
		Phone no.	( )

For Privacy Act and Paperwork Reduction Act Notice, see separate instructions. Cat. No. 11390Z Form **1065** (2008)

Partial Form 1065 (continued)

15. 1,700

Line 16a: The depreciation deduction of $1,700 is provided in the scenario.

16. 0

Line 16b: No depreciation is reported on Schedule A or elsewhere. The software calculates the amount (1,700) on Line 16c based on the information on lines 16a and 16b.

17. 0

Line 17: There is no depletion mentioned in the scenario.

18. 0

Line 18: There is no retirement plan expense mentioned in the scenario.

19. 0

Line 19: There is no employee benefit program expense mentioned in the scenario.

20. 24,000

Line 20: The other deductions of $24,000 is provided in the scenario. This includes supplies and utilities. The software calculates the amount (489,200) on Line 21 based on the information on lines 9 through 20. The software calculates the amount (185,550) on Line 22 based on the information on lines 8 and 21.

Communication (5 points)

To: TAX Partnership
From: John Preparer
Re: Leasehold Improvements

Several types of trade fixtures may be removed to the extent that the removal action does not materially damage the realty. To the extent that some of the planned renovations to your premises do not meet this criteria, they become part of the realty and **remain** with the **landlord** upon the termination of the lease. These commonly called leasehold improvements.

The tax code allows a **deduction** for the exhaustion of property used in a trade or **business** or held for production of income. Cost recovery deductions impact the **basis** of property; in other words, when the asset is sold, previous depreciation deductions enter into the calculation of gain or loss at that point. This applies both to trade fixtures which remain the partnership's property and the leasehold improvements.

Both types of property are **depreciated** over the class life assigned by the modified accelerated cost recover system (MACRS). For example, under this system, office furniture is assigned to a 7-year category and nonresidential real estate is assigned to a 39-year category. Most leasehold improvements will be considered **real estate.**

For tax purposes, a deduction for a **leasehold improvement** is determined in the same manner as for owned property; in other words, without considering the life of the lease. If the lease ends (and is not renewed) before the end of the MACRS recovery period, the partnership will have a **loss** for tax purposes in that year for the remaining **unrecovered** basis of the leasehold improvements.

Research (1 point)

Code Section Answer: §722

Code §722 states, "The basis of an interest in a partnership acquired by a contribution of property, including money, to the partnership shall be the amount of such money and the adjusted basis of such property to the contributing partner at the time of the contribution increased by the amount (if any) of gain recognized under Section 721(b) to the contributing partner at such time." Search terms: partner contribution

Post-Exam Diagnostics

The AICPA Board of Examiners' Advisory Grading Service provides state boards of accountancy with individual diagnostic reports for all candidates along with the candidates' grades. The diagnostic reports show the candidate's level of proficiency on each examination section. The boards of accountancy **may** mail the diagnostic reports to candidates along with their grades: candidates should contact the state board in their jurisdiction to find out its policy on this.

Remember that candidates are required to sign a statement of confidentiality in which they promise not to reveal questions or answers. Due to the nondisclosure requirements, Bisk Education's editors are no longer able to address questions about specific examination questions, although we continue to supply help with similar study problems and questions in our texts.

See the **Practical Advice** appendix for more information.

APPENDIX A
PRACTICE EXAMINATION

Editor's Note: There is only one practice (or final) examination. Do not take this exam until you are ready for it. If you did not mark the answers on the diagnostic exam, it can be used as a second "final" exam. The actual AICPA exam will be a total of 180 minutes long and may have 24 to 30 questions per multiple choice testlet.

Testlet 1 MULTIPLE CHOICE QUESTIONS (36 to 48 minutes)

1. Under the ethical standards of the profession, which of the following positions would be considered a position of significant influence in an audit client?
   a. A marketing position related to the client's primary products
   b. A policy-making position in the client's finance division
   c. A staff position in the client's research and development division
   d. A senior position in the client's human resources division (7883)

2. To exercise due professional care, which **two** should an auditor do?
   a. Critically review the judgment exercised by those assisting in the audit
   b. Examine all available corroborating evidence supporting management's assertions
   c. Design the audit to detect all instances of illegal acts
   d. Notify the client when outside consultation is necessary
   e. Attain the proper balance of professional experience and formal education (8007)

3. According to the ethical standards of the profession, which of the following acts is generally prohibited?
   a. Issuing a modified report explaining a failure to follow a governmental regulatory agency's standards when conducting an attest service for a client
   b. Revealing confidential client information during a quality review of a professional practice by a team from the state CPA society
   c. Accepting a contingent fee for representing a client in an examination of the client's federal tax return by an IRS agent
   d. Retaining client records after an engagement is terminated prior to completion and the client has demanded their return (5871)

4. Under the Statements on Standards for Consulting Services, which of the following statements best reflects a CPA's responsibility when undertaking a consulting services engagement? The CPA must
   a. Not seek to modify any agreement made with the client
   b. Not perform any attest services for the client
   c. Inform the client of significant reservations concerning the benefits of the engagement
   d. Obtain a written understanding with the client concerning the time for completion of the engagement (5874)

5. Which of the following services is a CPA generally required to perform when conducting a personal financial planning engagement?
   a. Assisting the client to identify tasks that are essential in order to act on planning decisions
   b. Assisting the client to take action on planning decisions
   c. Monitoring progress in achieving goals
   d. Updating recommendations and revising planning decisions (6852)

6. Which of the following promises is supported by legally sufficient consideration and will be enforceable?
   a. A person's promise to pay a real estate agent $1,000 in return for the real estate agent's earlier act of not charging commission for selling the person's house
   b. A parent's promise to pay one child $500 because that child is not as wealthy as the child's sibling
   c. A promise to pay the police $250 to catch a thief
   d. A promise to pay a minor $500 to paint a garage (8437)

7. For which of the following contracts will a court generally grant the remedy of specific performance?
   a. A contract for the sale of a patent
   b. A contract of employment
   c. A contract for the sale of fungible goods
   d. A contract for the sale of stock that is traded on a national stock exchange (8452)

8. Thorn purchased a used entertainment system from Sound Corp. The sales contract stated that the entertainment system was being sold "as is." Under the Sales Article of the UCC, which of the following statements is(are) correct regarding the seller's warranty of title and against infringement?

I. Including the term "as is" in the sales contract is adequate communication that the seller is conveying the entertainment system without warranty of title and against infringement.
II. The seller's warranty of title and against infringement may be disclaimed at any time after the contract is formed.

a. I only
b. II only
c. Both I and II
d. Neither I nor II (8435)

9. On June 15, Harper purchased equipment for $100,000 from Imperial Corp. for use in its manufacturing process. Harper paid for the equipment with funds borrowed from Eastern Bank. Harper gave Eastern a security agreement and financing statement covering Harper's existing and after-acquired equipment. On June 21, Harper was petitioned involuntarily into bankruptcy under Chapter 7 of the Federal Bankruptcy Code. A bankruptcy trustee was appointed. On June 23, Eastern filed the financing statement. Which of the parties will have a superior security interest in the equipment?

a. The trustee in bankruptcy, because the filing of the financing statement after the commencement of the bankruptcy case would be deemed a preferential transfer
b. The trustee in bankruptcy, because the trustee became a lien creditor before Eastern perfected its security interest
c. Eastern, because it had a perfected purchase money security interest without having to file a financing statement
d. Eastern, because it perfected its security interest within the permissible time limits (0582)

10. Syl Corp. does **not** withhold FICA taxes from its employees' compensation. Syl voluntarily pays the entire FICA tax for its share and the amounts that it could have withheld from the employees. The employees' share of FICA taxes paid by Syl to the IRS is

a. Deductible by Syl as additional compensation that is includible in the employees' taxable income
b. Not deductible by Syl because it does **not** meet the deductibility requirement as an ordinary and necessary business expense
c. A nontaxable gift to each employee, provided that the amount is less than $1,000 annually to each employee
d. Subject to prescribed penalties imposed on Syl for its failure to withhold required payroll taxes (4781)

11. Kelly is single with no dependents. In Year 4, Kelly's principal residence was sold for the net amount of $400,000 after all selling expenses. Kelly bought the house in Year 1 and occupied it until sold. On the date of sale, the house had a basis of $80,000. What is the maximum exclusion of gain on the sale of the residence that may be claimed on Kelly's Year 4 income tax return?

a. $320,000
b. $250,000
c. $125,000
d. $0 (3342)

12. A capital loss incurred by a married couple filing a joint return

a. Is **not** an allowable loss
b. Will be allowed to the extent of capital gains, plus up to $3,000 of ordinary income
c. May be carried forward up to a maximum of five years
d. Will be allowed only to the extent of capital gains (9911)

13. Nell Brown's husband died in Year 0. Nell did not remarry, and continued to maintain a home for herself and her dependent infant child during Year 1, Year 2, and Year 3, providing full support for herself and her child during these three years. For Year 0, Nell properly filed a joint return. For Year 3, Nell's filing status is

a. Single
b. Married filing joint return
c. Head of household
d. Qualifying widow with dependent child (9911)

14. A calendar-year taxpayer files an individual tax return for Year 1 on March 20, Year 2. The taxpayer neither committed fraud nor omitted amounts in excess of 25% of gross income on the tax return. What is the latest date that the Internal Revenue Service can assess tax and assert a notice of deficiency?
a. March 20, Year 5
b. March 20, Year 4
c. April 15, Year 5
d. April 15, Year 4 (4623)

15. John Budd was 58 at the date of his death on July 1, 2007. Emma, his widow, received life insurance proceeds of $60,000 under a group policy paid for by John's employer, upon John's death. In addition, an employee death benefit of $7,500 was paid to Emma by John's employer, Toob Company. How much of the group life insurance proceeds should be excluded from taxable income?
a. $0
b. $ 5,000
c. $50,000
d. $60,000 (9911)

16. Don Wolf became a general partner in Gata Associates on January 1, Year 1, with a 5% interest in Gata's profits, losses, and capital. Gata is a distributor of auto parts. Wolf does not materially participate in the partnership business. For Year 1, Gata had an operating loss of $100,000. In addition, Gata earned interest of $20,000 on a temporary investment. Gata has kept the principal temporarily invested while awaiting delivery of equipment that is presently on order. The principal will be used to pay for this equipment. Wolf's passive loss for Year 1 is
a. $0
b. $4,000
c. $5,000
d. $6,000 (1566)

17. Smith, a single individual, made the following charitable contributions during the current year. Smith's adjusted gross income is $60,000.

Donation to Smith's church	$5,000
Art work donated to the local art museum. Smith purchased it for $2,000 four month's ago. A local art dealer appraised it for	3,000
Contribution to a needy family	1,000

What amount should Smith deduct as a charitable contribution?
a. $5,000
b. $7,000
c. $8,000
d. $9,000 (7082)

18. A civil fraud penalty can be imposed on a corporation that underpays tax by
a. Omitting income as a result of inadequate recordkeeping
b. Failing to report income it erroneously considered **not** to be part of corporate profits
c. Maintaining false records and reporting fictitious transactions to minimize corporate tax liability
d. Filing an incomplete return with an appended statement, making clear that the return is incomplete (5760)

19. In Year 1, Acorn Inc. had the following items of income and expense:

Sales	$500,000
Cost of sales	250,000
Dividends received	25,000

The dividends were received from a corporation of which Acorn owns 30%. In Acorn's corporate income tax return, what amount should be reported as income before special deductions?
a. $525,000
b. $505,000
c. $275,000
d. $250,000 (4147)

20. A corporation's capital loss carryback or carryover is
a. Not allowable under current law
b. Limited to $3,000
c. Always treated as a long-term capital loss
d. Always treated as a short-term capital loss (2489)

21. Pursuant to a plan of corporate reorganization adopted in July Year 1, Gow exchanged 500 shares of Lad Corp. common stock that he had bought in January Year 1 at a cost of $5,000 for 100 shares of Rook Corp. common stock having a fair market value of $6,000. Gow's recognized gain on this exchange was
a. $1,000 long-term capital gain
b. $1,000 short-term capital gain
c. $1,000 ordinary income
d. $0 (1637)

Items 22 and 23 are based on the following:

Max Finch was the sole stockholder of Burr, Inc., a company engaged principally in manufacturing operations. Total organization costs of $12,000 were incurred in January, Year 0, and are being amortized over a 12-year period for financial statement purposes. Burr's retained earnings at December 31, Year 2, amounted to $1,000,000. For the year ended December 31, Year 3, Burr's book income, before income taxes, was $300,000. Included in the computa tion of this $300,000 were the following:

Keyman insurance premiums paid on Finch's life (Burr is beneficiary)	3,000
Group life insurance premiums paid on employees' lives (employees' dependents are beneficiaries)	9,000
Amortization of organization costs	1,000

22. In computing taxable income for Year 3, how much can Burr deduct for keyman and group life insurance premiums?
a. $0
b. $ 3,000
c. $ 9,000
d. $12,000 (4584)

23. In computing taxable income for Year 0, what is the maximum deduction that Burr can claim for organization costs, assuming that the appropriate election was made on a timely basis?
a. $0
b. $1,000
c. $2,400
d. $5,000 (9911)

24. Roper Corp. had operating income of $200,000, after deducting $12,000 for contributions, but not including dividends of $20,000 received from a 40%-owned domestic taxable corporation. How much is the base amount to which the percentage limitation should be applied in computing the maximum allowable deduction for contributions?
a. $212,000
b. $216,000
c. $220,000
d. $232,000 (9911)

Testlet 2 MULTIPLE CHOICE QUESTIONS (36 to 48 minutes)

1. In which of the following circumstances would a CPA who audits XM Corporation lack independence?
a. The CPA and XM's president are both on the board of directors of COD Corporation.
b. The CPA and XM's president each owns 25% of FOB Corporation, a closely held company.
c. The CPA has a home mortgage from XM, which is a savings and loan organization.
d. The CPA reduced XM's usual audit fee by 40% because XM's financial condition was unfavorable. (9911)

2. While preparing a client's individual federal tax return, the CPA noticed that there was an error in the previous year's tax return that was prepared by another CPA. The CPA has which of the following responsibilities to this client?
a. Inform the client and recommend corrective action
b. Inform the client and the previous CPA in writing, and leave it to their discretion whether a correction should be made
c. Discuss the matter verbally with the former CPA and suggest that corrective action be taken for the client
d. Notify the IRS if the error could be considered fraudulent or could involve other taxpayers (8209)

3. Under the liability provisions of Section 11 of the Securities Act of 1933, a CPA may be liable to any purchaser of a security for certifying materially misstated financial statements that are included in the security's registration statement. Under Section 11, a CPA usually will **not** be liable to the purchaser
a. If the purchaser is contributorily negligent
b. If the CPA can prove due diligence
c. Unless the purchaser can prove privity with the CPA
d. Unless the purchaser can prove scienter on the part of the CPA (5190)

4. At a confidential meeting, an audit client informed a CPA about the client's illegal insider-trading actions. A year later, the CPA was subpoenaed to appear in federal court to testify in a criminal trial against the client. The CPA was asked to testify to the meeting between the CPA and the client. After receiving immunity, the CPA should do which of the following?
a. Take the Fifth Amendment and **not** discuss the meeting
b. Site the privileged communications aspect of being a CPA
c. Discuss the entire conversation including the illegal acts
d. Discuss only the items that have a direct connection to those items the CPA worked on for the client in the past (8189)

5. Union Co. possesses the following instrument:

Holt, MT $4,000 April 15, Year 4

Fifty days after date, or sooner, the undersigned promises to pay to the order of

Union Co.
Four Thousand Dollars
at Salem Bank, Holt, MT
Ten percent interest per annum

This instrument is secured by the maker's business inventory.

EASY, INC.
By: *Thomas Foy*
Thomas Foy, President

Assuming all other requirements of negotiability are satisfied, this instrument is
a. Not negotiable, because of a lack of a definite time for payment
b. Not negotiable, because the amount due is unspecified
c. Negotiable, because it is secured by the maker's inventory
d. Negotiable, because it is payable in a sum certain in money (0531)

6. Hunt has in his possession a negotiable instrument which was originally payable to the order of Carr. It was transferred to Hunt by a mere delivery by Drake, who took it from Carr in good faith in satisfaction of an antecedent debt. The back of the instrument read as follows, "Pay to the order of Drake in satisfaction of my prior purchase of a new video calculator, signed Carr." Which of the following is correct?

a. Hunt has the right to assert Drake's rights, including his standing as a holder in due course and also has the right to obtain Drake's signature.
b. Drake's taking the instrument for an antecedent debt prevents him from qualifying as a holder in due course.
c. Carr's endorsement was a special endorsement; thus Drake's signature was **not** required in order to negotiate it.
d. Hunt is a holder in due course. (0565)

7. Teller, Kerr, and Ace are co-sureties on a $120,000 loan with maximum liabilities of $20,000, $40,000, and $60,000, respectively. The debtor defaulted on the loan when the loan balance was $60,000. Ace paid the lender $48,000 in full settlement of all claims against Teller, Kerr, and Ace. What amount may Ace collect from Kerr?

a. $0
b. $16,000
c. $20,000
d. $28,000 (7658)

8. On May 1, Year 5, two months after becoming insolvent, Quick Corp., an appliance wholesaler, filed a voluntary petition for bankruptcy under the provisions of Chapter 7 of the Federal Bankruptcy Code. On October 15, Year 4, Quick's board of directors had authorized and paid Erly $50,000 to repay Erly's April 1, Year 4, loan to the corporation. Erly is a sibling of Quick's president. On March 15, Year 5, Quick paid Kray $100,000 for inventory delivered that day. Which of the following is **not** relevant in determining whether the repayment of Erly's loan is a voidable preferential transfer?

a. Erly is an insider.
b. Quick's payment to Erly was made on account of an antecedent debt.
c. Quick's solvency when the loan was made by Erly.
d. Quick's payment to Erly was made within one year of the filing of the bankruptcy petition. (0610)

9. Under Chapter 7 of the federal Bankruptcy Code, what affect does a bankruptcy discharge have on a judgment creditor when there is **no** bankruptcy estate?

a. The judgment creditor's claim is nondischargeable.
b. The judgment creditor retains a statutory lien against the debtor.
c. The debtor is relieved of any personal liability to the judgment creditor.
d. The debtor is required to pay a liquidated amount to vacate the judgment. (7115)

10. Part agreed to act as Young's agent to sell Young's land. Part was instructed to disclose that Part was acting as an agent but not to disclose Young's identity. Part contracted with Rice for Rice to purchase the land. After Rice discovered Young's identity, Young refused to fulfill the contract. Who does Rice have a cause of action against?

	Part	Young
a.	Yes	Yes
b.	Yes	No
c.	No	Yes
d.	No	No

(8194)

11. On January 2, 2004, Bates Corp. purchased and placed into service 7-year MACRS tangible property costing $100,000. On December 31, 2007, Bates sold the property for $102,000, after having taken $47,525 in MACRS depreciation deductions. What amount of the gain should Bates recapture as ordinary income?

a. $0
b. $ 2,000
c. $47,525
d. $49,525 (5011)

12. On March 1, Harry Beech received a gift of income-producing real estate having a donor's adjusted basis of $50,000 at the date of the gift. Fair market value of the property at the date of the gift was $40,000. Beech sold the property for $46,000 on August 1. How much gain or loss should Beech report for the current year?

a. No gain or loss
b. $6,000 short-term capital gain
c. $4,000 short-term capital loss
d. $4,000 ordinary loss (9911)

13. Grey, a calendar year taxpayer, was employed and resided in New York. On February 2, Grey was permanently transferred to Florida by his employer. Grey worked full-time for the entire year. Grey incurred and paid the following unreimbursed expenses in relocating:

Lodging and travel expenses while moving	$1,000
Pre-move househunting costs	1,200
Costs of moving household furnishings and personal effects	1,800

What amount was deductible as moving expense on Grey's tax return?
a. $4,000
b. $2,800
c. $1,800
d. $1,000 (5424)

14. Paul and Lois Kim, both age 50, are married and will file a joint return for 2008. Their adjusted gross income was $80,000, including Paul's $75,000 salary. Lois had no income of her own. Neither spouse was covered by an employer-sponsored pension plan. What amount could the Kims contribute to IRAs to take advantage of their maximum allowable IRA deduction in their 2008 tax return?
a. $0
b. $ 5,000
c. $10,000
d. $12,000 (9911)

15. In the current calendar year, Alan Cox provided more than half the support for the following relatives, none of whom qualified as a member of Alan's household: a cousin, a nephew, and a foster parent. None of these relatives had any income, nor did any of these relatives file an individual or a joint return. All of these relatives are U.S. citizens. Which of these relatives could be claimed as a dependent on Alan's current year return?
a. No one
b. Nephew
c. Cousin
d. Foster parent (8040)

16. Don Mills, a single taxpayer, had $70,000 in taxable income before personal exemptions. Mills had no tax preferences. His itemized deductions were as follows:

State and local income taxes	$5,000
Home mortgage interest on loan to acquire residence	6,000
Miscellaneous deductions that exceed 2% of adjusted gross income	2,000

What amount did Mills report as alternative minimum taxable income before the AMT exemption?
a. $72,000
b. $75,000
c. $77,000
d. $83,000 (5435)

17. Which of the following fiduciary entities are required to use the calendar year as their taxable period for income tax purposes?

	Estates	*Trusts (except those that are tax exempt)*
a.	Yes	Yes
b.	No	No
c.	Yes	No
d.	No	Yes

(2473)

18. Dale's distributive share of income from the calendar-year partnership of Dale & Eck was $50,000 in Year 4. On December 15, Year 4, Dale, who is a cash-basis taxpayer, received a $27,000 distribution of the partnership's Year 4 income, with the $23,000 balance paid to Dale in May, Year 5. In addition, Dale received a $10,000 interest-free loan from the partnership in Year 4. This $10,000 is to be offset against Dale's share of Year 5 partnership income. What total amount of partnership income is taxable to Dale in Year 4?
a. $27,000
b. $37,000
c. $50,000
d. $60,000 (1714)

19. Which one of the following statements regarding a partnership's tax year is correct?
a. A partnership formed on July 1 is required to adopt a tax year ending on June 30.
b. A partnership may elect to have a tax year other than the generally required tax year if the deferral period for the tax year elected does **not** exceed three months.
c. A "valid business purpose" can **no** longer be claimed as a reason for adoption of a tax year other than the generally required tax year.
d. Within 30 days after a partnership has established a tax year, a form must be filed with the IRS as notification of the tax year adopted. (1715)

20. A guaranteed payment by a partnership to a partner for services rendered, may include an agreement to pay

I. A salary of $5,000 monthly without regard to partnership income
II. A 25% interest in partnership profits

a. I only
b. II only
c. Both I and II
d. Neither I nor II (5447)

21. Smith, a partner in Ridge Partnership, had a basis in the partnership interest of $100,000 at the time Smith received a nonliquidating distribution of land with an adjusted basis of $75,000 to Ridge and a fair market value of $135,000. Ridge had no unrealized receivables, appreciated inventory, or properties that had been contributed by its partners. Which of the following statements is(are) correct regarding the distribution?

I. Ridge recognized a $60,000 capital gain from the distribution.
II. Smith's holding period for the land includes the time it was owned by Ridge.

a. I only
b. II only
c. Both I and II
d. Neither I nor II (7649)

22. The partnership of Marks & Sparks sustained an ordinary loss of $42,000 in Year 1. The partnership, as well as the two partners, are on a calendar-year basis. The partners share profits and losses equally. At December 31, Year 1, Marks had an adjusted basis of $18,000 for his partnership interest, before consideration of the loss. On his Year 1 individual tax return, Marks should deduct an(a)

a. Ordinary loss of $18,000
b. Ordinary loss of $21,000
c. Ordinary loss of $18,000 and a capital loss of $3,000
d. Capital loss of $21,000 (8058)

23. Anderson's basis in the SBF Partnership is $80,000. Anderson received a nonliquidating distribution of $50,000 cash, and land with an adjusted basis of $40,000 and a fair market value of $50,000. What is Anderson's basis in the land?

a. $50,000
b. $40,000
c. $30,000
d. $20,000 (7655)

24. Thompson's basis in Starlight Partnership was $60,000 at the beginning of the year. Thompson materially participates in the partnership's business. Thompson received $20,000 in cash distributions during the year. Thompson's share of Starlight's current operations was a $65,000 ordinary loss and a $15,000 net long-term capital gain. What is the amount of Thompson's deductible loss for the period?

a. $15,000
b. $40,000
c. $55,000
d. $65,000 (7086)

Testlet 3 MULTIPLE CHOICE QUESTIONS (36 to 48 minutes)

1. Thorp, CPA, was engaged to audit Ivor Co.'s financial statements. During the audit, Thorp discovered that Ivor's inventory contained stolen goods. Ivor was indicted and Thorp was subpoenaed to testify at the criminal trial. Ivor claimed accountant-client privilege to prevent Thorp from testifying. Which of the following statements is correct regarding Ivor's claim?
a. Ivor can claim an accountant-client privilege only in states that have enacted a statute creating such a privilege.
b. Ivor can claim an accountant-client privilege only in federal courts.
c. The accountant-client privilege can be claimed only in civil suits.
d. The accountant-client privilege can be claimed only to limit testimony to audit subject matter.
(5884)

2. Cable Corp. orally engaged Drake & Co., CPAs, to audit its financial statements. Cable's management informed Drake that it suspected the accounts receivable were materially overstated. Though the financial statements Drake audited included a materially overstated accounts receivable balance, Drake issued an unqualified opinion. Cable used the financial statements to obtain a loan to expand its operations. Cable defaulted on the loan and incurred a substantial loss. If Cable sues Drake for negligence in failing to discover the overstatement, Drake's best defense would be that Drake did **not**
a. Have privity of contract with Cable
b. Sign an engagement letter
c. Perform the audit recklessly or with an intent to deceive
d. Violate generally accepted auditing standards in performing the audit (2329)

3. An accounting firm was hired by a company to perform an audit. The company needed the audit report in order to obtain a loan from a bank. The bank lent $500,000 to the company based on the auditor's report. Fifteen months later, the company declared bankruptcy and was unable to repay the loan. The bank discovered that the accounting firm failed to discover a material overstatement of assets of the company. Which of the following statements is correct regarding a suit by the bank against the accounting firm? The bank
a. Cannot sue the accounting firm because of the statute of limitations
b. Can sue the accounting firm for the loss of the loan because of negligence
c. Cannot sue the accounting firm because there was **no** privity of contact
d. Can sue the accounting firm for the loss of the loan because of the rule of privilege (8184)

4. Which of the following requirements must an auditor meet to express an opinion on a public company's effectiveness of internal control over financial reporting as of a point in time and taken as a whole?

I. The auditor must obtain evidence that internal control over financial reporting has operated effectively for the entire period covered by the company's financial statements.
II. The auditor must test the design and operation effectiveness of controls that the auditor ordinarily would not test if expressing an opinion only on the financial statements.

a. I only
b. II only
c. Both I and II
d. Neither I nor II (8278)

5. The Securities Act of 1933 provides an exemption from registration for

	Bonds issued by a municipality for governmental purposes	*Securities issued by a not-for-profit charitable organization*
a.	Yes	Yes
b.	Yes	No
c.	No	Yes
d.	No	No (8425)

6. Dean, Inc., a publicly traded corporation, paid a $10,000 bribe to a local zoning official. The bribe was recorded in Dean's financial statements as a consulting fee. Dean's unaudited financial statements were submitted to the SEC as part of a quarterly filing. Which of the following federal statutes did Dean violate?

a. Federal Trade Commission Act
b. Securities Act of 1933
c. Securities Exchange Act of 1934
d. North American Free Trade Act (7050)

7. Which of the following is **least** likely to be considered a security under the Securities Act of 1933?

a. Stock options
b. Warrants
c. General partnership interests
d. Limited partnership interests (3998)

8. Under the provisions of the Employee Retirement Income Security Act of 1974 (ERISA), which of the following statements is(are) correct regarding employee rights?

I. Employers are required to establish either a contributory or noncontributory employee pension plan.
II. Employers are required to include employees as pension-plan managers.

a. I only
b. II only
c. Both I and II
d. Neither I nor II (8171)

9. On January 1, Chance bought a piece of property by taking subject to an existing unrecorded mortgage held by Hay Bank. On April 1, Chance borrowed money from Link Finance and gave Link a mortgage on the property. Link did not know about the Hay mortgage and did not record its mortgage until July 1. On June 1, Chance borrowed money from Zone Bank and gave Zone a mortgage on the same property. Zone knew about the Link mortgage but did not know about the Hay mortgage. Zone recorded its mortgage on June 15. Which mortgage would have priority if these transactions took place in a notice-race jurisdiction?

a. The Hay mortgage, because it was first in time
b. The Link mortgage, because Zone had notice of the Link mortgage
c. The Zone mortgage, because it was the first recorded mortgage
d. The Zone and Link mortgages share priority because neither had notice of the Hay mortgage (4025)

Items 10 and 11 are based on the following:

On March 1 of the current year, Lois Rice learned that she was bequeathed 1,000 shares of Elin Corp. common stock under the will of her uncle, Pat Prevor. Pat had paid $5,000 for the Elin stock ten years ago. Fair market value of the Elin stock on March 1, the date of Pat's death, was $8,000 and had increased to $11,000 six months later. The executor of Pat's estate elected the alternate valuation date for estate tax purposes. Lois sold the Elin stock for $9,000 on May 1, the date that the executor distributed the stock to her.

10. How much should Lois include in her current year individual income tax return for the inheritance of the 1,000 shares of Elin stock which she received from Pat's estate?

a. $0
b. $ 5,000
c. $ 8,000
d. $11,000 (1635)

11. Lois' basis for gain or loss on sale of the 1,000 shares of Elin stock is

a. $ 5,000
b. $ 8,000
c. $ 9,000
d. $11,000 (8035)

12. Which of the following sales should be reported as a capital gain?

a. Sale of equipment
b. Real property subdivided and sold by a dealer
c. Sale of inventory
d. Government bonds sold by an individual investor (8182)

13. A tax return preparer is subject to a penalty for knowingly or recklessly disclosing corporate tax return information, if the disclosure is made

a. To enable a third party to solicit business from the taxpayer
b. To enable the tax processor to electronically compute the taxpayer's liability
c. For peer review
d. Under an administrative order by a state agency that registers tax return preparers (5031)

14. Morris Babb, CPA, reports on the cash basis. In March, Babb billed a client $1,000 for accounting services rendered in connection with the client's divorce settlement. No part of the $1,000 fee was ever paid. In July, the client went bankrupt and the $1,000 obligation became totally worthless. What loss can Babb deduct on his tax return?
a. $0
b. $1,000 short-term capital loss
c. $1,000 business bad debt
d. $1,000 nonbusiness bad debt (9911)

15. Fred and Amy Kehl, both U.S. citizens, are married. All of their real and personal property is owned by them as tenants by the entirety or as joint tenants with right of survivorship. The gross estate of the first spouse to die
a. Includes 50% of the value of all property owned by the couple, regardless of which spouse furnished the original consideration
b. Includes only the property that had been acquired with the funds of the deceased spouse
c. Is governed by the federal statutory provisions relating to jointly held property, rather than by the decedent's interest in community property vested by state law, if the Kehls reside in a community property state
d. Includes one-third of the value of all real estate owned by the Kehls, as the dower right in the case of the wife or curtesy right in the case of the husband (1695)

16. The generation-skipping transfer tax is imposed
a. Instead of the gift tax
b. Instead of the estate tax
c. As a separate tax in addition to the gift and estate taxes
d. On transfers of future interest to beneficiaries who are more than one generation above the donor's generation (2486)

17. Under the unified rate schedule,
a. Lifetime taxable gifts are taxed on a noncumulative basis.
b. Transfers at death are taxed on a noncumulative basis.
c. Lifetime taxable gifts and transfers at death are taxed on a cumulative basis.
d. The gift tax rates are 5% higher than the estate tax rates. (2485)

18. Raff died in Year 0 leaving her entire estate to her only child. Raff's will gave full discretion to the estate's executor with regard to distributions of income. For Year 1, the estate's distributable net income was $15,000, of which $9,000 was paid to the beneficiary. None of the income was tax exempt. What amount can be claimed on the estate's Year 1 fiduciary income tax return for the distributions deduction?
a. $0
b. $ 6,000
c $ 9,000
d. $15,000 (1699)

19. Which of the following is subject to the Uniform Capitalization Rules of Code §263A?
a. Editorial costs incurred by a freelance writer
b. Research and experimental expenditures
c. Mine development and exploration costs
d. Warehousing costs incurred by a manufacturing company with $12 million in annual gross receipts (8459)

20. The following information pertains to treasury stock sold by Lee Corp. to an unrelated broker in the current year:

Proceeds received	$50,000
Cost	30,000
Par value	9,000

What amount of capital gain should Lee recognize in the current year on the sale of this treasury stock?
a. $0
b. $ 8,000
c. $20,000
d. $30,500 (8054)

21. On January 1, Year 1, Locke Corp., an accrual-basis, calendar-year C corporation, had $30,000 in accumulated earnings and profits. For Year 1, Locke had current earnings and profits of $20,000, and made two $40,000 cash distributions to its shareholders, one in April and one in September. What amount of these distributions is classified as dividend income to Locke's shareholders?
a. $0
b. $20,000
c. $50,000
d. $80,000 (6913)

22. Which one of the following will render a corporation ineligible for S corporation status?
a. One of the stockholders is a decedent's estate
b. One of the stockholders is a bankruptcy estate
c. The corporation has 150 unrelated stockholders
d. The corporation has both voting and nonvoting common stock issued and outstanding (9911)

23. Beck Corp. has been a calendar-year S corporation since its inception on January 2, Year 0. On January 1, Year 3, Lazur and Lyle each owned 50% of the Beck stock, in which their respective tax bases were $12,000 and $9,000. For the year ended December 31, Year 3, Beck had $81,000 in ordinary business income and $10,000 in tax-exempt income. Beck made a $51,000 cash distribution to each shareholder on December 31, Year 3. What was Lazur's tax basis in Beck after the distribution?

a. $ 1,500
b. $ 6,500
c. $52,500
d. $57,500 (6799)

24. An S Corporation has 30,000 shares of voting common stock and 20,000 shares of non-voting common stock issued and outstanding. The S election can be revoked voluntarily with the consent of the shareholders holding, on the day of the revocation,

	Shares of voting stock	*Shares of nonvoting stock*
a.	0	20,000
b.	7,500	5,000
c.	10,000	16,000
d.	20,000	0

(4626)

SIMULATIONS

Testlet 4 (20 to 30 minutes)

Rogue is self-employed as a human resources consultant and reports on the cash basis for income tax purposes. (4167)

For Items 1 through 11, select the appropriate tax treatment from the following list.

Tax Treatments

A. Taxable as other income on Form 1040

B. Reported in Schedule B—*Interest and Dividend Income*

C. Reported in Schedule C as trade or business income

D. Reported in Schedule E—*Supplemental Income and Loss*

E. Not taxable

Transaction	Answer
1. Retainer fees received from clients.	
2. Oil royalties received.	
3. Interest income on general obligation state and local government bonds.	
4. Interest on refund of federal taxes.	
5. Death benefits from term life insurance policy on parent.	
6. Interest income on U.S. Treasury bonds.	
7. Share of ordinary income from an investment in a limited partnership reported in Form 1065, Schedule K-1.	
8. Taxable income from rental of a townhouse owned by Green.	
9. Prize won as a contestant on a TV quiz show.	
10. Payment received for jury service.	
11. Dividends received from mutual funds that invest in tax-free government obligations.	

Scenario	Tax Treatment	Communication	Research

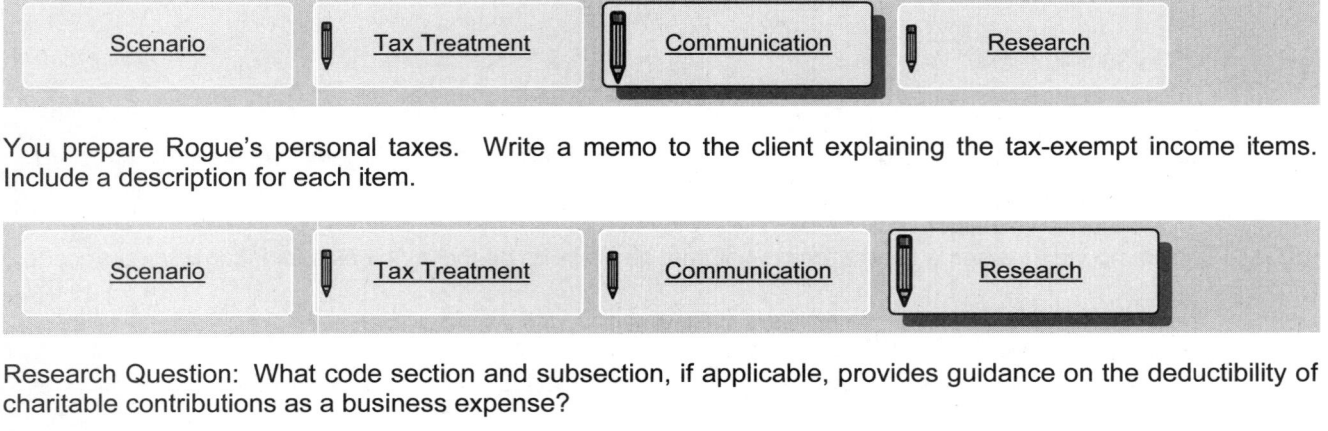

You prepare Rogue's personal taxes. Write a memo to the client explaining the tax-exempt income items. Include a description for each item.

Scenario	Tax Treatment	Communication	Research

Research Question: What code section and subsection, if applicable, provides guidance on the deductibility of charitable contributions as a business expense?

Section & Subsection Answer: §_____ (___)

Testlet 5 (20 to 30 minutes)

Anvil Corp., an accrual-basis calendar year C corporation, filed its Year 3 federal income tax return on March 15, Year 4. Anvil does not meet the definition of a small corporation for AMT purposes. Anvil elected out of bonus depreciation. (5504)

Items 1 through 6 each require two responses. Determine the amount of Anvil's Year 3 Schedule M-1 adjustment. Indicate if the adjustment (I) increase, (D) decrease, or (N) has no effect on Anvil's taxable income.

Transaction	Amount	Effect
1. Anvil's disbursements included reimbursed employees' expenses for travel of $100,000, and business meals of $30,000. The reimbursed expenses met the conditions of deductibility and were properly substantiated under an accountable plan. The reimbursement was not treated as employee compensation.		
2. Anvil's books expensed $7,000 for the term life insurance premiums on the corporate officers. Anvil was the policy owner and beneficiary.		
3. Anvil's books indicated an $18,000 state franchise tax expense for Year 3. Estimated state tax payments for Year 3 were $15,000.		
4. Book depreciation on computers for Year 3 was $10,000. These computers, costing $50,000, were placed in service on January 2, Year 2. Tax depreciation used MACRS with the half-year convention. No election was made to expense part of the computer cost or to use a straight-line method or the alternative depreciation system.		
5. Anvil's books showed a $4,000 short-term capital gain distribution from a mutual fund corporation and a $5,000 loss on the sale of Retro stock that was purchased in Year 0. The stock was an investment in an unrelated corporation. There were no other Year 3 gains or losses and no loss carryovers from prior years.		
6. Anvil's taxable income before the charitable contribution and the dividends received deductions was $500,000. Anvil's books expensed $15,000 in board-of-director authorized charitable contributions that were paid on January 5, Year 4. Charitable contributions paid and expense during Year 3 were $35,000. All charitable contributions were properly substantiated. There were no net operating losses or charitable contributions that were carried forward.		

For Items 7 through 10, indicate if the income is (F) fully taxable, (P) partially taxable, or (N) nontaxable for regular tax purposes on Anvil's federal income tax return. All transactions occurred during Year 3. Anvil filed an amended federal income tax return for Year 2 and received a refund that included both the overpayment of the federal taxes and interest.

Transaction	Answer
7. The portion of Anvil's refund that represented the overpayment of the Year 2 federal taxes.	
8. The portion of Anvil's refund that is attributable to the interest on the overpayment of federal taxes.	
9. Anvil received dividend income from a mutual fund that solely invests in municipal bonds.	
10. Anvil, the lessor, benefited from the capital improvements made to its property by the lessee in Year 3. The lease agreement is for one year ending December 31, Year 3, and provides for a reduction in rental payments by the lessee in exchange for the improvements.	

Write a memo to Anvil Corporation explaining whether the following items are deductible or not. Include a description for each item.

1. Anvil purchased theater tickets for its out-of-town clients. The performances took place after Anvil's substantial and *bona fide* business negotiations with its clients.

2. Anvil accrued advertising expenses to promote a new product line. Ten percent of the new product line remained in ending inventory.

3. Anvil incurred interest expense on a loan to purchase municipal bonds.

4. Anvil paid a penalty for the underpayment of Year 2 estimated taxes.

Research Question: What code section and subsection, if applicable, provides guidance on the allowable deduction for a net operating loss (NOL)?

Section & Subsection Answer: §_____ (___)

MULTIPLE CHOICE ANSWERS

Solution 1

Chapter 32: Accountant's Professional Responsibilities

1. (b) Independence is considered impaired if a spouse or dependent person (immediate family) of the member is employed in a position that allows significant influence over the client's operating, financial, or accounting policies. Independence is considered impaired if the position with the client involves activities that are audit-sensitive, even though the position is not one that allows significant influence. A person's activities would be considered audit sensitive if such activities are normally an element of, or subject to, significant internal controls; for example, the positions of cashier, internal auditor, accounting or finance supervisor, purchasing agent, or inventory warehouse supervisor. (CSO: I)

2. (a, d) Two responses are required for full credit. The standard of due care requires a critical review of the work done and the judgment exercised by those assisting in the audit. It also requires that the client be advised when a consultant must be engaged to perform the audit. (CSO: I)

3. (d) Retaining a client's records after an engagement is terminated prior to completion when the client has demanded their return is prohibited by the ethical standards of the profession. Issuing a modified report explaining a failure to follow a governmental agency's standards and revealing confidential client information during a state review of a professional practice are not ethically prohibited. Interpretation of Rule 302 provides that a contingency fee is permissible when a CPA represents a client in an *examination* by a revenue agent. (CSO: I)

4. (c) Under the Statements of Standards for Consulting Services, a CPA has the responsibility to inform the client of significant reservations concerning the benefits of the engagement. The Standards for Consulting Services do not require a CPA to obtain a written understanding with the client concerning the time for completion of the engagement. Nor do the Standards prohibit a CPA from modifying a client agreement or from performing attest services. (CSO: I)

5. (a) Personal financial planning engagement activities include defining the engagement objectives, planning specific procedures, developing a basis for recommendations, communicating recommendations to the client, and identifying action tasks for planning decisions. Assisting the client to take action on planning decisions, monitoring progress in achieving goals, and updating recommendations and revising planning decisions could also be part of a personal financial planning engagement but are not necessarily required. (CSO: I)

Chapter 34: Contracts

6. (d) Consideration is an act or a forbearance to act that causes a contracting party to suffer a legal detriment. The minor suffers a legal detriment (painting the garage) for the promise to pay. A preexisting duty and past consideration are not consideration as these cause the party to suffer no legal detriment. In the incorrect answer options, the real estate agent, the child, and the police have given no consideration for the promise to pay. (CSO: II)

7. (a) Specific performance typically is granted only when damages are insufficient, such as a contract for the sale of unique property. Specific performance rarely is granted if the contract requires personal services, such as employment. Fungible goods and stock that is traded on a national stock exchange could be purchased with an award of money. (CSO: II)

Chapter 35: Sales

8. (d) The warranty of title and against infringement may be disclaimed only by specific language or circumstances that give the buyer reason to know that the buyer is not receiving full title. The phrase "as is" may disclaim implied warranties, such as a warranty of merchantability, but not express warranties and the warranty of title and against infringement. An agreement to modify or rescind a sales contract need not be supported by consideration to be binding; however, the seller's warranties may not be unilaterally disclaimed. (CSO: II)

Chapter 37: Secured Transactions

9. (d) If a creditor takes a purchase money security interest in equipment and files a financing statement within 20 days of attachment, the creditor will have priority over other secured creditors. In this situation, Eastern filed the financing statement within the 20-day period and, thus, Eastern will have priority over the trustee in bankruptcy. In addition, filing the financing statement after commencement of the bankruptcy case is not a preferential transfer. This represents a contemporaneous exchange since value was given in exchange for the perfected security interest. (CSO: II)

Chapter 41: Other Regulations

10. (a) Where an employer pays an employee's share of FICA taxes, the amount of FICA taxes paid on behalf of that employee qualifies as taxable income to the employee and as an ordinary and necessary business expense to the employer. The FICA requires an employer to withhold and pay both the employer's and the employee's share of FICA taxes. An employer who fails to withhold the employee's share will be liable for payment of both the employer's and employee's share. There are no additional penalties imposed on an employer who voluntarily pays its employee's share. (CSO: II)

Chapter 43: Federal Taxation: Property & Other Tax Topics

11. (b) A single taxpayer may exclude up to $250,000 of gain from the sale of a principal residence provided the taxpayer occupied the home in two of the five preceding years. The exclusion may be applied once every two years. (CSO: IV)

12. (b) Under §1211(b), individuals are allowed to offset capital losses to the extent of capital gains plus up to $3,000 of ordinary income (assuming they have that much capital loss). For this purpose, married couples filing jointly are considered as one individual. Unused capital losses are carried forward indefinitely until they are absorbed. (CSO: IV)

Chapter 44: Federal Taxation: Individuals

13. (c) Since Nell's husband died more than two years ago, she cannot qualify as a surviving spouse. However, under §2(b), Nell will be a head of household because she was not married at the close of her tax year, was not a surviving spouse, and maintained her home as a household for her dependent child. (CSO: V)

14. (c) Section 6072(a) requires that the individual who uses a calendar year file his federal income tax return by April 15 of the following year unless the taxpayer receives an extension under §6081(a). Section 6501(a) provides that in general no assessment of additional taxes may be made after 3 years from the time the tax return was filed. However, §6501(b)(1) provides that a return that is filed early will be deemed to have been filed on its due date. Thus, the return filed on March 20, Year 2, is deemed to have been filed on April 15, Year 2, for purposes of §6501. Section 6501(a) then gives the IRS until April 15, Year 5, to assess additional taxes and assert a notice of deficiency. (CSO: III)

15. (d) Gross income does not include life insurance proceeds, if such amounts are paid by reason of the death of the insured [§101(a)(1)]. Thus, the entire $60,000 should be excluded. (CSO: V)

16. (c) A passive loss is any loss from activities involving the conduct of a trade or business in which the taxpayer does not materially participate. With respect to this partner, any loss generated from operations will be considered a passive loss since he is not a material participant. Passive loss is calculated as 5% (partnership percentage) × $100,000 = $5,000. This passive loss may generally be used only to offset income from passive activities. (CSO: V)

17. (b) Amounts actually paid to a qualified donee during the year are deductible subject to a percentage of AGI limitation. Smith can deduct the $5,000 cash contribution to the church under §170. The deduction of a charitable contribution of appreciated property depends on the status of the property. Appreciated property that would realize long-term capital gain if sold instead of donated is valued at fair market value. Other property (including short-term capital gain property) is valued at the lesser of basis or fair market value. Stock owned for four months would not realize a long-term gain. Qualified donees include domestic organizations and foundations operated exclusively for religious, charitable, scientific, literary, or educational purposes. (Individuals are not qualified donees.) Gifts to individuals, such as a gift to a needy family, are not deductible. (CSO: V)

Chapter 46: Federal Taxation: Corporations

18. (c) Section 6663 imposes a penalty of 75% of a tax underpayment attributable to fraud. Section 7454(a) places the burden of proof for fraud on the Secretary of the Treasury. Tax Court Rule 142(b) states that such burden is to be carried by clear and convincing evidence. Fraud implies that the taxpayer had bad faith, intentionally understated his tax liability, or had a sinister motive. To be guilty of fraud the taxpayer must have intentionally engaged in wrongful activities to avoid the payment of taxes. Maintaining false records and reporting fictitious transactions to minimize the corporate tax liability would be evidence of fraud. Omitting income as a result of inadequate recordkeeping would be indicative of negligence under §6662(b) and §6662(c), not fraud. Under Reg. §1.6662-3(b)(1) negligence includes any failure by the taxpayer to keep adequate books and records or to substantiate items properly. The penalty for negligence is 20% of the tax underpayment attributable to negligence under §6662(a). Failing to report income that the taxpayer did not consider to be included in gross income is

not fraud because there is no bad faith. Whether this action constitutes negligence depends on whether the taxpayer intentionally or recklessly disregarded rules and regulations. Likewise, filing an incomplete return with adequate disclosure is not fraud because there is no evidence of bad faith. (CSO: III)

19. (c) The dividends received deduction is a special deduction. The question asks for income before special deductions ($500,000 Sales + $25,000 Dividends received – $250,000 Cost of sales = $275,000 Income before special deductions). Cost of sales needs to be subtracted because it is not a special deduction. The dividends need to be included in income in total and then the appropriate percentage is subtracted as a special deduction. (CSO: VI)

20. (d) A corporation's carryback and carryforward capital losses are always treated as short-term capital losses in the year to which they are carried. Excess capital losses of a corporation can be carried back three years and forward five. The $3,000 limit for offsetting capital losses against ordinary income applies only to individuals. Unlike individuals, corporations only use capital losses to offset capital gains (not ordinary income). (CSO: VI)

21. (d) Section 354 provides for the nonrecognition of any gain or loss on property transferred to a corporation pursuant to a corporate reorganization in exchange solely for stock or securities of such corporation or in another corporation that is party to the reorganization. Because the taxpayer received only stock in the exchange, no gain or loss is recognized. (CSO: VI)

22. (c) In general, insurance premiums are a deductible business expense. However, §264(a)(1) provides that no deduction is allowed on life insurance premiums paid on a policy covering the life of any officer or employee if the taxpayer is the direct or indirect beneficiary under the policy. Thus, the key-person insurance premiums are not deductible, while the group life insurance premiums are deductible. (CSO: VI)

23. (d) Corporations may elect to deduct up to $5,000 of organization costs incurred in the tax year its business begins under §248. However, the $5,000 deduction is reduced on a dollar-for-dollar basis for those expenses in excess of $50,000. Burr's deduction is not affected by this limit. Any remaining balance must be amortized of 15 years. (Prior to AJCA '04, a corporation could elect to amortize organizational expenses incurred before the end of the first tax year in which the corporation is in business over a period of at least 60 months.) (CSO: VI)

24. (d) Section 170(b)(2) provides that total deductions for charitable contributions for the year cannot exceed 10% of the corporation's taxable income computed without regard to deductions for (1) charitable contributions, (2) dividends received, (3) NOL carrybacks, and (4) capital loss carrybacks. For purposes of computing the §170(b)(2) limitation, Roper must add to its $200,000 operating income both the $20,000 of unincluded dividends and the $12,000 of contributions already deducted. (CSO: VI)

Solution 2

Chapter 32: Accountant's Professional Responsibilities

1. (b) Independence is impaired with respect to a client if the CPA or her/his firm had any joint closely held business investment with the client or any officer, director, or principal stockholder of the client. The CPA's *nonfinancial* relationship to COD does not generally impair her/his independence with respect to XM. CPAs can have home mortgages from clients that are financial institutions without impairing independence. The CPA is not precluded from decreasing her/his audit fee. (CSO: I)

2. (a) The internal revenue code (IRC) provides penalties for disclosure of confidential information to person unnecessary to the preparation or filing of a taxpayer's return. (CSO: I)

Chapter 33: Accountant's Legal Responsibilities

3. (b) Under the provisions of Section 11 of the Securities Act of 1933, a CPA will be liable to a purchaser of securities if the financial statement either omits or misstates a material fact. The CPA may avoid liability by showing that s/he acted with due diligence. Pursuant to the 1933 Act, the purchaser need not prove privity or scienter to impose liability. Contributory negligence by the purchaser is not a defense under Section 11. (CSO: I)

4. (c) Professional ethics discourage disclosure of confidential information by a CPA except in select circumstances, such as when in compliance with an enforceable subpoena. Professional ethics require a CPA to act in a way that will serve the public interest and honor the public trust. The attorney-client privilege extends to federally authorized tax practitioners (including CPAs) relating to noncriminal tax matters (except tax shelters) before the IRS or in federal courts. (CSO: I)

Chapter 36: Negotiable Instruments & Documents of Title

5. (d) This instrument has all the requirements to be negotiable: it is in writing, contains an unconditional promise to pay, payable to the order of, a sum certain, payable at a definite time, signed by the maker, and it represents an unconditional promise to pay. This instrument is payable at a definite time. The amount due is specific. It is permissible to state that the instrument is secured by some asset; had the instrument stated it was subject to some other agreement, the note would be nonnegotiable. (CSO: II)

6. (a) Taking an instrument in payment of an antecedent debt satisfies the requirement that an HDC take the instrument for value. A special endorsement converts the instrument to order paper, requiring the endorsee's signature in order to be negotiable. An HDC must take by original issue or by negotiation. Order paper is negotiated by proper endorsement plus transfer of possession. In this situation, Drake transferred possession of the instrument, but did not endorse it. (CSO: II)

Chapter 38: Debtor & Creditor Relationships

7. (b) When there are two or more sureties (co-sureties), the right of contribution requires that a surety who pays more than her/his proportionate share on a debtor's default, may recover from the other co-sureties the amount paid above her/his obligation. Ace paid $48,000 in full settlement of the claims against the co-sureties. To determine each co-surety's proportionate share of the $48,000 liability, look at their maximum liabilities under the surety contract. Then divide the liability among the co-sureties according to their respective *pro rata* share in the surety contract. Kerr had a maximum liability of $40,000 on a surety contract with total liability of $120,000. Kerr's share of the liability is $16,000 [($40,000 / $120,000) × $48,000 = $16,000]. Therefore, Ace may recover $16,000 from Kerr. (CSO: II)

8. (c) Quick's solvency when the loan was made by Erly is not a relevant factor in determining whether the repayment of Erly's loan is a voidable transfer. Quick's solvency when the loan is repaid is a relevant factor. The fact that Erly is an insider, Quick's payment to Erly was for an antecedent debt, and Quick's payment to Erly was made within one year of the filing of the petition, are all relevant in determining if a voidable preferential transfer was made. (CSO: II)

9. (c) A discharge in a bankruptcy case under any chapter voids any existing and future judgments that are determinations of the personal liability of the debtor with respect to any discharged debt, and operates as an injunction against the commencement or continuation of an action at law, the employment of legal process, or any act (including telephone calls and letters) to recover, collect, or offset any discharged debt as a personal liability of the debtor or from the property of the debtor. (CSO: II)

Chapter 39: Agency

10. (a) When an agent is representing a partially disclosed principal, the contract generally binds both the principal and agent. After discovering the

identify of the principal, the third party may choose to hold the principal liable. (CSO: II)

Chapter 43: Federal Taxation: Property & Other Tax Topics

11. (c) On a sale of depreciable personal property, ordinary income under §1245 is generally equal to the lesser of (1) the total gain realized or (2) the accumulated depreciation. Section 1231 treats any remaining gain as a §1231 gain, which is not ordinary income under §64. The §1245 gain and the remaining §1231 gain are computed as follows. (CSO: IV)

Amount realized		$102,000
Cost	$ 100,000	
Less: Accum. depr.	(47,525)	
Less: Adjusted basis		(52,475)
Gain realized		$ 49,525
Sec. 1245 (ordinary) gain (lesser of $49,525 or $47,525)		$ 47,525
Sec. 1231 (capital) gain		2,000
Total gain realized		$ 49,525

12. (a) In general, the donee's basis in gifted property is the same as the donor's basis in such property. However, if, on the date of the gift, the FMV of the property is less than the donor's basis, the doe's basis for determining loss upon a subsequent disposition is the FMV on the date of the gift. Harry's "gain" basis for the real estate is $50,000 (the donor's adjusted basis in the property at the time of the gift). Harry's "loss" basis is $40,000 (the FMV of the property on the date of the gift). When property is sold or otherwise disposed of for an amount between the "gain" and "loss" basis, no gain or loss results. (CSO: IV)

Chapter 44: Federal Taxation: Individuals

13. (b) Section 217 allows an adjustment for moving expenses, but imposes tests that must be met before any deduction for moving expenses is allowed. The taxpayer's new place of work must be more than 50 miles further from the former residence than was the former place of work. The taxpayer must be employed full time for 39 weeks of the 12-month period following the move. The move from New York to Florida meets the 50-mile test. The taxpayer was employed from February 2 to December 31, meeting the time test. Section 217(b)(1) defines moving expenses as the reasonable expenses of moving household goods and the expense of traveling, including lodging, to the new residence. Pre-move house-hunting costs are not deductible. ($1,000 + $1,800) (CSO: V)

14. (d) Generally an individual may contribute the lesser of total earned income or $5,000. Individuals who are at least 50 by the end of the tax year have the contribution limit increased by $1,000. A taxpayer with a spouse with no earned income may set up a spousal IRS, with a combined contribution limit the lesser of double the individual limit or earned income. Since neither Paul nor Lois was covered by an employer-sponsored pension plan, the Kims could take a total IRA deduction of $12,000 in 2008, regardless of who earned the income. Editor's Note: This question differs from question ID 1589 in Chapter 44. (CSO: V)

15. (b) In order to qualify as a dependent, an individual must pass five tests. The first four, gross income, support, joint return, and citizenship or residence tests are passed by all of the relatives. However, the fifth test an individual must pass is the relationship test or the member of household test. Since none of the relatives qualified as a member of Alan's household, only the ones which pass the relationship test may be claimed as a dependent. Per §152, the following pass the relationship test: child or dependent of child; stepchild; brother or sister (including half-blood); stepbrother or stepsister; father, mother, or ancestor of either; stepfather or stepmother; nephew or niece; uncle or aunt; and brother-, sister-, father-, mother-, son-, or daughter-in-law. (CSO: V)

16. (c) Section 56(b)(1)(A)(i) disallows any deduction for an individual's miscellaneous itemized deductions in computing alternative minimum taxable (AMT) income. Section 56(b)(1)(A)(ii) disallows any deduction for taxes described in §164(a). Section 164(a)(3) includes state and local income taxes. Hence, state and local income taxes are not deductible in arriving at AMT income. Section 56(b)(1)(C)(i) disallows the deduction for qualified residence interest in arriving at AMT income. Instead §56(e) allows a deduction for qualified housing interest which includes interest on acquisition indebtedness but not other home equity loans, unless the taxpayer used the loan proceeds to improve the residence. Thus, the home mortgage interest on a loan to acquire a residence is deductible in arriving at AMT income and accordingly does not have to be added back to taxable income. Section 55(b)(2) defines AMT income as the taxable income of the taxpayer, determined with regard to the adjustments required by §§56 and 58 and increased by the preferences described in §57. Taxable income, as defined in §63(a), is gross income minus deductions. Section 56(b)(1)(E) disallows the standard deduction and deduction for personal exemptions in arriving at AMT income. (CSO: V)

Taxable income before personal exemption	$ 70,000
Add back: Miscellaneous itemized deductions	2,000
State and local income taxes	5,000
AMT income before the AMT exemption	$ 77,000

Chapter 45: Federal Taxation: Estates & Trusts

17. (d) Most trusts must adopt a calendar year. Only a trust which qualifies as a §501(a) tax-exempt organization or a charitable trust described in §4947(a) can elect to use a fiscal year. An estate has the option of choosing a fiscal or calendar year. (CSO: III)

Chapter 47: Federal Taxation: Partnerships

18. (c) Generally, a partner is taxed on the income of the partnership, regardless of distributions. (CSO: VI)

19. (b) Section 444 requires a partnership to use a calendar year or a year that does not create a deferral period which exceeds three months. A partnership formed during the year must elect to have a taxable year that ends in September, October, November, or December. A partnership can elect to have a taxable year other than a required taxable year as long as the deferral period does not exceed three months. The only form which must be filed with the IRS to adopt its tax year is Form 1065, U.S. Partnership Return of Income, which is due three and a half months after the end of its tax year. (CSO: III)

20. (a) Section 707(c) states that guaranteed payments are payments to a partner for services or for the use of capital to the extent determined without regard to the income of the partnership. The $5,000 monthly salary is guaranteed because it is not determined by any reference to the income of the partnership. The payment of 25% of the partnership's profits is not a guaranteed payment because it is determined by taking into account the income of the partnership. (CSO: VI)

21. (b) Section 731(a)(1) provides that a partner does not recognize gain on receiving a distribution from a partnership, except to the extent that any money distributed exceeds the adjusted basis of her/his partnership interest immediately before the distribution. Generally, partner's holding period for property received in a distribution from a partnership includes the holding period of the partnership respect to such property [Section 735(b)]. (CSO: VI)

22. (a) Because Marks and Sparks share profits and losses equally, Marks is allocated $21,000 of the ordinary loss (e.g., 50% of $42,000). Section 704(d) provides that a partner's distributive share of partnership loss is allowed only to the extent of the adjusted basis in that partner's partnership interest. Any loss disallowed under §704(d) will be allowed as a deduction at the end of the first succeeding taxable year to the extent that the partner's adjusted basis at the end of such year exceeds zero [Reg. §1.704-1(d)(1)]. Thus, Marks should deduct an ordinary loss of $18,000. The remaining $3,000 is carried forward and may be deducted in succeeding tax years. (CSO: VI)

23. (c) The basis of property distributed to a partner is generally its adjusted basis to the partnership immediately before the distribution. Section 732(a)(2) limits the adjusted basis to the adjusted basis of the partner's interest in the partnership reduced by any money distributed in the same transaction. ($80,000 – $500,000 = $30,000) (CSO: VI)

24. (c) Thompson's basis in the partnership interest is increased by the long-term capital gain under §705. Thompson's basis in the partnership interest is reduced, but not below zero, by cash distributions under §1367. Thompson's deductible loss for the period is the smaller of the basis before the loss or the ordinary loss or $55,000. (CSO: VI)

Basis at the beginning of the year	$ 60,000
Less: Cash distribution	(20,000)
Add: Long-term capital gain	15,000
Basis before loss	$ 55,000

Solution 3

Chapter 33: Accountant's Legal Responsibilities

1. (a) The Supreme Court has held that the U.S. Constitution's Fifth Amendment rights regarding self-incrimination do not extend to the CPA-client relationship. A number of states, however, do recognize such a privilege pursuant to state constitutional protections. Thus, Ivor can claim the privilege in those states that recognize such a privilege. There are no other instances in which a CPA-client privilege is recognized. The type of suit is irrelevant. (CSO: I)

2. (d) An auditor's best defense when sued for negligence is proof that the auditor did not violate generally accepted auditing standards in performing the audit. Lack of privity is not a valid defense with the client who engaged the auditor. A signed engagement letter is not a required part of the audit and the lack of such a letter would not be a valid defense for the auditor. Even if the auditor did not perform the audit recklessly or with an intent to deceive, it is still possible that the auditor failed to exercise reasonable care, under the circumstances, in conducting the audit. (CSO: I)

3. (b) Negligence is the failure to exercise that degree of care that a reasonable person would exercise under similar circumstances. An auditor failing to discover a material overstatement of assets during an audit generally is such a failure. The issue of whether the accountant knew that the audit of the financial statements was undertaken to obtain a loan from specific bank is unclear in this scenario; a known, specific bank is a third-party beneficiary and contractual liability extends to third-party beneficiaries. Fifteen months after the audit is unlikely to be past the time limit for bringing action; under federal securities law, actions must be commenced within one year of the time when the error or omission was discovered, but no later than three years after the security offering. The "rule of privilege" is inapplicable in this context; typically it concerns the attorney-client privilege; there is no widespread auditor-client privilege. (CSO: I)

4. (b) To express an opinion on ICOFR effectiveness as of a *point in time,* the auditor should obtain evidence that ICOFR has operated effectively for a sufficient period of time, which may be less than the entire period covered by the company's financial statements. To express an opinion on ICOFR effectiveness *taken as a whole,* the auditor must obtain evidence about the effectiveness of controls over all relevant assertions related to all significant accounts and financial statement disclosures. This requires the auditor to test the design and operation effectiveness of controls that the auditor ordinarily would not test if expressing an opinion only on the financial statements. (CSO: I)

Chapter 40: Federal Securities Regulation

5. (a) The Securities Act of 1933 exempts certain securities from its registration requirements. These exempted securities include those issued by not-for-profit charitable organizations and governments. (CSO: II)

6 (c) Corporations must file quarterly reports (Form 10-Q). Rule 10b-5 makes it unlawful to make any untrue statement of a material fact or to omit to state a material fact. A material fact is one where a reasonable person would attach importance to the fact in determining a choice of action. (CSO: II)

7. (c) Under the Securities Act of 1933, securities are defined broadly as any security that allows an investor to make a profit on an investment through the efforts of others rather than through her/his own efforts. Therefore, a general partnership interest would not likely be considered a security under the 1933 Act since partners in a general partnership have a right to manage and are considered active in the management of the business. Under the 1933 Act, securities are broadly defined to include stock options, warrants, and limited partnership interests. (CSO: II)

Chapter 41: Other Regulations

8. (d) ERISA does not require employers to have pension plans, but does set standards that employers must follow if they have a plan. These standards do not include employees as pension-plan managers. (CSO: II)

Chapter 42: Property

9. (b) A mortgage is recorded to give constructive notice of the mortgage and protect against subsequent mortgagees. Under a notice-race statute, if the first mortgage is not recorded, a subsequent mortgagee who has no knowledge of the first mortgage will have priority once s/he records. However, if the subsequent mortgagee did have notice of the first mortgage, s/he can't get priority. Thus, the Link mortgage has priority because Zone had notice of the Link mortgage. The first mortgage in time has priority only if it is recorded first. The Zone mortgage can't have priority since Zone knew about the Link mortgage. Although neither Zone nor Link had notice of the Hay mortgage, Link has priority because Zone had notice of the Link mortgage. (CSO: II)

Chapter 43: Federal Taxation: Property & Other Tax Topics

10. (a) Section 102(a) provides that gross income does not include the value of property acquired by gift, bequest, devise, or inheritance. Thus, Lois should not include any amount on her tax return for the inheritance of the stock. (CSO: IV)

11. (c) Section 1014(a)(2) provides that when the alternate valuation date is elected, the basis of property inherited by the decedent is equal to the value of the property as it is determined under §2032. Under §2032, the value of property distributed from the estate after the date of death, but before the alternate valuation date, is equal to the FMV on the date of distribution [§2032(a)(1)]. Thus, Lois' basis in the stock is $9,000 (e.g., the stock's FMV on the date of distribution). (CSO: IV)

12. (d) Section 1221 defines capital assets as property held by the taxpayer except for a number of items listed. Government bonds are not so listed. Section 1221(4) excludes accounts receivable from the sale of inventory from being treated as capital assets. Section 1221 excludes depreciable property used in a business and excludes inventory or property held primarily for sale to customers in the ordinary course of business from the definition of capital assets. Subdivided land sold by a dealer is inventory to the dealer. (CSO: IV)

13. (a) Section 6713 authorizes a civil penalty and §7216 authorizes a criminal penalty for the unauthorized disclosure by a tax preparer of information furnished to the preparer by a taxpayer. Reg. §301.7216-2(o) allow disclosure for the purpose of a quality or peer review. Reg. §301.7216-2(c) allows disclosure pursuant to an administrative order by a state agency that registers tax return preparers. Reg. §301.7216-2(h) allows disclosure for the purpose of processing the tax return, including electronic filing. Disclosure for the purpose of enabling a third party to solicit from the taxpayer is not an exception to the general prohibition. (CSO: III)

Chapter 44: Federal Taxation: Individuals

14. (a) A deduction is allowed for any debt which becomes totally worthless during the year. However, the deduction is only allowed with respect to debts that represent items which have been previously taken into income. A cash basis taxpayer does not take an item into income until payment is received. Since no part of the fee in question was taken into income, no deduction is allowed for the worthlessness of the debt. (CSO: III)

Chapter 45: Federal Taxation: Estates & Trusts

15. (a) The decedent's fractional share of property is included in the gross estate [Reg. §20.20401(a)(1)]. In this case, two individuals are involved; therefore, 50% of the value of property owned is included. The question of who furnished the original consideration is not considered. (CSO: V)

16. (c) The generation-skipping transfer tax is a separate tax imposed in addition to the gift tax and the estate tax. The generation-skipping transfer tax applies to transfers to beneficiaries who are more than one generation *below* the transferor's generation. (CSO: V)

17. (c) Under the unified transfer tax system, one transfer tax schedule is used to compute the gift tax as well as the estate tax. Transfers at death and lifetime taxable gifts are taxed on a cumulative basis. (CSO: V)

18. (c) As long as a distribution to a beneficiary does not exceed the distributable net income of the estate, the estate is allowed a deduction for the amount of the distribution that is subject to income tax on the beneficiary's return. Thus, the estate may claim a distribution deduction of $9,000 (e.g., $9,000 < $15,000) on its fiduciary income tax return. (CSO: V)

Chapter 46: Federal Taxation: Corporations

19. (d) In the case of property purchased for resale, a taxpayer is exempt from the uniform capitalization rules (UNICAP), if its average gross receipts for the preceding three years are $10 million or less. UNICAP rules generally apply to real and tangible personal property produced by the taxpayer for use in a trade or business or for investment purposes and to personal and real property purchased for resale to customers. (CSO: III)

20. (a) Under Section 1032, when a corporation exchanges its own stock (e.g., treasury stock) for property or money, no gain or loss is recognized on the exchange. Thus, Lee Corp. will recognize no gain on this sale. (CSO: VI)

21. (c) Dividends paid from earnings and profits (E&P) are income ($20,000 + $30,000 = $50,000). Dividends paid beyond E&P are a return of capital. (CSO: VI)

22. (c) An S corporation may not have more than 100 shareholders. If a corporation has 150 unrelated shareholders, it cannot elect S status. The estate of a decedent who was a shareholder can be

a qualifying shareholder. It is irrelevant if one of the shareholders is a bankrupt estate. In addition, the prohibition of having more than one class of stock does not prevent a corporation from issuing voting and nonvoting common stock as long as the stock is of the same class. (CSO: VI)

23. (b) Without debt transactions, a partner's adjusted basis in a partnership interest is the beginning basis plus income minus distributions. [$12,000 + 50% × ($81,000 + $10,000) – $51,000 = $6,500] (CSO: VI)

24. (c) Under §1362(d)(1)(B), an election to be an S corporation may be revoked voluntarily only if shareholders holding more than one-half of the shares of stock of the corporation on the day the revocation is made consent to the revocation. Reg. §18.1362-3 states that such shares include nonvoting shares. With 50,000 shares outstanding, shareholders holding more than 25,000 shares must consent to the revocation. The 10,000 voting shares and 16,000 nonvoting shares total 26,000 shares, which is greater than 25,000 shares. (CSO: VI)

PERFORMANCE BY TOPICS

The final examination questions corresponding to each chapter of the Regulation text are listed below. To assess your preparedness for the CPA exam, record the number and percentage of questions you correctly answered in each topic area. To simplify the self-evaluation, the simulations are excluded from the Performance by Topics. The point distribution of the multiple choice questions (not including the simulations) approximates that of the exam.

Chapter 32: Accountant's Professional Responsibilities

Question #	Correct √
1:1	
1:2	
1:3	
1:4	
1:5	
2:1	
2:2	
# Questions	7
# Correct	________
% Correct	________

Chapter 33: Accountant's Legal Responsibilities

Question #	Correct √
2:3	
2:4	
3:1	
3:2	
3:3	
3:4	
# Questions	6
# Correct	________
% Correct	________

Chapter 34: Contracts

Question #	Correct √
1:6	
1:7	
# Questions	2
# Correct	________
% Correct	________

Chapter 35: Sales

Question #	Correct √
1:8	
# Questions	1
# Correct	________
% Correct	________

Chapter 36: Negotiable Instruments & Documents of Title

Question #	Correct √
2:5	
2:6	
# Questions	2
# Correct	________
% Correct	________

Chapter 37: Secured Transactions

Question #	Correct √
1:9	
# Questions	1
# Correct	________
% Correct	________

Chapter 38: Debtor & Creditor Relationships

Question #	Correct √
2:7	
2:8	
2:9	
# Questions	3
# Correct	________
% Correct	________

Chapter 39: Agency

Question #	Correct √
2:10	
# Questions	1
# Correct	________
% Correct	________

Chapter 40: Federal Securities Regulation

Question #	Correct √
3:5	
3:6	
3:7	
# Questions	3
# Correct	________
% Correct	________

Chapter 41: Other Regulations

Question #	Correct √
1:10	
3:8	
# Questions	2
# Correct	________
% Correct	________

Chapter 42: Property

Question #	Correct √
3:9	
# Questions	1
# Correct	________
% Correct	________

Chapter 43: Federal Taxation: Property & Other Tax Topics

Question #	Correct √
1:11	
1:12	
2:11	
2:12	
3:10	
3:11	
3:12	
3:13	
# Questions	8
# Correct	________
% Correct	________

Chapter 44: Federal Taxation: Individuals

Question #	Correct √
1:13	
1:14	
1:15	
1:16	
1:17	
2:13	
2:14	
2:15	
2:16	
3:14	
# Questions	10
# Correct	________
% Correct	________

Chapter 45: Federal Taxation: Estates & Trusts

Question #	Correct √
2:17	
3:15	
3:16	
3:17	
3:18	
# Questions	5
# Correct	________
% Correct	________

Chapter 46: Federal Taxation: Corporations

Question #	Correct √
1:18	
1:19	
1:20	
1:21	
1:22	
1:23	
1:24	
3:19	
3:20	
3:21	
3:22	
3:23	
3:24	
# Questions	13
# Correct	________
% Correct	________

Chapter 47: Federal Taxation: Partnerships

Question #	Correct √
2:18	
2:19	
2:20	
2:21	
2:22	
2:23	
2:24	
# Questions	7
# Correct	________
% Correct	________

PERFORMANCE BY CONTENT SPECIFICATIONS

The final examination questions corresponding to the Regulation portion of the AICPA Content Specification Outline are listed below. To assess your preparedness for the CPA exam, record the number and percentage of questions you correctly answered in each topic area. To simplify the self-evaluation, the simulations are excluded from the Performance by Content Specifications. The point distribution of the multiple choice questions (not including the simulations) approximates that of the exam.

CSO I

Question #	Correct √
1:1	
1:2	
1:3	
1:4	
1:5	
2:1	
2:2	
2:3	
2:4	
3:1	
3:2	
3:3	
3:4	
# Questions	13
# Correct	
% Correct	

CSO II

Question #	Correct √
1:6	
1:7	
1:8	
1:9	
1:10	
2:5	
2:6	
2:7	
2:8	
2:9	
2:10	
3:5	
3:6	
3:7	
3:8	
3:9	
# Questions	16
# Correct	
% Correct	

CSO III

Question #	Correct √
1:14	
1:18	
2:17	
2:19	
3:13	
3:14	
3:19	
# Questions	7
# Correct	
% Correct	

CSO IV

Question #	Correct √
1:11	
1:12	
2:11	
2:12	
3:10	
3:11	
3:12	
# Questions	7
# Correct	
% Correct	

CSO V

Question #	Correct √
1:13	
1:15	
1:16	
1:17	
2:13	
2:14	
2:15	
2:16	
3:15	
3:16	
3:17	
3:18	
# Questions	12
# Correct	
% Correct	

CSO VI

Question #	Correct √
1:19	
1:20	
1:21	
1:22	
1:23	
1:24	
2:18	
2:20	
2:21	
2:22	
2:23	
2:24	
3:20	
3:21	
3:22	
3:23	
3:24	
# Questions	17
# Correct	
% Correct	

SIMULATION SOLUTIONS

Solution 4 Federal Taxation: Individuals

Tax Treatment (4 points)

1. C

Schedule C is used to report trade or business income and expenses. Retainer fees from clients are an example of trade or business income.

2. D

Schedule E is used to report income or loss from rental real estate, royalties, partnerships, S corporations, estates, and trusts.

3. E

Interest income on general obligation state and local government bonds is not taxable.

4. B

The interest income from a refund of federal taxes is an example of interest income which is taxable on Schedule B.

5. E

Death benefits from a life insurance policy are not taxable income.

6. B

Interest on U.S. Treasury bonds is taxable income and is reported on Schedule B.

7. D

Schedule E is used to report income or loss from rental real estate, royalties, partnerships, S corporations, estates, and trusts. Income from a limited partnership is an example of Schedule E partnership income.

8. D

Schedule E is used to report income or loss from rental real estate, royalties, partnerships, S corporations, estates, and trusts. Income from the rental of a townhouse is an example of taxable rental real estate income.

9. A

Prize money is an example of other income reported on Form 1040.

10. A

Payment received for jury service is taxable as other income on Form 1040.

11. E

Dividend income from mutual funds that invest in tax-free government obligations is not taxable.

Communication (5 points)

To: Mr./Ms. **Rogue**
From: Candidate
Re: Tax-Exempt Income Items

During the preparation of your income tax return, we found a few income items that are not taxable and, therefore, are not included on the tax return. The tax-exempt income items are as follows.

Interest income on **general obligation** state and local **government bonds** is not taxable.

Death benefits from a **life insurance** policy are not taxable income.

Dividend income from mutual funds that invest in tax-free government obligations is not taxable.

A copy of the income tax return is enclosed. Please keep the copy for your records.

Research (1 point)

Code Section Answer: §162(b)

Code §162(b) states, "No deduction shall be allowed for any contribution or gift which would be allowable as a deduction...were it not for the percentage limitations, the dollar limitations, or the requirements as to the time of payment, set forth in such section."

Solution 5 Federal Taxation: Corporations

Adjustments (3 points)

1. $15,000, I

Section 162(a)(2) allows a deduction for traveling expenses, including meals, incurred in a trade or business. Section 274(n)(1) limits the deduction for business meals to 50% of the cost of such meals. All of the travel cost and the cost of meals were deducted on Anvil's financial accounting books. Because 50% of the cost of business meals may **not** be deducted for tax purposes, such amount must be added back to the financial accounting income in arriving at taxable income ($30,000 × 50%).

2. $7,000, I

The $7,000 in life insurance premiums was deducted in arriving at financial accounting income. However, §264(a)(1) disallows any deduction for life insurance premiums paid on the life of a corporate officer when the taxpayer is the beneficiary of the policy.

3. $0, N

Under §461(a), the amount of any deduction is to be taken in the proper taxable year under the method of accounting used in computing taxable income. Because Anvil is an accrual basis taxpayer, the franchise tax expense is generally deducted in the year accrued. However, §461(h)(4) requires that all events have occurred that fix the fact of the liability and that the amount can be determined with reasonable accuracy. Also, §461(h)(1) states that the all-events test is not deemed to be satisfied until economic performance has occurred. Under Reg. §1.461-4(g)(6), economic performance occurs for a tax liability when the tax liability is paid. However, §461(h)(3)(A) provides an exception for recurring items. For recurring items, the economic performance test is waived if (1) the all-events test is satisfied, (2) economic performance occurs within the shorter of a reasonable time after the close of the tax year or 8½ months after the close of the tax year, (3) the item is recurring in nature and is consistently treated by the taxpayer, and (4) the item is not material or results in a better matching of income and deductions. The accrual of the franchise tax liability should meet the recurring item exception. Therefore, $18,000 should be deducted in arriving at Anvil's taxable income.

4. $6,000, D

Section 168(e)(3)(B)(iv) provides that any qualified technological equipment is 5-year property. Section 168(i)(2) includes computers in the definition of qualified technological equipment; thus, computers are 5-year MACRS property. Section 168(b)(1) requires the double-declining balance method, with a switch to the straight-line method when the straight-line method provides a greater deduction. Section 168(b)(4) states that salvage value is to be ignored. The straight-line depreciation rate would be 20% a year (100% / 5 years). Therefore, the double-declining balance rate is 40% (20% × 2). Section 168(d)(1) requires the use of the half-year convention. Section 168(d)(4)(A) states that the half-year convention treats all property placed in service during the year as placed in service at the mid-point of the year. Therefore, the MACRS deductions for these computers are determined as follows.

For tax Year 2: $50,000 × 40% × 1/2 = $10,000
For tax Year 3: ($50,000 – $10,000) × 40% = $16,000

The MACRS deduction is $6,000 ($16,000 – $10,000) more than the book depreciation.

5. $1,000, I

The $4,000 capital gain distribution was included and the $5,000 loss on the sale of the Retro stock was deducted in arriving at Anvil's financial accounting income. For tax purposes, §§165(f) and 1211(a) limit the deduction of a corporation's capital losses only to the extent of the corporation's capital gains. The $4,000 capital gain distribution is included in Anvil's gross income under §61(a). However, only $4,000 of the $5,000 capital loss is deductible in arriving at taxable income.

6. $0, N

Anvil would have deducted the $35,000 in charitable contributions made during Year 3 and the $15,000 in charitable contributions accrued in Year 3 and paid in Year 4 on its financial accounting books for Year 3. Section 170(a)(1) authorizes a deduction for charitable contributions paid during the taxable year. Also, §170(a)(2) authorizes a deduction for a corporation on the accrual basis of accounting for charitable contributions, authorized by its board of directors during the taxable year, if payment is made by the 15th day of the third month following the taxable year. Thus, Anvil has a potential deduction for charitable contributions of $50,000 ($35,000 + $15,000) for Year 3. However, §170(b)(2) limits a corporation's deduction for charitable contributions to 10% of its taxable income, determined without regard to charitable contributions, the DRD, any NOL carryback, and any net capital loss carryback. Since Anvil's taxable income before the charitable contributions and DRD was $500,000, Anvil's charitable contributions deduction is limited to $50,000 ($500,000 × 10%). The limit equals the potential deduction, and Anvil may deduct all $50,000 in charitable contributions for Year 3.

Income (1 point)

7. N

Section 275(a)(1) disallows any deduction for federal income taxes. When Anvil receives a refund of federal income tax that Anvil previously paid, the refund is excluded from gross income because Anvil received no tax benefit from paying the federal income taxes. Although not directly applicable because Anvil's payment of the federal income taxes was not deductible, see §111 relating to the tax benefit rule. Under this rule, an amount received as a refund of an item previously deducted is included in gross income only to the extent that the deduction provided a tax benefit in a previous tax year.

8. F

Interest income from the Internal Revenue Service is fully included in gross income under §61(a)(4).

9. N

Section 103(a) excludes from gross income the interest on any state or local bond. The income from the mutual fund retains its character under §852(b)(5).

10. F

In general, under §109 a lessor's gross income does not include any improvements made by the lessee on the lessor's property. However, the lessor will recognize gross income to the extent that the rental payments are reduced as a result of the improvements under Regs. §1.109-1(a), §61(a)(5), and §1.61-1(a). The lessor will also receive a basis in the improvements equal to the gross income recognized as a result of the reduction in rental payments.

Communication (5 points)

To: **Anvil** Corporation
From: Ima Preparer
Re: Deductibility of Select Items

During the preparation of Anvil's income tax return, we received questions from you regarding several items. The following is a short discussion of these items.

The **theater tickets** are deductible as an **ordinary** and **necessary** business expense. Anvil meets the requirement that the entertainment is **associated** with its business. However, the internal revenue code allows only **fifty percent** of the cost of **entertainment** (that is otherwise deductible) as a deduction.

Advertising expenses are fully deductible as an ordinary and necessary business expense in the year paid or incurred. The amount of any deduction is to be taken in the proper taxable year under the **method of accounting** used in computing taxable income. The fact that ten percent of the new product line remains in inventory is **irrelevant**.

The internal revenue code disallows any deduction for **interest** on indebtedness incurred to purchase or to carry **tax-exempt** obligations. Interest on municipal bonds is tax exempt.

The internal revenue code disallows any deduction for business expense for any **fine** or similar **penalty** paid to a government for the **violation** of any law. Such penalties include **civil** penalties that are additions to taxes.

If you have further questions regarding these issues, please contact us for greater detail.

Research (1 point)

Code Section Answer: §172(a)

Code §172(a) states, "There shall be allowed as a deduction for the taxable year an amount equal to the aggregate of (1) the net operating loss carryovers to such year, plus (2) the net operating loss carrybacks to such year."

APPENDIX B
PRACTICAL ADVICE

Your first step toward an effective CPA Review program is to **study** the material in this appendix. It has been carefully developed to provide you with essential information that will help you succeed on the CPA exam. This material will assist you in organizing an efficient study plan and will demonstrate effective techniques and strategies for taking the CPA exam.

SECTION ONE: GENERAL COMMENTS ON THE CPA EXAM

The difficulty and comprehensiveness of the CPA exam is a well-known fact to all candidates. However, success on the CPA exam is a **reasonable, attainable** goal. You should keep this point in mind as you study this appendix and develop your study plan. A positive attitude toward the examination, combined with determination and discipline, will enhance your opportunity to pass.

Purpose of the CPA Exam

The CPA exam is designed as a licensing requirement to measure the technical competence of CPA candidates. Although licensing occurs at the state level, the exam is uniform at all sites and has national acceptance. In other words, passing the CPA exam in one jurisdiction generally allows a candidate to obtain a reciprocal certificate or license, if they meet all the requirements imposed by the jurisdiction from which reciprocity is sought.

Boards of accountancy also rely upon other means to ensure that candidates possess the necessary technical and character attributes, including interviews, letters of reference, affidavits of employment, ethics examinations, and educational requirements. Boards' contact information is listed in this section of the **Practical Advice** appendix and on the web site of the National Association of the State Boards of Accountancy (http://www.nasba.org).

The CPA exam essentially is an academic examination that tests the breadth of material covered by good accounting curricula. It emphasizes the body of knowledge required for the practice of public accounting. It is to your advantage to take the exam as soon as possible after completing the formal education requirements.

We recommend that most candidates study for two examination sections at once, since there is a **synergistic** learning effect to be derived through preparing for more than one part. That is, all sections of the exam share some common subjects (particularly Financial Accounting & Reporting and Auditing & Attestation); so as you study for one section, you are also studying for the others. This advice will be different for different candidates. Candidates studying full-time may find that studying for all four sections at once is most beneficial. Some candidates with full-time jobs and family responsibilities may find that studying for a single exam section at once is best for them.

Score

A passing score for each exam section is 75 points. The objective responses are scored electronically. The written communication portions of simulations are graded manually as well as by computer. Scores are released to candidates by boards of accountancy. Scores are not available from the testing sites.

Format

The CPA exam is split into four sections of differing length.

1. **Financial Accounting & Reporting**—This section covers generally accepted accounting principles for business enterprises and governmental and nonprofit organizations. This section's name frequently is abbreviated as FAR. (4 hours)

2. **Auditing & Attestation**—This section covers the generally accepted auditing standards, procedures, and related topics. The CPA's professional responsibility is no longer tested in this area. This section's name often is abbreviated as AUD. (4½ hours)

3. **Regulation**—This section covers the CPA's professional responsibility to the public and the profession, the legal implications of business transactions generally confronted by CPAs, and federal taxation. This section's name commonly is abbreviated as REG. (3 hours)

4. **Business Environment & Concepts**—This section covers business organizations, economic concepts, financial management, planning, measurement, and information technology. This section's name typically is abbreviated as BEC. The AICPA has not specified when simulations will appear in this exam section, but it might be as early as late 2010. (2½ hours)

Schedule

There are four exam windows annually; the first one starts in January. A candidate may sit for any particular exam section only once during a window. Between windows there is a dark period of about a month when the exam is not administered. Once a candidate has a passing score for one section, that candidate has a certain length of time (typically 18 months) to pass the other three exam sections, or lose the credit for passing that first exam section. Candidates should check with the governing Board of Accountancy concerning details on the length of time to pass all four sections. Exam sites typically are open Mondays through Fridays; some are open on Saturdays as well.

January	February	March
April	May	June
July	August	September
October	November	December

Writing Skills Content

Written communications are used to assess candidates' writing skills. Only those writing samples that generally are responsive to the topic will be graded. No credit will be given for a response that is off topic or offers advice that clearly is incorrect. Written communication responses are scored holistically, by hand as well as by computer. Scores are based on three general writing criteria:

1. Organization
2. Development
3. Expression

Additional information is included in the **Writing Skills** appendix.

Reference Materials

All the material you need to review to pass the CPA exam is in your Bisk Education *CPA Comprehensive Review* texts! However, should you desire more detailed coverage in any area, you may consult the actual promulgations. Individual copies of recent pronouncements are available from the FASB, AICPA, SEC, etc. To order printed materials from the **FASB** or **AICPA** contact:

FASB Order Department	AICPA Order Department	
P.O. Box 5116	P.O. Box 1003	
Norwalk, CT 06856-5116	New York, NY 10108-1003	
Telephone (203) 847-0700	Telephone (800) 334-6961	www.aicpa.org

The AICPA has made available, to candidates with their Notice to Schedule (NTS), a **free** six-month's subscription to some of the databases used in the exam. Bisk Education is unable to fill orders for these subscriptions; they are available only through the AICPA exam web site (www.cpa-exam.org).

If you do not yet have your NTS, the FASB offers a student discount that varies depending on the publication. The AICPA offers a 30% educational discount, which students may claim by submitting proof of their eligibility (e.g., copy of ID card or teacher's letter). AICPA members get a 20% discount and delivery time is speedier because members may order by phone. Unamended, full-text FASB statements are available without charge in PDF format on the FASB Web site (www.fasb.org/st). Bear in mind that these statements are not provided in a searchable format, nor are they the only authoritative literature used in the research element of simulations.

STATE BOARDS OF ACCOUNTANCY

Certified Public Accountants are licensed to practice by individual State Boards of Accountancy. Application forms and requirements to sit for the CPA exam should be requested from your individual State Board. IT IS EXTREMELY IMPORTANT THAT YOU COMPLETE THE APPLICATION FORM CORRECTLY AND RETURN IT TO YOUR STATE BOARD BEFORE THE DEADLINE. Errors and/or delays may result in the rejection of your application. Be extremely careful in filling out the application and be sure to enclose all required materials. Requirements as to education, experience, internship, and other matters vary. If you have not already done so, take a moment to call the appropriate board for specific and current requirements. Complete the application in a timely manner. Some states arrange for an examination administrator, such CPA Examination Services [a division of the National Association of State Boards of Accountancy (NASBA), (800) CPA-EXAM (272-3926)], to handle candidate registration, examination administration, etc.

It may be possible to sit for the exam in another state as an out-of-state candidate. Candidates wishing to do so should also contact the Board of Accountancy in the state where they plan to be certified. NASBA has links (**http://www.nasba.org**) to many state board sites.

At least 45 days before you plan to sit for the exam, check to see that your application to sit for the exam has been processed. DON'T ASSUME THAT YOU ARE PROPERLY REGISTERED UNLESS YOU HAVE RECEIVED YOUR NOTICE TO SCHEDULE (NTS). You must present your NTS and proper identification to be admitted to the testing room at an exam site. Contact the applicable board of accountancy if you have any doubts about what constitutes proper ID.

The AICPA publishes a booklet entitled *Uniform CPA Examination Candidate Bulletin: Information for Applicants,* usually distributed by Boards of Accountancy to candidates upon receipt or acceptance of their applications. To request a complimentary copy, contact your **state board** or the **AICPA,** Examination Division, 1211 Avenue of the Americas, New York, NY 10036. This publication is also available on the AICPA's exam web site: www.cpa-exam.org.

Candidates requiring medication during the exam should make sure to notify the state board and other examining entities as appropriate during registration.

Contacting Your State Board

CPA Examination Services, a division of the National Association of State Boards of Accountancy (NASBA) administers the examination for 25 states. Contact CPA Examination Services at (800) CPA-EXAM (272-3926), (615) 880-4250, or www.nasba.org.

CO	CT	DE	FL	GA	HI	IA	IN	KS	LA	MA	ME	MI	MN	MO	MT
NE	NH	NJ	NM	NY	OH	PA	PR	RI	SC	TN	UT	VA	VT	WI	

Castle Worldwide at (800) 655-4845 administers the examination for WA.

Following are the telephone numbers for the boards in the other states.

AK	(907) 465-2580	IL	(217) 333-1565	OK	(405) 521-2397
AL	(334) 242-5700	KY	(502) 595-3037	OR	(503) 378-4181
AR	(501) 682-1520	MD	(410) 333-6322	SD	(605) 367-5770
AZ	(602) 255-3648	MS	(601) 354-7320	TX	(512) 305-7850
CA	(916) 263-3680	NC	(919) 733-4222	VI	(340) 773-2226
DC	(202) 442-4461	ND	(800) 532-5904	WV	(304) 558-3557
GU	(671) 477-1050	NE	(402) 471-3595	WY	(307) 777-7551
ID	(208) 334-2490	NV	(775) 786-0231		

The web sites for the state boards that administer the exam themselves are listed here. Each address has www. as a prefix, except WY. The Bisk Education web site **(www.cpaexam.com)** has links to the AICPA and NASBA. These numbers and addresses are subject to change without notice. Bisk Education doesn't assume responsibility for their accuracy.

AK	dced.state.ak.us/occ/pcpa.htm	MT	discoveringmontana.com/dli/bsd
AL	asbpa.state.al.us	NE	nol.org/home/BPA
AZ	accountancy.state.az.us	NV	accountancy/state.nv.us
AR	state.ar.us/asbpa	NH	state.nh.us/accountancy
CA	dca.ca.gov/cba	NC	state.nc.us/cpabd
DC	dcra.org/acct/newboa.shtm	ND	state.nd.us/ndsba
FL	myflorida.com	OK	state.ok.us/~oab
GU	guam.net/gov/gba	OR	boa.state.or.us/boa.html
ID	state.id.us/boa	SD	state.sd.us/dcr/accountancy
IL	illinois-cpa-exam.com/cpa.htm	TX	tsbpa.state.tx.us
KY	state.ky.us/agencies/boa	UT	commerce.state.ut.us
MD	dllr.state.md.us/license/occprof/account.html	VI	usvi.org/dlca/licensing/cpa.html
MN	boa.state.mn.us	WV	state.wv.us/wvboa
MS	msbpa.state.ms.us	WY	cpaboard.state.wy.us

COMPUTER-BASED TESTING (CBT)

The information presented here is intended to give candidates an overall idea of what their exam will be like. This information is as accurate as possible; however, circumstances are subject to change after this publication goes to press. Candidates should check the AICPA's web site (www.cpa-exam.org) 45 days before their exam for the most recent bulletin.

Registration Process

To sit for the exam, candidates apply to the appropriate state board of accountancy. Some state boards contract with NASBA's service to handle candidate applications. Once a state board or its agent determines that a candidate is eligible to sit for the exam, the board informs NASBA of candidate eligibility and NASBA adds the candidate to its database. With a national database, NASBA is able to ensure that no candidate can sit for the same exam section more than once during a single exam window. Within 24 hours, NASBA sends Prometric a notice to schedule (NTS). At that point, a candidate can schedule a date and time to sit for the exam with Prometric. With a NTS, a candidate also can subscribe to electronic databases of professional literature for free through the AICPA's exam website, www.cpa-exam.org. Please note that at Prometric's call center, Monday tends to have the longest wait times.

Scheduling

Candidates to whom taking the exam on a particular day is important should plan to schedule their exam dates **45 days** in advance. Upon receipt of the NTS, candidates have a limited amount of time to sit for the specified exam sections; this time is set by states. The exam is called on-demand because candidates may sit at anytime for any available date in the open window.

Candidate Medical Condition

If any medical conditions exist that need to be considered during the exam, candidates should supply information about that situation when scheduling. Ordinarily, candidates may not bring anything into the exam room—including prescription medications.

Granting of Credit

Once candidates have been granted credit for one exam section, they typically have 18 months to pass the three other exam sections. As this issue is decided by 54 boards of accountancy which are independent of each other, the length of time varies among jurisdictions.

Prometric

Prometric, a commercial testing center, has facilities at different security levels; the CPA exam is administered only at locations that have the highest restrictions. In other words, not all Prometric facilities may administer the CPA exam. These locations have adjustable chairs, 17-inch monitors, and uninterruptible power supplies (UPS). Prometric generally is closed on Sundays. A few locations are open on Saturdays. Candidates can register either at individual Prometric locations or through Prometric's national call center (800-864-8080). Candidates may schedule, reschedule, cancel, or confirm an exam as well as find the closest testing location online at www.prometric.com. Prometric doesn't score the exam. Candidates do not know their scores when they leave the exam site. Prometric sends a result file to NASBA that includes candidate responses, attendance information, and any incident reports.

Incident Reports

Prometric prepares an incident report for any unusual circumstances that occur during the exam. While Prometric has UPS available at qualified testing centers, if some problem similar to a power outage should occur, an incident report is included with the information that Prometric sends to NASBA after the candidate is finished with the exam. An incident report would be filed for such events as missing scratch sheets or a mid-testlet absence from the testing room.

Exam Day

On the day of their exam, candidates sign in and confirm their appointments. An administrator checks notices to schedule and **two** matching forms of identification. Digital photos are created. Candidates stow their belongings in designated locations. Note that test-site lockers are very small. Candidates may not bring purses, watches, bottles of water, tissues, etc. into the exam room. Each candidate may receive six pages of scratch paper. Candidates may exchange used sheets for six more sheets. Candidates must account for the six pages at the conclusion of the exam. After the exam, candidates complete a survey to provide feedback.

Fees

States inform candidates of the total applicable fee. The total fee includes fees for NASBA, AICPA, Prometric, the state board, and the digital photo. Cancellations in advance generally result in a partially refunded fee. Cancellations (as opposed to a missed appointment) with no notice result in no refund. If a candidate misses an appointment, there generally is a $35 to $50 rescheduling fee unless due to circumstances beyond the candidate's control. Those situations are decided on a case-by-case basis. Some states structure their fees to provide incentive for taking more than one exam section in the same exam window.

Testing Room

Ordinarily, candidates are not permitted to bring any supplies into the testing room, including pencils, water, or aspirin. Candidates requiring medication during the exam should make sure to notify the state board as appropriate during the registration process. Exam proctors supply "scratch" or note paper. These pages must be returned to proctors before leaving the examination site.

Testlets

Multiple choice questions and simulations are grouped into testlets. A testlet typically has either from 24 to 30 multiple choice questions or a single simulation. The typical exam has three multiple choice testlets and two simulation testlets. Candidates may not pick the order in which they answer testlets. In other words, candidates cannot choose to answer the simulation testlets first and then the multiple choice question testlets. Within any one testlet, questions cover the entire content specification outline and are presented in random order.

Adaptive Testing

Each testlet is designed to cover all of the topics for an exam section. After the first testlet is finished, the software selects a second testlet based on the candidate's performance on the first testlet. If a candidate did well on the first testlet, the second testlet will be a little more difficult than average. Conversely, if a candidate did poorly on the first testlet, the second testlet will be a little less difficult than average. The examiners plan on adaptive testing eventually allowing for less questions, resulting in more time for testing skills.

Initially, testlets with different levels of difficulty will have the same number of questions; however, the point value of a question from an "easy" testlet will be less than a question from a "difficult" testlet. Thus, some candidates may think that they are not doing well because they are finding the questions difficult; when in reality, they are getting difficult questions because of exceptional performance on previous testlets. Other candidates may think that they are doing well because they are finding the questions easy; when in reality, they are getting easy questions because of poor performance on previous testlets.

The BEC exam section is not yet adaptive. The AICPA has not announced when this will change. Simulations are not adaptive.

Breaks

Once a testlet is started, a candidate ordinarily may not leave the workstation until that testlet is finished. Once a testlet is finished, a candidate may not return to it to change responses. After each testlet, a candidate has the option to take a break, but the clock still is running; a candidate's time responding to questions is reduced by the amount of time spent on breaks.

For a well-prepared candidate, time should not be an issue. Candidates will receive a five or ten minute warning. The software stops accepting exam responses at the end of the exam time automatically. All information entered before that time is scored.

Multiple Choice Questions

If there are six answer options and a candidate is told to choose one, the software will allow the selection of a second option and automatically unselect the previously selected option. If there are six answer options and a candidate is told to choose two, the software will not allow the selection of a third option without the candidate unselecting one of the other selected options.

In Bisk Education's printed book, letter answers appear next to each answer option to simplify indicating the correct answer. In the exam, a radio button appears instead of this letter. During the exam, candidates will indicate their response by clicking the appropriate radio button with a mouse device.

Simulations

A simulation is a case study with a variety of tasks, some of which require searching databases, writing communications, and working with spreadsheets or forms. Simulations typically are 30% of the exam score for FAR, AUD, and REG. This usually is 10% for written communications and 20% for all other simulation aspects. The BEC exam section currently does not have simulations; BEC simulations are not expected until November 2010 at earliest.

Simulation Appearance Simulations generally appear as a collection of tabbed pages. Each tab requiring a candidate response will be designated by a pencil icon that changes appearance when any response is entered on that tab. Candidates should be alert to the fact that the altered icon does not indicate that all responses on that tab are entered, but rather that one response is entered.

Scenario Elements Simulations generally have one or two scenarios providing the basis for answers to all of the questions in the simulations.

Objective Response Elements Simulations may require candidates to select answers from drop-down lists or to enter numbers into worksheets or tax forms. Tax forms or schedules may appear on the REG exam section, but not all simulations on tax topics will include tax forms. Candidates don't need to know how to create a spreadsheet from scratch to earn full points on the exam; they do need to know how to categorize, determine value, and add to a previously constructed worksheet.

Written Communication Elements Written communication elements are graded electronically and manually. The score focuses primarily on writing skills. The content must be on topic to earn the full point value, but the examiners plan to focus on testing content in the objective response questions. Candidates should use their own words in these responses; excerpts pasted from the standards may result in a zero score for this element.

Word Processor Tool There is a word processor tool with limited features in some simulations. The word processor tool has cut, paste, copy, do, and undo features. Spell check likely will be available. The word processor intentionally does **not** have bold, underline, or bullet features; the examiners don't want candidates spending much time on formatting.

Spreadsheet Tool The exam has a blank spreadsheet for use like a piece of electronic scratch paper. Anything in such a spreadsheet generally is not graded. In other words, if a candidate calculates an amount in a spreadsheet, it must be transferred to the appropriate answer location in order to earn points.

Research Elements At least one simulation in the FAR, AUD, and REG exam sections will have a research element, probably for one point. With an estimated two simulations per exam section, this means that the point value on any one of these three exam sections for the research element of a simulation will total two percent of that section's point value, at most. The AICPA has not announced yet when simulations, let alone research elements, first will appear in the BEC exam section.

A research element involves a search of an electronic database of authoritative literature for guidance. The examiners devise research questions with references unlikely to be known, requiring candidates to search the material. No written analysis of the reference is required; candidates merely provide the most appropriate reference(s) to a research question. Each research question will specify the number of references to provide.

The research skill evaluation distills down to the ability to structure a search of an electronic database and select the appropriate guidance from the "hits" generated by that search. Candidates may search using **either** Boolean protocols or the table of contents of the relevant guidance. Qualified candidates may get a **free** six month subscription to the databases used in the FAR and AUD exam sections from the AICPA and NASBA. Any difficulties candidates encounter in accepting the joint AICPA-NASBA offer should be brought to the attention of AICPA or NASBA. Qualified candidates may subscribe at www.cpa-exam.org. Only candidates who have applied to take the exam, been deemed eligible by one of the 54 boards of accountancy, and have a valid Notice to Schedule (NTS) may have access to this complimentary package of professional literature. Further information may be found at www.cpa-exam.org. For further inquiries after subscribing at this site, candidates may contact either: AICPA, 212.596.6111; or NASBA, 615.880.4237.

Tutorial

The AICPA provides a web-based tutorial for the CBT. This tutorial has samples of all the different types of simulation elements. The examiners believe that an hour spent with this tutorial will eliminate any point value loss due merely to unfamiliarity with the CBT system. It is important that you become familiar with the latest version of the AICPA testing software. The simulations use both a word processor and a spreadsheet program; however, these applications are not Microsoft Excel™ or Word™. It may be unsettling to encounter an unfamiliar interface on your exam day. This tutorial is **not** available at the exam sites.

Advice to Candidates

Arrive at the testing center **at least** ½ hour before your appointment. Midweek appointments probably will be easiest to schedule. If taking the exam on a certain day is important, **schedule 45 days in advance.** Prometric doesn't overbook like airlines do—that is why there is a rescheduling fee for missed appointments.

Don't go to the exam without spending at least an hour with the practice materials (also called a tutorial) available on the AICPA exam web-site, www.cpa-exam.org. This tutorial is intended to familiarize candidates with the features of the exam software, so that when they take the exam, they are not worried about functionality and, hence, can concentrate on the content. The AICPA does **not** intend its tutorial to demonstrate content. The Bisk Education editors recommend viewing this tutorial at least a month before taking the exam and again a second time a week before your exam date.

THE NONDISCLOSED EXAM

Exam Disclosure

The Uniform CPA Examination is nondisclosed. This means that candidates are not allowed to receive a copy of their examination questions after the test. Also, candidates are required to sign a statement of confidentiality in which they promise not to reveal questions or answers. Only the AICPA have access to the test questions and answers. (In the past, the AICPA has released a small number of questions with unofficial answers from each nondisclosed exam; it makes no guarantees that it will continue this practice.) Bisk Education's editors update the diagnostic, study, and practice questions, based upon content changes, items from previously disclosed tests, and the teaching expertise of our editors. Due to the nondisclosure requirements, Bisk Education's editors are no longer able to address questions about specific examination questions, although we continue to supply help with similar study problems and questions in our texts.

The AICPA no longer discloses the exam in order to increase consistency, facilitate computer administration of the test, and improve examination quality by pretesting questions. Because the examination is no longer completely changed every year, statistical equating methods are more relevant, and the usefulness of specific questions as indicators of candidates' knowledge can be tested.

Time Management

Approximately 20% of the multiple choice questions in every section of every exam are questions that are being pretested. These questions are not included in candidates' final grades; they are presented only so that the Board of Examiners may evaluate them for effectiveness and possible ambiguity. The Scholastic Achievement Test and the Graduate Record Exam both employ similar but not identical strategies: those tests include an extra section that is being pretested, and test-takers do not know which section is the one which will not be graded. On the Uniform CPA Examination, however, the extra questions are mixed in among the graded questions. This makes time management even more crucial. Candidates who are deciding how much time to spend on a difficult multiple choice question must keep in mind that there is a 20% chance that the answer to the question will not affect them either way. Also, candidates should not allow a question that seems particularly difficult or confusing to shake their confidence or affect their attitude towards the rest of the test; it may not even count. This experimental 20% works against candidates who are not sure whether they have answered enough questions to earn 75%. Candidates should try for a safety margin, so that they will have accumulated enough correct answers to pass, even though some of their correctly answered questions will not be scored.

Post-Exam Diagnostics

The AICPA Board of Examiners' Advisory Grading Service provides boards of accountancy with individual diagnostic reports for all candidates along with the candidates' grades. The accountancy boards may mail the diagnostic reports to candidates along with their grades. Candidates should contact the state board in their jurisdiction to find out its policy on this issue. Grades are mailed in the first month of the next exam window; the examiners plan to reduce this waiting time gradually as they speed up the grading process.

Question Re-Evaluation

Candidates who believe that an examination question contains errors that will affect the grading should contact the AICPA Examinations Division, in accordance with the AICPA's *Uniform CPA Examination Candidate Bulletin: Information for Applicants* within **four days** of taking the examination. The Advisory Grading Service asks candidates to be as precise as possible about the question and their reason for believing that it should be re-evaluated, and, if possible, to supply references to support their position. Since candidates are not able to keep a copy of examination questions, it is important to remember as much detail as possible about a disputed question.

TEN ATTRIBUTES OF EXAMINATION SUCCESS

1.	**Positive Mental Attitude**	6.	**Examination Strategies**
2.	**Development of a Plan**	7.	**Examination Grading**
3.	**Adherence to the Plan**	8.	**Solutions Approach™**
4.	**Time Management**	9.	**Focus on Ultimate Objective—Passing!**
5.	**Knowledge**	10.	**Examination Confidence**

We believe that successful CPA candidates possess these ten characteristics that contribute to their ability to pass the exam. Because of their importance, we will consider each attribute individually.

1. Positive Mental Attitude

Preparation for the CPA exam is a long, intense process. A positive mental attitude, above all else, can be the difference between passing and failing.

2. Development of a Plan

The significant commitment involved in preparing for the exam requires a plan. We have prepared a study plan in the preceding **Getting Started** section. Take time to read this plan. **Amend it to your situation.** Whether you use our study plan or create your own, the importance of this attribute can't be overlooked.

3. Adherence to a Plan

You cannot expect to accomplish a successful and comprehensive review without adherence to your study plan.

4. Time Management

We all lead busy lives and the ability to budget study time is a key to success. We have outlined steps to budgeting time in the **Personalized Training Plan** found in the **Getting Started** section.

5. Knowledge

There is a distinct difference between understanding the material and knowing the material. A superficial understanding of accounting, auditing, and the business environment is not enough. You must know the material likely to be tested on the exam. Your Bisk Education text is designed to help you acquire that essential knowledge.

6. Examination Strategies

You should be familiar with the format of the CPA exam and know exactly what you will do when you enter the examination room. In Section Two, we discuss the steps you should take from the time you enter the testing room, until you hand in your note (or scratch) sheets. Planning in advance how you will spend your examination time will save you time and confusion on exam day.

7. Examination Grading

An understanding of the CPA exam written communication grading procedure will help you to maximize grading points on the exam. Remember that your objective is to score 75 points on each section. Points are assigned to written communication responses by the human grader who reads your exam. In Section Three, we explain AICPA grading procedures and show you how to tailor your answer to the grading guide and thus earn more points on the exam.

8. Solutions Approach™

The Solutions Approach™ is an efficient, systematic method of organizing and solving questions found on the CPA exam. This Approach will permit you to organize your thinking and your written answers in a logical manner that will maximize your exam score. Candidates who do not use a systematic answering method often neglect to show all their work on free form response questions—work that could earn partial credit if it were presented to the grader in an orderly fashion. The Solutions Approach™ will help you avoid drawing "blanks" on the exam; with it, you always know where to begin.

Many candidates have never developed an effective problem-solving methodology in their undergraduate studies. The "cookbook" approach, in which students work problems by following examples, is widespread among accounting schools. Unfortunately, it is not an effective problem-solving method for the CPA exam or for problems you will encounter in your professional career. Our Solutions Approach™ teaches you to derive solutions independently, without an example to guide you.

Our **Solutions Approach™** and grader orientation skills, when developed properly, can be worth at least 10 to 15 points for most candidates. These 10 to 15 points can often make the difference between passing and failing.

9. Focus on the Ultimate Objective—Passing!

Your primary goal in preparing for the CPA exam is to attain a grade of 75 or better on all sections and, thus, **pass the examination**. Your review should be focused on this goal. Other objectives, such as learning new material or reviewing old material, are important only insofar as they assist you in passing the exam.

10. Examination Confidence

Examination confidence is actually a function of the other nine attributes. If you have acquired a good working knowledge of the material, an understanding of the grading system, a tactic for answering simulations, and a plan for taking the exam, you can go into the examination room **confident** that you are in control.

SECTION TWO: EXAMINATION STRATEGIES

The CPA exam is more than a test of your knowledge and technical competence. It is also a test of your ability to function under psychological pressure. You easily could be thrown off balance by an unexpected turn of events during the days of the exam. Your objective is to avoid surprises and eliminate hassles and distractions that might shake your confidence. You want to be in complete control so that you can concentrate on the exam material, rather than the exam situation. By taking charge of the exam, you will be able to handle pressure in a constructive manner. The keys to control are adequate preparation and an effective examination strategy.

Overall Preparation

Advance preparation will arm you with the confidence you need to overcome the psychological pressure of the exam. As you complete your comprehensive review, you will cover most of the material that will be tested on the exam; it is unlikely that any question will deal with a topic you have not studied. But if an unfamiliar topic **is** tested or a familiar topic is presented in an unfamiliar manner, you will not be dismayed because you have learned to use the **Solutions Approach™** to derive the best possible answer from the knowledge you possess. Similarly, you will not feel pressured to write "perfect" written communication answers, because you understand the grading process. You recognize that there is a limit to the points you can earn for each answer, no matter how much or how well you write.

The components of your advance preparation program have previously been discussed in this appendix. Briefly summarizing, they include the following.

1. Comprehensive review materials such as your Bisk Education CPA Review Program.

2. A method for pre-review and ongoing self-evaluation of your level of proficiency.

3. A study plan that enables you to review each subject area methodically and thoroughly.

4. A **Solutions Approach™** for each type of examination question.

5. An understanding of the grading process and grader orientation skills.

CPA Exam Strategies

The second key to controlling the exam is to develop effective strategies for the days you take the exam. Your objective is to avoid surprises and frustrations so that you can focus your full concentration on the questions and your answers.

You should be familiar with the format of the CPA exam and know exactly what you will do when you enter the testing room. Remember to read all instructions carefully, whether general or specific to a particular question. Disregarding the instructions may mean loss of points.

On the following pages, we discuss the steps you should take on exam day. Planning in advance how you will spend your examination time will save you time and confusion.

Examination Inventory

You should spend the first few minutes of the exam planning your work. **Do not** plunge head-first into answering the questions without a plan of action. You do not want to risk running out of time, becoming frustrated by a difficult question, or losing the opportunity to answer a question that you could have answered well. Your inventory should take no longer than a minute. The time you spend will help you "settle in" to the examination and develop a feel for your ability to answer the questions.

1. Carefully read the "Instructions to Candidates."
2. Note the number and type of testlets, as well as any other information provided by the examiners.
3. Devise a time schedule on your "scratch" paper, taking into account the number and type of testlets.

Order of Answering Questions

Objective questions comprise a majority of the point value of each section. Because of their objective nature, the correct solution often is listed as one of the answer choices. (The exception is when a numeric response is required.) By solving these questions, not only do you gain confidence, but they often involve the same or a related topic to that covered in any written communications that may appear in the simulations.

A very effective and efficient manner of answering the objective questions is to make **two passes** through the questions. On the first pass, you should answer those questions that you find the easiest. If you come across a question that you find difficult to solve, note it on your scratch paper and proceed to the next one. This will allow you to avoid wasting precious time and will enable your mind to clear and start anew on your **second pass.** On the second pass, you should return and solve those questions you left unanswered on the first pass. Some of these questions you may have skipped over without an attempt, while in others you may have been able to eliminate one or two of the answer choices. Either way, you should come up with an answer on the second pass, even if you have to guess! Once you leave a testlet, you may not return to it. Before leaving a testlet, make sure you have answered all of the individual questions. Be careful not to overlook any items; use particular care in simulations.

Written communication responses should be worked only through an outline on the first pass. Then take a fresh look at the question and return to write your solution.

Examination Time Budgeting

You must **plan** how you will use your examination time and adhere faithfully to your schedule. If you budget your time carefully, you should be able to answer all parts of all questions. You should subtract a minute or two for your initial inventory on each section. Assuming you will use the **Solutions Approach™** and there will be two simulations in all sections except BEC, your time budgets may be similar to these. Your actual exam may differ from this scenario. You may benefit by taking more breaks than are included in this schedule. Be sure to adjust your time budget to accommodate the number and type of questions asked as well as your individual needs and strengths.

	Minutes			
	FAR	AUD	REG	BEC
Inventory examination	1	1	1	1
Answer multiple choice question testlet	51	58	33	49
Answer multiple choice question testlet	51	58	33	50
Answer multiple choice question testlet	51	58	33	50
Break	6	5	0	0
Answer simulation testlet	40	45	40	n/a
Answer simulation testlet	40	45	40	n/a
	240	270	180	150

Your objective in time budgeting is to avoid running out of time to answer a question. Work quickly but efficiently (i.e., use the **Solutions Approach™**). Remember, when you are answer a written communication element, a partial answer is better than no answer at all. If you write nothing, how can a grader justify giving you any points?

Page Numbering

Identify and label your scratch pages to avoid confusing yourself during the stress of the exam.

Psychology of Examination Success

As stated previously, the CPA exam is in itself a physical and mental strain. You can minimize this strain by avoiding all unnecessary distractions and inconveniences during your exam week. For example, consider the following.

- **Use the AICPA's free tutorial and sample examination** at www.cpa-exam.org at least a week before your examination. Because the exam interface is subject to change, re-visit the site to be sure that you are familiar with the current interface if you took an exam in a previous window. The site also has the most current *Uniform CPA Examination Candidate Bulletin,* a publication with useful information for candidates. These are **not** available at the test center.

- **Carefully register for the examination.** You must bring two forms of identification and your notice to schedule to the test center on the day of your exam. The name you use to make the appointment must match **exactly** your name on the identification and your notice to schedule (which also must match each other exactly).

- **Make any reservations for lodging well in advance.** If you are traveling, it's best to reserve a room for the preceding night so that you can check in, get a good night's sleep, and locate the exam site well before the exam.

- **Stick to your normal eating, sleeping, and exercise habits.** Eat lightly before the exam. Watch your caffeine and alcohol intake. If you are accustomed to regular exercise, continue a regular routine leading up to your exam day.

- **Locate the examination facilities** before the examination and familiarize yourself with the surroundings and alternate routes.

- **Arrive early for the exam.** Allow plenty of time for unexpected delays. Nothing is more demoralizing than getting caught in a traffic jam ten minutes before your exam is scheduled to begin. Your appointment time is the time that the actual examination process is scheduled to start, not the start of the test center pre-exam procedures: identification verification, digital photography, storage locker assignment, etc. The examiners recommend that you arrive **at least** 30 minutes before your scheduled appointment. If your examination doesn't begin within 30 minutes of your scheduled start time, you may have to reschedule. This means that if you show up 30 minutes after your scheduled start time, you may have to reschedule—pre-exam procedures are neither instantaneous nor factored into your scheduled appointment.

- **Avoid possible distractions,** such as friends and pre-exam conversation, immediately before the exam.

- In general, **you should not attempt serious study on the nights before exam sessions.** It's better to relax—watch a movie, exercise, or read a novel. If you feel you must study, spend half an hour or so going over the chapter outlines in the text. Some candidates develop a single page of notes for each chapter (or each exam section) throughout their review process to review for a few minutes during the evening before the exam. This single page includes only those things that are particularly troublesome for that candidate, such as the criteria for a capital lease or the economic order quantity formula.

- **Don't discuss exam answers with other candidates.** Not only have you signed a statement of confidentiality, but someone is sure to disagree with your answer, and if you are easily influenced by his or her reasoning, you can become doubtful of your own ability. If you are writing more than one exam section within a two-month exam window, you will not have the reliable feedback that only your score can provide from your first section before you sit for the second section. Wait and analyze your performance by yourself when you are in a relaxed and objective frame of mind.

- **Avoid self-evaluation** of your exam performance until after you receive your official score. The Bisk editors have heard from several candidates who were sure that they failed by a large margin, only to receive subsequent messages rejoicing in scores in the 80s and 90s. Self-evaluation without an official score is unreliable. Not all of the examiners' questions are the same point value. Further, approximately 20% of multiple choice questions are not scored; candidates have no reliable way to know which questions are not scored. Instead of speculating, focus on preparing for your next exam section.

General Rules Governing Examinations

1. Read carefully any paperwork assigned to you; make note of numbers for future reference; when it is requested, return it to the examiner. Only the examination number on your card shall be used on your exam for the purpose of identification. If a question calls for an answer involving a signature, **do not** use your own name or initials.

2. Use the exact same name as on your notice to schedule (NTS) when scheduling your appointment. Two pieces of identification are required; one must have a photo. The name on your identification must match your name on your notice to schedule **exactly.**

3. Seating during the exam is assigned by Prometric.

4. Supplies furnished by the Board remain its property and must be returned whether used or not.

5. Any reference during the examination to books or other matters or the exchange of information with other persons shall be considered misconduct sufficient to bar you from further participation in the examination.

6. The only aids most candidates are permitted to have in the examination room are supplied by the proctors. Wallets, briefcases, files, books, phones, watches, and other material brought to the examination site by candidates must be placed in a designated area before the start of the examination. Candidates get a key to a **small** storage locker. The test center is not responsible for lost items.

7. Do not leave your workstation during a testlet. Breaks are allowed only before starting and after finishing testlets.

8. Smoking is allowed only in designated areas away from the general examination area.

9. No telephone calls are permitted during the examination session.

10. Answers must be completed in the total time allotted for each exam section. The fixed time for each session must be observed by all candidates. One time warning is given five or ten minutes before the end of the exam. The testing software will end the test at the end of the specified time.

CPA Exam Week Checklist

What to have on hand for exam week:

1. CPA exam notice to schedule (NTS) and **two** forms of identification that exactly match your name on the NTS.

2. If traveling, your hotel confirmation and an alarm clock. (Don't rely on a hotel wake-up call.)

3. Cash and/or a major credit card.

4. An inexpensive watch (will not be allowed in the testing room) to facilitate your timely arrival at the exam site.

5. Comfortable clothing that can be loosened to suit varying temperatures. What is worn into the testing room must be worn throughout the testing period. Once at the testing center, you can remove a coat, for instance, before entering the testing room.

6. Appropriate review materials and tools for final reviews during the last days before the exam.

7. Healthy snack foods (will not be allowed in testing room).

Evenings before exam sections:

1. Read through your Bisk Education chapter outlines for the next day's section(s).

2. Eat lightly and monitor your intake of alcohol and caffeine. Get a good night's rest.

3. Do **not** try to cram. A brief review of your notes will help to focus your attention on important points and remind you that you are well prepared, but too much cramming can shatter your self-confidence. If you have reviewed conscientiously, you are already well-prepared for the CPA exam.

The morning of each exam section:

1. Eat a satisfying meal before your exam. It will be several hours before your next meal. Eat enough to ward off hunger, but not so much that you feel uncomfortable.

2. Dress appropriately. Wear layers you can loosen to suit varying temperatures in the room.

3. Arrive at the exam center at least 30 minutes early.

What to bring to the exam:

1. Appropriate identification (two forms, one with a picture) and notice to schedule (NTS). Your name on the identification must match your name on your NTS **exactly.** Use the exact same name when scheduling your appointment.

2. An inexpensive watch (to be left outside of the exam room) to ensure that you arrive at least **30 minutes** early.

3. Take only those articles that you need to get to and from the exam site. Avoid taking any articles that are not allowed in the exam room, especially valuable ones. There are **small** storage lockers outside of the testing room to hold purses, etc. The test center is not responsible for lost items. Watches, phones, pencils, purses, tissues, candy, and gum are not allowed in the exam room. Even medication is not allowed except by previous arrangement.

During the exam:

1. Always read all instructions and follow the directions of the exam administrator. If you don't understand any written or verbal instructions, or if something doesn't seem right, ASK QUESTIONS as allowed. Remember that an error in following directions could invalidate your **entire** exam.

2. Budget your time. Always keep track of the time and avoid getting too involved with one question.

3. **Satisfy the grader.** Remember that the grader cannot read your mind. You must explain every point in written communications. Focus on key words and concepts. Tell the grader what you know, don't **worry** about any points you don't know.

4. Answer every question, even if you must guess.

5. Use **all** the allotted time. If you finish a testlet early, go back and reconsider the more difficult questions.

6. Get up and stretch between testlets, if you feel sluggish. Walk around as allowed. Breathe deeply; focus your eyes on distant objects to avoid eye strain. Do some exercises to relax muscles in the face, neck, fingers, and back.

7. Do not leave your workstation. except between testlets. Leaving your workstation during a testlet may invalidate your score.

8. Take enough time to organize written communications. Well-organized responses will impress the grader.

9. Remember that you are well-prepared for the CPA exam, and that you can **expect to pass!** A confident attitude will help you overcome examination anxiety.

SECTION THREE: EXAMINATION GRADING ORIENTATION

The CPA exam is prepared and graded by the AICPA Examinations Division. It is administered by a commercial testing center, Prometric. Candidates register for the exam through various State Boards of Accountancy.

An understanding of the grading procedure will help you maximize grading points on the CPA exam. Remember that your objective is to pass the exam. You cannot afford to spend time on activities that will not affect your grade, or to ignore opportunities to increase your points. The following material abstracted from various editions of the AICPA's *Uniform CPA Examination Candidate Bulletin: Information for Applicants* booklet summarizes the important substantive aspects of the Uniform CPA Examination itself and the AICPA grading procedures.

Security

The examination is prepared and administered under tight security measures. The candidates' anonymity is preserved throughout the examination and grading process. Unusual similarities in answers among candidates are reported to the appropriate state boards.

Objective Questions

Objective questions consist of multiple-choice questions and objective format questions in simulations, which includes: yes-no, true-false, matching, and questions requiring a numerical response. Objective questions are machine graded. It is also important to understand that there is **no grade reduction** for incorrect responses to objective questions—your total objective question grade is determined solely by the number of correct answers. Thus, you **should answer every question.** If you do not know the answer, make an intelligent guess.

The point to remember is to avoid getting "bogged down" on one answer. Move along and answer all the questions. This helps you avoid leaving questions unanswered or panic-answering questions due to poor budgeting of test time.

Written Communications

Written communications also appear on the computer-based exam, as components of simulations. On the actual exam, written communications are graded partly by computer and partly by people. These responses are graded mainly for writing skills, but the content must answer the question that the examiners asked. Written communications questions are graded by CPAs and AICPA staff members, using the following procedures.

First Grading

The first grading is done by graders assigned to individual questions. For example, each written communication in the Regulation section will be graded by a different grader. A grader assigned to a single question becomes an expert in the subject matter of the question and in the evaluation of candidates' answers. Thus, grading is objective and uniform.

The purpose of the first grading is to separate the candidates' papers into three groups: obvious passes, marginal, and obvious failures.

Second Grading

Upon completion of the first grading, a second grading is done by reviewers. Obvious passes and failures are subjected to cursory reviews as part of the grading controls. Marginal papers receive an extensive review.

The graders who make the extensive reviews have had years of experience grading the CPA examination. They also have participated in the development of the grading bases and have access to item analysis for objective questions, identifying concepts as discriminating (those included by most candidates passing the exam) or as rudimentary (those included by candidates both passing and failing the exam). An important indicator of the competence of the candidate is whether grade points were earned chiefly from discriminating concepts or from rudimentary concepts.

Third Grading

After the papers have been through the second grading for all parts of the examination, the resultant grades are listed by candidate number and compared for consistency among subjects. For example, if a candidate passes two subjects and receives a marginal grade in a third, the marginal paper will receive a third grading in the hope that the candidate, now identified as possessing considerable competence, can have the paper raised to a passing grade by finding additional points for which to grant positive credit. This third grading is done by the section head or a reviewer who did not do the second grading.

Fourth Grading

The Director of Examinations applies a fourth grading to papers that have received the third grading but have grades that are inconsistent. The Director knows that the papers already have been subjected to three gradings, and that it would be difficult to find additional points for which the candidates should be given credit. Obviously, very few candidates are passed in this manner, but this fourth grading assures that marginal candidates receive every possible consideration.

Written Communication Example—Grading Guide

Remember, written communication responses are graded mainly for writing skills, but the content must answer the question that the examiners asked.

To address the content aspect of writing skills, consider the following factors. Through a grading of sample papers, a list of key concepts related to each question is accumulated. A key concept is an idea, thought, or option that can be clearly defined and identified. A candidate would not have to provide all the key concepts to get the maximum available points. Conversely, a candidate cannot receive more points even if s/he provides more than the standard number of key concepts for any particular written communication element.

FYI: While it is unlikely that any one written communication on the current computer-based exam would be worth so many points, the Bisk Education editors continue to use large point essays from previous exams for two main reasons. First, previous exams provide the best indication of the nature of the written communications on the computer-based exams. Second, the responses to written communication elements provide an alternate review of the content that candidates should know whether responding to multiple-choice or free-response questions.

To illustrate the grading procedure and the importance of using key concepts in your answers, we will develop a hypothetical grading guide for a question adapted from a past Regulation exam. We will assume that the entire question is worth 10 points.

Example 1—Sample Written Communication

Hardaway Lending, Inc., had a 4-year $800,000 callable loan to Superior Metals, Inc., outstanding. The loan was callable at the end of each year upon Hardaway's giving 60 days written notice. Two and one-half years remained of the four years. Hardaway reviewed the loan and decided that Superior Metals was no longer a prime lending risk and it, therefore, decided to call the loan. The required written notice was sent to and received by Superior 60 days prior to the expiration of the second year. Merriweather, Superior's chief executive officer and principal shareholder, requested Hardaway to continue the loan at least for another year. Hardaway agreed, provided that an acceptable commercial surety would guarantee $400,000 of the loan and Merriweather would personally guarantee repayment in full. These conditions were satisfied and the loan was permitted to continue.

The following year the loan was called and Superior defaulted. Hardaway released the commercial surety but retained its rights against Merriweather and demanded that Merriweather pay the full amount of the loan. Merriweather refused, asserting the following:

- There was no consideration for his promise. The loan was already outstanding and he personally received nothing.
- Hardaway must first proceed against Superior before it can collect from Merriweather.
- Hardaway had released the commercial surety, thereby releasing Merriweather.

Discuss the validity of each of Merriweather's assertions, setting forth reasons for any conclusions stated.

Now let's look at the unofficial answer. Notice that we have boldfaced the key concepts in the answer. Later, as we develop a grading guide for the answer, you will see the importance of using key concepts to tailor your answer to parallel the grading guide.

Solution: Consideration/Liability of Debtor and Surety

The **first two defenses** asserted by Merriweather are **invalid**. The **third defense** is **partially valid**.

Consideration on Hardaway's part consisted of **foregoing the right to call the Superior Metals loan**. The fact that the loan was already outstanding is irrelevant. By permitting the loan to remain outstanding for an additional year instead of calling it, Hardaway **relinquished a legal right**, which is **adequate consideration** for Merriweather's **surety promise**. **Consideration need not pass to the surety**; in fact, it usually primarily benefits the principal debtor.

There is **no requirement** that the creditor first proceed against the debtor before it can proceed against the surety, unless the surety undertaking **expressly provides such a condition**. Basic to the usual surety undertaking is the **right of the creditor to proceed immediately against the surety**. Essentially, that is the reason for the surety.

Hardaway's **release of the commercial surety from its $400,000 surety undertaking partially released Merriweather**. The release had the legal effect of **impairing Merriweather's right of contribution against its co-surety** (the commercial surety). Thus, Merriweather is **released to the extent of 1/3 [$400,000 (commercial surety's guarantee) / $1,200,000 (the aggregate of the co-sureties' guarantees)] of the principal amount ($800,000), or $266,667**.

Example 2—Grading Guide for Written Communication

The grading guide consists of a list of the key concepts relevant to the question, both in key word form and in detailed phrases. Concept may be assigned point value. Points also are given on many questions for neatness and clarity of answer (including the use of proper formats, schedules, etc.). A hypothetical grading guide for our sample question follows.

STATE ____________________
CANDIDATE NO. ____________

POINTS	KEY WORD CONCEPTS
2	Consideration was foregoing the right to call the loan
1	Irrelevant that the loan was outstanding
2	Consideration need not pass to the surety
1	No requirement to proceed against the creditor first
2	Hardaway's release of the commercial surety partly releases Merriweather
2	Ratio of partial release is 1/3 of $800,000
10	

GRADE CONVERSION CHART: POINTS TO GRADE

POINTS	1	2 3	4 5	6 7	8 9 10
GRADE	1	2	3	4	5

Concepts to Consider

First, the answer is written in standard English, with clear, concise sentences and short paragraphs. A simple listing of key words is **unacceptable**; the concepts and their interrelationships must be logically presented.

Secondly, remember to follow instructions. If the instructions are to write a memo or letter, your response should be a memo or letter, respectively.

Thirdly, remember that while an unofficial answer represents an acceptable solution to a question, this is not to say that alternative answers are not considered, or that other answers are not equally as acceptable. During the accumulation of grading bases, many concepts are added to the original "correct answer." Additionally, a response that is near the passing mark receives a third (and perhaps fourth) grading, at which time individual consideration is given to the merits of each answer.

A grading guide similar to the one in Example 2 is attached to every candidate's work, with grading bases for each question. On the first grading, answers may be scanned first, then read carefully. The process is repeated by the second grader and subsequent graders if necessary (i.e., borderline responses).

The unofficial answer closely conforms to the grading guide, making the grader's task simple. In turn, the unofficial answer also conforms to the format of the question. That is, each answer is numbered and lettered to correspond to the requirements. This should be your standard format.

Parenthetically, we should mention that—to the extent available—the Bisk Education CPA Review written communications and problems are solved using the unofficial AICPA answers. Thus, you have ample opportunity to accustom yourself to the favored answer format.

Research Questions—Accountant's Responsibilities

For candidates with a Notice to Schedule (NTS), the AICPA & NASBA offer **free** six-month online subscriptions to professional audit and accounting literature through www.cpa-exam.org. The package includes AICPA Professional Standards, FASB Current Text, and FASB Original Pronouncements. The cost to include these copyrighted databases in Bisk Education's CPA Ready software is prohibitive and eligible candidates can obtain these subscriptions for free; consequently, these databases are not included in the CPA Ready software.

Expect all REG simulations on the CPA exam to include a research element. This type of element probably will be about 2% of the point value for an exam section with simulations. (Initially, the BEC exam section will not have simulations.) Candidates unfamiliar with the professional standards are advised to read the "How Professional Standards Is Organized" portion of the professional literature.

The research element of the simulation is completed when the candidate narrows the search (to answer the question asked) down to a paragraph reference. In other words, the paragraph or its reference is the answer that the examiners seek. The candidate doesn't provide commentary or conclusions. Some exam sections require candidates to transfer the reference number to the answer field; others require candidates to transfer the guidance. The examiner's "transfer-to-answer" feature works like "cut-and-paste" features common in word processors and spreadsheets, but doesn't allow for subsequent modification.

Candidates who would like more practice with the professional literature than is provided by the research questions in the Bisk materials and the AICPA tutorial might take some of the references from the Bisk text material and questions and locate them in the codification of standards. If you do this, use at least one reference from Bisk Chapters 32 and 33. This also will help you become familiar with the standards.

In their current form, research questions merely are objective questions. The only response is a reference to the professional literature. The candidate doesn't provide any commentary or analysis of the guidance. Please note the following statements from the FAQ pages of the AICPA exam website (www.cpa-exam.org).

> CPA candidates are expected to know how to use common spreadsheet and word processing functions, including writing formulae for spreadsheets. They must also have the ability to use a four-function calculator or a spreadsheet to perform standard financial calculations. In addition, candidates will be asked to use online authoritative literature. Many of the question types used in the simulations are based on familiar computer interface controls (e.g., text entry, mouse clicks, highlighting, copy and pasting). In order to become familiar with the electronic tools provided for research questions, further practice may be required.
>
> All CPA candidates are strongly encouraged to review the exam tutorial at http://www.cpa-exam.org/lrc/exam_tutorial.html. The tutorial explains the design and operation of the computer-based test, and reviews the types of questions and responses used in the new exam. Sample tests that contain a few sample multiple-choice questions and a sample simulation for each applicable section (BEC will not contain simulations at launch) will be available at www.cpa-exam.org. The sample tests will use the same software that is used for the operational examination. Neither the tutorial nor the sample test will be available at the test centers.

Please note the tree control on the left-hand side of the AICPA's website. Under AICPA Online Publications, you will find AICPA Literature, under which you will find Professional Standards. Under this last option, you will find the following table of contents (note the abbreviations). If you are using a printed codification, you will find a similar table of contents.

How Professional Standards Is Organized
Cross-References to SASs
U.S. Auditing Standards [AU]
Attestation Standards [AT]
Public Company Accounting Oversight Board [PC]
Accounting and Review Services [AR]
Code of Professional Conduct [ET]
Bylaws of the American Institute of Certified Public Accountants [BL]
Consulting Service [CS]
Quality Control [QC]
Peer Review [PR]
Tax Services [TS]
Personal Financial Planning [PFP]
Continuing Professional Education [CPE]

Candidates cannot avoid the research merely by answering the question; they must provide the reference to the authoritative literature that answers the question. The search can be made either by using the table of contents feature or by using the search engine and Boolean operators. Most candidates will find the table of contents easier to use than a Boolean search, once they become familiar with the professional literature database.

The three Boolean operators are OR, AND, and NOT. Boolean operators can be combined to refine searches. For example, the following parameters would find information on letters to a client's attorney inquiring about litigation, claims, and assessments: (attorney OR lawyer) AND (letter OR inquiry). If you get too many or too few results from a search, refine your search parameters until you find what you need. The exam doesn't limit candidates from repeating searches with refined parameters. A review of Boolean operators is provided here.

A search using "accounting OR auditing" will find all documents containing either the word "accounting" or the word "auditing." OR typically is used to search for terms that are used as synonyms, such as "management" and "client." As more terms are combined in an OR search, more documents are included in the results.

A search using "accounting AND auditing" will find all documents containing both the word "accounting" and the word "auditing." All other things being equal, a search using AND typically will find fewer documents than a search using OR, but more than a search using NOT. As more terms are combined in an AND search, fewer documents are included in the results.

A search using "accounting NOT auditing" will find all documents containing the word "accounting" except those that also contain the word "auditing." All other things being equal, a search using NOT typically will find the fewest documents. As more terms are combined in a NOT search, fewer documents are included in the results.

Research Question Example

What authoritative reference provides guidance on a member of the profession who permits another to make materially false and misleading entries in the records of an entity?

If you have difficulty with Boolean searches, consider using the table of contents instead. Research is a very instance-specific activity; search skills are developed with practice. Any particular search will have little value for you when you are confronted with what likely will be a different research question on the exam. Use the process illustrated here to refine your search process; do not memorize the answer to this particular example.

Avoid using a search phrase such as "guidance on materially false and misleading entries in records." Anything that you find in the standards will be guidance; furthermore, the term "guidance" might not be in the reference that you seek. Also, eliminate words such as "on" and "in" unless you are seeking an exact phrase that you are sure includes them.

This leaves "materially false misleading entries records." Typically, search engines default to the Boolean search connector "OR" for all words, which probably would give us many irrelevant hits with this phrase, so modify it to "materially" AND "false" AND "statements."

Why not include "misleading" in this search phrase? If "false" is in the reference, "misleading" probably will be there also. If "misleading" is in the reference without "materially" that reference is likely irrelevant. In other words, the word "misleading" does little to narrow the search. However, if there are too few hits using "materially" AND "false" AND "statements," try ("material" AND "false" AND "statements") OR ("materially" AND "misleading" AND "statements"). The standards are not always consistent with their use of words; the guidance might use both "material" and "materially."

Once you have narrowed the responses to a few hits (responses to a search) read through the most likely ones to determine which answers the question at hand.

Once you find the guidance, determine the reference from your selection on the Professional Standards menu. (In the printed version of the codification, the section numbers are in the page margins, usually the footer.)

Please note the following note from the top of the page of the Section 500 guidance: AICPA Literature/ Professional Standards/Code of Professional Conduct [ET]/ET Section 500 - Other Responsibilities and Practices, followed by ET Section 501, Acts Discreditable. This is how you know that the section number is 501.

The rest of the reference comes from the paragraph number. For instance, the paragraph labeled ".05" reads as follows. (In the printed version of the codification, each paragraph also has a paragraph number.)

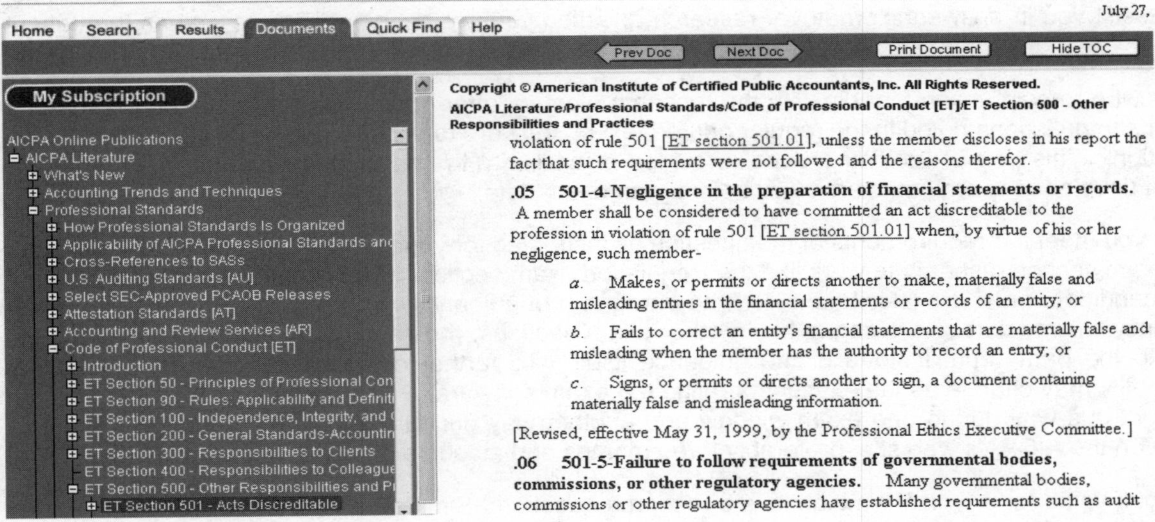

Copyright © American Institute of Certified Public Accountants, Inc. All Rights Reserved.

AICPA Literature/Professional Standards/Code of Professional Conduct [ET]/ET Section 500 - Other Responsibilities and Practices

violation of rule 501 [ET section 501.01], unless the member discloses in his report the fact that such requirements were not followed and the reasons therefor.

.05 **501-4-Negligence in the preparation of financial statements or records.** A member shall be considered to have committed an act discreditable to the profession in violation of rule 501 [ET section 501.01] when, by virtue of his or her negligence, such member-

a. Makes, or permits or directs another to make, materially false and misleading entries in the financial statements or records of an entity; or

b. Fails to correct an entity's financial statements that are materially false and misleading when the member has the authority to record an entry; or

c. Signs, or permits or directs another to sign, a document containing materially false and misleading information.

[Revised, effective May 31, 1999, by the Professional Ethics Executive Committee.]

.06 **501-5-Failure to follow requirements of governmental bodies, commissions, or other regulatory agencies.** Many governmental bodies, commissions or other regulatory agencies have established requirements such as audit

Response: To summarize, the reference for the preceding paragraph is ET section 501.05, 501-4 or ET §501.05, 501-4.

Research Questions—Federal Taxation

The AICPA has not specified the exact taxation database; however, the AICPA has stated that the database provided during a Regulation simulation will:

- Be used by candidates in answering the research element
- Include certain portions of the Internal Revenue Code (IRC)
- Include all necessary information to complete the research element

CPA exam candidates can get a free six-month subscription to professional literature used in the computerized CPA examination; however, this online package only includes accounting and auditing literature. The AICPA does not provide exam candidates with access to the IRC or any portion thereof to be included in the taxation database used for the CPA exam. Nor have the examiners specified a commercially available database as the one it will use. Therefore, candidates have no way of learning, before the exam, the exact contents or search functionality of the database. This makes preparing for the research element of a REG simulation slightly more challenging than for the FAR or AUD exam section, but there are still ways that candidates can and should prepare.

The search engine functionality of the taxation database used on the CPA examination is likely to resemble the functionality in the fee-based subscription databases used most widely by tax professionals. If you cannot gain access to a fee-based subscription database, you can access and search the IRC as part of the United States Code from good, free Internet editions. A good one to use is the electronic edition of the United States Code posted free on the Internet by the House of Representatives at: http://uscode.house.gov. Select the "search" feature once at this site. The IRC is Title 26 of the United States Code, so use this information in the Title field to limit your search to the IRC.

Whatever resource you use, the important thing is that you become comfortable with finding tax citations using appropriate search terms. It is not important that you have the most cutting edge tax research software to practice this basic skill.

Additional Research Comments

The editors strongly recommend that you practice answering research questions on your own. Bear in mind, given the vast numbers of questions that the examiners could ask, it is highly unlikely that you will encounter any one particular research question on your exam. The skills that you develop while answering these questions, however, will assist you in answering whatever research question you get on your exam as well as throughout your career.

For candidates who remain uncomfortable with the research element after other exercises, find the paragraphs and explanations to questions noted in the regular printed text or software to either a printed or electronic version of the codification. This sort of "poking around" provides a familiarity that facilitates research. As this easy familiarity is not developed overnight, start it well before your exam date.

Make sure that you meet the requirements of the question as instructed for your exam. Don't expect the Auditing & Attestation exam section research to work like the Regulation exam section. For instance, in some sections of the exam, the candidate must "transfer-to-answer" the paragraph of guidance. The software will not permit you to transfer-to-answer only part of a paragraph. In other exam sections, the candidate must transfer-to-answer the reference to the paragraph, instead of the guidance itself. To further complicate matters, the research feature functionality may change as the examiners refine the exam software. For instance, the Regulation exam section may work one way during one exam window and another way during another exam window. Practice with the tutorial on the AICPA's web site, preferably three months and a couple of weeks before your exam.

One-tenth of point value for a typical simulation is a research question. Simulations are about 30% of the point value. For most candidates, these are relatively easy points. Don't worry if you get a difficult research question on your exam. Move on after a few minutes.

Research skills are not something you can acquire instantly. If you don't have them already, you must practice these skills. Start familiarizing yourself with the professional standards and practicing research well before your exam date. For instance, as you encounter references in the text and question explanations, find those references in the professional standards.

Grading Implications for CPA Candidates

To summarize this review of the AICPA's grading procedure, we can offer the following conclusions that will help you to **satisfy the grader** and maximize your score:

1. Attempt an answer on every question.
2. Respond directly to the requirements of the questions.
3. Use schedules and formats favored by the AICPA examiners.
4. Answer all requirements.
5. Develop a **Solutions Approach™** to each question type.
6. Written communication question elements: Label your solutions parallel to the requirements. Offer reasons for your conclusions. Emphasize key words by underlining them. Separate grading concepts into individual sentences or paragraphs. Use of a well-chosen example is an easy way of expressing an understanding of the subject or supporting a conclusion. Do **not** present your answer in outline format. Note that the editors strongly recommend **against** cutting-and-pasting excerpts from the professional literature provided for research questions.
7. Allocate your examination time based on AICPA point value, if provided.

SECTION FOUR: THE SOLUTIONS APPROACH™

The **Bisk Education Solutions Approach™** is an efficient, systematic method of organizing and solving questions found on the CPA exam. Remember that all the knowledge in the world is worthless unless you can communicate it to others. Conversely, a little knowledge can go a long way if you use a proper approach. The **Solutions Approach™** was developed by our Editorial Board in 1971; all subsequently developed copies trace their roots from the original "Approach" that we formulated. Our **Solutions Approach™** and grader orientation skills, when properly developed, can be worth at least 10 to 15 points for most candidates. These 10 to 15 points often make the difference between passing and failing.

We will suggest a number of steps for deriving a solution that will help maximize your grade on the exam. Although you should remember the important steps in our suggested approach, don't be afraid to adapt these steps to your own taste and requirements. When you work the questions at the conclusion of each chapter, make sure you use your variation of the **Solutions Approach™**. It is also important for you to attempt to pattern the organization and format of your written solution to the unofficial answer reprinted after the text of the questions. However, DO NOT CONSULT THE UNOFFICIAL ANSWER UNTIL YOU FINISH THE QUESTION. The worst thing you can do is look at an old question and, before answering it, turn to the answer without working the problem. This will build false confidence and provide **no** skills in developing a **Solutions Approach™**. Therefore, in order to derive the maximum number of points from a written communication, you should **first** apply the **Solutions Approach™** to reading and answering the question, and **secondly**, write an answer using an organization and format identical to that which would be used by the AICPA in writing the unofficial answer to that essay question.

Solutions Approach™ for Written Communications

Our **six steps** are as follows:

1. Scan the text of the question for an overview of the subject area and content of the question.
2. Study the question requirements slowly and thoroughly. Note portions of the requirements on your scratch paper as needed.
3. Visualize the unofficial answer format based on the requirements of the question.
4. Carefully study the text of the question. Note important data on your scratch paper.
5. Outline the solution in key words and phrases. Be sure to respond to the requirements, telling the grader only what s/he needs to know. You must explain the reasons for your conclusions.
6. Write the solution in the proper format based upon your key word outline. Write concise complete sentences. Do not forget to proofread and edit your solution, but don't waste time on formatting your response.

Written Communication Question Example

To illustrate the **Solutions Approach™** for essay questions, we consider a question from a past examination.

Example 3—Sample Written Communication

Debco Electronics Inc. sells various brands of computer equipment to retail and business customers. An audit of Debco's Year 1 financial statements has revealed the following transactions:

- On September 1, Year 1, a Debco salesperson orally agreed to sell Rapid Computers, Inc. eight TMI computers for $11,000, to be delivered on October 15, Year 1. Rapid sells computers to the general public. The Debco salesperson sent Rapid a signed confirmation of the sales agreement. Rapid received the confirmation on September 3, but did not respond to it. On October 15, Year 1, Debco tendered delivery of the computers to Rapid. Rapid refused to accept delivery, claiming it had no obligation to buy the computers because it had not signed a contract with Debco.

- On October 12, Year 1, Debco mailed TMI Computers, Inc. a signed purchase order for certain specified computers for delivery by November 30, Year 1. The purchase order also stated the following: This purchase order will not be withdrawn on or before October 31, Year 1. You must accept by that date or we will assume you cannot meet our terms. Ship F.O.B.—our loading dock.

  TMI received the purchase order on October 15, Year 1.

- On October 25, Debco mailed the following signed correspondence to TMI, which TMI received on October 29:

  Cancel our October 12, Year 1, purchase order. We have found a better price on the computers.

- On October 31, Year 1, TMI mailed the following signed correspondence to Debco, which Debco received on November 3:

  We have set aside the computers you ordered and turned down other offers for them. Therefore, we will ship the computers to you for delivery by November 30, Year 1, F.O.B.—your loading dock with payment terms 2/10; net 30.

  There were no further communications between TMI and Debco.

  TMI shipped the computers on November 15, and Debco received them on November 29. Debco refused to accept delivery. In justifying its refusal to accept delivery, Debco claimed the following:

- Its October 25 correspondence prevented the formation of a contract between Debco and TMI;

- TMI's October 31 correspondence was not an effective acceptance because it was not received by Debco until November 3;

- TMI's October 31 correspondence was not an effective acceptance because it added payment terms to Debco's purchase order.

Debco, Rapid, and TMI are located in a jurisdiction that has adopted the UCC.

a. State whether Rapid's claim is correct and give the reasons for your conclusions.

b. State whether Debco's claims are correct with regard to the transaction involving TMI and give the reasons for your conclusions.

Applying the Solutions Approach™

Let's look at the steps you go through to arrive at your solution:

In **Step 1**, you scan the question. Do not read thoroughly, simply get an overview of the subject area and content of the question. You notice the question addresses a UCC sale of goods consisting of several transactions.

In **Step 2**, you study the question requirements thoroughly. **Part a** addresses Rapid's claim, while **Part b** refers to the various claims made by Debco. Note key phrases and words.

In **Step 3**, you visualize the format of your solution. The solution will be in paragraph form. **Part a** will discuss Rapid's claim, whether it is correct, and why. **Part b** will discuss Debco's claims (note that there are several), whether they are correct, and why. It will be important to identify each of these claims in the text of the question to aid in organizing your thoughts.

In **Step 4**, you carefully study the text of the question, given the requirements you want to satisfy (e.g., read the question carefully, noting Rapid's claim and each of Debco's three claims). You should to note important information.

In **Step 5**, you outline your answer in keyword form. This will include an answer of "correct" or "incorrect" for the claim in **Part a** and each of the claims in **Part b** plus additional key concepts you want to include in your final answer. In your exam preparation, as you work Regulation written communications, notice that sometimes you are not asked to make a decision or reach a conclusion, but rather you are asked to identify and discuss all important factors in the situation.

Outline Answer

a. Rapid's claim—incorrect
 - UCC Statute of Frauds is satisfied for oral contract between two merchants if
   - Confirmed in writing
   - Within reasonable period of time
   - Signed by the party sending it
   - Received by the other party
 - Both parties are bound unless receive written objection within 10 days

b. Debco's first claim—incorrect
 - Purchase order is firm offer
   - Debco is merchant
   - Purchase order is in writing and signed
   - States will not be withdrawn for time specified

 Debco's second claim—incorrect
 - Acceptance effective when dispatched (mailed)

 Debco's third claim—incorrect
 - UCC provides acceptance will form a contract
   - If definite and timely expression
   - Even if terms are different
   - Unless acceptance is made conditional on accepting the different terms

In **Step 6**, you write your solution in a format similar to the unofficial answer. Notice how clear and concise the AICPA unofficial answers are. There is no doubt as to their decision or the reasoning supporting the decision. Notice also how they answer each requirement separately and in the same order as in the question. Be sure to proofread and edit your solution.

In general, each requirement in Business Law is designed to elicit from you at least one rule of law which is different from any other rule of law covered by any other part of the question. Finally, if you discuss two sides of an issue, be sure to indicate that this is what you are doing so that it does not appear that you have inconsistencies in you answer.

Example 4—Unofficial Answer

a. **Rapid's claim** is **incorrect**. Both **Debco and Rapid** are **merchants under** the **UCC** because they both deal in the type of goods involved in the transaction (computers).

The UCC provides that a **confirmation satisfies** the **UCC Statute of Frauds**, if an **oral contract between merchants** is:

- **Confirmed in writing** within a **reasonable period of time**, and
- The confirmation is **signed by the party sending it** and **received by the other party**.

Both parties are bound even though the party receiving the confirmation fails to sign it. This is correct **unless** the party receiving the confirmation submits a **written objection within 10 days of receipt**. Rapid will be bound even though it did not sign the confirmation because no written objection was made.

b. **Debco's first claim**, that its October 25 correspondence prevented the formation of a contract, is **incorrect**. Debco's **October 12 purchase order** will be regarded as a **firm offer** under the UCC because:

- Debco is a **merchant**.
- The **purchase order is in writing and signed**.
- The purchase order **states** that it will **not be withdrawn for the time specified**.

Because Debco's October 12 purchase order is considered a firm offer, **Debco cannot revoke** it, and its October 25 **attempt to do so is ineffective**.

Debco's second claim, that TMI's October 31 correspondence is not an effective acceptance because it was not received until November 3, is **incorrect.** An **acceptance of an offer** is **effective when dispatched** (in this case, when **mailed**), provided that an **appropriate mode of communication** is used. The UCC provides that an offer shall be construed as inviting acceptance in any manner and by any medium reasonable in the circumstances. In this case, Debco made its **offer by mail**, which, if **adequately addressed** with **proper postage** affixed, would be considered a reasonable manner and medium for acceptance. As a result, TMI's acceptance was effective when mailed on October 31.

Debco's third claim, that TMI's acceptance is not effective because it added payment terms to Debco's offer, is also **incorrect**. The **UCC** provides that a **definite and timely expression** of **acceptance** of an offer **will form a contract, even if** the **terms** of the acceptance are **different** from those in the offer, **unless acceptance is expressly made conditional on accepting the different terms**. Therefore, TMI's October 31 correspondence, which expressly stated that TMI would ship the computers ordered by Debco, was an effective acceptance, and a contract was formed despite the fact that TMI added payment terms.

Solutions Approach™ for Objective Questions

The **Solutions Approach™** is also adaptable to objective questions. We recommend the following framework:

1. Read the "Instructions to Candidates" section on your particular exam to confirm that the AICPA's standard is the same. Generally, your objective portion points will be determined by the number of correct answers with no penalty for incorrect answers.

2. Read the question carefully, noting exactly what the question is asking. Negative requirements are easily missed. Note key words and note when the requirement is an exception (e.g., "except for...," or "which of the following does **not**..."). Perform any intermediate calculations necessary to the determination of the correct answer.

3. Anticipate the answer by covering the possible answers and seeing if you **know** the correct answer.

4. Read the answers given.

5. Select the best alternative. Very often, one or two possible answers will be clearly incorrect. Sometimes, more than one answer is a correct statement, but only one such statement answers the question asked. Of the other alternatives, be sure to select the alternative that **best answers the question asked**. Mark the correct answer.

6. After completing all of the individual questions in a testlet, **go back** and double check your answers—making sure the answer and sequence are correct. READ THE INSTRUCTIONS CAREFULLY.

7. Answer the questions in order. This is a proven, systematic approach to objective test taking. You generally are limited to a maximum of 2 to 2½ minutes per multiple choice question—or even less time. Under no circumstances should you allow yourself to fall behind schedule. If a question is difficult or long, be sure you remain cognizant of the time you are using. If after a minute or so you feel that it is too costly to continue on with a particular question, select the letter answer you tentatively feel is the best answer and go to the next question, noting the question number on your scratch paper. Return to these questions at a later time and attempt to finally answer them when you have time for more consideration. If you cannot find a better answer when you return to the question, use your preliminary answer because your first impressions are often correct. However, as you read other question(s), if something about these subsequent questions or answers jogs your memory, return to the previous tentatively answered question(s) and make a note of the idea for later consideration (time permitting).

A simulation includes a group of objective questions based on one hypothetical situation. A simulation is particularly challenging format for many candidates. In this case, you should consider skimming all the related questions (but not answer possibilities) before you begin answering, since an overall view of the problem will guide you in the work you do.

Note also that many incorrect answer choices are based on the erroneous application of one or more items in the text of the question. Thus, it is extremely important to **anticipate** the answer before you read the alternatives. Otherwise, you may be easily persuaded by an answer choice that is formulated through the incorrect use of the given data.

Let's consider a multiple choice question adapted from a past examination.

Example 5—Sample Objective Question

Migrane Financial does a wide variety of lending. It provides funds to manufacturers, middlemen, retailers, consumers, and homeowners. In all instances, it intends to create a security interest in the loan transaction it enters into. To which of the following will Article 9 (Secured Transactions) of the Uniform Commercial Code **not** apply?

a. A second mortgage on the borrower's home
b. An equipment lease
c. The sale of accounts
d. Field warehousing

Applying the Solutions Approach™

Let's look at the steps you should go through to arrive at your objective question solution.

In **Step 1**, you must carefully read the "**Instructions**" that precede your particular objective CPA exam portion.

In **Step 2**, you must read the question and its requirements carefully. Look out for questions that require you to provide those options **not** applicable, **not** true, etc…

In **Step 3**, you must anticipate the correct answer **after** reading the question **but before** reading the possible answers.

In **Step 4**, you must read the answer carefully and select the alternative that best answers the question asked. Ideally, the best alternative will immediately present itself because it roughly or exactly corresponds with the answer you anticipated before looking at the other possible choices.

In **Step 5**, you select the best alternative. If there are two close possibilities, make sure you select the **best** one in light of the **facts** and **requirements** of the question.

In **Step 6**, you must make sure you accurately mark the **correct answer** in the proper sequence. If **anything** seems wrong, stop, go back and double check your answer sheet. As a fail safe mechanism, circle the correct letter on the exam sheet first, before you move it to the answer sheet.

In **Step 7**, you must make sure you answer the questions on the answer sheet in order, with due regard to time constraints.

Example 6—Unofficial Answer

Solution: The answer is (a). Uniform Commercial Code (UCC) 9-109 states that the UCC applies to any transaction intended to create a security interest in **personal property** or **fixtures**. Expressly excluded from Article 9 UCC coverage are liens (mortgages) on real property. Answers (b), (c), and (d) are all forms of personal property, whereas answer (a) is clearly a real property interest.

Benefits of the Solutions Approach™

The **Solutions Approach™** may seem cumbersome the first time you attempt it; candidates frequently have a tendency to write as they think. Such a haphazard approach often results in a disorganized answer. The Solutions Approach™ will help you write a solution that parallels the question requirements. It also will help you recall information under the pressure of the exam. The technique assists you in directing your thoughts toward the information required for the answer. Without the Solutions Approach™, you are apt to become distracted or confused by details that are irrelevant to the answer. Finally, the Solutions Approach™ is a **faster** way to answer exam questions. You will not waste time on false starts or rewrites. The approach may seem time-consuming at first, but as you become comfortable using it, you will see that it actually saves time and results in a better answer.

We urge you to give the **Solutions Approach™** a good try by using it throughout your review. As you practice, you may adapt or modify it to your own preferences and requirements. The important thing is to develop a system so that you do not approach exam questions with a storehouse of knowledge that you can not put down on paper.

SECTION FIVE: CONTENT SPECIFICATION OUTLINE

The AICPA Board of Examiners has developed a **Content Specification Outline** for each section of the exam to be tested. These outlines list the areas, groups, and topics to be tested and indicate the approximate percentage of the total test score devoted to each area. The content of the examination is based primarily on results of national studies of public accounting practice and the evaluation of CPA practitioners and educators. Exposure drafts of new content and skills specification outlines were issued in 2008. A final practice analysis report is scheduled, tentatively, to be issued in December 2010.

REGULATION

I. Ethics and Professional and Legal Responsibilities (15% - 20%)

A. Code of Professional Conduct

B. Proficiency, Independence, and Due Care

C. Ethics and Responsibilities in Tax Practice

D. Licensing and Disciplinary Systems Imposed by the Profession and State Regulatory Bodies

E. Legal Responsibilities and Liabilities

1. Common Law Liability to Clients and Third Parties
2. Federal Statutory Liability

F. Privileged Communications and Confidentiality

II. Business Law (20% - 25%)

A. Agency

1. Formation and Termination
2. Duties and Authority of Agents and Principals
3. Liabilities and Authority of Agents and Principals

B. Contracts

1. Formation
2. Performance
3. Third-Party Assignments
4. Discharge, Breach, and Remedies

C. Debtor-Creditor Relationships

1. Rights, Duties, and Liabilities of Debtors, Creditors, and Guarantors
2. Bankruptcy

D. Government Regulation of Business

1. Federal Securities Acts
2. Other Government Regulation (Antitrust, Pension and Retirement Plans, Union and Employee Relations, and Legal Liability for Payroll and Social Security Taxes)

E. Uniform Commercial Code

1. Negotiable Instruments and Letters of Credit
2. Sales
3. Secured Transactions
4. Documents of Title and Title Transfer

F. Real Property, Including Insurance

III. Federal Tax Procedures and Accounting Issues (8% - 12%)

A. Federal Tax Procedures

B. Accounting Periods

C. Accounting Methods Including Cash, Accrual, Percentage of Completion, Completed Contract, and Installment Sales

D. Inventory Methods, Including Uniform Capitalization Rules

IV. Federal Taxation of Property Transactions (8% - 12%)

A. Types of Assets

B. Basis of Assets

C. Depreciation and Amortization

D. Taxable and Nontaxable Sales and Exchanges

E. Income, Deductions, Capital Gains and Capital Losses, Including Sales and Exchanges of Business Property and Depreciation Recapture

V. Federal Taxation—Individuals (12% - 18%)

A. Gross Income—Inclusions and Exclusions

B. Reporting of Items from Pass-Through Entities, Including Passive Activity Losses

C. Adjustments and Deductions to Arrive at Taxable Income

D. Filing Status and Exemptions

E. Tax Computations, Credits, and Penalties

F. Alternative Minimum Tax

G. Retirement Plans

H. Estate and Gift Taxation, Including Transfers Subject to the Gift Tax, Annual Exclusion, and Items Includible and Deductible From Gross Estate

VI. Federal Taxation—Entities (22% - 28%)

A. Similarities and Distinctions in Tax Reporting Among Such Entities as Sole Proprietorships, General and Limited Partnerships, Subchapter C Corporations, Subchapter S Corporations, Limited Liability Companies, and Limited Liability Partnerships

B. Subchapter C Corporations

1. Determination of Taxable Income and Loss, and Reconciliation of Book Income to Taxable Income
2. Tax Computations, Credits, and Penalties, Including Alternative Minimum Tax
3. Net Operating Losses
4. Consolidated Returns
5. Entity/Owner Transactions, Including Contributions and Distributions

C. Subchapter S Corporations

1. Eligibility and Election
2. Determination of Ordinary Income, Separately Stated Items, and Reconciliation of Book Income to Taxable Income
3. Basis of Shareholder's Interest
4. Entity/Owner Transactions, Including Contributions and Liquidating and Nonliquidating Distributions
5. Built-in Gains Tax

D. Partnerships

1. Determination of Ordinary Income, Separately Stated Items, and Reconciliation of Book Income to Taxable Income
2. Basis of Partner's Interest and Basis of Assets Contributed to the Partnership
3. Partnership and Partner Elections
4. Partner Dealing With Own Partnership
5. Treatment of Partnership Liabilities
6. Distribution of Partnership Assets
7. Ownership Changes and Liquidation and Termination of Partnership

E. Trusts

1. Types of Trusts
2. Income and Deductions
3. Determination of Beneficiary's Share of Taxable Income

APPENDIX C
WRITING SKILLS

CONTENTS

INTRODUCTION

Before skipping this appendix, review at least the following writing samples and the "Writing an Answer to an Exam Question" starting on page C-5. Be sure to take the Diagnostic Quiz on C-8.

An assessment of written communication skills is incorporated into simulations. The written communication elements require candidates to write memoranda, letters to clients, or other communications an entry-level CPA would write on the job. Simulations with written communication elements currently are presented in the Financial Accounting & Reporting, Auditing & Attestation, and Regulation exam sections, but not the Business Environment & Concepts (BEC) exam section. The examiners have yet to announce an implementation date for the current plan to have communication elements in the BEC exam section only.

For this element, candidates read a description of a situation and then write an appropriate document relating to it. The instructions will state in what form the document should be presented and its focus. The candidate's response should provide the correct information in writing that is clear, complete, and professional. Only those writing samples that are in your own words and responsive to the topic will be graded. Credit will not be given for a response that is off-topic or offers advice that clearly is incorrect.

Constructed responses will be scored holistically. Scores will be based on three general writing criteria: organization, development, and expression.

1. **Organization:** The document's structure, ordering of ideas, and linking of one idea to another:

   Overview/thesis statement
   Unified paragraphs (topic and supporting sentences)
   Transitions and connectives

2. **Development:** The document's supporting evidence/information to clarify thoughts:

   Details
   Definitions
   Examples
   Rephrasing

3. **Expression:** The document's use of conventional standards of business English:

   Grammar (sentence construction, subject/verb agreement, pronouns, modifiers)
   Punctuation (final, comma)
   Word usage (incorrect, imprecise language)
   Capitalization
   Spelling

WRITING SKILLS SAMPLES

The following questions taken from past exams are answered in various ways to illustrate good, fair, and poor writing skills.

Essex Company has a compensation plan for future vacations for its employees. What conditions must be met for Essex to accrue compensation for future vacations? FAR Problem—From Chapter 7—Liabilities

Good: Essex must accrue compensation for future vacations if all of the following criteria are met. Essex's obligation relating to employees' rights to receive compensation for future vacations is attributable to employees' services already rendered. The obligation relates to rights that vest or accumulate. Payment of the vacation benefits is probable. The amount can be reasonably estimated.

Explanation: This essay is coherent, concise, and well organized. The first sentence uses the wording of the question to introduce the elements of the answer. Each point is then made clearly and concisely. There are no unnecessary words or elements. The language and vocabulary are appropriate, and there are no mistakes in grammar or spelling.

Fair: In order for Essex to accrue compensation for future vacations, they must attribute their obligation to employees services already rendered, recognize that the obligation relates to vested and accumulated rights, and that payment is probable and the amount can be reasonably estimated.

Explanation: This passage is also coherent and concise; however, it lacks the clarity and detail of the previous answer. The language is appropriate, but the grammatical construction is somewhat weak.

Poor: It is based on accrual. The employees must have vested or accumulated rights. They must be able to estimate amounts of compensation and their payment. Vested rights means that the employer must pay the employees even if he is fired or quits.

Explanation: This answer is so poorly worded and disorganized as to be virtually incoherent. There are also some grammar mistakes. The final sentence is additional information but not necessary to answer the question.

PARAGRAPHS

The kind of writing you do for the CPA exam is called **expository writing** (writing in which something is explained in straightforward terms). Expository writing uses the basic techniques we will be discussing here. Other kinds of writing (i.e., narration, description, argument, and persuasion) will sometimes require different techniques.

Consider a paragraph as a division that consists of one or more sentences, deals with one point, and begins on a new, indented line. Paragraphs provide a way to write about a subject one point or one thought at a time.

Usually, a paragraph begins with a **topic sentence.** The topic sentence communicates the main idea of the paragraph, and the remainder of the paragraph explains or illuminates that central idea. The paragraph sometimes finishes with a restatement of the topic sentence. This strategy is easily read by the exam graders.

Often the topic sentence of the first paragraph is the central idea of the entire composition. Each succeeding paragraph then breaks down this idea into subtopics with each of the new topic sentences being the central thought of that subtopic.

Let's take a look at a simple paragraph to see how it's put together.

> The deductibility of home mortgage interest has been under recent review by Congress as a way to raise revenue. There have been two major reasons for this scrutiny. First, now that consumer interest is nondeductible and investment interest is limited to net investment income, taxpayers have been motivated to rearrange their finances to maximize their tax deductions. Second, most voters do not own

> homes costing more than $500,000 and, therefore, putting a cap on mortgage loans does not affect the mass of voters. Given the pressure to raise revenue, two major changes have occurred in this area.

The first sentence of the example is the **topic sentence.** The second sentence introduces the supporting examples which appear in the next two sentences beginning with *first* and *second.* The final sentence of the paragraph acts as a preview to the contents of the next paragraph.

Now, let's examine the makeup of a single paragraph answer to a written communication question from a previous CPA Exam.

> Question: Dunhill fraudulently obtained a negotiable promissory note from Beeler by misrepresentation of a material fact. Dunhill subsequently negotiated the note to Gordon, a holder in due course. Pine, a business associate of Dunhill, was aware of the fraud perpetrated by Dunhill. Pine purchased the note for value from Gordon. Upon presentment, Beeler has defaulted on the note.
>
> Required: Answer the following, setting forth reasons for any conclusions stated.
>
> 1. What are the rights of Pine against Beeler?
> 2. What are the rights of Pine against Dunhill?

Examples of possible answers:

> 1. The rights of Pine against Beeler arise from Pine's having acquired the note from Gordon, who was a holder in due course. Pine himself is not a holder in due course because he had knowledge of a defense against the note. The rule wherein a transferee, not a holder in due course, acquires the rights of one by taking from a holder in due course is known as the "shelter rule." Through these rights, Pine is entitled to recover the proceeds of the note from Beeler. The defense of fraud in the inducement is a personal defense and not valid against a holder in due course.

The first sentence of the paragraph is the topic sentence in which the basic answer to the question is given. The third and fourth sentence explains the rule governing Pine's rights. (The *shelter rule* would be considered a *key phrase* in this answer.) The final sentence of the paragraph is not really necessary to answer the question but was added as an explanation of what some might mistakenly believe to be the key to the answer.

> 2. As one with the rights of a holder in due course, Pine is entitled to proceed against any person whose signature appears on the note, provided he gives notice of dishonor. When Dunhill negotiated the note to Gordon, Dunhill's signature on the note made him secondarily liable. As a result, if Pine brings suit against Dunhill, Pine will prevail because of Dunhill's secondary liability.

The first sentence of this paragraph restates the fact that Pine has the rights of a holder in due course and what these rights mean. The second sentence explains what happened when Dunhill negotiated the note, and the third sentence states the probable outcome of these results.

Note that in both answers 1. and 2., the sentences hang together in a logical fashion and lead the reader easily from one thought to the next. This is called coherence, a primary factor in considerations of conciseness and clarity.

Transitions

To demonstrate how to use **transitions** in a paragraph to carry the reader easily from one thought or example to another, let's consider a slightly longer and more detailed paragraph. The transitions are indicated in italics.

> A concerted effort to reduce book income in response to AMT could have a significant impact on corporations. *For example,* the auditor-client relationship may change. *Currently,* it isn't unusual for corporate management to argue for higher rather than lower book earnings, *while* the auditor would argue for conservative reported numbers. Such a corporate reporting posture may change as a consequence of the BURP adjustment. *Furthermore,* stock market analysts often rely on a price/earnings ratio. Lower earnings for essentially the same level of activity may have a significant effect on security prices.

The first sentence of the paragraph is the topic sentence. The next sentence, beginning with the transition *for example,* introduces the example with a broad statement. The following sentence, beginning with *currently,* gives a specific example to support the basic premise. The sentence beginning *furthermore* leads us into a final example. Without these transitions, the paragraph would be choppy and lack coherence.

What follows is a list of some transitions divided by usage. We suggest you commit some of these to memory so that you will never be at a loss as to how to tie your ideas together.

Transitional Words & Phrases

One idea plus one idea:

again	equally important	in addition	likewise	similarly
also	finally	in the same fashion	moreover	third
and	first	in the same respect	next	thirdly
and then	further	last	second	too
besides	furthermore	lastly	secondly	

To show time or place:

after a time	at that time	immediately	presently	thereafter
after a while	at the same time	in due time	second	thereupon
afterwards	before	in the meantime	shortly	to the left
as long as	earlier	lately	since	until
as soon as	eventually	later	soon	when
at last	finally	meanwhile	temporarily	while
at length	first	next	then	
	further	of late		

To contrast or qualify:

after all	at the same time	however	nevertheless	on the other hand
although true	but	in any case	nonetheless	otherwise
and yet	despite this fact	in contrast	notwithstanding	still
anyway	for all that	in spite of	on the contrary	yet

To introduce an illustration

for example	in particular	incidentally	specifically	to illustrate
for instance	in other words	indeed	that is	
in fact	in summary	namely	thus	

To indicate concession

after all	I admit
although this may be	naturally
at the same time	of course
even though	

To indicate comparison:

in a likewise manner
likewise
similarly

WRITING AN ANSWER TO AN EXAM QUESTION

Now that we have examined the makeup of an answer to an exam question, let's take another question from a past CPA Exam and see how to go about writing a clear, comprehensive answer, step by step, sentence by sentence. A question similar to the one that follows would very likely be one the examiners would choose to grade writing skills.

Question:

Bar Manufacturing and Cole Enterprises were arch rivals in the high technology industry, and both were feverishly working on a new product that would give the first to develop it a significant competitive advantage. Bar engaged Abel Consultants on April 1, for one year, commencing immediately, at $7,500 a month to aid the company in the development of the new product. The contract was oral and was consummated by a handshake. Cole approached Abel and offered them a $10,000 bonus for signing, $10,000 a month for nine months, and a $40,000 bonus if Cole was the first to successfully market the new product. In this connection, Cole stated that the oral contract Abel made with Bar was unenforceable and that Abel could walk away from it without liability. In addition, Cole made certain misrepresentations regarding the dollar amount of its commitment to the project, the state of its development, and the expertise of its research staff. Abel accepted the offer.

Four months later, Bar successfully introduced the new product. Cole immediately dismissed Abel and has paid nothing beyond the first four $10,000 payments plus the initial bonus. Three lawsuits ensued: Bar sued Cole, Bar sued Abel, and Abel sued Cole.

Required: Answer the following, setting forth reasons for any conclusions stated.

Discuss the various theories on which each of the three lawsuits is based, the defenses that will be asserted, the measure of possible recovery, and the probable outcome of the litigation.

Composing an Answer:

<u>Analyze</u> requirements.

<u>Plan</u> on one paragraph for each lawsuit. Each paragraph will contain four elements: theory, defenses, recovery, and outcome.

Paragraph one:

Step 1: Begin with the first lawsuit mentioned, Bar vs. Cole. Write a topic sentence that will sum up the theory of the suit.

Topic sentence: Bar's lawsuit against Cole will be based upon the intentional tort of wrongful interference with a contractual relationship.

Step 2: Back up this statement with law and facts from the question scenario.

The primary requirement for this cause of action is a valid contractual relationship with which the defendant knowingly interferes. This requirement is met in the case of Cole.

Step 3: State defenses.

The contract is not required to be in writing since it is for exactly one year from the time of its making. It is, therefore, valid even though oral.

Step 4: Introduce subject of recovery (damages).

Cole's knowledge of the contract is obvious.

Step 5: Explain possible problems to recovery.

The principal problem, however, is damages. Since Bar was the first to market the product successfully, it would seem that damages are not present. It is possible there were actual damages incurred by Bar (for example, it hired another consulting firm at an increased price).

Step 6: Discuss possible outcome.

It also might be possible that some courts would permit the recovery of punitive damages since this is an intentional tort.

Paragraph one completed:

Bar's lawsuit against Cole will be based upon the intentional tort of wrongful interference with a contractual relationship. The primary requirement for this cause of action is a valid contractual relationship with which the defendant knowingly interferes. The requirement is met in the case of Cole. The contract is not required to be in writing since it is for exactly one year from the time of its making. It is, therefore, valid even though oral. Cole's knowledge of the contract is obvious. The principal problem, however, is damages. Since Bar was the first to market the product successfully, it would seem that damages are not present. It is possible there were actual damages incurred by Bar (for example, it hired another consulting firm at an increased price). It also might be possible that some courts would permit the recovery of punitive damages since this is an intentional tort.

Paragraph two:

Step 1: Discuss second lawsuit mentioned, Bar vs. Abel. Write a topic sentence that will sum up the theory of the suit.

Topic sentence: Bar's cause of action against Abel would be for breach of contract.

Step 2: State defenses. [Same as for first paragraph; this could be left out.]

The contract is not required to be in writing since it is for exactly one year from the time of its making. It is, therefore, valid even though oral.

Step 3: Introduce subject of recovery (damages).

Once again, [*indicating similarity and tying second paragraph to first*] damages would seem to be a serious problem.

Step 4: Explain possible problems to recovery.

Furthermore, punitive damages rarely would be available in a contract action. Finally, Bar cannot recover the same damages twice.

Step 5: Discuss possible outcome.

Hence, if it proceeds against Cole and recovers damages caused by Abel's breach of contract, it will not be able to recover a second time.

Paragraph two completed:

Bar's cause of action against Abel would be for breach of contract. [The contract is not required to be in writing since it is for exactly one year from the time of its making. It is, therefore, valid even though oral.] Once again, damages would seem to be a serious problem. Furthermore, punitive damages rarely would be available in a contract action. Finally, Bar cannot recover the same damages twice. Hence, if it proceeds against Cole and recovers damages caused by Abel's breach of contract, it will not be able to recover a second time.

Paragraph three:

Step 1: Discuss third lawsuit mentioned, Abel vs. Cole. Write a topic sentence that will sum up the theory of the suit.

Topic sentence: Abel's lawsuit against Cole will be based upon fraud and breach of contract.

Step 2: State defenses.

There were fraudulent statements made by Cole with the requisite intent and that were possibly to Abel's detriment. The breach of contract by Cole is obvious.

Step 3: Back up these statements with law and facts from the question scenario.

However, the contract that Cole induced Abel to enter into and which it subsequently breached was an illegal contract, that is, one calling for the commission of a tort.

Step 4: Explain possible problems to recovery and possible outcome.

Therefore, both parties are likely to be treated as wrongdoers, and Abel will be denied recovery.

Paragraph three completed:

Abel's lawsuit against Cole will be based upon fraud and breach of contract. There were fraudulent statements made by Cole with the requisite intent and that were possibly to Abel's detriment. The breach of contract by Cole is obvious. However, the contract that Cole induced Abel to enter into and which it subsequently breached was an illegal contract, that is, one calling for the commission of a tort. Therefore, both parties are likely to be treated as wrongdoers, and Abel will be denied recovery.

Paragraph Editing:

After you have written your response, review your work to check for the six characteristics that the AICPA will be looking for; coherent organization, conciseness, clarity, use of standard English, responsiveness to the requirements of the question, and appropriateness to the reader.

DIAGNOSTIC QUIZ

The following quiz is designed to test your knowledge of standard English. The correct answers follow the quiz, along with references to the sections that cover that particular area. By identifying the sections that are troublesome for you, you will be able to assess your weaknesses and concentrate on reviewing these areas. If you simply made a lucky guess, you'd better do a review anyway.

Circle the correct choice in the brackets for items 1 through 17.

1. The company can assert any defenses against third party beneficiaries that [they have/it has] against the promisee.

2. Among those securities [which/that] are exempt from registration under the 1933 Act [are/is] a class of stock given in exchange for another class by the issuer to its existing stockholders without the [issuer's/issuer] paying a commission.

3. This type of promise will not bind the promisor [as/because/since] there is no mutuality of obligation.

4. Under the cost method, treasury stock is presented on the balance sheet as an unallocated reduction of total [stockholders'/stockholders/stockholder's] equity.

5. Jones wished that he [was/were] not bound by the offer he made Smith, while Smith celebrated [his/him] having accepted the offer.

6. [Non-cash/Noncash] investing and financing transactions are not reported in the statement of cash flows because the statement reports only the [affects/effects] of operating, investing, and financing activities that directly [affect/effect] cash flows.

7. Since [its/it's] impossible to predict the future and because prospective financial statements can be [effected/affected] by numerous factors, the accountant must use [judgment/judgement] to estimate when and how conditions are [likely/liable] to change.

8. A common format of bank reconciliation statements [is/are] to reconcile both book and bank balances to a common amount known as the "true balance."

9. Corporations, clubs, churches, and other entities may be beneficiaries so long as they are sufficiently identifiable to permit a determination of [who/whom] is empowered to enforce the terms of the trust.

10. None of the beneficiaries [was/were] specifically referred to in the will.

11. Either Dr. Kline or Dr. Monroe [have/has] been elected to the board of directors.

12. The letter should be signed by Bill and [me/myself].

13. Any trust [which/that] is created for an illegal purpose is invalid.

14. When the nature of relevant information is such that it cannot appear in the accounts, this [principal/principle] dictates that such relevant information be included in the accompanying notes to the financial statements. Financial reporting is the [principal/principle] means of communicating financial information to those outside an entity.

15. The inheritance was divided [between/among] several beneficiaries.

16. Termination of an offer ends the offeree's power to [accept/except] it.

17. The consideration given by the participating creditors is [their/there] mutual promises to [accept/except] less than the full amount of [their/there] claims. Because [their/there] must be such mutual promises [between/among] all the participating creditors, a composition or extension agreement requires the participation of at least two or more creditors.

Follow instructions for items 18 through 20.

18. The duties assigned to the interns were to accompany the seniors on field work assignments and the organization and filing of the work papers.

    Fix this sentence so that it will read more smoothly. ______________________________

    ____

    ____

19. Circle the correct spelling of the following pairs of words.

liaison laison	privilege priviledge	paralleled paraleled
achieve acheive	occasion occassion	accommodate accomodate

20. Each set of brackets in the following example represents a possible location for punctuation. If you believe a location needs no punctuation, leave it blank; if you think a location needs punctuation, enter a comma, a colon, or a semicolon.

    If the promises supply the consideration [ ] there must be a mutuality of obligation [ ] in other words [ ] both parties must be bound.

ANSWERS TO DIAGNOSTIC QUIZ

Each answer includes a reference to the section that covers what you need to review.

1. it has	Pronouns—Antecedents, p. C-27.
2. that; is; issuer's	Subordinating Conjunctions, p. C-30; Verbs—Agreement, p. C-23; Nouns—Gerunds, p. C-26.
3. because	Subordinating Conjunctions, p. C-30.
4. stockholders'	Possessive Nouns, p. C-25.
5. were; his	Verbs, Mood, p. C-22; Nouns—Gerunds, p. C-26.
6. Noncash; effects; affect	Hyphen, p. C-20; Syntax: Troublesome Words, p. C-13.
7. it's; affected; judgment, likely	Syntax: Troublesome Words, p. C-13; Spelling: Troublesome Words, p. C-22; Diction: List of Words, p. C-11.
8. is	Verbs—Agreement, p. C-23.
9. who	Pronouns, Who/Whom, p. C-26.
10. were	Verbs—Agreement with Each/None, p. C-24.
11. has	Verbs—Agreement, p. C-23.
12. me	Pronouns, that follow prepositions, p. C-27.
13. that	Subordinating Conjunctions, p. C-30.
14. principle; principal	Syntax: Troublesome Words, p. C-12.
15. among	Diction: List of Words, p. C-10.
16. accept	Syntax: Troublesome Words, C-12

17. their; accept; their; there; among; Syntax: Troublesome Words, p. C-12; Diction: List of Words, p. C-10.

18. Two possible answers: Parallelism: p. C-15.

    The duties assigned to the interns were *accompanying* the seniors on field work assignments and *organizing* and filing the work papers.
    or
    The duties assigned to the interns were to accompany the seniors on field work assignments and *to organize* and *file* the work papers.

19. In every case, the **first choice** is the correct spelling.
    Refer to Spelling: Troublesome Words, p. C-21.

20. If the promises supply the consideration [,] there must be a mutuality of obligation [;] in other words [,] both parties must be bound. Refer to Punctuation, p. C-16.

Scoring

Count one point for each item (some numbers contain more than one item) and one point for question number 18 if your sentence came close to the parallelism demonstrated by the answer choices. There are a total of 40 points.

If you scored 37-40, you did very well. A brief review of the items you missed should be sufficient to make you feel fairly confident about your grammar skills.

If you scored 33-36, you did fairly well—better than average—but you should do a thorough review of the items you missed.

If you scored 29-32, your score was average. Since "average" will probably not make it on the CPA exam, you might want to consider a thorough grammar review, in addition to the items you missed.

If you scored below average (28 or less), you **definitely** should make grammar review a high priority when budgeting your exam study time. You should consider using resources beyond those provided here.

SENTENCE STRUCTURE

A sentence is a statement or question, consisting of a subject and a predicate. A subject, at a minimum is a noun, usually accompanied by one or more modifiers (for example, "The Trial Balance"). A predicate consists, at a minimum, of a verb. Cultivate the habit of a quick verification for a subject, predicate, capitalized first word, and ending punctuation in each sentence of an essay. A study of sentence structure is essentially a study of grammar but also moves just beyond grammar to diction, syntax, and parallelism. As we discuss how sentences are structured, there will naturally be some overlapping with grammar.

DICTION

Diction is appropriate word choice. There is no substitute for a diversified vocabulary. If you have a diversified vocabulary or "a way with words," you are already a step ahead. A good general vocabulary, as well as a good accounting vocabulary, is a prerequisite of the CPA exam. Develop your vocabulary as you review for the Exam.

An important aspect of choosing the right words is knowing the audience for whom you are choosing those "perfect words." A perfect word for accountants is not necessarily the perfect word for mechanics or lawyers or English professors. If a CPA exam question asks you to write a specific document for a reader other than another accountant or CPA, you need to be very specific but less technical than you would be otherwise.

Accounting, auditing, and related areas have a certain diction and syntax peculiar unto themselves. Promulgations, for instance, are written very carefully so as to avoid possible misinterpretations or misunderstandings. Of course, you are not expected to write like this—for the CPA exam or in other situations. Find the best word possible to explain clearly and concisely what it is you are trying to say. Often the "right word" is simply just not the "wrong word," so be certain you know the exact meaning of a word before you use it. As an accountant writing for accountants, what is most important is knowing the technical terms and the "key words" and placing them in your sentences properly and effectively. Defining or explaining key words demonstrates to graders that you understand the words you are using and not merely parroting the jargon.

The following is a list of words that frequently either are mistaken for one another or incorrectly assumed to be more or less synonymous.

Among—preposition, refers to more than two
Between—preposition, refers to two; is used for three or more if the items are considered severally and individually

> If only part of the seller's capacity to perform is affected, the seller must allocate deliveries *among* the customers, and he or she must give each one reasonable notice of the quota available to him or her.
> *Between* merchants, the additional terms become part of the contract unless one of the following applies. (This sentence is correct whether there are two merchants or many merchants.)

Amount—noun, an aggregate; total number or quantity
Number—noun, a sum of units; a countable number
Quantity—noun, an indefinite amount or number

> The checks must be charged to the account in the order of lowest *amount* to highest *amount* to minimize the *number* of dishonored checks.
> The contract is not enforceable under this paragraph beyond the *quantity* of goods shown in such writing.

Allude—verb, to state indirectly
Refer—verb, to state clearly and directly

> She *alluded* to the fact that the company's management was unscrupulous.
> She *referred* to his poor management in her report.

Bimonthly—adjective or adverb; every two months
Semimonthly—adjective or adverb; twice a month

> Our company has *bimonthly* meetings.
> We get paid *semimonthly.*

Continual—adjective, that which is repeatedly renewed after each interruption or intermission
Continuous—adjective, that which is uninterrupted in time, space, or sequence

> The *continuous* ramblings of the managing partner caused the other partners to *continually* check the time.

Cost—noun, the amount paid for an item
Price—noun, the amount set for an item
Value—noun, the relative worth, utility, or importance of an item
Worth—noun, value of an item measured by its qualities or by the esteem in which it is held

> The *cost* of that stock is too much.
> The *price* of that stock is $100 a share.
> I place no *value* on that stock.
> That stock's *worth* is overestimated.

Decide—verb, to arrive at a solution
Conclude—verb, to reach a final determination; to exercise judgment

Barbara *decided* to listen to what the accountant was saying; she then *concluded* that what he was saying was true.

Fewer—adjective, not as many; consisting or amounting to a smaller number (used of numbers; comparative of few)
Less—adjective, lower rank, degree, or importance; a more limited amount (used of quantity—for the most part)

My clients require *fewer* consultations than yours do.
My clients are *less* demanding than yours are.

Good—adjective, of a favorable character or tendency; noun, something that is good
Well—adverb, good or proper manner; satisfactorily with respect to conduct or action; adjective, being in satisfactory condition or circumstances

It was *good* [adjective] of you to help me study for the CPA exam.
The decision was for the *good* [noun] of the firm.
He performed that task *well* [adverb].
His work was *well* [adjective] respected by the other accountants.

Imply—verb, to suggest
Infer—verb, to assume; deduce

Her report seems to *imply* that my work was not up to par.
From reading her report, the manager *inferred* that my work was not up to par.

Oral—adjective, by the mouth, spoken; not written
Verbal—adjective, relating to or consisting of words
Vocal—adjective, uttered by the voice, spoken; persistence and volume of speech

Hawkins, Inc. made an *oral* agreement to the contract.
One partner gave his *verbal* consent while the other partner was very *vocal* with his objections.

State—verb, to set forth in detail; completely
Assert—verb, to claim positively, sometimes aggressively or controversially
Affirm—verb, to validate, confirm, state positively

The attorney *stated* the facts of the case.
The plaintiff asserted that his rights had been violated.
The judge *affirmed* the jury's decision.

SYNTAX

Syntax is the order of words in a sentence. Errors in syntax occur in a number of ways; the number one way is through hasty composition. The only way to catch errors in word order is to read each of your sentences carefully to make sure that the words you meant to write or type are the words that actually appear on the page and that those words are in the best possible order. The following list should help you avoid errors in both diction and syntax and gives examples where necessary.

Troublesome Words

Accept—verb, to receive or to agree to willingly
Except—verb, to take out or leave out from a number or a whole; conjunction, on any other condition but that condition

Except for the items we have mentioned, we will *accept* the conditions of the contract.

Advice—noun, information or recommendation
Advise—verb, to recommend, give advice

The *accountant advised* us to take his *advice.*

Affect—verb, to influence or change (**Note:** affect is occasionally used as a noun in technical writing only.)
Effect—noun, result or cause; verb, to cause

The effect [noun] of Ward, Inc.'s decision to cease operations affected many people.
He quickly *effected* [verb] policy changes for office procedures.

All Ready—adjectival phrase, completely prepared
Already—adverb, before now; previously

Although the tax return was *all ready* to be filed, the deadline had *already* passed.

All Right; Alright—adjective or adverb, beyond doubt; very well; satisfactory; agreeable, pleasing. (Although many grammarians insist that **alright** is not a proper form, it is widely accepted.)

Appraise—verb, set a value on
Apprise—verb, inform

Dane Corp. *apprised* him of the equipment's age, so that he could *appraise* it more accurately.

Assure—verb, to give confidence to positively
Ensure—verb, to make sure, certain, or safe
Insure—verb, to obtain or provide insurance on or for; to make certain by taking necessary measures and precautions

The accountant assured his client that he would file his return in a timely manner.
He added the figures more than once to *ensure* their accuracy.
She was advised to *insure* her diamond property.

Decedent—noun, a deceased person
Descendant—noun, proceeding from an ancestor or source

The decedent left her vast fortune to her *descendants.*

Eminent—adjective, to stand out; important
Imminent—adjective, impending

Although he was an *eminent* businessman, foreclosure on his house was *imminent.*

Its—possessive
It's—contraction, **it is**

The company held *its* board of directors meeting on Saturday. *It's* the second meeting this month.

Lay—verb, to place or set
Lie—verb, to recline

He *lies* down to rest.
He *lays* down the book.

Percent—used with numbers only
Percentage—used with words or phrases

Each employee received 2 *percent* of the profits.
They all agreed this was a small *percentage.*

Precedence—noun, the fact of preceding in time, priority of importance
Precedent—noun, established authority; adjective, prior in time, order, or significance

The board of directors meeting took *precedence* over his going away.
The president set a *precedent* when making that decision.

Principal—noun, a capital sum placed at interest; a leading figure; the corpus of an estate; adjective, first, most important
Principle—noun, a basic truth or rule

Paying interest on the loan's *principal* [noun] was explained to the company's *principals* [noun].
The principal [adjective] part of...
She refused to compromise her *principles.*

Than—conjunction, function word to indicate difference in kind, manner, or identity; preposition, in comparison with (indicates comparison)
Then—adverb, at that time; soon after that (indicates time)

BFE Corp. has more shareholders *than* Hills Corp.
First, we must write the report, and *then* we will meet with the clients.

Their—adjective, of or relating to them or themselves
There—adverb, in or at that place

There were fifty shareholders at the meeting to cast *their* votes.

Modifier Placement

Pay close attention to where modifiers are placed, especially adverbs such as **only** and **even.** In speech, inflection aids meaning but, in writing, placing modifiers improperly can be confusing and often changes the meaning. The modifier should usually be placed before the word(s) it modifies.

She *almost* finished the whole report.
She finished *almost* the whole report.

Only she finished the report.
She *only* finished the report.
She finished *only* the report.

Phrases also must be placed properly, usually, but not always, following the word or phrase they modify. Often, **reading the sentence aloud** will help you decide where the modifier belongs.

Fleming introduced a client to John with a counter-offer. (*With a counter-offer* modifies *client,* not *John,* and should be placed after *client.)*
The accountant recommended a bankruptcy petition to the client under Chapter 7. (*Under Chapter 7* modifies *bankruptcy petition,* not *the client,* and should be placed after *bankruptcy petition.)*

Split Infinitives

Infinitives are the root verb form (e.g., to be, to consider, to walk). Generally speaking, infinitives should not be split except when to do so makes the meaning clearer.

Awkward: Management's responsibility is to clearly represent its financial position.
Better: Management's responsibility is to represent its financial position clearly.

Exception: Management's responsibility in the future is to better represent its financial position.

Sentence Fragments

To avoid sentence fragments, read over your work carefully. Each sentence needs at least (1) a subject and (2) a predicate.

> Unlike the case of a forged endorsement, a drawee bank charged with the recognition of its drawer-customer's signature. (The verb *is*, before the word *charged,* has been left out.)

PARALLELISM

Parallelism refers to a similarity in structure and meaning of all parts of a sentence or a paragraph. In parallelism, parts of a sentence (or a paragraph) that are parallel in meaning are also parallel in structure. Sentences that violate rules of parallelism will be difficult to read and may obscure meaning. The following are some examples of different **violations** of parallelism.

(1) A security interest can be effected through a financing statement or the creditor's taking possession of it. (The two prepositional phrases separated by **or** should be parallel.)

Corrected: A security interest can be effected through a financing statement or through possession by the creditor.

(2) The independent auditor should consider whether the scope is appropriate, adequate audit programs and working papers, appropriate conclusions, and reports prepared are consistent with results of the work performed. (The clause beginning with **whether** (which acts as the direct object of the verb **should consider**) is faulty. The items mentioned must be similarly constructed to each other.)

Corrected: The independent auditor should consider whether the scope is appropriate, audit programs and working papers are adequate, conclusions are appropriate, and reports prepared are consistent with results of the work performed.

(3) The CPA was responsible for performing the inquiry and analytical procedures and that the review report was completed in a timely manner. (The prepositional phrase beginning with **for** is faulty.)

Corrected: The CPA was responsible for performing the inquiry and analytical procedures and ensuring that the review report was completed in a timely manner.

(4) Procedures that should be applied in examining the stock accounts are as follows:

(1) Review the corporate charter…
(2) Obtain or preparing an analysis of…
(3) Determination of authorization for… (All items in a list must be in parallel structure.)

Corrected:

1. Review the corporate charter…
2. Obtain or prepare an analysis of…
3. Determine the authorization for…

There are many other types of faulty constructions that can creep into sentences—too many to detail here. Furthermore, if any of the above is not clear, syntax may be a problem for you and you might want to consider a more thorough review of this subject.

NUMBERS

1. The basic rule for writing numbers is to write out the numbers ten and under and use numerals for all the others. More formal writing may dictate writing out all round numbers and numbers under 101. Let style, context of the sentence and of the work, and common sense be your guide.

The partnership was formed 18 years ago.
Jim Bryant joined the firm four years ago.
Baker purchased 200 shares of stock.

2. When there are two numbers next to each other, alternate the styles.

three 4-year certificates of deposit 5 two-party instruments

3. Never begin a sentence with numerals, such as:

1989 was the last year that Zinc Co. filed a tax return.

This example can be corrected as follows:

Nineteen hundred and eighty-nine was the last year that Zinc Co. filed a tax return. (For use only in very formal writing)
or
Zinc Co. has not filed a tax return since 1989.

CAPITALIZATION

This section mentions only areas that seem to cause particular difficulties.

1. The first word **after a colon** is capped only when it is the beginning of a complete sentence.

We discussed several possibilities at the meeting: Among them were liquidation, reorganization, and rehabilitation.
We discussed several possibilities at the meeting: liquidation, reorganization, and rehabilitation.

2. The capitalization of titles and headings is especially tricky. In general, the first word and all other important words, no matter what length they are, should be capped. Beyond this general rule, there are several variations relating to the capitalization of pronouns. The important thing here is to pick a style and use it consistently within a single document, article, etc.

For example, the following pair of headings would both be acceptable depending on the style and consistency of style:

Securities to which SFAS 115 Applies **or** Securities to Which SFAS 115 Applies
Issues for Property other than Cash **or** Issues For Property Other Than Cash

PUNCTUATION

PERIOD

Probably the two most common errors involving periods occur when incorporating quotation marks and/or parentheses with periods.

1. When a period is used with closing quotation marks, the period is always placed **inside,** regardless of whether the entire sentence is a quote or only the end of the sentence.

2. When a period is used with parentheses, the period goes **inside** the closing parenthesis if the entire sentence is enclosed in parentheses. When only the last word or words is enclosed in parentheses, the period goes **outside** the closing parenthesis.

(See Chapter 34, Contracts.)
The answer to that question is in the section on contracts (Chapter 34).

EXCLAMATION POINT

An exclamation point is used for emphasis and when issuing a command. In many cases, this is determined by the author when he or she wants to convey urgency, irony, or stronger emotion than ordinarily would be inferred.

COLON

A colon is used to introduce something in the sentence—a list of related words, phrases, or items directly related to the first part of the sentence; a quotation; a **direct** question; or an example of what was stated in the first part of the sentence. The colon takes the place of **that is** or **such as** and should never be used **with** such phrases.

> The accountant discussed two possibilities with the clients**:** first, a joint voluntary bankruptcy petition under Chapter 7, and second,…

> The following will be discussed**:** life insurance proceeds; inheritance; and property.

> My CPA accounting review book states the following**:** "All leases that do not meet any of the four criteria for capital leases are operating leases."

Colons are used in formal correspondence after the salutation.

> Dear Mr. Bennett**:**
> To Whom it May Concern**:**

Note: When **that is** or **such as** is followed by a numeric list, it may be followed by a colon.

When writing a sentence, if you're not sure whether or not a colon is appropriate, it probably isn't. When in doubt, change the sentence so that you're sure it doesn't need a colon.

SEMICOLON

A semicolon is used in a number of ways:

1. Use a **semicolon in place of a conjunction** when there are two or more closely related thoughts and each is expressed in a coordinate clause (a clause that could stand as a complete sentence).

   > A marketable title is one that is free from plausible or reasonable objections**;** it need not be perfect.

2. Use a **semicolon** as in the above example **with a conjunction** when the sentence is very long and complex. This promotes **clarity** by making the sentence easier to read.

   > Should the lease be prematurely terminated, the deposit may be retained only to cover the landlord's actual expenses or damages**;** ***and*** any excess must be returned to the tenant.

   > An assignment establishes privity of estate between the lessor and assignee**;** ***[and]*** therefore, the assignee becomes personally liable for the rent.

3. When there are commas in a series of items, use a **semicolon** to separate the main items.

   > Addison, Inc. has distribution centers in Camden, Maine; Portsmouth, New Hampshire; and Rock Island, Rhode Island.

COMMA

Informal English allows much freedom in the placement or the omission of commas, and the overall trend is away from commas. However, standard, formal English provides rules for its usage. Accounting "language" can be so complex that using commas and using them correctly and appropriately is a necessity to avoid obscurity and promote clarity. Accordingly, we encourage you to learn the basics about comma placement.

What follows is not a complete set of rules for commas but should be everything you need to know about commas to make your sentences clear and concise. Because the primary purpose of the comma is to clarify meaning, it is the opinion of the editors that in the case of a complex subject such as accounting, it is better to overpunctuate than to underpunctuate. If you are concerned about overpunctuation, try to reduce an unwieldy sentence to two or more sentences.

1. Use a comma to **separate a compound sentence** (one with two or more independent coordinate clauses joined by a conjunction).

   Gil Corp. has current assets of $90,000**,** but the corporation has current liabilities of $180,000.
   Jim borrowed $60,000**,** and he used the proceeds to purchase outstanding common shares of stock.

   Note: In these examples, a comma would **not** be necessary if the **and** or the **but** were not followed by a noun or pronoun (the subject of the second clause). In other words, if by removing the conjunction, the sentence could be separated into two complete sentences, it needs a comma.

2. Use a comma after an introductory word or phrase.

   During 1992**,** Rand Co. purchased $960,000 of inventory.
   On April 1, 1993**,** Wall's inventory had a fair value of $150,000.

   Note: Writers often choose to omit this comma when the introductory phrase is very short. Again, we recommend using the comma. It will never be incorrect in this position.

3. Use a comma after an introductory adverbial clause.

   Although insurance contracts are not required by the Statute of Frauds to be in writing**,** most states have enacted statutes that now require such.

4. Use commas to separate items, phrases, or clauses in a series.

   To be negotiable, an instrument must be in writing**,** signed by the maker or drawer**,** contain an unconditional promise or order to pay a sum certain in money on demand or at a specific time**,** and be payable to order or to bearer.

   Note: Modern practice often omits the last comma in the series (in the above example, the one before **and**). Again, for the sake of clarity, we recommend using this comma.

5. In most cases, use a comma or commas to separate **a series of adjectives.**

   Silt Co. kept their inventory in an old**,** decrepit**,** brick building.
   He purchased several outstanding shares of common stock. (*No* commas are needed.)

When in doubt as to whether or not to use a comma after a particular adjective, try inserting the word **and** between the adjectives. If it makes sense, use a comma. (In the second example, above, **several and outstanding,** or **outstanding and several** don't make sense.)

6. Use a comma or commas to set off any **word or words, phrase, or clause that interrupts the sentence** but does not change its essential meaning.

   SLD Industries**,** as drawer of the instrument**,** is only secondarily liable.

7. Use commas to set off **geographical names** and **dates.**

   Feeney Co. moved its headquarters to Miami**,** Florida**,** on August 16**,** 1992.

QUOTATION MARKS

Quotation marks are used with **direct quotations; direct discourse and direct questions;** and **definitions or explanations of words.** Other uses of quotation marks are used rarely in the accounting profession and, therefore, are not discussed in this review.

HYPHEN

1. Use a hyphen to separate words into syllables. It is best to check a dictionary, because some words do not split where you might imagine.

2. Modern practice does not normally hyphenate prefixes and their root words, even when both the prefix and the root word begin with vowels. A common exception is when the root word begins with a capital letter or a date or number.

prenuptial	nonexempt	semiannual
pre-1987	nonnegotiable	non-American

3. Although modern practice is moving away from using hyphens for **compound adjectives** (a noun and an adjective in combination to make a single adjective), clarity dictates that hyphens still be used in many cases.

long-term investments	two-party instrument
a noninterest-bearing note	short-term capital losses

4. Use a hyphen **only** when the compound adjective or compound adjective-adverb **precedes the noun.**

   The well-known company is going bankrupt.
   The company is well known for its quality products.

Note: There are certain word combinations that are always hyphenated, always one word, or always two words. Use the dictionary.

5. **Suspended hyphens** are used to avoid repetition in compound adjectives. For example, instead of having to write **himself or herself,** especially when these forms are being used repeatedly as they often must be in our newly nongender-biased world, use **him- or herself.**

10-, 15-, and 18-year depreciation	first-, second-, and third-class

SPELLING

Just as many of us believe that arithmetic can be done always by our calculators, we also believe that spelling will be done by our word processors and, therefore, we needn't worry too much about it. There is no doubt that these devices are tremendous boons. However, sometimes a spell-checker cannot tell the difference between words that you have misspelled which are nonetheless real words, such as **there** and **their.** (See the list in this section of words often confused.)

Let's hit some highlights here of troublesome spellings with some brief tips that should help you become a better speller.

1. **IE** or **EI**? If you are still confused by words containing the **ie** or **ei** combinations, you'd better relearn those old rhymes we ridiculed in grade school.

   "**i** before **e** except after **c.**" (This works only for words where the ie-ei combination sounds like **ee.**)

ach**ie**ve	bel**ie**ve	ch**ie**f
ceiling	re**cei**ve	re**cei**pt

Of course there are always **exceptions** such as:

either	neither	seize	financier

When **ie** or **ei** have a different sound than **ee**, the above rule does not apply. For example:

fr**ie**nd	s**ie**ve	effic**ie**nt
for**ei**gn	sover**ei**gn	surf**ei**t

2. **Doubling final consonants.** When an ending (**suffix**) beginning with a vowel is added to a root word that ends in a single consonant, that final consonant is **usually doubled**.

lag—lagging	bid—bidding	top—topped

The exceptions generally fall under three rules.

First, double only after a short vowel and **not** after a double vowel.

big—bigger	tug—tugging	get—getting
need—needing	keep—keeping	pool—pooled

Second, a **long** vowel (one that "says its own name"), which is almost always followed by a silent **e** that must be dropped to add the suffix, is **not** doubled.

hope—hoping	tape—taped	rule—ruled

Note: Sometimes, as in the first two examples above, doubling the consonants would create entirely new words.

Third, with root words of two or more syllables ending in a single consonant, double the consonant **only** when the last syllable is the **stressed syllable.**

Double:	be**gin**—beginning, beginner	pre**fer**—preferred, preferring
	re**gret**—**regretted**, regrettable	ad**mit**—admitted, admittance
Don't Double:	pro**hi**bit—prohibited, prohibitive	**ben**efit—benefited, benefiting
	de**vel**op—developing	**pref**erence—preferable

3. **Drop** the silent **e** before adding a suffix **beginning with a vowel.**

store—storing	take—taking	value—valuing

Keep the **e** before adding a suffix **beginning with a consonant,** such as:

move—movement	achieve—achievement

Again, there are **exceptions**.

e:	mile—mileage	dye—dyeing	
No e:	argue—argument	due—duly	true—truly

4. Change **y** to **ie** before adding **s** when it is the single final vowel.

country—countries	study—studies	quantity—quantities

Change **y** to **i** before adding other endings **except s.**

busy—business	dry—drier	copy—copier

Exceptions: Keep **y** for the following:

copying studying trying

Y is also usually preserved when it follows another vowel.

delays joys played

Exceptions:

day—daily lay—laid pay—paid say—said

5. **Forming Plurals.** The formation of some plurals does not follow the general rule of adding **s** or **es** to the singular. What follows are some of the more troublesome forms.

Some singular nouns that end in **o** form their plurals by adding **s**; some by adding **es**.

ratio**s** zero**s** hero**es** potato**es**

Many nouns taken directly from **foreign languages** retain their original plural. Below are a few of the more common ones.

alumnus—alumni
criterion—criteria
basis—bases
datum—data
crisis—crises
matrix—matrices

Other nouns taken directly from foreign languages have **two acceptable plural forms:** the foreign language plural and the anglicized plural. Here are some of the more common:

medium—media, mediums
formula—formulae, formulas
appendix—appendices, appendixes
memorandum—memoranda, memorandums

Finally, in this foreign language category are some commonly used Latin nouns that form their plurals by adding **es.**

census—censuses
hiatus—hiatuses
consensus—consensuses
prospectus—prospectuses

Troublesome Words: Spelling

Spelling errors occur for different reasons; probably the most common reason is confusion with the spelling of similar words. The following is a list of commonly misspelled words. You will find those you may have misspelled in taking the Diagnostic Quiz, and you may recognize others you have problems with. Memorize them. (Note: some of these words may have acceptable alternative spellings; however, the spellings listed below are the preferred form.)

accommodate
achieve
acknowledgment
balance
bankruptcy
deferred
existence
fulfill
irrelevant
judgment
liaison
occasion
paralleled
privilege
receivable
resistance
skillful
supersede
surety
trial

GRAMMAR

This section on grammar is intended to be a brief overview only. Consequently, the authors have chosen to focus on items that seem to cause the most problems. If you did not do well on the Diagnostic Quiz, you would be well advised to go over all the material in this section and consider a more thorough grammar study than provided here.

VERBS

The verb is the driving force of the sentence: it is the word or words to which all other parts of the sentence relate. When trying to analyze a sentence to identify its grammatical parts or its meaning, or when attempting to amend a sentence, you should always identify the verb or verbs first. A verb expresses action or being.

Action: The accountant *visits* his clients regularly.
Being: Kyle *is* an accountant.

Voice

1. The **active voice** indicates that the subject of the sentence (the person or thing) does something. The **passive voice** indicates that the subject is acted upon.

   Active: *The accountant worked* on the client's financial statements.
   Passive: The client's financial statements *were worked on by the accountant.*

2. The most important thing to understand about voice is that it should be consistent; that is, you should avoid shifts from one voice to another, especially within the same sentence as below.

   Taylor Corporation *hired* an independent computer programmer to develop a simplified payroll application for its new computer, and an on-line, data-based microcomputer system *was developed.*

   Use the active voice for the entire sentence:

   Taylor Corporation *hired* an independent computer programmer to develop a simplified payroll application for its new computer, and he *developed* an on-line, data-based microcomputer system.

Mood

1. Common errors in syntax are made when **more than one mood** is used in a single sentence. The first example that follows begins with the **imperative** and shifts to the **indicative.** The second example corrects the sentence by using the imperative in both clauses, and the third example corrects the sentence by using the indicative in both clauses. The fourth example avoids the problem by forming two sentences.

   Pick up (imperative) that work program for me at the printer, and then we will go (indicative) to the client.
   Pick up that work program for me at the printer, and then go to the client with me.
   After you pick up that work program for me at the printer, we will go to the client.
   Pick up that work program for me at the printer. Then we will go to the client.

2. There are three moods: the indicative, the imperative, and the subjunctive. We do not examine the subjunctive. Most sentences are **indicative:**

   The percentage of completion method is justified. Declarative indicative.
   Is the percentage of completion method justified? Interrogative indicative.

3. Sentences that give a command are called **imperative** sentences:

   Pick up your books!
   Be sure to use the correct method of accounting for income taxes.

Tense

1. Tense is all about *time.* If the proper sequence of tenses is not used, confusion can arise as to what happened when. Consider:

   Not getting the raise he was expecting, John was unhappy about the additional work load. [???]
   Having not gotten the raise he was expecting, John was unhappy about the additional work load. [Much clearer]

2. The **present tense** is used to express action or a state of being that is taking place in the present. The present tense is also used to express an action or a state of being that is habitual and when a definite time in the future is stated.

   Dan *is taking* his CPA exam.
   Robin *goes* to the printer once a week.
   The new computer *arrives* on Monday.

3. The **present perfect tense** is used to indicate action that began in the past and has continued to the present.

   From the time of its founder, the CPA firm *has celebrated* April 16 with a fabulous dinner party.

4. The **future tense** is used to indicate action that takes place in the indefinite future.

   A plan of reorganization *will determine* the amount and the manner in which the creditors *will be paid*, in what form the business *will continue,* and any other necessary details.

5. The **future perfect tense** is used to indicate action that has not taken place yet but will take place before a specific future time.

   Before Susan arrives at the client's office, the client *will have prepared* the documents she needs.

6. The **past tense** is used to indicate an action that took place in the past. The **past tense** is also used to indicate a condition or state occurring at a specific time in the past.

   The predecessor auditor *resigned* last week.
   The company *contacted* its auditor the first of every new year.

7. The **past perfect tense** is used to indicate an action that is completed before another action that also took place in the past.

   The work load *had been* so heavy that she was required to work overtime. (Not *was*)

Agreement

1. The first element of agreement to examine is **verb** and **subject.** These two components must agree **in number.** Number is just one of several things to consider when examining the agreement of the components of a sentence.

2. The subject of the sentence is the noun or pronoun (person, place, or thing) doing the action stated by the verb (in the case of the active voice) or being acted upon by the verb (in the case of the passive voice). Although the subject normally precedes the verb, this is not always the case. Thus, you must be able to identify sentence elements no matter where they happen to fall. This is not a difficult matter, at least most of the time. Consider:

   (1) Lewis, Bradford, Johnson & Co. [is or are] the client with the best pay record.

   (2) For me, one of the most difficult questions on the exam [was or were] concerned with correcting weaknesses in internal controls.

In both examples, the first choice, the singular verb form, is correct. In sentence (1), Lewis, Bradford, Johnson & Co. is considered singular in number because we are talking about the company, not Lewis, Bradford, and Johnson per se. In sentence (2), the verb is also singular because **one** is the subject of the sentence, not **questions. Questions** is the object of the preposition **of.** If this seems confusing, rearrange the sentence so that the prepositional phrase appears first, and the agreement of subject and verb will be clearer. Thus:

Of the most difficult questions, one *was concerned* with correcting weaknesses in internal controls.

We will address special problems associated with prepositional phrases in other sections.

3. Beware of the word **number.** When it is preceded by the word **the,** it is always singular, and when it is preceded by the word **a,** it is always plural.

   The number of listings generated by the new EDP system *was* astounding.
   A number of listings *were generated* by the new EDP system.

4. A **compound subject,** even when made up of nouns singular in number, always takes a plural verb.

   The balance sheet, the independent auditor's report, and the quarterly report *are lying* on the desk. (Not *is lying)*

5. Continuing now with **compound subjects,** let's address the problem of when there are two or more subjects—one (or more) singular and one (or more) plural. When the sentence contains subjects connected by **or** or **nor,** or **not only...but also,** the verb should agree with the subject nearer to the verb.

   Either the auditors or the partner *is going* to the client.
   Not only the partner but also the auditors *are going* to the client.

   In the case of the first example above, which sounds awkward, simply switch the order of the subjects **(the partner; the auditors)** and use the verb **are going** to make it read better.

6. When one subject is **positive** and one is **negative,** the verb always agrees with the positive.

   The partner, and not the auditors, *is going* to the client.
   Not the partner but the auditors frequently go to the client.

7. You should use singular verbs with the following: each, every, everyone, everybody, anyone, anybody, either, neither, someone, somebody, no one, nobody, and one.

   Anybody who wants to go *is* welcome.
   Neither the accountant nor the bookkeeper ever *arrives* on time.
   One never *knows* what to expect.

> Watch out for the words **each** and **none.** They can trip up even careful writers.

8. Improper placement of **each** in the sentence will confuse the verb agreement.

   The balance sheet, the income statement, and the statement of cash flows each [has/have] several errors.

   In this example, we know that the verb must be **has** (to agree with **each**), but then again, maybe it should be **have** to agree with the subjects. The problem is that we have a sentence with a compound subject that must take a plural verb, but here it is connected with a singular pronoun (each). This is a very common error. This particular example may be fixed in one of two ways. First, if the word **each** is not really necessary in the sentence, simply drop it. Second, simply place the word **each** in a better position in the sentence. In the example below, placing the word **each** at the end of the sentence properly connects it to **errors;** also it no longer confuses verb agreement.

The balance sheet, the income statement, and the statement of cash flows *have* several errors *each.*

9. The word **none** has special problems all its own. Not too many years ago, it was the accepted rule that every time **none** was the subject of the sentence, it should take a **singular verb.** Most modern grammarians now agree that the plural may be used when followed by a prepositional phrase with a plural object (noun) or with an object whose meaning in the sentence is plural.

    None of the statements *were* correct.

    When **none** stands alone, some purists believe it should take the singular and others believe that the plural is the proper form when the meaning conveys plurality. Consequently, in the following example, either the singular or plural is generally acceptable.

    All the financial statements had been compiled, but none *was* ***or*** *were* correct.

> When in doubt, use **not one** in place of **none** (with a singular verb, of course).

NOUNS

Nouns are people, places, and things and can occur anywhere in the sentence. Make sure that, when necessary, the nouns are the same in number.

Do the exercises at the end of each chapter by answering the *questions* true or false. (Not singular *question*)
At the end of the engagement, everyone must turn in their *time sheets.* (Not singular *time sheet*)

Possessive Nouns

1. The basic rule for making a **singular noun** possessive is to add an **apostrophe and an s.** If a singular noun ends in s, **add apostrophe and an s.** To make a **plural noun** possessive, add an **apostrophe alone** when the plural ends in **s** or an **apostrophe and an s** when the plural does not end in an **s.**

Singular:	client*'s*	system*'s*	beneficiary*'s*	*Chris'*
Plural:	clients*'*	systems*'*	beneficiarie*s'*	

2. A common area of difficulty has to do with **ownership,** that is, when two or more individuals or groups are mentioned as owning something. If the ownership is **not common** to all, apostrophes appear after each individual or group. If the ownership **is common** to all, only the last individual or group in the series takes an apostrophe.

    Not common to all: The accountant's and the attorney's offices…
    Common to all: Robert, his brother, and their sons' company…

> Most of the confusion associated with possessives seems to be with the plural possessive. Remember to make the noun **plural** first and **possessive** second.

3. Modern usage tends to make possessive forms into adjectives where appropriate. Thus:

    Company's (possessive) management becomes *company* (adjective) management.
    A *two weeks'* (possessive) vacation becomes a *two weeks* or *two-week* (both adjectives) vacation.

> In most instances, either the possessive form or the adjectival form is acceptable. Go with the form that seems most appropriate for that particular sentence.

Gerunds

1. A gerund is a verb changed to a noun by adding **ing.** A noun preceding a gerund must be possessive so that it may be construed as **modifying the noun.**

   Caroline's telecommuting was approved by the partner.

   In this example, the subject of the sentence is **telecommuting,** not Caroline or Caroline's. Since we know that nouns cannot modify nouns, Caroline must become **Caroline's** to create a possessive form that can modify the noun **telecommuting.**

2. The same holds true for **gerunds** used as **objects of prepositions:**

   The partner objected to *Caroline's telecommuting.*

   In this example, **telecommuting** is the object of the preposition **to.** Caroline's is an appositive (or possessive) form modifying **telecommuting.**

PRONOUNS

Like Latin where most words have "cases" according to their function in the sentence, English **pronouns** also have cases. Sometimes you may be aware that you are using a case when determining the proper form of the pronoun and sometimes you may not.

He met *his* partner at *their* office.

1. Let's begin by tackling everybody's favorite: **who** and **whom.** We're going to take some time reviewing this one since it seems to be a major area of confusion. There is little or no confusion when **who** is clearly the **subject** of the sentence:

   Who is going with us?

   And little or no confusion when **whom** is clearly (1) the **object** of the sentence or (2) the **object** of the preposition.

   (1) Jenny audited *whom*? *Whom* did Jenny audit?

   (2) Jenny is working for *whom*? For *whom* is Jenny working?

> If you are having difficulty with **questions,** try changing them into declarative sentences (statements) and substituting another pronoun. Thus: Jenny audits **them** (objective), obviously not **they** (subjective), or Jenny is working for **her,** obviously not **she.**

2. **Who** or **whoever** is the subjective case, and **whom** or **whomever** is the objective case. Common errors occur frequently in two instances: (1) when **who or whoever** is interrupted by a parenthetical phrase and (2) when an entire clause is the subject of a preposition.

   (1) *Whoever* she decides is working with her should meet her at six o'clock.

   In this example, **she decides** is a parenthetical phrase (one that could be left out of the sentence and the sentence would still be a complete thought). When you disregard **she decides,** you can see that **whoever** is the subject of the sentence, not **she.** The error occurs when **she** is believed to be the subject and **whomever,** the object of **decides.**

   (2) Jenny will work with *whoever* shows up first.

   This example represents what seems the most problematic of all the areas relating to who or whom. We have been taught to use the objective case after the preposition (in this case **with**). So why isn't **whomever** the correct form in this example? The answer is that it would be the correct form if the sentence ended with the word **whomever.** (**Whomever** would be the object of the preposition **with**.) In this case, it is not the last word but, rather, it is the **subject** of the clause **whoever shows up first.**

Again, make the substitution of another pronoun as a test of whether to use the subjective or objective case.

Let's look at a few more examples. See if you are better able to recognize the correct form.

(1) I'm sure I will be comfortable with [*whoever/whomever*] the manager decides to assign.

(2) To [*who/whom*] should she speak regarding that matter?

(3) He always chooses [*whoever/whomever*] in his opinion is the best auditor.

(4) She usually enjoys working with [*whoever/whomever*] the partner assigns.

(5) [*Who/Whom*] should I ask to accompany me?

Let's see how well you did.

(1) **Whomever** is correct. The whole clause after the preposition **with** is the object of the preposition, and **whomever** is the object of the verb **to assign.** Turn the clause around and substitute another pronoun. Thus, **the manager decides to assign *him*.**

(2) **Whom** is correct. **Whom** is the object of the preposition **to.** Make the question into a declarative sentence and substitute another pronoun. Thus, **She should speak to *him* regarding that matter.**

(3) **Whoever** is correct. The entire clause **whoever is the best auditor** is the object of the main verb **chooses. Whoever** is the subject of that clause. **In his opinion** is a parenthetical phrase and doesn't affect the rest of the sentence.

(4) **Whomever** is correct. The entire clause **whomever the partner assigns** is the object of the preposition **with,** and **whomever** is the object of the verb **assigns.** Again, turn the clause around and substitute another pronoun. Thus, **the partner assigns *him*.**

(5) **Whom** is correct. **Whom** is the object of the main verb **ask.** Turn the question into a regular declarative sentence and substitute another pronoun. Thus, **I should ask *her* to accompany me.**

3. Pronouns that follow prepositions are always in the **objective case,** except when serving as the subject of a clause, as discussed above. The most popular misuse occurs when using a pronoun after the preposition **between.** (**I, he, she, they,** are never used after **between,** no matter where the prepositional phrase falls in the sentence.)

   Between you and me, I don't believe our client will be able to continue as a going concern.
   That matter is strictly between her and them.

Antecedents

1. An antecedent is the word or words for which a pronoun stands. Any time a pronoun is used, its antecedent must be clear and agree with the word or words for which it stands.

   The accountant placed *his* work in the file.

   In this example, **his** is the pronoun with **the accountant** as its antecedent. **His** agrees with **the accountant** in person and number. **His** is used so as not to repeat **the accountant.**

2. Confusion most often occurs when using indefinite pronouns such as **it, that, this,** and **which.**

   The company for *which* he works always mails *its* paychecks on Friday.

In this example, the pronouns **which** and **its** both clearly refer to **the company.** Consider the next example. Since it is not clear what the antecedent for **it** is, we can't tell for sure whether the company or the paycheck is small.

The company always mails my paycheck on Friday and *it* is a small one.

3. So far in our discussion of antecedents, we have talked about agreement in person. We have not addressed agreement in **number.** The following examples demonstrate pronouns that **do not agree** in number with their antecedents.

   The company issued quarterly financial reports to *their* shareholders. (*Its* is the correct antecedent to agree in number with *company*.)

   Each of the methods is introduced on a separate page, so that the student is made aware of *their* importance. (*Its* is the correct antecedent to agree in number with *each*.) **Note: Importance** refers to **each,** the subject of the sentence, not to **methods,** which is the object of the preposition **of.**

4. When a pronoun refers to singular antecedents that are connected by **or** or **nor**, the pronoun should be **singular.**

   Joe or Buddy has misplaced *his* workpapers.

   Neither Joe nor Buddy has misplaced *his* workpapers.

5. When a pronoun refers to a singular and a plural antecedent connected by **or** or **nor**, the pronoun should be **plural.**

   Neither Joe nor his associates can locate *their* workpapers.

6. Pronouns must also agree with their antecedents in **gender.** Because English language has no way of expressing gender-neutral in pronoun agreement, it has been the custom to use **his** as a convenience when referring to both sexes. To avoid this "gender bias" in writing, there is a growing use of a more cumbersome construction in order to be more politically correct.

   Old: When a new partner's identifiable asset contribution is less than the ownership interest *he* is to receive, the excess capital allowed *him* is considered as goodwill attributable to *him.*

   New: When a new partner's identifiable asset contribution is less than the ownership interest *he or she* is to receive, the excess capital allowed *the new partner* is considered as goodwill attributable to *him or her.*

   You will note in the above example that **he or she (he/she)** and **him or her (him/her)** have been used only once each and the antecedent **new partner** has been repeated once.

The idea is to not overload a single sentence with too many repetitions of each construction. When it seems that **he/she** constructions are overwhelming the sentence, repeat the noun antecedent where possible, even if it sounds a bit labored.

7. **Reflexive pronouns** are pronouns that are used for **emphasizing their antecedents** and should **not be used as substitutes** for regular pronouns. The reflexive pronouns are **myself, yourself, himself, herself, itself, ourselves, yourselves, and themselves.**

   The financing is being handled by the principals *themselves.* (Demonstrates emphasis)
   The partner *himself* will take care of that matter. (Demonstrates emphasis)
   My associate and *I* accept the engagement. (Not my associate and *myself*...)
   I am fine; how about *you*? (Not how about *yourself?)*

ADJECTIVES & ADVERBS

1. Most of us understand that adjectives and adverbs are **modifiers,** but many of us can't tell them apart. In fact, there are many words that can be used as either depending on their use. Consequently, differentiating adjectives from adverbs is really not very important as long as you know how to use them. Understanding, however, that **adjectives modify nouns or pronouns,** and **adverbs modify verbs** and adjectives will help you choose the correct form.

   Falcone Co. purchased *two* computers from Wizard Corp., a very *small* manufacturer. (*two* is an adjective describing the noun *computers, very* is an adverb modifying the adjective *small*, and *small* is an adjective describing the noun *manufacturer.*)

   Acme advised Mason that it would deliver the appliances on July 2 as *originally* agreed. (*originally* is an adverb describing the verb *agreed.*)

2. In writing for the CPA exam, avoid colloquial uses of the adjectives **real** and **sure.** In the following examples, adverbs are called for.

   I am *very* (not *real*) sorry that you didn't pass the exam.
   He will *surely* (not *sure*) be glad if he passes the exam.

3. **Comparisons** using adjectives frequently present problems. Remember that when comparing two things, the **comparative** (often **er)** form is used, and when comparing more than two, the **superlative** (often **est**) form is used.

   This report is *larger* than the other one.
   This report is the *largest* of them all.
   This report is *more* detailed than the others.
   This report is the *most* detailed of them all.

4. **Articles** are adjectives. **An** precedes most vowels, but when the vowel begins with a **consonant sound,** we should use **a.**

   a usual adjustment...
   a one in a million deal...

   Similarly, when **a** or **an** precedes abbreviations or initials, it is the next **sound** that we should consider, not the next letter. In other words, if the next sound is a vowel sound, **an** should be used. Usually, your reader will be reading the abbreviations or initials and not the whole term, title, etc.

   An S.A. will be used to head up the field work on this engagement.
   An F.O.B. contract is a *contract* indicating that the seller will bear that degree of risk and expense that is appropriate to the F.O.B. terms.

CONJUNCTIONS

There are three types of conjunctions: coordinating, subordinating, and correlative.

Coordinating Conjunctions

Coordinating conjunctions are conjunctions that connect equal elements in a sentence. These conjunctions include **and, but, for, yet, so, or,** and **nor.** Examples of common problems involving coordinating conjunctions:

1. Leaving out the **and,** leading to difficulties with comprehension and clarity.

   The accountant studied some of management's representations, marked what she wanted to discuss in the meeting. (The word *and* should be in the place of the comma.)

Mike's summer job entails opening the mail, stamps it with a dater, routing it to the proper person. (Should be: ...opening the mail from other offices, *stamping* it with a dater, *and* routing it to the proper person. **This example also demonstrates a lack of parallelism,** which is addressed in an earlier section.)

2. Omission of **and** is correct when the sentence is a compound sentence (meaning that it contains two independent clauses), in which case a semicolon takes the place of **and.** When the semicolon is used, the ideas of each independent clause should be closely related.

    The security is genuine**;** it has not been materially altered.

3. Although the rules for **or** and **nor** have become less strict over time, you should understand proper usage for the sake of comprehension and clarity. Most of us are familiar with **either**...**or** and **neither**...**nor:**

    Either the creditor must take possession *or* the debtor must sign a security agreement that describes the collateral.

The company would neither accept delivery of the water coolers, nor pay for them, because Peterson did not have the authority to enter into the contract.

Subordinating Conjunctions

Subordinating conjunctions are conjunctions that introduce subordinate elements of the sentence. The most common and the ones we want to concentrate on here are **as, since, because, that, which, when, where,** and **while.**

1. **As; Since; Because**

    Because is the only word of the three that **always** indicates cause. **Since** usually indicates **time** and, when introducing adverbial clauses, may mean either **when** or **because. As** should be avoided altogether in these constructions and used only for comparisons. We strongly recommend using the exact word to avoid any confusion, especially when clarity is essential.

    Attachment of the security interest did not occur because Pix failed to file a financing statement. (Specifically indicates *cause.*)
    Green has not paid any creditor since January 1, 1992. (Specifically indicates *time.*)

    The following example is a typical misuse of the conjunction **as** and demonstrates why **as** should not be used as a substitute for **because:**

    As the partners are contributing more capital to the company, the stock prices are going up.

    The meaning of this sentence is ambiguous. Are the stock prices going up **while** the partners are contributing capital or are the stock prices going up **because** the partners are contributing more capital?

2. **That; Which**

    Many people complain about not understanding when to use **that** and when to use **which** more than just about anything else. The rule to follow requires that you know the difference between a restrictive and a nonrestrictive clause. A **restrictive clause** is one that must remain in the sentence for the sentence to make sense. A **nonrestrictive** clause is one that may be removed from a sentence and the sentence will still make sense.

    That is used with restrictive clauses; *which* is used with nonrestrictive clauses.

    (1) An accountant who breaches his or her contract with a client may be subject to liability for damages and losses *which* the client suffers as a direct result of the breach.

(2) As a result, the accountant is responsible for errors resulting from changes *that* occurred between the time he or she prepared the statement and its effective date.

(3) A reply *that* purports to accept an offer but which adds material qualifications or conditions is not an acceptance; rather, it is a rejection and a counter-offer.

In example (1) above, the clause beginning with **which** is nonrestrictive (sentence would make sense without it). In examples (2) and (3), the clauses that follow **that** are restrictive (necessary for the meaning of the sentence).

> If you can put commas around the clause in question, it is usually nonrestrictive and thus takes **which.** Occasionally, there will be a fine line between what one might consider restrictive or nonrestrictive. In these cases, make your choice based on which sounds better and, if there is another **which** or **that** nearby, let that help your decision. (Unless truly necessary, avoid two or three uses of **which** or two or three uses of **that** in the same sentence.)

3. **When; Where**

The most common incorrect usage associated with these words occurs when they are used to define something.

(1) Exoneration is *where* the surety takes action against the debtor, which seeks to force the debtor to pay his or her debts.

(2) A fiduciary relationship is where the agent acts for the benefit of the principal.

(3) Joint liability is *when* all partners in a partnership are jointly liable for any contract actions against the partnership.

The above three examples are **faulty constructions.** The verb **to be** (**is,** in this case) must be followed by a predicate adjective (an adjective modifying the subject) or a predicate nominative (a noun meaning the same as the subject), **not** an adverbial phrase or clause. These sentences should be rewritten as follows:

(1) Exoneration is *an action* by the surety against the debtor, which seeks to force the debtor to pay his or her debts.

(2) A fiduciary relationship is *the association* of the agent and the principal whereby the agent acts for the benefit of the principal.

(3) Joint liability is *the liability* of all partners in a partnership for any contract actions against the partnership.

4. **While**

Formerly, **while** was acceptable only to denote time. Modern practice accepts **while** and **although** as nearly synonymous. In example (1), either while or although is acceptable. In example (2), **while** is **not** a proper substitution for **although.**

(1) *While/Although* Acme contends that its agreement with Mason was not binding, it is willing to deliver the goods to Mason.

(2) Under a sale or return contract, the sale is considered as completed *although* it is voidable at the buyer's election.

Correlative Conjunction

The third type of conjunction is the **correlative conjunction.** We have briefly mentioned and presented examples of **either...or** and **neither...nor** earlier in connection with nouns, verbs, and agreement. Now we want to discuss these correlatives in connection with **parallelism.**

1. **Not only** should be followed by **but (also).**

   In determining whether a mere invitation or an offer exists, the courts generally will look *not only* to the specific language *but also* to the surrounding circumstances, the custom within the industry, and the prior practice between the parties.

2. Watch out for **placement of correlatives.** Faulty placement leads to faulty construction and obstructs clarity.

   The lawyer *either* is asked to furnish specific information *or* comment as to where the lawyer's views differ from those of management.

Below is the same sentence in much clearer form. Note that the phrases introduced by *either* and *or* are now in parallel construction: *either to furnish...or to comment.*

> The lawyer is asked *either* to furnish specific information *or to* comment as to where the lawyer's views differ from those of management.

APPENDIX D
MACRS TABLES

200% Declining Balance

150% Declining Balance

APPENDIX D

Table 1 Method: 200% Declining Balance (Switching to Straight Line*)
Recovery Period: 3, 5, 7, 10, 15, and 20 Years
Convention: Half-Year

Year	Recovery Period in Years					
	3-Year	5-Year	7-Year	10-Year	15-Year	20-Year
1	33.33%	20.00%	14.29%	10.00%	5.00%	3.750%
2	44.45	32.00	24.49	18.00	9.50	7.219
3	14.81*	19.20	17.49	14.40	8.55	6.677
4	7.41	11.52*	12.49	11.52	7.70	6.177
5		11.52	8.93*	9.22	6.93	5.713
6		5.76	8.92	7.37	6.23	5.285
7			8.93	6.55*	5.90*	4.888
8			4.46	6.55	5.90	4.522
9				6.56	5.91	4.462*
10				6.55	5.90	4.461
11				3.28	5.91	4.462
12					5.90	4.461
13					5.91	4.462
14					5.90	4.461
15					5.91	4.462
16					2.95	4.461
17						4.462
18						4.461
19						4.462
20						4.461
21						2.231

Table 2 Method: 150% Declining Balance (Switching to Straight Line*)
Recovery Period: 3, 5, 7, 10, 15, and 20 Years
Convention: Half-Year

Year	Recovery Period in Years					
	3-Year	5-Year	7-Year	10-Year	15-Year	20-Year
1	25.0%	15.00%	10.71%	7.50%	5.00%	3.750%
2	37.5	25.50	19.13	13.88	9.50	7.219
3	25.0*	17.85	15.03	11.79	8.55	6.677
4	12.5	16.66*	12.25*	10.02	7.70	6.177
5		16.66	12.25	8.74*	6.93	5.713
6		8.33	12.25	8.74	6.23	5.285
7			12.25	8.74	5.90*	4.888
8			6.13	8.74	5.90	4.522
9				8.74	5.91	4.462*
10				8.74	5.90	4.461
11				4.37	5.91	4.462
12					5.90	4.461
13					5.91	4.462
14					5.90	4.461
15					5.91	4.462
16					2.95	4.461
17						4.462
18						4.461
19						4.462
20						4.461
21						2.231

Table 1-A Method: 200% Declining Balance (Switching to Straight Line)
Recovery Period: 3, 5, 7, 10, 15, and 20 Years
Convention: Mid-Quarter
Placed in Service: First Quarter

Year	Recovery Period in Years					
	3-Year	5-Year	7-Year	10-Year	15-Year	20-Year
1	58.33%	35.00%	25.00%	17.50%	8.75%	6.563%
2	27.78	26.00	21.43	16.50	9.13	7.000
3	12.35	15.60	15.31	13.20	8.21	6.482
4	1.54	11.01	10.93	10.56	7.39	5.996
5		11.01	8.75	8.45	6.65	5.546
6		1.38	8.74	6.76	5.99	5.130
7			8.75	6.55	5.90	4.746
8			1.09	6.55	5.91	4.459
9				6.56	5.90	4.459
10				6.55	5.91	4.459
11				0.82	5.90	4.459
12					5.91	4.460
13					5.90	4.459
14					5.91	4.460
15					5.90	4.459
16					0.74	4.460
17						4.459
18						4.460
19						4.459
20						4.460
21						0.557

Table 1-B Method: 200% Declining Balance (Switching to Straight Line)
Recovery Period: 3, 5, 7, 10, 15, and 20 Years
Convention: Mid-Quarter
Placed in Service: Second Quarter

Year	Recovery Period in Years					
	3-Year	5-Year	7-Year	10-Year	15-Year	20-Year
1	41.67%	25.00%	17.85%	12.50%	6.25%	4.688%
2	38.89	30.00	23.47	17.50	9.38	7.148
3	14.14	18.00	16.76	14.00	8.44	6.612
4	5.30	11.37	11.97	11.20	7.59	6.116
5		11.37	8.87	8.96	6.83	5.658
6		4.26	8.87	7.17	6.15	5.233
7			8.87	6.55	5.91	4.841
8			3.33	6.55	5.90	4.478
9				6.56	5.91	4.463
10				6.55	5.90	4.463
11				2.46	5.91	4.463
12					5.90	4.463
13					5.91	4.463
14					5.90	4.463
15					5.91	4.462
16					2.21	4.463
17						4.462
18						4.463
19						4.462
20						4.463
21						1.673

Table 1-C Method: 200% Declining Balance (Switching to Straight Line)
Recovery Period: 3, 5, 7, 10, 15, and 20 Years
Convention: Mid-Quarter
Placed in Service: Third Quarter

Year	Recovery Period in Years					
	3-Year	**5-Year**	**7-Year**	**10-Year**	**15-Year**	**20-Year**
1	25.00%	15.00%	10.71%	7.50%	3.75%	2.813%
2	50.00	34.00	25.51	18.50	9.63	7.289
3	16.67	20.40	18.22	14.80	8.66	6.742
4	8.33	12.24	13.02	11.84	7.80	6.237
5		11.30	9.30	9.47	7.02	5.769
6		7.06	8.85	7.58	6.31	5.336
7			8.86	6.55	5.90	4.936
8			5.53	6.55	5.90	4.566
9				6.56	5.91	4.460
10				6.55	5.90	4.460
11				4.10	5.91	4.460
12					5.90	4.460
13					5.91	4.461
14					5.90	4.460
15					5.91	4.461
16					3.69	4.460
17						4.461
18						4.460
19						4.461
20						4.460
21						2.788

Table 1-D Method: 200% Declining Balance (Switching to Straight Line)
Recovery Period: 3, 5, 7, 10, 15, and 20 Years
Convention: Mid-Quarter
Placed in Service: Fourth Quarter

Year	Recovery Period in Years					
	3-Year	**5-Year**	**7-Year**	**10-Year**	**15-Year**	**20-Year**
1	8.33%	5.00%	3.57%	2.50%	1.25%	0.938%
2	61.11	38.00	27.55	19.50	9.88	7.430
3	20.37	22.80	19.68	15.60	8.89	6.872
4	10.19	13.68	14.06	12.48	8.00	6.357
5		10.94	10.04	9.98	7.20	5.880
6		9.58	8.73	7.99	6.48	5.439
7			8.73	6.55	5.90	5.031
8			7.64	6.55	5.90	4.654
9				6.56	5.90	4.458
10				6.55	5.91	4.458
11				5.74	5.90	4.458
12					5.91	4.458
13					5.90	4.458
14					5.91	4.458
15					5.90	4.458
16					5.17	4.458
17						4.458
18						4.459
19						4.458
20						4.459
21						3.901

Table 2-A Method: 150% Declining Balance (Switching to Straight Line)
Recovery Period: 3, 5, 7, 10, 15, and 20 Years
Convention: Mid-Quarter
Placed in Service: First Quarter

Year	Recovery Period in Years					
	3-Year	5-Year	7-Year	10-Year	15-Year	20-Year
1	43.75%	26.25%	18.75%	13.13%	8.75%	6.563%
2	28.13	22.13	17.41	13.03	9.13	7.008
3	25.00	16.52	13.68	11.08	8.21	6.482
4	3.12	16.52	12.16	9.41	7.39	5.996
5		16.52	12.16	8.71	6.65	5.546
6		2.06	12.16	8.71	5.99	5.130
7			12.16	8.71	5.90	4.746
8			1.52	8.71	5.91	4.459
9				8.71	5.90	4.459
10				8.71	5.91	4.459
11				1.09	5.90	4.459
12					5.91	4.460
13					5.90	4.459
14					5.91	4.460
15					5.90	4.459
16					0.74	4.460
17						4.459
18						4.460
19						4.459
20						4.460
21						0.557

Table 2-B Method: 150% Declining Balance (Switching to Straight Line)
Recovery Period: 3, 5, 7, 10, 15, and 20 Years
Convention: Mid-Quarter
Placed in Service: Second Quarter

Year	Recovery Period in Years					
	3-Year	5-Year	7-Year	10-Year	15-Year	20-Year
1	31.25%	18.75%	13.39%	9.38%	6.25%	4.688%
2	34.38	24.38	18.56	13.59	9.38	7.148
3	25.00	17.06	14.58	11.55	8.44	6.612
4	9.37	16.76	12.22	9.82	7.59	6.116
5		16.76	12.22	8.73	6.83	5.658
6		6.29	12.22	8.73	6.15	5.233
7			12.23	8.73	5.91	4.841
8			4.58	8.73	5.90	4.478
9				8.73	5.91	4.463
10				8.73	5.90	4.463
11				3.28	5.91	4.463
12					5.90	4.463
13					5.91	4.463
14					5.90	4.463
15					5.91	4.462
16					2.21	4.463
17						4.462
18						4.463
19						4.462
20						4.463
21						1.673

Table 2-C Method: 150% Declining Balance (Switching to Straight Line)
Recovery Period: 3, 5, 7, 10, 15, and 20 Years
Convention: Mid-Quarter
Placed in Service: Third Quarter

Year	Recovery Period in Years					
	3-Year	5-Year	7-Year	10-Year	15-Year	20-Year
1	18.75%	11.25%	8.04%	5.63%	3.75%	2.813%
2	40.63	26.63	19.71	14.16	9.63	7.289
3	25.00	18.64	15.48	12.03	8.66	6.742
4	15.62	16.56	12.27	10.23	7.80	6.237
5		16.57	12.28	8.75	7.02	5.769
6		10.35	12.27	8.75	6.31	5.336
7			12.28	8.75	5.90	4.936
8			7.67	8.74	5.90	4.566
9				8.75	5.91	4.460
10				8.74	5.90	4.460
11				5.47	5.91	4.460
12					5.90	4.460
13					5.91	4.461
14					5.90	4.460
15					5.91	4.461
16					3.69	4.460
17						4.461
18						4.460
19						4.461
20						4.460
21						2.788

Table 2-D Method: 150% Declining Balance (Switching to Straight Line)
Recovery Period: 3, 5, 7, 10, 15, and 20 Years
Convention: Mid-Quarter
Placed in Service: Fourth Quarter

Year	Recovery Period in Years					
	3-Year	5-Year	7-Year	10-Year	15-Year	20-Year
1	6.25%	3.75%	2.68%	1.88%	1.25%	0.938%
2	46.88	28.88	20.85	14.72	9.88	7.430
3	25.00	20.21	16.39	12.51	8.89	6.872
4	21.87	16.40	12.87	10.63	8.00	6.357
5		16.41	12.18	9.04	7.20	5.880
6		14.35	12.18	8.72	6.48	5.439
7			12.19	8.72	5.90	5.031
8			10.66	8.72	5.90	4.654
9				8.72	5.90	4.458
10				8.71	5.91	4.458
11				7.63	5.90	4.458
12					5.91	4.458
13					5.90	4.458
14					5.91	4.458
15					5.90	4.458
16					5.17	4.458
17						4.458
18						4.459
19						4.458
20						4.459
21						3.901

APPENDIX E
RECENTLY RELEASED AICPA QUESTIONS

In September 2008 and April 2009, the AICPA released several REG questions labeled as "Year 2007 Disclosed Questions" and "Year 2008 Disclosed Questions," respectively. For both sets of questions, Problem 1 was labeled "moderate" by the AICPA examiners and Problem 2 was labeled "more difficult." The REG questions and the related unofficial solutions are reproduced here, along with the exclusive Bisk Education explanations. The criteria for release of a question was that it would not be used for future exams; thus, candidates should not be surprised by obsolete questions. The AICPA did not state whether these questions were assigned points on any exam or whether they merely were questions being pre-tested that earned no points. These questions are intended only as a study aid and should not be used to predict the content of future exams. It is extremely unlikely that released questions will appear on future examinations.

Unlike some other exam sections, the AICPA made no reference to cognitive skills for the questions released in 2008. The simulation released in 2008 was re-labeled as Problem 5. The questions released in 2009 were re-labeled from Problems 1, 2, and 3, to Problems 3, 4, and 6, respectively.

Problem 1 MULTIPLE CHOICE QUESTIONS (30 to 40 minutes)

1. Taylor, an unmarried taxpayer, had $90,000 in adjusted gross income for year 13. During year 13, Taylor donated land to a church and made no other contributions. Taylor purchased the land in year 1 as an investment for $14,000. The land's fair market value was $25,000 on the day of the donation. What is the maximum amount of charitable contribution that Taylor may deduct as an itemized deduction for the land donation for year 13?
a. $25,000
b. $14,000
c. $11,000
d. $0 (R/08, REG, 0048T, #1, 8658)

2. Forrest Corp. owned 100% of both the voting stock and total value of Diamond Corp. Both corporations were C corporations. Forrest's basis in the Diamond stock was $200,000 when it received a lump sum *liquidating* distribution of property as a result of the redemption of all of Diamond stock. The property had an adjusted basis of $270,000 and a fair market value of $500,000. What amount of gain did Forrest recognize on the distribution?
a. $0
b. $ 70,000
c. $270,000
d. $500,000 (R/08, REG, 0743T, #2, 8659)

3. Nare, an accrual-basis, calendar-year taxpayer, owns a building that was rented to Mott under a 10-year lease expiring August 31, year 3. On January 2, year 1, Mott paid $30,000 as consideration for canceling the lease. On November 1, year 1, Nare leased the building to Pine under a five-year lease. Pine paid Nare $5,000 rent for each of the two months of November and December, and an additional $5,000 for the last month's rent. What amount of rental income should Nare report in its year 1 income tax return?
a. $10,000
b. $15,000
c. $40,000
d. $45,000 (R/08, REG, 0787T, #3, 8660)

4. Molloy contributed $40,000 in cash in exchange for a one-third interest in the RST Partnership. In the first year of partnership operations, RST had taxable income of $60,000. In addition, Molloy received a $5,000 distribution of cash and, at the end of the partnership year, Molloy had a one-third share in the $18,000 of partnership recourse liabilities. What was Molloy's basis in RST at year end?
a. $ 55,000
b. $ 61,000
c. $ 71,000
d. $101,000 (R/08, REG, 0949T, #4, 8661)

5. Fern received $30,000 in cash and an automobile with an adjusted basis and market value of $20,000 in a proportionate liquidating distribution from EF Partnership. Fern's basis in the partnership interest was $60,000 before the distribution. What is Fern's basis in the automobile received in the liquidation?
a. $0
b. $10,000
c. $20,000
d. $30,000 (R/08, REG, 0958T, #5, 8662)

6. Pope, a C corporation, owns 15% of Arden Corporation. Arden paid a $3,000 cash dividend to Pope. What is the amount of Pope's dividend-received deduction?
a. $3,000
b. $2,400
c. $2,100
d. $0 (R/08, REG, 1141T, #6, 8663)

7. Under the Negotiable Instruments Article of the UCC, a holder in due course in a nonconsumer transaction takes a negotiable instrument free from which of the following defenses that may be asserted by a party with whom the holder in due course had **not** dealt?
a. Fraud in the execution
b. Discharge in an insolvency proceeding
c. Breach of contract
d. Infancy, to the extent that it is a simple contract defense (R/08, REG, 1153L, #7, 8664)

8. Dunn received 100 shares of stock as a gift from Dunn's grandparent. The stock cost Dunn's grandparent $32,000 and it was worth $27,000 at the time of the transfer to Dunn. Dunn sold the stock for $29,000. What amount of gain or loss should Dunn report from the sale of the stock?
a. $0
b. $2,000 gain
c. $3,000 gain
d. $3,000 loss (R/08, REG, 1215T, #8, 8665)

9. Curator contracted to sell Train's painting. Train issued a $10,000 note to Curator that was payable within 10 days after Curator sold Train's painting. Curator sold the painting on May 1. Train, alleging that the note was not a negotiable instrument, refused to pay the note. Under the Negotiable Instruments Article of the UCC, which of the following statements is correct regarding the status of the note?
a. The note was **not** a negotiable instrument because it was **not** payable at a definite time.
b. The note was **not** negotiable because it was subject to another writing.
c. The note was negotiable because it was for a sum certain.
d. The note was negotiable because it was conditioned on an event that took place.
(R/08, REG, 1320L, #9, 8666)

10. U Co. had cash purchases and payments on account during the current year totaling $455,000. U's beginning and ending accounts payable balances for the year were $64,000 and $50,000, respectively. What amount represents U's accrual basis purchases for the year?
a. $441,000
b. $469,000
c. $505,000
d. $519,000 (R/08, REG, 1490T, #10, 8667)

11. Under the Code of Professional Conduct of the AICPA, which of the following is required to be independent in fact and appearance when discharging professional responsibilities?
a. A CPA in public practice providing tax and management advisory services
b. A CPA in public practice providing auditing and other attestation services
c. A CPA **not** in public practice
d. All CPAs (R/08, REG, 2579L, #11, 8668)

12. Which of the following is a miscellaneous itemized deduction subject to the 2% of adjusted gross income floor?
a. Gambling losses up to the amount of gambling winnings
b. Medical expenses
c. Real estate tax
d. Employee business expenses
(R/08, REG, A0044T, #12, 8669)

13. Which of the following transactions is subject to registration requirements of the Securities Act of 1933?

a. The public sale by a corporation of its negotiable 10-year notes
b. The public sale by a charitable organization of 10-year bearer bonds
c. The sale across state lines of municipal bonds issued by a city
d. Issuance of stock by a publicly-traded corporation to its shareholders because of a stock split

(R/08, REG, A0211L, #13, 8670)

14. Which of the following items is a capital asset?

a. An automobile for personal use
b. Depreciable business property
c. Accounts receivable for inventory sold
d. Real property used in a trade or business

(R/08, REG, A0221T, #14, 8671)

15. A C corporation has gross receipts of $150,000, $35,000 of other income, and deductible expenses of $95,000. In addition, the corporation incurred a net long-term capital loss of $25,000 in the current year. What is the corporation's taxable income?

a. $ 65,000
b. $ 87,000
c. $ 90,000
d. $115,000 (R/08, REG, A0388T, #15, 8672)

16. Which of the following professional bodies has the authority to revoke a CPA's license to practice public accounting?

a. National Association of State Boards of Accountancy
b. State board of accountancy
c. State CPA Society Ethics Committee
d. Professional Ethics Division of AICPA

(R/08, REG, A0569L, #16, 8673)

17. Jagdon Corp.'s book income was $150,000 for the current year, including interest income from municipal bonds of $5,000 and excess capital losses over capital gains of $10,000. Federal income tax expense of $50,000 was also included in Jagdon's books. What amount represents Jagdon's taxable income for the current year?

a. $185,000
b. $195,000
c. $205,000
d. $215,000 (R/08, REG, A0577T, #17, 8674)

18. Which of the following acts by a CPA is a violation of professional standards regarding the confidentiality of client information?

a. Releasing financial information to a local bank with the approval of the client's mail clerk
b. Allowing a review of professional practice without client authorization
c. Responding to an enforceable subpoena
d. Faxing a tax return to a loan officer at the request of the client

(R/08, REG, A0713L, #18, 8675)

19. A self-employed taxpayer had gross income of $57,000. The taxpayer paid self-employment tax of $8,000, health insurance of $6,000, and $5,000 of alimony. The taxpayer also contributed $2,000 to a traditional IRA. What is the taxpayer's adjusted gross income?

a. $55,000
b. $50,000
c. $46,000
d. $40,000 (R/08, REG, A1498T, #19, 8676)

20. Which of the following is a prerequisite for the creation of an agency relationship?

a. Consideration must be given.
b. The agent must have capacity.
c. The principal must have capacity.
d. The consideration must be in writing.

(R/08, REG, C02472R, #20, 8677)

Problem 2 MULTIPLE CHOICE QUESTIONS (30 to 40 minutes)

21. Which of the following areas of professional responsibility should be observed by a CPA **not** in public practice?

	Objectivity	*Independence*
a.	Yes	Yes
b.	Yes	No
c.	No	Yes
d.	No	No

(R/08, REG, 0805L, #21, 8678)

22. What is the standard that must be established to prove a violation of the anti-fraud provisions of Rule 10b-5 of the Securities Exchange Act of 1934?

a. Negligence
b. Intentional misconduct
c. Criminal intent
d. Strict liability (R/08, REG, 1141L, #22, 8679)

23. In June, Mullin, a general contractor, contracted with a town to renovate the town square. The town council wanted the project done quickly and the parties placed a clause in the contract that for each day the project extended beyond 90 working days, Mullin would forfeit $100 of the contract price. In August, Mullin took a three-week vacation. The project was completed in October, 120 working days after it was begun. What type of damages may the town recover from Mullin?
a. Punitive damages because taking a vacation in the middle of the project was irresponsible
b. Compensatory damages because of the delay in completing the project
c. Liquidated damages because of the clause in the contract
d. No damages because Mullin completed performance (R/08, REG, 1237L, #23, 8680)

24. Baker is a partner in BDT with a partnership basis of $60,000. BDT made a liquidating distribution of land with an adjusted basis of $75,000 and a fair market value of $40,000 to Baker. What amount of gain or loss should Baker report?
a. $35,000 loss
b. $20,000 loss
c. $0
d. $15,000 gain (R/08, REG, 1338T, #24, 8681)

25. Under the ethical standards of the profession, which of the following investments by a CPA in a corporate client is an indirect financial interest?
a. An investment held in a retirement plan
b. An investment held in a blind trust
c. An investment held through a regulated mutual fund
d. An investment held through participation in an investment club (R/08, REG, 1349L, #25, 8682)

26. Nolan designed Timber Partnership's new building. Nolan received an interest in the partnership for the services. Nolan's normal billing for these services would be $80,000 and the fair market value of the partnership interest Nolan received is $120,000. What amount of income should Nolan report?
a. $0
b. $ 40,000
c. $ 80,000
d. $120,000 (R/08, REG, 1375T, #26, 8683)

27. The CSU partnership distributed to each partner cash of $4,000, inventory with a basis of $4,000 and a fair market value (FMV) of $6,000, and land with an adjusted basis of $5,000 and an FMV of $3,000 in a liquidating distribution. Partner Chang had an outside basis in Chang's partnership interest of $12,000. In the second year after receiving the liquidating distribution, Chang sold the inventory for $5,000 and the land for $3,000. What income must Chang report upon the sale of these assets?
a. $0 gain or loss
b. $0 ordinary gain and $1,000 capital loss
c. $1,000 ordinary gain and $1,000 capital loss
d. $1,000 ordinary gain and $0 capital loss
(R/08, REG, 1455T, #27, 8684)

28. A couple filed a joint return in prior tax years. During the current tax year, one spouse died. The couple has no dependent children. What is the filing status available to the surviving spouse for the first subsequent tax year?
a. Surviving spouse
b. Married filing separately
c. Single
d. Head of household
(R/08, REG, 1570T, #28, 8685)

29. Under the Negotiable Instruments Article of the UCC, which of the following defenses generally may be used against all holders of negotiable instruments?
a. Breach of warranty
b. Fraud in the inducement
c. Minority of the maker
d. Lack of consideration
(R/08, REG, 1992L, #29, 8686)

30. Commerce Corp. elects S corporation status as of the beginning of year 2000. At the time of Commerce's election, it held a machine with a basis of $20,000 and a fair market value of $30,000. In March of 2000, Commerce sells the machine for $35,000. What would be the amount subject to the built-in gains tax?
a. $0
b. $ 5,000
c. $10,000
d. $15,000 (R/08, REG, 2009T, #30, 8687)

31. Rules issued under the Sarbanes-Oxley Act of 2002 restrict former members of an audit engagement team from accepting employment as a chief executive, chief financial or chief accounting officer, or controller of an audit client that files reports with the Securities and Exchange Commission. How many annual audit period(s) must be completed before such employment can be accepted?
a. One
b. Two
c. Three
d. Five (R/08, REG, 2450L, #31, 8688)

32. Under the Documents of Title Article of the UCC, which of the following correctly describes the standard of liability that must be established to hold a warehouser liable for loss or damage to stored property?
a. Strict liability
b. Ordinary negligence
c. Gross negligence
d. Deliberate destruction or theft
(R/08, REG, 2516L, #32, 8689)

33. Chris, age five, has $3,000 of interest income and no earned income this year. Assume the current applicable standard deduction is $950. How much of Chris's income will be taxed at Chris's parents' maximum tax rate?
a. $0
b. $1,100
c. $2,050
d. $3,000
(R/08, REG, A0038T, #33, amended, 8690)

34. Which of the following is allowed in the calculation of the taxable income of a simple trust?
a. Exemption
b. Standard deduction
c. Brokerage commission for purchase of tax-exempt bonds
d. Charitable contribution
(R/08, REG, A0209T, #34, 8691)

35. Which of the following statements about the child and dependent care credit is correct?
a. The credit is nonrefundable.
b. The child must be under the age of 18 years.
c. The child must be a direct descendant of the taxpayer.
d. The maximum credit is $600.
(R/08, REG, A0502T, #35, 8692)

36. Martin filed a timely return on April 15. Martin inadvertently omitted income that amounted to 30% of his gross income stated on the return. The statute of limitations for Martin's return would end after how many years?
a. 3 years
b. 6 years
c. 7 years
d. Unlimited (R/08, REG, A0987T, #36, 8693)

37. The individual partner rather than the partnership makes which of the following elections?
a. Election to amortize organizational costs
b. Nonrecognition treatment for involuntary conversion gains
c. Code section 179 deductions for tangible personal property
d. Whether to take a deduction or credit for taxes paid to foreign countries
(R/08, REG, A1046T, #37, 8694)

38. A taxpayer sold for $200,000 equipment that had an adjusted basis of $180,000. Through the date of the sale, the taxpayer had deducted $30,000 of depreciation. Of this amount, $17,000 was in excess of straight-line depreciation. What amount of gain would be recaptured under Section 1245 (Gain from Dispositions of Certain Depreciable Property)?
a. $13,000
b. $17,000
c. $20,000
d. $30,000 (R/08, REG, A1361T, #38, 8695)

39. Four years ago, a self-employed taxpayer purchased office furniture for $30,000. During the current tax year, the taxpayer sold the furniture for $37,000. At the time of the sale, the taxpayer's depreciation deductions totaled $20,700. What part of the gain is taxed as long-term capital gain?
a. $0
b. $ 7,000
c. $20,700
d. $27,700 (R/08, REG, A1538T, #39, 8696)

40. One of the elections a new corporation must make is its choice of an accounting period. Which of the following entities has the most flexibility in choosing an accounting period?
a. C corporation
b. S corporation
c. Partnership
d. Personal service corporation
(R/08, REG, C00359R, #40, 8697)

Problem 3 MULTIPLE CHOICE QUESTIONS (30 to 40 minutes)

41. Which of the following actions by a CPA most likely violates the profession's ethical standards?
a. Using a records-retention agency to store confidential client records
b. Retaining client records after the client has demanded their return
c. Arranging with a financial institution to collect notes issued by a client in payment of fees due
d. Compiling the financial statements of a client that employed the CPA's spouse as a bookkeeper (R/09, REG, 0001L, #1, 8851)

42. Under the liability provisions of Section 11 of the Securities Act of 1933, a CPA who certifies financial statements included in a registration statement generally will not be liable to a purchaser of the security
a. Unless the purchaser can prove scienter on the part of the CPA
b. Unless the purchaser can prove privity with the CPA
c. If the CPA can prove due diligence
d. If the financial statements were materially misstated (R/09, REG, 0123L, #2, 8852)

43. Camp orally guaranteed payment of a loan Camp's cousin Wilcox had obtained from Camp's friend Main. The loan was to be repaid in 10 monthly payments. After making six payments, Wilcox defaulted on the loan and Main demanded that Camp honor the guaranty. Regarding Camp's liability to Main, Camp is
a. Liable under the oral guaranty because the loan would be paid within one year
b. Liable under the oral guaranty because Camp benefited by maintaining a personal relationship with Main
c. Not liable under the oral guaranty because Camp's guaranty must be in writing to be enforceable
d. Not liable under the oral guaranty because of failure of consideration

(R/09, REG, 0394L, #3, 8853)

44. During the current year, Mann, an unmarried U.S. citizen, made a $5,000 cash gift to an only child and also paid $25,000 in tuition expenses directly to a grandchild's university on the grandchild's behalf. Mann made no other lifetime transfers. Assume that the gift tax annual exclusion is $12,000. For gift tax purposes, what was Mann's taxable gift?
a. $30,000
b. $25,000
c. $18,000
d. $0 (R/09, REG, 0553T, #4, 8854)

45. Wynn, a single individual age 60, sold Wynn's personal residence for $450,000. Wynn had owned Wynn's residence, which had a basis of $250,000, for six years. Within eight months of the sale, Wynn purchased a new residence for $400,000. What is Wynn's recognized gain from the sale of Wynn's personal residence?
a. $0
b. $ 50,000
c. $ 75,000
d. $200,000 (R/09, REG, 0996T, #5, 8855)

46. George and Suzanne have been married for 40 years. Suzanne inherited $1,000,000 from her mother. Assume that the annual gift-tax exclusion is $12,000. What amount of the $1,000,000 can Suzanne give to George without incurring a gift-tax liability?
a. $ 12,000
b. $ 24,000
c. $ 500,000
d. $1,000,000 (R/09, REG, 1129T, #6, 8856)

47. Kant, a cash-basis individual, owns and operates an office building. Kant received the following payments during the current year:

Current rents	$30,000
Advance rents for the next year	10,000
Security deposits held in a segregated account	5,000
Lease cancellation payments	15,000

What amount is included in gross income?
a. $30,000
b. $40,000
c. $55,000
d. $60,000 (R/09, REG, 1166T, #7, 8857)

48. Webster, a C corporation, has $70,000 in accumulated and no current earnings and profits. Webster distributed $20,000 cash and property with an adjusted basis and fair market value of $60,000 to its shareholders. What amount should the shareholders report as dividend income?
a. $20,000
b. $60,000
c. $70,000
d. $80,000 (R/09, REG, 1360T, #8, 8858)

49. Under the Secured Transactions Article of the UCC, for which of the following types of collateral must a financing statement be filed in order to perfect a purchase money security interest?
a. Stock certificates
b. Promissory notes
c. Personal jewelry
d. Inventory (R/09, REG, 1578L, #9, 8859)

50. Under the Secured Transactions Article of the UCC, what secured transaction document must be signed by the debtor?
a. Statement of assignment
b. Security agreement
c. Release of collateral
d. Termination statement
(R/09, REG, 1891L, #10, 8860)

51. Ames and Roth form Homerun, a C corporation. Ames contributes several autographed baseballs to Homerun. Ames purchased the baseballs for $500, and they have a total fair market value of $1,000. Roth contributes several autographed baseball bats to Homerun. Roth purchased the bats for $5,000, and they have a fair market value of $7,000. What is Homerun's basis in the contributed bats and balls?
a. $0
b. $5,500
c. $6,000
d. $8,000 (R/09, REG, 1891T, #11, 8861)

52. Sandy is the sole shareholder of Swallow, an S corporation. Sandy's adjusted basis in Swallow stock is $60,000 at the beginning of the year. During the year, Swallow reports the following income items:

Ordinary income	$30,000
Tax-exempt income	5,000
Capital gains	10,000

In addition, Swallow makes a nontaxable distribution to Sandy of $20,000 during the year. What is Sandy's adjusted basis in the Swallow stock at the end of the year?
a. $60,000
b. $70,000
c. $80,000
d. $85,000 (R/09, REG, 1965T, #12, 8862)

53. A $100,000 increase in partnership liabilities is treated in which of the following ways?
a. Increases each partner's basis in the partnership by $100,000
b. Increases the partners' bases only if the liability is nonrecourse
c. Increases each partner's basis in proportion to their ownership
d. Does not change any partner's basis in the partnership regardless of whether the liabilities are recourse or nonrecourse
(R/09, REG, 1999T, #13, 8863)

54. Under the Secured Transactions Article of the UCC, all of the following are needed to create an enforceable security interest, except
a. A security agreement must exist.
b. The secured party must give value.
c. The debtor must have rights in the collateral.
d. A financing statement must be filed.
(R/09, REG, 2151L, #14, 8864)

55. An individual received $50,000 during the current year pursuant to a divorce decree. A check for $25,000 was identified as annual alimony, checks totaling $10,000 as annual child support, and a check for $15,000 as a property settlement. What amount should be included in the individual's gross income?
a. $50,000
b. $40,000
c. $25,000
d. $0 (R/09, REG, A0730T, #15, 8865)

56. Bluff purchased equipment for business use for $35,000 and made $1,000 of improvements to the equipment. After deducting depreciation of $5,000, Bluff gave the equipment to Russett for business use. At the time the gift was made, the equipment had a fair market value of $32,000. Ignoring gift tax consequences, what is Russett's basis in the equipment?
a. $31,000
b. $32,000
c. $35,000
d. $36,000 (R/09, REG, A1487T, #16, 8866)

57. Dale was a 50% partner in D&P Partnership. Dale contributed $10,000 in cash upon the formation of the partnership. D&P borrowed $10,000 to purchase equipment. During the first year of operations, D&P had $15,000 net taxable income, $2,000 tax-exempt interest income, a $3,000 distribution to each partner, and a $4,000 reduction of debt. At the end of the first year of operation, what amount would be Dale's basis?

a. $16,500
b. $17,500
c. $18,500
d. $21,500 (R/09, REG, C03380R, #17, 8867)

58. The adjusted basis of Smith's interest in EVA partnership was $230,000 immediately before receiving the following distribution in complete liquidation of EVA:

	Basis to EVA	Fair market value
Cash	$150,000	$150,000
Real estate	120,000	146,000

What is Smith's basis in the real estate?

a. $146,000
b. $133,000
c. $120,000
d. $ 80,000 (R/09, REG, C04320R, #18, 8868)

59. A CPA in public practice may not disclose confidential client information regarding auditing services without the client's consent in response to which of the following situations?

a. A review of the CPA's professional practice by a state CPA society
b. A letter to the client from the IRS
c. An inquiry from the professional ethics division of the AICPA
d. A court-ordered subpoena or summons

(R/09, REG, ZA0804L, #19, 8869)

60. An S corporation engaged in manufacturing has a year end of June 30. Revenue consistently has been more than $10 million under both cash and accrual basis of accounting. The stockholders would like to change the tax status of the corporation to a C corporation using the cash basis with the same year end. Which of the following statements is correct if it changes to a C corporation?

a. The year end will be December 31, using the cash basis of accounting.
b. The year end will be December 31, using the accrual basis of accounting.
c. The year end will be June 30, using the accrual basis of accounting.
d. The year end will be June 30, using the cash basis of accounting.

(R/09, REG, ZA1555T, #20, 8870)

Problem 4 MULTIPLE CHOICE QUESTIONS (30 to 40 minutes)

61. Under which of the following circumstances is trust property with an independent trustee includible in the grantor's gross estate?
a. The trust is revocable.
b. The trust is established for a minor.
c. The trustee has the power to distribute trust income.
d. The income beneficiary disclaims the property, which then passes to the remainderman, the grantor's friend. (R/09, REG, 0620T, #21, 8871)

62. Brisk Corp. is an accrual-basis, calendar-year C corporation with one individual shareholder. At year end, Brisk had $600,000 accumulated and current earnings and profits as it prepared to make its only dividend distribution for the year to its shareholder. Brisk could distribute either cash of $200,000 or land with an adjusted tax basis of $75,000 and a fair market value of $200,000. How would the taxable incomes of both Brisk and the shareholder change if land were distributed instead of cash?

	Brisk's *taxable income*	*Shareholder's* *taxable income*
a.	No change	No change
b.	Increase	No change
c.	No change	Decrease
d.	Increase	Decrease

(R/09, REG, 0669T, #22, 8872)

63. Under the Negotiable Instruments Article of the UCC, which of the following parties has secondary liability on an instrument?
a. An acceptor of a note
b. An issuer of a cashier's check
c. A drawer of a draft
d. A maker of a note

(R/09, REG, 1247L, #23, 8873)

64. Train issued a note payable to Blake in payment of contracted services that Blake was to perform. Blake endorsed the note "pay to bearer" and delivered it to Reed in satisfaction of a debt owed Reed. Train refused to pay Reed on the note because Blake had not yet performed the services. Under the Negotiable Instruments Article of the UCC, must Train pay Reed?
a. No, Train does not have to pay Reed until the services are performed.
b. No, Train does not have to pay Reed because the note was issued to Blake.
c. Yes, Train has to pay Reed because the note was converted into bearer paper.
d. Yes, Train has to pay Reed because Reed was a holder in due course.

(R/09, REG, 1251L, #24, 8874)

65. Assuming appropriate disclosure is made, which of the following fee arrangements generally would be permitted under the ethical standards of the profession?
a. A fee paid to the client's audit firm for recommending investment advisory services to the client
b. A fee paid to the client's tax accountant for recommending a computer system to the client
c. A contingent fee paid to the CPA for preparing the client's amended income tax return
d. A contingent fee paid to the CPA for reviewing the client's financial statements

(R/09, REG, 1436L, #25, 8875)

66. Fox, the sole shareholder in Fall, a C corporation, has a tax basis of $60,000. Fall has $40,000 of accumulated positive earnings and profits at the beginning of the year and $10,000 of current positive earnings and profits for the current year. At year end, Fall distributed land with an adjusted basis of $30,000 and a fair market value (FMV) of $38,000 to Fox. The land has an outstanding mortgage of $3,000 that Fox must assume. What is Fox's tax basis in the land?
a. $38,000
b. $35,000
c. $30,000
d. $27,000 (R/09, REG, 1440T, #26, 8876)

67. Dart, a C corporation, distributes software over the Internet and has had average revenues in excess of $20 million dollars per year for the past three years. To purchase software, customers key-in their credit card number to a secure web site and receive a password that allows the customer to immediately download the software. As a result, Dart doesn't record accounts receivable or inventory on its books. Which of the following statements is correct?

a. Dart may use either the cash or accrual method of accounting as long as Dart elects a calendar year end.
b. Dart may utilize any method of accounting Dart chooses as long as Dart consistently applies the method it chooses.
c. Dart must use the accrual method of accounting.
d. Dart may utilize the cash basis method of accounting until it incurs an additional $10 million to develop additional software.

(R/09, REG, 1588T, #27, 8877)

68. Spinner, CPA, had audited Lasco Corp.'s financial statements for the past several years. Prior to the current-year's engagement, a disagreement arose that caused Lasco to change auditing firms. Lasco has demanded that Spinner provide Lasco with Spinner's working papers so that Lasco may show them to prospective auditors to help them prepare their bids for Lasco's audit engagement. Spinner refused and Lasco commenced litigation. Under the ethical standards of the profession, will Spinner be successful in refusing to turn over the working papers?

a. Yes, because Spinner is the owner of the working papers.
b. Yes, because Lasco is required to direct prospective auditors to contact Spinner to make arrangements to view the working papers in Spinner's office.
c. No, because Lasco has a legitimate business reason for demanding that Spinner surrender the working papers.
d. No, because it was Lasco's financial statements that were audited.

(R/09, REG, 1602L, #28, 8878)

69. The Simone Trust reported distributable net income of $120,000 for the current year. The trustee is required to distribute $60,000 to Kent and $90,000 to Lind each year. If the trustee distributes these amounts, what amount is includible in Lind's gross income?

a. $0
b. $60,000
c. $72,000
d. $90,000 (R/09, REG, 1709T, #29, 8879)

70. Sands purchased 100 shares of Eastern Corp. stock for $18,000 on April 1 of the prior year. On February 1 of the current year, Sands sold 50 shares of Eastern for $7,000. Fifteen days later, Sands purchased 25 shares of Eastern for $3,750. What is the amount of Sand's recognized gain or loss?

a. $0
b. $ 500
c. $1,000
d. $2,000 (R/09, REG, 1717T, #30, 8880)

71. Under the Negotiable Instruments Article of the UCC, which of the following instruments is classified as a promise to pay?

a. A check
b. A draft
c. A trade acceptance
d. A certificate of deposit

(R/09, REG, 1963L, #31, 8881)

72. Under Regulation D of the Securities Act of 1933, what is the maximum time period during which an exempt offering may be made?

a. Three months
b. Six months
c. Twelve months
d. Twenty-four months

(R/09, REG, 2289L, #32, 8882)

73. In April, A and B formed X Corp. A contributed $50,000 cash, and B contributed land worth $70,000 (with an adjusted basis of $40,000). B also received $20,000 cash from the corporation. A and B each receives 50% of the corporation's stock. What is the tax basis of the land to X Corp.?

a. $40,000
b. $50,000
c. $60,000
d. $70,000 (R/09, REG, A0104T, #33, 8883)

74. Which of the following is a capital asset?

a. Inventory held primarily for sale to customers
b. Accounts receivable
c. A computer system used by the taxpayer in a personal accounting business
d. Land held as an investment

(R/09, REG, A0122T, #34, 8884)

75. Aviary Corp. sold a building for $600,000. Aviary received a down payment of $120,000 as well as annual principal payments of $120,000 for each of the subsequent four years. Aviary purchased the building for $500,000 and claimed depreciation of $80,000. What amount of gain should Aviary report in the year of sale using the installment method?
a. $180,000
b. $120,000
c. $ 54,000
d. $ 36,000
(R/09, REG, A0741T, #35, 8885)

76. Which of the following payments would require the donor to file a gift tax return?
a. $30,000 to a university for a spouse's tuition
b. $40,000 to a university for a cousin's room and board
c. $50,000 to a hospital for a parent's medical expenses
d. $80,000 to a physician for a friend's surgery
(R/09, REG, A1227T, #36, 8886)

77. Which of the following groups may elect to file a consolidated corporate return?
a. A brother/sister-controlled group
b. A parent corporation and all more-than-10%-controlled partnerships
c. A parent corporation and all more-than-50%-controlled subsidiaries
d. Members of an affiliated group
(R/09, REG, A1316T, #37, 8887)

78. A 33-year-old taxpayer withdrew $30,000 (pre-tax) from a traditional IRA. The taxpayer has a 33% effective tax rate and a 35% marginal tax rate. What is the total tax liability associated with the withdrawal?
a. $10,000
b. $10,500
c. $13,000
d. $13,500 (R/09, REG, A1500T, #38, 8888)

79. A heavy equipment dealer would like to trade some business assets in a nontaxable exchange. Which of the following exchanges would qualify as nontaxable?
a. The company jet for a large truck to be used in the corporation
b. Investment securities for antiques to be held as investments
c. A road grader held in inventory for another road grader
d. A corporate office building for a vacant lot
(R/09, REG, A1731T, #39, 8889)

80. According to the AICPA Code of Professional Conduct, which of the following financial interests in the client during the period of the engagement impairs a CPA's independence?
a. All direct and indirect financial interests
b. Only direct financial interests
c. Only direct and material indirect financial interests
d. Only material financial interests
(R/09, REG, ZA0996L, #40, 8890)

SIMULATIONS

Problem 5 (20 to 30 minutes)

In the following simulation, you will be asked to complete various tasks. You may use the content in the **Information Tabs** to complete the tasks in the **Work Tabs**.

Information Tabs:

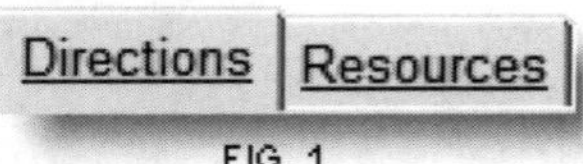

FIG. 1

- Go through each of the Information Tabs to familiarize yourself with the simulation content
- The Resources tab will contain information, including formulas and definitions, that may help you to complete the tasks
- Your simulation may have more Information Tabs than those shown in Fig. 1

Work Tabs:

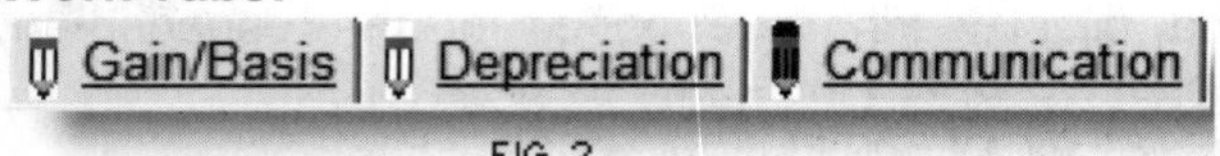

FIG. 2

- **Work Tabs**, to the right of the **Information Tabs**, contain the tasks for you to complete
- **Work Tabs** contain directions for completing each task—be sure to read these directions carefully
- The tab names in Fig. 2 are for illustration only—yours may differ
- Once you complete any part of a task, the pencil for that tab will be shaded (see **Communication** in Fig. 2)
- The shaded pencil does **NOT** indicate that you have completed the entire task
- You must complete all of the tasks in the **Work Tabs** to receive full credit

Research/Authoritative Literature Tab:

FIG. 3

- This tab contains both the Research task and the Authoritative Literature
- Detailed instructions for completing the Research task, and for using the Authoritative Literature, appear on this tab
- You may use the Authoritative Literature as a resource for completing other tasks

Note: If you believe you have encountered a software malfunction, report it to the test center staff immediately.

Editor's Note: This tab is one released by the AICPA. (R/08, REG, #41, 8748)

The Income Statement for the first year of operations of InterTax, Inc. is shown below.

Income Statement/Tax Return

	Tax	Book
Income		
Consulting fees	$1,880,000	$1,880,000
Tax-exempt interest	0	2,400
Interest income on bank accounts	16,400	16,400
Total income	$1,896,400	$1,898,800
Expenses		
Organization expenses	$ 5,707	$ 15,600
Officer salaries	800,000	800,000
Salaries and wages	240,000	240,000
Rent	76,800	76,800
Utilities	12,000	12,000
Advertising	30,000	30,000
Repairs	2,000	2,000
Taxes	10,000	10,000
Employee benefits	2,000	2,000
Interest	10,000	10,000
Office supplies	7,000	7,000
Depreciation	75,200	30,400
Total expenses	$1,270,707	$1,235,800
Net income before contributions	625,693	663,000
Charitable contributions	62,569	80,000
Pre-tax income	563,124	583,000
Federal tax expense	191,462	186,560
Net income	$ 371,662	$ 396,440

Note: There were no shareholder distributions during the year.

Complete Lines 1a – 30 on the IRS Form 1120, *U.S. Corporation Income Tax Return,* below for InterTax's first year of operations. Use the worksheet on the next tab (Line 26 Worksheet) to calculate the value for Line 26.

Form **1120** — Department of the Treasury, Internal Revenue Service

U.S. Corporation Income Tax Return

For calendar year 2007 or tax year beginning .... , 2007, ending .... , 20 ....

► See separate instructions.

OMB No. 1545-0123 — **2007**

A Check if:
- **1a** Consolidated return (attach Form 851) ☐
- **b** Life/nonlife consolidated return ☐
- **2** Personal holding co. (attach Sch. PH) ☐
- **3** Personal service corp. (see instructions) ☐
- **4** Schedule M-3 attached ☐

Use IRS label. Otherwise, print or type.
- Name
- Number, street, and room or suite no. If a P.O. box, see instructions.
- City or town, state, and ZIP code

B Employer identification number

C Date incorporated

D Total assets (see instructions) $

E Check if: **(1)** ☐ Initial return **(2)** ☐ Final return **(3)** ☐ Name change **(4)** ☐ Address change

Income

1a	Gross receipts or sales ____ **b** Less returns and allowances ____ **c** Bal ►	1c	
2	Cost of goods sold (Schedule A, line 8)	2	
3	Gross profit. Subtract line 2 from line 1c	3	
4	Dividends (Schedule C, line 19)	4	
5	Interest	5	
6	Gross rents	6	
7	Gross royalties	7	
8	Capital gain net income (attach Schedule D (Form 1120))	8	
9	Net gain or (loss) from Form 4797, Part II, line 17 (attach Form 4797)	9	
10	Other income (see instructions—attach schedule)	10	
11	**Total income.** Add lines 3 through 10 ►	11	

Deductions (See instructions for limitations on deductions.)

12	Compensation of officers (Schedule E, line 4)	12	
13	Salaries and wages (less employment credits)	13	
14	Repairs and maintenance	14	
15	Bad debts	15	
16	Rents	16	
17	Taxes and licenses	17	
18	Interest	18	
19	Charitable contributions	19	
20	Depreciation from Form 4562 not claimed on Schedule A or elsewhere on return (attach Form 4562)	20	
21	Depletion	21	
22	Advertising	22	
23	Pension, profit-sharing, etc., plans	23	
24	Employee benefit programs	24	
25	Domestic production activities deduction (attach Form 8903)	25	
26	Other deductions (attach schedule)	26	
27	**Total deductions.** Add lines 12 through 26 ►	27	
28	Taxable income before net operating loss deduction and special deductions. Subtract line 27 from line 11	28	
29	**Less: a** Net operating loss deduction (see instructions) **29a**		
	b Special deductions (Schedule C, line 20) **29b**	29c	

Tax and Payments

30	**Taxable income.** Subtract line 29c from line 28 (see instructions)	30	
31	**Total tax** (Schedule J, line 10)	31	
32a	2006 overpayment credited to 2007 **32a**		
b	2007 estimated tax payments **32b**		
c	2007 refund applied for on Form 4466 **32c** ( ) **d Bal** ► **32d**		
e	Tax deposited with Form 7004 **32e**		
f	Credits: **(1)** Form 2439 ____ **(2)** Form 4136 ____ **32f**	32g	
33	Estimated tax penalty (see instructions). Check if Form 2220 is attached ► ☐	33	
34	**Amount owed.** If line 32g is smaller than the total of lines 31 and 33, enter amount owed	34	
35	**Overpayment.** If line 32g is larger than the total of lines 31 and 33, enter amount overpaid	35	
36	Enter amount from line 35 you want: **Credited to 2008 estimated tax** ► **Refunded** ►	36	

Sign Here

Under penalties of perjury, I declare that I have examined this return, including accompanying schedules and statements, and to the best of my knowledge and belief, it is true, correct, and complete. Declaration of preparer (other than taxpayer) is based on all information of which preparer has any knowledge.

Signature of officer — Date — Title

May the IRS discuss this return with the preparer shown below (see instructions)? ☐ Yes ☐ No

Paid Preparer's Use Only

Preparer's signature — Date — Check if self-employed ☐ — Preparer's SSN or PTIN

Firm's name (or yours if self-employed), address, and ZIP code — EIN — Phone no. ( )

For Privacy Act and Paperwork Reduction Act Notice, see separate instructions. Cat. No. 11450Q Form **1120** (2007)

Use the spreadsheet below to calculate the value to enter on Line 26 of Form 1120, *Other Deductions.* Choose each deductible item that contributes to this value by double-clicking on a shaded cell in Column A and choosing an appropriate item from the dropdown list. Then enter the appropriate value for that deduction in Column B. The total deduction will automatically calculate at the bottom of the worksheet. Transfer the total value to Line 26 of Form 1120 on the previous tab. Some of the items on the list and some of the shaded lines may not be used.

Line 26 Deduction Worksheet:

	A	B
1		
2		
3		
4		
5		
7	Total deductions (transfer to Line 26)	

Dropdown list:

- Charitable contributions
- Federal tax expense
- Organization expenses
- Officer salaries
- Salaries and wages
- Rent
- Utilities
- Advertising
- Repairs
- Taxes
- Employee benefits
- Interest
- Office supplies
- Depreciation

Schedules M-1 & M-2 | Communication | Research

Complete Schedules M-1 and M-2 on the IRS Form 1120, *U.S. Corporation Income Tax Return,* below for InterTax's first year of operations. Note: To use a formula in the spreadsheet, it must be preceded by an equal sign, e.g., =A1+B1.

Form 1120 (2007) Page **4**

Schedule L Balance Sheets per Books

Assets	Beginning of tax year (a)	(b)	End of tax year (c)	(d)
1 Cash				
2a Trade notes and accounts receivable				
b Less allowance for bad debts	( )		( )	
3 Inventories				
4 U.S. government obligations				
5 Tax-exempt securities (see instructions)				
6 Other current assets (attach schedule)				
7 Loans to shareholders				
8 Mortgage and real estate loans				
9 Other investments (attach schedule)				
10a Buildings and other depreciable assets				
b Less accumulated depreciation	( )		( )	
11a Depletable assets				
b Less accumulated depletion	( )		( )	
12 Land (net of any amortization)				
13a Intangible assets (amortizable only)				
b Less accumulated amortization	( )		( )	
14 Other assets (attach schedule)				
15 Total assets				
Liabilities and Shareholders' Equity				
16 Accounts payable				
17 Mortgages, notes, bonds payable in less than 1 year				
18 Other current liabilities (attach schedule)				
19 Loans from shareholders				
20 Mortgages, notes, bonds payable in 1 year or more				
21 Other liabilities (attach schedule)				
22 Capital stock: a Preferred stock				
b Common stock				
23 Additional paid-in capital				
24 Retained earnings—Appropriated (attach schedule)				
25 Retained earnings—Unappropriated				
26 Adjustments to shareholders' equity (attach schedule)				
27 Less cost of treasury stock		( )		( )
28 Total liabilities and shareholders' equity				

Schedule M-1 Reconciliation of Income (Loss) per Books With Income per Return

Note: Schedule M-3 required instead of Schedule M-1 if total assets are $10 million or more—see instructions

1 Net income (loss) per books		7 Income recorded on books this year not included on this return (itemize): Tax-exempt interest $	
2 Federal income tax per books			
3 Excess of capital losses over capital gains			
4 Income subject to tax not recorded on books this year (itemize):		8 Deductions on this return not charged against book income this year (itemize):	
5 Expenses recorded on books this year not deducted on this return (itemize):		a Depreciation . . . . $	
a Depreciation . . . . $		b Charitable contributions $	
b Charitable contributions $			
c Travel and entertainment $		9 Add lines 7 and 8	
6 Add lines 1 through 5		10 Income (page 1, line 28)—line 6 less line 9	

Schedule M-2 Analysis of Unappropriated Retained Earnings per Books (Line 25, Schedule L)

1 Balance at beginning of year		5 Distributions: a Cash	
2 Net income (loss) per books		b Stock	
3 Other increases (itemize):		c Property	
		6 Other decreases (itemize):	
		7 Add lines 5 and 6	
4 Add lines 1, 2, and 3		8 Balance at end of year (line 4 less line 7)	

Form **1120** (2007)

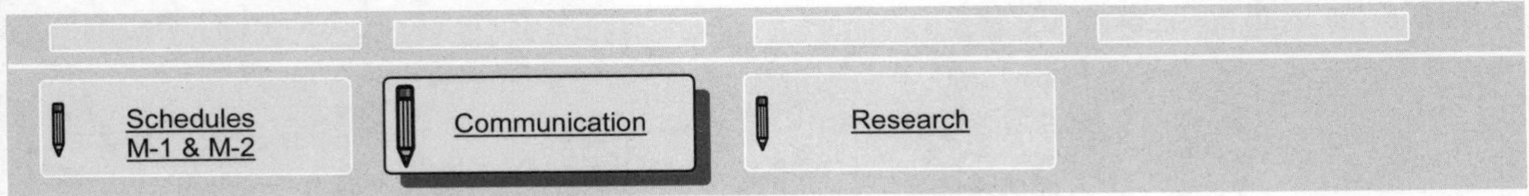

You are also the accountant for the company's CFO. Your client received the following notice from the Internal Revenue Service and sent it to you, asking for your assistance. As your client's CPA, write a letter to your client explaining the significance of the notice and telling them what information you need to respond to the IRS.

Type your communication in the response area below the horizontal line using the word processor provided.

REMINDER: Your response will be graded for both technical content and writing skills. Technical content will be evaluated for information that is helpful to the intended reader and clearly relevant to the issue. Writing skills will be evaluated for development, organization, and the appropriate expression of ideas in professional correspondence. Use a standard business memo or letter format with a clear beginning, middle, and end. Do not convey information in the form of a table, bullet point list, or other abbreviated presentation.

Department of the Treasury
Internal Revenue Service

Date of Notice: Oct. 9, 2003
Form: 1040 Tax Period: Dec. 31, 2002

James Dugan
42 Chestnut Street
Anytown, USA

WE CHANGED THE INCOME REPORTED ON YOUR TAX RETURN
YOU HAVE AN AMOUNT DUE

We changed your 2002 return. As a result of these changes, you owe $500. Our records show that you received a Form 1099-DIV from First Investors Brokerage showing ordinary dividend income in the amount of $2,000. If you think we made a mistake, please reply to this letter no later than October 30, 2003.

Indicate your answer by selecting the related radio button.

Research Question: In the subsequent year, InterTax, Inc. sold one of its stock investments and realized a loss. What code section and subsection provide the authority regarding the treatment by corporate taxpayers of this realized loss?

Editor's Note: Database interface appeared here.

Problem 6 (20 to 30 minutes)

In the following simulation, you will be asked to complete various tasks. You may use the content in the **Information Tabs** to complete the tasks in the **Work Tabs**.

Information Tabs:

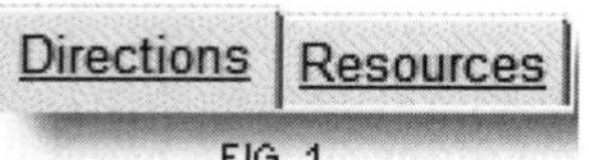

FIG. 1

- Go through each of the **Information Tabs** to familiarize yourself with the simulation content
- The **Resources** tab will contain information, including formulas and definitions, that may help you to complete the tasks
- Your simulation may have more **Information Tabs** than those shown in Fig. 1

Work Tabs:

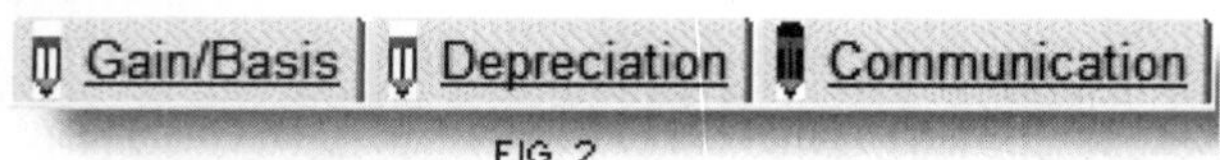

FIG. 2

- **Work Tabs,** to the right of the **Information Tabs,** contain the tasks for you to complete
- **Work Tabs** contain directions for completing each task—be sure to read these directions carefully
- The tab names in Fig. 2 are for illustration only—yours may differ
- Once you complete any part of a task, the pencil for that tab will be shaded (see **Communication** in Fig. 2)
- The shaded pencil does **NOT** indicate that you have completed the entire task
- You must complete all of the tasks in the **Work Tabs** to receive full credit

Research / Authoritative Literature Tab:

Research / Authoritative Literature

FIG. 3

- This tab contains both the Research task and the Authoritative Literature
- Detailed instructions for completing the Research task, and for using the Authoritative Literature, appear on this tab
- You may use the Authoritative Literature as a resource for completing other tasks

NOTE: If you believe you have encountered a software malfunction, report it to the test center staff immediately.

Miller, age 38, is a single taxpayer and is the sales manager of Standard Co., an auto stereo dealer. Miller's adjusted gross income (AGI) for the year is $67,000, which includes $4,000 of gambling winnings.

Miller's job is to oversee the sales operations of Standard Co. Miller has a private office at the dealership and is responsible for attracting new customers and retaining current customers. As the sales manager, Miller has the authority to hire and discharge sales personnel.

During the year, Miller attended several trade shows. While at these shows, Miller entertained clients, met with manufacturers, and spent some time gambling. During the year, Miller incurred and can properly document $5,000 of gambling losses.

Miller's mother incurred unreimbursed medical expenses during the year totaling $4,200. Because she was unable to pay these medical expenses herself, Miller paid them on her behalf. Miller cannot claim the mother as a dependent solely because her gross income is $10,000. (R/09, REG, #3, 8941)

During the year, Miller paid the business expenses shown in the following table. Miller's employer did not reimburse any of these expenses. In column C of the table, enter the amounts that are reportable unreimbursed business expense deductions, subject to a statutory percentage limitation, if any. If none of a particular unreimbursed expense is a reportable business expense deduction, enter a zero for that expense in column C. The total amount deductible on Schedule A, *Itemized Deductions,* of Form 1040, *U.S. Individual Income Tax Return,* as unreimbursed employee business expenses will automatically calculate.

Note: Disregard all AGI limitations, if any, in completing the first section of this table. Then follow the instructions in the table in completing the second section.

	A	B	C
1	**Expense**	**Amount**	**Amount reportable on Schedule A**
2	Unreimbursed airfares	2,200	
3	Dry cleaning costs for business suits worn at dealership	440	
4	Cost of meals during which business was discussed with potential customers	820	
5	Entertainment for clients, immediately after a business discussion	770	
6	Purchase of tuxedo to wear to trade show functions	400	
7	Cost of a business gift to a client	50	
8	Total	4,680	

In the following section, indicate the dollar amount of the limitations, if any, that apply to the expenses above. Enter any limitation as a negative number.

11	Total amount from table above	
12	Other miscellaneous deduction—gambling losses	
13	AGI limitation (in dollars)	
14	Total amount deductible on Schedule A	

During the year, Miller paid the expenses shown in the following table. The amount of each expense shown in the table is net of any insurance reimbursements received. In column C of the table, enter the amounts that are reportable unreimbursed medical expense deductions, subject to a statutory percentage limitation, if any. If none of a particular unreimbursed expense is a reportable medical expense deduction, enter a zero for that expense in column C. The total amount deductible on Schedule A, *Itemized Deductions,* of Form 1040, *U.S. Individual Income Tax Return,* as medical expense will automatically calculate.

Note: Disregard all AGI limitations, if any, in completing the first section of this table. Then follow the instructions in the table in completing the second section.

	A	B	C
1	**Expense**	**Amount**	**Amount reportable on Schedule A**
2	Medical insurance premiums paid with after-tax dollars	2,650	
3	Disability insurance premiums	720	
4	Vision correction surgery	2,400	
5	Hair transplant procedure	900	
6	Chin enhancement surgery to improve appearance	3,100	
7	Mother's medical expenses paid by Miller during the year	4,200	
8	Total	13,970	

In the following section, indicate the dollar amount of the limitations, if any, that apply to the expenses above. Enter any limitation as a negative number.

11	Total amount from table above	
12	AGI limitation (in dollars)	
13	Total amount deductible on Schedule A	

During the year, Miller made the interest payments shown in the following table. In column C of the table, enter the amounts that are reportable interest expense deductions, subject to a statutory percentage limitation, if any. If none of a particular payment is a reportable interest expense deduction, enter a zero for that expense in column C. The total amount deductible on Schedule A, *Itemized Deductions,* of Form 1040, *U.S. Individual Income Tax Return,* as interest expense will automatically calculate.

Note: Disregard all AGI limitations, if any, in completing the first section of this table. Then follow the instructions in the table in completing the second section.

	A	B	C
1	**Interest payment**	**Amount**	**Amount reportable on Schedule A**
2	Mortgage interest paid on principal residence	11,400	
3	Points on 30-year mortgage for the purchase of the principal residence paid on June 30 of the current year	4,200	
4	Mortgage interest paid on commercial rental property	2,150	
5	Interest paid on personal credit cards	470	
6	Interest paid to IRS for late filing of income tax return	25	
7	Interest paid on a $50,000 home equity loan; the FMV of the home exceeds the acquisition indebtedness by $70,000	475	
8	Total	18,720	

In the following section, indicate the dollar amount of the limitations, if any, that apply to the expenses above. Enter any limitation as a negative number.

11	Total amount from table above	
12	AGI limitation (in dollars)	
13	Total amount deductible on Schedule A	

During the year, Miller suffered the losses shown in the following table. In column D of the table, enter the amounts that are reportable casualty losses, subject to a statutory percentage limitation, if any. If none of a loss suffered is a reportable casualty loss deduction, enter a zero for that expense in column D. The total amount deductible on Schedule A, *Itemized Deductions,* of Form 1040, *U.S. Individual Income Tax Return,* as a casualty loss will automatically calculate.

Note: Disregard all AGI limitations, if any, in completing the first section of this table. Then follow the instructions in the table in completing the second section.

	A	B	C	D
1	**Loss suffered**	**Amount of loss**	**Insurance reimbursement**	**Amount reportable on Schedule A**
2	Damage to articles stored in basement due to water heater explosion	8,200	1,000	
3	Repair costs to prevent further roof deterioration from water damage	1,200	–	
4	Cost to rebuild detached garage due to damage from termites	5,500	2,100	
5	Total	14,900	3,100	

In the following section, indicate the dollar amount of the limitations, if any, that apply to the expenses above. Enter any limitation as a negative number.

8	Total amount from table above	
9	Casualty nonpercentage floor (in dollars)	
10	AGI limitation (in dollars)	
11	Total amount deductible on Schedule A	

A new individual client just received a substantial refund of state income taxes paid last year. The client wants to know how this refund will be treated on this year's federal income tax return. Write a letter to the client explaining that the answer depends on whether the client itemized deductions last year. Your explanation should include discussions of the following:

- Why the refund should not be included in this year's income if the standard deduction was taken last year.
- The circumstances under which the refund would be only partially included in this year's income if itemized deductions were taken last year.
- Why all of the refund must be included in income if itemized deductions were taken last year.

Type your communication in the response area below the horizontal line using the word processor provided.

REMINDER: Your response will be graded for both technical content and writing skills. Technical content will be evaluated for information that is helpful to the intended reader and clearly relevant to the issue. Writing skills will be evaluated for development, organization, and the appropriate expression of ideas in professional correspondence. Use a standard business memo or letter format with a clear beginning, middle, and end. Do not convey information in the form of a table, bullet point list, or other abbreviated presentation.

Research Question: Which section and subsection of the Internal Revenue Code describes the substantiation that a taxpayer must maintain in order to claim a valid business deduction for entertainment expenses?

Section & Subsection Answer §__________ (__)

Solution 1: Moderate

1. (a) Generally, the fair market value of appreciated property donated to a qualified public charity may be deducted if it doesn't exceed 50% of the donor's AGI. $25,000 < (50% × $90,000) (Chapter 44-4-6, CSO: 5.3.0)

2. (a) This event is a tax-free liquidation of a subsidiary. (Chapter 46-8-2, CSO: 6.2.5)

3. (d) Cancellation payments are rent to the landlord in the year received, so Nare must include the $30,000 received in cancellation of Mott's lease. Even accrual basis taxpayers must include rent in income when received rather than when earned under the claim of right doctrine; Nare must include the $5,000 received for the last month's rent. Nare also must include the $10,000 for November and December. $30,000 + $5,000 + $10,000 = $45,000 (Chapter 44-2-3, CSO: 3.3.0)

4. (b) Molloy's adjusted basis is the original contribution plus a share of any taxable income and partnership liabilities less any distributions and a share of losses. (Chapter 47-2-1, CSO: 6.4.2)

Original basis	$40,000
Plus: Share of income (1/3 × $60,000)	20,000
Less: Cash distribution	(5,000)
Plus: Share of liabilities (1/3 × $18,000)	6,000
Adjusted basis	$61,000

5. (d) As this is a liquidating distribution, Fern's adjusted basis in the automobile is Fern's basis in the partnership interest after deducting the cash. Neither the property's fair market value nor its basis to the partnership are used in this calculation. $60,000 – $30,000 = $30,000 (Chapter 47-2-2, CSO: 6.4.7)

6. (c) If a corporation owns less than 20% of another domestic corporation's stock, the corporate shareholder gets a 70% dividend-received deduction. 70% × $3,000 = $2,100 (Chapter 46-2-3, CSO: 6.2.1)

7. (c) A holder in due course generally takes a negotiable instrument free from personal, but not real, defenses. A breach of contract is a personal defense. Fraud in the execution, discharge in an insolvency proceeding, and incapacity (infancy) are real defenses. (Chapter 36-4-2, CSO: 2.5.1)

8. (a) If the property is acquired by gift, then the basis to the donee is determined at the time of disposal. When the property is later disposed of in a taxable transaction at a price between the fair market value at the date of the gift and the adjusted basis of the property in the hands of the donor, and the fair market value of the property at the date of the gift was less than the adjusted basis to the donor, then no gain or loss is recognized on the disposition. (Chapter 43-1-3, CSO: 4.5.0)

9. (a) Six prerequisites must be met to create a negotiable instrument: 1) the instrument must be in writing and signed by the maker (note) or drawer (draft or check); 2) the instrument must contain an unconditional promise or order to pay; 3) the amount of money must be a fixed amount; 4) the instrument must be made payable to order or to bearer (except for checks); 5) the instrument must be payable on demand or at a definite time; and 6) the promise or order may not have any other promise, order, obligation, or power given by the maker or drawer except as authorized by UCC Article 3. There is nothing in the given scenario to indicate the note was subject to another writing. The "sum certain" element is only one of several criteria. Conditions that already have been met still keep instruments from being negotiable, unless the holder can determine the event's occurrence from the face of the instrument. (Chapter 36-2-4, CSO: 2.5.1)

10. (a) With a beginning accounts payable (A/P) balance of $64,000 and an ending A/P balance of $50,000, there must have been $14,000 more payments to suppliers than accrual-basis purchases. With both cash purchases and payments on account totaling $455,000 and payments on account of $14,000, $455,000 – $14,000 = $441,000 of payments were for cash purchases. Editor's Note: This explanation assumes that all cash purchases are charged to the A/P account. The editors do not understand why this question was included in the REG exam section (rather than BEC) and do not expect a similar question to appear on future REG or BEC exams. (Chapter 46-4-1, CSO: 3.3.0)

11. (b) A CPA who provides auditing and other attestation services should be independent in fact and appearance. In providing all other services, an accountant should maintain objectivity and avoid conflicts of interest. A CPA need not be independent when providing tax and management advisory services. A CPA need not be independent when not in public practice. (Chapter 32-2-2, CSO: 1.1.0)

12. (d) An employee's unreimbursed business expenses are deductible as an itemized deduction from AGI. Section 67(a) states that miscellaneous itemized deductions are allowed only to the extent they exceed 2% of AGI. Section 67(b) states that

miscellaneous itemized deductions are those itemized deductions not listed in §67(b). Unreimbursed employee business expenses are not listed in §67(b). Medical expenses are subject to a 7.5% of AGI floor. Gambling losses to the extent of gambling winnings and real estate taxes are exempted specifically from the 2% of AGI floor. (Chapter 44-4-8, CSO: 5.3.0)

13. (a) The Securities Act of 1933 exempts certain securities from its registration requirements. Exempted securities include those issued by not-for-profit charitable organizations and domestic governmental organizations as well as stock given by the issuer to existing stockholders without a commission or other remuneration paid. (Chapter 40-2-3, CSO: 2.4.1)

14. (a) Section 1221 defines capital assets as property held by the taxpayer except for a number of items listed. Personal-use physical assets are not so listed. Section 1221 excludes depreciable and real property used in a business and accounts receivable from inventory sold from the definition of capital assets. (Chapter 43-3-2, CSO: 4.1.0)

15. (c) The taxable income is equal to the gross receipts plus other income less deductible expenses. A corporation may deduct capital losses only against capital gains. Individuals, but not corporations, may deduct up to $3,000 of capital losses annually. Since there are no capital gains, the entire capital loss is disallowed. A capital gain, not a capital loss, would be added to arrive at taxable income. $150,000 + $35,000 – $95,000 = $90,000 (Chapter 46-2-6, CSO: 6.2.1)

16. (b) It is individual state boards of accountancy that have the authority to grant CPA licenses to practice public accounting, and, thus, ordinarily would be the bodies to suspend or revoke such licenses. The National Association of State Boards of Accountancy (NASBA), state CPA societies, and the AICPA (including their committees and divisions) do not have authority to grant, suspend, or revoke CPA licenses. (Chapter 32-1-1, CSO: 1.4.0)

17. (c) Municipal bond interest is included in book income, but is exempt from federal income tax (FIT). Capital losses greater than capital gains are included in determining book income, but are not deductible for FIT purposes. FIT expense is included in determining book income, but is not deductible for FIT purposes. (Chapter 46-4-1, CSO: 6.2.1)

Book income	$150,000
Less: Municipal bond interest (tax-exempt income)	(5,000)
Add: Excess capital losses over capital gains (nondeductible)	10,000
Add: FIT expense (nondeductible)	50,000
Taxable income	$205,000

18. (a) ET 301 prohibits the disclosure of confidential information obtained in the course of a professional engagement without consent of the client, but does not prohibit review of a CPA's professional practices (including pertinent information) as a part of an AICPA authorized voluntary quality review program. While disclosing information at a client's request is allowed, mail clerks typically do not have authority to approve releases of financial information. ET 301 shall not be construed to affect in any way the member's obligation to comply with a validly issued and enforceable subpoena or summons, or to prohibit a member's compliance with applicable laws and government regulations. (Chapter 32-4-1, CSO: 1.6.0)

19. (d) Half of self-employment taxes paid, health insurance paid, alimony paid, and IRA contributions are all adjustments to arrive at adjusted gross income. There is no indication that the taxpayer does not qualify to claim these adjustments (health insurance available through an employer, alimony deemed child support or property settlement, or active participation in an employer retirement plan). $57,000 – (½ × $8,000) – $6,000 – $5,000 – $2,000 = $40,000. (Chapter 44-3-1, CSO: 5.3.0)

20. (c) A principal must have sufficient capacity to consent to the agency relationship. An agent need not possess legal capacity to contract because contracts properly negotiated as an agent will not bind the agent personally. Consideration is not necessary; a gratuitous agent is permissible. Generally, it is not necessary to have a written agency agreement; exceptions to this rule are if the agent's duties will involve the buying and selling of real property or if the agency agreement is to last more than one year. (Chapter 39-1-1, CSO: 2.1.1)

Solution 2: Difficult

21. (b) A CPA who provides auditing and other attestation services should be independent in fact and appearance. In providing all other services, an CPA should maintain objectivity and avoid conflicts of interest. (Chapter 32-5-1, CSO: 1.2.0)

22. (b) In order to recover a loss, a seller or purchaser of securities must prove the defendant acted with the intent to defraud (scienter). The SEC may base actions under Section 10(b) on a showing of reckless disregard of the truth (gross negligence) rather than establish specific fraudulent intent. The Rule 10b-5 standard is not negligence, criminal intent, or strict liability. (Chapter 40-3-3, CSO: 2.4.1)

23. (c) A liquidated damage is a specific amount provided in a contract to be recoverable in the event of breach. It is enforceable if actual damage would be difficult to assess and the amount appears reasonable at the time of contracting. If liquidated damages are excessive, a court may interpret them as a penalty and refuse enforcement. There are no punitive damages for a breach of contract. Compensatory damages are awarded to compensate for losses and lost profits suffered as a result of the breach; the town has not illustrated losses or lost profits suffered because of the breach. Failure to perform on time may be a material breach of contract, giving rise to an action for damages. (Chapter 34-7-2, CSO: 2.2.4)

24. (c) As this is a liquidating distribution, Baker's adjusted basis in the land is Baker's basis in the partnership interest. With the basis equal to the distribution, Baker has no gain. (Chapter 47-2-2, CSO: 6.4.7)

25. (c) If a member does not have the ability to direct investments, an investment in a client through a financial service product (such as a mutual fund) is considered an indirect financial interest and, hence, does not necessarily impair independence. Independence is considered impaired if a covered member owns stock in a client through an investment club, where presumably the member has the ability to direct investments, whether or not exercised, resulting in a direct financial interest. Independence is considered impaired even if a CPA has a material indirect financial interest in a client, whether or not it is placed in a blind trust. (Chapter 32-2-3, CSO: 1.2.0)

26. (d) Nolan has ordinary gross income from services rendered in an amount equal to the fair value of the property received as compensation under §61 and §83. (Chapter 47-2-1, CSO: 6.1.0)

27. (c) The basis of property other than money distributed to a partner in a liquidating distribution is equal to the adjusted basis of the partner's interest in the partnership as reduced by any cash received by the partner. In the case of liquidating distributions, the basis of the partner's interest in the partnership (as reduced by cash received) is allocated first to any unrealized receivables and inventory items in an amount equal to the adjusted basis of such receivables and inventory. Chang's basis first is reduced by the partnership's basis in the cash. Chang's remaining basis is allocated first to the inventory, in which the partnership's basis is $5,000. Sale of inventory generates ordinary income or loss. $5,000 – $4,000 = $1,000 After considering the impact of cash and inventory distributions, Chang's basis in the partnership is $12,000 – $4,000 – $4,000 = $4,000. This $4,000 becomes Chang's basis in the only remaining asset, the land. Sale of land generates capital gain or loss. $3,000 – $4,000 = ($1,000) (Chapter 47-2-2, CSO: 6.4.6)

28. (c) The surviving spouse status and the head of household status involve paying more than 50% to maintain a household that is the principal place of residence for the entire year of the taxpayer's child. Without such a child, an unmarried taxpayer's status is single. A spouse may file either married filing jointly or married filing separately in the year of the deceased spouse's death, but not in subsequent years. (Chapter 44-1-3, CSO: 5.4.0)

29. (c) A holder in due course generally takes a negotiable instrument free from personal, but not real, defenses. Incapacity (minority of the maker) is a real defense. A breach of warranty, fraud in the inducement, and lack of consideration are personal defenses. (Chapter 36-5-2, CSO: 2.5.1)

30. (c) There are some instances in which the S corporation is required to pay taxes at the corporate level, including built-in gains [the excess of the fair market value (FMV) of assets over their bases at the beginning of the first year in which the S corporation status is effective]. The FMV at the beginning of the first year in which the S corporation status is effective is greater than the basis at that time. The FMV at the date of sale is not included in this calculation. $30,000 – $20,000 = $10,000 (Chapter 46-10-4, CSO: 6.3.5)

31. (a) The final SEC rule (RIN 3235-AI73, part II., A.) deems an accounting firm to lack independence with respect to an audit client if a former lead partner, former concurring partner, or any former member of the audit engagement team who

provided more than ten hours of audit, review, or attest services to the issuer during the one-year period preceding the audit's initiation is employed by the issuer in a financial reporting oversight role. (Chapter 33-2-2, CSO: 1.2.0)

32. (b) A warehouser has a duty of care and is liable for loss or injury to goods caused by the failure to exercise such care as a reasonably careful person would exercise under like circumstances (ordinary negligence). A warehouser is not strictly liable for any loss on goods held in a warehouse. A claimant only need establish that a warehouser was negligent, not grossly negligent or that any destruction or theft was deliberate. (Chapter 36-9-5, CSO: 2.5.4)

33. (b) The net unearned income of a minor under the age of 14 is taxed at the parents' maximum tax rate to the extent it exceeds a threshold ($950 in 2009) plus the greater of the threshold amount or itemized deductions related to the production of the unearned income. $3,000 – ($950 + $950) = $1,100 (Chapter 44-5-1, CSO: 5.5.0)

34. (a) Estates and trusts may have a personal exemption. A standard deduction is available to individuals, not estates or trusts. A simple trust is a trust that requires all income to be distributed each year, does not make any charitable contributions, and does not make any distributions except out of current income; all other trusts are complex. Expenses relating to tax-exempt income are not deductible. (Chapter 45-4-1, CSO: 6.5.2)

35. (a) Section 26 limits the amount of any credits allowed in Subpart A of Part IV of Subchapter A of Chapter 1 to the excess of the taxpayer's regular tax liability over the tentative minimum tax. The child and dependent care credit is allowed by §21 (in Subpart A). Thus, the child and dependent care credit is not refundable. A child of any age physically or mentally incapable of caring for her- or himself is eligible. A dependant child qualifies without regard to descent. The maximum credit is $6,000 × 35% = $2,160. (Chapter 44-6-1, CSO: 5.5.0)

36. (b) Generally, all taxes must be assessed within three years after the later of the due date or the filing date. If the taxpayer omitted more than 25% when reporting gross income, this period is extended to six years. (Chapter 44-1-4, CSO: 3.1.0)

37. (d) IRC §702 specifically lists foreign taxes paid as a separately reported item. The election to amortize organizational costs, involuntary conversion treatment, and §179 deduction are decided at the partnership level. (Chapter 47-1-2, CSO: 6.4.3)

38. (c) On a sale of depreciable personal property, ordinary income under §1245 generally is equal to the lesser of (1) the total gain realized or (2) the accumulated depreciation. $200,000 − $180,000 = $20,000 < $30,000 (Chapter 43-3-4, CSO: 4.5.0)

39. (b) On a sale of depreciable personal property, ordinary income under §1245 is generally equal to the lesser of (1) the total gain realized or (2) the accumulated depreciation. Section 1231 treats any remaining gain as a capital gain. As the furniture was purchased four years ago, the gain is long term. The §1245 gain and the remaining §1231 gain are computed as follows. (Chapter 43-3-2, CSO: 4.5.0)

Amount realized		$ 37,000
Cost	$ 30,000	
Less: Accum. depreciation	(20,700)	
Less: Adjusted basis		(9,300)
Total gain realized		$ 27,700
Section 1245 (ordinary) gain (lesser of $20,700 or $27,700)		$ 20,700
Plus: Section 1231 (capital) gain		7,000
Total gain realized		$ 27,700

40. (a) For a C corporation, taxable income generally is computed on the basis of the taxpayer's annual accounting period, if it is a calendar or fiscal year. In this context, the term "annual accounting period" means the annual period on the basis of which the taxpayer regularly computes income in keeping the books. An S corporation generally is required to adopt a December 31 year end or a fiscal year that is the same as the fiscal year used by shareholders owning more than 50% of the corporation's stock. A partnership's taxable year generally is the same as that of its partners owning a majority interest in the partnership, unless a business purpose can be established for designating a different taxable year [IRC §706(b)(1)]. IRC §441(i)(1) states, "…the taxable year of any personal service corporation shall be the calendar year unless the corporation establishes, to the satisfaction of the Secretary, a business purpose for having a different period for its taxable year." (Chapter 43-6-2, CSO: 3.2.0)

Solution 3: Moderate

41. (b) Interpretation 501-1 generally requires an auditor to return a client's records after the client has demanded them. With adequate assurance of non-disclosure by a records-retention agency, use of such an agency does not violate confidentiality requirements. A CPA is not prohibited from collecting fees from clients. Compilation is a service that does not require the CPA's independence; also, the employment of the CPA's spouse as a bookkeeper (generally not considered a key employee) does not necessarily impair the CPA's independence. Editor's Note: Similar to question #12 (7862) in Chapter 32. (Chapter 32-5-1, CSO: 1.1.0, Skill: Understanding)

42. (c) A CPA's defense of due diligence is established by proving that after reasonable investigation the CPA had a reasonable basis for the belief that the registration statement was accurate and complete. Under the Securities Act of 1933, a purchaser needs to prove the financial statements were materially misstated and that the security purchases were offered through the inaccurate registration statement, but need not prove the CPA's scienter or privity with the CPA. Editor's Note: Similar to question #17 (8438) in Chapter 33. (Chapter 33-2-2, CSO: 1.5.2, Skill: Understanding)

43. (c) The Statute of Frauds applies to promises to answer for the debt of another regardless of how long the debt is to be outstanding. When a surety contract is contemporaneous with the primary contract, there is no need for any separate consideration beyond that supporting the primary contract to bind the surety. Contracts that are entered into primarily for the benefit of the surety, rather than the debtor, are held to be outside of the Status of Frauds; however, a personal relationship with the debtor is not sufficient to move the contract outside the Statute of Frauds applicability. (Chapter 38-4-1, CSO: 2.2.1, Skill: Analysis)

44. (d) Transfers to a qualified educational or medical care provider for tuition or medical care, respectively, are exempt from gift tax. As the $5,000 cash gift is well under the annual exclusion, Mann had no taxable gifts in the current year. (Chapter 45-5-2, CSO: 5.8.0, Skill: Analysis)

45. (a) Generally, a single individual may exclude up to $250,000 of the gain on the sale of a principal residence, regardless of whether a new home is purchased. The individual must have occupied the home as a principal residence in two of the five years immediately preceding a sale after 1997. After 2008, the exclusion is *pro rata* for the non-qualifying use. There is no indication that Wynn did not meet the requirements for the maximum exclusion. As the gain was $450,000 − $250,000 = $200,000, or less than the full exclusion, none of the gain is taxable income. (Chapter 43-3-8, CSO: 4.5.0, Skill: Analysis)

46. (d) There is an unlimited marital deduction from taxable gifts. (Chapter 45-5-5, CSO: 5.8.0, Skill: Analysis)

47. (c) Rent payments (including lease cancellation payments, nonrefundable deposits, and premiums) are taxable in the period received, regardless of the taxpayer's basis of accounting. Refundable security deposits are not rental income. $30K + $10K + $15K = $55K (Chapter 44-2-3, CSO: 3.3.0, Skill: Analysis)

48. (c) When a corporation distributes property to shareholders, the distribution is equal to the property's fair market value on the distribution date. The distribution amount is $20K + $60K = $80K. The distributions are treated as dividends to the extent of E&P, in this case, $70K. (Chapter 46-5-2, CSO: 6.2.5, Skill: Analysis)

49. (d) Of these items, only inventory requires the financing statement to be filed for perfection of a purchase money security interest (PMSI). Inventory also may be perfected by possession. The only way to perfect a security interest in stock certificates or promissory notes is by possession. Perfection is automatic with a PMSI in consumer goods (personal jewelry). (Chapter 37-2-2, CSO: 2.5.2, Skill: Understanding)

50. (b) A security interest is created when the debtor gives to the creditor possession of the collateral, a written security agreement signed by the debtor, or an authenticated security agreement. 'Statement of assignment' and 'termination statement' are not commonly used terms in this context. Generally, the creditor, not the debtor, would sign a release of collateral. (Chapter 37-1-2, CSO: 2.5.3, Skill: Understanding)

51. (b) No gain or loss is recognized if property is transferred to a corporation solely in exchange for stock if, immediately after the transfer, the transferors are in control of the corporation. There is no indication that anyone other than Ames and Roth are in control of the corporation. The corporation's basis in the property is the transferor's adjusted basis plus any gain recognized by the transferor on the transfer. $500 + $5,000 = $5,500 (Chapter 46-1-3, CSO: 6.2.5, Skill: Analysis)

52. (d) A shareholder's basis in S corporation stock is increased by all income (including tax-exempt income) and gains and reduced by distributions and losses (to the extent of basis). $60K + $30K + $5K + $10K − $20K = $85K (Chapter 46-10-7, CSO: 6.3.3, Skill: Analysis)

53. (c) An increase in partnership liabilities increases each partner's basis in proportion to his or her ownership, just as income, gains, and losses affect each partner's basis proportionately. The recourse or nonrecourse status of liability is important when determining when losses may offset taxable income, not when determining basis. (Chapter 47-2-3, CSO: 6.4.5, Skill: Understanding)

54. (d) A security interest is created when the debtor and creditor enter into an agreement giving the creditor rights in the debtor's property as collateral for a debt; however, a security interest is not enforceable against the debtor until it attaches. Attachment occurs when three events occur: (1) value is given by the creditor; (2) debtor has rights in the collateral; and (3) the debtor gives the collateral into the creditor's possession, or gives the creditor a signed written security agreement, or provides an authenticated security agreement. A financing statement is filed for perfection, not attachment, of a security interest. (Chapter 37-1-2, CSO: 2.5.3, Skill: Understanding)

55. (c) Alimony is included in gross income; child support and property settlements are not. Alimony must be (1) made pursuant to a divorce agreement; (2) consist of cash payments; (3) not be made to someone living in the same household; and (4) not continue after the recipient's death; (5) not be designated as anything other than alimony, such as child support or property settlement. Nothing in the given information indicates that the payments are mislabeled. (Chapter 44-2-3, CSO: 5.1.0, Skill: Analysis)

56. (a) Bluff's basis at the time of the gift was the cost (including improvements) less any depreciation ($35K + $1K − $5K = $31K). Ignoring gift tax consequences, if the fair market value exceeds the basis at the time of the gift, the donee's basis in the property is the donor's basis. (Chapter 43-1-3, CSO: 4.2.0, Skill: Analysis)

57. (c) As a 50% partner, Dale's basis is changed by a *pro rata* share of changes in liabilities. Dale's basis is increased by a *pro rata* share of both taxable and tax-exempt income and decreased by distributions received. $10,000 + (50% × $10,000) + (50% × $15,000) + (50% × $2,000) − $3,000 − (50% × $4,000) = $18,500 (Chapter 47-2-3, CSO: 6.4.2, Skill: Analysis)

58. (d) Smith's basis in the property cannot exceed Smith's adjusted basis in the former partnership. After adjusting for the cash distribution, Smith's basis in the partnership is $230K − $150K = $80K. (Chapter 47-2-2, CSO: 6.4.7, Skill: Analysis)

59. (b) A CPA may not disclose confidential client information regarding auditing services in a letter to the client from the IRS. A CPA's duty of non-disclosure does not apply when disclosure is made pursuant to a voluntary quality review, pursuant to a professional ethics division review, or in compliance with an enforceable subpoena or court order. Editor's Note: The editors are not sure how or why a CPA would disclose any information regarding auditing services in a letter from the client to the IRS and, thus, do not expect this question to appear on the exam in the future. (Chapter 32-4-1, CSO: 1.6.0, Skill: Understanding)

60. (c) C corporations may choose either a calendar or a fiscal year. Once a tax year is established, an entity may change the period only with IRS consent. C corporations generally are barred from using the cash basis of accounting; exceptions exist for entities with annual gross receipts of less than $1 million and personal service corporations with annual gross receipts of less than $5 million. Neither of these exceptions applies in this case. (Chapter 43-6-2, CSO: 3.3.0, Skill: Analysis)

Solution 4: Difficult

61. (a) To the extent that a decedent retained ownership of any property, it is included in the decedent's gross estate. Hence, a revocable trust is included in the grantor's gross estate. Trusts are irrevocable unless the grantor retains a revocation right. A presumably irrevocable trust for a minor would not allow for ownership retention by the grantor. A trustee's power to distribute trust income does not affect ownership retention by the grantor. A presumably irrevocable trust with an income beneficiary who disclaims the property in favor of a remainderman other than the grantor would not allow for ownership retention by the grantor. (Chapter 45-5-4, CSO: 5.8.0, Skill: Understanding)

62. (b) As the land has a basis of less than its fair market value, if the land is distributed, the corporation recognizes gain on the land's disposition. If the cash is distributed, the corporation does not recognize any gain. A C corporation shareholder recognizes dividend income (to the extent of the E&P) for the fair value of the cash or property received. As E&P exceeds the distribution, the shareholder has the same dividend income regardless of whether cash or land is distributed. (Chapter 46-5-2, CSO: 6.2.5, Skill: Judgment)

63. (c) Drawers and endorsers of negotiable instruments are parties that are secondary liable. A maker of a note and an acceptor (drawee) of a draft are primary parties. A cashier's check is a check drawn by a bank on itself. As a check is a special form of a draft, the issuer of a cashier's check is both the drawer and the drawee of a draft; thus, this issuer is primarily liable. (Chapter 36-7-1, CSO: 2.5.1, Skill: Understanding)

64. (d) A holder in due course (HIDC) generally takes an instrument free from all personal defenses of any party with whom he or she has not dealt. There is nothing to suggest that Reed is not a HIDC: Reed apparently took the instrument for value in good faith without notice. The given facts do not indicate the note was contingent on Blake's performance. The given facts do not indicate the note was nonnegotiable, making the fact that Reed was not the original holder irrelevant. The status as bearer or order paper does not influence whether Train must pay Reed. (Chapter 36-4-2, CSO: 2.5.1, Skill: Understanding)

65. (b) A CPA may recommend a product to a tax client, provided the fee paid to the CPA is disclosed to the client. A CPA may not recommend or refer any product or service to an audit client, for a fee. A CPA may not accept a fee contingent upon the outcome of an original or amended tax return or claim for refund or an audit or review of financial statements. (Chapter 32-5-3, CSO: 1.1.0, Skill: Analysis)

66. (a) The shareholder's basis in the land is its fair market value (FMV) on the distribution date. The amount of any related debt does not influence the shareholder's basis in the land. The corporation's basis in the land before the distribution does not influence the shareholder's basis in the land. (Chapter 46-5-2, CSO: 6.2.5, Skill: Analysis)

67. (c) C corporations generally are barred from using the cash basis of accounting; exceptions exist for entities with annual gross receipts of less than $1 million and personal service corporations with annual gross receipts of less than $5 million. Neither of these exceptions applies in this case. (Chapter 43-6-2, CSO: 3.3.0, Skill: Understanding)

68. (a) Under common law and in the absence of an express agreement to the contrary, an accountant owns his or her work papers. There is no requirement that a former client direct prospective auditors to a previous auditor. While a CPA generally may not disclose work papers without the client's permission, there is no requirement for disclosure at the client's demand, despite the client's financial statement audit being the subject of the work papers. (Chapter 33-3-1, CSO: 1.6.0, Skill: Analysis)

69. (c) A recipient's taxable income is the lesser of the amount of a *pro rata* share of distributable net income (DNI) or the distribution received. As total distributions ($60K + $90K = $150K) were greater than DNI, Lind's portion of the DNI was [$90K / $150K)] × $120K = $72K. (Chapter 45-4-2, CSO: 6.5.3, Skill: Analysis)

70. (c) A loss from the sale of securities is disallowed if substantially the same securities are purchased during a time period 30 days prior to or 30 days after the sale date. On February 1, Sands sold 50 shares at a loss of $180/share − $140/share = $40/share. Sands purchased 25 shares of the same stock within 30 days of the sale date. The loss on 25 of the shares is disallowed in the current year, but the loss on the other 25 shares is allowed.

$40/share × 25 shares = $1,000 (Chapter 43-4-1, CSO: 4.5.0, Skill: Analysis)

71. (d) A certificate of deposit is a bank's written acknowledgment of the receipt of a stated sum of money with a promise to repay it. A draft is a written order from one person directing a second person to pay a sum certain in money to the order of a third person or to the order of the bearer. Both trade acceptances and checks are special forms of drafts. (Chapter 36-1-2, CSO: 2.5.1, Skill: Understanding)

72. (c) Rules 504 and 505 of Regulation D of the 1933 Act permit companies to offer securities for sale without registration and disclosure requirements within a 12-month period. (Chapter 40-2-4, CSO: 2.4.1, Skill: Understanding)

73. (c) No gain or loss is recognized if property is transferred to a corporation solely in exchange for stock if, immediately after the transfer, the transferors are in control of the corporation. While the transferors are in control, B's receipt of boot (cash) triggers gain recognition to the lesser of the boot received ($20K) or the gain realized ($70K − $40K = $30K). The corporation's basis in the property is B's adjusted basis ($40K) plus B's recognized gain ($20K). (Chapter 46-1-3, CSO: 6.2.5, Skill: Analysis)

74. (d) Section 1221 defines capital assets as property held by the taxpayer except for a number of items listed. Land held for investment is not so listed. Section 1221 excludes inventory, accounts receivable, and depreciable property used in a business from the definition of capital assets. (Chapter 43-3-2, CSO: 4.1.0, Skill: Understanding)

75. (d) The amount of gain taxable each year of an installment sale is computed by multiplying the payments received that year by the gross profit percentage (total estimated gross profit / total contract price). The total estimated gross profit is the price ($600K) less the adjusted basis ($500K − $80K = $420K). ($180K / $600K) × $120K = $36K (Chapter 43-3-3, CSO: 3.3.0, Skill: Analysis)

76. (b) As the $40,000 payment for room and board is well over the annual exclusion amount of $12,000, the donor must file a gift tax return. Transfers to qualified educational or medical care providers for tuition or medical care, respectively, are exempt from gift tax. Also, there is an unlimited marital deduction from taxable gifts. (Chapter 45-5-2, CSO: 5.8.0, Skill: Understanding)

77. (d) Affiliated groups include only parent-subsidiary corporations. Both brother-sister corporations and parent-subsidiary corporations are controlled groups. While controlled groups are treated as one corporation for purposes of income tax brackets, the AMT exemption, and the accumulated earnings credit, only affiliated groups may elect to file consolidated tax returns. Partnerships generally do not file consolidated returns with corporations. The percentage ownership of a controlled group is 80%, not 50%. (Chapter 46-9-3, CSO: 6.2.4, Skill: Analysis)

78. (d) Any additional income will be taxed at the taxpayer's marginal tax rate. Unqualified distributions are subject to a 10% excise tax in addition to the regular income tax. (35% + 10%) × $30,000 = $13,500 (Chapter 44-3-2, CSO: 5.5.0, Skill: Analysis)

79. (d) A like-kind exchange is an exchange of property of the same nature or character (real property for real property or personal property for personal property). Like-kind exchange rules defer recognition of gain on the exchange for tax purposes, but do not apply to assets held as inventory, investment securities, or assets held for personal use. Editor's Note: The editors believe answers 'a' and 'd' to be equally valid. The editors do not expect this question to appear on the exam in the future. (Chapter 43-3-2, CSO: 4.4.0, Skill: Judgment)

80. (c) Direct or material indirect financial interest in an audit client during the period of a professional engagement is held to impair a CPA's independence. (Chapter 32-2-3, CSO: 1.2.0, Skill: Understanding)

Solution 5: Form 1120 & Schedule M-1

Taxable Income (2 points)

Line	1a	Gross receipts	1,880,000
	1c	Net receipts	1,880,000
	3	Gross profit	1,880,000
	5	Interest	16,400
	11	Total income	1,896,400
	12	Compensation of officers	800,000
	13	Salaries and wages	240,000
	14	Repairs and maintenance	2,000
	16	Rents	76,800
	17	Taxes and licenses	10,000
	18	Interest	10,000
	19	Charitable contributions	62,569
	20	Depreciation	75,200
	23	Advertising	30,000
	25	Employee benefit programs	2,000
	26	Other deductions	24,707
	27	Total deductions	1,333,276
	28	Taxable income before NOL & special	563,124
	30	Taxable income	563,124

Line 26 Worksheet (1 point)

	A	B
1	Organization expenses	5,707
2	Utilities	12,000
3	Office supplies	7,000
4		
5		
7	Total deductions (transfer to Line 26)	24,707

Schedules M-1 & M-2 (1 point)

Schedule M-1

Line	1	Net income (loss) per books		396,440
	2	Federal income tax		186,560
	3	Excess of capital losses over capital gains		
	5	Expenses recorded on books not deducted on return		
	5a	Depreciation	0	
	5b	Contributions carryover	17,431	
	5d	Organization expenses	9,893	
	5e			27,324
	6	Add Lines 1 through 5		610,324
	7	Income recorded on books this year not included on this return		
	7a	Tax-exempt interest	2,400	
	7c			2,400
	8	Deductions on this return not charged against book income this year		
	8a	Depreciation	44,800	
	8b	Contributions carryover	0	
	8e			44,800
	9	Add Lines 7 and 8		47,200
	10	Income (Line 28, page 1)—Line 6 minus Line 9		563,124

Schedule M-2

Line			
	1	Balance at beginning of year	0
	2	Net income (loss) per books	396,440
	3c		0
	4	Add Lines 1, 2 and 3	396,440
	5a	Distributions: a) Cash	0
	5b	b) Stock	
	5c	c) Property	
	6	Other decreases	
	7	Add Lines 5 and 6	0
	8	Balance at end of year Line 4 less Line 7)	396,440

Communication (5 points)

October 10, 2003

James Dugan
42 Chestnut Street
Anytown, USA

Dear Mr. Dugan:

The October 9 notice of Late Filing & Payment of Taxes states that your 2002 return was incorrect. I believe the Internal Revenue Service is incorrect, but it is necessary to verify the accuracy of the facts as presented in the notice. I need copies of any documentation that you have from First Investors Brokerage. This includes account statements and transaction notices as well as any Form 1099.

Please deliver such documentation to my office the items described above no later than October 17, so I can resolve this matter as soon as possible. It is imperative that this issue be addressed by October 30, 2003, to avoid any additional interest and penalties that will begin to accrue if payment is not received by that date.

Sincerely,

Irma Preparer, C.P.A.

Editor's Note: The AICPA did not provide a solution for the contents of the Communication tab. This solution was developed by Bisk Education.

Research (1 point)

Code Section Answer: §1211(a)

Code §1211(a) states, "CORPORATIONS.—In the case of a corporation, losses from sales or exchanges of capital assets shall be allowed only to the extent of gains from such sales or exchanges."

Solution 6: Schedule A, Itemized Deductions

Unreimbursed Business Expenses Tab (estimated 1 point)

1. $2,200

Line 2: Transportation is a qualified employee business expense.

2. $0

Line 3: While cleaning of uniforms may be deductible, cleaning of clothing suitable for personal use is not a qualified employee business expense.

3. $410

Line 4: Only 50% of the cost of meals at which business is discussed with potential clients is a qualified employee business expense.

4. $385

Line 5: Only 50% of the cost of entertainment immediately after a business discussion with clients is a qualified employee business expense.

5. $0

Line 6: While uniforms may be deductible, clothing suitable for personal use is not a qualified employee business expense.

6. $25

Line 7: A gift to a client, limited to $25 per gift, is a qualified employee business expense.

7. $4,000

Line 12: Gambling losses, to the extent of gambling winnings, are deductible as miscellaneous itemized deductions not subject to the 2% limitation.

8. $1,340

Line 13: Unreimbursed employee business expenses are deductible as miscellaneous itemized deductions that, in aggregate, are subject to the 2% of adjusted gross income (AGI) limitation. $67,000 × 2% = $1,340

Medical Expenses Tab (estimated 1 point)

1. $2,650

Line 2: Medical insurance premiums paid with after-tax dollars are a qualified medical expense.

2. $0

Line 3: Disability insurance premiums are not a qualified medical expense.

3. $2,400

Line 4: The cost of vision correction surgery is a qualified medical expense.

4. $0

Line 5: The cost of most cosmetic surgery is not a qualified medical expense.

5. $0

Line 6: The cost of most cosmetic surgery is not a qualified medical expense.

6. $4,200

Line 7: The medical expenses of a medical dependent are a qualified medical expense. A medical dependent is someone who would otherwise qualify as a dependent except that he or she did not pass the gross income test.

7. $5,025

Line 12: Medical expenses are deductible as an itemized deduction to the extent that the aggregate exceeds 7.5% of the taxpayer's AGI. $67,000 × 7.5% = $5,025; $9,250 − $5,025 = $4,225

Interest Expenses Tab (estimated 1 point)

1. $11,400

Line 2: Interest paid on a loan with the taxpayer's primary or secondary home as collateral is qualified acquisition interest expense to the extent that the debt does not exceed the lesser of $1,000,000 or the home's fair market value.

2. $4,200

Line 3: All of the points paid on the acquisition mortgage when a home is purchased are qualified interest expense in the year of the home purchase.

3. $0

Line 4: Mortgage interest paid on rental property is not reported on Schedule A. Instead, it is reported on Schedule E.

4. $0

Line 5: Personal interest, such as typically incurred on credit cards for purchases of assets for personal use, is not interest expense qualified for a deduction. Interest expense reported on Schedule A is limited to home acquisition indebtedness, home equity indebtedness, and—to the extent of net investment income—investment indebtedness.

5. $0

Line 6: Personal interest, such as a payment to the IRS on a late personal income tax return, is not interest expense qualified for a deduction.

6. $475

Line 7: As the FMV of the home exceeds the acquisition indebtedness by $70,000, the interest on the home equity loan of $50,000 is deductible.

7. $0

Line 12: Qualified interest expense is deductible as an itemized deduction without a specific limitation based on AGI.

Casualty Losses Tab (estimated 1 point)

1. $7,200

Line 2: A sudden, unexpected, or unusual loss of property not connected with a trade of business or a transaction entered into for profit is allowable as a deduction to the extent the loss exceeds the gains from other personal casualties and thefts, subject to thresholds.

2. $0

Line 3: A casualty loss must be due to a sudden, unexpected, or unusual cause. Water damage generally does not qualify as it is not sudden. Water damage due to a flood or hurricane would qualify as this would be sudden. Editor's Note: Presumably, this item is unconnected to the water heater explosion mentioned on line 2—a presumption reinforced by the description, "roof deterioration."

3. $0

Line 4: A casualty loss must be due to a sudden, unexpected, or unusual cause. Damage due to termites is not sudden.

4. $500

Line 9: Casualty and theft losses are deductible as an itemized deduction to the extent that the aggregate exceeds 10% of the taxpayer's AGI, after deducting a $500 floor per event (not per damaged or stolen item). Editor's Note: As released by the AICPA, this answer was $100. EESA '08 generally changed this answer to $500, for 2009 only.

5. $6,700

Line 10: Casualty and theft losses are deductible as an itemized deduction to the extent that the aggregate exceeds 10% of the taxpayer's AGI, after deducting a $100 floor per event (not per damaged or stolen item). $67,000 × 10% = $6,700; $7,200 − $500 − $6,700 = $0

Communication Tab (estimated 5 points)

Editor's Note: As the AICPA examiners declined to provide an unofficial solution for this element, the Bisk Education editors wrote this solution.

April 15, Year 3

Tom Neu
123 Elm Street
Anytown USA 99999

Re: State Income Tax Refund

Dear Mr. Neu:

The treatment of the refund of state income taxes paid last year depends on whether you itemized your deductions last year and, if so, the extent of your federal tax benefit from using these state income taxes to claim an itemized deduction.

If an expenditure for which a taxpayer received a federal **tax benefit** is refunded, the taxpayer must report the refund, to the extent of the federal tax benefit, as **income** in the year of **receipt**. The tax code **requires** this treatment rather than reducing the current year's total amount for that type of expenditure or amendment of a previous year's return.

If you claimed the **standard deduction,** then you received no federal tax benefit from overpayment of your state income taxes and, hence, the payment is merely a non-taxable refund of your overpayment.

On the other hand, if you claimed an itemized deduction for the amount of the overpayment, your federal income tax was reduced by the amount of the overpayment or, in other words, you received a federal tax benefit. In this case, there are two possibilities for the treatment of the refund: either **partially** or **fully** included in taxable income. In the following discussion, net state income tax is the total state income taxes paid less the overpayment.

If your itemized deductions for last year had been calculated using the net state income taxes and that amount is **less** than last year's standard deduction, then the federal tax benefit is the **difference** between last year's standard deduction and the itemized deduction actually taken. Thus, only the **part** of the refund that provided the federal tax benefit would be included in taxable income.

If your itemized deductions for last year had been calculated using the net state income taxes and that amount still is the same or **greater** than last year's standard deduction, the full amount of the refund provided a federal tax benefit. Thus, the full amount of the refund must be included in income in the current year.

If this response doesn't address your concerns adequately, please contact me again regarding this issue.

Sincerely

Ima Preparer, CPA

Research Tab (estimated 1 point)

Answer: IRC Section 274(d)

IRC Section 274(d) states, "SUBSTANTIATION REQUIRED.—No deduction or credit shall be allowed—274(d)(1) under section 162 or 212 for any traveling expense (including meals and lodging while away from home), 274(d)(2) for any item with respect to an activity which is of a type generally considered to constitute entertainment, amusement, or recreation, or with respect to a facility used in connection with such an activity, 274(d)(3) for any expense for gifts, or 274(d)(4) with respect to any listed property (as defined in section 280F(d)(4)), unless the taxpayer substantiates by adequate records or by sufficient evidence corroborating the taxpayer's own statement (A) the amount of such expense or other item, (B) the time and place of the travel, entertainment, amusement, recreation, or use of the facility or property, or the date and description of the gift, (C) the business purpose of the expense or other item, and (D) the business relationship to the taxpayer of persons entertained, using the facility or property, or receiving the gift. The Secretary may by regulations provide that some or all of the requirements of the preceding sentence shall not apply in the case of an expense which does not exceed an amount prescribed pursuant to such regulations. This subsection shall not apply to any qualified nonpersonal use vehicle (as defined in subsection (i))."

INDEX

A

B

C

D

E

F

G

H

I

J

K

L

M

N

O

P

Q

R

S

T

U

V

W

Education Requirements

Most states (and other jurisdictions) now require candidates to obtain 150 semester hours of education prior to taking the examination.

Delaware, New Hampshire, and Vermont currently don't have a 150-hour requirement.

Some jurisdictions with 150-hour requirements may substitute experience for some education. Others may allow candidates to sit for the exam without the experience required for the license. Naturally, this information is subject to change without notice. Contact the jurisdiction in question for all applicable requirements to sit for the exam.
